# WORLD ENCYCLOPEDIA OF PEACE

## (SECOND EDITION)

# WORLD ENCYCLOPEDIA OF PEACE

## (SECOND EDITION)

## VOLUME I

Honorary Editor-in-Chief

**Javier Perez De Cuellar**

Editor-in-Chief

**Young Seek Choue**

**OCEANA PUBLICATIONS, INC.®**
**NEW YORK**

·

**SEOUL PRESS**

#4l488803

## World Encyclopedia of Peace (Second Edition)

Published in the United States of America in 1999 and distributed
exclusively throughout the world, except in Korea, by
Oceana Publications Inc.
75 Main Street
Dobbs Ferry, New York 10522
Phone: (914) 693-8100
Fax: (914) 693-0402

ISBN: 0-379-21399-0 (Volume I)
ISBN: 0-379-21398-2 (Set)

Library of Congress Cataloging-in-Publication Data

World encyclopedia of peace / honorary editor-in-chief, Javier
Perez de Cuellar, editor-in-chief, Young Seek Choue. -- 2nd ed.
    p. cm.
    Includes bibliographical references and indexes.
    ISBN 0-379-21398-2 (clothbound set : alk. paper)
    1. Peace Encyclopedias. I. Perez de Cuellar, Javier, 1920-
II. Young Seek Choue, 1921-
JZ5533 .W67 1999
327.1'03--dc21                                          99-34811
                                                            CIP

Published simultaneously in the Republic of Korea in 1999 by
Seoul Press
Jin Wang Kim, Publisher
Room 303, Jeodong Bldg., 7-2, Jeodong, Chung-ku
Seoul 100-032, Korea
Phone: (02) 2275-6566
Fax: (02) 2278-2551

ISBN: 89-7225-097-X    94330 (Volume I)
ISBN: 89-7225-096-1 (Set)

Printed in the Republic of Korea by Seoul Press

# CONTENTS

# DEDICATION TO THE SECOND EDITION

In the late twentieth century, peace is increasingly understood not just in military terms, and not just as the absence of conflict, but as a multi-dimensional phenomenon encompassing economic development, social justice, environmental protection, democratization, disarmament and respect for human rights. These pillars of peace are interrelated and mutually reinforcing.

Building peace in an interdependent world requires the full participation of every citizen, every nation, every continent. Governments, non-governmental organizations, private sector businesses and industries, academic institutions, trade unions and other members of civil society are all players on the international stage. At the United Nations, all can come together in common cause to address today's complex global problems and to work towards shared goals.

Education plays a central role in this effort. The first ingredient of political stability is an informed citizen. The first ingredient of economic progress is a skilled worker. And the first ingredient of social justice is an enlightened society. Education is thus the key to global peace, well-being and understanding. In that spirit, I commend to all readers this *World Encyclopedia of Peace* (Second Edition).

Kofi A. Annan
Secretary-General
United Nations

# DEDICATION TO THE FIRST EDITION

The promotion and maintenance of peace has been a primary concern since the earliest days of human civilization. The fostering of a true and lasting peace is necessarily a multidimensional process, for no single path can guarantee its ultimate and universal attainment. As an organization created for the maintenance of peace, the United Nations reflects this reality, consistently seeking to improve international security and human welfare through its efforts in diverse fields. Breadth of vision, together with dedication and sustained effort, are among the keys to the effective promotion and maintenance of peace.

The Editors of the *World Encyclopedia of Peace* have provided a useful tool for consideration of the many aspects of peace in today's world. The Encyclopedia reflects the diversity of its authorship and offers insight into various dimensions of peace as well as possible approaches for its attainment. In preparing the Encyclopedia, the Editors have not sought to provide a unified perspective on peace, but have surveyed many existing and even contradictory views with the aim of providing a basis for further discussion and research.

I am pleased to welcome the timely initiative which has been taken with the publication of the first *World Encyclopedia of Peace*. The Encyclopedia will serve as a lasting resource on this vital issue, opening the way for further reflection and research by readers and researchers around the world.

Javier Pérez de Cuéllar
Secretary-General
United Nations

# PREFACE

The *World Encyclopedia of Peace* is published in its second edition in order to keep the information contained herein abreast with the epochal changes that have been occurring since more than a decade ago. These changes, which are significantly altering the global peace and security landscape, are going to further affect the events that will occur in the new millennium. The task of revising was began in 1996 to commemorate the tenth anniversary of the International Year of Peace (IYP). This large-scale revision entails adding and updating a significant number of articles to reflect the changing conceptual perspective of peace. Likewise, more information are added to better assist the student, scholar and practitioner in their practical needs. Nevertheless, the original goals behind the publication of the Encyclopedia remain as the prime motivation for this revision job.

The publication of the *World Encyclopedia of Peace* has been promoted by our deep concern for world peace—an objective that seems increasingly elusive and complicated despite the expectations that it would be easier to attain it now that the Cold War had been dismantled. The remaining challenges to peace and the new forms of peacelessness are equally imposing the necessity to advance knowledge in keeping with the fast changing international environment. However, we maintain our original belief that peace need not be a totally elusive goal if the people of the world can work together toward that end. The first steps in this process must be to define peace correctly and, at the same time, to educate people so that they can agree on this common goal.

In retrospect, the task of assembling a comprehensive encyclopedia of peace has been clearly an ambitious undertaking. But there were reasons why the attempt was made. Firstly, there was no single encyclopedia devoted to peace, although there was a plethora of reference works on other subjects. Secondly, we are convinced that the Encyclopedia would contribute greatly to the promotion of peaceloving ideas among the peoples of the world, and would provide a fertile source of materials both for policymakers as well as for peace researchers. Finally, the publication of the first edition of the Encyclopedia was a fitting commemoration of the fortieth anniversary of the United Nations and of the 1986 IYP, and this current revision commemorates the Thirteenth anniversary of the IYP.

The revolutionary compression of time and space by the ever-continuing advance of science and technology has brought about profound changes in humankind's environment and consciousness. Internationalism promoted by the spread of democratic ideals has homogenized the consciousness of humankind and transformed every individual into a member of the community of common destiny. Today, every human being is one component of a greater unit—that is, a member of world society. As a result, men are organically linked to one another and, therefore, closely interdependent.

Man is changing the course of his march away from a divisive centrifugal direction toward an integrative centripetal one. The creation of the League of Nations after the First World War and of the United Nations after the Second World War are indications of the necessity of change in this direction. The information revolution has irrevocably made the world an interdependent international cooperation society and created a "human familism."

The most urgent, critical problem in our contemporary world society is the problem of peace, upon which the survival and prosperity of humankind totally depend. Peace is precious; it is essential to humankind. In spite of this, prospects for peace are dim, because, first of all, we do not make a clear distinction between ideals and realities, and, secondly, because we have varying concepts of peace.

Despite such trends toward global interdependence, nationalistic power struggles and group conflicts continue to prevail, thereby, increasing the danger of large-scale genocide. In view of this anachronism and its danger, we ought to build world peace through cooperation and understanding among the peoples of the world. To realize this imperative goal, we have embarked on this revision work of the *World Encyclopedia of Peace*. We hope that this task will contribute to making the world a safer and more secure place to live in for every human being.

Finally, I would like to express profound gratitude to the former and current editors who devoted themselves to the planning, editing, revising and complementing of the Encyclopedia; to the global leaders and scholars who contributed articles to it; to Pergamon Press which published the first edition of the Encyclopedia, Oceana Publications Inc., which is one of the most prestigious publishing companies in the world, and Seoul Press, an outstanding English printer and publisher in Korea, for undertaking the publication of the Encyclopedia.

Young Seek Choue
Founder-Chancellor
Kyung Hee University System

# USER'S GUIDE TO THE ENCYCLOPEDIA

## I

The World Encyclopedia of Peace is the first attempt of its kind to present an integrated body of information on peace in all its aspects. The introductory essay, Peace "Encyclopedias" of the Past and Present, charts the history of past efforts to compile an authoritative work of reference on peace. This Encyclopedia is intended to complement these earlier works and to provide the basis for a truly comprehensive study of peace.

The Encyclopedia has two predominant themes: peace research and peace activism. In combining these two themes, the Editors have sought to demonstrate the interrelationships between them and the ways in which they have fostered each other. Consequently, peace is discussed in these volumes from a very broad spectrum of perspectives: from the idealist to the realist; from the global to the subnational; from the cultural to the economic; from the religious to the feminist; from the historical to the contemporary.

Inevitably, the Encyclopedia cannot be truly exhaustive in its scope. The first constraint upon this ideal lies in the language in which it is published. The second lies in the fact that peace research is still heavily concentrated in North America and Europe. The contents and authorship of the Encyclopedia reflect this bias to a degree.

Every effort has been made to demonstrate—and celebrate—the diversity of approaches to peace, seeking to favor no one approach over any other. A final constraint is the unavoidable one of history overtaking events. The Editors have sought, with the aid of database publishing techniques, to make the Encyclopedia as up-to-date as possible but developments in this area are rapid.

The study of peace is interdisciplinary by its nature. It is not yet possible to impose a rigid structure upon peace research and peace activism, as indeed it is not yet possible to prescribe a structure for a just world order. It is hoped, however, that the Encyclopedia will demonstrate the value of the study of peace and will go some way to refute the aphorism of Ambrose Bierce that peace is "a period of cheating between two periods of fighting."

## II

The Encyclopedia has been organized in such a way that information on a variety of topics is readily accessible. Volumes I to V comprise articles organized alphabetically by title; Volume VI comprises treaties of the 20th century related to peace; Volume VII contains chronological, descriptive and directorial data on events, personalities and organizations; and Volume VIII comprises basic reference data organized thematically—it also includes the indices to the first seven volumes.

The main body of the Encyclopedia consists in the ARTICLES in Volume I, II, III, IV and V. The Executive Editors—in consultation with their advisers—commissioned the articles on the basis of the following subject classification:

(a) Theories of conflict, aggression, and war.

(b) Theories of, and approaches to, dispute and conflict resolution.

(c) The modern states system—ideologies, structures, and individuals which have shaped it; how these have influenced the current instability of the world.

(d) Attempts to regulate the states system—through international law and through institutional frameworks.

(e) International conflict—and related issues of nuclear war and the militarization process.

(f) The North-South conflict—and related issues of development, nonalignment, and world economic order.

(g) World order and internationalism.

(h) Integration—theory and practice.

(i) Disarmament and arms control.

(j) Peace movement—history and contemporary.

(k) Pacifism.

(l) Religion and peace.

(m) Feminism and peace.

(n) Nonviolence—theory, practice, and pioneers.

(o) Human rights and social justice.

(p) Peace research—pioneers and theories.

(q) Peace education.

(r) Peace—history, advocates, plans, psychology, sociology.

Although in many respects it was seen as desirable to order the articles under these headings, an alphabetical organization was eventually adopted because of the extent of overlap between the subject areas. To overcome the disadvantages of the alphabetical organization, a comprehensive system of cross-referencing was employed so that readers may easily find articles in related areas of interest. Readers are also advised to make full use of the Subject Index in Volume VIII.

Volume VI is composed of the past and current treaties of the twentieth century. The TREATIES represent the legal and institutional effort to "enlarge" peace by circumscribing war: at a practical level by imposing limits upon the way in which it is fought, the weapons which may be deployed, and the geographical areas which may be affected; at a normative level by seeking to prohibit aggression and to outlaw war. Since the attempt to elevate international law to the status of a regulatory mechanism in the international system is of recent origin, all treaties have been selected from the twentieth century. Volume VII includes the CHRONOLOGY OF THE PEACE MOVEMENT; the PROFILES OF THE UNITED NATIONS SECRETARIES-GENERAL; articles on the NOBEL PEACE PRIZE LAUREATES; NOBEL PRIZE awardees; descriptions of UN's SPECIALIZED AGENCIES and descriptions of INTERNATIONAL PEACE INSTI-TUTES AND ORGANIZATIONS. The chronology of the peace movement provides details of the development of the "unofficial"—but by no means "unorganized"—search for peace since the beginning of the nineteenth century. Here can be seen not only the attempt to mobilize popular support against war but also the first stimulus to peace research and peace education. The profiles of the United Nations Secretaries-General give the reader a deeper understanding of the accomplishments of the men that have held the highest position in the world intergovernmental peace organization in keeping and making the peace among nations. The articles on the Nobel Peace Prize Laureates pro-vide a historical perspective upon the diversity of approaches to "peacemaking": the Nobel Committee has recognized the work of both institutions and individuals, both statesmen pursuing power-political routes to peace and activists practicing nonviolent direct action. The choices of the Nobel Committee, though scarcely radical, reflect the steady broadening of the definition of peace which has developed within both the peace activist and the peace research communities during the course of the twentieth century. The profiles of the awardees of the Nobel Prizes in medicines, economics, physics and literature allow a wide knowledge of the achievements of the "best" men and women in the selected fields or professions. Both the descriptions of UN specialized agencies and international peace research institutions and organizations offer more than just a directo-rial familiarity of the organizations working for international understanding, cooperation and peace.

Volume VIII has five sections: BIBLIOGRAPHY, JOURNALS, LIST OF CONTRI-BUTORS, and the NAME and SUBJECT INDEXES. Each of these sections has been categorized for ease of access and together they provide a valuable reference source. The bibliography comprises an alphabetical listing of references in the literature of peace studies and peace research. The final three sections of this volume complement the con-tents of all the volumes. The list of contributors presents, in alphabetical order, the names of all authors who have written articles for the Encyclopedia. The name index is an essential resource for readers who wish to locate all the references to a particular indi-vidual throughout the Encyclopedia. The subject index has been compiled as a guide to readers who are interested in finding all the references to a particular subject area.

## III

Spelling and punctuation throughout the Encyclopedia follow both the British and American styles to allow originality of the authors. Most articles in the Encyclopedia include a list of notes and a bibliography giving sources of further information. Contri-butors were requested to favor sources in the English language but many other languages are represented in addition to English. Each bibliography consists of general items for further reading and/or references which cover specific aspects of text. Where appropri-ate, authors are cited in the text using a name/date system as follows:

According to Smith (1985) . . .

. . . as was recently reported (Jones 1985).

All authors cited in the Encyclopedia are listed in the Name Index in Volume VIII. This gives details of the text page on which the author is cited and also the page on which full bibliographic details can be found. It can therefore be used to look up the name of an author known to have published material relevant to the subject of interest.

The compilation of the Encyclopedia has been greatly assisted by the use of advanced computer technology for processing all its sections through the various stages of production. This has enabled the Encyclopedia to be produced far more rapidly than would have been possible with traditional editorial and printing techniques. Since all material in the Encyclopedia is held on a database, it will also be possible to update, revise, and supplement its contents in the future. This facility is particularly appropriate for a subject area which is continuously changing and developing with the pace of current events.

# INTRODUCTION

More than a decade has passed since the publication of the first edition of the *World Encyclopedia of Peace* which was a fitting tribute to the declaration of the 1986 International Year of Peace (IYP). In that decade epochal changes had occurred in the international scene so much so that notions, ideas, and concepts on global peace need recasting and redefining. It is thus fitting once again that the revised and enlarged edition of the *World Encyclopedia of Peace* is published to commemorate the thirteenth anniversary of the IYP. With this second edition, it is hoped that the world community will better understand in a timely manner the conceptual underpinnings of the events that shape the lives of nations and peoples. Much of these events have been influenced to a certain extent by the consequences of the 1986 IYP.

In retrospect, the 1986 IYP was an idea of Dr. Young Seek Choue who, in 1981, while serving as president of the International Association of University Presidents (IAUP) presented a resolution to that body for the holding of the International Day, Month and Year of Peace. While in congress at Costa Rica the more than 600 members of IAUP adopted the resolution unanimously. The IAUP turned for support to the Costa Rican government through then President Rodrigo Carazo-Odio to present the resolution as an agenda to the United Nations. Costa Rica managed to present a draft resolution sponsored by twenty member-countries recommending the General Assembly to declare 1986 as the IYP. The Economic and Social Council adopted this resolution without a vote. Finally, on November 30, 1981 the resolution declaring 1986 as the IYP (A/36/L.29/Rev.1) was approved by the General Assembly without a vote, that is by "unanimous adoption" or "adoption by consensus."[1]

As contained in the UN Secretary General's report of October 14, 1987 (A/42/487/Add. 1) various commemorative activities for the IYP were held. Over a thousand commemorative activities were held by member and non-member states of the United Nations of which 99 countries held commemorative peace ceremonies, 92 countries issued commemorative stamps and 46 countries participated in the first Earth Run. Many other countries also issued commemorative coins, postcards, and posters and held various kinds of commemorative concerts, cultural and athletic events.[2]

Considered as the real thrust of the commemoration of 1986 IYP were the activities initiated by hundreds and thousands of individuals, groups and organizations around the world in which the information received from 140 countries indicated the understanding of the message of the festivities being that peace is an issue for everyone's concern and the role of the United Nations in bringing peace to the world is to be underscored. Social organizations and individuals commemorated the event in various ways which were most visible in Australia, Canada, New Zealand, Scandinavia, and several Latin American countries. In the United Kingdom, NGO Year of Peace Council brought together more than 1,000 organizations in England and a similar number in Scotland. Over 300 representatives of national, regional and international non-governmental organizations attended "Together for Peace Conference" in Geneva.[3]

Immediately before and during the celebration of the IYP, events that were occurring in the international arena have been signalling the advent of a more peaceful era for humankind. The US-Soviet Summit in Geneva in 1985 signalled the dismantling of the bipolar world. On New Year's day in 1986, leaders of the two superpowers exchanged messages and referred to the coming year as the Year of Peace. Several heads of states including Pope John Paul II addressed the Year of Peace in their new year's messages. The IYP was inaugurated by the Security Council at a special session.[4]

In October of that year, President Gorbachev and President Reagan met at Reykjavik, Iceland. The ensuing events led to the signing of the 1987 INF treaty that abolished all intermediate nuclear missiles. In the same year, the President of the then Soviet Union declared Glastnost and Perestroika as the implementing principle of the "New Thinking." It was the beginning of the metamorphic collapse of the Cold War system which found realization in the cataclysmic events of 1989, culminating in the breakdown of the "iron curtain" and the virtual dissolution of the Soviet Union in 1992. During his visit to Korea, former Soviet President Gorbachev was quoted to have said "Without the UN International Year of Peace and the Reykjavik Summit, there could not be the world of today . . . ." He likewise said, "If not for the UN International Day and Year of Peace, the peaceful mood for the summit meetings between the former USSR and the USA could not have been possible and there would not have been the world of reconciliation and cooperation that we see today."[5]

Thus, with the UN IYP serving as a watershed, a new era was ushered in amidst expectations of a more integrated and peaceful world. Metamorphic changes occurred in the global architecture. The Soviet Union did implode with the separation of the former Soviet satellites states, majority of whom have moved towards liberal democracy. With the socialist system amply rejected, all of these societies are moving towards market capitalism. Likewise, the basic processes and institutions of liberal democracy are undergoing development.

Moreover, the breakdown of the Cold War divide brought the international community closer to integration. The successful conclusion of the Gulf War in 1991, showed a new partnership and alliance among the major powers through the operations of the United Nations. The reaffirmation of a world system of collective security paved the way for the UN to take on the task of peacekeeping in troubled areas around the world which erupted due to the outburst of nationalism, ethnic secessionism and intra-state conflicts.

Furthermore, through the consensus shown in the Earth Summit at Rio in 1992, majority of humankind has reached the common resolve that the environment needs to be protected lest a catastrophic collapse of the biosphere would bring devastation to human life. The world community agreed that only a sustainable development will guarantee a continuance of economic growth without unduly sacrificing more the environment. Agenda 21 stipulates the programs to be undertaken by nation-states in concert to stave off further deterioration of the ecosphere. Likewise, the successful conclusion of the Uruguay Round gave birth to the World Trade Organization which is tasked to level the playing field for economies to compete in the world market. The international economic system is being reshaped to promote freer trade. These two events are charting the future course of global economic development.

In early 1995, the Social Summit in Copenhagen strengthened the resolve of world leaders to combat poverty, unemployment and social disintegration. The most radical proposal was the formation of an Economic Security Council in the United Nations, which reflected the new conception of peace and security beyond the outmoded realist view of war prevention.[6] The world community now stands more resolute to wage war against income inequality, dearth of income-generating activities, economic dependence and social disorder. The regressive pressure of overpopulation, receding resources, dissatisfaction of basic human needs and self-centeredness provides hurdles for social planners and developers.[7]

Beyond the 13th anniversary of the IYP, the world looks forward to a new millennium that will mark a new epoch in the development of human civilization. As human societies move towards the threshold of the present century, new paradigms are being sought to anticipate the growth of new knowledge in a new era. Peace is at the center of the challenge that lies ahead of humankind for without peace, the human species is in danger of extinction given the preponderance of knowledge, techniques and resources for making weapons of mass destruction. In understanding the multi-faceted demands of a peaceful human life in the 21st century, a compendium of knowledge is necessary to serve as reference for conceptualization. The second edition of the *World Encyclopedia of Peace* may well serve the purpose, along with other books of knowledge, of "defending the peace in the minds of men."

## Notes

1. Krysztof Ostrowski, "International Year of Peace: Initiative, Program, Effects," paper presented at the International Peace Conference in Commemoration of the 10th Anniversary of the UN International Year of Peace (1986) and the 15th UN International Day of Peace held on September 17 to 19, 1996 in Seoul, Korea, p. 8.

2. Young Seek Choue, "Peace Strategy for a Global Common Society and the Role of the United Nations in the 21st Century," Keynote speech delivered at the International Peace Conference in commemoration of the 10th Anniversary of the UN International Year of Peace (1986) and the 15th UN International Day of Peace held on September 17 to 19, 1996 in Seoul, Korea, p. 11.

3. Ostrowski, *Ibid.*, p. 35-36.

4. *Ibid.*, p. 24.

5. Young Seek Choue, "HCP Activities Report X," submitted to the Executive Committee Meeting of the IAUP held in San Francisco, USA in July 1996.

6. Pedro B. Bernaldez, "The 1986 UN International Year of Peace and Its Future Tasks: Building Positive Peace in the 21st Century," paper presented in the International Peace Conference in commemoration of the UN International Year of Peace and the UN International Day of Peace held in Seoul, Korea on September 17-19, 1996, p. 5.

7. *Ibid.*

Jae-Shik Sohn
Director
Institute of International Peace Studies

# Peace "Encyclopedias" of the Past till 1985

## An Introductory Essay

It is perhaps surprising to find that among the multitude of subjects for which encyclopedias exist the subject of peace is conspicuously absent. This is curious for at least two reasons: in the first place because peace, as an idea and ideal, has preoccupied humankind for a considerable part of its history. Throughout history we find the theme of peace adumbrated in the words and works of theologians and philosophers, statesmen and soldiers, poets and preachers. The Christian civilization was inaugurated, almost two thousand years ago, by the coming of Jesus Christ, the Prince of Peace, and peace has been an aspiration in other civilizations and in other religions (see *Religion and Peace*). The changes in warfare which social and technical developments have brought about in the past few hundred years (especially the Industrial and the French Revolutions) have brought the issue of peace even more fully to the forefront of humanity's consciousness, so much so that today it has become the single most important question upon which the future of the planet itself depends. Thus we are not dealing with an obscure, abstract, neglected, or unimportant idea.

In view of both the historical and contemporary concern about peace it is puzzling that no encyclopedia has been compiled on this subject. In Erasmus's *The Complaint of Peace* (1517)—which Roland Bainton has called "the first book in European history devoted entirely to the cause of pacifism"—Peace protests her banishment from all parts of society, being welcomed nowhere (see *Erasmus, Desiderius*). To the extent that no encyclopedia has been devoted to peace in the 450 years since Erasmus's passing, her banishment extends also to this literary genre. Since Erasmus wrote, a change has occurred which was the emergence of an organized peace movement after the Napoleonic wars. Independently of one another, American and English peace societies were established in 1815 and were followed by the creation of similar bodies in other countries. It was the first time that the broad reform movement of the eighteenth and nineteenth centuries which encompassed so many social concerns and found its expression in societies of various kinds, had also affected the opposition to war. From then, the peace movement became organized: societies (local, national, and international) sprang up whose members organized petitions and congresses and issued pamphlets and journals (see *Peace Movements of the Nineteenth Century*). Thus by the time of the First World War, after a century of organized peace efforts, a vast literature had come into existence. Although there have been disappointments and although peace organizations have come and gone, the twentieth century has witnessed their continued growth. The literature on peace has grown accordingly. Here, then, is the second reason for surprise: the lack of an encyclopedia in this voluminous library. To be specific, a recent extensive bibliography on war and peace contains in its subject index some 1,800 categories but one looks in vain for the subject "peace encyclopedia" (Carroll et al. 1983; for the full publication details of this and other books discussed in this essay see the bibliography at the end).

Nevertheless a number of literary works do exist which may be reckoned to display encyclopedic features. This essay draws attention to some 50 works, which can be grouped broadly into five categories (see Tables 1 and 2). Firstly, a number of major bibliographies exist; these help in the exploration of the field and can be regarded as the primary tools with which an encyclopedia on the subject should be fashioned. Secondly, several biographical reference works which detail the life and thought of individuals who have been important for the cause of peace supplement these guides to the literature. These biographical dictionaries provide another useful means for studying peace: although it is true that this field cannot be adequately depicted by the combined biographies of peace leaders yet their field cannot be adequately depicted by the combined biographies

**Table 1**
Thematic overview

| Author | Bibliography | Biography | Encyclopedic: Aspects | Encyclopedic: General | Other |
|---|---|---|---|---|---|
| Adler | | | 1952 | | |
| Beales | | | | 1931 | |
| Beckwith | | | | | 1847 |
| Bernhardt | | | 1981 | | |
| Boulding et al. | 1979 | | | | |
| Bouthoul | | | 1970 | | |
| Brock | | | 1968-72 | | |
| Carroll et al. | 1983 | | | | |
| Clarke | | | 1966 | | |
| Constantinescu-Bagdat | | 1924-28 | | | |
| Cook | 1969 | | | | |
| Cook et al. | | | | | 1971 |
| Cooney and Michalowski | | | | | 1977 |
| de Bloch | | | 1898-1900 | | |
| de Ligt | | | 1931-34 | | |
| Dougall | 1982 | | | | |
| Fried | | | | 1911-13 | |
| Galtung | | | 1975-80 | | |
| Gourevitch | | | | | 1955 |
| Haberman | | 1972 | | | |
| Hemleben | | | | | 1943 |
| Hershberger | | | | | 1944 |
| Hinsley | | | | | 1963 |
| Holl and Donat | | 1983 | | | |
| Huxley | | | | | 1937 |
| Josephson | | 1985 | | | |
| Kuehl | | 1983 | | | |
| La Fontaine | 1904 | | | | |
| Lange-Schou | | | | 1919-63 | |
| Lynd | | | | | 1966 |
| Marriott | | | | | 1937 |
| Mayer | | | | | 1966 |
| Molhuysen | 1916-63 | | | | |
| Norwegian Nobel Institute | 1912 | | | | |
| Ruyssen | | | | 1954-61 | |
| Sharp | | | 1973 | | |
| Sibley | | | | | 1963 |
| Silberner | | | 1939-57 | | |
| Singer et al. | | | 1972 | | |
| Société Jean Bodin | | | | 1961 | |
| Stawell | | | | | 1929 |
| ter Meulen | | | | 1917-40 | |
| ter Meulen | 1934-36 | | | | |
| Upham | | | | | 1836 |
| Verdoorn | | | 1972 | | |
| Weinberg and Weinberg | | | | | 1963 |
| Woito | 1982 | | | | |
| Wright | | | 1942 | | |
| Wynner and Lloyd | | | 1944 | | |
| York | | | | | 1919 |

*Table 2*
Chronological overview

| Period | Year | Author | Other editions and reprints |
|---|---|---|---|
| Nineteenth century | 1836 | Upham | 1842 |
| | 1847 | Beckwith | 1971 Garland repr. |
| | 1898-1900 | de Bloch | 1973 Garland repr. |
| pre-1914 | 1904 | La Fontaine | 1891 1st edn. |
| | 1912 | Norwegian Nobel Institute | |
| | 1911-13 | Fried | 1972 Garland repr.; 1905 1st end. |
| First World War | 1916-66 | Molhuysen | |
| | 1917-40 | ter Meulen | |
| Interbellum | 1919-63 | Lange-Schou | |
| | 1919 | York | |
| | 1924-28 | Constantinescu-Bagdat | |
| | 1929 | Stawell | |
| | 1931 | Beales | 1971 Garland repr. |
| | 1931-34 | de Ligt | |
| | 1934-36 | ter Meulen | |
| | 1937 | Huxley | 1972 Garland repr. |
| | 1937 | Marriott | |
| | 1939-57 | Silberner | 1972 Garland repr. of 1939 and 1946 volumes |
| Second World War | 1942 | Wright | 1965 2nd edn. |
| | 1943 | hemleben | 1972 Garland repr. |
| | 1944 | Hershberger | 1969 3rd edn. |
| | 1944 | Wynner and Lloyd | 1946 2nd pr. |
| 1950s | 1952 | Adler | 1977 21st pr. |
| | 1954-61 | Ruyssen | |
| | 1955 | Gourevitch | |
| 1960s | 1961 | Société Jean Bodin | |
| | 1963 | Sibley | |
| | 1963 | Weinberg and Weinberg | |
| | 1963 | Hinsley | |
| | 1966 | Lynd | |
| | 1966 | Mayer | Penguin edn. |
| | 1968-72 | Brock | |
| | 1969 | Cook | |
| 1970s | 1970 | Bouthoul | New edn.; 1951 1st edn. |
| | 1971 | Cook et al. | |
| | 1972 | Haberman | |
| | 1972 | Verdoorn | |
| | 1972 | Singer et al. | |
| | 1973 | Sharp | |
| | 1975-80 | Galtung | |
| | 1977 | Cooney and Michalowski | |
| | 1979 | Boulding et al. | 2nd edn.; 1974 1st edn. |
| 1980s | 1981 | - | Bernhardt |
| | 1982 | Dougall | |
| | 1982 | Woito | 6th edn.; 1967 1st edn. |
| | 1983 | Carroll et al. | |
| | 1983 | Holl and Donat | |
| | 1983 | Kuehl | |
| | 1985 | Josephson | |

of peace leaders yet their lives constitute an essential aspect of the study of peace. Similarly, our third category of works are encyclopedic in scope and structure but not in terms of content since they do not deal with all aspects of the subject. Taken as a whole, the literature in this category forms an impressive "collage" but in order to arrive at a veritable encyclopedia it would be necessary to integrate these works into a coherent scheme and to incorporate still other aspects of the subject on which no detailed studies yet exist. Some peace topics have been thoroughly investigated, for instance such relevant phenomena as pacifism, antimilitarism, nonviolent action, and nonresistance. We have compilations of peace plans of the past and also, especially since the emergence of peace research in the post-Second World War period, a growing body of peace theory. It is obvious that several studies which focus in a major way on war and on the question of armament and disarmament belong in this group. In a fourth category are studies which differ from the above in that they aim to provide an overview not so much of one aspect of peace as of the entire subject. Although half a dozen works have been put into this category, none is really an encyclopedia in the proper sense. Finally, a fifth category comprises literature of various types, including anthologies of peace, which treat the subject in an encyclopedic manner. Our review starts with two books in this last category.

## 1. A Misnomer: The Encyclopedias of Huxley and Gourevitch

It appears that in all the literature on peace only two books include the word "encyclopedia" in their title. They are Aldous Huxley's *An Encyclopaedia of Pacifism* (1937) and Boris Gourevitch's *The Road to Peace and to Moral Democracy: An Encyclopedia of Peace* (1955). It is therefore ironic that neither is an encyclopedia as that term is usually defined, namely "a literary work giving information on all branches of knowledge or of one subject." The only things that these books have in common is that they are called encyclopedias and that this description is rather misleading. Their format is as different as their content: Huxley's "Encyclopaedia" is a small, 126-page pamphlet in which 54 subjects are discussed in alphabetical order (hence the title) whereas Gourevitch's work more nearly resembles, at least in its outward form, an encyclopedia since it comprises two bulky volumes consisting of over 2,500 pages. Huxley writes as a convinced pacifist and his subject as the title indicates is pacifism, not peace (see *Pacifism*). This pamphlet was written for the Peace Pledge Union (founded by Dick Sheppard) which Huxley joined in 1935 (see *Peace Pledge Union (PPU)*). A recent critic,[1] finding that the pamphlet was "apparently written in great haste and more with an eye for journalistic simplicity than with a view towards profound permanence," draws attention to the platitudes and a tendency to slogan-eering, as well as to instances of Huxley's "extraordinary innocence"—which Huxley himself was to recognize in later years. Although many sections of the work are outdated and superficial, other parts have retained their value and insight which make it "a worthwhile addition to any library concerned with war and peace." However, Huxley's pamphlet rather than being a real encyclopedia is indicative of his "encyclopedic interests"—in this instance of his lifelong interest in peace.

Likewise Gourevitch's book is too seriously flawed in its overall conception and organization to constitute a true encyclopedia. The author wishes to lay a firm foundation for peace based on "the unification of all moral forces of our world in order to realize a thorough reform consisting in a reorganization of International Law towards the protection of the human person by the community of nations and towards the limitation of national sovereignty" (Gourevitch 1955 vol. 1, p. 16). The author, who was founder of the Union for the Protection of the Human Person by International Social and Economic Co-operation, argues for an alliance of the churches with moderate socialists, the labor unions, and democratic parties to achieve fundamental social reforms (including a reform of international law and of the United Nations Organization) since ". . . only the road to moral democracy can prevent wars and revolutions" (p. 12). Gourevitch's experience explains his passionate dedication to the ideals of peace and freedom of which this extensive study is convincing testimony. Most of his study is concerned with contemporary international events and here so much factual material, often irrelevant to the argument, is adduced that the major principles which he wishes to emphasize have become obscured. The whole is even more disorganized by the interspersion of historical material in this chronicle of contemporary events. Since it is neither a systematic exposition of a particular thesis on world peace nor a comprehensive and easily accessible reference work, Gourevitch's massive study thus falls short of what an encyclopedia should be.[2]

## 2. Two Nineteenth Century Christian Peace Manuals: Upham and Beckwith

More truly encyclopedic were the two *Manuals* published by two leading American advocates of peace more than a century before: Thomas Upham's *The Manual of Peace* (1836) and George C. Beckwith's *The Peace Manual* (1847). The first one is, in the words of Peter Brock, "a kind of encyclopedia of peace, a century before Aldous Huxley's attempt at something similar in the 1930s and on a much more ambitious scale. (It runs to more than 400 pages.) It is, in fact, one of the first attempts to give a full-scale exposition of pacifist ideology. In this aim it is not altogether successful, but it is as a pioneer work that it must be judged and its defects assessed" (Brock 1968 p. 507). Upham's manual essentially consists of three parts: an exposition of the wastefulness, futility, and moral evil of war; an outline of reforms which would mitigate the effects of war and ultimately eliminate war itself (reforms affecting international law and involving the setting up of a "congress of nations"—i.e., an embryonic world organization); and an extensive discussion of the principles and practice of "nonresistance" as applied to both individual and state behavior. The author, who was professor of moral philosophy at Bowdoin College, came very close to being an absolute pacifist since he regarded the doctrine of nonresistance as "the core of the peace idea" (p. 508). The institutional reforms which he advocated were no substitute for this doctrine but merely reflected his realization that most people were not yet convinced of the necessity of conscientious objection and nonresistance (see *Conscientious Objection*). These alone, however, accorded with the precepts of Christianity (p. 510). Although Upham made no original contributions to the theology of Christian pacifism and wrote within the rigid framework of the fundamentalist, literalist viewpoint "his work is important . . . for the systematic way in which he presents, from the complete pacifist position, many of the ideas which had been the stock in trade of peace advocates for at least two decades" (p. 510).

The original edition sold out within a few months; in 1842 a second and much slimmer edition of Upham's manual was published "for the purpose of bringing before a much larger number of readers the portions most important to the cause of Peace." The words are those of George Beckwith, the secretary of the American Peace Society under whose imprint the new edition was published. In his introduction he spoke of it as "a noble and eloquent contribution from one of the first writers of the age" and the reader was now offered "in a small compass, probably the best general view of the subject that can be found in the English or any other language" (Upham 1842 pp. 14-15). Beckwith wrote in his introduction that the Bible was "the great manual of peace" (p. 11) and although this was exemplified in Upham's argument, yet it is interesting to note the following passage in which he highlights the paradox of the neglect of the study of war (such a momentous and widespread phenomenon) and in which he makes, in effect, an early plea for peace research: "Shall the attention of the whole scientific and intellectual world be directed to the comparatively trifling circumstances of the discovery of a new plant, to the fall of a meteoric stone, or to some atmospheric phenomenon,—and shall war, that great moral phenomenon, so inexplicable as to strike angels with astonishment, and to fill even the spirits of darkness with wonder, be deemed of so little consequence as to arrest no thought, excite no feeling, and secure no spirit of inquiry?" (pp. 33-34).

In the preface to Beckwith's own manual, published in 1847, we read: "This little work is designed to furnish the most important facts, arguments and explanations, on the main topics embraced in the cause of peace." His argument against war proceeds in three stage: the physical evils of war, the moral evils of war, and remedies for war. Although is is very similar to Upham's manual it was to some extent written "to counteract some dangerous notions to be found in the earlier *The Manual of Peace*" (Brock 1968 p. 650). These dangerous notions concerned the views of absolute pacifists and nonresisters who denied the admissibility of defensive war or the right of governments to coerce in internal politics. This issue had caused serious divisions in the American Peace Society in the previous decade; under Beckwith's leadership the moderates established their authority. The essence of their argument is to be found in Beckwith's preface: "The cause of peace aims solely to do away the custom of international war; and I trust there will be found in this book nothing that does not bear on this object, nor anything that interferes with the legitimate authority of government. As a friend of peace, I am of course a supporter of civil government, with all the powers requisite for the condign punishment of wrong-doers, the enforcement of law, and the preservation of social order . . . . I condemn *only* THE GREAT DUEL OF NATIONS" (Beckwith 1847). Two years before, Beckwith had published *The Book of Peace: A Collection of Essays on War and Peace* (1845)—a volume to which he drew attention since he regarded it as "altogether the best thesaurus or encyclopedia of information on Peace that can be found in the English or any other language"(preface). The growth of the organized peace movement in the United States in the first half of the nineteenth century, the vigorous discussions which took place in it, and the need to present a comprehensive and coherent view on the subject (in order to convince outsiders but also, as with Beckwith's *Manual*, to impose some order and discipline within the peace movement itself), had thus resulted in a number of works which were self-consciously encyclopedic in character. They were, however, all written from a rather narrow, Christian point of view and were deliberately propagandistic. The next work that we consider emerged half a century later in Europe and was also propagandistic but in quite another way.

### 3. The Emergence of Scientific Peace Research at the Turn of the Century: De Bloch and Fried

It is appropriate that the first work that may be considered fully encyclopedic is Jean de Bloch's *La Guerre* (which was summarized and translated into English as *The Future of War*).[3] The scope of this study, its methodology, its objective, and the personality of its author all combine in making this book and its author, not only from a historical but equally from a contemporary point of view, highly important. The scope of the study is truly vast and can be gauged from its physical characteristics: it consists of six sturdy volumes, amounting to some 4,000 pages. Its methodological starting point was an empirical investigation of the nature of modern weapons and modern warfare; this modern approach, which involved many tests and experiments is already visible at first glance in the numerous statistical and other tables, folding-out in the peace movement which traditionally had been based largely on religious and ethical precepts in order to bring about a change in attitude and had stressed the un-Christian nature of warfare. At a time when quantitative methods and techniques were still a rarity in any of the social sciences it was all the more surprising to see them adopted, in such detail and so extensively, in antiwar propaganda. To the extent that one of the characteristics of modern peace research is its emphasis on the need to be scientific *La Guerre* must be regarded as an early and impressive example of peace research *avant la letter*.

   De Bloch's ingenious and laborious effort was meant to serve one purpose (not so much at the outset, it must be said, as when the work unfolded and the results of a future great war became increasingly obvious to him): to demonstrate that war between the Great Powers had become "impossible"—that is, senseless, futile, irrational, or, to use the title of Norman Angell's famous book of 1910, *The Great Illusion* (see Nobel Peace Prize Laureates: *Norman Angell*). The author believed that this illusion had been sufficiently demonstrated in his study and if this was made widely known (especially in political and military circles where decisions about war and peace were taken), the recourse to war as a rational instrument of policy or as "the continuation of diplomacy by other means" (Clausewitz) would finally be renounced. De Bloch became one of the leaders of the peace movement during the closing year of the twentieth (he died early in 1902). In this brief period his other peace endeavors rivaled his unique research: his efforts to educate and enlighten both policy makers and the general public on the nature of future warfare turned him into an untiring peace educator. He was an important influence behind the decision of the Russian Czar to call a peace conference at the Hague in 1899, and he conceived of, and paid for, a remarkable institution, the International Museum of War and Peace in Lucerne (see *Peace Museums*). De

Bloch appears to us today as a tireless and ingenious peace activist as well as a scientific peace researcher.[4] The means of destruction which the last world war brought in its wake have made his thesis about the "impossibility" of war between the Superpowers and his prophecy about the suicidal nature of modern warfare even more realistic than they were in their own day. If de Bloch was unsuccessful, it certainly was not for want of effort; the present generation cannot afford to fail.

There was no greater admirer of de Bloch and no greater propagandist of his ideas than the Austrian journalist and peace activist Alfred H. Fried (apart from the English journalist and social reformer W.T. Stead who was responsible for the publication of a one-volume summary edition of de Bloch's book in English). Like Stead, he introduced de Bloch to the West and Central European public through interviews with him and the popularization of de Bloch's thesis. In order to enhance the usefulness of de Bloch's great work Fried also constructed a subject index of it which was first published in 1905. In addition, Fried's own desire to make pacifism scientific and to argue against war on the basis of rational rather than religious foundations, made him all the more eager to promote de Bloch's kindred ideas. But it is as the author of an important encyclopedic work that Fried is included here (see Nobel Peace Prize Laureates: *Alfred Fried*).

His *Handbuch der Friedensbewegung* (Manual of the Peace Movement), first published in 1905 (Vienna and Leipzig, p. 464) was based on a series of six lectures which he had given for the Academic Peace Society of Vienna at the start of 1904 and formed an "Introduction to the Peace Movement." Bertha von Suttner (see Nobel Peace Prize Laureates: *Bertha von Suttner*) encouraged Fried to publish these lectures and, in the preparation for publication, Fried expanded the material so considerably that the end product was something quite different. In the foreword he wrote: "The need for a manual which deals with the entire peace movement has been felt for a long time by those active in peace propaganda. Rich as the literature on peace may be, up to now it has lacked—and not only in the German language—a work which presents the main ideas, the aims, the successes, the present nature and the historical development of the peace idea and the peace movement, in such a volume would also be a useful reference work for members of the movement." Fried did not flatter himself that he had fully achieved this goal and expected his friends to help him to improve a future edition. This was an exciting time for the movement which had recently witnessed the calling of the (first) Hague Peace Conference and was now seeing the preparations for a follow-up meeting. Fried felt that changes were occurring so quickly that the book was becoming outdated as he wrote it. This was the best proof that the peace movement was not merely a transitory phenomenon, nor utopia, but a development that was intimately related to the requirements of the new age whose growth was steady and irreversible. The *Handbuch* was intended to reinforce this historic process and convince skeptics that the cause of peace was the cause of the future.

Whereas the authors of the two previously considered peace manuals based their argument for peace wholly on their Christian beliefs, Fried "deliberately, and certainly against his better instinct, eschewed all moral opposition to war, and denounced all Christian or Tolstoyan criticism of war as 'utopian'."[5] In an article written in 1910 on the occasion of the death of Tolstoy, Fried criticized the latter's belief that "through the practical application of the teachings of Christianity the unfriendly relations between states could be overcome." Against such "romantic pacifism" Fried argued that it was only when "pacifism undertook to demonstrate peace as material interest, that it was able to win the hearts of the masses and the minds of political leaders." He concluded that Tolstoy (see *Tolstoy, Leo*) failed like others before him because he "believed too much in the power of morality." To a large extent Fried was able to substitute materialism for morality as the driving force that would bring about peace because of the large-scale industrialization and the accompanying process of internationalization (in the economic, technical-scientific, as well as other fields) which had characterized the latter decades of the nineteenth century. These were developments which had been only dimly perceived by the leaders of the American peace movement during the first half of that century.[6]

The second edition of the *Handbuch* which was published within a decade, was twice the length of the original one, necessitating its publication in two separate volumes. This new edition was not merely an expanded version but in many ways a completely new book. Of the works considered in this review, Fried's *Handbuch* perhaps comes nearest to being a true encyclopedia of peace. We have already quoted his own views on the kind of work he had in mind; they indicate that the various elements which make a work encyclopedic would be included in it. One of the most interesting and valuable features of the *Handbuch* is its last part, "The peace movement and its organs," which comprises 200 pages. It consists of three sections: an annotated list of international and peace organizations (divided into official and nonofficial bodies), a section entitled "'Who is Who?' of the Peace Movement" which comprises over 300 concise biographies, and a guide through the literature on peace (divided into a section on periodicals and one on books and pamphlets). A detailed subject index and an index of names (together amounting to 30 pages) make the vast quantity of data contained in the 750-odd pages of the book readily accessible. The reader cannot help but be impressed by the thoroughness with which each of these sections has been composed and this part of the Handbuch is even today a unique and most useful overview of the peace movement of the pre-First World War period.

## 4. The Bibliography of Peace (1904-16): Monaco, Oslo, The Hague

The optimism that Fried and other peace advocates displayed during the period preceding the First World War was encouraged by the support, both moral and material, they received from some of the leading industrialists of the age who were also great philanthropists: Jean de Bloch, Alfred Nobel, and Andrew Carnegie devoted considerable parts of their enormous fortunes to the cause of peace. For the first time material resources were made available for the establishment of permanent institutes of peace which enhanced the professionalism of the movement and the regard in which it was held by society. Some of the most important reference works on peace have been undertaken by, or have been associated with, the Nobel Institute in Oslo (founded in 1904) and the Peace Palace in the Hague (opened in 1913, and made possible through the gifts of Carnegie). Peace advocates were also proud to count among their number members of royalty: first and foremost Prince Albert of Monaco whose interest in the peace question had been stimulated by leading French pacifists such as Charles Richet and especially Gaston Moch. This resulted in the establishment in Monaco of the International Institute of Peace in 1903 in order to document the trend towards peace and internationalism. The first few volumes of Fried's *Annuaire de la vie international* were published under the auspices of the Institute. Of greater interest for our purpose, however, was publication by it of Henri La Fontaine's *Bibliographie de la paix et de l'arbitrage international* (1904) which is now regarded as "the first major bibliography on peace and the peace movement" (Carroll et al. 1983 p. 230). This volume dealt only with the peace movement as it was the first volume of a projected, much larger work. La Fontaine identified over 2,000 items—a considerable improvement on his earlier *Essai de bibliographie de la paix* (1891) which listed nearly 500 items. In the second edition of his *Handbuch*, Fried noted that La Fontaine's *Bibliographie* was only the first part of a grandly conceived work "whose continuation we have been awaiting a very long time already" (p. 434). No more volumes were to appear however, and the Institute itself, which was moved to Paris in 1912, apparently did not survive the war.

The first volume of the *Catalogue of the Library of the Norwegian Nobel Institute*, entitled "Pacifist Literature," and published in 1912, is very similar to La Fontaine's bibliography, except that it is larger by 500 titles and moreover it is (as the title implies) a description of the contents of a single, highly important, collection. The Institute is the scientific organ of the Nobel committee of the Norwegian parliament and was set up by the Committee in 1904 to assist it in its task of awarding the Peace Prize. It is interesting to note that the library, which is now an integral part of the Institute, was already in existence in 1902, having been suggested by Christian L. Lange (the first secretary of the Committee and from its foundation until 1909 also the first director of the Institute). In introducing the catalogue, Lange's successor, R. Moe, wrote: "Since the collection of the Norwegian Nobel Institute is undoubtedly the most complete in the world, and no book of any importance is missing from it, it was felt appropriate to subtitle the catalogue 'Bibliography of the

Peace Movement.'"

Both the La Fontaine and the Nobel Institute bibliographies are unsurpassed and are still the prime guides to the historical literature on peace. They need to be supplemented, however, by the bibliographical publications issued for many years by the Peace Palace at the Hague. Ironically, the latter had been inaugurated in the year preceding the outbreak of the First World War, and the development of the library in the first few years was obviously hindered by the war. It is all the more surprising, therefore, that the first catalogue of the library of the Peace Palace was published as early as 1916. This, as well as the first supplement which followed in 1922, was largely the work of Philipp C. Molhuysen, the deputy librarian. Both the catalogue and the supplement were massive volumes, each comprising about 10,000 items. Throughout the 1930s, and again in the 1950s and 1960s, various supplements and indexes were published, the whole comprising a most impressive and useful guide to the literature on peace and, particularly and increasingly, international law. Much of this work was undertaken by Jacob ter Meulen, the librarian of the Peace Palace from 1924 until 1952 whose term of office was characterized by a great expansion of the library. He acquired large quantities of ephemeral publications on pacifism and antimilitarism and this stimulated the compilation of the *Bibliography of the Peace Movement Before 1899*. The first part, covering the period 1776-1899, was published in 1934; the second part, for the period 1490-1776, in 1936. The first list is estimated to contain some 3,500 items, the second one almost 500 (Carroll et al. 1983 pp. 238-40). These lists are unique not only because of their exhaustive nature (and, as regards the second list, the antiquity of the period considered) but also because of the chronological arrangement of the items contained in them. The above works, together with his definitive bibliography of Grotius, make ter Meulen the undisputed bibliographer of peace. He was also instrumental in making the Peace Palace library the world's foremost collection of historical peace literature (it presently contains 600,000 volumes, five times more than the Nobel Institute library). Impressive as the achievements of ter Meulen and Lange are, their bibliographical work covers only one aspect of our subject. Both ter Meulen and Lange deserve our further attention because they are among the few authors of encyclopedic works on peace and internationalism.

## 5. The Development of Internationalist Thought: Ter Meulen, Lange-Schou, Ruyssen

Jacob ter Meulen's great work, *Der Gedanke der Internationalen Organization in seiner Entwicklung* (The Development of the Idea of International Organization), is the first of a remarkable trio of studies which show striking similarities in their overall approach and in the scale on which they have been conceived, each study consisting of three volumes. Ter Meulen studied at the University of Zurich under Max Huber who had made a strong impression on him at the second Hague Peace Conference (1907). In January 1914 ter Meulen obtained his doctorate in law with a thesis entitled *Beitrag zur Geschichte der Internationalen Organization 1300-1700* (Contribution to the History of International Organization), whose publication was delayed until 1916 because of the War. The following year saw the publication of the first volume of *Der Gedanke* in which the period covered to a description and analysis of 29 detailed projects, chronologically arranged, starting with that of Pierre Dubois (1306) and ending with that of Immanuel Kant (1795)—20 of these plans having been formulated in the eighteenth century. This central part is preceded by a historical introduction of 100 pages which reviews the development of the international idea, and is followed by a comparison of the various schemes.

The second volume, published in 1929, covers the French Revolution, the Congress of Vienna, the period of the Restoration until 1848, and the period from 1848 to 1870. The author briefly discusses the peace policy of the French Revolution and reviews individual French, German, Swiss, and other projects of the period. In the main part he details the several peace projects that emerged within the growing Anglo-American peace societies and those associated with the French utopian socialists. The series of European peace congresses in the middle of the century and a number of individual peace societies and those associated with the French utopian socialists. The third volume, published in 1940, traces the development of the peace idea up to 1889, that is, a century after the French Revolution. The projects discussed here are becoming increasingly legalistic, which is a reflection of the growth of international law societies and of international arbitration movements. Ter Meulen concludes the volume with a substantial overview of the projects discussed in the entire work.

Ter Meulen's massive enterprise was highly regarded by the community of students of international law and organization. In the immediate aftermath of the First World War, one reviewer wrote about the first volume: "The immemorial desire for permanent international peace, quickened by the unprecedented and incalculable cost of the recent war, has not only produced many plans for the better organization of the world, but has also stimulated the study of earlier efforts to solve the same problem. The most complete and, in many respects, the best review of these efforts is that given us by... ter Meulen."[7] Commenting on the same volume, the reviewer of the *Times Literary Supplement* found it "a most valuable treasure-house of material" and found "the very wide knowledge which it shows and the clearness and precision with which it is written" all the more remarkable in view of the author's youth. The reviewer was critical, however, of the author's failure to discuss the importance of the subject matter itself: "These projects spring not from those who are actually concerned in the conduct of affairs, but from the students, the thinkers, the preachers, the prophets, the philosophers." And this observation invited another one: "It is because these plans spring not from the actors but the onlookers that they have been so ineffective."[8] The writer of the first-mentioned review also commented upon the authorship of the peace plans but in a directly opposite manner: "It is interesting to note that the majority of the authors were not primarily philosophers, scholars or literary men, but men of affairs" and he went on to indicate that the list contained "a king, a pope, several other statesmen, half a dozen jurists and two or three military men."

The question of the practical relevance of these theoretical programs for international government was also raised by Pitman Potter of the University of Wisconsin. He was, however, full of praise for the first two volumes which "constitute a truly monumental if not a definitive history of the idea of international organization from the Renaissance to recent times." "The vigorous and comprehensive scholarship of Dr. ter Meulen," he continued, "has provided us with a work which is at the same time encyclopedic as to facts—in spite of the author's modest disclaimer—and very suggestive in analysis."[9] It is likely that ter Meulen did not need to be urged by commentators before he addressed himself to the question of the significance of his enterprise. He considered the value of studying hundreds of peace plans explicitly in the epilogue to his final volume: "The answer may be that the value of such an overview finally is to be found in the plans themselves, not in the value of each one separately but all of them together. Together they form a power whose influence so far has been small, a power which temporarily can be forced back, possibly can appear in new forms, but can never completely disappear. For it is a fact that the human consciousness contains not only a sense of the real but also of the ideal. Both elements are necessary for the organization of human society. They are also vital for the future shaping of the relations between peoples" (ter Meulen 1940 p. 353). It was tragic that the first and third volumes of his great study were published during the most catastrophic wars of the century; however, the wars may have strengthened his conviction that this task, to which he devoted 30 years of his life, was really necessary. Hans Wehberg, the editor of *Die Friedens-Warte*, elaborated this theme in a highly appreciative review which in its length and thoroughness did full justice to ter Meulen's *magnum opus*.[10]

The second work in the trio that we are considering took even longer than ter Meulen's and was not completed until half a century after its initiation. Christian L. Lange published the first volume of his *Histoire de l'internationalisme* in 1919 but he died in 1938 when he had finished only part of the second volume. Lange was not only a scholar and administrator (like ter Meulen) but also a diplomat, and his duties as secretary general of the Interparliamentary Union (until 1933) and especially as a member of the Norwegian delegation to the League of Nations (from 1920 until his death) so burdened him that he could return only occasionally to his research and writing (see Nobel Peace Prize Laureates: *Christian Lange*). After the Second World War, the Lange family requested August Schou to undertake the task of finishing the volume that Lange had started by working from the latter's notes and adding the fruits of his own study. Lange had conceived of the work and had initiated it, writing the first volume and part of the second; Schou continued and completed it by writing most of the second and all of the third volume. These circumstances explain the long delays involved in the publication of this work, particularly its second installment. These delays must have been especially disappointing to A. W. Ward who apologetically wrote in his review of the first—"this deeply interesting"—volume, two years after it had appeared: "Our delay in noticing this important work has in so far not been unfortunate, that we may now look forward to its speedy completion, and have it before us as a whole."[11] Likewise, William I. Hull concluded his review of "this, the standard, History of Internationalism" by looking forward to the unfolding of the story that Lange had traced so masterly "in the author's much-anticipated Volume II."[12]

Lange had conceived his work on an even grander scale than ter Meulen had, since his first volume covered the period from classical antiquity to the Peace of Westphalia. The volume opens with a discussion of Hellenic federation and arbitration, and the international and humanitarian ideas of a number of thinkers of the Graeco-Roman world. This is followed by an analysis of the internationalist ideas of primitive Christianity, the Christian Church and the medieval sects. Advocates of internationalism or universality of the Holy Roman Empire, of the Renaissance, and of the Protestant sects of the seventeenth century are considered next. The latter part of the volume traces the emergence and development of international law and discusses the ideas of a small number of important thinkers of the end of the period considered. This first volume thus details the beginnings of a long chain of ideas reaching from antiquity to the present and attempts to demonstrate the continuity of the idea at issue by establishing the various links in this chain. The second volume identifies and discusses the ideas of some 300 writers—philosophers, publicists, political, religious, and literary figures—from Hobbes to Kant, from the Age of Absolutism to the Age of Revolutions. Moreover, in the works of one reviewer: "Scattered through the chapter sections which expose the ideas of this galaxy of writers are summaries of the political aspects of society which together constitute as perspicacious an analysis of the evolution of political thought of the period as can be found."[13] The final volume encompasses the shortest period (the century preceding the First World War) and is the most lengthy one. This period saw the emergence of the organized peace movements as well as the establishment of international organizations in most areas of social life—economic, technical and scientific, humanitarian. Rapid progress was also made in the codification of international law and the use of arbitration procedures, and the first great peace conferences took place at the turn of the twentieth century. The entire study forms a comprehensive and most impressive treatment of the history of internationalist ideas.

In his chapter on the organized peace movement after 1871, Schou devoted a few pages to the ideas and activities of Théodore Ruyssen, who came to prominence in France as the moving force of *La Paix par le droit* (Lange-Schou 1963 pp. 352-54). This peace society had been set up by a group of university students from Nantes in 1887 and 10 years later Ruyssen became its president and its foremost publicist. He is the author of the third work we are considering in this section. His achievement is perhaps the most amazing of all: within the span of only seven years (1954-61) his three-volume work on the doctrinal sources of internationalism was published. As we have seen, 44 years separated the first and third volumes of the Lange-Schou study, and 23 years those of ter Meulen. The extraordinary nature of Ruyssen's achievement and career are even better demonstrated by the fact that he was born a year before Lange in 1868.[14] Ruyssen saw the publication of the first volume of his *magnum opus* in his 88th year, and its completion when he was 95! More than 50 years before Ruyssen's death, Fried had already devoted half a page to him in his "'Who is Who?' of the Peace Movement" (Fried 1913 pp. 403-04).

It is interesting to note that 1954 saw the publication of both the first installment of Ruyssen's work and the second installment of that of Lange-Schou. Until the latter's publication the Frenchman was unaware that the study started by Lange was being continued by Schou and it may well be that in his old age he boldly conceived the idea of reexamining and successfully concluding Lange's project. In the opening pages of his first volume Ruyssen informs the reader that he is honored to have been a friend of Lange and that the present work owes much to him. He also writes that Lange's study has unfortunately been left unfinished and that his "monumental" book, more than three decades later, appears in certain respects incomplete and dated (Ruyssen 1954 pp. 7-8). Ruyssen's work closely resembles that of Lange-Schou in its conception and execution. Whereas ter Meulen had confined himself largely to a history of plans for world peace, both Ruyssen and Lange-Schou charted the development of internationalist thought in which such plans were only a part. Unlike Schou, Ruyssen decided to finish his history by the middle of the nineteenth century because his concern was confined to the origins and the precursors of internationalism. As he explains: "In this age [nineteenth century], which is palpably that of the first private international congresses and the first public international institutions, the interdependent nature of the life of all peoples of the world has indeed become a reality of such conspicuousness and such magnitude that henceforth it imposes itself on all" (p. 6).

The most ancient sources of Ruyssen's history are formed by the Bible, Graeco-Roman civilization, and early Christianity. Like Lange, he does not extend his enquiry beyond the frontiers of Western thought since "the matrix of modern internationalism is clearly the civilization of the West" (p. 15). Although half of humanity belongs to the civilizations of China, India, and Islam, only Western civilization with its expansionism and future-oriented approach has assumed the role if not of fusion, at least of liaison and coordination of these diverse cultures. Even from a purely religious point of view the global predominance of Christianity and its role in shaping a world civilization cannot be disputed. Ruyssen uses these and other arguments in a stimulating introduction to justify his conviction that the precursors of internationalism will not be found outside Western culture (pp. 17-18). He discusses more "internationalists" from a wider background than Lange-Schou. Apart from being the most encyclopedic of the trio of works on the history of internationalism, Ruyssen's study also provides the most detailed documentation of the sources used. Whereas the volumes by ter Meulen and Lange-Schou contain extensive bibliographies (in ter Meulen's work regrettably only in the first volume), bibliographical sections of varying lengths conveniently accompany each chapter or paragraph in Ruyssen's work. The comments of S. Mack Eastman on the second volume of Ruyssen which he found "almost a *magnum opus* in itself" may be applied to the work in its entirety: "an excellent reference book. Such an erudite, well organized and interestingly written volume should be made available to all serious students of the history of international doctrines and relations."[15]

## 6. Surveys of Peace in English (1919-44)

The comment by Eastman just quoted may be applied in turn to the other two works discussed in the previous section and presupposes a knowledge of French or German on the part of the serious student. It is not surprising that these voluminous studies have not been translated into English; ter Meulen, moreover, wrote in a language which was not his own, and Schou had his Norwegian manuscript translated. What is remarkable is the absence of a study in English even remotely approaching their scope and comprehensiveness. Among books available in English on the subject is Elizabeth York's *Leagues of Nations: Ancient, Mediaeval, and Modern*, published in 1919. This opens with a chapter on the ancient Greek leagues and continues with a discussion of the ideas for a "league" of only nine individuals, from Dante to Alexander I, in as many chapters. This study limited itself to peace plans and the author found ter Meulen's work (only the first volume of which had appeared) "very useful" (York 1919 p. VI). The next book in English that we wish to consider was published 10 years later and closely resembles in its aim and title the works by Lange-Schou and Ruyssen. F. Median Stawell traces *The Growth of International Thought* in the Hellenic and Hebraic cultures, in the Roman Empire and early Christianity, in the Middle Ages, the Renaissance, and the Reformation. The only work she annotated in the short bibliography is Lange's (first) volume, "an invaluable book for the student" (Stawell 1929 p. 247). The most "encyclopedic" work in English to appear in the interbellum was, however, A.C.F. Beales's *The History of Peace: A Short Account of the Organized Movements for International Peace.* The book is a fairly detailed history of the first century of the peace movement from 1815 to 1914. The author was well-aware of the originality of the task he had set himself and of the significance of his study. He wrote in the preface of his book: "The history of Peace has at present only four prominent historians at work on it: Dr. Chr. L. Lange at Geneva, Dr. M. E. Curti in the United States, Dr. Jacob ter Meulen at the Hague, and Professor Paul Koht in Norway. The only 'History of the Peace Movement' already in existence, Alfred H. Fried's *Handbuch der Frieden sbewegung*, has not been translated, nor re-issued since its second edition in 1911. Apart from this monumental manual there is no work except the present which surveys the whole ground" (Beales 1931 p. VI). By taking a subject wider than the history of plans for peace (ter Meulen) but more specific than the history of internationalist ideas (Lange-Schou), Beales's history of the organized peace movement is a most useful complement to these works. Ruyssen wrote: "Concerning the history of pacifism, the best account is *The History of Peace*, written by an erudite Englishman" (Ruyssen 1961 p. 541, note 2). Here we must bear in mind that in English "pacifism" denotes a narrow aspect of peace whereas in French it refers to the advocacy of peace generally. As we shall see in the next section, the best history of pacifism in the "English" sense has in recent years been written by another erudite writer in the English language, Peter Brock. Since he has not covered exactly the same ground Beales's book retains its value.

Lastly, we mention three surveys of peace plans which were published within a few years of each other in England and in the United States and which are still useful because of their comprehensiveness and analysis. They are Sir John A. Marriott's *Commonwealth or Anarchy? A Survey of Projects of Peace from the Sixteenth to the Twentieth Century* (1937); Sylvester John Hemleben's *Plans for World Peace Through Six Centuries* (1943) and Edith Wynner and Georgia Lloyd's *Searchlight on Peace Plans* (1944). Hemleben's work is based on a thorough study of the literature as is evidenced by the copious references and an extensive bibliography. A recent reviewer rightly points out that his lucid summary of the chief plans makes his book an excellent introduction which, moreover, provides valuable bibliography aids for further study.[16] Like Hemleben's, Wynner and Lloyd's survey of peace plans of the past was meant to enlighten public opinion in its search for a workable plan which would make further wars impossible. The authors assembled some 200 specific proposals to unite nations dating from 1306 to 1944 claiming that theirs is "the most complete collection of specific peace plans ever assembled." The plans include not only theoretical ones but also practical attempts at international organization. "In the brief descriptions of the old plans (before 1914),"they write, "we present a great many that are not mentioned in any English compilation we have examined," and they record their indebtedness to ter Meulen (Wynner and Lloyd 1946 p.8). However, they included only those plans that contained adequate structural details of world organization, especially with regard to membership, representation, and methods of enforcement. The authors hoped that by extracting specific details from a multitude of plans and by analyzing and comparing the details, a fuller understanding would result of the advantages and disadvantages of the various plans proposed. In this way they aimed to clarify the issues facing those involved in the forthcoming peace settlement. Finally, to bring this survey up to date, it may be mentioned that the best discussion available in English on the theory and practice in the history of relations between states is F.H. Hinsley's *Power and the Pursuit of Peace* (1963).

## 7. Direct, Nonviolent Action and Pacifism: De Ligt, Brock, Sharp

The interest in plans for international organization (both historical and contemporary) in the interwar period was only one expression of the search for peace. This period also witnessed an upsurge of interest in the role of the individual in war prevention. Radical antimilitarism, expressing itself in direct action against war and preparation for war, was regarded by the "bourgeois" pacifists and internationalists who failed to trace the roots of warfare back to social institutions such as the state, the church, and the capitalist economy. The No More War Movement, which grew out of the demand for the recognition of conscientious objection during the First World War, and the War Resisters' International, both founded in the early 1920s and initially centered in England and Holland, were among the main organizations in the field. "One of the outstanding intellectual leaders of the pacifist movement between the two wars,"[17] who was intimately involved with these movement, as a thinker, writer, and organizer, was Bart de Ligt. He was not only a prolific and gifted publicist but also a great scholar. His *Vrede als Daad* (Peace as Deed), published in two volumes in 1931 and 1933, is an encyclopedic study of the theory and practice of direct action against war from the eighth century BC to the present. De Ligt first traces the emergence of the idea of direct action on behalf of peace in the ancient civilizations of China, India, and the Arab world as well as in the Judaeo-Christian and Graeco-Roman cultures. This is followed by an exhaustive account of the principles and practice of religiously inspired direct action and direct action inspired by "sociological" and humanist motivations. He noted in his preface that the rich, varied, and universal experience of this phenomenon has largely been forgotten—even by those in the peace movement who today work in the same tradition—and ignored or suppressed by officialdom because of its subversive quality. De Ligt sees his work as a first attempt to set the record straight: his aim is to pay homage to (and bring back into our consciousness) numerous individuals who have been neglected or maligned. Adopting a revolutionary antimilitary vantage point necessitates a principled rewriting of various aspects of the history of religion, of philosophy, as well as of socialism. He avers that the main objective of such an enterprise is to arouse (by means of a revision of the bourgeois notion of history and of revolutionary tactics) in all progressive thinkers a deeper sense of responsibility and to instill a stronger desire for direct action—not merely *against* war but also *for* peace and freedom (de Ligt 1931 p. 8).

An expanded version of the first part of de Ligt's book was published in French in 1934 in two volumes under the title *La Paix créatrice: Histoire des principes et des tactiques de l'action directe contre la guerre*. Two more volumes were planned but de Ligt died before they could be completed. The publisher announced *La Paix créatrice* in a separate prospectus which did full justice to its importance: the 16-page prospectus devoted 10 pages to a detailed table of contents and several more to highly favorable reviews and press comments which had greeted the book's original publication. The publisher asserted that "this encyclopedic work" was highly regarded not only in revolutionary antimilitary and radical pacifist circles but also in the scientific-scholarly world and that it would be the foundation of the new science of peace.[18] In a rare review in English, Oscar Jászi wrote: "The moral force doctrine, the direct action, individual and collective, against war, has never been treated so comprehensively as in this book."[19] In his *Encyclopedia of Pacifism* Aldus Huxley provided one of the few other references in English, calling it "the most complete history of Pacifist ideas and practice"(Huxley 1937 p. 18). Later in the same year he wrote in his introduction to de Ligt's *The Conquest of Violence*: "Bart de Ligt is the author of two books which are among the most important contributions to the literature of pacifism. The first is a comprehensive history of pacifist thought and action from the earliest times to the present day. This work has appeared in its entirety in Dutch, and a new and enlarged edition in French is in process of publication. Two volumes have already appeared under the title, *La Paix créatrice*, and two more are to be issued in the near future. *La Paix créatrice*, and two more are to be issued in the near future. *La Paix créatrice* is a work of wide and profound learning, indispensable to those who would study the history of peace and of 'the things that make for peace.' It is much to be hoped that, in due course, it will find an English translator and publisher."[20] Barely a year after these words were written, de Ligt died during one of his many journeys, having physically exhausted himself in the antimilitarist campaign. While discussing *The Conquest of Violence*, the only one of de Ligt's books that was published in English, Nicholas Walter observed: "Bart de Ligt also wrote a much longer book called *Creative Peace*, which for some reason has never been translated into English."[21] De Ligt's demise is the single most important factor which helps to explain this circumstance. He had, in fact, brought *La Paix créatrice* to the attention of his English publishers in his first letter to them.[22]

De Ligt's *magnum opus* brings us to today's leading historian of pacifism. In his *Pacifism in Europe to 1914*, Peter Brock starts the "Bibliographical Notes" (a section of 40 pages of small print which is as impressive and overwhelming as the volume to which it is appended) as follows: "No general history of pacifism has hitherto been published. The nearest to such a study comes from the pen of the Dutch anarchist Bart de Ligt: *Vrede als Daad* . . . De Ligt's work represents a truly pioneering venture; I am happy to acknowledge the inspiration which the French edition gave me, when I read it thirty years ago, to study the subject further." Brock continues in a more critical vein: "The author concentrates mainly, as his title indicates, on tracing the antecedents of the idea of 'direct action against war.' Unfortunately, in places the narrative is marred by a tendency toward erratic historical interpretation and a rather doctrinaire approach" (Brock 1972 p. 505).[23] Brock's own study is in its scope and detail superior to de Ligt's and the three volumes which comprise his "A history of pacifism" should be regarded as the definitive work on the subject. This subject, however, is fairly specific and Brock delineates its scope when he writes: "I have not attempted to write a general history of the peace movement in the sense of all efforts aimed at achieving international peace and organization: this is a noble theme but one which far transcends the more modest limits of my study. Nor have I tried to give an historical analysis of the theory and practice of nonviolence though its development is closely related to the history of pacifism. Again, the history of conscientious objection to war figures prominently in the pages of all three volumes, yet that topic by no means exhausts their contents. My main concern has been to explore the ideas and activities of individuals and of groups of people who . . . have rejected participation in all forms of war" (pp. IX-X)

The pacifism that Brock is interested in is further specified in the opening paragraphs of the Introduction where he writes: "although at times a longing for international peace and human brotherhood appeared in the thought patterns of some early civilizations . . . pacifism in the strict sense of an unconditional renunciation of war by the individual is, so far as we can tell, a little less than two thousand years old. The first clearcut renunciation of this kind appears among the early Christians" and he goes on to quote Henry J. Cadbury who wrote that pacifism and antimilitarism are "historically speaking, original with Christianity" (p. 3). The introductory chapter "Antimilitaryism in the early Christian church" is followed by a dozen chapters, each of which deals with a Christian pacifist sect, starting with the Czech Brethren and ending with the Tolstoyans. This period of almost five centuries also saw the emergence of the Anabaptist, the Polish Antitrinitarians, the Dutch and German Mennonites, and the British Quakers (to whom three chapters are devoted). From the way that de Ligt and Brock have defined their subjects and approached their tasks, it will be clear that they are addressing themselves only partly to the same question, and that their works overlap to a limited extent.

Brock's second volume, *Pacifism in the United States: From the Colonial Era to the First World War*, published in 1968, is even more lengthy and detailed than the book mentioned above.[24] Again, we may use the author's opening words to gauge its scope and purpose: "The history of pacifism in British colonial America and in the American Republic to the outbreak of war in Europe in 1914 has not been conceived as a general history of the American peace movement during this period. Its aim is narrower: to tell the story of the religious groups whose members refused military service on the basis of their objection to war, and of that section of the organized peace movement which from its beginnings in 1815 repudiated all war" (Brock 1968 p. VII). Brock divides his story according to the great events in American history: part one deals with pacifism in colonial America and in the American peace movement from its origins in 1815 to the Civil War; part four analyzes pacifism in the American Civil War—although a short period, 200 pages are devoted to it; the final part brings the story up to the outbreak of the First World War. The history of pacifism since then is covered in the author's third book, *Twentieth Century Pacifism*. The focus is, again, on "advocacy of personal nonparticipation in war of any kind or in violent revolution with an endeavor to find nonviolent means of resolving conflict." Brock draws attention to the different interpretations of "pacifism" in the West which we have discussed already: "On the European continent, 'pacifism' includes all efforts to achieve international peace and understanding. In Anglo-American usage, the term is normally limited to the definition given above; the adjective 'absolute' or 'integral' might well be used for the type of pacifism with which I am mainly concerned in this book" (Brock 1970 p. V). Conscientious objection in both world wars, Gandhian philosophy, pacifism in the interwar period, and nonviolent protest in the nuclear era are the main subjects covered in a slim volume which is far less definitive when compared with the two previous volumes. As the author writes elsewhere, "I have depicted the twentieth century with a more sweeping brush than earlier centuries and have painted the American scene with greater intensity than the European" (Brock 1972 p. IX), and *"Twentieth century Pacifism* deals largely, though by no means exclusively, with Great Britain and the United States" (p. 536). It is perhaps too early to expect a history of twentieth century pacifism conceived on the same grand scale as the author's other works.

A word must be said about the bibliographical references in these works because they are so numerous and derive from so many different sources that, by themselves, they constitute an impressive contribution to scholarship in the area of peace and pacifism. This is especially true for the 40-page bibliographical essay which replaces footnotes and references in *Pacifism in Europe*. While others may have been awaiting an English translation of de Ligt's *La Paix créatrice*, Brock has mastered not only French, German, and Dutch, but also Czech, Polish, and Russian as his many references to the relevant literature in these languages make clear. Indeed, a command of these languages may be regarded as a prerequisite for undertaking a scholarly history of European pacifism, and therefore it is unlikely that his superb achievement will be equalled. *Pacifism in the United States* is extensively annotated, and the 35-page bibliography is certainly, as the author hopes, "generally useful as a guide to the printed sources for the history of American pacifism before 1914"(p. VII). One well-known historian of Quakerism and pacifism wrote that with this bibliography Brock "has gone a long way toward preparing a definitive reference for future scholars."[25]

In conclusion, we return to an issue which was mentioned at the beginning of this brief discussion of Peter Brock's encyclopedic work, namely its origins and inspiration. The author was inspired to undertake a history of pacifist thought and practice after reading Bart de Ligt's work (see above) during the Second World War, when Brock was a conscientious objector in Great Britain. Shortly after the War, from 1946 to 1948, he worked with the Anglo-American Quaker Relief Mission in Poland. Practical peace witness and work was followed by research on "The political and social doctrines of the unity of Czech Brethren in the fifteenth and early sixteenth centuries." One of the figures Brock deals with in this study, published in 1957, is Peter Chelčický who, he says, "should . . . rank as the first European pacifist of note" (Brock 1972 p. 509). We may assume that the scholarly foundation was thus laid for Brock's later work on pacifism. Apart from his own personal convictions (as well as scholarly interests), another factor stimulated him in his enterprise. In the conclusion to *Pacifism in Europe* we read: "The problem of war and violence . . . has been more pressing today than ever before, and consideration of the various ways proposed for achieving lasting harmony between men, pacifism included, will continue to occupy the attention of concerned persons. The present volume, together with its two sequels on the United States before 1914 and on the twentieth century, will be able to make, I hope, a modest contribution to this quest"(p. 487).

The year following the completion of Brock's "History of pacifism" saw the appearance of another important work in three volumes: Gene Sharp's *The Politics of Nonviolent Action* which was the culmination of a study begun, like Brock's, over two decades before. Its author was similarly a conscientious objector (this time in the United States) which led in 1953 to his imprisonment.[26] "This study was begun," Sharp writes, "out of a view that alternatives to violence in meeting tyranny, aggression, injustice and oppression are needed. At the same time it appeared evident that both moral injunctions against violence and exhortations in favor of love and nonviolence have made little or no contribution to ending war and major political violence. It seemed to me that only the adoption of a substitute type of sanction and struggle as a functional alternative to violence in acute conflicts . . . could possibly lead to a major reduction of political violence in a manner compatible with freedom, justice and human dignity" (Sharp 1973 pp. V-VI). Whereas the individuals and groups in Brock's account are on the whole representatives of a "passive" pacifism, those Sharp deals with are advocates and examples of an "active" pacifism. Whereas Brock could be satisfied with tracing the history of pacifism, Sharp uses history in order to identify the methods and to analyze the dynamics of nonviolent action. As a political theorist and sociologist, he uses the historical material primarily "in assisting the inductive construction of the analyses, theories, and hypotheses" concern the nature of the technique of nonviolent action and its potentialities as a substitute for political violence (p. V). Having made this subject his own, the author can justifiably write: "This volume is . . . the most comprehensive attempt thus far to examine the nature of nonviolent struggle as a social and political technique, including its view of power, its specific methods of action, its dynamics in conflict and the conditions for success or failure in its use" (p. V). Sharp has listed here the main components of his study, each being the subject of a separate volume.

Part one, *Power and Struggle*, deals with the nature and control of political power and introduces nonviolent action (NVA) as an active technique of struggle. Sharp inquires into the social roots of power, considers the reasons for obedience and consent, and formulates a theory of nonviolent control of political power. He goes on to specify the characteristics of NVA and to provide illustrations from the past. He writes that NVA is "a neglected type of struggle" and this neglect is shown by "a lack of attention to the history of NVA [although] this technique has been widely used. It has a long history" (p. 72). Sharp notes the distinct contrast in the attention given to war and to NVA: "For the many forms of military struggle an overall conceptual tool has long existed, and this itself may have contributed to the detailed attention which wars have received. Attention to war has included historical and strategic studies which could help in future wars. But, until recently, NVA has had no comparable self-conscious tradition" (p. 73).[27] In the second part the author presents a classification of *The Methods of Nonviolent Action*. He examines in detail 198 specific methods of this technique, broadly classed as nonviolent protest and persuasion, noncooperation (social, economic, and political), and nonviolent intervention. He writes, "This catalog of methods of NVA has no precedent in the literature" (p. 116, note 4). When, in 1960, he published the first version of this listing in which 63 methods were identified it was itself "vastly longer than any previous integrated list" (pp. 433-34 and p. 445, note 300). The enumeration of specific methods of NVA and an exploration of their characteristics are invaluable yet by themselves insufficient for the development of a politics of NVA. Hence, factors such as the dynamics of the technique in struggle, its mechanisms of change, the specific elements which determine whether a given campaign will be a success or a failure, are analyzed in *The Dynamics of Nonviolent Action*, the final part of Sharp's trilogy. He discusses how a challenge to the established order brings repression and how the latter can be fought by solidarity and discipline, and he analyzes three ways in which success may be achieved, namely through the mechanisms of conversion, accommodation, and nonviolent coercion. The nonviolent technique, if successful, will result in the redistribution and decentralization of power, the subject of his final chapter.

It is not surprising to find that Sharp's extraordinary, 900-page work received fulsome praise. Its significance was recognized by both social and political scientists and also military experts. It is, indeed, "a monumental piece of work," "an extraordinary reference work," "an encyclopedic treatment of the theory and practice of nonviolence." Its author was hailed alternately as the Machiavelli of nonviolence" or "the Clausewitz of non-warfare." The reviewer in the *American Journal of Sociology* regarded it as "one of the most important books on social change and nonviolence in this century." Lastly, Herbert Kerman of Harvard University wrote: "It is doubtful that there is anyone—certainly among American scholars—who has given more thorough, systematic and thoughtful attention to the analysis of nonviolent action techniques than Gene Sharp . . . . I would not be surprised if nonviolent action and civilian defense became one of the lasting contributions of this violent century to the political life of the future."[28]

Events such as the civil rights movement under the leadership of Martin Luther King in the 1950s and 1960s (see Nobel Peace Prize Laureates: *Martin Luther King, Jr.*), and opposition to nuclear testing and the Vietnam War stimulated, especially in the United States, an interest in the theory and practice of nonviolent action and also brought about an awareness of its rich tradition (see *Nonviolence: Philosophy and Politics of*). We conclude this section by merely listing the most important anthologies on peace and nonviolence which were published in the United States in the decade before Sharp's work was published. In 1963 appeared Mulford Q. Sibley (ed.), *The Quiet Battle: Writings on the Theory and Practice of Nonviolent Resistance* and Arthur and Lila Weinberg (eds.), *Instead of Violence: Writings by the Great Advocates of Peace and Nonviolence Throughout History*. Two similar volumes were published in 1966: Staughton Lynd (ed.), *Nonviolence in America: A Documentary History* and Peter Mayer (ed.), *The Pacifist Conscience*. Mention must also be made of Robert Cooney and Helen Michalowski (eds.), *The Power of the People: Active Nonviolence in the United States* which is unique in being a visual history of the practice of nonviolence in the United States (as well as having an excellent text and bibliography). Finally, Guy F. Hershberger's *War, Peace, and Nonresistance*, a study which was commissioned by the Peace Problems Committee of the Mennonite Church in United States and was heralded upon its first publication in 1944 as "the standard handbook in the field" (Harold S. Bender, in his foreword), has come to be accepted as a classic, meriting continued publication (see *Civilian-based Defense; Nonviolence*).

## 8. Peace Research—General, Quantitative, and Historical: Wright, Boughoul, Galtung, the Garland Library

If the nineteenth century saw the emergence of an organized peace movement, the twentieth century witnessed the foundation of organized peace research. As we have seen, as early as the turn of the century such figures as de Bloch and Fried were able advocates and exponents of a scientific approach to peace. In the interwar years various isolated initiatives were taken to stimulate further this endeavor. For instance, Bart de Ligt shortly before his death in 1938 established an international Peace Academy for whose opening he wrote *Introduction to the Science of Peace*.[29] Scholars such as Lewis F. Richardson and Pitirim A. Sorokin started major investigations, the first ever, of war as a social phenomenon (see *Richardson, Lewis Fry; Sorokin, Pitirim*). The most significant of these projects was an original, large-scale investigation initiated by Quincy Wright (see *Wright, Quincy*) at the University of Chicago in 1926. In that year its Social Science Research Committee established a subcommittee on the causes of war (under the chairmanship of Wright) and over the next seven years provided funds for 25 research assistants who produced 66 studies, many of which were accepted for Master's or Doctor's degrees in the University of Chicago. "When the mass of manuscripts had been completed, it fell to the present writer," Wright says, "to attempt to digest them, as well as such portions of the vast literature of the field as he could examine, into a logical and useful system."[30] Quincy Wright's *A Study of War*, published in 1942 in two volumes, was the end-product of this investigation, "begun in the hopeful atmosphere of Locarno and completed in the midst of general war" (Wright 1965 p. VIII).

In order to convey the nature and merits of this book we can do no better than quote from the eloquent preface to the second edition (published in one volume in 1965) by Karl W. Deutsche, entitled "Quincy Wright's contribution to the study of war": "In the age of nuclear weapons, if we do not abolish war, war is likely to abolish most of us . . . . War, to be abolished, must be understood. To be understood, it must be studied. No man has worked with more sustained care, compassion, and levelheadedness on the study of war, its causes and its possible prevention, than has Quincy Wright . . . and in his great book . . . he has gathered, together with his collaborators, a larger body of relevant facts, insights, and far-ranging questions about war than any other man has done. . . . *A Study of War* offers an unparalleled collection of relevant data and facts and a unique survey of the important literature. All this information is clearly organized and focussed to one purpose: the understanding and control of war and its eventual prevention. This book offers the reader the best single foundation for the advanced study of international conflict that has appeared so far" (Wright 1965 pp. XII-XIII). Another student of Wright, William T.R. Fox, wrote: "Thought its two volumes did not quite match in size Arnold Toynbee's similarly titled ten-volume *(A) Study of History*, Quincy Wright drew his data from as many different civilizations as did Toynbee and drew on the techniques of a far greater number official science disciplines." He goes on to describe *A Study of War* as "a kind of nonalphabetical encyclopedia on the institution of war."[31]

The encyclopedic nature of Wright's *Study* is reflected at the outset in the analytical table of contents which runs to 16 pages. The 50 illustrations range from "Dates and casualties of battle of classic civilization (500 BC-AD 500)" to "Fluctuations in friendliness among the great powers, 1937-41." Almost half of its 77 tables come under the following three headings: "List of wars of modern civilization, 1480-1941), the duration in days of battles, their seasonal distribution, and so on. The study is essentially in two parts dealing with the history and the analysis of war. All of these tables, and most of the illustrations are to be found in the 44 appendices which are grouped at the end of each of the two main parts. Together these appendices comprise some 400 pages (one quarter of the book), and they not only contain the "raw" data but a considerable amount of analysis as well. Wright's *Study* is meticulously and abundantly annotated: the number of footnotes exceeds 3,000. These notes contain the sole references to the vast literature consulted; one's only regret is the absence of a bibliography which was omitted, no doubt, because it would have amounted to an entire volume by itself.

Deutsche has likened the significance of *A Study of War* to Grotius's *On the Law of War and Peace*, published over three centuries earlier during the Thirty Year's War: "As Grotius's book became a basis for the study of what later became known as 'international law,' so Quincy Wright's book marks the beginning of much that nowadays has become known as 'peace research;'" (Wright 1965 p.XII). Wright was nominated for the 1970 Nobel Peace Prize by a committee of 15 preeminent American scholars, who wrote in their letter to the Nobel Committee: "More than any other living scholar, he may be considered the founder of systematic research for peace. . . . *A Study of War* . . . represents the most serious and sustained research effort undertaken thus far, to bring together the knowledge of social scientists, historians, and students of politics on the causes of war, and on possible ways to abolish war as a social institution."[32] His death in October 1970 unfortunately precluded him from consideration for this honor.[33]

It may be useful to stress that whereas there is general agreement that peace research is beneficial to peace, the relationship between pacifism and peace is highly controversial. Wright found, "Peace propaganda has frequently in times of crisis urged particular groups to isolate themselves from areas of contention in order to avoid war and has thereby disintegrated the international community and assured the initiation and subsequent spread of war. In an interdependent world, propaganda of isolationism, neutrality, and absolute pacifism, however honestly pursued in the name of peace, have been causes of war" (Wright 1965 p. 1098). Furthermore, pacifism can be an obstacle to peace research (as well as to peace) as has been frequently observed by Gaston Bouthoul, the founder of the discipline in France (see *Bouthoul, Gaston; Polemology*). He writes: "To establish itself, polemological research has had to overcome several major obstacles. Paradoxically, the most important of those obstacles was—and still is—pacifism of the traditional type. Such pacifism, which goes on clinging to methods that have always proved a complete failure, assumes the problem of knowing about war to be resolved and continues to act as if all that is necessary is a little goodwill in order to put an end to wars once and for all. Pacifists . . . can conceive no other way of fighting against [war] except the old magical processes of incantation and imprecation. But what would be thought of a medicine which banned laboratories and tended the sick by making them shout together: 'Away with sickness, long live good health!'?"[34]

The first results of Bouthoul's research on war were published in 1939; his *magnum opus, Traité de polémologies: Sociologic des guerres*, appeared in 1970. Bouthoul argued that the time was ripe to substitute for the roman maxim "If you want peace, prepare for war" the new formula, "If you want peace, understand war." The objective, scientific study of war as a social phenomenon had been largely ignored in the past since the traditional study of war in military academies concerned mainly its technical aspects and the tactics and strategy involved in this "art." In order to avoid any possible misunderstanding, and to draw attention to the novelty of his approach, Bouthoul coined the word "polemology." He enshrined it in the name of what was possibly the first peace research institute, the Institute Francis de Polemologies, which he founded in Paris in 1945. His *Traite* was a revised version of the book first published in 1951, *Les Guerres—éléments de polémologies*. Although it cannot stand comparison with *A Study of War*, the *Traite* is nevertheless an impressive, encyclopedic study of war from a polemological perspective.

Bouthoul firmly believes that "Only through the study of wars will the establishment and preservation of peace be achieved" (Bouthoul 1970 p. 534) and this is also the leitmotif in the work of J. David Singer, one of the leading practitioners of the scientific study of war today. The "Correlates of War" project which he initiated with colleagues at the University of Michigan in Ann Arbor in the 1960s is, in certain ways, a continuation of Wright's project on the causes of war. Singer writes: "Until war has been systematically *described*, it cannot be adequately *understood*, and with such understanding comes the first meaningful possibility of controlling it, eliminating it, or finding less reprehensible substitutes for it. In our judgement, the important turning point is marked by the rise of scientific (and therefore quantitative) analyses of war, manifested primarily in the work of Quincy Wright and Lewis Fry Richardson beginning in the 1930s" (Singer et al. 1972 p. 4). An early result of the "Correlates of War" project is J. David Singer and Melvin Small's *The Wages of War 1816-1965: A Statistical Handbook*. According to the authors, the data collected in their book "represent a significant advance in accuracy and comparability over any prior compilation" (p. 12) which should encourage further research on the causes, characteristics, and consequences of war.

While the studies by Quincy Wright and Gaston Bouthoul pioneered peace research, including its institutional development, in North America and Western Europe, the publications of Johan Galtung had a similar effect in Scandinavia and beyond. In 1959 he founded the International Peace Research Institute in Oslo and five years later its *Journal of Peace Research*. The originality and fecundity of his thought, as well as his proficiency as a writer, are best gauged from his *Essays in Peace Research*, a series of five volumes averaging over 500 pages each. They were published between 1975 and 1980, and bring together 100 of his essays written over a period of 15 years, from 1958 until 1974. Of great importance are the introductions to each volume in which the author discusses the origins of many essays and the concepts treated in them, as well as the subsequent development of his views. Although critical of some of them, Kenneth Boulding, an equally important figure in contemporary peace research, wrote in his review of the first two volumes of Galtung's *Essays*: "The papers . . . reveal Galtung as a major world thinker in the field of peace research and conflict studies."[35] Whereas in the works of Wright and Vouthoul the focus is on war, in Galtung's writings the emphasis is often on peace. No writer has analyzed this concept as frequently, as thoroughly, and from as many angles as he (see *Peace Theory: An Introduction*). In his article on "Peace" for the *International Encyclopedia of the Social Sciences* (1968) and reprinted in his *Essays* he observed, "Social science has uncovered more knowledge about war than about peace" (Galtung 1975 p. 29). This no longer fully applies because of his work and that of others who have been inspired by it.

In its first issue, Galtung defined the aims of the *Journal of Peace Research* as follows: "to make an ever so small contribution to social science in general, to peace research in particular and—perhaps—even to peace policy."[36] The reality of these achievements so far, certainly with respect to the first two goals, can be seen in the extensive literature which peace research has brought forth within a relatively short period. The *Bibliography on World Conflict and Peace* (1979) compiled by Elise Boulding, J. Robert Passmore, and Robert Scott Gassler presents, in its main listing, over 1,000 entries organized in 26 major categories in the fields of conflict and peace studies. Equally useful is a bibliography of bibliographies, *Peace and War: A Guide to Bibliographies* (1983) by Berenice A. Carroll, Clinton F. Fink, and Jane E. Mohraz.[37] This bibliography, which covers a period from 1785 until 1980, identifies nearly 1,400 bibliographies grouped in three parts: Peace and war; Peace; and War. Each part in turn is divided into about 10 subject categories, making for 34 subject sections in all. A much more refined subject index comprising some 1,800 categories makes the material contained in the volume readily accessible. The meticulous annotations of many of the items enhance its value and provide the reader with a most useful indication of the precise content of the reference. These bare facts provide sufficient explanation for the praise which Michael Keresztesi, the president of the Association for the Bibliography of History, expresses in his foreword: "Publication of the present work must be considered a significant event in the annals of peace research. Aiming to identify, describe, and organize the hitherto unsorted multitude of bibliographical works in the field, the compilers have opened up broad vistas for research and analysis. No bibliographic instrument of comparable chronological and topical scope has been constructed so far . . . this guide [is] an exceptional research aid" (Carroll et al. 1983 pp. XI-XIII).[38]

The *Guide* covers the bibliographic literature on war and peace of the last two centuries although only 23 of the bibliographies listed in it were published before 1900 (p. XVII). Another bibliography attempts to show explicitly that peace research does have a history and this is Blanche Wiesen Cook's *Bibliography on Peace Research in History* (1969) which lists over 1,100 items. It was published under the auspices of the Conference on Peace Research in History (CPRH), an organization formed by American historians. The realization that peace efforts and peace writings of the past had been relatively neglected and that contemporary peace research provided the stimulus for rediscovering them has resulted, within the last two decades, in the bibliographies mentioned and in associations for the historical study of peace. It has also led to a major publishing venture: *The Garland Library of War and Peace*. This collection of 360 titles, published in the period 1971-76 (under the editorship of Blanche Wiesen Cook, Charles Chatfield, and Sandi Cooper, all prominent members of the CPRH), was designed "to make available a significant body of out-of-print literature dealing with man's efforts to cope with war and violence" (Cook et al. 1971 p. 7). The variety of these efforts is fully reflected in the judicious selection of books which are grouped in the *Catalogue*[39] into the following 12 sections:

(a) Proposals for peace: a history;

(b) Histories and problems of the organized peace movement, and biographies and memoirs of peace leaders;

(c) The character and causes of war;

(d) The political economy of war;

(e) Labor, socialism, and war;

(f) The control and limitation of arms;

(g) International organization, arbitration, and law;

(h) Nonresistance and nonviolence;

(i) Conscription and conscientious objection;

(j) Religious and ethical positions on war;

(k) The artist on war;

(l) Documentary anthologies.

A brief review of the authors and titles shows how accurately the collection reflects that the concern for peace has not been confined to any one place, time, or group of authors. Although the vast majority of the books are in English, some important texts in French and German are also included. The value of each volume is enhanced by extended essays. Moreover, closely related pamphlets and periodical material have been included with the original titles, which makes the series much more than a simple exercise in large-scale reprinting. Merle E. Curti, the doyen of American peace historians, writes in his introduction to the *Catalogue*: "It remains to be seen the extent to which the history of pacifism establishes useful modern guidelines, but clearly the search for an end to war cannot afford to ignore precedents. With the publication of *The Garland Library of War and Peace* a large body of essential reference material will now be readily available to students, scholars, and men of good will" (Cook 1971 p. 10). In our survey of peace encyclopedias, many of which are unique, the *Garland Library* must itself occupy a unique place.[40] We end this section by mentioning a most useful textbook, Robert Woito's *To End War* (1982), the sixth edition of a work first published in 1967 as an annotated bibliography. It concerns ideas and actions to end war and incorporates an annotated bibliography of over 2,000 books.

*9. The Biography of Peace: Josephson, Kuehl, Haberman*

Peace historians from the American Conference on Peace Research in History have been heavily involved in conceiving and producing several of the reference works discussed in the previous section; they have initiated two major biographical dictionaries which have appeared recently. The *Biographical Dictionary of Modern Peace Leaders* (1985), edited by Harold S. Josephson, provides concise biographies of 750 individuals who have distinguished themselves in the cause of peace. As the editor comments, "Given the diversity of peace leadership and the broad range of perspectives, the process of deciding who should be included in a biographical dictionary of modern peace leaders proved challenging" (p. XV). Only individuals alive after 1800 but not after 1980 have been included. The latter date gives the volume an historical dimension (and enabled the editor to sidestep the onerous task of deciding on the status of present-day peace figures); the former date reflects the fact that only with the modern period has the organized peace movement become a reality. Although figures from many countries and all parts of the world are included, the vast majority originate from the United States and Europe, the areas where the organized peace movement has been most developed. The general reader will encounter some individuals who are well-known but many more who are not. The editor explains: "Peace leaders are relatively obscure because most have not held political power; indeed, many have been sharp social critics or dissidents. nevertheless, their relative obscurity does not make these individuals less significant. Frequently their analysis of international relations, their perception of reality, and the policy prescriptions they offered were far more sophisticated and accurate than those who held political power" (p. XIV).

Well-known figures, however, can be found in the companion volume edited by Warren F. Kuehl, the *Biographical Dictionary of Internationalists* (1983), which concentrates on individuals who have played leading roles in the movement toward internationalism, regional and world integration, and world order. Among the 560 "internationalists" are to be found many well-known presidents, prime ministers, foreign secretaries, and international civil servants, more so than in the volume of "peace leaders." Most of the internationalists represented were born in the second half of the nineteenth century and reached their adulthood in the period which saw a rapidly increasing internationalization of the world culminating in the League of Nations. Kuehl identifies various categories of activity such as (in order of importance) the League of Nations, the United Nations, European unity, international law. Other categories which are well-represented are international labor, religious ecumenism, world federalism. Of all individuals included 70 percent come from the United States alone. The entries in both volumes follow a standard format: an introductory paragraph giving biographical data; a description of the subject's contribution to peace or internationalism; and a section providing bibliographical details of works by, and about, the subject. Both editors had the collaboration of some 250 authors, drawn from several nations but mainly from the United States. These two works, which necessitated much original research, provide invaluable reference tools for those interested in peace.

Another addition to the biographical literature is a German-language lexicon on the historical peace movement which focuses, appropriately, on the organized peace movement in Germany, Austria, and Switzerland. Karl Holl and Helmet Donat, leading peace historians from the former Federal Republic of Germany have edited the *Hermes Handlexikon Die Friedenbewegung* which provides biographical portraits of 160 leading peace figures as well as 100 articles on relevant ideas, organizations, and journals. The entries are arranged in alphabetical order and illustrated with over 300 photographs and documents which make an attractively presented encyclopedia of peace in the German-speaking world. *Die Friedensbewegung*, which concentrates on the last few decades of the nineteenth century and the first three decades of the twentieth, aims to rehabilitate German peace leaders, restore the moral dignity of the movement of the past, and so contribute to the historical and political education of the younger generation. Holl rightly places his volume in the "tradition of great German-language manuals of the peace movement" and he pays his respects, first and foremost, to Fried (Holl and Donat 1983 p. 14).

The comprehensive dictionaries of Josephson, Kuehl, and Holl-Donat have not made superfluous another work containing biographical information which appeared over a decade earlier. This brings together people (and institutions) who are united by the single honor of the Nobel Peace Prize (see *Nobel Peace Prizes*). The *Nobel Lectures: Peace*, edited by Frederick W. Haberman, contains for each Nobel laureate the lecture as well as the speech of presentation (delivered by the chairman of the Norwegian Nobel Committee), the biography (or the history of the institution), and a bibliography. The presentation speeches, with few exceptions, are published here in English for the first time and so are most of the 22 lectures by laureates (or organizational representatives) which were delivered in languages other than English. These three volumes, sponsored by the Nobel Foundation and the Nobel Committee of the Norwegian parliament, constitute the first complete collection of the speeches of presentation and of the Nobel Peace Prize lectures themselves (Haberman 1972 vol. I, p. X) and have been meticulously annotated. Haberman writes: "These lectures . . . constitute an important part of the historical record of twentieth century man's attempts to live in peace. These responses to the wars, economic depressions, and political catastrophes of this century vary from analysis of the problems to proposed answers, from defense of existing institutions to proposals for new ones, from statements of individualized ethics to pleas for united world action" (p. X). These volumes are thus a definitive record of the Nobel Peace Prize and at the same time an excellent guide to peace thought and action of the first seven decades of this century. They are a monument to the past as well as a beacon for the future. It is surprising to find that this fascinating work of excellent scholarship and on a subject of the highest importance has been apparently utterly ignored by the reviewers in the major journals.[41]

We conclude this section by referring to another large-scale attempt to treat the history of peace in a biographical manner, namely Elise Constantinescu-Bagdat's *Etudes d'histoire pacifists*. The three volumes which appeared in the period 1924-28 dealt with Erasmus, Vauban to Voltaire (this second volume including, for example, Fénélon, Saint-Pierre, Montesquieu, Rousseau), and Boyle. A fourth volume, Rabelais to La Bruyère, is mentioned as being in preparation but it apparently never appeared; possibly more volumes were planned. Her studies are noteworthy for their thoroughness and scholarship, and they contain much interesting source material as well as extensive bibliographies.

## 10. Encyclopedic Treatments of Peace in Economics, History, Medicine, Literature, Law

In this last section we draw attention to a few important studies which approach the question of war and peace from a variety of perspectives. These studies have special merit because they treat their subject in a systematic, exhaustive manner. The works we will be briefly reviewing belong to the following disciplines: economics, history, medicine, literature, and international law.

Although Edmund Silberner wrote in the preface to his *La Guerre et la paix dans i'histoire des doctrines économiques* (1957), "All those who are interested in the relationship between war and political economy know that so far no work has been devoted to this question"(p. VII), yet almost 20 years earlier, in 1939, he had published the first work on the subject, *La Guette dans la pensée économique du XVIe au XVIIIe siècle*. He found that from the end of the sixteenth until the end of the eighteenth century, two main currents manifested themselves in the history of economic thought concerning war: bellicist mercantilism and pacifist liberalism. The bellicist tendency predominated from the end of the sixteenth until the beginning of the eighteenth century; pacifist liberalism started to prevail from the middle of the eighteenth century. Silberner traced and impressively documented this evolution in his earlier work. His later book extended the analysis to the nineteenth century and the incorporation of an extensive summary of his work on the earlier period made the new study a comprehensive survey which encompassed economic thought of three centuries. For the nineteenth century he discussed the views on war and peace of the English classical economists (e.g., Malthus, Ricardo, the Mills), French liberals (Say, Bastiat, de Molinari), German protectionists and adherents of the historical school (especially List), and French and German socialists (Saint-Simon, Fourier, Marx and Engels). The title of the later book accurately included "peace" as well as war since Silberner examined the ideas of nineteenth century economists on topics such as the economic conditions for a durable peace, the economic consequences of disarmament, the relationship between world peace and economic factors. He wryly noted in his preface that the publication of his book had been delayed as a result of war (Silberner 1957 p. VIII). The manuscript was ready for publication in 1944 but the book, now in a considerably revised version, was published only several years later. The original manuscript appeared, however, in an English translation in 1946 as *The Problem of War in Nineteenth Century Economic Thought.*

One of the mercantilists whose views Silberner discusses is Jean Bodin for whom war is a providential institution which maintains the honor and virtue of the nation. In *Les Six Livres de la République* (1576) Bodin was the first to expound the notion of the sovereignty of the state. The institution of war and the sovereignty of the state are the subjects covered by the two volumes entitled *La Paix* which were the proceedings for 1961 of the "Jean Bodin Society for the Comparative History of Institutions." Thirty-six historians present, in as many chapters, a multifaceted survey of peace from ancient times to the present. The first volume analyzes the organization and maintenance of peace in primitive societies, in the Hindu world and in Japan, in the ancient civilizations of the Middle East, in the Graeco-Roman world, and in various places and at various times in the Middle Ages. The second volume continues the historical account with analyses of peace in the British Isles and in the German Empire in the Middle Ages. Subsequent chapters deal with the role of the papacy in the settlement of conflicts between states in the thirteenth- and fourteenth-centuries, the just war theory, the ideas of prominent thinkers such as Lully, Vives, Victoria, and Grotius, and the thoughts on peace of some Polish and Czech writers. There are, finally, chapters on the Holy Alliance, the League of Nations, the United Nations, and on arbitration and conciliation. The last chapter is an early survey of female efforts on behalf of peace in the nineteenth and twentieth centuries.[42] Although perhaps eclectic rather than encyclopedic, *La paix* presents a comprehensive overview of the most important aspects of peace in various civilizations and at different historical periods. This work is a rare example of the response of European historians to the imperative of peace in the nuclear era which stimulated their American colleagues to place the same topic at the head of their agenda (see above).

In view of the suffering that war has always brought about, in recent times on a scale as never before, it is surprising that the medical world has never been prominently involved in peace activities. This is strange because many philosophers (albeit a minority) from ancient times to the present have characterized war as a "disease"—and for many who have used this phrase it meant more than a metaphor. One of the earliest attempts to interest physicians in the problem of war and to alert them to their special responsibility for its prevention dates from the beginning of the century. In 1904 the French doctor Joseph Riviera founded the Association Medicable International Contre la Guerre in Paris and he detailed its activities in a volume published in 1910, *Actes et manifestations divers de l'Association* (etc.). When Fried listed the Association in his Handbuch he mentioned that it numbered 6,000 doctors from many nations. The First World War not only prevented a large conference which Rivièra had planned but also put an end to the organization itself. His idea was taken up by the Dutch doctor J. Roorda in 1930. As a result, the Netherlands Medical Association, consisting of over 4,000 doctors, instituted a Committee for War-prophylaxis which made Holland the first country where the problem of the prevention of war was officially accepted by the national federation of doctors as an integral part of their professional work. Among its notable initiatives was the *Letter to the Statesmen* (1935) which was signed by 340 leading psychiatrists from 27 countries, and the volume *Medical Opinions on War.*[43] At that time England was the only other country where women doctors regarded the elimination of war as an essential part of their work. Whereas these initiatives were revived in England soon after the Second World War with the establishment of the Medical Association for Prevention of War in 1951, it was not until 1969 that Dutch doctors founded the Dutch Society for Medical Polemology. One of its leading figures was Dr. J. A. Verdoorn, the author of *Arts en Oorlog* (Doctor and War). This work was intended to fill a lacuna in the history of medicine whose literature is otherwise very extensive. But the work is more than an historical account (as the subtitle—*Medical and Social Care for Victims of War in the History of Europe: Introduction to Medical Polemology*—indicates): it is also an introduction to medical peace research since Verdoorn argues that medical peace researchers regard war as a social-pathological phenomenon for which the profession has to take its responsibility. The theme is treated in the first volume from the ancient world until the twentieth century and in the second volume from the First World War until the present time. As B. V. A. Rölling, the founder of peace research in Holland, writes in the introduction, Verdoorn has written an impressive book on the fascinating history of medical care for war victims (Verdoorn 1972 pp. I-VI).

The themes of war and peace figure prominently in the literature of the Western world and have often provided the background against which a story—whether fictitious, mythological, or historical—is unfolded: from Homer to Tolstoy, from Thucydides to Gibbon, from Virgil to Shakespeare, from Machiavelli to Freud. This literature, from Homer to Freud, is collected together in the series *Great Books of the Western World* (whose 51 volumes comprise 443 works by 74 authors) and we are able to select passages on war and peace from this literature by using the two companion volumes entitled *The Great Ideas: A Syntopicon of Great Books of the Western World*. This work identifies 102 themes, one of which is War and Peace and this theme is divided into some 30 topics whose main headings are as follows: (a) War as the reign of force: the state of war and the state of nature; (b-e) the kinds, rights, causes, and effects of war; (f) The conception of war as a political instrument; (g) The inevitability of war: the political necessity of military preparations; (h) The desirability of war: its moral and political benefits; (i) The folly and futility of war; (j) The military arts and the military profession: their role in the state; and (k) The nature, causes, and conditions of peace. For each of the topics, references are given to the relevant works and passages in *Great Books*. Mortimer Alder, the editor of the *Syntopicon*, writes: "By serving as a guide to the syntonical reading of the great books, it does more than transform them from a mere collection of books into a unified whole; it translates them into a new kind of encyclopedic whole—a new kind of reference library" (Alder 1952 p. XII). In the *Syntopicon* one can follow the continuous discussion between the greatest minds of 30 centuries of Western civilization on war and peace.

A recent and more conventional publication which lists and annotates works of prose, drama, and poetry that illuminate the problem of war is Lucy Dougall's *War and Peace in Literature* (1982). The whole history of Western warfare, from the Trojan War to Vietnam, is covered in the 354 works listed. Like the previous source, this is not an introduction to antiwar literature but something more: "It is a listing of works which hold a mirror up to war, revealing the ways in which it enhances and even ennobles, as well as destroys and degrades, those subject to its demands" (Robert Pickups, president of the World Without War Council, in the foreword, p. 2). The author sees her book as a first step to a more complete compilation which would include other genres and traditions. One genre that Dougall does not include is imaginary works dealing with wars of the future. This is the subject of I. F. Clarke's fascinating and original study *Voices Prophesying War 1763-1984*. Most of these voices were raised not in order to prevent war but in order to alert the nation to the shape of future warfare, draw attention to the wickedness of the opponent, and urge preparation for defense and victory. The imaginary wars in Clarke's book are thus very different from, for example, Jean de Bloch's *The Future of War*, a contrast which Clarke briefly comments upon (Clarke 1966 p. 134). Not only is de Bloch's forecast factual whereas the literature described by the author is fictitious, but also the two kinds of work differ in both intent and effect. These works of the literary imagination had a pernicious influence on actual politics. Clarke writes: "There can be no doubt that the authors of the many tales of future warfare whaled in the responsibility for the catastrophe that overtook Europe. [These authors] helped to raise the temperature of international disputes. . . . During the 43 years from 1871 to the outbreak of the First World War the device of the imaginary war had become an established means of teaching every kind of aggressive doctrine" (p. 135). Stories of the coming conflict between Britain and Germany reached a peak in the decade leading up to August 1914. According to Clarke, "it is clear that the device of the imaginary war had begun to affect international relations in a way never known before" (p. 136). For the student of peace Clarke's book is important because it suggests the effects of perceptions and predictions and the workings of the self-fulfilling prophecy mechanism. Moreover, its "Checklist of Imaginary Wars, 1763-1965" (pp. 227-49) makes the book particularly valuable as a reference work for this topic.

Of all the established disciplines none has focused on the question of war and peace more clearly than international law; Grotius's *On the Law of War and Peace* (1625) is generally regarded as the beginning of its systematic study. The literature concerning this subject was already so extensive by 1785 that the German scholar Ompteda was able to devote a voluminous bibliography to it.[44] The task of selecting from the literature one or more appropriate encyclopedic works has been made easier with the recent appearance, exactly 200 years after Ompteda, of the *Encyclopedia of Public International Law*. This work also originates from Germany and is published under the auspices of the Max Planck Institute for comparative Public Law and International Law in Heidelberg under the direction of Rudolf Bernhardt. The *Encyclopedia* is, however, in English, and is the first of its kind in that language. It is being published in 12 installments, each one treating a specific subject area and containing, on average, over 100 entries arranged in alphabetical order. Since 1981, seven installments have appeared dealing with the following subjects: (a) Settlement of disputes; (b) Decisions of international courts and tribunals; (c) and (d) Use of force, war and neutrality, peace treaties; (e) International organizations; (f) Regional cooperation; (g) History, foundations and principles, and sources of international law. The remaining volumes, to be published within the next few years, will deal with (h) Human rights, international economic relations; (i) International relations in general, diplomacy, and consular relations; (j) States; (k) Laws of the sea, air, and space; and (l) Geographic issues. Eventually, the *Encyclopedia* will be complemented by an edition (in five volumes) in which all the articles are arranged alphabetically. This work will prove to be very useful not only for the student and practitioner of public international law but also for the student of peace and moreover, for the latter, it is likely to be the most relevant of all existing encyclopedias.[45]

This survey of encyclopedic treatments of peace leads to the conclusion that there are few areas of human enquiry that have excluded it. Indeed, it is necessary to draw on the sum of human knowledge in order to comprehend the phenomena of war and peace. What a famous writer on war asserted two centuries ago with respect to military science is as true today when applied to the study of peace:

> Only military science constitutes an encyclopedia. It is the most interesting of the sciences, whether one looks at it from the point of view of the variety of its detail, or the importance of its aim, or the glory and the high stakes which are involved. (Jacques A H de Guibert 1773 *Essai général de tactique*. Liège, Vol. 2, p. 220)[46]

*Notes*

1. Milton Birnbaum in his introduction to the 1972 Garland reprint, pp. 5-13. The first German edition of Huxley's *Encyclopedia* has recently been published in *Plädoyer für den Weltfrieden und Enzyklopädie des Pazifismus* (1984, Knaur, Munich, pp. 45-151). A reprint of Huxley's work forms the first part of Robert A. Seeley's *The Handbook of Nonviolence* (1986, Lawrence Hill, Westport, Connecticut and Lakeville Press, Great Neck, New York). In the second and main part of his book Seeley provides additional articles (following the format of Huxley's *Encyclopedia*). Regrettable his selection is arbitrary and inadequate.

2. It is interesting to note that reviewers were unanimous in their opinion of the book's main weakness: "Unfortunately, the organization of the book prevents its handy usage" (*Jewish Social Studies*, Vol. 18, 1956, p. 235); "his chief points become lost as fact is piled upon fact" (*Political Science Quarterly*, vol. 72, no. 1, March 1957, p. 154); "the vast amount of information seems to have dominated the form and structure, and to this degree one must regret to report that the admirable purpose and lofty ideals behind the volumes are not served in the most effective manner" (*The Annals of the American Academy of Political and Social Science*, vol. 308, Nov. 1956, p. 176).

3. For details of editions in several languages see my *A Bibliography of the Pacifist Writings of Jean de Bloch* (1977, Housmans, London).

4. On these various aspects of de Bloch's activities see the following studies by the present writer: "The International Museum of War and Peace at Lucerne" in *Schweizerische Zeitschrift für Geschichte/Revue Suisse D'Histoire* (vol. 31, no. 2, 1981, pp. 185-202); *The Making of Peace: Jean de Bloch and the First Hague Peace Conference* (1983, California State University, Center for the Study of Armament and Disarmament, Los Angles); "Jean de Bloch: a Nineteenth century peace researcher" in *Peace Research: The Canadian Journal of Peace Studies* (vol. 15, no. 3. Sept. 1983, pp. 21-27).

5. Daniel Gasman in his introduction to the 1972 Garland reprint of the *Handbuch's* second edition, p. 9. The quotes from Fried which follow are taken from the same source.

6. Fried was not alone in taking such an attitude. This is what a prominent French peace advocate wrote: "One should read and reflect on the 'Annuaire de la vie international' published by A. H. Fried .... This is merely an annual in which there is no place for philosophy, philanthropy, morality, *and other stupidities* [emphasis added] in this collection of documents, figures, statistics, and names. The number of international associations . . . is over 170.

What better example could one give to prove that Europeans resolutely desire European unity? Facts are more eloquent than phrases." cf. Charles Richet, *Le Passé de la guerre et l'avenir de la paix* (1907, Paul Ollendorff, Paris, pp. 389-90, note 1).

7. *Political Science Quarterly* (vol. 34, no. 2, 1919, p. 351).

8. *Times Literary Supplement* (8 March 1917, p. 111).

9. *Political Science Quarterly* (vol. 45, no. 1, 1930, p. 116).

10. "Die Entwicklung des Gedankens der internationalen Organisation: Zur Vollendung des Grossen Werkes von Jacob ter Meulen" in *Die Friedens-Warte* (vol. 41, no. 5/6, 1941, pp. 217-36).

11. *English Historical Review* (vol. 36, July 1921, pp. 461-63).

12. *The American Journal of International Law* (vol. 14, 1920, pp. 483-86).

13. *The American Journal of International Law* (vol. 49, 1955, pp. 434-35).

14. According to the information in Fried (1913p. 403) and in Kuehl (1983 p. 647); Schou (1963 p. 352) gives the date as 1866.

15. *International Journal* (vol. 14, 1959, p. 143).

16. Walter F. Bense in his introduction to the 1972 Garland reprint, p. 7.

17. Harold Bing in *Pacifists over the World* (1943, Peace News, London, p. 4).

18. *Vient de paraître: La paix créatrice* (1934, Marcel Riviera, Paris, pp. 1-2).

19. *American Political Science Review* (vol. 31, no. 2, April 1937, pp. 368-69).

20. Bart de Ligt, *The Conquest of Violence* (1937, George Rutledge and Sons, London, p. IX).

21. *Nonviolent Resistance: Men Against War* (1963, Nonviolence 63, London, p. 28).

22. Peter van den Dungen, Herman Noordegraaf and wim Robben *Bart de ligt (1883-1938): Peace Activist and Peace Researcher*. 1990 Foundation for Information on Active Nonviolence, zwolle, pp. 27-47.

23. Further on the same page Brock writes: "There are two monumental histories of the wider peace movement" and he refers to the works of ter Meulen and lange-Schou. Apparently Ruyssen's work is unknown to him.

24. Shortly afterwards two smaller volumes appeared which consisted of chapters extracted from it; *Radical Pacifists in Antebellum America* (1968, Princeton University Press, Princeton), which were chapters 10-17 of the larger work, and *Pioneers of the Peaceable Kingdom* (1970, Princeton University Press, Princeton), which were seven chapters from the original work dealing with the Quaker Peace Testimony.

25. Edwin B. Bronner, reviewing *Pacifism in the United States* in *The Annals of the American Academy of Social and Political Science* (vol. 384, 1969,p. 142). It is a pity that the review by Robert Scharf of *Pacifism in Europe* in the same journal was incompetent and inappropriate (vol. 407, 1973, p. 210). J. R. Pole thought *Pacifism in the United States* an "immense [but] undisciplined book" and stressed the "mines of information" provided by Brock and "the weight of his scholarship" (*History*, vol. 56, 1971, p. 491). A. J. A. Morris, reviewing *Pacifism in Europe*, wrote: "On the whole, Professor Brock has succeeded in writing an exhausting study without exhausting the Reader" (*History*, vol. 56, 1974, p. 293). Other reviews had similar comments.

26. The author was imprisoned for nine months of a two-year sentence. His stance led to an interesting correspondence with Einstein. cf. Otto Nathan and Heinz Norden (eds.) *Einstein on Peace* (1968, Schocken Books, New York, pp. 543-45, and p. 676, note 2).

27. Here and elsewhere we find clear echoes of de Ligt whose *La Paix créatice* is nowhere mentioned by Sharp (although de Ligt's *The Conquest of Violence* is referred to on a few occasions).

28. For these and other commendations see the back covers of Sharp's volumes.

29. Peace Pledge Union, London, 1939. For a brief analysis of this and other early proposals for a science of peace see my "Varieties of peace science: An historical note" in the *Journal of Peace Science* (vol. 2, no. 2, Spring 1977, pp. 239-57).

30. For a detailed description of "The Causes of War project at the University of Chicago" see appendix I in Wright 1965, pp. 409-13.

31. William T. R. Fox, "'The truth shall make you free': One student's appreciation of Quincy Wright" in the *Journal of Conflict Resolution* (vol. 14, no. 4, Dec. 1970, p. 450). This was a memorial issue for Wright.

32. The full text of this letter is given by Allen S. Whiting in "In memoriam: Quincy Wright, 1890—1970—a symposium" (*Journal of Conflict Resolution*, vol. 14, no. 4, pp. 445-46).

33. cf. Martin B. Travis's article on Wright in *International Encyclopedia of the Social Sciences* (vol. 18, 1979, p. 817), Biographical Supplement.

34. Gaston Bouthoul, "Polemology and the solution of conflicts" in *Impact of Science on Society* (vol. 18, no. 2, April—June 1968, p. 105).

35. "Twelve friendly quarrels with Johan Galtung" in the *Journal of Peace Research* (vol. 14, no. 1, 1977, p. 75).

36. "An editorial—what is peace research?" in the *Journal of peace Research* (vol. 1, no. 1, 1964, p. 4).

37. It appears as no. 16 in the excellent War/Peace Bibliography Series under the general editorship of Richard Dean Burns. For details of the Series see Carroll et al. 1983, pp. V-VII.

38. The Guide is not, however, without serious shortcomings as I have pointed out elsewhere. cf. "Review essay: The biography of internationalists and the bibliography of peace" in *International Journal on World Peace*, Vol. 3, no. 4, October-December 1986, pp. 103-122

39. This *Catalogue* accompanies the collection and constitutes, by itself, a most useful work of reference. Carroll et al. rightly say that it is "perhaps the most interesting and informative introduction to the field" (p. 3).

40. Of note are also the "International Library" founded in 1905 by the Boston publisher and peace educator

Edwin Ginn and published from 1909 by the World Peace Foundation under the editorship of Edwin D. Mead; the *Encyclopédie Pax* published in Paris during the interwar period under the direction of J. de Romanet-Beaune by Les Editions Internationales; and the *Bibliothèque de la Paix* published in Paris in the 1860s by the Ligue Internationale et Permanente de la Paix.

41. Whereas the Nobel lectures on other subjects were reviewed when they were published (in the 1960s), not a single review for these volumes on peace was noted! In his excellent article "The transformation of the Nobel Peace Prize," Irwin Abrams called them a "valuable collection" (*Peace and Change*, vol. 10, no. 3/4, Fall/Winter 1984, p. 23, note 4).

42. "Les efforts féminine pour l'organisation de la paix aux XIXe et XXe siècles" by W. H. Posthumous van der Goot (pp. 581-610). For a fuller treatment see the same author's *Vrouwen vochten voor de vrede* (Women fought for peace) (1961, Van Loghum Slaterus, Arnhem).

43. Elsevier for the Netherlands medical Association, Amsterdam, 1938, 72 pp. The *Letter to the Statesmen* is reprinted in it.

44. This bibliography is the earliest entry in Carroll *et al.* (1983) and the editors comment that its publication suggests "that the need for bibliographies was felt much earlier in the field of international law than in other fields represented here" (Carroll et al. 1983 pp. 4 and 92).

45. Still useful, however, are such reference works as Fred L. Israel, (ed.) *Major Peace Treaties of Modern history, 1648-1967* (1967, Chelsea House, New York, in four volumes with a fifth, covering the years 1967-79, published in 1980) or Peter H. Rohn (ed.) *World Treaty Index* (1985, ABC-Clio, Santa Barbara/Oxford, 2nd edn., in five volumes). Although the Encyclopedia deals with arms control and disarmament it is likely that some of the major reference works on these subjects (e.g. the SIPRI Yearbooks), which we had to exclude from our survey, will equally retain their value.

46. A similar sentiment was expressed by Edwin Paxton hood in his *An Encyclopedia of Facts, Anecdotes, Arguments and Illustrations, from History, Philosophy and Christianity, in Support of the Principles of Permanent and Universal Peace* (1846, William Irwin, Manchester and Charles Gilpin, London, 289 pp.). In the conclusion of his work Hood wrote: "Let us hope that literature and philosophy, and government, and theology, will all unite together to disturb and agitate public opinion" (p. 267). His book, devoid of literary merit was "but a compilation—a handbook," but one which he hoped would contribute to this goal: "In trust . . . that it may serve a purpose which no other book with which I am acquainted can serve; and open up to the mind of the reader, a view of the exciting interest and vast extent of its great subject" (p. iii). This work is a bibliographical curiosity as yet found only in the great peace collections in Oslo and the Hague.

## Bibliography

Adler M J (ed.) 1952 *The Great Ideas: A Syntopicon of Great Books of the Western World.* [War and Peace. Vol. 2, Chap. 98, pp. 1010-37] Encyclopedia Britannica, Chicago, Illinois

Beales A C F 1931 *The History of Peace. A Short Account of the Organised Movements for International Peace.* Bell, London, 355 pp.

Beckwith G C 1847 *The Peace Manual: Or, War and its Remedies.* American Peace Society, Boston, Massachusetts, 252 pp.

Bernhardt R (ed.) 1981 *Encyclopedia of Public International Law.* North-Holland, Amsterdam

Bounding E, Passmore J R, Gassler R S (comp.) 1979 *Bibliography on World Conflict and Peace*, 2nd edn. Westview Press, Boulder, Colorado, 168 pp.

Bouthoul G 1970 *Traité de polémologie: Sociologie des guerres*, New edn. Payot, Paris, 560 pp.

Brock P 1968 *Pacifism in the United States. From the Colonial Era to the First World War.* Princeton University Press, Princeton, New Jersey, 1,005 pp.

Brock P 1970 *Twentieth Century Pacifism.* Van Nostrand Reinhold, New York, 274 pp.

Brock P 1972 *Pacifism in Europe to 1914.* Princeton University Press, Princeton, New Jersey, 556 pp.

Carroll B A, Fink C F, Mohraz J E 1983 *Peace and War: A Guide to Bibliographies.* ABC-Clio, Santa Barbara/Oxford, 580 pp.

Clarke I F 1966 *Voices Prophesying War 1763-1984.* Oxford University Press, Oxford, 254 pp.

Constantinescu-Bagdat E 1924-28 *Etudes d'histoire pacifists*, 3 vols. [Vol. I 1924 *La 'Querela Paris's d'Erasme (1517)*, 218 pp.; Vol. II 1925 *De Vauban à Voltaire*, 464 pp.; Vol. III 1928 *Bayle (1647-1706)*.] Presses Universitaires de France, Paris

Cook B W (ed.) 1969 *Bibliography on Peace Research in History.* ABC-Clio, Santa Barbara/Oxford, 72 pp.

Cook B W, Chatfield C, Cooper S (eds.) 1971 *The Garland Library of War and Peace*, (Catalogue). Garland, New York, 136 pp.

Cooney R, Michalowski H (eds.) 1977 *The Power of the People: Active Nonviolence in the United States.* Peace

Press, Culver City, California, 240 pp.

de Bloch J 1898-1900 *La Guerre: Traduction de l'ouvrage russe 'La guerre future aux points de vue technique, économique et politique'*, 6 Vols. [Vol. I *Description du mécanisme de la guerre*, 663 pp.; Vol. II *La Guerre sur le continent*, 726 pp.; Vol. III *La Guerre navale*, 443 pp.; Vol. IV *Les Troubles économiques et les pertes matérielles que déterminera la guerre future*, 524 pp.; Vol. V *Les Efforts tendant á supprimer la guerre; les causes des différends politiques; les conséquences des pertes*, 391 pp.; Vol. VI *De l'Ouvrage entier; conclusions générales*, 388 pp.] Guillaumin, Paris

de Ligt B 1931-33 *Vrede als Daad: Beginselen, geschiedenis en strijdmethoden van de direkte aktie tegen oorlog*, 2 Vols. [Vol. I 1931 332 pp.; Vol. II, 1933, 389 pp.] Van Loghum Slaterus, Arnhem

de Ligt B 1934 *La paix créatrice: Histoire des principes et des to tactiques de l'action directe contre la guerre*, 2 Vols. [Vol. I *Caractère de l'action directe: L'Avènement de l'idée de la paix créatrice*, pp. 1-221; Vol. II *L'Action directe religieuse pour des motifs strictement religieux*, pp. 222-536.] Marcel Rivière, Paris

Dougall L (comp.) 1982 *War and peace in Literature: Prose, Drama and Poetry which Illuminate the Problem of War*. World Without War Publications, Chicago, Illinois, 171 pp.

Fried A H 1911-13 *Handbuch der Friedensbewegung*, 2nd edn., 2 Vols. [Vol. I 1911 *Grundlagen, Inhalt und Ziele der Friedensbewegung*, 269 pp.; Vol. II 1913 *Geschichte, Umfang und Organisation der Friedensbewegung*, 492 pp.] Verlag der 'Friedens-Warte', Berlin and Leipzig

Galtung J 1975-80 *Essays in Peace Research*, 5 vols. [Vol. I 1975 *Peace: Research, Education, Action*, 406 pp.; Vol. II 1976 *Peace, War and Defense*, 472 pp.; Vol. III 1978 *Peace and Social Structure*, 564 pp.; Vol. IV 1980 *Peace and World Structure*, 736 pp.; Vol. V, 1980 *Peace Problems: Some Case Studies*, 499 pp.] Christian Ejlers, Copenhagen

Gourevitch B 1955 *The Road to Peace and to Moral Democracy: An Encyclopedia of Peace*, 2 Vols. [Vol. I 1,083 pp.; Vol. II 1,540 pp.] International Universities Press, New York

Haberman F W (ed.) 1972 *Nobel Lectures—Peace*, 3 Vols. [Vol. I *1901-25*, 418 pp.; Vol. II *1926-50*, 474 pp.; Vol. III *1951-70*, 496 pp.] Elsevier (for the Nobel Foundation) Amsterdam

Hemleben S J 1943 *Plans for World Peace Through Six Centuries*. University of Chicago Press, Chicago, Illinois, 227 pp.

Hershberger G F 1969 *War, Peace, and Nonresistance*, 3rd edn. Herald Press, Scottdale, Pennsylvania, 382 pp.

Hinsley F H 1963 *Power and the Pursuit of Peace: Theory and Practice in the History of Relations Between States*. Cambridge University Press, Cambridge, 416 pp.

Holl K, Donat H (eds.) 1983 *Die Friedensbewegung. Organisierter Pazifismus in Deutschland, Oesterreich und in der Schweiz*. ECON Taschenbuch Verlag, Düsseldorf, 432 pp.

Huxley A (ed.) 1937 *An Encyclopedia of Pacifism*. Chatto and Windus, London, 126 pp.

Josephson H (ed.) 1985 *Biographical Dictionary of Modern Peace Leaders*. Greenwood Press, Westport, Connecticut, 1,133 pp.

Kuehl W F (ed.) 1983 *Biographical Dictionary of Internationalists*. Greenwood Press, Westport, Connecticut, 934 pp.

La fontaine H 1904 *Bibliographie de la paix et de l'arbitrage international*. [Vol. I *Movement pacifique*, 280 pp.] Institute International de la Paix, Monaco

Lange C L, Schou A 1919-1963 *Histoire de l'internationalisme*. [Vol. I Lange 1919 *Jusqu'à la Paix de Westphalie (1648)*, 517 pp.; Vol. II Lange and Schou 1954 *De la Paix de Westphalie jusqu'au Congrès de Vienne (1815)*, 482 pp.; Vol. III Schou 1963 *Du Congrès de Vienne jusqu'à la Première Guerre Mondiale (1914)*, 565 pp.] Aschehoug, Kristiania (Oslo) [Publications de l'Institut Nobel Norvégien, Vols. IV, VII, VIII]

Lynd S (ed.) 1966 *Nonviolence in America: A Documentary History*. Bobbs-Merrill, Indianapolis, Indiana, 535 pp.

Marriott J A 1937 *Commonwealth or Anarchy? A Survey of Projects of Peace from the Sixteenth to the Twentieth Century*. Philip Allan, London, 225 pp.

Mayer P (ed.) 1966 *The Pacifist Conscience*. Holt, Rinehart, and Winston, New York, 473 pp.

Molhuysen P C, Oppenheim E R 1916 *Bibliothèque du Palais de la Paix*, Catalògue. [Supplements and indexes 1922-66] Sijthoff, Leiden, 1,576 cols.

Norwegian Nobel Institute 1912 *Bibliographie du movement de la paix: Litérature pacifists dans la Bibliothèque de l'Institut Nobel Norvégien*. Aschehoug, Kristiania (Oslo), 226 coals. and pp. 227-38

Ruyssen T 1954-61 *Les Sources doctrinales de l'internationalisme*, 3 vols [Vol. I 1954 *Des Origines à la Paix de Westphalie*, 500 pp.; Vol. II 1958 *De la Paix de Westphalie à la Révolution Française*, 646 pp.; Vol. III 1961 *De la Révolution Française au milieu du XIXe siècle*, 592 pp.] Presses Universitaires de France, Paris

Sharp G 1973 *The Politics of Nonviolent Action*, 3 Vols. [Vol. I *Power and Struggle*, pp. 1-105; Vol. II *The Methods of Nonviolent Action*, pp. 106-445; Vol. III *The Dynamics of Nonviolent Action*, pp. 446-902] Porter Sargent, Boston, Massachusetts

Sibley M Q (ed.) 1963 *The Quiet Battle: Writings on the Theory and Practice of Non-violent Resistance*. Doubleday/ Anchor, Garden City, New York, 390 pp.

Siberner E 1939 *La Guerre dans la pensée économique du XVIe au XVIIIe siècle*. Sirey, Paris, 301 pp.

Silberner E 1946 *The Problem of War in Nineteenth Century Economic Thought*. Princeton University Press, Princeton, New Jersey, 332 pp.

Silberner E 1957 *La Guerre et la paix dans l'histoire des doctrines économiques*. Sirey, Paris, 212 pp.

Singer J D, Small M 1972 *The Wages of War 1816-1965: A Statistical Handbook*. John Wiley, New York, 419 pp.

Societe Jean Bodin Pour l'Histoire Comparative des Institutions, Recueils de la 1961 *La Paix*. [Vol. I, 554 pp.; Vol. II, 610 pp.] Editions de la Librairie Encyclopédique, Brussels

Stawell F M 1929 *The Growth of International Thought*. Butterworth, London, 252 pp.

ter Meulen J 1917-40 *Der Gedanke der Internationalen Organisation in seiner Entwicklung*, 3 Vols. [Vol. I 1917 *1300-1800*, 397 pp.; Vol. II *1929 1789-1870*, 371 pp.; Vol. III *1940 1867-1889*, 373 pp.] Martinus Nijhoff, the Hague

ter Meulen J 1934 *Bibliography of the Peace Movement Before 1899 (Provisional Lists): Period 1776-1898*. Library of the Palace of Peace, The Hague, 124 coals.

ter Meulen J 1936 *Bibliography of the Peace Movement Before 1899 (Provisional Lists): Period 1480-1776*. Library of the Palace of Peace, The Hague, 24 pp.

Verdoorn J A 1972 *Arts en oorlog: Medische en sociable zorg voor oorlogsslachtoffers in de geschiedenis van Europa: Inleiding in de medische polemologie*, 2 Vols. [Vol. I *Van de antieke wereld tot de twintigste eeuw*, pp. 1-474; Vol. II *Van de eerste wereldoorlog tot de tegenwoordige tijd*.] [Doctor and war. Medical and social care for victims of war in the history of Europe. Introduction to medical polemology. Vol. I, From the ancient world to the twentieth century; Vol. II, From the First World War to the present.] Lynx, Amsterdam

Weinberg A, Weinberg L (eds.)1963 *Instead of Violence: Writings by the Great Advocates of Peace and Nonviolence Throughout History*. Grossman, New York, 486 pp.

Woito R S 1982 *To End War: A New Approach to International Conflict*. Pilgrim Press, New York, 755 pp.

Wright Q 1965 *A Study of War*, 2nd edn. University of Chicago Press, Chicago, Illinois, 1,637 pp.

Wynner E, Lloyd G (eds.) (1944) 1946 *Searchlight on Peace Plans: Choose Your Road to World Government*. Dutton, New York, 532 pp.

York E 1919 *Leagues of Nations: Ancient, Mediaeval, and Modern*. Swarthmore Press, London, 337 pp.

PETER VAN DEN DUNGEN

# Encyclopedic Works on Peace, 1986-1996

If a compilation of 'peace encyclopedias of the past and present' was a problematic and perhaps foolhardy enterprise when it was first undertaken (more than ten years ago)—if for no other reason than what constitutes 'peace' and 'encyclopedia' is by no means clear, and a broad definition of both would make the relevant literature virtually limitless—it is obvious that in the rapidly changing world of the post-Cold War era such an exercise must be fraught with even more difficulties. Then we concluded by quoting from one of the first encyclopedic works on peace, published 150 years ago. Its author wanted to make the reader aware "of the exciting interest and vast extent" of its subject. Never before has interest in peace been as great, the extent of the subject as wide—and as a result of both, publications as numerous—as is the case today. To gain a comprehensive overview of it has become impossible, and any selection will of necessity be somewhat arbitrary and reflect the author's own preferences and limitations. In what follows our modest aim has been, firstly, to attempt to update where applicable the encyclopedic works discussed in the original essay, and secondly, to introduce a few new ones. They will be briefly introduced in an order which only broadly follows that of the original essay, starting with the topics of nonviolent action and pacifist history.

## 1. Nonviolence

*Protest, Power, and Change: An Encyclopedia of Nonviolent Action from ACT-UP to Women's Suffrage* (1997) was conceived as "a standard reference work for an important domain of human behavior that has been well studied but incompletely identified" (p. XI). The editors define nonviolent action "as a distinctive form of conflict behavior—one that eschews violence and physical force" and argue that the phenomenon is much more widespread than is generally held to be the case (see *Nonviolence*). Nonviolent action is not confined to the campaigns of Gandhi or M.L. King but has also been used by "people as varied as members of medieval guilds, African-American slaves, and upper-class English women" (p. XI). But marginalization and misunderstanding have until now prevented the phenomenon from achieving its proper identity and coherence. The encyclopedia aims to map out the terrain through case studies of more than 100 campaigns (ranging from the Abolition Movement in the US to the Zambian Anti-colonial Movement), profiles of some seventy individuals (from Jane Addams to Betty Williams) and forty organizations (from ACT-UP to Women's International League for Peace and Freedom), as well as descriptions of forty different methods of nonviolent action (from Air Raids to Withdrawal) and presentation of as many topics related to nonviolent action (from Ahimsa to Women and Nonviolent Action). The encyclopedia proper consists of 300 articles arranged in alphabetical order and is preceded by a helpful listing which groups entries into the five broad analytical categories referred to. Among the individuals profiled is Gene Sharp, whom the editors acknowledge as having provided the inspiration for their project. His pioneering work, stretching out over four decades, has doubtlessly similarly inspired many of the contributors to the volume.

## 2. Peace History

The significance of Gene Sharp for the history (and theory) of nonviolence is paralleled by that of Peter Brock for the history of pacifism. To the pioneering trilogy of works discussed above can now be added, amazingly, another trilogy published at the beginning of the 1990s, and representing a comprehensive history of pacifism to 1914. *Freedom From Violence: Sectarian Nonresistance from the Middle Ages to the Great War* (1991) deals with the various Christian sects in Europe and North America which rejected both the violence involved in wars and in the government of states. Brock devotes individual chapters to such sects as the Waldenses, the Bohemian

**Table 1**
Thematic overview

| Author | Bibliography | Biography | Encyclopedic: Aspects | Encyclopedic: General | Other |
|---|---|---|---|---|---|
| Adler | | | 1952 | | |
| Beales | | | | 1931 | |
| Beckwith | | | | | 1847 |
| Bernhardt | | | 1981 | | |
| Boulding et al. | 1979 | | | | |
| Bouthoul | | | 1970 | | |
| Brock | | | 1968-72 | | |
| Carroll et al. | 1983 | | | | |
| Clarke | | | 1966 | | |
| Constantinescu-Bagdat | | 1924-28 | | | |
| Cook | 1969 | | | | |
| Cook et al. | | | | | 1971 |
| Cooney and Michalowski | | | | | 1977 |
| de Bloch | | | 1898-1900 | | |
| de Ligt | | | 1931-34 | | |
| Dougall | 1982 | | | | |
| Fried | | | | 1911-13 | |
| Galtung | | | 1975-80 | | |
| Gourevitch | | | | | 1955 |
| Haberman | | 1972 | | | |
| Hemleben | | | | | 1943 |
| Hershberger | | | | | 1944 |
| Hinsley | | | | | 1963 |
| Holl and Donat | | 1983 | | | |
| Huxley | | | | | 1937 |
| Josephson | | 1985 | | | |
| Kuehl | | 1983 | | | |
| La Fontaine | 1904 | | | | |
| Lange-Schou | | | | 1919-63 | |
| Lynd | | | | | 1966 |
| Marriott | | | | | 1937 |
| Mayer | | | | | 1966 |
| Molhuysen | 1916-63 | | | | |
| Norwegian Nobel Institute | 1912 | | | | |
| Ruyssen | | | | 1954-61 | |
| Sharp | | | 1973 | | |
| Sibley | | | | | 1963 |
| Silberner | | | 1939-57 | | |
| Singer *et al.* | | | 1972 | | |
| Société Jean Bodin | | | | 1961 | |
| Stawell | | | | | 1929 |
| ter Meulen | | | | 1917-40 | |
| ter Meulen | 1934-36 | | | | |
| Upham | | | | | 1836 |
| Verdoorn | | | 1972 | | |
| Weinberg and Weinberg | | | | | 1963 |
| Woito | 1982 | | | | |
| Wright | | | 1942 | | |
| Wynner and Lloyd | | | 1944 | | |
| York | | | | | 1919 |

*Table 2*
Chronological overview

| Period | Year | Author | Other editions and reprints |
|---|---|---|---|
| Nineteenth century | 1836 | Upham | 1842 |
| | 1847 | Beckwith | 1971 Garland repr. |
| | 1898-1900 | de Bloch | 1973 Garland repr. |
| pre-1914 | 1904 | La Fontaine | 1891 1st edn. |
| | 1912 | Norwegian Nobel Institute | |
| | 1911-13 | Fried | 1972 Garland repr.; 1905 1st end. |
| First World War | 1916-66 | Molhuysen | |
| | 1917-40 | ter Meulen | |
| Interbellum | 1919-63 | Lange-Schou | |
| | 1919 | York | |
| | 1924-28 | Constantinescu-Bagdat | |
| | 1929 | Stawell | |
| | 1931 | Beales | 1971 Garland repr. |
| | 1931-34 | de Ligt | |
| | 1934-36 | ter Meulen | |
| | 1937 | Huxley | 1972 Garland repr. |
| | 1937 | Marriott | |
| | 1939-57 | Silberner | 1972 Garland repr. of 1939 and 1946 volumes |
| Second World War | 1942 | Wright | 1965 2nd edn. |
| | 1943 | hemleben | 1972 Garland repr. |
| | 1944 | Hershberger | 1969 3rd edn. |
| | 1944 | Wynner and Lloyd | 1946 2nd pr. |
| 1950s | 1952 | Adler | 1977 21st pr. |
| | 1954-61 | Ruyssen | |
| | 1955 | Gourevitch | |
| 1960s | 1961 | Société Jean Bodin | |
| | 1963 | Sibley | |
| | 1963 | Weinberg and Weinberg | |
| | 1963 | Hinsley | |
| | 1966 | Lynd | |
| | 1966 | Mayer | Penguin edn. |
| | 1968-72 | Brock | |
| | 1969 | Cook | |
| 1970s | 1970 | Bouthoul | New edn.; 1951 1st edn. |
| | 1971 | Cook et al. | |
| | 1972 | Haberman | |
| | 1972 | Verdoorn | |
| | 1972 | Singer et al. | |
| | 1973 | Sharp | |
| | 1975-80 | Galtung | |
| | 1977 | Cooney and Michalowski | |
| | 1979 | Boulding et al. | 2nd edn.; 1974 1st edn. |
| 1980s | 1981 | – | Bernhardt |
| | 1982 | Dougall | |
| | 1982 | Woito | 6th edn.; 1967 1st edn. |
| | 1983 | Carroll et al. | |
| | 1983 | Holl and Donat | |
| | 1983 | Kuehl | |
| | 1985 | Josephson | |

Hussites, Czech and Swiss Brethren, German and Polish Anabaptists, German, Dutch and Russian Mennonites, and to Mennonites and Brethren in America. The author has devoted a separate volume to the Quakers: *The Quaker Peace Testimony, 1660 to 1914* (1990) surveys the peace witness of the Society of Friends not only in North America and the British Isles but also on the European continent (France, Prussia, Norway) and in Australia and New Zealand. The work thus represents the first comprehensive account of Quaker peace history since Margaret Hirst first attempted this in 1923. *Freedom from War: Nonsectarian Pacifism 1814-1914* (1991) "deals primarily with the ideas and activities of those 'absolute' pacifists who did not belong to a religious body collectively espousing pacifism" (p. VIII). Brock documents here how the pacifist impulse, which before 1814 was almost exclusively sectarian, in the course of the Nineteenth century expanded beyond its narrow origins and gained adherents also in other denominations (as well as among those not subscribing to any religion). Taken together, these three volumes provide a detailed and original documentation and analysis of the rebirth and evolution of 'the pacifist impulse' which until 1914 was largely derived from the Christian faith.

To celebrate the publication of this landmark historical synthesis of worldwide pacifism, an international conference was held in May 1991 at the University of Toronto in honor of its author. The papers delivered on that occasion were published as a *Festschrift* to Peter Brock on his seventy-fifth birthday (1995): *The Pacifist Impulse in Historical Perspective* (Toronto: University of Toronto Press, 1996). In his opening chapter, entitled "Peter Brock as a Historian of World-Wide Pacifism: An Appreciation," Harvey L. Dyck, the editor, calls Brock "the doyen of peace history" whose pioneering and scholarly writings on pacifism "cut across the ages and circle the globe;" his latest three-volume work "does no less than define for our generation the sub-field of peace history to 1914."[1]

*3. Disarmament*

The early 1990s also saw the publication of the first part of another three-volume history on a very different aspect of peace and collectively entitled *The Struggle Against the Bomb*. 1914 was a watershed both in the history of the world and of the pacifist phenomenon, and this explains why Brock finishes each of his studies with the year which has become synonymous with the start of World War I. 1945 constitutes no less a watershed in both respects; the birth of the nuclear age also witnessed the emergence of a new kind of pacifism: nuclear pacifism. Lawrence S. Wittner's *One World or None: A History of the World Nuclear Disarmament Movement Through 1953* (1993) is the opening volume in what will be the first comprehensive history of the global movement against the development, possession and use of nuclear weapons. One of the factors which inspired Wittner to embark on his ambitious project was the wish to find an explanation for a paradox: even though nuclear disarmament (see *Nuclear Weapons Abolition*) has been widely regarded as desirable, little progress has been made towards achieving that goal. As regards the scale of his project, the author rightly argues that "the story is so vast, important, and little-known" that it deserves to be the subject of a multi-volume work. In his first volume Wittner has examined the anti-nuclear activities of scientists, pacifists, world-government advocates, religious leaders, Japanese atomic bomb survivors (*hibakusha*), and other concerned citizens in dozens of nations. One part of the book is devoted to the communist-led movement against the bomb, and the problems this posed for non-communist abolitionists. The second volume will trace the history of the global nuclear disarmament movement to 1970, with the third one bringing the story up to the present time. Reviewers of the first volume have been unanimous in their praise of this "monumental undertaking."[2]

Wittner argues that the history of the world-wide struggle against the Bomb deserves serious study because, despite the end of the Cold War, the nuclear menace "remains alive and well... Annihilation continues to beckon" (p. X). The struggle must continue, and is likely to be more effective in so far as lessons from past experience can be drawn and will be heeded. Richard Dean Burns, Editor in Chief of the three-volume *Encyclopedia of Arms Control and Disarmament* (1993), indicates that his encyclopedia likewise was motivated by the desire to enable academics, diplomats, journalists, military officers and even professional arms controllers "to look to the past for insight" (p. XI). He, too, points out that the need for arms control and disarmament—not only in the nuclear but also in the conventional field—persists in the post-Cold War era. He argues that, given the growing importance which arms control and disarmament have assumed since 1945 (because of the increasing destructiveness of weapons), scholars and policymakers alike have been in need of a comprehensive and reliable survey of all those processes "that seek to prevent or ... contain war and ameliorate its violence" (p. XI).

The first volume comprises two parts, one dealing with country and regional surveys (from Africa to the US), and one with themes and institutions (from Arms Control Treaty Compliance to the US Arms Control and Disarmament Agency). The second volume focuses on arms control from both historical and contemporary perspectives. The historical section ranges from Restraining Violence in Early Societies to Regulating Submarine Warfare 1919-45. The contemporary section contains essays which deal with, e.g., the disarming and rearming of the Axis powers of World War II, and essays which survey their subject, be it, e.g., Test Ban Proposals or Confidence-Building Measures, from the beginning to the present. The final volume contains the texts of important treaties, with editorial notes and comments. The documents are presented in six categories: (a) Limitation of weapons and personnel; (b) Demilitarization, denuclearization and neutralization; (c) Regulating and outlawing weapons and war; (d) Controlling arms manufacture and traffic; (e) Rules of war; and (f) Stabilizing the international environment. For each category, the texts of several dozen agreements are given; on most occasions they span a period of two millennia or more. For example, treaties in the second category range from Limiting Use of War Elephants in 202 B.C. to the UN Resolution Prohibiting Iraqi Possession of Weapons of Mass Destruction (1991). The fourth section surveys its subject from the control of Israel's 'Blacksmiths' in 1100 B.C. to the Big Five Initiative on Arms Transfer and Proliferation Restraints (1991). These few examples are suggestive of the thoroughness of the enterprise, and the unexpected and fascinating detail which especially the historical sections frequently reveal. Each essay has been contributed by a recognized expert on the subject, making this unique encyclopedia a most impressive and useful reference work on a subject which is so vital to the achievement of peace.

Important as they are, disarmament and arms limitation are of course not the only, or a sufficient, road to peace. *Peace/Mir: An Anthology of Historic Alternatives to War* (1994) documents the long search for peace in the history of Western civilization. Some 160 key documents, spanning a period from 400 B.C. to 1945, and drawn from many societies and authors, are used to illustrate the rich variety of peace approaches and proposals, including absolute pacifism, arbitration, international organization, citizen peace action, and state diplomacy.[3] The volume is the fruit of cooperation between US and Russian historians, and was made possible through the financial support of the US Institute of Peace (see *US Institute of Peace*) and the Russian Academy of Sciences (Institute of Universal History). It is, in the field of peace history, the first such collaborative effort which the end of the Cold War has made possible. The editors recognize that, for all their diversity, the ideas of peace in Western civilization do not exhaust the world's approaches to peace. They express the hope that their volume "will be followed by others clarifying the peace traditions of Asian, African, and indigenous American cultures" (p. XVI). Such a series would indeed constitute a veritable world encyclopedia of peace ideas and would confirm that today's global search and yearning for peace are fully reflected and foreshadowed in that of the past.

## 4. Nobel Peace Prize

If pacifists and war resisters have traditionally been minorities and outsiders, it can not be denied that the twentieth century has witnessed a steady growth in the peace (if not strictly pacifist) sentiment—no doubt largely in response to the increasing destructiveness of modern war. The Nobel Peace Prize can be regarded as a typically twentieth century manifestation of this evolution in the traditional attitudes towards war and peace. Whereas the notions of honor and glory, and heroism, have always been identified in national cultures with war and military exploits (and their opposites with peace and pacifism), this is no longer the case. In fact, today the Nobel Peace Prize has by general agreement "come to represent the most prestigious world prize for service to humanity" (Abrams, XI). The words are those of Irwin Abrams to whom we owe the most scholarly and authoritative study on the subject: *The Nobel Peace Prize and the Laureates: An Illustrated Biographical History, 1901-1987* (a revised and updated edition is forthcoming). Since 1962, when he published the first critical analysis of the correspondence between Alfred Nobel and Bertha von Suttner (the Austrian baroness who inspired Nobel to become a Maecenas for peace), Abrams has been researching and writing on the prize, making him the world's foremost scholar of it.[4] We would like to endorse the view of one prominent reviewer of Abrams' biographical history who wrote: "For scholars of peace, the work should be a basic reference book that will stand alongside the *Biographical Dictionary of Internationalists* (1983) ... and the *Biographical Dictionary of Modern Peace Leaders* (1985) ... Extraordinarily useful for scholars, it should also inspire men and women of good will everywhere."[5]

It is fitting that Abrams was appointed to edit the two-volume *Nobel Lectures in Peace* for the period 1971-1990 which supplement the original volumes edited by Frederick Haberman mentioned above. Given the importance of the peace efforts which are honored by the Nobel award, and the growing interest in the prize and in the subject of peacemaking generally, it is convenient to have also the more recent Nobel lectures, presentation and acceptance speeches, and laureates' biographies collected and published together (see *Nobel Peace Prizes*). The editor sums up well the significance of his volumes: "Altogether the contributions collected here represent an unrivaled documentation of the many ways in which some of the noblest spirits of our time have worked on the most crucial problem facing humanity today, the restraining of violence and the building of peace based upon human solidarity" (pp. IX-X).

The realization that the Nobel peace laureates constitute a pantheon of contemporary heroes and heroines, who provide inspiring role models for the young generation of today, has prompted Abrams to reach out beyond the scholarly community to a wider audience. This is also the rationale underlying the publication of a unique reference work on 'The Nobel Peace Prize from 1901 to Today': *Der Friedens-Nobelpreis von 1901 bis heute*. Written by leading historians and biographers and profusely illustrated, the twelve-volume work was conceived so as to appeal especially to younger readers. The often moving and exciting stories of individual laureates, told in an engaging manner, and enlivened by colorful illustrations, are meant to leave a mark on readers who are in search of an image of the world and of their future in it. As the publishers wrote in an extensive and appealing prospectus announcing the venture: "What once was a longing of many, now has become a condition for the survival of all. ... The experiences and the ideas of the Nobel peace laureates are the capital we would like to draw on today."[6] The series was conceived to present the twentieth century from a new perspective, namely through the collective biographies of those individuals and institutions that have struggled to replace war and violent conflict by peace, human rights, and justice. Through sponsorship, the publishers aimed to equip every school and public library in the country with a complimentary set. Thus, this unique encyclopedia was accompanied by a peace education initiative without parallel. The twelve volumes were published in the period 1987-93, comprising laureates from 1901 to 1988, and plans exist to bring out supplementary volumes so as to keep the work up to date. It is a matter for regret that so far no translations of this excellent work have appeared.

The increasing recognition of the importance of the work of the Nobel laureates in the search for peace today, and in the building of a culture of peace, is further demonstrated by the support of UNESCO, the Norwegian Nobel Institute, and the Norwegian Institute of Human Rights for a voluminous anthology comprising abridged versions of all the Nobel lectures and speeches. In *Peace! By the Nobel Peace Prize Laureates* (1995), editor Marek Thee has organized the material in seven thematic parts so as to be able to emphasize the different approaches and perspectives to peace which the laureates represent. Following a section on the meaning of peace, they are: instruments for peace policies (international law and arbitration, international organizations, and international understanding and cooperation); the peace movement and the pacifist world-view; armament and disarmament; human rights, welfare and social justice; humanitarian challenges; and regional conflicts (South Africa, Middle East). Within each of these thematic parts, the chronological order has been maintained (1901-94). As UNESCO Director-General Federico Mayor writes in a preface: "In its efforts to establish the foundations of a genuine culture of peace, UNESCO could not hope to find a richer source of inspiration than the work initiated by Alfred

Nobel nearly a century ago . . . . The Nobel Peace Prizes serve to signpost possible paths to peace" (p. 5). This volume, constructed around the most significant signposts, is a helpful guide.

## 5. Medical Peace Movement

It is, in many ways, also a hopeful guide—as exemplified in the remarkable success story of the 1985 laureate, International Physicians for the Prevention of Nuclear War (IPPNW) (see Nobel Peace Prize Laureates: *International Physicians for the Prevention of Nuclear War*). Its US cofounder, Dr. Bernard Lown, mentioned in his December 1985 Nobel lecture that the organization was also celebrating at this same time "only the fifth anniversary of our founding" (in Thee, op. cit., p. 343). IPPNW is a telling example of the truth of a favorite observation of Lown's (borrowed from Margaret Mead), namely, "that a small group of thoughtful, committed citizens can change the world."[7] Although IPPNW itself is a young organization, its roots go back at least to the beginning of the century, when Joseph Rivière founded the International Medical Association Against War in Paris, in 1905 (it has been regarded as the world's first professionally based peace organization).[8] But well before this, individual physicians had pointed out the responsibility of their profession for helping to prevent what is, after all, the greatest destroyer of human life and health. Thanks to an initiative in the 1980s of the East and West German branches of IPPNW to uncover the history of the medical peace movement, we have now available the most detailed and comprehensive study yet: Thomas M. Ruprecht and Christian Jenssen (eds.), *Aeskulap oder Mars? Aerzte gegen den Krieg* (Asclepius or Mars? Doctors Against War). Consisting of some thirty chapters, grouped in five chronological sections (starting with the period 1848-1914), the book profiles all of the leading figures of the medical peace movement of the last one and a half century as well as the various medical peace initiatives and organizations they have created in order to promote the cause. Since the volume started out as a German-German initiative, and was also meant to be an exercise in practical bridge-building across the East-West divide, the medical peace movement in the German-speaking world predominates[9] but developments elsewhere are given their full due. This volume is indeed, as one reviewer has commented, "an indispensable historical source book"[10] which provides a truly encyclopedic coverage of its subject.

## 6. International Law

An example of IPPNW's imaginative, practical and productive approach to peacemaking has been its central involvement in the early 1990s (together with two other international non-governmental peace organizations, International Association of Lawyers Against Nuclear Arms, and the International Peace Bureau) in the World Court Project. This was the (successful) attempt to have the World Health Organization, as well as the General Assembly of the UN, request an advisory opinion from the International Court of Justice (see *International Law; International Court of Justice*) in The Hague on the question of the legality of the use or threat of nuclear weapons. Just as the medical profession has become increasingly involved in the peace movement, so the latter has increasingly recognized the importance of the legal approach (and the opportunities inherent in it) in efforts to strengthen peace and disarmament. It is thus fortuitous that the twelve-volume *Encyclopedia of Public International Law* is now available in its entirety. Given the ambitious nature of the project, it is not surprising that its completion has taken a full decade, from publication of the first installment in 1981 to the last one in 1990.[11] And yet, this is only the first phase of the project.

As we mentioned already in the original essay above, the thematically organized Encyclopedia will also appear in a format which is strictly alphabetical. Of the five projected volumes, two have so far been published. The first one (1992) comprises entries ranging from Aaland Islands to Dumbarton Oaks Conference; the second one (1995) deals with topics ranging from East African Community to Italy-US Air Transport Association. Articles have been carried over unchanged from the thematic to the alphabetical version but where necessary and possible, short addenda have been provided which contain information on recent developments, new documents, and supplementary literature. A few entirely new articles are also included; these and other changes are carefully noted in the new version. The *Encyclopedia's* editor, Rudolf Bernhardt, writes in the preface of the 1992 volume: "The last decade of the twentieth century promises to bring about many new developments in the various fields of public international law. It is hoped that these can be dealt with later in a revised edition of the Encyclopedia" (p. VII).

## 7. United Nations

It is a happy coincidence that the full *Encyclopedia of Public International Law* has become available at the start of the decade of international law—one of the aims of which is to promote a better understanding of its nature and role among a wider public (a purpose which the Encyclopedia is well able to serve). Several of its more than 450 authors have also contributed to a less ambitious but still "extremely useful"[12] quasi-encyclopedic two-volume reference guide entitled *United Nations: Law, Policies and Practice* (1995). In 162 chapters, starting with "ABC-weapons" and ending with "WTO-World Tourist Organization," the work attempts to describe fully all the institutions, functions, and activities undertaken by the UN and its specialized agencies. The work finds its origins in the German Handbook of the UN, first published in 1977 and fully revised in 1991. The present volume is a further revised and updated version of the 1991 edition, now for the first time translated into English. Its editor in chief, Rüdiger Wolfrum, is chairman of the German United Nations Association (UNA), whose financial support of the publication (appearing during the UN's 50th anniversary) is acknowledged. However, a more substantial reason than the celebration of the anniversary underlies the publication: as Wolfrum points out, the impact of the United Nations on world politics has increased greatly following the end of the Cold War, and in consequence the UN has acquired "renewed prestige as the pre-eminent force in international relations" (p. V).[13]

Ten years before the publication of Wolfrum's edited volumes, the first proper encyclopedia on the UN was published on the occasion of the 40th anniversary of the ratification of the UN Charter. This was Edmund Jan Osmanczyk's *The Encyclopedia of the United Nations and International Agreements.* The distinguished author and internationalist completed a second, updated, edition just before his death in 1989—the year in which he was elected to the reestablished Senate of his native Poland.[14] Published in 1990, the *Encyclopedia* not only contains information on the UN, its specialized agencies, and the many organizations which cooperate with the UN, it also contains entries on several thousand international agreements, conventions and treaties which are quoted in full or in part. The rationale for including the latter in a work on the UN is explained in the foreword: "The UN System arose and continues to develop in a nexus of bilateral and multilateral arrangements (see *Status and Role of the United Nations*). Without guidance in these agreements it is impossible to understand the UN System and its role in world relations" (p. XI). The then Secretary-General, Javier Pérez De Cuéllar, hailed the *Encyclopedia* as a "remarkable accomplishment" by "a most thoughtful analyst and supporter of the UN" (p. IX).

## 8. International Organizations

The UN, like so many other international organizations, has its own *Yearbook*, prepared by the Department of Public Information.[15] The rapid growth in recent years, both in number and importance, of international and regional organizations (of an inter-governmental or nongovernmental nature) has resulted in the publication of many guides, directories and dictionaries which aim to survey this phenomenon.[16] From this literature we single out only the undisputed pioneer work which is truly encyclopedic and awesome in its scope and detail. The *Yearbook of International Organizations*, first published in 1948, is today published in four heavy tomes (33rd edition 1996/97); the volumes, which have been increasing in weight and number over the decades, provide a visible yardstick for the growth of the organizations it deals with. The *Yearbook* is the best known of the documentation sources provided by the Union of International Associations (UIA). In the early years of this century, long before Brussels would become a byword for European unification, the city was at the center of various proposals and initiatives to become the international capital; the UIA was established when the first World Congress of International Associations took place in Brussels in 1910.[17] An independent research institute, the UIA has worked closely with the League of Nations and the United Nations in documenting and coordinating the work of international organizations, both official and private. The *Yearbook* is, above all, the world's most complete and authoritative inventory of international organizations. Beyond this, the tens of thousands of organizations which are profiled in it (divided into more than 3,000 categories) provide an inexhaustible data base for research on the specifically twentieth century phenomenon of the international organization.

The UIA also produces an encyclopedia which it regards as a companion to the *Yearbook*: the *Encyclopedia of World Problems and Human Potential*. This unique and ambitious reference work aims to be a comprehensive sourcebook for information on recognized world problems (the third edition, published in 1991, contained entries on more than 13,000!), their interconnectedness, and the human resources available to analyze and ultimately respond to them. Deriving much of its information from the UN and other international agencies, the Encyclopedia identifies and juxtaposes the many conflicting perceptions and priorities which constitute the dynamic reality of world society. A reviewer of its most recent edition (the 4th), published in three volumes in 1994, has critically noted: "The main problem is that the dominant perspective expressed ... merely sustains the orthodoxy of the international agencies. Moreover, the cases relating to the possibilities for ameliorating social and political distress are few and say little about the grassroots work done by many international agencies"[18] or by indigenous political and social movements across the globe.

## 9. *Peace Encyclopedias in Languages other than English*

Several of the authors of classical plans for world peace and of blueprints for a world organization, among other details also discussed the question of the language in which the business of the proposed organization should be conducted. For example, William Penn specified that the European Parliament which he proposed in 1693 use Latin or French; Saint-Pierre wanted his European Senate (1712) to deliberate "in the language which finds itself the most used and which is the most common one in Europe among the living languages." Whereas in the eighteenth century French started to supplant Latin as the language of international diplomacy, the growth of the British Empire in the nineteenth century and the rise of the US as a world power in the twentieth, have combined to make English the indisputable *lingua franca* of today. It is significant that the *Encyclopedia of Public International Law*, although initiated in Germany and with a collective authorship which is almost wholly drawn from the German-language area, is nevertheless published in English. The present *World Encyclopedia of Peace*, although conceived in Korea, appears in the same language. This 'bias' is also reflected in the coverage of the literature discussed above.

It seems especially important, however, when addressing the question of how different nations and cultures interpret the concept of peace and the various ways to achieve it, not to ignore the relevant literature in languages other than English. Limitations of a practical kind have prevented any systematic effort which would have allowed its inclusion here. By way of illustration, two such "peace encyclopedias" will be briefly introduced. A team of researchers at the Institute of International Relations at the University of Warsaw headed by Professor J. Kukulka published the first 'Peace Lexicon' (*Leksykon Pokoju*), comprising some 370 entries, in 1987. Appearing at a time when the Cold War was thawing but not yet over, this collective work still shows strongly the ideological attitudes of the time. A sympathetic yet not uncritical reviewer deplored the "doctrinal approach" which was reflected in a "tendency to treat all the initiatives of the socialist States as peaceful from the very definition and an opposite tendency when the politics of the capitalist States [are] presented."[19]

The second work to consider also displays a particular viewpoint but of a very different kind. The Japanese 'Peace Encyclopedia' or 'Dictionary' (*Heiwa Jiten*) aims to provide the reader with the necessary information and knowledge for understanding peace issues, taking the experience of Hiroshima and Nagasaki as its starting-point. The work was prepared at the independent Hiroshima Peace and Culture Centre (Hiroshima Heiwa Bunka Centre). As the only country to have suffered the effects of atomic bombing, it would be surprising if Japan's perspective on international relations was not dominated by that tragic experience. First published in 1985, a second and expanded edition appeared in 1991. More than 100 experts contributed to the volume's twenty-one thematic chapters. They frequently take the form of 'Peace and X', whereby 'X' in turn stands for politics, economic development, education, art, international law, etc. Other chapters deal with military and strategic issues, nuclear weapons and disarmament. Among the wealth of peace and peace research literature in their language, Japanese scholars regard this book as the most comprehensive and reliable introduction to issues of war and peace available.[20]

## 10. Some Other Encyclopedias

Apart from the encyclopedic works which focus on peace or aspects of peace which have been briefly reviewed above, recent years have also seen the publication of many encyclopedias on subjects which have an obvious bearing on peace. Its complex, multi-faceted nature means that few areas of human knowledge and enquiry can be ignored (an observation with which we concluded the original introductory essay, above). Human rights, development, and the environment are among the most urgent and keenly debated issues of the contemporary world; their central importance in efforts to make the world more peaceful is widely accepted. It is, however, not the intention to present here encyclopedic treatments of these and similar subjects. This article concludes more modestly by drawing attention to a few examples of recent encyclopedias which the serious student of peace should be aware of.

It has rightly been said that the twentieth century has been the 'American century'; the US has played a foremost role in shaping that century—no matter whether the issue is economy, science and technology, popular culture, or international relations. The *Encyclopedia of US Foreign Relations* (1997), produced under the auspices of the US Council on Foreign Relations, provides a comprehensive historical survey of US foreign policy and diplomacy since the American independence. The four volumes of alphabetically arranged entries range from brief biographical sketches to major essays on critical issues of US foreign policy. Reflecting both the remarkable international involvement of the US, as well as the formidable expansion of the foreign relations agenda in the twentieth century, the *Encyclopedia* explores a wide range of topics: from treaties and accords, conferences and commissions, and politicians and peacemakers, to military conflicts and defense strategies, international commerce and trade negotiations, and environmental and health issues. It constitutes in some ways an update of the earlier *Encyclopedia of American Foreign Policy*. Sub-titled 'Studies of the principal movements and ideas,' and edited by Alexander De Conde, this 3-volume work comprises almost 100 essays.[21] Written by leading US experts, they range from 'Alliances, Coalitions and Ententes' to 'Unconditional Surrender.' Among the topics of the alphabetically arranged essays are conscription, disarmament, internationalism, international law, international organization, military-industrial complex, pacifism, peace movement.

The twentieth century is also characterized by stark contradictions such as that between the growth and spread of democracy and human rights on the one hand, and totalitarianism and genocide on the other. The four-volume *Encyclopedia of Democracy* (1995) deals with its subjects in over 400 articles, which have been contributed by 250 authors. Equally voluminous and useful is the *Encyclopedia of the Holocaust* (1990). It is perhaps appropriate to introduce as the last work one which is not only forthcoming, but also an ambitious attempt to bring the current state of knowledge and research on violence, peace, and conflict together in a single reference work. *The Encyclopedia of Violence, Peace, and Conflict*, scheduled for publication in 1998, will contain some 300 essays grouped into thematic thematic categories. The latter consist of the main disciplinary fields relevant to the subject, and range from such fields as Anthropological and Biomedical Studies, via Cultural, Economic, and Ethical Studies, to Psychological, Sociological, and War Studies. The main alphabetical arrangement is according to discipline name, as indicated; the articles in each disciplinary section are likewise arranged in alphabetical order. This encyclopedia thus adopts an interesting formula which marries the two usual formats for organizing and presenting its subject, the alphabetical and the thematic approach.

## Notes

1. The volume contains a bibliography of Brock's writings on peace history from 1957 to 1994.

2. The words are those of another leading American historian of our nuclear predicament, Paul Boyer. See the back-cover of Wittner's first volume for this and similar comments. In his review, LeRoy Moore refers to 'a deeply documented ... trail-blazing history' which 'whets the appetite.' *Peace and Change*, Vol. 20, no. 1, January 1995, pp. 141-146.

3. As the enthusiastic reviewer of this 'very interesting book' in the *Journal of Peace Research* commented: 'The book is not really about alternatives to war so much as an anthology of the history of ideas about war and peace.' Vol. 32, no. 2, 1995, p. 374.

4. See 'Profile of a Peace Historian: Irwin Abrams,' in *Organization of American History (OAH) Magazine of History*, Spring 1994, pp. 40-41.

5. Calvin D. Davis, in *Peace and Change*, Vol. 14, no. 4, October 1989, pp. 470-471.

6. *Der Friedens-Nobelpreis von 1901 bis heute: Projekt-information.* Zug and Munich: Edition Pacis, 1986, 31 pp. (at pp. 2-3). The project met with wide public acclaim, as is testified by several pages of commendations.

7. Bernard Lown & Eugene I. Chazov, 'Physician Responsibility in the Nuclear Age,' *Journal of the American Medical Association*, Vol. 274, no. 5, 2 August 1995, pp. 416-419 (at p. 416).

8. See Nick Lewer & Peter van den Dungen, 'Joseph Rivière: Physician and Peace worker,' in *Medicine and War*, Vol. 6, no. 2, April-June 1990, pp. 94-104.

9. Even before this book was published, one student of the medical peace movement was able to write: 'In the German Federal Republic a flourishing literature on the social history of medicine in Germany, under the pressure of war and in peace, was born in the 1980s. This is related partly to the stimulus of the IPPNW movement, but mainly to the German medical profession's need for a thorough self-examination. ... The anti-war movement of physicians in Germany spans many generations—as does that country's history of militarism, which is better known! Cf. Ilkka Taipale, 'German Physicians Against War Since 1870,' in *Medicine and War*, vol. 6, no. 4, October-December 1990, pp. 269-274 (at pp. 269-70).

10. Jack Boag, review in *Medicine and War*, Vol. 9, no. 2, April-June 1993, pp. 161-163.

11. The 12th and final thematic instalment is entitled 'Geographic Issues' and covers 96 cases, from Aaland Islands to Walvis Bay. More extensive coverage of the same theme can be found in Alan Day, John B. Allcock *et al.*, *Border and territorial disputes* (Harlow, Essex: Longman, 3rd ed. 1992, 630 pp.) The introduction to this very useful work makes clear that since 1989 and the collapse of the Soviet Union, Europe has once again become a focal point of conflict and tension and that as a result the coverage for Europe has more than doubled compared with the previous editions (when border and territorial disputes were largely an issue affecting the developing world).

12. Thus, Vera Gowlland-Debbas in her detailed review entitled 'United Nations A-Z' in *Security Dialogue*, Vol. 27, no. 3, September 1996, pp. 352-354 (at p. 354).

13. The most notable development of all UN activities (in both quantitative and qualitative terms) has been in peacekeeping. An essential reference work is *The Blue Helmets: A Review of United Nations Peacekeeping*. New York: UN Dept. of Public Information, 3rd ed., 1996, 808 pp. For a judicious review, see Anthony McDermott in *Security Dialogue*, Vol. 28, no. 2, June 1997, pp. 247-248.

14. With a name like his, Osmanczyk was perhaps destined to become an internationalist, and an expert on the UN. He was the descendant of a Turkish soldier who had settled in Poland after being captured by the Poles during the last siege of Vienna in 1683. See the interesting obituary by Jan Ciechanowski in the *Encyclopedia* (pp. XIII-XIV).

15. The most recent *Yearbook of the UN* is vol. 48, covering the year 1994 (The Hague: Martinus Nijhoff, 1995, 1564 pp.) In the same year, the same publisher brought out a special edition: *Yearbook of the UN: UN Fiftieth Anniversary 1945-1995* (464 pp).

16. By way of examples, we simply list a small selection of such works which have all appeared since 1990; while some cover much the same ground, others, by focusing on a region or specific type of activity, set themselves apart and manage to be more original. Giuseppe Schiavone, *International Organizations: A Dictionary and Directory* (London: Macmillan, 3rd ed., 1992, 337 pp.); Sheikh R. Ali, *The International Organizations and World Order Dictionary* (Santa Barbara, CA & Oxford: ABC-Clio, 1992, 283pp.); Hans-Albrecht Schraepler, *Directory of International Organizations* (Washington, DC: Georgetown University Press, 1996, 424 pp.); Richard Owen, *The Times Guide to World Organisations* (London: Times Books, 1996, 254 pp.); Richard Fredland, *A Guide to African International Organizations* (London: Hans Zell, 1990, 316 pp.); Mark W. Delancey & Terry M. Mays, *Historical Dictionary of International Organizations in Sub-Saharan Africa* (Metuchen, N.J.: Scarecrow Press, 1994, 517 pp.); Derek W. Urwin, *Historical Dictionary of European Organizations* (Metuchen, N.J.: Scarecrow Press, 1994, 390 pp.); Bernard Colas, ed., *Global Economic Co-operation: A Guide to Agreements and Organziations* (Didcot, Oxfordshire: Management Books 2000, 2nd ed., 1994); N.J. Rengeer with John Campbell, *Treaties and Alliances of the World* (London: Cartermill, 6th ed., 1995, 538pp.). This last publication is also available on CD-ROM in an expanded version. The present survey of 'peace encyclopedias' has been limited to traditional print-media, ignoring publications on microfiche, CD-ROM, and the internet. Some of the publications listed above acknowledge their indebtedness to the reference work which is introduced next. 424 pp.); Richard Owen, *The Times Guide to World Organisations* (London: Times Books, 1996, 254 pp.); Richard Fredland, *A Guide to African International Organizations* (London: Hans Zell, 1990, 316 pp.); Mark W. Delancey & Terry M. Mays, *Historical Dictionary of Interna-

*tional Organizations in Sub-Saharan Africa* (Metuchen, N.J.: Scarecrow Press, 1994, 517 pp.); Derek W. Urwin, *Historical Dictionary of European Organizations* (Metuchen, N.J.: Scarecrow Press, 1994, 390 pp.); Bernard Colas, ed., *Global Economic Co-operation: A Guide to Agreements and Organziations* (Didcot, Oxfordshire: Management Books 2000, 2nd ed., 1994); N.J. Rengeer with John Campbell, *Treaties and Alliances of the World* (London: Cartermill, 6th ed., 1995, 538pp.). This last publication is also available on CD-ROM in an expanded version. The present survey of 'peace encyclopedias' has been limited to traditional print-media, ignoring publications on microfiche, CD-ROM, and the internet. Some of the publications listed above acknowledge their indebtedness to the reference work which is introduced next.

17. Further details on the UIA are contained in the entries for Peace Museums (Vol. 2) and Henri La Fontaine (Novel Peace Prize Laureate 1913, Vol. 3) in the present encyclopedia.

18. Ray Bush, review in *Security Dialogue*, Vol. 28, no. 1, March 1997, pp. 124-125.

19. J. Kukulka (ed.), *Leksykon Pokoju*, Warsaw: KAW, 1987, 250 pp. Review by Andrzej Harasimowicz in *Polish Peace Research Studies*, Vol. 2, no. 1, 1989, pp. 119-121 (at p. 119).

20. *Heiwa Jiten*, Hiroshima: Keiso Shobo, 1991, 604 pp. I am grateful to Kiyohiko Toyama for information about this publication.

21. New York: Charles Scribner's, 1978, 1201 pp.

## Bibliography

Abrams I 1988 *The Nobel Peace Prize and the Laureates: An Illustrated Biographical History, 1901-1987*. G.K. Hall Boston

Abrams I (ed.) 1997 *Nobel Lectures—Peace*, 2 vols. World Scientific (for the Nobel Foundation), Singapore

Bernhardt R (ed.) 1981-1990 *Encyclopedia of Public International Law*, 12 vols. North-Holland, Amsterdam

Bernhardt R (ed.) 1992 *Encyclopedia of Public International Law*. North Holland, Amsterdam

Brock P 1990 *The Quaker Peace Testimony, 1660 to 1914*. Sessions, York

Brock P 1991 *Freedom from Violence: Sectarian Non-resistance from the Middle Ages to the Great War*. Toronto University Press, Toronto

Brock P 1991 *Freedom from War: Nonsectarian Pacifism, 1814-1914*. Toronto University Press, Toronto

Burns R D (ed.) 1993 *Encyclopedia of Arms Control and Disarmament*, 3 vols. Charles Scribner's Sons, New York

Chatfield C, Ilukhina R (eds.) 1994 *Peace/Mir: An Anthology of Historic Alternatives to War*. Syracuse University Press, Syracuse, New York

Gutman I (ed.) 1990 *Encyclopedia of the Holocaust*, 4 vols. Macmillan, New York

Jentleson B, Paterson T (eds.) 1997 *Encyclopedia of U.S. Foreign Relations*, 4 vols. Oxford University Press, New York

Kurtz L (ed.) (forthcoming) 1998 *Encyclopedia of Violence, Peace, and Conflict*. Academic Press, San Diego, California

Lipset S M (ed.) 1995 *The Encyclopedia of Democracy*, 4 vols. Congressional Quarterly, Washington, DC; Routledge, London

Neumann M (ed.) 1987-1993 *Der Friedens-Nobelpreis von 1901 bis heute*, 12 vols. Edition Pacis, Zug and Munich

Osmanczyk E J (ed.) 1990 *The Encyclopedia of the United Nations and International Agreements*, 2nd edn. Taylor and Francis, London

Powers R, Vogele W (eds.) 1997 *Protest, Power, and Change: An Encyclopedia of Nonviolent Action from ACT-UP to Women's Suffrage*. Garland, New York

Ruprecht T, Jenssen C (eds.) 1991 *Aeskulap oder Mars? Aerzte gegen den Krieg*. Donat Verlag, Bremen

Thee M (ed.) 1995 *Peace! By the Nobel Peace Prize Laureates. An Anthology*. UNESCO, Paris

Union of International Associations (UIA) (ed.) 1996 *Yearbook of International Organizations 1996/97*, 33rd edn. 4 vols. K.G. Saur, Munich

Union of International Associations (UIA) (ed.) 1991 *Encyclopedia of World Problems and Human Potential*, 3rd edn. 2 vols. K.G. Saur, Munich, (1994, 4th edn. 3 vols.)

Wittner L 1993 *The Struggle against the Bomb*, Vol. I. *One World or None: A History of the World Nuclear Disarmament Movement through 1953*. Stanford University Press, Stanford, California

Wolfrum R (ed.) 1995 *United Nations: Law, Policies and Practice*, 2 vols. Martinus Nijhoff, Dordrecht

PETER VAN DEN DUNGEN

# A

## Acheson, Dean

Dean Gooderham Acheson (1893-1971), United States Secretary of State under President Harry Truman, was one of the principal architects of United States foreign policy in the years following the Second World War.

Acheson graduated from Yale University in 1915 and went on to Harvard Law School, where he obtained his degree in 1918. He then went to Washington, where he practiced law from 1921 to 1941, taking six months out in 1933 to serve as Undersecretary of the Treasury. Acheson's law practice acquainted him with numerous international issues, and he returned to government in 1941 as Assistant Secretary of State. During the Second World War he became a major voice in the formation of United States policy, using his influence most effectively to encourage an active United States role in creating a prosperous, economically and politically stable Europe after the defeat of Nazism. His efforts bore fruit after the war with the dispatch of United States aid to Greece and Turkey early in 1947, aid which played a vital role in stopping those countries' drift into anarchy and possible Soviet domination. Acheson was also a strong and effective adherent of the Marshall Plan, which committed the United States to massive aid to Europe, later in 1947.

In 1949, Truman made Acheson his Secretary of State. International tensions then stood at an uncomfortably high level, particularly in the relationship between the United States and the former Soviet Union. The United States had never accepted the Soviet takeover of Eastern Europe after the Second World War, and the Soviets, deeply suspicious of Western intentions, were sparing no effort to undercut the Marshall Plan. Berlin, a lonely Western outpost behind the "Iron Curtain," was then under Soviet blockade, being precariously kept alive by a massive airlift. In Asia, China was in the process of falling into communist hands. Acheson, though not a militant anti-Soviet hardliner, concluded that the differences between the former Soviet Union and the United States were too great to be bridged. Rather than seek an end to the conflict,

he concluded that the only wise course of action was to make the West as strong and united as possible, so that it would be able to deter or resist Soviet pressure.

Acheson was instrumental in the creation of the North Atlantic Treaty Organization (NATO) alliance in 1949, which committed the United States, Canada, France, the United Kingdom, and other European democracies to come to one another's aid if attacked. His adroit diplomacy is credited with forging NATO into a strong and effective bloc. By 1952 he had even convinced the reluctant French to end their occupation of German territory, then to allow the Federal Republic of Germany to rearm, paving the way for a vastly strengthened alliance.

Acheson's record in Asia is more controversial. He argued successfully against using United States military power to shore up Chiang Kai-shek's tottering anticommunist régime in China, thereby provoking a great deal of conservative resentment. Then in January 1950, he gave a speech in which he defined United States security interests in Asia in such a way that only Japan and the Philippines appeared to enjoy United States military protection. This was later denounced for perhaps contributing to the communist invasion of the Republic of Korea that June.

Once Korea was attacked, though, Acheson quickly decided that to give way here would be to repeat the disastrous "appeasement" policies which had led to the Second World War. He enthusiastically supported the decision to fight in Korea, so much so that here too his actions remain controversial. Reacting to a wave of anticommunist feeling, he reversed United States policy by extending US military protection to Taiwan, thereby saving that island from communism but virtually guaranteeing that China's Civil War would be prolonged indefinitely. He also failed to foresee that a counter-invasion of the Democratic People's Republic of Korea would provoke Chinese intervention in the Korean War, thus condemning Korea to two added years of bloody and futile stalemate. By the end of his tenure as Secretary of State, Acheson had done much to lock the United States into a rigidly anti-Chinese stance in Asia that it would take decades to reverse.

Acheson retired as Secretary of State in 1953, when the Eisenhower Administration took office, and never held public office again. He spent the last 18 years of his life writing, lecturing, and serving as an increasingly respected adviser to the United States government on foreign policy issues. Even in retirement, it would never be Acheson's lot to escape controversy. Although conservative suspicion that he was not sufficiently anticommunist died down considerably after the 1950s, a new generation of critics soon began to assail him from the other direction. In the 1960s and 1970s, scholars searching for the roots of the Vietnam tragedy began to regard Acheson with hostility as one of the creators of the United States' disastrous Asian policy. Indeed, Acheson did encourage the Truman Administration to support the French effort in Vietnam after the Korean War broke out, and he later approved of the Johnson Administration's deepening of the United States commitment in Vietnam in the 1960s. By 1968, though, he had concluded that the US effort in Vietnam was futile, and began to call for the United States to cut loose.

Throughout his career, Acheson always maintained that, when it came to questions of war and peace, it was best to err on the side of peace. The dangers inherent in the nuclear age, he felt, made this particularly important.

Acheson, who produced eight highly regarded books and numerous columns and articles, was a prolific and graceful writer. His general views of war and peace can best be studied in his *Power and Diplomacy*, and his account of his years as Secretary of State in *Present at the Creation*.

*Bibliography* ———————————————

Acheson D 1958 *Power and Diplomacy*. Harvard University Press, Cambridge, Massachusetts
Acheson D 1965 *Morning and Noon*. Houghton Mifflin, Boston, Massachusetts
Acheson D 1969 *Present at the Creation*. Norton, New York
Acheson D 1971 *The Korean War*. Norton, New York
McLellan D S 1976 *Dean Acheson*. Dodd Mead, New York
Smith G 1972 *Dean Acheson*. Cooper Square, New York

GARRETT L. MCAINSH

# Acton, John

John Emerich Edward Dalberg Acton (1834-1902), best remembered for his passionate defense of individual rights against the power of the state, was one of the most prominent intellectual figures of Victorian England. Born into an aristocratic English Catholic family, Acton remained a devout Catholic all his life, though his liberalism often put him at loggerheads with the Church leadership. Acton won election to Britain's House of Commons in 1859, and was given a seat in the House of Lords ten years later by his good friend, Liberal Prime Minister William Gladstone (see *Gladstone, William Ewart*). However, he was far more active in historical scholarship than in politics. Though he published little on history during his lifetime, his erudition and conceptual abilities were highly respected. His talents were recognized by his appointment as Regius Professor of Modern History at Cambridge University in 1895, and by his being chosen to launch the ambitious, multi-volume *Cambridge Modern History* project a year later.

At the center of Acton's concept of history is the assertion that people are motivated predominantly by their ideas: therefore it is ideas which shape events and make history. The most significant idea of the modern world, he argued, was the concept that every individual has inalienable, God-given rights. It was basically this idea, he said, which had caused the American and French Revolutions, and which was moving people to throw off the shackles which tyranny had imposed on them all over the world. This struggle for freedom was the most important trend of modern history, Acton maintained. The historian's task was not simply to describe it, but to celebrate it. Those people and events which helped to secure human freedom should be praised, those subverting it pitilessly exposed.

Acton saw human freedom as constantly challenged by the state, and regarded leaders chosen by modern democratic methods as nearly as likely to abuse their power and trample on the rights of those they governed as were dictators or hereditary monarchs. "Power tends to corrupt," he warned in his most famous maxim, "and absolute power corrupts absolutely." Acton believed that the highest law for individuals should be their conscience, rather than society's expectations or even the government's laws and commands. Racism, nationalism, and socialism, all of which tended to subordinate the individual to the requirements of the group, he angrily rejected as inimical to human freedom. Nationalism in particular, which he felt encouraged intolerance and provoked wars, he regarded as dangerous. He hoped that his *Cambridge Modern History* would be so devoid of nationalistic prejudice that, even in its accounts of European wars, readers would be unable to tell whether the author was English, French, or German.

Acton agonized over the fact that individual freedom which he so valued, could apparently only be won through warfare and violence, which he abhorred. He was particularly distressed by the fact that, with rare exceptions, in the modern world the inevitable violent struggle for liberty resulted not in freedom, but in renewed tyranny. Few people have raised the question of whether noble ends can be justified by violent, warlike means more eloquently than Acton.

*Bibliography*

Acton J 1948 *Essays on Freedom and Power*. Beacon Press, Boston, Massachusetts
Butterfield H 1959 *The Whig Interpretation of History*. AMS Press, London
Himmelfarb G 1962 *Lord Acton: A Study in Conscience and Politics*. University of Chicago Press, Chicago, Illinois

GARRETT L. MCAINSH

# Aesthetic Value and Restoration of Humanity in the Technological Society

Political, economic, and social changes in the nineteenth century in the West raised in a new form the Platonic problem of the artist's relation to his society, his possibly conflicting obligations to his craft and to his fellow men. At that time, an important part of aesthetic thinking was concerned with this problem. One solution to the problem was to think of the artist as a person with a calling of his own; the artist, because of his superiority, or higher sensitivity, must be alienated from society, and carry his course as a pride. Eventually, it became the doctrine of "art for art's sake," an expression of aestheticism, according to which art or aesthetic value is more important than anything else.

In this paper, my intention is not to construct a contemporary version of aestheticism, but to call attention to the significance of aesthetic value, which may be unexpectedly valuable in dealing with the problem of identity crisis and restoration of human value in the contemporary situation. In order to do this, I shall be mainly concerned with the analysis of aesthetic value as distinguished from other values, although they mutually influence, and its relation to the structure of our society, which is characterized as the product of capitalistic commercialism, individualistic liberalism, and technological scientism. The point is that we need an aesthetic sensibility to tell us, whether man's most recent creations of himself cohere in a healthy pattern of wholeness or apart into schizoid decadence.

It is sometimes said that man's identity crisis in the contemporary situation is mainly due to the technological development of modern science. The wider implications of modern science as its ways of work and its general concepts seriously affect our worldviews. In the broadest sense, there can be no doubt that scientific attitudes toward nature and natural laws, and scientific skepticism toward the supernatural, have added powerfully to the modern drive toward rationalism, positivism, and materialism. Science continues to promote the worldview we have seen arising in early modern times. Indeed, many scientists have managed to make of the pursuit of scientific knowledge itself a kind of religion. In this respect, Ludwig Wittgenstein may be right, when he claims that we live in a dark age, in which the Medieval religious value has been replaced by the scientific cognitive one.[1]

On the influence of technology, Herbert Marcuse claims that the technical apparatus of production and distribution functions, not as the sum-total of mere instruments which can be isolated from their social and political effects, but "rather as a system which determines *a priori* the product of the apparatus as well as the operations of servicing and extending it." He says;

> As the project unfolds, it shapes the entire universe of discourse and action, intellectual and material culture. In the medium of technology, culture, politics, and the economy merge into an omnipresent system which swallows up or repulses all alternatives.[2]

"The productivity and growth potential of this system," adds Marcuse, "stabilize the society and contain technical progress within the framework of domination. Technological rationality has become political rationality."[3]

On the other hand, the strictly scientific view of man does not consider the realm of science to extend beyond the objective "facts" as disclosed by the various sciences. Man differs from the other animals by his "advanced anatomical and physiological complexity" and his more elaborate behavioral patterns. The scientific outlook may lead to the assertion that man and all his activities are determined by the laws of physics, chemistry and biology. These sciences have furnished us with a mass of facts or descriptive material regarding man's life and relationships. They give us valuable and expert information about segments of man's life and relationships. For example, knowledge of our metabolism, our allergic sensitivity, the Mendelian laws of heredity, defense mechanisms, and our intelligence quotients is important. There is great quantity of technical knowledge we could not gain by other methods. We need more, rather than fewer, such facts to live well.

The scientific view of man is one which can be accepted as far as it goes, and no limitations or barriers to the study of its proper subject matter should be placed in its way.

However, as Harold H. Titus points out, "where it is deficient it is usually not because it is false, but because it is incomplete."[4] He says:

> There is the danger that we may "reduce" the rich qualities of human personality to the functioning of the biological organism, and then attempt to interpret the organism according to physical and chemical action and reaction. The sciences, with their emphasis on objectivity, are likely to neglect what is distinctively human about man.[5]

"The knowledge furnished us by the sciences," adds Titus, "is related to our everyday experiences somewhat as road map is related to the country through which one travels. In attempting to be objective, impersonal, and quantitative, the sciences emphasize certain aspects of man and his life and ignore others."[6] To be sure, this procedure is unobjectionable if the investigator does not forget what he has done.

From the above analysis of the technological society and the scientific view of the man, it may be reasonable to say this: the identity crisis of man in the contemporary situation has been resulted directly from scientism and technological rationality, in which cognitive value is idolized, just as religious value was dominant in the Medieval age. If this is the case, it may be also true that the problem is an inevitable consequence of the mistaken view of man and human value. In this respect, presumably the most desirable way to begin philosophizing the problem of identity crisis and the restoration of humanity would be an immediate turn to a proper analysis of human value. In other words, one of the philosophical problems we have to tackle is to find an answer to

such questions as: Is there a single absolute value? Or are there certain intrinsic values which are absolutely free and unconditional? Then what are they, how are they related to one another?

There is a line of thought, constantly and variously asserted or assumed, which runs contrary to the position that there is no single absolute value, but claims there are certain intrinsic values which are absolutely free and unconditional. There has arisen a very important distinction between intrinsic and instrumental values. Intrinsic value is prized for its own sake—it is inherent in the value itself; instrumental value is prized as a means or a cause of intrinsic value. Economic value is one type of instrumental value, whereas beauty is an example of intrinsic value. Among the intrinsic values there is a distinction generally made between the higher and the lower. The development of all sides of experience— the maintenance of life as a whole—means that one must often choose humble tasks and lowly values if the whole is to grow in right proportion. Roughly the intrinsic values may be classified as follows. Lower intrinsic values are recreational play, bodily health, social association, and economic labor among others, whereas higher intrinsic values, or "cardinal values" are cognitive truth, moral goodness, aesthetic beauty, and religious holiness. According to Melvin Rader, these basic values are also absolutely free and unconditional. He says:

> Traditionally, these are the religious, the moral, and the intellectual, and the aesthetic—the holy, the good, the true, and the beautiful. They are respectively affirmed as absolutes in such familiar doctrines as righteousness for righteousness's sake, the sacred uncontaminated by the profane, truth as eternal and absolute, and pure art—art for art's sake.[7]

It is important to note the relations of these two points of view for interpreting the value experience. Most intrinsic values may also be instrumental in producing further value experience; and many, if not all, instrumental values may also be enjoyed as intrinsic. However, when man treats that which is primarily instrumental—like money or property—as being intrinsic, the proper development of human life or humanity is destroyed and the man is called a miser. Thus holiness, goodness, truth, and beauty are intrinsic and spiritual values and are not subject to the conditions and determinations of physical values like felt pleasures or bodily satisfactions. Nevertheless, without instrumental values the intrinsic would disappear, for without causes there would be no effects. But also without the intrinsic, the instrumental would obviously be meaningless.

On the other hand, there is no intrinsic value that stands alone. Realization of all the other values is dependent on moral values; the cheat destroys fun or truth, the aesthetic or religion. Attempt to define any one value as utterly alone and apart from all the others. What value can stand without truth? What value is completely defined if its aesthetic aspects are omitted? What is the value of religion when the good, the true, and the beautiful have been removed from it? The values, then, interpenetrate. No values can be fully appreciated without taking all other values into account. Since every person is a member of society, it is necessary to go further and take the entire society into account. However, since society itself is dependent on the world in which it lives, and since value experiences arise through interaction between society and its environment, an even wider "environment" must be considered. In other words, one's values can only be understood and must always be interpreted and criticized in the light of one's world view. Thus human values not only interpenetrate each other, but value and all reality, it would seem, also mutually interpenetrate.

However, here I am not concerned with a justification of any theory of value. I am mainly concerned with an analysis of value and its relation to the problem of identity crisis in our technological society. From the above consideration in this respect, it may be reasonable to say this; the identity crisis of man in the contemporary situation is mainly due to the fact that scientific truth as prototype of cognitive value has dominated the world of value, and consequently the cardinal values appear to be subject to the conditions and determinations of instrumental values like felt pleasures or bodily satisfactions. It follows that there can be physiological psychology of piety; virtue has a price; and there is occasional truth and relative beauty. In a word, there can be economic determination of the spiritual or intrinsic values. If this is the case, it would be desirable to correct the mistaken view of human value by means of a careful examination of scientific knowledge. However, at this juncture, I shall claim that the most desirable way to begin with is to call attention to the significance of aesthetic value and aesthetic attitude. Then what is the nature of aesthetic value and the characteristics of aesthetic attitude?

In general, the aesthetic attitude, or the aesthetic way of looking at the world, is most commonly opposed to the practical attitude, which is concerned mainly with the utility of the object in question. The real estate agent who views a landscape only with an eye to its possible monetary value, for example, is not viewing the landscape aesthetically. As John Hospers points out, to view a landscape aesthetically one must "perceive for perceiving's sake," not for the sake of some ulterior purpose.

He says:

> One must savor the experience of perceiving the landscape itself, dwelling in its perceptual details, rather than using the perceptual object as a means to some further end.[8]

One might object, as he admits, that even in aesthetic contemplation we are regarding something not "for its own sake" but for the sake of something else, namely, enjoyment. We would not continue to attend to the perceptual object if doing so were not enjoyable; hence, enjoyment would be the end in the aesthetic case. However, "there is a difference between savoring the perceptual experience itself and merely using it for purposes of identification, classification, or further action," Hospers says, "as we commonly do in daily life when we do not really look at the tree but perceive it only clearly enough to identify it as a tree and then walk around it if it is in our path."[9] Thus the distinction remains, and only the mode of describing it is subject to clarification.

On the other hand, particularly interesting feature is that the aesthetic attitude is also distinguished from the cognitive. For example, those who are familiar with the history of architecture are able to identify quickly a building or a ruin, in regard to its time and place of construction, by means of its style and other visual aspects. "This kind of ability," says Hospers, "may be important and helpful, but it is not necessarily correlated with the ability to enjoy the experience of simply viewing the building itself." He adds:

> The analytical ability may eventually enhance the aesthetic experience, but it may also stifle it. People who are interested in the arts from a professional or technical aspect are particularly liable to be diverted from the aesthetic way of looking to the cognitive.[10]

This leads us directly into a further distinction. Thus the aesthetic way of looking is also antipathetic to the aesthetic object so as to absorb what it has to offer him, considers its relation to himself. With regard to this criterion, the term "disinterested" is used to express a quality of a good judge and occurs when he is impartial. To be sure, as Immanuel Kant (see *Kant, Immanuel*) points out, aesthetic judgement is essentially disinterested. For him, a judgment of taste "in which the least interest mingles, is very partial and is not a pure judgements of taste."[11] Here it is important not to confuse the words "disinterested" and "uninterested." To be disinterested is to be free from bias and from the influence of selfish interest; one can be "disinterested" and yet very interested. A spectator at a football game can be disinterested, in the very strong sense of not caring which side wins, and yet very interested in the game.

It may be evident from the above consideration that we can be more or less free from the practical attitude, which is concerned with the utility of the object in question, without mainly relying on a scientific interpretation of man and the world. Besides, it may be also important to note that aesthetic value does not impose itself upon us with biding necessity unlike other intrinsic or cardinal values. If this is the case, there is a good reason why we have to call attention to the aesthetic aspect of life in the contemporary situation, in which the restoration of humanity or harmonization of human value is urgent.

When Kant said that the aesthetic attitude characteristically is disinterested and reflective, he also points out that it tends to unify and structure its subject matter. For this reason, Arthur Schopenhauer interpreted this to mean that in art and aesthetic value the faculties are detached from all willing, most particularly from sexual desire. With his doctrine of art as escape from the will Schopenhauer took the aesthetic state to be a pure will-less contemplation in which sensuality is put out of action.[12] And, presumably, when we are in the museum, the cathedral, or the concert hall, we are disinterested and tend to concentrate more on what we are seeing or listening to than we normally do.

The question arises: Why can we not be like this all of the time? Many people would dismiss this question by saying we cannot spend all our waking day in museums and concert halls, or that the practical demands of life require that our states of mind normally be non-aesthetic. But this answer is not conclusive. If we were willing to make demands on ourselves by exerting ourselves aesthetically, at the same time worrying less about the practical needs of life, we could make most or all of our experience aesthetic. This aesthetic appreciation is one of the goals of such movements as transcendental meditations. There is abundant testimony that it can work, although it requires considerable sustained effort. The reward of this effort is more thoroughly aesthetic waking life, and also, of course, tranquility and a thoroughly collected mind. Zen practician would say,

for example, we are arbitrarily reserving our aesthetic experiences for certain objects and certain moments. If a sunset in the mountains deserves an aesthetic experience, why does not an ordinary tree with snow on its branches also deserve one? Why exclude the sky on an ordinary day, or trash cans waiting for collection, or the side of beef that stimulated Rembrandt to paint it?

Man may live his life totally on a biological level, where he seeks to satisfy his appetites and desires, or he may live it on a distinctly human level. Unless he consciously seeks to live on the higher level and maintains deep-rooted ideals of personal honor and responsibility, he is likely to revert to the animal level. Man is a creature of necessity determined by the forces of nature and by his biological impulses, but he transcends those natural processes and manipulates them. In order to live on the higher level and transcend our biological impulses, we must be prepared to pay attention to aesthetic value, since aesthetic attitude may be the most desirable way to quicken our sensitivity to our needs for a balanced and whole human existence in the age of anxiety. In short, aesthetic sensibility should become an arbiter of true and false needs for restoration of humanity in the contemporary technological society.

*Notes*

1. Wittgenstein, Ludwig, *Philosophical Investigations*, trans. G.E.M. Anscombe (NY: The Macmillan Co., 1968), vi.

2. Marcuse, Herbert, *One-Dimensional Man* (London: Routledge, Kegan Paul Ltd., 1964), pp. 1-2.

3. *Ibid.*, p. 2.

4. Titus, Harold H., *Living Issues in Philosophy* (N.Y.: Van Nostrand Reinhold Co., 1970), p. 135.

5. *Ibid.*

6. *Ibid.*

7. Rader, Melvin, and Jessup, Bertram, *Art and Human Values* (N.J., Englewood Cliffs: Prentice-Hall, Inc., 1976), p. 296.

8. Hospers, John, "Problems of Aesthetics," in *The Encyclopedia of Philosophy*, Vol.I, ed. P. Edwards (NY: Macmillan Pub. Co., Inc., 1967), p. 36.

9. *Ibid.*

10. *Ibid.* pp. 36-37.

11. Kant, Immanuel, *The Critique of Judgment*, trans. J. H. Bernard (N.Y.: Hafner Press, n.d.), sec 2, p. 39. For Kant, it is involved in aesthetic reflective judgments about the beautiful and sublime, distinguished from a mark of moral goodness.

12. Schopenhauer, Arthur, *The World as Will and Idea*, R. B. Haldane and J. Kemp, trans.,(London: Routledge, 1948), Vol.I, pp. 281-287.

JUNG SIK UM

# Aggression

In common parlance, "aggression" refers to actions intended to harm others. In the 1930s, a decade marked by the rise of virulent militarism in Italy, Germany, and Japan, "aggression" entered the lexicon of international relations to designate an unprovoked attack by one state on another.

The growing destructiveness of weapons induced increasing concern about the recurring phenomenon of war and inspired investigations into its origins and etiology. Already in 1920, Freud, deeply disturbed by the ordeal of the First World War advanced his pessimistic hypothesis of a "death wish" residing in the human psyche. He supposed, further, that aggressive impulses against self, generated by the "death wish" were opposed by a life-preserving instinct and redirected against others (Freud 1948) (see *Freud, Sigmund*).

There being no way to test this hypothesis, it could not be regarded as a basis for a scientific theory. Theories of aggression, less sweeping but more or less supported by evidence, were subsequently developed primarily by psychologists and ethologists. These theories comprise three main currents of thought. One places "instinct" or "drive" at the center of attention. Another views aggression as a reaction to specific experiences, for instance, frustration or being the target of aggression by another. The third current emphasized the role of social learning in manifestations of aggression. In this view, aggressive behavior, like any form of human behavior, is learned. Whether or not it occurs and, if it does, in what circumstances and in what form depends primarily on what has been learned in the process of socialization.

## 1. Instinctual or Drive Theories of Aggression

Explaining aggressive behavior by reference to an "aggressive instinct" amounts to hardly more than putting a label on the phenomenon to be explained. Labeling something may induce an impression that what has been labeled has been explained by making it seem more familiar. Clearly, however, explanations of this sort cannot be accorded scientific status.

The term "instinct" does acquire some substance if it can be shown that a behavior pattern is apparently innate and could have been selected for in the process of evolution, because it confers a survival advantage.

Arguments to the effect that aggressive behavior does confer a survival advantage on the species in which it is genetically imbedded have been ethologists' contribution to the instinctual theories of aggression (Lorenz 1966).

Aggression directed at members of one's own species is commonly observed in vertebrates. Typical fighting encounters occur in the process of contending for a mate or over a territory. Assuming that the stronger contender acquires the mate or the territory fought over, we can suppose that the overall vigor of the species is enhanced thereby. In the case of contests for a mate, it is the genes conducive to vigor that win the opportunity to reproduce themselves. The same result can be assumed in the case of a contest for a territory, since the activities necessary for producing offspring able to survive to reproductive age often depend on available living space free of competitors.

The easily imagined linkage between prowess in combat and reproductive success may suggest that ever-increasing aggressiveness would continue to be selected for in animals competing for mates or territory. However, extensive observations by ethologists have by no means supported this conclusion. Patterns of combat encounters are extremely varied. In some cases, such encounters are quite perfunctory, often limited to gestures or displays without bodily contact. Upon some reflection, evolution of mild forms of aggressive behavior becomes understandable. Severe forms of combat may have easily been selected against, because the resulting injuries could confer a reproductive handicap rather than an advantage on genetic carriers of a predilection to intense violence.

Evidence for the evolution of restraint in intra-specific aggression is seen in the circumstance that conflict between animals possessing formidable weapons, such as teeth, horns, or claws are very seldom fatal. The backward-swept horns of some mountain goats, for example, seem to have been designed with the view of making it more difficult to inflict serious injury (Maynard Smith and Price 1973). Fights between wolves often end when the defeated animal assumes a posture of submission, exposing his jugular vein, as if inviting the victor to kill him. The gesture seems to inhibit further aggression. In contrast, animals ordinarily thought of as "peaceful," when subjected to severe stress, as in being confined to an exceedingly crowded area, often fight to the death, presumably because inhibitions against killing their own kind had not evolved in their behavior.

Relevant to theories of human aggression is the question to what extent aggressive behavior is part of man's psychological make-up, in particular, whether an "aggressive instinct" exists in humans.

In the light of the long history of violence perpetrated by human beings against human beings, it is easy to assume that man is just "naturally cruel." Some anthropologists purport to see the origin of this supposed trait in man's biological heritage, passed down from our direct primate ancestor, *Australopithecus africanus*, who lived about three million years ago (Freeman 1964). This creature changed from a vegetarian to a flesh eater. The cruelty of his descendants is attributed to the psychological predilection necessary for catching and killing prey.

This explanation of "man's inhumanity to man" is weak on two grounds. First, with proper selection of examples, human beings could be easily described as gentle, nurturing, and cooperative as well as vicious, rapacious, and exploiting. "Human nature," if, indeed, it makes sense to speak of it at all, is much too complex and its manifestations are much too diverse to be subsumed under a single character trait.

Second, the allusion to carnivorous habits as facilitating aggression misses the important distinction between aggression and predation. Predation may be associated with behavior that reminds us of aggression, for example killing prey, but it need not be related to aggression understood as behavior directed at harming others. Surely a frog snapping at a fly is not committing "aggression" in this sense, nor is an angler catching a fish. Killing in the process of predation is only a by-product of the function it serves, namely, nutrition. Only in the context of intraspecific aggression, directed against members of own species can we speak of behavior "as if" directed toward inflicting harm or, at least, threatening to inflict harm.

In sum, there is little justification for ascribing the evermore destructive outbursts of aggression among humans (as in wars) to an inherent propensity. First, it is difficult to conceive of such a propensity as conferring survival advantage on the species (which a genetically determined propensity must do in order to be incorporated in an organism in consequence of natural selection). Second, there are alternative reasonable explanations of this form of behavior.

## 2. Reactive Theories of Aggression

Reactive theories seek to explain aggression by linking instances of it to specific stimuli or experiences. Thus, the frustration-aggression theory (Dollard et al., 1939) is based on the hypothesis that aggressive behavior in human beings is triggered by thwarted attempts to satisfy needs. Such behavior tends to be directed at the perceived source of frustration. If the source is not present or if aggression against it is inhibited, aggression may be directed at some other target (a "scapegoat").

As it stands, the hypothesis is as difficult to corroborate convincingly as it is to refute. Practically every one has at one time or another experienced frustration and has at one time or another behaved aggressively. Thus, any number of instances can be cited when aggression was preceded by frustration or when frustration was followed by aggression. But for this very reason, the corroborations are less than convincing. A genuine test of a hypothesis can be made only when the hypothesis is in principle falsifiable, that is, when it is *a priori* uncertain whether it will be corroborated or refuted. Such tests can be made in the context of laboratory experiments, in which subjects are put into situations specifically designed to induce a frustrating experience followed by an opportunity to commit aggression. In this context, the frustration-aggression hypothesis generates a specific prediction: persons subjected to such and such experiences (which the experimenter regards as frustrating) are likely to behave in such and such a manner (which the experimenter interprets as aggressive). The method requires also an accompanying control experiment, in which persons are not subjected to "frustration" in the expectation that these persons will not behave "aggressively" (or will behave less aggressively) than the presumably frustrated persons.

Many experiments designed to test the frustration-aggression theory were performed by social psychologists, mostly in the United States. On the whole, statistically significant connections could be established between induced "frustrations" and observed "aggression." It should be kept in mind, however, that in the laboratory the sorts of experience interpreted as "frustration" and the sorts of behavior interpreted as "aggression" are for obvious reasons severely limited. Thus, it is difficult to assess the contribution of the theory to the understanding of aggression as a pervasive pattern of human behavior on scales far transcending casual encounters between individuals in a laboratory. In particular, the simple extension of the stimulus-response model of behavior on which the frustration-aggression theory is based, hardly accounts for the most pervasive and severe modes of aggression perpetrated by human beings against human beings, as in war, persecutions, and genocide. Theories of social learning appear to shed more light on these phenomena.

## 3. Socially Learned Aggression

Unlike the behavior patterns of non-humans, those of

humans can be transmitted to succeeding generations independently of their genetic determinants. The mechanism of transmission is social learning, that is, acquisition of behavior patterns, skills, attitudes, images of reality, and so on by imitating others or believing what one has been told. That a child acquires the language of the community in which it lives and, for the most part, adopts its values regardless of its biological heritage is *prima facié* evidence that such transmission occurs.

The diversity of behavior patterns, complexes of attitudes, and so on so acquired is incomparably larger than the variability associated with fluctuations in the genetic profile. Not only the vast variety of behavior patterns but also the modes of acquiring them can be learned in this manner. For example, "obedience" is not a specific behavior pattern. It is a rule governing the acquisition of behavior patterns. Such rules are also transmitted to succeeding generations.

There is reason to believe that humans learn aggressive behavior (Berkowitz 1968). Moreover, it is possible to learn to commit acts of aggression without necessarily acquiring the effect ordinarily associated with aggressiveness. For a soldier, killing human beings becomes a normal occupation, learned in the course of acquiring other skills associated with soldiering. This process, that is, inducing people to acquire matter-of-fact attitudes toward killing people, has been tremendously facilitated by the development of war technology.

Before the advent of firearms, soldiers killed each other in close bodily contact. It is possible that the human being, far from harboring an "aggressive instinct" (that could presumably associate killing with the satisfaction of a need like hunger or the sexual urge), on the contrary possesses inhibitions against killing his own kind (Andreski 1964). As the development of war technology made killing at ever greater distance possible, progressively less effort was required to overcome such inhibitions. The purpose of military training may be precisely that: to facilitate overcoming inhibitions against lethal intraspecific aggression.

Evidence for this conjecture was obtained in experiments conducted by Milgram (1963). Subjects were led to believe that they were participating in an investigation into the effects of punishment in learning situations. The role of the "teacher" was assigned to a subject, and the role of the "learner" to a person who, although posing as another subject, was actually a confederate of the experimenter. Learning consisted in associating nonsense syllables. The "teacher" was instructed to administer electric shocks to the

"learner" each time the latter made a mistake (unknown to the subject, the shocks were fictitious). With each successive error the severity of the "shocks" had to be increased well into the range of severe pain, possibly serious injury. As evermore severe shocks were given, increasingly urgent signs of distress were heard from the "learner," supposedly strapped in a chair in another room, culminating in pleas to stop and finally in silence. A considerable proportion of the subjects, urged by the experimenter to go on, continued to increase the intensity of the "shocks" all the way into the region of clear danger.

Milgram's experiments can be regarded as a demonstration of the abrogation of personal responsibility. Compulsion "to obey orders" seems to have overridden inhibitions against inflicting injury on an innocent human being. That such inhibitions exist was evidenced by the extreme anxiety manifested by some subjects as they nevertheless followed orders. That the compulsion to obey orders does not necessarily depend on fear of punishment (the soldier's situation) was evidenced by the fact that the subjects could not seriously expect to be severely punished by the experimenter.

The only reasonable conclusion seems to be that "obeying orders of a superior" had been learned in the process of socialization. Moreover, practically all forms of behavior, including behavior that is normally regarded as grossly immoral, can, evidently, be learned under proper circumstances.

This finding puts the phenomenon of war in a new light. While war in its gross aspect appears as the epitome of aggression, psychological states concomitant to aggression need not play a significant part in the behavior of the millions of individuals whose actions "add up" to a modern war. As we have seen, modern war technology has completely "uncoupled" the killer from the victim. The scientist "improving" a nerve gas need not commit "aggression" in its usual sense on anyone. In his work the scientist is immersed in actions and deliberations quite similar to those of a scientist engaged in a search for a life-giving drug. The offices of a ministry of defense (formerly ministry of war) resemble in all essential features the offices of any institution or enterprise. None of the component activities of preparing and launching war need involve any action that could be called "aggression." Only the integrated end result of all these actions amounts to a vast act of aggression, possibly on a scale that can exterminate the human race.

This insight into what modern war has become suggests that the connection between war and aggression, usually taken for granted, ought to be reexamined. The key to the problem of war may be not at all in the psychological roots of "aggression" related to the struggle for existence (as aggression is depicted by ethologists) or to stimulus-response chains (as aggression is depicted in frustration-aggression theories) but rather in the way civilized people have become an adjunct to the autocatalytic growth of military technology coupled with institutional and conceptual inertia. It is apparently extremely difficult for human beings to readjust their modes of thought and to redesign their institutions, no matter how urgently these changes are needed for continued survival.

## 4. Failure to Outlaw Aggression by States

Institutional and conceptual inertia seems to be also at the root of the failure so far to remove the chronic threat of war by legalistic procedures. In the 1930s, attempts were made to organize a common front against aggressions committed by Italy (in Africa), Japan (in Asia), and Germany (in Europe). The then foreign commissar of the Soviet Union, Litvinov, offered a lucid definition of "aggression" in terms of unmistakably recognizable overt actions (Litvinov 1939). The League of Nations had been organized after the First World War, presumably for the purpose of preventing wars, and a clear definition of "aggression" seemed to assure unambiguous recognition of an aggressive, hence "unjustified" war. War waged "in self-defense," however, remained justified. Thereby all onus could be removed from any war, at least in the estimation of those who started it, by the simple expedient of calling it "defensive." The former Soviet Union, once the most eloquent accuser of "aggressor" states, having signed a nonaggression pact with the principal "aggressor" in Europe (Nazi Germany), proceeded to participate in the partition of Poland and to attack Finland. In the decades following the decisive victory of the "peace-loving" states over the "aggressor" states, the United States, the outspokenly "peace-loving' state committed overt aggression against Cuba in 1961 and 1962, against the Dominican Republic in 1965, and against Grenada in 1984. The United Kingdom and France joined Israel in attempted aggression against Egypt in 1956. The former Soviet Union invaded Czechoslovakia in 1968 and Afghanistan in 1979.

These events throw doubt on any characterization of states as inherently "aggressive" or "non-aggressive" and so on any theory that emphasizes psychological determinants or predispositions to aggression. Indeed, the concept of "aggression" itself appears to be of questionable relevance to the problem of war.

However, the very failure to establish necessary connections between the determinants of aggression and those of war may have been the most valuable result of the extensive research on aggression. Thereby ideological, institutional, and above all, technocratic determinants of war have come to the forefront of attention.

Since the end of the Cold War (widely perceived as a consequence of the dissolution of the Soviet Union), the most prominent manifestations of aggression appeared in contexts apparently unrelated to wars between states. Civil wars and rebellions, typically accompanied by massive rapes and massacres of civilians, predominantly in the impoverished world, appeared to be instigated by highly aggravated aggressive urges, much more so than the destruction wreaked by the ultrasophisticated weapons in wars between "civilized" states throughout recent history.

In the light of these events, psychologically rooted instigation of violence gains credence. The outbursts of rage can now be reasonably assigned to aggressive drives that had been suppressed by authorities now no longer in power. Also the frustration-aggression theory applied to massive violence now finds some sources of support. Nevertheless, the ideological-institutional-technocratic determinants of horrendously destructive violence still retain their significance, partly in view of the fact that the "advanced" states continue to supply the "backward" masses with the most effective means of homicide and destruction for reasons that have little to do with the psychology of aggression, such as pursuit of profit or geopolitical considerations.

See also: *Conflict: Inherent and Contingent Theories; Just War; Nuremberg Principles; Psychology of Peace; Structural Violence and the Definition of Conflict; War: Environmental and Biological Theories*

*Bibliography*

Andreski S 1964 Origins of war. In: Carthy J D, Ebling F J (eds.) 1964 *The Natural History of Aggression*. Academic Press, New York

Berkowitz L 1968 The frustration-aggression hypothesis revisited. In: Berkowitz L (ed.) 1968 *Roots of Aggression: A Reexamination of the Frustration-Aggression Hypothesis*. Atherton, New York

Dollard J, Doob L W, Miller N E, Mowrer O M, Sears R R 1939 *Frustration and Aggression*. Yale University Press, New Haven, Connecticut

Freeman D 1964 Human aggression in anthropological perspective. In: Carthy J D, Ebling F J (eds.) 1964 *The Nat-*

*ural History of Aggression.* Academic Press, New York

Freud S 1948 *Beyond the Pleasure Principle.* Hogarth Press, London

Litvinov M 1939 *Against Aggression.* International Publishers, New York

Lorenz K 1966 *On Aggression.* Methuen, London

Maynard Smith J, Price G R 1973 The logic of animal conflict. *Nature* 246

Milgram S 1963 Behavioral study of obedience. *J. Abnormal and Social Psychology* 67

ANATOL RAPOPORT

# Agricultural Trade Development and Assistance Act of 1954 (United States)

Adopted by the Congress of the United States on July 10, usually known as "Public Law 480" (P.L.480), also called "Food for Peace Act," it is the major legislation under which food aid by the United States is distributed.

## 1. Content

According to the "Declaration of Policy," the main objectives were:

(a) to expand international trade;

(b) to develop and expand export markets for agricultural commodities from the United States;

(c) to combat hunger and malnutrition by using the abundant productivity of US agriculture;

(d) to encourage economic development in the developing countries, in particular to improve their own agricultural production; and

(e) to promote in other ways the foreign policy of the United States.

By the 1975 amendment some declarations on food aid and rural development were added.

The main part of the P.L. 480 legislation (Title I) concerns the "sale of agricultural commodities for foreign currencies and long-term-dollar-credit" to provide for the sale of dollars on easy credit terms (interest rate two-three percent over 30 to 40 years) or for inconvertible local currencies. That means that despite the nominal sale, the program was virtually a free gift to countries which otherwise would have had to spend scarce foreign exchange for foodstuffs, or else do without. The smaller part of the proceeds were used by the US government and US business firms to meet local expenses while the remaining receipts could be given or lent to the purchasing countries (counterpart funds). Furthermore, their governments were allowed to sell the commodities commercially in the home market. In agreement with the United States, the proceeds not set aside for US use could be spent directly on investment projects or in defense budgets. By the 1971 amend-

ment all Title I local-currency sales were switched to hard-currency sales; exceptions were made for South Vietnam and Cambodia.

The other important part of P.L. 480 (Title II) concerns "famine relief and other assistance and donations of food." The US government was authorized to send US agricultural commodities for free food aid programs on a government-to-government basis, through voluntary organizations, and through the United Nations system, in particular the United Nations World Food Program (WFP). Title III concerned barter of strategic raw materials in exchange for food; today it is no longer of importance.

In the mid-1970s the legislation was complemented and reformed. The emergency provisions were improved by assuring a minimum level of assistance, some continuity in aid programs, and some recourse to a multilaterally determined criterion of emergency. A new chapter under the keyword "Food for Development Program" established the use of the funds accruing from the local sale of US agricultural commodities to finance poverty-oriented development measures, particularly in rural development.

## 2. Implementation

Responsibility for making sales was lodged in the Department of Agriculture (USDA); the Commodity Credit Corporation (CCC) was to carry out the program. The political responsibility was delegated to the secretary of state.

Wheat exports under P.L. 480 averaged 12 million metric tons from 1960 to 1966, then fell to about 5 million tons in the early 1970s. In 1977-78, the US food aid in grain reached 7.6 million tons, and in the early 1980s fell back again to about 5 million tons. Food aid was surpassed by commercial sales. Whereas 30 percent of all US food exports was shipped as aid in the mid 1960s, this dwindled to 4 percent in 1974. In 1961, 68 percent of all US wheat exports referred to P.L. 480; in the early 1980s just less than 5 percent. From 1954 to 1962 about 10 billion US dollars were spent under P.L. 480. The net payments for all US food aid in 1980 reached up to nearly 700 million dollars. The food aid of the United States in general amounts to two-thirds of all food aid given by surplus countries in the early 1980s, while about 55 percent of the world exports of grain grew up on US farms, which is more than 110 million tons a year.

## 3. Reasons

The main political reason for establishing the P.L. 480 legislation was the need to manage the abundant surplus of the US farm sector with the principal aim of serving domestic interests. While government costs of storing were reduced, the sales helped the American farmers by keeping up the home prices. Public Law 480 was also instrumental in opening up new markets for US agricultural products. As a governmental report of 1968 declares, the program was in fact very successful in making new markets accessible: people having never seen bread learned to use American wheat.

At the same time the program seemed to be of great humanitarian value. Millions of hungry people could be fed by an otherwise useless and undesired surplus. Public Law 480 has been an imaginative combination of self-interest and idealistic help based on an ideal of remaking the world in the image of wheat-eating Americanism, of feeding the hungry and selling wheat.

After the early 1970s, the most important economic goal changed from one of reducing the agrarian surplus to reducing the growing deficit of the balance of payments by selling more food for dollars. The domestic agricultural policy had been changing too: unsalable surplus production now had to be cut back according to market conditions. The contradiction between the humanitarian motive and the aims of domestic farm policy became most evident when in the early 1970s the US food aid dwindled down just at the very moment of the worldwide food shortage: in 1974 the quantity of food aid provided reached just up to one-third of the 1972 volume. Thus, while the P.L. 480 program shifted from a "countercyclical" to a "procyclical" pattern, food was more and more seen as a political resource. The reduced food aid was now distributed even more strategically.

## 4. Food Politics

Public Law 480 has been an instrument of foreign policy from the beginning. The aid was always allocated according to political considerations rather than by the criterion of the real need of the people, as a short look at the distribution patterns shows. Although US food aid is shipped to more than 80 countries around the world, the great bulk of US surplus grain has subsidized budgets in only a few countries which are of great political and strategic importance for the US state department. Public Law 480 is also an instrument for the US government to circumvent opposition by the Congress, as happened in the case of the Vietnam war: "friendly" regimes can be supported by P.L. 480 means more than Congressmen or public opinion would concede. By the amendments of the mid-1970s three-quarters of the program are bound to be given to most seriously affected countries.

Because dependence on food assistance may expose the recipient country to political interference by the donor, P.L. 480 is, on the one hand, a political tool with regard to foreign affairs by offering food as a carrot and denying it as a stick (see *Food Weapon*); on the other hand, more than being a mere diplomatic leverage or an element of producing external dependence, food aid under P.L. 480 could be used to influence structures in the recipient countries themselves. So in principle, generosity with food so closely related to the daily needs of so many people improved attitudes toward the United States. More concretely, the counterpart funds gave the donor a set of possibilities to use influence on the policies of any recipient government, in particular the design of the course of economic and social development.

## 5. Results for the Recipients

Food aid usually functions as budgetary support. So, it is a support to friendly regimes and favored elites, too. The foreign exchange thus released from payment for imported agricultural products can be spent either unproductively on foreign military hardware and consumptions goods or productively on social reforms and development measures. Generally, one may say that food aid like P.L. 480 in the long run benefits other purposes than feeding the poor or even developing agriculture because the need of reforms and substantial development measures is lessened by the easy availability of foreign food. A kind of relief mentality and the political intention to lower urban food prices, both reduce the necessary incentives for the domestic producers, implying that growing cheap food does not pay. The readier availability of food aid encouraged most countries to emphasize nonagricultural production both in economic planning and in investment programs. If their own agriculture failed to produce, food could be obtained from the United States to fill the need. In particular, indiscriminate food aid may breed economic elitism, corruption, agricultural complacency, and bureaucratic inertia. There were no guarantees that those commodities provided under P.L. 480, which were to be sold commercially by the recipient governments, really reached the people who needed them—those who suffer hunger do not have much purchasing power.

## 6. Conclusions

On account of such general problems of food aid the FAO, for example, calls for raising food aid in toto but passing a greater proportion of it through multilateral channels. But this is not very popular with the US administration because it would mean renunciation of both an economically and a politically successful national instrument. On the other hand, neither the United States nor the other industrialized countries with an agricultural surplus will be able to feed the hungry of the world in the long run.

Therefore, most experts argue that concern over the malnourished must be turned toward the development of their own local food-producing ability and, simultaneously, the development of their purchasing power. Food aid under P.L. 480 has, without doubt, been of substantial assistance in meeting the urgent food problems of many developing nations, and in the 1950s and 1960s the program provided a collective benefit of food security to the world; some emergencies arising from food shortages could be avoided or at least relieved. Public Law 480 also might have been a serious development program in the sense of abolition of lasting poverty and structural hunger, if only its political potential had been used to change structures in agriculture instead of maintaining them.

See also: *Food Weapon*

## *Bibliography*

Annual Reports on Activities Carried on under P.L. 480, Washington, DC
Hopkins R F 1977 How to make food work. *Foreign Policy* 27
Kaplan J J 1967 *The Challenge of Foreign Aid.* New York
Maxwell S, Singer H 1979 Food Aid to Developing Countries: A Survey. *World Development* 7
Postel S 1996 *Dividing the Waters: Food Security, Ecosystem Health, and the New Politics of Scarcity.* Washington, DC
Rothschild E 1976 Food politics. *Foreign Affairs* 54
Toma P A 1967 *The Politics of Food for Peace: Executive-legislative Interaction.* Tucson
Uvin P 1994 *The International Organization of Hunger.* London/New York
Wallerstein M B 1980 *Food for War, Food for Peace: United States Food Aid in a Global Context.* Cambridge/Mass.
Wiedemann H H 1978 *American Grain Export Policy: The Evolution of Public Law* 480. Geneva

REINHARD WESEL

# Alliance

In the interactions between states there are times when close coordination of efforts is desired in order to reach security goals vis-à-vis other states. An alliance exists between two or more countries whenever the basis for close coordination of foreign military policies is made explicit and fulfillment of the joint goal requires the active participation of the partners of the alliance in competition with non-alliance countries. In an alliance, two or more states exchange explicit pledges regarding the use of war, either between themselves or in connection with an external threat. The pledges can involve a promise of immediate support from allies, an agreement to consult in the event of attack, or a commitment not to use force in relations among members of the same alliance.

Several types of cooperative arrangements are similar to alliances (Sullivan 1974). A coalition is a cooperative effort for attaining short-range, issue-specific objectives in times of war. Countries that fought together during the First and Second World Wars often did so because they had joint enemies rather than because of previous alliance commitments; these wartime coalitions quickly faded away at the end of the fighting and are not considered to be alliances because no explicit agreements formalized the relationship between the coalition partners. An informal alignment exists when two or more countries develop stable expectations concerning how much cooperation to expect from one another under various circumstances. Deutsch and associates (1957) refer to informal alignments that entail war avoidance as pluralistic security communities. The United Nations provides collective security through a treaty, in which there is a pledge to come to the aid of any victim of aggression in the world; but no specific adversary is identified, even implicitly, so collective security is not the same as a policy of alliance pursued by specific states (see *Collective Security and Collective Self-defense*).

Alliances can be bilateral (with two partners) or multilateral (three or more partners). Alliances can also be kept secret, a practice decried by Woodrow Wilson in his Fourteen Points, which argued that arrangements between states should be "open covenants, openly arrived at." But all alliances have one objective in common—to augment the power of an individual state through the collective resolve of one or more other states in coping with an international adversary.

Alliances have not always existed in the world polity. Until the rise of the Greek city-states (Bozeman 1960) ancient empires tended to seek world domination rather than treating each other on an equal basis. However, Greek states also warred with their neighbors. Although they tended to sign treaties to conclude war and to regulate the subsequent peace among former belligerents, enduring alliances were not considered to be necessary until some states grew so powerful that they threatened to endanger the system of city-states by establishing imperial control. In the latter half of the sixth century BC, Sparta organized the Peloponnesian League among the states of the Peloponnesus, a military alliance that lasted until 371 BC (Boak 1921 p. 378). Athens organized the Ionian maritime states under the Delian League in 477 BC to deter an attack from the rising Persian Empire, and the alliance lasted about 100 years (Boak 1921 pp. 378-79; Bozeman 1960 p. 79). These are two of the earliest and longest alliances on record.

Some entities called "alliances" have been pseudo-alliances—that is, not alliances at all. After the defeat of Napoleon due to the alliance between Austria, England, Prussia and Russia in 1814, the autocratic regimes of Austria, Prussia and Russia signed a Declaration of Christian Principles on September 26, 1815 with the aim of establishing a mechanism for regular consultation in case monarchies and other "legitimate" regimes were in danger of being overthrown. Known as the Holy Alliance, this collective security arrangement eventually had the concurrence of most European rulers and a body called the Concert of Europe was established, which was to meet as needed when countries perceived a threat to the balance of power in Europe (see *Balance of Power*). A second pseudo-alliance is the Alliance for Progress approved at the 1961 Conference of the Organization of American States in Punta del Este. With the backing of President John Kennedy, the ten-year program called for an investment of US$20 billion in the region as a means for achieving a 2.5 percent growth rate. Latin American countries, as a condition of investment assistance under the so-called Alliance for Progress, were to undertake land and tax reforms. There was no pledge concerning military action on either side, so there was no alliance as that term is generally defined.

Small and Singer (1969) have compiled a list of some 183 alliances formed between 1815 and 1965. Their compilation is based only on countries that had diplomatic relations with two major powers.

There are several types of alliances. All are based on treaties or executive agreements. Small and Singer have 91 defensive alliances, 49 non-aggression pacts, and 43 ententes in their listing.

A defensive alliance, according to Small and Singer, exists when a treaty commits the ratifying countries to deploy military forces in case of an armed attack on any member of the alliance or, in some cases, when there is a threat of such an attack. The North Atlantic Treaty Organization (NATO) is the most important defensive alliance today.

A nonaggression pact is an agreement among states not to fight each other, even when one becomes involved in war with a country external to the alliance. Prior to the Second World War, Nazi Germany signed nonaggression pacts with Poland (1934), Denmark (1939), and Estonia (1939) in order to provide a false sense of its peaceful intentions; all three alliances were terminated by German aggression in 1939.

In an entente, two or more governmental leaders agree merely to consult together in case of an attack on one of the partners. The South-East Asia Collective Defense Treaty of 1954, which formed the basis for the now-defunct South-East Asia Treaty Organization (SEATO), is an arrangement for joint consultation. Although the treaty is still in force, the Bangkok-based secretariat no longer exists and the ministerial-level Council no longer meets. The alliance remains on paper but in fact is defunct.

There is some uncertainty as to whether alliances promote war or peace. President Wilson believed that alliances encouraged war; his proposal for a League of Nations aimed to provide security for all nations through a collective guarantee of peace. According to a careful empirical analysis by Singer and Small (1968), the evidence does not provide consistent support for Wilson's belief. They find that alliances tended to serve as deterrents to war during the nineteenth century, whereas alliance activity has been especially brisk just before wars of the twentieth century.

*Bibliography*

Boak A E R 1921 Greek interstate associations and the League of Nations. *Am. J. Int. Law* 15

Bozeman A B 1960 *Politics and Culture in International History.* Princeton University Press, Princeton, New Jersey

Deutsch K W et al., 1957 *Political Community and the North Atlantic Area.* Princeton University Press, Princeton, New Jersey

Singer J D, Small M 1968 Alliance aggregation and the onset of war, 1815-1945. In: Singer J D (ed.) 1968 *Quantitative International Politics.* Free Press, New York

Small M, Singer J D 1969 Formal alliances, 1818-1965: An extension of the basic data. *J. Peace Res.* 6 (3)

Sullivan J D 1974 International alliances. In: Haas M (ed.) 1974 *International Relations.* Chandler, San Francisco, California

MICHAEL HAAS

# Alternative Defense

Alternative defense—term coined in the 1980s to denote a defense policy in which nuclear states, such as the United Kingdom or France, or alliances, such as the North Atlantic Treaty Organization (NATO), would rely on conventional warfare, territorial defense in depth, and/or guerrilla warfare or nonviolent "social resistance" as an alternative to depending on nuclear weapons, or in which non-nuclear states would move to an unambiguously defensive or nonviolent strategy.

The debate about an alternative, non-nuclear, strategy was at its most intense in the early to mid 1980s following the deployment of US Cruise and Pershing missiles in Western Europe, and of SS20 missiles on the Soviet side, the intensification of Cold War rhetoric, and the revival of a mass peace movement in response to these developments. Interest in the topic has diminished with the ending of the Cold War. Yet the exploration of morally defensible and strategically sound defence alternatives which would contribute to, rather than undermining, stability in international relations remains a task of prime importance.

The most radical of the alternative defence proposals is civilian (or civilian-based) defense—sometimes also referred to as social defense. This envisages the use of systematic non-cooperation by the civilian population, and various forms of civil disobedience and nonviolent direct action in place of armed resistance. Ideally this would be combined with international sanctions against the aggressor, and international assistance to the unarmed resistance. Debate on such an approach long predates the nuclear era and goes back to at least the mid-nineteenth century when an organised peace movement began to take shape in the US and parts of Europe. But it was only in the twentieth century that civilian defense as such began to be explored in a systematic way.

In 1915, Bertrand Russell (see *Russell, Bertrand*), in an article in the *Atlantic Monthly*, suggested that "after a generation of instruction in the principles of passive resistance" the United Kingdom might disband its armed forces and respond to any invasion with a campaign of noncooperation; however, he expressed skepticism that this would be accepted and was inclined therefore to favour collective security.

In the interwar years the impact of Gandhi's campaigns of non-cooperation against the British Raj (see *Gandhi, Mohandas Karamchand*), and the defeat of the attempted Kapp Putsch in Germany in 1920 by means of a general strike, excited renewed interest in Europe and the United States in the possibilities of nonviolent resistance as a form of national defence. A number of pacificist writers, notably Aldous Huxley in the United Kingdom, Bart de Ligt in the Netherlands, and Richard Gregg in the United States argued for the feasibility of nonviolent defense. Gandhi himself talked about this possibility for an independent India and shortly before his death (1948) founded the Shanti Sena—peace army—whose volunteers would be specially trained in nonviolent techniques and imbued with the spirit of nonviolence (see *Nonviolence*). In Europe, the military strategist and political commentator Commander Stephen King-Hall suggested to the Danes in 1938 that they should make preparations for nonviolent resistance against a possible German attack on the grounds that they could not realistically hope to put up a successful military resistance given the size and strength of Hitler's armies.

During the Second World War, resistance in occupied Europe took the form of both guerrilla warfare and civil resistance. In Norway, sustained non-cooperation by the teachers defeated the plans of the Quisling regime to introduce a Nazi-style curriculum into the schools; and churches, trade unions, and cultural and sporting organizations withheld cooperation from the regime. Strikes, go-slows, public demonstrations, and other acts of passive resistance were also common in other occupied countries. In Denmark, clandestine organizations succeeded in smuggling 95 percent of the Jewish population to safety in neutral Sweden.

The moral and strategic dilemmas posed by the

development of nuclear weapons gave rise in the late 1950s both to a popular anti-nuclear campaign and to renewed interest in alternative defense. In the United Kingdom Stephen King-Hall published a book in 1958 entitled *Defence in the Nuclear Age* in which he argued that the United Kingdom and Western Europe should forgo any reliance on nuclear weapons and make preparations for nonviolent resistance the central element in defense planning. He argued that once the use of nuclear weapons had been ruled out, it would be pointless preparing to fight a major war against a nuclear armed opponent, and that therefore there needed to be a fundamental shift in thinking about defense. He called for the establishment of a Royal Commission to investigate the possibilities of this approach.

This suggestion was not taken up, but a number of academics, peace activists, and strategists took part in a conference on the subject at St. Hilda's College, Oxford in 1964. Three years later a collection of essays based on contributions to the conference was published under the title *The Strategy of Civilian Defence*. The spectacular nonviolent resistance of Czechs and Slovaks to the Soviet and Warsaw Pact invasion of Czechoslovakia in 1968, though ultimately defeated, provided an illustration in practice of the kind of resistance to invasion and occupation that many of the contributions advocated. In 1969 the book was reissued in a paperback edition under the title *Civilian Resistance as a National Defence* with a new introduction by its editor, Adam Roberts, which took account of the Czechoslovak events.

During the 1970s a number of studies on civilian defence or "social defense" were published in several European countries, some of them—in Sweden, Denmark, and Holland—under government sponsorship. Of these, Boserup and Mack's *War Without Weapons* remains essential reading. In 1985 the French government, despite its commitment to the nuclear Force de Frappe, decided to fund a research institute to study the nonviolent resolution of conflicts. In the same year the Fondation pour les Etudes de Defense Nationale published a study by three researchers entitled *La Dissuasion Civile*. In the (then) Federal Republic of Germany the Green Party adopted a defence police in which civilian resistance figured as the central element.

Other contributions to the literature in the 1980s included a report of a government-sponsored commission in Sweden in 1985 on "social resistance" as a complementary form of defense for that country, and a study published in the same year by the American pioneering specialist in the field, Gene Sharp, of "civilian-based defense" for Europe entitled *Making Europe Unconquerable*. This received a highly favor-

able review by George Kennan, former United States Ambassador to the Soviet Union, in *The New York Review of Books* in February 1986, who emphasized that any major war in Europe, even if it remained conventional, would have catastrophic consequences for the population, and that Sharp's proposals needed to be judged against the stark alternatives that Europe faced (see *Civilian-based Defense*). Among subsequent publications in English have been Gene Sharp's *Civilian-Based Defense: A Post-Military Weapons System* (Princeton University Press, 1990) and Peter Ackerman and Christopher Kruegler's *Strategic Nonviolent Conflict*.

The successes of civilian resistance—or "people power"—in overthrowing autocratic and dictatorial regimes in many parts of the world underlined the potential of this form of struggle. 1979 had seen the overthrow of the Shah of Iran in a massive, largely unarmed, insurrection. In August of the following year Solidarity was formed in Poland, posing a major challenge to the centralised power of a Leninist state within the Soviet sphere of influence, and hence also to the legitimacy and stability of Soviet hegemony throughout Eastern and East Central Europe. Even after the suppression of Solidarity in December 1981, Polish society was never the same again. However, it was the overthrow of the Marcos regime in the Phillippines that marked the beginning of a series of spectacular successes for "People Power", culminating in the collapse of communist rule across Eastern Europe in 1989, a freedom struggle in the Baltic States influenced in some degree by the writings and ideas of Gene Sharp, the successful resistance to an attempted coup in the Soviet Union in 1991, and finally the collapse of the Soviet system itself. (The repression of the democracy movement in China, however, in June 1989 demonstrated that civil resistance brought no guarantee of success.)

Despite these victories, the new governments in Eastern Europe, with the exception of the now independent Baltic republics, have shown little interest in incorporating preparations for civilian defence into their defense plans and have instead sought membership of NATO as the means of strengthening their security. The Gulf War of 1991, the internecine strife that accompanied the break-up of ex-Yugoslavia, the wars within and between successor states of the Soviet Union, and the conflicts in Chechnya, Somalia, Rwanda, Sierra Leone and elsewhere underlined the precariousness of the post-Cold War world and doubtless prompted states to err on the side of caution with respect to their defence arrangements.

However, already in the 1980s the focus of alternative defense studies had shifted away from the idea of replacing military defence with preparations for nonviolent resistance and towards the concept of developing a viable and realistic military strategy without nuclear weapons. The notion of civilian defense was retained in many of the proposals from this period, but it was usually seen as a complementary, or fall-back strategy. A pioneering study along these lines, entitled *Defence without the Bomb* was published by the Alternative Defence Commission in the United Kingdom in 1983. The Commission, based at the School (now Department) of Peace Studies at Bradford University, examined possible defense strategies for a United Kingdom and Western Europe that had rejected all reliance on nuclear weapons. It also drew on studies by American and other European strategists who were considering ways in which NATO might fundamentally reduce the extent of its reliance on nuclear weapons—though without forgoing it altogether—by increasing the effectiveness of conventional defense

The key concept in these proposals was that of Non-Offensive Defence (NOD) and the related concept of "defensive deterrence." The discussion at the time was conducted chiefly in terms of the security problems of the Cold War, and the possibilities of alternative non-nuclear (or minimally nuclear) strategy for NATO or for individual countries within it. However, its wider relevance in other contexts and geographical areas was not altogether ignored. The aim of NOD and defensive deterrence is to provide a country or alliance with a system of defense that could threaten the destruction or defeat of invading forces without strategic offensive operations against the aggressor state, and, above all, without threatening the mass destruction of the opponent's society.

A fundamental critique at the strategic level of reliance on nuclear weapons made by its opponents was that it severed the traditional linkage between deterrence and defense. All previous military systems could offer some measure of genuine protection for a country if deterrence failed. With nuclear weapons—at least in the context of the East-West confrontation—this was no longer true. All the eggs were placed in the deterrence basket, and if deterrence were to break down the result would be total catastrophe for both sides and possibly for the whole planet. The critics urged that the balance must be redressed at least to the extent of ensuring that nuclear weapons played only a minimal role in deterring a nuclear attack by the other side and adopting the policy that conventional attack would only be met at the conventional level. This would imply as a minimum the acceptance of a No

First Use of Nuclear Weapons Policy (see *Nuclear Weapons, No First Use of*), and the removal of "battlefield" nuclear weapons—that is, nuclear mines, shells, and short-range rockets—whose deployment carried the implication that nuclear weapons were to be regarded not as an ultimate deterrent but as just another and more powerful addition to the conventional armoury.

Criticisms of NATO's willingness to use nuclear weapons first under some circumstances (which, as of February 1999, it has still not abandoned) and of the deployment of battlefield nuclear weapons, came from otherwise orthodox strategists and political commentators on both sides of the Atlantic. Moreover, two major European political parties, the SPD in the Federal Republic of Germany and the British Labour Party, committed themselves in 1984 to supporting a No First Use policy by NATO and to the withdrawal of Cruise and Pershing II missiles. The Labour Party policy document also committed it to the rejection of British nuclear weapons and to advocating a non-nuclear and defensive system by NATO, though this did not extend to a rejection of a minimal United States nuclear guarantee to Europe to deter the possibility of a Soviet nuclear attack. More radical critics of current policy argue that any use of nuclear weapons, even in a second strike, would be immoral and pointless and that an alternative strategy must be one that rejects any reliance on weapons of mass destruction. For western Europe this would imply not simply the physical removal of nuclear weapons but the explicit decoupling of European defense from the United States nuclear system. However, the Labour Party, following a succession of electoral defeats, jettisoned its anti-nuclear commitment and the Labour government elected in 1997 continues to maintain—and expand—the Trident nuclear arsenal. The SPD—Green Coalition Government in Germany which took office in the autumn of 1998 is still (1999) pressing for NATO to adopt a No First Use policy. In the meantime Ground Launched Cruise and Pershing II missiles, together with battlefield nuclear weapons, have been removed from Europe, and the whole context of the defence debate has changed.

The argument that a country or alliance could aim to establish a viable system of non-offensive defence, and defensive deterrence, rests on the traditional insight of military strategists since Clausewitz that the defense enjoys certain inherent advantages over the offense. Military commanders usually work on the assumption that a three-to-one numerical or equivalent advantage is necessary to be reasonably sure of success in an offensive operation at the battlefield level; at the "theater" level, which might encompass a whole country or several countries, the advantage is even more heavily weighted to the defender due to such factors as shorter supply lines, knowledge of the terrain and of political and social conditions, and strong motivation for resistance by the population whose country is under attack. Thus a country or alliance that wished to be strong in a defensive mode would not need to match a potential opponent's forces tank for tank or soldier for soldier and could concentrate on different types of armaments better-suited to a defensive strategy.

Advocates of defensive deterrence recognize that no weapon, and no military system, is entirely incapable of being used in an offensive capacity. Moreover, even a military system with a clearly defensive purpose would require some capability for offense at the tactical level in order to mount counterattacks within the territory in the event of invasion. But the number and disposition of forces, and the type of armaments deployed, could reduce to a minimum the possibility of any major strategic offensive being launched against another state. Thus a country which had no long-range bombers or missiles, limited the number of its tanks, and concentrated on building up its capability to repel attack with fighter aircraft, anti-tank and antiaircraft weapons, and, where appropriate, a defensive naval force would pose a minimal threat to its neighbours. Sweden, Finland, Switzerland, and Austria are examples in Europe of states that have a clearly defensive military system and are not seen by other states as posing a military threat.

The toughest question faced by advocates of a non-nuclear alternative defence policy was how a country which had adopted it could respond to nuclear blackmail or nuclear attack—perhaps in the course of a conventional war where the nuclear-armed opponent was facing defeat. They pointed out, however, that there were strong moral and political inhibitions to the use of nuclear weapons against non-nuclear states, and that if, for example, the former Soviet Union—the only plausible contender for playing such a role at that time—were seriously to contemplate the use of such weapons against a non-nuclear Western European country, or against a non-nuclear Western Alliance in Europe, it would know that such a course of action would earn it unique opprobrium throughout the world and cost it heavily in political terms. Such inhibitions would not operate to anything like the same extent where both sides had nuclear weapons and for this reason non-nuclear states like Sweden or Switzerland were in much less danger of suffering a nuclear attack than any of the NATO countries that either possessed nuclear weapons themselves or relied

on the US "nuclear deterrent." However, it was acknowledged that the ultimate vulnerability of non-nuclear states to nuclear escalation or blackmail pointed up the need for a fall-back strategy of guerrilla warfare or nonviolent resistance. Today, the possibility of nuclear escalation, or nuclear blackmail, has receded though it could reemerge as a live issue in the future. And the use, or threatened use, of chemical or biological weapons raises similar questions and could become a more immediate concern.

A claim frequently made in the 1980s was that developments in conventional military technology had enhanced the advantages of the defense. In particular precision-guided munition systems (PGMS) had made tanks, aircraft, and major ships like aircraft carriers more vulnerable than in the past. While there is some truth in this claim, the 1991 Gulf War—and the US-UK bombardment of Iraq in December 1998 without the loss of a single life or single ship or plane—demonstrated how military technology could shift the advantage in the other direction. In 1991, the intensive bombardment of Iraqi positions in Kuwait quickly overwhelmed them, and in 1998, an initial bombardment by cruise missiles substantially reduced the threat to subsequent attacks by US and British bombers. Moreover, the aircraft themselves were better equipped than in the past both to evade anti-aircraft missiles and to use precision weapons to destroy Iraqi radar equipment and anti-aircraft weapons.

Proponents of alternative defense—with one or two exceptions—have never claimed that a non-offensive defence system would make a country invulnerable, whatever the circumstances. No system of defence can do that. The size and military strength of the belligerent states, including their degree of industrial and technological development, has to be taken into account. Indeed this was the other major reason—in addition to the nuclear threat—that led to the inclusion in most models of alternative defence of plans for a fall-back strategy of territorial defence in depth, guerrilla warfare or civil resistance. What one can reasonably look for from a defense system is the ability to threaten an attacker with defeat under all but the most extreme circumstances—such as an all-out attack by a large, heavily-armed power on a small state—or at least to signal to any hostile state that an attack would involve heavy costs in military and/or political terms. Even in relation to Iraq it should be noted that while its forces were driven out of Kuwait in 1991 with relative ease, the alliance ranged against it stopped short of trying to occupy Iraq itself and depose Saddam Hussein. Legal considerations were a factor here, but it is clear from statements by political and military leaders both in 1991 and again in 1998 that it was also recognized that to attempt an invasion would require massive ground forces and involve a heavy loss of life on both sides.

What the 1991 Gulf War demonstrates most dramatically is that a system of collective military security system under existing circumstances requires a massive offensive capability, at the disposal of the UN—which in practice means in the hands of one or more member states acting, or claiming to act, in its name. For if Iraqi forces were driven out of Kuwait at short shrift once the fighting started, this operation nevertheless required the deployment of one of the most formidable offensive forces ever assembled, and a massive bombardment of Iraqi forces.

Clearly, then, non-offensive defence cannot meet all the requirements of national and international security. It has limited applicability in the kind of internecine wars that have proliferated in recent decades, and it cannot provide the basis for collective security, at any rate while there continue to be heavily armed states able and willing to attack smaller and less powerful neighbours. (This point holds even if one takes the view that the particular military action taken against Iraq in 1991 was not justified and/or that a peaceful solution could have been arrived at.) However, in regions of potential conflict, a shift towards a non-offensive posture, preferably on the part of all protagonists, could prove a vital confidence-building measure and a means of preventing future wars. Ultimately defence systems of themselves cannot ensure international security. This—in so far as it is attainable at all—requires also political initiatives, including an end to the trade in offensive weapon systems, a huge reduction in the level of armaments worldwide, and the building of a more equitable global economy.

See also: *Deterrence; Unilateralism*

*Bibliography* ———————————————

Ackerman P, Kruegler C 1994 *Strategic Nonviolent Conflict.* Praeger, Westport, Connecticut, and London

Afheldt H 1978 Tactical nuclear weapons and European Security. In: SIPRI 1978 *Tactical Nuclear Weapons: European Perspectives.* Taylor and Francis, London

Alternative Defence Commission 1983 *Defence without the Bomb.* Taylor and Francis, London

Alternative Defence Commission 1985 *Without the Bomb.* Granada, London

Alternative Defence Commission 1987 *The Politics of Alternative Defence.* Paladin, London

Baylis J (ed.) 1983 *Alternative Approaches to British Defence Policy.* Macmillan, London

Boserup A, Mack A 1974 *War Without Weapons.* Frances Pinter, London

Galtung J 1984 *There Are Alternatives. Four Roads to Peace and Security.* Spokesman, Nottingham

Holst J J 1990 *Civilian-Based Defense in a New Era.* Albert Einstein Institution, Monograph Series No.2, Cambridge, Mass

Kennan G 1986 A new philosophy of defense. *The New York Review of Books* 33(2)

King-Hall S 1958 *Defense in the Nuclear Age.* Gollanz, London

Mellon C, Muller J-M, Semelin J 1985 *La Dissuasion Civile.* Foundation pour les Etudes de Defense Nationale

Nolte W 1984 Autonomous protection. In: Tromp H, de Vries K (eds.) *Non-nuclear War in Europe.* Groningen University Press, Groningen

Randle M 1990 *People Power: The Building of a New European Home.* Hawthorn Press, Stroud

Randle M 1994 *Civil Resistance.* Fontana

Roberts A (ed.) 1967 *The Strategy of Civilian Defence.* Faber and Faber, London

Roberts A (ed.) 1969 *Civilian Resistance as a National Defense.* Penguin Books, Harmondsworth

Semelin J 1991 *Unarmed Against Hitler: Civilian Resistance in Europe 1939-1943.* Praeger, Westport, Connecticut and London

Sharp G 1985 *Making Europe Unconquerable: The Potential of Civilian-based Deterrence and Defence.* Taylor and Francis, London

Sharp G (with the assistance of Bruce Jenkins) 1990 *Civilian-Based Defense: A Post-Military Weapons System.* Princeton University Press

The Program on Nonviolent Sanctions in Conflict and Defense (?) *Transforming Struggle: Strategy and the Global Experience of Nonviolent Direct Action.* The Center for International Affairs, Harvard University

Moeller B (ed.) *NOD & Conversion* (The quarterly international research newsletter).The Copenhagen Peace Research Institute

MICHAEL RANDLE

# Alternative Dispute Resolution

There has been a recent rapid growth within Western countries of experimental measures for the resolution of conflicts of all types. It has taken the form of a "movement" away from formal legal settlement in favor of more subtle localized forms of managing disputes. This movement, although responding to new pressures typical of developed industrial societies, takes its cue from much older pre-legal mechanisms still in evidence in many non-Western nations.

The modern pressures from which the movement derives its momentum are the increasing use of the law (amounting to a virtual crisis caused by overloading of the justice systems in a number of Western nations), the increasing bureaucratization and depersonalization of social life, and the continual threats of internal strife, disorder, and violence to which accelerating economic development seems to be prone. These factors are not unrelated and indeed may all be manifestations of an increasing alienation between individuals and the major social institutions, which appears to be a common feature of large-scale national societies.

Although these ills go much deeper in the socioeconomic structure, and cannot simply be adduced to the law, it is to the latter that resort is most readily and frequently made in an effort to stem such social unrest. The fact that the law itself partakes of just these same characteristics of depersonalization and formalism, and does so *par excellence* among all social institutions, is therefore ironic.

These features, moreover, are those that give strength to the law as a means of dispute settlement. They enable the judicial apparatus to be seen as impartial in judgment, unscrupulously fair in procedure (due process), and independent of other social or political influences in application. The law is a powerful contributor to peace in society in so far as it can maintain its credibility as a completely just arbiter whose decisions are accepted by both parties, loser as well as winner. It is also conducive to peace by taking conflict or retaliation out of the hands of individual parties and thus minimizing the violence and disorder that might otherwise arise.

In practice, although in many ways the law is able to live up to its promise, its most valuable features are precisely the ones that limit its success in a range of cases. (There are many works dealing with the limitations of the law; see for example Levin and Wheeler 1979, and Marshall 1985.) These are cases in which the assignment of blame for an isolated past offense is a minor consideration in relation to the untangling of a whole history of conflict between the parties, and the establishment of better relations for the future. While the law is ideally constructed in theory to defuse conflicts arising over offenses committed by strangers, such as a burglary, or a traffic incident, or specific disagreements occurring between persons who normally get along (e.g., over the building of an extension that shades a neighboring garden), it can be less than perfect when the presenting issue is only one of an extended series of accusations and counter-accusations. In such cases its very impersonality, formality, and refusal to entertain "extraneous" considerations can obviate any attempt to obtain a useful and realistic settlement.

Realization of this problem of the limited relevance of the law to conflict resolution has led to a search for alternatives which stress the personal participation of the parties and reduce procedural formality in favor of greater flexibility. At a minimum, this shift away from the judicial has taken the form of arbitration, which preserves the independence of the judge or arbitrator as the ultimate decision maker, but allows parties freedom to present their own cases in the way they wish, introducing any considerations they believe relevant. This has proved successful particularly in specialist areas of law, such as contract disputes between commercial firms. At a maximum, the rejection of judicial forms would entail abdication from third party intervention altogether, taking Christie's (1977) argument to the extreme when he says that conflicts are the property of the parties themselves and should not be forcefully taken away from them. Of course, people's natural skills at interpersonal negotiation cannot be expected to be perfect, and conflict may escalate beyond their intentions because of poor communication, misunderstanding, or emotional commitment. In such cases access to some form of third party assistance may be able to save considerable individual distress, time, and effort, let alone any adverse social ramifications that may ensue from unresolved disputes.

This middle range of alternatives to the judicial, variously termed "mediation," "conciliation," or "conflict management consultancy," has taken many different forms, all based on the principle of the third party not as arbiter but as facilitator of negotiation between the parties, who themselves retain the power to formulate a mutually acceptable agreement or not to agree at all (see *Arbitration, International*).

Some of the earliest and most systematic attempts to provide community-based alternatives to courts this century were made in socialist countries, beginning with the Workers' Court of the former Soviet Union, which dealt with petty offenses within the workplace, and expanded into a variety of "comrade courts" based on individual neighborhoods in East Europe, China, Cuba, Tanzania, etc. Although these "courts" typically had decision-making powers and state sanctions, their major intention was to persuade parties to obey the rules by means of the application of social pressure. The court bench consisted of elected local lay representatives, but they were in practice loaded with party "*apparatchiks.*" Although a central tenet of communism was the return of control of social institution to the people, the courts were really used as means of ideological indoctrination and were highly unpopular. They have since been abandoned throughout East Europe and the former Soviet Union, and have resulted in considerable distrust of "alternatives dispute resolution" in those nations. This highlights the dangers of extra-legal procedures without safeguards for individual rights and democratic control.

Apart from the socialist countries, the urge to develop alternatives to the law for dispute settlement has been most prominent among those countries adopting the Anglo-American forms of law especially the United States, because of its particular tendency to excessive legalism (Liebermann 1981) compared with the more "inquisitorial" nature of legal justice in Western Europe, where judges have more scope for investigating contextual circumstances and questioning parties. The long and spasmodic history of attempts to reassert community control over local conflicts in North America has been documented by Auerbach (1983).

The most recent manifestation of this movement has its origin in three seminal academic papers published in US legal journals in the mid-1970s, and summarized in McGillis and Mullen (1977). The first of these, by Richard Danzig, referred to the "community moot" model of justice, thought to typify the process of law in small tribal societies, in which the emphasis is upon community involvement, consensus decisions rather than a single arbiter's judgement, reconciliation of the parties rather than singling one out for blame, social relationships rather than legal norms, and future harmony rather than past faults. The second model, by Eric Fisher, was closer to the "community court" of socialist countries and is an extension of the law rather than a complete alternative. Lastly, Frank Sander opted for an intermediate model, the "dispute resolution center," which avoided the potential coercion of Fisher's, but would not rely entirely on community control.

It was this last approach which was encapsulated in an experimental program of three Neighborhood Justice Centers set up by the Department of Justice in 1977. Since then many more such centers have opened up throughout the country. Typically they receive cases directly from parties, or on referral from community and criminal justice agencies, such cases being conflicts or minor offenses between parties in some form of ongoing relationship. Mediators are local lay volunteers who receive around 40 hours' training for the task. The centers vary considerably in their degree of attachment to and dependence on the legal justice system, some being virtually restricted to cases diverted from the police or the courts, others accepting only community referrals before any legal action is taken. The bulk of centers have a mixed caseload but tend to be heavily weighted towards minor offenses diverted from criminal justice agencies, while the "on-going relationship" between the parties which all hold to may be as tenuous as customer-business or landlord-tenant relations.

Most of the cases dealt with by Neighborhood Justice Centers derive from neighbor squabbles, but the movement towards mediation has been effective in other types of dispute, too. Labor relations constituted the first problem area, not only in the United States, but also in the United Kingdom, Europe, and elsewhere, to give rise to formal arbitration and mediation arrangements (see German 1979 on the United States, and Aaron 1969 on Western Europe). The resolution of divorce-related family disputes (over access to children, for instance) was another issue to which mediation has been widely applied in the United States and the United Kingdom, Australia, and elsewhere (see Roberts 1983). Newer problem areas within which mediation appears to be finding a fruitful role, especially in the United States, are environmental issues and race relations (or intergroup conflicts more generally). While such schemes are based in local neighborhoods or established (in the case of labor relations, etc.) on a national basis, individual organizations are also finding mediation techniques useful for the settlement of internal conflicts in, for example, schools, prisons, and commercial corporations (see *Mediation*).

While most neighborhood mediation is carried out by community-based programmes, there has been a considerable expansion in the 1980s and 1990s of commercial mediation services, often staffed by retrained lawyers, who particularly provide mediation for contract disputes, divorce settlements, and environmental issues. While the fees for mediation may not be much less than those for legal services, the speed of mediation compared to going to court, plus the advantage that it allows the parties to maintain, or re-establish, their relationship, may mean that it is both more economical and the preferred option for parties themselves. Overviews of mediation, particularly of the commercial kind, are provided by Brown & Marriott (1993) and Mackie (1991).

In the United Kingdom (Marshall and Walpole

1985) mediation developed in the 1980s in several directions. One of these was towards community-based services, influenced by US models, and by the establishment in 1980 in New South Wales, Australia, of similar Community Justice Centers (Institute of Criminology, University of Sydney 1982). These services use specially trained volunteers recruited from the local communities to mediate disputes brought by local people themselves, or referred by local agencies such as Citizens Advice Bureaux, the police, housing departments and environmental health officers. After a slow initial development, such services proliferated in the 1990s when local authorities discovered that funding them saved considerable amounts of their own officer's time, and that more disputes were resolved, and resolved more completely, than before. Some housing departments and housing associations provide their own internal mediation service. Many local mediation services also train school staff and pupils to conduct their own conflict resolution.

The other major direction taken in Britain is the development of mediation in criminal justice, either in association with diversion from prosecution, or alongside prosecution and complementing it (see Marshall and Merry 1990). This "victim-offender mediation" helps resolve the issues that remain between victim and offender as a result of the commission of an offense. It helps victims express their feeling and explain their hurt, provides the offender with an opportunity to apologize and give their own perspective, and allows both to negotiate a reparation agreement. It provides help to victims beyond what the judicial system can offer, and also has a more substantial impact on the offender because of the personalized and participatory nature of the experience. Such programmes were influenced in origin by North American ones, including VORPs (Victim-Offender Reconciliation Projects) (see PACT Institute of Justice 1984) and "reparation schemes" for negotiating compensation to victims by offenders (see Galaway and Hudson 1990). "Family group conferences" began in New Zealand (see Brown & McElrea 1993) and have since spread in different forms to Australia, North America and Britain. These involve not only the victim and offender but other relatives or supporters of each, and they attempt a general resolution of each crime by consensus, including the negotiation of compensation, sanctions and a rehabilitation program. So far they have only been used for juvenile offenders, but thought has been given to extending them to adults as well (For a full description of programmes in Britain, see Marshall 1996).

In some other European countries there have been similar developments. These include the Norwegian community-based "conflict councils" (based on a model developed by Nils Christie); French *juges conciliateurs,* now replaced by "penal mediation" for adults, on referral by public prosecutors (similar arrangements apply in Belgium), "reparation" for juveniles, and *maisons de justice et du droit,* which are community-based mediation programs for disadvantaged communities; extensive mediation for juvenile offenders in Germany and Austria; and variations on these ideas in Finland and elsewhere (see Wright 1996 for more details on European developments).

Mediation in a criminal justice context has given rise to new ideas about justice, generally under the term "restorative justice," arguing that a purely legal approach is insufficient because it does not focus sufficiently in victims' interests, the need to restore communities, and the importance of giving offenders a chance to regain their good name. Restorative justice proposes greater public participation and a problem-solving orientation to crime as a means of achieving effective prevention and putting right the harm caused. Similar ideas are also being used in schools to deal with problems of persistent misbehavior, truancy and bullying. The classic text on restorative justice is that by Zehr 1990, but there has since been a burgeoning literature on the topic, including Cragg 1992, Umbreit 1994, and Marshall 1994 and 1996.

The recent proliferation of the "alternative dispute resolution" movement has spawned a confusing array of different organizations and techniques, and the movement is characterized currently by an equally considerable variety of aims, intentions, and hopes, ranging from religious notions of pacification (see Kraybill 1982) to hard-headed concern with the costs of legal justice and a search for cheaper forms of dispute settlement. There is still great ferment and debate over standards and methods, and the evangelical literature of the earlier years (mid-1970s to early 1980s) is now being supplemented by cogent critiques of many of the practices (especially Tomasic and Feeler 1982, and Vermont Law School 1984). In particular, the applicability of notions of "community" in modern societies has been questioned, while many schemes have uncritically adopted forms based on traditional small-scale societies; the problem of unequal power in many relationships (customer-business, husband-wife, citizen-government) also raises the question of whether mediation outside the procedural protection of the law can ever be "fair" in such cases; the possibility of "informal justice" degenerating into mindless vigilantism is a further worry of many commentators; while some are concerned that the movement is being exploited by governments to off-load a mass of minor cases from legal justice for the sake of mere economy (thereby creating a stratum of second-class justice), others stress the danger of social control being extended further into areas of social life and individual freedom beyond the reach of the established law.

These are real problems that will need to be addressed as the movement unfolds, but there appears little doubt that mediation will continue to play a role, if only because personal involvement is valued by many parties and because the formal processes of the law could not possibly cope with the mass of conflicts and disputes that are a continuing part of everyday life. Mediation is a natural process within any community (see Cain and Kulcsar 1983), and Marshall (1985 ch. 7) argues that this should be built upon, and supported by, more formal schemes involving semiprofessional intervention.

There are many forces within modern societies towards the creation and escalation of conflict, and a tendency towards adversarial confrontation and disregard for the social consequences, which might be tempered by an approach that advocates cooperative problem solving. Insofar as dispute settlement (whether by legal justice or alternative means) is aimed at suppression of conflict by the encouragement of compromise for its own sake, by employing social pressures, however discrete, and individuals' own dislike of overt conflict to persuade them to accommodate their aims beyond what in the longer term is satisfactory to them, the peace and order thus gained will be illusory and will only stoke the fires of greater conflicts in future. Insofar, however, as dispute settlement is achieved in a creative manner, attempting to satisfy all parties without undue compromise of reasonable aims, and with a readiness to tackle extrinsic barriers to resolution (see Folger and Poole 1984), a real peace may ensure, or at least the conflict may proceed without distortion by emotional overtones and violence (On the relation to "peacemaking," see National Forum 1983). In the process everyone may become wiser in the social skills necessary to live their own lives fully while enabling their neighbors to do likewise.

See also: *Crime Trends and Crime Prevention Strategies; Confidence Building in International Diplomacy; Conflict Resolution, History of; Negotiations, Direct; Problem Solving in Internationalised Conflicts*

Organizations Able to Supply Further Information

*Canada*

The Network Interaction for Conflict Resolution, Grebel College, Waterloo, Ontario N2L 3G6.

*United States*

Conflict Resolution International Inc, 2205 E Carson St, Pittsburgh PA 15203-2107.
Institute for Conflict Analysis & Resolution, George Mason University, Fairfax, Virginia 22032.
National Institute for Dispute Resolution, 1726 M St NW, Suite 500, Washington DC 20036-4502.
Program on Negotiation, 516 Pound Hall, Harvard Law School, Cambridge, MA 02138.
RESOLVE, 2828 Pennsylvania Avenue NW, Suite 402, Washington DC 20007.
Victim Offender Mediation Association, 777 S Main St, Suite 200, Orange, CA 92868-4614.

*United Kingdom*

Advisory, Conciliation and Arbitration Services (ACAS), 27 Wilton Street, London SW1X 7AZ.
Centre for Dispute Resolution, (CEDR), 7 StKatherines Way, London EL 9LB.
ENCORE (European Network for Conflict Resolution), Friends House, Euston Road, London NW1 2BJ.
Environmental Resolve, The Environment Council, 21 Elizabeth Street, London SW1W 9RP.
MEDIATION UK, Alexander House, Telephone Avenue, Bristol BS1 4BS.
National Coalition Building Institute, PO Box 411, Leicester LE4 8ZY.
National Family Mediation, 9 Tavistock Place, London WC1H 9SN.
Quaker Peace and Service, Friends House, Euston Road, London NW1 2BJ.

*Bibliography*

Aaron B (ed.) 1969 *Dispute Settlement Procedures in Five Western European Countries*. Institute of Industrial Relations, University of California, Berkeley, California

Auerbach J S 1983 *Justice Without Law?* Oxford University Press, London

Brown BJ, McElrea FWM 1993 *The Youth Court in New Zealand*. Legal Research Foundation, Auckland

Brown HJ, Marriott AL 1993 ADR *Principles and Practice*. Sweet & Maxwell, London

Cain M, Kulcsar K (eds.) 1983 *Disputes and the Law*. Akademiai Kiado, Budapest

Christie N 1977 Conflicts as property. *Br. J. Criminol.* 17(1)

Cragg W 1992 *The Practice of Punishment.* Routledge, London

Folger J P, Poole M S 1984 *Working Through Conflict: A Communication Perspective.* Scott, Foreman, Glenview, Illinois

Galaway B, Hudson J 1990 *Criminal Justice, Restitution and Reconciliation.* Criminal Justice Press, Mousey, NY

Getman J G 1979 Labor arbitration and dispute resolution. *Yale Law J.* 88

Institute of Criminology, University of Sydney 1982 *Proc. Seminar on Community Justice Centers.* Government Printing Offices, Canberra

Mackie, KJ (ed.) 1991 *A Handbook of Dispute Resolution.* Routledge, London

Marshall TF 1994 Grassroots initiatives towards restorative justice. In: Doff A et al., (eds.) *Penal Theory and Practice.* Manchester University Press, Manchester

Marshall TF 1996 The evolution of restorative justice in Britain. *European J. on Criminal Policy and Res.* 4(4)

Marshall TF, Merry S 1990 *Crime and Accountability.* HMSO, London

Umbreit M 1994 *Victim Meets Offender.* Criminal Justice Press, Mousey, NY

Wright M 1996 *Justice for Victims and Offenders,* 2nd edn. Open University Press, Milton Keynes

Zehr H 1990 *Changing Lenses.* Herald Press, USA

TONY F. MARSHALL

# Ambassadors

The documents of Medieval Europe refer to the agents sent back and forth between rulers to negotiate treaties and agreements as "ambassadors." Rather than live in foreign countries, medieval ambassadors would be sent abroad to accomplish a specific purpose. Once this had been done, they would return home. They also appear to have been concerned only with peaceful relationships. For declarations of war, different agents, known as heralds, would be sent.

The functions of ambassadors changed dramatically during the fifteenth and sixteenth centuries, a period which essentially gave birth to modern diplomacy. In the fifteenth century, the fiercely competing Italian city-states found it to their advantage to appoint permanent representatives in neighboring capitals. The monarchies of the rest of Europe copied this practice of exchanging permanent resident ambassadors in the sixteenth century. In 1815 the Congress of Vienna confirmed that ambassadors, along with papal nuncios and legates, were the highest ranking representatives which one state could send to another, and established that their order of precedence in any capital would be based on the length of their service there. Since the nineteenth century this system of diplomacy, characterized by resident ambassadors being exchanged by sovereign states, has spread throughout the entire world. In 1815 only representatives sent from one monarchy to another were normally given ambassadorial rank, but by the end of the nineteenth century republics such as the United States of America were also sending and receiving ambassadors. Since the Second World War, virtually all permanent heads of diplomatic missions have been given the rank of ambassador. In addition, representatives sent to international bodies such as the United Nations are now typically given ambassadorial rank.

Once an ambassador has been selected, he or she may then be accepted, or declared persona grata (welcome) by the head of state of the country to which he or she has been sent. Once accredited, he or she can function as ambassador and enjoys diplomatic immunity. This last means that ambassadors are immune from legal prosecution under the laws of the country to which they have been sent. Such immunity is designed to protect ambassadors and other diplomats from the threat of arrest being used to exert pressure on them as they carry out their duties. If an ambassador is thought to have abused this immunity, the head of state of the host country can declare him or her persona non grata (unwelcome) and expel him or her. The complexities of the diplomatic immunity and privileges of ambassadors and other diplomats were codified in the Vienna Convention on Diplomatic Relations in 1961, which has been signed by nearly all of the world's nations.

The last 150 years have seen enormous changes in the characteristics of ambassadors. Where previously ambassadors were almost always wealthy, aristocratic male amateurs, their ranks have increasingly been broadened to include professionally trained diplomats, including women, who have been selected on the basis of their ability rather than birth or wealth. Alexandra Kollontay, who became the Soviet ambassador to Mexico in 1926, was the first of a growing number of female ambassadors. In addition, twentieth century ambassadorial ranks have frequently included distinguished persons from a variety of walks of life. Examples drawn from the United States, which makes more use of such distinguished nonprofessional diplomats than any other major country, include Shirley Temple Black, actress, ambassador to Ghana from 1974 to 1976; John Kenneth Galbraith, Professor of Economics, ambassador to India from 1961 to 1963; and Leonard Woodcock, labor leader, ambassador to the People's Republic of China from 1979 to 1981.

The functions and duties of ambassadors have also undergone extensive changes over the past century or so. Modern communications, which permit ambassadors to convey information and receive instructions from their own governments instantly, have greatly lessened the importance of ambassadors as negotiators. While ambassadors still carry on negotiations with the host governments, final decisions about important matters are now almost invariably made by foreign ministers and heads of government, rather than by the ambassadors who represent them. The ambassador's role in negotiations is now predominantly one of presenting and defending his or her country's position to the government to which he or she is accredited, and conveying that government's positions and arguments back to his or her own government.

Beyond negotiations, ambassadors also play a very important role in keeping their own governments informed about the land to which they have been accredited. They report not only about its government and its capabilities and intentions, but about the country's general economic, political, social, and military trends. In order to do so, ambassadors are expected to cultivate ties with a wide variety of contacts and to keep themselves well-informed about the country to which they have been sent.

Ambassadors also serve as the representatives of their own countries abroad. Through cultivating friendships and participating in ceremonies, and through social and charitable activities, they attempt to give the government and people of the host country a favorable impression of their own nation and its government. The role of the Papal Nuncio, or diplomatic representative of the Vatican, is particularly important in this respect in many countries with predominantly Roman Catholic populations.

In the Middle Ages ambassadors were regarded as servants of peace, and the establishment of friendly ties and the settlement of differences through peaceful negotiation are still among their most common functions. It should be recognized, however, that ambassadors also can and have been used to undermine the governments to which they have been accredited, to spy, and even to lay the groundwork for war. Modern ambassadors must be seen as the servants of the governments which send them—not of peace. They are responsible for carrying out the policies of their governments, which may or may not be peaceful ones. The maxim of Ermolao Barbaro, Venetian ambassador to Rome in the late fifteenth century, is still worth noting today: "The first duty of an ambassador is . . . to do, say, advise, and think whatever may best serve the preservation and aggrandizement of his own state." In the same vein, the seventeenth-century English statesman Sir Henry Wotton wryly described the moral ambiguity of the modern diplomat by telling a friend that "an ambassador is an honest man sent to lie abroad for the good of his country."

Wholehearted dedication to the interests of their own governments has frequently led to ambassadors being regarded with suspicion, hostility, and even fear. In recent years it has not been uncommon to see diplomats, including those of the former Soviet Union, the People's Republic of China, and the United States, expelled from the countries to which they have been accredited, following accusations that they had been engaged in subversion, espionage, and other activities hostile to the interests of the host government.

The concept of diplomatic immunity has also been severely strained recently by the activities of some small, radical states. The "People's Bureaus" or embassies of Libya offer particularly vivid examples of such activities. In 1980 Libyan diplomats in Western Europe and the United States were strongly suspected of using their privileged positions to harrass and even murder Libyan dissidents in the countries to which they were accredited, and a number of them were expelled. Four years later, in 1984, a policewoman was killed by a bullet fired from the Libyan People's Bureau in London. Since the Libyan representative could claim diplomatic immunity, the frustrated British government was unable to prosecute the murderer, though it did sever relations with Libya and expel its diplomats. It remains to be seen whether outrage over such abuses of diplomatic privilege will result in major changes in the status and activities of ambassadors and their staffs.

See also: *Diplomatic Recognition*

*Bibliography* ————————————————————

Denza E 1976 *Diplomatic Law*. Oceana, New York
Green L C 1981 Trends in the law concerning diplomats. *19th Canadian Yearbook of International Law*
Ikle F 1967 *How Nations Negotiate*. Harper and Row, New York
Nicolson H 1964 *Diplomacy*. Galaxy Books, New York
Satow E 1957 *A Guide to Diplomatic Practice*. New York

GARRETT L. MCAINSH

# Anarchy, International

The term "anarchic" (or "anarchical") is derived from the classical Greek word *anarchos*. This word has two meanings which are still relevant: (a) without a leader; (b) procedure to settle conflicts outside courts of law. These meanings make it clear why contemporary world society can be described as an "anarchic society." Anarchy in the terminology of political science does not mean "chaos" but the absence of a formal legal order (courts) and of a central monopoly of violence (a leader) which can enforce peaceful conduct of the members of a society with respect to each other. To maintain internal peace is precisely the basic function of the state. States among each other, however, have not yet found their Leviathan. They still find themselves in what in eighteenth-century social contract philosophy was called the "state of nature." Before state-societies were established, the natural condition of men was one of "war of every man against every man" in the words of Hobbes. Hobbes has also described quite well the persistent consequences of the lack of a central monopoly of violence at the world level:

> Yet in all times Kings and Persons of Sovereign Authority, because of their Independency, are in continual jealousies, and in the state and posture of Gladiators; having their weapons pointing and their eyes fixed on one another; that is their Forts, Garrisons and Guns, upon the Frontiers of their Kingdomes; and continually Spyes upon their neighbours; which is a posture of war.

The anarchic structure of world society thus forces states into a situation in which the memory or the threat of war is always present. Memories and expectations of war produce feelings of insecurity and often what more dispassionate analysis would consider as exaggerated enemy images, popular fears, and defense panics.

The anarchic character of competitive state systems presents states with a continuous security dilemma: the absence of a central monopoly of violence which can force states to settle their conflicts within courts of law implies that states can never be completely certain that they will not be attacked by other states or that the superior military power of an opponent will not compel them to make political or economic concessions which threaten their independent survival. In order not to be forced to submit, states will therefore be inclined to arm themselves, as well as they can or to ally themselves with other (stronger) states. However, such defensive armament programs or alliances will be perceived by other states as a threat to their own security. They will in turn feel forced to strengthen their own arms capacity or to form their own alliances. So even if no single state actually intends to attack another state, the coercive dynamic set in motion by international anarchy keeps the drift towards war in existence and arms production and arms acquisition in full swing.

Double bind may be a more precise concept than the anarchy metaphor. States form double-bind figurations and processes (Elias 1985):

> Human groups which are interdependent, because each of them is without redress, without a chance to appeal for protection to any superior force or to a binding code of self-restraint of civilized conduct, are exposed to the possible use of violence by the other group. Wherever human groups are arranged in such a form they are with great regularity drawn into a power struggle and, if they form the top of an interstate hierarchy, into a hegemonial struggle with a strong self-perpetuating tendency.

Participants in a double-bind process are tied in two ways: to their rivals and the threat of their uncontrolled rivalry as well as to their own fears and emotions which prevent them from analyzing the threat in a more detached and realistic manner. As can be seen quite clearly in situations which have been called "Cold War" (see *Cold War*), high levels of perceived danger produce high levels of emotional responses and vice versa, preventing realistic assessment of the nature of the threat and realistic practice in order to mitigate it. It is a circular process which is very difficult to break through. In such situations it is always the opponent—its supposed expansionism or innate aggressiveness—that is blamed for the threat instead of perceiving the anarchic or double-bind situation of interstate relations itself as the main source of danger. The double-bind situation which results from the anarchic structure of interstate relations is thus not just a matter of political and military-strategic relations, it also has deep-seated emotional and psychological implications. That is why arms control and crisis management negotiations are so difficult and so often fail.

International anarchy does not mean that interstate relations are not structured. Relations between states are structured and to some extent regulated by the power balances between them. But again, there is no power strong enough to effectively claim the right to use violence and physical coercion to maintain the peace between competing states and make them comply with the rules and regulations of international law. The structure and "order" of the relations between states is therefore primarily a function of the relative power ratios between them, usually called "the balance of power" (see *Balance of Power*). Great Powers can function as a partial substitute for a central monopoly of violence. They can fulfill certain pacifying and regulating functions on an international scale, such as the pacification of the relations within their own alliances, or the coordination of international monetary relations. But such substitutes are only partial. The question is therefore whether more promising substitutes or functional equivalents for the central monopoly of the state at the world level can be found.

International anarchy is the major explanation for keeping the world in a state of potential war but might, at the same time, be the key toward a more durable peace. The only conceivable possibility is an extension of the restraint into which nuclear weapons at present force the Great Powers, which has resulted in a period of 40 years' peace between them. Especially during the past 30 years, when both major nuclear powers possessed an invulnerable nuclear arsenal, making retaliation possible after any kind of attack, they have behaved so prudently that even political crises were kept at a low level, below the alert level in any case. But the double-bind situation prevented them until now from drawing the conclusions from that situation with respect to arms procurement policies and nuclear strategy. Further development of nuclear restraint would imply, on the one hand, that the dangers of accidental and unintended nuclear war have to be nearly eliminated through extended and comprehensive negotiations between the nuclear powers and, on the other hand, that nuclear weapons would make it ever more impossible for the Great Powers, and later also for other states, to use violence in order to settle their conflicts, because any war could in theory still escalate into a nuclear war. Nuclear weapons would then assure peaceful conduct amongst states and no longer make the term "anarchic" applicable to world society. But precisely the double-bind character of the relations between the Great Powers makes such a development regrettably still utopian.

*Bibliography* ———————————————

Bull H 1977 *The Anarchical Society*. Macmillan, London
Elias N 1985 *Problems of Involvement and Detachment*. Oxford
Hobbes T 1962 *Leviathan*. Everyman, London
Hoffmann S 1965 *The State of War: Essays in the Theory and Practice of International Politics*. Praeger, New York
Mandelbaum M 1981 *The Nuclear Revolution*. Cambridge University Press, Cambridge
van Benthem van den Bergh G *The Taming of the Great Powers*.
Waltz K N 1979 *Theory of International Politics*. Addison-Wesley, Reading, Massachusetts

G. van Benthem van den Bergh

# Ancien Regime

Ancien Regime is the French term for the monarchical government that existed before the French Revolution. It has since been applied to the political regimes of all dynastic states in the period of so-called absolutism. It thus describes the European political regimes during roughly the period between 1648 (the Treaty of Westphalia) and 1789 (the French Revolution). In that sense Ancien (or old) Regime has only a descriptive meaning. But more often than not the term denotes not only a former regime but also an obsolete one. It then stands for a government and political structure that has outlived itself but is unable to change itself through conscious reforms. An Ancien Regime in short, then, is a blocked system in which any reform of its structure and power relations will affect the roots of its power and undermine its foundations to such an extent that it may topple.

The Ancien Regime in France can be seen as the model of such a system, because France was the most highly developed dynastic state and its monarchy the most clear example of absolutism (leaving aside Czarist Russia, which had a very different pattern of development from the Western European dynastic states). That kind of regime had its origin in the development of the relations between the monarch and the two major classes (estates) in society, the aristocracy and the bourgeoisie, though these social classes themselves changed drastically in character over the centuries. When the position of the landed—originally feudal—warrior-aristocracy became weakened, primarily as a consequence of the inflation caused by the inflow of precious metals, the King, Louis XVI, became capable of pursuing a careful balancing strategy. He compelled the aristocracy to take up residence at his court (Versailles) by giving its members pensions and/or court functions. The warrior-aristocracy was thus transformed into a court aristocracy dependent on the favors of the King, its members not being allowed to engage in commercial activities. In remembrance of their former way of life this court aristocracy in France was called *Noblesse de l'Épée*, the sword-carrying aristocracy. But the King gave members of this aristocracy, apart from court functions which they monopolized, only a limited number of functions in the state organization, primarily in the diplomatic service and the military. Most functions in the state administration, such as tax collecting and the administration, of the state budget, were reserved for members of the upper strata of the urban bourgeoisie, and these also often received noble titles. There thus developed a *Noblesse de Robe*, an aristocracy of the "gown," next to the court aristocracy, which was in command of the most important administrative and judicial functions in the state. The *Noblesse de Robe* was in fact a state bourgeoisie which derived its power resources not so much from control over the means of production as from privileged access to the monopolized control over the means of violence and taxation. Wealthy members of the town bourgeoisie could buy administrative offices and thus secure for themselves both a noble title and a guaranteed part of the tax revenues. The values of the French bourgeoisie therefore were less oriented to accumulating capital than to acquiring enough money to buy a title and an office.

For the aristocracy however, as for the King, expenses to maintain their status and prestige necessarily came before income. Many aristocratic families therefore ruined themselves. The Count de Montesquieu, himself a member of the *Noblesse de Robe*, developed on the basis of this observation one of the very first sociological theories, a model of the circulation of families within and between estates. The court aristocracy could not engage in commerce, and therefore could not increase its wealth. Families ruined themselves by keeping up their status. Their ruin enabled some families of the *Noblesse de Robe* to be elevated into the court aristocracy. In turn, positions in the *Noblesse de Robe* became available for wealthy merchants to buy. In that manner the social division between the estates could remain and be combined with sufficient social mobility of individual families. It also stimulated merchants to do their utmost in order to leave their lowly status behind. Thus, according to Montesquieu, everybody will do what they should do to make the state function in the best way possible.

As long as the King could balance off the court aristocracy and the state bourgeoisie against each other by giving both specific privileges and power,

but not sufficiently for any class to become predominant, his power was absolute in the sense that no-one within the state could challenge it. The King's power was thus a function of the competition between the two most powerful classes in society. These classes, however, had a common interest in the maintenance of institutionalized privilege as such. This situation prevented attempts by the new aristocracy to overturn the old, as such attempts might well have led to a further redistribution of power in society. They thus had an ambivalent relationship: envious of each other yet forced to take a common stand against the lower classes in society. In the eighteenth century, however, the figuration which Montesquieu described in terms of a moving equilibrium in fact became a frozen situation. As Elias (1983) has described it:

> We encounter here a situation which has a certain significance as a model. We see a figuration of ruling élites who are imprisoned in the antagonism of their mutual tensions as if it were a trap. Their values and goals are so oriented towards their opponents that every move of themselves or their opponents is seen in the light of the advantages or disadvantages that it could bring to themselves or to their opponents.

Reform movements having the development of society at large in view had to fail in such a situation. The *Noblesse de Robe* became more and more closed and more and more separated from the merchant, banking, and industrial bourgeoisie in the towns. The balancing strategy of the King implied such a distribution of state revenues that consumption of luxury goods instead of productive investment was stimulated. Reform movements developed within the court administration, such as the physiocrats, and outside of it the broad intellectual movement of the Enlightenment emerged. Even when the economy improved, there remained rising dissatisfaction with the blocked political system. The pre-industrial élites bound to their rival class perspectives were unable to perceive the changing power balances in society and therefore could not make the concessions necessary to avert violent struggle. They became more and more locked in the deadly embrace of their ambivalent relationship. It is in that characteristic of the Ancien Regime that we find the long-term origin of the French Revolution.

In fact, certain aspects of eighteenth century development in France show great similarities with developments in contemporary ancien regimes like that of Haile Selassie's Ethiopia and the Shah's Iran. So, for example, de Tocqueville wrote: "though the reign of Louis XVI was the most prosperous period of the monarchy, this very prosperity precipitated the outbreak of the Revolution" and "the spirit of revolts was promoted by well-intentioned efforts to improve the people's lot." Modernizing policies can promote revolution as well as prevent it. As long as an Ancien Regime with its obsolete privileges and power monopolies is not reformed, modernization and economic growth will primarily fuel revolutionary sentiment.

The blockages of the Ancien Regime also have international implications, as became all too clear in the revolutionary wars which upset the previous "balance of power" system that had existed in Europe. Drastic internal political transformations often provoke or lead to international conflicts. Ethiopia and Iran also became involved in wars after their Ancien Regimes had been deposed.

The Ancien Regimes in Europe did, however, make a major international achievement in further developing the ancient concept and policy of balance of power. In fact, the Ancien Regime in Europe after 1648 is co-terminant with "Europe's classical balance of power." This classical balance of power was based on "such an equal distribution of power among the Princes of Europe, as makes it impracticable for the one to disturb the repose of the other" (Europe's Catechism), and on the conception that all states had an interest in the preservation of the balance. The former was not a durable given, however. Such a power balance had to be maintained by continual combination and recombination, and flexibility in forming alliances—and, when a balance threatened to break down, through quickly forming war coalitions (even among previous enemies) against aspiring hegemonists. Balance-of-power policy was different from a policy based on reason of state (*raison d'état*) which recognized no higher interest than that of the individual state. Balance-of-power policy was in fact an early attempt to develop procedures and institutions for the limitation and control of international violence. It saw the relations between states as a structure with regularities and a dynamic of its own and accepted that states have to act upon a shared conception of the nature of that balance rather than on a narrow view of the immediate interests of the individual state. The control of violence would be facilitated if the member states of a balance of power shared the same kind of (Ancien) Regime. Such a balance was of course fragile because if an increasingly powerful state with a different kind of regime, such as Revolutionary and Napoleonic France, neither recognized the balance as such nor respected its rules anymore it would break down.

Balance-of-power policy as practiced by Ancien Regimes after 1815 gave rise to the practices of the Concert of Europe through which a large number of conflicts in Europe were settled peacefully. It prevented major wars in Europe between 1815 and 1914. The Ancien Regime thus had some lasting significance for the development of a more peaceful world.

See also: *Balance of Power*

*Bibliography* ─────────────────────────

Elias N 1983 *The Court Society.* Oxford
Gulick E V 1955 *Europe's Classical Balance of Power: A Case History of the Theory and Practice of One of the Great Concepts of European State Craft.* Ithaca, New York
Moore B Jr 1966 *Social Origins of Dictatorship and Democracy.* Boston, Massachusetts
de Tocqueville A 1966 *The Ancien Regime and the French Revolution.* Fontana, London
Williams E N 1970 *The Ancien Regime in Europe: Governments and Societies in the Major States 1648-1789.* New York

G. VAN BENTHEM VAN DEN BERGH

# Anglican Church of Canada

In relation to peace, Anglicans in Canada are influenced by two fundamental realities: the geographical and political presence of the United States as next door neighbor, and their heritage as members of a relatively conservative Christian body. The developing peace policy of the Anglican Church of Canada thus arises out of interaction between these two factors and the church's increasing moral and spiritual autonomy.

Anglicans are Christians whose churches are descended from the historic national churches of the British Isles, and who are in communion with the Archbishop of Canterbury, senior bishop of world Anglicanism. The first recorded moment in Anglican history in Canada was an act of worship celebrated in 1578 at Frobisher Bay, North-West Territories. In 1749 the first Anglican parish was formed (St. Paul's, Halifax, Nova Scotia). Canada's first Anglican bishop, Charles Inglis, himself a refugee from the American War of Independence, was consecrated in 1787. In 1893, bishops, priests and laypersons from across Canada gathered to form the General Synod (GS) or national assembly of what was then called the Church of England in Canada. The name was changed to the Anglican Church of Canada (ACC) in 1955, in recognition that many members of the church were of other than English origin.

According to official church figures of the early 1980s, Anglicans on parish rolls represented some four percent of Canada's population of some 25,000,000. Census figures from 1981, however, indicate that some three times this number call themselves Anglicans. The Anglican Church is the third largest Christian community in Canada, coming after the Roman Catholic Church, which comprises just over half the population, and the United Church of Canada, which comprises about a fifth. However, because of relatively high levels of education and income among Anglicans over the years, and because of the early entry of Anglicans into the development of national life, Anglicans, at least until recently, have occupied a recognized position in the mainstream of Canadian life out of proportion to their numbers. Whether this will to any large extent continue beyond the 1980s remains to be seen.

## 1. The Post-Hiroshima Period I: 1945-63

In England, though not in the other countries of the United Kingdom, the Church of England is the "established" or official church of the land. Among Canadian Anglicans, therefore, many of whom have valued their own connection and the connection of their church with England, there has often been an assumption that church and nation work together for the same goals, and with this a corresponding reluctance to criticize the government, especially on "patriotic" issues such as national security or disarmament. Until the Second World War the ACC relied on the Church of England or on the Lambeth Conference (of bishops in communion with Canterbury, held every ten years: the next one is scheduled for 1988) for the formulation of concerns about war and peace. A landmark in this regard is Resolution 25 of Lambeth 1930, reaffirmed many times since, which states that "war as a method of settling international disputes is incompatible with the teaching and example of our Lord Jesus Christ."

Since 1945, however, the ACC has taken full responsibility for addressing its own membership, other Christians, the government of Canada and the wider community on war and peace. A booklet issued in the mid-1960s by the church's Council for Social Service (CSS) summarized the immediate postwar position of the ACC on peace as follows:

(a) War as a means of settling disputes is incompatible with the teaching of our Lord Jesus Christ.

(b) It is the duty of governments of nations to work

for general reduction and control of armaments.

(c) Weapons of mass destruction should be universally banned under international agreement and control.

(d) The United Nations and its related agencies should be given full support as instruments of collective security and justice.

(e) It is the responsibility of Christians to work and pray continually for world peace.

(f) There must be greater aid to under-developed [*sic*] countries and a greater recognition of the need to extend fundamental human rights if world tensions are to be reduced. (*Warfare, Armaments and Christian Responsibility* p. 3)

During this same period other specific points were made in resolutions of the CSS (carrying the authority of that subordinate body only), the Executive Council (later the National Executive Council: EC. NEC), which speaks officially for the church between meetings of the General Synod, and the GS itself, the highest legislative authority of the church. These included the following: 1947—a "fundamental change in spirit" urged if progress toward peace was to take place (CSS); 1948—Marxism condemned by reason of its atheistic and totalitarian nature, and a serious consideration of the communist critique of Western society called for (CSS); 1950—the statement of the World Council of Churches (WCC) condemning the hydrogen bomb endorsed, and thankfulness expressed for the UN's multinational military operation "against aggression in Korea" (CSS); 1952—the conviction expressed that Canada should work for peace in a particular way through its membership in the Commonwealth (GS); 1958—endorsement of Resolution 106 of Lambeth 1958, declaring the use of nuclear weapons to be "repugnant to the Christian conscience," and Resolution 107, calling on Christians "to subject to intense prayer and study their attitudes to the issues involved in modern warfare" (CSS, EC); 1960—support registered for the government's policy on the cessation of all forms of nuclear testing (tests in the atmosphere, in space, underwater and underground were specified) (CSS); 1962—the view stated that "the only sane course open to humanity is never to use nuclear weapons," and attention called to the "moral influence of those nations who refuse to have nuclear weapons" even though they have the capacity for them, a reference to Canada's 1945 decision not to proceed with the development of its own nuclear weapons (GS); and 1963—a welcome for the

Limited Test-Ban Treaty, and a request to the Canadian government to work for similar agreements on other nuclear issues (CSS, EC).

A statement of May 22, 1963 (*Warfare, Armaments and Christian Responsibility* p. 9) by Archbishop Howard Clark, primate (chief pastor and executive officer) of the ACC, sums up Anglican views in this first post-Hiroshima period. The statement was issued in response to a vote in the House of Commons supporting the newly elected minority government of Liberal Prime Minister Lester Pearson in its nuclear policy under which Canada, as a member of the North Atlantic Treaty Organization (NATO), was committed to use tactical nuclear weapons in Europe. As the church's chief pastor, he stated then that the first use of such weapons in response to a non-nuclear attack had no moral justification, and urged the Canadian government to press for a change in NATO policy. He also recorded the fact that, at that time, Anglicans, like other Christians, were divided on the morality of the use of nuclear weapons in retaliation for nuclear attack.

## 2. The Post-Hiroshima Period II: 1963 to the Present

In the later 1960s and early 1970s, a period of relative détente internationally, there was a corresponding lessening of peace-related activities and resolutions in the ACC and in Canada in general. By the end of the 1970s and the beginning of the 1980s, however, international tension was again on the rise. For Canadians, this was particularly noticeable in the US presidential campaign which resulted in the election of Ronald Reagan in 1980, and in the subsequent references of his administration to "limited nuclear war." It may be soberly stated that these statements, together with the reaction to them in Canada and elsewhere, had the effect of bringing many Anglicans and other Canadians into active membership in the peace movement.

In 1979 the NEC had proposed that a consultation of Anglicans be held on a subject of world importance for which the ACC had no current developed policy. This proposal was referred to the church's Unit of Public Social Responsibility, which agreed that disarmament was such an issue. The consultation, "Anglicans and Peacemaking," held in Burnaby, British Columbia, in November 1982, considered the arms race in general and Canadian involvement in it in particular, and brought to this consideration a thorough biblical and theological response. Out of this gathering, which included participants from developing countries and from sister churches in Canada, the

Unit took statements and strategies which were incorporated into a draft resolution. This resolution was discussed at a number of diocesan synods in the spring of 1983 and was presented to the GS of June 1983 in Fredericton, New Brunswick.

Resolution 111, as finally passed with a large majority, now represents the developed peace policy of the ACC. Based on the biblical understanding that "shalom—peace with justice, freedom and true security for all—is the future God intends" for the human race, and on the Risen Christ as the personal expression of this shalom, the Resolution calls on all members of the ACC to respond in hope and witness to the world's need for peace. It reaffirms earlier GS statements on the arms race (1955, 1962, 1965), and declares the "development, production or use of nuclear weapons or other weapons of mass destruction . . . [to be] contrary to the will of God and the mind of Christ." It thereby goes beyond the 1963 statement of Archbishop Clark by renouncing the use of nuclear weapons even in retaliation for a nuclear attack, so demonstrating a decisive change in Anglican opinion in the intervening two decades. It also asks the government "to take initiatives toward mutual, balanced and verifiable disarmament," to reassess Canadian use and sale of nuclear technology, to commit the nation to "alignment with other nations pursuing nonviolent methods for the resolution of conflict," to continue the participation of Canadian forces in peacekeeping operations, to attempt to persuade the United States and the former Soviet Union to redirect funds used for weapons toward economic and social development, and to redouble its efforts to persuade other countries to accept and abide by the Nuclear Non-Proliferation Treaty (see *Non-Proliferation Treaty (NPT)*).

The resolution also commits the church itself to helping Canadians to achieve a fuller understanding of God as creator of all, of the nature of global citizenship, and of the implications of Christian love for political life; to working with persons from all over the world in the creation of a just and participatory society as the basis for peaceful international relations; and to developing an effective theology and ministry of peacemaking at all levels of its life. It further asks the theological colleges in which Anglican priests are educated to ensure that "within their courses proper attention is paid to resources and training in human conflict resolution and in ministries of peacemaking"; asks the parishes and diocese of the church to commit themselves "to giving peacemaking a primary place in [their] liturgy and program;" gives GS endorsement to the work of Project Ploughshares (see below); recommends that Anglicans involve themselves at all levels of society in attempts to reduce violence; and directs the GS Program Committee to assist local groups across the church in the implementation of the resolution as a whole.

Further resolutions on peace were passed by large majorities at Fredericton, the first (Resolution 79) urging the government to pass private member's bill C-678 declaring Canada a nuclear weapon free zone; the second (Resolution 82) urging the universal outlawing of chemical and biological weapons; and the third (Resolution 83) asserting the particular immorality of the first use of nuclear weapons in any future war, and further stating the conviction that a moral obligation rests on all countries, NATO members included, to forswear such use.

## 3. Ecumenical Relationships

Resolutions comparable to those summarized above were approved in 1982 by the national legislative bodies of the other major churches of Canada and of the Canadian Council of Churches (CCC). Together with the Anglican resolutions, they have been collated and published by Project Ploughshares. This ecumenical peace coalition was founded in 1976 by representatives of the ACC and other Canadian churches, and now carries on its work under the general sponsorship of the CCC. It acts on behalf of the churches in undertaking research on issues of peace and security, in coordinating ecumenical representations to the government, and in working to have Canada declared a nuclear weapon free zone. Of particular significance in its recent work are the two statements of December 1982 and December 1983 prepared for the leaders of the Anglican, Lutheran, Presbyterian, Roman Catholic, and United Churches and of the CCC for presentation to the prime minister. Perhaps most critical in the 1982 statement was the request to the government to cancel the permission granted to the US armed forces to test the Cruise missile over Canadian territory. This request, representing the views of a majority of the Canadian people (52 per cent according to the Gallup poll taken close to the time of the meeting), was rejected, and the first such test took place in March 1984. The 1983 statement, written after Prime Minister Pierre Trudeau had begun his personal peace initiative, encouraged him in his efforts. But in language much stronger than that of the 1982 statement it also asked him to take steps to disengage the Canadian government from what many Christians and other Canadians perceived as a less than sufficiently critical support of US foreign and military policy, while at the same time the necessity of maintaining a close relation with the United States which it described as "Canada's principal ally."

On a wider ecumenical horizon, the ACC has given strong support to the peace initiatives of the WCC since the foundation of that body in 1948. The connection with the WCC has become closer in recent years, with the then primate of the ACC, Archbishop Edward Scott, having served as moderator of the Central Committee (1976-83), and with the holding of the WCC's Sixth Assembly in Vancouver in 1983. Of Archbishop Scott it should be mentioned that he has given strong support, both official and personal, to the churches' peace witness both in Canada and throughout the world.

## 4. Prospects

Since about 1980, peace and justice groups have formed in many parishes and among ecumenical groups of churches in local neighborhoods. Canadian Anglicans also joined secular peace groups during this time, and were thereby in many cases impelled to integrate their peace concerns as citizens with their Christian understanding of God's intentions for humankind. Given the spread of the peace movement in the church and in Canadian society, it is probable that both these undertakings will continue to grow. It is also possible that, if the clauses on theological education in the churches' resolutions are taken seriously, peace and justice ministry could become the focus for the renewal of the theological curriculum, particularly if it is integrated with the renewal of spirituality. As the 1980s continue, the ACC may also be expected to work with the other churches through Project Ploughshares in pressing upon the government the need for a stronger national commitment to unilateral initiatives for peace, and for the rejection both of deterrence as a sufficient basis for national security and of support for the use of nuclear weapons by Canada's allies. The years coming will also very likely see an increasing acquaintance of the ACC's members with the church's policy on peace as expressed in Resolution 111. This will in all probability lead to intensification of internal conflicts in many parts of the church before the consensus expressed at GS 1983 is accepted by the church at large.

Nonetheless, the 1983 resolutions, as the fruit of a long process of consultation, reflection and legislative decision, represent in a way in which no previous enactments do the church's considered policy, offered as such to the church's members for their moral, social and political guidance. Canadian Anglicans thus possess a sufficiently broad policy on the basis of which to work for peace and disarmament until the coming of God's shalom.

See also: *Religion and Peace*

*Bibliography* ————————————————

Anglican Church of Canada 1983 *Report on Anglicans and Peacemaking: A Consultation on Disarmament.* Anglican Church of Canada, Toronto, Ontario

Anglican Church of Canada Council for Social Service 1964 *Warfare, Armaments and Christian Responsibility.* Anglican Church of Canada, Toronto, Ontario

Judd W W (ed.) 1951 *A Positive Programme for Peace.* Angli-can Church of Canada Council for Social Service, Toronto, Ontario

Project Ploughshares 1983a *Brief to the Prime Minister of Canada.* Project Ploughshares, Waterloo, Ontario

Project Ploughshares 1983b *Resolutions and Statements on Disarmament Issues by Canadian Church Leaders.* Project Ploughshares, Waterloo, Ontario

Rankin W W 1983 Anglican attitudes and behaviors concerning war. In: Elmen P (ed.) 1983 *The Anglican Moral Choice.* Morehouse-Barlow, Wilton, Connecticut

Regehr E, Rosenblum S (eds.) 1983 *Canada and the Nuclear Arms Race.* Lorimer, Toronto, Ontario

DONALD GRAYSTON

# Appeasement Policy

During the late 1930s, as Nazi Germany and Fascist Italy behaved more and more belligerently on the international scene, the British government adopted the strategy of trying to buy peace by "appeasing" the dictators whenever it appeared that resisting them might lead to war. It was hoped that if the dictators were allowed to take what they wanted peacefully, they would be appeased, or satisfied, and thus the world would be spared the horrors of a new war. This policy, which allowed Nazi Germany to arm itself, contrary to its obligations under the Versailles Treaty of 1919, and to absorb several of its weaker neighbors, is now almost universally regarded as having been both immoral and ineffectual. In the end it not only failed to keep the peace, but meant that when war did come Britain's enemies were in a far stronger position than they otherwise would have been.

The appeasement policies of the 1930s have many of their roots in Britain's First World War experiences. The horrors of that conflict, in which an entire generation—around two and a half million of the six million Britons who fought became casualties—was decimated, left many convinced that anything was preferable to another such slaughter. During the 1930s, recalled British historian R. H. Tawney, "the loathing of war was unquestionably the most powerful, the most general and the most constant of political emotions" in England. Such emotions were reinforced by fears that the rapid development of military aircraft would make the next war even more ghastly than the last one. Military staff estimates of huge numbers of civilian casualties and the apocalyptic visions of science fiction writers such as H. G. Wells fanned popular imaginations and sobered political leaders.

The historical research which was carried out in the 1920s and 1930s contributed to these antiwar sentiments by indicating that none of the Great Powers had really wanted a general European war in 1914. The war appeared to have been caused not by some militaristic plot, but by the unwillingness of everyone concerned to back down in the crisis which preceded it. Everyone had clearly seen the dangers of appeasing their foes, but no one had appreciated that war, which turned out to be the alternative, was infinitely more dangerous. The lesson of history seemed to be that patience, compromise, even a willingness to retreat—in other words appeasement—stood a far better chance of preserving peace than did stubborn rigidity in the face of foreign provocations.

This new feeling of shared responsibility for the origins of the First World War also helped to discredit the settlement which had followed it. The war had produced great hatred for Germany in Britain and throughout the Western world, hatred which was amply reflected in the Versailles Treaty which Germany was forced to sign in 1919. In that treaty Germany was blamed for having deliberately started the war, was deprived of territory, was saddled with reparations payments, and was forbidden to rearm. As passions cooled over time, and as the idea that German guilt in starting the war had been grossly exaggerated won increasing acceptance, many in Britain concluded that the treaty had been unduly harsh and unjust. Thus when Hitler began unilaterally to break the Versailles Treaty—by reintroducing conscription and openly rearming in 1935, and by remilitarizing the Rhineland in 1936—Britain protested but did not feel inclined to take action. There was a strong feeling that any true peace must be based on justice, and that Hitler, reprehensible as he was, was simply securing belated justice for Germany.

The Great Depression which began in 1929 and crippled Western economies through the 1930s also played an important role in shaping the policies of appeasement. Extremely high unemployment placed stringent budgetary restrictions on the governments of Britain and the other Western democracies. Tax revenues were falling at the very moment when the cost of programs aiding the jobless was going through the roof. This meant that there was great reluctance to increase military spending, no matter what the provocation, and military weakness pointed toward a cautious, conciliatory foreign policy. Indeed, Britain's opposition Labour Party was even more adamantly opposed to military spending than were the Conservatives who dominated the government and installed the policy of appeasement. In the elections of 1935, Conservative Prime Minister Stanley Baldwin and Chancellor of the Exchequer Neville Chamberlain, two of the chief architects of appeasement, were actually branded as warmongers by Labour when they argued in favor of modest increases in defense spending.

British anti-communism also played a significant role in appeasement. Fear and suspicion of Soviet Russia made many Britons very happy to see Hitler and Mussolini build a band of strength across Central Europe to serve as a bulwark protecting the West from Stalin. According to their logic, Britain should strive for friendship with Nazi Germany and Fascist Italy at all costs, for the only beneficiaries of war between these authoritarian states and the Western democracies would be the Soviet Union and communism.

Appeasement thus had elements which appealed to people all across the political spectrum, from right-wing anti-communists to people with social consciences which recoiled at the thought of scarce resources being spent on guns instead of on the needs of the poor, from adherents of international justice to outright pacifists. Only a minority of the British people and their leaders had the ability to see clearly that unless the insatiable appetites of Hitler and Mussolini were resisted stubbornly, they would cause problems infinitely worse than anything else the West had to face. Among the leaders who did attack appeasement, Conservatives Winston Churchill, Harold Nicolson, and Anthony Eden; and Labourites Ernest Bevin and Hugh Dalton stand out for the courage with which they opposed the popular consensus.

Many historians argue that the first episode of appeasement came with Britain's failure to do more than mount ineffectual diplomatic protests when Japan invaded Manchuria in 1931. It is difficult, however, to see what other course could have been taken in this case. The other powers in the League of Nations, despite their supposed commitment to collective security, were too preoccupied with their own problems to have any desire to become embroiled with Japan. Since Britain alone had neither the military power nor the economic leverage to force the Japanese to withdraw from Manchuria, unilateral action would have been an exercise in futility. Nonetheless, this episode was a dramatic demonstration that aggression was still possible in a world which had supposedly agreed to ban it.

Although economic sanctions were briefly and half-heartedly tried when Mussolini invaded Ethiopia in 1935, the basic British reaction was again to appease the aggressor by not taking strong action against him. Here the British fleet had the military power to halt the Italian invasion without much difficulty, but the British government worried that such an action would drive Mussolini into Hitler's arms. In fact, the weakness of the Western response to his belligerence left Mussolini so contemptuous of the democracies that he formed an alliance with Hitler anyway, in 1936.

In the spring of 1938 Hitler annexed the republic of Austria, again scorning Germany's treaty obligations. Once again Britain and the other Western powers chose to allow this unilateral breaking of the Treaty of Versailles and destruction of a small and weak state; once again it was argued that allowing a dictator to have what he wanted would appease him and preserve world peace.

The climax of the policy of appeasement came in the fall of 1938, when Hitler ordered Czechoslovakia to cede the Sudetenland provinces, insisting that he would go to war against the Czechs if he were refused. France had a treaty committing it to declare war on Germany if it invaded Czechoslovakia, but felt too insecure to honor this obligation without British support. The decision of whether to risk war over the Sudetenland or appease Hitler once again rested on the shoulders of Neville Chamberlain, who had become Britain's prime minister in May, 1937.

Chamberlain and other leaders felt that to begin a war with Germany over the Sudetenland would be a disastrous folly. Such a conflict would certainly lead to millions of deaths, just to preserve the integrity of a distant and rather questionable border. In addition, they could not militarily prevent Germany's conquest of the entire Czech state if war came; nor could they seriously threaten Germany itself, with its newly fortified Western frontier. Even those who were coming to believe that war was inevitable argued vigorously that Britain needed more time to arm and prepare itself for the ordeal.

Chamberlain reluctantly ordered the British fleet to

mobilize when Hitler threatened war, but then leapt to accept Hitler's last-minute suggestion of an international conference in Munich to discuss the crisis. There, at the end of September, 1938, he attempted to preserve the peace by agreeing that Hitler could have the Sudetenland. In return, Hitler gave his solemn promise that the Sudetenland was his "last territorial demand."

Though today Munich is regarded as a shameful betrayal of a small nation, Chamberlain was given a hero's welcome on his return to England, as the man who had secured "peace in our time." It was not until the spring of 1939, when Hitler annexed the rest of Czechoslovakia and began demanding territory from Poland, that the folly of trying to preserve the peace by appeasing Hitler became apparent. When Hitler invaded Poland that September, Britain and France both declared war on Germany, thus abandoning the policy of appeasement.

The appeasers later claimed that their policies had been wise in that they gave Britain and France much-needed time to rearm before embarking on war with Nazi Germany and Fascist Italy. They also argued that their patience in dealing with the dictators resulted in the Western populations becoming convinced that there was no alternative to war, thus giving the Western governments solid popular backing for the war effort. There is some truth to these arguments. However, critics point out that Germany was rearming at a much faster rate than the Western powers, so that the military gap between them actually widened, rather than narrowed, as the war approached. In addition, Munich deprived the West of the help of Czechoslovakia's excellent army in the war, and also convinced Stalin that his interests lay in allying with Germany rather than the West. In short, the appeasement policy can only be regarded as a military and moral disaster for the democracies.

*Bibliography*

Chamberlain N 1939 *In Search of Peace*. Putnam, New York

Churchill W 1948 *The Gathering Storm*. Cassell, London

Fuchser L W 1982 *Neville Chamberlain and Appeasement*. Norton, New York

Gilbert M 1967 *The Roots of Appeasement*. New American Library, New York

Gilbert M, Gott R 1963 *The Appeasers*. Houghton Mifflin, Boston, Massachusetts

Wheeler-Bennett J W 1948 *Munich: Prologue to Tragedy*. Macmillan, London

GARRETT L. MCAINSH

# Arab-Israeli Conflict: Peace Plans and Proposals

The Arab-Israeli conflict has generated numerous and diverse efforts for its resolution and the attainment of peace and tranquility. In 1979, more than thirty years after the United Nations first focused its attention on the Palestine problem, Israel and Egypt signed a Treaty of Peace. Despite this achievement, the relative tranquility established in one sector of the region, and the resolution of some of the issues in the conflict, it was not until the 1990s that this was mirrored elsewhere, and still many differences between Israel and the Arabs remain unresolved. While it is not possible to review all the proposals, public and private, official and unofficial, which have been advanced, it is the intention here to present the more salient and significant proposals put forward by the parties to the conflict and by the major outside powers (including the United Nations and its organs), and to identify those that have determined the direction of the quest for peace in the Arab-Israeli conflict.

*1. To the Six Day War of June 1967*

The focus of the Arab-Israeli conflict has been the status of the territory known as Palestine, that came under British control with the demise of the Ottoman Empire at the end of the First World War and which the British subsequently divided into Transjordan and Palestine. In the period between the two World Wars the territory west of the Jordan river was administered by Britain as the mandate of Palestine. That area became the subject of international controversy and United Nations deliberations following the Second World War, when the British decided to relinquish control and the international community sought to find a solution acceptable to both the Arabs and Jews of Palestine, as well as the Arab states.

The issue came before the United Nations on April 2, 1947 when the United Kingdom formally requested consideration of the Palestine question by the General Assembly. The United Nations established a Special Committee on Palestine (UNSCOP) which met from May to September 1947 when it submitted its proposals for a solution to the General Assembly. The main recommendations were that the mandate be terminated and that independence be granted at the earliest practicable date. The committee differed, however, on specific elements of the problem. A majority recommended a plan for the partition of Palestine into an Arab state and a Jewish state bound together in an economic union. The City of Jerusalem, including Bethlehem, was to be placed under trusteeship, with the United Nations as the administering authority. A minority plan proposed a single independent state comprising both Arab and Jewish entities under a federal government. Representatives of the Arab Higher Committee and of the Arab League (see *League of Arab States*) rejected the committee's recommendations, advocating instead the establishment of one Arab state comprising the whole of Palestine. The Jewish Agency, representing the Jewish community of Palestine, stated their readiness, despite reservations, to accept the majority plan with some modifications.

On November 29, 1947 the UN General Assembly adopted Resolution 181 (II), which embodied the majority plan, by a vote of thirty-three to thirteen with ten abstentions. The plan was never implemented, however, as violent clashes between Arabs and Jews persisted until the British, themselves under sporadic attack, finally withdrew and the violence that had characterized relations between the communities in Palestine erupted into the first Arab-Israeli war in May 1948 (see *Arab-Israeli Wars*).

Even before the formal outbreak of war, the UN General Assembly responded to the persistent hostilities with Resolution 186 (S-2) (see *United Nations Peacekeeping Operations*), by which it appointed a United Nations mediator in Palestine to assure the protection of the Holy Places and to "promote a peaceful adjustment of the future situation of Palestine." The war which followed Britain's withdrawal and Israel's proclamation of independence was halted by a truce which went into effect on June 11, 1948. The mediator, Count Folke Bernadotte, subsequently appealed to the parties to extend the truce, but the hostilities were resumed in early July. The mediator reported to the Security Council that the suggestions for a solution which he had presented to the parties on June 28, 1948 had not been acceptable either to the Jews or the Arabs, and since he had exhausted all the powers available to him, he called on the Council to intervene (see *Mediation*). On September 17, 1948 Bernadotte was assassinated.

In December 1948 the General Assembly established a Conciliation Commission for Palestine (CCP) consisting of France, Turkey, and the United States of America to assist the parties to arrive at a settlement. Meanwhile, fighting in the region was halted by another truce. The United Nations acting media-

tor, Dr Ralph Bunche, presided over negotiations on the island of Rhodes (see Nobel Peace Prize Laureates: *Ralph Bunche*). By the spring of 1949 the negotiations produced armistice agreements between Israel and each of the contiguous Arab states (Egypt, Syria, Jordan, and Lebanon). The armistice agreements were to "remain in force until a peaceful settlement between the parties is achieved . . . ." They were not regarded as a solution to the problem; they provided for further negotiations for the achievement of peace. Efforts to move from armistice to peace thus became the major objective and the focus of all subsequent proposals and activity.

The CCP invited Israel and the Arab governments to send delegations to Lausanne. The Commission reported, however, that it was not possible to arrange direct negotiations under its auspices because of the Arab insistence that they negotiate as a united bloc, whereas Israel preferred to deal with each question separately, with the state or states immediately concerned. Nevertheless, the CCP continued in its efforts. Having sought to act as intermediary at Lausanne in the spring of 1949, the following year at Geneva, the Commission attempted to bring about direct negotiations through the medium of mixed committees. In Paris, in 1951, the CCP submitted to the parties for their consideration a set of specific proposals to deal with the problem of the refugees created as a consequence of the war, and to turn the armistice into broader and more permanent arrangements. Ultimately, the CCP had to report that although it had employed "all the procedures which were at its disposal" it "has been unable to make substantial progress in . . . assisting the parties to the Palestine dispute towards a final settlement of all questions outstanding between them." The United Nations proved unable to improve upon these efforts of the CCP and confined its role primarily to the maintenance of the original armistice agreements and the provision of subsistence to the Arab refugees.

As the armistice agreements failed to give way to more permanent arrangements and an arms race began to develop between the parties, the Great Powers became more directly involved. On May 25, 1950, Britain, France, and the United States issued the Tripartite Declaration that reaffirmed their desire to maintain the stability of the region and to regulate the flow of arms to the area. They declared "their deep interest in and their desire to promote the establishment and maintenance of peace and stability in the area." Despite this general declaration of intent, no specific actions and plans to promote the desired peace and stability were forthcoming. In the wake of the initial failures to convert the armistice agreements into more permanent arrangements, and with the view that the problem was not likely to be resolved soon, efforts to deal with elements of the problem, rather than the entire complex of issues, soon became the prevailing approach. Underlying this shift of emphasis were two perceptions: (a) that amelioration of portions of the problem might provide a step in the direction of a general solution, and that, (b) in the interim, the partial steps would improve conditions for the Arab refugees and might help to promote regional stability. Among the earliest of these efforts was that of the United Nations Economic Survey Mission, under the chairmanship of Gordon Clapp, which was established by the CCP in 1949. It was to "examine the economic situation arising from the recent hostilities, and to make recommendations to the CCP concerning ways of reintegrating the refugees and of "creating the economic conditions which will be conducive to the establishment of permanent peace." Although there were some benefits from its activities (including the creation of UNRWA—the United Nations Relief and Works Agency for Palestine Refugees—which was established to alleviate the refugee problem) the movement toward peace was not facilitated.

In a similar vein the United States produced a scheme of its own. Eric Johnston was sent to the Middle East by President Dwight Eisenhower in 1953. Among other tasks, he was to undertake discussions concerning the mutual (Arab-Israeli) development of the water resources of the Jordan River in a practical effort to benefit all the people of the area. It was believed that a comprehensive Jordan Valley development project would facilitate economic progress, reduce tension, contribute to stability, and perhaps foster accommodation. The scheme produced no tangible results, and President Eisenhower complained: "At times the effort seemed promising, but prejudice and resentments on both sides caused rejection of the plan which had achieved agreement among the engineers; no progress was made." Rather than let the Jordan Valley plan fall completely by the wayside, the United States sought to devise some further steps to promote a settlement.

In August 1956 US Secretary of State John Foster Dulles (see *Dulles, John Foster*), in an address before the Council on Foreign Relations in New York, outlined what he saw as the three principal problems: the plight of the refugees, the pall of fear hanging over Israelis and Arabs alike, and the lack of fixed permanent boundaries between Israel and its Arab neighbors. Dulles suggested a multifaceted approach.

To resolve the refugee problem he proposed a combination of resettlement and repatriation, to be facilitated by the creation of more arable land through water development projects. The necessary funds would partly be made available by the United States, which would also participate substantially in an international loan, to enable Israel to pay compensation to the Arab refugees. In an effort to replace the fear existing between the Arabs and Israelis with a sense of security, the United States would "join in formal treaty engagements to prevent or thwart any effort by either side to alter by force the boundaries between Israel and its Arab neighbors." Dulles expressed the hope that other powers and the United Nations would join such a security guarantee providing collective measures "which commit decisive power to the deterring of aggression." He suggested that the United States would be willing to assist the parties to the dispute to find a permanent solution to the boundary problem that would replace the temporary lines fixed by the 1949 armistice agreements.

Israel's reaction to Dulles' proposals was mixed. While welcoming the understanding of Israeli problems which he had shown, Israel was skeptical about Dulles' plans for the refugees and, in particular, the question of where to fix the international boundaries. Israel maintained that these should be based on the 1949 armistice lines, although it conceded that in the context of negotiated peace treaties it might be willing to make minor border adjustments. Arab opposition, meanwhile, was based on Dulles' omission of reference to United Nations resolutions which, they maintained, embodied a return to prewar arrangements: the partition of Palestine as proposed in 1947, the internationalization of Jerusalem, and the right of the refugees to return to those areas now under Israel's control (see *Problem Solving in Internationalized Conflicts*).

The Prime Minister of Britain, Sir Anthony Eden (see *Eden, Anthony*), offered a proposal similar to that of Dulles, in an address on November 9, 1955. He stated that Britain would help guarantee mutually accepted arrangements concerning borders, along with the United States and other powers; that it would, also along with others, provide aid to the refugees; and that Britain would provide assistance to reconcile the differences between the Arab position based on the 1947 partition plan and the Israeli insistence on basing the negotiations on the 1949 armistice lines. Arab leaders seemed encouraged, but Israeli spokesmen denounced the proposal.

The Dulles and Eden proposals were overshadowed by the arms deal between Czechoslovakia and

Egypt and the concomitant increase in regional tension. The outbreak of the Suez War in 1956 and its aftermath actually brought little change in the nature of the conflict and the quest for peace. Israel was required to withdraw from the territory it had occupied during the conflict (i.e., the Gaza Strip and the Sinai Peninsula) and there was a return to the *status quo ante*.

There were two matters that were to be of later consequence. A United Nations Emergency Force (UNEF) was established and put in place between Israel and Egypt (see Nobel Peace Prize Laureates: *United Nations Peacekeeping Forces*). It helped to ensure the tranquility of that sector until its precipitous removal in May 1967. Also, as part of the reassurances that led Israel to withdraw from the Sinai Peninsula and the Gaza Strip, United States Secretary of State John Foster Dulles presented an aide-mémoire to Israel in February 1957. In it the United States noted its belief that the Gulf of Aqaba "comprehends international waters and that no nation has the right to prevent free and innocent passage in the Gulf and through the Straits giving access thereto." When Egyptian President Nasser announced, in May 1967, the blockade of the Strait of Tiran, this became a factor in the subsequent hostilities.

Between the 1956 and 1967 Arab-Israeli Wars, one of the more noteworthy efforts to devise a solution was proposed under the administration of John Kennedy in the United States. Joseph E. Johnson, President of the Carnegie Endowment for International Peace, was appointed as a special representative of the CCP, in August 1961, and was charged with exploring "practical means of seeking progress on the Arab refugee problem." His consultations led him to suggest that the refugees should be enabled to express their wishes on resettlement in private, that Israel should be entitled to refuse reentry to Arabs regarded as security risks, and that the United Nations should set up a fund to aid both repatriation and resettlement. Johnson's proposals did not meet with the approval of the parties to the conflict and he reported that, at that time, there was no possibility of a settlement of the refugee problem that was not also a part of an overall settlement. This was the last significant effort under the auspices of the CCP.

## 2. After the Six Day War

The Arab-Israeli War of 1967 significantly changed the climate and circumstances governing the search for a solution to the Arab-Israeli conflict. For the Arabs, especially those states bordering Israel that

had lost territory to it, the war was humiliating. For Israel, meanwhile, it generated some optimism about the prospects of more substantive negotiations for peace. By the closing of hostilities, Israel had occupied the Golan Heights, the West Bank of the Jordan River, East Jerusalem, the Gaza Strip, and the Sinai Peninsula to the bank of the Suez Canal.

In the immediate aftermath of the war the United States and the former Soviet Union came into direct conflict with regard to the appropriate goals of diplomatic activity. The United States sought to secure a peace settlement and noted that a return to the old state of belligerency was intolerable. The former Soviet Union, on the other hand, sought a return to the situation that existed before the conflict and especially a withdrawal by Israel to the prewar lines. Soviet Premier Alexei Kosygin came to the United States shortly after the war. In essence he sought to avenge the Arab defeat and to salvage the Soviet position and investment in the area. In the first instance he orchestrated a diplomatic effort in the United Nations where he sought to have Israel condemned for aggression and ordered to withdraw from territories occupied in the conflict. In a press conference at the United Nations on June 25, immediately after the Glassboro summit meeting with President Lyndon Johnson, Kosygin made clear the Soviet view and in so doing showed the wide divergence between the US and Soviet positions. He emphasized that the primary objective was Israeli withdrawal and that Israel should be condemned and punished through the payment of reparations. After the Israeli withdrawal other matters could be raised. In mid-June the United Nations accepted a Soviet request for an emergency special session of the General Assembly. The former Soviet Union sought the meeting as a means to help save face in light of the Arab defeat and to secure an Israeli withdrawal. The United States opposed the idea on the grounds that it would not help, and might hinder, the cause of peace, since it was anticipated that the session would accomplish nothing and would become primarily a propaganda forum.

The earliest and most fundamental statement of the United States approach, in the wake of the Six Day War, was made by President Johnson on June 19, 1967. Johnson proposed, and committed the United States to, an Arab-Israeli peace based on five fundamental principles: (a) "every nation in the area has a fundamental right to live and to have this right respected by its neighbors;" (b) "justice for the refugees;" (c) "the right of innocent maritime passage must be preserved for all nations;" (d) "limits on the wasteful and destructive arms race;" and (e) "respect for political independence and territorial integrity of all the states of the area." The overall goal of the United States was to achieve a durable peace. Johnson rejected a return to the situation as of June 4, since, he claimed, "this is not a prescription for peace but for renewed hostilities."

Johnson's "Principles for Peace" were pronounced just prior to Kosygin's presentation of the Soviet perspective before the United Nations. Kosygin proposed a resolution in which Israel would be condemned for aggression, its withdrawal from occupied territory would be immediate and unconditional, and it would pay reparations to the Arab states. The United States offered a resolution embodying Johnson's five principles. The General Assembly, on July 4, 1967, approved a resolution appealing for funds for refugee and war relief and another resolution asking Israel not to change the status of Jerusalem, but a formula for the drawing of borders was not agreed. In the latter part of July, after five weeks of debate, the General Assembly turned the matter over to the Security Council.

After much debate about an appropriate procedure and the offering of several alternative resolutions the UN Security Council adopted a resolution that, inter alia, provided for the appointment of a UN special representative to assist in peace efforts based on the principles stipulated in the resolution. The resolution, Security Council Resolution 242 of November 22, 1967, has continued to be the focus of peace efforts in the Arab-Israeli conflict. It contained the formula for a just and lasting peace that should include the application of both the following principles:

(a)  withdrawal of Israeli armed forces from territories occupied in the recent conflict; and

(b)  termination of all claims or states of belligerency and respect for and acknowledgment of the sovereignty, territorial integrity, and political independence of every state in the area and their right to live in peace within secure and recognized boundaries free from threats or acts of force.

It also affirmed the necessity:

(a)  for guaranteeing freedom of navigation through international waterways in the area;

(b)  for achieving a just settlement of the refugee problem; and

(c)  for guaranteeing the territorial inviolability and political independence of every state in the area, through measures including the establishment of demilitarized zones.

This resolution established the mandate and framework for a mission entrusted to the Swedish Ambassador to Moscow, Gunnar Jarring, which sought a working arrangement that would lead to a peaceful settlement. The year 1968 might well be characterized as that of the Jarring Mission. Not only was Jarring especially active, but the major powers permitted him to assume the central role in the effort to achieve a settlement. Despite the intensive initial activity of the Jarring Mission, its tangible accomplishments were slight, although Jarring assisted in bringing about an exchange of war prisoners. No substantial progress toward peace was made.

The Jarring Mission (which ended its useful activity in 1971) was often overshadowed by new developments and the efforts of other parties, some of which were parallel in concept and timing. All were based on the view that they were to facilitate the Jarring effort and the implementation of Resolution 242.

In the fall of 1968, there was a low-key and non-public initiative by US Secretary of State Dean Rusk. It sought an end to the state of war between Israel and Egypt; withdrawal of Israeli forces from Sinai; resolution of the refugee problem through the individual decision of each refugee; free navigation through international waterways; restrictions on arms supply; a United Nations force to be positioned at Sharm el Sheikh; and the signatures of Israel and Egypt to the agreement.

The former Soviet Union also developed a framework for peace in the Middle East. In a note to the United States on December 30, 1968 (and, apparently, in similar notes presented to the British and French governments), the former Soviet Union proposed a plan. The preamble berated Israel, emphasized the need for a political solution, and urged that United States influence be used on Israel. The package proposal proffered by the Soviets, based on Resolution 242, called for total Israeli withdrawal in stages from occupied territory, for which a timetable was envisaged. In a first stage Israel would withdraw 30-40 kilometers from the Suez Canal to permit clearing operations. Later it would withdraw to the pre-1967 war lines. The canal would be reopened. Israel would have freedom of navigation in the region's international waterways. After total Israeli withdrawal, all parties would make written renunciations of belligerency, ending the state of war, to the United Nations and would convey their willingness to respect the political independence and territorial integrity of each state within the secure and recognized boundaries called for in Resolution 242. United Nations observers, with Egyptian permission, would be stationed along the lines to be established. A refugee settlement would be included. It was envisaged as a settlement achieved by contacts through Ambassador Jarring, and not by direct Arab-Israeli negotiations.

The Soviet plan was accompanied by a flurry of activity. Bilateral meetings were held in Paris, London, and Washington. The United States administration seemed uncertain about the Soviet actions and was hesitant to act so close to the end of Johnson's tenure in office and the Nixon inauguration. It sought clarification of the content and intent of the Soviet plan.

While propounding their own proposals, the former Soviet Union also rallied behind a French proposal for four-power talks. The French argued that the Middle East situation required the combined and concerted effort of the four powers (the United States, the former Soviet Union, Britain, and France) in order to make progress toward implementation of Resolution 242. The French pointed out that this idea had originated with President Charles de Gaulle as early as the May 1967 crisis when he counseled that amelioration of the situation and prevention of war could be attained if the powers would act together. France continued to press for four-power talks and suggested, in January 1969, that the representatives of the four to the UN Security Council should meet to discuss the means of "establishing a just and lasting peace in the Middle East." The Soviet and the French proposals awaited the response of the Nixon Administration in Washington.

The view of President Richard Nixon, as articulated at his January 27, 1969 news conference, suggested that a Great Power attempt to find a solution would be an acceptable approach and that the dangers would be greater if the powers did not make an attempt at settlement than if they did. Nixon announced that he saw a need for new initiatives and new suggestions to defuse what he depicted as the "powder keg" of the situation in the Middle East. Nixon agreed to the French proposal for four-power talks, if such talks proved to be warranted by a preliminary series of talks among the four powers—particularly the United States and the then Soviet Union.

The permanent representatives to the United Nations of France, the former Soviet Union, the United Kingdom, and the United States met on April 3, 1969 "to begin consideration of how they can contribute to a peaceful political settlement in the Middle East." They based their approach on Resolution 242 and reaffirmed their support for the Jarring Mission. The four-power talks were begun after the bilat-

eral exchanges had indicated that a point of some consensus had been reached—enough points of agreement had been established and the areas of disagreement had been sufficiently clarified.

From the outset, the four-power meetings produced no discernible progress and the general expectation was that it would take a good deal of time for the powers to reach some accommodation, if at all. Simultaneously with the talks at the United Nations, a series of bilateral talks also took place between the United States and the former Soviet Union. Underlying these discussions was the assumption that the Superpowers shared a desire to see the Middle East situation stabilized. In May 1969 the United States gave some concrete points to the Soviets and these apparently formed a basis for the discussions between Soviet Foreign Minister Gromyko and Egyptian President Nasser in Cairo on June 11 and 12, which dealt with the positions reached in the bilateral and four-power talks to that date. A Soviet-Egyptian joint communiqué issued on June 13 called for full Israeli withdrawal from all occupied territory and for implementation of all the provisions of Resolution 242. The former Soviet Union made this the basis of their response to the United States position. This seemed to conclude a first phase of efforts by the powers, and on July 1, 1969 the four powers announced an indefinite recess of their talks at the United Nations on the Middle East. The next round of talks and consultations was thus left to be undertaken in the US-Soviet Union bilateral realm.

Bilateral discussions continued into the fall of 1969. At the beginning of November, Undersecretary of State Elliot Richardson commented that the United States and former Soviet Union "have reached a substantial degree of agreement on the principles on which a settlement might be achieved," but "there remain still a number of unresolved substantive questions."

Despite the previous lack of progress in that forum, the four-power talks resumed on December 2, 1969. In a communiqué issued at the end of the meeting, the ambassadors confirmed "that they regard the situation in the Middle East as increasingly serious and urgent and reaffirmed their conviction that this situation must not be permitted to jeopardize international peace and security." They restated their objective of supporting Resolution 242 and its implementation as a "package deal." At the same time as of reporting on the status of the Great Power discussions, Secretary of State William Rogers, publicized much of the United States proposals that had been considered by the powers in their secret discussions, in the form of a new initiative.

## 3. The Rogers Plan

Speaking on December 9, 1969, Secretary Rogers announced a United States plan for a "just and lasting peace." The rationale was that "an agreement among other powers cannot substitute for agreement among the parties;" that "a durable peace must meet the legitimate concerns of both sides;" that "the only framework for a negotiated settlement was one in accordance with the entire text of the United Nations Security Council Resolution," and that "a protracted period of no war-no peace, recurrent violence, and spreading chaos would serve the interests of no nation, in or out of the Middle East." Rogers called for Israeli withdrawal from territories occupied in the 1967 war and an Arab commitment to peace based on a "binding agreement." He said that peace must be defined in specific terms and that demilitarized zones and security arrangements should be worked out by the parties themselves. New boundaries, which should be secure and recognized, should reflect only "insubstantial alterations required for mutual security" in the preexisting boundaries. He did not provide a specific plan for resolving the refugee problem, but noted that a "just settlement must take into account the desires and aspirations of the refugees and the legitimate concerns of the governments of the area." On the status of Jerusalem, Rogers recommended that it be a "unified city" with both Jordan and Israel participating in the "civic, economic and religious life of the city." He also said that Jerusalem should be accessible to all, and that a design for its administration should take into account the interests of all its inhabitants and of the Jewish, Islamic, and Christian communities.

Israel's reaction was strongly negative. It objected to the scope of the judgments made in the plan prior to actual negotiation, which smacked of an imposed solution and seemed to preclude direct negotiations on the most sensitive questions between Israel and its neighbors. Perhaps more significantly, Israel objected to most of the substantive positions concerning withdrawal, secure borders, refugees, and Jerusalem. These objections were to remain central to the Israeli negotiating position between the 1967 and 1973 wars. It was the incompatibility of the positions of the parties which allowed a gradual degeneration into the War of Attrition along the Suez Canal. President Nixon, meanwhile, sought to reassure Israel of United States support, which effectively terminated the Rogers initiative.

The War of Attrition was initiated by President Nasser of Egypt, as a way of convincing Israel to reconsider its position along the Suez Canal, without launching an actual military advance. Hostilities began in spring 1969, and escalated to the point where the danger of Superpower confrontation was envisaged. Soviet pilots flew combat aircraft over the Canal, in support of the Egyptian defenses, after Israel initiated deep penetration raids into Egyptian territory. The perception of President Nixon and his National Security Adviser Henry Kissinger was that this situation was potentially very dangerous, since it could lead to a confrontation between the Superpowers, as each sought to assist its ally, and thus produce the potential for a general war. Responding to this danger, Secretary of State Rogers launched a "political initiative" on June 25, 1970. He sent letters to the foreign ministers of Egypt and Jordan in which he proposed that Egypt, Israel, and Jordan restore the cease-fire for 90 days, that they agree to discussions under Jarring, and that they use Resolution 242 as the basis for "a just and lasting peace" based on acknowledgment of "sovereignty, territorial integrity and political independence, along with withdrawal from occupied territories." Nasser responded favorably. Israel transmitted its formal acceptance on August 4, but after an initial negotiating session, refused to participate further until Egyptian-Soviet violations of the standstill cease-fire had been "rectified." The United States used its influence to reassure Israel and succeeded in bringing it back to acceptance of the Jarring mediation in December 1970. The Jarring Mission was reactivated the following January.

Jarring tried to break the prevailing deadlock between the parties, on February 8, 1971, by seeking parallel and simultaneous prior commitments from both Israel and Egypt, on the major issues in dispute. He asked Israel to "give a commitment to withdraw its forces from occupied United Arab Republic territory to the former international boundary between Egypt and the British Mandate of Palestine," and Egypt to "give a commitment to enter into a peace agreement with Israel," making explicit to Israel, on a reciprocal basis, "various undertakings and acknowledgments arising directly or indirectly from paragraph 1(ii) of . . . Resolution 242 . . ." (which was the section dealing with the recognition of the rights of states in the area). Responding on February 15, 1971, Egypt insisted on total Israeli withdrawal from Sinai and the Gaza Strip and Israel responded that it would not return to the lines of the pre-Six Day War period.

The Jarring approach seemed to highlight, rather than resolve, the differences. Israel argued that it could not accept his approach because it involved preconditions to negotiations and that Israel would have to agree to total withdrawal from occupied territories prior to discussions. It held that the designation of the lines to which it should withdraw must be settled as a result of negotiation. Egypt criticized Israel for not being responsive to the Jarring initiative and for not providing the prior commitment on withdrawal. The Jarring Mission ended in practice in March 1971 when Ambassador Jarring, convinced that the negotiations under his auspices between Israel and the United Arab Republic (Egypt) would continue to be deadlocked until Israel agreed to formulate a new position on borders, returned to his post as Sweden's Ambassador to Moscow. Two diplomatic initiatives in the course of 1971 were aimed at facilitating the resumption of the Jarring talks: a United States attempt to promote an interim agreement for the reopening of the Suez Canal and a mission of inquiry on behalf of the Organization of African Unity (OAU) (see *Organization of African Unity (OAU)*).

"Rogers Plan C," as the American proposal for an interim agreement became known, was presented by the Secretary of State at a press conference on March 16, 1971. Based on earlier suggestions by both Israeli Defense Minister Moshe Dayan, and Egyptian President Anwar Sadat, the plan entailed the reopening of the Suez Canal, the extension of the cease-fire separation of the combatants, and a partial Israeli withdrawal, as a step in the direction of implementing Resolution 242. The initiative failed, partly as a result of the reluctance of Sadat to accept it.

In June 1971, at its summit conference in Addis Ababa, the OAU formed a Middle East Peace Commission. This Commission dispatched a delegation of four presidents of African states to the Middle East to "promote a dialogue" between Israel and Egypt. The presidents (Leopold Senghor of Senegal, Yakubu Gowon of Nigeria, Ahmadou Ahidjo of Cameroon, and Joseph Mobutu of Zaire) visited Israel and Egypt in November in an effort to stimulate a renewed search for a settlement. The African presidents sought the revival of the Jarring Mission and the application of Resolution 242. After the visit of the four presidents to Israel and Egypt, the OAU Middle East Commission met in Dakar from November 10 to 12. At the end of that meeting it was announced that a new mission consisting of President Senghor and General Gowon and representatives of Presidents Mobutu and Ahidjo would return to the Middle East to make new proposals to Egypt and Israel. After their return to the area and additional meetings with Egyptian and Israeli officials, the OAU committee

reported on December 2, 1971 to UN Secretary-General U Thant (see United Nations Secretaries-General: *U Thant*), at the time the General Assembly was debating the Middle East. The UN General Assembly subsequently adopted a resolution calling for reactivation of the Jarring Mission and for Israel, "to respond favorably" to the Jarring memorandum of February 8, 1971. Egypt backed the resolution, but Israel voted against the resolution and the United States abstained. Israel had indicated it could not accept the resolution and that its passage would prolong the stalemate in the negotiations process. Israel's primary objection was to the paragraph calling on it to respond favorably to Jarring's memorandum in which he asked for an Israeli commitment to withdraw to the pre-Six Day War lines. The resolution did not reflect the OAU mission nor did it, in the final analysis, provide the basis for restarting the Jarring effort. The mission of the African heads of state came at a time when other efforts at a Middle East settlement seemed to be in a state of suspended animation. The Jarring Mission had not made any real progress since the exchange of memorandums in the early spring of 1971. The Rogers' proposals for an interim settlement seemed similarly moribund.

During 1972 the Middle East remained uncharacteristically quiet, with no crises drawing international attention. US-Soviet summit meetings achieved little, with regard to the Arab-Israeli conflict. Various consultations, meetings, and discussions in the region and elsewhere failed to generate any real momentum, and the process seemed to reflect the complacency of some of the participants, notably the United States and Israel. United States efforts to promote proximity talks for an interim settlement continued during the spring and summer and into the fall of 1973, while regional developments were moving in a different direction. By the end of the summer, the question of oil and its potential importance in the Arab-Israeli equation came under increased scrutiny and gained additional attention. Henry Kissinger became Secretary of State, and in a press conference at the beginning of September 1973, Nixon noted that "we have put at the highest priority moving toward making some progress toward settlement of that dispute." It seemed likely that the United States would make additional efforts to deal with the issue, but there appeared to be no sense of urgency. There was an air of confidence, in the United States administration, and in Israel, that there was plenty of time to pursue the process in a deliberate and orderly way. The October War changed this thinking and provided a markedly altered environment for the peace process.

## 4. Aftermath of the October War

Egypt's President Sadat claimed that the launching of an Arab military offensive in October 1973 was necessitated by the failure of all previous peace plans and proposals to have any practical effect. Renewed warfare did not enable the Arabs to win back the territory lost in 1967, but the initial successes of the Egyptian and Syrian forces in putting the Israelis on the defensive and in recapturing some territory (albeit while losing other land), shifted the psychological atmosphere in the region by ending a period of apparent invincibility for the Israelis. As had happened in 1967, a cease-fire was agreed in the form of a United Nations Security Council Resolution, which set the stage for subsequent endeavors. Resolution 338 called for a cease-fire, the implementation of Resolution 242, and for negotiations for peace between the parties concerned. This was a new departure in terms of the requirement that negotiations take place between the combatants. The cease-fire proved successful after an initial breakdown and the adoption of Resolutions 339 and 340 to supplement and endorse 338.

During the course of the 1973 war the then Soviet Union and the United States played concurrent roles as sources of emergency supplies to the combatants (to the Arabs and to Israel, respectively), at the same time as monitors of the conflict who eventually pressured the combatants to halt hostilities. The superpowers were in contact with each other over the "hot line" during the war and both put their own forces on a state of alert. Both pledged their support for Resolution 338 and the Geneva Conference which it inspired. Yet it was United States Secretary of State Henry Kissinger who became the crucial mediator in postwar talks which produced disengagement agreements between Israel and Egypt in January 1974 and between Israel and Syria in May 1974, and beyond these the Sinai II agreement between Egypt and Israel of September 1975.

After the Security Council mandated cease-fire became effective, Kissinger concentrated on pragmatic first steps: the stabilization of the cease-fire and the disengagement of hostile forces. Initially he focused on Egypt because of its importance in the Arab world and because of the unstable military situation resulting from the post-hostilities troop deployments along the Suez Canal. Israeli and Egyptian officers met at Kilometer 101 on the Cairo-Suez road on October 28, 1973, and agreed to permit relief for the encircled Egyptian Third Army. Subsequently, and with Kissinger's mediation, Egypt and Israel

concluded an agreement to implement Resolution 338 and to stabilize the cease-fire, which was signed on November 11, 1973. Most of the provisions of this agreement were carried out, but the problem of disengagement and the separation of forces remained when the Geneva Conference opened on December 21, 1973.

The Geneva Conference was convened in fulfillment of the third clause of Resolution 338, which required that, "immediately and concurrently with the cease-fire, negotiations start between the parties concerned under appropriate auspices aimed at establishing a just and durable peace in the Middle East." The United States and the former Soviet Union presided jointly though they asked UN Secretary General Kurt Waldheim (see United Nations Secretaries-General: *Kurt Waldheim*) to serve as convener of the conference and to preside in the opening phase. Jordan and Egypt were represented at the conference, but Syria boycotted the meeting. The initial round of the Geneva Conference was devoted to general policy speeches. It ended on December 23. The basic positions of the parties were presented in their opening policy statements. One side sought the recovery of sovereignty and the redress of grievances suffered by a displaced people. The other, Israel, sought security and recognition as a nation.

Egyptian Foreign Minister Ismail Fahmi told the conference that Egypt sought peace and stressed five essentials: total withdrawal of Israel from Arab territories occupied since the 1967 war; liberation of the Arab city of Jerusalem; Palestinian self-determination; the right of every state in the region to enjoy territorial inviolability and political independence; and international peace and security in the area guaranteed by the major powers or the United Nations or both. He noted that these points were in conformity with the decisions of the Arab summit at Algiers. Jordanian Prime Minister Zaid Rifai attacked Israeli expansionist policy and stressed the need for Israeli withdrawal, the legitimate rights of the Arab people of Palestine, and the restoration of Arab sovereignty in the Arab sector of Jerusalem.

Israeli Foreign Minister Abba Eban, noted that Israel's aim was the achievement of a peace treaty—not a cease-fire or an armistice—which would define future Arab-Israeli coexistence. Israel sought permanent boundaries and would not agree to a return to the 1949-67 armistice lines. He reiterated Israel's position that the refugee problem could be solved, and the view of Jerusalem as "Israel's capital, now united forever." He said that Israel would make detailed peace proposals but declared the first priority to be a disengagement along the Suez Canal. At the end of the initial round the participants agreed to a communiqué in which they noted the establishment of a military working group to deal with the disengagement of forces. The Geneva conference at the foreign ministers' level would reconvene as needed. The conference itself had lasted only two days, and despite innumerable suggestions for subsequent meetings, it did not reconvene.

The conference was followed by negotiations on disengagement that continued into January 1974, with little success. Kissinger left Washington on January 10 to begin his Egypt-Israel shuttle that culminated in an Egypt-Israel Disengagement Agreement on January 17. The full extent of assurances made by and to Kissinger remained secret. A similar exercise in shuttle diplomacy was undertaken by Kissinger in May 1974, which produced the Syria-Israel Disengagement Agreement.

The achievement of the two disengagement agreements reduced the threat of war, in part, by restructuring the complex of troop deployments and providing for a United Nations Emergency Force (UNEF) to be deployed between Egypt and Israel, and for a United Nations Disengagement Observer Force (UNDOF) to buffer positions between Israel and Syria (see *Peacekeeping Forces*). Although these were limited agreements dealing with pressing military problems and did not involve central political concerns of the parties, they provided the basis for further efforts. The second stage however, was to prove more difficult. United States efforts to develop second-phase agreements began in the summer of 1974 with consultations in Washington, but these were overshadowed by the Nixon-Brezhnev summit meeting, the Cyprus crisis, and finally Nixon's resignation, and did not produce any immediate results. Further progress was then thrown into question as a result of the decision of the Arab League summit in Rabat in October 1974 to endorse the Palestine Liberation Organization (PLO) as the sole legitimate representative of the Palestinian people. This was perceived as problematic because Israel had said it would not negotiate with the PLO and the PLO had consistently refused to recognize Israel's right to exist. Seeking to avert the collapse of the step-by-step approach Kissinger visited the Middle East in early February 1975, and again in March, to seek an arrangement between Egypt and Israel, but further reconciliation between the Arabs and Israelis was not forthcoming. The failure of the third Kissinger shuttle ended a period of considerable optimism, following the October War, in which two important, but primarily technical (and, critically, apolitical), agreements were reached.

## 5. Another Step: Sinai II

The impasse in the diplomatic endeavors of Secretary Kissinger led to a brief flirtation with the idea of using the Geneva Conference to work for an overall settlement. This was soon discarded in a renewed effort for another interim Egyptian-Israeli agreement. The United States, Israel, and Egypt were soon ready to revert to a step-by-step approach with Kissinger's mediation. President Gerald Ford ordered a "reassessment" of United States policy to determine appropriate next steps in light of new developments in the international environment, including the communist victories in Vietnam and Cambodia. The reassessment also served to influence Israel to modify its position and move closer to that of Egypt, thus allowing a United States effort to bridge the gap. Following a period of "reversed shuttle" diplomacy, in which the parties sent their views, and sometimes their representatives, to Kissinger in Washington, Ford met Egyptian President Sadat in Europe, and later Israeli Prime Minister Yitzhak Rabin (see Nobel Peace Prize Laureates: *Yitzhak Rabin*), in Washington in June. Following yet another round of Kissinger shuttle diplomacy in the Middle East, the Sinai II Accords were signed in Geneva on September 4, 1975.

The Sinai II agreements provided for Israeli withdrawal from territory in Sinai (including the Mitla and Gidi passes and the Abu Rudeis oilfields) in exchange for Egyptian political concessions, and pledges of support from the United States. Israel and Egypt agreed to observe the cease-fire on land, sea, and in the air, and to refrain from the threat or use of force or military blockade; they established a new buffer zone and agreed to the limitation of the numbers of military forces that each side was permitted to station adjacent to the zone, and agreed that the mandate of the United Nations Emergency Force should be renewed annually, rather than for shorter periods. They also agreed to continue negotiations for a final peace agreement and Egypt pledged that non-military cargoes to or from Israel would be permitted to use the Suez Canal. An annex spelled out some details for the implementation of the agreement. There was also a United States proposal providing for an early warning system in which up to 200 US civilian volunteers would participate and would report to both Israel and Egypt. In addition to the formal agreement released by the US Department of State, other arrangements were subsequently made public by the

US Senate Committee on Foreign Relations. These involved assurances by the United States to Israel and to Egypt on various matters, including military and economic assistance, coordination between the United States and Israel on the reconvening of the Geneva Conference, and United States assurances concerning oil for Israel.

Sinai II was a United States accomplishment. It resulted from extensive and intensive US involvement: the shuttles, the proposals, the pledges, and the commitments, for which the parties were not prepared to allow any other power or instrumentality to serve as substitute. Although substantial and complex issues remained, for the first time Israel and Egypt (the leading Arab state) went beyond previous agreements which were primarily cease-fires or armistices (military in nature and content) and reached accord on matters with political and psychological overtones which moved them in the direction of an overall settlement. Sinai II clearly engaged United States prestige, presence, participation, and expenditure in the continued search for peace. The direct, formal, and essentially irreversible United States involvement marked the inauguration of a new era in the search for a resolution of the Arab-Israeli conflict.

After the conclusion of Sinai II the problem was to identify an appropriate next step, given the realities of the situation in the region. Neither Syria nor Jordan was an appropriate choice, the former being unwilling to negotiate with Israel on the basis of Resolution 242 and the latter having lost its mandate as a result of the Rabat Arab summit decisions of 1974. The Kissinger step-by-step approach to peace was soon overshadowed by the Lebanese civil war and associated developments.

## 6. Renewal of the Search for a General Peace

Soon after his inauguration in January 1977, President Jimmy Carter began to involve his administration in the Arab Israeli problem. Within a few months there evolved a Carter "plan" which was made public in a series of statements and signals. The Carter approach sought to replace the step-by-step diplomacy with an effort to achieve a general settlement, to be attained through direct negotiations at a rejuvenated Geneva Conference. The immediate goal was to reconvene the conference and to establish a set of general principles as a basis for negotiation. Three elements were identified as central and indispensable: the definition and assurance of permanent peace, the question of territory and borders, and the Palestinian question. Carter defined peace as "a

termination of belligerence toward Israel by her neighbors, a recognition of Israel's right to exist, the right to exist in peace, the opening up of borders with free trade, tourist travel, cultural exchange between Israel and her neighbors . . . ."

The second element was the establishment of permanent and mutually recognized borders. Precise lines were not identified, but the principles involved were clear. There would be substantial Israeli withdrawals from the territories occupied in the 1967 War, and minor adjustments in the pre-1967 War lines. The final lines would have to be negotiated and agreed between Israel and the Arabs.

The Palestinian element was to prove the most controversial. Under the Carter approach the political facets (rather than the refugee-humanitarian or the terrorist aspects of the Palestinian question) became dominant. His earliest views were that the legitimate interests of the Palestinian people had to be incorporated in a settlement (this was later altered to the legitimate rights of the Palestinian people). Carter believed that there should be a Palestinian homeland or entity, whose political status would have to be negotiated, but his preference was that such an entity be linked with Jordan. To achieve a settlement Carter believed that the Palestinians had to have a stake in peace—they would have to be involved in the negotiating process and to be represented at Geneva.

When the Geneva Conference first convened after the October War in December 1973 it had been presided over by both the United States and the former Soviet Union serving as co-chairs. Subsequently, Kissinger had effectively excluded the former Soviet Union from direct involvement in the peace process, apparently in keeping with the preferences of both Israel and President Sadat. It was "informed but not involved." President Carter, however, sought Soviet participation in connection with the effort to reconvene the Geneva Conference. The Soviets were apparently prepared to take a more active role and on October 1, 1977 the United States and the former Soviet Union issued a joint communiqué in which they set forward the following guidelines for a comprehensive peace settlement in the Middle East:

(a) Both governments are convinced that vital interests of the peoples of this area as well as the interests of strengthening peace and international security in general urgently dictate the necessity of achieving as soon as possible a just and lasting settlement of the Arab Israeli conflict. This settlement should be comprehensive, incorporating all parties concerned and all questions.

The United States and the former Soviet Union believe that, within the framework of a comprehensive settlement of the Middle East problem, all specific questions of the settlement should be resolved, including such key issues as withdrawal of Israeli armed forces from territories occupied in the 1967 conflict; the resolution of the Palestinian question, including the legitimate rights of the Palestinian people; termination of the state of war and establishment of normal peaceful relations on a basis of mutual recognition of the principles of sovereignty, territorial integrity and political independence.

The two governments believe that, in addition to such measures for insuring the security of the borders between Israel and the neighboring Arab states as the establishment of demilitarized zones and the agreed stationing in them of United Nations troops or observers, international guarantees of such borders as well as of the observance of the terms of the settlement can also be established, should the contracting parties so desire. The United States and the former Soviet Union are ready to participate in these guarantees subject to their constitutional processes.

(b) The United States and the Soviet Union believe that the only right and effective way for achieving a fundamental solution to all aspects of the Middle East problem in its entirety is negotiation within the framework of the Geneva Peace Conference, specifically convened for these purposes, with participation in its work of the representatives of all parties involved in the conflict, including those of the Palestinian people, and legal and contractual normalization of the decisions reached at the conference.

In their capacity as co-chairmen of the Geneva Conference, the US and the USSR affirm their intention through joint efforts and in their contacts with the parties concerned to facilitate in every way the resumption of the work of the Conference not later than December 1977. The cochairmen note that there still exist several questions of a procedural and organizational nature which remain to be agreed upon by the participants to the Conference.

(c) Guided by the goal of achieving a just political settlement in the Middle East and of eliminating the explosive situation in this area of the world, the US and the USSR appeal to all the parties in the conflict to understand the necessity for careful consideration of each other's legitimate rights and interests and to demonstrate mutual readiness to act accordingly.

The statement was designed to accelerate the efforts toward reconvening the Geneva Conference and to demonstrate that the two Superpowers were capable of working cooperatively on matters of crucial international importance. This communiqué generated concern on the part of Israel, and its supporters in the United States, and also Egypt, and the Carter Administration soon abandoned the joint communiqué as the basis of its approach. By contrast, the then Soviet Union, after 1977, sought to restore the essentials of the communiqué as the central focus of the quest for peace in the Middle East.

## 7. The Sadat Initiative

On November 9, 1977 President Anwar Sadat of Egypt made his historic announcement that he was prepared to go to the Israeli Knesset to discuss, directly and in person, the Arab-Israeli conflict, with the Israelis. This marked a significant shift—it was the first time an Arab leader had proposed face-to-face, direct, and official negotiations with Israel to resolve the Arab-Israeli conflict. Even though his gesture took the international community by surprise, Sadat was to reveal later that it was a carefully calculated decision to make public contacts with Israel that had already begun in secret through Romania and Morocco, as a way of both heightening the psychological pressure on Israel to make territorial withdrawals and also shifting the focus away from the joint Soviet-US initiative, about the prospects of which he was not optimistic. He was also concerned by the renewed position of the USSR in the efforts to resolve the conflict.

In the years since Israel's establishment, no Arab state had recognized Israel nor officially acknowledged negotiations with it. Now Egypt, the most powerful and populous Arab state, reversed this approach by the sudden visit of its president to Jerusalem and his address to the Knesset, in which he proclaimed: "We welcome you among us with full security and safety," and "we accept to live with you in permanent peace based on justice."

Sadat's initiative was to instigate the drawing up of two sets of proposals for settlement of the Arab-Israeli conflict. The Egyptian proposals were outlined by Sadat in his address to the Knesset on November 20, 1977 and they constituted, essentially, a restatement of established positions. He wanted, he said, a peace agreement based on:

First: ending the Israeli occupation of Arab territories occupied in 1967. Second: achievement of the fundamental rights of the Palestinian people and their right to self-determination, including their right to establish their own state. Third: the right of all states in the area to live in peace within their boundaries, in addition to appropriate international guarantees. Fourth: commitment of all states in the region to administer the relations among them in accordance with the objectives and principles of the United Nations Charter, particularly the principles concerning the non-resort to force and the solution of differences among them by peaceful means. Fifth: ending the state of belligerency in the region.

Israeli Prime Minister Menachem Begin, meanwhile, presented the Israeli plan at Ismailia on Christmas Day 1977, and made its contents public in a speech to the Knesset on December 28. The plan, to be "instituted upon the establishment of peace," proposed that there be demilitarization in the Sinai; that the Egyptian army would not move beyond its positions on the Gidi and Mitla passes; that between the Suez Canal and that line there would continue in effect the limited forces agreement arranged in Sinai II; that Israeli settlements in Sinai would remain, would be linked to Israeli administration and law, and would be defended by an Israeli force; that during a transition period of a few years, Israeli forces would hold a defense line in the middle of Sinai and would maintain air bases and early warning mechanisms: they would later withdraw to the international frontier; that freedom of navigation in the Tiran Straits would be guaranteed either by a UN force or by joint Egyptian-Israeli units. In Judea, Samaria, and the Gaza district (i.e., the West Bank and the Gaza Strip) the military government would be abolished and replaced by "administrative autonomy of the residents, by and for them." Security and public order in these areas would be the responsibility of the Israeli authorities. All residents would be granted free choice of either Israeli or Jordanian citizenship. Various matters concerning legislation and immigration would be determined by committees composed of representatives of Israel, Jordan, and the administrative council. "Israel stands by its right and its claim of sovereignty to Judea, Samaria and the Gaza district. In the knowledge that other claims exist, it proposes for the sake of the agreement and the peace, that the question of sovereignty be left open." The holy places and Jerusalem would be considered in a special proposal.

Clearly, the Begin and Sadat proposals were not fully compatible, but negotiations soon began for their consideration. By July 1978 the peace negotiations had produced disagreements between the United States and both Egypt and Israel, but no substantial progress toward peace. The discord between Egypt and the United States focused on the nature of the US role and on the Egyptian proposal for a settlement, which the Carter Administration did not regard as a suitable basis for negotiations. The disagreements between Israel and the United States which at times became caustic, concerned Begin's interpretation of UN Security Council Resolution 242 as not necessarily applying to the West Bank and Israel's policy of establishing Jewish settlements there. The deadlock threatened to halt the negotiations and alarmed the United States because it would be a setback for Sadat and the peace process, and might renew tensions between Egypt and Israel, thus increasing the danger of war. There was also concern because the term of the United Nations force in Sinai, to which Egypt had committed itself in the 1975 Sinai II Accords, was about to expire. These factors led Carter to try to break the deadlock through a new and dramatic initiative.

## 8. The Camp David Accords

On August 8, 1978 the United States announced that Sadat and Begin had accepted President Carter's invitation to come to Camp David, Maryland, "for a meeting with the President to seek a framework for peace in the Middle East." The three leaders met for their historic negotiations in virtual secrecy, and were closeted in complex and intensive discussions for a lengthy period, between September 5 and 17, 1978. The negotiations are memorable for the direct personal involvement of the heads of state. The stakes were clearly high and the need to achieve an agreement obvious.

The Camp David Accords (see *Camp David Accords*) were signed ceremoniously on September 17, and became the basis for the peace negotiations which followed. The Accords did not constitute a peace treaty, but instead consisted of two documents: "A Framework of Peace in the Middle East" and "Framework for the Conclusion of a Peace Treaty between Egypt and Israel."

The Middle East framework set forth general principles and some specifics for a comprehensive peace settlement between Israel and its Arab neighbors. It dealt with the Palestinian problem and the future of the West Bank and Gaza, calling for a transitional period of not more than five years. In order to provide "full autonomy to the inhabitants of those areas, the Israeli military government would be withdrawn upon the creation of a self-governing authority freely elected by the inhabitants of those areas, although the

Israeli military would remain in specified areas of the West Bank and Gaza to protect Israel's security interests. "Egypt, Israel, Jordan and the representatives of the Palestinian people should participate in negotiations on the resolution of the Palestinian problem in all its aspects." It called for negotiations to resolve the final status of the West Bank and Gaza, and Israel's relations with Jordan, based on Resolution 242 and Israel's right to live within secure and recognized borders.

The Israel-Egypt framework provided for a peace treaty in which Israel would withdraw from Sinai, including its settlements and airfields, in phases according to a timetable to be determined, and for normal and peaceful arrangements to be established between the two states. Egypt agreed to normalization of relations, an exchange of ambassadors, and the opening of the Suez Canal to Israeli shipping.

The Camp David Accords met with caution and skepticism in both Egypt and Israel, and the reaction of the Arab world was overwhelmingly negative. Arab opposition to Sadat, which had begun during his negotiations with Israel that led to Sinai II, intensified as a result of his initiative and the Camp David Accords.

The United States sought support for the Camp David Accords and for Sadat's position elsewhere in the Arab world. In this regard the critical states were seen as Jordan and Saudi Arabia, and it was to these states, among others, that Secretary of State Cyrus Vance, traveled after Camp David. But they did not join in the negotiations, nor did they endorse the peace process. The only recourse was to proceed without the participation of other parties to the conflict. After intense negotiations in Washington a draft for a treaty between Egypt and Israel was drawn up, yet various points remained subject to disagreement. Owing to the persistence of the differences between the parties, the December 1978 deadline set at Camp David for the conclusion of the Egypt-Israel Treaty was not met. Finally, by the end of March 1979, a treaty was attained, but not before President Carter himself had engaged in shuttle diplomacy between Cairo and Jerusalem. The formal signing of the Egypt-Israel Peace Treaty on March 26, 1979 in Washington bore witness to the value of persistent diplomatic effort to attain peace (see *Negotiation, Direct; Conflict Resolution, History of*).

By the terms of the treaty, Egypt and Israel ended the state of war, established peace, renounced the use of war to settle disputes, and pledged mutual recognition. Israel agreed to withdraw its armed forces and civilians from the Sinai Peninsula in stages, to a line running from El-Arish to Ras-Muhammad, after nine months, and to the international frontier (essentially from Rafah to the Gulf of Aqaba) after three years. Within a month of the completion of the first stage (the "interim withdrawal"), Israel and Egypt would exchange ambassadors, end economic boycotts, and open commerce between the two states. Sinai would be divided into zones with limitations on Egyptian military personnel and equipment, and a United Nations force verifying compliance would be stationed in the zone adjacent to the Israeli border. United Nations observers would ensure Israeli compliance on its side of the border as well. Israel was to have the right of free passage through the Suez Canal, and the Gulf of Aqaba and Strait of Tiran would be regarded as international waterways, open to all nations for unimpeded freedom of navigation. A joint commission would oversee the withdrawal, and a claims commission would deal with any outstanding financial claims and arbitrate disputes. The United States agreed to continue surveillance flights over Sinai and to create an international force if the United Nations failed to do so.

The treaty also provided that one month after ratification, Israel, Egypt, the United States, Jordan, and representatives of the Palestinians living in the West Bank and Gaza would begin negotiations, to be completed within one year, for a self-governing authority in the West Bank and the Gaza Strip. The protocols, letters, annexes, and maps attached to the Egypt-Israel Peace Treaty dealt in detail with the phased Israeli withdrawal from the Sinai, the security arrangements and the specific details for further negotiations on trade, economic, cultural, transportation, telecommunications, and other agreements between the two countries.

President Carter agreed to expand the American security, economic, and political commitment to Egypt and Israel, as a means of facilitating the peace process. United States loans and grants to Egypt and Israel and specific American assurances to Israel that reaffirmed and broadened the assurances provided in the 1975 Sinai II agreements were important adjuncts to the Peace Treaty.

### 9. Implementing Camp David Accords

During the period between the signing of the Egypt-Israel Peace Treaty in March 1979 and the spring of 1982, the parts of the treaty which pertained to the withdrawal of Israel from Sinai and the normalization of relations between Egypt and Israel were gradually implemented. The full withdrawal of Israel from Sinai, including the dismantling of settlements, was carried out as scheduled. As to the normalization of relations, ambassadors were exchanged, and various technical arrangements made for free passage and exchange across the borders. After the initial excitement, however, relations failed to grow in warmth or frequency of contacts, and a "cold peace" developed that included the recall of the Egyptian ambassador from Tel Aviv in the wake of the Israeli invasion of Lebanon in June 1982 and the massacres at Shatila and Sabra refugee camps in September 1982.

The signing of the treaty by Sadat was almost universally condemned by other Arab leaders. The Arab League, meeting at the end of March 1979, expelled Egypt from membership and rejected any cooperation with the peace treaty or the autonomy talks. The Arab League countries (except for Sudan and Oman) and the Palestine Liberation Organization (PLO), severed diplomatic relations with Egypt and voted to impose an economic boycott. This general ostracism of Egypt endured beyond the assassination of Anwar Sadat, the accession of Hosni Mubarak to the Presidency of Egypt, the implementation of the Israeli withdrawal from Sinai, and the degeneration in Egyptian-Israeli relations following the Israeli invasion of Lebanon. Nevertheless, Egypt was never fully isolated from the Arab world and improvements in its formal ties included such actions as the restoration of diplomatic relations with Jordan, at the initiative of King Hussein, in September 1984.

Despite the dramatic reaction of the Arab world, the negotiations concerning implementation of the Camp David "Framework for Peace in the Middle East" opened as scheduled on May 25, 1979. The goal of the first stage of the negotiations was full autonomy for the inhabitants of the West Bank and Gaza under a freely elected, self-governing authority that would serve for a transitional period of not more than five years. The final status of the West Bank and Gaza was reserved for a second stage of negotiations, to begin as soon as possible, but not later than three years after the self-governing authority was inaugurated. The so-called "autonomy talks" involved only Egypt, Israel, and the United States.

May 1980 had been designated as a deadline by which agreement on steps towards autonomy should be reached. Not only was agreement not reached in time, but Sadat suspended Egyptian participation in the talks on the grounds that the Israeli parliament was considering confirming the status of Jerusalem as Israel's capital. The autonomy talks were resumed again in July, but were suspended again by Sadat in early August 1980. The stated rationale was that Israel's Knesset had adopted a "Basic Law" confirm-

ing Jerusalem's status as Israel's "eternal and undivided capital." The autonomy talks were stalled on a number of counts. Israel argued that autonomy should be limited to the inhabitants of the territories, while Egypt believed that it should extend to the actual territory. Israel saw the self-governing authority as an administrative council, while Egypt wanted this authority to have full legislative and executive powers as well as control of the administration of justice. Egypt sought a self-generating authority and the transfer to it of all powers from the military government. Israel sought to limit the powers of the authority through negotiation and believed that the military government should be the source of authority. There was also discord on the sharing of the scarce water resources of the West Bank, the right of the Arabs of East Jerusalem to vote on questions relating to the self-governing authority, the status and use of private and public lands, and Jerusalem's final status.

Israel saw an autonomy agreement as a practical solution to the Palestinian question and as responsive to Israel's need for security, Egypt's wish to adhere to the Arab cause, and the Palestinian Arabs' desire to govern their own affairs. Israel's proposed autonomy plan would allow the Arab inhabitants fully to manage "areas of legitimate internal administration" while Israel "will retain those powers and functions which are essential to her defense and security." By contrast Israel opposed Egypt's autonomy proposals partly because they "would set in motion an irreversible process which would lead to the establishment of an independent Arab-Palestinian state." Egypt, meanwhile, sought total Israeli withdrawal from the occupied territories (including East Jerusalem), the dismantling of Israel's settlements, and the right of the Palestinians to self-determination. It sought to safeguard its position in the Arab world and to remain a part of the Arab community. It was important to Egypt to demonstrate that Sadat's approach was practical.

The negotiations were suspended between December 1980 and September 1981, at which time they were resumed, but without high-level involvement by the Reagan Administration. On October 6, 1981 Sadat was assassinated by Islamic militants in Cairo. His successor, Hosni Mubarak, pledged to continue the process but no new ground was broken before Israel's invasion of Lebanon and the subsequent suspension of the talks by Egypt.

In the spring of 1982, when the last of Israel's forces were withdrawn from the Sinai Peninsula, the commitment of both Egypt and Israel to implementing the terms of the Egypt-Israel Peace Treaty was established. The treaty had dealt strictly with matters pertaining to bilateral relations between Israel and Egypt and it proved practicable. The issue of autonomy for the Palestinians was not characterized by the same level of agreement between the parties, and the autonomy talks did not produce a settlement.

During the early months of the first Reagan Administration, United States attention was focused elsewhere—on security issues in the Persian Gulf sector of the Middle East and on preoccupation with a perceived Soviet threat. There was little feeling in Washington that circumstances were appropriate for a new breakthrough in the Arab Israeli peace process.

The perception in the Arab world, and among other observers in the international community, that the Camp David Accords had failed to produce a framework for a general settlement of the Arab-Israeli conflict that was acceptable to all the parties, produced two alternative proposals that are noteworthy; one by the European Community, the other by Crown Prince Fahd of Saudi Arabia.

## 10. The Venice Declaration

In June 1980 the leaders of the nine member states of the European Community (see *European Political Community*) met in Venice, to exchange views on all aspects of the situation in the Middle East, including the state of negotiations resulting from the agreements signed between Egypt and Israel in 1979. They agreed that growing tensions affecting the region constituted a danger and rendered more pressing the need for a comprehensive solution to the Arab-Israeli conflict. The nine members regarded themselves as obliged to play a special role and to work in a more concrete way toward peace, because of the "traditional ties and common interests which link Europe to the Middle East." At the conclusion of the conference the participants issued the Venice Declaration, on June 13, 1980, which, they claimed, was based on Resolutions 242 and 338 as well as statements made on behalf of the Community since June 1978. The Declaration asserted the need to promote the recognition and implementation of the two principles of the right to security of all the states in the region, including Israel; and justice for all the peoples, which, they noted, implies the recognition of the legitimate rights of the Palestinian people.

Articles six and seven of the Venice Declaration stated:

Article 6. A just solution must finally be found to the Palestinian problem, which is not simply one of refugees. The Palestinian people, which is conscious of existing as such, must be placed in a position, by an appropriate process defined within the framework of the comprehensive peace settlement, to exercise fully its right to self-determination.

Article 7. The achievement of these objectives requires the involvement and support of all the parties concerned in the peace settlement which the Nine are endeavoring to promote, in keeping with the principles formulated in the declaration referred to above. These principles apply to all the parties concerned, and thus the Palestinian people, and to the Palestine Liberation Organization, which will have to be associated with the negotiations.

The proposal to include the PLO in the peace process marked a difference in the perspective of Europe and of the United States. The Nine also declared themselves ready to participate in a system of international guarantees for secure and recognized borders in the region. They criticized the continuing Israeli presence in the West Bank and designated Israeli settlements in the occupied territories illegal under international law. In conclusion, the Nine declared it their intention to make contact with all the parties concerned, to ascertain their positions with respect to the Declaration and "in the light of the results of this consultation process to determine the form which such an initiative on their part could take."

The official reaction to the Venice Declaration by Israel was to reject it, with an explicit condemnation of the proposal to involve the PLO, and declare its commitment to the Camp David process. The Palestine Liberation Organization, in a statement issued by its Executive Committee on June 16, 1980, announced its rejection of the Venice Declaration, on the grounds that it was "an attempt aimed at peddling the Camp David designs and the autonomy conspiracy." The Egyptian reaction to the European initiative was, however, more favorable. On June 16, Foreign Minister Boutros Ghali pronounced the statement in keeping with the goals of the Camp David agreements and incorporating a number of the fundamental principles of Egyptian diplomacy. Egyptian approval was not, however, sufficient encouragement by itself for the Europeans to press their initiative, and they bowed, albeit reluctantly, to resumption of United States leadership in the peace process when President Reagan issued his initiative in September 1982.

## 11. The Fahd Plan

The plan for the Arab Israeli conflict which was

devised by then Crown Prince (and later King) Fahd of Saudi Arabia, was initially made public through the Saudi press agency on August 8, 1981. The text of the plan was as follows:

First, that Israeli should withdraw from all Arab territory occupied in 1967, including Arab Jerusalem. Second, that Israeli settlements built on Arab land after 1967 should be dismantled. Third, a guarantee of freedom of worship for all religions in the holy places. Fourth, an affirmation of the right of the Palestinian people to return to their homes and to compensate those who do not wish to return. Fifth, that the West Bank and the Gaza Strip should have a transitional period, under the auspices of the United Nations, for a period not exceeding several months. Sixth, that an independent Palestinian state should be set up with Jerusalem as its capital. Seventh, that all states in the region should be able to live in peace. Eighth, that the United Nations or member states of the United Nations should guarantee to execute these principles.

The reception of the plan was mixed.

On October 29, 1981, the United States administration "welcomed certain elements" of the plan, such as the suggestion that all nations should live in peace, but viewed others as problematic. This contrasted with the initially dismissive US official response to the plan. Prime Minister Begin described the plan as an obstacle to peace and as a plan "to liquidate Israel in stages," particularly since it called for a Palestinian state under PLO control with Jerusalem as its capital. Begin expressed concern over the fact that there were those in the United States and Europe who supported parts of the plan, and suggested that it was a deviation from the Camp David Accords.

The Arab states and the PLO were to hold a summit meeting at Fez, Morocco in late November 1981, to consider the Fahd proposal, but that meeting ended without any decision. Saudi Arabia was embarrassed and the United States was disappointed. King Hassan of Morocco announced that the summit would be resumed at a later date, and it considered the proposal, along with the new regional situation and the Reagan initiative at the reconvened Fez Summit in September 1982.

## 12. Reagan's "Fresh Start" Initiative

In the aftermath of Israel's invasion of Lebanon, launched on June 6, 1982, the United States defined an opportunity for a new initiative for a peace settlement. On September 1, 1982 President Reagan announced the new initiative and set forth the posi-

tion of his administration on some of the central and critical aspects of the Arab-Israeli conflict. This was not a plan for resolution of the conflict, and the administration was careful to distinguish between the proposals and a detailed blueprint for action which would include specific methods and timetables. Reagan sought to take advantage of the strategic alterations in the region, and specifically the evacuation of the PLO from Beirut. It was an attempt to get the regional states to think in terms of a peace process and, to this end, to help them with United States ideas. While building on UN Security Council Resolution 242 and the Camp David Accords, it sought to bring together Jordan, under King Hussein, and representatives of the Palestinians in negotiations directly with Israel to work out a solution for the future of the West Bank and Gaza. It was based on the perspective that the Arab world should recognize that the option of going to war to defeat Israel no longer existed; that guerrilla/terrorist activity would not serve the Arab purpose; and that if the Palestinians hoped for a secure future in the region, the most effective means was to negotiate for a settlement.

Reagan outlined his position by saying that in the West Bank and Gaza, neither of the alternatives preferred by the parties would be acceptable. He opposed Israeli sovereignty and he opposed an independent Palestinian state in the West Bank. He believed that Israel should stop building settlements and suggested that there be a self-governing West Bank under Palestinian control, associated with Jordan. He proposed that Jerusalem remain undivided, but that its future be negotiated by the parties.

The immediate reactions to the "fresh start" initiative were varied. On September 2, the Israeli cabinet rejected the proposal on a number of grounds, although a major argument was that it departed from the conceptual framework agreed at Camp David, and that it seemed to determine prematurely the outcome of negotiations on several points, including the status of Jerusalem as the capital of Israel and the future of the West Bank and Gaza. Israel was also concerned at the absence of prior consultations with the United States about the initiative, contrary to bilateral understandings established at the time of the Sinai II Accords in 1975, and reiterated at Camp David.

Implicit in the distinctive features of the Reagan initiative are three assumptions which are crucial to understanding the basis of the Reagan peacemaking approach and its fate.

The initiative envisaged Palestinian self-government in association with Jordan, thus making Hussein central to the process on the Arab side. Hussein was invited to join in the peace talks with the view that such a decision would constitute a significant breakthrough. In a sense, Reagan was trying to identify a role for Hussein similar to the one played previously by President Sadat of Egypt. Prior to identifying the role for Hussein there were consultations with him, in late August 1982, which elicited the view held in the administration that he was prepared to participate in the process provided that the appropriate mandates might be secured from the Arab states and/or the PLO. The Reagan Administration clearly believed that Jordan could be drawn into the process with appropriate American incentives and the backing of some Arab leaders. The timing of the initiative immediately prior to the projected Fez Arab summit meeting sought to take advantage of that opportunity for Hussein to secure the essential mandate for participation in the new process.

A second key assumption involved Israeli participation. Although it was obvious that the Reagan view was incompatible with Prime Minister Begin's view concerning Israel's control of the West Bank, it was believed that there might be a mechanism which would alter this situation. The initiative seemed to assume (although the administration did not articulate it) that there could be an alteration in the policies of the Begin government (or even in the government itself) under appropriate circumstances.

A third assumption was of a link between the situation in Lebanon and the initiative. The basic goals of the United States were to secure the withdrawal of all foreign forces from Lebanon, extend and secure the sovereignty of the government throughout the territory of Lebanon, and achieve the economic and social reconstruction of the country. This was seen as a relatively straightforward process whose earliest elements could be achieved readily. Thus, the sequence of events envisaged at the time when the Reagan initiative was first issued was: the withdrawal of all foreign forces from Lebanon, the building up of the Lebanese army and the reconstruction of the country, the promotion of stability and the extension of effective governmental sovereignty to the entire territory of Lebanon, and the inauguration of negotiations to implement the various elements of the Reagan peace initiative.

The main and initial Arab response to the Reagan initiative came at the Fez Arab summit later the same month, where the Arab leaders restated the designation of the PLO as the sole legitimate representative of the Palestinians. They refused to grant King Hussein the necessary mandate to negotiate on behalf of the Pales-

tinians, which United States policy had apparently hoped would be forthcoming on the basis of its earlier consultations with Hussein and other Arab leaders.

In addition to the Reagan initiative, various Arab proposals were considered by the Arab leaders meeting at Fez in September 1982. King Hassan of Morocco, King Hussein of Jordan, King Fahd of Saudi Arabia, and President Hafez al-Assad of Syria conferred in secret about both the Fahd plan of 1981 and a Tunisian proposal dating from 1965, which called for Arab acceptance of the 1947 United Nations proposal to partition Palestine into Jewish and Arab sectors. The Fez summit concluded its proceedings with a statement which endorsed a modified version of the Fahd plan. The Fez summit peace proposal, which followed closely the eight points of the Fahd plan, called for the establishment of an independent Palestinian state, and envisaged international guarantees for "all" states in the region. The summit also endorsed the PLO as sole legitimate representative of the Palestinians and required the return of territories occupied by Israel. The plan contained no explicit indication of whether the state of Israel was included in its provision of international guarantees, which left the question of recognition of Israel ambiguous. Israel dismissed the plan as a basis for a settlement.

## 13. Peace Strategy of the Soviet Union

The former Soviet Union was highly critical of the Camp David Accords and the Egypt-Israel Peace Treaty, claiming, among other objections, that neither arrangement made provision for the self-determination of the Palestinians and Israeli withdrawal from all the occupied territories. On September 15, 1982, in a speech at a dinner in honor of President Ali Nasser Muhammed of the People's Democratic Republic of Yemen, President Leonid Brezhnev criticized the Reagan initiative in the same vein and outlined the principles upon which the former Soviet Union would wish to see the peace process based. Brezhnev specified the following six principles for "a just and lasting peace in the Middle East:"

> In the first place, the principle of the inadmissibility of seizing foreign lands through aggression should be strictly observed, and this means that all territories occupied by Israel since 1967 . . . must be returned to the Arabs. The borders between Israel and its Arab neighbors must be declared inviolable.
>
> Second, the inalienable right of the Arab people of Palestine to self-determination, to the creation of their own independent state on the Palestinian lands which will be freed from the Israeli occupation on the

West Bank of the Jordan River and in the Gaza sector must be ensured in practice. The Palestinian refugees must be granted the opportunity envisaged by the UN decisions to return to their homes or get appropriate compensation for the property left by them.

Third, the eastern part of Jerusalem, which was occupied by Israel in 1967 . . . must be returned to the Arabs and become an inseparable part of the Palestinian state. Free access of believers to the holy shrines of the three religions must be ensured in all of Jerusalem.

Fourth, the right of all states of the area to safe and independent existence and development must be ensured, of course, with the observance of full reciprocity, as it is impossible to ensure the security of some people while violating the security of others.

Fifth, an end must be put to the state of war, and peace must be established between the Arab states and Israel. And this means that all sides in the conflict, including Israel and the Palestinian state, must commit themselves to mutually respect each others' sovereignty, independence and territorial integrity and resolve cropping up disputes through peaceful means, through talks.

Sixth, international guarantees of settlement must be drawn up and adopted, the role of guarantors should be assumed, let us say, by the permanent members of the Security Council or by the UN Security Council as a whole.

Brezhnev added that such a settlement could be drawn up and implemented only with the participation of the PLO as the sole legitimate representative of the Arab people of Palestine.

The Soviet principles for peace, announced in September 1982, were an expression of the enduring perspective of the former Soviet Union on the elements of the Arab-Israeli conflict and reiterated early proposals. This perspective was unacceptable to Israel, and thus crucial to the failure of the Soviet approach to produce a breakthrough. The perception in the Arab world, meanwhile, has been that the involvement of the United States at the center of any peace process is necessary if Israel is to be persuaded to negotiate.

## 14. After the War in Lebanon

The Reagan initiative became stalled over the remaining two and a half years of the first Reagan Administration. Repeated attempts to bolster the existing Lebanese government failed to help it win control of the country outside Beirut and its environs, or to unite Lebanon's political and religious factions behind it. Having tried to contribute to greater stability as part of a multinational force (composed of Unit-

ed States, French, Italian, and British troops), and having suffered attacks on both its embassy and marine base, the United States reduced its presence in Lebanon to skeleton strength.

Following the War in Lebanon (1982), Israel and Lebanon negotiated under the auspices of the United States, with the substantial involvement of Secretary of State George Shultz, concerning the withdrawal of foreign forces from Lebanon and related arrangements. After months of discussion an agreement was reached and was signed on May 17, 1983.

The agreement did not constitute a "peace treaty" but the two parties agreed "to respect the sovereignty, political independence and territorial integrity of each other" and to "confirm that the state of war between Israel and Lebanon has been terminated and no longer exists." The "existing international boundary between Israel and Lebanon" was to be the border between the two states. Israel undertook "to withdraw all its armed forces from Lebanon." And, they agreed to refrain from various hostile actions against each other.

The agreement foundered and was eventually abrogated by the Lebanese, largely because of the failure of the agreement to incorporate the Syrians in its calculations in a way acceptable to the Syrian government.

The position of Israel's government on the initiative did not soften and the 1984 elections produced a coalition government, the absorbing priority of which appeared to be dealing with economic difficulties and the withdrawal of Israel's forces from Lebanon. Attempts by King Hussein of Jordan, meanwhile, to attain the backing of Yasser Arafat (see Nobel Peace Prize Laureates: *Yasser Arafat*) as a form of mandate to act on the Palestinians' behalf, failed to produce any positive results. No Arab interlocutor was willing to participate in the negotiations for peace with Israel. Apparently disenchanted with the venture and disillusioned by the losses of American lives in Lebanon, the Reagan Administration downgraded the Arab-Israeli conflict as a foreign policy priority in the last months of its first term and reaffirmed traditional ties of friendship with Israel. The other extant peace proposals that had been put forward by various parties remained similarly moribund.

In the period after the abrogation of the Israel-Lebanon agreement of May 17, 1983 in March 1984 by Lebanon under heavy pressure from Syria, little progress was made in resolving the conflict, although there were several efforts toward that end.

On February 11, 1985, Jordan's King Hussein and the PLO's Yasser Arafat joined in an agreement in an effort to create momentum in resolving the Palestinian issue. They agreed to a number of points as a framework for a comprehensive peace.

"The Government of the Hashemite Kingdom of Jordan and the Palestine Liberation Organization have agreed to march together towards the realization of a just and peaceful settlement of the Middle East problem and to put an end to the Israeli occupation of the Arab occupied territories, including, Jerusalem, in accordance with the following principles: (a) Land in exchange for peace as cited in the UN resolutions, including the Security Council resolutions. (b) The Palestinian people's right to self-determination when the Jordanians and Palestinians manage to achieve this within the framework of an Arab Confederation that it is intended to establish between the two states of Jordan and Palestine. (c) Solving the Palestinian refugee problem in accordance with the UN resolutions. (d) Solving all aspects of the Palestine question. (e) Based on this, peace negotiations should be held within the framework of an international conference to be attended by the five UN Security Council permanent member states and all parties to the conflict, including the PLO, which is the Palestinian people's sole legitimate representative, within a joint delegation—a joint Jordan-Palestinian delegation."

This proposal achieved little and in February 1986 King Hussein suspended his ties with the PLO citing a lack of progress toward peace talks and the PLO's continued refusal to accept United Nations Security Council Resolutions 242 and 338.

In July 1986, Israeli Prime Minister Shimon Peres (see Nobel Peace Prize Laureates: *Shimon Peres*) visited King Hassan II in Morocco. Hassan and Peres met a number of times during the visit. They reportedly made an in-depth examination of the situation in the Middle East and of the matters of "form and substance" of peace in the region. King Hassan focused on the Fez Plan and Peres provided his reactions to the proposals. They also noted that the meeting was designed to be exploratory and "never for a moment aimed at the start of negotiations." No further discussions followed.

No substantial progress was made in achieving an Arab-Israeli peace in the ensuing period. The process was moribund. US Secretary of State George Shultz, in light of the Lebanon failure, seemed reluctant to commit the United States to any significant effort unless some positive outcome could be identified, and other powers were similarly reluctant. This situation seemed to await some regional or other development that might change the environment and generate a new set of proposals. This occurred with the outbreak of the *intifada* in December 1987.

## 15. The Intifada

The *intifada* began in December 1987 with demonstrations in the Gaza Strip that soon spread to the West Bank. Within a few months it generated a renewed effort by George Shultz.

Arab uprising in the West Bank and Gaza Strip that began in December 1987 in strong and violent opposition to continued Israeli occupation of those territories. The Palestinian uprising became a test of wills and policy between Palestinians in the territories occupied by Israel in the Six Day War and Israel. Israel sought to end the uprising and to restore law and order. The Palestinians saw the uprising as a means to end Israeli occupation and to promote an independent Palestinian state. Palestinians sought to accelerate the political process and, in particular, to gain a representative role for the Palestine Liberation Organization (PLO) in negotiations with Israel and the United States. Confrontation and violence marked the evolution of the *intifada*, with a growing toll of casualties on both sides. For the Palestinians, the *intifada* seemed to provide a catharsis but also a high cost in casualties, imprisonment, loss of education and employment, and growing divisions within the Palestinian population. For Israel, the *intifada* posed a major challenge on a number of counts, including damage to its international image, divisions within the body politic on how to respond, the monetary costs of increased military reserve duty, and the costs of other disruptions of the economy (see *Gulf Conflict: Domestic Protest and Political Terrorism*).

The *intifada* began with a series of incidents, including the stabbing to death of an Israeli by a Palestinian in Gaza City, a traffic accident in which four Palestinians were killed, and subsequent riots in the Jabaliya refugee camp in early December 1987. Over the ensuing period the violence grew and gained increasing international attention for the status of the Palestinians in the West Bank and Gaza Strip. Eventually, Israeli defense minister Yitzhak Rabin argued that this was not classical terrorism but civilian violence carried out by a considerable portion of the Palestinian population by means available to every individual, such as stones, Molotov cocktails, barricades, and burning tires (see *Terrorism*). The difficulty was to devise a means to defuse the violence. For both sides the *intifada became a test of political wills portending continuation over time* (see *Psychological Causes of Oppositional Political Terrorism: A Model*).

On March 4, 1988, United States Secretary of State George Shultz, partly in response to the *intifada*, put forward a plan for resolving the Arab-Israel conflict. Schultz delivered a letter to Israeli Prime Minister Yitzchak Shamir. Similar letters were delivered to Jordanian King Hussein, Syrian President Hafez al-Assad, and Egyptian President Hosni Mubarak. In the case of the West Bank and Gaza, the proposal called for transitional arrangements negotiations interlocked in timing and sequence with final status talks, based on UN Security Council Resolutions 242 and 338. The initiative was designed to produce direct, bilateral Arab-Israeli negotiations to achieve comprehensive peace based on the provisions and principles of United Nations Security Council Resolution 242. The United States supported a properly structured international conference that would launch a series of bilateral negotiations. All attendees at the conference would be required to accept United Nations Security Council Resolutions 242 and 338 and to renounce violence and terrorism. The conference would be specifically enjoined from intruding in the negotiations, imposing solutions or vetoing what had been agreed bilaterally. The Schultz plan was similar to previous United States peace initiatives in that it sought to achieve a comprehensive solution through direct, bilateral Arab-Israeli negotiations.

Reaction to the plan was generally negative. Shamir opposed it as he was adamantly against the idea of an international conference and felt the central concept was contrary to Camp David. The Palestinian leaders were concerned that they were the junior partner to Jordan. King Hussein was ambivalent. The former Soviet Union thought the international conference was only symbolic and that they did not have a real role in the negotiating process. Syria also opposed the initiative. Only Egypt's President Hosni Mubarak endorsed the plan.

On November 15, 1988, at the session of the Palestine National Council in Algiers, Algeria, PLO Chairman Yasser Arafat issued a formal "Declaration of Independence for the State of Palestine."

Arafat asserted that there existed an eternal bond between the land of Palestine, its people, and their history. That, despite being deprived of their political independence, Palestinian self-determination was rooted in their history as a nation as well as in United Nations General Assembly Resolution 181 (II), which partitioned Palestine into one Arab and one Jewish state. Arafat noted that "by virtue of natural, historical, and legal rights . . . and relying on the authority bestowed by international legitimacy as embodied in the resolution of the United Nations since 1947 . . . . The Palestine National Council, in the name of God, and in the name of the Palestinian

Arab people, hereby proclaims the establishment of the State of Palestine on our Palestinian territory with its capital Jerusalem."

In a political communiqué issued the same day, the Palestine National Council formally committed the PLO to arrive at a comprehensive settlement with Israel that involved a two-state solution. The PNC affirmed its support for an international peace conference based on United Nations Security Council Resolution 242 and 338; Israeli withdrawal from all Arab territories occupied since 1967, including Arab Jerusalem; the annulment of all measures instituted by the Israeli government during occupation; questions of Palestinian refugees to be settled in accordance with relevant United Nations resolutions; and Security Council guarantees for security and peace between all the states concerned, including that of Palestine.

The PNC meeting occurred as the *intifada* had thrust the Palestinian issue to the center of international attention. Then, on July 31, 1988, King Hussein renounced Jordan's claim to the West Bank, followed by an announcement that Jordan would no longer be party to future joint Palestinian-Jordanian delegations.

The Declaration received wide attention, Israel and the United States rejected it and the United States continued to refuse to open a direct dialogue with the PLO. It was not until after Arafat's December 13, 1988 address to the UN General Assembly and his subsequent press statement clarifying the PLO's position that the United States lifted its ban on dealing with the PLO.

As part of the Sinai II Accords process, a Memorandum of Agreement between the Governments of Israel and the United States, *inter alia*, spelled out the United States position concerning dealings with the PLO: "The United States will continue to adhere to its present policy with respect to the Palestinian Liberation Organization, whereby it will not recognize or negotiate with the Palestinian Liberation Organization so long as the Palestinian Liberation Organization does not recognize Israel's right to exist and does not accept Security Council Resolutions 242 and 338." Later, in the Carter Administration, renunciation of terrorism was added to the requirements. In December 1988, Yasser Arafat, in a speech to the United Nations suggested that the PLO had decided to meet those requirements. But, the statement was not unambiguous. On December 14, Arafat, in a press conference in Geneva, Switzerland, clarified his position.

In response, the United States announced that it

was prepared to hold a substantive dialogue through US Ambassador to Tunisia, Robert Pelletreau.

> The Palestine Liberation Organization today issued a statement in which it accepted UN Security Council Resolutions 242 and 338, recognized Israel's right to exist in peace and security and renounced terrorism. As a result, the United States is prepared for a substantive dialogue with PLO representatives.
> I am designating our Ambassador to Tunisia as the only authorized channel for that dialogue. The objective of the United States remains as always, a comprehensive peace in the Middle East. In that light, I view this development as one more step toward the beginning of direct negotiations between the parties which alone can lead to such a peace.
> Nothing here may be taken to imply an acceptance or recognition by the United States of an independent Palestinian state. The position of the US is that of the status of the West Bank and Gaza cannot be determined by unilateral acts of either side, but only through a process of negotiations. The United States does not recognize the declaration of an independent Palestinian state.
> It is also important to emphasize that the United States commitment to the security of Israel remains unflinching.

The new Bush administration sought to start negotiations between Israel and the Palestinians in the spring of 1989.

During a visit to Washington between April 12 and 16, 1989, Israeli Prime Minister Yitzhak Shamir, prodded by the Bush administration, offered a peace proposal containing several elements: Israel, Egypt and the United States would renew their commitment to Camp David and peace; the United States and Egypt would ask the Arab states to end their hostility to Israel and accept negotiations; the United States would lead an international effort to solve the Palestine refugee problem; and Palestinians from the West bank and Gaza Strip would be elected to form a delegation to negotiate an interim agreement and then a final settlement with Israel. The initiative was formulated by Shamir and Yitzhak Rabin and represented the consensus of Israel's national unity government. On May 14, 1989, the Israeli government formally approved the proposal to initiate negotiations between Israel and Palestinian representatives.

Despite the efforts of the Bush administration to promote Arab-Israeli negotiations on the basis of Israel's spring 1989 plan, progress was slow. In July 1989 Egyptian President Hosni Mubarak sought to facilitate the process with a ten-point plan.

> 1. All Palestinians in the West Bank, the Gaza Strip

and East Jerusalem should be allowed to vote and run for office. 2. Candidates should be free to campaign without interference from the Israeli authorities. 3. Israel should allow international supervision of the election process. 4. Construction or expansion of Jewish settlements would be frozen during this period. 5. The army would withdraw from the area of polling places on election day. 6. Only Israelis who live or work in the occupied territories would be permitted to enter them on election day. 7. Preparation for the elections should not take longer than two months; Egypt and the United States would help form the Israeli-Palestinian committee doing that work. 8. The Israeli Government should agree to negotiate the exchange of land for peace, while also protecting Israel's security. 9. The United States and Israel should publicly guarantee Israel's adherence to the plan. 10. Israel should publicly agree in advance to accept the outcome of the elections.

In October 1989 (although formally released on December 6, 1989), United States Secretary of State James Baker announced a five-point plan to clarify Egyptian President Hosni Mubarak's ten-point proposal and thereby to advance the prospects for movement in the peace process.

> 1. The United States understands that because Egypt and Israel have been working hard on the peace process, there is agreement that an Israeli delegation should conduct a dialogue with a Palestinian delegation in Cairo. 2. The United States understands that Egypt cannot substitute itself for the Palestinians and Egypt will consult with Palestinians on all aspects of that dialogue. Egypt will also consult with Israel and the United States. 3. The United States understands that Israel will attend the dialogue only after a satisfactory list of Palestinians has been worked out. 4. The United States understands that the Government of Israel will come to the dialogue on the basis of the Israeli Government's May 14 initiative. The United States further understands that Palestinians will come to the dialogue prepared to discuss elections and the negotiating process in accordance with Israel's initiative. The US understands, therefore, that Palestinians would be free to raise issues that relate to their opinion on how to make elections and the negotiating process succeed. 5. In order to facilitate this process, the US proposes that the Foreign Minister of Israel, Egypt, and the US meet in Washington within two weeks.

## 16. The Madrid Conference and Afterward

The end of the Cold War and the Gulf War suggested new possibilities in the quest for an Arab-Israel peace. United States President George Bush and Secretary of State James Baker noted that the new world order facilitated such an effort. Baker made eight trips to the region in the spring and summer of 1991 in an effort to convene a peace conference. In October, the United States and the former Soviet Union issued invitations to Israel, Lebanon, Syria and the Palestinians to an opening session in Madrid, Spain. The co-sponsors' letter laid out the framework for negotiations and provided details on the sessions and the approach to be followed. It reflected compromises by all sides developed in the course of Baker's shuttle diplomacy.

The Arab-Israeli peace conference convened in Madrid, Spain on October 30, 1991. It began ceremonially with a three-day session where all parties were represented by official fourteen-member delegations. The Jordanian/Palestinian delegation had fourteen representatives from each. The Palestinians also sent a six-member advisory team that had no official standing but coordinated policy with the PLO. Presidents George Bush and Mikhail Gorbachev (see Nobel Peace Prize Laureates: *Mikhail Gorbachev*) opened the conference. Bush called for peace based on security for Israel and fairness for the Palestinians. He said "territorial compromise is essential for peace" and that only direct talks between Israelis and Arabs could bring peace about; the superpowers could not impose it. Israeli Prime Minister Yitzchak Shamir recounted the history of the Jews and argued that the cause of conflict is not territory but Arab refusal to recognize the legitimacy of Israel. He did not mention the occupied territories or Israeli settlements. Palestinian delegation head Haidar Abd al-Shafi asserted that the Palestinians were willing to live side by side with Israelis and accept a transitional stage, provided it led to sovereignty. He called on Israel to give Palestinian refugees displaced since 1967 the right to return and to stop settlements. Abd al-Shafi referred to the unnamed PLO as "our acknowledged leadership." Jordan Foreign Minister Kamal Abu Jaber, rebutting a common Israeli view, declared that Jordan has never been and will not be Palestine. Syrian Foreign Minister Farouk Al-Sharaa contended that Resolutions 242 and 338, or the "land for peace" formula, should be implemented. The opening session was followed by bilateral negotiations between Israel and each of the Arab delegations. The conference was an important step on the road to peace in that it involved direct, bilateral, public and official peace negotiations between Israel and its Arab neighbors.

The new and innovative contribution of Madrid was its multilateral component—a series of sessions focusing on functional areas of concern. The functional meetings were to be coordinated from Moscow and sessions dealing with five subject areas have been held at various locations worldwide—environment, regional economic development, water, refugees and arms control and regional security. These talks have included the regional players—Israel, Jordan, Lebanon, Syria, the Palestinians—as well as some other Arab states and various other states.

The concept was that progress on issues of a functional nature might reinforce the efforts for peace and help to build the Middle East of the future.

Parallel to the multilateral sessions on functional issues were bilateral negotiations on the central political issues of the conflict. These began in Madrid immediately after the public plenary sessions. And, after an initial round the bilateral talks shifted to Washington with the United States as the host.

The talks in Washington were held in secret. In each set of negotiations only the parties were present. The venue was provided by the Department of State. The Israelis met separately with the Lebanese and the Syrians and, initially, with a Jordanian-Palestinian delegation that later divided into two parts.

The talks in Washington were primarily left to the parties—outside proposals were not introduced in any systematic way to the process. Outsiders did not participate directly in the negotiations—they were not in the room.

Despite a substantial number of sessions, no agreements emerged from these sessions. It was during this Washington-based bilateral process that the super-secret talks between Israel and the PLO began in Europe—the talks generally referred to as the Oslo talks/process.

The Oslo talks involved a very small number of Israelis and Palestinians who met in secret and eventually agreed on a declaration of principles and accompanying letters.

In the final analysis, the Israel-Palestinian sector remains at the core of the Arab-Israeli conflict and the focus of efforts to achieve peace. Since the Madrid Conference and its subsequent peace process the Israel-Palestinian/PLO component has emerged as the focal point.

At the end of the War in the Gulf in the Spring of 1991, President George Bush and Secretary of State James Baker spoke of opportunities to create a New World Order after defeat of the aggression by Saddam Hussein in Kuwait. Among the identified elements of this New World Order was the idea of resolving the Arab-Israeli conflict. To this end Baker made a series of trips to the region between the spring and fall of 1991 to organize a peace conference to deal with the Arab-Israeli conflict. Although no specific plans for resolution of the conflict were proffered, the conference itself inaugurated a new set of approaches to the problem.

After an initial plenary session at which each of the central players presented its position, the Conference at Madrid gave way to a series of bilateral and multi-lateral negotiating sessions.

## 17. Israel, the Palestine Liberation Organization (PLO), and the Declaration of Principles (DOP)

Bilateral negotiations between Israel and the Arabs begun at Madrid continued in 1992 and 1993, albeit with interruptions. In early 1993 Israel and the Palestine Liberation Organization (PLO) conducted secret negotiations in Oslo which culminated in the signing of Israel-PLO Declaration of Principles (DOP) in Washington, DC on September 13, 1993. As part of the arrangement, Israel recognized the PLO as the representative of the Palestinian people. For its part, the PLO recognized Israel's right to exist in peace and security, accepted United Nations Security Council Resolutions 242 and 338, and renounced the use of terrorism and violence. Israeli Foreign Minister Shimon Peres and PLO Executive Committee member Mahmoud Abbas (Abu Mazen) signed the DOP in a ceremony on the White House lawn, witnessed by United States Secretary of State Warren Christopher and Russian Foreign Minister Andrei Kozyrev, in the presence of United States President Bill Clinton, Israeli Prime Minister Yitzhak Rabin and PLO Chairman Yasser Arafat.

In addition to the main text, there were four annexes: Annex I: Protocol on the Mode and Conditions of Elections; Annex II: Protocol of Withdrawal of Israeli Forces from the Gaza Strip and Jericho Area; Annex III: Protocol on Israeli-Palestinian Cooperation in Economic and Development Programs; and Annex IV: Protocol on Israeli-Palestinian Cooperation Concerning Regional Development Programs. There were also agreed minutes providing more details and specifics concerning various articles of the declaration. The agreement entered into force on October 13, 1993 and negotiations on implementation began.

On September 13, 1993, Israel and the PLO—represented by Shimon Peres and Abu Mazen—signed a Declaration of Principles on the White House lawn in Washington. The venue and the ceremony were consciously designed to imitate the 1979 signing of the Egypt-Israeli Peace Treaty. This became a worldwide media event of substantial proportions facilitated by and contributing to a sense of euphoria that this would lead to an Israeli-Palestinian peace to be followed by a broader Israeli-Arab peace.

## 18. After the DOP

After the signing of the Israeli-PLO Declaration of Principles (DOP) on the White House lawn in September 1993, the nature of the Arab-Israeli peace process took on a new set of characteristics. With a new regional situation in place, characterized or marked by a new peace efforts, the need for peace plans and proposals was altered to create a situation where broad plans and proposals, especially by outside powers, were essentially replaced by a need for specific ideas for rather narrow issues at the heart of on-going negotiations and for mechanisms to expedite the process itself. Broad peace plans and proposals were, in essence, replaced by the agreements reached by the parties which set the agendas in place for future talks. Thus, after the Oslo accords were signed (as the DOP) in Washington the peace plans and proposals become focused on each sector individually.

In the case of Israel and Lebanon the agenda of issues to be resolved and proposals for dealing with them have been essentially in place since the Israel-Lebanon accord of May 1983, albeit with modifications to take into account regional changes. No new plans or proposals have emerged nor are they likely until there is movement on the Israel-Syrian front.

In the case of Israel and Syria the agenda has been in place for a substantial period and plans and proposals for dealing with these agenda items have similarly been available. The issues include the status of the Golan Heights, the matter of peace and normalization of relations, the security of water resources and the status of Lebanon. Where the borders will be drawn between the two states and what limitations may be imposed on armaments on the Golan Heights become elements of the equations. While numerous plans and proposals to deal with each of the elements of the agenda exist, negotiating them to a point of accord and agreement becomes the test of the peace process.

Peace talks between Israel and Syria have been sporadic with occasional useful discussions and longer periods of rancor and discord. A second session of Syrian-Israeli peace talks conducted under the auspices of the United States were held at the Wye River Conference Center in Maryland in late January 1996. The meeting focused mainly on security arrangements to be covered in an Israeli-Syrian Peace Treaty. These followed an initial round of Wye talks in late December 1995 and early January 1996.

In the case of Israel and Jordan, the plans that had been developed over years of secret encounters between the parties as well as by outside parties such as the US and various other bodies, were used to good avail during the 1993-94 negotiations between Israel and Jordan that led to their 1994 peace treaty. Plans and proposals generated decades earlier were modified to fit revised regional and bilateral circumstances and were supplemented by proposals focusing on specific elements of the identified problems.

On September 14, 1993, Israel and Jordan signed a substantive common agenda providing their approach to achieving peace between them. On October 1, 1993, Jordanian Crown Prince Hassan and Israeli Foreign Minister Shimon Peres met at the White House with President Bill Clinton. They agreed to set up a bilateral economic committee and a US-Israeli-Jordanian trilateral economic committee. The first meeting of the trilateral committee was held on November 4, 1993 in Paris and a second was held in Washington on November 30, 1993.

As Israel and the PLO continued their efforts to implement the Declaration of Principles, Israel and Jordan conducted negotiations to achieve peace along the lines of their 1993 Agreed Common Agenda. On July 25, 1994, King Hussein of Jordan and Prime Minister Yitzhak Rabin of Israel signed the Washington Declaration in Washington, DC. The end result was the successful conclusion of a treaty of peace that was signed in 1994 and implemented with relative expedition thereafter. As with most peace treaties, it was not implemented without difficulty and periodic negotiations between the parties were required to devise proposals and solutions to deal with the specific problems at hand.

On October 17, 1994 Israel and Jordan initialed a peace agreement in Amman, Jordan. The signing ceremony took place on October 26, 1994 in the Jordan Valley. Prime Minister Abdul-Salam Majali of Jordan and Prime Minister Yitzchak Rabin of Israel signed the treaty while United States President Bill Clinton served as a witness. The peace treaty comprises thirty articles and includes five annexes which deal with security, boundary demarcations, water issues, police cooperation, environmental issues and mutual border crossings, and the establishment of normalized relations. The border was to be based on maps drawn up by the British Mandate. Jordan agreed to lease back to Israel (for twenty-five years with an option to renew) cultivated lands which Israel agreed to return to Jordan. Israel agreed to transfer water to Jordan from existing sources and

they will jointly operate new water purification plants. Both parties agreed not to join, aid or cooperate with a party whose goal is to attack the other side and neither will allow any military force or equipment which may harm the other side to enter into their territory. They pledged to cooperate in combating terrorism and to solve the refugee problem. They will establish peace and full diplomatic and normalized relations. Israel will also recognize Jordan's special role with respect to the Muslim holy places in Jerusalem. They will seek economic cooperation as a pillar of peace as noted various areas of potential effort, especially tourism.

The signing of the Israel-Jordan Peace Treaty was followed by a series of meetings and bilateral agreements dealing with issues devolving from the peace agreement between them. Among other topics, these included scientific and cultural cooperation, postal services, telecommunications, and a maritime border accord. They also reached accord on transforming the Aqaba-Eilat region into a single district for cooperation in tourism, industry, trade and environment.

The remaining sector—that of Israel and the Palestinians—remains the most complex with a multifaceted agenda of difficult problem that require plans and proposals not simply to foster continuation of the process but also to address the issues in contention.

On August 24, 1994 an agreement on the early transfer of certain civil responsibilities in the West Bank from Israel to the Palestinian Authority was initialed in Cairo. This early empowerment agreement was a provision of the Israeli-Palestinian Declaration of Principles and was signed by Major General Danny Rothschild of the Israeli Defense Forces (IDF) and Palestinian Authority member Nabil Shaath in a ceremony at the Erez crossing between Israel and the Gaza Strip on August 29, 1994.

The Agreement on Preparatory Transfer of Powers and Responsibilities provides for the transfer of powers to the Palestinian Authority in five spheres: (a) Education and culture: responsibility over higher education, special education , cultural and educational training activities, institutions and programs, and private, public non-governmental or other educational or cultural activities or institutions. (b) Health: authority over all health institutions. (c) Social Welfare: authority over governmental and non-governmental organizations and institutions, including charitable societies and institutions and voluntary and non-profit organizations. (d) Tourism: regulating, licensing, grading, supervising and developing for the tourist industry. (e) Direct taxation and indirect taxation: Authority for the income tax and for Value Added Tax.

The educational system was transferred to the Palestinian Authority on August 28, 1994. On November 15, 1994 Israel transferred authority in the fields of welfare and tourism to the Palestinians. On December 1, 1994 Israel transferred responsibility for health and taxation to the Palestinian Authority. This completed the implementation of the early empowerment agreement.

The Interim Agreement between Israel and the PLO signed in Washington on September 28, 1995 constituted a new and important stage in the transition from conflict to reconciliation between Israel and the Palestinians through further implementation of the DOP.

The main object of the Interim Agreement was to broaden Palestinian self-government in the West Bank by means of an elected self-governing authority (the Palestinian Council). This will allow the Palestinians to conduct their own internal affairs, reduce points of friction between Israelis and Palestinians, and open a new era of cooperation and co-existence based on common interest, dignity and mutual respect. At the same time it protects Israel's vital interests, and in particular its security interests, both with regard to external security as well as the personal security of its citizens in the West Bank.

The Interim Agreement between Israel and the PLO, including its various annexes, comprises some 400 pages, setting forth the future relations between Israel and the Palestinians. To the main body of the agreement are appended six annexes dealing with security arrangements, elections, civil affairs (transfer of powers), legal matters, economic relations, and Israeli-Palestinian cooperation.

The agreement states that a Palestinian Council will be elected for an interim period not to exceed five years from the signing of the Gaza-Jericho Agreement (i.e., no later than May 1999). The negotiations on the permanent status arrangements were to begin no later than May 1996. The permanent status negotiations will deal with the remaining issues, including Jerusalem, refugees, settlements, security arrangements, borders, relations and cooperation with neighboring countries, etc.

The Palestinian Council to be established following the elections will assume various powers and responsibilities in security and civil spheres in the West Bank and Gaza. With the establishment of the Council, the Israeli military government will be withdrawn and the Civil Administration dissolved. The Council will assume responsibility for all rights, liabilities, and obligations in the spheres transferred to it. At the same time Israel will retain those powers and responsibilities not transferred to the Council.

The IDF will redeploy in the West Bank according to the timetables set out in the agreement. In the first stage, designed to facilitate the holding of elections, the IDF will withdraw from the populated areas of the West Bank: the six cities—Jenin, Nablus, Tulkarm, Kalkilya, Ramallah and Bethlehem (in the city of Hebron special security arrangements will apply as provided in the agreement)—and 450 towns and villages. At the end of this redeployment, there will be almost no IDF presence in Palestinian population centers.

In general, throughout the West Bank and the Gaza Strip, Israel will have overall responsibility for external security and the security of Israelis and settlements.

With regard to internal security and public order, the agreement establishes different arrangements for three types of area. Area "A" comprises the six cities listed above. In these areas, the Palestinian Council will have full responsibility for internal security and public order, as well as full civil responsibilities. Area "B" comprises the Palestinian towns and villages of the West Bank. In these areas, which contain some 68 percent of the Palestinian population, the Council will be granted full civil authority, as in Area "A." The Council will be charged with maintaining public order, while Israel will have overall security authority to safeguard its citizens and to combat terrorism. This responsibility shall take precedence over the Palestinian responsibility for public order. Twenty-five Palestinian police stations will be established in specified towns and villages to enable the Palestinian police to exercise its responsibility for public order. The agreement contains provisions requiring that the movement of Palestinian police be coordinated and confirmed with Israel. In Area "C," which comprises the unpopulated areas, areas of strategic importance to Israel and the Jewish settlements, Israel will retain full responsibility for security and public order. The Council will assume all those civil responsibilities not related to territory, such as economics, health, education, etc.

In addition to the redeployment of Israeli military forces described above, the agreement provides that a series of further redeployments are to take place at six-month intervals following the inauguration of the Council. In the course of these redeployments, additional parts of Area "C" will be transferred to the territorial jurisdiction of the Council, so that by the completion of the redeployment phases, Palestinian territorial jurisdiction will cover West Bank territory except for the areas where jurisdiction is to be determined under the final status negotiations (settlements, military locations, etc.).

The agreement contains an undertaking to revoke those articles of the Palestinian Covenant calling for the destruction of Israel, within two months of the inauguration of the Council.

The agreement provides for the establishment of a strong police force, that will constitute the only Palestinian security force. The Security Annex specifies the deployment of the police force, the approved equipment and its modes of action.

The Security Annex specifies the commitment of Israel and the Palestinian Council to cooperate in the fight against terrorism and the prevention of terrorist attacks. Both sides, in accordance with this agreement, will act to insure the immediate, efficient and effective handling of any incident involving the threat, or acts of terrorism, violence or incitement, whether committed by Palestinians or Israelis. To this end they will cooperate in the exchange of information and coordinate policies and activities. Joint security committees will be established to coordinate between the IDF and the Palestinian police. Regional offices will operate twenty-four hours a day. Joint patrols will ensure free and secure movement on designated roads in Area "A." Joint Mobile Units will serve as rapid response units in case of incidents and emergencies.

The agreement sets out the arrangements for the transfer of agreed upon civil powers and responsibilities from the Civil Administration to the Council.

Responsibility over sites of religious significance in the West Bank and Gaza will be transferred to the Palestinian side. In Area "C" this will be transferred gradually during the "further redeployment phase," except for the issues which will be negotiated during the permanent status negotiations. Both sides shall respect and protect religious rights of Jews, Christians, Moslems and Samaritans: (a) Protecting the holy sites. (b) Allowing free access to the holy sites. (c) Allowing freedom of worship and practice. Jewish holy sites are listed in the agreement. The agreement guarantees freedom of access to and freedom of worship at the holy sites, and defines access arrangements for the holy places located in Areas "A" and "B." With regard to Rachel's Tomb in Bethlehem and Joseph's Tomb in Nablus, special arrangements are set out in the agreement which will also guarantee freedom of access and freedom of worship.

In view of the Jewish presence in the heart of Hebron and the sensitive historical and religious aspects involved, special arrangements will apply in this city. These arrangements will enable Palestinian police to exercise responsibilities vis-à-vis Palestinian residents while at the same time Israel will retain the powers and responsibilities necessary to protect Israeli residents living in Hebron and visiting the holy places. There will be a redeployment of Israeli military forces in Hebron, except for places and roads where arrangements are necessary for the security and protection of Israelis and their movements. This redeployment will be completed no later than six months after the signing of this agreement. Israel will continue to carry the responsibility for overall security of Israelis for the purpose of safeguarding their internal security and public order. The status quo at the Tomb of the Patriarchs will remain unchanged, for the time being.

There will be a temporary international presence in Hebron.

The agreement contains an undertaking on the part of Israel to increase the amount of water allocated to the Palestinians by 28 million cu.m. Any further addition to either side will be based on an increase in the available water resources to be developed through international funding and channels, among them the tripartite American-Palestinian-Israeli forum which will hold its first meeting after the signing of the Interim Agreement. The agreement provides for the establishment of a joint water committee that will manage water resources and enforce water policies, protecting the interests of both parties by the prevention of uncontrolled drilling and enforcing standards, etc.

See also: *Conflict Formation, Elements in; Field Diplomacy: A New Conflict Paradigm; Local Wars since 1945; Pan-Arabism; Problem Solving in Internalized Conflicts; Pacific Settlement of International Disputes*

*Bibliography* —————————————————

Bickerton I J, C L Klausner 1995 *A Concise History of the Arab-Israeli Conflict*, 2nd edn. Prentice-Hall, Englewood Cliffs, NJ

Carter J 1982 *Keeping Faith: Memoirs of a President*. Bantam Books, New York

Kissinger H 1979 *White House Years*. Little Brown, Boston, Massachusetts

Reich B (ed.) 1996 *An Historical Encyclopedia of the Arab-Israeli Conflict*. Greenwood Press, Westport, Connecticut

Reich B (ed.) 1995 *Arab-Israeli Conflict and Conciliation: A Documentary History*. Greenwood Press, Westport, Connecticut and London

Reich B 1977 *Quest for Peace: United States-Israel Relations and the Arab-Israeli Conflict*. Transaction Books, New Brunswick, New Jersey

Reich B 1984 *The United States and Israel: Influence in the Special Relationship.* Praeger, New York

Tessler M 1994 *A History of the Israeli-Palestinian Conflict.* Indiana University Press, Bloomington and Indianapolis

United States Congress, House, Committee on Foreign Affairs 1979 *The Search for Peace in the Middle East: Documents and Statements, 1967-69.* Government Printing Office, Washington, DC

United States Congress, House, Committee on Foreign Affairs 1982 *Documents and Statements on Middle East Peace, 1979-82.* Government Printing Office, Washington, DC

United States Congress, Senate, Committee on Foreign Relations 1975 *Select Chronology and Background Documents Relating to the Middle East.* Government Printing Office, Washington, DC

United States Congress, House, Committee on Foreign Affairs 1989 *Documents on Middle East Peace, 1982-88.* Government Printing Office

United States Department of State 1984 *The Quest for Peace: Principal United States Public Statements and Related Documents on the Arab-Israeli Peace Process 1967-83.* Government Printing Office, Washington, DC

BERNARD REICH; ROSEMARY HOLLIS; JASON FUIMAN

# Arab-Israeli Wars

The Arab-Israeli wars emerged out of the twentieth century conflict over the country that historically was called Palestine. This is defined as the area between the Mediterranean Sea and the Jordan River. In terms of present-day political divisions, Palestine encompasses the State of Israel and the Israeli-occupied West Bank and Gaza Strip (in some areas of which a partially autonomous Palestinian Authority emerged during the 1990s).

By most conventional counts, there have been five Arab-Israeli wars to date: the First (or 1948) War (also known as the Palestine War and, by Israelis, the "War of Independence"), the Second (or 1956) War (also called the Sinai or the Sinai-Suez War), the Third (or 1967) War (sometimes also called the June War or the Six-Day War), the Fourth (or 1973) War (also called the Ramadan War, from the Islamic month in which it occurred, mainly by pro-Arab writers; the Yom Kippur War, from the Jewish holiday on which it began, usually by pro-Israeli writers; or the October War, typically by neutral observers); and the Fifth (or 1982) War (perhaps better known as the Lebanon War). However, it is arguably more accurate to speak of the above merely as major clusters of battles in a continuing struggle that dates back to the 1920s—but not much earlier, as the popular myth of an "age-old conflict" between Arabs and Jews lacks substance.

## 1. Origins of the Conflict

The twentieth century has seen a conflict between two rival claims to Palestine. On the one side are the Palestinians—or, to be more precise, the Arab Palestinians. For centuries Palestine was an overwhelmingly Arab country and hardly underpopulated (except for the Negev Desert in the south). It is estimated that its slightly more than 10,000 square miles had a population of 740,000 in 1914, only 60,000 of whom were Jews even after over two decades of Jewish immigration. The Arab Palestinians seem to be an amalgam of all the peoples living in the country since ancient times (including Jews), who were assimilated to Arab culture and identity mainly since the seventh century AD.

The Arab Palestinians' claim has been backed by the Arab world generally. Arab governments were increasingly drawn into the conflict by the late 1930s. For a long time, particularly between 1948 and 1967, the Palestinians themselves tended to rely on the independent Arab countries to pursue their cause. But some leaders of Arab states came at times to be accused of substituting rhetoric to appease anti-Israeli publics for any real commitment to the struggle while using this as a weapon in inter-Arab propaganda and even secretly collaborating with the Israelis.

The second claim to Palestine is that of the Zionist movement on behalf of the Jewish people of the world. The Jews are defined in terms of adherence (at least formally) to Judaism, but, despite racial heterogeneity that points to their being a product of conversion over the centuries, it is usually taken for granted that they are a people as well as a religious sect and that they are a continuation of the Jews whose homeland was in Palestine in ancient times. In any case, Jews who lived throughout the world (but mostly in Europe, particularly the eastern parts, including Russia, and to a lesser extent in the modern period in various Middle Eastern countries, not to mention their eventual settlement in North America) maintained a strong attachment to Palestine over the centuries and a belief in their historical destiny eventually to "return." However, it was not until the end of the nineteenth century that a political movement—

nationalist like the other ethnic movements in Eastern Europe at the time but also colonialist in that it called for settlement in a non-European country and tended to overlook the rights or even the existence of the indigenous people (whose "transfer" outside Palestine they sporadically called for)—arose under the name of Zionism to establish a Jewish society and a Jewish state in Palestine.

Despite the unwillingness of the Ottoman Empire (which included Palestine) to cooperate with them, the Zionists had minor successes in establishing Jewish settlements before the First World War. But it was the British commitment in 1917, the Balfour Declaration, in favor of a Jewish "national home" in Palestine—despite its intentional ambiguity and even contrary assurances to the country's "non-Jewish communities," not to mention the United Kingdom's previous promise to back Arab independence—that represented a real breakthrough for the Zionist movement. This was especially true in light of the fact that the United Kingdom was to rule Palestine—eventually as the mandatory power under the authority of the League of Nations—for the next three decades.

Under British rule, Palestine experienced large scale Jewish colonization, particularly after the Nazis came to power in Germany. Many peasants were uprooted from their villages when absentee landlords sold land to the Zionists, and Arabs feared that they would be removed from the country to make way for a Jewish state. Arabs rioted against British rule and Jewish settlement several times during the 1920s, and a Great Rebellion by the Arab peasantry against British rule and British-sponsored colonization (which perhaps deserves to be considered the first Arab-Israeli War) began in 1936 but was extinguished by the end of the decade. Following the dispatch of several British commissions of inquiry, the United Kingdom limited its support for Zionism after 1939. Even as late as 1948, about two-thirds of the population of Palestine was Arab. But Zionist demands for turning the country into a Jewish state intensified and involved terrorism against both Arabs and British.

A partition plan was adopted by the UN General Assembly in November 1947, as the British prepared to leave Palestine. However, the Arabs at least publicly rejected this plan on the ground that it allotted most of the country to the Jewish minority, and, as civil war intensified, the Zionists—who had proclaimed their acceptance of partition—also occupied some areas the UN had designated for the Arabs. Fear induced by massacres by Zionist organizations such as the Stern Gang and the Irgun, especially in the village of Dayr Yasin in April 1948, as well as outright expulsion in some areas by the main Jewish force, the Haganah, started a mass flight of the Arab population from the country. Jewish volunteers from all over the world joined their co-religionists in Palestine, while volunteers from Arab countries joined an Arab Liberation Army.

## 2. The 1948 Arab-Israeli War

Leaders of the Jewish community declared the existence of a State of Israel on May 14, 1948, as the British completed the gradual withdrawal of their forces from the country and terminated the mandate. Armed contingents from five Arab States (Transjordan, Egypt, Syria, Lebanon, and Iraq) immediately entered Palestine, purportedly to support the Arab Palestinians. They had some initial successes, but a truce went into effect on July 11, and during its short duration the Israelis built up their forces and went on the offensive on July 8. The remainder of the war witnessed sporadic advances by Israeli forces, who not only represented a modern European settler society as opposed to the underdeveloped Arab countries but actually always greatly outnumbered the Arab troops sent to Palestine. Also, the Arab leaders were competing with each other as much as with the Israelis. A careful examination of what happened shows that Transjordan, which was careful not to enter areas the UN had designated for the Jewish state, was collaborating with the Israelis in dividing up the territories the UN allotted to an Arab Palestinian state (which consequently did not come into existence), while the main Egyptian aspiration was to thwart Transjordanian ambitions.

Israel concluded a series of separate armistices with the adjacent Arab countries in 1949. These left about 77 percent of Palestine under Israeli control, with the Egyptians now administering the small Gaza Strip and with another area (subsequently called the West Bank) annexed by Jordan (formerly Transjordan). The city of Jerusalem was left partly under Israeli and partly under Jordanian control.

With advancing Israeli forces driving the Arabs out of most areas, the new state attained an overwhelmingly Jewish population. Only a small Arab minority remained. Roughly 775,000 Arab Palestinians were now refugees, dreaming of returning to their lost homeland.

## 3. The 1956 Arab-Israeli War

Movements toward Arab-Israeli peace were recurrently aborted after 1949. Arab leaders sometimes engaged in empty talk about a future "second round," but documentary evidence now reveals that they often were quietly amenable to proposals for peace, while it was the Israelis who preferred to wait and repeatedly sabotaged moves toward a peaceful settlement. Numerous small incidents occurred, and the Israelis carried out sporadic raids into Arab territory, sometimes killing dozens of civilians. Israel also occupied some of the areas that the armistice agreements had demilitarized. And Egypt sometimes forbade Israeli access to the Suez Canal and to the Gulf of Aqaba, whose entrance was in Egyptian waters. A major Israeli raid into the Gaza Strip in February 1955 began an intensified phase of the conflict, with Egypt now turning to the former Soviet Union to buy arms and training Palestinian guerrillas to raid Israel. France increasingly armed Israel during the mid-1950s in the belief that Egyptian support was responsible for the anti-colonial rebellion in Algeria.

Egypt's nationalization of the Suez Canal Company in July 1956 evoked strong opposition in both the United Kindgom and France and led them to join Israel in an attack on that country. Israel attacked first, on October 29, and proceeded to occupy the Gaza Strip and the Sinai. British and French troops entered the Suez Canal zone on November 5, but US opposition forced the invaders to stop and then to withdraw entirely (by March 1957, in Israel's case). With a United Nations Emergency Force (UNEF) (see *United Nations Peacekeeping Operations*) patrolling the armistice line (though never allowed on the Israeli side), the Egyptian-Israeli frontier came to be relatively quiet, and, with the UNEF also at the entrance to the Gulf of Aqaba, Israel also now gained access to that waterway. Otherwise, the conflict was not abated.

## 4. The 1967 Arab-Israeli War

Clashes continued on the Israeli-Syrian and the Israeli-Jordanian frontiers, and from 1964 on the conflict intensified. Israel's diversion of the waters of the Jordan River was one aggravating factor. A Palestine Liberation Organization (PLO) emerged (then under team leadership which was designed to make it ineffective while giving legitimacy to the Arab regimes that created it), as did a more serious Palestinian guerrilla organization called Fatah, which carried out small-scale raids against Israel. In November 1966 the Israeli army destroyed a Jordanian village, and an air attack on Syria ensued in April 1967. During a period of intensified inter-Arab cold war, Egypt found itself taunted by conservative Arab

leaders for "hiding behind" the UNEF, which would also hinder Egyptian support for Syria if the invasion of that country being talked about at the time by the Israelis were carried out.

The removal of the UNEF (following Egypt's original request for a partial removal), the subsequent declaration that the Gulf of Aqaba was again closed to the Israelis, and the movement of Egyptian troops to Sinai to deter a possible Israeli attack provided the immediate prelude to the 1967 War. A surprise (if predicatable) Israeli air attack destroyed the Egyptian air force on June 5. Several other Arab states entered the war with varying degrees of seriousness (although the total number of Arab troops committed to combat was still smaller than those of Israel) but, without air cover, were no match for the enemy. When the battles ended six days later, Israel had occupied Sinai, the Gaza Strip, the West Bank (including Arab Jerusalem), and part of southwestern Syria (the Golan Heights). A few hundred thousand additional Arabs became refugees.

Again, there was no progress toward a settlement. Although Israel at first proclaimed the intention of trading the newly occupied territory for peace, it gradually began to indicate that it would not withdraw completely. Arab Jerusalem was unilaterally annexed. Palestinians intensified their guerrilla war against Israel but ultimately failed, in large part because Israeli retaliation forced Arab regimes to suppress them or to curtail their activities. There was also sporadic fighting between Israeli and Arab armies, with Egyptian artillery fire across the Suez Canal escalating to a War of Attrition in March 1969. This was met by Israeli raids deep inside Egypt early in 1970, followed by another Egyptian-Israeli ceasefire in August. Although most of the Arab states involved increasingly indicated their willingness to make peace with Israel in return for full withdrawal, again there was no progress in that direction.

## 5. The 1973 Arab-Israeli War

The 1973 War began with a surprise attack by Egypt and Syria on the Israeli forces occupying their territories. The offensive proved to be remarkably successful at first, but the Syrians were eventually pushed back; although Egypt was able to hold a strip of territory in Sinai, the Israelis also occupied an area on the western side of the Suez Canal. Again, several Arab states entered the war on at least a small scale; of perhaps greater potential significance, the Arab oil producers announced a cutback in production and a boycott of countries supporting Israel. The primary goal of Egypt and Syria in beginning this offensive had been to prod the major powers into a peace initiative, and this seemed to have succeeded, as US Secretary of State Henry Kissinger's good offices helped to produce disengage agreements on both fronts.

A peace conference met briefly in Geneva in December 1973, but there were quarrels over the representation of the PLO and also a desire by some parties to avoid Soviet participation in the process (the United States and the former Soviet Union jointly chaired the conference). Also, Washington seemingly preferred partial measures that would result in separate peace agreements between Israel and specific Arab states (a "peace process" that others saw as an attempt to obstruct real peace) to a comprehensive approach. Inter-Arab quarrels intensified, and a civil war that flared up in Lebanon in 1975 was in part a spin-off of the Arab-Israeli conflict in that one facet of the Lebanon conflict was the attempt of rightist Maronite Christians to suppress the increasing numbers of Palestinian guerrillas in that country and soon involved Israeli intervention on the side of the rightist Maronites. Egypt eventually opted for a separate peace in 1979 that led to Israel's withdrawal from Sinai. But there was no progress on the Palestinian front as a more nationalistic Israeli government under Prime Minister Menachem Begin accelerated the process of creating Israeli settlements and rejected the idea of ever withdrawing.

## 6. The 1982 Arab-Israeli War

Israeli forces invaded southern Lebanon in March 1978 but withdrew three months later, leaving local clients in control of some areas. Air raids on PLO forces in Lebanon took place from time to time, and a major escalation occurred in July 1981, with Israel bombing Beirut and Palestinians retaliating by bombarding northern Israel. A ceasefire then went into effect that generally was effective until Israel launched a full-scale invasion of southern Lebanon in June 1982 and moved north to besiege and repeatedly bomb Beirut. This was the first Arab-Israeli War to involve mainly the Israelis versus the Palestinians, and the latter held out longer than had the Arab states' armies in previous conflicts (taking the truces in the 1948 War into account), but in August Palestinian forces finally evacuated Beirut.

Israel had succeeded in weakening the PLO, thus seemingly facilitating the policy of absorbing the West Bank and the Gaza Strip (the major Israeli goal in launching the war). But the goal of putting a friendly government in power in Lebanon proved

elusive. Furthermore, the Shi'ite Muslims of southern Lebanon became increasingly embittered by the Israeli occupation and, inspired by the Islamic Revolution in Iran, proved to be a formidable enemy. With its casualties continuing to mount, Israel gradually withdrew its soldiers from Lebanon except for a few who stayed on as advisers to a local client force, the South Lebanon Army (SLA), that continued to control a strip along the border.

The Iranian-inspired Party of God has continued to mount resistance to the Israelis and the SLA in southern Lebanon. Israel's war against the Lebanese guerrillas has escalated on several occasions, particularly in 1993 and 1996, which involved massive artillery fire destroying towns and villages and temporarily expelling the population of the southern part of the country. None of these occurrences has been added to conventional lists of "Arab-Isreali wars," apparently because only Arab guerrillas, not official armies, fought on the Arab side.

Another outbreak that has not been added to the conventional list of wars was the massive Uprising (Intifadah) that erupted at the end of 1987 in the West Bank and the Gaza Strip. The weapons of the Intifadah were stones thrown at the occupying forces, as well as various other kinds of organized disobedience. Particularly after the leaders of the PLO entered into an arrangement with their former enemy to establish limited self-government in parts of the occupied territories that many Palestinians saw as a form of collaboration, religious zealots on both sides have periodically carried out dramatic acts of violence.

## 7. Impact on Peace and War

As the above account makes obvious, the Arab-Israeli conflict has produced warfare almost continuously since the 1940s and even earlier. Almost all the countries of the Middle East have been drawn in at times. It is possible that it will increasingly involve non-Arab Mulsim states as well as the Arabs, and indeed revolutionary Iran has become the most militant opponent of Israel, at least verbally, at a time that many Arab regimes and even the PLO have made peace with the Jewish state. The issue of the Muslim holy places in Jerusalem may be particularly potent in the long run in bringing in increasing Muslim involvement. Furthermore, as the example of Lebanon shows, the Arab-Israeli conflict has tended to aggravate conflicts within the Arab world itself.

The potential violence of the Arab-Israeli conflict has intensified as more sophisticated weapons have been introduced. It is partly because of this conflict that the region has become one of the most heavily armed parts of the world, at least in terms of conventional weapons. Furthermore, Israel is known to have developed a substantial nuclear weapons capacity, thus creating the specter of future horrors for the world. Other states in the region, including Iran, may acquire such nuclear weapons within a few years.

During the Cold War, the Arab-Israeli conflict pulled the Superpowers and other major powers in as supporters of one side or the other. Arab-Israeli Wars had the potential of setting off a world war. As a case in point, the United States put its forces on alert throughout the world in 1973 to deter the despatch of Soviet troops to help Egypt. Observers repeatedly concluded that no other situation in the world was as likely to start a Third World War as was the Arab-Israeli conflict.

Israel is formally at peace now with its immediate neighbors, except on the Syrian and Lebanese front. But such a situation is shaky in light of the popular feeling on the part of many Arabs that this is a kind of peace based on acquiescence by their own authoritarian regimes—themselves potentially unstable—to superior power. The Israelis also are divided, and could conceiveably plunge into an internecine civil war of their own if their government ever accepted terms that the Arabs—and the Palestinians in particular—considered reasonably just. It is hard to determine whether the Arabs and Israel are now on the road to true peace or whether the underlying conflict is building up to new levels of violence.

See also: *Arab-Israeli Conflict: Peace Plans and Proposals; Camp David Accords; Local Wars Since 1945; Pan-Arabism*

## Bibliography

Flapan S 1987 *The Birth of Israel: Myths and Realities*. Pantheon Books, New York

Khouri F J 1985 *The Arab-Israeli Dilemma*, 3rd edn. Syracuse University Press, Syracuse, New York

Lustick I (ed.) 1994 *Arab-Israeli Relations: A Collection of Contending Perspectives and Recent Research*, 10 vols. Garland, Hamden, Connecticut

Morris B 1987 *The Origins of the Palestinian Refugee Problem, 1947-1949*. Cambridge University Press, New York

Morris B 1990 *1948 and After: Israel and the Palestinians*. Clarendon Press, Oxford

Neff D 1988 *Warriors Against Israel*. Amana Books, Brattleboro, Vermont

Neff D 1981 *Warriors at Suez*. Linden Press, New York

Neff D 1984 *Warriors for Jerusalem: Six Days that Changed the Middle East*. Linden Press, New York

Ovendale R 1984 *The Origins of the Arab-Israeli Wars*. Longman, New York

Palumbo M 1987 *The Palestinian Catastrophe: The 1948 Expulsion of a People from their Homeland*. Faber and Faber, London

Pappe I *The Making of the Arab-Israeli Conflict, 1947-1951* I B Tauris, London Parker, R B (ed.) 1996 *The Six-Day War: A Retrospective*. University Press of Florida, Gainsville

Shlaim A 1988 *Collusion Across the Jordan: King Abdullah, the Zionist Movement, and the Partition of Palestine*. Columbia University Press, New York

Smith C D 1996 *Palestine and the Arab-Israeli Conflict*, 3rd edn. St. Martin's, New York.

Tessler M *A History of the Israeli-Palestinian Conflict*. Indiana University Press, Bloomington

GLENN E. PERRY

# Arbitration, International

International arbitration is a process for settling disputes between states by a judicial procedure based on respect for law, using judges, and on terms chosen by the parties to the dispute. It is a sophisticated process reflecting the wish of the parties to have their dispute settled by judicial rather than diplomatic processes. Modern international arbitration has developed from the practice of states and from the rules to be found in bilateral and multilateral treaties. In modern times international arbitration has not been chosen frequently, but it has played a role in the settlement of territorial and similar delimitation disputes between traditionally friendly states. Recourse to international arbitration may be the result of a general undertaking to refer future disputes to arbitration or of a specific agreement (*compromis*) relating to a specific dispute. In addition to choosing the judges and the procedures, the parties may specify the basis upon which the arbitration is to determine the dispute. This is often the rules of international law (see *International Law*) as encompassed in Article 38 (1) of the Statute of the International Court of Justice, but may also include—either in the absence of any settled rules of international law or as an alternative to them—settlement on an equitable basis as provided for under Article 38 (2) of the Statute of the International Court of Justice.

Arbitration awards are binding on the parties, though they are not necessarily final. Either party may, if the *compromis* permits, take further proceedings to seek the interpretation, revision, or rectification of the award and in all cases may challenge the decision as a nullity if it is flawed by some failure to comply with the requirements of the *compromis.* Indeed there are many instances of lengthy legal disputes concerning the meaning of effect of awards. Yet there have been few outright repudiation of awards, the most famous recent example being the repudiation by Argentina of the award in the Beagle Channel Arbitration (see below).

This article reviews the historical development of international arbitration, refers to some modern examples of the process, and explains its place in the maintenance of international peace and security. Though there has been an increasing use of arbitration between large commercial concerns and states in recent years for the resolution of disputes concerning economic interests, this article is concerned only with arbitrations between states.

## 1. Historical Development

Modern international arbitration is often said to date back to the Jay Treaty of 1794 whereby the United States and the United Kingdom established a number of mixed commissions consisting of commissioners from each state to resolve disputes between the two states which arose following the gaining of independence by the United States. These early commissions were a mixture of judicial and diplomatic processes aimed at providing a machinery for determining what was in effect a negotiated settlement. But the idea of mixed commissions took hold and the judicial aspects of the process soon came to predominate. In particular, the success of the Alabama Claims in 1872, again between the United States and the United Kingdom, settled the model for future arbitrations. These claims related to allegations that the United Kingdom had not remained neutral during the American Civil War by allowing the South to have boats built and fitted out in British shipbuilding yards. These vessels, including the *Alabama* which gave its name to the arbitration, had caused much damage to the commerce of the North. Once the Civil War was over, the United States sought compensation from the United Kingdom for its failure to remain neutral. The arbitral tribunal consisted of representatives

appointed by the heads of states of Italy, Brazil, and Switzerland sitting with a representative appointed by each of the disputing parties. The arbitration resulted in the award of US $15.5 million to the United States. Although the United Kingdom protested the legality of the award, it was nevertheless met. One commentator describes the Alabama Claims arbitration as "a turning point in the history of arbitration, marking its definitive breakthrough." Such successes led to the proposal that some permanent system of international arbitration should be established.

The principal attempts to establish a permanent system were the Hague Conventions of 1899 and 1907 for the pacific settlement of international disputes (see *Pacific Settlement of International Disputes*). These treaties resulted from a conference called by Czar Nicholas II in an attempt to limit the armaments race of the day and provide a viable alternative to "an appeal to arms." All the major powers of the day attended the conference. The two Conventions are still in force and have attracted widespread ratifications. Contracting states recognized the importance of international arbitration as a means of settling their disputes, but there is only a moral obligation to refer disputes to arbitration. The 1899 Convention describes international arbitration "as the most effective, and at the same time as the most equitable, means of settling disputes which diplomacy has failed to settle." The absence of any legal duty to refer disputes to arbitration is a defect of the Conventions, but it should be remembered that it was not until 1928 that the Kellogg-Briand Pact sought to outlaw recourse to force in the settlement of disputes. The Conventions established the inappropriately named Permanent Court of Arbitration, which is neither permanent nor a court. Indeed, there is only machinery in the form of the International Bureau, housed in the Peace Palace at The Hague, for establishing arbitral tribunals to hear specific cases. The Administrative Council consists of the contracting states and the International Bureau acts as a registry when states wish to set up an arbitral tribunal to settle a dispute. Contracting states nominate for terms of six years up to four persons of known competence in questions of international law, of the highest moral reputation, and disposed to accept the duties of arbitrators to a panel which is maintained by the International Bureau. If contracting states wish to use the machinery, each party to the dispute nominates two arbitrators from the panel, only one of whom may be a national of the nominating state. The four arbitrators then nominate a fifth person to act as umpire. The 1907 Convention added a Summary Procedure involving only three arbitrators and a wholly written procedure. The Convention machinery has also produced a rudimentary system of procedural rules for submission of disputes to arbitration which are frequently adopted by states resorting to arbitration. Between 1900 and 1932, the Permanent Court of Arbitration dealt with 20 cases, but since then only three cases have involved use of the machinery. The decline in its use is partly accounted for by the establishment of the Permanent Court of International Justice, later to become the International Court of Justice (see *International Court of Justice*).

The major significance of the Hague Conventions is that they are the only treaties which commit the Soviet Union to any form of international adjudication, though it has to be noted that the former Soviet Union has taken no part in the running of the Permanent Court of Arbitration since the First World War. Today, the Permanent Court of Arbitration offers little advantage over a well-drafted *compromis* in an ad hoc arbitration, though the premises, staff, and facilities of the International Bureau at the Peace Palace at The Hague appear to be a resource often overlooked by states.

The creation of the Permanent Court of International Justice in 1920 and its replacement with the International Court of Justice in 1946 did not spell the death knell for international arbitration, though it has diminished its incidence. Attempts were made in the General Act for the Pacific Settlement of International Disputes in 1928, and by its revision in 1949, to persuade states to accept compulsory reference of disputes to judicial settlement either by the Court, or, if the states agreed, by international arbitration. Neither attempt was successful. Today, the vast majority of states accept the international legal duty to resolve their disputes by peaceful means but assiduously reserve to themselves the choice of means, of which judicial settlement is but one.

In 1949 the International Law Commission set about preparing a draft code of arbitral procedure. The result was that in 1953 the International Law Commission proposed a general multilateral convention on arbitral procedure based on its draft code. This was designed to ensure the effectiveness of undertakings to refer disputes to arbitration. Under the proposed convention, once a binding undertaking to refer a dispute to arbitration was established, a state party to the dispute could not frustrate the arbitration by refusing to agree on procedural matters. The convention would take over the establishment of the arbitration, removing this aspect from the consent of the par-

ties in dispute. Such an approach was not acceptable to states and a watered-down form of the International Law Commission's proposals became draft articles which states could use as Model Rules on Arbitral Procedure in concluding bilateral and multilateral treaties or in agreeing on the reference of a dispute to arbitration. These draft articles were presented to the General Assembly in 1958. In the weak General Assembly Resolution 1262 of November 14, 1958, the General Assembly merely took note of the draft articles and drew the attention of member states to them. These draft articles have had less impact than the procedural rules of the earlier Hague Conventions.

## 2. Modern Examples

The most cursory examination of modern instances of international arbitration shows that they are almost invariably the product of ad hoc arbitration agreements. Such agreements, not all of which are as full and complete as is necessary, commonly define the issues for arbitration, and the constitution, powers, and procedures of the tribunal. Such special agreements are of great significance, because the arbitrators only have authority to deal with the issues referred to them under the agreement on the basis set out in the agreement. Any failure to respect the terms of the agreement can result in any award being challenged as a nullity. Arbitrations between states resulting from ad hoc arbitration agreements have not been numerous, possibly because in the era of the United Nations Charter, most states choose to implement the obligation to settle their disputes by peaceful means by using the private diplomatic processes of negotiation, conciliation, inquiry, and good offices rather than judicial processes.

A number of regional treaties recognize the value of international arbitration as a method of settling disputes, but few go beyond the obligations set out in Article 2 (3) and Chapter VI of the United Nations Charter, which stress that states have an unfettered freedom to choose any peaceful means to settle their disputes. This principle of freedom of choice is also enshrined in bilateral treaties between states which contain obligations to settle disputes by peaceful means. Consequently few examples can be found of international arbitrations being based on obligations in such treaties. But the figure may be artificially low because the obligation in the bilateral treaty may have been the catalyst which led to the special agreement to refer the dispute to international arbitration. Finally, a preference for arbitration for disputes concerning the law of the sea is reflected in the Law of the Sea Convention of 1982 which establishes a new International Tribunal for the Law of the Sea.

Some examples of international arbitration will add substance to this description and illustrate the willingness of states, if the circumstances are right, to refer a variety of issues affecting vital national interests to arbitration.

The Island of Palmas arbitration of 1928 concerned a dispute between the United States and the Netherlands about the ownership of the Island of Palmas. The United States claimed title on the basis of the Treaty of Paris under which Spain had ceded all its territory in the region to the United States. The crucial question therefore became the nature of Spain's rights over the territory in 1898 when the Treaty of Paris came into force. The sole arbitrator was the Swiss Professor Max Huber, whose decision is still today a leading authority on principles of international law relating to title to territory. The arbitrator held that it was vital to look not just at claims to title but to the actual display of peaceful and continuous sovereignty over the territory. His extensive consideration of the relative claims of Spain and the United States as its successor, and of the Netherlands, established that there had been unchallenged acts of peaceful display of sovereignty by the Netherlands from 1700 to 1906 (the date the dispute between the United States and the Netherlands arose) and this was sufficient to establish the title of the Netherlands to the island.

The Trail Smelter arbitration of 1941 between the United States and Canada is another landmark arbitration, because it established a principle of good neighborliness concerning air pollution at a time when there was no international law concerning protection of the environment. The dispute concerned air pollution from a lead and zinc smelter operated by a Canadian company which caused damage in the United States. The arbitration agreement enabled the Tribunal to consider the liability of Canada and to establish and monitor emissions from the smelter for the future. No other form of adjudication could have established the obligations of Canada toward the United States.

The Rann of Kutch arbitration of 1968 is a good example of the use of arbitration to resolve a dispute which had already resulted in hostilities between the parties. For centuries there had been boundary disputes concerning 3,500 square miles of territory known as the Rann of Kutch. This dispute was inherited by India and Pakistan when they attained statehood. The territory is salt desert for part of the year and flooded territory for the remainder of the year. In April 1965 India and Pakistan had engaged in hostil-

ities over the territory and in the ceasefire agreement of June 1965 agreed to refer the dispute to international arbitration. Each side chose an arbitrator: India chose a Yugoslavian judge, and Pakistan chose the Iranian former President of the General Assembly. The Secretary General of the United Nations chose judge Lagergren of Sweden as the President of the Tribunal. The arbitrators went to great pains to assemble the facts supporting each side's claims to the territory and the arbitration took the familiar form of adjudicating between the competing claims. On some issues the evidence was finely balanced. The award of the Tribunal gave some territory to each side, and enabled the parties to the dispute to fix a boundary by the erection of 847 pillars and the execution of final maps. It is especially significant that the decision to award certain territory to Pakistan was based on the consideration that it would "promote peace and stability in the region." The arbitration provides a modern illustration of the use of the process to resolve a dispute which has been the cause of the use of force between large states, though it should be noted that the character of the territory made its loss to either side not particularly significant.

The Beagle Channel arbitration (1977) between Chile and Argentina is a rare example of an arbitration resulting from a long-standing treaty obligation to refer disputes to arbitration by the British Government. The Queen as Head of State appointed five members of the International Court of Justice to act as her advisers and to produce a report on the disputed title to certain islands in the Beagle Channel. The Tribunal reported substantially in favor of Chile. The Queen adopted the report and declared it as her award under the terms of the treaty. But the award was not acceptable to Argentina which comprehensively repudiated it for reasons which had little merit. The repudiation very nearly led to hostilities between Chile and Argentina, which were only averted by the skillful diplomacy of the papal envoy, Cardinal Samore. The whole unedifying episode illustrates the weakness of long-term treaty commitments to refer disputes to arbitration and the wisdom of the modern approach of preferring ad hoc references to arbitration.

The happier example is of the 1977 arbitration between the United Kingdom and France over the delimitation of the continental shelf boundary in the English Channel and in the Western Approaches. The arbitrators were charged with the actual delimitation of the boundary on a chart. The successful outcome has been important not only for the parties but also for the contribution it has made to international law on the delimitation of maritime zones.

The Case concerning the differences between New Zealand and France arising from the Rainbow Warrior affair is unique because the Secretary-General of the United Nations acted as the arbitrator by agreement between the two countries involved.

On July 10, 1985 a civilian vessel, the Rainbow Warrior belonging to Greenpeace Organization, not flying the New Zealand flag, was sunk at its moorings in Auckland harbor, New Zealand, as a result of extensive damage caused by two high explosive devices. In the process a Netherland citizen, Mr. Fernando Pereira, was killed. The Rainbow Warrior was then operating in the Pacific to oppose the French nuclear tests on Mururoa. The Government of France officially admitted that the act was committed by Major Alain Mafart and Captain Dominique Prieur of the French Armed Forces, the agents of French Directorate General of the External Security (DGSE), on official orders from the French Government, who were subsequently arrested and prosecuted by New Zealand authorities. On November 4, 1985, they pleaded guilty in the district court of Auckland to charges of manslaughter and willful damage to a ship and sentenced to ten years' imprisonment each.

The Government of New Zealand argued that the attack was indisputably a serious violation of basic norms of International Law and more specifically involved a serious violation of New Zealand sovereignty and of the Charter of the United Nations. New Zealand sought reparations in the form of: (a) A formal and unqualified apology by France; and (b) Compensation no less than US$9 million.

Eventually, the Secretary General of the United Nations ruled, *inter-alia*, that: (a) the Prime Minister of France should convey to the Prime Minister of New Zealand a formal and unqualified apology; (b) the French Government should pay the sum of US$7 million to the Government of New Zealand as compensation for all the damages it has suffered; (c) Major Mafart and Captain Prieur should be transferred to the French military facility on the isolated island of Hao in French Polynesia under certain conditions; and (d) the two Governments should conclude and bring into force binding agreements incorporating all of the Secretary-General's rulings and further agree that any differences that may arise about the implementation of the agreements can be referred for binding decision to an arbitral tribunal.

As a side issue, trade matters were brought up by New Zealand, namely, New Zealand claimed and France denied that the French Government has introduced certain trade issues into dispute in connection with EEC imports of New Zealand products. The Secretary-General also ruled on this topic to the effect that France should not oppose continuing imports of New Zealand butter into the United Kingdom and should not take measures that might impair the implementation of the European Economic Community's agreement with New Zealand in regard to the imports of mutton, lamb and goatmeat from New Zealand.

The case attested to the new role of the Secretary-General of the United Nations that he could take advantage of the prestige and neutrality of his office to act as an arbitrator in a dispute, if the Member States concerned could agree to entrust him with the task and also agree to be bound by his rulings.

Finally, as another example of successful arbitration resolving a very complex territorial dispute, the Case concerning the Location of Boundary markers in Taba between Egypt and Israel (Taba Case, 1988) may be mentioned. The factual background of the case goes back beyond the 19th century when the territories of present-day Egypt and Israel were both contained in the Ottoman Empire.

After several exchanges of lengthy memorials with numerous appendices between Egypt and Israel, the Arbitral Tribunal composed of five eminent jurists rendered an award on September 29, 1988 by 4 to 1 votes that the boundary pillar No. 91 was at the location advanced by Egypt and marked on the ground as recorded in the Appendix of the *Compromis*. The Dissenting Opinion of Professor Ruth Lapidoth is also quite instructive. Basically, the value of the award lies in the fact that the case threw some useful lights on evidentiary rules applicable to complex territorial disputes such as "preponderance of evidence" rule, evidentiary value of publications, etc., as well as the principle of *non licet* (*non licet quod dispendio licet*), estoppel and acquiescence.

What then is the contribution of international arbitration to the maintenance of international peace and security? It provides a valuable, though infrequently used, process for the resolution of disputes. It is clearly not a process to be thrust upon the parties, as the unfortunate Beagle Channel case illustrates. Ultimately its effectiveness rests on the political will of states both to refer the dispute to arbitration and to honor the award resulting from the arbitration.

See also: *International Judicial Settlement; Mediation*

*Bibliography* ————————————————

Fox H 1972 Arbitration. *International Disputes—The Legal Aspects*. Europa Publications, London

Johnson D H N 1986 International arbitration—Back in favor? *Yearbook of World Affairs*

Lagergren G 1988 *Five Important Cases on Nationalisation of Foreign Property Decided by the Iran-United States Claims Tribunal.* Raoul Wallenberg Institute, Lund, Sweden

Lillich R B, Brower C N (ed.) 1994 *International Arbitration in the 21st Century: Towards "Judicialization" and Uniformity?: Twelfth Sokol Colloquium.* Transnational Publishers, Irvington, New York

Merrills J G 1984 *International Dispute Settlement.* Sweet and Maxwell, London

Muller S (ed.) 1994 *The Flame Rekindled: New Hopes for International Arbitration.* M Nijhoff, Netherlands

Reisman W M 1992 *Systems of Control in International Adjudication and Arbitration: Breakdown and Repair.* Duke University Press, Durham, North Carolina

Rubino-Sammartano M 1990 *International Arbitration Law.* Kluwer

Sanders P 1990 *International Arbitration.* Martinus Nijhoff, The Hague

Simpson J L, Fox H 1959 *International Arbitration.* Stevens, London

Sohn L B 1963 The function of international arbitration today. *Hague Review* 108 (1)

United Nations *Reports of International Arbitral Awards*, Volumes I - XXI. New York

Wetter J G 1979 *The International Arbitral Process: Public and Private.* Oceana, New York

Wilson G C 1990 *The Hague Arbitration Cases: Compromis and Awards with Maps in Cases Decided under the Provisions of the Hague Conventions of 1899 and 1907 for the Pacific Settlement of International Disputes and Texts of the Conventions.* F B Rothman, Littleton, Colorado

ROBIN C. A. WHITE; WOONSANG CHOI

# Aristophanes

Thucydides, the historian and general, described the Peloponnesian war of 431-404 BC as the largest and most significant conflict that Greece had ever known. His account of the causes and course of the war is particularly valuable because he was contemporary with the events. The paucity of historical evidence for this exciting period in Greek history inveigles the modern historian to grasp at any potential source which can help to shed light on those areas not covered by Thucydides or to confirm those which he did cover, and this motivation has led many an historian to dissect the remains of a completely different literary genre: comedy.

While numerous fragments from other fifth century BC comic poets have been collected (generally from citations by later authors), the only complete plays at our disposal are attributable to Aristophanes. Of the 40 plays attributed to Aristophanes, 11 survive, spanning the years 425-388 BC. Nine of these extant plays were written during the years of the Peloponnesian war and fall into the category of what we call Old Comedy. The distinctive characteristics of Old Comedy are its topicality and its "parrhesia," or nearly unbridled freedom of expression.

Thucydides wrote in the first chapter of his *History* that his work should "serve as a possession for all time rather than a performance for today" (1.22.4). He intended his work for those who would learn from his assessment of the enduring principles of interaction between individuals, factions, and city-states. The ostensible purpose of the comic playwrights is just the converse of the statement by Thucydides. These plays were performed at specific festivals in competition with four (sometimes only two) other entries. They were not intended as enduring reference works, and it was rare that a play would be given a repeat performance. The great topicality of the comic plays makes jokes and allusions often obscure to the modern reader; in all likelihood even some members of the original audiences must have found certain allusions difficult to understand. At the same time, it is this topicality which makes Old Comedy so attractive to the modern historian; Old Comedy was concerned not only with recent events, but more so with individuals, such as leading politicians, generals, philosophers and poets—people who would be sitting in the audience.

Historians have long debated the reliability of the comic plays as historical evidence, and even those who would use them maximally for this purpose recognize the need to handle this particular source of information with extreme caution. Part of the problem is comic distortion. Satire, parody, travesty, and burlesque, the comic weaponry, distort the pictures of individuals and events. Also, it is the license of the comic poet to seem to be in earnest when in fact he is not, and we cannot accept a statement unquestionably as the point of view of the poet simply because it is spoken by a character who seems to be the hero of the drama. Thus, although few would doubt Aristophanes' familiarity with contemporary events and personages, it is a precarious and frustrating task to pin down the poet's views. And yet we cannot disregard the question entirely. However distorted the poet's treatment of the facts may be, however grotesque the comic mask, there is bound to be a background of "truth" (as perceived by the poet) upon which the comedy is built. If we can peer through the comic mask, perhaps we can catch a glimpse of the expression on Aristophanes' face.

There are three extant plays which deal primarily with the theme of peace: *Acharnians*, produced in 425 BC; *Peace*, 421 BC; and *Lysistrata*, 411 BC.

In 425 BC the Peloponnesian war had entered its seventh year. Sparta had followed the policy of invading Attica (now for the fifth time), laying waste the crops, and withdrawing. But the Athenians had withstood the attacks, generally by following the program of Pericles which called for abandoning the outlying territories in Attica and concentrating their strength in and around the city of Athens. This overcrowding probably contributed to the outbreak of plague in Athens in 430-429 BC and yet the Athenians made advances by sea, and in 425 they posted a victory over a Spartan garrison at Pylos, capturing nearly 300 troops on the island of Sphacteria close by Pylos. Peace could have been at hand, but the opponents of reconciliation in both camps kept this possibility from becoming a reality. It was in this atmosphere that Aristophanes produced the *Acharnians*.

*Acharnians* opens with the hero, Dicaeopolis (the name means literally, Just City), sitting on the Pnyx awaiting the start of the assembly, in which he is determined to let only the subject of peace be raised. In para-tragic language he chides the city for its indolence in bringing an end to hostilities.

> But as for peace, they show no regard for
> how it shall be brought about; O city! City!
> (26-27)

> So this time I've come fully prepared to
> shout and interrupt and rail at the orators if
> anyone speaks of anything put peace!
> (37-39)

Receiving no satisfaction from the assembly, Dicaeopolis makes a private peace with Sparta, a 30-year truce, which—playing on the world for truce, *sponde*, which also means a wine libation—is represented on stage by a wine flask. First Dicaeopolis is given a sip of five- and ten-year *spondai*, to which he reacts:

> I don't like this one, because it smells of
> pitch and naval works. (189-90)

And this one smells really pungent, like emissaries who are sent to other cities to wear out our allies (i.e., representatives sent to collect tribute from the allies). (192-93)

But in response to the 30-year truce, Dicaeopolis exclaims:

> O Feast of Dionysus! This one smells of
> ambrosia and nectar, and of not having to
> keep an eye on three days' worth of
> provisions; this one says to the mouth, "go
> wherever you wish." (195-98)

> Freed now from war and its evils, I'll go
> inside and direct the rural Feast of Dionysus.
> (201-202)

Aristophanes' language of peace concerns food, drink freedom of speech, and the arts: in short, what the Dionysiac festivals (at which the dramatic competitions were held) were all about.

In a long speech to the chorus of Acharnians, who are angered by his private peace, Dicaeopolis claims that the war arose from a sordid affair involving the kidnapping of a couple of prostitutes. His scenario is a comic one, but at the same time he is making a point about the foolishness of the politicians who allowed their personal motives to embroil the whole of Greece in this war.

Aristophanes does not present us with a plan for peace in any practicable sense; there is no depth of analysis on the causes of the conflict between the two Superpowers of his day. We can, however, appreciate his sensitivity toward a peaceful society, expressed, as it were, through his "poetics of peace," which preach that all that is good is attached to peace.

In 421 BC, after ten years of warring and witnessing the advantage waver between the Athenians and the Spartans, and after the deaths of Brasidas and Cleon, the most belligerent politicians and generals of Sparta and Athens respectively, the two sides were ready to conclude a truce. Aristophanes' *Peace* was performed shortly before the declaration of the truce (the so-called Peace of Nicias), but negotiations had been going on for months and the news must have been in the air already. The play reflects this situation.

The hero, Trygaios (whose name means "Harvester"), is fed up with the war and directs his complaint to Zeus. Imitating the myth of Perseus' flight towards Olympus on Pegasus, Trygaios soars to Olympus on the back of a dung-beetle. His intention is to persuade Zeus to bring peace to Greece. He arrives only to learn from Hermes that all the other gods have abandoned Olympus and that Polemos ("War" personified) now rules in their stead. Moreover, Polemos has buried the goddess "Peace" in a cave so that Greece may never again see her.

When Trygaios asks why the gods have abandoned Greece to destruction, Hermes gives a reply that describes well the course of the war:

> Because while the gods tried often to make
> peace you always chose war. If the Spartans
> ever gained a slight advantage, they would
> say something like, "By god, now we'll make
> those men of Attica pay!" But if you men of
> Attica should somehow get the upper hand,
> and the Spartans come to sue for peace,
> straightaway you cry out, "By Athena, we're
> being tricked! By Zeus, don't believe them!
> They'll come again if we hold on to Pylos."
> (211-20)

Peace is then rescued through an effort which begins as a pan-Hellenic invocation and ends as the sole struggle of the farmers of Attica. But the pan-Hellenic note has been struck, and that appears as something new in the comedies of Aristophanes. Along with Peace, two other allegorical figures are pulled from the cave, Opora—goddess of fruits—and Theoria—goddess of festivals. These attendants of Peace recall the metaphors for artistic and agricultural prosperity which pervaded *Acharnians*. Turning to Theoria, Trygaios becomes ecstatic,

> What breath you have! So pleasant to my
> heart! Such a sweet fragrance of myrrh and
> disarmament! . . . aroma of harvesting,
> invitations to dinner, Festivals of Dionysus,
> flute melodies, dramas, songs of Sophocles,
> thrushes, catchy phrases of Euripides . . . ivy
> wreaths, strained wine, bleating lambs,
> women running to the fields, a drunken
> slave-girl, an empty bottle, and many other
> blessings.

In 411 BC the situation was more desperate for the Athenians. Following the disaster of the Sicilian expedition (415-413), at the start of which excursion hopes had run so high in Athens, her main task was keeping her own allies from defecting. This time the struggle for peace takes a different form in Aristophane's play. *Lysistrata* (literally "disbander of armies") is not focused against particular warmongers, the Cleons and Lamachuses of the earlier plays; this time the women of Greece band together in a truly pan-Hellenic union

to take the initiative in bringing about peace. "Together we women shall save Greece" (41, cf. 29-30). Through a general sex strike the women of Greece succeed in securing an end to all hostilities, and their prayer to Athena that "the Athenians and Greece be delivered from war and madness" (342) is fulfilled.

In 404 BC Athens capitulated, and her Long Walls were pulled down. One year before the end, Aristophanes had written one of his most brilliant comedies, *Frogs*, in which the god of the theater himself, Dionysus, descends into Hades to retrieve one of the great tragedians. "I have come down here to get a poet," says Dionysus. "And for what reason? So that the city might be saved and maintain its choruses" (1418-19). Thus the god of both tragedy and comedy unites the welfare of the state with the preservation of the arts, a union which would have been completely understandable to the audience, for it was the role of the poet to instruct society and to improve it. The mission turns into a battle between Aeschylus and Euripides to determine who is the best tragedian, and the debate is finally settled by their responses to Dionysus' question about how to save the state; that is, in the final analysis literary merit plays no part, rather political acumen decides the victor.

The last two extant plays of Aristophanes are dated to the years 392 and 388 BC. In these we witness the decline in the role of the chorus (the last play, *Wealth*, is devoid of choral lyrics) and a shift from the topicality of the earlier plays to a more universal sort of social comedy. The battle to save the state and its choruses had been lost; there is a sadness behind the mask of the poet in the final two plays, a lack of the old vitality and incisiveness. Perhaps Athens was too impoverished now to maintain the choruses, but the poet makes no joke about this situation or about the altered form and content of the comic plays. One might ponder what Edgar Allen Poe described in *The Masque of the Red Death:*

> Even with the utterly lost, to whom life and death are equally jests, there are matters of which no jest can be made.

## Bibliography

Croiset M 1906 *Aristophane et les partis a Athenes.* Fontemoing, Paris [1909 *Aristophanes and the Political Parties at Athens.* Macmillan, London]

Dover K J 1972 *Aristophanic Comedy.* University of California Press, Berkeley, California

Ehrenberg V 1951 *The People of Aristophanes: A Sociology of Old Attic Comedy.* Blackwell, Oxford

Gomme A W 1938 Aristophanes and politics. *Classical Review* 52
Murray G T 1933 *Aristophanes: A Study.* Oxford University Press, Oxford
Norwood G 1931 *Greek Comedy.* Methuen, London
Pickard-Cambridge A W 1962 *Dithyramb, Tragedy and Comedy.* Clarendon Press, Oxford

Taillardat J 1962 *Les Images d'Aristophane, études de langue et de style.* Les Belles Lettres, Paris
Whitman C H 1964 *Aristophanes and the Comic Hero.* Harvard University Press, Cambridge, Massachusetts

BRUCE H. KRAUT

# Arms Control, Evolution of

Humankind has for centuries dwelled on the question of war, peace, and order. Arms control and disarmament, therefore, are phenomena which have long manifested themselves in international negotiating fora. For some individuals, a first acquaintance with the terms "arms control" and "disarmament" may stimulate no inquiry and they may even appear to describe the same phenomenon. Indeed, the definitions of the above terms overlap each other to some extent and are controversial. Yet, disarmament is a measure that significantly lowers the levels of armaments or leads to the abolition of such military assets (Bloomfield et al., 1965). The concept of arms control, however, connotes an approach to armament policy which encompasses quantitative amounts and qualitative kinds of weapons in being, as well as development, deployment, and utilization of such forces. Furthermore, arms control includes the possibility of disarmament, "either in limited or extensive ways," or the possibility of "arms limitation," which may or may not constitute a reduction of forces (Brennan 1961). Hence these distinctions should be considered when analyzing the evolution of negotiations concerning military assets (weapons).

A detailed review of the evolution of these phenomena would be long and tedious, requiring both space and a firm determination to examine historical facts and interpretations. The goal of this article, however, does not lie in this approach. Instead, it will attempt to review only the efforts directed towards arms control and disarmament after the Second World War. In doing so, it will review certain initiatives which have generated the negotiations undertaken in this period. Such a review will cast some light on the much debated issue of the successes and failures involved. The ultimate goal is to enable the layreader to arrive at his or her own conclusions as to whether there are some lessons yet to be learned on this subject by both states and people, and whether the process of arms control has gradually developed or has frozen itself into the quagmire of diplomatic history.

## 1. The Early Postwar Years

A great concern among scientists, politicians, military personnel, and scholars alike stimulated discussions on the need to disarm and/or to control the spread of atomic weapons in the postwar years. This concern was based upon a belief that, unlike other weapons invented up to that time, the atomic bomb—the "absolute weapon"—was an instrument of a unique destructiveness and offered no adequate defense. Hence initiatives were taken to pursue this goal on a multilateral basis. Among the early legal initiatives were the American Baruch Plan (or "Lilienthal Plan") of June 14, 1946 (see *Baruch Plan*), the Soviet "Draft International Convention"(1946), and a Soviet proposal made on June 11, 1947.

The Baruch Plan proposed, through the United Nations Atomic Energy Commission (UNAEC), the creation of an International Atomic Development Authority (IADA). This would have had powers of control or ownership, and of inspection, and would license atomic activity over all phases of the development and use of atomic energy. Shortly thereafter, the US stock of atomic bombs would be destroyed. The rationale was that, once this international body had such a potential source of power under control, the use of atomic energy for destructive purposes would be eliminated.

Nevertheless, the Baruch Plan did not find support from the former Soviet Union, which presented a counter-proposal containing an atomic energy control plan differing fundamentally from the US plan. On the one hand, ownership and management would be left in the hands of states and not of the IADA, while control would be subject to extensive but periodic inspection. On the other hand, such control would only begin after, and not before, the Americans had destroyed their stock of atomic bombs (see United Nations Atomic Energy Commission 1947 for an extensive discussion of these differences).

An impasse developed as a result of the debates involving both the US and the Soviet proposals.

Although the will to negotiate agreements to ban certain classes of weapons might have been strong across the negotiating table, the multilateral forum set up to address arms control and disarmament faced several obstacles which rendered negotiations long and complex. The efforts toward disarmament then became polemical. What seemed to be a rationally and commonly sought step to disarm suddenly became unreasonable, implicitly and explicitly woven within the fabric of international relations. Proposals were tabled and debates went on for over a decade and it was not until 1959 that the first postwar arms control agreement was finally reached, initiating a new phase in the evolution of arms control and disarmament.

## 2. From Disarmament to Arms Control

In the late 1940s East-West negotiations emphasized a need to pursue the direction of disarmament. However, a series of events, starting with the explosion of the Soviet Union's first atomic device (1949), continuing with the explosion of hydrogen bombs (early 1950s), and ending with the launching of Sputnik (1957), led to a political climate which effectively ensured that arms control agreements would dominate the nature of negotiations in the 1960s and beyond. This change of emphasis was basically the result of perceptions about both the international climate and the role nuclear weapons would play in international security. Fundamentally, there was an unavoidable feeling of mistrust and considerable international tension among states. As a consequence, there appeared a concern that the accumulation of production of fissionable material could not be traced back and/or controlled. This was for the first time formally accepted by the Soviets in a disarmament plan proposed on May 10, 1955:

> Thus, there are possibilities beyond the reach of international control for evading this control and for organizing the clandestine manufacture of atomic and hydrogen weapons, even if there is formal agreement on international control. (United Nations Disarmament Commission 1946-55)

It is therefore not surprising that the "Ban the Bomb" slogan of the late Stalin period faded away. Nor is it surprising to see atomic weapons being firmly interwoven in US defense policies with the creation of the so-called "deterence" theory. Yet, negotiations continued on both the bilateral and multilateral levels. Proposals and conferences from 1954 to the end of the decade focused on two major issues. One was the

creation of some kind of nuclear early-warning system to reduce the danger of attack or miscalculation, or to detect a massive "surprise attack"; in this respect, both the "Open Skies Plan" (1955) and the "Surprise Attack Conference" (1958) stand as unsuccessful attempts to lessen the fear of a nuclear confrontation. The other issue concerned the Soviet reluctance to see nuclear weapons proliferate in Central Europe; this was reflected in the development of what became known as the "Atom-Free Zone" (AFZ). Although neither initiative succeeded in yielding an agreement in the 1950s, they were to be tackled again in the 1960s in a new political climate conducive to negotiations—the decade of détente.

## 3. Negotiations Gain Momentum

The last 26 years of arms control and disarmament negotiations offer several lessons as to how states view world order and consequently their own security. Disarmament appears to have lost currency as a realistic goal. Arms control is the dominant phenomenon. A glance at the major postwar agreements (see Table 1) confirms this. Of these 12 agreements only one—the Biological Weapons (BW) Convention—is clearly a disarmament measure, which rightly according to its definition has led to the abolition of a whole class of armaments. In fact, this convention (if fully observed by the contracting parties) has gone beyond eliminating an entire class of weapons from the arsenals of nations. What it has also done, although seldom mentioned, is limit the horrors of war since it deals with a weapon of mass destruction. Here, success in the nature of this agreement is unquestionable. Efforts toward a convention concerning a related class of weapons—chemical weapons—accomplishing the same goal have been under way in the Committee on Disarmament as well as in a bilateral forum. While success is not immediately in sight, much work has been done on the scrutiny of complex and profound divergences embedded in a sound disarmament measure. Issues such as feasibility of verification of compliance and the timing for destruction of existing stockpiles are at the center of the debates.

Differing from disarmament measures, arms control agreements by their very nature induce much polemic on several accounts. First, arms control poses a serious problem as to how to measure asymmetrical weapons capabilities; this problem has manifested itself, in particular, in the US-Soviet Strategic Arms Limitation Talks (SALT). A second problem seriously affecting arms control is that of so-called "trade-offs." Thirdly, the term arms control can be misleading in the sense that quantitative control of arms may not reflect qualitative control of the weapons' destructive power, thus defeating its own purpose. These and other arguments are raised in the literature of arms control, and are a source of disappointment for some individuals. Nevertheless, one should not judge arms control agreements only upon these intricacies. In order to make an accurate judgment of arms control it is necessary to look at both the successes and failures of individual agreements as well as the overall impact made collectively by such undertakings. Furthermore, it is also essential to make a clear distinction between type I arms control, which deals with central weaponry issues, and type II arms control, which is lateral to the main issue of destructive power, but nonetheless helps reduce bipartite or multipartite insecurity.

### 4. Achievements of Arms Control and Disarmament Agreements

Among the achievements of arms control is the Antarctic Treaty. The significance of this 1959 treaty is at least threefold. First, it was the earliest of the postwar arms limitation agreements and thus had effect in demonstrating that the long-sought arms control and relaxation of tension (from the Cold War) were feasible and worth pursuing. Second, this treaty has a special character in that it is of a "preclusive" nature; in other words, it governs or controls an environment (the Antarctic), preventing its militarization before it developed. Third, it paved the way for other agreements with a similar character such as the Outer Space Treaty, the Latin America Nuclear Free Zone Treaty, and the Sea-Bed Treaty. It is important to note that these preclusive agreements made an important contribution to international relations; for by themselves, and more so in aggregate terms, they have "made the military relationships between East and West more calculable, and therefore [more] stable . . ." (Bertram 1978).

Judging arms control also involves considering agreements which are lateral to the main issues of weaponry. In this connection one should consider type II agreements which have dealt with communi-

*Table 1*
Major postwar security agreements

| Agreement | Date | Nature |
|---|---|---|
| Antarctic Treaty | Dec. 1, 1959 | P |
| Limited Test Ban Treaty | Aug. 5, 1963 | L |
| Outer Space Treaty | Jan. 27, 1967 | P |
| Latin America Nuclear Free Zone Treaty | Feb. 14, 1967 | P |
| Non-Proliferation Treaty | July 1, 1968 | L |
| Sea-Bed Treaty | Feb. 11, 1971 | P |
| Biological Weapons Convention | April 26, 1972 | D |
| SALT I—Interim Agreement—ABM Treaty | May 1972 | L |
| Threshold Test Ban Treaty | July 3, 1974 | L |
| Peaceful Nuclear Explosions Treaty | May 28, 1976 | L |
| Environmental Modification Convention | May 18, 1977 | L |
| SALT II | June 18, 1979 | L |
| South Pacific Nuclear Weapons Free Zone Treaty | Aug. 6, 1985 | P |
| INF Treaty | Dec. 8, 1987 | L |
| CFE Treaty | Nov. 19, 1990 | D |
| START Treaty | July 31, 1991 | L |
| Open Skies Treaty | Mar. 24, 1992 | L |
| CFE 1A Agreement | July 10, 1992 | L |
| START II Treaty | Jan. 3, 1993 | L |
| Chemical Weapons Convention | Jan. 13, 1993 | L |
| African Nuclear Weapons Free Zone Treaty | April 11, 1996 | P |
| Comprehensive Nuclear Test-Ban Treaty | Sep. 24, 1996 | L |
| Ottawa Treaty | Dec. 4, 1997 | L |

D= disarmament, L= arms limitation, P= arms control of a preclusive nature
Source: For a compilation of these treaties, see United States Arms Control and Disarmament Agency (1998)

cation. This was the fundamental theme in the decade of détente—a theme which found expression in the signing of an agreement establishing a direct communication link between the United States and the Soviet Union, the so-called "Hot Line" Agreement (1963). Albeit coming about with a "push" from a serious preceding event (the Cuban missile crisis), it responded to the need for a prompt and direct communication link between heads of states—particularly nuclear weapons states. Further, a reevaluation of the need to improve communication between states yielded both the "Accident Measures" and the "Hot Line" modernization agreements (1971). All three agreements, while not central to the question of armaments did play a significant role in improving US-Soviet communication, and proved their validity in the 1973 Middle East war. The agreements are "confidence-building" measures insofar as they reduce the risk of war by misunderstanding, misinterpretation, and the like. In short, they affect the overall climate of inter-state relations.

Other type II initiatives are the Helsinki Final Act of 1975 and the following CSCE process (see *Organization for Security and Cooperation in Europe (OSCE); Confidence Building in International Diplomacy*). Basically the Helsinki Final Act was initiated as a multi-dimensional security regime. However, in its operational terms, the most discernible sub-regime was an arms control regime codified in the Helsinki Final Act in which information measures such as CBMs played an important role. Parallel to this arms control regime, a primitive verification regime was created by implementing procedures for voluntary observation. The arms control and verification regime took a further step forward when the second generation of CSBMs and on-site inspection mechanisms were adopted at the Stockholm Conference in 1986. In particular, the second generation of CSBMs is characterised by the incorporation of constraining measures. The CSCE arms control regime was transformed at the Vienna Follow-up Meeting in 1989 by incorporating a structural measure, namely the CFE, into the mandate of the CSCE. After the advent of the post-Cold War era, the CSCE arms control regime began to lose its relevance and significance as the possibility of war between the two military superpowers diminished. Since the Paris Summit in November 1990, the CSCE has gained a new dynamism, finally resulting in a transformation of the regime from merely a 'process' into an 'international organisation.' This transformation was highlighted in the Budapest Review Meeting of 1994 by changing the name from the CSCE (Conference on Security and Cooperation in

Europe) to the OSCE (Organisation for Security and Cooperation in Europe). A new task, a new framework and a new role to play in managing new types of security issues are all required. As a result, in place of the arms control regime, conflict prevention spearheads the activities of the OSCE in the field of peace-building for long-term conflict prevention and preventive diplomacy for short-term preventive action (Ki-Jun Hong 1997).

The importance of the Limited Test Ban Treaty (LTBT) should not be neglected in any study of the evolution of arms control. The treaty directly prohibits nuclear weapons tests (as well as any other nuclear explosion) in three environments: (a) the atmosphere, (b) outer space, and (c) underwater. To some extent, indirectly, it also prohibits such tests underground. It came about as an effort to avoid radiological fallout and the possibility of cumulative contamination of the environment. The LTBT stands as a particularly important treaty, serving as the starting point for limiting nuclear tests. This goal was further advanced in the course of the 1970s. For instance, in 1974 the Treaty on the Limitation of Underground Nuclear Weapons Test established a "threshold" on nuclear tests, thus limiting the explosive force of new nuclear weapons. Subsequent efforts to this end led in 1976 to a treaty governing underground nuclear explosions for peaceful purposes being signed.

Other arms control agreements which should not be neglected are the Nuclear Weapons Free Zone and the Sea-Bed Treaties. Aside from its preclusive nature, the former became a new option in confronting the problem of the horizontal (i.e., geographical) proliferation of nuclear weapons. Since general and complete disarmament seemed not to be an attainable goal, plans were readily made for the creation of nuclear weapons free zones. Such plans include Africa, Latin America, the Middle East, South Asia, and the South Pacific. Today, Latin America, South Pacific and Africa enjoy this status (see *Nuclear-Weapon-Free Zones: A History and Assessment*).

Another option was to agree on a treaty prohibiting the proliferation of nuclear weapons. The Non-Proliferation Treaty (1968) was a response to the concern that more nuclear weapons states would entail a more complex structure of power and higher destruction levels should war occur. Furthermore, it promotes the development of the applications of nuclear energy for peaceful purposes. Thus it contributes to peace by having both a negative and positive aspect: nonproliferation of nuclear weapons, and proliferation of nuclear energy for peaceful use. In spite of these contributions, though, critics claim that the Treaty is dis-

**Table 2**
The State of Nuclear Proliferation as of May 1998

| | |
|---|---|
| Recognised Nuclear Weapon States | China, France, Russia, UK, US |
| Unrecognised Nuclear Weapon States | India, Israel, Pakistan |
| States of Immediate Proliferation Concern | North Korea, Iran, Iraq, Libya |
| Recent Converts to Nuclear Non-Proliferation | Algeria, Argentina, Belarus, Brazil |
| | Kazakhstan, South Africa, Ukrain |

criminatory because it makes legal the attitudes desired by the Superpowers—that is, it prohibits horizontal proliferation without placing serious restrictions upon vertical proliferation within the nuclear weapons states. While open for discussion, this criticism presents an interesting argument. In fact, it could partly explain why potential nuclear weapons states such as India, Israel, and Pakistan have not signed the Treaty thus far. But, in the final analysis, one could conclude that the criticism does not, at best, degrade the value of the Treaty (see *Non-Proliferation Treaty (NPT)*). Table 2 illustrates the state of nuclear proliferation as of now.

On the bilateral level, the apogee of détente was marked by the SALT I and II agreements. It is perhaps here, most of all, that a certain confusion leads the layperson to an unclear understanding of the forces acting in arms control agreements. It is easy to take sides and criticize the Soviets or the Americans for the many shortcomings and unfounded expectations of the negotiations. However, one must also consider that arms control talks between such parties imply debate on at least two levels: the political/ideological level and the practical/technological one. The former calls for the reconciling of deep-stated differences in approach. Political suspicion between parties can greatly curb negotiations. In addition, on the American side, the Arms Control and Disarmament Agency (ACDA)—which has no counterpart in the Soviet system—finds itself often in disagreement with the views of the Department of Defense.

The second level required, the practical/technological one, compels much effort toward flexibility from both parties. Complex technical problems include "trade-offs" that have to be made between asymmetrical weapons capabilities. This essentially means that choices have to be made to sacrifice (in terms of limiting or disarming) a given number or class of weapons. Since the weaponry of both sides is divergent in many respects (warhead number, payload per missile, weapons function and performance, etc.), trade-offs are a serious internal problem of arms control. For example, proposals envisaging 50 percent reductions of land-based ICBMs (intercontinental ballistic missiles), while appearing legitimate, are subject to question: how could the Soviets accept the principle of such proposals if most of their distructive power has been developed in land-based ICBMS while that of their opponents lies in air power? Hence there is more to reaching agreement than just the determination to negotiate. The problem of security is complex and cannot be judged unidimensionally.

An analysis of agreements which have sought quantitative and/or qualitative limitations and reductions of existing weapons arsenals does not, in fact, reveal very clear, concrete, positive results. SALT I and II have, perhaps, slowed the pace of a massive nuclear build-up, and if this is indeed the case then all the efforts of the long years of negotiations are commendable. Yet, serious concerns about treaty violations and noncompliance ping-pong from the White House to the Kremlin. Among them are the Soviet deployment of a new ICBM, the SS-X-25, prohibited by SALT II. In response, the Americans have planned the deployment of the Midgetman small ICBM. Further, there is the question of whether or not the Soviets had violated SALT II in regard to the prohibition on deploying SS-16 ICBMS.

There has been a debate concerning the success of the 1972 ABM (Anti-Ballistic Missile) Treaty. At the heart of this debate is the question of whether or not the Soviets had assimilated the American wisdom of "stability" theory and mutual vulnerability. There are some who argue that the Soviets had in fact accepted the validity of the above concepts, thus implying that the Treaty had been successful. However, the core of their argument seems to be overshadowed by reports that the Soviets had never abandoned Ballistic Missile Defense (BMD). But it seems that whether the former or the latter is more nearly true is not of primary importance. The basic importance of the ABM Treaty today, as it was in the late 1960s, is to diminish the interest in the proliferation of offensive nuclear forces. The idea is that if ABM systems were widely developed a "monkey-see monkey-do" situation would lead to ever higher and more cost-deficient levels of offensive weapons. It is erroneous, therefore, to judge arms control agreements only in terms of their physical reduction or of limitation of weapons systems in the field, while forgetting their intrinsic value to limit potential armaments build-up.

Unfortunately, there are other ways and reasons to foster weapons build-up. In 1960 the United States had a four-times higher number of megatons in its nuclear stockpile than in 1980. This condition has been reached through replacing aging nuclear weapons and by exploiting improved accuracy with new technology, but it has hardly been a product of arms control. The number of US strategic warheads increased during the SALT and START (Strategic Arms Reduction Talks) period (1970-84) from approximately 2,200 to 7,600, while increases on the Soviet side have been said to be from 1,400 to 8,700 warheads (Pipes 1984).

The treaty on Conventional Armed Forces in Europe (CFE), signed on 19 November 1990, is a major accomplishment in conventional arms control. As the first real disarmament measure in the area of conventional forces, the CFE Treaty set equal ceilings for the two groups of countries on the five most important categories of conventional weapons. In an area that stretches from the Atlantic to the Urals, the two groups are limited to 20,000 battle tanks, 30,000 armoured combat vehicles, 20,000 pieces of artillery, 6,800 combat aircraft and 2,000 attack helicopters. Within these overall limits, the Treaty established regionally defined sub-ceilings. The so-called "sufficiency rule" provides that no single State may have more than 13,300 tanks, 20,000 armoured combat vehicles, 13,700 pieces of artillery, 5,150 combat aircraft and 1,500 attack helicopters. The CFE Treaty entered into force de facto on July 17, 1992 after the original 22 signatories plus seven former Soviet republics with territory in the ATTU zone of application had signed the Provisional Application of the CFE Treaty on July 10, 1992 (Ki-Joon Hong 1997).

After almost 10 years of difficult negotiations, the United States and the former Soviet Union signed the Strategic Arms Reduction Treaty (START I) July 31, 1991. START mandates substantial reductions in the number of strategic ballistic missiles and heavy bombers and their attributed nuclear warheads. Reductions are to take place in three phases and must be completed in seven years. Each side must reduce to 1,600 deployed ballistic missiles and heavy bombers, 6,000 warheads on those missiles and bombers and no more than 4,900 warheads on the ballistic missiles. Launchers associated with those missiles must also be eliminated. In addition to the elimination of missiles, their launchers and bombers, START has prohibitions on locations, training, testing and

modernization. It also includes an intrusive verification regime consisting of a detailed data exchange, extensive notifications, 12 types of on-site inspection, and continuous monitoring activities designed to help verify that signatories are complying with their treaty obligations. The collapse of the Soviet Union delayed START's entry into force nearly three and a half years until Belarus, Kazakstan and Ukraine, which had inherited strategic nuclear weapons from the former Soviet Union, ratified START and joined the Nuclear Non-Proliferation Treaty as non-nuclear states (http://www.osia.mil/ pub_afrs/star. html, Dec. 10, 1998).

The START I talks led to the June 1992 "framework agreement" for the US-Russian Treaty on Further Reduction and Limitation of Strategic Offensive Arms (START II) signed by Presidents George Bush and Boris Yeltsin on January 1993. It includes the elimination of all ground-based, multiple-warhead intercontinental ballistic missiles (ICBMs, the area of greatest Russian investment and, arguably, advantage), while permitting the retention of substantial numbers of such missiles at sea (where the USA enjoys a substantial advantage) (Walker 1994).

Recently, codifying commitments made at the Helsinki Summit in March 1997, the United States and Russia signed a set of agreement related to START II on September 26, 1997 as part of a joint effort to obtain approval of the treaty by the Russian Duma. The START II extension protocol shifts the deadline for the completion of strategic nuclear force reductions by five years: from January 1, 2003 to December 31, 2007. In addition, Secretary of State Madeleine Albright and Russian Foreign Minister Yevgeniy Primakov exchanged letters formalizing the Helsinki commitment to "deactivate" by the end of 2003 all strategic nuclear delivery vehicles to be eliminated under START II.

The Open Skies Treaty, signed in March 24, 1992, in Helsinki, Finland, is to promote openness and transparency in military activities through reciprocal, unarmed observation overflights. Designed to enhance security confidence, the Treaty gives each signatory the right to gather information about the military forces and activities of other signatories. The Treaty specifies the maximum number of overflights that each signatory must accept annually. During the first three years of implementation, signatories must accept only 75 percent of their full quota. After full implementation, the United States is obligated to accept up to 42 flights per year.

It should be noted that one of the most important nuclear non-proliferation agreements in decades will be the Comprehensive Test Ban Treaty (CTBT) which was signed on September 24, 1996. The CTBT was negotiated over a period of two-and-a-half years in the Conference on Disarmament (CD) in Geneva. The purpose of the CTBT is to constrain the development and qualitative improvement of nuclear weapons; end the development of advanced new types of nuclear weapons; contribute to the prevention of nuclear proliferation and the process of nuclear disarmament; and to strengthen international peace and security. However, the CTBT was challenged by the nuclear tests conducted by India and Pakistan in May 1998. Right after the test, India said it would be prepared to consider being an adherent to some of the undertakings of the CTBT provided certain conditions were met. Pakistan has maintained it would be prepared to sign the CTBT if India does. To date, three of 44 CD members—India, Pakistan, and North Korea—have not yet signed.

The most recent development in the evolution of arms control is the Ottawa Landmine Convention signed by 121 states on December 3-4, 1997. Formally titled the Convention on the Prohibition of the Use, Stockpiling, Production and Transfer of Anti Personnel Mines and on Their Destruction, the Ottawa treaty is a succinct legal instrument that will obligate each state party to eliminate landmines from its offensive arsenal and territory within a time-bound framework, in addition to outlawing the use of such weapons. As of February 27, 1998, there were 124 signatories and five states parties to the treaty. However, many countries, including the United States, Russia and China as well as states in regions of tension such as the Middle East and South Asia, did not sign the treaty. Ultimately, the treaty's effectiveness as a global norm will depend on the actions of both non parties as well as states parties.

## 5. Reflections

It is evident that arms control—as opposed to disarmament—has been used as an instrument to assist in ensuring secure relations among states. Where disarmament has failed, arms control has attempted to succeed. But the security problem is not a simple one. Arms control alone does not suffice to solve it. Consequently arms control is a means to an end, and not an end in itself.

Arms control agreements risk becoming a perpetual phenomenon as weapons technology improves and new ideas bring innovations to the arsenals of nations. If this is so, have we learned from the available empirical evidence? In the absence of disarmament, both approaches to arms control seem crucial to world security.

Other arms control agreements, such as the ones governing strategic weapons limitation, have presented some questions as to their validity. But are there not positive aspects in such agreements? If not, should all arms control initiatives be judged upon the basis of one or two agreements? Here we should be cautious and perhaps decide whether the "whole is worth more than the sum of the parts."

See also: *Arms Race, Dynamics of; Disarmament and Development; Military Research and Development, Role of; Multilateralism; Strategic Weapons in the Cold War Era; Unilateralism*

*Bibliography*

Bertram C 1978 Arms control and disarmament technological changes: Elements of a new approach. *Adelphi Paper* 146

Bloomfield L P et al., 1965 *Soviet Interests in Arms Control and Disarmament: The Decade of Khrushchev 1954-1964.* Center for International Studies (Massachusetts Institute of Technology), Cambridge, Massachusetts

Brennan D G 1961 Setting objectives and goals of arms control. *Arms Control and Disarmament: American View and Studies.* Cape, London

Goodby J E 1985 Address before the American Association for the Advancement of Science in Los Angeles on May 30, 1985

Hong K J 1997 *The CSCE Security Regime Formation: An Asian Perspective.* Macmillan, London

Pipes R 1984 How to cope with the Soviet threat: A long term strategy for the West. *Commentary* 78(2)

Walker J 1994 *Security and Arms Control in Post-Confrontation Europe.* Oxford University Press, New York

United Nations Atomic Energy Commission 1947 *A.E.C.O.R., 2nd Year, Special Supplement.* Second report to the Security Council, Sept. 11

United Nations *Disarmament Commission* 1946-55 DC/SC. 1/PV. United Nations, New York

United States Arms Control and Disarmament Agency 1980 *Arms Control and Disarmament Agreements: Texts and History of Negotiations.* US Arms Control and Disarmament Agency, Washington, DC

Weinberger C W 1984 *Annual Report to the Congress: Fiscal Year 1985.* Department of Defense, Washington, DC

KI-JUN HONG; PÉRICLES GASPARINI ALVES

# Arms Control, Modeling of

## 1. Introduction

One of the first writers dealing with this subject (Saaty 1968) defined arms control as the attempt of States to impose arbitrary limits on the instruments and consequences of conflict. This included the possibility both of limited or of comprehensive disarmament or merely of arms limitation which may or may not constitute a reduction of forces. In this spirit, for our purposes we will generally only use the term arms control, using it in the broadest possible sense.

Quantitative models in the social sciences play a different role than those in the natural sciences. In particular in politics, they have to provide criteria to test for the existence of certain qualitative concepts. Examples for such concepts are stability and consistency which are basic to the interpretation of various interactions in human relations.

Models for arms control and disarmament, being of just such a quantitative nature, certainly have to include methods for the collection and processing of numbers of items and parameters. Examples of these are troops, tanks and aircraft; range, throw-weight and accuracy of missiles and many other factors that are somehow indicative of armament or disarmament efforts of States or alliances.

More important, however, is the fact that arms control models have to provide numerical information for the investigation of answers to questions like the following:

(a) What mutual states of armament represent equilibria?

(b) How stable are those equilibria?

(c) Which armament and arms control strategies enhance stability?

(d) Are there possibilities to attain stable equilibria eventually without a temporary destabilisation during the establishment of the respective systems?

These questions indicate that the concepts of *equilibrium* and *stability* are invariably connected with those of arms control (see *International Conflicts and Equilibria*). In fact, in addition to the many stability definitions in security politics, like arms race stability, crisis stability, first strike stability, there is also the idea of *arms control stability*. A stable arms control regime exists precisely when a participating State or alliance has no reason to fear that some other State or alliance will endanger its security by developing new weapons systems.

In order to characterize once more the role of formal models in arms control analysis, let us quote Mathematica authors (1963), who distinguish between the mathematical and the political styles of verification studies: "The mathematical style models the questions of inspection effort, cheating strategies, effectiveness within a given, closed, fully delineated set of conditions. These questions are studied, as a quantifiable relationship between the number of opportunities to violate and the number of inspections allowed (see *Game Theory*). The political style examines the psychological and political milieu within which the decisions to cheat or comply are made. Therefore, such complicating variables as incentive to cheat, incentive to detect, longer-term objectives, deterioration of existing weapons systems, political repercussions, and the domestic political system must be taken into account when assessing how much inspection is needed."

From a categorization point of view, arms control models may be classified as being either *static or dynamic*. The former define, mostly by means of some additive utility functions on both sides, indices which reflect the respective force capabilities. The latter take into account the dynamic interactions of the opposed forces in war in order to provide estimates of conflict outcomes.

The most prevalent form of analysis seems to be of the static type. However, static analysis results imply, among other things, a more or less symmetric situation on both sides, especially with regard to the opponents' geographic situations. This may be true for the nuclear armament of the superpowers, but it is clearly not a very realistic prerequisite in any kind of conventional confrontation on land. In addition, static analysis techniques are by their very nature incapable of addressing questions related to the stability of force balances. The main reason for their rather widespread use in spite of such shortcomings appears to be their inherent simplicity. The results are simple sums of numbers of items weighted by their marginal capability indices, the underlying assumptions of which are supposedly easy to check, at least in a formal sense. This is certainly not the case for the assumptions underlying most of the richer dynamic analysis models, in which items interact in more or less complex ways. Thus, for every analysis problem there is a tradeoff between the adequacy and the communicability of the model being used and its results.

The *methodological* tools which are used for formulating and analyzing arms control models are taken from the area of game theory, since that theory deals with conflict situations in general, from probability theory and statistics in order to take into account stochastic elements of any kind and finally from operations research in order to determine numerical solutions for equilibria, optimal policies etc. In particular simulation methods are used for the determination of outcomes of realistic warfare models.

Finally, arms control models may be classified according to their *purpose*. The first category, let us call them *basic* models, consists of very simple models, mostly using low-game theory in the sense of O'Neill (1989). These models try to explain fundamental features of arms control in general, such as trust and distrust, threat, communication and bargaining and so on. Second, there are very complicated models, let us call them *realistic*, which use highly complex simulation methods with thousands of input data. Their purpose is to support politicians domestically and diplomats taking part in international negotiations, demonstrating the consequences of concrete disarmament measures. In between, there are *special* models which deal with well-defined, but special problems, e.g., in the area of verification. They may turn out to be mathematically more sophisticated than the basic models, but less data and computer-oriented than the realistic category. In general, they cannot be applied to other problem areas (see *Field Diplomacy: A New Conflict Paradigm*).

Following the historical development, an overview will now be provided of all categories of arms control models mentioned here and published in the open literature: strategic and conventional arms control models which fall into the realistic category, as discussed above, will be treated generally, without describing their methodologies in detail. The basic and special models will be presented thereafter.

## 2. History

Typically, as pessimists may say, arms race models were developed first and disarmament models only later. L. Richardson (1939) formulated a system of differential equations for the general description of arms races and applied them to the naval arms race between England and Germany at the beginning of this century. It was probably only the confrontation of the superpowers after the second world war and in particular the pending danger of a global "all out"

nuclear war that stimulated arms control and disarmament efforts on a large scale and, as a by-product, the development of quantitative models (see *Arms Control, Evolution of*). Incidentally, just before that time, J. v. Neumann and O. Morgenstern (1953) published their seminal work which provided the methodological foundations for modeling of arms control.

Even though a large number of different approaches was worked out in the fifties, one may identify three essential sources for the subsequent development of quantitative arms control models. One of these sources involves the work of American social scientists, culminating in Schelling's book (1960), the influence of which is still to be felt: For the first time, central aspects of international conflicts, such as the establishment of arms control regimes, were analysed quantitatively with the help of game-theoretical methods. These aspects included threats and promises, communication and bargaining, surprise attack and disarmament, and the attention was drawn not only of a wider circle of scientists, but also of diplomats and politicians.

A second source is given by the research performed over a period of several years in the sixties by Mathematica scholars (1963, 1965) on behalf of the United States Arms Control and Disarmament Agency (USACDA). All aspects of arms control were treated with game theoretical and statistical methods. It should be mentioned that over the years, verification problems became the central issue of their work, and more theoretical aspects, such as the impact of incomplete information, were analyzed in considerable detail.

A third source of quantitative modeling is the development of battlefield models, starting with Lanchester's differential equations for attrition in battles (1914), and followed by a large amount of analytical and numerical work on models for conventional warfare, see e.g., Taylor (1983) and Huber (1990). This work formed the basis for the very elaborate computer simulation models for conventional arms control models, especially for the European theatre.

## 3. Strategic Arms Control Models

In view of the enormous destructive potential of nuclear weapons, in the beginning of the seventies static analyses of threats in form of comparisons of nuclear arsenals became less important than estimations of aggregated destructive power. The nuclear strategies of the superpowers developed over time in a complicated way. The central deterrence concept became the second strike capability (see *Deterrence*).

The adversary is deterred from a first strike, if the targeted power, after having suffered a first strike, still manages to keep enough forces to destroy the attacker (see *Deterrence*). So-called nuclear exchange models are studied. With their help, and on the basis of data of carrier systems, warheads accuracy etc., nuclear wars may be simulated by the computer. Simulations of this kind were performed on a large scale, both in military and in scientific circles, see, e.g., Akimov (1991) or Oelrich and Bracken (1988).

A reduction of nuclear arsenals can be achieved in peacetime by appropriate disarmament agreements, or in time of war, by use of global Ballistic Missile Defense (BMD) systems. In the former case a major problem, partly because of changing political conditions and technological progress, is the determination of stable upper limits. How much is enough ? The search for *sufficient* nuclear arsenals dominated the discussion of the eighties (see *Nuclear Strategy*). Obviously, the question of the nuclear deterrence in multipolar systems is even more complicated.

In 1983, United States' President Reagan, with his announcement of the Strategic Defense Initiative (SDI), opened a new era, one which may be interpreted as a move from mutual assured destruction to mutual assured survival, see, e.g., Bracken (1990). Apart from other problems, the introduction of such systems requires simultaneous steps of both superpowers in order to avoid transition instabilities: If only one side uses a partial BMD system, then it could be tempted to perform a first strike. The partial BMD system could reasonably be expected to counter the resulting second strike more effectively than a hypothetical first strike, to which it would of course be especially vulnerable, see e.g., Gronlund and Wright (1992).

In 1987, the Intermediate Nuclear Forces (INF) Treaty was signed by the two superpowers. This treaty foresaw the destruction of all land-based nuclear missiles with ranges between 500 and 5,500 km, and prohibited the production of new ones. After the end of the East-West confrontation new proposals for the disarmament of strategic forces were discussed on the basis of new models (see *Proliferation of Nuclear Weapons, Ending the*). New problems are now posed by the nuclear forces of the successor states of the former Soviet Union such as the Ukraine, Kazakstan and Belarus. After the success of the second Strategic Arms Reduction Talks (START-I) the search for lower limits of strategic forces for a mutual deterrence has become less important. Proposals have been worked out by the United States' Congressional Budget Office (1991), which extend from a

world without nuclear weapons up to reduced upper limits of 1,000, 3,000 or 6,000 warheads for each of the two superpowers (see *Disarmament and Development*).

## 4. Conventional Arms Control Models

The negotiations on Mutual Balanced Force Reductions (MBFR) in Europe, which were opened in Vienna in 1973, did not make any progress for many years. Therefore, it is not surprising that during that time no substantial arms control models for conventional forces were made public, even though detailed calculations were performed by all parties involved.

Only after the speech of Soviet Union's President Gorbachev at the United Nations General Assembly in 1988, when the new negotiations on the subject started, were calculations finally published. These negotiations, by the way, terminated successfully in the agreement on the Conventional Forces in Europe (CFE) Treaty in 1990. The purpose of the calculations was to demonstrate how far conventional forces might be reduced without affecting conventional (crisis) stability. They went beyond the determination of static force equilibria; in fact, potential battle scenarios and equivalent dynamic scenarios were taken into account. All these models assumed, in accordance with the North Atlantic Treaty Organization (NATO) (see *North Atlantic Treaty Organization (NATO)*) viewpoint, a conventional attack of Warsaw Treaty (WT) forces. Details of Soviet models were not published.

Posen (1989) investigated the problem of whether or not WT forces were able to defeat NATO defense units; he used an "Attrition Forward Edge of the Battle Area" method. For the estimation of the success of an attack he took into account factors like relative military strength, impact of air forces on ground battle, force-to-space-ratio, attrition and exchange rates, advancing speed of ground forces. Furthermore, various scenarios, for example the speed of mobilization, were considered.

Whereas Posen drew favorable conclusions for the NATO side, Thomson and Gantz (1987) got different results. Assuming that deterrence would work only if NATO forces could stop an attack after 40 km and could defend its lines for 30 days, they saw NATO with the force ratios as given at that time in a very difficult situation. Therefore, they advocated asymmetrical force reductions in the CFE negotiations in Vienna. Other models were published by Epstein (e.g., 1990), who developed his "Adaptive Dynamic Model" as an alternative to the Lanchester model. His work was used by the United States' Congressional Budget Office (1988) in order to test potential improvements of NATO defense in Europe.

## 5. *Prisoners' Dilemma*

Whereas in a concrete political situation there are many reasons for two States to arm or to disarm, a general explanation will take into account the observation that the benefits and costs to each other are dependent on what both States do. Hence, the conflict situation posed by the armament or disarmament race between two States has to be formulated as a non-cooperative two-person game in the sense of von Neumann and Morgenstern (1953). The game most frequently proposed as an appropriate model for this kind of conflict is the famous *Prisoners' Dilemma*.

Of course any model that assumes that States as players have only two strategies which lead to well-defined payoffs is a drastic oversimplification. However, this simplified model has the advantage that it exhibits, in a strikingly simple way, an explanation of the fundamental intractability of an arms race based only on rational behaviour by the participants.

The Prisoners' Dilemma may be described as follows: Let two potential adversaries, as stated, have only the two strategies, armament (A) or disarmament [$\overline{A}$]. Since the payoffs to the two States for all possible outcomes are measured in utilities, only their relative values matter. Thus, if the first nation arms and the second disarms, the first gets its best, and the second its worst payoff, $a_1$ and 0, or 0 and $a_2$ for the first and second State, respectively. If both States disarm, their payoffs are $b_1$ and $b_2$, and if both arm $c_1$ and $c_2$. It is assumed $a_i > b_i > c_i > 0$ for i = 1, 2. This produces the bimatrix game shown in Table 1.

In the original story that gives Prisoners' Dilemma its name, two persons suspected of being partners in a crime are arrested and placed in separate cells so that they cannot communicate with each other. Without a confession from at least one suspect, the district attorney does not have sufficient evidence to convict them for the crime. To try to extract a confession, the district attorney tells each suspect the consequence of their actions of confessing or not confessing, thus leading to the payoffs given in Table 1.

The solution of this game is defined as that pair of so-called equilibrium strategies that have the property, that any unilateral deviation does not improve (in general worsens) the payoff of the deviating side. Now it can be seen easily that (A, A) is such a pair of equilibrium strategies, and is in fact the only such pair. It leads to payoffs $(c_1, c_2)$. The unfortunate consequence is that both States, by choosing A, are

***Table 1*** The armament-disarmament game for two States. The arrows indicate the preference directions. (Arm, Arm) is the unique pair of equilibrium strategies

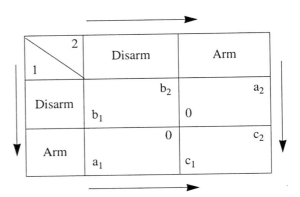

worse off than if they could somehow reach an arms control agreement and choose $\overline{A}$ instead, which would lead to a payoff of $(b_1, b_2)$, greater than $(c_1, c_2)$ for both. But this pair of strategies is unstable—it is not an equilibrium.

Is there another kind of logic that offers more hope? Not at first sight. Instead, the historical evidence at many occasions seems to give one little reason to be sanguine. On the contrary, the reasoning presented here seems to confirm the situation as it was and is. Nevertheless, optimists do not consider the situation as hopeless. Several variants have been proposed. One is to include the intelligence capabilities of the involved states, which allow predictions about the adversary's likely choices.

The most important variant has been discussed by Axelrod (1984) who considers the conflict not as a one step game, but rather as a sequence of games. In technical terms, he dealt with an extensive form game between the states which is played over time. Axelrod found that when many computer programs playing different strategies were matched against each other in computer tournament plays of Prisoners' Dilemma, the program playing *tit-for-tat* did better than any other program. The tit-for-tat strategy is to start out by cooperating, but to retaliate on the next round with non-cooperation if the other player does not cooperate initially—and then to imitate the opponent's previous-round behaviour in all subsequent plays. Tit-for-tat does better on average than most other strategies, including the one of never cooperating.

Prisoners' Dilemma and its many variants have been used very often for the explanation of military conflict of States in peace and war. Examples include the cease-fire negotiations of the United States and the former Soviet Union in the Yom Kipur War, and their nuclear arms race and disarmament efforts in the sixties and seventies, see, e.g., Brams (1985).

## 6. Verification

According to Kokoski and Koulik (1990) the objectives of the verification of arms control and disarmament agreements may be defined as follows: " The most obvious [purpose] is to *detect* violations of an agreement, thereby to provide early warning to deny any advantage to a violator. The second purpose is to *deter* violations by the fact that verification increases the risk of detection. The third main purpose is to *build confidence*, not only among treaty partners but also within domestic political communities. Finally, verification aims to *clarify uncertainty*."

The quantitative analysis of verification procedures seeks to determine optimal inspection schemes, ideally those which will induce the inspected party to legal behaviour, under the assumption that the potential illegal action is carried out strategically. Thus one considers a non-cooperative two-person game in which the two players are the inspection authority and inspected State.

Inspection games should be distinguished from two related topics: Inspection for quality control, or for prevention of other kinds of random accidents, for which there is no adversary acting strategically, and inspections that are search problems, where an adversary attempts to escape a searcher with well-defined and legitimate strategies, for example a submarine escaping a destroyer. Neither situation is described by an inspection game in the sense of arms control. The salient feature here is that the inspection authority tries to prevent the inspectee from behaving illegally in terms of the agreement.

Three phases of development in the application of such models to arms control and disarmament may be identified. In the first of these, roughly from 1961 through 1968, studies that focused on inspecting a nuclear test ban treaty emphasized game theory, with less consideration given to statistical aspects associated with data acquisition and measurement uncertainty. The second phase, from 1968 to about 1985, involved work stimulated by the Treaty on the Non-Proliferation of Nuclear Weapons (NPT). Here, the verification principle of material accountancy came to the fore, along with the need to include the formalism of statistical decision theory within the inspection models in order to cope with measurement errors of all kinds . The third phase, 1985 to the present, has been dominated by challenges posed by such far-

reaching verification agreements as the INF Treaty, the CFE Treaty and the Chemical Weapons Convention (CWC), as well as by perceived failures of the NPT system in Iraq and North Korea.

The sequential and the statistical verification models which were developed for NPT safeguards are mathematically too complicated for a short and intuitive exposition—in our previous classification scheme they would belong to the third rather than to the second category, see also Avenhaus et al., (1996). The CFE treaty on the other hand poses the problem of the allocation of limited numbers of inspections across sites associated with different utility for both sides. This problem is easier to handle and provides valuable insight. Therefore, it will be outlined here as an example.

Suppose that a State can choose to comply or to violate the CFE agreement either at site 1 or 2, and that the authority's inspector is committed to inspect at exactly one of the two sites. Take both players' utilities to be 0 if there is legal behaviour, and—$a_i$ to the inspector and—$b_i$ to the nation if there is a violation of the inspected site i, i = 1, 2. The violation is assumed in this case to be detected with certainty. If, on the other hand, there is a violation at site i but that site is not inspected, let the utilities be—$c_i$ to the inspector, and $d_i$ to the State. We assume $0 < a_i < c_i$ , $0 < b_i$ , $0 < d_i$ . This leads to the bimatrix game shown in Table 2.

Let us consider first the illegal game, i.e., the game where the State is determined to violate the agreement. Since the preference directions are circular, there exists an equilibrium only in *mixed strategies*. The State will violate at site 1 or 2 with probability q or 1-q, respectively. The inspector will inspect site 1 or 2 with probability p or 1-p, respectively. In equi-

*Table 2* A simple two-site inspection game. The arrows indicate the preference directions in the illegal game.

| State \ Inspector | Violate at 1 | Violate at 2 | Comply |
|---|---|---|---|
| Inspect 1 | $-b_1$ / $-a_1$ | $+d_2$ / $-c_2$ | 0 / 0 |
| Inspect 2 | $+d_1$ / $-c_1$ | $-b_2$ / $-a_2$ | 0 / 0 |

librium, these probabilities are given by

$$p = \frac{d_1 + b_2}{d_1 + b_1 + d_2 + b_2}, \quad q = \frac{c_1 - a_2}{c_1 - a_1 + c_2 - a_2},$$

the equilibrium payoffs to the inspector and to the State are, furthermore,

$$I_1 = \frac{c_1 c_2 - a_1 a_2}{c_1 - a_1 + c_2 - a_2}, \quad I_2 = \frac{d_1 d_2 - b_1 b_2}{d_1 + b_1 + d_2 + b_2}.$$

Now let us take into account the possibility that the State will comply. This in fact occurs, if the State's expected utility in case of compliance is larger than in the case of violation. This in turn is true if

$$b_1 b_2 > d_1 d_2,$$

i.e., if the sanctions to the State in case of detected violation are larger than the gains in case of undetected violation. It should be mentioned that here, the equilibrium probabilities of inspection are not unique. Rather, the probability of inspection at site 1 is given by the range

$$\frac{d_1}{b_1 + d_1} < p < \frac{b_2}{b_2 + d_2}.$$

Since the equilibrium probability of inspecting site 1 in the illegal game lies in this interval, the inspector is well advised to keep that probability in order to cover all possibilities.

This simple site selection game, which is due to Kilgour (1992) has been generalized in many directions: More than two sites, imperfect inspection, more than just one inspected site etc.; see, e.g., Avenhaus and Canty (1996). However, this simple game already shows how "political" parameters, such as level of punishment (sanctions) for a detected violation, can affect behaviour. When the situation is favourable, there can be considerable flexibility in the technical choice of where to inspect; in unfavourable circumstances the inspector may not be able to deter violations, but only to minimize their impact.

## 7. Conclusion

Are formal arms control models of any use for the progress of arms control itself? Are there examples which explicitly demonstrate their value? Or, on the contrary, are there important aspects which the models developed thus far have not taken into account? What has to be done in the future?

It is difficult to answer these questions if, for example, one has in mind the negotiations of the two superpowers on the reduction of their strategic arsenals, since only the results of these negotiations were made public. In case of the negotiations on conventional forces, for example those leading to the CFE Treaty, there are pessimistic views which dispute any measurable contribution of models like those described above to the success of such negotiations. Nevertheless, figures have been fixed in the CFE Treaty, which could not have been achieved without any supporting quantitative argument.

Put more strongly, very detailed provisions, like those on verification, cannot be agreed upon if there are no quantitative concepts. These results are less spectacular, of course, being quite technical in nature. Thus the questions raised above tend to miss the point.

An answer to the last two questions has been given by O'Neill (1995) who defended formal (game) models against the argument that goes along the lines: "If they even do not apply to a simple context like gambling, they must be irrelevant to complicated international issues." O'Neill replies by saying: "In fact, they clarify international problems exactly because they are more complicated. Unlike card games the rules of interaction are uncertain, the aims of the actors are debatable and even basic terms of discourse are obscure. What does it mean to show resolve? What constitutes escalation ? What assumptions imply that cooperation will emerge from international anarchy? The contribution of (game) models is to sort out concepts and figure out what the game might be."

See also: *World Peace Order, Dimensions of a; Economics of Disarmament: Certain Premises; Emerging Tool Chest for Peacebuilders*

*Bibliography* —————————————————

Akimov V 1991 Strategic stability and the "ASK" computer system (in Russian). *Nauka* 2
Avenhaus R, Canty M 1996 *Compliance Quantified—An Introduction to Verification Theory.* Cambridge University Press, Cambridge, UK
Avenhaus R, Canty M, Kilgour M, Stengel B V, Zamir S 1996 Inspection games in arms control. Invited Review, *European J. Oper. Res.* 90
Axelrod R 1984 *The Evolution of Cooperation.* Basic Books, New York
Bracken J 1990 Stable transitions from mutual assured destruction to mutual assured survival. *Canadian J. Information*

*Systems and Oper. Res.* 28

Brams S 1985 *Superpower Games*. Yale University Press. New Haven and London

CBO 1988 Congressional Budget Office, *U.S. Ground Forces and the Conventional Balance in Europe*. Washington, DC

CBO 1991 Congressional Budget Office, *The START Treaty and Beyond*. Washington, DC

Epstein J 1990 *Conventional Force Reductions—A Dynamic Assessment*. The Brookings Institution, Washington, DC

Gronlund L, D Wright 1992 Depressed trajectory submarine launched ballistic missile: A technical evaluation and arms control possibilities. *Science and Global Security* 1-2

Huber R K (ed.) 1990 *Military Stability : Prerequisites and Analysis Requirements for Conventional Stability in Europe*. Nomos, Baden-Baden

Kilgour D M 1992 Site selection for on-site selection in arms control. *Arms Control* 13

Kokoski R, Koulik S (eds.) 1990 *Verification of Conventional Arms Control in Europe*. Westview Press, Boulder and London

Mathematica 1963 *Applications of Statistical Methodology to Arms Control and Disarmament*. Final Report, submitted to the USACDA under Contract No. ACDA/ST-3 by Mathematica Inc., Princeton, NJ

Mathematica 1965 *The Application of Statistical Methodology to Arms Control and Disarmament*. Final Report, submitted to the USACDA under Contract No. ACDA/ST-37 by Mathematica Inc., Princeton, NJ

v Neumann J, O Morgenstern 1953 *Theory of Games and Economic Behavior*, 3rd edn. Princeton University Press, Princeton

Oelrich I, J Bracken 1988 A Comparison and Analysis of Strategic Defense, Transition Stability Models. Institute for Defense Analysis, *IDA Paper* P-2145, Washington, DC

O'Neill B 1989 Game theory and the study of deterrence of war. In: Stern P, Axelrod R, Jervis R, Radner R (eds.) *Perspective in Deterrence*. Oxford University Press, New York

O'Neill B 1994 A survey of game theory models on peace and war. In : R Aumann, S Hart (eds.) *Handbook of Game Theory*, Vol.II. Elsevier, Amsterdam

Posen B R 1989 Correspondence : Reassessing net assessment. *Int'l Security* 13 (4)

Saaty Th 1968 *Mathematical Models of Arms Control and Disarmament-Application of Mathematical Structures in Politics*. Wiley, New York

Schelling Th 1960 *The Strategy of Conflict*. Harvard University Press, Cambridge, Mass

Taylor J G 1983 *Lanchester Models of Warfare*, Vol I and II. Military Applications Section, Operations Research Society of America, Arlington, VA

Thomson J A, Gantz N 1987 *Conventional Arms Control Revisited Objectives in the New Phase*. The RAND Corporation, Santa Monica, CA

RUDOLF AVENHAUS

# Arms Conversion

## 1. Background and Status

Insofar as there is a popular notion of the concept of arms conversion it is generally associated with that of beating swords into plowshares, an idea derived from old Testament prophecies and one which offers the vision of a society without war, where military industries and armed forces could be turned to peaceful purposes. There is, though, no widely accepted formal definition of "arms conversion" in recent history. Most scholars on western Europe have generally used the abbreviated term "conversion" while reference to arms conversion itself is most widespread in the United Kingdom. In the United States the phrase most commonly used by writers on the subject is that of "economic conversion." To avoid confusion these terms must be carefully differentiated from related concepts like "diversification" and, indeed, "economic conversion" in the broader, non-military sense of the phrase. This lack of harmonization amongst the various terms used in the literature

has been noted in a major review by Albrecht (Wallensteen 1978).

Arms conversion (conversion or economic conversion) refers to the process by which a part of the military-industrial capacity would move completely from military to civilian activities. It is a special case of a process which is going on in the economy all the time, embracing the broader definition of economic conversion, whereby a part or all of given industries firms, and other facilities are changed from one set of activities to a completely different set in response to shifts in the structure of total demand, public and private. As opposed to arms conversion, diversification involves the entry of a firm into a substantially different business field, either through internal changes or through acquisition, without abandoning its original business field. In the case of military firms this implies alternating military and non-military work to fill excess capacity.

The difficulties over terminology combined with an understanding that the nature of arms conversion must alter with changing military technologies, as well as economic and political circumstances, necessitates applying the term to an historically specific period if more than a very abstract notion of the concept is to be achieved. Since the end of the Second World War, interest in arms conversion has, at various stages, been greater than ever before and it is this period which will, therefore, form the background to a modern treatment of the subject. This interest has been engendered by the establishment of permanent war industries in the major, industrialized countries, particularly in the United States and the former Soviet Union, to support a global arms race of unprecedented size and strength (Ball arid Leitenberg 1983, United Nations 1982). Since, in the early 1960s, just seven countries accounted for about 85 percent of global military expenditure, increasing concern was expressed that the main industrialized countries could not afford to disarm because too many vested interests depended on the maintenance of defense spending and the arms industries. The literature that emerged as a result was concentrated in just a few countries, most notably the United States, but with significant contributions later from the Scandinavian countries, the former Federal Republic of Germany, the United Kingdom and Benelux countries. Soviet discussion of the subject tended to be limited to either western problems in converting arms industries or the link with development issues. This latter aspect has brought about, especially through the United Nations, a continuing interest in conversion from underdeveloped countries for whom global disarmament might be expected to hold out the prospect of increased development assistance from the developed states. However, it must be stressed, that most arms conversion literature relates to the western market economies. The comparable structure of the main defense industries in these economies, despite the much greater size of the United States defense sector, allows these countries, in general terms, to draw on each other's conversion studies and experience.

A brief mention should be made of the "reconversion" experiences of the United Sates and the United Kingdom after the end of the Second World War when millions of men and women in the armed forces were demobilized while millions more, engaged in arms manufacture, were either transferred to civilian production or left the labor force entirely. (The term reconversion is, on the whole, more appropriate in this context since many firms and other facilities returned to civilian activities in which they had previously been engaged before the war began.) These experiences demonstrated that where favorable circumstances pre-

vail a disarmament program of far greater proportions than would now be entailed could be implemented without causing an economic depression. However none of the factors prevailing in 1945 are present today including: a backlog of demand arising from the war years; savings running at high levels due to lack of wartime spending opportunities; political commitment and a planning apparatus to support the reconversion program; a climate of postwar optimism and radicalism, while this is not to say that arms conversion programs cannot or will not be carried out, it is necessary to emphasize that the question should be examined in the context of more recent history.

Growing worldwide anxiety about the nuclear and conventional arms race on which technology is the driving force, and the consequent emergence of modern peace movements in many of the western democracies, provided the impetus—from the late 1950s and especially the 1960s, for many studies on the economics of disarmament and arms conversion. The literature, with substantial inputs from the peace research and United Nations traditions as well as government experts, was mostly technical in nature in that it assumed that the political will for disarmament or major reductions on military spending existed and so proceeded to investigate the economic consequences and how they might best be handled, the empirical studies in the 1960s and early 1970s were usually based, as would be expected, on a Keynesian macroeconomic approach. Saltman (1972) in a review of this research, covering some 160 different publications, pointed to the overwhelming consensus that the economic problems of disarmament could be successfully met as long as there was sufficient advance planning. This would be required to deal with the two main problems attendant upon disarmament; and meeting structural adjustments affecting the regions and industries in which defense work is concentrated. Such planning, in which the role of governments would be paramount, would not only avert economic disaster but would ensure unprecedented growth and development, nationally and internationally, directed at civilian needs. These studies, she added, reveal how over time the economic feasibility of conversion has been gradually replaced as the focal point of concern by a deep recognition that political feasibility is the major problem.

This literature reached its zenith in the mid-1960s, before the United States became fully involved in the Indochina war. Thereafter the number of studies declined until the prospect of a "peace dividend" arising from American withdrawal in the early 1970s renewed interest in the economics of disarmament and arms conversion. In the event there were few economic gains for the United States as inflation and new military equipment programs absorbed much of the potential peace dividend.

However by this time a new strand of defense economics was being developed which was to have an important impact on approaches to conversion. Previously, studies on the economics of disarmament had pointed to the alternative uses of military expenditure in meeting human needs and overcoming social deprivation but they had given scant attention to the apparently harmful long-run consequences of high levels of military spending on the economy. The view that military spending is good for the economy and jobs was to be increasingly challenged from the mid to late 1960s onwards. Econometric analysis was used by many economists, within and outside the peace research tradition, to explore various aspects of this matter and formed a major part of Albrecht's review of conversion literature (Wallensteen 1978). This review examined not only the various methodologies employed in econometric analysis but also those used in focusing on the political and social problems of conversion. He, too, noted the paucity of studies on the most formidable conversion problem: the political one.

Melman's work (1974), although not dependent on econometric analysis itself, provides one of the most comprehensive theories of conversion linking the damaging economic and social consequences of the arms race to the need for economic conversion from military to civilian activities. The findings of econometric studies, by no means unanimous or conclusive, can provide only partial support for Melman's thesis which, unlike many earlier conversion studies, covers every aspect of the issue including political, ideological, and motivational factors as well as economic, industrial, and technological questions. His many books and articles pertaining to conversion span a period of about 25 years and have been a significant influence on the United States and, probably, beyond.

The arms conversion perspective was implicitly and explicitly criticized during the latter half of the 1960s onwards by Marxists who argued that high military spending was essential to the maintenance of a capitalist system in the United States. Melman (1974) confronted the "monopoly capitalism" thesis of Baran and Sweezy, which was one of the first of various under-consumptionist theories developed in the Marxist tradition. The more advanced of these theories, for instance that of Reich (discussed by Albrecht in Wallensteen 1978), argued a propensity, rather than a necessity, for arms production in a capi-

talist society and formed a part of the debate during this period about the military-industrial complex and the extent to which the combined interests of military institutions and defense establishments can exert influence over the civilian government. The implications of these interrelated matters have a bearing on what Albrecht calls "systemic compatibility" (Wallensteen 1978), that is, the degree of change acceptable to the social system. So if high military spending were essential to the capitalist economic system or if the military-industrial complex were not amenable to democratic control then arms conversion plans could never be implemented. On the whole, though, most scholars, including some Marxist ones, are agreed that neither of these extreme propositions hold true. Nevertheless these theories do suggest some causes of the political difficulties in implementing conversion programs.

A major new perspective was brought to bear on the arms conversion question as a result of the activities of shop stewards and workers at Lucas Aerospace, a major United Kingdom aerospace manufacturer with heavy reliance on defense work. In 1976 the Lucas Aerospace combine shop stewards committee announced its alternative corporate plan, the centerpiece of its strategy to reverse the drastic decline on jobs at their company and to counter the threat of further job losses as a result of cutbacks of various military contracts (Wainwright and Elliott 1982). The Lucas plan proposed a range of alternative "socially useful" products which the company could work on using mostly existing skills and equipment rather than making further workers redundant. Although management rejected the plan, and no alternative civilian production occurred, it did provide an important model for conversion activity which not only stimulated other trade unionists to initiate conversion campaigns, in the United Kingdom and abroad, but provided a new worker-oriented, microeconomic approach to arms conversion activities to supplement the previous emphasis on macroeconomic issues. It also highlighted the problem of managerial lack of interest in, or opposition to, diversification or conversion programs. Finally, it provided a new link between labor and peace movement activists and the beginnings of a fruitful dialogue where previously there had often been mistrust and misunderstanding.

In the most recent phase in the development of ideas on arms conversion, from the late 1970s and into the 1980s, the level of interest in conversion planning and policies has been greater than at any time since the mid-1960s while the sophistication of the related analysis has also been much greater, scholarly works, like that of Tuomi and Vayrynen (1983), not only linked the economic consequences of the arms race to the economics of disarmament but began to place greater emphasis on acquiring a detailed knowledge of the defense industry which is itself the focus of conversion efforts. The data collected on national defense industries was increasingly disaggregated, reflecting in part the greater interest in company- and factory-based conversion initiatives. One notable study not only compared the structure of the main Western and Eastern defense industries, within the constraints of state and commercial secrecy, but included sections on those of smaller and developing countries as well (Ball and Leitenberg 1983). Again, though the political barriers to arms conversion were regarded as serious in many of the countries investigated although conversion of military resources to civilian purposes was economically feasible.

The United Nations (1982) study on the relationship between disarmament and development was the most detailed examination of disarmament issues carried out to date by that organization. It concluded that military expenditures have a generally negative effect on the economy through preventing investment in civilian projects, reducing development assistance, creating less employment than investment in the civilian sector, contributing to inflation, and distorting research and development work. The Secretary-General's Expert Group advocated a policy of linking disarmament with development so as to reduce tensions between East and West while creating opportunities for a dialogue between North and South. Moreover, conversion was held to be technically and economically feasible and governments were recommended to plan in advance the transfer of resources from the military to the civilian sector.

As a direct result of this study the Swedish government appointed its own special expert to undertake a similar project from a national perspective. A very thorough report was produced on two volumes (Thorsson 1984 and 1985) which is one of the most comprehensive commissioned by any national government since various United States government studies, especially those of the United States Arms Control and Disarmament Agency, were sponsored to investigate the economics of disarmament in the 1960s and early 1970s. The Swedish government's expert concluded that the effects of disarmament would be manageable, provided defense-sector conversion was well-planned and carried out gradually. The expert argued that government, defense producers, and unions all needed to be involved on this process, adopting a long-term perspective. Thorsson

(1985) contains a review by Ball of conversion experience outside of Sweden in which the major conversion-related problems confronting national and local governments, specific industries, and defense employees are discussed, drawing on available research since the early 1960s.

However it should not be thought that the critical attitudes adopted toward arms conversion in earlier years have disappeared even within the peace research tradition. Oberg argued (Tuomi and Vayrynen 1983) that as long as conversion was set in the context of existing notions of a weapons-based national security concept it was very unlikely to lead to disarmament. It needed to be seen not as an independent goal of its own but as a substrategy in a wider framework encompassing a changed attitude among decision makers as to what security is about, democratic control over those social forces behind the armaments build-up, and development achieved through structural transformation and dissolution of those destructive elements which result in war.

Despite the extensive literature which has emerged since the late 1950s, pertaining to conversion matters, little progress has been made so far in implementing arms conversion programs. In part this is a reflection of the lack of success at the international level in achieving disarmament or even many arms control agreements. However, while there are only isolated examples of defense-industry conversion, the office of Economic Adjustment in the United States Department of Defense (president's Economic Adjustment Committee 1981) can claim many successful military-base economic adjustment projects over a 20-year period. This was achieved with only limited technical resources and no capital funds of its own. The need for conversion planning, though, has not yet gained widespread acceptance in the United States or elsewhere.

## 2. Programs and Accomplishments (1985-1996)

Nevertheless, in the last few years an economic conversion movement has arisen in the United States and in some parts of Western Europe (Gordon and McFadden 1984). These grassroots campaigns have, in the United States, provided a degree of popular support which, while still of very limited strength, has been much less evident and organized over the long period, traced by Leitenberg, stretching back to 1963 of failed efforts to persuade congress to enact conversion legislation (Tuomi and Vayrynen 1983). While current proposals in congress still have a long way to go. Dumas argues that such legislation has a potentially pivotal role to play (Gordon and McFadden 1984).

The International Economic Conversion Conference held in Boston, Massachusetts in June 1984 brought together trade unionists, peace activists, and representatives from churches and groups working for economic justice. Participants came from 13 different countries. While the significance of this international meeting should not be exaggerated, it did at least demonstrate beyond doubt that job losses in the defense industries, occurring anyway because of the increasingly capital- and technology-intensive nature of the business and altered procurement requirements, had produced a common interest between some workers, who no longer regarded military spending as the source of economic security—and peace activists, who through adopting a policy of economic conversion hoped to win the support of defense workers and others for disarmament. Currently conversion policies and strategies are being adopted more widely within various peace and labor movement campaigns. The Freeze campaign, in the United States, unilateral nuclear disarmament in the United Kingdom and various trade union campaigns to save jobs in several Western countries have all, to differing extents, included arms conversion as a part of their overall strategy. The work of the Boston Study Group in the United States and the Alternative Defence Commission in the United Kingdom, both involving a different approach to questions of national security and defense policy, has included some attention to the jobs impact and the question of alternative employment.

Most activities inspired by the Lucas workers' plan have taken place in the United Kingdom (Thorsson 1985). At various times since the late 1970s workers at Vickers (involved in tank manufacture), the Royal Dockyards, and a Royal Ordinance Factory have been involved in Lucas-type initiatives. The most recent project, the Barrow Alternative Employment committee, has employed a full-time worker to help shop stewards at Vickers Shipbuilding and Engineering consider defense conversion potential in the event of cancellation of the Trident nuclear missile program, as the shipyard at Barrow-in-Furness would be heavily involved on building the submarines. The Alternative Employment Study Group, which is community- rather than workplace-based, is also assessing the employment impact, on the Clyde Submarine Base and the local economy, of the United Kingdom abandoning its independent nuclear force. Other projects have been supported in London by the Greater London conversion council, a local government organization with trade union, peace movement, and technical representation which has also commissioned research into the local defense industry. Further research support for conversion-related activities has been undertaken by the School of Peace Studies, University of Bradford, which has produced several peace research reports on various aspects of this subject. In other parts of Europe significant conversion research has been carried out by the International Peace Research Institute in Oslo the Tampere Peace Research Institute in Helsinki, and the universities of Bremen and Hamburg supported by I. G. Metall, the German metalworkers' union.

The future of this embryonic conversion movement, nationally and internationally, remains an open question. However the significance of arms conversion itself to the broader issues of peace and security seems to be threefold: firstly, it provides a basis for a wider definition of the concept of security, at national and global levels, by giving greater priority to economic security and the need to reduce excessive military spending in order to meet human and development needs; secondly, conversion planning is needed to reduce political opposition to disarmament, especially from within the military-industrial complex, by demonstrating that viable alternatives to military production exist; finally, even before disarmament occurs it is desirable, from the point of view of society as a whole, that wherever possible human and technical resources be transferred from military to peaceful purposes in order to secure jobs and improve the prospects of the civilian economy. While views differ as to the centrality of arms conversion amidst the many other pressing social and peace issues of our time, its significance has clearly been enhanced by the way it has been linked—in several western countries, to various disarmament and labor movements and brought within the ambit of the alternative defense and industrial policies which some political and research organizations are developing.

## 3. Effects and Implications (1985-date)

The Bonn International Center for Conversion has monitored arms conversion in the last 15 years or so and has come up with a list of effects of conversion activities.

### 3.1 Reallocation of Financial Resources

Conversion may contribute to fostering the disarmament process and strengthening the political will to reallocate financial resources to non-military use. Global military expenditures decreased by 30 percent between 1985-94 average and the year 1995, when they amounted to about US$697 billion. The reductions were most pronounced in Eastern Europe including Russia, Africa, Western Asia and Western Europe. If one adds up to annual differences between military expenditures in 1986-1994 and the peak of US$1.2 trillion reached in 1986, one arrives at savings of about US$1.5 trillion. The prospect of these savings generated hopes in the late 1980s for a peace dividend that would be available for distribution, both domestically and internationally. Unfortunately these savings were partly illusory and partly lost in economic recessions. Reductions in military efforts also produce costs that partially offset military expenditure reductions. Such costs include pensions for demobilized soldiers, unemployment benefits, investment in base reuse and funds for weapons disposal. The net savings have predominantly been used not for purposes advocated by proponents of the peace dividends such as increases in social expenditures or development aid. In Germany, they became part of the investment in unification. The most frequent use appears to have been reduction of government deficits. Interestingly, the use of savings from military expenditures adds considerable support to the view that a peace dividend exists not in the short run or detectable through reallocation within government budgets, but rather in the long run and observable through increases in the growth of economies and the welfare of individuals.

### 3.2 Reorientation of Military Research and Development

Military research and development (R&D) was at the heart of the technological arms race between East and West and still plays an important role in the modernization of armaments. Although detailed comparative figures on R&D are not publicly available, it is undisputed that military R&D is a major employer of scientific and technical personnel. Of the 5-7 million persons engaged in R&D worldwide in 1990, approximately 1.5 million were working in the military sector. At that time military R&D expenditures amounted to an estimated 12 percent of total military expenditures, thus equaling about US$110 billion worldwide. About 80 percent of the finances and personnel involved were accounted for during the Cold War period by the United States and the USSR alone. The significant change since 1990, as a result of the collapse of the former Soviet Union, has been a drastic reduction of the former Soviet Union's military R&D.

A number of Western countries also had to reduce their military R&D spending because of budget constraints. In contrast to procurement expenditures for weapons production, which fell significantly, cuts in R&D expenditure were moderate. This trend is the result of a policy of trying to maintain the capacity to develop state-of-the-art weapon systems while reducing the weapon building-rate. Programs for reorientation of military R&D can contribute to a number of different fields, including two of the major global challenges: underdevelopment and environmental pollution.

### 3.3 Conversion of Defense Industry

The changing security environment and general economic decline which precipitated the end of the Cold War have had tremendous implications for the nature and scale of defense production worldwide. Reductions in military expenditures beginning in the mid-1980s as a result of budgetary pressures and a reduction in East-West tensions have led not only to a significant decline in the global trade in conventional weapons and domestic procurement, with concomitant reductions in defense industrial employment, but also in many cases to a shrinkage in the overall size of the industry—through mergers and acquisitions, shutdowns, and diversification—and a reevaluation of its very nature and relation to commercial production. Employment in defense-related industry has declined from a 1987 high of 17.3 million to less than 11 million at present, with further redundancies only a matter of time.

This contraction in the market for military hardware and the resulting redundancies in defense-related employment have led to a variety of responses on the part of governments, firms and individual workers, in an effort to effectively redeploy resources to new and productive ends. This process, whether termed 'conversion,' 'diversification,' or 'industrial restructuring,' has met with mixed results. The imperative conversion—those underlying issues which made its consideration relevant immediately following the end of the Cold War—remains untouched.

### 3.4 Demobilization and Reintegration of Military Personnel into Civilian Life

The total number of armed forces worldwide has declined considerably over the past decade. The rising trend of the early 1980s continued from 28.2 million people in 1985 to its high of 28.8 million in 1987. Since then, the global trend has been downward, to 23.5 million in 1995, and an estimated 22.7 million in 1996. So, in one decade, the world's armies declined by more than six million soldiers or 21 percent. The largest troop reductions in the last decade took place in the region as of Americas and Europe. In absolute terms, the countries with the largest cuts were China, Iraq, Russia, Vietnam, and the United States. In relative terms, however, other countries also implemented significant demobilization, such as El Salvador, Eritrea, Ethiopia, Namibia, Nicaragua, and Mozambique, where more than half of the armed forces have been demobilized. Haiti mobilized its regular armed forces in 1995.

The reduction of the number of people employed by the military and their reintegration into civilian life has been seen as an important aspect of conversion. As in other facets of conversion, the positive impact of demobilization is neither automatic nor straightforward. The process clearly has its costs and benefits. In most countries that reduce the number of military personnel, special efforts are made to assist ex-combatants in returning to civilian life, in such a way that they do not become a security risk and that their skills benefit society.

### 3.5 Military Base Closure and Redevelopment

Military base closures have become a fact of life for thousands of communities wordwide as countries reduce military expenditures and armed forces. The closure of military facilities reduce the employment and income levels of affected regions inducing political pressure on governments to avoid closure or on local leaders to quickly replace the economic stimulus of a closed base. Obstacles to recovery include the presence of environmental contamination and abandoned military-specific infrastructures. In the long run communities benefit from the additional land and infrastructure that become available for civilian purposes.

There are implications of arms conversion in the post-Cold War era and these are recognized by military-oriented research outfits such as the BICC, as explained above. The calculus of arms conversion can be both economic or non-economic. Social implications are difficult to measure objectively except perhaps for those conversion schemes that redirect resources from the military to civilian sectors in terms of social services provisions. Nonetheless, the peace dividend advocates are able to stress that arms conversion do in fact help in increasing the society's capacity to provide for social projects and services as a result of arms conversion.

See also: *Alternative Defense; Disarmament and Development; Militarism and Militarization; Military-Industrial Complex*

### Bibliography

Ball N, Leitenberg M (eds.) 1983 *The Structure of the Defense Industry.* Croom Helm, Beckenham

Bonn International Center for Conversion 1998 Military Expenditures and Defense Budgets. http://bicc.uni-bonn.de/budget/budget.html

Gordon S, McFadden D (eds.) 1984 *Economic Conversion: Revitalizing America's Economy.* Ballinger, Cambridge, Massachusetts

Melman S 1974 *The Permanent War Economy: American Capitalism in Decline.* Simon and Schuster, New York

President's Economic Adjustment Committee 1981 *Twenty Years of Civilian Reuse: Summary of Completed Military Base Economic Adjustmemt Projects, 1961-1981.* Washington, DC

Saltman J 1972 The economic consequences of disarmament. *Peace Res. Rev.* IV(5)

Thorsson I 1984, 1985 *In Pursuit of Disarmament—Conversion from Military to Civil Production in Sweden.* Liber, Stockholm

Tuomi H, Vayrynen R (eds.) 1983 *Militarization and Arms Production.* Croom Helm, Beckenham

United Nations, Report of the Secretary-General 1982 *The Relationship between Disarmament and Development* A/36/356. United Nations, New York

Wainwright H, Elliott D 1982 *The Lucas Plan: A New Trade Unionism in the Making.* Allison and Bushy, London

Wallensteen P (ed.) 1978 *Experiences in Disarmament.* Report No. 19. Uppsala University, Uppsala

PETER SOUTHWOOD; PEDRO B. BERNALDEZ

# Arms Race, Dynamics of

Arms races are historically and situationally conditioned. They are rooted in a given sociopolitical reality, take place in a specific cultural-psychological climate, and evolve in accordance with the level of material-economic advancement of the society in question. Therefore, their comprehension requires discrimination and concrete apposition in the socio-historical setting, in time, and in space. Crucial in this context is the state of technological development of society, especially the level of military technology.

In the course of the 20th century arms races and armaments continued unabated, though at time with different intensity, vigor and context, in line with the historico-political and economic circumstances, with shifting alliances and changing pairs of adversaries. Arms races preceded World War I, persisted fiercely in the interwar period, erupted with high bellicosity in the Cold War (see *Cold War*) era, to roll on in a more temperate fashion in the post-Cold War time, nurtured by the Cold War residuals and the new challenges of a turbulent multipolar world. The enduring trend throughout the century was the acquisition and employment of ever more sophisticated and deadly weapons technology.

A powerful boost to weapon modernization and proliferation in the 1990s came from the experiences and lessons of the Gulf War. Both successes and failures in the employment of most advanced conventional weaponry—in space, air, land and sea—resulted in a strong urge to modernize existing and develop new weapon systems. A new technological spiral in the arms race ensued.

In the political and historical literature, arms race rationales—their motivation, causation, and dynamics—are usually attributed to sets of interrelated material and behavioral factors. Most current are five theorems:

(a)  imperial and national rivalries, power politics, and expansionist schemes;

(b)  security dilemmas caused by real or tenuous, perceptionally internalized fears of aggressive or revindicative intentions on the part of neighbors or major powers;

(c)  systemic competition of a sociopolitical, ideological, or religious nature;

(d)  profit and vested interests related to pressures from the "military-industrial complex," and

(e)  the technological momentum driven by the push of modern military technology.

Obviously, such a complex phenomenon as arms races cannot be explained in a reductionist way, restricting motivation, causation, and dynamics to one class of agents only. Different stimulants tend to combine, interact, and overlap, even if at times one particular motive force may predominate. Also, there are a number of dependent functional variables common to almost all types of arms races: these include the inertia of bureaucratic structures, and the interactive dynamics of action-reaction and overreaction. Related to all theorems as well is the contingent impact of idiosyncratic, behavioral-psychological, and perceptual factors produced and shaped in the heat of confrontation. Threat perceptions, enemy images, extreme self-righteousness—these are some of the salient traits of the virulent dependent phenomena in the political-doctrinal superstructure of arms races.

Primary armaments determinants can be roughly divided into two categories: of an internal and external nature. With reference to the five arms theorems listed above, the first three can generally be classified as related to externally generated races, and the last two as related rather to races internally impelled. Given the weight of the particular factors, contemporary arms races between developed industrial countries would seem to be largely internally determined. Vested sociopolitical interests (military-industrial complex) (see *Military-Industrial Complex*) and the technological drive (military research and development) (see *Military Research and Development, Role of*) combine to produce a powerful self-sustaining armaments momentum. The impact from the international environment-technological competition, systemic-ideological variables, as well as threat perceptions—further heighten the vehemence of the race. Characteristically enough, international influences designed to decelerate the arms race—such as arms control agreements or the policy of détente—have not been in a position to countervail the force of internal impulsion. In recent decades, the arms race has continued, despite arms control negotiations and moments of détente (see *Détente*).

World military expenditures in 1985—according to *SIPRI Yearbook 1986*—amounted to US$663 billion (at 1980 prices and exchange rates) with the share of NATO being 49.4% and of the Warsaw Treaty Organization (WTO) 24.1%. In the following years world military expenditures grew considerably to flatten and decline in the post-Cold War period, primarily because of the collapse of the Soviet Union and the disintegration of the WTO. However, NATO expenditures remained approximately near the pre-Cold War level (see attached table) (see *North Atlantic Treaty Organization (NATO)*). At the same time military expenditures of the developing countries mushroomed vigorously. Reliable data for Russia and the Commonwealth of Independent States was absent because of high inflation, volatile exchange rates and lack of conclusive statistics. Yet Russian arms continued to flow into the world market. In fact, armaments persisted to have a distinct impact on international relations, not least because of the accumulation of large stocks of nuclear weapons. According to *SIPRI Yearbook 1996*, at the beginning of 1995, there were at least 20,000 nuclear warheads in the operational inventories of the nuclear weapons states, i.e., 7,770 strategic and several hundred tactical warheads for the USA, and 8,527 strategic and 2,000-6,000 tactical warheads for Russia and the Commonwealth of Independent States.

A typology of determinants of contemporary arms races may differentiate between factors of a structural, functional, and behavioral-doctrinal nature. The structural factors are rooted in the impact and operation of military technology, as well as the backing from the sociopolitical constituencies behind armaments. The functional agents lie in the political-administrative management of armaments, as reflected in bureaucratic politics and the surrender to competitive action-reaction dynamics. And behavioral-doctrinal factors mirror cultural-historical impulses and follow doctrines generated by the material-technological environment.

## 1. Military Technology and the Military-Industrial Complex

The structural determinants—military technology and the might of the vested interest groups—form the mainstay of today's arms races. These two determinants reflect the operative and political economy components of the armaments drive. Both rely on interlocked strong institutional backing in the form of a competitive alliance of four influential corporate constituencies, the military establishment, the military industry, the state political bureaucracy, and the scientific-technological community engaged in military research and development (R&D). These four interest groups constitute the military-industrial-bureaucratic-technological (MIBT) complex—the enlarged version of what is popularly termed the "military-industrial complex." The driving force and push of armaments is located in the intense and unceasing exertion of military R&D, while the MIBT complex offers the staying power.

Military R&D is the force and engine of armaments. The emergence of military R&D as a mammoth endeavor and crucial agent of the arms race is a new historical phenomenon, linked to the science-based revolution in military technology which started in the Second World War. Military R&D evinces specific traits which inherently tend to kindle to arms race, making it intense and vicious. Fundamentally, R&D visualizes the research process as an endless continuum with no end-solution to any particular problem. Applied to military R&D this necessitates, as a matter of expedience and scientific urge, constantly seeking improvement on any achievement in weapon development. Scientific curiosity is compounded by material favor and professional ambition, combining into an irresistible constitutional and temperamental drive for higher and higher levels of arms utility and efficiency.

The race in military technological innovation is turning into an end in its own right—as a crucial variable in

***Table 1*** *NATO military expenditures*, in constant price figures, 1986-95
Figures are in US$ m., at 1990 prices (CPI deflated) and exchange rates

| | 1986 | 1987 | 1988 | 1989 | 1990 | 1991 | 1992 | 1993 | 1994 | 1995 |
|---|---|---|---|---|---|---|---|---|---|---|
| NATO | | | | | | | | | | |
| *North America* | | | | | | | | | | |
| Canada | 11 233 | 11 488 | 11 631 | 11 536 | 11 547 | 10 413 | 10 482 | 10 433 | 10 191 | 9 430 |
| USA | 335 048 | 331 215 | 323 860 | 320 427 | 306 170 | 268 994 | 284 116 | 269 111 | 254 038 | 238 194 |
| *Europe* | | | | | | | | | | |
| Belgium | 4 984 | 5 017 | 4 806 | 4 732 | 4 644 | 4 579 | 3 760 | 3 571 | 3 551 | 3 568 |
| Denmark | 2 520 | 2 662 | 2 714 | 2 648 | 2 650 | 2 697 | 2 648 | 2 653 | 2 587 | 2 559 |
| France | 41 081 | 42 284 | 42 243 | 42 793 | 42 589 | 42 875 | 41 502 | 41 052 | 41 260 | 39 426 |
| Germany | 39 889 | 40 570 | 40 242 | 40 146 | 42 320 | 39 216 | 37 697 | 33 979 | 31 609 | 31 448 |
| Greece | 3 861 | 3 856 | 4 078 | 3 819 | 3 863 | 3 663 | 3 808 | 3 716 | 3 780 | 3 843 |
| Italy | 20 186 | 22 699 | 24 113 | 24 304 | 23 376 | 23 706 | 23 004 | 23 127 | 22 556 | 21 380 |
| Luxembourg | 78 | 89 | 101 | 93 | 97 | 107 | 111 | 102 | 112 | 108 |
| Netherlands | 7 461 | 7 598 | 7 561 | 7 636 | 7 421 | 7 217 | 7 174 | 6 590 | 6 358 | 6 278 |
| Norway | 3 234 | 3 442 | 3 279 | 3 369 | 3 395 | 3 293 | 3 569 | 3 326 | 3 473 | 3 375 |
| Portugal | 1 504 | 1 563 | 1 738 | 1 824 | 1 875 | 1 925 | 1 977 | 1 908 | 1 861 | 2 088 |
| Spain | 8 827 | 9 995 | 9 345 | 9 668 | 9 053 | 8 775 | 8 113 | 8 823 | 7 940 | 8 037 |
| Turkey | 4 532 | 4 316 | 3 802 | 4 398 | 5 315 | 5 463 | 5 747 | 6 355 | 6 213 | 5 336 |
| UK | 42 867 | 42 561 | 40 646 | 40 792 | 39 776 | 41 087 | 37 141 | 36 312 | 34 742 | 32 677 |
| NATO Europe | 181 025 | 186 653 | 184 668 | 186 223 | 186 375 | 184 601 | 176 253 | 171 513 | 166 043 | 160 114 |
| NATO Total | 527 305 | 529 356 | 520 159 | 518 185 | 504 092 | 464 008 | 470 851 | 451 057 | 430 271 | 407 738 |

Source: SIPRI Yearbook 1996

major power competition. Almost all armaments constituencies around the world have become captives of this race. The self-sustaining inner-induced technological push generated by military R&D subsequently channels into a competitive weapon-technological spiral which fuels the clash between the world giant military machines.

Military R&D is sustained and tended by the web of special interests of the military-industrial-bureaucratic-technological complex. These powerful corporate constituencies are bound together by an interest in continued armaments, their production, supply, and demand. In his celebrated 1961 farewell address, in which he coined the term "military-industrial complex," President Eisenhower pointed to the fact that "this conjunction of an immense military establishment and a large arms industry" exerts a profound influence—economic, political, even spiritual—"in every city, every state house, every office of the federal government." He said:

> We have been compelled to create a permanent armaments industry of vast proportions . . . . We recognize the imperative need for this development. Yet we must not fail to comprehend its grave implications . . . . In the councils of government we must guard against the acquisition of unwarranted influence, whether sought or unsought, by the military-industrial complex. The potential for the disastrous rise of misplaced power exists and will persist. We must never let the weight of this combination endanger our liberties or democratic processes.

The MIBT complex should not be oversimplified and seen as an absolute monolithic, like-minded solid block, opportunist and conformist, in pursuit of power, privileges, and profit. Within its ranks there are hawks and doves, dogmatic nationalists and pragmatists. Individual members and even large segments of the MIBT complex, especially among the scientific-technological community, experience split-personality dilemmas in confronting the mad momentum of the arms race and in thinking about its possible consequences, nationally and internationally. They may not be unreceptive to a rational critical assessment of armaments; they may particularly be sensitive to moral and ethical considerations. Indeed, in this heterogeneous nature of the MIBT complex lies one of the potentials for political and educational offsetting action to check its influence.

The MIBT complex is not an incidental and ephemeral phenomenon but a structural one. It reflects the transformation of modern societies into industrial giants, the revolution in science and explosion of technology, the concentration of economic and political power, the availability of abundant resources, the increasing control of the state over its citizens, and the growth of organized violence in internal and external affairs. Within this architecture, interest groups around the MIBT complex have acquired excessive power, and have come to play a crucial role in society. They guard military R&D like a sacred flame as the most treasured asset in the armaments drive.

## 2. Bureaucratic Politics

In addition to the technological momentum sustained by the MIBT web of special interests, the arms race is invigorated by the way the arms flow is handled on the political, administrative, and organizational levels—from their technological maturation, through acquisition until deployment. A long and complex decision-making process is involved. This engages many organizations, military services, industrial interests, and governmental institutions—as groups and individuals—all competing for solutions which would best serve their economic and political interests, their personal and corporate ambitions. The outcome in most cases is that, as a result of clash, bargaining, and compromise in the procurement and deployment process, the amounts and types of new weapons are levelled up to the highest common denominator. The management procedures, involving both bureaucratic inertia and aggressive rivalry, are subsumed under the term of bureaucratic politics sometimes portrayed as bureaucratic determinism.

Bureaucratic politics underline the fundamental feature of contemporary armaments: that their center of gravity has shifted from external to internal stimulation. Because of the technological momentum and the complex decision-making process, armaments have become geared to internal technological, organizational, and political pressures.

## 3. Military Doctrine and Behavioral Factors

The material and functional agents of the arms race are upheld and bolstered by a gamut of virulent factors in the political, ideological, perceptional, and behavioral superstructure. These contribute to the shaping of the climate of international relations, and in a circular way influence and mold the pace and intensity of the arms race.

Paramount among these factors today is the doctrine of nuclear deterrence (see *Nuclear Deterrence, Doctrine of*). This infuses threat and intimidation into international relations, as nuclear deterrence *par excellence* is based on the manipulation of fear and

*Figure 1*
Great power armaments dynamics

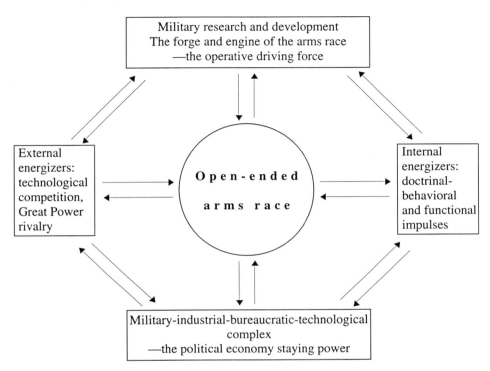

threat. This is epitomized by the "balance of terror" concept, a convoluted way of describing and stimulating the arms race. The "balance of terror" is not trusted by either side (see *Deterrence*). Each and every mutation of the military capability by one side, even of a defensive nature, will be interpreted by the other side as aggressive military and political intent. Eventually, nuclear deterrence locks the major powers into an open-ended race in all domains of armaments: nuclear and conventional, tactical and strategic—on land, sea, air, and in outer space.

It is widely assumed that part of the contemporary armaments dynamics stems also from ideological divergencies and systemic contradictions. However, a rational substantive analysis of the sociopolitical and economic motivations of either side in international affairs would rather question the immanence and fundamentality attributed to these factors. Faced up with a twentieth century perspective of development failures and sociopolitical disillusionment, ideology has landed in deep crisis. True, it is still exploited in political and psychological warfare, like religious fervor. It builds on deep-rooted self-righteousness and nationalism (see *Psychology of Peace; Cultural Roots of Peace*). But, as the improved US-Chi-

nese relations have demonstrated—relations which were at the time of the Vietnam war mutually portrayed in extreme ideological Good-Evil terms—ideological issues are no longer fundamental.

Of more basic import are certain intrinsic behavioral traits of major powers rooted in military-technological competition and the historical impulse. Two would seem to exert a substantial influence on armaments: the military imperative and the imperial drive.

The military imperative is a function of contemporary international relations, which essentially are power relations. The major powers, as the empiricism on the international scene again and again has proved, tend to act and react to any security dilemma and signs of conflict, not so much by seeking true and lasting political solutions, as by coercive action and the use of force. Conflicts and adversity are met by efforts of conflict suppression and domination. This, of course, does not resolve conflict, but perpetuates it (see *Conflict Formation: Elements in*). Even when political methods are tried, as in arms control negotiations, these are generally underpinned by a show of force. Politics from a position of strength have become a characteristic pattern of major power behavior. This reflects a basic reality: armaments are used as instruments of policy and diplomacy.

Parallel to the military imperative, major powers seem also impelled by an imperial historical drive. The histories of the United States and Russia are histories of expansion on the American and Euro-Asian continents respectively. After the Second World War, in step with the global reach of modern weapons, this historical drive expanded even into distant developing nations in pursuit of spheres of influence and economic positions. The "manifest destiny" (see *Manifest Destiny*) push over the Pacific has entangled the United States in the fateful Indochinese wars; the Russian unrelenting continental drive to the south has trapped the former Soviet Union into a protracted war in Afghanistan. Attempts have been made to justify these historical drives in terms of the pursuit of "vital national security interests" (see *Critical Security Studies*). But stretching these "vital interests" to almost all corners of the globe is tantamount to admitting an historical imperial expansionist impulsion. Protestations of defense have turned into political and strategic offense. Boosted by armaments and stimulating armaments, the historical drive remains an immanent feature of major power behavior (see *Power*).

Evidently, neither the military imperative nor the historical drive would have acquired such breath and vehemence without the availability of modern weapons and modern technology, which invests the major powers with unprecedented strategic mobility and coercive preponderance.

### 4. The General Scheme of Armaments Dynamics

A general paradigmatic scheme of contemporary major power arms race dynamics can be charted as in Fig. 2. This depicts a mainly inner-generated and inner-stimulated multivaried and interactive structure, with external impulses from the military-technological rivalry invigorating the arms race. The multiplicity of agents—structural, functional, and doctrinal-behavioral—intertwine and reinforce each other. The major power arms race is mainly the work of political and economic forces. Yet the operative gravitational center and prime mover of this system, sustained as it is by the MIBT complex, lies in the science-based and mission-oriented exertion of military research and development.

See also: *Militarism and Militarization*

*Bibliography* —————————————————————————

Allison G T, Morris F A 1975 Armaments and arms control: Exploring the determinants of military weapons. *Daedalus* 104(3)

Canton D, Shaerf C (eds.) 1975 *The Dynamics of the Arms Race*. Croom Helm, London

Gantzel K J 1973 Armaments dynamics in the East-West conflict: An arms race? *The Papers of the Peace Science Society (International)* 20

Gleditsch N P, Njolstad O (eds.) 1990 *Arms Races: Technological and Political Dynamics*. Sage, London

Gray C S 1976 *The Soviet-American Arms Race*. Saxon House Lexington Books, Lexington, Massachusetts

Holloway D 1983 *The Soviet Union and the Arms Race*. Yale University Press, New Haven, Connecticut

Myrdal A 1976 *The Game of Disarmament: How the US and Russia Run the Arms Race*. Panther Books, New York

Richardson L F 1960 *Arms and Insecurity: A Mathematical Study of Causes and Origins of War*. Quadrangle Books, Chicago, Illinois

Thee M (ed.) 1982 *Armaments. Arms Control and Disarmament. A UNESCO Reader for Disarmament Education*. Part 3: Armaments Dynamics. UNESCO Paris

Thee M 1986 *Military Technology, Military Strategy and the Arms Race*. The United Nations University, Tokyo Croom Helm, London

Thee M 1994 Armaments and disarmament in the post-cold war period: The quest for a demilitarized and nuclear-free world. In: Bonschier V, Lengyel P (eds.) *Conflicts and New Departures in World Society*, Vol. 3. World Society Foundation, Zürich

Wright Q 1965 *A Study of War*, 2nd edn. University of Chicago Press, Chicago. Illinois

York H F 1970 *Race to Oblivion: A Participant's View of the Arms Race*. Simon and Schuster, New York

MAREK THEE

# ASEAN Regional Forum

The ASEAN Regional Forum (ARF) is an annual foreign ministerial level dialogue and consultation among nations of East Asia and the Pacific on issues of regional peace and security. It is preceded by an ARF Senior Officials Meeting (ARF-SOM). Partially modeled on the Conference on Security and Cooperation in Europe (CSCE), the ARF's goal is to provide a forum to devise constructive and confidence building measures on security-related questions in the Asian region. The concept of security is comprehensively defined to include not only military aspects but also political, economic, and social. The first formal session took place on July 25, 1994 (see *Regionalism in Asia-Pacific, Organizational Forms of*).

## 1. The Organizational Framework

The ARF membership through 1996 included twenty-one nations: the seven members of the Association of Southeast Asian Nations (Brunei Darussalam, Indonesia, Malaysia, the Philippines, Singapore, Thailand, Vietnam), the three countries shortly to be added to ASEAN (Cambodia, Laos, Myanmar), along with ASEAN Observers, Consultative, and Dialogue Partners of ASEAN: Australia, Canada, China, the European Union, Japan, India, New Zealand, Papua New Guinea, the Republic of Korea, the Russian Federation, and the United States. At the third, July 23, 1996, ARF meeting it was agreed that candidates for future ARF membership would have to be sovereign states (thus excluding Taiwan) and would have to demonstrate an impact on peace and security in ARF's Northeast Asia, Southeast Asia, and Oceania "geographical footprint." Finally, all questions regarding future participants will be decided by consultation and consensus among the members. This leaves open the question of future membership for other South Asian or Pacific states, in particular Pakistan and Sri Lanka.

As a forum process, the annual ARF session takes place within the context of the ASEAN Ministerial Meeting (AMM) and its Post-Ministerial Conference (PMC). The AMM is the principal policy executive of ASEAN with its venue and chairmanship annually rotating through the membership. The annual host Chairman of the AMM is the Chairman of the ARF. The AMM is followed by the PMC during which the ASEAN ministers meet with their Consultative and Dialogue Partners on matters of mutual interest and concern. At the January 1992 ASEAN Fourth Summit Meeting, the ASEAN Heads of Government urged the enhancement of ASEAN's efforts to promote regional security cooperation. In their "Singapore Declaration," they called for an intensification of ASEAN's external dialogues on political and security matters by using the PMC. A Special Meeting of ASEAN Senior Officials on Regional Security was held in June 1992. This was followed in May 1993 by the first meeting of the senior officials of the ASEAN PMC which produced a "convergence of views" on the need for consultations on regional political and security issues. The first such "informal" consultations took place in Bangkok in July 1993, after the Singapore AMM. At that meeting the ARF in a separate institutional format was constituted.

The first "formal" ARF session took place in Bangkok on July 15, 1994, following immediately after the ASEAN PMC. In order to provide preparatory support and follow-up activity, the ARF-SOM was institutionalized, its membership consisting of both foreign ministry and defense officials of the ARF member states. Although the policy concerns of the ARF extend beyond the Southeast Asian geographical region, it has been agreed by the members of ARF that ASEAN "undertakes the obligation to be the primary driving force." ASEAN's organizational primacy resulted in part because the existing, well-established ASEAN structure was convenient for the institutional add-on of the ARF. Secondly, ASEAN's three decades of success in developing cooperative modes for its other areas of functional cooperation with non-ASEAN partners made ASEAN a natural home for the ARF. Finally, the ASEAN connection alleviates concerns that the multilateral structure of the ARF would be self-interestedly manipulated by one or another of the regional great powers.

## 2. Background to the ARF

For a decade from its inception in 1967, ASEAN leaders denied that security was one of the functional areas of concern of the grouping, although the underlying impetus for the organization had its roots in the security concerns of domestic communist insurgencies, Indonesia's undeclared war on Malaysia, and the American-Vietnamese Second Indochina War. ASEAN's response to the global US-USSR Cold War had been its 1970 Declaration of the Southeast Asian Zone of Peace, Freedom, and Neutrality (SEAZOPFAN) (see *Association of Southeast Asian Nations (ASEAN)*). It was not until the reunification of Vietnam and a perception of potential threat from communist Vietnam that the security concerns of ASEAN became manifest at the 1976 First ASEAN Summit on Indonesia's island of Bali. Two documents, the "Declaration of ASEAN Concord" and the "Treaty of Amity and Cooperation in Southeast Asia," spelled out the relationship between the stability of the ASEAN states and regional peace and security. They not only served to set the norms for regulating relations among the ASEAN states but also provided the framework for the integration of non-ASEAN Southeast Asian states into ASEAN as well as setting the parameters for ASEAN political relations with extra-Southeast Asian states. ASEAN political and security solidarity was tested by its response to the Vietnamese invasion and occupation of Cambodia in December 1978. For more than a decade ASEAN, with the support of China and the US, backed the Khmer Resistance against the Hun Sen regime installed by Vietnam, backed by the Soviet Union. The Vietnamese withdrawal from Cambodia followed by the UN Security Council-endorsed 1991 peace accord for Cambodia meant the end of great power linkages to conflict in Southeast Asia and paved the way for the expansion of ASEAN to eventually include all ten Southeast Asian states.

The ARF is the product of the post-Cold War strategic structure in East Asia in which the political and security rigidities of the bipolar US-USSR global confrontations and the regional PRC and USSR strategic tension, particularly manifest in Vietnam's invasion and occupation of Cambodia have been replaced by the uncertainties of a dynamically emerging multi-polar distribution of power that is characterized by three primary structural issues: the collapse of the USSR, growing Chinese military power and the concerns about possible ends to which it might be put, and questions about the scope and intensity of the future US political/military commitment to the region. These issues have to be addressed in a security environment in which at least three potential flashpoints for armed conflict with potential great power involvement persist: on the Korean peninsula, across the Taiwan Straits, and in the South China Sea territorial and jurisdictional competitions. In addition to the traditional threats to security of cross-border armed conflict, other security issues that have surfaced in an ARF context have included nuclear proliferation, arms control, and human rights violations, particularly in Myanmar.

Although security in a general sense provides the conceptual cement of the ARF, it increasingly appears that the political cement of ARF, at least from the ASEAN side, is the effort to constructively engage China in a functionally comprehensive multi-dimensional stable regional international system. This goal is also shared by Japan and the United States. To most of the Southeast Asian states, China's long run political ambitions in the region are a matter of concern. This is underscored by China's steady build-up of its military capabilities. The question of intentions is most obviously immediately of significance in the Chinese claims in the South China Sea that overlap with four of ASEAN's members and where China has demonstrated a willingness to use force. Although China had always insisted that its territorial and jurisdictional disputes were bilateral questions, ASEAN had already multilateralized the South China issue in its July 1992 "ASEAN Declaration on the South China Sea" which noted that "adverse developments" there

"directly affect peace and stability in the region." By engaging China in the ARF process, ASEAN hoped to dissuade further China from unilateralism.

For China itself, institutional engagement in ARF solidifies its political presence in Southeast Asia in a format that is independent of the policy framework of either the United States or Japan. Already in Southeast Asia China's bilateral political ties, particularly with Myanmar and Thailand, and its burgeoning economic relations with Singapore and Malaysia, have been complemented by a China-ASEAN dialogue process and Chinese involvement in the ASEAN backed Greater Mekong development scheme. The ARF is one more foreign policy instrument for China to demonstrate its non-threatening relationship to Southeast Asia despite the frictions in the South China Sea.

China's greater presence in the region has been paralleled by ASEAN concerns about perceptions of a diminished US political presence. This was made real by the reduction in the US's capability for forward deployment in Southeast Asia with the termination of the US military bases in the Philippines in 1991. Uncertainties about an even lower US regional presence have been heightened by the debate over the future of US deployments in Japan. From the Southeast Asian vantage point, for the US to be able to "balance" a growing China in the region, the US has to remain a regional presence. For ASEAN, therefore, the ARF was a vehicle to promote continued US involvement in the multilateral framework of engagement in the Southeast Asian security environment. Finally, in linking ASEAN to the security problems of Northeast Asia in the ARF, the ASEAN leadership has greater political influence in the wider region than it would otherwise possess. In particular, the ARF preempted the possible emergence of a security dialogue inside of the Asia Pacific Economic Cooperation (APEC) forum, the agenda of which would be independent of ASEAN.

A "regionalization" of the US presence in a multilateral format has historically run counter to the consistent US policy that has insisted on a loose bilateralism. It was not until the Clinton administration took office in 1993, that the US government became receptive to loose multilateralism in which American security interests were linked to economic growth and democratization as the pillars of a notional "Pacific Community." For the US, the ARF paired a loose security dialogue with the growing regional multilateral economic dialogue embodied in APEC. Even in the ARF, however, the US security strategy still is based on its core military alliance structure as the foundation for its regional security commitment.

## 3. Operation of the ARF

At its second, Brunei meeting, the ARF members agreed upon a three-stage approach to cooperation: (a) the promotion of confidence building; (b) development of preventive diplomacy; and (c) the elaboration of approaches to conflict. Although these stages are not necessarily sequential and can overlap, in fact, the ARF is in "stage one" and the central question of its future is whether it will be able to reach "stage two," let alone "stage three."

The implementation of its "stage one" is being carried out by a "two track" process. Track One involves intergovernmental activities. Track Two activities are non-governmental and involve security oriented regional research institutions and relevant non-governmental organizations. It is designed to support the official intergovernmental dialogue. With the inclusion of the China Center for International Studies and Hanoi's Institute for International Relations in December 1996, there were 14 full CSCAP members with a European and Indian Associate Member and the UN Regional Centre for Peace and Disarmament in Asia and the East Asia and Pacific Division of the UN's Department of Political Affairs in observer status. Individuals involved in the Track Two process do so in non-official capacity, and the Track Two organizations do not represent governments. The Track One and Track Two working groups have co-chairs from an ASEAN and non-ASEAN member country.

The work of Track One has been organized around an Inter-sessional Support Group (ISG) on Confidence Building; an Inter-sessional Meeting (ISM) on Peace-keeping Operations, and an ISM on Search and Rescue Coordination and Cooperation. A new ISM on Disaster Relief was convened in 1997, with Thailand and New Zealand the designated chairs. The ISG on Confidence Building Measure, chaired in 1995-96 by Indonesia and Japan, has focussed on a dialogue on security perceptions, defense policy publication, contacts and exchanges among national defence colleges, the UN Register of Conventional Arms, and notification of military exercises. The 1996-97 Chairs of the ISG are the Philippines and China. The ISM on Peace-keeping is led by Malaysia and Canada. Its agenda included ARF member states relations with UN Peacekeeping operations; training for peace support operations, and stand-by arrangements. The ISM on Search and Rescue was co-chaired by Singapore and the United States. Its emphasis was on shared training, standardization, and practical exercises. Its activities were continued under the same chairs in 1996-1997.

The principal Track Two activities are coordinated through the Council for Security Cooperation in the Asia Pacific (CSCAP) which since June 1993 has linked regional security and strategic studies "think tanks" and through them national committees made up of academics, security specialists, and former and current government officials in their private capacity. Its founding co-chairmen were from Indonesia's Center for Strategic and International Studies and the US's Honolulu-based Pacific Forum/Center for International and Strategic Studies. Malaysia's Institute of Strategic and International Studies served as the secretariat. The CSCAP is coordinated by a "steering committee" that meets biannually. CSCAP's work is carried out through International Working Groups (IWG). There are IWG's on Comprehensive and Cooperative Security, the North Pacific, Confidence and Security Building Measures (CSBMs), and Maritime Security Cooperation. The CSBM and Maritime Security Cooperation IWGs have been the most productive to date. Since it began its work in Fall 1994, the CSBM IWG, co-chaired by the US, Singapore, and the Republic of Korea had met six times through Spring 1997. It has given attention to expanded transparency measures, support of global treaty regimes, building on existing cooperation and the development of new multilateral approaches. In the latter area, the most significant initiative has been on new multilateral approaches to nuclear safety and non-proliferation including the possible formation of an Asia Pacific Atomic Energy Organization (PACATOM). The Maritime Security Cooperation IWG co-chaired by Indonesia and Australia has produced a draft "Guidelines for Regional Maritime Cooperation." This is suggested as a possible contribution to "soft law" in the region, that is an instrument that is not legally binding but represents broad agreement articulating basic ground rules for international behavior.

In addition to the work of CSCAP and its affiliated national committees, the Track Two ARF process has also seen a number of seminars including in 1995, a CSBM seminar in Canberra, a "Peacekeeping" seminar in Brunei, and a "Preventive Diplomacy" seminar in Seoul. In 1996, ARF-related seminars took place in Moscow on "Principles of Security and Stability" in the Asia Pacific; a German-Indonesian-Australian seminar on "Nuclear Nonproliferation" in Jakarta; and a second seminar on "Preventive Diplomacy" in Paris. In order to maximize the availability of human resources, the increasingly crowded ARF calendar is now divided between Track One in the first half-year and Track Two in the second.

## 4. The ARF Agenda

While useful in setting out the architecture for possible future institutional and legal arrangements, the functionally specific and technically differentiated tasks involved in both Track One and Track Two activities is not the stuff of ministerial meetings. The ARF as a "dialogue" and "forum" is not structured to address in specific terms current conflicts in a way that might lead to a contribution to conflict resolution. In part this is because the exclusive ASEAN-relatedness and membership ground rules are such that all interested parties are not part of the process. For example, the absence of Taiwan from the ARF and Track One and Track Two activities—at the insistence of China—precludes a useful exchange over peace in the Taiwan Straits. The non-participation of North Korea reduces any value that ARF's input might have in contributing to the resolution of security issues, including the nuclear issue, on the Korean Peninsula. In this respect the ARF becomes one additional target for the mobilization of support for the policies of ARF members.

It is obvious and intentional that the ARF is not designed to be a framework for negotiation or diplomatic initiative. The prepared statements of the ministers at the ARF sessions are restatements of their well known general positions. The ARF's final communique is a consensus document that reflects lowest common denominator on the principle of the desirability of peaceful settlement of disputes. Because of the political fragility of the assumed common interest in the ARF process itself, divisive and contentious issues are excluded from the formal agenda in order to avoid possible disruption. The ARF's commitment to consensus is designed to guarantee another organizational guideline, that "the ARF process shall move at a pace comfortable to all participants." What this means in practice is that no ARF final statement will include any substantive proposal for action that will touch specifically upon the security interests of a member state without that state's approval.

The inclusion of Myanmar in ARF underlines the problems of the ARF as an instrumentally meaningful forum. Myanmar has become an ARF member despite the definition of Myanmar's regime as part of the security problems of the region by US and other non-ASEAN participants. ASEAN's insistence on Myanmar's participation also throws into relief the different political values background that the diverse countries of the ARF bring to their appreciation of comprehensive security. More narrowly, the controversy over Myanmar will serve to enhance China's influence in the ARF and reduce the ARF's significance for key non-ARF members.

## 5. The Future of ARF

Consensus in ARF will become even more difficult in the future as the ARF has put on its agenda the issue of drug production and trade, environmental threats, and the other challenges of comprehensive security. The expansion of membership, the rule of consensus, and the broadening of the dialogue will probably mean a reduced effectiveness of ARF as a central focus for the management of regional security concerns. The ARF process will not replace the bilateral and other multilateral modes of conflict avoidance and resolution. This does not mean that the ARF is not a functional addition to the task of building in the Asia Pacific region. It is still in formative stage of development, and it is possible that in its developmental process it can find consensus on some useful CSBM and preventive diplomacy measures.

The fact that it probably will not be able to move from "stages one and two," to its goal of "stage three," "approaches to conflict," does not mean that the ARF cannot be a positive addition to the building of a more stable order in the region. The argument can be made that the ARF might be more useful as an inclusive pan-Asian security dialogue if it were decoupled from the ASEAN process which seems limited by the ASEAN-China nexus. In any case, the ARF is but one element, and certainly not the most important, in an Asia Pacific security complex that has as its controlling element the ability of the major powers to avoid major conflict.

See also: *Collective Security and Collective Self-defense; Security Regimes: Focusing on Asia-Pacific; Peace and Regional Integration; Multilateralism*

*Bibliography* ——————————————

Antolik M 1994 The ASEAN regional forum: The spirit of constructive engagement. *Contemporary Southeast Asia* 16(2)

ASEAN Secretariat, "Chairman's Statement," First, Second, and Third ASEAN Regional Forums

Leifer M 1996 *The ASEAN Regional Forum.* International Institute of Strategic Studies, *Adelphi Paper* 302, London

DONALD E. WEATHERBEE

# Asia Pacific Economic Cooperation (APEC)

## 1. Introduction

The Asia Pacific Economic Cooperation forum or APEC is the intergovernmental institution linking 18 of the most important and dynamically growing economies of the Asia Pacific region on the basis of their common commitment to trade liberalization, economic cooperation, and open regionalism. Its membership through 1997 consisted of Australia, Brunei Darussalam, Canada, Chile, China, Hongkong, Indonesia, Japan, Malaysia, Mexico, New Zealand, Papua New Guinea, the Philippines, Singapore, South Korea, Chinese Taipeh, Thailand, and the United States. At the subregional level, the six Southeast Asian countries were already joined in the Association of Southeast Asian (ASEAN). Canada, the US and Mexico are partners in the North American Free Trade Area (NAFTA); and Australia and New Zealand are paired in the Closer Economic Relations (CER) relationship that has forged links with ASEAN. Both the ASEAN Secretariat and the South Pacific Forum Secretariat are represented as "observers" in the APEC meetings (see *Regionalism in Asia-Pacific, Organizational Forms of*).

APEC grew out of the recognition of the intensifying interdependencies resulting from the rapid economic growth of Pacific Rim countries which now account for nearly half of the world's total economic output and nearly half of global merchandise trade. It was founded in 1989, after three decades of preparatory study and consultation. It has evolved to become the primary vehicle of regional economic multilateralism to promote liberalization of trade and investment in an open regional and global market so as to contribute to prosperity and opportunity for all of its members.

## 2. Background

Since the 1960s, a variety of initiatives have been taken for the development of multilateral channels of communication and consultation on matters of common interest to the market-oriented states of the Pacific region. The underlying rationale has been that the deepening economic and commercial interdependencies in the region have produced a complex system of relations in which the full realization of future promise and the resolution of new problems cannot be achieved by unilateralism or bilateral devices, but require a regional approach. While the idea that Pacific-region economic growth and development could be better promoted through some kind of associational community was attractive, issues of institu-

tionalization, scope, policy emphasis, and structural detail have meant that the maturation of the vision of Pacific regionalism has been politically gradual, at a pace determined by newly industrialized or industrializing countries of East and Southeast Asia, not by Japan and the United States.

The intellectual roots of the idea of a Pacific Economic Community are usually traced back to 1965, when Professors Kiyoshi Kojima and Kurimoto Hiroshi of Japan proposed a Pacific Free Trade Area modeled on the EEC. This influenced Prime Minister Takeo Miki's formulation in 1967 of an "Asian Pacific Policy" which had as its fruits the series of Pacific Trade and Development Conferences (PACTAD) that brought research economists together to consider issues of international economic policy affecting Asian and Pacific trading nations. The idea of a formal free trade area was not then further pursued. Many of Japan's smaller trading partners saw this as an effort to institutionalize the perceived trade inequalities already working to Japan's advantage. In 1979, Japan's Prime Minister Ohira appointed a Pacific Basin Cooperation Study Group, chaired by Saburo Okita, to find ways to promote the building of a Pacific Community. The Okita's committee's "Report on the Pacific Basin Cooperation Concept" was the basis for Ohira's 1980 Pacific Basin Initiative that called for a gradualist approach to community building which envisioned at some future point an intergovernmental organization to promote understanding and resolve conflict in all fields of economy, society, culture, transport, communications, and science and technology.

On the other side of the Pacific Ocean, Peter Drysdale and Hugh Patrick were paralleling the Japanese intellectual thrust with their own proposal in 1979 for an Organization for Pacific Trade and Development (OPTAD). The OPTAD model was the Organization for Economic Cooperation and Development (OECD) and provided for intergovernmental consultation on issues of regional trade and investment. Although given wide hearing in academic and government circles, many felt that OPTAD was an idea before its time since it presumed too broad and intense a level of regional interest and did explicitly advocate a move from the informal to the formal intergovernmental organizational format. It is important to note, however, that already before the full burst of economic energy that has transformed East Asia and the Pacific, the main policy themes of what in the 1990s became the APEC process were in circulation and being tested.

The constituency for Asian economic regionalism was broader than simply academics and government elites. The private sector has been a major promoter of region-wide consultation. The Pacific Basin Economic Council (PBEC) was founded in 1967 to provide regular consultation. Not surprisingly, its agenda was pragmatically modest, giving priority attention to short-term issues and avoiding visionary futurism. PBEC can be considered the ancestor of APEC's Business Advisory Council.

The tentative notional efforts towards regionalism began to assume a concrete form in September 1980 with the first of the Pacific Economic Cooperation Conferences (PECC). The line from PECC to APEC is clear with the PECC process producing the consensus around a cluster of issue areas necessary to move the consultative framework from the unofficial to the official. PECC I was convened in Canberra and endorsed by Australian Prime Minister Fraser and Japan's Ohira. The PECC process involved a tripartite dialogue between academics, businesses, and government officials acting in their "private" capacities (see *Track II Diplomacy*). PECC was given continuity through the creation of a Standing Committee and the establishment of Task Forces with specific functional study and reporting responsibilities. Already beginning with PECC II in Bangkok, the PECC agenda was to create a vehicle for converting its consensual output into meaningful input into regional governmental policies. National committees were established in each of the PECC participating countries with the same kind of tripartite membership. The national committees acted as domestic advocates for Pacific cooperation and expanded the official-unofficial exchange. PECC also linked up with other regionalist fora like PACTAD and PBEC. By PECC VI in Osaka in 1988, an evolutionary trend of great potential for Pacific regionalism was well underway with broadening private and public elite support. PECC's special role has been continued, and it is the only non-official organization to enjoy "observer" status at APEC meetings.

Continuing Japanese official interest in a formal multilateral forum was signalled in Prime Minister Nakasone's "Pacific Initiative" speech in March 1988, in which he proposed the establishment of a "Pacific Forum for Economic and Cultural Cooperation" based on the experience and activities of PECC. He explicitly stated that it could be a Pacific OECD. The OECD model also figured in American Secretary of State George Shultz's call in Jakarta in July 1988, for an intergovernmental grouping of like-minded countries of the Asia Pacific. This announcement of American official interest was echoed a year later by Secretary of State James Baker who advocated a new "Pacific Partnership" to give structure to Pacific rim economic cooperation. A major obstacle to such a "partnership" and other like proposals has been the reluctance of the six nations of ASEAN to commit themselves to any official region-wide structure whose agenda would be set by the two economic superpowers and in which ASEAN coherence and identity would be at risk. On the other hand, it was understood that ASEAN's participation was vital if the wider regionalism envisioned on both sides of the Pacific were to be realized.

By 1989, the momentum for structured official government to government consultations on Asian regionalism would carry along even the most hesitant nations, particularly the Southeast Asian nations, urged on by their respective national PECC participants. ASEAN's original misgivings were somewhat allayed by the active promotion of the concept by middle-range Korea and Australia who developed a non-threatening blueprint for regionalism. Although South Korean President Chun Doo Hwan's May 1982 call for a Pacific Basin Summit might have been premature, Korean President Roh Tae Woo had a more responsive audience when he raised the issue of a formal Asia Pacific cooperation agreement during his November 1988 trip through Southeast Asia. In February 1989, Australian Prime Minister Bob Hawke made a four-nation Asian tour, beginning in Korea, during which he proposed again that the countries of the region should look seriously at the OECD model. He invited the member states of ASEAN to join with Australia and South Korea in creating such a structure.

While the Australians were canvassing support for a regional ministerial meeting to discuss the Australian proposal for a limited Pacific OECD, Japan was lobbying to insure that such a ministerial meeting would be inclusive of the PECC membership including Canada and the United States so as not to be perceived simply as an Asian bloc reacting to the emergence of the European Union and the implications of NAFTA. The ASEAN states agreed only to an exploratory dialogue that did not commit them in advance to any particular institutional format or plan of action. Australia sent out the invitations for a November 1989 meeting of foreign trade and commerce ministers in Canberra, the first APEC Ministerial Meeting.

## 3. Structure and Processes

Over a period of five years (1989-1993) and five Ministerial Meetings (Canberra, Singapore, Seoul, Bangkok, and Seattle), APEC was organized and institutionalized. The first, Canberra APEC meeting consisted of 12 nations: the ASEAN 6 together with Australia, Canada, Japan, New Zealand, South Korea, and the United States. The question of China's membership was solved at the third, Seoul APEC meeting in 1991, with the entry of the People's Republic of China, Hong Kong, and Taiwan as Chinese Taipeh. With Hong Kong and Taiwan APEC became an organization of economies, not sovereign national states. In 1993, at the Bangkok meeting, Papua New Guinea, a longtime ASEAN observer, was added along with the US and Canada's NAFTA partner Mexico. Finally, Chile was brought in at the 1994 Jakarta meeting. At the 1993 Seattle meeting, a three year moratorium was declared on membership applications after Chile's 1994 admission.

The breadth of APEC concerns was illustrated by the agenda topics of the Canberra meeting: world and regional economic developments; the role of the Asia Pacific region in global trade liberalization; opportunities for regional cooperation in specific areas; and future steps towards Asia Pacific Cooperation. A major interest in the early APEC deliberations was to show support for a successful conclusion of the Uruguay Round of GATT negotiations and the strengthening of the open global trading system. Although no agreement was reached on any particular structure for a ministerial level forum or its support structure, it was clear from the suggested future work program that while the consultations themselves might be informal, the process would have to have structure and continuity.

At the third, 1991 Seoul APEC gathering the assembled ministers declared that the goals of APEC would be:

(a) to sustain the growth and development of the region for the common good of its peoples and, in this way, to contribute to the growth and development of the world economy;

(b) to enhance the positive gains, both for the region and the world economy, resulting from increasing economic interdependence, by encouraging the flow of goods, services, capital and technology;

(c) to develop and strengthen the open multilateral trading system in the interest of Asia-Pacific and all other economies;

(d) to reduce barriers to trade in goods and services and investment among participants in a manner consistent with GATT principles, where applicable, and without determent to other economies.

The Seoul APEC Declaration represents a commitment to an "open regionalism" designed to promote not only a reduction of intra-regional barriers to economic interactions but also the reduction of external barriers to economies not part of the the region. APEC's "open regionalism" stands in contrast to inward looking, closed trading blocs. The Seoul APEC Declaration is also noteworthy in its recognition of the role of the private sector in Asian Pacific economic success. The ministers promised to "enhance and promote the role of the private sector and the application of free market principles in maximising the benefits of regional cooperation" and encouraged private sector involvement in approriate APEC activities. It was agreed that the APEC mode of operation would be based on the principle of mutual benefit" and that there would be an open dialogue and consensus-building with equal respect for the views of all participants. The APEC mode of operation regionalized the existing ASEAN mode.

The Seoul APEC Declaration sketched the outline of an institutional structure that has been considerably fleshed out at succeeding meetings. Executive direction to APEC is given by the annual Ministerial Meeting and any additional ministerial meetings convened as necessary. The ministers set the work program to be carried out by committees and working groups with representation from every APEC participant. The responsibility for continuity in overseeing the APEC process lies with regular, four times a year, Senior Officials Meeting. The 1992 Bangkok APEC Ministerial agreed to establish a permanent APEC Secretariat in Singapore to support the work program of APEC's policy-based committees and sectoral Working Groups. The Executive Director of the Secretariat is annually seconded from the member economy currently the APEC Chair and serves one year. The Deputy Executive Director is appointed by the economy scheduled to succeed next to the Chair.

At the working level of APEC are three committees, an ad hoc policy group, and eleven sectoral Working Groups. These APEC fora are:

(a) *Committee on Trade and Investment* (CTI). This is an upgrade of the former Informal Group on Regional Trade Liberalization. It is based on the 1993 APEC Declaration on a Trade and Investment Framework to increase economic activity and facilitate the flow of goods and services among member economies.

(b) *The Economic Committee (EC).* This was established in 1994, transforming the former Ad Hoc

Group on Economic Trends and Issues into a formal APEC committee. It focuses on enhancing APEC's capability for analysis of economic trends and studies of specific economic issues. It is the research arm of APEC.

(c) *Budget and Administrative Committee* with general financial oversight of all APEC activities.

(d) *Eleven Working Groups.* The Working Groups are designed to promote economic and technical cooperation in broad functional areas. The groups are:

Trade Promotion Working Group
Trade and Investment Data Review Working Group
Industrial Science and Technology Working Group
Human Resource Development Working Group
Regional Energy Cooperation Working Group
Marine Resource Conservation Working Group
Telecommunications Working Group
Transportation Working Group
Tourism Working Group
Fisheries Working Group
[Agricultural Technical Cooperation Experts' Group]

As suggested by the Seoul APEC Declaration, business has an important role in APEC. In 1993, a Pacific Business Forum was set up by APEC consisting of one large and one small business representative from each member economy. This was enlarged and its mandate broadened in 1995 when the APEC Business Advisory Council (ABAC) was established to give input to APEC on specific business sector priorities.

Although APEC made considerable progress in the establishment of a cooperative climate of dialogue and exchange of views in its early years, its profile, both official and public, remained very low. There was little that APEC could claim in terms of innovative programs or measurable policy results. There was little movement beyond the general goals as laid out in the Seoul Declaration towards real policy objectives or practical targets. The 1992 Ministerial sought assistance in building a more concrete agenda by commissioning an Eminent Persons Group (EPG) to prepare a report on the future of APEC. The EPG, chaired by American economist C. Fred Bergsten, was composed of a distinguished representative from each APEC state. Its first report in November 1993 was titled "A Vision for APEC: Towards an Asia-Pacific Community" and set forth a recommended program of action and agreement that would transform the very nature of APEC from a consultative forum towards what Bergsten later described as "potentially the largest trade agreement in history."

## 4. The APEC Summit Process: From Vision to Action

The first EPG report coincided with the policy galvanizing impact of the first summit meeting of the leaders of the APEC states at Blake Island Washington in conjunction with the 1993 fifth, Seattle APEC Ministerial Meeting. The reinvigoration of APEC was in part a result of American President Bill Clinton's efforts to vitalize American engagement in Asia. In a speech in Japan in July 1993, President Clinton announced his intention to invite the leaders of the APEC nations to an informal summit on Blake Island, near Seattle, on November 20, immediately after the Seattle APEC meeting. The summit process inaugurated at Blake Island, although not officially part of APEC given the absence of two of its member economies (Hong Kong and Taiwan), nevertheless has supplanted the Ministerial Meeting both in terms of attention paid to it and the controlling policy guidelines announced at the summits. At Blake Island, with the EPG's report in hand, the APEC leaders, with the exception of Malaysia's Prime Minister Mahathir who had stayed away, pledged to reduce trade and investment barriers so that goods, services, capital, and investment could flow freely among the economies. Most significantly, the leaders in their Blake Island *"Vision Statement"* welcomed the challenge by the EPG to achieve free trade in the APEC region.

The following year at the 1994 Bogor Summit, following the Jakarta APEC Ministerial Meeting, the leaders, this time with Malaysia's Mahathir in attendance, indicated how they would meet the challenge. In the Bogor "Declaration of Common Resolve," the leaders set the goal of achieving free and open trade among the APEC nations to no later than 2010 for the industrialized economies and 2020 for the developing economies. This was essentially the recommendation of the EPG's second, 1994 report, "Achieving the APEC Vision: Free and Open Trade in the Asia Pacific Region." Not surprisingly, given the great diversity of interests represented in APEC, the political leadership at the Summit was cautious in terms of the EPG's suggestions with respect to APEC infrastructure development.

The blueprint for implementation of the Bogor Declaration was given at the third, Osaka APEC Summit in November 1995, in the *"Osaka Action Agenda."* With an EPG report, "Implementing the APEC Vision," at hand, the leaders, absent the American President, promulgated an elaborate and lengthy set of principles and guidelines to facilitate comprehensively achieving the goal of the Bogor Declaration. The Action Agenda has been described as standing on "three legs:" liberalization, facilitation, and cooperation. Each member economy was tasked with preparing its own "Action Plan" containing concrete and specific details as well as time frames for the near and medium term as to how they planned to achieve the 2010 or 2020 target dates. The APEC ministers were instructed to have ready for the 1996 Manila APEC Ministerial Meeting and Subic Bay Summit, their Individual Action Plans (IAP) as well as the proposals for APEC collective actions for sectoral liberalization.

In the Philippines in November 1996, the leaders agreed to implement their IAPs together with APEC's collective initiatives in the *Manila Action Plan for APEC* (MAPA) beginning 1 January 1997. This was viewed as the first step towards meeting the Bogor goals even though the IAPs varied widely in terms of comprehensiveness, detail, and quantification. With its IAPs, APEC is the only forum in the world to have developed a transparent mechanism for comparing liberalization progress made by diverse economies. It was made clear that the process was voluntary in the framework of consensus.

The Philippines APEC-related meetings were also important since they preceded the first WTO Ministerial Meeting held in Singapore in December 1996 (see *World Trade Organization (WTO)*). APEC wanted to go to Singapore united in a common goal of implementing the Uruguay Round commitments by each WTO member. Also at Manila, the US sought to enlist APEC's support in the WTO for a US-initiated liberal International Technology Agreement, one of the unfinished pieces of business of the Uruguay Round. The US proposal would have zero-tariff for items such as computers and software by the year 2000, a position not fully shared by APEC countries such as Malaysia, China, and Chile. A compromise was brokered with more ambiguous language in which the leaders called for an ITA that "would substantially eliminate tariffs by the year 2000," recognizing the need for flexibility as negotiations in Geneva proceed.

The Subic Bay conferees also had in their hands the ABAC's first report to APEC's leaders, titled "APEC Means Business: Building Prosperity for Our Community." The identification by ABAC of APEC as a "community" may be somewhat premature. An earlier EPG suggestion that the "C" in APEC stand for "Community" was not accepted by the leaders. Its institutional and infrastructural implications suggested a level of policy integration that most members are unwilling to commit to. This raises the question, however, of APEC's future direction and structure; that is whether "partnership" can be translated into a higher order of structural cooperation.

## 5. *The Future of* APEC

For the short and intermediate range the future APEC will continue to be concerned with the implementation and monitoring of the IAPs and the APEC collective initiatives as set forth in the MAPA, beginning at the Vancouver, Canada Ministerial Meeting in 1997. In addition to tracking progress towards the goals of free trade by 2010 and 2020, APEC will work to devise collective mechanisms to facilitate that progress. The question is how will the momentum from Blake Island to Subic be maintained? Can it be reasonably expected that the routinization of APEC progress can sustain an annual summit process that politically requires some new, dramatic announcement in order to be deemed a success? Moreover, it should be remembered that the APEC process takes place within the broader framework of the WTO. APEC leaders have constantly reiterated their full support for the Uruguay Round and the WTO. APEC has always viewed itself as a catalyst for global multilateralism. Ironically, already in 1997, a major trade disagreement between Japan and Indonesia over automobiles has been raised to the dispute resolution mechanism of the WTO. It can be expected that other intra-APEC problems will end up on the WTO's plate as the multiplicity of trade relationships leads to forum shopping.

The issue of APEC's expansion will impact both its direction and pace. Eleven Pacific region countries are knocking on APEC's door with the ending of the membership moratorium. Alphabetically ordered, they are Colombia, Ecuador, India, Macau, Mongolia, Pakistan, Panama, Peru, Russia, Sri Lanka, and Vietnam. Criteria for membership will be adopted at the Vancouver Summit. It is expected that Peru and Vietnam will become the first new members. This will be announced at the Malaysia Summit in 1998 for their participation in the 1999 New Zealand Summit. ASEAN's position in APEC even after Vietnam joins will be complicated by its own expansion from seven to ten when Cambodia, Laos, and Myanmar join it.

The APEC leaders at the Subic Summit repeated the formula that "the strength of APEC is derived from its diversity." While increased diversity through expansion may add to strength as measured by inclusiveness, it also complicates APEC's growth process. Decision making by consensus and equal weighting of members' views will become more complex, slower, and less specific as more differing interests have to be taken into account. For example, APEC's expansion will broaden the range of economic differences between the APEC members. ASEAN's experience is a good example of the kinds of problems that might be encountered.

ASEAN's own ASEAN Free Trade (AFTA) timetable for tariff reduction has been speeded up so as not to be overtaken by APEC, its goal of tariffs between 0 and 5 percent cut from 2003 to 2015. An ASEAN of ten will be three-tiered. The core six have given Vietnam until 2006 to meet AFTA's target, and plan to give Cambodia, Laos, and Myanmar until 2008. Even then it is understood that more time may be needed.

The "diversity" of interests goes well beyond levels of economic development and capacities. Prospective ASEAN member Myanmar is the object of unilateral economic sanctions by the United States because of the Myanmar government's gross violation of human rights. The ASEAN states and other APEC members, especially China, reject the injection of political criteria in trade matters. The chronic issue in the US of annual renewal of MFN status for China and US unwillingness to sign off on China's WTO application is another example of the political irritants that have entered the economic dialogue. There are also other aspects of a "social agenda" advanced by some APEC members, not just the US, with respect to such issue areas as worker's rights, gender equality, minimum pay, etc., the purpose of which is viewed by the proponents as helping to insure "a level of playing field" but is interpreted by others as being disguised protectionism.

It is East and Southeast Asian uncertainty about the political quality of APEC that has helped keep alive an alternative regionalist format, the East Asian Economic Caucus (EAEC) that would exclude the Western Hemisphere as well as Australia and New Zealand. The 1996 proposal that the ASEAN "informal summit" should also include Japan, China, and South Korea is the EAEC in different clothing. ASEAN members of APEC are also the most vigorous proponents of the newly institutionalized Asia Europe Summit Meeting (ASEM) to balance the trans-Pacific orientation of APEC (see *Association of Southeast Asian Nations (ASEAN)*). It might also be noted that the Asian leaders at the ASEM are also the EAEC.

There is no question that the APEC process has proved to be an important mechanism for heightening and making more policy relevant such as the multilateral dialogue on trade, investment and other related matters in the Asia Pacific Region. The new attention paid to facilitative technical matters such as harmonizing tariff categories, customs clearance procedures or investment guarantees is also attributable to APEC, especially its responsiveness to the private sector. APEC's existence certainly contributes to the stability

of the post-Cold War regional international order. With the ASEAN Regional Forum (ARF), APEC might be considered an element of the architecture of a Pacific Community. A true community, however, is part of an integrative process. Even if "free and open trade" is achieved by the year 2020, this does not necessarily mean that a "community" exists.

Real community is based on widely shared political values. Values are derived from culture and history. While there may be widely shared interests among the APEC states, there are immense value differences. This is what distinguishes the trans-Pacific process from the trans-Atlantic, or the intra-Asian pattern from the Western European. The APEC process is one of incremental adjustment and adaptation driven not by vision but by the dynamics of economic growth and the need to sustain and maximize it. The intrusion of politics whether the politics are of value differences, territorial disputes, spillovers of ethnic strife etc., can only detract from APEC's progress at the governmental level of association. Also, APEC's cement of interdependency has not been tested in times of economic slowdown.

After eight years and four summits, it seems clear that APEC is more than just an ongoing tariff-cutting negotiation. How much more will not become evident until we have an accurate measure of how fast and how far the APEC members do in fact move in the direction of "free and open trade" by the years 2010 and 2020. For that to happen, the leaders must remain engaged.

See also: *Economic Integration; Integration, Regional; Integration Theories; North American Free Trade Agreement (NAFTA); European Union; Peace and Regional Integration*

*Bibliography*

National Bureau of Asian Research 1995 APEC at the crossroads. *NBR Analysis* 6(1)

Symposium on the APEC Process 1995 *J. Northeast Asian Stud.* 14, Winter

United States Congress, House of Representatives 1995 *The Future of the Asia-Pacific Economic Cooperation Forum (APEC)*. Joint Hearing, July 18, before the Subcommittee on International Economic Policy, and Asia and the Pacific, House Committee on International Relations Hearings

DONALD E. WEATHERBEE

# Association of Southeast Asian Nations (ASEAN)

The Association of Southeast Asian Nations (ASEAN) was first established in August, 1967. Two earlier organizations—the Association of Southeast Asia (ASA) established in July 1961, by Thailand, Malaysia and the Philippines, and Maphilindo, created in 1963 by Malaya, the Philippines and Indonesia, had both failed to take root, but ASEAN was destined to survive and grow.

Initially, membership was confined to five countries—Indonesia, the Philippines, Thailand, Malaysia (now newly reconstituted) and Singapore. The purpose, according to the founders, was to promote economic, social and cultural cooperation. In reality, however, the early activities of ASEAN centered heavily upon politics. At this point, the broad political interests of the five members were similar in nature, namely, to combat Communism, whether in the form of domestic subversion or external intrusion; and to keep a balance among the major powers involved in the region, with a tilt toward the United States.

Over time, ASEAN evolved, with meetings of high officials scheduled and a modest institutional structure created. The first meeting of heads of state took place in Bali in February, 1976. Meetings of senior officials were subsequently regularized. Further, a permanent ASEAN Secretariat was established in Jakarta in June, 1976. Functional committees were created, and later, ASEAN accepted such major states as Japan, the United States and China as dialogue partners.

Political events dominated the ASEAN agenda for several decades after its establishment. The victory of the Communists in Vietnam heightened fears that the United States would withdraw from Asia, leaving the Communist powers ascendant. The ASEAN answer was complex. On the one hand, it declared its nonalignment in the Cold War, and proclaimed that Southeast Asia should be Zone of Peace, Freedom, and Neutrality (ZOPFAN). In this fashion, it hoped to ward off the greater intrusion of Communist powers. On the other hand, while calling for the abandonment of all foreign bases in the region (including the US bases in the Philippines), various ASEAN members accepted US military use of their port and airfield facilities as a gesture to keep the US in the area and as a hedge against external aggression.

Vietnam's incursion into Cambodia in the late 1970s sparked a new diplomatic offensive. ASEAN took the lead in condemning Vietnam at the United Nations, and in assisting the formation of an independent Cambodia.

In its early stages, ASEAN had served two primary political functions. First, it had brought leaders of the region together for wide-ranging dialogues, and served to reduce bilateral friction between various members. Second, it had served to enhance the voice of individual countries by making them a part of a collective organization forwarding policies on the basis of consensus. The latter process became known as the ASEAN way, available to others in resolving disputes.

Gradually, membership was slightly enlarged. Brunei joined in 1984, and more significantly, Vietnam became a member in 1995. By this time, concerns within Southeast Asia, and most particularly, in Vietnam, about China had risen. At an earlier point, Japan had been considered the expansionist power, not in political-military terms but as an economic giant. By the 1990s, however, China's dynamic economy and its militant nationalism combined to produce a growing fear of a Greater China, one that could draw into its economic orbit the Overseas Chinese in the region who controlled a high percentage of the ASEAN economies. Periodically, ethnic tensions erupted in violence within ASEAN states, notably Indonesia, displaying the deep sensitivity to this issue.

Thus, the proposal that all ten Southeast Asian nations be enrolled in ASEAN, including Cambodia, Laos and Myanmar, was on the table by 1996, with some differences of opinion as to timing and conditions preventing immediate action. Behind such a step were clearly strategic as well as economic reasons. A ten-member ASEAN would provide a formidable regional entity from which to deal with such issues as the controversy over the South China Sea atolls and other matters that might emerge as the strength of the major powers shifted. In sum, an enlarged ASEAN represented preparation for the 21st Century.

Even as its political-strategic role continued to be highly significant, the economic importance of ASEAN greatly increased in the 1990s. Negotiations with respect to creating an ASEAN Free Trade Area (AFTA) got underway, with an agreement among members to reduce tariffs on industrial and agricultural products to a maximum of 5 percent by the year 2003. The service industry has also been included in AFTA coverage, thereby encompassing virtually all economic intercourse among ASEAN members. It remains to be seen, however, whether the less developed Southeast nations now being considered for membership can adhere to the established schedule, or whether some time lag will be permitted.

Meanwhile, a broader organization dedicated to open regionalism emerged in 1989, namely, the Asia-Pacific Economic Cooperation forum (APEC). APEC was formed through the initiative of Australia, with strong backing from the United States, designed to support the GATT objective of an open global economy (see *Asia Pacific Economic Cooperation (APEC)*). Regional trade and investment liberalization were termed key objectives, with most favored nation treatment promised to all nations that were prepared to reciprocate.

The ASEAN attitude toward APEC has been complex and varied. Some ASEAN members feared that APEC would dilute the influence of ASEAN, or move too rapidly in opening Asia-Pacific markets, thereby disadvantaging the less developed nations. The United States in particular was regarded as pushing too fast, too hard. Thus, the proposals of the so-called Eminent Persons Group (EPG) for a two phase time-table for full liberalization, 2010 for the APEC advanced nations, 2020 for others, evoked concern on the part of certain ASEAN members.

Such a view was strongly held by Malaysia's Prime Minister Mahathir who had earlier proposed the creation of an East Asian Economic Group (EAEG) that would exclude all western nations including Australia and New Zealand. Mahathir's proposal was subsequently modified, termed the East Asian Economic Caucus (EAEC), and presented as a body that would work within APEC. Skepticism concerning the EAEC by such parties as Japan remained, however, given the strong opposition of the United States.

Meanwhile, through the post-ministerial conferences, and subsequently, through the creation of an ASEAN Regional Forum (ARF), ASEAN has played a prominent role in forwarding discussions on Asia-Pacific security issues, encompassing the entire region. In 1976, members had agreed to the ASEAN Treaty of Amity and Cooperation, an accord to which all members are supposed to adhere (see *ASEAN Regional Forum*). In 1992, ASEAN set forth the view that all parties concerned in the controversy over the potentially oil-rich South China Sea atolls should settle differences peacefully, refraining from violence. The adherence of Vietnam to ASEAN brings this issue to the fore, since the principal antagonists up to date have been Vietnam and China, although Malaysia and the Philippines are also involved. Even before it joined ASEAN, Vietnam had signified its adherence to the 1992 accord.

ASEAN's stance appeared to reap dividends when at the July 1995 ASEAN Post-Ministerial Conference, Qian Qichen, PRC Foreign Minister, agreed to multilateral discussions on the dispute involving ASEAN members. However, a resolution to the controversy is not in sight. In late 1994, the Law of the Sea Treaty came into effect, providing that littoral states hold a 200-mile exclusive economic zone (see *Oceans: The Common Heritage*).

Given the conflicting jurisdictions, this complicates rather than alleviates the problems.

The ARF represents the culmination of ASEAN efforts to expand its security role, with the initial meeting held in July, 1994. In essence, the ARF is a dialogue and consultative organization to promote confidence-building measures, and in the case of disputes, to advance possible remedies. Its membership includes virtually all of the East Asian states (North Korea and Myanmar up to date are not involved) as well as the United States.

Thus far, the ARF has had modest accomplishments. Given its heterogeneous membership, and the fact that most major disputes are essentially bilateral in nature, it lacks the capacity to be a decision-making body. It has provided a regularized opportunity for Asia-Pacific leaders to come into regular contact, and this has value. Sometimes, the between-session one-on-one discussions are the most useful, providing an understanding of views and establishing the basis for subsequent bilateral dialogue.

In any case, in the absence of a more effective peacemaking and peacekeeping regional organization, the ARF serves a purpose. At some point in the future, we may witness the emergence of a Northeast Asia Security Cooperation forum, as has been suggested by various parties. Already, a Track II forum of this type is in operation. Until that time, however, the ARF provides a platform for states to air their concerns and proposals.

Thus, as 1997 opened, ASEAN appeared to be stronger and more vital than at any time in its thirty-year history. Membership was being expanded to eventually include the ten states of the Southeast Asian region. Intra-ASEAN disputes were at a minimum, with those issues not yet resolved subject to dialogue. On the region-wide front, the ARF was serving a purpose, albeit, one somewhat limited by circumstances.

Significant progress had been made toward a free trade zone through AFTA, with the primary question being the capacities of newly acquired members. Through active participation in APEC, ASEAN members had made their collective voice heard with respect to the Asia-Pacific region as a whole. In sum, ASEAN appears destined to have a lengthy and fruitful existence, with the likelihood that it will play an important role in the early 21st Century, both with respect to economic and political-security issues.

See also: *Economic Integration; Regionalism in Asia-Pacific, Organizational Forms of; Regionalism, Economic Security and Peace: The Asia Pacific; Economic Integration; Security Regimes: Focusing on Asia-Pacific*

ROBERT A. SCALAPINO

# Augustus

Gaius Octavius (63 BC-AD 14), the founder of the Roman Empire, is best known by the honorific name Augustus, which was bestowed on him by the Roman senate in 27 BC. As a youth, his ability was noted by Julius Caesar, his mother's uncle, who adopted him and willed him most of his vast estate. Upon Caesar's assassination in 44 BC, Augustus used this legacy and the Roman army's loyalty to his adoptive father to become a major force in Rome's troubled politics. By 36 BC, after victory in several bloody civil wars, Augustus had become the master of the western part of the Roman state. Mark Antony ruled the east, but the relationship between the two became increasingly tense. They went to war against one another in 32 BC, a struggle which ended with Antony's defeat at Actium in 31 BC and his suicide (along with that of his ally and paramour, Egypt's queen Cleopatra) a year later.

These events left Augustus in undisputed control of the Roman state. Though he maintained Rome's traditional republican form of government, he gathered more and more power into his own hands. Though he was usually referred to as *princeps* (first citizen) rather than *imperator* (emperor), the term used for his successors, he was in fact the first of the Roman Emperors. Augustus prove to be an extraordinarily astute politician as well as a gifted administrator. Though his power rested at bottom on his control of Rome's army, he was careful to rule by persuasion and accommodation wherever possible, using force and the threat of force only as last resorts. He gave Rome a far more honest and efficient government than it had ever known, as well as allowing local government far more autonomy within the Roman state.

The key factor in the willingness of so many Romans to acquiesce to their loss of freedom under Augustus, though, was that he promised them peace. The last century of the Roman republic had been stained by increasingly bloody civil strife, culminating in a period of almost constant warfare between 49 and 31 BC. Rome's factional and social fissures had become so great that many despaired of ever healing them. They concluded that the wisest course of action was to give their loyalty to a strong man who could enforce order and bring peace back to their society.

Indeed, Augustus's defeat of Antony did signal the beginning of the "Pax Romana," a period of internal peace throughout the Mediterranean world which lasted nearly unbroken for two and half centuries.

Augustus's foreign policy was characterized more by conservatism and caution than by a desire to expand Roman power by military means. He successfully resisted pressure to wage a war of vengance against the Parthians, instead achieving a peaceful settlement of Roman Parthian differences in 20 BC. In Europe, though, his desire to safeguard the northern approaches to Rome did lead to a series of wars which pushed the boundary of the empire northward to the Danube River. He attempted, with a strike across the Rhine, to add Germany to the empire as well. This plan, however, was definitively frustrated by a disastrous defeat at the hands of Germanic tribesmen at the battle of the Teutoberg Forest in 9 AD.

Although his career was marked by a number of violent conflicts, Augustus could plausibly claim to be more a man of peace than a man of war. Certainly any conceivable alternative to his rule in Rome would have involved much more suffering from both civil strife and foreign war than Augustus's relatively humane policies produced. One of his proudest boasts, recorded in his testament, was that "the temple of Janus Quirinus, which our ancestors desired to be closed only when peace with victory was secured . . . throughout the entire empire of the Roman people, and which before I was born is recorded to have been closed only twice since the founding of the city, was during my rule three times ordered by the senate to be closed."

*Bibliography*

Buchan J 1937 *Augustus.* Houghton Mifflin, Boston, Massachusetts
Earl D C 1980 *The Age of Augustus.* Exeter Books, New York
Holmes T R 1977 *Architect of the Roman Empire.* AMS Press, New York
Rowell H 1962 *Rome in the Augustan Age.* University of Oklahoma Press, Norman, Oklahoma

GARRETT L. MCAINSH

# Autarky

Autarky refers both to a condition and to policies. A political community enjoys a condition of autarky to

the extent that it is self-sufficient in major commodities and resources needed to achieve welfare and foreign-policy goals. Autarky is economic independence. We must distinguish, however, between autarky as the result of geographic isolation, which is the predominant condition for most subsistence economics, and autarky that is achieved through government, policies in an otherwise interdependent or dependent world or regional economic structure. The isolated kingdoms of Nepal or Bhutan in the nineteenth century are examples of the former. Japan's strict exclusion of all foreign contacts until the mid-nineteenth century, Germany's economic planning to create economic self-sufficiency in the 1930s, and the former Soviet Union's drive to industrialization also in the 1930s are all examples of the latter.

Autarkic policies involve state intervention to build a self-reliant economy, particularly one that can sustain high levels of extraction and production in critical commodities, resources, and war material. They are often combined with stockpiling, so that should economic activity be interrupted by war, blockade (see *Economic Blockade*), or the loss of access to world markets, the state can continue to maintain necessary levels of economic and military production to achieve or defend its welfare, defense, and military goals. The search for self-reliance may also involve forms of economic imperialism, that is, obtaining guaranteed access, often of a monopolistic character, to selected foreign markets.

Autarky as a condition was predominant for most political communities prior to the Industrial Revolution. Low levels of military technology, combined with high degrees of self-sufficiency in food production, allowed most governments to build simple military machines and to sustain minimum requirements of life without recourse to, or reliance upon, foreign supplies. There were exceptions, of course, as in the case where in the seventeenth and eighteenth centuries dwindling supplies of certain types of wood prevented some governments from building large naval fleets.

Since most states today cannot by themselves produce highly sophisticated military hardware, and because a majority of countries are no longer self-sufficient in food production, policies aimed at achieving high levels of autarky would be extremely costly. Both the United States and Russia are relatively self-sufficient, but in the case of the former, it must stockpile large quantities of strategic minerals, including oil, while the latter would have considerable difficulty achieving self-sufficiency in food production. Other countries, such as the United Kingdom, Canada, Japan, the Republic of Korea, and many African nations could not hope to achieve even a modest degree of autarky, as trade constitutes up to 35 percent of their gross national product (GNP) and they are reliant on a broad range of essential imports.

Recent example of autarkic policies indicate that while a certain degree of economic independence, or self-reliance, can be achieved, it is done only at the cost of drastically declining output rates. Burma, which for two decades in the 1960s and 1970s virtually sealed itself off from the outside world, enjoyed its autarky at the cost of economic stagnation and near collapse. The autarkic policies of the People's Republic of China during the period of the Great Proletarian Cultural Revolution also demonstrated that even for a state well-endowed with natural resources, the attempt to become radically self-sufficient may lead to dramatic declines in economic output. Nazi Germany may be the last example of an industrial state that successfully followed a policy of autarky. It was able through radical state intervention in private economic decision making to build a highly self-reliant economy, one that could produce simultaneously a modern armed capability and goods sufficient to meet the minimum welfare needs of its population.

Germany's autarky was achieved by a combination of policies. These included stockpiling, currency manipulation, export and import licensing, import substitution and subsidies to local firms, and research and development to create synthetic substitutes for goods like rubber which had been available only through international trade. The Nazi government and German firms also employed preemptive buying to obtain such critical goods as iron ore and manganese from suppliers in neutral Spain, Turkey, and Sweden. The idea was to purchase these commodities on long-term contracts by offering highly inflated prices that could not be matched by the Allies.

Prior to the war, the Nazi government also penetrated the economies of the Balkan states and turned them into economic satellites. This was done through long-term trade agreements, usually in the form of barter exchanges, whereby the Germans offered guaranteed markets at above-world prices for Bulgarian wheat and Rumanian oil; payment was made by the sale of surplus German manufactured goods. The governments of the Balkan countries were initially pleased to obtain guaranteed markets in a time of world depression; later, they discovered that they had become locked into the German economic sphere, which of course had serious political and diplomatic repercussions. For most of the war, these countries provided a safe supply of commodities and foodstuffs to the Reich. Finally, autarky was buttressed by outright pillage, such as the grain transfers from occupied Ukraine, and by slave labor.

All of these policies provided Nazi Germany with a high degree of self-sufficiency, thus allowing it to prosecute the war with a minimum of economic disruption. Allied countermeasures, which included blockades, blacklists against those trading with Germany, sabotage, and preemptive buying all took their toll eventually, but with the possible exception of oil, the Nazi policies were sufficiently successful that the ultimate military defeat of the German armed forces was not caused by shortages of critical materials.

Theoretically, one can argue that a system of states characterized by relative independence and autarky is likely to be more peaceful than one in which a high level of economic interdependence exists (see *Interdependence, International*). The logic follows from the assumption that economic contacts between states often generate conflicts, particularly where transactions are highly asymmetrical and typically exploitative, or where there is extreme competition for markets and access to sources of supply. Contrary to much liberal thought in the nineteenth century, the argument continues, international trade leads to harmonious diplomatic relations only under very special conditions, conditions which have not been typical throughout most of human history. The case for autarky, as enunciated by Rousseau (see *Rousseau, Jean-Jacques*) and others, is that trade relations are inherently competitive—and often exploitative—suggesting that a condition of peace is likely to result only if states reduce external dependencies as much as possible.

The argument has merit only if one accepts the initial assumption about the competitive aspects of international economic relations. The historical record fails to support the thesis. Systems characterized by high degrees of autarky among their units, as was the case with the Greek states during the classical period, were nevertheless very war-prone. Similarly, the city-states of Italy during the Renaissance were relatively self-sufficient, but wars between the units were almost incessant. The aggressions of the 1930s by Italy, Germany, and Japan were launched against a background of falling levels of international trade and deliberate attempts by many states to achieve high levels of autarky. The explanation may be that wars and aggressions (see *Aggression*) influenced the declines in trade rather than the reverse, but most experts agree today that the search for eco-

nomic self-sufficiency in a period of depression or recession is likely to cause serious diplomatic conflicts, not peace.

The counterargument can also note that periods of high economic interdependence combined with expanding international trade have often been accompanied by diplomatic stability, as in the late nineteenth century and in the post-Second World War period. To the extent that states have relatively free access to markets and sources of supply, economic conflicts are less likely to become linked to security and territorial issues which, of course, are major sources of international crises and wars.

Autarky is related to war in the sense that states generally try to achieve high levels of economic self-sufficiency when they are either planning or anticipating war. These policies may not cause wars directly, but they are probably a good indicator of the state of diplomatic tensions at any given time. Stockpiling, preemptive buying, import substitution, and the search for guaranteed markets to the exclusion of others indicate that not all is well on the diplomatic front. They are also a form of insurance for those anticipating direct involvement in crises and war.

See also: *Self-reliance*

*Bibliography*

Buzan B 1984 Economic structure and international security. *Int'l Organization* 38(4)
Geldenhays D *Isolated States: A Comparative Analysis.* Cambridge University Press, Cambridge
Gordon D L, Dangerfield R 1947 *The Hidden Weapon: The Story of Economic Warfare.* Harper and Row, New York
Hirschman A O 1945 *National Power and the Structure of Foreign Trade.* University of California Press, Berkeley, California
Holsti K J 1982 *Why Nations Realign: Foreign Policy Restructuring in the Postwar World.* Allen and Unwin, London
Knorr K 1975 *The Power of Nations.* Basic Books, New York
Kohn L 1979 *Development Without Aid: The Translucent Society.* Schocken, New York
Vaughan C E (ed.) 1915 *The Political Writings of J-J Rousseau.* Cambridge University Press, Cambridge

K. J. HOLSTI

# Avoiding Conflict by Preventive Diplomacy: West New Guinea, 1951

The Netherlands West New Guinea crisis, which became acute during President Kennedy's administration, arose from the demands of President Sukarno of Indonesia that the Dutch evacuate and turn over this territory to Indonesia. The problem was assigned to me to handle as Under Secretary of State for Political Affairs, under the general supervision of the Secretary and Under Secretary. The President himself made the decision that we would take an active role in mediating the matter.

Although we had little sympathy for Sukarno or his objectives, it seemed to be in the Dutch interest, as well as the general interest, that the Dutch withdraw. In one discussion Secretary Rusk asked the Dutch Ambassador whether the Netherlands was willing to fight Sukarno to keep West New Guinea, and the answer was "no." "That's why we are not willing to keep it for you," replied Rusk. If the Dutch were not prepared to fight for their position in West New Guinea, there was no reason why we or others should.

We were, however, willing to risk some of our good will with the Dutch, if necessary, in order to bring about their withdrawal. From the beginning, it was hoped that this could be accomplished under the United Nations, so it would not appear that Sukarno had been rewarded for his aggressive and threatening behavior.

At an earlier stage, I had, as Counselor and head of Policy Planning of the Department, proposed a United Nations Trusteeship for the territory, but this idea was abandoned due to difficulties encountered in the Congo in paying the bill for United Nations actions of this type. As a result of the President's decision that we would play a more active role, Under Secretary George W. Ball and I agreed that we should ask Ambassador Ellsworth Bunker to serve as mediator, but in behalf of the United Nations rather than the US. Although Bunker had spent most of his life in the sugar business, having become president of the American Sugar Company, he had been a skillful Ambassador to Argentina, Italy, and India, combining persistence with patience. It was my responsibility to set up the conference and to follow its day-to-day proceedings. I persuaded George Brown of Houston to donate the use of his estate (which happened to be adjacent to mine, near Middelburg, Virginia), as a site for the secret conference, which the press never located and the local gentry ignored. The President was keenly interested in the conference, and I and others informed him daily of Bunker's progress.

Diplomatic failures make the headlines, diplomatic successes usually do not, especially when they are the result of quiet negotiations out of the public limelight. The resolution in 1962 of the long and bitter dispute between Holland and Indonesia over the future of West New Guinea was the result of patient labor by a skilled American diplomat acting as mediator between the two parties. I believe there is little doubt that had this effort not succeeded, there would have been war—the last of the wars of colonial withdrawal, with far-reaching consequences for the area and great cost to the Dutch.

As Chairman of the Policy Planning Council I had initiated a study of the West Irian (West New Guinea) problem early in 1961. The dispute, I contended, offered a classical opportunity to deflect two countries from what could only be described as a "collision course." The timing of an intervention to resolve a dispute is all-important. Early efforts to bring the parties together had failed because the crisis was not yet ripe (see *Crisis Management*). A later effort would probably have been too late. When John F. Kennedy became President in 1961, much futile effort had been expended on the problem by the UN, the US, and others, as well as by the parties concerned.

The recommendation of the Policy Planning Council that was submitted to Secretary of State Dean Rusk and by him to the President was based on a thorough study of the problem by career Foreign Service Officer Edward E. Rice. It concluded that the US should abandon its policy of neutrality in the dispute and offer its services as a mediator. We advocated a solution whereby a United Nations Trusteeship would serve as a way station, a fig leaf to cover the ultimate transfer to Indonesian sovereignty, which we considered inevitable. The President authorized me to consult with Senator J. William Fulbright, Chairman of the Senate Foreign Relations Committee, who promised his support. Averell Harriman, then Assistant Secretary for Far Eastern Affairs, skillfully obtained UN, Dutch, and Indonesian approval of our mediation under terms that offered hope for success.

Then there was the question of who would be the American mediator. Ball and I were convinced that the best possible mediator would be Ellsworth Bunker, then in temporary retirement. Although other possible mediators were considered, there was never any question that the Department's choice was Bunker. Ball and I talked with him, pointing out all the difficulties. He expressed willingness to undertake the task and was accepted by the two parties to the dispute.

The story of how Bunker went about his task is an interesting one. From March to August 1962, off and on, a series of negotiations were conducted near Middelburg, Virginia, and later in New York, Washington, The Hague, and Jakarta. Seemingly impossible obstacles were encountered, which necessitated the personal intervention of President Kennedy. These involved the difficult problem for the Dutch of fulfilling their perceived obligations to the Papuans for self-determination, and the Indonesian demand for a direct transfer of sovereignty. It was only due to the patience, understanding, tact, and quiet good sense of Bunker as "moderator," as he chose to call himself, that the negotiations succeeded.

During the six months of his mediation the threads of the discussions were always in Bunker's hands. At difficult times, he always had a suggestion for overcoming the impasse, some new tact to try, which he could put to the parties. In these efforts his combination of skill and integrity was all-important. In the race against war, diplomacy and Bunker won.

Ambassador Martin Herz edited a booklet published by the Institute for the Study of Diplomacy of Georgetown University, on the unique aspects of the negotiation, which follow in part.

The notion held by outsiders, that diplomatic negotiations involve two delegations sitting across from each other along a green, baize-covered table, addressing each other with stilted and perhaps overly polite phrases, mindful of all the niceties of diplomatic punctilio and protocol, enunciating carefully guarded legal formulations couched in even more guarded diplomatic circumlocutions, with the side that makes the more convincing arguments carrying the day—that notion is shattered by this account. And it is well that that notion should be shattered, because it never had much validity in the first place.

Neither, however, is the opposite kind of negotiation the rule, although it is, alas, a sufficiently frequent exception to justify analysis in a case study—with two sides talking past each other, or only pretending to understand each other's positions, or pretending to *misunderstand* each other's positions, failing to come to grips with the core problems in terms which are susceptible to adjustment, hardening their stance, making irrelevant concessions that are then touted as solutions, engaging in threats or insincere brandishments or personal attacks, failing to show up at meetings, or trying to involve outsiders in their positions, or going public with only portions of those positions, upping the ante when agreement seems in sight, etc.

Not all of the foregoing undesirable features were present in the Dutch-Indonesian negotiations, but many of them were; and many stemmed from the basic inequality of the two negotiating partners, which the author correctly brings out in his Preface: The Dutch wanted out and the Indonesians wanted in, the Dutch were far away and the Indonesians

close at hand, the Dutch talked in terms of principles and the Indonesians in terms of both principles and power. Why, then, did the negotiation take so long? Why was the role of the mediator so critical? Because the Dutch did not want (were not able, politically) to pull out of West New Guinea at any price, and the Indonesians preferred—at least for a time—a negotiated solution to one obtained by force.

The foremost goal of Ellsworth Bunker was to implement Washington's broad outline for a peaceful transfer of West New Guinea to Indonesia. The precise manner in which this plan could be effected was left to his own discretion. The breakdown of the March talks apparently convinced Bunker that a comprehensive formula had to be put to both parties. This formula, which formed the core of what later became known as the Bunker Plan, contained the minimum requirements of each side: West New Guinea would ultimately pass to Indonesia, and The Netherlands would receive face-saving guarantees with respect to Papuan free choice. Significantly, a framework for future negotiations had now been established; henceforth both sides had to address the points contained in this formula.

The key turning point in the mediation exercise occurred when Bunker, having failed to win Dutch acceptance of his proposals, decided to make his formula public. The initial reaction of The Hague was shock, and Dutch officials angrily charged that Bunker had himself become a party to the dispute. But this tactic was necessary and achieved its desired effect. By appealing to world opinion to judge the fairness of his proposals, Bunker generated additional pressure on the Dutch to accept his formula as the matrix for renewed negotiations.

When the negotiations finally resumed at Middelburg in July, Bunker resisted repeated Indonesian attempts to undermine his formula and pressed for a discussion of the practical aspects of his Plan. He also overcame the problem of Ambassador Malik's limited mandate by stressing that discussion of the details of transfer was "unofficial" and that any agreement on these points would thus be only tentative. Another device which Bunker used during the negotiations was to deal with the easiest issues first. This tactic had the advantage of enlarging the area of common ground between the two sides, thus creating a slightly improved mutual confidence and a sense of momentum. At a number of critical stages during the negotiations—most notably the July 26 crisis and the flag incident—Bunker appealed to higher authorities to break a deadlock.

During the final hectic days of the talks at the United Nations, when the Dutch negotiating stance virtually collapsed in the face of the threat of war, Bunker was forced to exert maximum leverage (through the US government and the UN Secretary General) on the Indonesians to win Sukarno's acceptance of Bunker's compromise formula for resolving the flag dispute. At one point in his talks with the Indonesian Foreign Minister, Bunker told Subandrio that the Indonesian position in this matter was "outrageous and incomprehensible." Such strong language from a diplomat noted for his imperturbability no doubt had an effect on Subandrio's decision to endorse the mediator's proposals—especially since Bunker had the support of both President Kennedy and Secretary General Thant.

See also: *Negotiations, Direct; Problem Solving in Internationalized Conflicts; Alternative Dispute Resolution; Arbitration, International*

GEORGE C. MCGHEE

# B

## Bahá'í Peace Program

The establishment of world peace is one of the cardinal objectives of the Bahá'í Faith and has occupied a central position in the activities of the Bahá'í community since its inception in 1844. The Bahá'í Peace Program is not centered upon the mere elimination of war as a means of the settlement of disputes among peoples and nations of the world. Rather, peace is viewed in the Bahá'í Faith as one fundamental outcome of an evolutionary transformation of human life on this planet—a transformation which occurs at the individual, institutional, and social levels. To provide an overview of the Bahá'í Peace Program it is thus necessary to first examine the Bahá'í concept of peace and then review the specific activities which the Bahá'í community continues to pursue in furtherance of peace.

### 1. The Bahá'í Faith: A Summary

The Bahá'í Faith is an independent world religion based on the teachings of Bahá'u'lláh. The religion began in Persia (now Iran) in 1844 and has since spread to 190 countries and 45 territories. Among the adherents of the Bahá'í Faith are people from all religions, nationalities, and racial and ethnic groups. Bahá'í literature has been translated into more than 802 languages and dialects and the Faith is established in over 119,276 localities around the globe.

The Bahá'í Faith teaches that religious truth is not absolute but relative, part of an unending progression of Divine Revelation, and that all the great religions, though differing in their social aspects, are in essence one. Their founders are regarded as having proceeded from one common Divine source, and their teachings have progressively united ever larger segments of the human family and provided the basis for all human civilizations. The revelation of Bahá'u'lláh, who is seen by Bahá'ís as the latest but not the last of the Divine educators, is scientific in its method and revolves around the principle that the organic unity of mankind represents the final, inevitable stage in the process of human evolution. Religion has as its

fundamental purpose the promotion of concord and harmony and, hand-in-hand with science, constitutes the sole and ultimate basis of a peaceful, ordered and progressive society. The Bahá'í teachings go so far as to say that if religion becomes the source of discord and conflict then it is better to be without it.

Unlike most other religious systems, the Bahá'í Faith has no clergy or religious leaders. Rather, its affairs are administered by democratically-elected spiritual assemblies on a local level in 17,148 villages, towns, and cities around the world and on a national level in 174 countries and territories. The international governing body of the Bahá'í Faith, the Universal House of Justice, is elected once every five years by the members of the National Spiritual Assemblies. (All statistics as of 12 June 1996)

### 2. The Bahá'í Concept of Peace

The Bahá'í peace program is based on a profound conceptual framework and a comprehensive practical plan for its implementation. Resting upon its religious foundations, the Bahá'í concept of peace is implicated in a larger process of the regeneration and transformation of all aspects of the life of humanity.

At the individual level the Bahá'í concept of peace calls for an ethical and spiritual lifestyle; universal in its outlook, unifying in its impact, and truth-seeking and truthful in its approach. World peace is dependent not only on international and inter-group unity, it also requires a citizenry that is peaceful. Inner peace and interpersonal and international peace all are interdependent. Inner peace is a reflection of the unity of human thoughts, feelings, and actions within the framework of the universal spiritual principle that govern human life. As such, the Bahá'í peace program requires individual spiritual transformation along with the institutional changes that are essential for creation of peace.

At the institutional level, the Bahá'í peace program is firmly established on the principle of Justice. Bahá'u lláh states that "*the purpose of Justice is the appearance of unity*"[1] among people and thus redefines the concept of justice in a most dramatic and profound manner. Justice, from a Bahá'í perspective, is both a social and individual quality and an ethical and spiritual phenomenon. For justice to be established there is need for equality, freedom from all forms of prejudice and bigotry, existence of a universal economic system aimed at eradication of the extremes of wealth and poverty, and creation of a civilization marked by the freedom of the individual and the maintenance of the social order.

The central role of justice in the creation of unity and peace assumes both its universality and practicality in the framework of the New World Order envisioned by Bahá'u'lláh. Within this Order, the democratically elected local, national and international institutions of the Bahá'í Faith, called respectively Local and National Spiritual Assemblies and the Universal House of Justice have the specific mandate to administer justice and promote unity. Within the Bahá'í peace program, force becomes an instrument of justice and the politics of power give way to the creative forces of unity.

The central feature of Bahá'í belief concerning peace is the principle of oneness of humankind expressed in the context of unity in diversity. Unity is the fundamental prerequisite for peace. In conjunction with the emergence of unity, the Bahá'í concept of peace is also based on its unique perspectives concerning the collective growth of humankind, the spiritual nature of human reality, and the necessary emergence of a new World Order shaped by new institutional arrangements based on the principle of Justice.

### 2.1 Unity: The Prerequisite for Peace

The pursuit of peace alone is not sufficient for its achievement. Peace is a natural and spontaneous outcome in human affairs once certain prerequisite conditions are met. At all levels of human interaction the most important condition which brings about peace is unity. Unity of husband and wife is the cause of peace in the family; unity among various segments of society brings peace to its citizens: and unity among the nations of the world will herald world peace. Bahá'u'lláh states that *"the well-being of mankind, its peace and security, are unattainable unless and until its unity is firmly established."*[2]

The Bahá'í concept of unity is both broad and specific. At the broad level the establishment of the unity of humanity is pursued as the prerequisite for world peace. Concurrently, however, many specific forms of unity must be established in order for any

lasting peace to evolve. The emancipation of women and their full participation in all fields of human endeavor is an example. The Bahá'í Writings state:

*So it will come to pass that when women participate fully and equally in the affairs of the world, when they enter confidently and capably the great arena of laws and policies, war will cease; for woman will be the obstacle and hindrance to it.*[3]

The harmony of science and religion is another example of a specific type of unity needed for world peace. Truth is one, whether it concerns the nature of the material world, the domain of science, or the social and spiritual realm which is the domain of culture and religion. The role of religious truth is to lead humanity to reject superstitious beliefs and practices based on blind faith. The Bahá'í Faith scientific in its method, sees religious strife as a result of the failure to apply those universal spiritual principles inherent in religion which call for mutual acceptance and forbearance rather than exclusivity and prejudice.

Bahá'ís see a number of other social principles as necessary adjuncts to any successful peace program: universal education and the elimination of ignorance, the principle cause of prejudice; legal measures to eradicate racism, a major barrier to peace; elimination of extremes of wealth and poverty, a source of acute suffering which now keeps the world in a state of instability; the replacement of unbridled nationalism with a wider loyalty to humankind as a whole; and adoption of an international auxiliary language to facilitate communication between peoples of the world.

### 2.2 The Concept of the Collective Growth of Humankind

While unity is the prerequisite for world peace, maturity is the prerequisite for that unity. As Shoghi Effendi, the Head of the Bahá'í Faith from 1921-1957 observes:

*The long ages of infancy and childhood, through which the human race had to pass, have receded into the background. Humanity is now experiencing the commotions invariably associated with the most turbulent stage of its evolution, the stage of adolescence, when the impetuosity of youth and its vehemence reach their climax, and must gradually be superseded by the calmness, the wisdom, and the maturity that characterize the stage of manhood .... Unification of the whole of mankind is the hall-mark of the stage which human society is now approaching. Unity of family, of tribe, of city-state, and nation have been successively attempted and fully established. World unity is the goal towards which a harassed humanity is striving. Nation-building has come to an end. The anarchy inherent in state sovereignty is moving towards a climax. A world, growing to maturity, must abandon this fetish, recognize the oneness and wholeness of human relationships, and establish once for all the machinery that can best incarnate this fundamental principle of its left.*[4]

The demilitarization and reconstruction of the world, as called for by Shoghi Effendi, is now possible because humanity is at last approaching its age of maturity. During childhood and adolescence, rivalries and competition abound and distrust and arrogance dominate human relationships under their less favorable conditions. In the same way, the prevalence of similar conditions in current world affairs development is facing some fundamental difficulties. It is in this light that the following invitation of the Universal House of Justice provides us a framework to approach this monumental task of transition:

*A candid acknowledgment that prejudice, war and exploitation have been the expression of immature stages in a vast historical process and that the human race is today experiencing the unavoidable tumult which marks its collective coming of age is not a reason for despair but a prerequisite to undertaking the stupendous enterprise of building a peaceful world.*[5]

## 2.3 The Spiritual Nature of Human Beings

A radically different and fundamentally positive view of man's spiritual nature is intrinsic to the Bahá'í concept of the collective growth of mankind. Spiritual qualities such as love, justice, enlightenment, truthfulness, and humility, all manifest themselves most powerfully in the context of a mature society, as they do in the mature individual. With the coming of age of humankind, these spiritual qualities will become more apparent and men and women will be able to free themselves from the bondage of instinctual forces. Ultimately, it is the ability to use the uniquely human capacities of knowledge, love and will within the parameters of the ethical and spiritual teachings of religion that will distinguish humanity from animals and will herald the era of a spiritual civilization characterized by justice, unity, and peace.

The view that human beings are essentially noble makes possible and entirely different reaction to violence, which has traditionally been countered by more violence, rationalization of violence, or passive resistance to it. The Bahá'í Faith offers a fourth approach to the problem of human violence, based on the view that contrary to common belief, the powers of kindness, peace and love are more powerful than those of violence, war and hatred. These latter qualities are, in fact, the absence of the former. Hatred is, in essence, the absence of love. In the presence of love, there is no hatred. Likewise, when peace is established, there is no war. Instead there is creativity, life and progress. From the Bahá'í perspective the solution to the ills of mankind comes by developing and nurturing these truly human qualities, and not by focussing on the conditions which emerge as result of the absence of these qualities.

At no time has humanity been faced with as great an opportunity to reaffirm its spiritual nature and thus become victorious over the forces of destruction. Simultaneously, at no time have we been as close to denying our essential reality, thereby delaying the course of our collective evolution. *Whether peace is to be reached only after unimaginable horrors precipitated by humanity's stubborn clinging to old patterns of behavior, or is to be embraced now by an act of consultative will, is the choice before all who inhabit the earth.*[6]

## 2.4 The World Order of Bahá'u'lláh

The creation of a new world order is long overdue, and its establishment must become the main objective of all. In their quest for peace various ideological and social movements have recognized the necessity for the establishment of such a world order, but their proposed methods for achieving and maintaining it have not led to any enduring success. Discrepancies in ideological perceptions or lack of the means necessary to achieve this goal are among the reasons for the failure of their vision.

However, in the Bahá'í Faith both the ideal and the means for the establishment of a new world order are clearly set forth. The ultimate goal of the World Order of Bahá'u'lláh has been delineated specifically in the following passage by Shoghi Effendi:

*The unity of the human race, as envisaged by Bahá'u'lláh, implies the establishment of a world commonwealth in which all nations, races, creeds and classes are closely and permanently united, and in which the autonomy of its state members and the personal freedom and initiative of the individuals that compose them are definitely and completely safeguarded. This commonwealth must, as far as we can visualize it, consist of a world legislature, whose members will, as the trustees of the whole of mankind, ultimately control the entire resources of all the component nations, and enact such laws as shall be required to regulate the life, satisfy the needs and adjust the relationships of all races and* peoples. *A world executive, backed by an international force, will carry out the decisions arrived at, and apply the laws enacted by, this world legislature, and will safeguard the organic unity of the whole commonwealth. A world tribunal will adjudicate and deliver its compulsory and final verdict in all and any disputes that may arise between the various elements constituting this universal system.*[7]

Obviously, such world institutions will require facilitating mechanisms such as a universal auxiliary language, a unified script, universal systems of weights and measures and currency, to be added to the technological capacity for communication and interaction which already exist.

During the last century, the Bahá'í world community has established its administrative order in the anticipation of the gradual evolution of the New World Order. The world-wide Bahá'í community is a prototype which merits close study by all students of peace and globalization.

## 3. The Bahá'í Peace Program 1844-1997

As the Bahá'í concept of peace implies, there are many diverse ways through which Bahá'ís feel they can assist the world in its progression toward peace. Generally the peace activities of the Bahá'í community could be grouped under the following headings: Peace Education and Creation of a Unity-Based Community.

### 3.1 Peace Education

Since its beginning, the Bahá'í Community has made a number of specific attempts to bring to the attention of the leaders and peoples of the world the fact that the greatest challenge before humanity is the achievement of world peace. These education efforts have addressed both the conceptual and the practical aspects of peace education. In regards to the development of a comprehensive conceptual perspective on peace, here we will refer only to a few of the many Writings from the pen of the central figures of the Bahá'í Faith.

The prophet-founder of the Bahá'í Faith Bahá'u'lláh, addressed a number of letters to the leaders and peoples of the world in 1867 calling upon them to focus their attention on the issue of peace. For example, in one of his letters to the kings of the world he observed:

*The time must come when the imperative necessity for the holding of a vast, an all-embracing assemblage of men will be universally realized. The rulers and kings of the earth must attend it, and, participat-*

*ing in its deliberations, must consider such ways and means as will lay the foundation of the world's Great Peace amongst men.*[8]

'Abdu'l-Bahá, the immediate successor to Bahá'u'lláh and the Center of His Covenant, likewise devoted his life and work to the cause of peace. In the years 1911-1913, soon after he was released from his forty year imprisonment, embarked upon a journey to Europe and North America, elaborating on various aspects of peace and unity in a series of talks which are published in the form of three books, *The Promulgation of Universal Peace, Paris Talks, and The Foundations of World Unity.* Furthermore, his book: *The Secret of Divine Civilization* provides profound insights into various aspects of the administration of human affairs in a peaceful and spiritually oriented world.

From the 1920's to 1950's, a period during which humanity struggled with the impact of two world wars, the Guardian of the Bahái Faith, Shoghi Effendi, provided the Bahá'í Community around the world with a penetrating and illuminating vision of a future world order. In his writings such as *The World Order of Bahá'u'lláh, The Promised Day has Come,* and *The Advent of Divine Justice,* he enumerated most of the unique characteristics and specific stages of the process of establishing this new world order.

In 1967, on the centenary of the proclamation of Bahá'u'lláh to the kings and rulers of the world, Bahá'ís brought once again the original peace message of Bahá'u'lláh to the attention of the world's leaders in the form of the book *The Proclamation of Bahá'u'lláh.*

In 1985, the Bahái community began its most direct and audacious campaign of Peace Education. The Universal House of Justice produced a statement entitled *The Promise of World Peace* which was actively disseminated to the leaders, as well as the masses, of humanity. *The Promise of World Peace* declares the Bahá'í belief in the inevitability of world peace and systematically delineates the prerequisites for the emergence of that peace.

At the practical level, the Bahá'í community has developed a systematic and comprehensive program of peace education. We have already referred to some of these educational activities at the individual and institutional levels. Here, we briefly discuss another essential peace education activity—Bahá'í consultation. Consultation is practiced by all individuals and institutions in the Bahá'í communities in all parts of the world: in villages, rural communities, and the metropolitan cities.

Throughout history of humanity and in all parts of

the contemporary world power has played a primary role in decision-making and conflict-resolution activities at the individual, interpersonal, institutional, and international levels. Power, however, is easily abused and the litany of abuses in the form of authoritarian and dictatorial practices and competitive and power-struggle approaches are too familiar to need any elaboration (see *Power*). The primacy of the role of power in the history of humanity has its roots in our biological and psychological evolution during the stages of our collective infancy, childhood, and adolescence. As humanity enters its age of collective adulthood the need for new and effective approaches to conflict-resolution and decision-making become increasingly acute. Consultation is a conceptual and practical approach to the creative resolution of conflict and creation of prerequisites of peace.

The basic goal of consultation is to find the best solution to the question at hand within the framework of unity in diversity and oneness of humanity. The objective is to engage those involved in the consultative process to resolve conflicts in a spirit of amity and with the objective of reaching decisions that are at the same time, just and unifying, specific and universal, compassionate and truthful, and free from the prevalent power-based practices we encounter in all segments of the life of the society. This new approach to conflict-resolution calls for mature and ethical standards to be observed both by the individuals and institutions of the society. In fact, consultation is both a mature tool for conflict-resolution and a conflict-free tool for maturation.

### 3.2 Creation of a Unity-Based Community

While Peace Education is fundamental, it is by no means enough. The real test of the efficacy of the Bahá'í concept of peace is its actual applicability and relevance to the needs of humanity. To this end, the first 150 years of the Bahá'í Faith have been focussed on the erection of the pattern of life and governance whose operational ethic is unity. By creation of patterns of community life based on unity, the circle of peace continues to grow and envelop the peoples of the world.

Accordingly, the Bahá'í Faith has directed its efforts toward the creation of the nucleus of a world community of people united in their views, and having as their common objective the fostering of a global civilization. Furthermore, with the establishment of a unique administrative machinery based on the principle of free elections, universal moral standards, and group consultation, the Bahá'í Faith has been able to create a prototype of a world community

capable of administering human affairs in a constructive and peaceful manner, one in which the motive of power-seeking and personal aggrandizement is being successfully channelled and controlled.

The worldwide Bahá'í community, with its several million adherents scattered in all corners of the globe and representing most of the nations, races, religions, and languages of the world, is an excellent example of a unified society committed to functioning according to the principles of justice, equality, and freedom. Furthermore, the unity of the Bahá'í community is comprehensive, seeing no separation between itself and the rest of humanity and functioning on the principle that *"the earth is but one country and mankind its citizens."*[9]

This is one reason why Bahá'ís refrain from participation in partisan politics, are enjoined to be law-abiding citizens as a demonstration of trustworthiness and do not, under any circumstances, become agents of anarchy, opposition, or war. Instead, they focus all their attention on building a new, united society and electing their administrative bodies by secret ballot without the use of propaganda, nominations, electioneering or divisive power politics.

The Bahá'í community thus provides a global society equipped to meet the challenges and opportunities inherent in establishing a New World Order where peace is an achievable reality rather than a utopian ideal. As such, its experience is worthy of study by individuals or organizations seriously investigating the issue of world peace.

### 4. Conclusion

Viewing the establishment of world order as one of the eventual and inevitable goals of human evolution, Bahá'ís see many favorable signs of progress in current world events which indicate that mankind is slowly moving in the direction of peace. Among them may be cited:

... *The steadily growing strength of the steps towards world order taken initially near the beginning of this century in the creation of the League of Nations, succeeded by the more broadly-based United Nations Organization; the achievement since the Second World War of independence by the majority of all the nations on earth, indicating the completion of the process of nation-building, and the involvement of these fledging nations with older ones in matters of mutual concern; the consequent vast increase in co-operation among hitherto isolated and antagonistic peoples and groups in international undertakings in the scientific, educational, legal, economic and cultural fields; the rise in recent decades of an unprecedented number of humanitarian international organizations; the spread of women's and youth movements calling for an end to war; and the spontaneous spawning of widening networks of ordinary people seeking understanding through personal communication. The scientific and technological advances occurring in this unusually blessed century portend a great surge forward in the social evolution of the planet, and indicate the means by which the practical problems of humanity may be solved. They provide, indeed, the very means for the administration of the complex life of a united world.*[10]

The challenge before humanity and its political, academic, and religious leaders is the need for a new mindset; universal in its outlook, inclusive in its approach, ethical in its principles, just in its administration, and unifying in its objectives. It is only through this process that a balance between the material and spiritual aspects of civilization can be achieved and our collective efforts to create a lasting international peace become both meaningful and practical.

Finally, it should be noted that the movement of humanity towards peace will be gradual. The most immediate and significant step for the creation of a civilization of peace—an agreement by the political leaders of the world to end war—now seems to be at hand. This is an opportune time for *"the holding of a vast, an all-embracing assemblage" of the "rulers and kings of the earth"* to *"consider such ways and*

*means as will lay the foundations of the world's Great Peace amongst men."*[11] Signing of such a treaty by the leaders of governments and the nations of the world, as called by Bahá'u'lláh over 130 years ago, will finally usher in the era of a lesser peace that will eventually be translated to a most great and enduring peace on earth.

See also: *Religion and Peace; World Order; Federalism, World; Peace Education; Global Ethic; World Peace Order, Dimensions of a*

## Notes

1. Bahá'í u'lláh, *Tablets of Baháu'lláh*, (Wilmette, Illinois: Bahá'í Publishing Trust, 1952). p. 67.

2. Bah'áu'lláh, *Gleaning from the Writings of Bah'áu'lláh*, (Wilmette, Illinois: Baháí Publishing Trust, 1952). p. 286.

3. "Abdu'l-Bahá, *The Promulgation of Universal Peace.* (Wilmette, Illinois: Bahá'í Publishing Trust, 1982). p. 135.

4. Shoghi Effendi, *The World Order of Bahá'u'lláh*, (Wilmette, Illinois: Bahá'í Publishing Trust, 1955). p. 202.

5. The Universal House of Justice, *The Promise of World Peace*, (Haifa: Bahá'í World Center, 1985), pp. 3-5.

6. *Ibid.*, pp. 1-2.

7. Shoghi Effendi, *The World Order of Bahá'u'lláh*, (Wilmette, Illinois: Bahá'i Publishing Trust, 1995). p. 203.

8. Bahá'u'lláh, *Gleanings from the Writings of Bahá'u'lláh*, (Wilmette, Illinois: Bahá'i Publishing Trust, 1953). pp. 249-250.

9. *Ibid.*, p. 250.

10. Shoghi Effendi, *The World Order of Bahá'u'*, (Wilmette, Illinois: Baháí Publishing Trust, 1955). pp. 1-2.

11. *Ibid.*, pp. 249-250.

H. B. DANESH

# Balance of Power

Passing references to the balance of power as a mechanism for preserving peace in a system of independent states are found in Greek writings of the classical period, in Chinese analyses of interstate relations during the later Chou period, and in the works of Kautilya, who advised statesmen of the Mauryan dynasty in India. But a formal theory of power-balancing in the conduct of diplomacy became highly developed only later in the fledgling European states system of the late seventeenth and early eighteenth centuries. The Treaty of Utrecht (1713) gave formal recognition to the idea of power balance as an important requisite for maintaining peace and stability in Europe. Although some philosophers and observers, such as Rousseau (see *Rousseau, Jean-Jacques*), were highly critical of the idea—claiming that the search for a mythical balance

led to war, not to peace—it has persisted in the vocabulary of diplomacy and theoretical writings on international politics up to the present day. The idea of a balance of power has thus guided statesmen in their search for peace, provided justifications for a variety of diplomatic maneuvers, including alliance formation and wars to "preserve" the balance, and has served propaganda purposes as well.

## 1. Theoretical Considerations

The assumptions of the theory are relatively simple:

(a) the maintenance of the sovereignty and independence of these communities is a primary goal of political and diplomatic life;

(b) some states will seek to augment their power by

territorial expansion, internal development, or the formation of coalitions with like-minded states;

(c)  it is in the interest of all states in the system not to allow a single state or coalition to achieve hegemony over the others;

(d)  hence, the most effective guarantee for the perpetuation of the system is to form countercoalitions or to call in a "balancer" to form a military-diplomatic counterweight against those who might seek hegemony; and

(e)  since policy makers are reasonably rational, they will not go to war unless they have a significant preponderance of power.

An approximate balance of power—meaning roughly equal military capabilities—should be sufficient to deter those who might seek hegemony (see *Hegemony*) over the system.

Alliances and technological innovation are the most important mechanisms for "redressing" the balance, should a hegemon approach preponderance. In the eighteenth century, many of the European states made and shifted alliances with startling rapidity, sometimes for very concrete reasons of state interest, but at others, for the more abstract reason of attempting to maintain an overall equilibrium of power on the Continent. The role of the smaller states in the system is to support the major actors in an attempt to maintain that distribution of power that is characterized as "balanced." In the theory of power-balancing, then, the critical variables are the military growth rates of the major powers, and the forging of diplomatic-military coalitions.

There is a reasonable consensus among academics that the balance of power is not merely a descriptive device, a shorthand for characterizing any distribution of power. Rather, it is a full theory of hypothesis about diplomatic life, which posits the necessary and sufficient conditions for preventing hegemony, and which describes the general strategies states must pursue in order to attain a rough equilibrium.

Despite straightforward assumptions, the theory is by no means a model of clarity. What, for example, does "balance" mean? In diplomatic usage, it has often referred to virtually any distribution of power between two or more actors, even if their military capabilities are far from equal. For example, observers of international politics in the 1950s and 1960s often spoke of the Soviet-United States "balance," despite the fact that during those decades the total United States military arsenal and all the

other bases of power, such as industrial output and modern technology, were vastly superior to those of the former Soviet Union, which had only an edge in troops and certain categories of conventional weapons. Another ambiguity: is it necessary to have a "balancer" for the system to maintain peace and stability? During the nineteenth century, some British statesmen held that it was always in the interest of the United Kingdom to intervene on the Continent on behalf of the weak power or coalition, should a single power seek domination of Europe. One version of the balance-of-power theory thus requires a relatively indifferent power which will always align with the weaker coalition against those seeking hegemony.

The dependent variable is war. The purpose of balancing, in some versions of the theory, is to prevent war. But what kind of war? Some writers have argued that it is to prevent all war. Rousseau's critique of the theory stems from his observation that in the eighteenth century, states sometimes undertook wars in the name of maintaining or restoring the balance. But if the balance is supposed to prevent war, how can wars be undertaken in its name? Rousseau alerts us to a fundamental distinction in various versions of the theory, one that is often misunderstood or not even acknowledged. For many writers, power-balancing is not designed to prevent all wars, but to sustain the essential characteristics of the states system, namely the continued independence and sovereignty of its members, and the various rules that have been developed to govern their mutual relations. This version of the theory does not hypothesize that all wars can be prevented, but only that balancing is necessary to prevent a potential hegemon from transforming the states system into a regional or universal empire. The coalitions against Louis XIV, Napoleon, Imperial Germany, and Nazi Germany were formed not so much to protect highly circumscribed territorial or commercial interests, but to defend the entire diplomatic order against those who wished to transform it into a French or German-centered world empire. Wars and interventions may be necessary to prevent such a system transformation. Thus the theory in its classical form does not prescribe the necessary conditions for perpetual peace; rather, it outlines the diplomatic and military steps—of which war may be one—that are necessary to preserve the essential characteristics of an interstate system. Other versions of the theory, on the other hand, argue that the purpose of power-balancing is to prevent all war, or at least wars between the major powers.

A final ambiguity refers to the status of balance of power as both an explanatory device and as a guide to policy. Kenneth Waltz (1978) has argued that the balance of power is an *automatic* consequence of a system of anarchy where there is no superior authority over individual states. Balances will form naturally regardless of the policies of particular leaders. Most other analysts insist that the balance of power is a human *contrivance*, designed and implemented by statespersons. Those who, like the British government in the 1930s, fail to pursue the appropriate balancing strategies will ultimately pay the price for their mistakes by having to fight wars against potential hegemons. The way to avoid such wars is to build counter-coalitions and to augment national capabilities. These actions must be planned, they do not just happen automatically.

## 2. Research Findings

How does contemporary research address these questions? The problem of the relationship between power distribution and peace has received considerable attention in recent years. Important works by Organski (1968), Organski and Kugler (1980), Gilpin (1981), Singer et al., (1972), Bueno de Mesquita (1978), and others suggest no firm conclusion. Gilpin and Organski, for example, have argued that preponderance, not balance, is the necessary condition for peace. The great *status quo* power must resist the challenges posed by rising powers. During the Cold War, the United States was seen as the preponderant power which maintained a diplomatic order descended from the European states system, but fundamentally transformed as a result of the Second World War. The former Soviet Union (and the People's Republic of China until the early 1970s) was the main challenger. According to Organski, the most dangerous time is when the distribution of military and other capabilities between these two states approaches equality. But a number of other studies show that war is more likely to break out when power is unequally distributed and, thus, that peace is more probable in a system characterized by rough equality among the main powers.

While these studies have added to our knowledge of the dynamics of international politics, it is difficult to assess them because they use different databases, statistical practices, research design, and historical periods. But the most significant problem remains the character of the dependent variable, that is, war. Most studies have linked power distribution to the incidence of all war in the system. But this tests only one version of the theory. A more appropriate question is whether balance or preponderance is linked to

hegemonic wars. Historically, the greatest challenges to the modern states system came from Louis XIV, Napoleon, possibly Imperial Germany, Nazi Germany, and on a regional basis, Japan in the 1930s. In none of these cases was war avoided, even when power was distributed relatively evenly, as in 1914. But the theory is supported in the sense that in each of these instances, those who sought to transform the system, whether into a Holy Roman Empire or a Thousand Year Reich, were defeated by a superior coalition of those who were committed to the maintenance of the states system. It is also possible to argue that had the *status quo* coalitions formed earlier, the onslaughts of those seeking hegemony might have been effectively deterred.

Whatever the case, it is clear that the theory as a predictor of actual behavior is limited. If there is some evidence that a relatively equal distribution of power in the system is associated with peace, it does not follow that the balance works automatically, or that in any sense it is a "law" of international politics. The available evidence allows us only to say that in a condition of relative equality, certain types of wars are less likely to occur. There are few statistical regularities in the available studies, so that neither case—balance or preponderance—is proven. Indeed, so many other variables help account for the incidence of wars, that the simple equation: balance=peace has to be approached with considerable skepticism. In a more limited form, however, the theory does explain the history of the modern states system quite well: those who seek to transform this system into a regional or world empire will sooner or later face a massive coalition of those who are committed to the values of sovereignty and independence. The theory thus tells us more about one of the essential mechanisms for preservation of the states system—even when it involves world wars—than it does about the incidence of war, or the conditions of peace.

## 3. The Utility of the Concept in the Nuclear Age

We might also raise the question of the explanatory and descriptive utility of the concept in the nuclear age. What are some of the essential differences between the techniques of balancing in the eighteenth and late twentieth centuries?

In the post-Second World War polarized system, military-technological buildup and innovation by each superpower were more significant means of maintaining or striving for balance than was the search for allies. The allies of the former Soviet Union and the United States played significant strategic roles, but none by itself was crucial to the overall distribution of military capabilities. Neither state vigorously sought to create new, formal, allies since Cuba joined the Soviet bloc in the 1960s. Both suffered a defection—the People's Republic of China's renunciation of its military agreement with the Soviet Union, and the withdrawal of France from the NATO command structure in the 1960s—but at no great loss to overall strength. Both sides relied instead on the development of nuclear capabilities, both by addition of numbers and by improvement of warheads and missile accuracy. Whereas in the eighteenth century, when all nations had military forces characterized by primitive technology, the number and quality of allies was critical in maintaining balances, today, adjustments to the balance can be made by the superpowers unilaterally.

As a guide to Cold War policies, the idea of balance of power suffered from serious difficulties. For example, neither Soviet Union nor United States policy makers reached a consensus on the empirical components or indicators of such terms as "balance," "inferiority," "superiority," or "parity." One party's search for parity was characterized by the spokespersons of the other as the attempt to attain superiority; for one side, a reasonable "balance" appeared to the other as a dangerous imbalance. Because of misperceptions, and for reasons of propaganda, prestige, and prejudice, it was unlikely that any balance, if achieved, would be stable in the sense that both sides would forgo future military innovation programs. The persistent temptation to improve old weapons and to develop new ones always rendered any balance precarious. Both sides maintained a retaliatory capacity that would make a first strike suicidal, but both dreaded the possibility that the opponent might ultimately develop a capability for a disarming first strike, the situation the Reagan Administration termed a "window of vulnerability." The balance therefore remained precarious, and each side lived with the nightmare of a technological breakthrough that could render it highly vulnerable. It is for this reason that during the Cold War, the balance of power was also termed the balance of terror.

One consequence of this state of affairs was that the Soviet-United States rivalry was conducted largely through means involving a relatively low probability of generating a superpower crisis. Subversion, foreign aid, propaganda, arms sales, support for guerrilla groups, and occasional direct intervention, as in Afghanistan and Grenada, were the main instrumentalities the superpowers used to protect or extend their interests.

## 4. The Balance of Power in the Post-Cold War Era

The end of the Cold War has given rise to further questions about the analytical utility of the balance of power concept. With the serious erosion of Russian military capabilities, morale, and organization since 1991, it is difficult to point to any balance among today's great powers. Some have argued that we are living in a "unipolar" world where the United States is the only superpower. Since the United States does not constitute a threat to the security of most other countries in the world, is there a need for a balancer? In an age when power and influence in international affairs are based more on technological, economic, and environmental leadership, does military capability mean very much? Others have argued that despite clear American predominance in the contemporary world, it cannot act as a true hegemon which, according to the eighteenth century international lawyer Emerich Vattel, can "lay down the law" to the rest of the world. In an age of interdependence, the United States can only lead a coalition of powers, as it did in dealing with the Iraq invasion of Kuwait in 1990. The appropriate metaphor to characterize today's power arrangements is not a balance, but a *concert* of powers that can collectively manage the international system.

Stephen Walt (1987) has made a further point that the critical variable in the relations between the great powers is not balances of capabilities, but of threats. In international relations it is quite possible, as history shows, that two or more states can have roughly equal or even predominant military capabilities. The critical question is whether those capabilities constitute a threat to others. The United States has vastly superior military capabilities, but it does not pose a threat of hegemony to the rest of the system. In contrast, contemporary relations between Greece and Turkey, or between Israel and Syria, involve perceived threats that require balancing and counterthreats.

A final observation is that the balance of power concept does not describe or explain relations between states in many regions of the world. Although there was a balance of power system in nineteenth-century South America, there is none today. Balancing is not a concept particularly relevant to the analysis of relations within the European Union, nor does it help us understand the dynamics of diplomacy within Africa. In Asia, by contrast, notions of balancing are prominent in both scholarly analysis and diplomacy. The ASEAN countries constitute an implicit counterweight to Chinese military expansion in the region, and United States-Japan and United States-South Korean security arrangements, designed originally to deal with the problems posed by the former Soviet Union and North Korea, today constitute some sort of balancing mechanism, also against China.

Given the ambiguities of the concept of balance of power, and its seeming irrelevance as characterization of post-Cold War international politics, it is difficult to sustain the argument that the idea is some sort of "law" of international politics, that it is ubiquitous, or that it is automatic. There remain areas of regional rivalry where balancing of capabilities and threats seems prudent and even necessary to maintain peace. But in the rest of the world, economic, environmental, technological, and other sorts of issues have largely replaced military rivalries. Finally, since 1945, we have witnessed a significant decline in the incidence of interstate wars. Today, wars within states are much more important. The concept of balance of power developed in a particular European and Cold War diplomatic system that no longer exists. We have in some respects a new type of international system where its dynamics will have to be explained and understood by new concepts.

See also: *Peace, Systems View of*

*Bibliography* ────────────────────

Bueno de Mesquita B 1978 Systemic polarization and the occurrence and duration of war. *J. Conflict Resolution* 22
Claude I 1962 *Power and International Relations*. Random House, New York
Gilpin R 1981 *War and Change in World Politics*. Cambridge University Press, Cambridge
Gulick E 1955 *Europe's Classical Balance of Power*. Cornell University Press, Ithaca, New York
Haas EB 1953 The balance of power: Prescription, concept, or propaganda? *World Politics* 5
Healy B, Stein A 1973 The balance of power in international history: Theory and reality. *J. Conflict Resolution* 17
Hume D 1948 Of the balance of power. In: Hendel CW (ed.) 1948 *David Hume's Political Essays*. Bobbs-Merrill, Indianapolis, Indiana
Kaplan M A 1957 *System and Process in International Politics*. Wiley, New York
Organski A F K 1968 *World Politics*. Knopf, New York
Organski A F K 1968 Balancing, stability, and war. *Int'l Studies Q.* 40
Singer J D, Bremer S, Stuckey J 1972 Capability distribution, uncertainty, and major power war, 1820-1965. In: Russett B M (ed.) 1972 *Peace, War and Numbers*. Sage, Beverly Hills, California
Walt S 1987 *The Origin of Alliances*. Cornell University Press, Ithaca
Waltz KN 1979 *Theory of International Politics*. Addison-Wesley, Reading, Massachussetts
Wight M 1973 The balance of power and international order. In: James A (ed.) 1973 *The Bases of International Order*. Oxford University Press, Oxford

K. J. HOLSTI

# Balzac, Honoré de

Honoré de Balzac was born in Tours on 20 May 1799. In time he would become heart and soul a Parisian, but he would always maintain a special attachment to his native province, Touraine. Notwithstanding the aristocratic *de* he inserted in his name, his background was very plebeian, very modest. Of the other three children, his favorite was a sister Laure, later Mme Surville, to whom many of his letters are addressed. Although said to have been involved in a scheme to rescue the imprisoned Queen Marie Antoinette during the French Revolution, his father, Bernard Francis Balzac, subsequently served Napoleon well as a military supplier. From 1807 to 1813 Honoré studied at the Oratorian Collège de Vendôme and at the Lycée de Tours. When Bernard Francis moved his family to Paris in 1814, his son's studies were continued at the Lycée Charlemagne.

While law did not attract him as a profession, Balzac became a law student in 1816 and worked as a law clerk until 1819, attending literature courses at the Sorbonne also. One of his professors at the Sorbonne was Abel François Villemain, who once declared, "Give me a country's map, its outline, its climate, its waters, its winds, its whole physical geography; give me its natural produce, its flora, its fauna, and I take it upon myself to tell you *a priori* what the man from this country will be like . . . , not accidentally but necessarily." Balzac agreed. To this lesson in basic determinism should be added other influences: Cuvier and Geoffroy St-Hilaire as well as Swedenborg, Gall, Mesmer, and Lavater—all of whose teachings, the nascent novelist believed, contributed to explaining human behavior.

Realizing that their son was not cut out to be a lawyer, Balzac's parents agreed in 1819 to allow him a small income for two years during which time he would endeavor to establish himself as a writer. The next few years were harsh. He wrote a verse tragedy, *Cromwell*, and, under a series of resounding pen names, a succession of bad novels. But he was learning his trade and was on his way to becoming the greatest novelist France has ever produced. Meanwhile, he had several overlapping tender attachments, mostly with women considerably older than he. The earliest was with Laure ("La Dilecta") de Berny, whose stepfather, like Balzac's father, had once tried to rescue the doomed Marie Antoinette. Mme de Berny was the model for the incomparable Mme de Mortsauf in *Le Lys dans la vallée* (1835). Another mistress was a novelist, the Duchesse d'Abrantès, who introduced him to salons where he met imperial warriors whose deeds, a little more than a decade earlier, had shaken Europe. There was also another duchess, Henriette de Castries, who belonged to France's oldest aristocracy. She fostered his conservatism and became the heroine of *La Duchesse de Langeais* (1834). With two or three other women he had rewarding platonic relationships. One of these was with the poetess Delphine de Girardin, whose enterprising husband Emile published *La Presse* and was in a position to print his work. Another valued friend was Zulma Carraud, a provincial army officer's wife, who gave him much-needed, levelheaded advice.

But exquisite, intellectual women did not make him wealthy. Both as an apprentice author and, later, as a mature artist, Balzac lived beyond his means. First one then another scheme to make money captured his volatile imagination. He started periodicals such as the *Chronique de Paris* and the *Revue parisienne*, which were short-lived. One or two publishing ventures likewise failed. His most foolhardy undertaking was a silver mine in Sardinia. From all of these he emerged owing more money than before but having acquired a firsthand knowledge of the workings, often sordid, of the financial world, a knowledge that, unfortunately, he was incapable of applying to his own business endeavors. If he was going to get rich, clearly he was going to have to do it with his pen.

With that pen he was already beginning to turn out a phenomenal number of short stories, novellas, novels, plays. Collectively they would bring in a great deal of money over the years, but their author always needed more than they earned. His first real success came in 1829 with an historical novel, *Les Chouans*.

Laid in 1799, it chronicles Catholic, royalist resistance to the First Republic in Brittany and Normandy during the last phase of the French Revolution. Balzac signed it with his own name. After serving a ten-year novitiate, all of a sudden he had attained artistic maturity. From then on a constant stream of masterpieces flowed from his pen. Some of these are brilliant short stories or *nouvelles* and include "L'Elixir de longue vie" (1830), "Le Réquisitionnaire" (1831), "La Femme abandonnée" (1832), "Le Curé de Tours" (1832), "Un Drame au bord de la mer" (1834), and "Facino Cane" (1836), which appeared in periodicals such as the *Revue de Paris*, the *Revue des Deux Mondes*, and *La Mode*. Balzac also wrote, imitating the language of the sixteenth century, some rather licentious tales which he called *Contes drolatiques*. But it was chiefly his novels that brought him to the reading public's lasting attention. *Louis Lambert, Le Médecin de campagne, Eugénie Grandet, Ferragus, La Recherche de l'absolu, Le Père Goriot, La Fille aux yeux d'or, Le Lys dans la vallée* and almost innumerable others appeared in quick succession. Balzac wrote hastily and, when reading his proofs, not only made countless corrections but inserted or added extensive new passages, a practice that must have driven his publishers to despair.

Perhaps too pretentiously, Balzac insisted that in his work he was conforming to scientific practice, classifying human beings according to habitat and profession more or less as one categorizes animals on the basis of species. Certain it is that he presented and analyzed for his readers a staggering variety of human exempla. Characters appearing in one work frequently turn up in others. Thus Claire de Beauséant, who in *Le Père Goriot* plays a secondary role as one of Paris' most fashionable hostesses, is the heroine of "La Femme abandonnée." Lucien de Rubempré, Mme de Bargeton's youthful protégé in *Illusions perdues*, is a principal character in *Splendeurs et misères des courtisanes*. Eventually it occurred to the writer that, in these stories and novels, he was painting a vast fresco of modern French society, and he decided to present them as such to the reading public. With an obvious allusion to Dante, as of 1841 he began calling them, collectively, the *Comédie humaine*. Explaining his idea in a preface to the 1842 edition, he classified them as well as the others he would write later under the headings of "scenes" or "studies." So it is that the approximately one hundred tales and novels that make up the *Comédie humaine* were distributed in the *Etudes de moeurs* and the *Etudes philosophiques*.

Most of the *Etudes philosophiques* involve the supernatural and include such works as *La Peau de chagrin* (1831), *La Recherche de l'absolu* (1834), and *Séraphita* (1835). Among the *Etudes de moeurs*, only the most indispensable titles can be mentioned since the overall grouping is so extensive. The category includes the subdivisions *Scènes de la vie privée* (*Le Père Goriot*, 1834); *Scènes de la vie de province* (*Eugénie Grandet*, 1833; *Le Lys dans la vallée*, 1835; *Illusions perdues*, 1837-43); *Scènes de la vie parisienne* (*César Birotteau*, 1837; *Le Cousin Pons*, 1847); *Scènes de la vie politique* (*Un Episode sous la Terreur*, 1844); *Scènes de la vie militaire* (*Les Chouans*, 1829); and *Scènes de la vie de campagne* (*Le Médecin de campagne*, 1833; *Le Curé de village*, 1839-41). Occasionally the author moved a work from one category to another, deciding that it had a more appropriate place in the second classification than it had had in the one to which he had previously assigned it. This happened to "Le Curé de Tours," which, having been one of the *Scènes de la vie privée*, came to rest in the *Scènes de la vie de province*. Sometimes the grouping in which the author placed a work seems altogether arbitrary. For example, the action of *Illusions perdues*, one of the scenes of provincial life, takes place in Paris as well as in the provinces. Similarly, "Le Réquisitionnaire" could take its place in the *Scènes de la vie militaire* quite as plausibly as it could in the *Etudes philosophiques*, which is where Balzac placed it.

Most of the *Comédie humaine* deals with the Restoration (1814-30), but both earlier and later periods are also shown. The author's viewpoint was conservative, and it was with pious conviction that he defended "the altar and the throne," holding that France's true interests lay in espousing Roman Catholicism and, despite the fact that almost all of the *Comédie humaine* was written during the July Monarchy, the fallen Bourbons. Nevertheless, Balzac was equitable in his judgments and did not attempt to conceal from his readers that there were bad priests like Abbé Trubert ("Le Curé de Tours"), nor did he seek to convince them that the Restoration had not made serious blunders (*Le Cabinet des antiques*).

Balzac has been labeled both a Romantic and a Realist, and neither label is inaccurate. Like his Romantic contemporaries, he had a taste for plots that often were too complicated, too melodramatic, too farfetched. Now and then a character or situation is overdone, pathos is abused. As did such Romantic authors as Victor Hugo, Balzac nurtured philosophical pretentions that, to most readers today, appear absurd. On the other hand, he was a Realist in his careful observation, his scrupulous documentation, and his accurate descriptions. He visited the places he described. Many of his characters are based upon people he knew (Louis Lambert had been a classmate at the Collège de Vendôme). On the whole, his psychology is excellent. Whereas Romantic writers generally created characters who are all good or all bad, those that Balzac conceived are seldom exclusively the one or the other, but, even when they are, the reader is made to understand why this is the case and the characters remain credible. Readers love Père Goriot, who is so kind, so deserving, yet so mistreated, and willingly overlook the fact that, at the outset, this gentle old man owed his fortune to the fact that he had sold flour to his fellow citizens at astronomical prices during a bread famine. But then, Goriot was trying to provide handsomely for his two daughters, whom he loved unreasonably. The astonishingly varied world Balzac leads us into is peopled with every kind of denizen, from princesses to prostitutes, from bankers to priests to criminals, all bearing the stamp of authenticity. Balzac believed, as we have seen, that an individual is the product of his environment, a belief the Realists were to share. Finally, Balzac is a Realist in the role he attributes to money. Anticipating the Realists and Naturalists, he realized its importance and made it the cornerstone of the *Comédie humaine's* social structure.

While the main body of Balzac's work is fiction, the author's ventures into theatre writing should not be forgotten. Several of the novels, such as *Illusions perdues* and *Splendeurs et misères des courtisanes*, take their reader into the entertainment world. It was a world Balzac found intriguing, and he wrote for it, though his successes in this domain were limited. *Vautrin* (1840) showed audiences new facets of a character made famous in *Le Père Goriot* and in *Illusions perdues*. Intentionally or otherwise, Frédérick Lemaître, who played the evil Vautrin, was made up to resemble King Louis Philippe, and the play was closed. *La Marâtre* (1848) is a good play, but bad luck pursued it. 1848 was a year of revolution, and political unrest was not conducive to good box office receipts. Moreover, to put on his play, Balzac had chosen Alexandre Dumas' notoriously mismanaged Théâtre Historique, which, in any event, was not interested in a long run, since it was planning to go on tour in Great Britain. In addition, Marie Dorval, scheduled to play the leading role, had withdrawn at the last minute. The frantic quest for money is the theme of *Mercadet*, Balzac's best play. When the author died, it had not been performed, but since his death it has enjoyed a certain amount of well-deserved success.

As pointed out above, Balzac's literary output, enormous as it was, never brought with it the wealth the writer constantly sought. Once or twice it looked as if marriage would reward him for what hard work had denied him, but these projects fell through, and several heiresses eluded his grasp. In 1832 a rich Polish countess, Eve Hanska, initiated a correspondence with him, at first signing her letters "the Foreign Woman." To both author and admirer the correspondence soon became vital, and Mme Hanska revealed her identity. Balzac visited her at various times. He traveled to Vienna to see her in May 1835, for instance. In 1843 he visited her in Russia and, in 1846, in Rome, after which he traveled with her in Germany.

She had become a widow late in 1841, but, due in part to the circumstance that her inheritance would be reduced in the event she should marry and live abroad, she hesitated to marry him. Finally, on 14 March 1850, in the Ukraine, she became Mme de Balzac. Balzac was ill at the time. With his bride he returned to Paris toward the end of May and died there on 18 August. Once more fortune had outdistanced him, but Mme de Balzac once again a widow, at least paid his enormous debts. Membership in the Académie Française had been denied him on several occasions, but the Academy's debt was never wiped out. Victor Hugo, who had attempted to see Balzac the evening he died, pronounced a moving oration at his friend's funeral.

Balzac had little interest in peace and claimed that the French, by nature, are a bellicose nation. As we have seen, one of his first literary endeavors was concerned with Cromwell. He had been born, after all, at a time when Revolutionary France was winning spectacular victories and occupying countries as far away as the Near East. The First Republic having given way to the First Empire, he spent his childhood and adolescence in an era when Napoleon was master of most of the European continent and when his own father was serving as a supplier to the French armies. Thus it would have been natural enough for him to admire France's man on horseback, and he

did. Even when, under Mme de Castries' tutelage, he renounced his youthful liberalism and became a conservative, he retained that admiration. Probably no one has ever praised Napoleon more glowingly than did Balzac in *Le Médecin de campagne* when he put into the mouth of an old soldier, Goguelet, a long account of Napoleon's political and military career. Interestingly enough, an officer present observes—and there is nothing to indicate that Balzac does not concur—"To me, military organization seems to be the model of all good civil societies. The sword is a people's guardian." On 31 May 1835 Balzac visited the Wagram battlefield, where in 1809 Napoleon had won one of his most brilliant victories. For himself, however, a military career had no interest, and he did his best to avoid serving in the National Guard. In 1835 he went into hiding so as not to be called up and the following year served a week in prison because of the incident. However, his unwillingness to do what was looked upon as his civic duty, far from springing from lofty moral convictions, represents rather a simple desire to avoid a personal inconvenience.

*Bibliography* ———————————————

Chollet R 1983 *Balzac Journaliste*. Klincksieck, Paris
Fernandez R 1980 *Balzac ou l'envers de la création romanesque*. Grasset, Paris
Guyon B 1967 *La Pensée politique et sociale de Balzac*. Armand Colin, Paris
Lotte F 1952 *Dictionnaire biographique des personnages fictifs de la Comédie humaine*. José Corti, Paris
Prendergast C 1978 *Balzac. Fiction and Melodrama*. Holmes and Meier, New York
Robb G 1994 *Balzac*. W.W. Norton & Company, New York
Saint-Paulien (Sicard, Maurice Ivan) 1979 *Napoléon Balzac et l'empire de la Comédie humaine*. Albin Michel, Paris
Sipriot P 1992 *Balzac sans masque*. Robert Laffont, Paris
Troyat H 1995 *Balzac*. Flammarion, Paris

HARRY REDMAN, JR.

# Bandung Conference

The Afro-Asian Conference of Bandung which took place between April 18 and 24, 1955 in Bandung (Indonesia), was initiated by the so-called Colombo States of Burma, Ceylon (now Sri Lanka), India, Indonesia, and Pakistan. It was significant in two ways. Firstly, it marked the entrance of the develop-

ing countries into world politics, a reality which could then no longer be ignored. Secondly, it is thought of as the forerunner to the nonalignment movement founded in Belgrade in 1961 (see *Nonalignment*).

Although recognized as a summit meeting between

heads of governments and heads of state, this was not the first international solidarity meeting of the developing nations. It was preceded by a series of other conferences without which the Bandung Conference would have been unimaginable and which therefore should be briefly outlined here.

The Asian Relations Conference of March 1947 was set up on Nehru's initiative in a private capacity with the help of the Indian Council of World Affairs. The Asian states were invited to this unofficial conference in India, which was then on the rise to independence. With the exception of the then still British colony of Pakistan, which turned down the invitation with the argument that the meeting would be an "instrument of Hindu imperialism," 248 delegates from 27 Asian states took part. The following topics were discussed in different work groups:

(a) Methods of achieving economic, cultural, and social advancement.

(b) Furtherance of industrial and economic development.

(c) Conversion of the colonial economy to a national economy.

Although few concrete results were produced at this meeting, its significance lies in the fact that the first contacts between the different national Asian leaders were made and the first statements on foreign policy and the role of Asia in world politics were developed. It was at the same time a manifestation of a self-educating community of all Asian people sharing the same fate and interests.

The conference over Indonesia was convened at Nehru's request in Delhi on January 20, 1949. Seventeen Afro-Asian states took part in this conference. The outlined aim of the program was to help put an end to the colonial war in Indonesia. President Sukarno summarized the significance of the conference in his opening speech in Bandung in 1955 with the words:

> Never before in the history of mankind has there been such solidarity among the peoples of Asia and Africa in delivering another Asian nation from danger . . . . Perhaps the same roots of today's conference are planted in that manifestation of Asian-African solidarity of 6 years ago.

The Colombo Conference was set up as a meeting of the prime ministers of Burma, Ceylon (now Sri Lanka), India, Indonesia, and Pakistan. Although even today this conference is often seen as a kind of working session in preparation for the Bandung Conference, it was in general concerned with other no

less important questions, which were also raised at the Bandung Conference. As well as discussing the possibilities of a non-aggression pact between the five states taking part, closer cooperation in the areas of culture and economy, a resolution against the use of the H-bomb, and the suggestion to admit the People's Republic of China to the United Nations Organization, the participants concerned themselves primarily with the conflict in Indochina, colonialism, the Cold War, and the dangers of the infiltration of communism. The suggestion of the Indonesian Prime Minister to call a bigger conference on an advisory basis as a "new positive force in international politics" which "should not aggravate the present day conflicts even more but positively influence world peace," was greeted by the participating states with enthusiasm, but the decision on it was deferred to the next meeting in Bogor (Indonesia) in December 1954, at which the conference place, aims, schedule, and the countries to be invited were also to be determined.

Although this conference brought few results as far as the topics dealt with were concerned, its significance lay among other things in the particular international political climate in which the conference took place, namely at the time of the climax of the conflict in Indochina, the breakdown of the Geneva Conference which met because of Korea and Indo-china, and the transition of the Cold War in Asia from "rollback" to the politics of "containment," in the course of which the United States attempted to establish a defense treaty in Southeast Asia, the South-East Asia Treaty Organization (SEATO). The conference also brought wider international recognition to the five premiers, who wished to raise their voices together in order to prevent them from becoming simply the objects of the rival Great Powers, especially in matters concerning themselves, for example, in Southeast Asia or in Asia in general.

One year later, practically all Afro-Asian nations invited[1] (comprising almost 65 percent of the world's population at that time) chose to attend the conference in Bandung. It was a milestone in the history of the emancipation of the colored nations. The aims and motives, that is to say the hope of the conference's initiators, can be summarized as follows:

(a) to promote goodwill and cooperation between the nations of Asia and Africa, to examine and promote their mutual and joint interests, and to establish and strengthen good neighborly relations;

(b) to advise the countries represented at the conference on social, economic, and cultural problems and relations;

(c) to consider the problems and special interests of Asian and African peoples, for example, problems concerning national sovereignty, the race question, and colonialism; and finally

(d) to examine the position of Asia and Africa and their peoples in the world, and the contribution they can afford to offer for the promotion of world peace.

Of course one cannot—due to the general wording—measure the real results of the conference against these aims; even less can one take the basic motive of the five initiators from it. The conference did serve to cut across barriers of communication and social development between the invited states. But it was also necessary for the conference participants to be reconciled to the fact that some of the states invited were already parties to pacts with a military component. These contradictions, due to the heterogeneity of the participating states, became especially clear during the dispute over the question as to which powers were to be regarded as colonialistic. While for the Iraqi delegate, Zionism and communism were considered "colonialism in the old style," the heads of the Iranian delegation called communism a "colonialism in new clothes." The suggestion of the Ceylonese (Sri Lanka) prime minister that the conference should demand an end to all forms of colonialism under which even the East European satellite states of the former Soviet Union might be claimed to suffer, was opposed by Iran, Iraq, the Lebanon, Libya, the Philippines, Turkey, and Ceylon. They demanded a resolution in which "all forms of colonialism including the international doctrine based on methods of violence, infiltration, and subversion" should be condemned. The Indian President Nehru on the other hand wanted to see the North Atlantic Treaty denounced as the protector of colonialism. As a result of these ideological and political differences it is not surprising that in order to demonstrate the unity of the congress, the conference delegates finally agreed on the vague formula that colonialism is "in all its forms an evil." In order not to endanger the cohesion of the conference by struggling for a mutual position on the question of world peace, they likewise accepted the "Five Principles" (*Pancha Shila*), as they had been negotiated in June 1954 during Zhou Enlai's visit to Nehru in New Delhi, namely:

(a) Mutual respect for territorial integrity,

(b) Non-interference in home affairs of other states,

(c) Equality and mutual support,

(d) Peaceful coexistence,

(e) Renunciation of all acts of aggression.

It should also be noted that the results of the Bandung Conference offered both the United States and the former Soviet Union equally the opportunity to make a positive judgment on the conference and, with reference to the final communiqué, to attempt to exert an influence on the nonaligned nations. The United States was satisfied by the aim for objectivity which had prevented a one-sided condemnation of Western colonialism while the former Soviet Union chose to emphasize its role in the struggle for independence of the young nations or those still under colonial rule.

Although at Bandung, as briefly outlined, no concrete or tangible results were recorded, world interest in this Afro-Asian conference and its special significance for the participating states would seem to lead back to the "symbolic or emotional context respectively" which it evoked in its participants. For these were nations which belong to the so-called colored nations and between them they had centuries of experience of—generally Western—colonialism. In 1955 they found themselves politically and culturally in the middle of a new orientation phase in their national existence. They were in search of a suitable policy and national identity. Economically they almost all belonged to the so-called developing countries and their aspirations toward economic development and social progress were similar.

Above all the conference was regarded by the participating heads of government and state, many of whom even shortly before had been imprisoned or exiled as revolutionaries by colonial rulers, as the fulfillment of their lives' aspirations. This also explains the very emotional treatment of the topics concerning Western and Eastern imperialism and colonialism, the equality of races, and world peace including problems such as peaceful coexistence, atomic weapons, and military treaties. The Bandung meeting was for them the symbol of the renaissance of the previously dependent nations of Asia and Africa into nations assertively determining their own fate. This feeling was expressed most effectively by the Indonesian Prime Minister Sukarno in his welcoming speech with these words:

> For many generations our nations were the silent ones of the world. We were not esteemed, we were the nations others . . . made decisions for, the peoples who lived in poverty and humility. Then . . . our peoples fought for independence and they won it . . . . We now

have a great responsibility to ourselves, the world and the as yet unborn generations . . . .

Carlos P. Romulo (1956) summarized these hopes and feelings with the following words:

To my first grandson
Carlos III,
that he may, as an Asian,
see and enjoy the full
flowering of our efforts
in Bandung.

## Notes

1. Burma, Ceylon (Sri Lanka), India, Indonesia, and Pakistan (as hosts) and Afghanistan, Egypt, Ethiopia, People's Republic of China, Ghana, Iraq, Iran, Japan, Yemen, Jordan, Cambodia, Laos, Lebanon, Liberia, Libya, Nepal, Philippines, Saudi Arabia, Sudan, Syria, Thailand, Turkey, Democratic Republic of Vietnam, Republic of Vietnam. North and South Korea to whom "independence" was denied, were not invited. Taiwan was excluded on account of Beijing's participation. South Africa was not considered because of her Apartheid poli-cy. Yugoslavia could not take part because the conference was restricted to Afro-Asian states.

## Bibliography

Brecher M 1963 International relations and Asian studies: The subordinate state-system of Southern Asia. *World Politics* (January)

Cousins N 1955 Report from Bandung. *Saturday Review*, May 21

Fifield R 1958 *The Diplomacy of Southeast Asia 1945-1958.* Harper, New York

Kahin G M 1965 *The Asian-African-Conference, Bandung, Indonesia, April 1955.* New York

Martin L (ed.) 1977 *Neutralism and Nonalignment: The New States in World Affairs.* Greenwood Press, London

Romulo C P 1956 *The Meaning of Bandung.* Chapel Hill, North Carolina

Spector I 1959 Russian and Afro-Asian neutralism. *Current History* 37

Wilcox F O 1962 The nonaligned states and the United Nations. *Neutralism and Nonalignment*

MIR A. FERDOWSI

# Baruch Plan

Just six weeks after the signing of the Charter of the United Nations (UN), pressure for control of atomic weapons was beginning to build up. In January 1946 the UN General Assembly adopted a proposal to establish an Atomic Energy Commission (AEC) to be composed of all the members of the Security Council plus Canada. The AEC was to submit to the Security Council plans for eliminating all atomic weapons, formulating regulations and safeguards, and ensuring the peaceful use of atomic energy.

When the AEC of the United Nations met on June 14, 1946, two proposals were presented to it. The United States proposal was presented by the US representative on the AEC, Bernard M. Baruch, a Wall Street tycoon, philanthropist, Wilsonian idealist, and public official. The United States proposal was commonly referred to as the Baruch Plan. The Soviet Union's proposal was presented by Andrei Gromyko. The two-phase proposal of the United States was based largely on the Acheson-Lilienthal Plan which had been drafted in the spring of 1946.

The first phase of the Baruch Plan called for the establishment of an International Atomic Development Authority which would exercise a monopoly over the ownership, production, and research for peaceful purposes of all atomic materials and which would operate all nuclear energy from mine to fin-ished product. This international authority would prohibit the manufacturing of any type of atomic weapon, would inspect all nuclear activities, and would impose severe penalties on any violator by veto-free Security Council actions. After an inspection and control system was adequately established, the second phase of the Baruch Plan was to be implemented which called for the cessation of all production of atomic weapons, the destruction of the American stockpile of atomic weapons, and the transfer of its scientific information on atomic processes to the International Atomic Development Authority.

The former Soviet Union denounced the Baruch Plan, insisting that the existing atomic weapons first be destroyed before discussion of controls, that atomic facilities be owned by individual states, that a nationally operated inspection system be established, and that the veto power be retained in the Security Council.

Although in December 1946 the AEC approved, with the Soviet and Polish members abstaining, the so-called First Report based on a series of proposals submitted by Baruch, this United States-Soviet difference over the control and disarmament of nuclear weapons remained as a basic problem throughout all ensuing negotiations between the two Superpowers. The Baruch Plan for the control of atomic energy remained however official US policy until the former

Soviet Union developed its own atomic bombs in 1949.

At the time the Baruch Plan was presented, the United States held the monopoly over atomic weapons. Thus the plan was in reality a suggestion that the then Soviet Union accept permanently a second-rank status as a non-nuclear power. If the Baruch Plan were accepted, the United States could have established a monopoly of basic knowledge in nuclear science and weapons by restricting the freedom of other countries in developing and testing an atomic weapon. The then Soviet Union was at that time developing its own nuclear capability—a process which culminated in its own test of an atomic weapon in 1949. The former Soviet Union thus rejected the US proposal.

See also: *Arms Control, Evolution of*

*Bibliography* ────────────────

Bennet A L 1980 *International Organizations: Principles and Issues*, 2nd edn. Prentice Hall, Englewood Cliffs, New Jersey

Rosenbloom M V 1953 *Peace Through Strength: Bernard Baruch and a Blueprint for Security*. New York

United States Department of State 1946 *The International Control of Atomic Energy: Growth of A Policy*. Department of State (Pub. 2702), Washington, DC

United States Department of State 1947a *The First Report of the United Nations Atomic Energy Commission to the Security Council*, Dec. 31, 1946. Department of State (Pub. 2737), Washington, DC

United States Department of State 1947b *The Second Report of the United Nations Atomic Energy Commission to the Security Council*, Sept. 11, 1947. Department of State (Pub. 2932), Washington, DC

United States Department of State 1948 *The International Control of Atomic Energy: Policy at the Crossroads*. Department of State (Pub. 3136), Washington, DC

KIM KWAN-BONG

# Baudelaire

Born in Paris on April 9, 1821, Charles Baudelaire was the second son of François Baudelaire, who died in 1827. In November of the following year, Mme Baudelaire remarried. Her new husband, Jacques Aupick, was a soldier who would end his career as a general, an ambassador, and a senator. Baudelaire's studies, begun in Paris, were continued in Lyon, where Jacques Aupick was stationed in 1831. Five years later Aupick was transferred to Paris, and there Baudelaire entered the Collège Louis le Grand, where he proved to be an exceptional student, winning a prize for a Latin poem. Later he would frequently give Latin titles to works written in French. He received the *baccalauréat* in the summer of 1839.

For a time in 1840 and 1841 he was, at least nominally, a student at the University of Paris Law School. At this time he met and began to spend time with Latouche, Nerval, and Balzac, as well as several less important writers. He also had an intimate affair with Sarah, a Latin Quarter prostitute who inspired several poems that would later appear in the *Fleurs du mal* ("Tu mettrais l'univers entire dans ta ruelle," "Une Nuit que j'etais près d'une affreuse juive") and in the *Poésies diverses* ("Je n'ai pas pour maitresse une lionne illustre").

General and Mme Aupick, alarmed at the young man's social connections and activities, not to mention his debts, decided to remove him from what they saw as the pernicious moral climate in which he was moving. At their insistence, he agreed to take a long voyage from Bordeaux to Calcutta. He sailed on June 9, 1841. En route he stopped on the island of Mauritius, where Mme Adolphe Autard de Bragard, who entertained him there, made an impression that resulted in the poem "Aune dame créole," which was eventually included in the *Fleurs du mal*. Resuming his trip, Baudelaire went as far as Reunion, then refused to proceed any farther. He returned to France, landing in February 1843. Henceforth, except for short reconciliations, his contacts with General Aupick would be strained, even unpleasant. Gone were the days, fairly harmonious ones, when he had traveled with the Aupicks in the Pyrenees Mountains (1838) and, seemingly, had enjoyed it.

Hardly was he back in Paris than Baudelaire reached the age of twenty-one and came into his inheritance, which he set about squandering. Soon he had his own lodgings on the Ile St-Louis and, a little later, in the Hôtel Pimodan and got involved with the first of several women who would exert a deep influence upon his personal and creative life. With his natural taste for the exotic, much heightened by his recent voyage, he could not resist the mulatto Jeanne Duval, a minor actress. A beautiful, lascivious shrew, she was devoid of intellect but gave him emotional thrills and torment, seasoned with a certain measure of sensual oblivion. Financially, she caused him disaster. From 1844 onwards, what remained of Baudelaire's inheritance was administered by a certain Me Ancelle, empowered, over the poet's protests, to handle his money. Baudelaire, in other words, received an allowance. Not all of his financial troubles were due to Jeanne Duval, but she was their major cause. In addition to this, Jeanne was vicious—on one occasion she poisoned her lover's cat—but she also had much to contend with. Whatever her merits and demerits, Baudelaire could live neither with her nor without her. Punctuated by separations, the relationship lasted until 1861. With all her faults, Jeanne nevertheless caused Baudelaire to write some of his best poems. It was of her that he was thinking when he wrote not only "Sed non satiata" but also "Le Balcon," "La Chevelure," and the awesome "Une Charogne."

Jeanne Duval was not faithful, but neither was Baudelaire. Already, in 1852, he was writing anonymous letters to Apollonie Sabatier, a fashionable courtesan as intelligent as she was beautiful. She had a salon, and her Sunday dinner parties were attended by important artists and writers. She has been immortalized in a number of statues and paintings. For this somewhat unlikely muse, Baudelaire nurtured a *sublimated*, ethereal, platonic devotion. His one sexual experiment with her (1860) was a disaster, but she remained a true friend. Inspired by her are such poems as "A celle qui est trop gaie," "Le Flacon," and the brilliant "Harmonie du soir." At some point Baudelaire met still another woman whom he found irresistible. This was the actress Marie Daubrun. With her, in 1854 and 1855, he had a liaison, terminated when Mlle Daubrun decided that her new lover would probably never write the play that would assure her a triumphant success on the Paris stage. Nevertheless, it was with her in mind that Baudelaire wrote such enduring poems as "Le Poison," "L'Irréparable," "Ciel brouillé," and the unforgettable "L'Invitation au voyage."

Partly in the hope that he could find there a publisher for his complete works, Baudelaire traveled to Belgium in the spring of 1864. He failed in his attempt to find the publisher but, in Brussels, gave a series of five lectures on Delacroix, Gautier, and narcotics as he had treated them in the *Paradis artificiels*. The lectures were not a great success and brought in appreciably less money than he had been led to expect. Quickly, he took a vigorous dislike to Belgium and Belgians, attacking them mercilessly in the barbed epigrams making up *Amoenitates belgicae* (1866) and in the prose *Pauvre Belgique*, not published in its entirety until 1952. The Belgian sojourn saw the poet's health begin to deteriorate. In March

1866 Baudelaire experienced an attack of aphasia and hemiplegia that left his mind generally intact but deprived him of the ability to speak. Mme Aupick took him back to Paris early in July and put him in a private clinic, the superintendent of which was named, curiously, Dr. Duval. It was there, more than a year later, that he died on August 31, 1867. The *Petits Poèmes en prose* began appearing that very day in the *Revue Nationale*. Baudelaire was buried at Montparnasse Cemetery beside General Aupick, who had died a little more than a decade earlier.

While Baudelaire is chiefly known for a single collection of poems, he wrote other things that richly deserve to be mentioned. His art criticism as embodied in the Salons of 1845, 1846, and 1859 and in his articles on Eugène Delacroix (1863) reveal a sensitive artistic temperament, alive to color and movement (he left sketches of his own, especially of Jeanne Duval). His keen musical esthetic, ahead of the times, comes out in "Richard Wagner et *Tannhauser* à Paris" (*Revue Européenne* 1861). Baudelaire praised Victor Hugo, but his correspondence reveals that, in private, his enthusiasm was a little less than appeared to be the case in print. Above all, his literary criticism declaims against the view that art must be didactic or utilitarian. Literature's only allegiance, he held, was to art[1], which no doubt explains why he admired Théophile Gautier as much as he did. Too much the Romantic to appreciate Realism as an approach to art, he found it personally distasteful but was nonetheless able to praise Flaubert's *Madame Bovary* (*L'Artiste*, October 18, 1857). Baudelaire's critical work was assembled and published, after the writer's death, in the two volumes *Curiosités esthétiques* (1868) and *L'Art romantique* (1868).

Baudelaire made several French translations of English prose and poetry. But he was particularly excited by the American writer Edgar Allan Poe (1809-49), whom he called "a vast mind, as deep as Heaven and Hell."[2] Poe's nervous sensitivity and dedication to art were consonant with Baudelaire's own attitudes and proclivities, and, with his awareness of opiates, the French writer could easily understand Poe's problems with alcohol. Baudelaire translated Poe's prose fiction, in book form, as *Histoires extraordinaires* (1856), *Nouvelles Histoires extraordinaires* (1857), *Histoires grotesques et sérieuses* (1865), and *Aventures d'Arthur Gordon Pym* (1858). He also translated *Eureka* (1864), which he considered an important philosophical treatise. Baudelaire's interest in Poe did more than any other single thing to bring the American writer to the attention of the Symbolist poets, who would see in him one of their great precursors. Baudelaire also wrote some original tales, such as "La Fanfarlo" (1847). *Les Paradis artificiels, opium et haschisch*, appeared in 1860. Baudelaire had had some experience with these narcotics but without having become an addict. In this work he drew heavily upon Thomas De Quincey's *Confessions of an English Opium-Eater* (1822) and *Suspiria de profundis* (1845), translating and commenting.

Baudelaire's most enduring claim to world celebrity rests upon the collection of poems *Les Fleurs du mal*, many of the individual poems having already appeared in various periodicals. Wrought with exquisite care, they reveal a plethora of moods and treat numerous themes, some of them morbid or sexual. Filled with subtle images and unexpected associations ("Correspondences"), the poems, as Victor Hugo would shortly declare, introduced "a new shiver" into French poetry. The volume appeared June 25, 1857. Because certain poems were considered immoral, available copies were seized and the author indicted. Tried on August 20, Baudelaire and his publishers were condemned and fined and told that six poems had to be deleted. From Guernsey, Hugo wrote the poet that the *Fleurs du mal* "shine and dazzle like stars." There was nonetheless no new edition until 1861. The deleted poems, plus seventeen new ones that had come out in periodicals, appeared in Brussels in 1866 as *Epaves*. Meanwhile, Baudelaire had written a number of prose poems similar in tone and workmanship to the *Fleurs du mal*. Collectively, these are the *Petits Poèmes en prose* (1869), which appeared in a volume of the author's posthumous complete works. Baudelaire did not create the prose poem, but his example gave considerable impetus to the genre.

Given General Aupick's vigorous but not very successful efforts to impose some kind of discipline upon his wife's son, Baudelaire could not be expected to have been drawn to war or to men who make war. War and peace are not topics that he wrote about, even though occasional allusions to them occur in his work. A violent heroine of the French Revolution, heedless of the deaths she might cause as she rushed up the stairs at Versailles Palace, is presented in one poem as being "in love with carnage"

("Sisina"). Now and then soldiers' pursuits other than war occurred to the poet. He admitted, for instance, that military brass band concerts, with soldiers as musicians, can "pour a bit of heroism into the hearts of citydwellers" ("Les Petites Vieilles"). But elsewhere he was severe in showing his readers a hardened quartermaster who seems to have procured himself a mistress by giving a woman the rations intended for hungry soldiers ("Portraits de maitresses"). In one famous poem, the author's dismal view of love is conveyed by means of military imagery. The poet's introducing two people in the act of love, described as "two warriors" who "have rushed upon one another," furious and yelling, was not intended to paint love as a pleasant experience ("Duellum"). The obvious, implied comment on fighting is eloquent. Still, Baudelaire did not excoriate war. In his correspondence he did little more than mention the Crimean War. Later he would speak of France's involvement in Piedmont's war with Austria as her involvement in "a great war" (May 16, 1859), and he could be glad when he observed that even in the midst of war people still read books (May 1, 1859). Had he lived to see the Franco-Prussian War, the terrible ordeal might have stirred him to see war as the scourge that horrified so many of his contemporaries.

*Notes*

1. See "Les Drames et les romans honnêtes" (*Semaine Théâtrale*, 27 November 1851) in *OEuvres complètes* (Paris: Gallimard, 1961)
2. "Hégisippe Moreau," *OEuvres complètes*

*Bibliography*

Ferran A 1968 *L'Esthétique de Baudelaire*. Nizat, Paris
Leakey F W 1969 *Baudelaire and Nature*. University of Manchester Press, Manchester
Pichois C, Ziegler J 1987 *Baudelaire*. Julliard, Paris
Poggenburg R P 1987 *Charles Baudelaire: une micro-histoire*. Vanderbilt University Press, Nashville
Starkie E 1988 *Baudelaire*. Paragon House Publishers, New York
Troyat H 1994 *Baudelaire*. Flammarion, Paris

HARRY REDMAN, JR.

# Bentham, Jeremy

Jeremy Bentham (1748-1832), renowned English philosopher and social reformer, is credited with being the father of the philosophic movement known as Utilitarianism. Bentham was a true radical, who spent his entire life in a state of profound and seething dissatisfaction with virtually every aspect of the society in which he lived. He concluded that its laws, ideas, values, family structure, morals, religion, and politics were based on nothing more than blind adherence to tradition. All, he insisted, should be swept away and refounded on the basis of strict adherence to reason. Rational laws and rational government, he argued in such seminal works as *A Fragment on Government* (1776) and *An Introduction to the Principles of Morals and Legislation* (1781), would produce rational behavior, permitting humankind to live in peace and harmony.

Only in such a rational society, said Bentham, could humankind ever hope to find true happiness. According to his calculations, happiness consisted in doing those things which give pleasure and avoiding those things which give pain. A rational society, therefore, would have laws, customs, and institutions designed to give the greatest pleasure to the greatest possible number of people.

Not surprisingly, Bentham castigated warfare as among the most irrational of all human activities. War, he pointed out, produced very little happiness, and that only for the few who enjoyed it or profited from it. This paltry happiness was gained only at the cost of an enormous amount of pain suffered by the infinitely greater number of war's inevitable victims. Warfare thus utterly failed his test of rationality: it was very definitely not something which gave "the greatest happiness to the greatest number." Thus, any rational society would eliminate war.

Bentham developed his ideas on this subject most fully in his influential tract, *Plans for an Universal and Perpetual Peace.* Here he pointed out that in making war, states act directly counter to their own rationally conceived self-interest. He maintained that if societies would base their decisions on reason, they would soon see the advantage of establishing rational international laws and international institutions to help them arbitrate their disputes peacefully. It is worth noting that in making this argument, Bentham coined the very word "international." Bentham was particularly interested in seeing an international court established which would settle all arguments between states on the rational basis of securing the greatest happiness for the greatest number of people involved. He also hoped to see the formation of an international legislative body to publicly review treaties, secure disarmament, and encourage the emancipation of colonies. Bentham fully appreciated how important colonial rivalries were as a cause of war in his own time.

Bentham's optimistic view that war, since in reality it was against the true interests of almost everyone, might actually come to be eliminated, was an inspiration for his many followers. His ideas were extremely important for the peace movements of the United Kingdom and the rest of the Western world in the nineteenth century.

*Bibliography* ————————————

Atkinson C M 1971 *Jeremy Bentham: His Life and Work.* AMS Press, New York

Bentham J 1948 *An Introduction to the Principles of Morals and Legislation.* Hafner, New York

Bentham J 1962 *Works,* 11 vols. New York

Davidson W L 1915 *Political Thought in England: The Utilitarians from Bentham to J. S. Mill.* Oxford University Press, Oxford

Mack M P 1962 *Jeremy Bentham: An Odyssey of Ideas.* London

GARRETT L. McAINSH

# Biological Weapons Convention: An Overview

Since ancient times, the use in war of poison and pathogenic agents has been considered a treacherous practice. It was condemned by international declarations and treaties, notably by the 1907 Hague Convention (IV) respecting the laws and customs of war on land.[1] Efforts to strengthen this prohibition resulted in the conclusion, in 1925, of the Geneva Protocol which banned the use of asphyxiating, poisonous or other gases, usually referred to as chemical weapons, as well as the use of bacteriological methods of warfare. The latter are now understood to include not only bacteria, but also other biological agents, such as viruses or rickettsiae which were unknown at the time the Geneva Protocol was signed. (On 1 January 1997, 132 States were party to this Protocol.) However, the Geneva Protocol did not prohibit the development, production and stockpiling of chemical and biological weapons. Attempts to achieve a complete ban were made in the 1930s in the framework of the League of Nations, but with no success.

Shortly after World War II, the United Nations called for the elimination of all weapons "adaptable to mass destruction."[2] Biological and chemical weapons were included in this category of arms along with atomic and radiological weapons.[3] Debates on their prohibition took place in the 1950s and 1960s in the context of proposals for general disarmament but, again, the debate remained inconclusive.

As a separate issue, the prohibition of chemical and biological weapons appeared on the agenda of the Eighteen-Nation Committee on Disarmament in 1968. One year later, the United Nations published an influential report on the problems of chemical and biological warfare,[4] and the question received special attention at the UN General Assembly. The UN report concluded that certain chemical and biological weapons cannot be confined in their effects in space and time and might have grave and irreversible consequences for man and nature. This would apply to both the attacking and the attacked nations. A report by the World Health Organization (WHO) on the health aspects of chemical and biological weapons, issued in 1970, stated that these weapons pose a special threat to civilians, and that the effects of their use are subject to a high degree of uncertainty and unpredictability.[5]

Although simultaneous prohibition of chemical and biological weapons had been considered for many years as both desirable and necessary, towards the end of the 1960s it became clear that such a prohibition was not achievable. In the Eighteen-Nation Committee on Disarmament, where the issue was under discussion, the United Kingdom and a few other Western countries adopted the view that biological weapons should be banned first. The Socialist and many neutral and non-aligned States were opposed to a separate treatment of these weapons, but finally accepted the Western approach. A factor which facilitated this development was the unilateral renunciation of biological weapons by the United States, announced on 25 November 1969, and the decision by the US government to destroy its stockpile of these weapons, irrespective of a possible future international agreement.[6] On 14 February 1970, the United States also formally renounced the production, stockpiling and use of toxins for war purposes. It stated that military programmes for biological agents and toxins would be confined to research and development for defensive purposes.[7] Subsequent negotiations on a global prohibition of biological weapons led to an international agreement. On 16 December 1971, the text of the convention worked out by the Conference of the Committee on Disarmament (CCD), the successor of the Eighteen-Nation Committee on Disarmament, was commended by the UN General Assembly.[8]

## 1. A Critical Analysis of the BW Convention

On 10 April 1972, the *Convention on the Prohibition of the Development, Production and Stockpiling of Bacteriological (Biological) and Toxin Weapons and on their Destruction* was opened for signature. It entered into force on 26 March 1975, after the deposit of the instruments of ratification by 22 signatory governments, including the governments of the Soviet Union, the United Kingdom and the United States, designated as depositories. By 1 January 1997, the BW Convention had been joined by 140 States, including all the permanent members of the United Nations Security Council.

### 1.1 Scope of the Obligations

The BW Convention prohibits the development, production, stockpiling or acquisition by other means, or retention of microbial or other biological agents or toxins, as well as of weapons, equipment or means of delivery designed to use such agents or toxins for hostile purposes or in armed conflict (Article I).

The Convention has not defined the prohibited items nor the targets to which the prohibitions relate. There exists, however, an authoritative definition of biological agents formulated by the WHO. In its 1970 report, mentioned above, the WHO described biological agents as those that depend for their effects on multiplication within the target organism and are intended for use in war to cause disease or death in man, animals or plants; they may be transmissible or non-transmissible. Toxins are poisonous products of organisms; unlike biological agents, they are inanimate and not capable of reproducing themselves. The Convention applies to all natural or artificially created toxins, "whatever their origin or method of production" (Article I). It thus covers toxins produced biologically, as well as those produced by chemical synthesis. Since toxins are chemicals by nature, their inclusion in the BW Convention was a step towards the projected ban on chemical weapons.

Since the signing of the Convention, there have been no disputes among the parties regarding the definition of biological agents or toxins, but the lack of definition of "weapons, equipment or means of delivery" led to a controversy. In ratifying the BW Convention, Switzerland reserved the right to decide for itself which items fall within the definition of weapons, equipment or means of delivery designed to use biological agents or toxins. The United States entered an objection to this reservation, claiming that it would not be appropriate for States to reserve unilaterally the right to take such decisions. In its opinion, the prohibited items are those the design of which indicates that they could have no other use than that specified in the Convention, or that they were intended to be capable of the use specified.[9] There are, however, few weapons, equipment or means of delivery which would meet such criteria.

Under the BW Convention, the prohibition to develop, produce, stockpile or otherwise acquire or retain biological agents and toxins is not absolute. It applies only to types and to quantities that have no justification for prophylactic, protective or other peaceful purposes. Retention, production or acquisition by other means of certain quantities of biological agents and toxins may thus continue, and there may be testing in laboratories and even in the field. According to the clarification given in the course of the negotiations, the term "prophylactic" encompasses medical activities, such as diagnosis, therapy and immunization, whereas the term "protective" covers the development of protective masks and clothing, air and water filtration systems, detection and warning devices, and decontamination equipment, and must not be interpreted as permitting possession of biological agents and toxins for defence, retaliation or deterrence.[10] The term "other peaceful purposes" has remained unclear. One can assume that it includes scientific experimentation.

There are no provisions in the BW Convention restricting biological research activities. One reason for this omission may be that research aimed at developing agents for civilian purposes is difficult to distinguish from research serving military purposes, whether defensive or offensive. Moreover, in the biological field it is difficult to draw a dividing line between research and development; a country can develop warfare agents in research facilities. Once developed, these agents can be rapidly produced in significant quantities. This circumstance and the express authorization to engage in production (for peaceful purposes) of biological agents and toxins that may be used in warfare create a risk that the provisions of the Convention will be circumvented. The stipulation that any development, production, stockpiling or retention of biological agents or toxins must be justified does not carry sufficient weight. There are no agreed standards or criteria for the quantities of agents or toxins that may be needed by different States for the different purposes recognized by the Convention. The parties are not even obliged to declare the types and amounts of agents or toxins they possess and the use they make of them. The system of material accountancy that is useful in the verification of certain measures of arms control is not practicable in the case of biological or toxin agents. It is thus not evident how much of a given prohibited substance stocked by a given country would consti-

tute a violation of the Convention. The secrecy surrounding biological research activities and, in particular, the maintenance of defensive preparations, which at certain stages may be indistinguishable from offensive preparations, could generate suspicions leading to allegations of breaches.

A separate article of the Convention prohibits the transfer of agents, toxins, weapons, equipment or means of delivery, specified above, to "any recipient whatsoever," that is, to any State or group of States or international organizations, as well as sub-national groups or individuals. The provision of assistance, encouragement or inducement to acquire the banned weapons is likewise forbidden (Article III). These non-proliferation clauses appear hard to reconcile with the commitment of the parties to engage in the "fullest possible" exchange of biological agents and toxins, and of equipment for the processing, use or production of such agents and toxins for peaceful ends (Article X). For all such materials and technologies, as well as expertise, are dual-use and as such widespread. To reduce the risk of misuse, an informal forum of industrialized countries, known as the Australia Group (after the country which took the initiative to convene it), decided to apply certain restrictions on transfers of items relevant to the BW Convention.[11] Many nations consider the control arrangements adopted by the Group as complementary to the BW Convention, because an export may be precluded if there is particular concern about its potential diversion for weapon purposes. Other nations consider these arrangements to be discriminatory, because they chiefly affect the developing world. The latter would like to see the Australia Group disbanded and have all export restrictions that might be agreed among all parties incorporated in a legally binding verification document.

Parties to the BW Convention have undertaken to cooperate in the further development and application of scientific discoveries in the field of biology for the prevention of diseases or for other peaceful purposes (Article X). However, since the Convention is essentially a disarmament treaty, it can hardly serve as an effective instrument for such cooperation. The participants in the latest BW Convention Review Conference acknowledged the existence of an increasing gap between the developed and developing countries in the field of biotechnology, genetic engineering, microbiology and other related areas.[12]

The most remarkable feature of the BW Convention is the disarmament obligation of the parties: to destroy or divert to peaceful purposes all agents, toxins, weapons, equipment and means of delivery

(Article II). The BW Convention was the first treaty providing for the abolition of an entire category of arms. The envisaged destruction or diversion was to take place not later than nine months after entry into force of the Convention, it being understood that for States acceding to the Convention after its entry into force the destruction or diversion was to be completed upon accession. All the necessary safety precautions are to be observed during the destruction operations to protect "populations" (that is, not only the population of the country carrying out these operations) as well as the environment in general. The United States was the only State to announce that its stockpile of biological and toxin agents and all associated munitions had been destroyed, except for small quantities for laboratory defensive research purposes. It also made it known that former biological warfare facilities had been converted to medical research centres.[13] No other State has made such an announcement. The United Kingdom said that it had no stocks of biological weapons.[14] The former Soviet Union stated that it did not possess any biological agents or toxins, weapons, equipment or means of delivery, as prohibited by the Convention,[15] but this statement turned out to be untrue (see below).

## 1.2 Relationship with the 1925 Geneva Protocol

The BW Convention does not expressly prohibit the use of biological or toxin weapons. It only states that the obligations assumed under the 1925 Geneva Protocol, which prohibits such use, remain valid (Article VIII). However, adherents to the BW Convention are not necessarily parties to the Geneva Protocol. Moreover, the Convention stipulates that nothing in its provisions shall be interpreted as in any way limiting or detracting from the obligations assumed by States under the Geneva Protocol. This implies that the reservations to the Protocol, which form part of the obligations contracted by the parties, continue to exist. Insofar as the reservations concern the right to employ the banned weapons against non-parties or in retaliation against a party violating the Protocol, they are incompatible with the obligation of the parties to the Convention never "in any circumstances" to acquire biological weapons (Article I). They also contradict the parties' expressed determination to exclude "completely" the possibility of biological agents and toxins being used as weapons (ninth preambular paragraph). It is for this reason that, in acceding to the BW Convention in 1984, China declared that the absence of an explicit prohibition on the use of biological weapons was a defect which should be corrected "at an appropriate time." Indeed,

over the years, a number of States have withdrawn their reservations to the Geneva Protocol, either with regard to biological weapons alone, or to both biological and chemical weapons.[16] They have thereby recognized that since the retention and production of biological weapons are banned, so must, by implication, be their use, because use presupposes possession.

Nonetheless, in 1996, Iran proposed that the Convention (its title and Article I) be amended so as to make the ban on use explicit rather than implicit.[17] An amendment submitted by a party enters into force for each State accepting it upon its acceptance by a majority of the parties (Article XI). However, the Iranian proposal is opposed by many States which fear the risks of having other provisions of the Convention opened up for renegotiation as well. Some are apprehensive that States not accepting the Iranian-proposed amendment would appear to condone the use of biological weapons under certain circumstances, and since use would be possible only after breaking the BW Convention, the absolute character of the Convention prohibitions would be called into question. What seems less objectionable than an amendment is a solemn declaration of understanding by all parties that the use of microbial or other biological agents or toxins in any way that is not consistent with prophylactic, protective or other peaceful purposes, would be a violation of the Convention.

## 1.3 Verification of Compliance

No specific measures are set forth in the BW Convention to verify compliance with the obligation not to develop, produce, stockpile or otherwise acquire or retain biological agents or toxins for "hostile purposes." Indeed, hostile intentions, like any other intentions, cannot be verified. As mentioned above, the parties are not obliged to declare biological agents or toxins used in non-prohibited activities. Nor are they obliged to declare all laboratories engaged in research and development of substances that could be used as agents of warfare. This is a serious lacuna, because advances in biotechnology have made it possible to produce large quantities of potent toxic substances by a small number of people, in a short period of time, and in facilities which are difficult to identify. Such substances may be stored in inconspicuous repositories and eventually "weaponized," that is, filled into missiles, bombs or spray systems. Consequently, a violator could relatively easily break out from the Convention. What is even more incongruous, States joining the Convention are not required to declare the possession or non-possession of the banned weapons. Nor are States, which may have declared such possession, obligated to prove that they have destroyed the weapons or diverted them to peaceful purposes. The opening-up by the United States of some of its biological facilities for public inspection and international visitors, following the destruction of its stocks, was a voluntary act.[18]

National technical means of verification cannot be relied upon to verify in other countries the non-development and non-production of biological agents and toxins for hostile purposes, and there are at present no international means to perform such tasks. Illegal possession of the banned weapons could be demonstrated indirectly through investigations which the UN Secretary-General is authorized to carry out in response to reports that may be brought to his attention on the possible use of chemical and biological or toxin weapons entailing a violation of the Geneva Protocol or of any other applicable rule of international treaty or customary law.[19] However, such investigations, which may be initiated by UN member States (but not by individuals or non-governmental organizations), could also prove inconclusive, because the diseases allegedly caused by biological weapons might be similar to those occurring naturally, and because it might be difficult for the investigators to determine the identity of the aggressor.

Each party is obliged to take measures, in accordance with its constitutional processes, to prohibit and prevent the activities banned by the Convention from taking place within its territory and under its jurisdiction or control anywhere (Article IV). The term "measures" applies to legislative, administrative or regulatory measures, whereas the term "under its jurisdiction or control" (also used in Article II referred to above) extends the bans to non-self-governing territories administered by States parties, and to territories under military occupation. "Anywhere" implies that even transnational corporations operating in the territories of non-parties to the Convention are covered by the prohibitions if they remain under the jurisdiction or control of the parties. Not all parties, however, have taken the steps required to ensure domestic compliance with the Convention.[20] This is all the more regrettable in that biological agents appear to be becoming attractive, for terrorist purposes, to players other than States (see *Terrorism*). According to reliable reports, the Aum Shinrikyo sect, which released nerve gas in a Tokyo subway train, had also been working on the development of biological weapons and in 1995, shortly before the arrest of its leader, was close to completing this programme.[21]

On the international level, the parties have undertaken to consult one another and to cooperate in solving problems relating to the objective or the application of the provisions of the Convention. Such consultation and cooperation may also take place "through appropriate international procedures within the framework of the United Nations and in accordance with its Charter" (Article V). Since the Convention does not explain what "appropriate international procedures" amount to, the participants in the BW Review Conferences agreed that such procedures should include the right of any party to request that a "consultative meeting", open to all parties, be convened promptly at expert level.[22]

The parties have the right to lodge with the UN Security Council complaints regarding breaches of the Convention. They have undertaken to cooperate in carrying out any investigation which the Security Council may initiate on the basis of the complaint received, and they are entitled to be informed of the results of such investigation. Each complaint must contain "all possible evidence" confirming its validity (Article VI). However, only a few States have the means to collect such evidence. Others may not be in a position to do so, and could not always count on obtaining relevant information from foreign sources, even from their allies. There is thus a possibility that, for political or other reasons (for example, unwillingness to disclose the nature or the source of the evidence), certain powers will deliberately overlook transgressions committed by some States to the detriment of others. A State which suspects a violation, but lacks reliable information and therefore does not possess sufficient evidence, may have its request for consideration rejected by the Security Council. Even if the Security Council agreed to discuss a charge which did not satisfy the above requirement, there would always be a danger that the case would not receive proper examination. For the Council is not entitled (or equipped) by the UN Charter to check compliance with arms control agreements; nor is it empowered to take action against violators of such agreements. Only when the Council finds that the situation created by the violation can lead to international friction may it recommend, under Chapter VI of the UN Charter, "appropriate procedures or methods of adjustment" to the State or States concerned. This may not always be the case.

In 1992, the President of the UN Security Council stated, on behalf of its members, that proliferation of weapons of mass destruction, which include biological weapons, would constitute a "threat to international peace and security," and that appropriate action would be taken to prevent it.[23] That action could include the application of coercive measures under Chapter VII of the UN Charter. However, the statement of the President of the Security Council has no binding legal effect. Even if it were transformed into a formal decision of the Council to have such effect, it would not necessarily enable the Council to act in all pertinent instances. The power of veto possessed by the permanent members of the Council can always be used to protect violators of treaties, especially when the violator happens to be a great power. A suggestion, put forward during the BW negotiations, that the Security Council's permanent members should waive their right of veto at least with regard to resolutions concerning investigations of complaints, was not accepted. This is why proposals have been repeatedly made that a representative body of States parties—rather than the United Nations—should deal with investigations of alleged breaches of the BW Convention. If, in 1982, the UN General Assembly requested the UN Secretary-General to investigate alleged violations of the ban on use of chemical and biological weapons (see above), it did so primarily because the ban, as embodied in the 1925 Geneva Protocol, is widely considered to form part of international customary law to be observed by all States, parties and non-parties to relevant treaties alike.[24]

The circumstance that the fact-finding stage of the complaints procedure is not clearly separated from the stage of legal/political consideration and judgment is a serious shortcoming of the BW Convention. It makes it difficult to ascertain a violation. Moreover, a State under suspicion of having violated its obligations has no international impartial mechanism to turn to in order to free itself from that suspicion. Ill-considered allegations can therefore be made with impunity.

In the case of an established violation, parties would have to provide or support assistance, in accordance with the UN Charter, to a party which so requested, if the Security Council decided that this party had been exposed to danger as a result of the violation (Article VII). It appears from the negotiating history that assistance was meant primarily as action of a medical or other humanitarian or relief nature. In the understanding of at least the United Kingdom and the United States, it would be for each party to decide whether it could or was prepared to supply the requested aid.[25] In other words, assistance would be optional, not obligatory: it could be refused without incurring the charge of non-compliance.

The Convention provided for a review conference

of the parties to be convened five years after its entry into force (Article XII). Later, the parties decided to meet at least every five years; these Conferences review the operation of the Convention, taking into account the relevant scientific and technological developments.

### 1.4 Allegations of Non-compliance

Several allegations of non-compliance with the BW Convention have been made since the Convention entered into force.[26] Those which received most attention were the "Sverdlovsk" and "Yellow Rain" cases.

### 1.4.1 The Sverdlovsk Case

In March 1980, the United States accused the Soviet Union of maintaining an offensive biological weapons programme which included production, weaponization and stockpiling of biological warfare agents. The accusation was based on the suspected airborne release of anthrax spores from a Soviet biological facility, which caused an outbreak of anthrax in the city of Sverdlovsk in April and May 1979.[27] The former Soviet Union confirmed that there had been an outbreak of anthrax in the Sverdlovsk region, but attributed this occurrence to the sale of anthrax-contaminated meat in violation of veterinary regulations.[28] It provided little additional information. The issue was the subject of bilateral US/Soviet consultations, and various groups of scientists met to evaluate the Soviet account of the incident,[29] but the US government maintained its accusation.[30] In 1992, the Russian authorities admitted that a breach of the BW Convention had been committed. They undertook, under a decree issued by the President of the Russian Federation, to open secret military research centres to international inspection and convert them to civilian use.[31]

### 1.4.2 The "Yellow Rain" Case

In 1981, the US government accused the former Soviet Union of being involved in the production, transfer and use of trichothecene mycotoxins in Laos, Kampuchea and Afghanistan in violation of both the 1925 Geneva Protocol and the BW Convention.[32] The allegation was categorically rejected by the former Soviet Union. US charges were based on reports by alleged victims and eye-witnesses who stated that since the autumn of 1978 enemy aircraft had been spraying a toxic yellow material (hence the name of the case). Chemical analyses of samples of the yellow material and medical checks of the affected persons were conducted to substantiate the case. However, as the investigations proceeded, with the involvement of laboratories, in different countries and a careful scrutiny of the eye-witnesses' reports, the reliability of the evidence was increasingly questioned.[33] Some authoritative scientists found that the yellow substance consisted to a large extent of excrements of wild honeybees, and extensive analytical efforts in several laboratories failed to confirm the initial positive reports of trichothecenes.[34]

## 2. Assessment

As compared to other arms control agreements, the negotiations for the BW Convention—conducted separately from those on chemical weapons with which they had been associated for decades—encountered few obstacles and were concluded relatively quickly, in a common taboo on use. The reasons were as follows.

Biological weapons are unpredictable in their effects and of limited value in combat.[35] Since cheating under a BW Convention could not yield significant military advantages to the cheating party, a ban on biological weapons without verification of compliance was considered by the negotiators to be free of serious security risks. By contrast, chemical weapons are predictable, capable of producing immediate effects and, consequently, useful in combat. Banning their possession without elaborate and intrusive methods of verification was, therefore, deemed impossible. Most states which joined the BW Convention did so on condition that the complete prohibition of biological weapons would be recognized as a step towards a complete prohibition of chemical weapons (Preamble and Article XI).

The aim of the BW Convention was not so much to remove an immediate peril, as to eliminate the possibility that scientific and technological advances, modifying the conditions of production, storage or use of biological weapons, would make these weapons militarily attractive. Indeed, progress in biotechnology is making it increasingly possible to "improve" upon known biological agents. Normally harmless organisms which do not cause diseases can be modified so as to become highly toxic and produce diseases for which there is no known treatment. But the Convention is comprehensive enough to cover all relevant scientific and technological developments, including biological agents and toxins that could result from genetic engineering processes.

The disclosure by the UN Special Commission of an extensive biological weapons programme in Iraq,[36] as well as reports that certain other nations, too, have or are seeking to acquire a biological

weapon capability,[37] indicate that the threat of biological warfare remains real. Since the BW Convention has no instruments to check compliance, there is a need for verification machinery to deter would-be violators. Negotiations for a verification protocol, or another legally binding document strengthening the Convention with measures of control, have been going on in an ad hoc group of States, open to all parties, since January 1995. So far, however, agreement has proved elusive. Until it is reached, parties to the Convention are expected to implement the confidence-building measures they have agreed at their Review Conferences. The most important among them are measures enhancing the transparency of activities involving biological agents and toxins. They include exchanges of information on facilities and research programmes relevant to the Convention, on vaccine production, and on significant and unusual outbreaks of diseases.

Eventually, to make possible a differentiation between treaty-prohibited and treaty-permitted activities, the objects of the prohibitions will have to be more clearly defined, and the criteria necessary to assess compliance will have to be unambiguously established. Moreover, apart from short-notice visits to declared sites, on-site inspections of undeclared sites will have to be accepted without reservation by all parties. It is, of course, understood that sensitive commercial proprietary information and national security information, not directly related to the BW Convention, must be reliably protected. A special organization will be needed to oversee the implementation of the parties' obligations.

See also: *Disarmament and Development; Economics of Disarmament and Conversion; Economics of Disarmament: Certain Premises*

## Notes

1. For the text of this Convention, as well as the texts of the 1925 Geneva Protocol and the 1972 Biological Weapons Convention, which are discussed later in this article, see J. Goldblat, *Arms Control: A Guide to Negotiations and Agreements*, London, Thousand Oaks, New Delhi, PRIO and SAGE Publications, 1994, p. 257, 277 and 370, or D. Schindler and J. Toman (ed.), *The Laws of Armed Conflicts*, 3rd ed., Marinus Nijhoff Publishers/Henry Dunant Institute, Dordrecht/Geneva, 1988.
2. United Nations General Assembly Resolution No.1, 24 January 1946.
3. As decided in 1948 by the UN Commission on Conventional Armaments, a subsidiary body of the UN Security Council (United Nations document S/C.3/32/Rev.1).
4. United Nations, *Chemical and Bacteriological (biological) Weapons and the Effects of their Possible Use*, New York,

1969.

5. World Health Organization, *Health Aspects of the Use of Chemical and Biological Weapons*, Geneva, 1970.

6. ACDA, *Documents on Disarmament* 1969, Washington DC, 1970, pp. 592-93.

7. Office of the White House Press Secretary, Press release, Washington DC, 14 February 1970.

8. United Nations document A/2826(XXVI).

9. This interpretation was contained in the note of 18 August 1976 addressed by the US Secretary of State to the Swiss government.

10. Disarmament Conference document CCD/PV. 542.

11. The Australia Group was founded in 1985, in the aftermath of chemical weapons' use in the Iran-Iraq war, to constrain the trade in the technologies and materials of chemical warfare. In 1990, its purview was expanded to include bilolgical weapons.

12. Fourth Review Conference of the Parties to the BW Convention, document BWC/CONF.IV/9.

13. Disarmament Conference documents CCD/PV. 585 and 655.

14. Disarmament Conference document CCD/PV. 659.

15. Disarmament Conference document CCD/PV. 666.

16. Ireland (1972), Barbados (1976), Australia (1986), New Zealand (1989), Czechoslovakia (1990), Mongolia (1990), Bulgaria (1991), Canada (1991), Chile (1991), Romania (1991), United Kingdom (1991), Spain (1992), Russia (1992), South Africa (1996), France (1996), Belgium (1997).

17. Fourth Review Conference of the Parties to the BW Convention, document BWC/CONF.IV/COW/WP.2.

18. US Congressional Record-Senate, 9 March 1971.

19. United Nations Security Council Resolution 621 (1988). Guidelines and procedures for United Nations investigations were developed by a group of experts and endorsed by the United Nations General Assembly Resolution 45/57C (1990).

20. Even before the BW Convention entered into force, France—not a signatory—adopted a law (No. 72-467 of 9 June 1972) prohibiting biological and toxin weapons on its territory. The wording of its main provisions is almost identical to that of the Convention. Severe punishment of violators by fines and imprisonment is provided for, and elaborate procedures are intended to ensure that the prohibitions are respected. France acceded to the Convention only in 1984.

21. United States Senate Permanent Sub-Committee on Investigations, *Hearings on global proliferation of weapons of destruction: A case study on Aum Shinrikyo*, 31 October, 1995.

22. First and Second Biological Weapons Convention Review Conferences, documents BWC/CONF.I/10 and BWC/CONF.II/13.

23. United Nations Security Council document S/23500, 31 January 1992.

24. See S. Sur, "La résolution A.37/98 D du 13 décembre 1982 et les procédures d'enquête en cas d'usage allégué d'armes chimiques et bactériologiques (biologiques)", *Annuaire francais de droit international* (AFDI), 1984, pp. 93-109.

25. Disarmament Conference documents CCD/PV. 542 and CCD/PV. 544.

26. Descriptions of these allegations can be found in SIPRI *Yearbooks*. Allegations of use of biological means of warfare had also been made before the BW Convention entered into force.

27. *New York Times*, 19 March 1980.

28 First Biological Weapons Convention Review Conference document BWC/CONEI/SR. 12 para 29.

29. For detailed descriptions of the case see M. Meselson, "The biological weapons convention and the Sverdlovsk anthrax outbreak of 1979", *Federation of American scientists public interest report*, Vol. 41 (7), Washington DC, September 1988; E. Harris, "Sverdlovsk and yellow rain: Two cases of Soviet noncompliance?", *International Security*, Vol. 11(4), spring 1987, pp. 45-47; Ch. C. Flowerree, "Possible implications of the anthrax outbreak in Sverdlovsk on future verification of the Biological Weapons Convention: a US perspective"; S.J. Lundin (ed), *Views on possible verification measures for the Biological Weapons Convention*, SIPRI, Oxford University Press, Oxford, 1991; V. Issraelyan, "Possible implications of the anthrax outbreak in Sverdlovsk on future verification of the Biological Weapons Convention: a Soviet perspective", *ibid*.

30. The White House, *Report to the Congress on Soviet noncompliance with arms control agreements*, Washington DC, 23 February 1990.

31. *Chemical Weapons Convention Bulletin*, No.16, June 1992, pp. 18-19.

32. The allegation was in public for the first time by Secretary of State Haig in September 1981 (US Department of State, press release, 13 September 1981). More details were given in: US Department of State, *Chemical Warfare in Southeast Asia and Afghanistan*, Special Report No. 98, Report to the Congress from Secretary of State Alexander M. Haig, Jr., March 22, 1982; and US Department of State, *Chemical warfare in Southeast Asia and Afghanistan: An update*, Special Report No.104, by Secretary of State George P. Shultz, November 11, 1982.

33. A UN expert team, dispatched by the Secretary-General in 1981 and 1982, was not able to shed more light on the issue (UN documents A/36/613 Annex and A/37/259).

34. For an analysis of the Yellow Rain case, disputing the allegations, see J. P. Robinson, J. Guillemin, M. Meselson, "Yellow rain in Southeast Asia: The story collapses", S. Wright (ed.), *Preventing a biological arms race*, MIT Press, Cambridge Mass., 1990.

35. They might, perhaps, be militarily more useful for area denial.

36. United Nations Security Council document S/1995/864.

37. Statement by the Director of the US Arms Control and Disarmament Agency to the BW Convention Review Conference, 26 November 1996.

JOZEF GOLDBLAT

# Bouthoul, Gaston

Gaston Bouthoul (1900-80) was a French scientist who treated war as a scientific subject from a sociological point of view. He was the first, in his book

*Cent millions de morts* (1946), to call this field of research "polemology" (from the Greek "polemos" and "logos"), which means the "science of war." As a D.Litt. and D.Juris he became professor at the Sorbonne University in Paris and later practiced as a lawyer. His initial economic statistical research activities and his interest in demographic problems led him, at an early stage, to sociological studies, particularly in relation with the phenomenon of "war." His first study, published in 1939, dealt with the functions and the periodicity of warfare.

In 1945, under the double shock of the nuclear devastation of Hiroshima and Nagasaki and the atrocities of the Nazi concentration camps, Bouthoul decided to devote his further scientific research to a new approach to the study of war. In 1945 he founded and directed the Institut Français de Polémologie. In 1968 he started the publication of a scientific periodical, *Guerre et paix,* from 1971 on called *Etudes Polémologiques.*

According to Bouthoul, two major obstacles have hampered a scientific approach to war: (a) a lack of astonishment at and the acceptance of military conflict throughout the ages as self-evident, and (b) the erroneous belief in the exclusively voluntary and conscious character of warfare. This is why he rejected firmly the illusion of the short-term, therapeutic approach aiming at the regulation, prevention, or even abolition of war by judicial means, as if international conflicts could be compared to friction between individuals. He asked the question how would it be possible to legislate on a phenomenon that has not yet been studied in depth. Therefore he replaced the ancient Roman adage "If you want peace, prepare for war" with his own; "If you want peace, study war." This approach constitutes the basis of Bouthoul's scientific study of war.

Analyzing the religious and philosophical backgrounds of war, Bouthoul noticed that the idea of warfare is very ancient and goes back to classical mythology, where it is considered as a very important and highly honorable activity practiced, encouraged, and protected by the gods. In the Old Testament, God appeared frequently as the "god of the armies." According to the Koran, the propagation of Islam by armed force was a religious duty. Originally the Christians condemned violence but rapidly the Catholic Church, and particularly St. Thomas and his followers, developed the theory of a "just war" (see *Just War*) very close to the concept proclaimed by Moslems (see *Islam*).

Considering the philosophical approaches to war, Bouthoul concluded that only the Chinese, throughout the ages, firmly avoided exalting war, according to their conviction of being superior to the surrounding civilizations. Greek philosophers regarded war generally as part of the divine order. Among the more modern philosophers, Macchiavelli proclaimed that each war is just on the condition that it is necessary, particularly in the case of a preemptive war (see *Machiavellianism*). As a logical and necessary consequence of his "categorical imperatives," Kant condemned all warlike activities. He recognized, however, that such condemnations have an abstract character and therefore he looked for more practical and concrete conditions for the establishment of a perpetually peaceful world (see *Kant, Immanuel; Perpetual Peace*). On the contrary, Hegel considered war as a necessary evil that only could be brought to an end by achieving the "Absolute Spirit." Joseph de Maistre considered war as a "renovation of the blood of the civilizations" and as a "divine law regulating world order." In many of his works, Nietzsche exalted war and its hardships as an appropriate educational step toward the creation of the future type of human being, who should get used to suffering and death. Nietzsche's lyrical language is, however, ambiguous and it is not always clear if in glorifying war he was not referring more to moral struggles than to physical violence.

Clausewitz, one of the greatest theorists of warfare, analyzed this phenomenon, taking into account its aspects, objectives, and means. He demonstrated that war is "the continuation of politics by other means." He considered the armed forces as an instrument of politics, and war as an act of violence pushed toward its extreme limits.

Analyzing the sociological theories of warfare, Bouthoul came to the conclusion that these theories generally considered war as a "normal" element in the evolution of society. The pessimists considered war as an eternal phenomenon, frequently with beneficial effects. Their views stressed the instinctive cruelty of the human being and of the struggle for life, but without any scientific justification. The optimists (Saint-Simon, Comte, Spencer, Tarde, and Marx) were of the contrary opinion, viewing war as a product of social structure which would vanish when inevitable changes in society occur. Saint-Simon and Comte believed that the evolution of industry would eventually lead to the abolition of war. Marx and his followers denounced war as a ploy on the part of the leading social classes to divert the attention of the people from the class struggle.

According to Bouthoul, war is essentially a collective phenomenon, involving a subjective element, the intention, and a political element, the organization. War serves the interests of a political group. Bouthoul also stressed the juridical character of warfare. Consequently he defined war as an armed and bloody struggle between organized groups. It is a methodological and organized form of violence, limited in time and space, and regulated by particular juridical rules, which are extremely variable according to regions and historical periods. In Bouthoul's view, bloodshed and the destruction of human life were essential characteristics of war. Therefore he refused to use the term war to describe non-armed conflicts and the mere exchange of threats, such as the Cold War between East and West.

Bouthoul also analyzed the economic aspects of war. War supposes a preceding accumulation of capital, manpower, equipment, and logistics. In that sense Bouthoul characterized war as "an activity of luxury" and as an economic enterprise requiring an accumulation of material, money, and reserves. According to Bouthoul, preparations for war contribute to full employment, provoke an accelerated consumption, and involve shifts in wealth. It causes changes in economic and industrial structures and modifies the distribution of investments, capital, and export opportunities. Bouthoul considered economics as an essential cause of war, although not the only one. War is indeed a total social phenomenon, resulting from numerous aspects. He distinguished wars of economic shortages and economic abundance. In his view, history proves that nations are more eager to go to war in times of abundance, because preparation for war presupposes an accumulation of surplus in production. Among primitive societies, however, economic shortages are more likely to be the causes of war. Colonial warfare is a typical example of the rich fighting the poor. Wars fought with the aim of finding export possibilities are typical examples of armed struggle caused by surplus of production. In this context, liberal economics and commercial competition stimulate friction among nations which frequently leads to military conflicts.

Bouthoul attached great importance to the demographic causes and functions of war, which he considered to be predominant amongst all causes. He defined war as collective, organized, and finalized homicide. The main function of war, in Bouthoul's view was to restore the balance between a demo-economic structure having a large mass of turbulent youth and the requirements of economic production. In this sense he qualified war as a "deferred infanticide" and a "demographic relaxation," achieving the destruction of many young lives not required for an adequate functioning of the socioeconomic system. Thus wars are consciously destructive and biodemographically regulating institutions.

In analyzing the ethnological aspects of war, Bouthoul saw it as a supreme ceremony, an ostentatious destruction, with collective rites and aesthetic, social, and ludic expressions. The sacramental aspects of war transform mentalities and values. War imposes a Manichean mentality on society, polarizing activities and beliefs around mainly dualistic themes.

Finally, Bouthoul studied the psychological aspects of war, such as individual and collective aggression, and the psychoanalysis of warlikeness.

Considering pacifism, Bouthoul made a distinction between its origins (from political leaders or from the population) and its different forms (sacred and evangelical pacifism, moderated and warlike pacifism). Some kinds of pacifism condemn war but continue to consider it as an unavoidable and useful phenomenon in certain circumstances. Peace plans are generally limited by a preventive approach to the causes of war. Bouthoul concluded that there will always remain an irrational element in the war phenomenon. Therefore he advocated peace plans based upon scientific research and on an objective study of war. He rejected strongly the idea that peace can result from a world organization replacing the presently existing sovereign states. Interstate rivalries would then be replaced with conflicts between factions, armies, and other interest groups. On the other hand, he saw the achievement of peace through a power balance between states as a permanent source of war and violent competition.

The relevance of Bouthoul's studies to peace and security today lies beyond any doubt in the fact that he was the founding father of polemology. He was one of the first scientists to propose the view that war is an ordinary social phenomenon that needs to be demystified and treated as a subject of scientific inquiry so that it may be combated. He challenged historians to combine their reflections with the works of sociologists in the study of human conflicts. He proclaimed that the multidisciplinary study of the causes and functions of war, as a social phenomenon, is essential for achieving world peace. In his view the study object of polemology should be limited to war as an armed struggle between organized social groups ruled by judicial regulations and involving the destruction of human lives and material goods. In the discussion of the methodological approaches of the study of war and peace, he firmly rejected those scientists who focused their scientific research unilaterally on the study of peace. He strongly opposed peace researchers proposing mainly subjective, concrete solutions for the resolution of conflicts without having any answer to the essential questions of the causes and functions of war.

Bouthoul wrote over 30 books and hundreds of articles, and participated in numerous international seminars and conferences. His works influenced polemological thinking in the Netherlands, the United Kingdom, the Federal Republic of Germany, Switzerland, Italy, the Middle East, Canada, Mexico, Brazil, and Belgium, where he was made Doctor *honoris causa* in 1972. His periodical, *Etudes Polémologiques*, contains a detailed data bank on armed conflicts in the world and therefore constitutes an extremely valuable basis for further research. Unfortunately, though, his studies remain largely ignored by Anglo-Saxon social scientists and polemologists. This may be attributable to his biodemographical approach to war as a regulating factor in the restoration of the balance between population growth and economic requirements which, neglecting as it does other methods for neutralizing the traditional turbulence of youth, made him vulnerable to the criticism of different polemological schools.

See also: *Peace and Conflict Research Development; Polemology; War*

*Bibliography*

Bouthoul G 1962 *War.* Walker, New York
Bouthoul G 1968 Polemology and the solution of conflicts. *Impact of Science on Society* 18 (2)
Carrere R 1981 Gaston Bouthoul, homme de vérite et de paix. *Etudes polémologiques* 24
Corvisier A 1977 L'Etude de la guerre entre la sociologie et l'histoire. *Revue Historique* 257 (2)
Freund J 1981 Gaston Bouthoul, Sociologue de la guerre et de la paix. *Etudes Polémologiques* 24
Institut Francais de Polemologie (IFP) 1981 Méthode et spécificité de la polémologie. *Etudes Polémologiques* 24
Muraise E 1976 Polémologie et problématique mondiale. *Etudes Polémologiques* 6 (20-21)

IVO SCHALBROECK

# Brezhnev Doctrine

The principles of what became known as the Brezhnev Doctrine were first stated by the General Secretary of the Communist Party of the Soviet Union (CPSU) in a speech to the People's Party Rally of the United Polish Worker's Party on November 12, 1968. Leonid Brezhnev stated that:

It is common knowledge that the Soviet Union has really done a good deal to strengthen the sovereignty and autonomy of the socialist countries. The CPSU has always advocated that each socialist country determine the concrete forms of its development along the path of socialism by taking into account the specific nature of their national conditions. But it is well known, comrades, that there are common natural laws of socialist construction, deviation from which could lead to deviation from socialism as such. And when external and internal forces hostile to socialism try to turn the development of a given socialist country in the direction of restoration of the capitalist system, when a threat arises to the cause of socialism in that country—a threat to the security of the socialist commonwealth as a whole—this is no longer merely a problem for that country's people, but a common problem, the concern of all socialist countries.
It is quite clear that an action such as military assistance to a fraternal country to end—a threat to the socialist system is an extraordinary measure, dictated

by necessity; it can be called forth only by the overt actions of enemies of socialism within the country and beyond its boundaries, actions that create a threat to the common interests of the socialist camp. (*Pravda* November 13, 1968)

This doctrine, in addition to retroactively justifying the invasion of Czechoslovakia by Warsaw Pact troops in 1968, on the one hand served as the basis for future disciplining of Soviet satellite states, and on the other formed the ideological underpinning for the strengthening of efforts towards integration within the Warsaw Pact and the member states of the Council for Mutual Economic Assistance (COMECON). In fact, the doctrine found its ideological anchorage one month after the Soviet intervention in Czechoslovakia in an article by Kovalev, "Sovereignty and International Duties of Socialist Countries," published in *Pravda* on September 26, 1968. In this article Kovalev considered the future homogeneous political formation of ideas of the socialist community states on the international plane of the communist parties guaranteed through the principle of "proletarian internationalism." The ideas put forward, which were adopted by Brezhnev in his speech and became known as the Brezhnev Doctrine, can be condensed into the following theses—even when consideration is made of later statements by leading Soviet personalities.

(a) The socialist states are only conditionally sovereign: they may lay claim to the rights of a sovereign state insofar as they do not contravene the interests of the "socialist community and the worldwide revolutionary movement" which take priority over national interests.

(b) The socialist states have only limited powers of self-determination (see *Self-determination*). Breaking free from the "socialist state community" is therefore not possible as such a step would be detrimental both to themselves and to the interests of the other socialist countries and would justify the use of military force.

(c) Since the formation of a "socialist commonwealth" the dictatorship of the proletariat has adopted an international character. This implies a global claim to government on the part of the communist parties. The sovereignty of a socialist state has a class character which cannot be violated by acts of intervention of another socialist country. Sovereignty exists by law of the working people to establish a socialist, or communist, social order under the leadership of a communist party.

(d) If a communist party, while developing socialism, deviates or threatens to deviate from the Soviet model, then the "brother countries" are obliged, in accordance with the principles of proletarian internationalism, to intervene by means of military force. Consequently, through ideological divergences in the "Soviet commonwealth" (according to Soviet Foreign Minister Gromyko in October 1968 at the UN), the conception of the CPSU can be put into effect with the help of the armed forces of the Warsaw Pact should the diverging political line of a country bring the danger of a split in and the inner disintegration of the socialist commonwealth and the country in question is not itself able or willing to oppose the differences.

(e) The principles of peaceful coexistence (see *Peaceful Coexistence*), equality, respect for territorial integrity, and the state's independence in home affairs are, as far as relations between socialist countries are concerned (and in particular with regard to the Soviet Union), only partially effective.

(f) The defense of world socialism as a common achievement of the working people of all countries is the common cause of all communists and all progressive people on earth, first and foremost the working people of the socialist countries.

(g) Every communist party is responsible for its actions, even before all socialist countries and before the communist world movement.

These theses which are to be found in a similar form in the "Declaration of the 81st Communist and Workers' Parties of December 1960" (printed in *Pravda* December 6, 1960) reflect the restrictive principles of "proletarian socialist internationalism" of the Stalin era, and, as described by Korea (1969) also fit in with the principles of action of Comintern. Confirmation of this is to be found also in an essay by the Communist Party ideologue, A Sovyetov, (1968) in which he describes "Solidarity with the Soviet Union and its support in the international arena in the present situation as before as a fundamental component of proletarian internationalism."

Nonetheless, the Soviet conception of the principles of "proletarian internationalism" has, at least since the statement of the Brezhnev Doctrine, been rejected by communists of all shades who are not prepared to recognize such unlimited hegemony. On August 22, 1968, Nikolaf Ceausescu pointed out at the Great National Congress of Romania that the forces of the Warsaw Pact should in no way and under no circumstances be used for military actions against any of the socialist countries. The reaction from the People's Republic of China was particularly strong. It described the Brezhnev Doctrine as a "gangster theory" and accused the Soviets of "social fascism" and "social imperialism." An article by Kung Chun-Ping (1969) stated:

By putting out his theory of "international dictatorship," the Soviet revisionists intend first of all to justify their barefaced social-imperialist aggression and second, to fabricate a "theoretical" basis for their rapacious expansionist ambitions. We must expose this theory for what it is and lay bare the diabolical features of Soviet revisionist social-imperialism in the broad light of day.

The Soviet revisionist renegade clique glibly talks about "national dictatorship" and "international dictatorship." Let the question be asked: Which class exercises the "dictatorship" you speak of, and which class is subjected to this "dictatorship?"

By turning "national dictatorship" into "international dictatorship," the Soviet revisionists are out to extend their domestic counter-revolutionary bourgeois dictatorship abroad and, by plunder and aggression, exercise a counter-revolutionary dictatorship over the people of other countries.

Plunder, aggression, suppression of the people of

other countries, and even military occupation—this is the reactionary essence of the Soviet revisionists' so-called theory of "international dictatorship . . . ."

Today, under the pretext of "safeguarding the socialist gains," the Soviet revisionist renegade clique sends its troops marching into Czechoslovakia and imposes "international dictatorship" over the people of that country. Tomorrow, under the pretext of "safeguarding" something else, it can send aggressor troops marching into another of its "fraternal countries" in the "socialist community" or into countries outside this so-called "community" to violate their territorial integrity and sovereignty. In fabricating the theory of "international dictatorship," a theory for fascist aggression, the Soviet revisionist renegade clique has a completely vile purpose in mind . . . .

This, among other statements by communist critics of the Brezhnev Doctrine, shows clearly both the controversy surrounding the doctrine and the ferocity of political disputes within the communist state system.

Although opposed by Moscow's leadership, both the reformist communists and the "brother parties" insisted on a system of relations within the communist world, which was to have the character of a law of coordination rather than subcoordination. However, this claim did not materialize until the mid-eighties when Mikhail Gorbachev (see Nobel Peace Prize Laureates: *Mikhail S. Gorbachev*) was elected Secretary General of the KPDSU in March 1985; only then, in the course of 1987, did the bloc policy undergo a process of reorientation. In the face of enormous difficulties in one's own country, it was reasoned that a relaxed security policy should replace the vassal loyalty demanded up to now. The stations leading up to the surrender of the doctrine of superiority of the Soviet model can be chronologically summarized as follows:

(a) Speech on a rally of the Czechoslovakian Soviet Friendship on April 10, 1987 in Prague;
   "We are," so the Head of the Kremel, "far removed from calling upon anybody to copy us. Every socialist country has her specifics. While taking into account the national conditions, the fraternal parties assess the political course (. . .) Nobody has the right to claim a special status in the socialist world. We hold these principles to be self-evident: every party is autonomous, it is responsible for the people, and it has the right to solve the questions of the country's development with sovereignty (. . .) There is not a single party that possesses the monopoly on the truth."

(b) The XIXth All Unions Conference of the KPDSU and June 28, 1988 where Gorbachev lectured on

the freedom of peoples and states to choose their own social system;

(c) Gorbachev's speech to the UNO General Assembly on December 7, 1988 during which he emphasized once again that "for us (. . .) the binding force of the principle of free choice (is) beyond all about . . . ;" furthermore he interceded in favor of deideologizing the interstate relations;

(d) His communication at the Meeting of the Political Advisory Committee of the Warsaw Pact on July 7/8, 1989 in Bucharest in which he stated that "there are no universal models of socialism (. . .) The erection of a new society is a creative process. It is developed in every country according to its preconditions, traditions and requirements." Moreover, the need was stressed that the countries develop their relations autonomously on the basis of equality, independence and the right of each to utilize, without external interference, her political line, strategy and tactics. With this decision, and with a resolution made by the Committee of the Foreign Ministers of the Warsaw Pact States on October 26/27, 1989 in Warsaw, confirming to the "brother states" more strikingly yet full freedom of judgement in internal affairs, the Eastern Military Alliance once and forever deshelved the "Brezhnev Doctrine" formulated during the suppression of the "Prague Spring." Possibly triggered by this action were the "peaceful revolutions" to follow in East and Middle Europe which, in turn, did not only lead to the dissolution of the Warsaw Pact and East bloc, but may even have introduced the end of the Soviet imperium.

See also: *Socialism and Peace; Socialist International; Socialism, Scientific; Eastern Europe, Transformation of*

*Bibliography* ⎯⎯⎯⎯⎯⎯⎯⎯⎯⎯⎯⎯⎯⎯⎯⎯

Edmonds B 1983 *Soviet Foreign Policy: The Brezhnev Years.* Oxford University Press, New York
Korey W 1969 The Comintern and the genealogy of the Brezhnev Doctrine. *Problems of Communism* 3
Kung C P 1969 The theory of international dictatorship is a gangster theory of social imperialism. *Peking Review* 20
Meissner B 1969 *Die "Breshnew-Doctrine."* Köln
Sovyetov A 1968 The present stage in the struggle between socialism and imperialism. *Int'l Affairs* 11

MIR A. FERDOWSI

# Buddhism

Scholars, teachers, and practitioners of Buddha Dharma all agree that Buddhism is a religion fundamentally concerned with peace. There is however a wide range of opinion on the issue of whether the peaceful orientation of Buddhism is concerned with the individual's progress on the path to Nirvana or Enlightenment; or does the concern for peace have political, social and environmental implications for Buddhists. There is an implicit tension and sometimes an explicit debate between these two views of Buddhism. It is useful to distinguish accounts of Buddhism which are seeking to locate the tradition purely in its textual and historical context, and accounts which are focussed on the relevance of Buddha Dharma to contemporary life and issues. Having made that distinction, it should be pointed out that a particular view of the nature of early Buddhism, often informs a discussion of the contemporary role of Buddhism. It is also the case that a commentator's or teacher's commitment to a particular Buddhist ethical or social orientation, may influence his view of the nature of Buddhism in its textual and early historical expressions.

## 1. Three Approaches to Buddhism and Peace

An example of the first kind of approach can be found in Gombrich (1988 pp. 72-81), where the author characterises early Buddhism as form of religious individualism, with a new understanding of effective individual action (karma), which appealed strongly to an increasingly important mercantile class. Gombrich doubts whether the Buddha took an interest in politics or intended his teachings to have political consequences. He argues that the Buddha's insight that, "... societal status depends on man-made conventions had some consequences, which he neither foresaw nor intended" (1988 p. 81). This is in line with the view held by many scholars that early Buddhism was primarily a spiritual teaching concerned with the realising of Nirvana and directed specifically at monks. It must be said that guessing the Buddha's intentions is always going to be a difficult procedure.

A more socio-politically orientated view of early Buddhism is offered by Trevor Ling. He sees early Buddhism as a psycho-social philosophy which incorporates '... a theory of existence consisting of a diagnosis (of the human malaise) and the prescription for a cure' (1973 p. 120). He rightly takes the teaching of no-self as central to Buddhism, but interprets it specifically as a teaching designed to overcome the 'disease of individualism' (p. 124). He sees the communal life of the sangha as providing the context and environment where individualism can be most effectively broken down. On the issue of the relationship between sangha and lay society, Ling maintains that the Buddha consciously modelled the sangha's constitution and organisation on the methods of government of the tribal republics of north India, and that these principles were ideally seen as a model for government for society in general. His case for the latter largely rests on his interpretation of the 'conditions of welfare' passage in the Mahaparinibbana sutta, in which the survival of the Vajjian confederacy is said to depend on maintaining its regular process of collective decision making, and upholding its established traditions and institutions. In the text the Buddha compares this with the sangha's survival, which also depends on its observance of collective decision making and upholding its traditions (Ling 1973 pp. 128-133, Ling 1981 pp. 144-152) Ling concedes that in practice the early sangha (monastic order) had to come to terms with the reality of increasingly powerful centralised and expansionist monarchies in north India in the fifth and fourth centuries BC. The issue of the sangha and kingship will be addressed below. It is important to realise that whatever the broader intention behind the Buddha's teaching on governing, whether it was directed at kings or more specifically at governing the sangha (monastic order), by responding as he did in the immediate situation, he averted a major military conflict. This role of peacemaker is demonstrated by the Buddha more than once in early canonical texts. For example in his famous intervention between the Sakyans and Koliyas, who are about to go to war over irrigation rights. He simply asks them which is more valuable, the water they are disputing over or the lives of their finest warriors (Burlingame trans 1969, part 111 p. 71).

Despite the apparent differences between Ling and Gombrich in their characterisations of early Indian Buddhism, it is possible to reconcile significant aspects of their positions. One could argue that a soteriological religion of self help and individual responsibility, with its ethic of merit at a popular level and spiritual endeavour at the elite level, would be forced to confront the psychologically and spiritually damaging implications of its own individualism. Taking this process further, efforts of an individual and inherently 'self authenticating' kind must be made in order to overcome or uproot the notion of individualism and its attendant excesses. One can, of course, interpret this as an impossible and paradoxical vicious circle or one can assume the Mahayana Buddhist perspective of skillful means and see it as using a thorn to take out a thorn. The value of such an interpretation can be seen when the nature of the Buddhist understanding of karma (action, moral cause and effect) is discussed later in this article.

A third perspective on the issue of Buddhism and peace can be identified as the Engaged Buddhist view. In the latter half of the twentieth century Engaged Buddhism has emerged as a significant dimension of Buddhist expression and practice. Engaged Buddhism adopts Buddhist categories in analysing contemporary social, political and moral questions, and see Buddha-dhamma correctly understood and actively applied, as offering the means to peaceful progress. The order of Interbeing founded in 1964 by the Vietnamese monk Thich Nhat Hanh, sought to base social concerns and responsibilities around the practice of mindful awareness and non-violence (Thich 1967; Batchelor 1994 ch. 21). Engaged Buddhism now has a considerable international following with a wide range of projects such as conciliation services, environmental projects, projects for refugees, a Buddhist prison chaplaincy and visiting service (Batchelor 1994 ch. 21). Engaged Buddhists such as Ken Jones (1989,1993) and Joanna Macy (1983,1985,1991) often reflect considerable textual sophistication and see Buddhism as a living tradition with vital resources and perspectives to contribute to so many contemporary problems. Other Engaged Buddhists have been criticised for their lack of textual and historical sophistication. The suggestion that western, bourgeois, liberal values are being imposed on interpretation of ancient Buddhist concepts and institutions. An example of this charge can be seen in Gombrich's critique of the writings of A.T. Ariyaratane on Buddhist notions of development and the Sarvodaya movement. Apart from specific criticism of the misuse of Buddhist terms and the misrepresentation of traditional Sinhalese village life, Gombrich feels that the monastic core of traditional Buddhism and its other-worldly, Nibbanic orientation, is being neglected in Ariyaratna's account (Gombrich & Obeyesekere 1988 pp. 243-252).

## 2. *Interpreting Buddhism and Social Issues in Early Texts*

Buddhist scholarship tends to examine historical and textual accounts for an understanding of the relationship between Buddhism, monarchy and socio-political issues during the early development of Bud-

dhism. Gombrich doubts whether many canonical passages dealing with kingship and politics were meant to be normative or offer practical policies intended for rulers. He argues that many of the passages are intentionally mythological, and are dealing with "fantasy" kings, not practical guidelines for real kings. He suspects the "authenticity" of the famous Cakkavatti Sihanada-sutta (Digha Nikaya 111, Ling ed. 1981 pp. 115-128). He suggests that its lack of a context, unlike most suttas in the Digha Nikaya, and its exaggerated mythological content, make it unlikely to be the word of the Buddha. The text is however regarded as such by tradition, and its content must therefore be taken seriously. It describes a succession of strong and righteous rulers in ancient times whose merit and success was marked by a Celestial Wheel in the sky, and by the great longevity of them and their subjects. The average lifespan being forty thousand years. Periodically the wheel would slip, but provided the ruler at the time took counsel from the wisest hermit in the kingdom and acted accordingly, it was restored. Then one ruler began governing according to his own ideas, and ignoring the example of the previous ruler, and not taking counsel from the hermit. When a man was brought before him for stealing, the king gave him money to support his family. Other subjects heard of this and they also stole. The king realised that by rewarding theft, he was encouraging it, so he had the next offender executed. People by now had habituated to stealing, so that rather than stop, they armed themselves to prevent capture. When some were captured they lied about their crimes, and so society degenerated. Lying and stealing were rife and people became progressively coarser and shorter lived. Eventually society and values collapsed, people were killing their own families to eat, and the human lifespan dwindled to ten years. Then a small group resolved to abstain from violence and live cooperatively, and in doing so gradually improved the human condition and the lifespan, so once again people began to prosper and live in harmony, villages and towns developed all over India. Eventually a wise and righteous Universal Monarch (Cakkavatti) emerged and during his reign Metteya (Maitreya) the next Buddha will appear, to teach Dhamma (Dharma) throughout the world.

Even if we accept Gombrich's point about the inappropriate time-frame of the story and its undoubted mythic style, it does establish an important connection between the human conduct and Dharmic or ethical orientation. Human health, wealth and happiness, on material, ethical and spiritual levels are linked to the leadership of the ruler as well to individual's own actions. The story emphasises the important role of exemplary rulers and their need to listen to wise counsel. Though not a technical treatise, the story establishes that moral cause and effect or the working of karma are not merely individual processes, but have important social and cosmic dimensions. The story clearly emphasises the role of the righteous ruler in improving the social and moral environment in which virtue is rewarded and wrongdoing punished. And significantly, establishing the conditions in which Dhamma can operate.

In the Kutadanta-sutta (Digha Nikaya vol. 1, Ling 1981 pp. 91-100) the Buddha in a former life as religious advisor to a great king, that he can restore peace and order in his kingdom not by performing the traditional animal sacrifice, or by applying severe punishments to wrongdoers, but by ensuring that all those working in his kingdom are properly rewarded for their labours. The king is advised to supply traders and businessmen with capital, to help them prosper, and that wealthy brahmans, ksatriyas and householders should be encouraged to establish charitable foundations in all directions, to support the poor, and the wandering mendicants and wise teachers. The Buddha declares that after the king has done all this he can perform a non-violent sacrifice.

As Gombrich points out, the story is told to a Brahmin not a king, and it it seems to be more concerned with the nature of sacrifice, than be a practical outline of policy. Such policies would have been unthinkable to the real kings at the time of the Buddha. But their very articulation does represent something of a criticism of despotic and punitive rulers, and does offer radical alternative that might cause a more sympathetic ruler to re-consider his priorities. If the rulers of the kingdoms of north India were as despotic and pragmatic as Gombrich suggests, then it would have been unthinkable for the Buddha to offer such radical advice on the use of charity and the re-distribution of wealth. Then it becomes more credible that such ideas would be taught in the form of highly mythic and fantastic accounts. In other words, the Buddha or early Buddhists are using indirect means on tactical and expedient grounds to present some radical and challenging ideas.

We have seen that Buddhist textual and scholars and Engaged Buddhists tend to use Buddhist texts in quite different ways. Christoper Titmus, an Engaged Buddhist and Environmental campaigner, cites the Kutadanta-sutta, Cakkavati Sihanada-sutta and Aggana-sutta to support the view that "the social conscience of the Buddha was an integral part of his teach-ing" (Titmus 1995 p. 213). He regards the injunctions on kings to relieve the suffering of the poor, as an expression of loving kindness in action. Despite the mythic context, he regards the Buddha's analysis of the causes of suffering, violence and social collapse, as related to socio-economic as well as karmic factors as an intentional expression of Dharma. He interprets such injunctions as placing rulers under a serious obligation to reduce poverty and restore peace and justice as a legitimate expression of Buddhist teaching (1995 p. 211).

## 3. The Nature of Buddhist Teachings

To resolve the issue of whether Buddhist peace is a private spiritual matter or a condition with social and political implications, a consideration of the nature of Buddhist teachings is necessary. It soon becomes apparent that these teachings have considerable depth and flexibility . . . . Buddhist texts and authorities from all schools and traditions except models of spiritual understanding and moral attainment which are both developmental and hierarchical. Such models are implicit in the notion of "Path" itself. This means that beings at different levels of understanding and attainment are taught in ways and at levels appropriate to their understanding and attainment. The Buddha's and any enlightened teacher's skill in teaching consists in their capacity to identify and adapt to the level of those being taught. This explains why the Buddha's response to what appear to be the same questions could vary according to the situation and understanding of the questioner. One way of articulating this kind of differentiation is through the concepts of conventional truth (samvrtisatya) and ultimate truth (paramārtha-satya). This distinction is usually associated with Mahayana Buddhism, particularly the philosophical tradition of Madhyamika. Steven Collins has shown convincingly how it is equally appropriate to the Pali texts and the Theravada tradition. He applies it specifically to the various levels and types of discourse developed around the notions of person (pudgala/puggala) and no self (anātman/anatta), and relates these levels to the social categories in Theravāda Buddhist Societies and to the distinction between 'Kammatic Buddhism' and 'Nibbanic Buddhism' (Colins 1982 ch. 5). Given the variety of levels of discourse and the process of accommodation to different levels of attainment which are evident in Buddhist texts and teachings, it is apparent that definitive statements and generalisations about the nature of Buddhist ethics are extremely problematic. The tendency to evaluate generalised statements about Buddhist ethics, according to the standards of western ethical theories and assumptions is one which should be resisted. Buddhist ethics cannot be reduced to classical western ethical theory, but Buddhist ethical insights can illumine western notions of ethics, in both theoretical and practical ways. The importance of control and understanding of the mind is an important dimension of Buddhist ethical understanding from which moralists can learn.

## 4. The Centrality of Karma in Buddhist Theory and Practice

The Buddha's important contribution to the theory and concept of karma has been to give an ethical and psychological orientation to the Brahmanic notion of karma, which referred to effective ritual action. The emphasis in Buddhism is on the determining or volitional intention behind the action, and it is this which produces the seeds and tendencies which affect or determine future states and conditions. In the Buddhist context the meaning of karma has shifted from ritual act to volitional act or intention. 'It is choice or intention that I call karma—mental work—for having chosen, a man acts by body, speech and mind' (Anguttara Nikāya, quoted in Carrithers 1983 p. 67). This is reflected in the traditional Buddhist emphasis on the need for controlling and understanding the mind, if moral practice and spiritual training are to be cultivated to their higher levels. The emphasis on the psychology of intentions in traditional Buddhist ethical teaching and spiritual practice, should not lead to the undermining of physical behaviour and actual consequences. It would be incorrect to say that the intention or will to perform an unwholesome act, which was not actually carried out, would produce the same effect as the actual performance of such an act. The subtlety of levels of intention and the relationship between intention and behaviour is acknowledged. For example the casual thought, 'I wish X were dead,' is certainly unwholesome, and will produce some unfortunate result. But the results would be much more serious in the case of someone who wishes X dead and makes detailed plans for murder. The results would be even more grave in the case of someone who raised the initial thought, plans and then actually carries out the murder. The degree of intention or volition (saṃskāra/saṅkhāra) involved in the final scenario are clearly greater than those involved in the first two.

It is clear that the notion of karma permeates all levels of Buddhist teaching and practice. A generalised 'knowledge of the ownership of deeds' greatly facilitates cultivation of giving and moral conduct. It is also clear that a full understanding of the detailed operation of karma and its implications is only available at the highest levels of attainment and practice. It is interesting to note that it is only at this level of practice and attainment, when intentional acts producing harmful consequences are no longer performed, that a full understanding of the nature of that action and results is achieved (Robinson and Johnson 1977 p. 38-39). This does not mean that beings at this advanced level no longer act. The teaching career and activities of the Buddha and the Arhats (Worthy/Enlightened Ones) disproves this. It simply means that their acts are of such a quality that they no longer generate fresh tendencies and consequences in performing them.

## 5. Theory into Practice

The Engaged Buddhist perspective takes contemporary social, political and ethical issues as its starting point rather than particular texts or teachings. It does however view these in the light of Buddhist practice and a Buddhist analysis of the human condition. According to this analysis, human and sentient life in general is subject to suffering and imperfection. At the root of this suffering are the three poisons of greed, hate and ignorance. Beings are ignorant of the transitory nature of existence and consequently grasp after phenomena or states, believing them to be permanent. When things change or cease, then beings in a state of ignorance and grasping, suffer further. Graving, grasping and attachment to self as permanent, surviving separate entity, give rise to selfishness, obsessional states, attachments, competition, hostility and violence. The antidote to this vicious circle is the practice of the Four Sublime States (Brahmāvihāra) as a particular meditational discipline. These states of loving kindness, compassion, sympathy and even-mindedness were recommended by the Buddha for monks and lay people (Conze 1956 p. 118). The details of the practice with regard to loving kindness are discussed by saddhatissa (1970 pp. 90-99). As they are developed in meditation they permeate and are consciously applied to the individuals daily life and conduct (Ce Bary 1958 pp. 117-119, Horner (trans.) *1967 Middle Length Sayings* Vol.1 p. 166). The importance of even-mindedness is that only when it is developed and pervades the other states can they become truly impartial. Ultimately they must be practised without discriminating between friend or enemy, self or other.

It is clear that the Buddha's analysis and much

later Buddhist teaching, place considerable emphasis on the mental factors which give rise to anger, tension conflict and violence. This emphasis is particularly evident in the famous opening verses of the Dhammapada, which states that the mind is the source of all wholesome actions and of all unwholesome actions, and that thought, action and consequences are always associated (Mascaro (trans.) 1973). It is also clear that it is primarily on this mental or psychological level that problems are to be resolved and behaviour can be modified. Having indicated that the psychological and spiritual orientation of the Buddha's analysis of the human condition is paramount, the external manifestations of greed, hate and ignorance are not ignored. Specific prohibitions of acts of violence and retaliation are central to Buddhist ethical teachings. The first of the five precepts is to abstain from killing, which is expanded in one important text in the following way, "Do not kill a living being; You should not kill or condone killing by others; Having abandoned the use of violence you should not use force against either the strong or the feeble" (Saddhatissa 1970 p. 88). It is significant that the textual and commentarial discussions of the precept and its applications again emphasise the mental factors and motivations behind its abuse (ibid., pp. 87-101). The degree of non-violence and non-retaliation advocated by the Buddha and early texts is only possible when considerable progress in self discipline and meditation has been achieved. "But this was said by the Lord in the Parable of the Saw: 'If, monks, low down thieves should carve you limb from limb with a two handled saw, whoever sets his heart at enmity . . . is not a doer of my teaching. Unsluggish energy shall come to be stirred up by me, unmuddled mindfulness set up, the body tranquilised impossible, the mind composed and one-pointed. Now, willingly let blows from hands affect this body, let blows from clods of earth . . . from sticks . . . from weapons affect it; for this teaching of the Awakened Ones is being done." (Horner (trans.) 1967 a *Middle Length Sayings* Vol.I p. 232, cf. Vol.I p. 166. Vol.III p. 320).

There are important social and political implications for the above teachings; and although the primary emphasis is on the internal processes, motivations and conduct of the individual these wider implications are not ignored. For example, the teaching on Right Livelihood on the Eightfold Path prohibits a lay person from trading in weapons, human beings, flesh, intoxicants and poisons. Military service, hunting and fishing are effectively ruled out for lay followers in the early texts. Apart from condemning wars in general as futile and harmful and inconclu-

sive the Buddha instructed monks to avoid contact with military matters and personnel (Rhys Davids (trans.) 1969 *Dialogues of the Buddha* pt.1 pp. 3-5, 13, 20, Horner 1967 (b)). In a number of different discourses the Buddha gives detailed advice on the social and domestic responsibilities and duties of lay peoples and on the special responsibilities of the ruler in relation to the sangha (monastic order) and the rest of society (Ling (ed.) 1981 part II and Ling 1973 ch. 8). The general conclusions from all these discussions is that where the Dharma prevails, then a righteous, harmonious, cooperative, non-individualistic society will flourish.

The Engaged Buddhist perspective starts with the problems and issues and is therefore situational in a way similar to the context of the earliest Buddhist teachings, where the Buddha begins with a particular problem or crisis and addresses that person on a level appropriate to their understanding. When he uses hythopthetical cases, the Buddha frequently uses exaggerated ones, as in the mythological scenarios described in the Cakkavatti Sihanada-sutta and Kutadanta-sutta. In the hypothetical attack on the monk by bandits, described above, he deliberately exaggerates the violence of the attack in order to emphasise the importance of the mind remaining in equanimity and not retaliating even mentally, to the attack. A literal way of reading this passage would be in terms of the Christian teaching of "turn the other cheek." But note that the emphasis is on the mental response rather than the physical action. When personally confronted with violence, the Buddha response was different from the theoretical case, but was appropriate to the circumstances. When the bandit assassin Angulimala pursues the Buddha in order to kill him, the Buddha uses psychic powers to prevent Angulimala's attack and keep him at a distance until he has calmed the assassin's mind sufficient to teach him Dharma (Horner 1989 trans. Middle Length Sayings Vol. 11 pp. 285-286). In other words, the Buddha's response is always appropriate and it is unequivocally situational.

Returning the starting point of this account, the issue of whether Buddhism is to be seen as a private practice concerned with the individual's own spiritual advancement or whether it has social, economic and environmental implications which need to be acknowledged and pursued. I shall conclude that a fundamental relationship exists between meditative awareness and social action. I would argue that meditation and spiritual practice create a mental "breathing space" and a basis for reflection on alternatives to lives based around greed, hate and delusion. The ancient Buddhist sources considered do suggest a relationship between human awareness, access to Buddha Dharma and the presence of supportive and cooperative social structures, and the reduction of conflict and violence I shall conclude with a challenging quote from another engaged Buddhist, Peter Timmerman who reflects on the role of Buddhism in the modern world in a challenging and positive way,

*". . . to be a Buddhist today is a geopolitical act for the reason that every one of our acts now adds to or subtracts from the load of human affairs which burden the earth. It is also a geopolitical act because, given the continuing devotion to consumerism, one of the most radical acts we can perform in our society is to consume less, to sit quietly meditating in a room, or to try and think clearly about who we are trying to be. And finally Buddhism is a geopolitical act because it provides us with a working space within which to stand back from our aggressive culture and consider alternatives."* (Timmerman in Batchelor and Brown (eds.) 1992 p. 75)

See also: *Religion and Peace; Buddhism as a Principle of Peace and Tolerance*

*Bibliography* ———————————

Batchelor S, Brown K (eds.) 1992 *Buddhism and Ecology.* Cassell, London

Batchelor S 1994 *The Awakening of the West.* Aquarian/ Harper Collins, London

Burlingame E W 1969 *Buddhist Legends: Dhammapada Commentary*, Part 111. Pali Text Society, London

Carrithers M 1983 *The Buddha.* Oxford University Press

Collins S 1982 *Selfless Persons.* Cambridge University Press

Conze E 1956 *Buddhist Meditation.* Allen and Unwin, London

De Bary W T (ed.) 1958 *Sources of Indian Tradition.* Columbia University Press, New York

Gombrich R F 1988 *Theravada Buddhism.* Routledge, London

Gombrich R F, Obeyesekere G *Buddhism Transformed.* Princeton University Press, New Jersey

Hanh T N 1967 *Vietnam. The Lotus in the Sea of Fire.* SCM, London

Horner I B 1967a /1975 *Middle Length Sayings*, Vols. I & III (1967), Vol. II (1975). Pali Text Society, Luzac, London

Horner I B 1967b *Early Buddhism and the Taking of Life.* The Wheel Publication No. 104. Buddhist Publication Society, Kandy, Sri Lanka

Jones K 1989 *The Social Face of Buddhism.* Wisdom Publications, London

Jones K 1993 *Beyond Optimism: A Buddhist Political Ecology.* Jon Carpenter, Oxford

Ling T O 1973 *The Buddha.* Temple Smith, London

Ling T O 1979 *Buddhism, Imperialism and War.* Allen and Unwin, London

Ling T O 1981 *The Buddha's Philosophy of Man.* Dent, London

Macy J 1985 *Dharma and Development*, rev. edn. Kumarian Press, USA

Macy J 1983 *Despair and Personal Power in a Nuclear Age.* New Society Publisher, Philadelphia

Macy J 1993 *World as Lover, World as Self.* Rider, London

Mascara J 1973 *The Dhammpada.* Penguin, London

Rhys Davids T W 1969 *Dialogues of the Buddha.* pt.1. Luzac, London

Robinson R H, Johnson W L 1977 *The Buddhist Religion.* Dickenson, California

Saddhatissa H 1970 *Buddhist Ethics.* Allen and Unwin, London

Titmus C 1995 *The Green Buddha.* Insight Books, Totnes, England

STEWART MCFARLANE

# Buddhism as a Principle of Peace and Tolerance

*1. The Significance of the Contemporary World*

Buddhism has played a significant role in human history for a long time. Since the 6th century BC, Buddhism has cultivated and enriched with its long tradition, the wide diversity of cultures which can be found on the Asian Continent; from Kashmir in the west to Japan in the east, to the Mongolian desert in the north to tropical Java in the south.

Especially in Korea, Buddhism has played the positive role in her long history that no other religion did. Introduced in the 4th century AD to Korea, Buddhism determined the path of history for the ancient peninsula society. It is no coincidence that in the kingdom of Shilla, where Buddhism penetrated every state of the population, from the king to the commoners, it succeeded in establishing the first unified state and created the most glorious culture in the peninsula's five thousand years history.

For the one thousand and hundred years of the Shilla and Koryo Dynasty, Buddhism was the spiritual stay and the sole guidepost of life for the Korean people. Unfortunately, during this time Korean Buddhism, because of negligent study and the loss of its essential meaning, became corrupted. This led directly to anti-Buddhist policy of the Chosun Dynasty.

It should be remembered, however, that it was Buddhists, though under suppression, who defended the people and country from the alien aggressors at the time of the national crisis.

Now, because of the rapid structural changes in the world since World War II, the role and place of religion has faced serious trials and challenges.

We can sum up the phenomena which characterize the contemporary world as follows. First the most significant ideological change in the contemporary world is the surge of the materialistic way of thinking, a trend which has its root, on the one hand, in the doctrines of Socialism and on the other hand, in the egoistic desire incidental to the Capitalist economy. The result is that all over the world, the spiritual traditions of the past are entirely neglected. The emergence of the trend has become the serious threat to all the religions including Buddhism.

Secondly, the change in the way of thinking has made the behavior of contemporary man ruthless and aggressive. This makes it impossible to maintain or to expect a peaceful relationship of mutual trust and cooperation among people and nations. Violence is demonstrated even in the mass murder of fellow human beings and threatens to trigger at any moment the most ghastly war of destruction in the annals of mankind.

The trend toward antagonism and conflict is not limited to the domains of politics and economics. It has now invaded the domain of religion, the last fortress of conscience.

Thirdly, another world-wide phenomenon we can identify under these circumstances is the spiritual anxiety of contemporary man.

This anxiety has various causes; the unlimited pursuit of wealth, the blind indulgence in sensual satisfaction and immoral life amid material prosperity, the corruption of social justice, and the lack of hope and confidence. Hatred is prevalent among contemporary man. This could result in war at any moment, and a war caused in this way could, with today's unprecedented development of science and technology, destroy all mankind.

## 2. Violence and Buddhist Tolerance

In these circumstances, how should Buddhists act in seeking solutions to these urgent questions?

Violence has been part of human civilization since time immemorial. Santi in Buddhism meant to terminate violence, which was symbolized by *Ajatasatru, Angulimala,* and *Devadatta.* Compassion was highly regarded as a vehicle to cope with violence. But

today, man suffers from serious violence, for modern violence is systematic and even rational.

Nobody would object to the assertion that the technical term *pratitya-samutpada* is one entirely unique feature of Buddhism. The essential meaning of the term is; everything is produced inter-dependently and the entire world floats on this basis.

According to this truth, there is, therefore, no room for an unchanging, solid, self-sufficent, independent entity or an all powerful absolute being, beyond this law itself.

> Imasmim Sati idam hoti, imass' uppada idam uppajjti imasmim asati idam na hoti, iassa niroddha idam nirujjhati
> (Samyutta-Nikaya II p. 65)

"When 'this' exists, 'that' exists; when 'this' comes about 'that' comes about, when 'this' does not exist, 'that' does not exist; when 'this' does not come out, 'that' does not come about."

Based on these principles, tolerance is carried here to its ultimate, for no entity is irrelevant and threatens the other entity in the network of universal harmony.

The doctrine of *Pratityasamutpada* that encompasses not only human beings but also every creature, therefore, constitutes a principle for maintaining and implementing 'cooperation' built up mutually through whole-hearted, all-out efforts, which is neither simple compromise nor mere ingratiation. More over, it wholly transcends such unsavory elements as superior inferior relationships and extortion. These principles enable us to reflect deeply and to be keenly aware of the right path of peace and tolerance they support, lead and guide our efforts for peace and cooperation.

I am going to tell you of the spirit of boundless compassion and tolerance by quoting the teachings in the *Angulimara sutra.* Angulimara was a brutal bandit who murdered people without remorse but later became a disciple of Buddha. He led a thoroughly ascetic life and underwent exceptionally hard discipline to redeem his past evil deeds, but people harassed him when they learned he was Angulimara. One day, he came to Buddha badly beaten and bleeding and asked: "What is the most difficult thing in the world? I find it the most difficult not to hate someone when he is wielding his sword to kill me." Buddha replied with a smile, "Good, Angulimara! But there is a more difficult thing than that. Not to hate the person who is going to kill you is not enough. The most difficult thing in the world is to be able to say 'you are the Buddha' to him."

This shows us how far Buddhist tolerance should extend. A simple reverence for life is not enough. This teaching cannot be understood without first understanding that oneself and others are one. We believe everyone has the innate potential for this much tolerance, for this is how life was originally created. The multitudes, however, have forgotten their fundamental selves and lead a life of estrangement.

The Dharma, which penetrates all things of this universe, is none other than the rule of cause and effect. Individuals or objects, which appear to be of no relation to each other, actually exist through this circle of cause and effect. We might replace the upper three forms of the six forms of the Hua-Yen Sutra—the whole, the universal and the perfect—with the concept of the world and the lower three forms—the partial, the diverse and the disintegrating—with the concept of humanity. We can also equate the upper three with the Buddha and the lower three with the multitude.

Here we can conclude that the universal self and the individual self are but one. The self in me is thus a universal self. I am a living entity. The universe is filled with innumerable living entities and I am but a tiny speck in the enormous stream of lives in the universe. If I died, it would be a devastating event for me, my family and friends but it would not make any difference to the great stream of life. For the universal life is an endless repetition of birth and death. Right at this moment, a life is born and a life is dying, neither making a difference to the entire flow. If we can identify the individual self with the universal self, the life and the death will no longer make a difference. The Son masters realized this truth and led their lives based on their realization.

The grand motto World Peace should in truth be based on this philosophical introspection. The Western concept of peace seems to be an antonym of war. Peace, however, is not a world without war. We should understand the importance of inner peace, a world inhabited by people who have freed themselves from the chain of Three Poisons—greed, anger, folly. I believe the fundamental value of peace is an all embracing world where the universal and the individual are identified with each other.

The Hua-Yen Sutra emphasizes that the natural tendency to destroy Dharma stems from the ignorance of the sentient multitude. It can be explained with the example of a house in relation to the timber of which it is built. A thick, sturdy timber is used as a ridge-beam and a slender timber is used for the rafters. Good quality wood is made into a living room door and lower quality wood is made into a kitchen or toilet door. If all of the wood insisted on becoming a ridge-beam, the house would never get completed. It is only through the dedication and sacrifice of each part that order is achieved in the form of a completed house.

Nature observes this order completely. Lao-tzu (see *Lao Tzu*) says in his way of Tao that it is the law of nature to fill what is lacking and remove what is superfluous. Hence, the dialectic of the inacting nature, or nature perfect without the interference of humans.

This order is not observed in human society, however. Every human wants to play the role of the hero or heroine on the stage called the universe. Imagine a movie full of heroes and heroines with no supporting actors or extras. The Buddhist tolerance comes from its compassion for other people. It evokes thoughts that the Chinese character meaning "deception" comprises two characters which, when individually used, mean a "human deed." A Son Buddhist's expression here, however, would be "I am satisfied with what I am." We can interpret it as knowing one's own limitations.

Human prejudices destructive of the universal order can be summarized as the following two points. The first is a dichotomous way of dividing the world in relation to oneself. The black or white logic which is prominent in biased thinking is steeped in analytic knowledge, often at the risk of missing the comprehensive understanding. As the proverb goes, "one can't see the forest for the trees."

The second is the lack of determination to realize Dharma. As Vijnana Buddhism points out, it is a disease caused by justifying the progress of the selfish mind.

I believe it is necessary for us to understand ourselves in relation to the universal order and to endeavor to live an altruistic life. Such terms as mutual interrelation and mutual equality in the structural logic of Buddhism come to mind. Mutual interrelationship means that subjectivity and objectivity influence each other. Mutual equality thus means that both becomes one.

Monk Uisang (620-702) summed it up in *Hwa-om ilsung popgyedo*, his commentary on the Hua-Yen (Hwa-om) Sutra, that "a thought of an instant is for eternity." The ideal of Buddhism then is the realization of togetherness in Great Compassion.

## 3. Bodhisattva Ideals

In both Fundamental Buddhism and Theravada Buddhism, emphasis was placed on the Thirty-seven virtues of Bodhi, Eight noble Paths, as items of Practice. However, these items were aimed at the self-perfection of disciples and not at the enlightenment and salvation of society. It was for the purpose of correcting the egoism of the Sectarian Buddhism seeking their self-interest that Mahayana Buddhism emerged.

For this reason Mahayana Buddhism preaches altruism in addition to self-interest, with stress on their neighbors and society as a whole become peaceful and prosperity. The direction Bodhisattva set for himself is described with the explanation that one should help others cross before one crosses himself and that the act of awakening will become smooth when one awakens others after one at awakened. So Mahayana Buddhism revised the items of practice into Six Paramita including altruistic efforts for society such as alms giving (danna) and for bearance (ksanti).

As Mahayana Buddhism teaches, one who has become a Bodhisattva by dint of one's Bodhisattva Mind is promised to attain Buddhahood through rightful awakening. This indicates that the starting point toward the Mahayana faith is the realization that one should attain rightful awakening.

Mahayana Buddhism also does not make a distinction between priesthood and the laity. Any one who has became a Bodhisattva, ever a laymen, is regarded as having realized the path to awakening from the start. This means that the daily life of the Bodhisattva is identified with religious practice.

The *Sung-man-kyong* (Srimaledevi Sutra) quotes a statement of Bodhisattva ;

"I do not overlook those who practise vice and those who violate moral codes until I arrive at the final enlightenment. I will destroy those who rebel and accept those who follow morality, for such destruction (調伏) and acceptance (攝受) will help us maintain the true order."

We may see the 'acceptance' as corresponding to the face of 'Maitrey' and the face with white projected teeth, and 'destruction' as corresponding to the angry face in the eleven faces of *Avalokitesvara Bodhisattva*. According to Houei-Shao (慧超) those who should be dealt with by anger are: those who suffer pains because of their desire to relieve themselves from these pains, those who seek pleasure without knowing its harmful nature, and those who become attached to a disturbed condition while seeking peace. Those who believe in violence today are synonymous with these three Categories.

Under the influence of the positive social ethics stressed in *Sung-Man-Kyong*, Shilla people distinguised the object of 'Maitrey' from the object of

'Karuna.' They also believed in the wisdom of Prajna that embraces the masses. In the Shilla Kingdom, compassion was aimed at tapering the will of violence. Changing egotism into a selfless state of mind, and bringing reform to the speech, thought, and action of all people.

For a long time, humans have lived in the midst of conflicts and confrontations. In ancient societies, the cause of confrontations was differences in religious ideologies. A religious belief is a system of absolute conviction which offers absolute justification for one's own beliefs and condemns the beliefs of the other as utterly worthless. A good example is the Crusades in the Middle Ages. The bigotry of denouncing others' religion in adherence to one's own in the belief it is the one and only religion is a sad legacy born of prejudices.

On the other hand, the conflicts in the Middle Ages derived mostly from a desire for conquest. The competition of the so-called great men to acquire and expand their territories reduced the populace to perpetual anxiety and fear. Their vainglory was responsible for the colonization of the Orient by the Western countries and the adventurism of the imperialists, which resulted in the two World Wars. In the modern era, the mode of confrontation gradually took on the shape of proxy wars incited by ideologies, their most convincing examples being the tragedies of the Korean Peninsula and Vietnam. The misadventures of the 20th century summed up as the Cold War, however, seem to have come to an end. It appears the confrontations of the future will take the form of economic conflicts. The protectionism of advanced nations and the Uruguay Round are their harbingers. Futurists are already describing the economic confrontations as wars without swords and guns.

What will be the end of these confrontations going to be? Is it impossible after all to have a truly quarrelless world?

Here we need to remember again what motivated the Buddha to leave his home and enter the monkhood. Witnessing senseless killings in the secular world, Prince Siddhartha lamented:

"What makes living things harass and kill one another? Is it truly impossible for them to coexist peacefully?" (Ch'ulyogoyong Sutra) Later in his life, after achieving Enlightenment, he experienced numerous personal sorrows such as the rebellion of Devaddatta, the death of Riputra and Maudgaly Yana, the downfall of his Gautama tribe, and the endless condemning of Buddhism as a religion that ends family lines. He says: "I fight not with the world, ye monks. The world fights with me. He who proclaims the truth, the monks, fights with no one in the world." The end of confrontations pursued by Prince Siddhartha remains the quest of all humanity.

I have already summarized the Buddhist position in the matter in five points. What we need here is the determination and institutional support to put them into practice. Some complain Buddhist ideals are too unrealistic, much like the babbling of a dreamer, but we should endeavor to thwart such self-doubt and self-derogation. From the Fourfold Principles of Bringing Together to the Four Immeasurable Minds and Six Paranmita, there is nothing that is not idealistic in the path of a Bodhisattva. And there are many real examples of people who willingly and successfully took that harsh path of life.

We must, therefore, increase companions in faith who appreciate this way to the truth. Some people suggest that a constitutional government is what we need most to bring an end to the combativeness in our lives. However, the ideal way is to enlighten the entire populace. This is the justification of Buddhism. The propagation of Buddhism is the spreading of a mode of life ideal for humankind.

Obviously future society is going to be multi-religious. We cannot say a religion is superior to another because it has a greater number of believers, sanctums and clergy. The important point is how close it is to the world of truth it professes to strive to reach.

Buddhists should question constantly how close they are to the Bodhisattva mind they strive to attain. If we take pride in being the followers of Buddha, we should live his teachings. As proclaimed in the Lotus Sutra, we should be able "to reside in Buddha's room, wear Buddha's clothes and speak in Buddha's voice."

After all, the true nature of all living things is the Buddha. I firmly believe it is our spiritual assignment to enlighten our unfortunate neighbors of their Buddha nature of which they are unaware.

## 4. Conclusion

The present age we live in is often characterized by antagonism and competition and Buddhism should play a more important role than ever with its principle of peace and tolerance.

(a) Contemporary people are apt to be brainwashed by mistaken notion of peace and cooperation, and it is up to us, as Buddhists, to correct them and make them realize the basis for true peace and cooperation.

(b) Buddhism has much to say about contemporary economic justice, human rights, disarmament, and ethics, and we should be able to shed the light of truth on the various trends in the world. Buddhism possesses the basic principle to put us on the right path, making our everyday life into righteous one.

(c) The evil of sensualistic desire is a serious problem which religion continually cautions us about. Today we see everywhere the phenomena of degeneracy with increasing crime and disintergration of home and society due to the degradation of sexual morality. Religion seems to have given up the effort to check this trend. True Buddhism should endeavour to stop and correct this trend, however difficult it may be, because the increase of sensualism will surely lead to the degradation of man to that of an animal. This will be so because sensualism is a gross attitude which values carnal desire more than true feeling.

(d) Practice of Zen can overcome the spiritual crisis of contemporary man. Modern man has become feeble and weak for various reasons; anxiety and tension induced by egoistic competition, excessive work and lack of repose, various social injustices and lack of ability to correct them, and psychological and physical weakness from indulgence in the sensual life.

(e) Develop the educational ideals in religion. The new pedagogy, psychology, curriculum, and teaching method based on the educational ideals and methodology of Buddhism and we should examine it as a detailed, concrete way, not as an abstract principle.

These tasks does not mean a change of the principle of Buddhism itself but the adaptation of the principle to the changing times and environment. Contemporary society is entirely different from the type of society prevalent during the period which the Buddhist scriptures were written. In our rapidly changing society we must attempt to strike a new path for Bodhisattvas.

It is my firm belief that the destiny of mankind in the contemporary world is to be determined by the proper exercise of the life-force of Buddhism. We, who believe in the eternal truth of the Holy Teachings, should do our best to solve the problems of mutual concern, striving to realize the goal of Religion; the salvation of mankind.

See also: *Buddhism; Religion and Peace*

BYUNG JO CHUNG

# C

## Camp David Accords

On November 9, 1977, President Anwar Sadat of Egypt announced that he was prepared to go to the Israeli Knesset to discuss ending the Arab-Israeli conflict. This gesture marked a radical new departure in the history of that conflict: Sadat was the first Arab leader officially to offer to negotiate publicly and directly with Israel. His initiative set in motion a process which, almost a year later, yielded the Camp David Accords: two documents on the Arab-Israeli conflict, formulated and agreed to by Egypt, Israel, and the United States. The Accords generated a bilateral Egypt-Israel Peace Treaty and further negotiation concerning a broader peace in the region.

Sadat's initial gesture left Israel and the United States perplexed about Egyptian policy and Sadat's real intentions. The dominant US reaction was that Sadat's move might isolate him in the Arab world and jeopardize his political future. Sadat's initiative forced the United States to contend with the difficulty of supporting Sadat and helping him fend off his critics while keeping on friendly terms with Jordan and Saudi Arabia, both of which had significant objections to his policy. These considerations caused the United States to counsel caution to Sadat while urging Israel to make concessions in response to Sadat's initiative. Within a few days the Carter Administration had committed itself to participating in the Sadat-inspired negotiations process, but was unable to persuade other Arab governments to back Egypt's dramatic move. The government of Menachem Begin in Israel, meanwhile, tried to combine responding positively to Sadat with limiting the extent of commitments on the future of the occupied territories.

Sadat's initiative was to instigate the drawing up of two sets of proposals for settlement of the Arab-Israeli conflict: those of Egypt and those of Israel. The Egyptian proposals were outlined by Sadat in his address to the Knesset on November 20, 1977 and they constituted, essentially, a restatement of established positions. He wanted, he said, a peace agreement based on:

First: ending the Israeli occupation of Arab territories occupied in 1967. Second: achievement of the fundamental rights of the Palestinian people and their right to self-determination, including their right to establish their own state. Third: the right of all states in the area to live in peace within their boundaries, in addition to appropriate international guarantees. Fourth: commitment of all states in the region to administer the relations among them in accordance with the objectives and principles of the United Nations Charter, particularly the principles concerning the non-resort to force and the solution of differences among them by peaceful means. Fifth: ending the state of belligerency in the region.

Begin, meanwhile, presented the Israeli plan at Ismailia on Christmas Day 1977, and made its contents public in a speech to the Knesset on December 28. The plan, to be "instituted upon the establishment of peace," proposed that there be demilitarization in the Sinai; that the Egyptian army would not move beyond its positions on the Gidi and Mitla passes; that between the Suez Canal and that line, there would continue in effect the limited forces agreement arranged in Sinai II; that Israeli settlements in Sinai would remain, would be linked to Israeli administration and law and would be defended by an Israeli force; that during a transition period of a few years, Israeli forces would hold a defense line in the middle of Sinai and would maintain air bases and early warning mechanisms: they would later withdraw to the international frontier; that freedom of navigation in the Tiran Straits would be guaranteed either by a UN force or by joint Egyptian-Israeli units. In Judea, Samaria, and the Gaza district (i.e., the West Bank and the Gaza Strip) the military government would be abolished and replaced by "administrative autonomy of the residents, by and for them." Security and public order in these areas would be the responsibility of the Israeli authorities. All residents would be granted free choice of either Israeli or Jordanian citizenship. Various matters concerning legislation and immigration would be determined by committees composed of representatives of Israel, Jordan, and the administrative council. "Israel stands by its right and its claim of sovereignty to Judea and Samaria and the Gaza district. In the knowledge that other claims exist, it proposes for the sake of the agreement and the peace, that the question of sovereignty be left open." The holy places and Jerusalem would be considered in a special proposal. Clearly, the Begin and Sadat proposals were not fully compatible.

Begin and Sadat agreed to set up two committees to pursue negotiations: the Military Committee was to discuss the problems of Sinai, while the Political Committee was to seek agreement on a declaration of principles. However, a number of factors contributed to the persistence of the divisions between the parties. By July 1978 the peace negotiations had produced disagreements between the United States and both Egypt and Israel, as well as between Egypt and Israel. The deadlock threatened to halt the negotiations and alarmed the United States because it would be a setback for Sadat and the peace process, and might renew tensions between Egypt and Israel, thus increasing the danger of war. There was also concern because the term of the UN force in Sinai, to which Egypt had committed itself in the 1975 Sinai II Accords, was about to expire. These factors led Carter to try to break the deadlock through a new and dramatic initiative.

## 1. The Camp David Summit

On August 8, 1978 the United States announced that Sadat and Begin had accepted President Carter's invitation to come to Camp David, Maryland, "for a meeting with the President to seek a framework for peace in the Middle East."

The three leaders met for their historic negotiations in virtual secrecy, and were closeted in complex and intensive discussions for a lengthy period, between 5 and September 17, 1978. The negotiations are memorable for the direct personal involvement of the heads of state. The stakes were clearly high and the need to achieve an agreement obvious. The attainment of an agreement through the summit was clearly a hard-won achievement.

The Camp David Accords were signed ceremoniously on September 17, and became the basis for the peace negotiations which followed. The Accords did not constitute a peace treaty, but instead consisted of two documents: "A Framework of Peace in the Middle East" and "Framework for the Conclusion of a Peace Treaty between Egypt and Israel." The Middle East Framework set forth general principles and

some specifics for a comprehensive peace settlement between Israel and its Arab neighbors. It dealt with the Palestinian problem and the future of the West Bank and Gaza, calling for a transitional period of not more than five years to prepare "full autonomy" arrangements for the inhabitants of those areas. The Israeli military government would be withdrawn upon the creation of a self-governing authority freely elected by the inhabitants of those areas, although the Israeli military would remain in specified areas of the West Bank and Gaza to protect Israel's security interests. "Egypt, Israel, Jordan and the representatives of the Palestinian people should participate in negotiations on the resolution of the Palestinian problem in all its aspects." It also called for negotiations to resolve the final status of the West Bank and Gaza, and Israel's relations with Jordan, based on Resolution 242 and Israel's right to live within secure and recognized borders.

The Israeli-Egypt framework provided for a peace treaty in which Israel would withdraw from all of Sinai, including its settlements and airfields, in phases according to a timetable to be determined, and for normal and peaceful arrangements to be established between the two states. The United States agreed to construct airfields for Israel in the Negev. Egypt agreed to normalization of relations, an exchange of ambassadors, and the opening of the Suez Canal to Israeli shipping.

The Camp David Accords, although accepted by both Egypt and Israel, met with caution and skepticism from others concerned with the matter. The reaction of the Arab world initially was overwhelmingly negative. Arab opposition to Sadat, which had begun during his negotiations with Israel that led to Sinai II, intensified as a result of his initiative and the Camp David Accords. The final signing of Sinai II had spurred the formation of the Rejectionist Front composed of Syria, Iraq, Algeria, Libya, the People's Democratic Republic of Yemen, and the Palestine Liberation Organization (PLO). Following the Algiers summit of February 1978 this group broke political and economic ties with Egypt, and, in direct response to the Camp David Accords, reorganized as the "Front for Steadfastness and Confrontation" pledged to work for the collapse of the peace process.

The United States sought to secure support for the Camp David Accords and for Sadat's position elsewhere in the Arab world. In this regard the critical states were seen as Jordan and Saudi Arabia, and it was to these states, among others, that Secretary of State Cyrus Vance travelled after Camp David. But, they did not agree to join in the negotiations nor to endorse the peace process.

The only recourse was to proceed without the participation of other parties to the conflict. After another round of intense negotiations in Washington a draft for a treaty between Egypt and Israel was drawn up, yet various points remained subject to disagreement.

Owing to the persistence of the differences between the parties, the December 1978 deadline set at Camp David for the conclusion of the Egypt-Israel treaty was not met. Generally, Egypt sought to achieve the maximum linkage between the bilateral Egypt-Israel peace process and the overall, comprehensive peace process. Israel sought to reach agreement with Egypt on bilateral questions while reducing the connection between that agreement and the overall settlement of the Arab-Israeli conflict. For Sadat, movement toward Palestinian autonomy was crucial, as it would serve to reduce Arab criticism that he had made a separate peace with Israeli. For Begin, any movement toward Palestinian autonomy on the West Bank and Gaza would draw additional opposition from right-wing elements of his party and the religious parties, important elements of support for his government. Israel also feared that if the peace treaty were linked to a timetable for Palestinian autonomy, it could give the Palestinians an effective veto over an Egyptian-Israeli Peace Treaty merely by refusing to participate in any autonomy discussions and arrangements, thereby preventing the timetable from being met. The Egyptian demand for linkage between the two Camp David Accords, including a detailed timetable for Israel's relinquishing of its military rule over the West Bank and Gaza and a fixed date for the election of a Palestinian parliamentary council was rejected by the Israeli cabinet. Finally, by the end of March 1979, a treaty was attained, but not before President Carter himself had engaged in shuttle diplomacy between Cairo and Jerusalem. The formal signing of the Egypt-Israel Peace Treaty on March 26, 1979 in Washington bore witness to the value of persistent diplomatic effort to attain peace.

By the terms of the treaty, Egypt and Israel ended the state of war, established peace, renounced the use of war to settle disputes, and pledged mutual recognition. Israel agreed to withdraw its armed forces and civilians from the Sinai Peninsula in stages, to a line running from El-Arish to Ras-Muhammad, after nine months, and to the international frontier (essentially from Rafah to the Gulf of Aqaba) after three years. Within a month of the completion of the first stage (the "interim withdrawal"), Israel and Egypt would exchange ambassadors, end economic boycotts, and

open commerce between the two states. Sinai would be divided into zones with limitations on Egyptian military personnel and equipment, and a United Nations (UN) force verifying compliance would be stationed in the zone adjacent to the Israeli border. United Nations observers would ensure Israeli compliance on its side of the border as well. Israel was to have the right of free passage through the Suez Canal, and the Gulf of Aqaba and Strait of Tiran would be regarded as international waterways, open to all nations for unimpeded freedom of navigation. A joint commission would oversee the withdrawal from Sinai, and a claims commission would deal with any outstanding financial claims and arbitrate disputes. The United States agreed to continue surveillance flights over Sinai and to create an international force if the United Nations failed to do so.

The treaty also provided that one month after ratification, Israel, Egypt, the United States, Jordan, and representatives of the Palestinians living in the West Bank and Gaza would begin negotiations, to be completed within one year, for a self-governing authority in the West Bank and the Gaza Strip. The protocols, letters, annexes, and maps attached to the Egypt-Israeli withdrawal from the Sinai, the security arrangements, and the specific details for further negotiations on trade, economic, cultural, transportation, telecommunications, and other agreements between the two countries.

## 2. Implementing Camp David

During the period between the signing of the Egypt-Israel Peace Treaty in March 1979 and the Spring of 1982, the parts of the treaty which pertained to the withdrawal of Israel from Sinai and the normalization of relations between Egypt and Israel were gradually implemented. The full withdrawal of Israel from Sinai, including the dismantling of settlements, was carried out as scheduled. As to the normalization of relations, ambassadors were exchanged, and various technical arrangements made for free passage and exchange across the borders. After the initial excitement, however, relations between Egypt and Israel failed to grow in warmth and frequency of contacts, and a "cold peace" developed that included the recall of the Egyptian Ambassador from Tel Aviv in the wake of the Israeli invasion of Lebanon in June 1982 and the massacres at Shatila and Sabra refugee camps in September 1982.

The signing of the treaty by Sadat was almost universally condemned by other Arab leaders. The Arab League, meeting at the end of March 1979, expelled

Egypt from membership and rejected any cooperation with the peace treaty or the autonomy talks. The Arab League countries (except for Sudan and Oman) and the PLO, severed diplomatic relations with Egypt and voted to impose an economic boycott. This general ostracism of Egypt endured beyond the assassination of Anwar Sadat, the accession of Hosni Mubarak to the Presidency of Egypt, the implementation of the Israeli withdrawal from Sinai, and the degeneration in Egyptian-Israeli relations following the Israeli invasion of Lebanon. Nevertheless, Egypt was never fully isolated from the Arab world and improvements in its formal ties included such actions as the restoration of diplomatic relations with Jordan, at the initiative of King Hussein, in September 1984.

Despite the dramatic reaction of the Arab world, the negotiations concerning implementation of the Camp David "Framework for Peace in the Middle East" opened as scheduled on May 25, 1979. The goal of the first stage of the negotiations was full autonomy for the inhabitants of the West Bank and Gaza under a freely elected, self-governing authority that would serve for a transitional period of not more than five years. The final status of the West Bank and Gaza was reserved for a second stage of negotiations, to begin as soon as possible, but not later than three years after the self-governing authority was inaugurated. The so-called "autonomy talks" involved only Egypt, Israel, and the United States.

May 1980 had been designated as a deadline by which agreement on steps towards autonomy should be reached. Not only was agreement not reached in time, but Sadat suspended Egyptian participation in the talks on the grounds that the Israeli parliament was considering confirming the status of Jerusalem as Israel's capital. The suspension generated US concern and a flurry of diplomatic activity. The autonomy talks were resumed again in July, but were suspended again by Sadat in early August. The stated rationale was that Israel's Knesset had adopted a "Basic Law" confirming Jerusalem's status as Israel's "eternal and undivided capital." In any event, the autonomy talks were stalled on a number of counts. Israel argued that autonomy should be limited to the inhabitants of the territories, while Egypt believed that it should extend to the actual territory. Israel saw the self-governing authority as an administrative council, while Egypt wanted this authority to have full legislative and executive powers as well as control of the administration of justice. Egypt sought a self-generating authority and the transfer to it of all powers from the military government. Israel sought to limit the powers of the authority through negotia-

tion and believed that the military government should be the source of authority. There was also discord on the sharing of the scarce water resources of the West Bank, the right of the Arabs of East Jerusalem to vote on questions relating to the self-governing authority, the status and use of private and public lands, and Jerusalem's final status.

Israel saw an autonomy agreement as a practical solution to the Palestinian question and as responsive to Israel's need for security, Egypt's wish to adhere to the Arab cause, and the Palestinian Arabs' desire to govern their own affairs. Israel's proposed autonomy plan would allow the Arab inhabitants fully to manage "areas of legitimate internal administration" while Israel "will retain those powers and functions which are essential to her defense and security." By contrast Israel opposed Egypt's autonomy proposals partly because they "would set in motion an irreversible process which would lead to the establishment of an independent Arab-Palestinian state." Egypt, meanwhile, sought total Israeli withdrawal from the occupied territories (including East Jerusalem), the dismantling of Israel's settlements, and the right of the Palestinians to self-determination. It sought to safeguard its position in the Arab world and to remain a part of the Arab community. It was important to Egypt to demonstrate that Sadat's approach was practical.

The negotiations were suspended between December 1980 and September 1981, at which time they were resumed, but without high-level involvement by the Reagan Administration. On October 6, 1981 Sadat was assassinated. His successor, Hosni Mubarak, pledged to continue the process but no new ground was broken before Israel's invasion of Lebanon and the subsequent suspension of the talks by Egypt.

In the Spring of 1982, when the last of Israel's forces were withdrawn from the Sinai peninsula, the commitment of both Egypt and Israel to implementing the terms of the Egypt-Israeli Peace Treaty was established. The treaty had dealt strictly with matters pertaining to bilateral relations between Israel and Egypt and it proved practicable. The issue of autonomy for the Palestinians was not characterized by the same level of agreement between the parties and the autonomy talks did not produce a settlement.

Lack of progress made in implementing the comprehensive framework can be attributed to a number of factors. Among the more significant was the failure to involve other participants beyond Egypt, Israel, and the United States in the process. The initial hope, voiced in the Camp David Accords, that Jordan and representatives of the Palestinian people would participate in the peace process, soon proved to be little more than wishful thinking. Hussein objected to the Camp David process and his position was especially sensitive because of Jordan's sizable Palestinian population and because the role envisaged for him by the Camp David Accords in negotiations on Palestinian "autonomy" conflicted with the decisions of the Arab League summit in Rabat in 1974 which had designated the PLO as the sole legitimate representative of the Palestinian people. The overthrow of the Shah in Iran, the enhancement of the PLO's regional position, and the lack of any support for him to adopt an alternative stand, reinforced Hussein's rejectionist attitude.

The failure to broaden the peace process to include additional parties, including Jordan and/or representatives of the Palestinian people, envisaged in the Camp David Accords, characterized the period preceding the 1982 War in Lebanon. That war generated an intensified US effort to revitalize the Camp David process in the form of the Reagan "fresh start" initiative of September 1, 1982. Implicit in the Reagan initiative was the intention to draw Jordan into negotiations on behalf of the Palestinians, thus the United States sought to attain the element that had been crucially absent in the Camp David process.

The Camp David process failed to produce a comprehensive settlement of the Arab-Israeli conflict. It remains, however, that the Camp David Accords represent a major milestone in the history of the efforts to resolve the Arab-Israeli conflict and to achieve peace. This was recognized when Sadat and Begin were awarded the Nobel Peace Prize for their efforts.

See also: Nobel Peace Prize Laureates: *Anwar al-Sadat; Menachem Begin*

*Bibliography* —————————————

Brzezinski Z 1983 *Power and Principle: Memoirs of the National Security Adviser, 1977-81.* Farrar, Straus, Giroux, New York

Carter J 1982 *Keeping Faith: Memoirs of a President.* Bantam, New York

Reich B 1984 *The United States and Israel: Influence in the Special Relationship.* Praeger, New York

United States Congress, House Committee on Foreign Affairs 1979 *The Search for Peace in the Middle East: Documents and Statements, 1967-79,* Washington, DC

United States Department of State 1984 *The Quest for Peace: Principal United States Public Statements and Related Documents on the Arab-Israeli Peace Process, 1967-83,* Washington, DC

Vance C 1983 *Hard Choices: Critical Years in America's Foreign Policy.* Simon and Schuster, New York

BERNARD REICH; ROSEMARY HOLLIS

# Campaign for Nuclear Disarmament (CND)

The Campaign for Nuclear Disarmament (CND) is the major British organization protesting against nuclear weapons, but is part of a wider social movement. Its headquarters are in London, and its current address is: 162 Holloway Road, London, N7 8DQ.

The general aim of CND is to achieve worldwide nuclear disarmament, but its specific aim is complete nuclear disarmament by Britain. During the 1950s Britain had developed its own nuclear force and become the third nuclear power, so when CND was launched in February 1958 its first demand was that Britain should give a moral lead by abandoning its own Bomb. The most distinctive element in CND's policy was its insistence that Britain ought to give up its nuclear weapons unilaterally, and not wait upon multilateral negotiation. But unilateral action by Britain was seen as a means of promoting negotiated agreement between the United States and the former Soviet Union. Since the early years of CND several more countries have acquired either a nuclear arsenal or a nuclear weapons capacity, but CND still sees the abandonment of the British Bomb as an important measure to halt proliferation. This policy continued to be relevant in the 1990s. Despite the renewal in 1995 of the Non-Proliferation Treaty, Britain and the other nuclear weapon states have not taken seriously their obligations under the Treaty to scale down their own nuclear arsenals. The Indian nuclear bomb tests in 1998 and the threat of a nuclear arms race with Pakistan and China highlighted the urgency of wider nuclear disarmament.

In addition to its own nuclear force, Britain was closely linked to nuclear weapons strategy through the network of American nuclear bases on its territory. Since its inception, CND has insisted that nuclear disarmament by Britain must include removal of these bases. When CND gained renewed support and political influence after 1979, one of the central issues was opposition to the planned siting of cruise missiles. After the 1987 INF agreement between the

USA and USSR to dismantle intermediate range nuclear missiles, the cruise missiles were removed. Improvements in long-range weapons technology and the end of the Cold War have also meant that the USA has scaled down its British bases, which have ceased to be a primary focus for protest.

The third way in which Britain has been closely linked to nuclear strategy is through membership of the North Atlantic Treaty Organization (NATO) (see *North Atlantic Treaty Organization (NATO)*), which has relied on battlefield nuclear weapons and intermediate-range missiles, as well as being ultimately dependent on the American strategic nuclear force. CND decided in 1960 to extend its opposition to nuclear weapons to nuclear alliances, and so to include withdrawal from NATO in its policy; this meant that a non-nuclear Britain would become neutral or nonaligned. Since the break up of the Soviet bloc and the disintegration of the Warsaw Pact the role of NATO and its relations with East European countries and Russia have changed significantly. But it still remains a nuclear alliance.

The main emphasis of CND is on nuclear weapons, but it is also opposed to chemical and biological weapons of mass destruction, and supports the ultimate goal of general and complete disarmament. CND literature and speeches often make connections between the vast global expenditure on arms and the problems of famine, poverty and underdevelopment (see *Disarmament and Development*). Within Britain CND has campaigned vigorously against civil defense on the grounds that no real defense against a major nuclear attack is possible. CND extended its activities in the 1970s to expose the links between the civil and military uses of nuclear energy, and majorities at conferences have passed resolutions opposing all forms of nuclear energy. This has continued to be one focus of CND activity in the 1990s. CND also raises civil liberties issues that arise out of government moves to limit demonstrations at nuclear bases, surveillance of CND by intelligence services, and the emergency measures planned in the event of war.

## 1. Organization of CND

The organizational basis of CND has always been a national committee and office at the centre of a network of local groups. Originally the CND Committee was a self-selected group of individuals well-known on the Left of British politics. But as the Campaign grew, its organization was formalized—local groups were joined into regions, CND held an annual conference, and the National Council and Executive Committee were formally elected. Special sections for youth, students, and women, and a Christian group were formed within CND; so were professional grouping, for example for scientists. The basic structure of CND in the 1980s was similar to that of the 1960s, although since 1966 CND has also had a system of individual membership. The political and cultural movements of the last two decades have, however, had some impact on CND's style. There is, for example, less emphasis on having prominent personalities at the top.

CND's funds come largely from its local groups, its individual members, and from donations. The amount of its annual income and the size of its central office varies with the strength of the organization at various times. In 1961 CND had nearly 900 local groups and about 20 full-time works in its central office. During the CND revival of the 1980s individual membership rose to 110,000 national members by 1985, local groups to 1,000 and the full-time office staff to about 40. There were also around 1,500 affiliated organizations from churches, trade unions, and various professions.

CND as an organization is not involved in party politics and seeks support from all parties. But its membership and support does of course reflect the attitudes and views of Britain's various parties to the British Bomb and defense issues. CND has always had strong support among many Labour activists and Labour Members of Parliament. It won the Labour Party Conference over to a unilateralist position in 1960, but the determined opposition of the Labour leadership at that time swung the Conference against unilateralism a year later.

The Labour Party in office between 1964-70 and 1974-79 maintained and modernized Britain's Polaris nuclear force, but during the 1980s the Labour party in opposition adopted an anti-nuclear policy. After a confused presentation of its defense policy in the 1983 election (due to internal party divisions) the Party reaffirmed a more united commitment to abandon the British Bomb and remove American nuclear bases. After losing the 1987 election, the Labour leadership rejected a unilateralist policy, and the Labour Government elected in 1997 was committed to retain nuclear weapons.

CND originally had some support from Liberals (now Liberal Democrats), who then opposed a British Bomb although the Party supported NATO. CND has enjoyed strong backing from Scottish and Welsh Nationalist parties and the small Green Party. The Communist Party was initially cautious about a unilateralist and nonaligned movement, but gave support after 1960. A few individual conservatives have sympathized with CND, and a small group, Tories Against Cruise and Trident, was formed in the 1980s, but Conservatives tend to be opposed to both the ideas and the ethos and campaigning style of CND.

## 2. The Early Period of CND

The history of CND reflects the changing political and cultural attitudes and the changing fashions of protest in Britain and the West. The late 1950s saw a growing worldwide concern about nuclear testing and the development of popular movements in the West to oppose it.

As Cold War attitudes eased, nonaligned peace movements were able to campaign and to get a serious hearing. The background to CND was Britain's first H-bomb test in 1957. A National Committee for the Abolition of Nuclear Weapon Tests was created in February of that year, and this was the nucleus of the organization that became CND. The British H-Bomb test was also the focus for a group committed to nonviolent direct action who planned to send a protest ship from Japan into the testing area. This group later became the Direct Action Committee Against Nuclear War and was responsible for organizing the first Aldermaston March at Easter 1958. So the first phase of the nuclear disarmament movement began with a divergence between CND using constitutional forms of protest and a nonviolent direct action wing of the campaign.

The formation of CND was also influenced by developments in the Labour Party. Labour Members of Parliament and activists formed the Labour H-Bomb Campaign Committee, which put a resolution urging Britain to give up its nuclear weapons unilaterally on the agenda of the 1957 Labour Party Conference, where it was defeated.

The final catalyst to CND was an article by J.B. Priestley (popular novelist and radical essayist) in the socialist weekly the *New Statesman* in November 1957, which stimulated a major response and led to the creation of the CND Committee. The chairperson of the new body was Canon John Collins, but it included prominent members of the Labour Party like Michael Foot, and its secretary was Peggy Duff, a veteran of organizing pressure groups and a Labour Party activist. Whilst CND maintained a nonpartisan stance, its real political agenda in the view of many of its leaders and supporters was to win over the Labour Party.

CND's first phase of mass support and political significance lasted from its inception at a meeting in

London's Central Hall in February 1958, until the end of 1963. During this period it organized mass rallies and marches at a national level: the main annual demonstration of CND strength became the four-day Aldermaston March at Easter, which CND took over in 1959. The 1958 march had set out from Trafalgar Square in London and ended at the Aldermaston nuclear weapons research establishment. CND reversed the order of the march, stressing the movement's focus on the seat of government in Whitehall. In the years 1960-62 estimated numbers of 100,000 or more attended the final rally.

The Direct Action Committee that had initiated the march turned its attention to local campaigns and civil disobedience at the Thor missile bases being built in 1958 and 1959, and to agitation at factories producing aircraft and missiles for Britain's nuclear force. Civil disobedience was at this time very controversial, and CND distanced itself from the breaking of the law, even by nonviolent means. But under pressure from its rank and file the CND leadership extended qualified support to some Direct Action Committee protests.

The issue of direct action became more divisive in CND when the Committee of 100 was set up in 1960, with the aim of involving thousands in mass civil disobedience. The philosopher Bertrand Russell, who was already president of CND, became the most prominent figure in the Committee of 100, which he helped to found. The Committee held several sit-down protests in Whitehall, London, with numbers ranging from around 2,000 in February 1961 to 12,000 in September 1961, when there was a major confrontation with the police after the Committee had been denied the right to assemble in Trafalgar Square. A third of the members of the Committee had been imprisoned in advance of the September sit-down for two months; in December the six officers of the Committee were charged with conspiracy and sentenced to between a year and 18 months in prison. These arrests were made just before the Committee's first demonstrations at American nuclear bases in which 5,000 took part. After 1961, the committee organized a number of further protests in London and at bases and turned its attention to promoting industrial action against nuclear weapons. The Committee was strongly influenced by anarchist ideas. It reorganized itself into regional committees and members branched out into use of direct action for other causes. It gradually lost its national impact.

CND began to decline after 1963 for a number of reasons. The international protests against nuclear testing appeared to have some success when the

United States, the former Soviet Union, and Britain signed the Partial Test Ban Treaty in 1963, and a number of other arms control agreements followed. A second factor was the difficulty of any movement in maintaining mass support and momentum over a long period. A third important cause of the decline of CND was that the Labour Party came to power in 1964, many prominent Labour CND members withdrew and Labour activists were less willing to campaign against their own government.

During the later 1960s new movements attracted young people. The central political issue was the Vietnam War. CND did include opposition to American military policy in Vietnam in its activities, but the militant rhetoric and support for violent protests associated with the anti-Vietnam campaign was at odds with the quieter image of CND. The student protests, the hippy movement, and the evolution of radical feminism in this period were all strands in a new protest culture that seemed to leave the more traditional attitudes and methods of CND behind. During the 1970s the growing appeal of the "green" environmentalist groups reintroduced commitment to nonviolent forms of protest and provided a cause—the dangers of nuclear power—on which CND could begin to find common ground with environmentalists. But during the later 1960s and throughout the 1970s, support for CND was low and the press did not take CND seriously as a national body.

### 3. *CND in the 1980s*

The revival of CND after 1979 owed something to specifically British circumstances. The Conservative Government publicly stressed the need for a British independent nuclear force and committed itself to acquiring Trident missiles. The Government also gave new public emphasis to civil defense, thereby highlighting the gap between existing measures and the known results of a nuclear attack, and providing a favourable campaigning issue for CND. But the main reasons for the revival of CND were those that created at the same time a major public reaction throughout Western Europe: new fear of nuclear war in response to new missiles and the development of first strike technology, the collapse of détente and, after 1980, the policies and rhetoric of Reagan Administration. These factors also led to the mushrooming Freeze Campaign in the United States.

CND in the 1980s was the center of a much wider campaign. Groups parallel to CND were created in a number of professions: Teachers for Peace developed peace education; Lawyers for Nuclear Disarmament

examined the international legality of nuclear weapons; the Medical Campaign Against Nuclear Weapons assessed the effects of nuclear war; and Scientists Against Nuclear Arms criticized civil defense assumptions about the effects of a nuclear winter (see *Nuclear Winter*). Over 140 local councils had by 1982 declared themselves to be "nuclear free zones"—that is opposed to the production, siting, or transportation of nuclear weapons in their area, and usually opposed also to cooperation in civil defense exercises (see *Nuclear-Weapon-Free Zones: A History and Assessment*).

All the churches engaged in the nuclear debate about the moral implications of nuclear strategy. The most politically significant debate occurred in the Church of England, when a working party recommended in 1982 a policy of unilateral nuclear disarmament by Britain. The General Synod of the Church did not accept this recommendation, but did vote in favor of a NATO policy of "no first use" of nuclear weapons (see *Nuclear Weapons, No First Use of*).

CND was part of an international movement, but at an organizational level it was rather less involved in international cooperation than it was in the early 1960s, when CND helped to launch the International Confederation for Disarmament and Peace to link up antinuclear movements. One reason for CND's limited international role has been the existence of the European Nuclear Disarmament movement (END) created in 1980. The socialist historian E.P. Thompson was a key figure in launching END, which began with an appeal for a nuclear-free Europe signed by individuals from the United States and Western Europe but also sought signatures from independent individuals in the former Soviet Union and Eastern Europe.

END remained a relatively small grouping within Britain—it avoided competing with CND for local support—but joined with West European groups to organize a series of international congresses, and published a bimonthly journal of theoretical analysis and international news. END also developed links with opposition bodies in Eastern Europe (for example Charter 77) and with independent peace movements that emerged from the Protestant Church in the former German Democratic Republic, among students for a time in Hungary, and on a very small scale inside the Soviet Union—the Moscow Group for Establishing Trust. END also maintained a dialogue with the official Peace Committees in the Soviet Union and Eastern Europe. END's links with opposition groups in Eastern Europe were controversial in some CND circles, who wished to avoid linkage between human rights and peace issues or to concentrate on relations with the official Peace Committees.

But prominent figures in END were also active at the center CND, and there was no ideological division between the two organizations. The organizational separation enabled END to concentrate on international issues and CND, which spanned a wider range of political opinions, to concentrate primarily on campaigning in Britain.

CND was, however, spared in the 1980s the organizational and philosophical conflicts over direct action that caused problems in the 1960s. Nonviolent direct action had become much less controversial as a method of protest, and CND endorsed it in principle at national conferences. The peace camps at nuclear bases were independent, but CND also organized its own civil disobedience protests.

National demonstrations were CND's method of showing the extent of its support. The main attempt to pull out mass support centered on demonstrations in central London—the highest turnouts were in October 1981 and October 1983, when it was estimated 250,000 people took part. During 1982 CND launched "Operation Hard Luck" intended to dramatize the effects of a nuclear war in Britain, and succeeded with the help of many local authorities in achieving the cancellation of the government's proposed civil defense exercise "Hard Rock." CND also worked with trade unions and with Members of Parliament, and it has attempted to influence national elections within the strict limits set by electoral law.

### 4. CND in the 1990s

The end of the Cold War and the reduced fears of nuclear war meant a gradual decline in support for CND. Although as in the 1980s radical peace protest has often been undertaken by autonomous groups monitoring nuclear weapons convoys, holding peace camps or promoting civil disobedience, CND has remained active. It played a prominent part in opposing the Gulf War in 1991 and in protests against renewed French nuclear testing in the Pacific in 1995, which also boosted CND membership. The World Court advisory opinion in July 1996 that use or threat to use nuclear weapons would "generally be contrary to the rules of international law" was stressed by CND in its publicity, although the opinion did not cover possession of nuclear weapons. The British nuclear force has been CND's main focus for demonstrations, for example the Faslane Trident submarine base in Scotland and the Aldermaston nuclear weapons plant. Much of CND's activity has always occurred at a local level, involving leafleting, collecting signatures to petitions, literature sales, meetings and local demonstrations.

### Bibliography

Driver C 1964 *The Disarmers: A Study in Protest.* Hodder and Stoughton, London

Groom J 1974 *British Think about Nuclear Weapons.* Frances Pinter, London

Minnion J, Bolsover P (eds.) 1983 *The CND Story.* Allison and Busby, London

Pritchard C, Taylor R 1980 *The Protest Makers: The British Nuclear Disarmament Movement of 1958-65 Twenty Years On.* Pergamon, Oxford

Wittner L S 1997 *The Struggle Against the Bomb*, Vol 2. Stanford University Press, Stanford

APRIL CARTER

# Camus, Albert

Albert Camus (1913-60), the French author, was born in the village of Mondovi in Algeria, then a French territory, the son of a nearly illiterate and partly deaf mother of Spanish origin and of a farm laborer who was killed in 1914 in the First World War. Camus studied at an elementary school in Algiers and then, thanks to a scholarship, at the lycée and the University of Algiers, where he undertook work toward an advanced degree. He ultimately wrote a thesis on Plotinus (1936). An attack of tuberculosis at age 17 and recurring ill health led to a rethinking of his plans for the future, since he believed he could not have a teaching career because he would not meet the health requirements, and to reflections of a somber nature on the precarious physical and metaphysical position of human beings in a hostile universe. Slowing down his studies, he worked at odd jobs, in journalism, and in amateur theater. Throughout his career he remained interested in stagecraft and playwriting. He was briefly an active member of the Algerian Communist Party (1934-37), but disavowed it when it renounced its pro-Moslem policies. He was an early spokesman in the Algerian press for justice for the natives (Moslems and Kabyles). His essays, dating from 1939, which deplored the miserable economic, educational, and sanitary conditions in which the Algerian government allowed the natives to live and work, called for immediate and far-reaching reforms. (These essays have been collected as *Chroniques algériennes*.) Though he did not advocate independence for Algeria, he inevitably raised questions concerning French rights and responsibilities, particularly the French right to impose in their colonies a double standard of living (one for Europeans, one for natives) by exporting valuable raw materials and not putting the profits from that exploitation back into the territory.

Not called for military service in 1939 because of his ill health, Camus spent the years of the Second World War first in Algeria, then in France, where his two most famous works, *L'Etranger* and *Le Mythe de Sisyphe*, were published in 1942. These, like his well-known *Caligula* (1945) and *Le Malentendu* (1944), are concerned chiefly with the metaphysical position of human beings in a universe where they are condemned to suffer and die and there is no recognizable divine concern for them; they also stress personal, but not economic, alienation. Though not always in good health, Camus in 1943 joined the underground movement called *Combat* and was by the war's end the editor of its very important newspaper. The thrust of this movement was, of course, anti-German. However, after the war, his voice was one of the more moderate to be heard at a time of passionate vendettas against collaborationists. Though he had deplored as much as any of his fellow resistants the German occupation of France and the Nazi atrocities, he concluded that Germany alone was not responsible for the sort of attitudes which had led to the war, and that vengeance against the former enemy and vicious treatment of collaborators were unjustified and unconstructive. The theme of generalized guilt shared by modern Europeans is visible in *La Chute*, published in 1956. He had already published *Lettres à un ami allemand* (1943-44), the very title of which revealed his lack of animosity. Their thesis was that the idea of culture and humankind proposed by modern Germany was unacceptable: "Your nation has received from its sons only the love it deserved, and which was blind. One is not justified by just *any* love." "Rather than risking injustice, we [the French] preferred disorder." He also showed his early enthusiasm for a European ideal beyond petty nationalisms, which would lead to a unified Europe.

In post-Liberation France, Camus was active in various political circles and continued his journalistic and literary activity. He had hoped for a Europe at peace after the war, able to pursue the social justice that he had called for so eloquently in his writings.

He had not counted on its polarization into Soviet- and US-dominated spheres and the Cold War (see *Cold War*). While he found the division unfortunate, he was forced to take sides and his position was, with reservations, pro-NATO and anti-Soviet.

Liberals considered him to have sold out to capitalism and American warmongering. His own view was more shaded: he would have preferred a Europe without an Iron Curtain, military bases, and confrontations, but he could not approve of the Soviet takeover in Eastern Europe, and Soviet tyranny was worse, in his eyes, than that of the Western capitalistic democracies, so he had to be pro-Western. The invasion of Hungary in 1956 only confirmed this position.

While most of his major postwar works are only marginally concerned with the concrete problems of peace and war in Europe, some aspects of them are pertinent in this context. In the novel *La Peste* (1947), he showed eloquently the presence of natural, moral, and metaphysical evil in the world and made his heroes people who struggle against evil even if there seems to be no hope, rather than give in to it. The novel also has a political meaning: the plague is generally considered to be a symbol of the German occupation of France, a political evil which the French were right to fight against heroically. In *Les Justes* (1949), a play, he treated the subject of Russian anarchists in 1905, and though he showed his sympathy for the plight of the serfs under the Czars and the purposes of the anarchists, he illustrated the philosophical incompatibility between terrorism and a just cause, since terrorism always kills innocent bystanders. In *L'Homme révolté*, an essay dating from 1951, he compared revolution—that is, an organized political protest which tyrannizes in the name of freedom and imposes its will, becoming ultimately an oppressive totalitarian state—and rebellion, the condition of the individual struggling for freedom. Only the latter, he argued, could remain authentic. This essay was the occasion of Camus's public quarrel in the press with his friend Jean-Paul Sartre, who favored a socialist revolution in Europe.

While he was interested in the Cold War and its consequences, Camus also had to turn his attention perforce to other contemporary problems. One problem on which he wrote eloquently is capital punishment, of which he could never approve and which to him revealed the fundamental flaws in all societies which practiced it (*Réflexions sur la guillotine*). An even more urgent topic was Algeria. From the outbreak of the insurgency in Algeria on November 1, 1954 until his death in an automobile accident in 1960, Camus found himself in a very uncomfortable position. As an early partisan of social justice, as he defined it, for the natives, he understood their anger; but he could not bring himself to denounce the French presence as a whole in Algeria, even when he criticized certain specific policies and officials. To him, Algeria was French and should remain so politically as well as through its cultural heritage. Because of his great popularity as an author and journalist, he was repeatedly called upon to take a stand on Algeria. As a spokesman for the Resistance, he had been identified with the liberal Left, an identification that was certainly appropriate in some ways. But when he would not denounce the war France was waging against the Algerian rebels, those liberals who had not already condemned him for his anti-Soviet stand branded him a political traitor. Some observers, however, now believe that the position he took on Algeria was more realistic than that taken by Sartre, whom events have proven wrong in a number of ways. He was accused of racism, and indeed his fiction and theatre reveal what is doubtless an unintentional scorn of minority groups.

He continued to speak in the press about the war, trying especially to bring about in 1956 what he called a civil truce, which would then allow negotiations between the two sides to begin and would, meanwhile, put a stop to the bloodshed. But his personal intervention failed (he was ill-received when he tried to speak in Algeria) and he was denounced by the Right and the Left alike; he then curtailed his journalistic efforts on behalf of a cease-fire. When he was awarded the Nobel Prize for Literature in 1957, his acceptance speech turned into a scandal, because he condemned the rebels and their use of terrorism, stating that he loved justice but loved his mother (then still alive, and living in Algeria) more than justice. As well as having a personal meaning, the phrase was probably intended to signify that one's concern for the concrete individual must take precedence over devotion to an abstraction, but it was interpreted in the most narrow and unfavorable sense. In the last years of his life he withdrew from participation in the debate and turned his attention to plays and short stories, in some of which (e.g., "L'Hôte") one can see traces of the bitterness he experienced after failing to promote peace in Algeria.

Camus was not a systematic thinker, nor, according to some views, even a careful and rigorous one. His thought is not dialectical, and this separates him from many other thinkers who have wrestled with the problems of East-West confrontation and other political problems of this century. His philosophic essays *Le Mythe de Sisyphe* and *L'Homme révolté* deal in a very searching way with the human predicament but are not treatises on concrete social and political problems, such as war and peace. However, his journalistic writing deals repeatedly with war and social upheaval, and throughout it, as well as in his fiction and plays, one can sense his commitment to the sort of society in Europe and indeed in the whole world which would make warfare unnecessary. His position can be summed up roughly as that of an idealistic humanist. A famous statement in *La Peste* says that there is more in humankind to love than to despise. When Camusian heroes such as Dr. Rieux struggle to bring an end to suffering, whether on a wide scale or not, they do not despair; although the doctor says at the end of the novel that the plague is always with us, and there can be no definitive victory over evil, Camus shows that individual and collective struggle can sometimes bring about change. In any case, he insists, one must take sides with the victim, not the executioner. Camus was convinced that social justice and the resultant international peace for which his generation was hungry could be achieved only through understanding and enlightenment on an *individual* scale: like many French writers, he found moral progress within the person to be a necessary prelude to any lasting social improvement. For political and social changes to be dictated by a ruling revolutionary party is a contradiction, since if they are imposed, they do not represent genuine progress, and they destroy rather than enhance freedom. Thus Camusian writings link personal moral choice with social progress and ultimately with the sort of society in which hydrogen bombs would not be necessary; this is part of the message of *La Chute*.

This position is open to the criticism often made of liberal humanistic thinking: namely, that there is little reason to believe people will correct themselves or evil will vanish through a gradual process. Historical arguments can always be called upon to support this criticism. Camus is also open to the charge of refusing, idealistically, in the name of individual human values, to reckon in terms of numbers (for instance, to approve of the sacrifice of a few innocent bystanders in order to reach the aim of destroying Czarist power). Yet he was not a naive daydreamer either—certainly his very precise appeals for economic and social assistance for native Algerians before 1939 and his plan for cessation of terrorism in Algeria in 1956 were basically feasible, had the government wished to carry them out. Nor was he a philosophic pacifist (an uncommon position in France at the time of the war, but not unknown—a case in point is Jean Giono). Reluctantly but frankly,

Camus had to approve of the Allied struggle against Nazi Germany, because Germany would otherwise have destroyed the Western idea of humankind. That is, he recognized defensive war as a justifiable position, saying that if "the spirit can do nothing against the sword, the spirit united with the sword is the eternal conqueror of the sword drawn for its own sake" (*Essais* p. 244). He did not favor, either, peace at any price in Indochina or Algeria (despite his campaign for a truce), since he held that the French presence in these territories had some merit and that, should the French withdraw totally, the resulting political vacuum could be much worse than the French occupation. He did, however, call for a new basis of cooperation among interested parties to achieve peace in these territories. This call was based on appeals to reason and to such typical French republican ideals as liberty, fraternity, and equality. It supposed that peace could be achieved through social and political process, by people of goodwill negotiating in good faith after arms had been laid down. This position can be considered inadequate, to the degree that people of good faith are not always those in positions of power and that such ideals as equality may be understood differently. Yet it is a position which appealed to thousands of readers (to judge by Camus's popularity) who did not want social revolution in Europe but did want progress toward more just societies, less competitive nationalism, an end to violence, greater autonomy and freedom for former colonized territories, and increased international cooperation, leading to peace. Camus's views have been just as widely disseminated as those of his Marxist rivals such as Sartre, and, despite his critics, his reputation endures as a voice of reason and humanitarianism, calling for a Europe and a world in which violence would no longer be employed.

*Bibliography*

Brée G 1961 *Camus*. Rutgers University Press, New Brunswick

Camus A 1942 *L'Etranger*. Gallimard, Paris [1946 *The Stranger*. Knopf, New York; also, *The Outsider*. Hamish Hamilton, London]

Camus A 1942 *Le Mythe de Sisyphe*. Gallimard, Paris [1955 *The Myth of Sisyphus and Other Essays*. Knopf, New York]

Camus A 1944 *Le Malentendu; Caligula*. Gallimard, Paris [1958 *Caligula and Three Other Plays*. Knopf, New York]

Camus A 1946 Ni victimes ni bourreaux. *Combat*, Nov 1946 [1966 Neither Victims nor Executioners. In: Mayer P (ed.) 1946 *The Pacifist Conscience*. Hart-Davis, London]

Camus A 1947 *La Peste*. Gallimard, Paris [1948 *The Plague*. Modern Library, New York]

Camus A 1948 *Lettres à un ami allemand*. Gallimard, Paris [1961 *Resistance, Rebellion, and Death*. Knopf, New York]

Camus A 1950 *Les Justes*. Gallimard, Paris [1958 *Caligula and Three Other Plays*. Knopf, New York]

Camus A 1951 *L'Homme révolté*. Gallimard, Paris [1956 *The Rebel*. Knopf, New York]

Camus A 1958 *Actuelles III: Chroniques algériennes*. Gallimard, Paris [1961 *Resistance, Rebellion, and Death*. Knopf, New York]

Lottman H R 1979 *Albert Camus*. Doubleday, Garden City, New York

McCarthy P 1982 *Albert Camus*. Hamish Hamilton, London

Parker E 1965 *Albert Camus, the Artist in the Arena*. University of Wisconsin Press, Madison, Wisconsin

CATHARINE SAVAGE BROSMAN

# Caribbean Basin Initiative (CBI)

Central America and the Caribbean has become an area of vital importance to the United States to the point where it is spoken of as its fourth border and as a strategic and commercial zone. This is one of the main reasons why the Congress of the United States approved the Caribbean Basin Recovery Act, also known as the Caribbean Basin Initiative (CBI), which is aimed at rescuing the weakened economies of the small countries of the area in order to maintain their endangered political stability.

Central America as well as the Caribbean obviously represent only a marginal economic interest for the United States, in spite of their growing importance as an export market. Nevertheless, there are motives besides the aforementioned that induce the United States to take a special interest in the area. Among these is the considerable increase in Caribbean and Central American emigres, many of whom, due to their illegal alien status, are socially and economically disadvantaged. This has obliged the United States Government to take special measures to prevent them from becoming a social burden. Likewise, the United States is quite concerned about the use of certain countries as drug traffic routes to redirect cargoes to United States ports. To this end, the United States has offered surveillance and control assistance to prevent further increase in the use of these countries for illegal purposes.

## 1. Financing Component

At the beginning of the Reagan Administration a bipartisan commission presided over by Henry Kissinger was established to set the basis for a subregional preference scheme according to the political and strategic plans of the United States in the area. The recommendations of the Kissinger Commission Report are centered around the short-term emergency needs of a stabilization program, which includes complementary aid of us$400 million, official guarantees for Central American credits, as well as support for debt negotiation and for the Central American Integration Bank (CABEI).

The program aims to generate on a medium- and short-term basis us$8,000 million during a five-year period, as of 1985, as well as to create expansion of commercial opportunities, technical and financial support for export promotion programs, and the improvement of investment conditions through the establishment of a private capital company to promote them in Central America. On a long-term basis, the Kissinger Commission Report aims to set up an aid program for several years to transfer a considerable volume of resources into the area.

The Caribbean Basin Initiative is conceived as a program which combines fiscal and commercial advantages as well as greater assistance from the United States to promote economic and political stability in the Caribbean Basin through the expansion of different existing industries and the attraction of new investments.

The CBI is part of a campaign to obtain multilateral aid for the region with the participation of Canada, Colombia, Mexico, and Venezuela. The Caribbean Basin Act foresees also the temporary application of a franchise regime to all products originating from a beneficiary country, except for the following products: textiles and clothing subject to special agreements and protocols, shoes and leather articles, gloves, crude and refined oil, and canned tuna. A quantitative annual restriction on the imports of sugar from the region was also established.

The rules for the Caribbean Basin Initiative do not oppose the increase of imports from other developing countries. The free importation of products from the Caribbean and Central America has been restricted up to a limit of us$600 million as a consequence of the CBI. All these advantages are obtained by the Caribbean and Central American countries as a result of series of concessions, namely the acceptance of conditions regarding the exchange of banking and tax information as well as extradition and investment protection and promotion agreements. The countries of the Caribbean and those of the Central American area are aware that small states such as their own have special difficulties in the structural adjustments of their economies. Nevertheless, besides all the aforementioned problems, a concerted action from the international community is also needed to help these countries out in their commercial and development programs. This fact was considered in the First Lome Convention in 1975, as well as at the Fourth United Nations Conference on Trade and Development (UNCTAD) in 1974, where the concept of insular and small states was introduced. Within the framework of this aid policy and for all the previous reasons pointed out, the United States makes a reasonable effort in its aid programs and approves the Caribbean Basin Act.

Trade, transfer of technology, and improved access to the American capital market are the most important elements of the multilateral aid that Latin America needs as a whole. This was clearly outlined in the Declaration of Quito of January 1984, in which the Heads of States of the Caribbean and Latin American countries, as a token of solidarity, recognized that the Central American and Caribbean nations face special problems and are economically more vulnerable because of their size and structure and that, therefore, a more special and preferential treatment would be required for several years in order for these countries to participate efficiently in international markets.

Antigua, Bermuda, Bahamas, Barbados, Belize, Dominican Republic, Grenada, Guyana, Haiti, Jamaica, Saint Kitts-Nevis, Santa Lucia, Saint Vincent, Grenadines, Suriname, Trinidad and Tobago, as well as the following Central American countries: Guatemala, El Salvador, Honduras, Costa Rica, and Panama, are the countries which benefit from the CBI (Cuba and Nicaragua have been excluded as a result of antagonism between them and the United States).

The Central American and Caribbean Region must, nevertheless, be aware that in order to solve its problems, a much broader multilateral aid from the European countries, Japan, and other regional powers is highly desirable, although some of the Caribbean countries, as a result of the Lome Conventions, already have a special relationship to the European Union. To a certain extent this has a more practical aspect than that of the CBI, that is, the STABEX system, the spectrum of products with franchise, special agreements for certain goods such as sugar and bananas, as well as the relative absence of political conditions and multilateral consultations and negotiation procedures.

## 2. Trade Component

The Law for Economic Recovery of the Caribbean Basin of 1983, contains tariff and commercial measures, destined to the promotion of the economic revitalization and the expansion of the private sector of the Caribbean Basin Region. This Law became effective January 1, 1984. The main elements of the program are:

(a) Duty free entry into the United States of America (However, it must be taken into account that the products eligible for customs duty exemption, may be subject to federal taxes on consumption,

(b) Increase of the economic aid that the US provides to the region,

(c) Provide incentives for efforts that the Caribbean Basin Countries make on their own,

(d) Reduction of US's taxes, to those companies that hold conventions in acceptable countries, in order to increase tourism,

(e) A wide variety of promotional programs of the government of the US (e.g., Textile Access Program 807-A),

(f) Support of other commercial partners of multinational development institutions, such as: The Interamerican Development Bank (IDB), World Bank (WB), the implementation of the Caribbean Canada, since Canada grants benefits to the Caribbean, which are obtained through intervention of the CBI.

There are certain requisites that must be met by products to obtain CBI benefits. To enter the US, within CBI, a product must meet the following criteria:

(a) To be grown, produced or manufactured in one or more of the Caribbean Basin countries and exported directly to the US,

(b) If it is a product that has imported raw materials incorporated, the added value must be at least 35% of the product. However, if the product was manufactured partly with raw materials from the US, an additional 15% is considered, for the components from that country. In such cases, the national or regional added value of such article, may be 20%,

(c) The product being offered must be a commercial item, completely different from the foreign materials used to manufacture it, meaning that this transformation must show a significant effort in production,

(d) The article must be directly imported from a beneficiary country into the customs territory of the US or not undergo any changes in the countries it transits.

There are some products that are not eligible for duty free entry into the US, in accordance with the CBI, these are: (a) most textiles and clothing in general; (b) canned tuna; (c) oil and oil products; (d) shoes, except for disposable items and shoe parts, certain leather, rubber or plastic gloves; (e) luggage, hand bags and leather accessories; (f) certain clothing items made of leather; and watches and parts for watches.

In addition to the origin rules enumerated above, the Customs and Trade Act of 1990 added new criteria for duty-free eligibility under the Caribbean Basin Initiative.

First, articles which are the growth, product or manufacture of Puerto Rico and which subsequently are processed in a CBI beneficiary country, may also receive duty-free treatment when entered, if the three following conditions are met:

(a) They are imported directly from a beneficiary country into the customs territory of the United States,

(b) They are advanced in value or improved in condition by any means in a beneficiary country,

(c) Any materials added to the article in a beneficiary country must be a product of a beneficiary country or the US.

Second, articles which are assembled or processed in whole from US components or ingredients (other than water) in a beneficiary may be entered free of duty. Duty-free treatment will apply if the components or ingredients are exported directly to the beneficiary country and the finished article is imported directly into the customs territory of the United States.

*Bibliography*

CENTREX 1998 *Caribbean Basin Initiative—CBI.* http://www.elsalvadortrade.comsv/ i_tratados/html/cbi.html

Gonzalez P 1984 *Relaciones Economicas de lo Estados Unidos de America con el Caribe. Rev.* Capitulos del SELA 7

Kissinger H 1984 Kissinger Commission Report 1984

Lowenthal A F 1982 The Caribbean Basin initiative: Misplaced emphasis. *Foreign Policy* 47

Reagan R 1982 President Reagan's address at the OAS on the Caribbean Basin Plan. February, 1982

Tanzi V 1983 The underground economy. *Finance and Development* 23 (4)

Tourism Industrial Development Company 1998 Caribbean Initiative II (CBI II) http://sealus.umn.edu/untpdc/incubator/tto/tppos/miniti/tragtscbi.htm

Trade Point, USA 1995 Caribbean Basin Initiative (CBI). http://sys1.tpusa.com/ ir01/imprtgui/ch14.html

JORGE RHENAN SEGURA; PEDRO B. BERNALDEZ

# Caudillismo

The roots of caudillismo are found in the early days of Latin American independence from Spain. The breakdown of Spanish central authority permitted private armies and other irregular rural forces to attempt seizure of the nationwide political organization and establish successor governments serving the interest of local landed oligarchy.

In this context the term "caudillo" was first used by nineteenth century politicians to describe the new emerging self-proclaimed leader, usually a military officer, who became the agent of a new social order built on personalistic charismatic authority and with distinct counter-revolutionary tendencies.

In the twentieth century, the concept was gradually extended by various political and sociological analysts to refer to any kind of authoritarianism or political system controlled by military personnel in Latin America and other developing regions. The name caudillo now is applied to any charismatic leader ignoring the fact that there exist substantive differences between political systems and unique historical development. Thus the designation of Generalissimo Francisco Franco of Spain as "*El Caudillo de España por la Gracia de Dios*" reveals how far the concept has been taken away from its historical roots.

There exists a copious literature concerning the origins of "caudillismo" found in varying degree and at different times throughout nineteenth century Latin America. Interestingly enough some authors have even looked for racial components and hereditary psychological predispositions in Latin American societies to explain the "caudillo" as the natural consequence of the unruly Hispanic conquistador, the African regulus, or the aborigine "cacique." The Indian-derived "caciquismo" is used today to refer to the pattern of local leadership in the contemporary Latin American peasant movement.

Historically, the caudillo gained access to power in the independence movements of 1810-23 and the succeeding civil wars. Until the late eighteenth century, separatist ambitions in the New World were effectively handled by the crown of Spain because military units stood under the exclusive command of royal "peninsulares," that is native-born Spaniards. The growing weakness of the Spanish empire, however, forced Charles III of Spain in the 1760s to institute a series of imperial reforms that included the establishment of a colonial militia and the regularized commissioning of Latin-born "criollos" (members of the local aristocracy) as military officers of the Spanish crown. Being granted the full privileges of the Spanish officers—including the "fuero militar" exempting them from trials by civil courts—this "new generation" of officers was to play a decisive role in the internal struggle for political hegemony that finally led to the end of Spanish rule in the New World. Such men as Símon Bolívar, Francisco de Miranda, and José de San Martín, formerly trained in the Spanish army, became the leaders of the Latin American struggle for independence.

Despite the continental aspirations for political independence, these intellectual leaders and other upper class White members of local society were deeply divided on ideological grounds. Their attempt to carry through an authentic revolution in the countries of Latin America evoked a coalition of interest between the clericalist landowning conservatives and opponent military leaders now fighting for the preservation of the traditional social order. This conflict gave form to the politics of the continent until the 1860s and almost every country followed a path from independence to short-lived liberal victory to caudillismo.

Furthermore, the extended military contest led to a broader popularization of the officer corps opening it to persons of lower social status. Less idealistic aspirants to higher social positions now easily gained access to power and were in turn contested by hundreds of equally ambitious "little caudillos." Their praxis of "machete" and "machismo" combined with very close personal relationships with their subordinate soldiers made many of them very popular, however. Thus a caudillo of the Páez type felt himself responsible not only for the security of his troops but also for the well-being of their families; they in turn loved him like a "father." With the same personalistic attitude, the caudillo, when in power, was surrounded by an ever-present camarilla of mediating officials, and he subjected all legislative functions under his intimate and immediate control.

Some of the caudillos reigned for long periods. Gaspar Rodriguez Francia ruled in Paraguay from 1813 to 1840, Juan Manuel de Rosas in Argentina from 1829 to 1852, and José Antonio Páez, one of the predominant figures of counter-revolution, came into power in Venezuela in 1831, 1839, and 1861. Other well-known caudillos are Rafael Carrera (1844-48 and 1851-65) of Guatemala, Jean Pierre Boyer (1818-43) of Haiti, and Antonio López de Santa Anna (more or less from 1821 to 1855) of Mexico. In some cases the caudillos even developed specific schools of thought, and they have all left a deep imprint on their national histories and ideologies. By the 1860s, however, traditional caudillismo was dead.

Latin American historians have for a long time been divided over the political success or failure of the great caudillos with reference to the historical development of their countries. Salcedo-Bastardo speaks of two essential errors in caudillismo shaping the destiny of the continent: an ethical one, revealing the crisis of true patriotism, and an intellectual one, preventing the search for political and cultural identity. Against that, modernization theorists tend to emphasize the nation-building functions and modernizing force of caudillistic military rule and the meaning of caudillismo for contemporary events.

Critical contemporary research however, clearly distinguishes classical caudillismo (1810-60) from the subsequent (quasimilitary) autocracies (1870-1910; Porfirio Díaz in Mexico) and modern (military) dictatorships (Somoza in Nicaragua).

As each Latin American state is different, internally in the development of their social relations and externally in the degree of dependency on foreign hegemony, it appears false to regard caudillismo as a constant factor in Latin American political culture. Moreover, in view of the growing global interest in military-civil relations, the Latin American experience is more or less unique and any attempt to use it as a "case study" for other military regimes in developing countries will probably fail.

*Bibliography*

Beltrán V R 1970 *El papel politico y social de las Fuerzas Armadas en American Latina*. Monte Avila Editores, Caracas

Chapman C 1932 The age of the Caudillos: A chapter in Hispanic American history. *Hisp. Am. Hist. Rev.* 12

Hamill H M Jr (ed.) 1965 *Dictatorship in Spanish America*. Columbia University Press, New York

Humphreys R A 1969 *Tradition and Revolt in Latin America*. Columbia University Press, New York

Liewen E 1960 *Arms and Politics in Latin America*. Praeger, New York

Liewen E 1964 *Generals vs. Presidents. Neo-militarism in Latin America*. Praeger, New York

Johnson J 1964 *The Military and Society in Latin America*. Stanford University Press, Stanford, California

Schmitter P C (ed.) 1973 *Military Rule in Latin America*. Sage, Beverly Hills, California

Sotelo I et al., 1975 *Die bewaffneten Technokraten Militär und Politik in Lateinamerika*. Kohlhammer, Stuttgart

Waldmann P 1978 Caudillismo—Konstante der politischen Kultur Lateinamerikas? In: *Jahrbuch für Geschichte, von Staat, Wirtschaft und Gesellschaft*

Wolf E R 1966 Caudillo politics. A structural analysis. *Comp. Stud. Sociol. Hist.* 9

INGRID LANGER

# Changing Concept and Role of the UN in the 21st Century

## 1. Introduction

The United Nations has just started its second half century with great expectation, which extends to the twenty-first century. But the next century, which is also the opening of the third millennium, will be different from the twentieth century in many fundamental ways. It will present a new kind of challenges which call for international cooperation. In particular, technological revolution brings the peoples all over the world closer and closer, which has resulted in stressing the centrality of humanity in the increasingly interdependent relations of nations. This will significantly affect the development of the future status and role of the UN in world politics. Therefore, for the purpose of discussing the future status and role of the world organization, it is important to see how humanity will become the new major challenge in the next century. Before considering the new challenges of the future, however, we need to examine how the capabilities of sovereign states have declined in recent years, which has necessitated the strengthening of the United Nations (see *Status and Role of the United Nations*).

## 2. *From Independence to Interdependence*

In the sixteenth and seventeenth centuries the proliferation of nation-states resulting from divisions in Europe led to highly unstructured interstate relations. At the time the independence of states was regarded as absolute and most necessary to ensure their survival. International society, based on the Hobbesian state of nature, was composed of mutually exclusive and isolated states which were concerned only with the issues of war and peace. Its anarchical nature had remained essentially unchanged until the end of World War II. The twentieth century has been characterized by the uncontrolled behaviors of egoistic sovereign states which asserted their independence as the most important principle. But the principle has already begun to reveal its serious problems in the development of international relations. In this regard, it is not much different from the nineteenth century which historians have labelled as the age of nationalism.

The first half of the present century had abounded with the conflicts between sovereign states which had pursued the policy of expansionism. After the end of World War II, the Great Powers had dominated international politics, but this has steadily declined with the emergence of the Third World states which ushered in the age of new nationalism (see *Nationalism*). In this situation, sovereignty, war, independence, national interest, and ideology continue to be the important considerations in relations of states.

However, the traditional state-centered international society began to be transformed into a more organized world society as a consequence of new changes. And the development of world society based on the interdependence of states and the common interest of the world community has been sustained by the process of globalization which puts an end to nationalism as the guiding ideology. Globalization that changes the character of international relations has been accelerated by the following four developments (see *Globalization*).

First, technological revolution has made it possible to overcome the spatial limits of national boundaries. Revolutionary progress in transportation and communication has brought about the expansion and deepening of the interdependent relations of states. This has eroded the absoluteness of states and facilitated the formation of a common value system of the world community.

Second, the rise of global issues has presented new challenges to the nation-state system which has dominated interstate relations during the last five hundred years. Even the national problems of states have become increasingly globalized. But more important is that globalized issues are on the increase. Poverty, human rights violation, population explosion, resource shortage, environmental degradation, and South-North conflict over economic development are only a few examples of the new global concerns. If these global problems are left alone, it would ultimately threaten even human survival.

Third, economic problems which are global by nature have replaced the military concern as the central issue in international relations after the end of the Cold War. The primacy of economic issues has come to dominate interstate politics, while the importance of the military power declines as the instrument of problem-solving in the economic realm.

Fourth, the Third World states have changed the political context of international relations. They have exerted their influence in restraining the confrontational behavior of the two superpowers in UN politics and diplomacy; as a result, they helped promote the politics of public opinion and moral principle. The growing influence of the Third World has contributed to the strengthening of UN's function of collective legitimization, which also enhances its mediating role. More important, the South-North conflict (see *North-South Conflict*) has led to the development of new principles of the world community, such as the common heritage of mankind (see *Oceans: The Common Heritage*), which becomes the foundation for a global value system.

In these circumstances individual states are no longer capable of dealing with global problems and their own globalized national problems. They have often remained powerless and even irrelevant in the face of global problems which call for multilateral cooperation. The days of states as absolute sovereign entities are over which have unilaterally exercised dominant influence in international relations. They are called upon to actively participate in the efforts of international cooperation which needs a rational and multilateral approach.[1]

The growing interdependence of states has necessitated international cooperation for collective action in tackling global problems. Now, international cooperation becomes the controlling principle in managing world problems. It is no longer a matter of choice for states in the collective management of global issues; it has become a political necessity for common prosperity in the new world order. World politics has come to emphasize multilateral cooperation as the major consideration in the allocation of values among states, because a set of bilateral cooperation are neither adequate nor sufficient for managing global issues. Multilateral cooperation helps develop a strong sense of the world community (see *Multilateralism*). The deepening interdependence of states facilitates consensus-building within the global community, which also helps lay the foundation for their common value system.

International cooperation is a phenomenon that occurs in the process of searching for a solution to various issues of states. Conceptually, it is distinguished from collaboration. While the former contains a positive normative connotation, the latter that has a value-neutral meaning involves functional activities which accompany the active participation of two or more autonomous actors.[2] The collaboration of states is possible when diverse national interests coincide and when the need for coalition exists; and the quality of collaboration is dependent upon the level of perception of such interests.[3] On the other hand, international cooperation is more dictated by the need to solve the common problems of states (see *Interdependence, International*).

A new world order of the post-Cold War era may be given an important meaning because it has created a new international environment congenial for the promotion of multilateral cooperation amid the diffusion of power. The changing international realities have made sovereign states no longer adequate as the basic political units of the international system. The ability of states to deal with global issues has rapidly declined due to their inherent political and institutional limits that inhibit multilateral cooperation; in fact, the very nature of nation-states or state sovereignty has the inherent tendency of exclusiveness and localism. As a result, states have now come to recognize the need for global authority, which points to what Strobe Talbott called the birth of the global nation.[4] This, however, does not necessarily mean the creation of a world government; the common interests based on the interdependence rather than independence of states become the new basis of international relations. In this situation, the greater role of international organization is inevitable for the management of global commons.

## 3. The Evolution of International Organization

International organization has gradually developed as an institutional framework for international cooperation. It has come through three stages of development. At the first stage, it was established as an institution subservient to the interests of individual states, and its role was limited and passive. The League of Nations (1919-39) (see *League of Nations*) was such a case. At the time international society was underdeveloped which could support only a weak international organization. It was dominated by egoistic sovereign states whose independence was the most important concern and whose interactions were minimal and conflictual at best. It was more like a collection of billiard balls, where there was no recognition of a clearly defined common interest. In the circumstances, international cooperation was rather exceptional and limited, which was based on the calculated self-interest of states; consequently, international organization was overshadowed by dominant nationalism. But sovereign states began to change their perception of international organization after World War II.

At the second stage of development, international organization came to have its own independent political identity, apart form states which gave their consent to establish it. The United Nations of the period from 1945 to 1990 belongs to this category (see *United Nations: Achievements and Agenda*). However, its functioning had been made difficult by the development of the Cold War. On the other hand, the rise of the Third World states much contributed to the strengthening of the UN as a universal institution. The Third World greatly facilitated the development of world politics by de-Europeanizing the past Europe-centered international relations. As Secretary-General U Thant pointed out,[5] the new nations have injected "new blood and new attitudes" into international politics, which allowed the UN to acquire dynamism, new realism and the future-oriented senses. The Third World states also reinforced the moral influence of world public opinion, while acting as an important factor in the international balance of power in the General Assembly.[6] The result is that it has changed the character of international politics by transforming the bipolarity of political power into multipolarity in the United Nations. All these have helped the UN to strengthen its own distinctive identity.

The third stage of development may be said to have begun with the end of the Cold War. In the 1990s the UN has emerged as a viable independent political factor in international politics. It has played the central role in the global governance of common concerns of mankind, based on the principle of multilateralism. As a new concept, global governance involves more than formal institutions and organizations for the management of international problems. It requires the operation of command mechanism which provides stability, prosperity, order, consistency and continuity for the international social system.[7]

Now international organization, such as the United Nations, represents order, norms and rules. Once it is created, it comes to have its own life to sustain and develops as an independent entity which even the states that created it cannot dissolve at will. International organization has become a major factor which exercises its own independent political influence in international relations; its role will continue to increase in the politics of international cooperation as complex interdependence of states becomes deepened and expanded.

## 4. *The Issue Areas of the United Nations*

The nature of the issues that the United Nations deals with will condition the development of its future roles. For this reason, it is necessary to discuss the main issue area of the UN in order to understand the direction of its future roles (see *United Nations Reform: Historical and Comparative Perspectives*). But it should be noted that its central issue area has been shifting over the past years. The issue politics has changed in the world body when its power base moved from the superpowers to the Third World states in the 1960s and then to mankind as a whole in the 1990s. Therefore, it is possible to identify three different issue areas the UN has focused in the periods of the Cold War, the Third World, and the post-Cold War. This has been manifested in the transition of main issue areas from international peace to distributive justice and then to human dignity, which are closely interrelated.

The maintenance of mechanical or procedural international peace and security had been the central issue area during the early period of the UN, but this approach soon became difficult to achieve as the political context changed with the rise of the Third World states which have raised global economic and social problems. As a result, the main concern of the UN shifted to the area of economic and social problems involving the principle of distributive justice. The growing economic disparity between developed and developing countries has become a serious global concern, which calls for international cooperation. Thus, international peace and security would be inconceivable without the implementation of distributive justice, but distributive justice without humanity remains irrelevant in the interdependent world. So, the problem of humanity emerges as the important issue of the international community.

In the 1990s after the end of the Cold War, human dignity has become the primary concern of the UN, which is considered a more effective approach to international peace and distributive justice. It is because the well-being of individuals, not individual states, is the paramount consideration in the UN efforts to resolve global problems. This is well illustrated by the 1995 UN World Summit for Social Development in Copenhagen, where the world leaders discussed for the first time "poverty, employment and social integration" as the urgent problems of individuals rather than states, and unanimously adopted the Copenhagen Declaration and Action Programme to promote the quality of human life. The summit meeting marked the transformation of the hitherto state-centered history into the human-oriented one. Now, no other issue appears to be so important than human rights (see *Human Rights and Peace*). It is only natural that the issues of human rights have received increasing attention from all nations in recent years. For this reason, it seems necessary to discuss the major aspects of human rights concern.

Although human rights, development, the environment, market-oriented economy and democracy have been mentioned as the important concerns of the world community in recent years, human rights is regarded as the basic value for all other values; human values are the fundamental consideration in the activities of states in the global governance of common issues. There is no doubt that human rights will remain the basic value even in the twenty-first century. But it is important to note that the realization of human rights can be ensured by the progress of development. Secretary-General Boutros Boutros-Ghali has stressed development as the more important concern of all nations; he even stated that the twenty-first century should be the development century.[8] This assertion may be better understood when we see that development as a broad concept contains five dimensions which are inter-linked: peace as the foundation, the economy as the engine of progress, the environment as the basis of substantiality, justice as a pillar of society, and democracy as good governance (see *Global Ethic, Human Rights Laws and Democratic Governance*).[9]

Above all, the right to development makes the important part of fundamental human rights which is the most secure basis for peace.[10] Its relationship to human rights and democracy was set forth as mutually reinforcing at the World Conference of Human Rights held at Vienna in June 1993 (see *Peace and Social Development*). In the Vienna Declaration and Programme of Action, the Conference reaffirmed "the right to development, as established in the Declaration on the Right to Development, as a universal and inalienable right and an integral part of fundamental rights." In connection with this right, the following efforts also should be noted as important: the 1995 World Conference on Women in Beijing, the efforts of the Commission on the Status of Women (established in 1946), the Convention on the Elimination of All Forms of Discrimination against Women, the Convention on the Rights of the Child, and the Vienna Declaration of the World Conference of Human Rights for Women, and the Habitat II Conference on Human Settlement, the "City Summit" in 1996. The success of these efforts will greatly influence the shaping of the vision for the 21st century.[11]

Another related development is that human rights concerns have caused a major change in the structure of international law. As the present legal system is still too state-centric to accommodate new problems, its transformation into a global-oriented system becomes necessary to effectively respond to the changing needs of the world community. This change has already been shown in a movement from classical international law to world law (see *Global Ethic*). Given that globalism has superseded nationalism as the guiding principle of interstate relations, the transition is inevitable in the legal sphere. Indeed, writers have already used the term *world law* or *supranational law* to suggest a new direction for the development of international law. If international law is geared toward the coexistence of states in the age of nationalism, then world law refers to a system for the cooperation of states in the age of globalism.

The basic charateristic of world law lies in its human value-oriented system, where human dignity as the key value provides the political and legal framework for the activities of states. For this reason, Myres S. McDougal and Harold D. Lasswell have proposed a building of world public order based on human dignity which contains the egalitarian and democratic values of the world community.[12] Indeed, the emphasis on human dignity is the main feature of world law as the basic norm of global society.

However, one of the fundamental requisites for human dignity is the effective protection of individual human rights. So far, states have assumed the primary responsibility for the actual implementation of human rights law, but this is no longer acceptable in view of the current trend of growing human rights concerns. The international protection of the individual rights is essential which cannot be left solely to states, particularly if it is the state which has carried out the oppression and discrimination against the individual.

In this situation, we need a system that ensures the involvement of all main organs of the United Nations in human rights cases. The UN Charter (see *United Nations Charter*) provides the ample legal basis for intervention by the UN organs. After all, the Secretary-General represents the common interest of the world; the Security Council has the primary responsibility for the maintenance of international peace and security; the General Assembly has the power to discuss any matters within the scope of the UN Charter; the Economic and Social Council is entrusted with the actual responsibility to promote universal respect for, and observance of, human rights and fundamental freedoms. Although these organs clearly have the power and mandate to be actively involved in the promotion of human rights, however, their legal standing before international tribunals needs to be improved in human rights cases.

As part of efforts to provide effective international protection of human rights, the establishment of a regional court of human rights may be recommended for regions where such a court is unavailable. The United Nations Secretary-General, the General Assembly, the Security Council, and the Economic and Social Council should be given special rights and responsibility to present cases involving human rights violations before both a regional court and the International Court of Justice (ICJ) (see *International Court of Justice*). Secretary-General Boutros-Ghali has already made some recommendations for the increased use of the ICJ, such as endowing the Secretary-General with the power to utilize the advisory competence of the Court and the withdrawal of states' reservations to the jurisdiction of the Court by the end of this decade.[13]

All in all, it is undeniable that the protection of human rights has made some progress due to the conclusion of numerous multilateral agreements which create international obligations for states (see *International Law*). International norms and rules of human rights are spread throughout many different documents. The United Nations has helped produce about 70 instruments of the International Bill of Human Rights (see *International Bill of Human Rights*), which identify various rights and freedoms of the individual. Even so, the fact that international law provides norms and regulates compliance is far from enough for the promotion of human rights. The effective protection of human rights calls for the total involvement of the United Nations.

## 5. The Roles of the United Nations

Under the Charter, the UN is given the broad mandate and responsibilities to ensure international peace, economic and social justice, and respect for human rights. But its roles have been different, depending on which issue area it emphasizes as its primary concern. When the UN had focused on the maintenance of international peace and security as its primary concern during the Cold War period, its roles had been very limited and indirect, merely helping Member States settle their disputes in accordance with the procedures of the Charter. That is, the UN placed its emphasis on peace preservation, the promotion of friendly relations of states, and the harmonization of actions and policies of Member States. To achieve the objectives of these activities, the various approaches have been applied.

Above all, the UN has employed an approach to the resolution of conflicts by isolating and restraining the crisis situation, while developing conditions congenial for the peaceful resolution of them and putting political and moral pressures on the parties to the conflict. Its activities relating to the procedures of conflict resolution include the provision of normative prescription for Member States' behavior. The UN makes international regulation of armaments for Member States and seeks to contain the conflict, in which the UN Secretary-General is often delegated great responsibilities.[14]

The UN also facilitates mediation, negotiation, conciliation and agreement for the resolution of international disputes (see *Pacific Settlement of International Disputes*).[15] As Secretary-General Dag Hammarskjöld pointed out,[16] it could serve as the most effective instrument of conciliation diplomacy, if properly used. Being different from the form of traditional diplomacy, it provides a constitutional framework that encourages Member States to conduct concrete diplomatic negotiations. However, it should be noted that the UN cannot be a substitute for the efforts of normal mediation and conciliation procedures.

Another important role of the UN is to promote the moderation of states involved in disputes through debates; it could prevent the deterioration of disputes by providing the cooling-off period, and help states to make face-saving concessions for the resolution of disputes. But it should be warned that debates in the General Assembly are often directed to the domestic political audience more than to the persuasion of other parties to disputes.[17]

When the UN began to shift its major emphasis from international peace to distributive justice with the rise of the Third World states in the 1960s, however, its roles became more regulatory but indirect through the involvement of Member States. These are reflected in the following functions.

First of all, the United Nations articulates the common interest of the world community, and suggests the direction of action for states. It is useful as an ideal observation post for the exchange of information.[18] Indeed, the UN can be the good source of information and the place for initiating contact with many member states without political constraint. It offers the opportunities for Member States to evaluate national interest and a diplomatic arena inducing negotiation. It performs the function of collective legitimization by approving or disapproving the actions or policies of Member States.[19] It helps organize international cooperation by providing an institutional framework. The UN contributes to consensus-building of Member States on international issues; it plays a central role in setting the priority of issues. It facilitates constructive negotiations in various fields by assisting in perception, investigation and analysis of issues in advance.[20] The world organization serves as a forum for mobilizing world public opinion.

At present, international organization makes more and more decisions on international agenda, but in this process it helps activate political coalitions by bringing representatives and officials of governments together; and it plays an important part in making potential political coalition of governments a clear transgovernmental one by developing centralized authority through direct communication. In particular, international organization can serve as a useful arena for the political initiative of small and weak states because most of its norms emphasize equality, and social and economic equity of all states.[21] It has an important meaning as a forum where they could use linkage strategies to achieve their political objectives, using the majority power.[22] Indeed, the UN has played an important role in implementing distributive justice; it has been the center for promoting cooperation between developed and developing countries.

The United Nations represents an institutional manifestation of restraints that the international system imposes on states; it has acted as the systemic modifier of state behavior. By so doing, it has greatly contributed to the stabilization, flexibility and efficiency of international politics.[23]

However, as humanity becomes a new focal point in UN politics in the 1990s, the nature of the UN roles has changed to be direct and regulatory. It has increasingly assumed the main responsibility for the protection of human rights. For this, the UN plays a central role in developing world order values, devising concrete action programs based on global consensus, coordinating various activities, and defining the direction of multilateral cooperation. Now it has the major responsibilities in three issue areas—the maintenance of international peace, the implementation of distributive justice, and the promotion of human dignity. But if we look at the relationship of these three areas, it is easily seen that the UN seeks to discharge its responsibilities for global governance of peace and distributive justice within the framework of human dignity, which involves regulation and enforcement on the global level (see *Global Peace and Global Accountability*).

First, the global governance of humanity involves international rule-making. The UN collectively manages global problems through the provision of common behavioral rules for actors. It plays an important part in establishing norms and rules governing the behaviors and policies of states. Without these rules, their global relations would end in the state of anarchy. However, such rules of behavior are not made by states individually. These are the product of their collective decisions.

International law should be made more forward-looking if it is to remain effective in the changing global environment. As noted above, this calls for the transformation of the traditional state-centric international law system into a world law system which performs a dynamic role as the instrument of social engineering to realize the basic values of the world community—peace, distributive justice and human dignity. This function involves a process of clarifying and implementing common interests for the equitable allocation of values among the peoples, not states, of the world. The result is that the function of international law has changed from regulatory to protective and distributive.

Second, global governance calls for the enforcement of the UN decisions and international norms backed by sanctions. The effective enforcement of world law is a critical point. The international law of human rights, which has major implications for global peace and stability, cannot afford to continue as an unpracticed and disregarded system in the global community. For this reason, some minimal coercive measures are needed to uphold the system. Sanctions are an essential tool for enhancing the credibility of the United Nations as a champion of individual human rights. Past experiences with the use of sanctions have produced a great deal of political frustration. However, the new circumstances of the post-Cold War era have much improved the possibilities of application of sanctions as an effective measure. Now, sanctions are available at the diplomatic, economic and military levels, as stipulated in Articles 41 and 42 of the Charter. In many cases, however,

diplomatic and/or economic sanctions are sufficient to bring states into compliance with international norms and rules of human rights in an interdependent and economy-oriented world; and the current trends of world politics rarely require the use of controversial military sanctions.

In sum, when the UN focused on political and security issues, its role and approaches were essentially passive and indirect. As economic and social issues emerged as the major concern of the world organization in the 1960s and 1970s, its role had become more regulatory, which still remains important and necessary. And human dignity as the new issue area calls for the protective, distributive and regulatory roles of the UN in the 1990s. This means that the UN will have to perform more and more the functions of international regulation and enforcement for the global governance of common issues.

## 6. Conclusion

The dysfunctional political environment of the United Nations has much changed in recent years. Despite many difficulties, the world body will surely develop as the major institution capable of meeting the new challenges of the twenty-first century. This is important in view of the fact that the next century will be the age of international organization. International institutions will make more and more important decisions affecting the actions and policies of states. In particular, the UN will play the central role in protecting individual human rights as a human-oriented world order will develop in the twenty-first century. In this situation, the United Nations emerges as a focal point in international politics and diplomacy, and states will have to pursue their national interests within its framework. In this regard, it may not be too far-fetched to state that a new world order of the post-Cold War era is Pax UN. At present, humankind has no alternative other than the United Nations which will remain as a source of hope and aspiration for peace and prosperity in the next century.

*Notes* ————————————————

1. *General Assembly Official Records (*GAOR*): Thirty-Ninth Session*, 1984, Suppl. No.1 (A/39/1), p. 12
2. Jonathan B, Tucker, "Partners and Rivals: a model of international collaboration in advanced technology, " *International Organization*, Vol. 45, No. 1 (Winter 1991), pp. 83-120.
3. Ernst B. Haas, "Words can hurt you: or Who said what to when about regimes," Stephen D. Krasner (ed.), *International Regimes* (Ithaca and London: Cornell University Press, 1983), p. 44.

4. *Time*, July 20, 1992, p. 56.

5. The Secretary-General's Address to the UN Association of the United Kingdom, *UN Monthly Chronicle*, Vol. III, No. 5 (May 1966), p. 32; "Africa and the World Community," - Address by the Secretary-General in the Algerian National Assembly, February 4, 1964, *UN Review*, Vol. II, No.3 (March 1964), p. 14

6. Richard A. Falk, *Future Worlds*, Headline Series, No. 229 (February 1976), p. 4.

7. James N. Rosenau, "Governance in the Twenty-First Century," *Global Governance*, Vol, 1, No. 1 (Winter 1995), pp. 13-14.

8. Boutros Boutros-Ghali, *An Agenda for Development* 1995 (New York: United Nations, 1995), p. 2, 13, 17.

9. *Ibid.*, p. 20, 26, 31, 37, 44, 49.

10. *Ibid.*, p. 2, 13, 17.

11. *Ibid.*, p. 44, 57, 58.

12. Gray L. Dorsey, "AGORA: McDougal-Lasswell Redux : The McDougal-Lasswell Proposal to Build a World Public Order," *American Journal of International Law*, Vol. 82, No. 1 (January 1988); Myres S. McDougal & Harold D. Lasswell, "The Identification and Appraisal of Diverse Systems of Public Order," *American Journal of International Law*, Vol. 53 (1953), pp. 4-5.

13. Boutros-Ghali, *op. cit.*, pp. 53-54.

14. John G. Ruggie, "The United States and the United Nations: Toward a new realism," *International Organization*, Vol. 39, No. 2 (Spring 1985), p. 346.

15. General Assembly Official Records (GAOR): *Sixth Session*, 1951, Suppl. No. 1A (A/2141/Add.1), p. 2.

16. *GAOR: Twelfth Session, 1957, Suppl. No. 1A* (A/3594/Add.1) p. 3.

17. David W. Ziegler, *War, Peace, and International Politics* (Boston: Little, Brown and Co., 1977), p. 310.

18. Chadwick F. Alger, "Personal Contact in Intergovernmental Organizations," Robert W. Gredd and Michael Barkun (eds.), *The United Nations System and its functions* (Princeton, N.J. : J.Van Nostrand Co., Inc., 1965), p. 108.

19. Inis L.Claude, Jr., "Collective Legitimization as a Political Function of the United Nations," *International Organization*, Vol. 20, No. 3 (Summer 1966), p. 367.

20. Introduction to the Annual Report of the Secretary-General on the Work of the United Nations to the 38th Session, 1983, UN Chronicle, Vol, XX, No.9 (October 1983), p. 79.

21. Robert O. Keohane & Joseph S. Nye, Jr., *Power and Interdependence, World Politics in Transition* (Boston: Little, Brown and Co., 1977), p. 36, 54.

22. *Ibid.*, p. 36.

23. Herbert J. Spiro, *World Politics: The Global System* (Homewood, III: The Dorsey Press, 1966), 152-56.

CHI YOUNG PAK

# Channing, William Ellery

William Ellery Channing (1780-1842) was an ardent defender of human freedom and dignity and an opponent of slavery and war in the early nineteenth century United States. Born into a prominent New England family, he graduated from Harvard in 1798 and took employment as tutor to the children of a large, wealthy family in Richmond, Virginia. There he encountered the institution of Negro slavery, which he immediately condemned as an unnatural violation of a human being's inherent right to liberty. Even after his return to Boston in 1800 to study theology, opposition to slavery remained a major theme of his life and work.

In 1803 Channing became the minister of the Federal Street Congregational Church in Boston, a post which he was to hold for the rest of his life. However, Channing's growing belief in the essential dignity and morality of man, and his belief in a rational, knowable God increasingly put him at odds with the dour Calvinistic traditions of Congregationalism. Though he was loathe to break with the Congregationalists or to form a new sect, in 1820 he did assemble a group of like-minded clerics, forming the nucleus of what soon developed into the Unitarian Church. Unitarianism, which has had a large and influential following among American intellectuals, regards Channing as the principal founder of the denomination.

During his long career, Channing preached and wrote copiously on a wide variety of topics, including most of the social and political problems of his day. His interests included international relations, temperance, education, literature, and the condition of the working class, as well as slavery and theology. The importance of peace was a frequent theme of both his writings and his sermons, and he had a profound influence on the development of American pacifism. Indeed, the well-known Massachusetts Peace Society was founded by him in his own home.

Though the tone of his work was profoundly antimilitary, Channing was not a pacifist himself in the strictest sense of the word. He argued reluctantly that a nation is morally entitled to use military force in self-defense, but only if no other option remains open to it. Channing demonstrated the seriousness with which he held this position in 1812, when his own country declared war on Great Britain. He regarded this struggle as immoral and unjustified and preached eloquently and courageously against it.

Something of Channing's detestation of war can also be found in the lengthy article he wrote in 1827 reviewing a popular biography of Napoleon Bonaparte which had just appeared. Relentlessly he endeavored to strip the mighty conqueror of every vestige of glamor, concentrating instead on the bloodshed and misery which his career had entailed. War and those who waged it, in Channing's view, should never be made to appear glorious.

Channing's commitment to peace was stronger even than his commitment to the eradication of slavery. He incurred much criticism from zealots active in the movement for the abolition of slavery because of his prophetic warnings that too headlong a pursuit of that end could split the nation and lead to war. Civil war, he argued, would be so horrible that it must be avoided at all costs, even at the cost of perhaps prolonging the evil of slavery.

Channing's most complete development of his views on war and peace are contained in a lecture on war which he delivered in 1838. Again he relentlessly attacked the idea of military glory, stressing that war is a horror which should be entered into only as a last resort, if all other means of self-defense have failed. Such arguments, and the respect which his views inspired, have earned Channing a reputation as one of the founders of the peace movement in the United States.

*Bibliography*

Channing W E 1972 *Discourses on War.* Garland, New York

Edgell D P 1955 *William Ellery Channing: An Intellectual Portrait.*

Patterson R L 1952 *The Philosophy of William Ellery Channing.*

Ramsey P 1961 *War and the Christian Conscience.*

GARRETT L. MCAINSH

# Chateaubriand

François René de Chateaubriand was a Breton, born in St. Malo on September 4, 1768. A younger son, he seemed destined for minor orders in the Catholic Church but did not seem enthusiastic about them. Then his older brother, Jean Baptiste, procured him a commission as a second lieutenant in the Navarre Regiment and had him presented to King Louis XVI, giving a new orientation to his career plans. The coming of the French Revolution altered those plans, however. The Navarre Regiment was disbanded. With little else to do, in 1791 Chateaubriand visited North America, perhaps venturing into territories now included in the Gulf of Mexico states. Did he also, as he claimed, meet George Washington? At present such a meeting can neither be proved nor disproved. On returning to France, he married and, soon afterwards, leaving his new wife behind, joined the Army of the Princes, which hoped to restore the Old Regime. He saw action at Thionville and Verdun. Wounded, suffering from smallpox, he was discharged and chose to go into exile. Still sick, he made his way first to Jersey, then to England, arriving in May 1793. Here he remained, publishing in the meantime his *Essai sur les révolutions anciennes et modernes* (1797), until 1800.

Back in France, the Revolution had run its course by this time. As First Consul, Napoleon Bonaparte had restored order and was encouraging the exiles to return. It was believed that a concordat would be worked out with Rome and that the church doors, closed since the worst of the Revolution's excesses, would be reopened. At a friend's urging, Chateaubriand decided to return. He landed at Calais on May 8, 1800 and proceeded to the capital. Soon he was involved in its literary ferment. He appears to have begun his *Génie du christianisme* in England, and whatever portions of it he had written he brought with him. Anxious to acquire a reputation as quickly as possible, he detached an episode and, on April 2, 1801 published it as the novella *Atala.* The tale recounts the woes of an Indian princess, Atala, who frees her lover Chactas, scheduled to be executed by her tribe, and flees with him into the wilderness. Unsure that she can live up to a vow her mother once made that she remain a virgin, she drinks poison, repents, and dies beneath the eyes of Chactas and a kindly missionary, Fr. Aubry. Literary traditionalists scolded, but the story, couched in a resplendent new poetic prose, was a sensation, and Chateaubriand's literary career was launched. He took a mistress, Pauline de Beaumont.

On April 8, 1802 France's new concordat with Rome became the law of the land. Now traditional Catholicism, repressed during the Revolution, was not only permitted but fashionable. Six days after the concordat became law, the *Génie du christianisme,* which was to be Chateaubriand's most important work, appeared. The author was—and still is—accused of opportunism. Whether the accusation is deserved or not, certainly the book was timely. Divided into four parts dealing with Dogma and Doctrine, the Poetics of Christianity, Literature and the Arts, and Worship, it posits the thesis that Christianity is a "poetic" religion and that its themes and stories are better suited to inspire artistic and literary creativity than had been the myths, legends, and historical deeds of Greek and Roman antiquity, which had furnished so much subject matter for French classical art and literature. Chateaubriand's book was an esthetic presentation of Christianity, one in which doctrine counted less than sentiment and emotion. To illustrate one of his ideas, the author included in it the novella *René*, with which he created the French Romantic hero. René, with no deep religious beliefs and tormented by vague drives he does not understand and cannot channel, is unable to cope with life in a civilized social order and goes to live among a tribe of American Indians. Here, no happier than he had been earlier, he manages to get killed in a struggle between the Indians and a nearby colony of European settlers. Chateaubriand's avowed moral purpose, as Fr. Souël, a character in the novella, defines it, was to show that "Solitude is harmful for the individual who does not live in it with God." However, Chateaubriand made his hero so pathetic and so attractive that the message was lost on most readers, who chose to lament René's misfortunes rather than deplore his lack of character and direction.

As the book went to press, Chateaubriand wrote articles for the *Mercure*, biding his time and hoping. Soon the waiting was over, and he had the public's verdict. The *Génie du christianisme* was an enormous success. Overnight its author became the talk of the literary world in France and even outside of France. At about this time he also acquired two powerful protectors, the First Consul's sister and brother, Elisa and Lucien. Back in London, he had considered dedicating the book to the exiled Louis XVIII. In Paris he thought better of it and, starting with the second edition, dedicated it instead to the First Consul. As we have seen, the sympathetic treatment of Christianity coincided with the First Consul's policies. Soon Chateaubriand had been named French Embassy Secretary in Rome, serving under the first Consul's uncle, Cardinal Fesch. In Rome he committed blunder after blunder, living openly with Pauline de Beaumont, who died of tuberculosis, and alienating Cardinal Fesch. He was sent home. Named French Minister to the Valais, in Switzerland, he did not move on to his new post, finding a pretext to remain in Paris. In keeping with Mme de Beaumont's last wishes, however, he returned to his wife. He nonetheless learned to leave her at home when he went out. Mme de Chateaubriand accepted the situation and proved to be no hindrance to his social life. By now his current love was Delphine de Custine.

The First Consul became Emperor Napoleon I in 1804. Chateaubriand claims in his memoirs to have broken with Napoleon when the latter had the Duc d'Enghien, a Bourbon prince, kidnapped and executed. His correspondence shows that this was not the case and that he continued to court members of the imperial family. The Emperor intervened personally to have him elected to the Académie Française in 1811, although the new academician could not be formally installed because his acceptance speech was politically unacceptable. Napoleon also asked the Académie Française why it had not awarded the *Génie du christianisme* a prize. Nevertheless, despite these indications that he enjoyed imperial favor, Chateaubriand was offered no important post in the government, and he sulked.

Next he decided to write a prose epic called *Les Martyrs*, which would deal with the persecution of Christians under the Roman emperor Diocletian. To collect material, he needed to visit the Near East. Mme de Chateaubriand was allowed to go with him as far as Venice and was then sent home. With his servant Julien Chateaubriand sailed on July 28, 1806. He saw Greece, Constantinople, Bethelehem, Jerusalem, the Jordan River, the Dead Sea, Jaffa, the Nile, Alexandria, Cairo, the Pyramids, Tunis, and Cadiz. Throughout the trip, Spain had been as great an attraction as the Holy Land, for there he was to rendezvous with a new love, Natalie de Noailles, with whom he shared ecstatic moments in Granada, at the Alhambra. Travelling back to France, the lovers discreetly parted company at Bayonne, returning to Paris in separate conveyances. Chateaubriand reached home in June 1807. *Les Martyrs* appeared in 1809. With no allusions to Mme de Noailles, an *Itinéraire de Paris à Jérusalem* came out in 1811.

With the French invasion of Russia in 1812, Napoleon's star began to wane. Chateaubriand had not obtained as much as he would have liked from the fallen Emperor. He decided to try his luck with the Bourbons. When the Allies entered Paris in April 1814, he was ready with an opportune pamphlet, *De Buonaparte et des Bourbons*. As Lieutenant General of the Realm, Charles, Louis XVIII's brother, reached Paris on April 12, and Chateaubriand was presented to him. He was also on hand when Louis XVIII arrived several weeks later, presenting his people with a constitution he called a charter. The king wished to reward Chateaubriand for his pamphlet, and an ambassadorship was found at the court of Sweden. Paris was the new ambassador's social and intellectual center, however, and he was in no hurry to go to Stockholm. Besides, there might be more important prizes to be won if he remained under the King's eyes. Then, suddenly, Napoleon returned to France from exile on the island of Elba. In panic, Louis XVIII fled ingloriously to Ghent, and Chateaubriand went with him. There was no interior for him to manage, of course, but, during his new exile, he held the title Minister of the Interior all the same. Soon the Battle of Waterloo ended Napoleon's career for good, and the Second Restoration was in power. Louis XVIII named Chateaubriand a Peer of France but appointed him to no active post in the government, although he was a nominal Minister of State. Hurt, Chateaubriand grew critical, as was his habit, and wrote another pamphlet, *La Monarchie selon la charte*, which appeared on 9 September 1816. The police seized it, and Chateaubriand lost his title of Minister of State and, with it, the 24,000 francs a year that went with the title. He was now an outsider. He then founded the *Conservateur*, an opposition newspaper which, while monarchist, insisted that the Charter be scrupulously observed. The paper was suppressed. Financially, Chateaubriand, whose wisdom in money matters was never remarkable, was having problems. In the spring he had to sell his library. Soon he had to part with his beloved estate, the Vallée aux Loups. But not all was amiss in 1817. The authoress Claire, Duchesse de Duras, did not have charms seductive enough to make her his mistress, but, accepting her role as advisor, she could use her position as a *grande dame* to mention Chateaubriand's name where it was useful to do so, and mention it she did. Another advisor and protectress at this time was the Marquise de Montcalm. Most important of all, it was in 1817 that Chateaubriand became attached to the exquisite Juliette Récamier, who was to be his mistress for the rest of his life. Mme de Chateaubriand consoled herself by founding the Infirmerie Marie Thérèse, a hospice for aged ladies and retired priests.

For the remainder of Louis XVIII's reign, Chateaubriand was a leader of what might be called, generally, the loyal opposition, making speeches and writing pamphlets against government censorship and, in general, attacking policies that he viewed as unwise. Several diplomatic appointments, less to reward him than to get him out of Paris where his constant criticism could cause the government trouble, came his way. Thus he was Minister to Berlin in 1821 for a few months, intriguing the whole time to return to Paris as quickly as possible. In 1822 he was Ambassador to London. From there he succeeded in having himself named a plenipotentiary to the Congress of Verona, which convened in the autumn of 1822 and decided to send help to Spain's King Ferdinand VII, a prisoner of his parliament, which had forced a liberal constitution upon the hapless, stubborn monarch. France, it was decided, would send an army to his aid. In 1838 Chateaubriand would publish the *Congrès de Vérone*, then incorporate it into his memoirs. As Chateaubriand was preparing to return to London, the unexpected happened. The Minister of Foreign Affairs resigned, and he was offered his post. He accepted quickly and on January 1823 took possession of the Ministry. The French invasion of Spain, which we shall come back to later, followed.

During his tenure as Minister and despite his relationship with Mme Récamier, Chateaubriand found time to carry on a passionate liaison with Cordélia de Castellane and still another with Fortunée Hamelin. Then suddenly, on June 6, 1824, he was dismissed. Louis XVIII died three months later, and he hoped much from Charles X, the new king. At first these hopes seemed warranted, when censorship was temporarily abolished. But Charles proved no more anxious to have Chateaubriand in the government than his brother had been. Meanwhile, Chateaubriand was publishing an edition of his complete works that included the *Voyage en Amérique, Les Natchez*, and *Les Aventures du dernier Abencérage*, written much earlier and inspired by his visit to Grenada with Natalie de Noailles. In 1828 he worked on his tragedy *Moïse*, largely written in 1811 and 1812 but not published until 1831. In 1828 he was named Ambassador to Rome, where he remained until 1829. As usual, he had a romantic involvement while there, this one with a Frenchwoman then in Rome, Hortense Allart. While he was on leave in France the appointment of a new Minister of Foreign Affairs, the reactionary Prince Jules de Polignac, was announced. Chateaubriand resigned. Three months later Polignac was Prime Minister and, in less than a year, his policies, seconded by Charles's obstinacy, brought on the Revolution of 1830 and with it the Bourbon's overthrow.

With a revised Charter, the Bourbon's cousin, the opportunistic Duc d'Orléans, became king of the French, taking the name Louis Philippe. Hoping to add a measure of luster to his reign, he tried to coax Chateaubriand, whose prestige as a man of letters and whose position on the censorship question were known to all, to join his government. Loyally, Chateaubriand refused to serve a king he viewed as a usurper. His political career was over. He resigned his positions as Peer of France and Minister of State and the income that went with them, and the stipend he received as a member of the Académie Française he declined as well. It was a noble gesture—it left him penniless.

But the aura that surrounded him as France's most renowned literary figure nonetheless remained undiminished. Over the next few years he used it, writing brochures which, it was hoped, would help the exiled Bourbons regain their throne. The first of these was *De la restauration et de la monarchie élective* (1831). It was followed by *De la nouvelle proposition relative au bannissement de Charles X et de sa famille* (1831). When the Duchesse de Berry, Charles's widowed daughter-in-law, was captured while attempting a legitimist coup in favor of her son the Duc de Bordeaux (Comte de Chambord), Chateaubriand penned still another pamphlet, the *Mémoire sur la captivité de Mme la duchesse de Berry* (1833), that ended with the ringing words, soon to be famous, "Madam, your son is my king!" The July Monarchy put Chateaubriand on trial, covered itself with ridicule, and had to watch, impotent, while a jury acquitted him. However thankless the Bourbons had generally been toward him, Chateaubriand continued to work in their behalf. Several times he acted as the Duchesse de Berry's emissary in her taut relations with Charles X. As for his financial resources, these were as bad as they had ever been. Still, when Charles offered to resume his Peer of France pension, he refused, although he later accepted it from the Comte de Chambord.

Meanwhile, he finished some *Etudes historiques* and an *Histoire de France*. In 1836 he published a remarkable translation of Milton's *Paradise Lost*, which he had always revered, and with it a rather personal *Essai sur la littérature anglaise*. Still, his need for money did not abate. In June 1836 an association was formed to guarantee him (and Mme de Chateaubriand, should she survive him) and income. In return, his memoirs, which he had been working on intermittently since his days at the Vallée aux Loups, would belong to the association and the association would publish them after his death. When the association sold its rights to the newspaper entrepreneur Emile de Girardin in 1844, Chateaubriand was enraged to learn that his monumental work would appear in installments in a newspaper before coming out in book form, but there was nothing he would do. While he saw little likelihood that a Bourbon restoration would ever come about, he continued to lend his name to the cause. Twice, in 1843 (London) and 1845 (Venice), he attended Bourbonist conclaves that had as their object to promote the Comte de Chambord's claims to the throne.

Persuaded to do so by his spiritual advisor, in 1844 he published a *Vie de Rancé*, a biography of Armand Jean Le Bouthillier de Rancé, who in the seventeenth century had initiated the Trappist reform. Full of digressions, many of them personal, the book was received with only moderate praise when it came out, but today it is looked upon as containing passages representative of Chateaubriand's best work. Apart from *René*, so important because it created the French Romantic hero, perhaps Chateaubriand's most important work is the posthumous *Mémoires d'outre-tombe*. With their majestic language, their vivid though biased commentaries on people and events, their penetrating insights into the social and political movement of the late eighteenth and early nineteenth centuries, these memoirs, even without the *Génie du christianisme*, would assure Chateaubriand an eminent place in literary history. As their author had planned, they appeared after his death, which occurred on July 3, 1848. Although Chateaubriand was correct in suspecting that there would be no Bourbon restoration, he did live to see the July Monarchy overthrown and the Second Republic proclaimed.

A word remains to be said about Chateaubriand and his attitude towards war and peace. We have seen that, as a young man with no clearcut ideas as to what career he would choose, he allowed his brother to procure him a military commission. He was not meant to be a soldier, however. When he returned from America, he saw honorable service in the Army of the Princes. Recovering from the wounds and illness that this service entailed, he must have realized that, even for a cause he believed in, fate had not intended him to bear arms. He remained in exile, making no effort to join the counter-revolutionaries in the *Vendée*. But Chateaubriand was by no means opposed to war. He both admired and hated Napoleon, whose victories he could not deny but which he belittled, comparing them unfavorably to Louis XIV's conquests. It was with great pride that, having become French Minister of Foreign Affairs, he took responsibility for the French invasion of Spain in 1823. Bourbon France, he held, needed to show the world that it too, like Napoleon, could win victories. Setting out to prove that it could, he enjoyed referring to the invasion as "my" war.

## Bibliography

Castries René de La Croix de 1974 *Chateaubriand ou la puissance du songe*. Perrin, Paris

Diesbach Ghislain de 1995 *Chateaubriand*. Perrin, Paris

Dubé P H, Ann 1988 *Bibliographie de la critique sur François René de Chateaubriand, 1801-1986*. Nizet, Paris

Guillemin H 1964 *L'Homme des*. Mémoires d'outre-tombe. Gallimard, Paris

Markale J 1986 *Chateaubriand au-delà du miroir*. Imago, Paris

Ormesson Jean d' 1982 *Mon dernier rêve sera pour vous.* Clattès, Paris
Painter G D 1977 *Chateaubriand, a Biography*, I. Chatto & Windus, London
Porter C A 1978 *Chateaubriand. Composition, Imagination, and Poetry.* Anma Libri, Saratoga

Roulin J M 1994 *Chateaubriand. L'Exil et la gloire.* Honore Champion, Paris
Sedouy J A de 1992 *Chateaubriand, un diplomate insolite.* Perrin, Paris

HARRY REDMAN, JR.

# Chauvinism

Chauvinism denotes an extreme form of nationalism usually with militaristic and xenophobic tendencies. The eponym of the word was Nicholas Chauvin, a Frenchman born in Rochefort, France. He became a soldier and took part in many campaigns at the time of the Revolution and Napoleonic Wars. He suffered hardships, including physical wounds, in the battlefields, but remained simple-mindedly loyal to the end to the memory of Napoleonic exploits and to the glory of France, cherishing military honors and the meager pension which had been awarded him.

He was later made a symbol of the cult of military glory in post-Napoleonic France particularly among the veterans of the Napoleonic Wars. This kind of attitude was shortly to be an object of various forms of popular ridicule. When, in the course of the Third Republic, there were conflicts between the civilian and military authorities, the term came to be applied to the militaristic groups which were blamed for trying to militarize the whole society, being hostile to the democratic cause. Removed from the context of French politics at given times, it has been used to describe any kind of blind partriotism regardless of political creeds.

See also: *Jingoism; Nationalism*

*Bibliography* ——————————————

Coubertin P de 1898 *L'evolution française sous la troisième Republique.* London
Curtis M 1959 *Three Against the Third Republic.* Princeton University Press, Princeton, New Jersey
Osgood S M 1960 *French Royalism under the Third and Fourth Republic.* The Hague
Rémond R 1954 *La Droite en France.* Paris
Weber E 1966 France. In: Rogger H, Weber E (eds.) 1966 *The European Right: A Historical Profile.* University of California Press, California
Zevort G 1894 *La France sous le regime de suffrage universel.* Paris

JONG-YIL RA

# Chemical Disarmament

## 1. Introduction

Chemical Weapons (CW) are the subject of the most comprehensive disarmament treaty ever negotiated. The Chemical Weapons Convention (CWC), which entered into force in April 1997, offers the prospect that in a not too distant future an entire class of unconventional weaponry will be eliminated. Nonetheless, it took the international community almost a full century to achieve this result. Even today, some states in unstable regions appear to remain interested in CW. While chemical arms are probably not the most effective battlefield weapons, they can instill terror in entire populations and compel governments to strike preemptively against CW production and storage sites. The presumption of a CW capability in an adversary state can thus magnify the already existing condition of crisis instability.

Fortunately, CW were used in only a small fraction of the many wars this century. Chemical warfare as we understand it today—the military exploitation of the toxic properties of certain chemical compounds against man or his environment—began in 1915 as a means to overcome the stalemate on the Western front. By the end of World War I in November 1918 the novel mode of warfare had caused over a million casualties, including more than 100,000 fatalities. Since then, CW use was confirmed in some colonial wars. Some other major cases include employment by Italy in Abyssinia in the 1930s, by Japan in China in the 1930s and early 1940s, by Egypt in The Yemen in the 1960s and by Iraq against Iran and its own Kurdish population in the 1980-88 Gulf War. In 1995 the world witnessed the first major terrorist incident when an extremely toxic agent was released in the Tokyo underground system.

Banning CW moved from early restrictions on their use to their total prohibition and elimination. The process took almost one century to complete.

## 2. Chemical Disarmament: An Historical Overview

The abhorrence to the use of poison in war can be found in some of the oldest literature of several cultures. During the last century the international community began the codification of the usages and customs of war, which resulted in the 1899 and 1907 Hague Regulations Respecting the Laws and Customs of War on Land. Poison and poisoned weapons became unconditionally outlawed as an expression of the fundamental principles that the means of injuring an enemy are not limitless and that warfare is subject to the humanitarian law. By the end of the 19th century discoveries in organic chemistry pushed industrial development in Europe and the United States forward. Fear of the military exploitation of the toxic properties of some of the new compounds led to the adoption of the 1899 Hague Declaration (IV, 2) Concerning Asphyxiating Gases by which the contracting parties agreed to abstain from the use of projectiles the sole object of which is the diffusion of asphyxiating or deleterious gases. The reference to projectiles, however, enabled the Germans to claim that their first large-scale cylinder attack in April 1915 did not violate the laws of war as no shells were involved.

In hindsight, the 1899 Hague Declaration (IV, 2) raised some fundamental questions regarding the impact of emerging technology on warfare and the precise meaning of humanity in war. As technology was perceived to be value-neutral, no compelling necessity to restrain it as such was experienced. The moral judgement was reserved for its application in war. Consequently, the agreements of the time placed constraints on the use of certain types of weapons and did not apply to weapons themselves. Humanity in war also began to assume a double meaning. On the micro-level, the unnecessary suffering of the individual or non-combatant could be ameliorated by regulating certain modes of warfare or banning weapons that cause superfluous injuries or are perfidious. On the macro-level, modern technology offered the possibility of making war so violent and destructive that fighting could only be of short duration and therefore cause far fewer overall casualties. Humanity in war was thus transmuted into a statistic expressed as a tally of dead, wounded and recoveries from injuries. Based on these arguments, the United

States, for example, refused to accept the Hague Declaration (IV, 2) in 1899. The latter argument featured prominently among proponents of CW armament. The 1993 CWC halted most of the debate by delegitimizing the entire class of weapons. However, the calls for non-lethal technologies, which include incapacitating chemicals, demonstrate that the discussion has shifted yet again.

Following World War I, the major Allied powers attempted to translate the widespread revulsion against chemical warfare into an international prohibition on the use of such weapons. The 1922 Washington Treaty Relating to the Use of Submarines and Noxious Gases in Warfare, concluded between France, Italy, Japan, the United Kingdom and the United States, never entered into force because France refused to ratify it for reasons unrelated to chemical warfare. Feeling strongly about chemical warfare, the United States submitted a proposal to prohibit the trade in chemical munitions to the League of Nations 'Conference for the Supervision of the International Trade in Arms and in Implements of War' in 1925. The subsequent discussions led to the adoption of the Geneva Protocol for the Prohibition of Use in War of Asphyxiating, Poisonous or Other Gases, and of Bacteriological Methods of Warfare (see *Biological Weapons Convention: An Overview*). Until the entry into force of the CWC in 1997, the 1925 Geneva Protocol remained the sole document constraining the employment of toxic chemicals in war. It has some major shortcomings. First, several major contracting parties attached reservations. They declared that the Protocol binds them only as regards other states that have also signed, ratified or acceded to it. They also stated that the Protocol will cease to be binding on them if they were first attacked with CW by another contracting party or any of its allies. Thus reduced to a no-first-use statement, the agreement did not remove the justification for chemical armament and preparations for chemical warfare. Second, the document did not contain any verification mechanisms if use was alleged nor did it provide for sanctions in the case of a proven violation. The agreement nonetheless gained great moral authority and acted as a major constraint on preparations for and resort to chemical warfare. From the mid-1960s onwards, as a consequence of massive US employment of lachrymatory and anti-plant agents in the Viet Nam War, the United Nations General Assembly adopted several resolutions interpreting the scope of the Geneva Protocol and inviting states to accede to it so as to make it as universal as possible. Today, 132 states are parties to the Geneva Protocol. Several states have also withdrawn their reservations in recent years.

During the first half of the 1930s, negotiations were conducted in the League of Nations to reduce the levels of armaments. Several proposals contained clauses to prohibit the development and production of chemical and biological weapons in peacetime and to destroy existing stockpiles. A special committee was set up to deal with issues such as the definition of chemical and biological weapons, the verification of treaty compliance and the imposition of sanctions in case of violations. In March 1933 Great Britain submitted a far-reaching draft treaty containing a definition of CW that included lachrymatory and incendiary agents. In an entirely new development, the agreement would also have prohibited the use of CW against non-parties to the treaty. The right of retaliation was maintained. Resort to biological weapons, by contrast, would have been banned under all circumstances. The disarmament conference ceased its activities in January 1936 as a consequence of the worsening international climate in Europe and Asia. Italy resorted to CW in the Abyssinian campaign and the international community failed to take coherent action. Military thinkers all over the world began to realize the awesome potential of fleets of bombers armed with chemical bombs against enemy cities and several European powers instituted extensive civil defence programmes. The 1930s ended with great fears of massive employment of CW in the next war.

Apart from Japanese operations in China, CW were not used in World War II. After the defeat of the Axis powers the class of weapons was totally overshadowed by the advent of the atomic bomb. CW mostly disappeared from the disarmament scene until the late 1960s, when events in Viet Nam prompted the United Nations to prioritize chemical and biological disarmament. While the discussions in the 1930s obviously ended in failure, the British draft had sown the seeds for the Chemical and Biological Weapons (CBW) disarmament treaties in the latter part of the 20th century. In particular, it heralded the shift away from constraining their use in war to the total abolition of a particular class of arms in peacetime.

## 3. The 1993 Chemical Weapons Convention

On January 13, 1993 the Convention on the Prohibition of the Development, Production, Stockpiling, and Use of Chemical Weapons and on their Destruction was opened for signature in Paris. To date it is the most comprehensive disarmament treaty. It contains elaborate verification measures and lays down certain rules of interstate behaviour in peace and war. It entered into force on April 29, 1997, almost one century after the first agreement restricting the use of projectiles with asphyxiating and deleterious gases. As of February 28, 1997, 161 states had signed the CWC and 70 had ratified it.

Negotiations on the CWC began in 1968 within the framework of the UN Eighteen-Nation Committee on Disarmament (The forum changed name several times: the Conference of the Committee on Disarmament (1969-79), the Committee on Disarmament (1979-84), and, until now, the Conference on Disarmament). An agreement on CBW almost immediately proved difficult to achieve. A two-step approach was chosen instead, by which the issue of biological disarmament was addressed separately. Although the negotiations were still complex, especially in the cold war context in which countries aligned themselves in blocs, the Convention on the Prohibition of the Development, Production and Stockpiling of Bacteriological (Biological) and Toxin Weapons and on their Destruction (BTWC) was signed at London, Moscow and Washington on April 10, 1972, and entered into force on March 26, 1975. The convention, however, lacks verification measures. Violations or allegations of BW use have proved difficult to follow up. Four review conferences have meanwhile considered several confidence-building measures. In September 1994 an Ad Hoc Group of Governmental Experts (VEREX) reported to a Special Conference of States Parties that verification measures were possible. A new *ad hoc* group is now attempting to establish a supplementary Verification Protocol, which should be ready before the next review conference in 2001. Negotiations have been complicated by rapid progress in biotechnology and genetic engineering, which offer the distinct possibility of designer agents and antidotes that would make biological warfare controllable.

The BTWC also committed states parties to further negotiations on CW disarmament. During the late 1970s the marked deterioration of East-West relations added to the complexities of banning a proven weapon. The positions on politically sensitive issues such as the nature and extent of verification measures remained far apart. Nevertheless, individual states or groups of states submitted a large number of working documents, including draft conventions. A series of bilateral negotiations between the USA and the USSR in the late 1970s and early 1980s also failed to achieve a breakthrough. The slow progress of the negotiations led to the development of the idea of a CW-free zone in Europe. NATO rejected the proposal because it would have undermined its retaliatory option as NATO would have been forced to transport chemical munitions from across the Atlantic Ocean in the event of initiation of chemical warfare by the Warsaw Pact. The idea died silently when East-West relations improved greatly during the latter half of the 1980s and a global ban on CW became a distinct possibility. The extensive use of CW in the 1980-88 Iraq-Iran War added urgency to the talks in Geneva.

In 1984 an important milestone was reached when the negotiators agreed on the basic structure of a preliminary draft treaty, based on a proposal submitted by the United States. A second series of bilateral talks between the United States and the former Soviet Union between 1986 and 1991 gave impetus to the multilateral process. In particular, both parties began exchanging detailed information on their respective CW stockpiles and committed themselves to verified destruction. The USA also agreed to end the controversial programme for the production of binary chemical munitions, which it had begun in 1987. The experience of the threat of chemical warfare in the 1990-91 Gulf War enabled the negotiators at the Geneva Conference on Disarmament to reach final agreement.

The overall purpose of the CWC is to prevent the possibility of CW use. In contrast to the 1925 Geneva Protocol it does not allow for reservations. States parties can never under any circumstances engage in any military preparations for offensive chemical warfare, and therefore forego the option of in-kind deterrence or retaliation. The CWC also prohibits the use of riot control or anti-plant agents as methods of warfare.

A key element in defining the CWC's scope is the so-called 'general purpose criterion.' Not the objects themselves, but certain purposes to which they may be employed, are prohibited. The convention thus defines CW as any toxic chemical or its precursors intended for purposes other than those not prohibited by the CWC as well as munitions, devices or equipment specifically designed to be used with them. Permitted purposes include industrial, agricultural and medical applications, research and development of protection and defence against CW, and domestic law enforcement and riot control. Lachrymator agents or herbicides, for example, are not banned as long as their production and retention are consistent with the goals of the CWC. Some chemicals have essentially no purpose than except for use in the manufacture of chemical warfare agents. They are consequently banned entirely except for small quantities for medical research or the development of protective equipment.

The general purpose criterion affords two major advantages. First, the CWC is not restricted to compounds which are explicitly listed in the convention. Thus, the discovery of a new potential chemical warfare agent will not pose a threat to the CWC regime, because it will be automatically banned if it has no justifiable non-military purpose. Moreover, the research installation or production facility where the new CW agent was made can become the object of inspection under the CWC. Second, the general purpose criterion allows the international community to deal with dual-use commodities. Many of the chemicals covered by the convention have widespread civilian application. Because it becomes possible to distinguish between permitted and prohibited activities, it is not necessary to determine the intrinsic threat posed by a chemical compound.

One of the major objectives of the CWC is the verified destruction of all existing CW stockpiles and production and other CW-related facilities within ten years after entry into force. Not more than an extra five years may be granted in exceptional cases. Upon entry into force all activities at CW production facilities must cease immediately and the installations must be closed within ninety days. The destruction of these facilities is to begin within one year after entry into force of the CWC; destruction of the CW themselves is to begin within two years. A state party is responsible for the destruction of all CW, production and other CW-related facilities on its territory or under its jurisdiction and control, as well as for any CW it may have abandoned after 1925 on the territory of another state party without the consent of the latter. The destruction time frames are counted from the date of entry into force, and states which ratify later face progressively shorter deadlines. States which become parties after the ten-year period must destroy their CW and related installations as soon as possible, based on a schedule negotiated with the Organisation for the Prohibition of Chemical Weapons (OPCW), the international body based in The Hague that was set up by the CWC to organize and oversee implementation.

To ensure compliance, the CWC establishes a comprehensive verification regime which affects both the military sector and civilian chemical industry. It seeks to balance confidence in compliance with the protection of national security interests and industrial proprietary information. Verification consists essentially of regular reporting requirements, on-site inspections and, in the case of well-founded suspicions, challenge inspections.

Each state party must declare all of its CW and related facilities to the OPCW within 30 days after entry into force. It must specify their precise location and the quantities of chemicals involved and submit a general destruction plan. Declarations are also required for abandoned CW and old CW, which were either produced before 1925 or between 1925 and 1946, but have deteriorated to such an extent that they are no longer usable. Based on these declarations, all locations where CW are stored or destroyed will be subject to verification through on-site inspection and monitoring with on-site instruments.

The activities of the chemical industry are monitored through declarations and on-site inspections. The nature of an industrial facility's obligations depends on the types and quantities of chemicals it produces, processes, transfers and consumes. The convention categorizes chemical compounds of particular concern in schedules depending on their relative importance for the production of CW agents or for legitimate civilian manufacturing processes. Each list has different reporting requirements. Schedule 1 contains compounds that can be used as CW and that have few uses for permitted purposes. They are subject to the most stringent controls. Schedule 2 includes chemicals that are key precursors to CW but which generally have greater commercial application. Schedule 3 chemicals can be used to produce CW but are also used in large quantities for non-prohibited purposes. The convention also places reporting requirements on firms which produce discrete organic chemicals not on any of the schedules, and contains special requirements for firms that produce unscheduled discrete organic chemicals with the elements phosphorus, sulphur or fluorine.

If non-compliance with the CWC is suspected any state party has the right to request an on-site challenge inspection on the territory of another state party. The inspected state party may neither refuse an inspection nor improperly restrict the access of the inspection team. The challenge inspection is a politically delicate instrument and serves as a safety net should the routine system fail.

While the CWC attempts to banish chemical warfare, states parties can none the less be faced with a chemical threat or the use of CW by another political entity. The CWC therefore provides for a range of remedial or preventive measures. For instance, it explicitly authorizes states parties to equip themselves with the most efficient protection against CW agents. As chemical agents affect their target through environmental mediation, interposing a barrier will significantly reduce the military advantage an attacker might hope to gain from CW use and thus diminish their attraction. Moreover, the CWC stipulates that each state party has the right to request and receive assistance and protection against the use or threat of use of chemical weapons. The requests for assistance and protection must be made through the OPCW, a guarantee for universal application.

The CWC also deals with the transfer of chemicals among states parties and between states parties and states that are not parties to the convention. In the past, the inability to distinguish unambiguously between chemicals used as warfare agents and those that have peaceful industrial purposes rendered any ban on their trade or transfer impractical because of the impossibility to verify the end use in the recipient state. The general purpose criterion addresses this problem. Each state party is expressly forbidden to transfer chemical weapons, directly or indirectly, to other states parties, non-states parties or subnational entities under any circumstances. It further disallows any activity that would assist, encourage or induce anyone to engage in any undertaking that contravenes the convention. Specific legislation must be adopted by each state party to prevent any natural or legal person from undertaking any activity prohibited by the CWC or illegal activities on its territory.

In addition to their significance for verification and reporting routines, the three schedules of the CWC also form the basis of an export control regime among states parties and between states parties and non-states parties. The overriding criterion is that none of the transactions may contravene the basic purpose of the CWC. Schedule 1 chemicals can be transferred between any two states parties only for research, medicine, pharmaceutical use or protection and only in specified quantities. These chemicals cannot be retransferred to a third state. Such transactions are subject to detailed reporting requirements by both states parties. States parties will be allowed to transfer Schedule 2 chemicals only among themselves three years after the CWC's entry into force. These transactions, however, are not subject to stringent quantitative conditions or reporting requirements like those for Schedule 1 chemicals. During the three years, states parties may continue to transfer such chemicals to nonparties if they obtain an end-use certificate. The transfer of Schedule 3 chemicals is only discussed in relation to non-states parties: there are no quantitative limits. However, the exporting state party must ensure that they will not be used for purposes prohibited by the convention and an end-use certificate is required which meets the minimum stipulations imposed by the convention. Five years after the CWC's entry into force all states parties will meet to consider other measures regarding the transfer of Schedule 3 chemicals to non-parties. End use is the object of routine reporting by a state party or, if the need arises, of verification inspection.

The CWC thus makes a very sharp distinction between states parties and other countries regarding trade relations. States parties are granted overall rights for permitted chemical activities and international cooperation among them. By implication, other countries cannot fully enjoy such rights. This may be seen as an incentive for states to join the CWC.

## 4. Chemical Weapons Proliferation Concerns

CW proliferation is usually described as a lateral spread of precursor chemicals, dual-use high technology and expertise from developed to developing countries. The issue came to the fore in 1984 when it became clear that Iraq was systematically using chemical agents in its war against Iran. It was soon realized that companies from the developed world were knowingly or unknowingly involved in Iraq's CW programme. The governments of Western countries set up national export control policies and began to coordinate their efforts in the Australia Group in 1985. The Australia Group is an informal forum whose current objective is to limit the transfer of chemical precursors, equipment used in the production of chemical and biological weapons, and biological warfare agents and organisms. Sanitized intelligence information regarding proliferation threats is also shared. As of February 28, 1997, 30 states take part in the meetings, while the European Commission attends as an observer. The participants have agreed to apply the decisions of the group in their national export control systems. Initially, the nonproliferation policies were viewed as a temporary measure until the CWC would enter into force.

In January 1989, as the world's leaders were meeting in Paris to restore the authority of the 1925 Geneva Protocol following the Iraq-Iran War, global attention was fixed on Libya's large CW factory at Rabta. West European companies with the assistance from some firms in East Europe and Asia were deeply involved despite the existence of export controls. These events, together with the chemical and biological warfare threat during the 1990-91 Gulf War made governments of the industrialized world advocate a more permanent nonproliferation regime that supplements the CWC.

Nonproliferation policies have generally been directed at state actors. Although proliferation to terrorist or criminal organizations has been considered, it was not until the March 20, 1995 nerve agent attack in the Tokyo underground that the threat moved out of the theoretical realm. The attack caused over 5500 casualties, including twelve fatalities. The extremist religious group Aum Shinrikyo had also released a nerve agent in a residential area of the town of Matsumoto on June 27, 1994, killing 7 and injuring over 200 people. The police investigations revealed the extent to which the group had been able to build up a sophisticated CW production capability. This demonstration of the relative ease with which obscure groups can acquire lethal chemicals, together with the emergence or return of domestic terrorist violence in the United States and Great Britain, has prompted security and emergency services to prepare for the use of chemical or biological agents against unsuspecting people. Governments of several countries have reacted to the events in the Tokyo underground by passing legislation against the manufacture and possession of CW agents. However, strategies for dealing with sub-state actors at the international level still need to be developed.

It is difficult to assess the global CW proliferation threat. The spectacular nature of new information about CW armament programmes in some countries and preoccupation with strengthening export controls have nested the fact that, even according to the worst intelligence estimates, only approximately 13 per cent of all nations are believed to have engaged in some form of CW armament. In World War I reliable evidence indicates that only 17 percent of all nations possessed CW. The figure for World War II was 19 per cent. However, 13 percent is higher than most of the time since 1945. These comparisons may be misleading because available intelligence reports do not define CW capability. Moreover, it is not clear whether some of the alleged proliferators may in fact have chosen not to attempt to acquire an offensive CW arsenal. Despite the apparently rising number of proliferators, the mix of CW possessors may vary at different times. Assessments are further complicated by the indigenous acquisition of knowledge, expertise and technologies by developing countries as part of their legitimate industrialization programmes. Worldwide access to relevant technologies as the result of globalization characterizes much of the proliferation process.

A well-functioning chemical industry is recognized as one of the pillars of sustained economic development. Developing countries increasingly criticize export controls as unilateral, discriminatory measures and demand their abolition after the CWC enters into force. They argue that the CWC commits states parties to remove barriers that restrict or impede trade for legitimate purposes with other states parties and to review their national regulations in the field of trade in chemicals in order to render them consistent with the object and purpose of the CWC. Many developed countries, including the members of the Australia Group, maintain that under the convention they can not under any circumstances assist any state to acquire a CW capability. They argue that the nonproliferation regime supplements the CWC. The controversy has become highly emotional and will dominate the early phases of the implementation of the convention.

*5. Conclusion*

CW disarmament has progressed far since the first attempts approximately one hundred years ago to outlaw their use in war. The CWC is a new start. So far, only three states are publicly known to be holders of CW stockpiles. The US has a stockpile of about 30,000 tonnes of agents and Russia, as successor to the USSR, holds about 40,000 tonnes. Iraq was a major producer of CW, but the greatest part has so far been destroyed under supervision of the United Nations Special Commission on Iraq (UNSCOM) following the 1990-91 Gulf War. The magnitude of the destruction problem will only become clear when states parties to the CWC begin to declare their stockpiles and past chemical warfare related activities.

The CWC holds the best promises for reducing chemical warfare threats by building an environment of confidence and security. Some of its instruments are verification and inspections as well as aid and assistance in the area of chemical warfare defences and in case of an attack. In addition, the aim of the CWC to effectively ban all CW is complemented by the wish to promote the peaceful uses of chemicals. Once all chemical munitions are destroyed and verification has become part of the routine, the promotion of trade and international cooperation in the field of chemical activities to enhance the economic and technological development of states parties may well become the convention's most important function.

See also: *War: Environmental and Biological Theories; Military Restructuring and Convertion*

*Bibliography* ─────────────────

Perry Robinson J P, Stock T, Sutherland R G 1993 The Chemical Weapons Convention: The Success of Chemical Disarmament Negotiations. *SIPRI Yearbook 1993: Armaments, Disarmament and International Security.* Oxford University Press, Oxford
Stockholm International Peace Research Institute 1971-75 *The Problem of Chemical and Biological Warfare*, 6 vols. Almqvist & Wiksell, Stockholm
Zanders J P 1995 Towards Understanding Chemical Warfare Weapons Proliferation. *Contemporary Security Policy*, 16(1) April

JEAN PASCAL ZANDERS; SUSANNA ECKSTEIN

# Christian-Marxist Dialogue for Peace

For more than twenty years (1971-1993) representatives of Christian and Marxist thought have been carrying on a dialogue for peace from different ideological points of view.

This dialogue which started in hard times of the Cold War (see *Cold War*) gave obvious proof that in spite of considerable differences in ideological and political opinions, people of good will are able to understand each other and interact successfully if they take universal human values as a point of discussion.

The participants of this International East-West Dialogue concerning the fundamentals of peace in a pluralistic world were inspired by aspiration for ensuring peaceful periods of humanity's history to replace global military confrontations. The common efforts, as we know today, made contributions such as to the transformation of contacts between Soviet and American presidents into valuable partnership, and to the historical meeting of Soviet President Mikhail Gorbachev (see Nobel Peace Prize Laureates: *Mikhail Gorbachev*) with Pope John Paul II. It can be stated that this dialogue contributed to the peaceful transformation of the European political, military, economic and humanitarian order in 1989/90.

The practical basis for an informal but partly institutionalized dialogue between Christians and Marxists was delivered by the Second Vatican Council. In particular, the pastoral constitution, "The Church in the World of Today" underlined the importance of the dialogue with the aim of serving humankind in the spirit of the gospel.

An important follow-up was supplied by the Institute for Peace Research at the Catholic Theological Faculty of the University of Vienna, which had been founded in response to the initiatives of the Second Vatican Council. This Institute in cooperation with another Vienna-based organization, the International Institute for Peace, began a series of international symposia in 1971 between Christians and Marxists on a scientific and academic level which have since become a regular, almost annual, event. The official title of these "Vienna-based Dialogues" was "Christian-Marxist Dialogue for Peace—The Quest for Peace Beyond Different Ideologies." The participants included a wide spectrum of Christians and Marxists working in the field of peace research and disciplines related to peace research. The purpose of the discussions was a free exchange of information taking into account the different ideological positions. The organization of the symposia has always been in the hands of the two Vienna-based Institutes in cooperation with the institution hosting the actual conference. In 1977 the Institute for Peace and Understanding in Rosemont, Pennsylvania, headed by Professor Paul Mojzes joined the two permanent organizers of the symposia as a cosponsor. All together more than 20 symposia have been held. A list of them follows:

(a) 1971 Vienna: The Search for Peace from Different Ideological Points of View,

(b) 1973 Moscow: Ways and Means for Solving the Problems of Social Developments from Different Ideological Points of View,

(c) 1974 Salzburg (Austria): Weltanschauung and Peace,

(d) 1975 Tutzing (Germany): Peaceful Coexistence and Social Program,

(e) 1977 Philadelphia (USA): Problems of Educating the Youth for Peace and Peaceful Coexistence,

(f) 1978 Kishinyev (USSR): Problems of Disarmament from Different Ideological Points of View,

(g) 1979 Saltsjobaden (Sweden): Peaceful Coexistence from Different Ideological Points of View,

(h) 1980 Detroit (USA): The Quest for Peace Beyond Differing Ideologies,

(i) 1981 Madrid: Ways and Means of Delivering Humanity from the Danger of War and Mass Destruction from Different Ideological Points of View,

(j) 1982 Florence: Dialogue of Florence—Encounter of Different Ideologies for Peace,

(k) 1983 Vienna: Goals of Peace Politics in the World Today: Dialogue of World Views for Peace,

(l) 1984 Hamburg: Realism in Politics,

(m) 1986 Vienna: Problems of Militarization of Space from Different World Views,

(n) 1987 Strassbourg: Humanism and Peace Order—the Right to Live in Peace in the Framework of Human Rights,

(o) 1988 Moskau: Humanistic Internationalism from Different Ideological Points of View in the Framework of the New Political Thinking,

(p) 1989 Leusden (NL): The Human Dimensions of Contemporary Peace: Man, Society, State and International Community,

(q) 1990 York (USA): The Role of Ideology in an Interdependent World,

(r) 1991 Vienna: Political and Cultural Processes in Europe—Towards a New European Identity and Structure,

(s) 1992 Augsburg (Germany): The Political and Cultural Reconstruction of Europe: The Contribution of the Christian Social Teaching,

(t) 1993 Moscow: European Civilization on the Border of the Second Millenary—Democracy, Liberalism, Market and Common Fundamental Values.

As early as 1971, at the first symposium in Vienna, a theologian Professor of the Vienna University, raised the pertinent question, whether such a peaceful communication could not eventually lead to peaceful change. At the same symposium a definition of the principle of peaceful coexistence from the Soviet point of view was outlined by Professor Nikolaj Kowalsky of Moscow University. He said that peaceful coexistence (see *Peaceful Coexistence*) required as a prerequisite multilateral cooperation among states with different social systems. In order to further this principle it was of great importance to carry out educational work among the citizens of the countries in question. The common goal of European security, he said, could be achieved only through the development of all forms of cooperation among European states and peoples and the realization that they were all—to put it simply—in the same boat. Such initiatives on the part of Catholic theologians and Marxist scholars were not uncontroversial at the time. They had to face many difficulties and overcome suspicion in the early stages of the Marxist-Christian dialogue. Since then much has changed, for as the former Austrian Primate and President of the Vatican Secretariat for Non-Believers, Cardinal Franz Konig, put it: "Dialogue has become the key word of the consciousness of our time."

The participants in the symposia generally were academics from the East and West as well as representatives of religious or ideological groups. Originally, attendance was confined to delegates from Eastern and Western Europe. In the course of time the framework of participation was considerably extended. In 1977, when the symposium was organized at Rosemont, North Americans attended for the first time in large numbers. In 1981, at the Madrid symposium, for the first time a delegate from South America addressed the meeting. In 1980 Jewish and Moslem representatives were invited for the first time and did indeed participate in the debate. The number of participants was generally confined to 40 persons to permit the most efficient exchange of views. As for the composition of the participants, care was taken that they should come not only from Eastern and Western countries, but also be selected on the basis of their roots in Christian or Marxist circles. In practice, this meant that Marxist delegates from Western countries also could participate in the symposia. The composition of the Eastern delegates was naturally more uniform. American delegates were invited by the Institute of Peace and Understanding in Rosemont, participants from Western Europe by the University Center for Peace Research at the University for Vienna (formerly the Institute for Peace Research), and participants from Eastern Europe by the International Institute for Peace in Vienna. In the course of time, a team of scholars have emerged who participated in almost every symposium. They were joined by different newcomers in every dialogue whose contributions enriched the variety and quality of the debate.

Most of the discussions took place at plenary sessions. However, ad hoc working groups have been created, consisting of about a dozen participants, devoting themselves to specific subjects. Usually there have been not more than three sucn working groups at every symposium. In addition to these formal discussions it was necessary to stress the importance of informal discussions conducted in and around the symposia. It was in these informal meetings very often that delicate points were discussed which the delegates would hesitate to raise at the formal meetings. And, of course they served as a means for the delegates to get better acquainted and to learn something of the academic and personal background of their opposite numbers. There was no strict separation between theoretical and action-oriented discussions. Naturally, the former were necessary before the latter could be tackled and practical suggestions be worked out.

The basic principle of the symposia had been the recognition of the fact that there should be no attempt by either side to convince the other of the correctness or the superiority of its own point of view. This was put very succinctly at the Swedish symposium by the Lutheran Bishop of the Swedish capital, Ingmar Strom: "We Christians do not expect that determined Marxists will turn into pious Christians by virtue of the strength of our arguments. And we for our part do not intend to accept the Marxist ideology or become confirmed atheists. I believe that this is a sound and positive prerequisite for a practical dialogue. It is our objective to search for concrete solutions for common aims." Thus it can be stated that the symposia were intended for each side to establish the scope of the standpoint of the other and possibly to gain a better understanding of this point of view. The choice of the topics of the different symposia has shown quite clearly that the participants in the discussions were moving away more and more from generalities and were ready to tackle controversial and delicate subjects-topics which on previous occasions would have been avoided out of fear that the dialogue could turn into and unfriendly disputation. The last symposia have demonstrated clearly that such fears no longer existed. Both sides have responded positively to the phenomenon that both Christians and Marxists have learned to distinguish between the ideological and political sphere. They have joined hands in an effort to find ways and means to influence political developments, each of course in his or her own sphere. A most important development has been the adoption at the 1982 symposium in Florence of a set of guidelines for Christian-Marxist dialogue. These are as follows:

(a) Each participant must come to the dialogue with complete honesty and sincerity and must assume the same degree of honesty and sincerity in the dialogue partner(s).

(b) Each participant must be seen as an individual and also as a representative of a certain religious and/or secular world view. All world views represented in the dialogue must be deemed worthy of respect by the participants.

(c) Each world view must be defined only by a participant upholding that world view, that is, Christianity must be defined by a Christian and Marxism by a Marxist. Participants may state what they perceive their dialogue partners to be, but must not make definitive statements about a world view to which they do not subscribe.

(d) Dialogue is not a debate where each participant or group is seeking to gain victory over the other. It is to be understood as a supportive encounter in which each participant listens as openly, carefully, and sympathetically as he or she can to the partner(s), attempting to understand the other world views represented as precisely and deeply as possible.

(e) The primary requirement for authentic dialogue is trust. We cannot trust what we do not know. Therefore, in the earliest phase of dialogue we unlearn misinformation about each other and begin to know each other as we truly are. In the next phase of dialogue we begin to discern values in each other's traditions.

(f) The purpose of dialogue is to use our common positive resources in order to work together in several ways for the good of all humankind, striving particularly to eliminate all threats to world peace.

It turned out that these symposia were very worthwhile. They were a recognition by Marxists that world peace cannot be promoted without Christians and a similar recognition by Christians that they must engage in dialogue with Marxists, despite the general worldwide lack of confidence between individuals and nations holding different world views.

The above describe Christian-Marxist dialogue for peace helped to prepare for glasnost, perestroika and the new political thinking in the former Soviet Union (see *Glasnost and Perestroika*). It contributed to bring about the change in Europe in 1989/90. The change in Europe is still going on. We are confronted with a new European setting but we are far from a new European peace and security order. There is still a long and difficult way to go towards this new peace order in Europe and the world. The present situation for instance in the Balkans and the Middle East can be seen as a backward movement from the opportunity to open a period of stable peace in humanity's history.

Dialogue is the key word for peace of today. More than ever peace and security are based on a process of dialogue. Maybe the above described dialogue could be taken as an example for future dialogues whose specific aim should be to build confidence and trust first among the participants than among national entities and ultimately among nations.

See also: *Eastern Europe, Transformation of*

*Bibliography*

Abtheker H 1970 *The Urgency of Marxist-Christian Dialogue.* Harper and Row, New York

*Christliche Humanitat und Marxistischer Humanismus* (Christian Humanity and Marxist-Humanism) 1996 Paulus Gesellschaft Selbstverlag, Munich

*Christentum und Marxismus Heute* (Christianity and Marxism Today) 1996. Paulus Gesellschaft Selbstverlag, Munich

*Christen und Marxisten im Friedensgesprach* (Christian and Marxist Peace Dialogue) Part I, 1976, and Part II, 1979. Herder Verlag, Vienna

*Christliche und Marxistische Zukunft* (The Future of Christianity and Marxism) 1965 Paulus Gesellschaft Selbstverlag, Munich

Garaudy R, Quenth L 1968 *A Christian-Marxist Dialogue.* Doubleday, Garden City, New York

Girardi G 1968 *Christianity and Marxism.* Macmillan, New York

Mitrokin L 1971 *About the Dialogue of Marxists and Christians.* Voprosi Fillisofii

Mojzes P 1981 *Christian-Marxists Dialogue in Eastern Europe.* Augsburg, Minneapolis, Minnesota

Ogletree T 1968 *Openings for Christian-Marxist Dialogue.* Abingdon Press, Nashville, Tennessee

Piediscalzi N, Thobaben R 1974 *From Hope to Liberation: Towards a New Marxist-Christian Dialogue.* Fortress Press, Philadelphia, Pennsylvania

Pöllinger S 1974-84 Reports on the various dialogues. Wiener Blatter zur Friedensforschung, Nos. 1, 5, 7/8, 13/14, 18, 22/ 23, 26/27, 34/35, 38/39, 42/43, 48/49, 53, 58, 61, 65, 69, 74, 75, 77

Vree D 1976 *On Synthesizing Marxism and Christianity.* Wiley, New York

Weiler R 1976 International peace and peaceful coexistence in Europe and the world. In: *Christen und Marxisten im Friedensgespräch* (Christian and Marxist Peace Dialogue). Herder Verlag, Vienna

SIGRID PÖLLINGER

# Christianity

The brotherhood of man under the fatherhood of God, the basic ideal of Christianity, calls for the maturing of the human race. But in view of today's global international tensions and the unprecedented destructive power of modern weaponry, something like a global psychological metamorphosis would seem to be called for. More than 100 wars have been fought with conventional weapons since the Second World War was brought to a close by the atomic bombs dropped on Hiroshima and Nagasaki. It is highly doubtful that civilization could survive a war in which today's vastly more destructive nuclear weapons would be unleashed.

It is no wonder that all discussion of Christian ideas and ideals seems centered today on the nuclear menace. The possible end of civilization, and perhaps even the end of all human life on earth, is the vital issue facing us. Not that a nuclear freeze can be considered an end in itself. What is required, the churches agree, is unity and cooperation on a global scale in the things that can make for both universal peace and universal justice. The two are closely linked.

The race for nuclear superiority has induced a dangerous benumbment in many people. Yet it has also sparked numerous peace movements in which Christians are associated with others of different beliefs and ways of life who wish to do something about this global threat to life.

In the Bible there are no passages that would seem to have a direct bearing on war on the scale the twentieth century has seen, unless the references to war in Revelation (16:16) are interpreted in a prophetic sense, "Peace" is often used as a salutation or blessing, (Numbers 6:26), though it is derived from the idea of the absence of warfare, and is often associated with victory over enemies (Leviticus 26:6-7) (see *Hebrew Bible and Peace*). Even the slaughter of enemies is sometimes enjoined in the Old Testament, though captured enemy women were to be treated as wives (Deuteronomy 21 :10ff.). In the New Testament Jesus referred to peacemakers as "the children of God" (St Matthew 5:9). In the Epistles, frequent use is made of the phrase "the God of Peace." (see *Peace According to the New Testament*)

Pope John XXIII, in his wide-ranging encyclical letter addressed to all humankind titled *Peace on Earth*, referred to the enormous build-up of armaments, with its "vast outlay of intellectual and economic resources." Not only are the citizens of the nuclear powers "loaded with heavy burdens," but "other countries as a result are deprived of the collaboration they need in order to make economic and social progress."

He went on to say,

Justice, then, right reason and consideration for human dignity and life urgently demand that the arms race should cease; that the stockpiles which exist in various countries should be reduced equally and simultaneously by the parties concerned; that nuclear weapons should be banned; and finally that all come to an agreement on a fitting program of disarmament, employing mutual and effective controls.

He quoted a warning by Pius XII: "Nothing is lost by peace; everything may be lost by war."

Some cogent questions are raised in the Pastoral Statement of the United States Conference of Catholic Bishops: "May a nation threaten what it may never do? May it possess what it may never use? Who is involved in the threat each superpower makes: government officials? or military personnel? or the citizenry in whose defense the threat is made?"

The danger, they say, is clear, "But how to prevent the use of nuclear weapons, how to assess deterrence, and how to delineate moral responsibility in the nuclear age are less clearly seen or stated. Reflecting the complexity of the nuclear problem . . . our 'no' to nuclear war must, in the end, be definitive and decisive."

There is much serious study going on within and among the churches on the threat of a nuclear holocaust. This theme is echoed in the title of the World Council of Churches' paperback "Before it's Too Late," edited by Paul Abrecht and Ninan Koshy, which contains the complete record of the Council's public hearing on nuclear weapons and disarmament (see *Campaign for Nuclear Disarmament (CND)*).

## 1. No Peace Without Justice

This is a recurring theme among the churches. It is the title of an article by John B. Cobb Jr. of the School of Theology, Claremont, California. It is also the subject of the World Council of Churches' document PJ-4, 1983, which makes two closely related statements: "Never before has the human race been as close as it is now to total self-destruction," and "Never before have so many lived in, the grip of deprivation and oppression," Peace and justice are linked together closely by the Council, which points to the 1983 estimate of US$2 billion spent globally every day for armaments (see *World Council of Churches (WCC)*).

A commitment to both peace and justice is regarded as a spiritual obligation also by the World Alliance of Reformed Churches (Presbyterian and Congregational). In the Alliance's quarterly, *Reformed World*, it is stressed that peace is more than an absence of war (see *Positive versus Negative Peace*). Peace means living together as a community in mutual respect, solidarity, and justice. Hunger, poverty, exploitation, discrimination, and repression are all seen as related to the violation of human rights (see *Human Rights and Peace*).

The World Council of Churches, together with the Commission of the Churches on International Affairs, organized a public hearing on nuclear weapons and disarmament in Amsterdam in 1981. Two elements from the record of that hearing were important for the Sixth Assembly of the Council in Vancouver two years later. First, the Council unambiguously rejected the concept of nuclear deterrence (see *Nuclear Deterrence, Doctrine of*). Their report reads, in part, "We wish to state unequivocally that nuclear war fighting is morally wrong, whatever the circumstances." The further question remained "whether the possession of, preparation for the use of, and readiness to use, nuclear weapons should fall under the same condemnation as their actual use." The Vancouver Assembly's answer, in its "Statement on Peace and Justice," was as follows: "We believe that the time has come when the churches must unequivocally declare that the production and deployment as well as the use of nuclear weapons are a crime against humanity, and that such activities must be condemned on ethical and theological grounds." (Gill 1983)

The Board of Congregational Life of the Presbyterian Church in Canada issued a study booklet on *Nuclear Disarmament and the Church* (Maclean 1982). In the preface the Church's Outreach and Corporate Witness Committee stresses the fact that "there is no more crucial issue facing the world today than the threat posed by nuclear weapons," adding that "all other matters pale beside the possibility of extinction of the human race and the devastation of the creation."

## 2. Deterrence versus Disarmament

Deterrence is discussed by Friedhelm Solms in an article titled "Beyond Deterrence." Deterrence assumes that fear will lead the other side to rational political behavior (see *Deterrence*). Solms contends that the opposite is obviously the case.

Olle Dahlen, in the Anglican Consultative Council's "Christianity and Social Order" series, stresses that "what is new is that the Churches have found it impossible to involve themselves in the debate on peace and war without looking for alternatives to the present national security system." He points out that even St. Augustine's doctrine of a "just war," which sought to spell out the conditions under which it was acceptable for Christians to participate in a war, has come under fire from a number of Churches.

## 3. The Just War Doctrine

The roots of the Just War doctrine are to be found in Greek, Roman, and Jewish custom and law (see *Just War; Just War Theory*). Christians in the first three centuries normally abstained from military service, but after the conversion of the Roman emperor in the fourth century. Christian thinkers began to define the conditions under which Christians could fight in a war, namely that the war was just, and was fought with a right intention. It was deemed to be in the interest of the common good that coercion be used against unjust interference.

In discussing this question in the early 1980s, a working party of the Church of England, under the chairmanship of the Bishop of Salisbury stated that "unhappily, once it is accepted that war-making can be morally licit, it is easy to forget the limits which are built into this tradition. Parties to armed conflict have a tendency to abandon restraint and to adopt a stance more akin to that of the Holy War."

Countless individual Christians are today actively involved in peace movements, associating with others who may be of different beliefs and customs, but who wish to do something about the global threats to life. It is important that the individual and collective development and growth opportunities that this earth life affords be fully appreciated. The Christian ideal lends no credence to any notion that this life span is unimportant, or that any life is extendible. Dying for a good cause is noble, but only if it is accepted. Death imposed is murder. Nuclear war is simply murder compounded to the $n$th degree. Hiroshima and Nagasaki will remain an everlasting blot on human history.

## 4. Armageddon

Yet there is a widespread and dangerous belief in certain Christian circles that God is prepared to finish human history, and the "second coming of Christ" is at hand. This thesis was elaborated by Hal Lindsey in his book *The Late Great Planet Earth* which had, by 1985, sold some 20 million copies. Lindsey's book was strongly criticized by the Rev. Tom Harpur, author and broadcaster, as "fatalistic and inexorably violent theology that would see Russia as the source of all terrorism and evil." Harpur also pointed out that in a United States 1985 poll almost two out of five respondents believed that the reference in the Bible to Armageddon (Revelation 16:16) was a prophecy about the inevitability of nuclear war instead of a biblical figure of speech symbolizing that evil will eventually be conquered.

## 5. Implications of Faith in Continuity

Faith in continuity is one of the most cogent concepts essential to Christianity and to any religion that can claim to be universal. The emphasis here is on faith, not simply belief—faith in a progressing, expanding, and continuing personality beyond death.

It is true that even some church-going Christians do not believe in any survival of personality after death, and many more are in honest doubt on that point. But most of such people are expressing faith in continuity by the general tenor of their lives. Logically, a life with no such faith ought to be completely opportunist. Many who are skeptical about life after death, however, live as if they truly believe in it. And that is what matters.

A great deal has been written about life continuing after death, by Christians among others, based on experiences of communication with the departed that they could not deny. The main implication of such experiences for those who have seriously considered such testimony is not simply that life goes on, but the confirmation it affords that what we do, individually and collectively, with the challenges and growth opportunities of this life matters supremely. The "everlasting life" promised to believers in Christ (St. John 3:6) is surely not an undefined state of endless bliss, but an active life, continuous with our earth experiences, ultimately leading to individual and collective fulfillment beyond our present imagining. We will surely have a lot more work and growing to do when we leave this earth life behind. In this connection "reincarnation" is also a sobering Biblical concept (St. John 9:2) offering much food for thought.

Faith in continuity after earth life focuses attention on what we may be called upon to do, here and now Our Maker is not through with us, nor are we through with one another when our individual span of life on earth is finished. Faith in continuity is fundamental both to peace on earth and meaningfulness of life.

Christians hold fast to the idea that humankind was created that we may become "sons of God." But creation is a matter of individual and collective growth and development, effort, and pain. Christians believe that all the suffering involved in our earthly sojourn has a great and glorious purpose.

See also: *Pacifism; Religion and Peace*

*Bibliography*

Abrecht P, Koshy N (eds.) 1982 *Before it's too Late*. World Council of Churches, Vancouver, British Columbia
Church of England Board for Social Responsibility 1982 *The Church and the Bomb: Nuclear Weapons and Christian Conscience*. Hodder and Stoughton, London
Cobb J B 1984 No Peace without justice. *Religious Education* 79(4)
Dahlen O 1984 *Peace and Peacemaking*. Christianity and Social Order Study Series
Gill D (ed.) 1983 *Gathered for Life: Report of the Sixth Assembly of the World Council of Churches*. Vancouver
Harpur T 1985 Apocalypse now? *Toronto Star* (July 14)
Lindsey H 1971 *The Late Great Planet Earth*. Zondervan, Grand Rapids, Michigan
Maclean E M I (ed.) 1982 *Nuclear Disarmament and the Church—A Presbyterian Perspective*.
Pope John XXIII 1963 *Peace on Earth*. Vatican Polyglot Press, Rome
Solms F 1985 Beyond deterrence. *The Ecumenical Review of the World Council of Churches* 37(1)
United States Conference of Catholic Bishops 1983 *The Challenge of Peace: God's Promise and our Response*. United States Catholic Conference

JOHN HARWOOD-JONES

# Churchill, Winston

Winston Leonard Spencer Churchill (1874-1965), British statesman, is chiefly noted for having led his country from despair to victory in the Second World War.

Born into one of Britain's most aristocratic and politically prominent families, Churchill was educated at Harrow and at the Royal Military College at Sandhurst, graduating with a commission as second lieutenant in 1894. The following year he got his first view of war, as an observer of Spanish efforts to put down an insurrection in Cuba. By the end of the century he had also seen action as an officer in campaigns in India and the Sudan. In the latter he participated in one of the last great cavalry charges, at the battle of Omdurman. After this British victory, Churchill was scathing in his criticisms of the British commander over the inhumane treatment meted out to Sudanese wounded and prisoners. He was soon to get a closer view of the problems of prisoners of war. While acting as a war correspondent during the Boer War in 1899 he was captured by the enemy, but was able to effect a dramatic escape.

Churchill was elected to parliament as a Conservative in 1900. Switching to the Liberal Party in 1904, he helped to lay the foundations of Britain's twentieth century welfare state as Home Secretary in 1910 and 1911; then played a key role in modernizing the British fleet in the years just before the First World War, as First Lord of the Admiralty between 1911 and 1915. Forced from office in 1915 because of his identification with the Dardanelles debacle, he promptly volunteered for service with the army in France, seeing action on the Western front.

After the First World War Churchill served first as head of Britain's War Office (1919-21), then as head of its Colonial Office (1921-22). In these positions he was particularly instrumental in prolonging British military intervention in the Russian Civil War, in trying to ensure a pro-British Middle East, and in ending the violence in Ireland. By 1924, Churchill had returned to the Conservative Party and became Chancellor of the Exchequer, a post in which he served until 1929.

Churchill was out of office during the 1930s, his passionate intensity and dogmatic assertiveness having made him many enemies in all parties. Always a prolific writer, with an impeccable grasp of the English language's potential for grace and majesty, he wrote during this period a highly regarded biography of his famous ancestor, the first Duke of Marlborough, whose military genius had done much to save Europe from French domination.

During the late 1930s, Churchill became increasingly alarmed by the rapid increase in the belligerence and military power of Fascist Italy and Nazi Germany, and by the failure of the British government to take any effective countermeasures. Rather than build up its own military strength as a deterrent to aggression, the British government sought to preserve peace by letting the dictators take those things which they demanded. It was hoped that this "appeasement policy" would prevent war, but as Churchill saw, it only whetted the appetites of the dictators and made war inevitable (see *Appeasement Policy*). The Nazi attack on Poland in September 1939 vindicated Churchill, who was quickly restored to office as First Lord of the Admiralty. In the spring of 1940, with all Europe reeling before the Nazi onslaught, Churchill was made Prime Minister. France fell just a few weeks later, leaving Britain without allies, alone against the full fury of the Nazi war machine. Churchill brilliantly rallied the nation by his firm, steady leadership and his inspired oratory, strengthening British determination to fight on against apparently hopeless odds. He became a symbol of British unity and resolve, particu-

larly during the dark days of the Battle of Britain, when the Nazis launched an intensive air assault on Britain in the fall of 1940.

Churchill's stubbornness in refusing to admit defeat bore fruit in 1941, when first the former Soviet Union and then the United States joined Britain in the war. Churchill managed to subdue his intense hatred of communism enough to cooperate with Stalin in defeating Hitler's Germany, but by the war's end he was profoundly worried about the expansion of Soviet power into the heart of Europe. In 1944 he committed British troops to Greece, averting a communist takeover there.

Removed from office as the war came to an end in 1945 by the Labour party's overwhelming election victory, Churchill devoted himself in the next years to working for Anglo-American unity against Soviet aggressiveness, and for the cause of European unity. Having witnessed the European powers wage two exceptionally bloody conflicts during his lifetime, he hoped that through unity they could avoid a third such tragedy. Churchill's dream that a unified, peaceful Europe would emerge from the rubble of the Second World War was shattered by the former Soviet Union's conversion of the areas which its armies occupied into a separate communist bloc. In 1946 he called attention to this development with a vivid and soon famous metaphor. In a speech delivered at a small United States college he mourned that "an iron curtain has descended across the continent . . . . This is certainly not the Liberated Europe we fought to build up. Nor is it one which contains the essentials of permanent peace."

A Conservative victory at the polls made Churchill Prime Minister again in 1951, but failing health forced his resignation four years later. The ten years remaining to him after that were devoted to bringing out a four-volume study of the role which the English-speaking peoples have played in the history of the world.

While Churchill's greatness is indisputable, he has never been without detractors as well as admirers. His fervid opposition to freeing Britain's colonies, particularly India and Pakistan, have caused him to be branded as an unregenerate imperialist. This is indeed true, though it should be noted that the bloodshed and civil strife which he predicted would follow Indian independence did indeed come to pass.

On a more general level, his aggressiveness, his combative manner, and the fact that he seemed to thrive best and enjoy himself most when involved with a war has led to the charge that he was a warmonger—that he actually encouraged and welcomed war. There is no denying that Churchill found war, which gave such great scope to his energies and talents, to be challenging and perhaps even exciting, but the charge of warmongering seems exaggerated. Churchill himself always argued vehemently that his goal was always peace, rather than war. It was his contention, however, that ultimately peace is preserved by being well-armed and by signaling a willingness to fight if necessary.

*Bibliography* ———————————————

Churchill W S 1956-58 *A History of the English-Speaking Peo-* *ples*, 4 vols. Dodd, Mead, New York

Churchill W S 1971 *While England Slept: A Survey of World Affairs, 1932-38*. Books for Libraries Press, Freeport, New York

Gilbert M 1966-83 *Winston S Churchill*, 6 vols. Houghton Mifflin, Boston, Massachusetts

Manchester W R 1983 *The Last Lion: Winston Spencer Churchill*. Little, Brown, Boston, Massachusetts

Lord Moran 1966 *Churchill: The Struggle for Survival, 1940-1965*. Houghton Mifflin, Boston, Massachusetts

GARRETT L. MCAINSH

# Cicero, Marcus Tullius

Marcus Tullius Cicero (106-43 BC) was a leading statesman and philosopher of the last turbulent years of the Roman republic. Though his origins were below the highest, or senatorial class, Cicero's brilliance and finely burnished oratory made him a force in Roman politics while he was still in his thirties. In 63 BC, with the aid of the powerful Pompey, he was elected consul. It was almost unheard of for anyone outside of the highest aristocracy to hold this important office. As consul, Cicero sought to unify Rome's upper classes to restore stability to the violence-racked Roman state, and exposed and defeated the dangerous conspiracy of Catiline against the republic.

Rome's social and factional disputes were too great for even Cicero's skills, though. In 58 BC, the political situation turned against him when he was driven into exile for over a year. Even after returning to Rome in 57 BC, Cicero was never able to regain his former influence. He watched helplessly as Julius Caesar made himself the effective dictator of the Roman State, and was even reduced to making speeches praising Caesar, who had subverted the republican ideals which Cicero believed in so passionately. He was freed from this subservience by Caesar's murder in 44 BC, and attempted by fiery speeches in the Roman Senate to rally support for a restoration of Rome's traditional republican form of government. These efforts were to no avail, though, and Cicero was condemned to death and killed by Mark Antony's forces in December 43.

Cicero was a prolific writer as well as an active politician, and it is primarily for his exquisite Latin style, his intimate personal letters, and his solid, humane ideas, rather than for his political activities, that he is remembered as one of the greatest of all the ancient Romans. Though he was not a highly original philosopher, he holds a very important place in the history of Western ideas. Cicero played a crucial role in the development of the Western mind as the foremost transmitter of Greek philosophic concepts and terms to the Roman world, thus assuring them a central role in the development of Western civilization.

Though he was not tied exclusively to any one philosophic school, Cicero's work on political problems stands basically in the tradition of Stoicism. Thus he believed that a rational natural law governs the universe, and that all human relationships should be based on that law. Natural law, said Cicero, was the same for all people everywhere, and it was unchanging. It was also discoverable, since rational, through the exercise of human reason. Since all people everywhere live under the same law, he went on, they are all essentially equal. Cicero concluded from this that since no one has a natural right to have power over anyone else, all legitimate political authority must ultimately be based on the moral consent of the governed, rather than on brute force.

Another of Cicero's conclusions was that since all people are children of the God who authored this natural law, their relationship one to another is that of brother to brother. Hence warfare between them is nothing but fratricide. Cicero at one point, writing to his friend Atticus, condemned all war outright, saying "I cease not to advocate peace; even though unjust it is better than the justest war." In his famous work on political duties and ethics, *De Oficiis*, however, he drew back from such thoroughgoing pacifism. Here he argued that defensive war is legitimate, saying that "the only excuse for war is that we may live in peace unharmed." Returning to this theme a few chapters later, he added that "war should be undertaken in such a way as to show that its only object is peace."

On war as on many other points, Cicero's ideas meshed well with basic concepts of Christianity.

This, plus the incomparable grace of his Latin style, assured him a wide readership and a significant impact on posterity. In the Renaissance, in particular, he was fervently admired. Christian pacifists such as Erasmus of Rotterdam then drew sustenance from the ancient writings of Cicero.

See also: *Peace in the Ancient World*

*Bibliography* ———————————————————

Cicero M T 1912-58 *Works*. Loeb Classical Library, Cambridge
Hunt H A K 1954 *The Humanism of Cicero*.
Shackleton-Bailey D R 1971 *Cicero*.
Stasburger H 1931 *Concordia Ordinum: Eine Untersuchung zur Politik Ciceros*.

GARRETT L. MCAINSH

# Civil Society and Non-governmental Organizations

Many, some cautiously, celebrate events after the Cold War period as final triumph of capitalism and democracy. The state as the primary agent of social change is increasingly devalued because it is considered not only distant from its subjects, but also arbitrary. Positive social change is considered unlikely to emerge from efforts at the level of the 'nation-state,' but rather from the local and global levels. 'Civil society' is one of the dominant themes in current thinking about present and future in the social, economic and cultural change. Though the meaning and usage of civil society is extremely diverse and tendentious, it has a considerable analytical and practical power; it reflects myriad social processes and solutions to diverse problems faced by contemporary society. Non-governmental Organizations (NGOs) are an important institutional expression of this emerging world order.

There is no doubt that Marxist-Leninist and Maoist ideologies and related social movements are rapidly losing their legitimacy. Across the globe, the role of the state in social development is reduced, and therein responsibilities of the civil society are expected to increase. Paradoxically, for some observers, post-Cold War celebrations also mark the end of liberalism and democracy, what Emmanuel Wallerstein calls "the World after liberalism." The increased influence of religious fundamentalism, ethno-religious nationalism, and state intolerance of organizations that do not subscribe to the neo-liberal economic reforms are evident in many parts of the world. Consequently, the optimism and popularity of NGOs also coincides with a great deal of ideological confusion creating extensive fears and dismay about the emerging world disorder.

This paper argues that the 'nation-state' has not yet become a meaningless entity, but the globalization of the economy has contributed to a paradoxical relationship between the state and its citizens. On the one hand, economic integration has increased the responsibility of the state for creating the political stability necessary for capitalist development. On the other hand, the state's autonomy, flexibility and available resources that create such political conditions are reduced. NGOs as mediators between the state and society—members of society yet subject to state power—face increasing difficulties in representing the civil society. Politics of NGOs are self-limiting and they are becoming an extension of the state, not only because their institutional identity is defined by the state, but also their ability to realize the social and institutional pluralism of the civil society is defined by the state, but also their ability to realize the social and institutional pluralism of the civil society is predicated on the capacity of markets to broaden its control over territorial and the natural resource bases for endless profit-driven material progress. Put differently, the capacity of NGOs to realize the objectives of civil society is constrained by the logic of capitalism and the politics of the nation-state. Consequently, the capacity of the NGOs particularly the ones that are associated with transnational bodies to influence in the 'internal' affairs of the state is also reduced. What we are witnessing today is a rearticulation and consolidation of state power vis-à-vis the society where the state is disciplining, accommodating, and subordinating the politics of the civil society in ways detrimental to its interests.

The intention here is not to paint a gloomy picture of the capacity of NGOs to achieve the interests of the civil society. Neither is it to advocate rosy bromides. Rather, it is to explain the strategic social transformative potential of NGOs in relation to global capitalism and state power. Such an inquiry about the thrust of civil society organizations and imperatives of economic and political power are essential to understand and to formulate policies to maximize the strengths and limitations of NGOs in social change.

Precursors of NGOs go back to middle of the eighteenth century and even earlier. However, novelty of contemporary NGOs lies not so much in the discovery of values and goals they represent as in social, economic, and political context in which they function. Contemporary NGOs represent diverse social groups' reaction against economic stagnation, the erosion of pluralist democracy, repression, social violence, and the nuclear threat to global survival. During the last decade, the number of NGOs has increased in thousands. Some international donors and governments see NGO as more effective, credible and equitable agents; they are also to become a substitute for areas hitherto monopolized by the state. Some even go as far as describing NGOs as a 'parallel state.'

Among their many functions, NGOs are expected to act outside the government for one or more of the following ends: to act as mediators between antagonistic parties when conventional institutions and avenues of conflict resolution have lost their legitimacy; to formulate alternative plans of action; to deliver goods and services that are not effectively done by the state and the private sector or done dysfunctionally by the public sector; to function as a supplement or a substitute for the state in formulation and implementation of policies that are for the benefit of shared interests. Furthermore, they are expected to create an institutional environment conducive to empowerment of citizens to take part in the public life effectively. Finally, they are expected to act as pressure groups to make the state to be more accountable and transparent to its citizens.

NGOs derive their strengths mainly from two sources. First, NGOs are members of the civil society. Such location enables them to overcome some of the limitations of the state. Some of the defining characteristics of NGOs are that they represent the general interests of the society as opposed to the particularistic interests represented by political parties and bureaucracies. Their non-profit orientation makes their programs able to reach the most neglected members of society, and meaningful to people than those based on commercial profits and political power. Finally, the NGOs' ability to mobilize the citizen's participation and local resources make their programs more sustainable than those imposed from the top.

Second, NGOs are also members of transnational networks that have the capacity to challenge the hegemony of the nation-state. Optimists argue that solidarity between civil society groups in different countries can be a potent force in challenging the negative consequences of state policies on citizens. In many parts of the world, NGOs are able to realize their objectives when these transnational networks exert international pressure on governments concerned, rather than due to the support they get from their members whom they assist.

The concept of the civil society as a social collective independent of the state has been in existence from the early part of the seventeenth century. Its meaning has been subjected to various interpretations under Romans, Hegelians, Marxists, Gramscians, Frankfurt school and post-structuralists. In Latin, the notion of *Civilis societas* referred to communities that conformed to norms and values that rose beyond the laws of the state. The contemporary versions of the civil society are far more ambivalent and incorporates characteristics of all its predecessors: i.e., the plurality of associations (Hegel and Tocqueville); social solidarity (Durkheim); and the public sphere as an important arena of social development (Ardent and Habermas).

Civil society consists of diverse and sometimes contradictory social interests that are shaped to fit their respective constituencies, thematic orientation and types of activity (UNDP, 1993, 1). Moreover, as White points out, "civil society implies a certain power relationship between the state and society such that there are limitations on the state's capacity to pervade and control society, and certain power on the part of members of a society to insulate themselves from, and exert influence upon, the state" (White, 1993:65).

From Machiavelli, Locke, Kant, Hume, Hegel, and Marx, Habermas the central concerns of the debates on civil society has been on the meaning of public sphere (universal interests) and private sphere (private interests); and how the relationships between them are constituted; how notions of legality, morality and ethics, rights and virtue, rights and trust are constituted and placed between the universal and private interests. In the liberal political thought, the idea of the morally autonomous individual provided the basis for the civil society. The resolution of its contradictions was achieved through the balance of power between the state and the society. According to the classical Marxist tradition overcoming the contradictions of civil society requires a new unity between social and political life that can be achieved only under the conditions of socialized forces and relations of production.

The central concern of the contemporary civil society is also how and to what extent the conflicts between public and private interests can be overcome or resolved by forming dialogue between the state and the society within the context of capitalist economy and democratic governance. Civil society advocates argue that the structured plurality of the public sphere provides the possibility of articulating and defining the social life in the civil society in terms of participation and publicity. Such participation achieved through communicative interaction ensures the revitalization of the public sphere now colonized by institutions of contemporary capitalism. It is the practical application of this theory that makes the NGOs as important players.

Generally, the notion of civil society has been invoked during periods in which a given social formation is faced with a crisis of social order with the potential to lead to the total breakdown of existing equilibrium of the society. The systematic reconstruction and expansion of meaning and functions of the civil society have varied from one context to another in the light of the developments within the social, economic and political trends in a given period. The implication is that this would lead to a search for alternative paths of social change. These varying notions of the civil society have provided the background to the nature of politics in different periods.

What is new about the contemporary discourse on civil society is the heavy emphasis on minimum intervention of the State in social development. In theory, some conventional responsibilities of the state are expected to be taken over by the voluntary sector. In practice however, such functions are filled increasingly not by the NGOs, but by the private sector, if at all, while vital areas of the society are in the hands of the state. Even within the United Nations, which has since the late 1940s advocated the role of NGOs, the status and responsibilities of NGOs vis-a-vis the state remains unresolved. Moreover, new institutional configurations have begun to emerge between NGOs, commercial banks, and international donors where they appear to work within the parameters of capitalist development. Governments and international donors are subcontracting various tasks to NGOs, which then are forced to function according to the logic of capitalist development.

This has contributed to a significant programmatic shift within some of the mainstream NGOs. For example, the objective of micro-credit programs in Bangladesh is to empower Muslim women by creating an appropriate institutional environment. The rationale is that improvement in economic power is an essential prerequisite for social and political empowerment. However, current research demonstrates that the use of local institutions (e.g., peer group pressure as a substitute for conventional types of collateral) by the NGOs to guarantee the regular repayment of loans tends to legitimize the very institutions considered to be oppressive to those women NGOs meant to help. Thus, the high visibility of women in NGO programs does not necessarily indicate positive changes in their social status. Ironically, in the process the feminist critique of development and the language of empowerment has been subverted and being used to strengthen the very same forces responsible for the low status of women.

These developments have a number of consequences. First, there are conflicts between those organizations that are for and against micro-credit. Dissident organizations are marginalized within mainstream NGOs and thus struggle to survive. This further undermines coordinated action of NGOs when they are deemed necessary to counter state power. Second, NGOs are also faced with a serious dilemma. That is, on the one hand, claims about the social transformative capacities of NGOs are supported by their ability to mobilize local and traditional institutions as means of achieving their goals. On the other hand, some of these institutions are responsible for perpetuating oppressive systems of social stratification that the NGOs are supposedly fighting against. There is much ambiguity as to how NGOs could reconcile these contradictory objectives. However, the intense competition between NGOs for 'success,' measured in terms of financial self-sufficiency forces them not to antagonize the power relations in the communities they work.

NGOs are a diverse lot in terms of their ideological and operational orientation. While their institutional identity as 'Non-governmental' is defined by the state: NGOs are primarily accountable to the state. In the present contexts, the state and international donors do not tolerate the activities of a civil society that are not in accordance with the imperatives of the neo-liberal political economy. It is therefore, unlikely to provide much advantage for those organizations that purport to act contrary to such interests.

These developments have contributed to an increasing convergence of interests between the NGOs, the state and international donors. NGO activities have become potent means through which the state is able to generate 'social capital' necessary for capitalist development. The claims and practices of NGOs are couched in the language of 'anti-statism,' 'empowerment,' 'self-reliance,' 'participatory development,' and 'development from below' enable the state and the international donors. Such actions, therefore, appear to be emerging from below or from the society rather than imposed from above, i.e., government and Western donors. This contributes to simultaneous legitimization of the withdrawal of the state from providing basic welfare services of the increasing transfer of a greater burden on the dissenting social classes to look after their own interests and welfare. Consequently, the struggles within the civil society, which have emerged directly in reaction to uneven distribution of capitalist development, are ignored or given second priority, in the activities of NGOs. NGOs are yet to develop ways to deal with the relationship between the liberal economic reforms and diverse interests they represent. NGOs activities have led to delegitimization of the conventional social movements that have proposed radical social changes by transforming the 'capitalist' underpinnings of contemporary civil society and the state.

The constitution and relationship between the civil society and the state are complex and ambiguous, and vary from one country to another. The majority of the institutions of the civil society and the state in the developed countries evolved via a process different from that of the developing countries. In the latter case, both entities were a product of complex struggles between dominant and subordinate social groups and impositions by the colonial state. In most of the former colonies, the civil society organizations played a vibrant role during the colonial period by creating the social capital for the native elites and colonial government to consolidate and legitimize their power. However, towards independence, the activities of these organizations were subsumed by the national independence movements: NGOs were expected to postpone their 'specific' struggles and to focus on the 'general' interests of the society i.e., national interests until the 'nation' is liberated from the Colonial power. After independence, the vitality of NGOs faded away as the state assumed the leading role in social development. Thereafter, NGOs could function only within the context of boundaries set by the state.

NGOs activities became revitalized due to widespread dissatisfaction with the decades of state-driven development. NGOs during this period played an important role in denouncing human right violations and non-democratic forms of governance and introducing innovative approaches to address economic and political grievances of people. In fact, even the rapidly disintegrating political left considered NGOs as a possible means of mitigating the adverse consequences of capitalist development. Interestingly, these NGOs have increasingly bypassed the issue of linkages between neo-liberal development and social justice causes that they originally stood for. Hence, NGOs became major recipients of aid and advice of international development agencies. Subsequently, the aid-dependent development and foreign aid driv-

en advocacy for a civil society has tended to limit the autonomy of the civil society in the developing countries. As the state consolidated its position in terms of managing the social conditions necessary for the continuity of capitalist development the vitality of NGOs declined. Therefore, I argue, despite the claims to the contrary, since colonial period the activities of NGOs have led to consolidation and domestication of state power and corresponding limiting of the freedom of the civil society to achieve its own ends.

Moreover, currently most developing countries are forced to achieve multiple objectives simultaneously: they required stabilizing their macroeconomics, both domestically and internationally, and restructuring their economies at every sector of the economy. Furthermore these already daunting set of economic reforms need to be achieved against the background of political reform, moving away from the societal institutions that are considered to be inappropriate and in need of transformation. Democratic form of governance is expected to be achieved in parallel to economic growth. Ironically, developed countries and international donors do not take into account the different trajectories of state formation in developing countries when they exert pressure to implement economic and political reforms.

Consequently, the constitution and politics of contemporary civil society in developing countries is far more complex because they are shaped by symbiotic relationships between nationalism, development, and democracy. The present scenario, however, does not entirely subscribe to Samuel Huntington's thesis of multipolar and multi-civilizational world order where 'culture' has become the more dominant ideological force and global politics reconfigured along cultural lines. Neither does it follow Francis Fukuyama's notion of the end of history where liberal capitalism has triumphed, nor post-structuralist and post-modernist arguments regarding replacement of meta-paradigms of social change by multiple and fragmented ones, nor Wallerstien's thesis of the end of liberalism—rather an optimistic view of capitalist development and pessimistic view of possibilities of systemic challenges to capitalism. Rather it demonstrates, at least for the time being, the incredible capacity of capitalist economy and related state forms to discipline, accommodate and even subordinate politics of the civil society.

However, one cannot undervalue the impact of NGOs in representing the dissenting interests of the civil society during the periods in which the freedoms of democratic institutions were suppressed by the state. Even the political parties in opposition welcomed the activities of NGOs. While in opposition political parties use the concerns of NGOs to attack their incumbents, some even protest against the repression of NGOs by the incumbents. Such appropriation of the NGOs' criticisms of the state enables political parties to enhance the legitimacy of their claims as those representing 'general' interests of the 'civil society.'

Indeed, NGOs have contributed to the rise and fall of governments. However, after assuming power these political parties have suppressed the freedoms of the NGOs, when attempts to hold the state accountable to its election promises. Once elected, the legitimacy of political power depends on broader social processes e.g., ethno-religious nationalism and economic development that are capable of appealing to the interests of the majority, rather than on the concerns of the NGOs that are usually localized, fragmented and are not in a position to mobilize larger political movements.

One of the strengths of the civil society lies in its diversity. At the same time, diversity functions as a self-limiting character of the civil society. NGOs do not have a mechanism to create solidarity between different social groups struggling for equality: NGOs are not clear about how to reconcile the conflicting egalitarian objectives. NGOs are weak in the areas of making alliances between the groups that are struggling against distributional consequences of capitalist development (e.g., class based struggles) and struggling against forms of discriminations based on social and cultural forces (e.g., gender based struggles).

These developments suggest that one cannot be over optimistic about the capacities of civil society organizations in the post-Cold War period. The argument is that if the politics of diversity do not permit the NGOs to address aspirations that are common to different social groups, and when such common interests can create solidarity among them, then the political parties and the broader ideological forces such as socialism, political autonomy, religion will continue to function as important forces of social mobilization. Thus contrary to the claims of 'postructuralists' and 'post-modernists' who celebrate diversity and fragmentation, meta-narratives and megapolitics have yet to exhaust their potency as forces of social change.

Indeed, a vibrant civil society has the potential of preventing a few special interest groups from enjoying preferential treatment by the state. However, even in such situations the competitions between civil society organizations for professional recogni-

tion, international funding and governmental patronage have greatly reduced the possibility of them acting as a unified body capable of challenging the state power. Despite their commitment for diversity and plurality, it is often the case that in many countries only a few NGOs have access to large percentage of resources allocated to the voluntary. Consequently, it is often the case that only a few NGOs monopolize the representation of civil society at the state level and promote a parasitic dependence between the civil society and the state.

NGOs have played an important role in mediating between ethnic minorities and the majoritarian governments in situations where the communications between the two parties have broken down. In fact, in situations where the government's administrative system is paralyzed, NGOs are the only means through which the government can provide various services to minorities and thus legitimize its authority. However, NGOs are often placed in a difficult situation with respect to the demands of "nation-hood" by ethnic minorities. Given that institutional identity of the NGOs is defined and sometimes their activities are funded by the state the challenge NGOs face to build consensus between the "national interests," that gives priority to the aspirations of the majority community, and "minority interests."

For example, even the most progressive NGO in Sri Lanka that support the devolution of political power to the Tamils minority does not challenge the priority given to the interests of the Sinhala Buddhist majority in the constitution of the country as an important reason for the demand for a political separation by the Tamil militant groups. Similarly, NGOs involved in human rights and environmental issues in India do not provide a normative challenge to a possible relationship between the Hindu nationalism of the Baratiya Janatha Party (BJP) and the testing of nuclear weapons, civil war in Kashmir, and the demands for rights of self-determination by various minority groups in the country. Similarly, NGOs in Bangladesh who are in the forefront of supporting the rights of the Chakma tribe in the Chittagong Hill tract only go as far as to the accommodation of those tribal interests within the constitutional framework of an Islamic/Bangladeshi State. In other words, these NGOs do not advocate separation between state and religion. Thus, the politics and prerogatives of NGOs are still constrained by the boundaries of the nation state: NGOs struggle towards accommodation of minority interests within the majority interests, not towards equality. During these situations, however, the conflicts between the NGOs who subscribe to majority interests and who are sympathetic toward political demands of minorities have escalated. These conflicts in turn feed into conflicts between incumbent and opposition political parties. Consequently, once a political party is elected to power, their will to fulfill the promised solutions to grievances of minorities was subsumed and undermined by broader social processes such as ethno-religious nationalism.

My argument is that a civil society, as envisioned by the Western liberal political theory and by majority of the NGOs, and a State form that subscribes to any one ethno-religious orthodoxy (e.g., Buddhist State, Hindu State and Islamic State) are two contradictory goals. To state differently, Buddhist Civil Society, Islamic Civil Society, and Hindu Civil Society are oxymorons. What is happening today is that even the liberal and secular NGOs do not provide a normative challenge to ethno-religious identities of the state that conflict with the ideals of civil society. Any organization that proposes radical course of action loses its identity as legitimate representatives of the civil society and get outlawed as terrorists, subversives, naxelites, separatists, and communists. Perhaps, it is time to abandon the notions of 'liberalism' and 'secularism' as defining characteristics of, or even possible goals of, civil society and the state in the 'South' and to search for more realistic notions to guide the actions of NGOs. NGOs will be able to maximize their contribution to peace and democracy only if they come to terms with and device more realistic relationship with the social processes that shapes day-to-day relationships between the state and the society.

Globalization is another reason for current popularity about the civil society. Generally, it refers to simultaneous universalization of capitalism and democracy as two main characteristics of the post-cold war period. Though notion of globalization and the relationship between capitalism and democracy are ambiguous and tendentiously used, they are having enormous social and political power in shaping the affairs of the contemporary society as they promise to create a better social order for every social group.

Be that as it may, globalization has revitalized NGOs. Optimist argue that NGOs through their transnational civil society networks can transcend state power and create conditions necessary to achieve goals of globalization. In practice, however, most programs of the NGOs are subordinated to the foreign policy and economic interests of the powerful Western countries that provide the bulk of the financial and moral support for the NGOs. For example, there is a far-reaching outcry about the need for democracy in Iraq and Afghanistan where 'militant Islamic fundamentalism' functions as the dominant ideology of the state. However, political processes of other Islamic countries and non-Islamic countries are not evaluated or scrutinized to the same degree and reforms advocated according to similar democratic ideals that the NGOs espouse. Currently, Islam is invoked as the new enemy of democracy and development, and its role in international political scene appears to be no different from that of communism during the Cold War period. Unfortunately, humanitarian and peacemaking agendas of NGOs do not promise to transcend the religious politics of the post-Cold War period.

Two obstacles for the NGOs to realize their objectives are the absence of clarity about their responsibilities and status within the governmental and United Nations bodies and lack of appropriate mechanisms to coordinate the activities and structures of diverse NGOs in different countries. Consequently, although the representations of these institutions in these transnational bodies have increased, many of the vital areas are still in the hands of the national governments.

Moreover, globalization does not indicate declining importance of the nation-state and a movement towards a more egalitarian distribution of economic and political power between nations, and increasing flow of development assistant from developed countries to developing countries. On the one hand, local economies are rapidly integrated with the global economy. On the other hand, increasingly individual states are responsible for dealing with the social struggles resulting from the uneven distribution of fruits of capitalism. Consequently, Cold War economic inequalities between developed and underdeveloped countries have increased. The only option available for these countries is to maximize their gains from the world economy through economic liberalization, while developed countries do not necessarily comply with the free-market economic policies that they themselves impose on developing countries.

These economic changes are also accompanied by the widespread invoking of 'culture' as an important force of political mobilization. Some countries that most dearly follow the liberal economic reforms have elected governments that directly espouse ethno-religious nationalism. In addition, ethno-nationalist civil society organizations have become an important obstacle for governments that are willing to adhere to democratic principles of governance. This has important implications for the civil society organizations, as the economic content of social discontent driven by 'culture' is extremely difficult to deal with when

NGOs as they do not have the capacity to capitalist development. Traditionally, NGOs have had a rather problematic relationship with cultural underpinnings of a given state formation. On the one hand, cultural institutions are important sources of legitimacy of NGO claims. The 'civil societiness' of NGOs is partly derived from them being embedded in local institutions and traditions. On the other hand, NGOs purport to transform cultural values that are responsible for the marginalization of social groups they represent. Issues emerging from this dilemma are not resolved either at the 'national' and 'transnational level.' Perhaps this may be one of the reasons for an increasing reluctance on the part of NGOs and governments in North to interfere in the internal affairs of the south. This in turn creates difficulties for NGOs in the South to achieve their objectives as most effective NGOs in the South are able to increase their bargaining power over the state when they are supported by their allies in the North.

It appears that during the post-Cold War period the power of the nation-state to prevent external bodies from interfering in its 'internal matters' have been increased. This is one of the reasons for the continuing failure of the United Nations and NGOs to be effective in resolving the social conflicts since the 1980s. The nuclear testing by India, the Persian Gulf war and civil war in former communist bloc countries like Yugoslavia, the apathy of the international community towards civil war in Sri Lanka, and more recently the actions of Talibans in Afghanistan are some examples of the ineffectiveness of the transitional networks and new ways in which the state has been able to consolidate its power.

Indeed, the preceding argument does not disagree with those who suggest that the NGOs are a response to the legitimization crisis of the modern capitalism and represent a reaction against the "colonization of life words" and the penetration of the state into new areas of life. Nor is the social transformative capacity of NGOs entirely dismissed. Indeed, NGOs are not marginal expressions of social protest but are situated within and are counter-hegemonic forces of the contradictions of capitalism and undemocratic forms of governance. Marx noted that the emergence of civil society and the modern state was an 'increment of freedom.' Marx perceived their capacity to safeguard the universalistic norms of citizenship, sovereignty of people, autonomy, equality, democracy, the principle of political self-determination—a principle that is available to inform social movements against exclusion and political inequality (MEGA I/33 p. 288 op. cit. Bottomore, 37). Yet at the same time, the civil

society-state duality was the basis for the alienation of the modern society. That is, as a member of the state, the individual is both a citizen participating in the affairs of the society, and a subject, the privatized object of political regulation. And "as a member of civil society, despite or because of one's freedom to determine one's will, the individual is subject to those alien powers (economic laws) that determines his chances, impose interest structure onto his needs, and deny autonomy of social life."

Therefore, "the social stability attained through the institutionalization of voluntary associations as corporations requiring State recognition and representation of the state bureaucracy on their councils—that is, the closure achieved through group representation of civil society in the state via the estate system—fatally undermines independence of civil society, whose principles are individuality, free association, and self determination." The reasons for these limitations of the social transformative power of the civil society emerged from the capitalist character of social relations of the State whose primary concern is to create the conditions necessary for the continuity of capitalism. This implies an interesting paradox of civil society.

> The basis of the State in antiquity was slavery; the basis of the modern State is civil society and the individual of the civil society, that is independent individual, whose only link with other individuals is private interest and unconscious, natural necessity, the slave of the wage labor, the selfish needs of himself and others; the modern State has recognized this, its natural foundation, in the universal rights of man.

Therefore, civil society organizations' capacity for genuine self organization and political dissent is mainly limited by the fact that they neither have a notion of the state different from that one that characterizes the neo-liberal capitalist economy, nor they have a unified body similar to the United Nations to counteract the interests of transnational capital and the nation-state system when they are detrimental to the interests of the groups NGOs represent.

## Bibliography

Abutu M I M 1995c *The State, Civil Society and the Democratization Process in Nigeria.* Codesria, Dakar, Senegal

Bottomore T B (ed.) 1964 *Marxist Sociology: Selected Writings in Sociology and Social Philosophy.* Mcgraw Hill Press

Brynen R, Korany B, Noble P (eds.) 1996 *Political Liberaliza-*

tion and Democratization in the Arab World. Lynne Rienner Publishers, Boulder, Colo.

Chinn P L 1995c Peace and Power: Building Communities for the Future, 4th edn. National League for Nursing Press, New York

Cooper A H 1996c Paradoxes of Peace: German Peace Movements since 1945. University of Michigan Press, Ann Arbor

Fischer S, Rodrik D, Tuma E (eds.) 1993c The Economics of Middle East Peace: Views from the Region. MIT Press, Cambridge, Mass.

Fisher J 1998 Nongovernments: NGOs and the Political Development of the Third World. Kumarian Press, West Hartford, Conn

Forsythe D P 1993c Human Rights and Peace: International and National Dimensions. University of Nebraska Press, Lincoln

Fukuyama F 1989 The end of history. The National Interests 16 (Summer)

Gibbon P (ed.) 1995 Markets, Civil Society and Democracy in Kenya. Nordiska Afrikainstitutet, Uppsala, Sweden

Hall J A (ed.) 1995 Civil Society : Theory, History, Comparison. Polity Press, Cambridge, UK

Hann C M (ed.) 1990 Market Economy and Civil Society in Hungary. F. Cass, London, England; Portland, Or: F. Cass c/o International Specialized Book Services

Harbeson J W, Rothchild D, Chazan N (eds.) 1994 Civil Society and the State in Africa. L. Rienner Publishers, Boulder

Haynes J 1997 Democracy and Civil Society in the Third World: Politics and New Political Movements. Polity Press, Cambridge; Blackwell, Malden, Mass.

Huntington S P 1997 The Clash of Civilizations: Remarks of World Order. Touchstone Books, New York

Janoski T 1998 Citizenship and Civil Society: A Framework of Rights and Obligations in Liberal, Traditional, and Social Democratic Regimes. Cambridge University Press, Cambridge, UK; New York

Joseph P 1993 Peace Politics: The United States between the Old and New World Orders. Temple University Press, Philadelphia

Karsh E (ed.) 1996 Between War and Peace: Dilemmas of Israeli Security. Portland, Or, F. Cass, London

Macdonald L 1997 Supporting Civil Society: The Political Role of Non-governmental Organizations in Central America. Macmillan, Basingstoke; St. Martin's Press, New York

Monga C 1996 The Anthropology of Anger: Civil Society and

Democracy in Africa. Translated by Linda L. Fleck & Clestin Monga. Lynne Rienner Publishers, Boulder, Colo.

Ndegwa S N 1996 The Two Faces of Civil Society: NGOs and Politics in Africa. Kumarian Press, West Hartford, Conn.

Neocleous M 1996 Administering Civil Society: Towards a Theory of State Power. Macmillan Press, Houndmills, Basingstoke, Hampshire; St. Martin's Press, New York

Norton A R (ed.) 1995-1996 Civil Society in the Middle East. Brill, Leiden, New York

Ritchey-Vance M, Arlington Va 1993 The Art of Association: NGOs and Civil Society in Colombia. Inter-American Foundation, Washington, DC

Roper J et al., 1993 Keeping the Peace in the Post-cold War Era: Strengthening Multilateral Peacekeeping. A report to the Trilateral Commission. Trilateral Commission, New York

Runyon T (ed.) 1989c Theology, Politics, and Peace. Orbis Books, Maryknoll NY

Sachikonye L (ed.) 1995 Democracy, Civil Society, and the State: Social Movements in Southern Africa. SAPES Books, Harare

Salem P (ed.) 1997c Conflict Resolution in the Arab World: Selected Essays. American University of Beirut, Beirut, Lebanon

Seligman A (no date) The Idea of Civil Society. Free Press, New York; Maxwell Macmillan, Toronto, Canada

Sicherman H 1993 Palestinian Autonomy, Self-government & Peace/Palestinian Self-government (Autonomy). West view Press, Boulder

Sponsel L E, Gregor T A 1994 The Anthropology of Peace and Nonviolence. L. Rienner, Boulder

Tismaneanu V (ed.) (no date) In Search of Civil Society: Independent Peace Movements on the Soviet Bloc. Routledge, New York

Wallerstein E 1995 After Liberalism. New Press, New York

Weiss T G, Gordenker L (eds.) 1996 NGOs, the United Nations, and Global Governance. Lynne Rienner, Boulder, Colo.

Yamamoto T (ed.) Emerging Civil Society in the Asia Pacific Community: Nongovernmental Underpinnings of the Emerging Asia Pacific Regional Community. Institute of Southeast Asian Studies, Singapore; Japan Center for International Exchange in cooperation with the Asia Pacific Philanthropy Consortium (APPC), Tokyo

JUDE FERNANDO

# Civil Wars: Dynamics and Consequences

## 1. Introduction

Although civil wars constitute dramatic and painful life experiences for the people affected, and even though no major region on earth has been spared to witness in some way this form of collective catastrophe, it is a striking fact that social sciences have given only little attention to this subject. We are not talking of a lack of monographs on civil wars such as the North American or the Spanish one, but what is missing are systematic, comparative studies, where pervasive and general features of this form of war have been examined. This statement may be applied to the background and causes of civil wars as well as to their structural features and manifestations. But it is especially true as far as the consequences of civil wars are concerned. Very little general and comparative work has been done on this important subject.

That is why in the following article we cannot resume academic wisdom already laid down in broad overview studies but must go back to individual cases of civil wars. Our examples focus on two types of civil wars: Those with a social revolutionary background and those with an ethnical background. The examples of civil wars conditioned by social revolutions are all taken from Latin America, as is the case with the Mexican revolution (1910-20, although it was named revolution, this conflict resembled a civil war during most of its period), the civil wars in Colombia (with interruptions from 1948 to date) and in Peru (1980-90) (see *Revolution*). The case material on those civil wars which have been motivated by ethnic conditions stems mostly from Europe and the Middle East. It includes the Lebanese conflict (1975-90), the Northern Irish conflict (1969 to date) and the conflicts in Bosnia Herzegovina (1992 to 1996).

First we will focus on the immediate consequences of civil wars. The following section deals with the frightening auto-dynamics of violent processes. This in turn has repercussions on all other structural spheres of society, which will be dealt with in the last section.

## 2. Short Term Consequences of Civil Wars

Civil wars can start innocuously with a little shooting or an armed robbery. Often, however, there is an éclat at their beginning, a social explosion, where accumulated feelings of anger and hate abruptly explode. For instance, the Colombian "bogotazo" in 1949 was such a "bang," which has been described by some authors as the biggest urban upheaval in Latin America to date (G. Sanchez 1985 p. 211, 219). It was the onset of the Colombian civil war's first and particularly bloody phase, which was by and large, marked by the discord between the two major parties.

At the beginning of the conflicts a sudden change of the external appearance of these societies occurs. The ethnic-religious, political or social tensions that

had been present before in everybody's mind but had not determined everyday life, suddenly become visible and turn into the dominant principle which subjects all other spheres of life. A profound restructuring and reordering of society takes place as much in mental and political as in military-geographical respect.

The most accurate observation on the bizarre mental metamorphosis after the outbreak of a civil war, was made already 2,400 years ago with the occasion of the Peloponesian war: (Thukydides p. 262) "In times of peace and under happy circumstances cities and people have better convictions, because they are not caught up in involuntary coercive situations. The war however, which restrains the effortless needs of everyday life, swings the coercive whip of violence and guides the passions of the masses, as the occasion dictates it. Thus the cities were shaken by party struggles and the example of those who had started it, compelled their followers to ever bigger extravagances and encouraged them to make use of unheard means of clever party deals and satisfaction of revenge." Here is already a clear reference to a polarization of what Thukydides calls "party struggles," once it has taken possession of social life. In an extreme case it can provoke a change of all values, according to Thukydides: "Recklessness was now considered sacrificed standing up for one's friends, wise restrain was now disguised cowardice, those who kept measure were taken for effeminate, those who resorted to rational thinking, were basically considered lazy and comfortable, but those who beat blindly, were considered real men, etc" (Thukydides p. 263).

Our cases provide plenty of proofs for these sharp observations, which are as valid nowadays as they were at their time. Thereby, it is of secondary importance, whether the escalation of the conflict is caused by the initiative of rivaling political parties or by the animosities of wide sectors of the population, whether it is driven by cold calculation or by heated emotions. One can state that in all cases, after the outbreak of hostilities, conciliatory voices pledging for patience, tolerance and for willingness to talk, rapidly loose influence and audience. Instead, time has come for fanatics to demand radical solutions. Their line of argument always follows the same basic pattern; it appropriates the increasing fear which in the face of growing tensions takes possession of all groups, and is voiced more or less in the following way: One is running the risk of being oppressed and discriminated; the only way to escape this menacing destiny is to preempt the enemy and to resort to armed attack (Hanf 1990 p. 150).

Occasionally one can find testimonies of the shock which invades the peacefully minded groups of society in face of a seemingly irreversible escalation of the conflict. One such example is M. Cehajic, a respected and wealthy Bosnia Muslim, who wrote to his family after his deportation by the Serbs into a camp, and shortly before his assassination: "Since May the 23rd, when they came into our house to pick me up, I have lived in a different world. It seems, as if everything that has happened to me, was a nasty dream, a nightmare. And I simply can not understand, how such thing is possible" (Gutman 1994 p. 167).

The incapacity to understand in the face of the toughness of suddenly erupting contrasts, as voiced in Cehajic's letter, is particularly characteristic of academics and intellectuals. However, these groups of shocked people represent in many cases the social minority. Wide shares of the population from all social levels, cheer the escalation of conflict or at least believe it inevitable. Activists from militant milieus rapidly join all sorts of mushrooming militias. The reasons for joining a revolutionary army, a guerrilla organization or an association of militia can be manifold. For some of the voluntary "fighters" the prospect of using it as an outlet for their rage on defenseless civilians, triggers virtually a rush for power and blood. One gets this impression when reading, for example, the reports on assaults of Bosnian Serbs on Muslims in Bosnia-Herzegovina (see *Ethnic Conflict and International Relations*). Not only did the aggressors imprison and expel their alleged enemies from their long established domiciles, but thought of all sorts of tortures and humiliations before they killed their victims. Another pattern of motivation can be found in Northern Ireland. The attacks of Protestants against Catholics, who had dared to settle on their "territory," showed features of a quasi-sacred purgatory act, as if the gradual intermingling of confessional groups were equivalent to a profanation of the Protestant belief (Waldmann 1989 p. 86). Emotional arbitrariness and ideological fanaticism are, however, not always the main driving forces of the bloody conflict. As has been pointed out by H.W. Tobler, in the case of the Mexican revolution, in the end it were the material reasons which made brigades and officials eventually join the rebels (Tobler 1984 p. 217, 224). The concrete advantages, which may derive from the participation in military campaigns (which are mostly predatory acts), should generally not be underestimated when compared to the often emphasized political and religious motives.

We have thus already tackled the second aspect of the sudden polarization of forces after the outbreak of a civil war, which is the military-geographic one. It is the component which, strikingly enough, makes conflicts irreversible, as it does not allow to return to the status quo ante after the beginning of a conflict. Each of the conflicting parties takes quickly and determinedly possession of specific regions, with the consequence that a territory previously controlled and united by the state will soon break up.

This process of spatial division is particularly visible in the case of ethnic conflicts. The ungloriously famous measures of "ethnic purge" taken in the Yugoslavian conflict are by no means exclusively typical of the Yugoslavian situation. Instead, these processes of segregation can be found everywhere where ethnic societies clash violently (Waldmann 1989 Ch. 4).

The general tendency is to build homogenous territorial blocks which are safe against attacks from within as from outside (Hanf 1990 p. 418, 429). The blocks are mostly formed from territorial bases, where the respective ethnic group is demographically dominant. These plans are all the more difficult to practice the higher the ethnically mixed zones are in number, and the closer interwoven the different ethnic groups live together. Particularly, bigger cities which have grown as a consequence of a consecutive inflow of different ethnic groups, turn into a focus of conflicts after the outbreak of hostilities. The increasing animosities provoked by the spatial concentration of different groups of population can in some cases only be contained by walls that divide a city into several sectors, as is the case in Belfast where the wall is euphemistically called "peace-line."

Generally, the desire of each group to consolidate its territory as quickly as possible, generates an aggressive hecticism at the start of civil wars. Later on, when prospects of gaining territory become exceptional—for instance in the case of external help, then initial attacks give way to a strategy of defense since the different groups no longer allow to be run over.

The division of a country into different zones, each respectively controlled by a civil war fraction, is of far reaching importance to each single citizen. Depending on where he lives and works, he may feel safe with his family or may be well advised to leave his home and to move to the home territory of the group to which he belongs. Civil wars always provoke massive migrations. Already the War of Thirty Years in Germany (1618-48) led to a major migration of the rural population into the cities, where the walls gave a feeling of safety (Schreiner 1985 pp. 39-

90). In the first phase of the Colombian war, which was marked by the conflicts between the two big parties (liberal and conservative), the safety of a person depended decisively on whether "his" party was, militarily speaking, dominant in the area where he was living. Liberal minded farm holders whose lands were located in a conservative area, were keen to move away quickly and to rent or sell their land. Apparently, two million Columbianes, that is approximately a sixth of the national population at the time, moved home because of political persecutions between 1949 and 1953 (Ortiz Sarmiento 1986 p. 267).

The figure shows that the share of an ethnic group or an entire population which is expelled or voluntarily seeks a new home during a civil war can be considerable. During the Lebanon conflict about half of the population, that is roughly 1.5 million people, moved temporarily or definitely away from their original home. Many of them were forced to migrate afterwards again. In the case of Bosnia Herzegovina, the estimated figures of migration are similarly high with 1.5 to 2 million expulsions within 2.5 years, of the whole population of 4.5 million inhabitants (Calic 1993 p. 55).

When the zones of dominance of the conflicting fractions in a civil war are clear, the options for migrating masses are clear and compulsive: They must leave the area where they represent only an unsheltered minority and they have to move to the respective rural or urban area where either their party, their confessional or ethnic group constitutes a .majority able to defend itself. However, it also happens sometimes that there are no clear cut border lines and zones of influence, since several groups claim the same territory. All commentators agree that unclear conditions of this sort carry the greatest risk for the population, as people at risk to be subjected and exploited by both sides or to be punished because of alleged alliance with the enemy. A good example are the highland regions in Peru, which in the early 80s were successively occupied by guerrilla and state security forces. Because of the vexations to which they were exposed by both sides, most of the province's population migrated into the safe anonymity of larger cities (Waldmann 1989a p. 184).

To be able to move away may be considered a privilege when hostilities have reached the point where people of the other side are indiscriminately locked up or killed. Civil wars are known to represent an especially cruel form of warfare. This cruelty manifests itself in the high number of victims as well as in the fact that most of these victims are civilians

who are not directly involved in the conflict.

That civil wars cause high casualties in terms of human lives is well known since the Thirty Years War in Germany in the 17th century, which reduced the population from 16 to 11 million people. Nevertheless, the number of victims may vary considerably. The Northern Ireland conflict, where about 3,000 people have been killed within 25 years (that means 8 persons per 100,000 habitants year) is a "low intensity war" in the true sense of the term, while the fights in Bosnia Herzegovina, where 145,000 persons died within 2.5 years (i.e., 1,300 per 100,000 habitants within one year) definitely does not deserve this name. The number of victims is independent of the cause of the war. Both basic forms of civil war, those with an ethnic-nationalist background and those with a social-revolutionary background, can go on relatively smoothly or develop into general bloodshed.

The high number of civilians among the victims has a lot to do with the arbitrariness of violence which is a typical trait of civil wars. In some regions the conflicting parties themselves use slogans which point to this tendency. For instance in Northern Ireland the formula "tit for tat" means, that after a terrorist attack of the IRA, in which people died, protestant vigilant groups will eventually kill the first catholic individual which happens to cross their way (see *Problem Solving in Internationalized Conflicts*). In the Lebanon the so called "passport murders" had a similar function: Whenever a person of the "wrong" side had the bad luck of crossing the border immediately after one of the guardians was shot, he was executed in an act of revenge. The term "arbitrariness" must not be given too strict a meaning in this context. While from a Western point of view, these murders violate all moral and humanitarian standards, they may well correspond to a certain degree of more archaic notions of justice according to which individuals are held responsible for any act of their own community, even if they did not participate in it or approve it.

The amount of violence used in civil wars does not escalate continuously. Its characteristic unpredictability (a result of its arbitrariness) finds one of its most important expressions in its non-continuous development. In the same way as certain villages remain completely unaffected while others are badly haunted by the horrors of the war, civil wars have phases in their development where the dynamic decreases strongly and then suddenly escalates again forcefully pushing towards a new climax. These waves may be determined by interventions of external powers, but they can also be explained to some extent as an expression of the circular auto-dynamic that violence has in civil wars. The next section will deal with this auto-dynamic process.

### 3. The Dynamics of Violence

The idea that violence in civil war develops a dynamic of its own is not new. It can be found in most monographs on civil wars used for this article (Tobler 1984 p. 225, 454; Hanf 1990 p. 416; Mansilla 1993 p. 148 etc.). However, the question arises as to what terms like "the independization of unleashed violence" or "violence as an end in itself" exactly mean. Can one already say that violence is becoming self-sustaining when civil war armies or guerrilla groups start to claim taxes in a region they have occupied? Has violence become an end in itself when battles are carried out, although their original political and ideological goals have already lost importance? Is it tenable to state in general terms that violence is practiced only for its own sake as the term "end in itself" suggests?

In order to answer such questions, it is useful to draw a scheme of the different levels on which violence gradually becomes detached from political restrictions and taboos. Such a scheme can only represent ideal types. The concrete cases underlying our considerations do not necessarily belong to only one level but contain elements of several levels or move up and down the "ladder of levels." The starting point is generally a situation where the state possesses the monopoly of violence which inevitably drives political dissidents with radically diverging political ideas to resort to the use of weapons in order to make their goals come true. This starting point is also fictitious. The assumption that violence is merely used as an indispensable means for a specific end, renders it easier for us to pursue and to understand the process of independization of violence. Thereby, we distinguish three levels of escalation of violence. We shall refer to them as "independization of the apparatus of violence," "privatization of violence" and "commercialization of violence."

The transition from a merely serving function to the first level, the self independization of violence, occurs almost innocuously and automatically. The functional logic underlying this development can be described in the following way: Political movements of resistance require long term planning in order not to disappear without effect. For, the further the goals of the rebels are away, the less likely it becomes for them to reach these goals in one move. This again

means that the enemy will adopt measures to face the menacing danger and to arm himself against it. Therefore, one can assume that the conflict will be of long duration and will consume huge amounts of energy and means on both sides. The rebels stand a chance to survive such a conflict only if their leaders operate cleverly, if they are well equipped and supplied, if the material and logistical infrastructure is secure, that means, in short, if they are well organized and if they proceed in an organized fashion. It is, however, a well known fact that organizations lead a life of their own, and that they have their own interests, mainly to preserve themselves. Be it a terrorist cell, militia, a guerrilla movement or a revolutionary army, all these organizations of violence tend to develop in the same way (see *Revolution*). Once they have been created they tend to develop a dynamic of their own and tend to degenerate to apparatuses of violence (Waldmann 1990).

The moment that triggers this process is generally the financial need of the rebellious movement. If it starts in a province which has its own fees and troops as was the case in the North Mexican movement, then it is already enough for the rebels to increase both (Tobler 1984 p. 201, 206). If outspoken enemies of the insurgents dwell in the region taken by the rebels, their land and belongings can be confiscated and its gains can be used for the revolutionary army. When such easily accessible, political and morally unproblematic resources are absent, the rebels are often forced to resort to dubious methods of raising money. This happens when they claim taxes from their followers in "their" areas, when they improve their financial situation with bank robberies, kidnapping or bribery, or when they engaged in shady businesses such as gambling or drug trafficking. Even if those unorthodox forms of organizing money might seem justified to their followers as a means and as a response to the difficult situation, they still have two defects which influence fatally the further development: For one, it is a burden which is not accepted by the respective population but is in fact imposed because of the power monopoly of the rebelling organization. Furthermore, these unconventional financing practices forecast a mingling of political and private forms of violence which eventually lead to a complete blurring of the distinction between these two forms.

If the conflicts have been going on for a reasonable long time, all rebellious organizations, no matter what they are fighting for, must face the question as to how they can justify their existence (Burton 1987 p. 82, 88). The responses to this problem can vary.

One answer consists in permanently reaffirming that the danger has not diminished for the group. The argument then goes, that as long as the revolution has not finished or the ethnic possessions have not been confirmed, a counterattack with unpredictable consequences could occur. The best conditions to perpetuate the privileges of irregular fighting groups are situations of power patt between different civil war parties (Mansilla 1992 p. 148). If the counterpart shows first signs of weakness or seems even willing to pull in, a quick provocation makes sure that it will defend itself. Thus in fact, under the pretense of mutual attack, a "balance of horror" is established in which different militant groups help each other to stay alive.

A less macabre possibility for rebellious organizations to legitimize their existence consists in assuming quasi-state functions. The logic of this step is obvious: Once these groups have appropriated an important part of State power by protecting a population group from an external enemy, they seek to replace the weak or inactive official state also in other spheres, for instance in the control of public security and order. The IRA, for instance, has assumed in the catholic areas of Belfast and Londonderry important police-like and judicial functions. It punishes criminals, resolves family conflicts, supervises the traffic and takes truant schoolchildren back to school (Darby 1990 p. 83, 94).

Finally, rebellious organizations can respond to the growing alienation from the bases by ignoring and repressing possible protests. This is also the easiest response since it applies the principle most familiar to those organizations which is that of making use of coercion instead of respecting the voluntary consensus. By so doing, they approach the second level of escalation of violence.

One can generally observe that the close connection of organizations of violence with the supporting popular sectors of the rebellion, be it of social revolutionary or of ethnic nature, grants that the long term goals do not get out of sight. Both things are typical for the first step of escalating violence. Even though, the apparatus of violence is established and proceeds ruthlessly and without measure, on the first level the obligation towards the high goals of the movement remains unaffected. In contrast, on the next step, this connection breaks up or becomes at least very unstable. Violence becomes available for various purposes which are not necessarily of political or social nature. Violence becomes "private." There are several indicators that hint at the fact that civil wars have reached the second step of escalation:

(a) The tensions *within* the political or ethnic war parties increase, often battles between rivaling fractions break out which exceed the scope the conflict had with the original enemy. Guerrilla leaders leave their troops and offer their armed services to everyone who pays enough. The entire military-political constellation starts flowing, alliances are quickly established and dissolved depending only on tactical considerations.

(b) The original claims and long term goals for the sake of which the struggle had been started loose importance. Thus, a grotesque imbalance is generated between the relatively modest claims and the effort and money-consuming campaign of violence which is meant to help that these claims be fulfilled. The population is no longer taken seriously in terms of social backing and is not included in the political decision-making process. Instead, it becomes an object of exploitation, bribery and forced recruitment. In this new context no longer a basic distinction is made between population groups that belong to the enemy's or to one's own fraction. Also, the latter are occasionally looted and ill-treated.

(c) Violence is used overtly and wildly, without restrain for private purposes. Many individuals use it to make money. But this is not all. Desire for revenge, envy and jealousy can also be triggering moments for acts of violence. The borderline between political violence and ordinary violence associated with criminality becomes increasingly blurred. The same armed group can at one moment appear as a group of fighters for liberation and at another time it may act as gang of bandits. As a consequence of organized coercive violence, real feudal courts come into being, which live on services and taxes of their "subjects." The right of the strongest becomes the dominant means of socially imposing one's will.

Most features we have presented here are present as much in the Mexican revolution, as in the civil war in Peru, Colombia, Yugoslavia and Lebanon. We will limit ourselves to show these in the case of Lebanon, the situation of which has been characterized by T. Hanf towards the end of the war as a rule of mercenaries in allusion to the War of Thirty Years (Hanf 1990 p. 423).

He observes that the militia, originally recruited from different confessional groups have meanwhile become independent and have developed a style and procedure very similar to one another. They have repeatedly split apart and are incessantly engaged in bloody conflicts with each other, they have taken control of administration and parties, they claim taxes from their respective confessional group without bothering about their steadily declining popularity. In short: They have established themselves as a "state within a state." S. Khalaf goes even further by asserting that after a decade of war, violence has penetrated all pores of Lebanese society (Khalaf 1987 p. 238). This is evident from the arbitrariness with which objectives and alliances amongst the militia change, but even more so from the fact that violence has become a common means of making and imposing decisions also outside ethic conflicts. He points at the alarming increase of crimes of violence of all sorts which stretch from vandalism to robbed murder. More and more frequently, armed gangs of thieves enter the scenario and take away from the citizens the few things they have rescued from the civil war.

As we can see from the assertions made by both authors, the expansion of violence on this level of civil war generates strong feelings of disapproval and of indignation. A horror vision of a society á la Hobbes is created where everyone is permanently wary of everyone, but where it also is of great importance that many citizens still vividly remember the times when the norms of behavior were dictated by law and not by violence.

On the third step of escalation and diffusion of violence, this memory is by far extinguished. In Colombia, which is a paradigmatic case for this third level, scandals related to violence are no longer conceived as such. And this is the case, although more than 25,000 people die of unnatural causes or murder in this country every year, more than anywhere else on earth. Many attempts have been made to explain this steady augmentation of violence in Colombia. The most recent theory argues that the drug trafficking is responsible for it since it has transformed the use of violence into a business. There might be a bit of truth in this argument, but the drug cartels constitute, as we shall see, only one amongst many organizations of violence. It is likely that in the course of 50 years of permanent political and social conflicts people have got so much used to violence as a means of imposing one's will that they tolerate and use it as if it was something normal.

When comparing Colombia to other countries which are also not free of violence, we can identify three features which distinguish the Colombian situation from others. It is first the high number of actors of collective violence, second the trivialization and third the closely linked commercialization of violence. As for the first feature, in the case of Colombia one is already impressed at first sight by the abundance of groups which are involved in one or another way in violent activities and who mostly make their living with it. Let us briefly list up the most important ones amongst them (Sánchez/ Peñarando 1986; Bergquist 1992). Apart from the military and the police which are instances of violence recognized by the state, group violence is extorted by: paramilitary groups who allegedly fight on the countryside against left wing sympathizers; para-police death squads who proceed in bigger cities against criminals and marginal groups (homosexuals and prostitutes); mercenaries and bodyguards in the service of drug traffickers; guerrilla organizations; criminal gangs of youths; groups of self protection which are formed by citizens who chase young criminals; militia who have been hired by farmers for their own protection.

The enumeration gives an idea of how violence, on an organizational level, permanently reproduces and renews itself: A closed oligarchic system of party control, which excluded political outsiders from participation in the political decision taking process, generated violent protest at some point. Since this protest was not listened to, it condensed to a guerrilla organization which operated on the countryside and in the cities. On the countryside, it imposed taxes on farmers who defended themselves by forming militias for self-defense. In the cities, they trained young "fighters for freedom" in the use of weapons. Once the guerrilla groups got on the defensive, these fighters used their ability to offer their services as bodyguards and killer bands to the newly emerging drug cartels. Besides, it is interesting to note that the Colombian law not only allows for this diffusion of violence, but stimulates it conscientiously by ordering its armed forces to assist groups of self defense in their formation.

The ubiquity of actors of violence and of violence in general in Colombia has led to the fact that violence as a medium, which in other societies is restrained by prohibitive norms and affective barriers, has here turned into a "normal" instrument of imposing one's will, a means that provokes no public outrage. Nothing is more appropriate to illustrate this everyday, unspectacular feature of even massive actions of violence than the proliferation of massacres in this country (Uribe 1994). The term massacre refers to murders which include at least four victims. Between 1980 and 1992, 1030 massacres have taken place throughout all provinces of Colombia. Most of them happened at night in rural areas and caused the death of entire families, most of which were peasants. What strikes most, is the instrumental character of these collective killings. Only rarely accumulated emotions or political or ideological fanatism come into play. By far, the most frequent variant are massacres driven by "social" or "economic" motives. That's what is meant by "trivialization" of violence in this stage.

The possibility to have someone killed by commission constitutes a third important difference with the preceeding phase. While the use of violence on the second step of escalation opened new opportunities for personal enrichment and acquisition of certain privileges, it has now become a commercial service, a professional business. A person who is after someone else's life does no longer have to kill him in person, but can commission someone to do the job for him. Just in Medellin, meanwhile also in Cali, there are dozens of "bureaus," which live from such commissions (Prieto Osorno 1993; Salazar 1990). It is sufficient to give them a photo of the prospective victim and to pay in advance half of the agreed price, which may vary considerably depending on the rank and the bodyguard situation of the indicated person. The "bureaus" takes care of everything else. Several thousand professional killers, called *sicarios*, live in the big cities of Colombia. Most of them are youngsters between 13 and 25 years of age, who dream of the great "Coup," the murder that will make them rich from one day to the other.

The Colombian case shows that the spectacular deviation of violence away from the political sector as it is typical for the second step, is followed in a further step by the profanation of violence and its pervasion of human interaction in every day life. Therefore the stepwise sequence of diffusion of violence must not be understood as a continuous process of independization and of loss of function, but should instead be looked at as a process of spiral and dialectic development: Violence, initially contained in the political area transcends in a first step the borders of its restrictions ("privatization"), in order to acquire on a second step a predictable, fixed value in the sense of a purchasable service on the exchange market of social relations.

It goes without saying that this development is not inevitable and that when taking place it is neither fast nor goal-oriented. The multi-step scheme serves to illustrate that it would be misleading to deny a civil war any dynamics, to look at it only as a meaningless massive extinction of people which follows no rules

and carries on until all participants are tired and return to the table of negotiations. Civil wars have a dynamics of their own which explains itself from the particular logic of self perpetuating and expanding processes of violence. And again, these processes of violence exert their impact on the structures of society, economy, politics and culture. These impacts shall be tackled in the following section.

## 4. Structural Consequences

Opinions agree by far with respect to the economic consequences of civil wars: Almost without exception they are considered negative. The War of Thirty Years seems so far a warning historical precedence. Not only did it leave behind a dramatically diminished population, but also empty treasuries burdened with debts, destroyed cities, looted and destroyed monuments and devastated stretches of land, which often took decades to be colonized again (Schreiner 1985).

However, we have to make distinctions. Not all regions of a country are affected to the same extent by a civil war. Civil wars vary according to their degree of intensity. Depending upon the scope and the density of the fighting, they interfere more or less deeply in the network of production and commerce of a country. Also the economic structure of a state is of importance. A small country specialized on commerce, financial services and tourism, as is the case in Lebanon, suffers far more from the enduring bloody conflicts than the geographically vast Mexico with its still little differentiated economic structure at the time of the revolution. The impact of the civil war in the case of former Yugoslavia and particularly Bosnia-Herzegovina was virtually catastrophic (Calic 1993 p. 16; Reuter 1993 p. 257, 266). In this case we have to keep in mind that the Yugoslavian economy was already declining before the outbreak of the uproars and that this emergency situation soon got dramatically worse in consequence of the internationally imposed embargo. Independently from that it has to be stated that a civil war that raged so furiously and destructively as it was the case in this core republic located in a breaking up Balkan state, inevitably paralyzed the entire economy. The industrial production, commercial and service sector, banks, transport, everything was unable to function, only the shadow economy flourished.

Similar but less devastating news came for a long time from Lebanon (see *Arab-Israeli Conflict: Peace Plans and Proposals*). In contrast to Yugoslavia, this country had been known for decades as a sort of

"Switzerland" of the Middle East, because of its diligent inhabitants and its privileged position as a center for commerce and finance. The fighting soon led to the loss of this privileged position. Too big were the damages left behind by the military conflicts as they included the destruction of the infrastructure (harbor, streets, airport), the division of a formerly flourishing capital city and the depopulation of vast areas of the hinterland. At the end of the struggle that had lasted 15 years the state was deeply indebted, since the militia now kept its tax income for themselves, the Lebanese currency had fallen to a fraction of its former value, the trade balance was negative and the average living standard was half of what it was in 1975 (Hanf 1990 p. 449).

The list of states whose economy has been badly damaged by civil wars could be extended. Not all of them had to pay as badly for the wars as Yugoslavia and Lebanon. The negative economic consequences of the enduring unrest in Northern Ireland and Peru, two certainly not too wealthy countries, are probably bearable, and with respect to Mexico, H.W. Tobler writes that the revolution has reduced only little the average living standard, since the lack of production in some sectors could be compensated by increased production in other economic sectors (Tobler 1984 p. 478).

The case of Colombia shows a totally different picture, which confirms its exceptional position with respect to the development and the consequences of violence: Colombia is one of the economically most stable and dynamic countries of Latin America in spite of the internal conflicts that have meanwhile been going on for decades (Stockmann 1989 p. 451; Mansilla 1993 p. 145). In contrast to most countries of the region it has a positive trade balance, the state debts are limited, the GDP grows steadily, likewise does the flow of foreign investment. In short, all economic indicators have an upward tendency. This does not mean however, that without the bloody internal conflicts economic growth would not have advanced faster. The question arises, as to whether the overall positive balance is perhaps a consequence of a general immunization of the economy towards acts of violence. If this is the case, then we can hardly expect any impulses from Colombian economic circles, that would contribute to diminishing the level of violence in the country.

When comparing the evaluation of economic consequences with the assessment of social consequences of civil wars, the latter turn out to be much more diverse. Some authors make references to the leveling-out effect, others hold occasionally that civil wars are no equalizers, but on the contrary that they make differences grow between rich and poor. Those are probably not real contradictions, both assertions may be correct depending on the area we look at.

If we look at the public sector, one can hardly doubt that it is always badly affected by civil wars and that all citizens suffer from this decline of quality of public life. When, for instance, an artillery attack provokes a power cut, water has to be rationed, central traffic lines are closed, public schools close or, because of lacking state control, gangs of burglars increase their activities in consequence, the entire population suffers, no matter which social class people belong to. At the beginning, the wealthier amongst them manage perhaps to partly compensate for the negative repercussions with increased private investment (private teaching, bribery); however, because of the steady impoverishment of the entire society, which includes all social classes, this initial advantage melts away quickly in the course of a long lasting civil war.

The decisive leveling-out factor derives from the threat that oneself may become a victim of the violence that menaces everyone. In the face of the unpredictability of violence of civil wars no one is safe from this threat, as long as he stays in the country.

The scenario changes when one looks at the private "sphere" of distribution of possessions. In this case the social inequality is generally greatly enhanced by civil wars. For the major part of the population it causes a considerable reduction of offer of commercial articles, a deterioration of life conditions and in some cases terrible poverty. These negative consequences can be observed throughout all strands of society, even though they may vary gradually. With the collapse of the state and the economy the traditional upper class suffers a noticeable loss of chances of development. If a person belonging to the upper class does decide not to leave the country, then she has to be contented with a considerable reduction of income and at least temporarily with a loss of political power. The same applies to the middle classes, which additionally often lack the means for a quick and smooth change of domicile abroad. Particularly affected are the "new," academically trained middle classes, who are normally employed in big private or public organizations, and who depend on regular salaries. They are often forced to look for new jobs which are far below their academic qualifications. The most affected of the troubles of the war are the lower class groups even when civil wars officially claim to promote their liberation and to improve their material standards. They generally lack material reserves and do not possess the mental flexibility to quickly adapt to the new situation and to adjust to it appropriately. The price, they have to pay for the conflict, be it in terms of expulsions or in terms of wounded and dead people, is far higher than the losses other social sectors have to suffer.

Nevertheless, in all societies affected by civil wars there is one social group, which knows how to make its benefit from the troubles (Tobler 1984 p. 206, 449; Hanf 1990 p. 456; Gutman 1994 p. 161: Calic 1993 p. 70; Hobsbawm 1985 pp. 13-23). Some of its members stem directly from the leadership of newly formed militia associations and mercenary groups, some of them emerge from the shadows of violent conflicts and are composed by speculators, merchants with confiscated or cheaply purchased grounds and civil servant cadres for the newly created administrative units. Most of these newcomers who stem from lower middle classes, do not fear to take risks, are unscrupulous and have in common a talent for improvisation and organization. These features and the shameless way of showing off with their newly acquired wealth is probably one of the main reasons why they are disliked by the majority of the population and negatively described in the literature: as beneficiaries of the war, members of the Mafia, typical representatives of a prospering shadow economy, who had no shame to take advantage of the general misery for their own benefit. Seen from an objective perspective, we can simply state that civil wars do not basically differ from other forms of accelerated social change: They increase the mobility of social ascent or descent. This is even more true for societies with rigid quasi-feudal social structures, as was the case in Spain before 1936, where the civil war suddenly opened for entire strands of the population new opportunities to move up socially (López-Casero 1982 p. 342).

In the context of these processes of social mobility the question arises as to the transformation of power structure in the course of civil wars. With respect to the conflicting parties we need to distinguish external and internal aspects. As for the external aspect concerning the relations between the different fractions of a civil war, the changes of power resulting from years of wrestling with each other are small. At the end of the war the conflicting militias, armies and guerrilla groups are often not far from the point where they had started (Pizarro Leongómez 1994 p. 29; Hanf 1990 p. 414). The decisive military advantages are generally achieved in the first phase when energies are still fresh and chances great to surprise an unprepared enemy who can be cornered. Later on a "power patt" establishes itself, a term which is fre-

quently used in civil war literature. Apparently, all civil war parties are from a certain moment no longer interested in extending their territorial assets undergoing considerable risks, but seek to maintain them. Civil war militia are excellent for the defense, but weak aggressors, particularly when they have to fight an enemy who struggles for survival instead of a defenseless population.

Paradoxically, the important changes of power in civil war do not refer to the relationship between the different conflicting parties. Instead, they arise from changes of relationship within these parties. This result is paradoxical, because the traditional elites of power who had provoked the conflict in order to obtain a little advantage, generally turn out to be the main losers. Some reports and analyses do even give the impression that the ruling elite changes completely. They say that traditional decision takers are discharged since their skills as mediators have become redundant in the face of an armed conflict; they are replaced by a new ruling elite which recruits itself from military associations and with them closely connected new military cadres. Such analyses might jump to conclusions too quickly. It might be true that the traditional political elite is relegated to a second position, while instead 'homines novi' acquainted with questions of war tactics come to have a say in their place. But traditional power elites are a very tough species, very difficult to eliminate. After some time, when people have become tired of fighting, these traditional elites can recuperate lost political territory. In the long run, a fusion of new and traditional upper class takes place. Only those political elites survive who take into account the interest of both shares of the newly constituted upper class.

We shall now finally turn to the cultural and moral developments of civil war societies. Opinions in this area are generally clear cut and agree in condemning the consequences these conflicts have on people's emotions and ethics. One example for a comparatively moderate judgment is the passage quoted from H.C.F. Mansilla's book on the civil wars in Colombia and Peru: "The general insecurity, the diminished agricultural production, the downfall of prices for houses, grounds and landownership in the fighting zones as well as the apparent devaluation of human lives, open the way for a collective demoralization, since now the future seems bleak and life chances precarious. Benefits from savings, the necessity of a predictable economic and social behavior, and even the value of family and friendship links are thrown into question. This painful relativizing of central norms and guiding images, which are not being replaced by new value concepts, drives the militarized population into a deep socio-cultural and ethnic crisis" (Mansilla 1993 p. 152). Most authors make similar assessments. Can one therefrom conclude that periods of civil war are times of moral decay?

Such generalizations are dangerous, as one can see from studies on Northern Ireland which prove that one can hardly speak of a lowering of moral standards and of a relaxation of social control within the two confessional groups after 1969 (Waldmann 1989 p. 343). When posing the question on the development of morals and ethics it is important to distinguish between the social norms of behavior on the one side, and the principal ideas on good and bad on the other side. A certain loosening of social control in civil wars is evident from growing rates of criminality which go along with the conflicts. The much criticized increasing egotism, the ever growing rudeness of social forms of behavior, the proliferation of fear, of distrust and of a 'survival of the fittest' mentality, they all are not so much a sign of moral vulnerability of people in general terms, but are forcefully requested as strategies of adjustment to changed conditions, as is the growing insensibility against human pain.

The other question is, whether the people who are affected by such external pressures will change their deep convictions. This reaction may occasionally occur, but cannot be taken as a general rule. We know from other situations, when norms are extremely shaken as in times of hyperinflation, that they do not alter deeper rooted concepts of value and guiding ideas of behavior, but on the contrary, tend to cement preexisting values (Waldmann 1987). As it is impossible to eliminate from the collective memory of societies which have never experienced a definite state monopoly of violence the option to resort to armed self defense is just as difficult to erase peaceful forms of civilized social behaviour in times of chronic violence. In this deep entrenched knowledge of the possibility of a better, more human life, lies the principal hope and main chance for those trying to reestablish peace, to reconcile the conflicting parties and to reconstruct society.

See also: *Human Security; Conflict Impact Assessment (CIAS); Theoretical Traditions of Peace and Conflict Studies; Power; Crisis; Crisis Management*

*Bibliography* ———————————————

Bergquist C et al., (eds.) 1992 *Violence in Colombia: The Contemporary Crisis in Historical Perspective*. Wilmington

Burkhardt J 1992 *Der Dreißigjährige Krieg*. Frankfurt

Burton F 1978 *The Politics of Legitimacy. Struggles in a Belfast Community*. London

Calic M-J 1993 *Der Krieg in Bosnien-Herzegowina*. Ursachen, Verlaufsformen und Lösungsmöglichkeiten, Ebenhausen

Darby J 1990 Intimidation and interaction in a small belfast community: The water and the fish. In: J Darby et al., (eds.) *Political Violence. Ireland in a Comparative Perspective*. Belfast

Gutman R 1994 *Augenzeuge des Völkermordes*. Reportagen aus Bosnien, Göttingen

Hanf T 1990 *Koexistenz im Krieg*. Staatszerfall und Entstehung einer Nation im Lebanon, Baden-Baden

Hobsbawm E J 1985 *La anatomia de "la Violencia" en Colombia*. In: G Sanchez (ed.) *Once Ensayos sobre la Violencia*, Bogota

Khalaf S 1987 *Lebanon's Predicament*. New York

Lopez-Casero F 1982 *Die Generation des Umbruchs. Veränderungen der Lebensund Produktionsformen in einer spanischen "Agrarstadt."* In: P Waldmann et al., (eds.) *Die geheime Dynamik autoritärer Diktaturen*. München

Mansilla H C F 1993 *Ursachen und Folgen Politischer Gewalt in Kolumbien und Peru*. Frankfurt

Ortiz S, Miguel C 1986 *"La Violencia" y los Negocios, Quindio Años 50 y 60*. In: Reñaranda SR (ed.) *Pasado y Presente de la Violencia en Colombia*. Bogota

Pizarro Leongómez E 1994 Insurgencia sin Revolución. *Violencia Politica y Proceso de Paz en Colombia*. Paper presented in Lima in April

Prieto Osorno, Alexander 1993 *Die Mörder von Medellin*. Todeskult und Drogenhandel, Frankfurt

Rathfelder E 1992 *Die Bosnische Tragödie*. In: Ders (ed.) Krieg auf dem Balkan, Hamburg

Reuter J 1993 Wirtschaftliche und soziale Probleme im neuen Jugoslawien. In: *Südosteuropa* 42(5)

Salazar A 1990 *No nacimos pa semilla, La cultura de las bandas juveniles de Medellin*. Bogota

Sanchez G 1985 La violencia y sus efectos en el sistema politico colombiano. In: Ders. u.a., *Once Ensayos sobre la violencia*. Bogota

Sanchez G, Peñaranda R (eds.) 1987 *Pasado y Presente de la Violencia en Colombia*. Bogota

Schreiner K 1985 Die Katastrophe von Nördlingen. In: *Historischer Verein für Nördlingen und das Ries* 27. Jahrbuch (1985), Nördlingen

Stockmann R 1989 Die Neue Violencia: Kolumbien in der Tradition der Gewalt. In: *Ibero-Amerikanisches Archiv*, N.F. 15(3)

Thykydides *Der Peleponnesische Krieg*. Essen

Tobler H W 1984 *Die Mexikanische Revolution*. Frankfurt

Uribe M V 1978 *Matar, Rematar y Contramatar. Las Masacres de le Violencia en el Tolima 1948-1964*. Bogota

Uribe M V 1994 Colombia, una construccion social violenta.

Paper presented in Lima in April

Waldmann P 1989 *Ethnischer Radikalismus*. Ursachen und Folgen gewaltsamer Minderheitenkonflikte, Opladen

Waldmann P 1989 *Guerillabewegungen in Lateinamerika*. Das Beispiel des Sendero Luminoso (Peru). In: D. Langewi-esche (ed.) *Revolution und Krieg*. Paderborn (1989a)

Waldmann P 1990 *Militanter Nationalismus im Baskenland*. Frankfurt

PETER WALDMANN

# Civilian-based Defense

Civilian-based defense is a defense policy to preserve a society's freedom against both internal threats (such as *coups d'état*) and external threats (such as invasions) by preparing in advance to resist such usurpations with nonviolent struggle applied by the whole population. The aim is to deter or to defeat such attacks, not simply by altering the will of the attackers but also by making successful usurpations impossible through massive and selective noncooperation and defiance by the citizens. This policy has also been called civilian defense, nonviolent defense, non-military defense, defense by civil resistance, and social defense.

Civilian-based defense applies political, social, economic, and psychological weapons in place of military ones to resist internal or international aggression. This is the adoption and adaptation of the technique of nonviolent action to develop a national defense policy as a practical substitute for military defense and nuclear deterrence. The term "civilian" indicates its nonmilitary character and also its aim of defending the independence and democratic nature of the society and its principles by action of the civilian population.

## 1. Origins of the Policy

The policy of civilian-based defense has four major origins. The first comprises the improvised cases of nonviolent noncooperation and defiance against *coups d'état* and foreign occupations. These include Hungarian resistance to Austrian rule, 1850-67; Finnish resistance to Russification, 1898-1905; resistance to the Kapp *Putsch* in Germany, 1920; German government-sponsored nonviolent resistance to the French and Belgian occupation of the Ruhr, 1923; various cases of anti-Nazi resistance during the Second World War including especially Norway, the Netherlands, and Denmark; various cases of resistance to save Jews from the Holocaust, as in Norway, the Netherlands, Denmark, Bulgaria, and even Berlin; French resistance to the 1961 generals' *Putsch* in Algiers; Czechoslovak nonviolent resistance to the Soviet and Warsaw Pact invasion and occupation, 1968-69; and various cases of nonviolent resistance in Eastern Europe (especially Poland since 1980) and nonviolent insurrections against established dictatorships (in Latin America, Thailand, the Philippines, and elsewhere).

The second origin is the thinking of military strategists, such as Sir Basil Liddell Hart and Commander Sir Stephen King-Hall (both now deceased), about how to achieve effective defense when military options suffer from serious disadvantages while nonviolent resistance has impressive capacities.

The third origin is the general policy projections of various practitioners of nonviolent action (including M. K. Gandhi) and social radicals (as in the Netherlands in the 1930s) that defense against foreign invasions could be effectively waged by the general population using nonviolent forms of struggle, including political noncooperation and labor strikes.

The fourth origin is the work, since about 1964, of a small number of academics and strategists of nonviolent struggle who have sought to develop the policy. A major example of their efforts was the 1964 Civilian Defence Study Conference in Oxford. These scholars have refined the general concept, analyzed its problems, explored possible strategies of defense, sketched political strategies for partial or full adoption of the policy, contributed to examination of the policy by political, military, and governmental bodies, and identified areas for future research and policy analysis.

Nonviolent resistance components have already been included in the official security policies of Switzerland, Austria, and former Yugoslavia. Some type of governmental or military consideration of the possible role of nonviolent resistance in defense has also been undertaken in Finland, Norway, Sweden, Denmark, the Netherlands, and France.

## 2. Improvised and Prepared Defense

In the past, use of nonviolent struggle for defense against coups and occupations, in revolts against dictatorships, and in resistance to other oppression has always been largely or completely unprepared, in contrast to the use of military means. Nonviolent struggles have sometimes even begun without advance decision, and almost always have been conducted without benefit of planning, preparations, and training of the participants. Nevertheless, there have been some successes and partial successes along with the failures. While building on the improvised prototype struggles of the past, civilian-based defense cannot be fully evaluated on the basis of their achievements alone because of their unrefined and improvised character.

In contrast, this policy is proposed to operate on the basis of prior research, policy analysis and decisions, contingency planning, preparations of diverse types, and extensive training of the population. Since these elements were not present in past improvised struggles, no cases of civilian-based defense in combat—successful or otherwise—can be cited at this point. This situation is shared with many innovations in military weaponry. Analysts see that the addition of the above elements would increase the effectiveness of a civilian-based defense policy significantly beyond the capacities demonstrated in past improvised cases of nonviolent struggle.

## 3. Civilian-based Deterrence

Civilian-based defense is projected to be capable of deterring potential attackers. Both internal usurpation and foreign invasions are undertaken to achieve some objective, argue strategists of this policy. Such attacks are therefore likely to be rationally calculated acts, rather than to grow out of fits of rage or be acts of simple destruction. Consequently, it is reasoned, potential attackers usually will calculate the odds of achieving their intended goal and decide whether it is worth the anticipated costs. If the chance of success is small, and the costs excessively high, then although the goal may still be desired, the attack is not likely to be launched; the potential attackers will have been deterred. The deterrence capacity of civilian-based defense is therefore based directly upon an actual defense capacity. Deterrence can thus occur within the context of strictly nonviolent means.

Whether, and to what degree, civilian-based defense can provide deterrence in a specific situation will depend on two main factors: (a) the actual capacity of the society to deny the attackers their desired objectives, and also to impose unacceptable costs (alone or in cooperation with others); and (b) the potential attackers' perception of this capacity.

If civilian-based defense preparations fail to deter, then, unlike nuclear deterrence, the result is not annihilation but application for the first time of the policy's actual defense capacity.

## 4. The Capacity to Defend

The capacity of civilian-based defense to defend against an attack rests on that same ability to deny to the aggressors their objectives and to inflict unusual and extensive domestic and international costs. The defenders should not be surprised to encounter severe repression and brutalities. In response the defenders must persist in their resistance and maintain their nonviolent discipline.

The effectiveness of civilian-based defense in resisting attack depends on at least six factors:

(a) the population's will to defend against the attack;

(b) the internal strength of the attacked society;

(c) the ability of the population and institutions to retain control of their sources of power and to deny them to the attackers;

(d) the defenders' ability to deny to the attackers their objectives;

(e) the defenders' capacity to fulfill the requirements for effective nonviolent struggle, including maintaining nonviolent discipline and persisting in struggle despite repression; and

(f) the defenders' skill in aggravating the weaknesses of the attackers' system and regime.

No single blueprint exists or can be created to plan deterrence and defense capacity by civilian-based defense for all situations. The political, social, economic, and psychological weaponry applied in any given case needs to be adjusted to relate directly to the specific issues at stake, the attackers' objectives, and the selected defense strategies.

## 5. Initial Defense Strategies

When an invasion or internal usurpation occurs, initial civilian-based defense action is likely to take one of two main forms. It may be a nonviolent *Blitzkrieg*, a massive demonstration of resistance and defiance—such as a short general strike or a temporary complete paralysis of the whole society—which might (the odds are not great) induce the aggressors' quick retreat or even capitulation. The other form of initial defense may be dramatic actions intended primarily to warn the attackers that resistance will be strong and of a particularly insidious type. These methods may include: filling the streets with demonstrators or leaving them completely empty; defiant publication of newspapers and dissemination of broadcasts with news of the attack and resistance; massive defiance of curfews; holding of street parties for all including the hostile troops; persistently carrying on of "business as usual" both economically and politically on the basis of the legitimate laws and practices; and massive attempts to subvert the loyalty and reliability of the attackers' troops and minor functionaries. The attackers' countermeasures to these initial forms of resistance may range from the extremely mild to the brutal. The defenders must be prepared to carry on the defense, in the assumption that the struggle could be extended and difficult. An initial nonviolent *Blitzkrieg*, a campaign of communication and warning, or a combination of both, is simply the opening phase of a defense effort which, like the military alternatives, may require a longer period of intense struggle to achieve victory.

## 6. Substantive Defense

In facing the strategic problems of longer range defense, the civilian defenders can apply one of two major strategies: either a massive campaign of total noncooperation similar to an extended nonviolent Blitzkrieg, or some form of selective resistance. The defenders may also use each of these major strategies at different times to meet special defense needs.

Massive, total resistance, consisting of campaigns of comprehensive noncooperation and defiance by the whole society against the attackers' regime and its policies as a whole may be appropriate at certain limited stages of the substantive defense. However, such total resistance is exceptionally difficult to apply except for special restricted periods. Total non-cooperation may be used at certain points to achieve specific objectives within a grand strategy that relies predominantly on selective resistance. Total resistance may also be applied toward the end of a longer defense struggle by selective resistance. The aim of total resistance at that point is to strike a knockout blow to defeat or disintegrate the attackers' regime or controls, to destroy their ability to continue the whole venture, and to restore the society's independence and freedom.

With those exceptions, the main thrust of the society's defense instead must be—most analysts agree—the strategy of selective resistance. This strategy concentrates resistance on particular points or objectives which are especially important for the defense effort. This strategy has several advantages. For example, it enables the defense to be concentrated, instead of diffused on a great variety of objectives and issues. This strategy is also less exhausting to the defending population, since in most cases the major responsibility for waging defense will shift from one section of the population to another as specific issues and points of resistance change.

In choosing the points for selective resistance the following factors should be considered: how to deny the attackers' main objectives; how to prevent the attackers from controlling the state apparatus; how to maintain the autonomy of the society's independent institutions; how to concentrate defense capacity on vulnerable points of the attackers' system; how to use the defenders' strongest capacities; and how to select for resistance specific, obviously justifiable, issues (such as freedom of religion or speech, independence of the schools, and use of national symbols) that are crucial for the whole defense effort.

## 7. Resisting Repression

The attackers cannot, of course, be expected to accept such vigorous defense efforts or passively to submit. On the contrary, these various civilian-based defense strategies will be correctly perceived as dangerous to the attackers' goals, system, and venture. At times, the response may be irrational rage. At other times it may be calculated repression. The civilian defenders must be prepared to withstand all such countermeasures and to persist in their defense struggle. By maintaining nonviolent discipline in the face of violent repression, the defenders can alienate still more groups from the opponent, turning the effects of the repression against the attackers themselves by the process of "political *jiu-jitsu*"—increasing the extent of resistance, arousing international efforts in support of the defenders, and provoking opposition in the opponents' own camp.

The combination of the direct effects of resistance and of the impact of political *jiu-jitsu* can make the costs of the venture unacceptable, deny the attackers their objectives, and force a halt to the attack or even dissolve the attacking forces and regime. As the attackers weaken and the defenders grow in strength, selective resistance campaigns of various types may progressively bring the defenders closer to victory.

It is important that the defenders develop and apply specific plans to bring the defense struggle to a final successful conclusion. The defenders may then adjust their strategy toward increasingly general resistance and a final campaign of total noncooperation to provide a knockout blow to the attackers' venture, or the defenders may develop a different strategy to bring victory.

In response, the attackers may intensify the repression. If that fails, they may inflict brutalities on the resisting population, but this may only accelerate the process of political *jiu-jitsu*. If the attackers remain rational and flexible, they may seek a way to extricate themselves from the situation, with minimal damage and perhaps even with some gains. More rigid opponents may defiantly continue their ever-more unsuccessful and counterproductive efforts, until the venture unravels as the resistance becomes evermore massive, the attackers' international friends disappear, and their own administrative and repressive forces dissolve.

## 8. Failure and Success

Not every attempt to apply civilian-based defense will succeed. This type of struggle, like any other, must fulfill certain requirements if success is to follow. If those requirements are not developed sufficiently to produce victory, then—to the degree that the resistance spirit and the resilience of the society's independent institutions are maintained—the population can renew the defense struggle at a later time.

## 9. Transarmament

As knowledge of civilian struggle spreads, it is probable that the number of societies will grow in which nonviolent struggle will be improvised in face of foreign attacks or internal usurpations. It is not a long jump from these situations and the past cases to new instances in which people, institutions, and governments carefully examine the options and begin preparations and training prior to attacks in order to become more able to deter and defend against future possible aggression.

Transarmament—the process of changeover—to civilian-based defense does not require any prior transformation of the international system, the disappearance of military threats, or universal adoption of the policy. Nor does it require prior fundamental change in the social system—much less a change in "human nature." Indeed, initial research, policy development, evaluation, and public consideration of civilian-based defense begins while present policies for deterrence and defense are fully intact.

Civilian-based defense is designed to deter and defend against attacks. Assuming its effectiveness, therefore, this policy can be adopted by single countries, groups of countries, or alliances, without any wider agreement in the international community, much less the participation of potential attackers. This is essentially the same principle which applies

when new military weapons or weapons systems are adopted because they are perceived to be superior to earlier ones and those of possible attackers. (It is possible to imagine a planned phased adoption of the policy by agreement of all countries in a region—such as Central Europe—with or without United Nations involvement, but that is unlikely to be the typical model.)

When the society and government of a country decide to begin to transarm to civilian-based defense, the initial preparations and training would begin on a relatively modest basis, while the existing military capacity is still in place. This civilian-based defense component of the overall defense posture is then expanded in stages. Some countries might keep both capacities permanently. The general model presented by civilian-based defense theorists, however, is for a full transarmament to the policy over a period of some years. During transarmament the military capacity would not be downgraded or eliminated until the society and government were sufficiently confident of the capacities of the new policy and of its advantages over a military posture.

In those very few countries—like Iceland and Costa Rica—which do not have standing armies, and in several others in which the military system is largely symbolic and incapable of serious military defense against potential attackers, a different model of transarmament may be possible. One possibility is a much more rapid build-up of civilian-based defense capacity determined officially on the governmental level. The other possibility is that the population and private institutions of the society could on their own initiative evaluate the proposed defense policy and prepare plans for their roles in a comprehensive civilian-based national defense effort against potential aggressors. These preparations could proceed prior to or parallel with governmental evaluation and decision making.

## 10. Conditions and Motives

Civilian-based defense does not require ideal social conditions for its adoption and practice. Past improvised applications of nonviolent struggle for defense against coups d'état and foreign invasions and occupations have occurred in highly imperfect societies, with serious internal injustices, elite or class rule, ethnic or linguistic heterogeneity, and extreme social and political conflicts. The opposite conditions—social harmony, diffused effective power, and vibrant democracy—would be more conducive to the use and success of such action, but they are not prerequisites.

This does not mean, however, that all governments and systems can be defended by civilian-based defense, without changes prior to or during the transarmament period or the defense struggle itself. Severe dictatorships ruling a deeply alienated population by terror ought not to expect a public outpouring of popular and strong resistance to defend the regime and system. The people would lack the will to defend, and the society would lack the resilience capable of repelling the attack.

In most societies the motives for waging civilian-based defense will be the same ones that apply in military defense: love of one's own country; opposition to international aggression, internal usurpations, and foreign domination; and belief in one's duty to protect one's homeland and people.

While an ideal society is not required as a prerequisite for use of civilian-based defense, a long-term link does exist between that technique and "democracy"—that is, a political system with popular participation in decision making. That type of system will contribute to increased effectiveness of civilian-based defense. Conversely, this policy and nonviolent struggle in general will contribute to the diffusion of effective power and democratic participation.

Given the will, civilian-based defense is possible under present domestic and international conditions. In all countries not subject to imminent attack, there is time for reasoned evaluation and decision making, and then for planning, preparations, and training to increase future effectiveness of this policy. Countries facing imminent attack which have military options with a reasonable chance of repelling invaders are likely to continue to rely predominantly on military means, but even they could add civilian-based defense components. A few countries without significant military options—such as Austria—have in civilian-based defense a serious alternative to impotent violent gestures risking massive destruction and casualties and to passive submission in face of aggression by military giants. Countries that are especially vulnerable to *coups d'état*—such as Spain or Thailand—might add this policy to deal with that threat alone. Other countries may move by small incremental steps to examine the policy and progressively add civilian-based defense components, which could be gradually expanded.

## 11. International Activities

Countries with civilian-based defense policies could participate in a great variety of international activities on bilateral, multilateral, regional, and global bases.

These activities could reduce the number and intensity of future international conflicts. Some of the international cooperation and mutual assistance among these countries will focus directly on the preparations for, and conduct of, civilian-based defense. This makes possible widespread sharing of knowledge and know-how among countries that have already adopted the policy and countries which are still investigating it. Research results, policy developments and analyses, plans and experience in preparations and training, insights into the nature and goals of potential attackers—all can be shared with mutual benefit. So too can studies of strategy, of responses to particular types of attack, of means of maximizing effectiveness, methods of maintaining resistance in face of repression, and measures to meet the society's survival needs during a defense struggle.

Research, policy studies, development and evaluation of means of preparation and training could be initially conducted by individual countries, private institutions, and interstate arrangements—by cooperating countries, treaty partners, regional organizations, or United Nations agencies.

These same bodies could also, on the basis of advance decision and planning—as by treaty arrangements—or in response to particular crises, provide various types of nonmilitary assistance to civilian-based defense countries facing attack. Appropriate and potentially beneficial types of assistance in such cases include:

(a) printing and broadcasting facilities for the attacked country;

(b) food and medical supplies;

(c) communication to the outside world of news about the defense struggle and the attackers' actions;

(d) mobilization of international economic and diplomatic sanctions against the attackers;

(e) communication to the attackers' troops, functionaries, and population of information about the attack, the issues at stake, and news of resistance, repression, and dissent among the attackers' usual supporters, as well as reports of pleas for help in ending the attack and in restoring international friendship and cooperation.

All such international assistance is extremely important, but the main burden of the defense must be borne by the population of the attacked society itself. No substitute exists for self-reliance, sound preparations, and genuine strength in civilian-based defense.

## 12. Potential Benefits

The policy of civilian-based defense has the potential in the long run to produce various beneficial results not possible with military policies. These include the following:

(a) By shifting the decisive factor from military to societal strength, it would increase the capacity for self-reliance in defense and security matters, even by smaller and medium-sized countries. This would help to depolarize the international situation.

(b) By its nonmilitary nature, civilian-based defense provides the deterrence-defense capacities of military systems without their attack-suppression capacities, thereby reducing international and internal anxieties and dangers. This would largely put an end to the problem that military preparations that are intended to be purely defensive by one country are often seen by its neighbors as intended for aggression.

(c) This policy can reduce the incidence of international aggression as potential attackers are deterred by civilian-based defense preparations.

(d) The policy may reduce nuclear proliferation by providing an alternative route to achieve self-reliance in security policies where conventional military means are perceived to be inadequate or impracticable.

(e) The policy is likely to reduce *coups d'état* and other usurpations because, in contrast to military systems, civilian-based defense does not build up an internal capacity for carrying out such attacks and instead creates a deterrence and defense capacity against them.

(f) Civilian-based defense, in common with nonviolent struggle more generally, tends to result in fewer casualties and less destruction than comparable military conflicts.

(g) Civilian-based defense countries—being incapable of launching nuclear attacks—are far less likely to be threatened or attacked with nuclear weapons than are countries with military policies, especially with nuclear weapon, which may stimulate targeting and even preemptive attacks.

(h) This policy is likely to contribute to development of a foreign policy concerned with human needs and rights, because defense is not tied to military requirements or alliances. It is also advantageous for countries with civilian-based defense policies to adopt policies that win friends and help to resolve international problems short of open conflict.

(i) Domestically, a civilian-based defense policy, not requiring military hardware or military systems, would reduce the size of government and the expense of deterrence and defense. The policy would also remove the centralizing influences endemic to military systems and introduce decentralizing influences associated with nonviolent sanctions.

(j) By placing responsibility for the defense on the people themselves, this policy would encourage citizens to recognize qualities of their society that are worthy of defense, and to examine the society's principles, way of life, and institutions, as well as means of improving it.

(k) By providing deterrence and defense by nonviolent struggle, this policy enables countries to abandon military means as no longer needed while increasing their capacity to ward off and withstand the dangers of the contemporary world.

## 13. Steps in Consideration

Significant evidence exists that the potential of civilian-based defense may be substantial and could successfully deter and defend against attackers. Its exponents and strategists have presented this alternative policy for thorough research, investigation, and consideration.

The development, evaluation, and implementation of civilian-based defense policies for particular countries require a series of distinguishable steps. These include basic research, problem-solving research, policy studies, public education and consideration, planning for preparations and training, development of contingency plans, comparative evaluation, decision making, and phased introduction of the policy. These activities can be variously conducted by independent institutions, special commissions, governmental agencies, and international organizations.

See also: *Alternative Defense; Nonviolence; Nonviolence, Philosophy and Politics of*

*Notes*

1. The following bibliography comprises only a selection of titles in the English language from a much larger bibliography of relevant works in English and several other languages.

*Bibliography* ───────────────────

Alternative Defence Commission 1983 *Defence Without the Bomb*. Taylor and Francis, London

Atkeson E B 1976 The relevance of civilian-based defense to US security interests. *Military Review* 56(5); 56(6)

Boserup A, Mack A 1974 *War Without Weapons: Non-Violence in National Defence*. Francis Pinter, London

Galtung J 1976 On the strategy of nonmilitary defense: Some proposals and problems. In: *Essays in Peace Research*, Vol. 2: *Peace, War and Defense*. Christian Ejlers, Copenhagen

Geeraerts G (ed.) 1977 *Possibilities of Civilian Defence in Western Europe*. Swets and Zeitlinger, Amsterdam

Kennan G 1958 *Russia, the Atom and the West*. Oxford University Press, Oxford

Keyes G 1981 Strategic non-violent defense: The construct of an option. *J. Strategic Studies* 4(2)

King-Hall S 1958 *Defence in the Nuclear Age*. Gollancz, London

King-Hall S 1960 *Common Sense in Defence*. K-H Services, London

King-Hall S 1962 *Power Politics in the Nuclear Age: A Policy for Britain*. Gollancz, London

Kritzer H Nonviolent national defense: Concepts and implications. *Peace Res. Rev.* 5(5)

Mahadevan T K, Roberts A, Sharp G (eds.) 1967 *Civilian Defence: An Introduction*. Gandhi Peace Foundation, New Delhi

Roberts A (ed.) 1967 *The Strategy of Civilian Defence: Nonviolent Resistance to Aggression*. Faber and Faber, London

Roberts A 1972 *Total Defence and Civil Resistance: Problems of Sweden's Security Policy*. FOAP Rapport C8335/M. Försvarets Forskningsanstalt, Stockholm

Roberts A 1975 Civil resistance to military coups. *J. Peace Res.* 12(1)

Roberts A 1980 *Occupation, Resistance and Law: International Law on Military Occupations and on Resistance*. Försvarets Forskningsanstalt, Stockholm

Roberts A, Frank J D, Naess A, Sharp G 1964 *Civilian Defence*. Peace News, London

Sharp G 1970 *Exploring Nonviolent Alternatives*. Porter Sargent, Boston, Massachusetts

Sharp G 1973 *The Politics of Nonviolent Action*, 3 vols. Porter Sargent, Boston, Massachusetts

Sharp G 1979 *Gandhi as a Political Strategist*. Porter Sargent, Boston, Massachusetts

Sharp G 1980 *Social Power and Political Freedom*. Porter Sargent, Boston, Massachusetts

Sharp G 1985a *Making Europe Unconquerable: The Potential of Civilian-based Deterrence and Defence*. Taylor and Francis, London/Ballinger, Cambridge, Massachusetts

Sharp G 1985b *National Security Through Civilian-based Defense*. Association for Transarmament Studies, Omaha, Nebraska

GENE SHARP

# Civilizational View of History

The civilizational view of history was originally conceived by Young Seek Choue in his book *The Creation of a New Civilized World* (1951). It is a human-centric view of history with the fundamental aim to create a new civilized world by way of establishing and realizing cultural norms which humans as cultural beings should observe. This view of history rests upon a broad conceptualization of the notion 'civilization' which includes culture. Here the term 'civilizational' stands for the Korean expression 'munhwa' which is used to be translated literally into English as 'culture' and 'cultural.' But as Norbert Elias clarified the formation process of the notions 'civilization' and 'culture' in Europe in his book *Über den Proze der Zivilisation*, these two notions had been used without any essential difference of meaning in Europe until the mid-18th century in which the contrast between the two notions emerged in Germany. At that time the term 'Kultur' ('culture' in German) began to be related to the spiritual and intellectual achievements of a nation or people whereas 'civilization' was associated

in German minds with something useful and material. But this kind of contrast between these two terms has remained in general to be a specific German phenomenon. Except the German cultural area, the term 'civilization' was not so much differentiated in its meaning from the term 'culture.' Moreover it is used more broadly and comprises the notion 'culture' in English. That's why we translate the Korean expression 'munhwa sagwan' as the "civilizational view of history."

In the civilizational view of history, the term 'civilization' stands for the overall process in which mankind uses nature to achieve an ever higher level of life. In this sense, the notion of 'civilization' means generally what Ernst Cassirer writes when he defines 'human culture.' "Human culture" taken as a whole may be described as the process of man's progressive self-liberation. Language, art, religion, science, are various phases in this process. In all of them man discovers and proves a new power—the power to build up a world of his own, an 'ideal' world" (Ernst Cassirer, *An Essay on Man: An Introduction to a Philosophy of Human Culture*, New Haven: Yale Univ. Press, 1944 p. 228). As for the civilizational view of history, this 'ideal' world is 'Oughtopia,' that is a spiritually beautiful, materially affluent, and humanly rewarding society. 'Oughtopia' is a compound word of "Ought to (be or do)" and "Topia," and it connotes the meaning of what "ought to be" in society. Oughtopia is a society of what "ought to be" in which human beings are able to lead a meaningful and humane life with correct understanding of cosmic reality and human nature. Among the theories of ideal society, there are many models such as Thomas More's *Utopia* and Tommaso Campanella's *The City of the Sun*. Those models, however, do not apply to the drastically transformed society of today. Oughtopia is a societal model designed for the third millennium, and differs from the previous models of an ideal society by constructing a feasible ideal type of society from reality. It is a new civilized world in which humanity will achieve perfection through self realization, society allows humans to enjoy their lives worth while to live, and happiness will result from a harmony of spirit and material affluence (see Choue, Young Seek, *Oughtopia*, Oxford: Pergamon Press, 1979).

The civilizational view of history criticizes not only the spiritualistic view of history which finds the essence of human being in the spirit and regards human history purely as the history of spirit, but also the materialistic view of history which tries to explain the driving force of human history solely with the human desires for material goods. The civilizational view of history comprehends the human history "cubically," that is, from the holistic viewpoint integrating both the material and spiritual aspects of human life. Its central message about the course of the human history is that the driving force of social change and historic progress is not the power of natural law, but 'cultural' norms and values which the human being creates. As a general rule, the natural world proceeds according to the nature's providence, the world of animals according to their own instincts and intrinsic reaction of conditional reflex, and the human society according to reason and social norms founded upon humanness.

Regardless of the forms of government, our political society has been founded on such human attributes and nature since the ancient times. The legitimacy of such political systems ever since was based on the divine right, the natural law, and the absolute authority of the people, state and classes, whereas the norms supporting such political systems were set forth by the absolute or reason-oriented view of his-

tory which are in fact derived from the natural norms. The problem with such norms is that they are simply based on the theory of force stemming from the belief in the supremacy of power. Therefore, it can be said that human history up to now is a history of natural law and power. Until now humans have been controlled by the order imposed by the law of nature. The civilizational view of history—as a comprehensive view of history through a combination of spiritual culture and material civilization—claims that such a problematic situation of human life under the control of the natural law of power should be transformed into a new civilized world in which humans, being able to discern right from wrong and good from evil, live a civilized life as cultural beings with mutual respect and cooperation.

The civilizational view of history upholds that man as the master of history and civilization is the center of society. It is based on the idea of 'humancentrism,' which conceives that all things in human society must be considered as factors and instruments to serve human life by creating human happiness and values. Differentiated from both humanism and anthropocentrism, humancentrism neither denies God nor despises animals. A human being with an independent personality, however, is a real spiritual being distinct from both God and animals, whose inherent ability permits him/her to be the master of his/her own destiny. The civilizational view of history lays emphasis on the possibility of such an active role of human being. The conscious leadership of a 'person' as the master of one's own destiny is the ability to control one's body and mind, through which a human being becomes the master of his/her social and natural environment, social structure and institution and his/her own life through self-determination. It is also the ability to take responsibility for his/her choices and actions. For this reason, human being should not be subordinate to anything else. Every social and natural entity should serve the human being insofar as the harmony between human choices and social and natural environments is maintained. In contemporary society, institutions, money, power, technology, etc., however, dominate and subordinate human beings instead of operating as means to further human happiness. Humancentrism seeks to reverse the relations of power to create a humancentered society, placing humans in position to be the masters of their own destiny. To realize a humane and civilized welfare society based upon humancentrism, which places special importance on human dignity, the civilizational view of history calls for the adoption of a new set of cultural norms which will combine Oriental and Occidental views of values, harmonize material values with spirituality, reconcile individual interests with communal ethics, and foster a sense of mutual equality and cooperation grounded in 'mankind-consciousness.' As for the establishment of such a new set of cultural norms, the civilizational view of history suggests the following five determinative criteria by which right can be discerned from wrong, and good from evil.

First of all, since 'good' is 'good of human society,' anything that is truly humane and beneficial to human life is good. Anything that is neither humane nor beneficial to human life is evil.

Second, since man should be a civilized being, anything that gives rise to civilization and anything that protects and preserves it are good. And anything that destroys it is evil.

Third, because we live today in a democracy that is rooted in the principle of popular sovereignty, anything that is not for exclusivism but for universal democracy is good. In other words, all things that contribute to the securing of universal freedom, equality and co-prosperity and to the preserving of equal rights and coexistence of all states big or small alike are good. And anything that is against it is evil.

Fourth, man lives a collective social life. Since man has to live in the domains of family, work place and country, he is in fact incapable of living outside of society. Man's capability of creating and developing civilization and his enjoyment of a happy life is attributable only to his cooperative social life. So, anything that fosters cooperative social life is good, and anything that obstructs or destroys it is evil.

Fifth, whatever preserves and furthers the above four criteria of good and evil is good (see Choue Young Seek, *Magna Carta of Global Common Society: Grand Vision of Human Society Toward the New Millennium*. Keynote Speech at the International Peace Conference for the 17th Anniversary of the UN International Day of Peace held from September 24 to 26, 1998).

With these five determinative criteria of right and wrong as well as good and evil, the civilizational view of history offers the guidelines for the realization of a new civilized world as a combination of humane society, cultural welfare society, and universal democratic society. It intends to guide humankind in restraining the excesses of materialism and of science and technology, and in breaking away from the trends of human alienation, human depreciation, and moral decay toward the construction of a humancentered society where humans become masters of their own history.

The current age marks a turning point in the human history toward an entirely new society, thanks to drastic improvements in communication technology, enabling the development of a borderless society, namely the global common society. With the insight that a time of great metamorphosis has arrived in human history, and for the cause of the Oughtopian reconstruction of human society, the civilizational view of history as a holistic view proposes the Second Renaissance Movement, which should enlighten the whole world again through the rediscovery of the true nature of human being and lead to the rebirth of humankind through the restoration of humanity and morality.

*Bibliography* ————————————————

Choue Y S 1951 *The Creation of a Civilized World*. Moonsungdang, Taegu (In Korean)

Choue Y S 1979 *Oughtopia*. Pergamon Press, Oxford

Choue Y S 1998 *Magna Carta of Global Common Society. Grand Vision of Human Society Toward the New Millennium*. Keynote Speech at the Commemorative Ceremony and International Peace Conference for the 17th Anniversary of the UN International Day of Peace held from Sept. 24-26, 1998

Cassirer E 1944 *An Essay on Man. An Introduction to a Philosophy of Human Culture*. Yale Univ. Press, New Haven

Elias N 1991 *Über den Proze der Zivilisation. Soziogenetische und Psychogenetische Untersuchungen*, 2 vols. a. M. Suhrkamp Frankfurt

HYONG-SIK YUN

# Clark, Grenville

Toward the end of his long life in 1967, when the goal of the rule of law in world affairs seemed more remote than ever, Grenville Clark reflected on the future of world federalism. The great factor in the future, he thought, probably would not be an actual, nuclear Third World War. It would be popular repudiation of the policies of deterrence, of programs of national preparedness *tending* to nuclear war. He wrote:

It may well be that a new series of shocks will be needed—famines, revolutions, confrontations. But whether or not these occur, I cannot but believe that worldwide understanding of the adverse effects of the arms race—tangible and intangible—will steadily increase to a point where the general sentiment of mankind will declare: "This arms race has become intolerable. Even if we knew that its 'balance of terror' could last indefinitely, its other evils are no longer to be borne." (A better ordered world—Hope or illusion? 1966, Clark Papers 21.33[1])

To end the arms race, Clark concluded, the people in every nation would have to abandon the "near chaos of the power politics system" and create a "better ordered world."

For Grenville Clark, who, with Harvard professor of law Louis B. Sohn, had written *World Peace Through World Law*, a better ordered world meant one in which all nations had voluntarily abolished their national armaments and had agreed to establish judicial and political conciliation tribunals of enforceable world law, to take the place of the former system of wars. This meant a thoroughly reformed United Nations Organization. The General Assembly would have to be made a representative world legislature empowered to enact law binding on individuals—subject to strict constitutional limitations to protect the freedoms and rights of individuals and minorities. The Security Council should then be transformed into an executive of the laws of the world legislature. The World Court, in turn, would have to be greatly enlarged and granted compulsory jurisdiction for the trial of cases involving individuals, as well as states, under the law (see *International Court of Justice*).

These reforms, in principle, would amount to transformation of the United Nations into a limited, federal world government. But they went deeper. They implied a commitment, a determination, on the part of the world's peoples and their national leaders, to continue politically the processes of interdependence and unification that were already so advanced on the economic, industrial, communications, transportation, and even military planes. What was needed was an act of will—the general will of humanity—to bring the nations out of a state of anarchy, which is a state of war, and into a civil state, which is one of law, or ordered freedom national sovereignty had to give way to the sovereignty of the people.

Whether popular demands for an alternative to the nuclear arms race would result in such a change in the direction of world politics, or would merely be sidetracked in new military solutions, depended, Clark thought, on a continuing international education program. Its goal should be to inform the public

in all lands about the nature of international anarchy and the consequent race for military superiority as a security measure (quite apart from any expansionist "intentions"). It should make plain the need for new world political institutions analogous to those of strong national or federal states. Clark remained hopeful that the world's diverse peoples would take the initiative—or at least would lend their firm support to wise national leaders who took the initiative—to unite under a limited, federal world government. He liked to quote Abraham Lincoln, who said during the crisis of the American union, "The people will save their government, if the government itself will do its part only indifferently well."

Grenville Clark became the elder statesman of the movement to strengthen the United Nations along the lines of federal world government. He never held public office and is not popularly known, but, as Norman Cousins has written, "It is doubtful if any other private American contributed more to the peace in the past half century." The character of the man—"a man for all seasons"—is conveyed by the volume of reminiscences from his many friends entitled *Memoirs of a Man* (Cousins and Clifford 1975).

Clark was born into the New York aristocracy in 1992. Like Franklin D. Roosevelt, he grew up with every advantage of wealth and schooling, and like him, too, his greatest work was in public service. Clark heard the maxims of Abraham Lincoln from a grandfather who had known the magnanimous president. Before Clark had graduated from Harvard, he had met Theodore Roosevelt. Elihu Root, Sr. was general counsel of his Wall Street law firm. He advised Roosevelt about the National Economy Act of the first New Deal. He brought Henry Stimson into the War Department and led a citizens' committee in favor of a selective service law when Roosevelt could not act in 1940. In short, Clark had many friends at the highest levels of US government and earned for himself the unofficial title of "statesman incognito."

In 1944, on the advice of Stimson, Clark began to devote himself primarily to world statesmanship. He worked for federal world government to the end of his life. Clark is significant among world federalists for his realism, timeliness, and practical wisdom.

Clark was realistic in a much more whole sense than is now usually understood by that term. He recognized that world politics was a struggle for power; he saw that human beings tend to be united most widely on the basis of their "interests." But he also recognized that the definition of interests was usually provided by national leaders, who utilized ideal and even moral conceptions, and he knew that the whole purpose of government is to establish order in accordance with some vision of the good life. Both realism and idealism are needed in theory and found in fact—idealism to guide political action, realism to act at all. He was as realistic, or as idealistic, as Hamilton, Madison, and Jay, the authors of *The Federalist Papers*.

Clark was convinced that, in the dangerous and interdependent world of the mid-twentieth century, federal world government was a realistic proposal. It was an adequate design for an international security organization. The rule of world law would be far safer than the continued play of power politics or the half measure of collective security. It was consistent with US political traditions and with the practice of federalism and the rule of law in many other nations. Moreover nuclear weapons and economic interdependence have made a world union necessary. If the world community were not yet ready, a clear statement of the goal, such as *World Peace Through World Law*, could help prepare people for the step. Once taken, even on a minimal basis, the functional operations of an effective federal world government would help to build the world community, just as national governments have gradually developed national communities.

Clark maintained four principles of an initial, effective world government: (a) universal membership; (b) weighted, popular representation in a unicameral world legislature; (c) delegation of only those sovereign powers necessary to provide for the common defense; and (d) a transition guided by official national policy and completed by negotiated agreement. The third principle meant that the government be federal in form (not unitary); the second, that its decisions have the character of law reaching to individuals (not recommendations to states). What was essential was that states renounce the right to wage war and accept some carefully guarded form of majority rule in the world legislature for the enactment of laws binding on individuals. At the very least, the amendment process should be flexible enough so that at regular intervals (say every ten years) the world community could reexamine the structure of its international organization.

Timeliness was the second of Clark's virtues, and it was connected with his realism. Historically, the period of opportunity for going beyond a league of sovereign states to a limited world federation was greatest during the years 1944-46. Clark had the most practical and well-thought out proposals ready at that time. Clarence Streit's Atlantic Union proposal was

conceived earlier, but it was not a universal plan and soon became part of the armory of anti-communism. Borgese's *Preliminary Draft of a World Constitution*, which provided for maximal powers in practically a unitary government, did not appear until 1948, after the Czech coup. The federalist movement remained weak and divided; the mainstream US organization, United World Federalists, which united only five groups, was not formed until 1947. Clark led the criticism of the Dumbarton Oaks plan, contributed to some liberalization of the amendment provisions (Art. 109, para. 3) of the UN Charter, sponsored the Dublin conference which called for federal world government in response to atomic energy, and tried to develop the Baruch Plan into an adequate plan for the international control of atomic energy (see *Baruch Plan*).

Grenville Clark's capacity for friendship, his commitment to law, the nobility of his character struck all those who knew him. As a federalist, he was the leading proponent of limited world government— limited in the sense of being "according to the constitution," as well as limited to powers for preservation of the peace. He had the American sense of a constitution as charter of individual rights *against* government. He wanted a world government strong enough to keep the peace, yet not so strong as to endanger the liberties of the people. He disagreed deeply, in his characteristically modest way, with Borgese that a "maximal" world government aimed at justice could be the next step beyond a league of sovereign states. As the years went on, and his attention turned to revision of the UN Charter, he recognized the need for an increased measure of socialism in the general government. He provided for a world development authority with powers to make grants in aid or interest-free loans to governments or organizations for economic and social projects considered necessary for the "creation of conditions of stability and well-being." Even so, he estimated the total budget—for international security as well as economic development—as only thirty to forty billion dollars. Clark was convinced that the rule of law could accommodate ecopolitical systems as antithetical as capitalism and communism. He knew that, apart from their ideologies, both East and West had mixed systems. What was necessary for real peace was that they renounce the right to appeal to force; then they could coexist under conditions of peaceful competition. He believed that timely citizens' action could initiate the change. He noted that many people believed that world government was inevitable because of the need for it, but he liked to remind them of Justice Oliver

Wendell Holmes' remark: "The mode by which the inevitable comes to pass is through effort."

See also: *Federalism, World; United Nations Reform: Historical and Contemporary Perspectives*

*Notes* ————————————————

1. Quote reproduced by permission of Finn Larrssen, Director, Institute for Global Policy Studies.

*Bibliography* ————————————————

Baratta J P 1985 *Grenville Clark, World Federalist*. Occasional Paper No. 3. Institute for Global Policy Studies, Amsterdam

Bogdanov O 1965 A Soviet view of disarmament. *World Federalist* (January)

Clark G 1944a New world order—The American lawyer's role. *Indiana Law J.* 19

Clark G 1944b The Dumbarton Oaks proposals—An analysis. *Am. Bar Assoc. J.* 30

Clark G 1946 An atomic energy authority and world government. *New York Times* 23 June 1946 (Letter to the Editor)

Clark G 1050 *A Plan for Peace*. Harper, New York

Clark G 1961 World order: The need for a bold new approach. *Ann. Am. Acad. Polit. Social Sci.* 336

Clark G, Sohn L B 1958 *World Peace Through World Law*. Harvard University Press, Cambridge, Massachusetts

Clark G, Cranston A, Mahony T H (Dublin Conference Committee) 1946 *Proposals for Amendment of the United Nations Charter: A Petition to the General Assembly of the United Nations*. Council for Limited World Government, New York

Cousins N, Clifford J G (eds.) 1975 *Memoirs of a Man: Grenville Clark*. Norton, New York

Kahn H 1963 World government vs. thermonuclear war. *War/Peace Rep*. March 3-7

Larson A 1962 Development of a world rule of law. *Social Education* 26

Sohn L B 1965 Basic problems of disarmament. *Notre Dame Lawyer* 41

Wright Q 1969 The Foundations of a Universal International System. *Notre Dame Lawyer* 44

JOSEPH P. BARATTA

# Cobden, Richard

Richard Cobden (1804-65) was an important advocate of social reform, free trade, and peace in early Victorian England. Born into a poor farming family, Cobden became wealthy through his own endeavors as a businessman in the 1820s and 1830s. He traveled widely in connection with his business activities, visiting Western Europe, the Middle East, and the United States during the 1830s. Such travel, and his considerable reading, convinced him that trade, not military power, was the key element in international relations. Britain, therefore, he insisted, should endeavor to expand its influence through the encouragement of free trade, rather than through imperialism and the might of its fleet.

For nearly a decade, from 1838 to 1846, Cobden's life was dominated by the struggle to eliminate the Corn Laws, which were the greatest bastions of anti-free-trade protectionism in nineteenth century England. The Corn Laws attempted to protect British farmers from foreign competition by imposing heavy tariffs on cheap imported grain. Cobden, who became the leading figure in the influential Anti-Corn-Law League, argued persuasively that the Corn Laws were in effect a government subsidy to England's politically powerful and wealthy landowning aristocracy. He showed that such subsidies were ulti-

mately paid for by the English working person in the form of expensive bread, and by society as well. In addition, he pointed out that if foreign nations could sell their grain to Britain more easily, they would be more able and more willing to buy the goods being turned out by Britain's matchless factories. Cobden won election to parliament in 1841 to further his work against the Corn Laws, and saw his efforts crowned with success in 1846, when after a bitter struggle the laws were finally repealed.

Cobden's passionate advocacy of free trade went deeper than concerns about economic utility or social justice. He firmly believed that free trade could unify the nations of the world in a great, interdependent network of supply and demand, thus promoting world peace. Nations which prospered by trading with one another freely, he insisted, would not wish to cripple such beneficial relationships by going to war with their trading partners. Cobden was as strong an opponent of militarism and war as he was of tariffs, and became a bitter opponent of the often bellicose policies pursued by Lord Palmerston and other Victorian leaders.

As early as 1836, in two pamphlets, "England, Ireland, and America" and "Russia," he argued that British policies should put peace first. The United States, he pointed out, was inevitably going to become a strong economic competitor. To meet this competition, Britain must not only embrace free trade, but must keep itself free from the economic burdens of war. In particular, he urged his country-men to abandon their attempts to hang on to Ireland and to resist the temptation to militarily oppose the expansion of Russia in the Eastern Mediterranean. As a member of parliament he repeatedly introduced motions calling for peaceful arbitration of interna-tional disputes and for reductions in armaments. Again and again he denounced the various colonial wars in Asia and Africa through which Victorian England was expanding its empire.

His most courageous stand against war came in the early 1850s, when he vigorously condemned British participation in the Crimean War. This conflict was just what Cobden had warned against back in the 1930s: a British attempt to block Russian expansion in the Mediterranean by military force. Even though public opinion strongly supported the government and the war, Cobden bravely refused to compromise his principles. He paid for his stand by being defeat-ed in the parliamentary elections of 1857.

Even after this setback, Cobden's political life was far from over. In 1860, as a representative of the British government, he struck a last blow for free trade. In that year he successfully negotiated a treaty between Britain and France which swept away most of the tariffs and trade barriers which had long exist-ed between the two neighbors. One feature of this treaty was a provision that neither signatory would impose any limitations on trade with the other that did not apply to other nations as well. This "most favored nation" concept has become a standard fea-ture of international economic agreements.

Cobden's concern for international peace contin-ued literally until his death. Even though his health was failing in the spring of 1865, he insisted on working against a government proposal to expand armaments. The effort proved to be too much, and he died on April 2 of that year.

*Bibliography*

Cobden R 1870 *Speeches*. William Ridgway, London
Cobden R 1973 *The Political Writings of Richard Cobden*. Garland, New York
Hobson J A 1918 *Richard Cobden: The International Man*, Unwin, London
McCord N 1958 *The Anti-Corn-Law League*. Unwin, London
Read D 1967 *Cobden and Bright: A Victorian Political Part-nership*. Edward Arnold, London

GARRETT L. MCAINSH

# Cold War

Cold War is the term used to characterize United States-Soviet Union relations in the post-Second World War period. Those relations were hostile, involving a number of serious conflicts and the for-mation of opposing alliances, but they did not include the use of force against each other. Thus, the condition was one of neither war nor peace. The Cold War began in Europe in 1947, spread through-out much of the world, and ended in Europe in 1989. It included phases of intense hostility relieved by moments of lessened tensions. Greater antagonism distinguished the years before 1963, while dimin-ished animosity characterized the later period.

These two vast countries entered the Second World War in 1941, each having been attacked by an enemy, Germany in the case of the former Soviet Union and Japan in the case of the United States. Together with the United Kingdom, they formed the Grand Alliance against Germany in the Second World War. In conformity with the Yalta Agreement (February 1945) the Soviet Union entered the war against Japan in August, shortly before the final sur-render. As the end of the war approached, disagree-ments between East (Soviet Union) and West (United States, United Kingdom, and allies) about post-war arrangements began to emerge, specifically over the issues of Poland and Germany.

Britain and France had gone to war in 1939 over Poland, and London had been the base for a Polish government in exile. The American conception of a postwar arrangement included the ideas of national self-determination, free elections as well as other democratic practices, and free trade based upon the principles of market economics. In contrast, the Sovi-ets had collaborated with Nazi Germany in 1939 in partitioning Poland. For the Soviets, Poland was a security buffer against the possibility of a resurgent Germany, and the former Soviet Union insisted upon having a Polish government it could control. Because Poland was occupied at the end of the war exclusive-ly by the Soviet army, the Soviet view prevailed and a Communist government was installed.

After considering and then rejecting the permanent partition of Germany, the wartime allies agreed to temporary zones of occupation. Berlin, the capital, which was located well inside the Soviet zone, was controlled by a four-power (US, USSR, UK, France) military command but occupied in sectors by the armed forces of the respective powers. A critical disagreement, which produced substantial tensions between the former allies, concerned reparations. Having been severely damaged by Germany, the former Soviet Union sought compensatory reparations, but extractions from the Western zones of occupation were resisted by the United States out of concern that the German standard of living would have to be subsidized by the United States. Soviet requests for the continuation of lend-lease, a program of material goods transfer, after the end of the war had already been turned down by the United States government.

Although the victors of the Second World War concluded peace treaties with the lesser allies of Germany, they were unable to agree to terms of a peace treaty dealing with Germany itself. There had been tentative agreements on the rearrangement of territorial boundaries by which the former Soviet Union took Polish territory, and Poland in turn was compensated with German land.

As the former Soviet Union established control over most of the Eastern European countries, Western attitudes reacted with intense hostility. In 1946, with President Harry S. Truman on the platform, British wartime leader Winston Churchill (see *Churchill, Winston*) called attention to the growing division of Europe, saying that an "iron curtain" was falling across Central Europe as a result of Soviet policies. Shortly thereafter, Soviet troops were removed from Iran where they had remained longer than wartime agreements provided for. Meanwhile, the civil war in China between the Kuomintang and the Communists resumed. As these and other problems proved intractable, revealing the difficulty of managing the world through the United Nations—which had been premised on cooperation among the Second World War victors—attitudes became increasingly hostile. These were fed in the West by revelations that the former Soviet Union was engaging in espionage to help develop its nuclear weapons program.

What had been fluid in 1945 and 1946 became firm in 1947 and 1948 and then rigid in 1949. In 1947 when Britain, by then an obviously declining power, notified the United States that it would no longer be able to shoulder its traditional burden of support for the Greek government, which was the object of a guerrilla war by Greek Communists, and for Turkey, which was the object of diplomatic pressure by the former Soviet Union, the American presi-

dent responded with a call for assistance for those two governments in what came to be known as the Truman Doctrine (see *Truman Doctrine*). This was an expansive statement which applied a general principle to the specific cases of Greece and Turkey: that the United States should "support free peoples who are resisting attempted subjugation by armed minorities or by outside pressures" (Truman 1956).

By spring 1947 it had also became apparent that recovery from the war was not proceeding vigorously, and economic conditions particularly in Western Europe were feared by governments to be providing opportunities for communist gains in the 1948 elections in France and Italy. Another major initiative by the United States—the Marshall Plan—was undertaken to speed recovery. Requiring that the recipient countries organize for joint control over the distribution of funds, the United States agreed to transfer massive amounts—over US$12 billion was spent between 1948 and 1953—to Europe. At first the former Soviet Union considered joining the enterprise but then decided against it on grounds that the requirements for joint planning would infringe on its sovereignty.

The Truman Doctrine and the European Recovery Program—the official name of the Marshall Plan— as well as other aspect of United States policy, which are treated below, were given conceptual underpinning by the idea of containment (see *Containment*). First published anonymously in 1947 under the title, "The Sources of Soviet Conduct," this conception authored by the then State Department analyst George F. Kennan held that a policy of flexible but firm counter pressure against the former Soviet Union's expansionist actions would result eventually in a mellowing of Soviet policy.

Convinced of the former Soviet Union's ambitions by a communist *coup d'etat* in Czechoslovakia in early 1948, the Western occupying powers began moving toward the creation of a West German state, first by imposing a currency reform in their zones. Responding to this action, the Soviets began to place restrictions on access to Berlin, finally in June 1948 completely blockading surface access routes to the western sectors of Berlin. The effective American counter-response was the implementation of an airlift which supplied the beleaguered city with food, fuel, and supplies throughout the next year until the blockade was lifted. Events had moved the respective powers to consolidate their positions, however, and two German states were created in 1949, giving rigidity to the division of Europe.

Meanwhile, building upon the Dunkirk Treaty (March 1948 between Britain and France) and the

Brussels Treaty (March 1948 among these and the Benelux countries), the Western Europeans negotiated with the United States and Canada the North Atlantic Treaty which was signed in April 1949 by the powers mentioned plus Denmark, Norway, Iceland, Italy, and Portugal. The North Atlantic Treaty Organization (NATO) gave emphatic expression to the idea of containment, and by early 1950 the United States, which had largely dismantled its armed forces at the end of the war, decided upon a rearmament program (see *North Atlantic Treaty Organization (NATO)*).

Two other events in 1949 increased the hostility between East and West. First, the former Soviet Union exploded its own atomic bomb, thus depriving the United States of its monopoly (see *Nuclear Strategy*). Second, the Chinese civil war came to a substantial conclusion as the Communists took power and the Kuomintang retreated to the island of Taiwan. Following difficult negotiations the new Chinese government concluded a treaty of alliance with the former Soviet Union. At this time, also, the United States began to give financial support to its ally France for the conduct of its war in Indo-China against the Viet-Minh, a communist organization fighting for the independence of the Southeast Asian French colonies.

Deepening the hostility between East and West was the Korean War which began in 1950 and ended only in 1953 after the death of Stalin, the Soviet leader who had authorized the invasion that set it off. The invasion by North Korea was thrown back by United States and allied forces fighting alongside South Korean troops under the auspices of the United Nations. Thereupon the United States decided to invade North Korea and, despite warnings from the People's Republic of China, advanced toward the Yalu River, the boundary of Korea and China. In response, China entered the war, and the adversaries fought to a standstill along a line approximately at the 38th parallel which had been the temporary boundary between North and South Korea. After long negotiations, a truce was agreed. In the midst of the war, the United States and many allies, but not the former Soviet Union, signed a peace treaty with Japan.

During the first half of the 1950s both the United States and the former Soviet Union developed thermonuclear weapons, which had much greater explosive power than atomic bombs. Moreover, they both worked on related technologies that resulted in the major innovation of the late 1950s, the intercontinental ballistic missile (see *Arms Race, Dynamics of*).

Following the death of Stalin, attempts were made to reduce tensions and reach agreements on some issues. There was a summit conference in Geneva in 1955, with two diplomatic achievements. A peace treaty with Austria providing for a neutral state was signed (see *Neutrality*). At the United Nations an agreement was reached to allow the admission of new members, which had been blocked in earlier years by ideological conflict. On the other hand, proposals such as the Rapacki Plan for a nuclear-free zone in both Germanies, Poland, and Czechoslovakia were turned down.

Meanwhile, the superpowers augmented their alliances. Greece and Turkey joined NATO in 1951, and the former Federal Republic of Germany joined in 1955. The East responded in 1955 to this latter action by the formation of the Warsaw Treaty Organization, an alliance of the former Soviet Union, Poland, Czechoslovakia, Hungary, Romania, Bulgaria, and Albania. The United States promoted the Southeast Asia Treaty Organization and the Baghdad Pact and signed bilateral alliance agreements with several other states, including Thailand, the Philippines, Taiwan, and Pakistan, thus encircling the former Soviet Union and China with formal alliances. Although not creating such formal structures, the former Soviet Union in this period sought to gain influence in parts of the world not under its control, and its first breakthrough was an arms agreement with Egypt in 1955.

One of the central features of the Cold War was the American objection to Soviet control over Eastern Europe. During the Eisenhower Administration beginning in 1953, the United States articulated the concepts of liberation of the peoples of Eastern Europe and of a roll-back of communism. However, in 1956 when the Hungarians fought for their country's independence against Soviet troops, this was shown to be merely a declaratory policy without substance. Later, in 1968 when the Warsaw Treaty Organization occupied Czechoslovakia to suppress a movement to present "Communism with a human face" the United States did not intervene. At this time, Soviet leader Leonid Brezhnev proclaimed that the former Soviet Union had a responsibility to intervene with force to uphold communist regimes, a position that was known as the Brezhnev Doctrine.

Important in the period before 1962 were the extended crisis over Berlin and the Sino-Soviet dispute. Premier Nikita Khrushchev, the Soviet leader, announced in November 1958 his wish to "normalize" the situation in Berlin and created a crisis atmosphere by setting a deadline for the signing of a separate peace treaty with the former German Democratic Republic. By shifting ground on his terms, Khrushchev kept the Berlin situation at a crisis point until in August 1961 the former German Democratic Republic was sealed off from West

Berlin—which had been a haven for refugees—by barbed wire and then a wall. Simultaneously, immense strains between the former Soviet Union and the People's Republic of China had been developing, The dispute between the two large communist countries was deep and intense, leading eventually to an armed clash in 1969 and to a complete split in the 1970s.

With these events as the main features, and a background that included United States-Soviet Union tension over nuclear testing, the shooting down of an American spy plane over Soviet territory, and the Bay of Pigs invasion of Cuba by United States CIA-backed exiles, the Soviet surreptitiously introduced nuclear missiles on Cuban territory. Upon their discovery, United States President John F. Kennedy demanded their removal and imposed a naval blockade to prevent any further shipment of missiles to Cuba. The most intense crisis of the Cold War ensued for two weeks, ending with Soviet agreement to dismantle and remove the offending missiles and an American pledge not to invade Cuba. In addition, the United States removed its missiles from Turkey.

Thereafter, the two superpowers made attempts to reduce the hostility of their relationship, reaching such agreements in 1963 as a Partial Nuclear Test Ban Treaty, a "hot-line" agreement, and modest trade and cultural exchanges. One observer (Shulman 1966) referred to their relationship as a "limited adversary" one. Despite the Soviet Union's invasion of Czechoslovakia and the United States' war in Vietnam, this new mode of interaction took on a more formal character with the Western policy of détente in the Richard M. Nixon administration and the equivalent Soviet promotion of peaceful coexistence in the early 1970s.

Among the agreements between the superpowers, a Basic Principles Agreement designed to govern their relations did not last beyond the 1973 war in the Middle East. On the other hand, the 1972 Anti-Ballistic Missile Treaty remained even after the end of the Cold War a centerpiece of nuclear arms control. In addition, the two signed Strategic Arms Limitation Agreements in 1972 and 1978; and they extended their commercial and cultural exchanges. By 1974, however, it was clear that the former Soviet Union was unwilling to accept American conditions attached to a normal trading relationship. Moreover, relaxation in tensions faced difficulties when the United States and China moved toward normal diplomatic relations after 1972. Tensions grew in the 1970s in the face of a continued arms race between the superpowers and increasing Soviet activity in Ethiopia and Angola in Africa. A new level of stress in the Cold War was reached when the former Soviet Union inter-

vened militarily in Afghanistan, the first large-scale troop deployment outside the area reached by the Soviet Union in 1945. Additionally, the former Soviet Union extended assistance to Nicaragua following its revolution in 1979. In response to what it perceived as new threats, the United States under President Jimmy Carter embarked on a major expansion of its military power, imposed economic sanctions on the former Soviet Union, and launched, under President Ronald Reagan, a vigorous rhetorical campaign of hostility against the former Soviet Union. In the early 1980s, also, the Reagan administration announced a new initiative to research and develop a system of defense against strategic missiles and nuclear warheads.

By the mid-1980s the Cold War began to recede. After enduring the death of three leaders in the early 1980s, the Soviet regime chose a reformer, Mikhail Gorbachev (see Nobel Peace Prize Prize Laureates: *Mikhail S. Gorbachev*), who began to address a number of severe problems faced by his country. Since the early 1970s the former Soviet Union's economy began a slow decline, made especially apparent by its inability to adapt to the new phase of the industrial revolution launched by the computer and other new information technologies. Thus, the country was falling behind developments in the West. Moreover, its economic weaknesses made it especially difficult to compete with the United States in a new phase of the nuclear arms race. Finally, it had become apparent in both the former Soviet Union and the Eastern European countries that Communism's legitimacy had become severely exposed, most obviously in Poland where a labor union, *Solidarity*, drew a membership of ten million in opposition to the Communist rulers who supposedly ruled on behalf of the working class.

Gorbachev initiated a program of reforms at home, and he offered what he called "new thinking" with regard to foreign policy (see *Glasnost and Perestroika*). This course led to the withdrawal of Soviet assets from abroad and to engagement in peaceful relations with all countries. Meeting in a series of summit meetings with United States President Reagan, Gorbachev agreed to American positions in arms reductions both in the European theater and in strategic arsenals.

It was in Eastern Europe that the Cold War came to a definitive end in 1989. Restiveness among the populations of the Eastern European countries had been apparent throughout most of the Cold War period, but popular aspirations had been denied either by such repressive practices as the Polish government's imposition of martial law in 1981 or by Soviet military intervention as in East Germany in 1953, in

Hungary in 1956, and in Czechoslovakia in 1968. Communist rule began to collapse quickly in 1989 when, in the face of an exodus of East Germans through Hungary to West Germany, Gorbachev announced that the former Soviet Union would no longer intervene to uphold communist rule. Without Soviet backing, the East German government decided not to crack down on demonstrators, and soon the Berlin Wall was breached, eventually to be torn down (see *Eastern Europe, Transformation of*). The former Soviet Union had withdrawn from hostile competition with the United States and the West.

In the aftermath, the Cold War adversaries agreed to the unification in 1990 of the two Germanies under the (West) German Basic Law and to United Germany's membership in NATO. Continued reform in the former Soviet Union itself prompted a failed coup attempt in August 1991, which was shortly followed in December by the disintegration of the former Soviet Union into fifteen successor states.

Over time, explanations for the origins of the Cold War have varied, and the issue of why it occurred is a matter of some controversy, particularly among American historians. Shortly after the Second World War the orthodox interpretation followed the views of American policy makers, holding that the Cold War was the result of Soviet expansionism which was met by a Western defensive response. This interpretation argued that Stalin's personality together with communist ideology and Soviet security fears led to consolidation of Soviet rule over an empire in Eastern Europe, to the turmoil in Greece and diplomatic pressure on Turkey, and to an attempt to dislodge the Western allies from Berlin and Germany. Such American actions as the Truman Doctrine, the Marshall Plan, NATO and other alliances, and policies such as foreign aid were regarded as maneuvers designed to defend the "free world" from further communist encroachment (see *Peace, Historical Views of*).

Later, other historians provided a revisionist interpretation which held that the Cold War originated in American imperialism, with the former Soviet Union a defensive power simply providing for its own security. Some writers dated American expansionism from the country's founding, while others regarded the Spanish-American War and Open Door Notes of 1898 and 1899, respectively, as the turning point. Others focused on Western hostility to the Russian Revolution of 1917. Whatever the precise date for the beginning, this interpretation often includes the view that the United States dropped the atomic bomb on Japan in August 1945 not to end the war but to impress the Soviets and to prepare the way for a

diplomacy that would intimidate the former Soviet Union (Alperovitz 1994). The war in Vietnam marked the high point of American imperialism but programs such as aid to Western Europe also demonstrated United States' expansionism.

Still another view—which can be termed the realist interpretation—employs a more complex and interactive analysis of the origins of the Cold War. With a fundamental bipolar structure in the world, the superpowers were placed inevitably and unintentionally in a position of conflict. An additional factor driving the conflict was the clash of opposing ideologies—authoritarian communist politics and centrally planned economies versus liberal democratic politics and market economics—which had very different visions of how public life should be organized. Personalities also, in this interpretation, played a role, as did security considerations, specifically Soviet interests in Eastern Europe and American involvement in Western Europe. Other factors contributing to the Cold War, from this perspective, were the American political system with its checks and balances and American public psychology which demanded a return to "normalcy" at the end of the war and which is infused with moralism. Finally, this interpretation attributes part of the Cold War to blunders, mistakes, and miscalculations on the part of the political leaders of both superpowers.

In retrospect, some observers regard the Cold War as "the long peace" (Gaddis 1986), for no war broke out between the major powers for a greater length of time than any other in the modern period. Thus, the Cold War can be cited as an object lesson of adversarial relations of Great Powers conducted with prudence and restraint. Even while the former Soviet Union sought advantage, it never pushed such issues as Berlin and the missiles in Cuba to the point of war. Similarly, the American policy of containment sought limited goals that fell far short of war with the former Soviet Union.

With respect to the issue of war and peace, specifically to confront the question of why war did not occur, two theoretical responses have been given. First, the bipolar structure of international politics, a new development in modern politics, provided less uncertainty than the multipolar structure that had preceded it. With only one adversary that could do it substantial harm, each superpower reacted to the other, with little miscalculation. Second, after both powers were armed with nuclear weapons, deterrence induced great caution among leaders out of fear of the devastation that would be caused by the use of the weapons.

See also: *East-West Conflict*

## Bibliography

Acheson D 1969 *Present at the Creation*. Norton, New York

Alperovitz G 1994 *Atomic Diplomacy: Hiroshima and Pots-dam*: The case of the atomic bomb and the American confrontation with Soviet power, 2nd expanded edn. Pluto Press, London

Feis H 1957 *Churchill, Roosevelt, Stalin: The War They Waged and the Peace They Sought*. Princeton University Press, Princeton, New Jersey

Feis H 1960 *Between War and Peace: The Potsdam Conference*. Princeton University Press, Princeton, New Jersey

Feis H 1966 *The Atomic Bomb and the End of World War II*. Princeton University Press, Princeton, New Jersey

Fleming D F 1961 *The Cold War and Its Origins, 1917-1960*. Doubleday, Garden City, New York

Gaddis J L 1972 *The United States and the Origins of the Cold War, 1945-1947*. Columbia University Press, New York

Gaddis J L 1986 The Long Peace: Elements of stability in the postwar international system. *Int'l Security* 10 (Spring)

Gaddis J L 1987 *The Long Peace: Inquiries into the History of the Cold War*. Oxford University Press, New York

Garthoff R L 1985 *Détente and Confrontation: American-Soviet Relations from Nixon to Reagan*. Brookings Institution, Washington, DC

Garthoff R L 1994 *The Great Transition: American-Soviet Relations and the End of the Cold War*. Brookings Institution, Washington, DC

George A L 1983 *Managing US-Soviet Rivalry*. Westview, Boulder, Colorado

Halle L 1967 *The Cold War as History*. Harper and Row, New York

Kennan G F 1947 The sources of Soviet conduct. *Foreign Affairs* 25 (4)

LaFeber W 1971 *The Origins of the Cold War, 1941-1947*. John Wiley & Sons, New York

McNeill W H 1970 *America, Britain and Russia: Their Cooperation and Conflict, 1941-1946*. Johnson Reprint Company, New York

Schlesinger A M Jr 1967 Origins of the cold war. *Foreign Affairs* 46 (1)

Seton-Watson H 1960 *Neither War Nor Peace: The Struggle for Power in the Postwar World*. Praeger, New York

Shulman M D 1966 *Beyond the Cold War*. Yale University Press, New Haven, Connecticut

Starobin J 1969 Origins of the cold war: The communist dimension. *Foreign Affairs* 47 (4)

Truman H S 1956 *Memoirs*. Doubleday, Garden City, New York

Ulam A 1968 *Expansion and Coexistence: A History of Soviet Foreign Policy, 1917-67*. Praeger, New York

Waltz K N 1979 *Theory of International Politics*. Addison-Wesley, Reading, Massachusetts

HOWARD H. LENTNER

# Collective Security and Collective Self-defense

The term "collective security" is used with a wide variety of meanings, often embracing almost every form of collective action used in dealing with threats to peace. It is based on the fundamental principle that one of the most effective ways to deter would-be aggressors, or to deal with aggression if this actually occurs, is to confront the aggressor with the concerted power of states determined to resist aggression and to keep the peace. Yet in a more precise and technical sense the concept is very complex and elusive. It involves a degree of commitment to which many states give lip-service but which few, if any, are willing to live up to when the test comes.

Thus we are faced with the paradox that collective security is espoused by many, and yet it has never been fully applied. So-called efforts to develop an effective system of collective security, of which the League of Nations (see *League of Nations*), the United Nations (see *United Nations Governance*), and the North Atlantic Treaty Organization (NATO) (see *North Atlantic Treaty Organization (NATO)*) are out-standing institutional examples, have fallen far short of the central objective for which they were formed. Other calls for such a system, such as the Kellogg-Briand Peace Pact (the Pact of Paris) of 1928 and Leonid Brezhnev's call in 1969 for "a system of collective security in Asia," have not moved beyond selective and limited endorsement and only nominal and inadequate efforts at implementation.

Collective security is, therefore, a term that should be used with caution by serious students of international relations, even though its basic idea is a commendable one. To present a charitable interpretation, it is possible to say that it is a desirable goal that is impossible to achieve without fundamental changes in the existing international system. It is, therefore, important to remember that it is used loosely and frequently to apply to methods of collective action which in fact fall far short of real collective security. For real collective security is based on certain underlying assumptions and basic requirements that no states, or groups of states, have thus far been willing, or able, to accept or implement in real world situations, however frequently they may subscribe to them in principle.

Collective security implies far-reaching commitments and obligations on the part of the majority of the nations of the world, including all, or at least most, of the Great Powers. The states involved in a collective security system must be willing to take whatever action may be necessary, including even the use of armed force, with the concomitant risk of involvement in a major war, to deter a would-be aggressor or aggressors, or to deal with aggression if it in fact occurs. Moreover, they must be in agreement on the identity of the aggressor, and such agreement is often lacking. In real world situations the threats to peace are many and varied, and these usually occur under such complicated circumstances that responsibility for provocative actions can seldom be clearly assessed or agreed upon. Even if there is agreement, many states may shy away from the implications of such agreement, and collective security is therefore undermined even before it can be effectively initiated. Even if this initial barrier is overcome, the collectivity must be stronger than any would-be aggressor, and its members must be both willing and able to mobilize, and if necessary employ, their preponderant power.

Thus formulated, collective security goes far beyond the well-established, if not universally agreed-upon, principle in international law of the right of collective self-defense with the concomitant right to resort to various forms of collective action or collective measures to meet threats to the peace. In this sense, as a noted international lawyer, Julius Stone, has observed, "Collective defense is a substitute for, not a consequence of, collective security." It is a right that is often resorted to because an effective system of collective security is lacking.

The right of collective self-defense was specifically recognized in such important international documents as the Covenant of the League of Nations, the Kellogg-Briand Pact, and the Charter of the United Nations (see *United Nations Charter*). Article 1 of the United Nations Charter calls for "effective collective measures for the prevention and removal of threats to the peace, and for the suppression of acts of aggression or other breaches of the peace," and Chapter VII of the Charter specifies in great detail what these "effective collective measures" may be. The last article in Chapter VII is the famous Article 51, which clearly states: "Nothing in the present Charter shall impair the inherent right of individual or collective self-defense if an armed attack occurs against a Member of the United Nations, until the Security Council has taken the measures necessary to maintain international peace and security."

Since the Security Council is unable to discharge effectively its primary function, mainly because of the "veto" privilege of the permanent members and the limitations incorporated in its mandate, several efforts have been made to make the United Nations a more effective instrument for collective action against threats to peace by giving a greater role in this vital area to the General Assembly. The outstanding example is the Uniting For Peace Resolution, adopted by the General Assembly in November, 1950, during the height of the Korean crisis. This resolution provided for immediate consideration by the General Assembly of any situation involving an act of aggression or other threats to the peace, if the Security Council failed to exercise "its primary responsibility." It also provided for a Peace Observation Committee and a Collective Measures Committee. Although this resolution has been invoked in several international crisis situations since 1950, it has done little more than extend a broader mantle over the generally ineffective efforts of the United Nations to be helpful in dealing with major international crises and over the more extensive efforts of directly affected states to take other measures of individual and/or collective self-defense. Because of its very nature, as a limited instrument of the nation-state system, the United Nations can hardly be regarded as an effective agency for collective self-defense, and certainly not as an effective agency for collective security, even though this term is often used with reference to its responsibilities and activities.

The United Nations-sponsored collective action in the Korean War (1950-53) is often cited as a test case of collective security—sometimes as the leading test case. But although it was sanctioned by the UN Security Council (with the Russian representative absent), it fell far short of a genuine collective security effort. Fewer than 20 member states contributed military forces, and most of these were of a token variety. Ninety percent of the non-South Korean military commitment was provided by a single nation, the United States, and the "United Nations forces" operated under American command.

As a universal organization, the United Nations is concerned with the maintenance of peace and security on both global and regional levels. Much of the responsibility on regional levels falls on various regional organizations and arrangements, such as the North Atlantic Treaty Organization (NATO), the Organization of American States (OAS) (see *Organization of American States (OAS))*, and the Organization of African Unity (OAU) (see *Organization of African Unity (OAU)*). But while the UN and some regional arrangements have had some limited success as instruments for collective action, they have been quite ineffective as instruments for collective security.

While the UN charter clearly recognizes the right of collective self-defense, "the precise scope" of this right, as Brierly (1963) has pointed out, "is the subject of controversy." The Uniting for Peace Resolution, for example, was one of the most controversial, as well as one of the most dramatic, resolutions that the General Assembly has ever adopted, and it was immediately challenged by several members of the UN, especially by the former Soviet Union and other communist states.

Brierly is one of the international legal experts who insist that "self-defense, properly understood, is a strictly limited right." "The need to keep self-defense within strict limits," he writes, "has been demonstrated very often in recent history . . . [N]early every aggressive act is sought to be portrayed as an act of self-defense." He calls attention to the fact that the German and Japanese leaders who were defendants in the war crimes trials after the Second World War pleaded the right of self-defense as justification for the "war crimes" and "crimes against humanity" of which they were accused. This plea was rejected by the War Crimes Tribunals (see *Nuremberg Principles*). But the question of the extent of the right of self-defense is still an unanswered one. The Nuremberg Tribunal itself observed that "whether action taken under the claim of self-defense was in fact aggressive or defensive must ultimately be subject to investigation and adjudication if international law is to be enforced." The Tribunal asserted that the minimum condition for a resort to armed force in self-defense must be "an instant and overwhelming necessity for self-defense, leaving no choice of means and no moment for deliberation." Brierly states that there are precedents for this interpretation, which he believes was originally formulated by Daniel Webster, then United States Secretary of State, in 1837. But certainly the right of self-defense is usually regarded by political leaders, if not by international lawyers, as much less limited. It is in any event frequently invoked by aggressors to justify their action and by states that seek to oppose these aggressors; and such actions are a consequence of the failure of the United Nations or any other international organizations and arrangements to provide an effective substitute, and of the failure of the world community to develop a real collective security system.

Measures for collective self-defense, therefore, may be regarded as either a substitute for, or an imperfect form of, collective security. They will undoubtedly continue to be widely employed, out of necessity until and unless a more genuine collective security system, either within or outside the framework of the United Nations, becomes an operating reality.

In this broader sense, collective security may be regarded, and often is so regarded, as one of two main approaches to "the maintenance of international peace and security," the other being measures for the peaceful settlement of international disputes. It is not a mere coincidence that the chapter in the UN Charter on the "Pacific Settlement of Disputes" (Articles 33-38) is followed by the chapter on "Action with Respect to Threats to the Peace, Breaches of the Peace, and Acts of Aggression" (Articles 39-51) (see *Pacific Settlement of International Disputes*).

Nor was it a coincidence that these two chapters were followed by a chapter on "Regional Arrangements" (Articles 52-54). These arrangements were conceived of as complementary, not contradictory, to the more universal provisions for peaceful settlement of disputes and collective action in the two previous chapters of the Charter. Presumably mutual security arrangements, such as NATO, would not be justifiable, or even necessary, if an effective system of collective security existed.

The same observation could be made about the balance of power (see *Balance of Power*), one of the central themes and practices in international relations for the past several centuries. Collective security is clearly incompatible with balance of power policies, except under most unusual conditions of balanced stability over long periods of time. Yet, as Quincy Wright has observed, "The relations of the balance of power to collective security have . . . been at the same time complementary and antagonistic." In any event, in Wright's words, "the fundamental assumptions of the two systems are different" (see *Wright, Quincy*).

Similar interpretations could be advanced regarding the relation of collective security to such very different foreign policy orientations as neutrality (see *Neutrality*) and nonalignment (see *Nonalignment*), and to various proposals and methods not yet translated into reality, for arms control and disarmament.

It is important to distinguish between collective security as a concept and collective security as a system. As a general concept the idea of collective security is an appealing one. It has often been remarked that the alternative to collective security is collective insecurity, and this is an intolerable situation in an increasingly dangerous world. As a concept, collective security is a pervasive theme in contemporary international relations; as a system it does not, in fact, exist. As Inis Claude has observed, "in the era of the United Nations, statesmen have been unable to discard the idea of collective security and unwilling to implement it."

Innumerable proposals have been made for the establishment of a genuine system of collective security, on a universal or regional basis. Many of these envision a fundamental transformation of the United Nations, and/or of regional arrangements. Others view the United Nations system as basically flawed, and therefore propose very different approaches. Most point in the direction of significant limitations on state sovereignty—which would probably necessitate the abandonment of the present nation-state system—and the transfer of sovereignty to some form of regional or world government. All such proposals are designed to achieve "a working peace system," to use David Mitrany's famous term. Some have received rather widespread verbal acceptance, but none has led to any basic transformation in the existing nation-state system, whose very nature makes a real system of collective security virtually impossible.

Since, in its real meaning, collective security has never been an operating reality, and has certainly not been developed as a system, it is obvious that even while working toward a desirable but hitherto-unachieved goal it is necessary for peace-loving nations and peoples to seek other means, well short of real collective security, to promote as much cooperation for mutual ends, including the basic ends of security and survival, as circumstances permit.

*Bibliography*

Brierly J L 1963 *The Law of Nations*, 6th edn. Oxford University Press, New York

Claude I Jr 1962 *Power and International Relations*. Random House, New York

Southeast Asia Treaty Organization 1963 *Collective Security: Shield of Freedom*, rev. edn. Southeast Asia Treaty Organization, Bangkok

Goodrich L M, Simons A P 1955 *The United Nations and the Maintenance of International Peace and Security*. Brookings Institution, Washington, DC

Haas E B 1955 Types of collective security: An examination of operational concepts. *Am. Polit. Sci. Rev.* 49

Henkin L 1968 *How Nations Behave*. Praeger, New York

Martin A 1952 *Collective Security*. UNESCO, Paris

Organski A F K 1968 *World Politics*, 2nd edn. Knopf, New York

Stone J 1954 *Legal Control of International Conflicts*. Rinehart, New York

Thompson K W 1953 Collective security reexamined. *Am. Polit. Sci. Rev.* 48

Wright Q 1942 *A Study of War*. University of Chicago Press, Chicago, Illinois

NORMAN D. PALMER

# Colombo Plan

Prospects for world peace and human survival will be greatly enhanced by substantial economic and social development in the developing nations, where the majority of the world's people live. Many international and interregional organizations, as well as many governments, are working to achieve this goal. Among these one of the most important, and one of the least known, is the Colombo Plan for Cooperative Economic and Social Development in Asia and the Pacific.

In its origin the Colombo Plan was a creation of the Commonwealth of Nations. It was proposed at a meeting of Commonwealth Foreign Ministers in Colombo, the capital of Ceylon (now Sri Lanka), in January 1950. Foreign ministers of Australia, the United Kingdom, Canada, Ceylon, India, New Zealand, and Pakistan took part in this meeting, and the countries they represented were therefore the original members of the Colombo plan. Later in 1950 a Consultative Committee was formed; and in March 1951 a Council for Technical Cooperation was established. The Plan became fully operational in July 1951. Until 1977 it was known as the Colombo Plan for Cooperative Economic Development in South and South-East Asia. It was then renamed the Colombo Plan for Cooperative Economic and Social Development in Asia and the pacific, reflecting the expansion of its programmatic and geographic scope.

It also expanded greatly in membership. By 1983 the original membership of seven Commonwealth nations had increased to 26 countries. Before the end of the 1950s Burma, Cambodia (now Kampuchea), Indonesia, Japan, Laos, Malaysia, Nepal, the Philippines, Thailand, South Vietnam, and the United States had joined. In the 1960s Afghanistan, Bhutan, Iran, the Maldives, Singapore, and the Republic of

Korea also became members. Since then Bangladesh, Fiji, and Papua New Guinea have joined. South Vietnam, of course, has ceased to exist, and the new communist government of Vietnam has not retained Vietnam's membership. Most of the countries of South and Southeast Asia are members, and most of the assistance provided under Colombo Plan auspices has gone to these countries.

Originally the Plan was adopted for a period of only six years, and on four subsequent occasions it was renewed for a similar period. In 1980, however, at the meeting of the Consultative Committee in Jakarta, it was finally placed on a more permanent basis, with an extension of its life for an indefinite period.

The Plan is primarily an instrument for the promotion of interregional economic and social cooperation and development, rather than an operating agency. It has limited funds at its disposal, and it has a relatively small organizational structure. It has four main organs: (a) a Consultative Committee; (b) a Council for Technical Cooperation; (c) a Colombo Plan Staff College for Technical Education; and (d) a Colombo Plan Bureau.

The Consultative Committee, in which representatives of all member countries participate, is the main policy-making and supervisory body. It meets at the ministerial level once or twice a year (biennially in recent years) in one of the member countries. All decisions and recommendations must be by consensus. It works closely with the United Nations, and with various international organizations and agencies within and outside of the United Nations system. Representatives of the International Bank for Reconstruction and Development, the United Nations Development Fund, the World Health Organization, the United Nations Educational, Scientific, and Cultural Organization, the Economic and Social Commission for Asia and the Pacific, and other international organizations attend meetings of the Consultative Committee as observers.

All members of the Plan are also represented on the Council for Technical Cooperation, which meets frequently in the Plan headquarters in Colombo. This is a very active agency for promoting and improving technical cooperation in and among member countries, and for disseminating information and ideas. It works closely with the many technical training institutes in all countries receiving assistance under the Plan, and it assists these countries in making arrangements for sending many of their nationals to more economically advanced member countries for technical training. It also has a special interest in the Colombo Staff College for Technical Education, which opened in Singapore in March 1975. This is the first multilateral project undertaken under Colombo Plan auspices. The College provides a variety of courses and training programs, organizes conferences, assists technical and other relevant institutions in member countries, sponsors research on matters relating to technical education and training, and serves as a clearing house for technical information and resources.

The Colombo Plan Bureau, based in Colombo, is the secretariat of the Plan. It has a small staff, headed by a Director. It provides staff assistance for the Consultative Committee and for a wide range of Plan programs and activities. It issues a large number of publications, of both a technical and general nature, highlighting the programs and achievements of the Plan. Since 1973 it has sponsored a Drug Advisory Program, which seeks to assist various national and international agencies in the efforts to control the widespread traffic in drugs, especially in the countries of South and Southeast Asia.

In its essence the Colombo Plan has been described as being "multilateral in approach but bilateral in operation." It is a forum for the exchange of views, the development of proposals, and the encouragement of cooperation among its members; but all negotiations for economic or technical assistance are on a bilateral basis, carried on directly between a potential donor and a potential recipient country.

The main forms of assistance, as in most programs of aid for economic and social development, are capital assistance and technical cooperation. Major fields of assistance include education, public administration, engineering, medicine and health, food and agriculture, and forestry. As the original name of the Plan indicated, the main focus of the Plan was, and still is, on economic development in the countries of South and South east Asia, almost all of which are Plan members. India, Pakistan, and Indonesia have been the major recipients of assistance under the auspices of the Colombo Plan. Up to 1981 donor members, mainly outside the area of immediate concern, with the United States by far the largest donor, had provided what might be called Colombo Plan aid of approximately US$65 billion.

Although it is a relatively inconspicuous actor in the contemporary world, and is limited in its organization and resources, the Colombo Plan has been quite active and effective in encouraging and promoting cooperation and assistance in areas of greatest need in regions where cooperation has been unusually difficult and disappointing. It is concerned with basic aspects of development—economic and social—in crucial areas of the developing nations. It is therefore centrally involved in the struggle for peace and human betterment. It deserves to be better known, and more widely appreciated.

*Bibliography* —————————————————————

Benham F C 1956 *The Colombo Plan, and Other Essays.* Royal Institute of International Affairs, London

Cohen J B 1951 The Colombo Plan for Cooperative Economic Development. *Middle East Journal* 5

Colombo Plan for Cooperative Economic and Social Development in Asia and the Pacific 1983/84, *Yearbook of International Organizations*, 20th edn. Saur, Munich

Colombo Plan Newsletter (Annually) Colombo Plan for Cooperative Economic and Social Development in Asia and the Pacific, Colombo

James C W 1955 The Colombo Plan passes halfway. *Australian Outlook* 9

Singh L P 1963 *The Colombo Plan: Some Political Aspects.* Department of International Relations, Research School of Pacific Studies, Australian National University, Canberra

Symon A C B 1952 The Colombo Plan. *Royal Central Asia Society Journal* 39

Norman D. Palmer

# Colonialism

Colonialism is the establishment and maintenance of rule for an extended time over an alien people that is separate from and subordinate to the ruling power. In a narrow sense, the concept refers to the direct political and military control exercised by the European states (or states settled by Europeans) over peoples of different races in Africa, Asia and America, and also to similar forms of rule by the United States and Japan. This classical definition excludes both the rule of states over other people within Europe and present forms of strong political hegemony (see *Hegemony*); strictly speaking also excepted is the relationship between mother countries and pure settlement colonies (after having exterminated or at least widely decimated the original population) like the British dependencies in Northern America and Australia. Colonialism is characterized by:

(a) domination by an alien minority, asserting racial and cultural superiority, over a materially inferior native majority;

(b) contact between a machine-oriented civilization with Christian origins, a powerful economy, and a rapid rhythm of life and a non-Christian civilization that lacks machines and is marked by a backward economy and a slow rhythm of life;

(c) great real differences between parent states and dependent territories in regard to political and social civil rights and possibilities;

(d) economic exploitation of the colonies by the metropolitan powers.

## 1. Chronology

From 1492 until 1807 the European expansion was directed to America, India (including Indonesia), and Siberia (mercantilist colonial empires). From 1878 to 1914 the Middle East, East Asia, and particularly Africa were the objects of the European powers' quest for new colonies (imperialist colonial empires). Between these main epochs of offensive colonialism there was a pause during which direct colonial rule seemed to soften. Since the Second World War, colonialism as a form of direct political control has come to an end in all former dependencies (decolonization).

The mercantilist era of colonialism was pioneered by Spain and Portugal following the discovery of America and the sea route to the Indian Ocean. After about 1600, England and Holland (the United Provinces) advanced in the Spanish and Portuguese sphere and France established her influence in Canada and the Caribbean. In the eighteenth century, Great Britain controlled the market of the trade of African slaves shipped to America; Russia expanded her territory to the East; and in the latter part of the century North American settlement colonies abolished British rule by founding the United States of America. Having prohibited the slave trade in 1807, the hegemonic sea power, Great Britain, actually stopped her colonial expansion, except in India. Britain abolished slavery in all of her colonies in 1838, and France followed in 1848. The colonies in Latin America became independent from their parent states Spain and Portugal; Chile was first in 1810. This short colonial pause was mainly the result of the new economic belief in free trade, but the economic depression following 1873 shook this belief.

The Continental countries, in particular France, feeling handicapped in comparison to England with respect to sea power, started the "scramble for Africa" which soon reached China and the Middle East as well. While China, Latin America, Persia, and the Ottoman Empire maintained a kind of semicolonial but informal dependent status, in Africa and Asia clearly delineated formal colonial empires were established or maintained. As a result of the First World War Germany lost her dependent territories to the allied forces but the colonial system itself was maintained until after the Second World War. After 1945, in most colonies national liberation movements emerged. The demand for political independence— also supported by strong anti-colonial opposition in Europe—became overwhelming and was finally accepted by the colonial powers. Only Holland in Indonesia (1945-49), France in Vietnam (1946-54) and Algeria (1954-62), and Portugal in her African colonies (1961-74) tried to withstand this process by military means. In all cases the former mother country decided to a large extent who was to take over political power upon achieving independence. Only the internal colonialism in South Africa has been consolidated as a form in its own rights for more than four decades.

## 2. Political Patterns

Colonies were established for the following reasons:

(a) *Settlement.* The dependencies could absorb the surplus population of the European people; this worked effectively only in North America, Australia, and New Zealand where colonialism ended in the nineteenth century.

(b) *Strategic importance.* Military colonies helped to control other dependent territories or to secure strategically important sea routes.

(c) *Economic purposes.* This has been regarded as the primary motivation for colonialism. The economic motive was considered quite legitimate by the colonizers. Private capital was most frequently the main force behind the establishment of colonial rule (for example the East India Companies of England and Holland), even though in the case of France the mercantilist state was economically most active.

The main types of colonial rule were:

(a) *Self-government* in settlement colonies which soon led to independence, as happened in the American Revolution.

(b) *Integration* with the mother country which also nullified colonial rule in the long run.

(c) *Direct rule* was the most usual method of colonial control. The dependencies were governed by civil servants of the mother country and/or by its military forces. Even the more democratic colonial powers ruled their colonies in a totalitarian way.

(d) *Indirect rule* was developed especially by Britain as a more sophisticated system of colonial rule and was established when the financial resources of the imperial state were not capable of covering the costs of systematic direct rule. Traditional political structures and local leaders of the colonized people were functionally integrated without any real sovereignty in the overall control by the colonial power.

## 3. Economic Patterns

The colonized people in the mercantilist period suffered death, enslavement, robbery, and—economically most significant—forced trade within the respective colonial empire. This colonial trade was secured by protectionist and monopolistic practices, but normally the colonial rulers did not methodically influence the methods of production. Noble metals were merely stolen or obtained by forced labor in great amounts in order to serve the financial needs of the European mercantilist states. The import of luxury consumer goods and later of agricultural raw materials proved incalculable advantages in favor of the development of the European economies. A very lucrative business was the triangular trade transactions between Africa, America, and Europe, especially Britain: cheap African slaves were shipped to America and the Caribbean and sold as urgently needed labor for large-scale agricultural production; from there, sugar, spices and herbs, rum, tobacco, cotton, and other goods were shipped to Europe. According to the mercantilistic economic philosophy, the colonial powers entirely excluded foreign ships from colonial ports; virtually all colonial exports and imports were routed through the ports of the mother country; specified manufactures or processing of raw materials were banned in the dependencies. By these means the mother country should retain a monopoly of colonial bullion and raw materials and as well a guaranteed colonial market for manufacturers. In fact, the main colonial profit arose from commercial monopoly because the colonies had to pay higher prices for their imports and received lower returns for their exports than under a free-trading system.

In the first half of the nineteenth century, Britain gradually adopted free-trade practices at home and extended them to the colonies. Other colonial powers slowly followed. Spain and Portugal never completely removed mercantile controls but largely liberalized them for their dependencies. By 1870, no imperial power obtained economic advantages from its dependencies that were not available to others. In this period, however, the classical principle of colonial economy was fully established (*pacte colonial* as the French called it): the colonies had to provide (mainly agricultural) raw materials and tropical consumer goods mostly produced in huge monocultural plantations, while the European metropolitan economies exported industrial products. It was this lucrative mechanism of unequal division of labour—the economic practice since about 1880—that secured the resurgence of limited protectionism in a "neomercantilist" form. During the last phase of European colonialism, most colonial powers adopted some form of preferential system within their colonial empires.

## 4. Theories and Justifications

Theories on the advantages and the best methods of colonial rule were normally based on the political and economic practice of the parent state. Colonial practices usually followed the practice at home. Before 1660, as expansion proceeded more experimentally, no general theory of colonialism was needed and no attempt was made to select or provide a rationale for it. Then, in the classical age of mercantilistic thought, there was still some lack of clarity of aims, but the primary considerations were considered to be economic advantage and value of colonial trade; the economies of the colonies were to be made entirely complementary to the special needs of each metropolitan country's economy. In 1776, Adam Smith attacked the mercantilist colonial concept by applying his theory of the division of labor to colonial production and trade, demanding that the colonies should be liberated and their trade opened to the world. In the modern imperialist period, the need to export surplus capital and the need for controlled export markets were stressed; by the early twentieth century, such arguments were widely accepted while at the same time new criticism arose and the modern theories of imperialism were created.

Political arguments and ideological justifications of colonial rule cover a wide range. Normally colonialism has been accepted as a consequence of the axiom that the strong dominate the weak. The usual presumption has been that every colony does or ought to exist for the benefit of the mother country which was frequently rationalized by the argument of the right of the conqueror. This was often bolstered

by the claim of racial superiority and strong missionary elements. The myth of anthropological and racial inferiority of colored people served ideologically and emotionally as the key argument of colonialist thinking. If the interests of the dependent people were taken into account it was held that an extended period of guardianship was necessary to enable them to meet the challenges of the modern world. The French *mission civilisatrice* or the English *white man's burden* marked this ideology of colonial rule as the universal instrument for the spread of civilization. Particularly in the free-trade period and in the early twentieth century significant European and United States criticism of colonialism has to be noted. Since the beginning of the decolonization process, by the foundation of the United Nations and because of the emergence of the developing nations as the self-conscious new majority of nations (most of them having been colonies) the phenomenon and the term "colonialism" has become naturally assessed as extremely negative. The contemporary term "neocolonialism" expresses both this and the present significance of the historical colonial rule.

## 5. Historical and Present Significance

Today, there is little consensus regarding the real reasons for colonialism or regarding its most important results and effects. The value of the economic yield of the colonial mother countries has always been questioned. Indeed, there can be no simple answer because such questions are beyond mere reckoning—they are essentially theoretical and political issues. Although most colonies seem to have been of less importance to the world trade of their parent state—particularly in the last imperialist period—than is often assumed, the lasting socioeconomic importance of colonialism is to be seen in the basic change and continuous foreign determination of the economic activities and structures of the dependencies. No matter whether colonial exploitation was necessary or at least helpful for the economic development of the European countries or not, for reasons of the long-term effects of persisting structures established in the colonial era, colonialism today is not at its end as is often claimed.

The colonial heritage is to be seen in present structural problems that are obstacles to development and threats to peace:

(a) agricultural monostructures that exist for the monofunctional economic orientation of a specialized supplier, resulting in trade disadvantages and food problems by separating agriculture from nourishment;

(b) political and economic dominance by an elitist minority which was for the most part not ended by the decolonization process since only the staff changed;

(c) national borders deriving from colonial borders or mere administration units often contradict the ethnic distribution of the populations which can cause both territorial conflicts between the post-colonial states and inner unrest;

(d) problematic social and ethnic strata which often give rise to racial conflicts or expulsions (important examples are the Black population in America or the Indians in Africa);

(e) international trade patterns and a division of labor which disadvantage the economies of the new states.

See also: *Neocolonialism; Imperialism; Maldevelopment; Conflict and Peace: Class versus Structural School*

*Bibliography* —————————————

Albertini R V 1982 *European Colonial Rule 1880-1940: The Impact of the West in India, South Asia and Africa.* Oxford

Brougham H 1970 *An Inquiry into the Colonial Policy of the European Powers.* New York

Darby P 1998 *The Fiction of Imperialism: Reading between International Relations and Post-colonialism.* London/ Washington, DC

David M D 1988 *Western Colonialism in Asia and Christianity.* Bombay

Deschamps H 1953 *Les methodes et les doctrines coloniales de la France de XVIe siecle a nos jours.* Paris

Easton S C 1964 *The Rise and Fall of Western Colonialism: A Historical Survey from the Early Nineteenth century to the Present.* London

Fieldhouse D K 1973 *Economics and Empire 1830-1914.* London

Grimal H 1978 *Decolonization: The British, French, Dutch and Belgian Empires 1919-1963.* Boulder

Grove R 1997 *Ecology, Climate and Empire: Colonialism and Global Environmental History, 1400-1940.* Cambridge

Healy C 1997 *From the Ruins of Colonialism: History as Social Memory.* Cambridge

Knorr K E 1963 *British Colonial Theories: 1570-1850.* Toronto

Kolarz W 1955 *Russia and her Colonies.* New York

Larraín J 1989 *Theories of Development: Capitalism, Colonialism, and Dependency.* Cambridge

Osterhammel J 1996 *Colonialism: A Theoretical Overview.* Princeton

Parry J H 1940 *The Spanish Theory of Empire in the Sixteenth Century.* Cambridge/Mass.

Schuyler R L 1945 *The Fall of the Old Colonial System: A Study in British Free Trade, 1770-1870.* New York

Spybey T 1992 *Social Change, Development and Dependency: Modernity, Colonialism and the Development of the West.* Cambridge

Townsend M E 1930 *The Rise and Fall of Germany's Colonial Empire: 1884-1918.* New York

Wallerstein I 1981 *The Modern World System,* 2 vols. New York

Wesseling H L 1997 *Imperialism and Colonialism: Essays on the History of European Expansion.* Westport

Winch D N 1965 *Classical Political Economy and Colonies.* London

REINHARD WESEL

# Commission of Investigation and Conciliation

The Commission of Investigation and Conciliation is a body established under the American Treaty of Pacific Settlement (Pact of Bogotá) of 1948. The Pact is one of a number of inter-American agreements which supplement the Charter of the Organization of American States (OAS). States party to the Treaty may invoke its assistance in settling disputes by requesting either inquiry into the facts or suggestions for settlement of a dispute. The title "Commission of Investigation and Conciliation" actually covers two sets of bodies; standing Commissions created by bilateral agreement among states party to the Treaty, and ad hoc Commissions established by the OAS Council when requested by disputing states. A standing bilateral Commission has five members, two chosen by each party and a chairperson chosen by the other four members. If states decide to create a standing Commission, they may choose one of their own nationals as a member. An ad hoc Commission's five members are chosen from among a list of conciliators maintained by the OAS Secretariat. In this case, parties still appoint two of the members, but may not choose one of their own nationals; the four members thus chosen select the chairperson.

Any party to the Treaty may unilaterally initiate investigation or conciliation by requesting the OAS

Council to convene a standing or ad hoc Commission. If the disputants have named a standing Commission, the Council need only specify when and where it will first meet. If they have not, they must appoint the members before the Council can summon it. In either case, Article XVI of the Treaty provides that "the controversy between the parties shall be suspended, and the parties shall refrain from any act that might make conciliation more difficult."

If the disputants decide that the controversy relates solely to questions of fact, the Commission's role is confined to inquiry into the facts and reporting the results of inquiry to the disputing governments. As usual in procedures of inquiry, the Commission is not empowered to suggest further steps in or substantive bases for settlement. If the disputants seek conciliation, Article XXII of the Treaty authorizes the Commission to "clarify the points in dispute between the parties and to endeavor to bring about an agreement between them on mutually acceptable terms." When pursuing conciliation, the Commission may decide on its own that certain facts should be investigated. It may also hear oral testimony from experts and others with relevant information, as well as request relevant documents and written evidence. Unless the parties to a dispute agree to extend the deadline, the Commission must report the results of its inquiry or conciliation efforts within six months of its first meeting.

The Pact of Bogotá is unusual among treaties establishing procedures for peaceful settlement in that it makes explicit provision for disputes among more than two states. Article XXI provides that, if two or more states involved in a dispute have an identical interest in the outcome, they will together appoint two members of the Commission. If they have different interests, then the Commission is enlarged so that each may appoint two members.

The Commission of Investigation and Conciliation is only one of the mechanisms for peaceful settlement of disputes established in the Pact of Bogotá. The Pact also provides for submission of disputes to mediation, arbitration, or adjudication by the International Court of Justice. However, only 14 of the OAS's 28 members are party to the Pact, many with reservations that severely limit its application. None of the 14 have acted to establish a standing Commission, and no dispute has been submitted to either a standing or an ad hoc Commission. Nor have the other mechanisms established in the Pact ever been used.

The relatively small number of parties limits the potential effect of the Pact of Bogotá. It cannot even serve as a regional mechanism since so many Western hemisphere states have remained aloof from it. Further, Western hemisphere governments, like others, prefer to deal with disputes through direct negotiation or resort to more politically oriented bodies. Therefore dispute settlement efforts have been concentrated in special OAS Meetings of Consultation attended by foreign ministers of member states, the OAS Council and the Inter-American Peace Committee.

See also: *Arbitration, International; International Judicial Settlement; Mediation; Pacific Settlement of International Disputes; International Court of Justice*

*Bibliography* —————————————————

American Treaty of Pacific Settlement (Pact of Bogotá). Text in *United Nations Treaty Series* 30:55

M. J. PETERSON

# Commission of Mediation, Conciliation, and Arbitration

The Commission of Mediation, Conciliation, and Arbitration serves as a mechanism for resolution of disputes among the members of the Organization of African Unity (OAU). Article XIX of the OAU Charter provides that: "Member states pledge to settle all disputes among themselves by peaceful means and to this end decide to establish a Commission of Mediation, Conciliation and Arbitration." Details of Commission function, structure, and procedure are set out in a Protocol to the OAU Charter. These provide distinct procedures depending on whether the Commission serves as mediator, conciliator, or arbitrator.

The Commission consists of 21 individuals chosen from among candidates nominated by OAU member states. They are elected by the OAU Assembly of Heads of State and Government to serve five-year terms. The only limits on the Assembly's choice are that no two members can be nationals of the same state. The Assembly also decides which of the 21 should serve as the president and two vice-presidents of the Commission, full-time officers charged with being available at all times to assist member states preparing to submit disputes. The other 18 members serve as needed in the settlement of particular disputes.

Disputes can be submitted to the Commission by certain OAU organs or by OAU member states. The OAU

Council of Ministers or Assembly of Heads of State and Government can decide that a dispute initially referred to them was better handled by the Commission. Alternatively, disputing states may decide to invoke the Commission's assistance directly. Commission proceedings are not compulsory. Though Article XIII of the Protocol allows unilateral submission of a dispute to the Commission, a state wishing to avoid it can stop proceedings by refusing to consent to the appointment of mediators or conciliators, or by refusing to sign a *compromis d'arbitrage*.

The authorized OAU organs or disputing states decide whether the dispute will be submitted to mediation, conciliation, or arbitration. If they choose mediation, the Commission's president, with the consent of the disputing states, names one or more Commission members as mediators. As in all mediation, the authority of the members selected as mediators extends only to the making of non-binding suggestion; in the language of Article XXI(1) of the Protocol, "the role of the mediator shall be confined to reconciling the views and claims of the parties." Disputing states are free to adopt or reject the mediator's suggestions.

For conciliation, a five-member Board of Conciliators is established. Three members, including the chairperson, are named by the Commission president, and one by each disputant. Such a Board proceeds in quasi-judicial fashion. The parties submit a written statement of the nature of the dispute. They send agents, assisted as needed by counsel and experts, to make supplemental oral presentations. The Board has authority to undertake inquiries into facts or circumstances relevant to the dispute on its own initiative, and to hear oral testimony from any person with information relevant to the dispute. At the end of its proceedings, the Board must submit a written report indicating either the terms of agreement reached by the disputants or the fact that no settlement was reached. The Board has no authority to suggest any further measures if the parties still fail to agree after conciliation has been attempted.

If arbitration is invoked, a three or five-member Arbitral Panel is set up to hear the case. The members of the Tribunal are chosen in the normal way from among those Commission members with legal training. If the disputants decide to establish a three-member Tribunal, each chooses one arbitrator and the two persons thus chosen select a third to serve as chairperson. If the disputants opt for a five-member Tribunal, each chooses one member, those two select the chairperson, and the Commission president chooses the final two. Arbitrators may not be nationals of, domiciled in, or employed by the government of any disputant. Nor can

they have previously served as mediators and conciliators in earlier efforts to settle the dispute.

Selecting arbitration also requires conclusion of a *compromis d'arbitrage*. This sets out the subject matter of the dispute, a definition of the applicable law, a time limit for decision by the Tribunal, and whether the Tribunal was authorized to rule *ex aequo et bono*. Arbitration is binding; Article XXVIII of the Protocol states that "recourse to arbitration shall be regarded as submission in good faith to the award of the Arbitral Tribunal."

The Commission provides the OAU with a flexible mechanism for peaceful settlement of disputes, one fully capable of providing all the dispute settlement assistance developed in international practice while simultaneously ensuring respect for the OAU norm that disputes among African states ought to be settled in African fora rather than taken outside the region. OAU members have stressed their interest in providing for such local mechanisms by including provision for resort to the Commission when disputes arise under African regional or subregional agreements, such as the Convention on the Exploitation of the Lake Chad Basin of 1964, the African and Malagasy Sugar Agreement of 1966, and the African Convention on the Conservation of Nature and Natural Resources of 1968.

Despite its great flexibility, the Commission has not been used. Most of the disputes arising between OAU members involve highly political issues, such as aid to subversives, foreign participation in civil wars, or territorial disputes, which have seldom been submitted to mediation, conciliation, or arbitration by any state. Instead, governments have used political methods of dispute settlement through the OAU Council of Ministers, the OAU Assembly of Heads of State and Government, or the diplomatic initiatives of individual African leaders.

See also: *Arbitration, International; International Judicial Settlement; Mediation; Organization of African Unity (OAU); Pacific Settlement of International Disputes*

*Bibliography* ⸺⸺⸺⸺⸺⸺⸺⸺⸺⸺⸺

Charter of the Organization of African Unity. *United Nations Treaty Series* 479

Protocol to the OAU Charter of the Commission of Mediation, Conciliation, and Arbitration. Text in *International Legal Materials* 3: 1116 (1964)

M. J. PETERSON

# Commission on Global Governance

The Commission on Global Governance was responsible for putting forward, through its report, '*Our Global Neighbourhood,*' a comprehensive set of proposals for creating a more cooperative and more democratic international order. Issued in 1995, the year the United Nations marked its fiftieth anniversary, the report centred on—but was not concerned exclusively with—the reform of the UN system. It became an important text in the study of international institutions and discussion of institutional change. First published in English, the report was soon issued in over a dozen other languages.

The Commission, an independent group of 28 eminent persons from a variety of backgrounds and countries, was formed in 1992. Mr Ingvar Carlsson, twice Prime Minister of Sweden, and Sir Shridath Ramphal of Guyana, a former Secretary-General of the Commonwealth, were its Co-Chairmen. It was the outcome of an initiative by the late West German statesman Willy Brandt, who convened a meeting in 1990 in Konigswinter to assess the opportunities for international cooperation that the end of the Cold War may have created. Discussions at this gathering led to a more formal meeting of some three dozen public figures in 1991 in Stockholm; they issued a statement "Common Responsibility in the 1990s: The Stockholm Initiative on Global Security and Governance." One of their recommendations was that an independent international commission should explore in greater depth the possibilities for creating a more effective system of world governance and cooperation, taking advantage of the post-Cold War improvement in the climate of international relations.

The Commission may be seen as following in the tradition of independent inquiries into major global issues that were a feature of the 1980s. These started with the Independent Commission on International Development Issues, formed as the result of a suggestion by the then President of the World Bank, Robert MacNamara, and chaired by Willy Brandt. It was followed by the Independent Commission on Disarmament and Security Issues, headed by Sweden's Olof Palme, the World Commission on Environment and Development, headed by Gro Harlem Brundtland of Norway, and the South Commission, with Julius Nyerere of Tanzania as Chairman.

The title the Commission gave its report, '*Our Global Neighbourhood,*' serves as a metaphor for the kind of world order to which it aspires. It is meant to be more than simply a description of the contemporary world, made smaller by advances in communications technology and more interdependent by the globalization they have facilitated. It is also a call for neighbourly behaviour to make the world "a satisfactory home for all its citizens." The title underlines the Commission's concern with people, as distinct from states; while it recognises the continuing relevance of the nation-state system, a desire to secure wider respect for the rights of people—and a larger role for them in the world's governance—is a prominent thrust of its report.

## 1. Call for a Global Ethic

The Commission's detailed proposals for improving the framework of global governance, including suggestions for additions to the existing institutional structure, were preceded by a call for an ethical underpinning of governance systems. Besides urging commitment to the values of internationalism and the rule of law worldwide, the Commission asserted that both organisations and laws should rest on a foundation "made strong by shared values··· informed by a sense of common responsibility for both present and future generations." It suggested that upholding a set of core values—respect for life, liberty, justice and equity, mutual respect, caring and integrity—could enable "a global neighbourhood based on economic exchange and improved communications" to be transformed into "a universal moral community in which people are bound together by more than proximity, interest or identity." It went on to advocate support for a global ethic consisting of a set of "common rights" balanced by a set of shared responsibilities.

## 2. A Wider Concept of Security

In addressing peace and security issues, the Commission called for a focus on the security of people and of the planet. It said that global security should "extend beyond the protection of borders, ruling elites and exclusive state interests to include the protection of people." It pointed out that preserving the security of the state had often been used in the past as a shield to cover policies that violated the security of people, and that the security of people should be treated as important as the security of states (see *Comprehensive Security*). Although the rights of states to security must continue to be upheld and states protected against external threats, the international community should also make the protection of people and their security an objective of global security policy.

The Commission was exercised by the increase in violent conflicts within countries relative to the incidence of interstate conflicts and by the extent to which the security of people was violated by conflicts that are internal in character. It called for recognition of the right of the international community to intervene in such situations when there is gross violation of the rights of people and for this recognition to be made explicit through an amendment of the Charter of the United Nations (see *United Nations Charter*). The Charter has barred UN intervention in matters "which are essentially within the domestic jurisdiction of any state" (Article 2.7), allowing intervention only for the purpose of maintaining or restoring "international peace and order." The Commission argued that quite often there were threats to the security of people that justified international action though they did not constitute threats to international peace and security, and a domestic conflict might assume such proportions that it ceased to be purely a domestic issue.

Despite the prohibition expressed in Article 2.7, the Security Council had on a few occasions authorised intervention in internal situations on humanitarian grounds, as in Somalia or in Rwanda (see *Intervention*). The Commission's view was that if the Council was to disregard Article 2.7, it should only be "in circumstances clearly defined" by a Charter amendment. The present practice of selective intervention was detrimental to world order under law. It accordingly proposed an amendment that would permit intervention but restrict it to "cases that constitute a violation of the security of the people so gross and extreme that it requires an international response on humanitarian grounds." The Commission observed that "the line separating a domestic affair from a global one cannot be drawn in the sand, but we are convinced that in practice virtually all will know when it has been crossed."

### 3. Preventing and Responding to Crises

The Commission's report called for greater international attention to action that could prevent conflicts from erupting in violence, noting that preventive action had received far less priority than the costlier action to stop wars once they had started. Strategies to deal with the underlying causes of conflict should be complemented by action to identify, anticipate and resolve conflicts before they degenerate into violent confrontations. As part of efforts to strengthen its capacity in this area, the United Nations was urged to develop a more comprehensive system to gather information on situations that may lead to

humanitarian tragedies, with the UN Secretary-General making greater use of the facility to send fact-finding missions to potential trouble-spots (see *Crisis Management*). The Commission also favoured the Security Council making more use of the power to call upon parties to a dispute to seek a solution through one or other of the mechanisms for peaceful settlement indicated in Chapter VI of the UN Charter.

Several recommendations of the Commission were designed to strengthen the UN's capacity to act more quickly and effectively when the Security Council decides on action under Chapter VII of the Charter to maintain or restore peace. It threw its weight behind the proposal for equipping the UN with a Volunteer Force to be available for rapid deployment, envisaging a force with a maximum strength of 10,000; it also called for the reactivation of the Military Staff Committee, which the Charter envisaged as a group providing advice and assistance to the Security Council on all military matters.

### 4. Eliminating Weapons of Mass Destruction

The Commission sought renewed international commitment to the progressive elimination of nuclear and other weapons of mass destruction, which it did not accept as legitimate instruments of national defence; it pointed out that the end of the Cold War provided an opportunity for moving towards a total prohibition of these weapons. It urged support for a programme to secure a complete end to such weapons within a ten-to-fifteen year period. It advocated the indefinite renewal of the Nuclear Non-Proliferation Treaty (NPT) (see *Non-Proliferation Treaty (NPT)*) and, in calling for the conclusion of a treaty to end all nuclear tests, it said that "no single act would symbolize more clearly the commitment of the international community to eliminate nuclear weapons."

Voicing disappointment at the failure to put an end to chemical and biological weapons, the Commission urged the many countries that had not done so to ratify the relevant conventions.

### 5. Demilitarization

The Commission's report noted that while there had been a decline in world military expenditure after the Cold War came to an end, there were important regional exceptions to the general trend. Arms spending continued at a high level in the Middle East, along the Persian Gulf and in South Asia, while nations in East Asia were engaged in a major arms build-up, with several countries also establishing large domestic defence industries. Advocating a global plan to address the economic and social as well as the military aspects of demilitarization, it called for attention to such matters as reallocation of financial resources and military installations, reorientation of military research, restructuring of industry, reintegration of military personnel into civilian work and alternative uses for or scrapping of surplus weapons.

Besides suggesting that governments should agree to annual reductions in military budgets and that institutions and governments providing development aid should discourage recipient nations from undertaking excessive military spending, the Commission recommended that a demilitarization fund should be set up to support defence conversion activity in developing countries willing to reduce their military establishments to levels consistent with self-defense needs. It pointed out that large standing militaries, far from offering security, often created threats to the security of people in their own countries. Governments, however, even when they recognised this danger, found it difficult to scale down their armies without financial support to ease the return of soldiers to civilian life.

Further recommendations envisaged negotiations towards an international convention on the curtailment of the arms trade that would, among other objectives, make reporting requirements under the UN Arms Register mandatory and prohibit or heavily circumscribe government financing or subsidization of arms exports. The Commission also endorsed the proposal for a worldwide ban on the manufacture and export of land mines. There was now a need not only to demilitarize international relations but to demilitarize international society, it observed in its report. Militarization—and the growth of a culture of violence—had become a global social phenomenon, evidenced by "the rampant acquisition and use of increasingly lethal weapons by civilians—whether individuals seeking a means of self-defence, street gangs, criminals, political groups, or terrorist organizations." This culture of violence had become a major source of insecurity to people everywhere in the world, and efforts should be made at the local and community levels as well as at the international level to reverse the trend and to plant the seeds of a culture of non-violence.

## 6. Global Economic Governance

The Commission was concerned that, while global interdependence had grown, political structures that could "articulate a sense of common interest and mediate differences" had not kept pace (see *Interdependence, International*). Opportunities for creating wealth had been multiplied but the chances of destabilising shocks being transmitted from one economy to another had also increased. Increasing affluence coexisted with a marginalised global underclass. Though there had been much economic and social progress, several indicators of poverty and deprivation were as chilling as they had been 25 years earlier. High unemployment—and the associated evils of growing poverty and social deprivation—affected many industrial countries. In both rich and poor countries large numbers of people had not been able to realise their potential due to unemployment, poor health and education facilities, discrimination against women or minorities, and other factors (see *Human Security*).

The world community had no satisfactory forum to address global economic problems in the round and the linkages between economic, social, environment and security issues in the widest sense. In a polycentric world, economic decision-making had become concentrated in the hands of the United States, Europe and Japan, countries with a little over one tenth of the world population. This was reflected in the distribution of power within the Bretton Woods institutions, and even more in the Group of 7, the nearest to an apex body having oversight of the world economy. The G-7 was far from representative of the world's population, and it gave low priority to development issues that concern most of that population. The world's economic centre of gravity was shifting as major developing countries grew faster than Western industrial countries; when national GDP was reckoned on a purchasing power parity basis, China, India, Brazil and Russia were among the world's ten largest economies. Yet none of them were in the G-7 and they were also under-represented in terms of votes in the Bretton Woods institutions.

## 7. An Economic Security Council

The Commission's principal recommendation for improving economic governance was accordingly a call for establishing, within the United Nations, an Economic Security Council, at the same high level as the existing Security Council but with deliberative rather than executive powers, to provide leadership and promote consensus on major issues in the economic, social and environmental fields. The Council's primary function was seen not so much as tackling crises but as looking at the main trends in the world economy and giving signals to guide the world community in achieving stable, sustainable development.

The Council's tasks were set out as follows:

(a) to continuously assess the overall state of the world economy and the interaction between major policy areas;

(b) to provide a long-term strategic policy framework in order to promote stable, balanced and sustainable development;

(c) to secure consistency between the policy goals of the major international organizations, particularly the main multilateral economic institutions (the Bretton Woods bodies and the proposed World Trade Organization), (see *World Trade Organization (WTO)*) while recognising their distinct roles;

(d) to promote consensus-building dialogue between governments on the evolution of the international economic system, while providing a global forum for some of the new forces in the world economy-such as regional organizations.

It was envisaged that the world's largest economies would have a place on the Council—with the Commission suggesting that GDP figures based on a purchasing power parity (PPP) basis should be used in ranking economies—together with some of the smaller economies, with attention given to the need for regional balance and the possibility of strong regional economic groupings participating on behalf of their members. It was suggested that total membership should be no larger than 23, the figure the Commission proposed for a reformed Security Council. The Commission stressed that the design of the body was less important than the concept. It said: "Without a representative high-level body developing an international consensus on critical economic issues, the global neighbourhood could become a battleground of contending economic forces, and the capacity of humanity to develop a common approach will be jeopardized."

## 8. Reform of the Security Council

In addressing the reform of the Security Council, the Commission was concerned to underline the need for the Council to command legitimacy in the eyes of the UN's members; this need had become all the greater as the Council had become far more active after the ending of the Cold War, during which tension between the two superpowers had tended to constrain the Council. From the beginning of 1990 the pace of Council activity had markedly increased, as reflected in the number of formal meetings, informal consultations and resolutions as well as in the extent of peacekeeping activity. The UN had been conducting eight peacekeeping operations with a total of 10,000 troops at the end of 1990; by the middle of 1994, it was fielding more than 70,000 troops in seventeen operations (see *Peacekeeping Forces*). The Council was faced with the challenge of "making its membership structure more equitable, while preserving the capability and political support necessary for it to play a major role," according to the Commission.

The Commission saw the Council's legitimacy as closely linked to its representative character. It felt that the position of the original permanent five had become increasingly anachronistic, and the Council had failed to take adequate note of the expansion in UN membership or of changes in the relative standing of nations in the past few decades. The last—and only—change in the structure of the Council was an increase in the number of non-permanent seats, held by members elected to serve for terms of two years, from six to ten (with a consequential increase in the minimum number of votes required for a decision from seven to nine). This enlargement of the Council took place in 1963 when membership of the United Nations had climbed from the 51 at the time of its founding to 113. The number of members had since risen to 184.

Neither permanent membership nor the power to veto Council decisions which has so far been a privilege of such membership found favour with the Commission. "Permanent membership limited to five countries that derive their primacy from events fifty years ago is unacceptable; so is the veto," it observed. While it accepted that the world had not reached the stage when it might be feasible to do away with permanent membership, it was against investing more members with the right to sit in the Council permanently. It was also against enlarging the ranks of veto-wielding members and called for some self-imposed restraint on the use of the veto by those who possessed it. The Commission proposed a two-stage scheme for reforming the Council; its main elements were:

(a) The creation of a new class of 'standing' members, without veto powers. The first group of five 'standing' members—two from industrial countries and three from developing countries—would be elected to serve until a full review of Council membership and structure in 2005,

(b) Agreement by the permanent members not to use

the veto save in exceptional circumstances related to their national security,

(c)  An increase in the number of non-permanent seats from ten to thirteen (raising total Council membership from fifteen to twenty-three and requiring the minimum number of votes necessary for a decision of the Council to be raised from nine to fourteen.),

(d)  The question of permanent membership and the role of the veto to be among the issues to be considered in the review proposed for 2005 to usher in the second phase of reforms.

## 9. Strengthening the United Nations

Side by side with the reform of the Security Council, the Commission recommended other measures to strengthen the United Nations, including changes to enable the General Assembly play a more vigorous role as a universal forum of the world's nation states. While the Assembly was only a deliberative organ and could only discuss and recommend without the authority to take binding decisions, the Commission pointed out that it was the one forum where the voice of every member could be heard. "The opportunity for countries to ventilate issues, bring complaints to the floor in the General Debate, and suggest new ideas in Committees of the Assembly is of vital importance to the health of global society," said its report. The Assembly had been dwarfed by the Security Council but it had played a key part in advancing progress on many issues of world concern, human rights, apartheid, Namibia and Palestine among them. It had also been a launchpad for such initiatives as that by Malta in 1967 that led eventually to the Law of the Sea Convention.

The Commission suggested that the Assembly should use the authority vested in it by the Charter to approve the UN budget to strengthen its role in global governance. It deplored the fact that the Assembly had allowed industrial countries, as the larger contributors to the UN's budget, to constrain the exercise of the Assembly's collective authority. These countries had persuaded the Assembly that decisions on the budget should be made by consensus; the Commission felt that while this could be a sound procedure in principle, it was objectionable "because of the de facto threat of a rich-country veto." The Assembly should therefore reassert its rightful authority.

Other suggestions for revitalising the Assembly included measures to enhance the role of its President, reduce and rationalize its agenda, limit the number and frequency of reports requested from the Secretary-General, and to merge and restructure the committees of the Assembly.

With the setting up of an Economic Security Council, the Commission suggested, the UN Economic and Social Council—ECOSOC—should be disbanded. It argued that ECOSOC had not been allowed to play the coordinating and direction-setting role envisaged for it and had been devalued into a sterile debating chamber. Recent changes had resulted in some improvement in its functioning, but the proposed Economic Security Council would be "altogether more promising machinery for addressing major economic and social issues." The Commission also called for a review of the positions of the UN Conference on Trade and Development (UNCTAD) and the UN Industrial Development Organisation (UNIDO). It felt these two agencies had provided significant support to developing countries in the past but circumstances had now reduced their utility and those of their functions that were still useful could be handled by other agencies. The Commission wanted its recommendations on economic governance to be treated as a package, including, in particular, the proposal for an Economic Security Council, which was designed to be "more responsive to the interests of developing countries than existing arrangements for global economic governance," and changes in the allocation of votes in the Bretton Woods institutions to give developing countries a larger voice in their governing bodies.

## 10. Trusteeship of the Global Commons

The Commission saw a new use for the Trusteeship Council which had exhausted its mandate of overseeing the progress of trust territories to independence. It suggested that the Council should be given a fresh lease of life as a custodian of the global commons including the atmosphere, outer space, the oceans beyond national jurisdiction, and the related environment and life-support systems that contribute to sustaining human life. It held that "prudent and equitable management of the global commons" was "crucial to the future well-being and progress, perhaps even the survival, of humanity." The management of the commons, including development and use of their resources in the collective interests of humanity, including future generations, was best pursued by a body acting on behalf of all nations, and it was appropriate that this body should be a principal organ of the United Nations.

The Commission envisaged the Trusteeship Council in its new role becoming the chief forum on global environmental and related matters, with its functions including the administration of environmental treaties. In its original role, the Council's membership was related to the number of territories in trusteeship. The Commission suggested a fixed number of members, determined by the General Assembly, would be suitable in its new role, and that governments in nominating representatives to the Council should be free to name public officials or persons from civil society.

## 11. An Enlarged Role for Civil Society

That the institutions of governance, notably the United Nations, should take greater note of civil society and provide more space for it was one of the thrusts of the Commission's report. It urged the international community to create public-private partnerships to enable non-state actors to contribute to global governance. Conceding that the non-governmental sector, national or international, was not without imperfections, the Commission held that nevertheless the wider involvement of civil society organisations could benefit governance by bringing knowledge, skills, enthusiasm, a non-bureaucratic approach and grassroots perspectives, attributes that would complement the resources of official agencies.

The Commissions's specific suggestions for enhancing the role of civil society in governance included a proposal for a Civil Society Forum to be convened ahead of the annual sessions of the United Nations General Assembly—and in the Assembly chamber— to discuss some issues on the Assembly's agenda and provide its views as an input to the deliberations of national delegations within the Assembly. The Commission envisaged the Forum consisting of the representatives of 300 to 600 organisations, with the possibility of regional forums being arranged to allow a wider variety of bodies to make a contribution. It suggested that civil society itself should be involved in determining how the participating organisations should be identified and that the General Assembly and civil society should take steps to develop the idea of the Forum.

Another proposal made by the Commission that would provide a new window for civil society organisations was designed to improve protection for the security of people. The Commission recommended that a Council for Petitions should be formed within the United Nations through which civil society organisations concerned with humanitarian issues could draw international attention to situations within countries in which there was cause to fear that people's security could be extensively violated.

The Commission's case was that governments, which are the only bodies entitled to bring matters to the attention of the Security Council, generally fight shy of fingering other governments for transgressions that might be considered matters of domestic jurisdiction. In emerging situations, in particular, civil society organisations working within the country concerned were much more likely to be able to sound an alarm, and a Council of Petitions would provide the machinery for them to alert the world community to looming danger and activate the UN's potential for taking preventive measures. The Council would be empowered to refer such petitions, after due consideration, to the Secretary-General, the Security Council or the General Assembly.

The Commission envisaged the Council as a high-level panel of five to seven persons, serving in their personal capacity and independent of governments; members would be appointed by the Secretary-General with the approval of the General Assembly.

## 12. Improving the UN Secretariat

Several recommendations made by the Commission were designed to improve the way the post of Secretary-General and other senior UN positions, including those of heads of UN agencies, are filled. It was quite critical of the procedure for appointing the world's number one civil servant, describing it as "haphazard and disorganized." Observing that there was "no organized search for suitable candidates, no interview, no systematic assessment of the qualifications required or presented by candidates," the Commission claimed that no company would "dream of appointing its chief executive officer in this manner." It suggested, inter alia, that the Security Council should organise a worldwide search for candidates, candidates should be barred from canvassing, the appointment should be for a single term of seven years, and that permanent members of the Security Council should not be able to apply the veto against any candidate but should be free to sponsor nationals of their countries. The procedure for selecting heads of UN agencies, programmes and funds should also be similarly improved, the Commission said.

Urging the need for greater professionalism, the Commission sought improvements in the procedures for selecting staff for UN positions. It called for a less rigid adherence to national quotas so that the Secretary-General could have greater freedom to choose the best candidates. It wanted an end to the practice of seeking clearance from governments before their nationals are appointed and the topping up by some governments of the salaries of nationals taking up UN appointments. The Commission also frowned on "governmental lobbying for or blackballing of candidates." It asked the UN General Assembly to rule that barring very exceptional circumstances, no person serving in a country's permanent mission to the UN should be recruited to the UN before a stated interval had elapsed after such service.

## 13. Financing the United Nations

The financial difficulties caused to the United Nations by governments delaying payment of agreed contributions as well as the wider issue of securing adequate funds to achieve globally agreed objectives engaged the Commission's attention. On the former question, it was blunt in stating, "Withholding contributions has even become a destructive way of exerting influence. It is essential that it must not pay not to pay. Those who choose not to adhere to the financial rules should be deprived of the right to vote, in accordance with Article 19 of the UN Charter." It went on to remark that it was unhealthy for the UN to depend on one country paying as much as 25 per cent of its regular budget, and to suggest that a new scheme of assessments should be worked out under which no country would pay more than an agreed percentage, which would be set at less than 25 per cent and which could be adjusted from time to time. The Commission recalled that in 1985 Olof Palme, then Prime Minister of Sweden, had suggested a lower ceiling for the US contribution, but the Reagan administration had opposed the proposal, "anxious to maintain the leverage that its level of contribution seemed to buy." It seemed to sense a shift in the position in Washington as the Clinton administration had indicated it wished to see its contribution to the UN's peacekeeping budget brought down from its then level of 30 percent.

On the wider issue, the Commission was convinced that it was time for a start to be made in providing the UN with an additional stream of income, independent of but complementary to contributions from national treasuries, to finance specific global undertakings. It pointed out that there was a "widening gap between the requirements of programmes widely supported in principle and the money actually made available through traditional channels," citing inadequate financing for agreed peacekeeping operations as one of the more glaring examples. The Commission made it clear that it was not proposing that the UN should have a supranational tax-raising authority. It indicated that, while proposals could be initiated in the UN, any new revenue arrangements would have to be agreed globally and introduced through an international treaty or convention which would then have to be approved and ratified by governments before it came into effect. It also proposed "stringent arrangements for allocation of global resources and accountability for their disbursement and use."

As one of the main measures for raising global revenue, the Commission favoured a tax on foreign currency transactions. It urged the UN and the Bretton Woods institutions to explore the feasibility of a Tobin tax—so-named after the US Nobel economist who first suggested it as a means of moderating speculative currency movements—and of a variant, a network of foreign currency exchanges generating revenue through user charges. The Commission identified charges for the use of the global commons as another suitable source of global revenue. It pointed out that these commended themselves on grounds of conservation and economic efficiency besides being attractive for their revenue potential. It urged examination of charges on a variety of activities involving use of the global commons: air travel, ocean transport, ocean fishing, commercial operations in Antarctica, satellite parking in space, and use of the radio spectrum.

## 14. The Rule of Law

Ways to strengthen international law also engaged the attention of the Commission. "The global neighbourhood of the future must be characterized by law and the reality that all, including the weakest, are equal under the law and none, including the strongest, is above it," said it in its report.

Several recommendations sought to give the International Court of Justice—the World Court—an enhanced position within the world system. Observing that in an ideal world, acceptance of the Court's compulsory jurisdiction would have been a condition of UN membership, the Commission urged all nations that have not done so to accept the Court's compulsory jurisdiction. If they could not immediately accept the Court's jurisdiction in all matters, they were encouraged to start by doing so in specific areas in which the Court had established its expertise and there was now a mature body of case law, as in disputes over the boundaries of continental shelves and exclusive economic zones. The possibility that disputes over boundaries could lead to conflict between states and endanger peace was an additional reason why states should be ready to accept the Court's universal competence on such issues. Noting some of the concerns voiced by countries that had shown a lack of confidence in the Court, the Commission suggested changes to the Court's chamber procedure to increase its appeal to states and to avoid damage to the Court's integrity.

The Commission expressed itself in favour of the Security Council making more frequent use of the World Court as a source of advisory opinions; it was concerned that the Council should "wherever possible, avoid being the judge in disputes on what international law may or not be in particular cases." It also favoured the UN Secretary-General being empowered to refer the legal dimensions of disputes to the Court. It felt that the Court in turn should treat such matters as of high priority and introduce faster procedures for handling them, and that such changes might encourage governments to seek rulings from the Court.

The Commission considered the desirability of the Council's decisions being made subject to review by the Court, at least on procedural matters, and of allowing states to ask the Court for its opinion on action proposed by the Security Council. It decided against recommending either step on the ground that changes of that kind could give rise to friction between Council and Court. But it went on to suggest that, in order to minimise the risks of illegality in Council decisions, the Council should have a distinguished legal person as its independent adviser, performing a role somewhat similar to that of an Attorney General in a parliamentary democracy.

Proposals for improving the standing of the International Court of Justice further included the suggestion that its judges should be limited to one term only, with the term extended from nine to ten years. The Commission sought by this means to end what it called "the demeaning spectacle" of judges canvassing support for their reappointment, and even, in some instances, seeking support from states with cases before the Court, and also to end room for suspicion that a judge's conduct had been influenced by thoughts of re-election. "The choice of judges for the World Court has assumed too high a level of politicization," said the report.

The Commission expressed strong support for the establishment of a permanent International Criminal Court, saying that the absence of such a court discredits the rule of law. It rejected arguments favouring ad hoc tribunals, pointing out that the delays in agreeing on a court to deal with crimes committed during the conflict in the former Yugoslavia illustrated the desirability of a permanent institution. A

standing court would avoid both the problem of delays—"justice delayed can be justice denied," said the Commission—and the danger of selectivity inherent in a case-by-case approach. The court should have an independent prosecutor or panel of prosecutors "of the highest moral character, as well as the highest level of competence and experience in investigating and prosecuting criminal cases," who would act independently without receiving instructions from any government or other source. It should be possible for the Security Council to refer cases to the Court when it believed that a crime was a threat to international peace and security.

## 15. Reactions to Commission's Report

Early, enthusiastic reactions to the Commission's report came from such world figures as Gro Harlem Brundtland of Norway, Vaclav Havel of the Czech Republic, and Nelson Mandela of South Africa. The diversity of languages in which editions of *Our Global Neighbourhood* were brought out reflected wide interest in the Commission's views and recommendations. There was special interest among non-governmental organizations concerned with international affairs; many organised discussions of the report and a few went to the extent of undertaking its publication in the local language, in full or in a summarised form. Academic interest was also significant, with a number of universities adopting it as a text on relevant courses and several journals carrying review articles.

Decisions on institutional reform have been slow to emerge from the international system, slower than advocates of change, focusing on the UN's completion of five decades in 1995 and the approach of a new millennium, had hoped. Within the United Nations, a cluster of working groups of the General Assembly have been engaged in discussions on reform but progress has been tardy. A change of pace was, however, signalled on a key issue, the reform of the Security Council, in March 1997; Razali Ismail, Malaysia's Permanent Representative to the United Nations and President of the Assembly, as chairman of the working group dealing with the reform of the Council, presented a set of proposals for enlarging the Council together with a time-table for Assembly action that envisaged final decisions being taken by March 1998. These proposals for reforming the Security Council were in almost all important respects similar to those put forward by the Commission on Global Governance.

Earlier, the concept of a Forum of Civil Society, an

important component of the Commission's strategy to enlarge the role of civil society (see *Non-governmental Organization (NGOS)*) in world governance, had attracted support within another of the working groups of the General Assembly. The proposal for an International Criminal Court moved a step forward with the General Assembly deciding to convene a world conference in 1998 to consider a draft convention to set up a court.

See also: *Human Security; Future of Humanity; Security Regimes: Focusing on Asia-Pacific; Global Ethic; Global Ethic, Human Rights Laws and Democratic Governance; Peace and Democracy; Crisis; Non-Proliferation Treaty (NPT): Disarmament and Development; United Nations Reform: Historical and Contemporary Perspectives; Social Progress and Human Survival; Global Neighborhood: New Security Principles*

SHRIDATH RAMPHAL

# Commission to Study the Organization of Peace

The Second World War began on September 1, 1939, and on September 3, President Roosevelt stated that in the future "the influence of America should be consistent in seeking for humanity a final peace which will eliminate as far as it is possible to do so, the continued use of force between nations." He asked that the American people "adjourn" partisanship so that "national unity be the thought that underlines all others." Within two weeks the state Department had appointed Leo Pasvolsky as a Special Department Assistant to Secretary of State Cordell Hull to work on the problems of peace, and within two months six of the most prestigious foreign policy groups started study groups for the purpose—the Council of Foreign Relations in New York City, the Foreign Policy Association, the Federal Council of Churches, the Woodrow Wilson Foundation, the Carnegie Endowment for International Peace, and the League of Nations Association.

The League of Nations Association was headed by James T. Shotwell, Professor of the History of International Relations at Columbia University, who had served on the US delegation in Paris in 1919, had played an important part in negotiating the Kellogg-Briand Pact of 1928, and had just completed editing the Carnegie Endowment's set of 150 volumes on the social and economic causes of the First World War. Shotwell resigned as chairman at the outbreak of war in 1939 to form what he called the Commission to Study the Organization of Peace (CSOP). He chose this somewhat cumbersome title because the term "organized peace" had come to have a special meaning for many. He took with him the executive director of the League of Nations Association, Clark Eichelberger (who would remain Executive Director of the CSOP for 35 years), and Clyde Eagleton as director of studies (Eagleton was Professor of International Law at New York University).

Shotwell secured the interest of about 100 of the leading US internationalists 28 of whom attended the first meeting in New York, on November 5, 1939. Among them were Virginian Guildersleeve (President of Barnard College at Columbia University, who was later to be one of the five US delegates to the San Francisco Conference that wrote the UN Charter), John Foster Dulles (later to become Secretary of State), William Allen Nielsen (President of Smith College), Monsignor John A. Ryan, and Orientalist-educator-journalist Owen Lattimore, together with two other distinguished journalists, Max Lerner and William Allen White. The membership of the Commission was heavily loaded with college professors from the Ivy League and other eastern colleges, but had a generous sprinkling of businessmen, lawyers, doctors, and as noted, journalists. They saw their first function as educating the leaders of American public opinion on the importance of "organization peace"— meaning something to take the place of the failed League of Nations (see *League of Nations*). The Commission functioned through a series of reports and statements carefully prepared and accepted by all or most of the members before being distributed to public information leaders throughout the United States. The first of these reports was issued in November 1940 in 100,000 copies. The third report, "The United Nations and the Organization of Peace" (1943), was of a particular importance in the process of developing support among the American people for a United Nations.

The membership of the Commission had influence, and it is worth noting that, at the San Francisco conference in 1945, 45 members of the Commission served either as delegates, consultants, or members of the secretariat. After the war the Commission drew many important citizens as members, including Eleanor Roosevelt, John Foster Dulles, Sumner Welles, Ralph Bunche, Arthur Sweetster, Frank Graham, Henry Steele Commager, Walter Reuther,

Charles P. Taft, Quincy Wright, James Warburg, and Luther Evans.

The chairmen of the Commission were: James T. Shotwell (1939-47); Clark M. Eichelberger (1948-55); Arthur T. Holcombe, Professor of Government at Harvard (1955-64); Clark M. Eichelberger (1964-68; Louis B. Sohn, Professor of International Law at Harvard (1968-69); Richard at W. Swift, Professor of International Relations at New York University (1970); and Louis B. Sohn (1971-81).

From 1940 to 1981 the Commission drafted about 50 reports and statements, the subjects depending upon what the Commission believed to be particularly pertinent problems facing the UN, but with special emphasis in the economic and social and trusteeship fields. There were studies on the role of the Secretary-General, on strategic bases, on universal membership, on human rights, and, during later years, on the law of the sea. The Commission's 1960 report was actually one of the first published drafts of the law of the sea.

Membership in and activity of the Commission declined in the 1970s when American public interest in the UN declined as the character of that organization changed. On May 9, 1981, the Commission's Executive Committee put the Commission on "standby" for the time being, largely because of lack of financial support. During the 42 years of its existence, particularly during the Second World War, the Commission contributed to the formulation of US foreign policy.

*Bibliography*

American Association for the UN 1948 *Commission to Study the Organization of Peace: A Ten Year Record 1939-1949*. American Association for the UN, New York
Department of State 1949 *Post War Foreign Policy Preparation 1939-1945*. Department of State, Washington, DC

WALDO CHAMBERLIN

# Common Foreign and Security Policy (CFSP) of the European Union

The Common Foreign and Security Policy (CFSP) of the European Union (EU) was established by the Treaty of Maastricht (or Treaty on the European Union) of February 1992. The objective of the Member States of the European Union was to create a new framework which would allow the EU to become a more efficient actor in international relations. In this article we first analyse European Political Cooperation which preceded CFSP as well as the reasons for the creation of CFSP. Next we focus on the objectives and instruments of CFSP, the decision-making and institutional framework, the relationship with the Western European Union, and the development of a structural foreign policy of the European Union.

## 1. From EPC to CFSP

Starting in the early 1970s, cooperation on foreign policy matters and coordination of the national foreign policies of the Member States of the European Communities (EC) was organized on the basis of "European Political Cooperation." As one part of the attempt to relaunch European integration and give a political dimension to the European Communities growing economic importance, in 1970 the EC Member States accepted the "Luxembourg Report" or "Davignon Report" which established European Political Cooperation (EPC). This put an end to the taboo on foreign policy in the process of European

integration since the failure to create a European Defense Community in 1954 and to agree on the Fouchet Plan in 1962. The Luxembourg Report underlines "the need to intensify their political cooperation and provide in an initial phase the mechanism for harmonising their views regarding international affairs." The objective was "to cooperate in the sphere of foreign policy." Firstly, the Member States were to "ensure, through regular exchanges of information and consultations, a better mutual understanding on the great international problems." Secondly, they had "to strengthen their solidarity by promoting the harmonisation of their views, the coordination of their positions, and, where it appears possible and desirable, common action."

In contrast to the European Defense Community and the Fouchet Plan, European Political Cooperation did not have great ambitions. It was not to restrict the Member States in having national foreign policies. European Political Cooperation was based on intergovernmental cooperation and was to operate beside and independent from the more supranational European Community. The intergovernmental approach implied that the ministers of foreign affairs and the heads of state and government bore full responsibility for European Political Cooperation and that the European Parliament, the Commission and the Court of Justice, which all played a role in the European Community, were not involved in European Political Cooperation.

What was the impact of European Political Cooperation? It resulted in a better exchange of information among the national Foreign Offices of the Member States, to common declarations on specific events in world politics, and to more coordination in some fields of international relations. Several dimensions of foreign policy remained, however, taboo for European Political Cooperation (i.e., Africa, relations with the US, military matters). Moreover, EPC allowed active participation and intervention in international affairs in only a limited number of cases. European Political Cooperation could be influential when the main Western forum of consultation and policy harmonisation, that is the North Atlantic Treaty Organisation (NATO), was less active. This became clear during the Conference on Security and Cooperation in Helsinki at the beginning of the 1970's. European Political Cooperation was unsuccessful when NATO or the USA dominated (i.e., the Middle East crisis in 1973-74). Other crises, such as the Soviet invasion in Afghanistan in 1979 and the Poland crisis in 1980-82, illustrated the inefficient procedures, the problems resulting from the noncommittal nature of European Political Cooperation and the problems arising from the artificial division between European Political Cooperation and the European Community and between the economic, political, and military aspects of security.

The Copenhagen Report (1973), the London Report (1981), and the Solemn Declaration of Stuttgart (1983) widened the scope of European Political Cooperation and improved its procedures, without fundamentally changing its original structure. Its limitations were not eliminated when the Single European Act of 1986 (which amended the European Community's founding Treaty of Rome) institutionalized European Political Cooperation. The Single European Act linked European Political Cooperation with the European Community through Title III: "Treaty provisions on European Cooperation in the sphere of Foreign Policy." In this Title, the Member States accepted for the first time coordination to align more closely their positions on the political as well as economic aspects of security. They also accepted some involvement of the Commission and the European Parliament, without changing the intergovernmental character of European Political Cooperation. These changes, however, did not change the principle obstacle: Member States' national interests still stood in the way of a common approach. This, together with the inadequate procedures and the need for unanimity, prevented the "Twelve" from reacting efficiently to international crises.

Several developments in 1989-91 resulted in growing pressure to fundamentally reform European Political Cooperation. The plans for the creation of an Economic and Monetary Union (EMU) led to demands for a parallel move towards more political integration. More important, the fall of the communist regimes in Eastern Europe and German unification strengthened the idea that a qualitative move was needed in the field of foreign and security policy. An Intergovernmental Conference on European Political Union resulted in the establishment of the "Common Foreign and Security Policy" (CFSP) as part of the European Union which was created by the Treaty of Maastricht of 1992. The objective of the Common Foreign and Security Policy is to define a "common" policy, not a "single" policy. This points to the non-exclusive nature of CFSP. The policy of the Union is to complement the national foreign and security policies of the Member States, not to replace it.

This Common Foreign and Security Policy replaced European Political Cooperation but did not really result in a fundamental change in the capacity of the EU to act as an efficient foreign policy actor. The lack of qualitative changes becomes obvious when we analyse the structure of the EU. The "Common Provisions" in the Treaty of Maastricht mention that the European Union "shall be served by a single institutional framework" and that it shall "ensure the consistency of its external activities as a whole in the context of its external relations, security, economic and development policies." The Treaty of Maastricht is, however, characterized by a pillar system, with a first pillar which includes EC matters (Title II to IV of the Maastricht Treaty), a second pillar which includes CFSP matters (Title V), and a third pillar which includes matters concerning justice and internal affairs. The transfer of competences from the Member States to the EU is very different in the three pillars and, in addition, the institutions in this allegedly single institutional framework have different competences in each of the three pillars. This lasting separation between the EC provisions and CFSP provisions indicates that, in the Treaty of Maastricht too, the foreign and security policy is considered an intergovernmental affair which is to be handled separately from the more supranational process of integration. The lasting divide between the EC and CFSP, with the external economic relations and development policy falling under Title II and the foreign and security policy under Title V, is one of the main reasons for the weakness of the European Union's external actions. The lack of a single decision-making centre and a centralised political leadership as well as the artificial division between the different dimensions of external relations inevitably produces a negative influence on the external capabilities of the European Union.

Disappointment with the CFSP was one reason for a new Intergovernmental Conference in 1996-97, which resulted in the Treaty of Amsterdam, signed in October 1997. The changes in the CFSP provisions did not result in fundamental changes and, consequently, will probably not be able to provide a structural solution for the weakness of CFSP. Nevertheless, it includes some adaptations which in the long run might strengthen the external capabilities of the EU. In 1998, it is impossible to foresee exactly what the impact will be of changes such as the establishment of a policy planning and early warning unit, the creation of the post of a High Representative for CFSP, the increased possibility of majority voting, and the mention of specific tasks for the Western European Union (WEU).

## 2. Objectives

One of the general objectives of the European Union, as defined by one of the common provisions of the Maastricht Treaty, is "to assert its identity on the international scene, in particular through the implementation of a common foreign and security policy including the eventual framing of a common defence policy, which might in time lead to a common defence." The first article of Title V of the Maastricht Treaty states that the "Union and its Member States shall define and implement a common foreign and security policy, . . . covering all areas of foreign and security policy." This includes not only the economic and political aspects of security (as in European Political Cooperation), but also the military dimension of security.

The Maastricht Treaty remains vague on the specific objectives of CFSP. Article J.2(2) defines five objectives, but these can be considered more as general principles than as precise objectives. These objectives are to safeguard the common values, fundamental interests and independence of the Union; to strengthen the security of the Union and its Member States in all ways; to preserve peace and strengthen international security, in accordance with the principles of the United Nations Charter as well as the principles of the Helsinki Final Act and the objectives of the Paris Charter; to promote international cooperation; and to develop and consolidate democracy and the rule of law, and respect for human rights and fundamental freedoms.

The European Council in Lisbon in June 1992 accepted a document which defines the objectives more precisely. This document points to the basically non-comprehensive character of CFSP. Although mutual consultation and policy coordination can focus on any event in international politics, genuine CFSP actions will be focused on a limited number of regions (the European continent, the Mediterranean, and the Middle East) and a limited part of the security dimension (such as confidence-building measures, non-proliferation and other topics of international conferences and talks). An analysis of this document also underlines the specific nature of the initial objectives and the initial role definition of the CFSP: they are in the first place focussed on promoting collective interests through dialogue and cooperation (rather than promoting the traditional national self-interest through coercion and the use of military instruments).

## 3. CFSP Instruments

The treaties foresee different instruments and procedures to pursue the objectives of the CFSP. On the first level, there are the principles of, and general guidelines for, the Common Foreign and Security Policy, which are defined by the European Council. The Council takes the decisions necessary for defining and implementing the CFSP on the basis of the general guidelines defined by the European Council. The second level, which was created by the Amsterdam Treaty of 1997, consists of "common strategies" to be implemented by the Union in areas where the Member States have important interests in common. Common strategies set out their objectives, duration, and the means to be made available by the Union and the Member States. The Council recommends common strategies to the European Council and implements them, in particular, by adopting joint actions and common positions. These are the two following levels of CFSP instruments, which were created by the Maastricht Treaty. "Joint actions" address specific situations where operational action by the Union is deemed to be required. The decisions on joint actions lay down their objectives, scope, the means to be made available to the Union, if necessary their duration and the conditions for their implementation. Joint actions commit the Member States in the positions they adopt and in the conduct of their foreign policy activities. "Common positions" define the approach of the Union to a particular matter of a geographical or thematic nature. Member States must ensure that their national policies conform to the common positions.

On the final level (which existed previously under EPS), CFSP objectives are pursued by strengthening systematic cooperation between Member States in the conduct of policy. Member States must inform and consult one another within the Council on any matter of foreign and security policy of general interest to ensure that the Union's influence is exerted as effectively as possible by means of concerted and convergent action. The diplomatic and consular missions of the Member States and the Commission Delegations in third countries and international conferences, and their representations to international organisations, must set up cooperation by exchanging information and carrying out joint assessments. They also cooperate in ensuring that the common positions and joint actions adopted by the Council are complied with and implemented. The Member States coordinate their actions and uphold the common position in international organizations and at international conferences. Member States which are also members of the UN Security Council will concert and keep the other Member States fully informed. Member States which are permanent members of the Security Council will, in the execution of their functions, defend the positions and the interests of the Union, without prejudice to their responsibility under provisions of the UN Charter. The latter indicates the ambiguous nature of this obligation, which results in Paris and London emphasising their specific responsibilities (and thus independence).

The Treaty underlines that Member States must support the Union's external and security policy actively and unreservedly in a spirit of loyalty and mutual solidarity, that they must work together to enhance and develop their mutual political solidarity, and that they must refrain from any action which is contrary to the interests of the Union or likely to impair its effectiveness as a cohesive force in international relations. These obligations and the creation of "joint actions" and "common positions" as legal instruments were intended to increase the legally binding nature of the CFSP. Nevertheless, in practice, the binding character of CFSP remains in essence political, with the Council the only actor able to evaluate the extent to which CFSP commitments have been respected. This implies that the Member States are responsible for evaluating and controlling their own adherence to CFSP policy, which shows the limited binding nature of CFSP.

## 4. Decision-making

Any member state or the Commission may refer to the Council any question relating to the common foreign policy and may submit proposals to the Council. In cases requiring a rapid decision, the Presidency, of its own motion, or at the request of the Commission or a member state, convenes an extraordinary Council meeting within forty-eight hours or, in an emergency, within a shorter period. The problem with this system of divided responsibility for the formulation of policy proposals is that there is no mechanism and no actor which assures that policy proposals are formulated systematically on each important policy issue. The absence of a formalized proposal organ partially explains the lack of EU action in several policy areas.

The Maastricht Treaty envisaged that decisions are taken by the Council acting unanimously. Decisions by qualified majority were possible in two cases: procedural matters and decisions to implement joint actions if the Council, when adopting the joint action, defined those matters on which decisions can be taken by a qualified majority. The latter implied that the Council had to decide unanimously whether or not to decide on certain matters by qualified majority. This made it possible for any member state to block the use of this new possibility of majority voting, which explains why this possibility has never been used in CFSP decision-making under the Maastricht regime. The unanimity rule was one of the main constraints on the development of an effective Common Foreign and Security Policy. It explains why the EU was often unable to agree quickly on specific actions and often had to limit its interventions to vague declarations. This is one of the reasons for the new, complex procedural provisions in the Amsterdam Treaty which try to make majority voting possible in practice. The principle of unanimous decision-making remains the basis of CFSP decision making. Nevertheless, decision-making and thus EU-action, should become easier as a result of the three following new provisions.

Firstly, abstentions by Member States will not prevent the adoption of decisions. When abstaining in a vote, any member of the Council may qualify its abstention by making a formal declaration. In that case, it is not obliged to apply the decision, but it must accept that the decision commits the Union. The member state concerned must refrain from any action likely to conflict with or impede Union action based on that decision and the other Member States must respect its position. However, if the members of the Council qualifying their abstention in this way represent more than one third of the votes weighted in accordance with the Treaty establishing the EC (in which the large states have more votes than small states), the decision will not be adopted.

Secondly, the Council will act by qualified majority when adopting joint actions, common positions or taking any other decision on the basis of a common strategy and when adopting any decision implementing a joint action or a common position. If a member of the Council declares that, for important and stated reasons of national policy, it intends to oppose the adoption of a decision to be taken by qualified majority, a vote will not be taken. The Council may, acting by a qualified majority, request that the matter be referred to the European Council for decision by unanimity. This possibility of qualified majority voting is excluded for decisions with military or defence implications. Thirdly, for procedural questions, the Council will act by a majority of its members.

A major question is how these complex provisions will be put into practice. Under the Amsterdam regime, it becomes less easy for a member state to block a decision. Nevertheless, Member States are still able to block a decision. Moreover, as experience with decision-making in the European Community proves, the formal possibility of majority voting does not guarantee that the Council will make use of this possibility, as the preference of Member States is to decide by consensus. Moreover, the complexity of the provisions might result in new procedural problems and disagreements which can undermine the decision-making potential of the EU.

## 5. Institutional Framework

The previous analysis demonstrates that the central actors in CFSP are the two institutions which represent the Member States of the European Union: the European Council (the heads of state and government of the Member States) and the Council of Ministers (their Ministers of Foreign Affairs). The Council takes the decisions and also has to ensure the unity, consistency and effectiveness of action by the Union. A Political Committee, which under the Maastricht regime consisted of Political Directors of the different Ministries of Foreign Affairs, monitors the international situation in all areas covered by Common Foreign and Security Policy. It contributes to the definition of policies by delivering opinions to the Council at the request of the Council or on its own initiative. It also monitors the implementation of agreed policies. The Presidency (held in turn by each member state in the Council for a term of six months) represents the Union in matters falling within the Common Foreign and Security Policy. It is responsible for the implementation of common measures and for expressing the position of the Union in international organizations and international conferences. In

these tasks, the Presidency can be assisted by the High Representative for the CFSP, by the Commission and, if need be, by the next member state to hold the Presidency.

The function of High Representative for the CFSP is, together with the policy planning and early warning unit, one of the major novelties introduced by the Amsterdam Treaty in the field of the CFSP. The High Representative, who will also be the Secretary-General of the Council, assists the Council in matters coming within the scope of the CFSP, in particular, through contributing to the formulation, preparation and implementation of policy decisions, and, when appropriate and acting on behalf of the Council at the request of the Presidency, through conducting political dialogue with other countries and other international organisations.

The policy planning and early warning unit, which is foreseen in a Declaration added to the Amsterdam Treaty, will be established under the responsibility of the High Representative for the CFSP, in the General Secretariat of the Council. It consists of personnel drawn from the General Secretariat, the Member States, the Commission and the WEU. The tasks of the unit are to monitor and analyse developments in areas relevant to the CFSP, to provide assessments of the Union's foreign and security policy interests and to identify areas where the CFSP could focus in future, to providing timely assessments and early warning of events or situations which may have significant repercussions for the CFSP, and to produce policy options papers to be presented under the responsibility of the Presidency as a contribution to policy formulation in the Council.

The new function of High Representative for the CFSP and the establishment of a policy planning and early warning unit are answers to several weaknesses of the CFSP during the Maastricht regime: the absence of information and analysis capabilities, of a proposal unit, of a credible and full-time representative, of continuity in the policy analysis, in policy formulation and in external representation. The two innovations of Amsterdam will contribute to solving these problems to some extent. They will not, however, be able to solve some of the most fundamental problems of CFSP such as the absence of institutionalized leadership, the absence of an efficient and fast decision-making mechanism, and the absence of adequate policy instruments.

In CFSP, the Commission does not possess the same competences as in the European Community, where it has the exclusive power of initiative and an important role in elaborating and implementing decisions.

The treaty provision which notes that the "Commission shall be fully associated with the work carried out in the Common Foreign and Security Policy field" does not guarantee that the Commission is considered an equal partner by the Member States. The impact of the Commission is larger than the treaty provisions indicate. The Common Foreign and Security Policy often needs to use EC instruments to implement CFSP decisions (e.g., economic sanctions, financial and technical support, expertise about specific countries and regions), which implies the involvement of the Commission.

The European Parliament plays no role in the decision-making procedures of the Common Foreign and Security Policy. The treaties only contain the rather noncommittal provisions that the Presidency will consult the European Parliament on the main aspects and the basic choices of the CFSP and will ensure that the views of the European Parliament are duly taken into consideration. The European Parliament may ask questions of the Council or make recommendations to it. Despite the lack of powers, the European Parliament can indirectly influence the Common Foreign and Security Policy because it is part of the EU's budgetary authority (which is important for financing the CFSP) and because certain agreements with third countries or groups of countries require the consent of the Parliament. The Court of Justice, which plays a crucial role in the European Community, did not have its jurisdiction extended to the CFSP.

An important conclusion from a comprehensive analysis of CFSP practice is that EC instruments, EC procedures and EC actors such as the Commission and the EP play a much more important role in making possible the major actions of the second pillar than was foreseen when the Maastricht Treaty was accepted. This indicates that, in practice, the functioning of the CFSP reveals a partial symbiosis of the first pillar and the second pillar of the Maastricht regime.

## 6. Western European Union (WEU)

One of the innovations of the Maastricht Treaty was that it established for the first time a link between the European Union and the Western European Union (which includes most but not all EU Member States). The EU was allowed to request the Western European Union to elaborate and implement decisions and actions of the Union which have defence implications. This provided a formal basis for the European Union to underpin its policy with the military instruments which are badly needed to get the CFSP taken seriously (as was proved in the crisis in ex-Yugoslavia). How-

ever, the ambiguous wording of the treaty provisions and of the WEU Declaration which was added to the treaty, showed the lasting disagreement among EU Member States about the nature of the Western European Union. In the opinion of some Member States, the WEU was an instrument to implement the Union's security policies and which should gradually be absorbed by the European Union. Other Member States defended the idea that the WEU should remain an independent organisation which is both the military arm of the European Union and the European arm of the Atlantic Alliance. This disagreement is, together with the operational weakness of the WEU, one of the main reasons why the formal provisions on the EU-WEU were not translated in operational terms. With the exception of the EU Administration of the city of Mostar in Bosnia-Herzegovina, the EU never received operational support from the WEU. Consequently, the EU did not manage to overcome the limitations of the status of a civilian power.

The Amsterdam Treaty did not resolve all the questions and ambiguities in the EU-WEU relationship. This is already clear from the following fundamental provision: "The common foreign and security policy shall include all questions relating to the security of the Union, including the progressive framing of a common defence policy . . . which might lead to a common defence, should the European Council so decide." Nevertheless, some of the new provisions indicated that the Member States agreed on the principle that the WEU should provide the Union an operational military capability in the context of the so-called Petersberg tasks: humanitarian and rescue tasks, peace-keeping tasks and tasks of combat forces in crisis management, including peace-making. An important innovation is that Member States of the EU which are not members of the WEU are also allowed to contribute to these tasks and to participate fully and on an equal footing in planning and decision taking in the WEU. This is important because practice revealed that the so-called neutral states of the EU (such as Sweden, Finland and Austria) were sometimes more eager to participate in international peacekeeping tasks than the WEU Member States within the EU.

The questions also arises in this context about how these new formal possibilities will be translated in practice and how it will be possible to overcome the existing operational weakness of WEU and the remaining ambiguity on the EU-WEU-NATO relationship. In this context it is remarkable that the provisions on security policy emphasize that the EU policy on security shall not prejudice the specific character of the security and defence policy of certain Member States (such as the neutral status of Ireland). They respect the obligations of the Member States of the European Union that are also members of the North Atlantic Alliance and they are compatible with the common security and defence policy established within that framework. The treaty provisions do not prevent the development of closer cooperation between two or more Member States on a bilateral level (such as Franco-German cooperation), in the framework of the Western European Union and the Atlantic Alliance, provided such cooperation does not run counter to or impede the CFSP provisions in the Treaty on European Union. In conclusion: the precise position of the CFSP within this Western security architecture is not very clear.

## 7. CFSP or Structural Foreign Policy?

An analysis of the policy of the CFSP from November 1993 (the entry into force of the Maastricht Treaty) till December 1997 reveals the limited external impact of the CFSP and the limited added value of the CFSP in comparison with the situation before 1993. This appears from the limited use that has been made of the new legal instruments (joint actions and common positions), from the limited scope of these joint actions and common positions and, more importantly, from the limited importance of most these CFSP decisions. The joint actions and common positions focused particularly on the former Yugoslavia (the subject of 40 percent of all joint actions and common positions), on sanctions and embargos against third countries and on non-proliferation and disarmament talks (each nearly 20 percent), on support for the Palestinian Authority and on the African Great Lake region. The only joint actions which had some external impact were those on the Stabilization Pact in 1993-94 (which helped to solve some security problems among the Central European countries) and, to a lesser extent, the joint actions on the EU Administration of the city of Mostar in Bosnia-Herzegovina, on anti-personnel mines and on nuclear non-proliferation.

Disappointment dominates most evaluations of CFSP. The main explanations given for the limited added value of the CFSP are the complexity of the new procedures, bureaucratic problems within and between the diverse institutions, and the limited 'political will' of the Member States to develop and respect CFSP. The most important explanation is the existence of fundamentally different views by the Member States on the external environment and on the way that an European actor can or should intervene in this external environment.

The conclusion that CFSP failed does not, however, mean that the foreign policy of the European Union as a whole failed. When we broaden our focus from the CFSP or the second pillar as such to the external actions of the EU as a whole, then it becomes clear that the initial CFSP objectives have been pursued and (partially) realized, not within the second pillar (as intended), but from the end of 1994 on through general EU strategies, partnerships, and action plans vis-à-vis other regions and countries. The interests of the Member States in the external actions of the EU shifted in 1994 from the CFSP to the development of comprehensive strategies and partnerships vis-à-vis other areas (such as Central and Eastern Europe, Russia, the Mediterranean countries, and the Palestinian Territories). This change of interest became very obvious from the European Council of December 1995 in Madrid onwards.

These strategies and partnerships, which transcend the pillar structure of the EU, point to the development of what we call a "structural foreign policy." This structural foreign policy is not focused on the traditional national self-interests. It tries to promote collective interests and 'other-regarding interests' through EU support for structural long-term changes and regional stabilization in other areas in the world and through EU support for the (partial and varying) adoption by other regions of 'European' ordering principles in the field of politics, economics and security. Anno 1998, the development of an EU structural foreign policy is still in its initial stage and both its future scope and depth remain unclear. Nevertheless, several factors explain both the emphasis of the EU on the elaboration of general strategies and partnerships and the relative success of this emerging structural foreign policy. They also explain why the prospects are brighter for a further elaboration of this structural foreign policy than for the further elaboration of the CFSP.

The first factor is the added value for the Member States of a structural foreign policy that focuses on 'new' common interests and objectives (in particularly the stabilization of other areas in the post cold-war period), which is in contrast to a CFSP which is seen as competing with national foreign policies. Next comes the relationship between national foreign policy and structural foreign policy as a positive-sum game and the incorporation of the structural foreign policy in (and its respect for) the existing international architecture. Another explanation is the usefulness and external relevance of a 'politicized' EC method which links the leading political role of the large Member States with the leading conceptual and implementing role of the Commission. The last explanation for the emphasis of the Member States on structural foreign policy, however, points to the limitations of a structural foreign policy of a non-military actor: the structural foreign policy can also be seen as an escape by the EU from reality in the face of the CFSPs failure to develop a daily foreign policy with a military dimension. This explains why a further development of the CFSP and of the CFSP-WEU relationship is important for the efficiency and the further development of the structural foreign policy of the EU.

## Bibliography

CFSP-*Forum*. Institut für Europäische Politik, Bonn

*European Foreign Affairs Review*. Kluwer Law International, London

Eliassen K (ed.) 1998 *Foreign and Security Policy in the European Union*. Sage, London

Hill C (ed.) 1996 *The Actors in European Foreign Policy*. Routledge, London

Holland M (ed.) 1997 *Common Foreign and Security Policy: The Record and Reforms*. Pinter, London

Keukeleire S (forthcoming) *The Structural Foreign Policy of the European Union*

Nuttall S 1992 *European Political Co-operation*. Claridon Press, Oxford

Peterson J, Helen S (eds.) 1998 *A Common Foreign Policy for Europe? Competing Visions of CFSP*. Routledge, London/New York

Piening C 1997 *Global Europe: The EU in World Affairs*. Lynne Rynner, Boulder/London

Pijpers A, Regelsberger E, Wessels W (eds.) 1988 *European Political Cooperation in the 1980's*. Martinus Nijhoff Publishers, Dordrecht

Regelsberger E, Schoutheete de Tervarent P, Wessels W (eds.) 1997 *Foreign Policy of the European Union. From EPC to CFSP and Beyond*. Lynne Publishers, Boulder

Smith H 1998 *The Foreign Policy of the European Union*. Macmillan, London

White B 1998 *European Foreign Policy*. Westview Press, Boulder

Zielonka J (ed.) 1998 *Paradoxes of European Foreign Policy*. Kluwer Law International, Dordrecht

STEPHAN KEUKELEIRE

# Communication: Key to World Peace

The scientific developments in space exploration, which took part in the latter part of the twentieth century, have put the world in the midst of a global communication explosion.

For the first time in the history of *homo sapiens*, human beings are beginning to look at their planet Earth the way it really is—a tiny blue watery pebble floating perpetually in the abyss of the universe. Astronauts and cosmonauts have been amazed to realize that in such a tiny object there has been a shameful history of human conflicts . . . conflicts that stem from artificial boundaries created by people themselves. These boundaries are of various sorts: political, national, ethnic and racial just to mention a few.

Through political set ups, iron curtains were built that segregated relatives and friends from each other. Through national fanaticism, the seeds of hatred have been implanted in the hearts of people and has led to rebellion and death. Through ethnic factions isolated groups are formed where hypocrisy and deceit replaces genuine love and human concern. Due to the color of their skin, people have been segregated and deprived of their rightful dignity and place (see *Race and Racial Prejudice*).

## 1. Sources of Conflict

When people create boundaries that hinder human communication at the national and international level, then the first steps to an inevitable war are taken (see *Conflict: Inherent and Contingent Theories*). According to the French educator, Gaston Berger, war could eventually stem from any of the following three sources:

*1.1 Individual or National Pride*—This constitutes the pride either of those who feel they are minor powers and want to increase their importance, or of those who already feel powerful but who wish to extend their power.

*1.2 Individual or National Fear*—This amounts to a kind of fear that is always a bad counselor. Fear sets little dogs barking and snapping and tends to make them really dangerous. One of the best antidotes of fear is knowledge which brings understanding and a clear view of things.

*1.3 Individual or National Poverty*—This involves a kind of poverty that when it weighs heavily it develops a spirit of revolt. When people draw the line, nothing will stop them from achieving their goals and objectives.

Scientific development can help us vanquish poverty. It can also help us eliminate fear through the provision of proper information and better usage of common sense. Although pride could be considered as the most difficult to crack, it can be controlled through an effective medium known as education (see *Education for Global Citizenship*).

Defects of responsible people in society, that inflict great harm on the human race are usually not academic in nature. They consist of various kinds of discrimination which in the realm of morality are described as *abuses of power*. These kinds of defects generally constitute a social crime that slowly but surely demolishes highly qualified potentials to the detriment of everyone involved. The tragedy of this crime lies in the fact that in theory it seems non-existent because the written policies of the state, institution, or organizations involved condemn explicitly any kind of discrimination.[1]

## 2. Learning for Communication

Good education depends also on the kind of teaching methods we use to achieve our ultimate goal: *world stability and international peace through communication as a key.*

What does education really achieve in having a student graduating with straight A's in courses as History, Government, and Human Relations, when the student does not actually learn how to utilize in his daily life the knowledge acquired and communicate it to others? In the sixties, Duane Pope, a highly respected student at the University of Nebraska, was considered as an "ideal American citizen" because of his high grades and his good behavior on campus. A few weeks after graduation he entered a bank, killed three people on the spot, and wounded five others in an attempted robbery. Is this the kind of "ideal American citizen" that teachers who give high grades try to produce? The principle conveyed here is applied equally well to teachers of schools in all countries around the world.

Lamentations are often heard in various communities about "poor parents, poor teachers, poor administrators, and poor schools." Maybe our attention has not been properly focused on the real source of the consequences! As a matter of fact, we do have good parents, good teachers, good students, good administrators, and good schools. But we just lack *communication* because in our school days we were simply tested on

"how much we know" rather than on how much we can *communicate* to others of what we know.

All strifes and conflicts that result in wars within the family, the community, the state, the nation and the world, stem from a *lack of communication*. If a lack of communication is the source of all evil, then it is the job of education to do something about it. In this way, human beings can set a precedent for peace that would contribute, for the first time in the recorded history of civilization, constructive ways of approaching the solution of problems that have degenerated into a mess through insubordination, rebellion and death.

Our lack of capability in training and testing for communication is bringing chaos in our families, communities, states, and nations everywhere. Such a lack of capability as revealed in the schools of today, has been regretfully explained by highly respected educators with such a phrase as "the generation gap." There is no such thing as "the generation gap," and the sooner we realize this, the better. As educators, we are simply guilty of perpetuating the mistakes of our predecessors when "communicating" to each other.

Education today needs revision. It needs a reevaluation of priorities based on an understanding of human nature. Dating back to Socrates, philosophers and later ascetics tell us that human nature has two strong urges that are in constant conflict: *rationality versus instinct*. When a human being acts on the basis of what he actually *ought* to do, then rationality dominates instinct . . . then prevails what could be termed "the decent person." On the other hand, when a human being behaves on the basis of what he *feels* like doing, then instinct overrules rationality. In this regard, one reduces himself below the level of human dignity and tends to act on the level of animals.

To illustrate this: A man may *feel* like taking sugar because he has always liked it since early childhood. But if he finds he is seriously sick with diabetes, he *ought not* to take it. Another man may find himself dying in a hospital of some serious disease, but if the only way for him to survive is to take a prescribed bitter pill, he *ought* to take it even though he does not feel like it.

Through careful study we can easily find out that the actual source of educational chaos that leads to many world problems could be traced to *a lack of understanding* of human nature in the manner explained above.

## 3. Problem of Priorities

After having achieved a clear understanding of human nature, we should then deal seriously with the problem of priorities. Such a problem has been getting bigger and bigger over the decades for the simple reason that we have formed the habit of viewing a problem by concentrating primarily on the accidental or unessential with little regard to the actual essential.

A human being could be nicknamed American, Russian, or Chinese because of the fact that he was accidentally born in a global area that was in turn nicknamed America, Russia, or China. Hence, in our reevaluation of educational priorities, especially in terms of human relations, the nationality we carry, the political party to which we claim we belong, as well as the customary set ups attached to our ethnic creeds should, for all practical purposes should, be considered of secondary and not of primary importance.

In this way, the problem of communication will diminish considerably. The conflicts that may remain among humans, will then take shape of those existent in the ordinary family. No matter how much brothers and sisters quarrel, litigate, and fight with each other—they will all end up eating at the same table and sleeping under the same roof in protection and security.[2]

## 4. Sound Educational Philosophy

Our philosophical outlook on life needs reevaluation. First, a human being is a sacred person with a unique identity of one's own. Second, a human being is what one habitually presents oneself to be through one's actions—a good, honest, reliable person, or a bad dishonest, unreliable individual.

The pragmatic approach in human relations needs to be tried. Educators should learn to stand side by side in search for *what* is right and not for *who* is right. Our concern is the actual solution of an involved problem. The best available solution is followed regardless of who furnished it. Trouble usually starts when we approach each other with the preconceived notion of *the whole world could be saved with my own ideas.* For such an attitude builds a Berlin wall in social relations that germinates the seeds of war.

Our hope in developing communication as a key to world peace lies primarily in education with a good philosophy of life (see *Peace Education for Youth*). After all, as General Eisenhower said to the students of Colombia University on March 23, 1990: *Peace is more the product of our day-to-day living than a spectacular program, intermittently executed.*

In addition, national and global conflicts have always started with people who had a distorted outlook of life (see *Human Nature Theories of War*). This explains why in the preamble of UNESCO it is

stated: *Since wars begin in the minds of men, it is in the minds of men that the defenses of peace should be constructed.* Moreover, a sense of responsibility and awareness of human needs must be emphasized. We need to concentrate more on the service than the reward. In this regard, President Kennedy pleaded with the American people: *Ask not what your country can do for you but what you can do for your country.*

Speaking on the same topic, President Truman in 1949 made the following remark: *One of the difficulties with our institutions is the fact that we've emphasized the reward instead of the service . . . but I think the fundamental purpose of our educational system is to instill a moral code in the rising generation and create a citizenship which will be responsible for the welfare of the Nation.* President's Truman's statement could as well be made by responsible leaders of all countries throughout the world.

The rapid modern means of communication will prove itself to be a great step toward creating a global family community spirit (see *Emerging Tool Chest for Peacebuilders*). Humans will soon look at each other not as "separate" individuals but as members of a *same* entity—humankind. To hurt one's toe is to lead one's whole body into lack of comfort, to hurt one's fellow man is to hurt oneself. This is the basic philosophy we face today. It will enable us to use all kinds of technical means to communicate with each other effectively in the interest of world peace.

The human long quest for peace may be difficult but not impossible to achieve. Recent scientific developments in space exploration have brought people closer together than ever before. Breaking through the barriers of communication is becoming increasingly an international necessity. World peace will eventually become the prerogative of the space age era that started in the late fifties of the 20th century and continued through the rapid development of space age technology which brought about a global communication explosion.[3]

## 5. Problem of Communication

The problem of communication is rather complex due to the fact that it may stem from a variety of sources for a variety of reasons. Lack of proper communication may derive from language barriers. If people experience difficulty in communicating with members of the same family when using the same language, imagine how much more complicated it becomes to communicate with people that have a different mode of self-expression. Hence, the importance of foreign languages to be taught in all schools at all levels (see *Language and Peace*).

Another leading problem of communication comes from the news media which relate to us statements made by politicians and self-interested groups. The news media never tell us the possible motivations behind political or civic statements. The tenure of politicians depends largely on public consent, and total exposure would shorten many careers substantially. Politicians are under no compulsion to keep the public fully informed of their activities (see *Peace and Democracy*).

News dissemination is also a media problem. News media are, in the first place, business enterprises, dependent for their existence on making a profit. State-owned media often fail to give news because of censorship. They feel no obligation to keep the public adequately informed. Dramatizing the news makes it more interesting and attracts a large audience which, in turn, increases media desirability to advertisers.

Communication as a key to world peace is a primary objective of the peace education curriculum (see *Peace and Peace Education: A Holistic View*). Success in the field of economics depends, to a large extent, on effective communication in everything imaginable, including business enterprises. The military-industrial complex in the United States, Russia, China, the United Kingdom, France and several other countries, has succeeded to force their respective governments to invest billions of dollars on unneeded weaponry systems (see *Military-Industrial Complex*).

By way of contrast, the medical profession has not succeeded to convince governments to invest equal amount of money for the purpose of finding perpetual cures to such deadly diseases as cancer, AIDS, and other malignancies that claim the lives of millions every year. Preventive medicine has been pretty much ignored because of communication problems existent in our earthly society. Thus, we may conclude that we have a distorted concept of priorities in the world which has brought untold harmful consequences.

This has been witnessed in nuclear incidents which have created a global environment that has become a threat to human survival itself.

Through proper and effective dialogues, we may communicate with responsible government officials in a way as to make human survival a top priority of each nation's agenda. Hence, the scientific advancements of recent years should be utilized to communicate to the various segments of our earthly society the best ways and means available to help solve most of our problems through preventive measures, the sooner the better (see *Social Progress and Human Survival*).

See also: *Intercultural Relations and Peace Studies; Peace Education; World Citizenship*

*Bibliography*

Ferencz B B, Keyes K Jr 1991 *Planethood: The Key to Your Future*. Love, Line Books, Coos Bay, OR
Harris E E 1993 *Prescription for Survival: One World or None*. Humanities Press International, Inc., NJ
Henderson M 1994 *All Her Paths are Peace: Women Pioneers in Peacemaking*. Kumarian Press, Inc., West Hartford, CN, USA
Merryfield M M, Remy R C 1995 *Teaching about International Conflict and Peace*. State University of New York Press, Albany, NY
Ruggiero V R 1995 *Beyond Feelings: A Critical Guide to Critical Thinking*. Mayfield Publishing Co., Mountain View, CA
Social and Human Sciences Documentation Centre 1992 *World Directory of Human Rights Research and Training Institutions*. Imprimerie de la Manutention, UNESCO, Mayene, France
Spangler M (ed.) 1996 *Cliches of Politics*. The Foundation for Economic Education, Irvington-on-Hudson, NY
Thompson W S et al., 1991 *Approaches to Peace: An Intellectual Map*. United States Institute of Peace, Washington, DC

CHARLES MERCIECA

# Community and Autonomy

The term "peace"—unless it is understood only in its negative sense as the absence of war—can be given a number of different interpretations. Taken in its social and sociological sense, it means a lasting coexistence of individuals, that is, some kind of community, which, not only maintains its own autonomy but also safeguards it for its members. Consequently, the problem in this context consists in the correlation between community and autonomy.

Community and autonomy are terms conditioning and, at the same time, excluding or at least limiting each other. They are conditioned by each other because in a community certain elements fuse, and these necessarily have a certain degree of autonomy. At the same time they necessarily act also as factors limiting each other, and that is where the problem arises in the sociohistorical view. A precondition of the birth of a community is the adoption by its members of a common value, norm, purpose, or any kind of common denominator, yet this will in every case set limits to their autonomy—whereas the enforcement of their autonomy sets limits to the self-assertion of the community.

Hence, the two terms will have to be examined according to their dialectical unity. Their unity and their difference certainly persist in every situation, but their mutual proportion may be questioned, and the purpose or objective may be formulated as the optimum relationship between the two tendencies.

This however, is only a logical treatment of the problem, irrespective of the concrete historico-social time and space. In historical development this same question recurs in many forms and obtains different solution. So much so that we may even ask to what extent we are entitled to use the term "unity of community and autonomy" and whether it is not necessary first to distinguish the different kinds of community and autonomy.

The types and forms of the community—or, to use the sociological and socio-psychological term, the group—is studied by sociology. A general classification distinguishes two kinds of groups or communities: human associations of a primary and of a secondary character. In German-speaking areas the same distinction is known as *Gemeinschaft* and *Gesellschaft* (after Tönnies 1923); these classifications are more or less congruent.

Primary communities are characterized by the fact that their numbers take part in them with their entire personality, all member know all other members, and there are no secrets and individual ways. In sociology, this relationship is referred to as having a face-to-face character. There are usually few possibilities of change in such communities—if any, they are of an extremely limited character: in most cases the individual is born into a given group, and this fact or some other circumstance such as residence, his or her individual endowments determines his or her place in the community. There are several types of primary communities. The family is the most outstanding among the traditional ones, but children being brought up together or adults taking part in some work of a workshop character also constitute examples.

The criteria of secondary communities contradict the above features. The members are engaged with only part of their personality, and the community itself does not endeavor to encompass the totality of life, but rather centers its activity on some special task. The face-to-face character disappears and one-dimensional relationships become the norm. The group to which an individual belongs can be selected to a much greater extent than in the case of primary communities. Hence,

the principle of contract does not rely on a "natural" situation (on common descent or on territorial distribution) but is determined by social convention(s). Secondary communities evolve, for instance, in modern factories, in urban settlements, and in state organizations. Whereas the members of a primary community are limited in number, the membership of a secondary community is—at least theoretically—unlimited.

As far as historical development is concerned, the first thing to be realized is that primary communities appeared at the lowest level of human evolution. Herbert Spencer's famous statement "Society is prior to man" applies to them. On the other hand, secondary communities are relatively new formations, created by modern large-scale commodity-producing societies. In the past 500 or so years, they have undergone wide differentiation and turned into a force penetrating and determining all of society—so much so that sociologists at one time thought that primary communities had an altogether anachronistic character and were mere remnants of a past age. Later, however, the process of rehabilitating or—to use Lazarsfeld's term—rediscovering primary communities was started. It has been proved that—behind the secondary organization on the surface of society—a diversity of primary communities are actively surviving and thriving.

The problem of autonomy can be examined in this context. In traditional primary communities we cannot detect the autonomy of the individual in the sense the term is used today. The individual has the feeling of being one with the community, does not wish to detach him/herself from it, looking upon its limits and confines as natural, as determined from the very outset by fate or by God. Since there is no wish for resistance, the issue of autonomy rarely arises. Those opposing this frame are seen as deviants, and they are punished accordingly.

A radically different situation came to pass after the appearance of secondary communities. The omnipotence of the traditional communities declined, and the individual became detached from the "umbilical chord" (Marx) of the natural communities. The evolution of autonomy displays at this time two intertwined tendencies. The first is the relative independence of the smaller communities from the larger social units, and the other is, the independence of the individual in the smaller communities. The two tendencies are valid together and constitute unity. Autonomy thus makes its appearance in life itself, and is an economic necessity in the structure of commodity-producing society.

Autonomy, however, does not necessarily, in every circumstance and in all senses, mean something good. The balance between community and autonomy has two scales: the gain of one involves losses or at least risks for the other. The materialization of autonomy is pregnant with the possibility of alienation, wherein the individual finds him/herself in something akin to a vacuum. We are doomed to freedom, said Sartre (1973), which may be paraphrased by saying we are doomed to autonomy. Autonomy achieved becomes a problem.

This system of contradictions is one of the great problems of our age—at least from the angle of social psychology, that is, of the life of society. But the importance of this fact should also be emphasized when examining the foundations of social development as a whole and when delineating its boundaries. Direct economic and political problems very often assume spectacular forms and the specialists studying them are liable to disregard the subjective problems of society: public atmosphere, daily values. Nevertheless, these deep layers of social reality penetrate social life through thousands of ties which transmit their impacts upon the whole structure because they determine the desires, the will, the opportunities of human beings. These factors cannot be neglected when studying issues of peace.

When examining communities from the angle of autonomy, however, the above-described classification in sociology (primary and secondary communities) seems to be insufficient. The autonomy of the individual is not developed in primary groups, while secondary groups are already characterized by autonomy. It is necessary to distinguish a third type of community—one in which autonomous people consciously unite into a community. This type cannot be called either primary or secondary, but may be appropriately termed tertiary. (It should be emphasized that in this case the terms secondary and tertiary do not mean second-rate and third-rate either in value or in importance.)

The direction and purpose of social development is in every case to find an equilibrium wherein individuals who have achieved autonomy may harmoniously unite into communities, while the small communities that have achieved autonomy may equally harmoniously adapt themselves to a wider social reality. At the present level of social development, this is a task and an objective; it cannot yet crystallize into reality. Hence the actual situation is pregnant with the possibilities of conflicts in every layer of society. Such conflicts produce great tensions and may propel societies forward, but also contain dangers. The solution can only be achieved through further social development. And, if it is true that humankind has throughout history only set itself aims that could be attained, then today the objective of uniting community and autonomy harmoniously can no longer be regarded as unrealizable.

Such socio-human tensions are Janus faced. They stimulate people to solve their own problems, and thus also the problems of society, even while they may intensify conflicts and thereby endanger social peace. The assessment of the problem in its true magnitude may promote the achievement of the more positive of these alternatives.

See also: *Social Conflicts and Peace*

*Bibliography* ————————————————

Lazarsfeld P J, Katz E 1955 *Personal Influence*. Free Press, New York

Marx K 1973 *Grundrisse: Foundations of the Critique of Political Economy*. Penguin, Harmondsworth

Sartre J-P 1973 *Existentialism and Humanism*. Eyre Methuen, London

Spencer H 1897-1906 *Principles of Sociology*, Vols. 1-3. Williams Norgate, London

Tönnies F 1923 *Gemeinschaft und Gesellschaft*, Berlin

MÁRIA SÁGI

# Comprehensive Nuclear Test Ban Treaty (CTBT)

After China and France ended their nuclear testing programmes, the comprehensive nuclear test ban treaty (CTBT) was completed and opened for signature in 1996. This historic event was made possible by a watershed in Chinese security policy making, the military's recommendation for continued testing having been overruled at the highest level. By the end of the year, the majority of states had signed it and only one—India—had declared unconditionally that it would not (see *CTBT in Indian Perception*). India's refusal to sign the CTBT could prevent the treaty from achieving its full legal force, although the international norm against testing it embodies is universally accepted.

## 1. The Endgame in 1996

On September 10, 1996, the UN General Assembly

voted overwhelmingly to adopt the CTBT as negotiated at the CD. The vote was 158-3 with five abstentions. The three states that voted against the resolution were India, Bhutan and Libya. Two weeks later, on September 24, the first 74 states signed the treaty at a ceremony in New York. On October 10, Fiji became the first state to ratify the CTBT. On November 20, a Preparatory Commission of the then-134 signatories met to discuss implementation of the treaty prior to its entry into force.

## 2. The Failure of the CD to Reach Consensus

The 1996 session of the CD's Ad Hoc Committee on the Nuclear Test Ban resolved a number of difficult issues and produced a draft treaty that nearly gained consensus. In the end, this process was stymied by only one of India's many reservations, but at least four other issues reviewed in this section may have a long-term effect on the treaty's entry into force and long-term viability: Peaceful Nuclear Explosions (PNES), inspections, the use of data from National Technical Means (NTM) of verification in decision making, and the composition of regional groups.

## 3. India

After more than a year of constructive work in the ad hoc committee, India reversed course and began to play a blatantly obstructive role in the negotiations, tabling new proposals for treaty language months after other CD members had agreed not to. In November 1995, the efforts of the Indian Defense Ministry and Department of Atomic Energy and sympathetic editorial writers to portray the CTBT as a threat to India's nuclear option finally resulted in a policy crisis. Although the proposition that India cannot maintain the option without testing and would not be free to withdraw from the treaty in a crisis anyway is hard to credit, the Congress (I) Government of Prime Minister P. V. Narasimha Rao was under pressure from the stridently pro-nuclear Bharatiya Janata Party (BJP) during a national election campaign. Though many observers believe Narasimha Rao himself supported the CTBT, he bowed to political necessity. Congress lost the election anyway.

India staked out a radical new position, putting forward new proposals on the treaty's scope and verification procedures that undid compromises made by China, Indonesia and others. India also argued that the CTBT should include a commitment to negotiate complete nuclear disarmament by a date certain. Ultimately, Ambassador Arundhata Ghose signalled

a willingness to stand aside and let the treaty pass by consensus as long as India was not required to sign it, a proposal that was unacceptable to at least four other CD members: China, Pakistan, Russia and the UK (see *CTBT Negotiations: Analysis and Assessment*).

## 4. The List of 44

The requirement that India sign and ratify the treaty for it to enter into force is rooted in the perception that the treaty must capture the nuclear programmes of a certain minimum set of states to be effective. The United States and others opposed this logic on the grounds that the CTBT would be sufficiently effective with only the five nuclear weapon states party to the 1968 Nuclear Non-Proliferation Treaty (NPT), although the participation of others certainly was desirable. Observers differ as to whether the four that insisted on a list of 44 countries intended mainly to ensure the treaty's non-proliferation benefits or were cynically attempting to prevent its entering into force.

In any event, India refused to allow a consensus on the treaty at the CD on the grounds that it violated the sovereignty of the 44 states listed. Most of the other states appear not to have been concerned, and only North Korea and Pakistan have not yet signed, Pakistan on the grounds that it can only do so when India does.

## 5. China

At the beginning of 1996, China's positions on many issues were so far from the emergent consensus that observers began to wonder whether the Chinese delegation in Geneva was not simply buying time for the test programme. In fact, once the decision to stop testing was announced in June, China quickly made a number of important compromises. Some of these apparently are still contested by critics of the CTBT in China and could be grist for debate before ratification.

China relaxed its demand that PNES be permitted in exchange for the assurance that they could be reassessed at periodic review conferences. China's nuclear establishment continues to express interest in PNES, however, and is still discussing their potential contribution to economic development with Russian colleagues. This interest is not sufficiently widespread that they have been able to secure funding from the Chinese Government, however.

The primary means for verifying compliance with the CTBT will be an International Monitoring System (IMS) of seismic, atmospheric monitoring, hydroacoustic and infrasound stations feeding data to national and international data centres, an infrastructure that is expected to cost US$80 million a year to maintain once it is up and running. The relatively low cost of the IMS is not an accident, but a strict design requirement that pervaded the negotiations. This low-cost approach was opposed by China (as well as India and others) on the grounds that some decisions on inspections would have to be made on the basis of information from sources other than the IMS, including the NTM of the most technologically advanced states.

Finally, the Chinese military is uneasy about inspections to verify that tests have not taken place. This concern is aggravated by the risk that the controversies over permitted activities and inspections will lead to requests for inspections of sensitive laboratories. Nuclear tests would most likely be conducted far from settled areas, but permitted activities like sub-critical tests could in principle be undertaken in laboratories. Even in a society as open as the USA, it may not be possible to fully reassure all treaty partners that sub-critical tests are not hydronuclear experiments or even low-yield tests. The difficulties in states with more secretive nuclear establishments like China, Israel and Russia will be all the greater. Other states parties will then have to decide whether to request inspections in spite of the specific assertions of China and Israel in the negotiating record that such activities were not grounds for inspection. Whether the result is a vote in favour of inspection or the requesting state party is rebuffed, confidence in the treaty could be undermined.

## 6. Israel and Its Region

A final concern arose regarding the definition of geographic regions for the sake of distributing appointments. Reflecting both historical animosities in the region and the deterioration of the Middle East Peace Process, a number of states in the region objected to Israel's being grouped with them. Although ultimately even Iran (the last hold out on the issue) stood aside in the negotiations, a number of predominantly Muslim states—including Iraq, Lebanon, Libya, Pakistan, Saudi Arabia, and Syria—have yet to sign the treaty.

## 7. The Treaty Completed and Opened for Signature

Of the controversies discussed above, only India's inclusion on the list of 44 threatened to prevent consensus on the treaty text. Despite India's objections, the text was presented to the UN General Assembly, adopted, and opened for signature on the same timetable as it would have been if consensus had been

achieved, although it had to be presented by Australia on behalf of 'Friends of the Treaty' rather than forwarded by the CD (see *CTBT Negotiations: Analysis and Assessment*).

## 8. Implications for the Nuclear Regime

The importance of the CTBT has become a source of debate from both sides. Critics of various stripes have dismissed it as worse than useless: those who think the CTBT goes too far say it cannot stop cheating or proliferation, whereas those who think it does not go far enough say it cannot stop modernization and does not contribute to disarmament but serves only as a distraction. The debate over the list of 44 has added an additional element of uncertainty about the treaty's status. Nevertheless, the treaty's advocates point out that the norm against testing is now universally accepted regardless of legal technicalities. Although modernization of delivery systems has become more important than modernization of warheads, the CTBT does have an important effect on both established arsenals and proliferation. It may also have an enabling effect on further disarmament measures. This section considers the status of the CTBT if it does not enter into force promptly.

Once China stopped testing, the norm of not testing was effectively accepted by every state in the international system. This universal acceptance of the norm is unprecedented in the history of the nuclear age, and could only be strengthened by the completion of the CTBT and its signature by the majority of states. Even non-signatory states have said they will not test for the foreseeable future and the norm can be seen as having the power of customary law. There remain two items of unfinished business, however: securing the ratifications of signatories and completing the conditions for the treaty to enter into force. While it is desirable that both of these items be accomplished, it is not clear that failure to do so will necessarily lead to the unravelling of the test ban.

Doubts about the willingness of key states to ratify the CTBT linger. The strengthening of the Republican majority in the 1996 US Senate elections—particularly the reelection of Foreign Relations Committee chair Jesse Helms—was a blow to the CTBT's chances for ratification, despite enthusiasm for the treaty in the Clinton Administration, including the nuclear weapon establishment. Helms is one of the most deeply anti-arms control members of the legislature and the Republican campaign platform condemned the CTBT.

The CTBT is also the object of legislative derision in Russia, where—unlike START-2—it has no real supporters to balance strong opposition from the Ministry of Atomic Energy. Some members of the Chinese National People's Congress reportedly have criticized the treaty, too, although they are likely to ratify it after a waiting period if Russia and the USA do. Israel stands by its position of insisting on widespread acceptance of the treaty in its region.

For the treaty to enter into force, not only must the 41 signatories with nuclear reactors ratify it, but India, North Korea and Pakistan must sign and ratify it, too. Several US officials have expressed optimism that India would respond positively to warm persuasion and perhaps gentle pressure, and sign as soon as 1998, the earliest that the treaty could enter into force in any event. Persuading India to sign is seen as less difficult than convincing China, Pakistan, Russia and the UK—the four states that insisted on the list of 44—to amend the treaty and allow entry into force without India.

Even if it is not possible to bring the treaty into force for the time being, many of the treaty's essential features will be in place. The treaty-mandated IMS and International Data Center will be operating on a trial basis and, combined with information available from other sources, should be able to detect any illegal tests, which are unlikely in any case. If an ambiguous event were detected, a conference of signatories could be convened and might reasonably expect to be invited to inspect the relevant site. In any case, the ultimate authority for assessing the response to non-compliant or unresolved suspicious behaviour will be the same with or without entry into force: the UN Security Council (see *United Nations Reform: Historical and Contemporary Perspectives*).

## 9. Prospects

Although the norm of not testing is now universally accepted and can only be strengthened by more signatures and ratifications of the CTBT, it is still possible that the regime could be undermined by a state resuming its nuclear test programme. This could come as the result of either of two developments, both of which are quite different from the traditional concern with large-scale covert testing that complicated the debate during the Cold War.

The first concern is that the political situation could change either within a state or at the international level so that a government would reverse its decision not to test. This could come as the result of greater influence on the part of the nuclear weapon establishment that still saw a requirement for testing, or if a state saw its security situation deteriorating.

The second concern is that weapons already in the arsenal cannot be maintained reliably and safely without testing. The US Department of Energy (DOE) readily admits that its US$4-billion-a-year stewardship programme is technologically risky and could fail. In effect, the DOE has grounds for an open-ended demand for funds and might still fail to certify the reliability, safety and security of the arsenal after its annual review some years from now, even if its budget is maintained in the face of declining spending for most other military and scientific activities. The other nuclear weapon states face tighter budget constraints and perhaps less political opposition to nuclear weapons and testing.

See also: *Campaign for Nuclear Disarmament (CND); Economics of Disarmament and Conversion; Disarmament and Development; Nuclear Weapons Abolition; North Korea's Nuclear Activities and US-North Korea Accord of 1994*

ERIC ARNETT

# Comprehensive Security

## 1. Introduction

The term 'comprehensive security' can be understood in at least two ways. Its narrower meaning refers to ideas that underpin the national security policies of several East Asian states. Its wider meaning refers to a range of ideas and concepts that seek to take the understanding of 'security' beyond both the purely military and the purely national. Since the wider meaning incorporates the narrower one, this essay will focus on it (see *Security Regimes: Focusing on Asia-Pacific*).

At issue in the general debate about the meaning of security is whether the concept should be defined by, and largely confined to, military relations between states, or whether it should be given a wider application. There are two, sometimes overlapping, ways in which this wider application can be pursued. One is to allow issues other than military ones into the discourse of security. This is what people do when they talk about economic security or environmental security or societal security (see *Human Security*). The other is to allow referent objects other than the state to be the focus of security thinking and policy. The term international security, for example, often carries the implication that there are referent objects other than the state, such as international society, and the international economic order. At the other end of the scale, individual security is often posed against the state. Much of the talk about economic and environmental security does not have the state in mind as its referent object, but the wider systems that comprise the world economy and the planetary ecosphere. 'National' security, in its literal meaning, refers to the security of the nation, which is often not the same thing as the security of the state, especially where the territorial boundaries of the state are not coterminous with the identity boundaries of nations.

For more than a decade there has been a lively debate about wider versus narrower conceptions of security. For most of the Cold War, the narrow interpretation was dominant, and at least in the West, became a well-established orthodoxy. Challenges to this orthodoxy began to arise during the 1980s, and continue today. In this essay I will sketch in the historical background of how the narrow view became the orthodoxy, and why it came under attack during the 1980s. I will review the current debate and sketch out the requirements for a comprehensive concept of security. The essay ends with brief sketches of some of the main terms currently in use: *collective security, common security, cooperative security, international security, security community* and *comprehensive security*.

## 2. History

In a longer historical perspective it can be argued that the main stream of thinking about security has been more in the wider than in the narrower mould. Before 1945, as exemplified in works from Cobden, through Hobson, Lenin, and Polanyi, to E.H. Carr, there was no question that the subject matters of what we now think of as international political economy (IPE) and international security were closely intertwined. Liberal free traders of the 19th century wanted to demilitarize relations between states by pursuing the logic of economic interdependence between them, and democratization within them. Both liberals and Marxists understood Western imperialism to reflect deep linkages between modes of economic organization (capitalism), and the spread of political control beyond national boundaries (empire). Marxists also had a political-economy theory of war, most clearly set out in Lenin's idea of imperialism as the phase in which capitalist powers move into conflict over the

redivision of the global market. In these perspectives, classes were almost as important as states in thinking about the dynamics and purposes of security (see *Imperialism*). This blending of IPE and security thinking resurfaced during the 1980s in the work of Robert Gilpin (1981) and Paul Kennedy (1988), and also in schools of thought such as those about interdependence and about the linkage between democracy and peace.

The rapid sequence of three world wars (first, second and cold), and the advent of nuclear weapons in 1945, steadily raised the profile of military security concerns to the point where by the early 1950s the security debates of the major powers were almost exclusively about military issues. After the first world war, the focus shifted to collective security as a way of preventing war (see *Collective Security and Collective Self-defense*). Immediately after the second world war, the concept of national security first crystallized in the United States, seeming initially to embrace a wider understanding of security. A wide range of activities were to be integrated from the perspective of security, and the National Security Council was set up to advise the President with respect to the integration of domestic, foreign and military policies relating to the national security. In the early years of the Cold War, when the concept of national security first came into fashion, the security problem for the West was how to respond to a broad spectrum challenge from the former Soviet Union. This challenge was not just military, but also ideological, social and economic. The Cold War was about a rivalry between two mutually exclusive systems of political economy over the future of industrial society (see *Cold War*). But this initially wide conceptualisation of security quickly narrowed down to a largely military focus under the pressure of a nuclear arms race marked by rapid, sustained, and strategically important improvements in technology. Right through to the 1980s, this arms race, and the theories of deterrence interwoven with it, dominated the discourse on security (see *Deterrence*). It led to the construction of Security Studies as a sub-discipline almost wholly in the military terms during the 1950s, 60s and 70s. Within Security Studies and International Relations, security became increasingly seen as synonymous with military, and a division of labour evolved, where IPE was seen as low politics, largely separate from security questions (see *Intercultural Relations and Peace Studies*). Only during the last decade of the Cold War did the wider agenda re-emerge, and by then its non-military aspects had acquired a quite different character. It is this peculiar period of the Cold War, and not any longer-term historical tradition, that has led to the close identity of security with military being seen as normal.

By the 1980s, the decline of military-political security issues at the centre of security concerns was visible in the growing awareness that war was disappearing, or in some cases had disappeared, as an option in relations amongst a substantial group of states. The core group of this emergent security community was Western Europe, Japan and North America. The effectiveness of nuclear deterrence between East and West made it possible to think that the former Soviet Union could also, in an odd way, be included in this sphere, an outlook that became much stronger once Gorbachev assumed power and embarked on an explicit demilitarisation of the Cold War (see *Deterrence*). After the Vietnam war, there was also an increasing tendency in the West to question whether war was a cost-effective method for achieving a wide-range of political and economic objectives. If war was fading away as a possibility amongst many of the leading powers in the system, then realist assumptions about the primacy of military security became questionable. Adding to this shift was the increasing securitization of two issues that had traditionally been thought of as low politics: the international economy and the environment.

In the case of the environment, the securitization process can be traced back to the 1960s. Starting from a concern about pesticides, this grew steadily into a wide range of interconnected issues including climate change, biodiversity, resource depletion, pollution, and the threat from meteorites (see *Green Security*). The underlying problem was a combination of rising human numbers and rising industrial activity within a finite planetary ecosystem. Concern was split between a potentially arcadian desire to make the environment itself the referent object of security, to preserve things as they had been before humans disturbed them, and a more pragmatic worry that if humans exceeded the carrying capacity of the ecosystem in too many ways, they would endanger the supporting conditions of their own prosperity, civilisation, and possibly existence (see *Global Environment and Peace*). There was also a growing awareness that nature itself could still deliver huge blows against humankind whose density and urban concentration made it increasingly vulnerable to major disruptions of trade and production.

In the case of the economy, the securitization process arose in part from the relative economic decline of the United States, and in part from reactions to the increasing liberalisation of the world economy. Relative American decline was an inevitable result of both the exaggerated position of global dominance that it held in 1945, and the imperial overstretch that set in with the Vietnam war. The US dominance was challenged both by Europe and Japan recovering from the Second World War, and by some newly decolonised countries finding effective paths to modernisation. By the 1970s some in the United States were already beginning to feel threatened by dependence on imported oil, by trade deficits, and by pressure on the dollar. Alongside US decline was the growing liberalisation of the global economy, first in trade, and from the 1970s also in finance. This meant that national economies became progressively more exposed to competition from other producers in a global market, and to ever more powerful transnational corporations, banks and financial markets (see *Globalization*).

When the Cold War finally unravelled at the end of the 1980s, these underlying developments towards widening were suddenly thrown into prominence by the rapid collapse of virtually the whole of the narrow military-political security agenda that had dominated the world for over forty years. As the former Soviet Union first withdrew its military and ideological challenge, and then imploded, the political-military rationale of the Cold War security system evaporated. With the ideological confrontation consigned to history, nuclear forces suddenly had little to deter, and conventional forces little to contain. But offsetting this positive development was the image of a new world disorder which quickly began to dominate perceptions of the future, bringing with it a wider security agenda.

This new security agenda is as yet much less clear than the old one. Like some vast condemned building, the collapse of the Cold War raised a huge cloud of dust which has not yet settled sufficiently to offer a clear view. Nevertheless, it seems safe to say that the relative simplicity of structure and certainty of purpose of security during the Cold War, has been replaced since the early 1990s by extreme complexity of structure and profound uncertainty about purpose. There is no longer any obviously dominant source of threat attached to a clearly identifiable actor. Instead, we are confronted by threats such as nuclear proliferation, economic turbulence, migration, pollution, climate change, and the possibility of large rocks in space hitting the earth. These threats seem more to be embedded in the structures and processes of complex systems, both natural and manmade, than to be identified with a particular 'enemy' actor. Neither is there any single pattern of threat strong enough to dominate the whole international system. Instead there is a much more decentralised pattern, though this could change quickly if either the global economy or the planetary environment shifted into crisis. For example, some scientists argue, on the basis of drill cores from the Greenland ice cap, that serious climate change in the past sometimes occurred with great swiftness, major changes in temperature (and therefore in glaciation and sea level) occurring within a few years. Many of the new security issues could become major, but they could just as well remain marginal, or of high concern only to a few actors (see *Future of Humanity*).

Since the operation of these complex systems is often either or both of poorly understood and beyond the control of existing policy machinery, difficult choices arise about whether to attempt large scale cooperative security policies in an attempt to address the problems, or to concentrate on specific local measures in an attempt to deal with the consequences. Does one try to stop global warming, or start raising the level of one's sea walls? Many of the new threats have a global systemic quality, but the extent and nature of their impact are very unevenly distributed. Some states might benefit from a bit of global warming (Canada, Russia) whereas others would face disaster (Bangladesh, Maldives, Netherlands). Some states do very well out of the liberal trading and financial system (Japan, Germany, South Korea, Saudi Arabia) whereas others are, in one way or another, ruined by it (Nigeria, Zaire, Russia, Mexico, and the long list of debt-crisis countries). Some are heavily affected by migration (US, EU, South Africa, Mexico) and the drugs trade (Colombia, Burma, Peru, US, Thailand), while others are largely bypassed.

Unless events take a turn which pushes some issue to the centre of global security concerns, there is a good case for thinking that the new security agenda will be considerably less monolithic and global, and considerably more diverse, regional and local, in character than the old one, despite the global quality of many of the new threats and referent objects. This diversity, of course, makes it exceedingly difficult to generalise. Although there will be some shared issues, in the post-Cold War world the security agenda will vary markedly from actor to actor in terms of both the issues and the priorities (see *Global Neighborhood: New Security Principles*).

Compounding this diversity is the much commented upon differentiation in the character of the states composing the international system. Now that the Cold War no longer obstructs the view, it is clear that there are at least three distinct classes of state in the international system: (a) postmodern states, defined by democracy, broad spectrum openness, and high levels of sociopolitical cohesion; (b) modern states, defined by strong government control over society and restrictive attitudes towards openness; and (c) premodern states, defined by low levels of sociopolitical cohesion and poorly developed structures of government. Because of their internal differences, these types of state are likely to have different views and priorities on what defines their security agendas (see *Peace, Systems View of*).

## 3. The Current Debate

The breakdown of the Cold War focus on military security generated a debate between wideners and traditionalists about the legitimate content of the concept of security. Wideners wanted to add a whole range of economic, environmental and societal issues to the security agenda, while traditionalists wanted to keep the security discourse centred on military questions. This debate was stimulated first by the rise of the economic and environmental agendas in international relations during the 1970s and 80s, and by the rise of concerns with identity issues, and transnational crime during the 1990s. This issue-driven widening eventually triggered its own reaction, creating a plea for confinement of Security Studies to issues centred around the threat or use of force. A key argument here was that progressive widening endangered the intellectual coherence of security, putting so much into it that its essential meaning became void. This perhaps masked a generally unspoken political concern that allowing non-military issues to achieve security status would have undesirable and/or counterproductive effects on the whole fabric of social and international relations. The example of the late Soviet Union demonstrates powerfully the negative consequences of excessive securitization and the closure that goes with it (see *Militarism and Militarization*). In addition, moves to securitize a wide range of things go against the general trend of liberal Western society for more than 150 years to try to narrow down the range of things defined as security issues, and to cultivate more open relationships within and between societies.

The defence of the traditionalist position got underway as the Cold War unravelled. As the main task of the strategic community—analysis of East-West military confrontation—evaporated, there was a period of disorientation. The function, and therefore the status and the funding, of the whole edifice of strategic studies built up during the Cold War seemed to be at risk, and consequently the military focus of strategic analysis seemed extremely vulnerable to pressure from the wideners. Indicative of this period was the 1989 issue of *Survival* (31: 6) devoted entirely to 'non-military aspects of strategy.'

Traditionalists fought back by reasserting conventional arguments about the enduring primacy of military security (Gray 1994). In varying degrees they accepted the need to look more widely at non-military causes of conflict in the international system, and there was little explicit attempt to defend the centrality of the state in security analysis at a time when so many non-state actors were playing vigorously in the military game. Most traditionalists insist on *military* conflict as the defining key to security, while being prepared to loosen their state-centrism. Some (Chipman 1992) argued that there was simply a return to the natural terrain of the subject after the artificial nuclear narrowing of the Cold War. Stephen Walt gives probably the strongest statement of the traditionalist position. He argues that Security Studies is about the phenomenon of war, and that it can be defined as 'the study of the threat, use, and control of military force.' Against those who want to widen the agenda outside this strictly military domain, he argues that this:

> runs the risk of expanding "Security Studies" excessively; by this logic, issues such as pollution, disease, child abuse, or economic recessions could all be viewed as threats to "security." Defining the field in this way would destroy its intellectual coherence and make it more difficult to devise solutions to any of these important problems. (Walt 1991 pp. 212-3)

Walt (1991 p. 227) does allow economics and security into his picture, but only as it relates to military issues, and not as economic security *per se*.

The traditionalists' criticism of the wideners that they risk intellectual incoherence can be a powerful point. The wider agenda certainly does extend the range of knowledge and understanding necessary to pursue Security Studies. More worryingly, it also does two other things. First, given the political function of the word security, it extends the call for state mobilization to a wide range of issues. As Deudney (1990) has pointed out, this may be undesirable and counterproductive in the environmental sector, and this argument could easily be extended into other sectors. Second, the wider agenda tends, often unthinkingly, to elevate 'security' into a kind of universal good thing—the desired condition towards which all relations should be moved. But as Wéver (1995) has argued, this is a dangerously blinkered view. At best, security is a kind of stabilization of conflictual or threatening relations, often through

emergency mobilization of the state. While security in relations may generally be better than insecurity (threats against which no adequate countermeasures are available), a securitized relationship is still one in which serious conflicts continue to exist, albeit ones against which some effective countermeasures have been taken. Even this degree of relative desirability can be questioned: liberals, for example, argue that too much economic security is destructive to the workings of a market economy. Security should not too easily be thought of as always a good thing. Better, as Wéver argues, is to aim for desecuritization: the shifting of issues out of emergency mode and into the normal bargaining processes of the political sphere.

At the time of writing, this debate continues between traditionalist defenders of a narrow conceptualization of security, and a whole variety of wideners. As suggested in the previous section, the actual unfolding of security policy concerns in the post-Cold War world leans in the direction of the wideners. Concern about military threats has declined overall (though still vigorous in some places), while concern about non-military threats has tended to rise. Since comprehensive security by definition engages with the wider view of security, it is worth examining just what the wider agenda embodies.

## 4. A Comprehensive Approach to Security

What does it mean to adopt a more diversified agenda in which economic, societal, and environmental security issues play alongside military and political ones? Thinking about security in terms of non-military sectors simply grew up without benefit of much reflection during the later decades of the Cold War as new issues got added to the military-political agenda. Embracing the wider security agenda means that one needs to consider both what one understands by security and what that means when applied to the wider range of non-military issues.

Security is about survival. It is when an issue is presented as posing an existential threat to a designated referent object (traditionally, but not necessarily, the state, incorporating government, territory and society). The special nature of security threats justifies the use of extraordinary measures to handle them. The invocation of security has been the key to legitimizing the use of force, but more generally it has opened the way for the state to mobilize, or to take special powers, in order to handle existential threats. Traditionally, by saying 'security' a state representative declares an emergency condition, claiming a right to use whatever means are necessary to block a threatening development. 'Security' is the rhetorical move that takes politics beyond the established rules of the game, and frames the issue either as a special kind of politics, or as above politics. Using this perspective it is possible to retain both the wider agenda and a coherent concept of security (Buzan, Wëver and de Wilde 1997, esp., ch. 2). Taken sector by sector, this more comprehensive view of security can be unfolded as follows.

Military security is about relationships of forceful coercion. It concerns the two-level interplay of the armed offensive and defensive capabilities of actors in the international system, and actor's perceptions of each other's intentions. In the military sector, the referent object is usually the state, though it may also be other kinds of political entity. It is also possible to imagine circumstances in which threats to the survival of the armed forces would elevate them to referent object status in their own right, perhaps serving to justify a coup against the existing government and its policy (whether of disarmament or of hopeless conflict). Traditional Security Studies tends to see all military affairs as security, but this may not be the case. For many of the advanced democracies, defence of the state is becoming only one, and perhaps not even the main de facto, function of the armed forces. For many European countries it is not clear that any significant national defence function in the traditional sense remains. Their militaries may be increasingly trained and called upon to support routine world order activities, such as peacekeeping or humanitarian intervention, that cannot be viewed as concerning existential threats to their states, or even as emergency action in the sense of suspending normal rules (see *Security and Cooperation in Europe*).

Political security is about relationships of authority, governing status and recognition. It concerns the organizational stability of states or other systems of governance, and the ideologies that give them legitimacy. In the political sector, existential threats are traditionally defined in terms of the constituting principle—sovereignty, but sometimes also ideology—of the state. Sovereignty can be existentially threatened by things that question recognition, legitimacy, or governing authority. Amongst the ever more interdependent and institutionalised relations characteristic of the West (and increasingly of the international system as a whole), a variety of supranational referent objects are also becoming important. The European Union can be existentially threatened by things that might undo its integration process. International regimes, and international society more broadly, can be existentially threatened by things that undermine the rules, norms and institutions that constitute them.

Economic security is about relationships of trade, production and finance. Generally, it might be taken to concern access to the resources, finance and markets necessary to sustain acceptable levels of welfare and political power. But in a liberal market economy, which depends on competition and the possibility of failure, it is illogical to securitize these things. Because of this, in the economic sector, the referent objects and existential threats are harder to pin down. Firms are most commonly existentially threatened by bankruptcy, and sometimes also by changes to the law that make them illegal or unviable (as after communist revolutions). But in the market economy firms are, with a few exceptions, expected to come and go, and only seldom do they try to securitize their own survival. National economies have more claim to the right of survival, but only rarely will this type of threat (national bankruptcy, or an inability to provide for the basic needs of the population) actually arise apart from wider security contexts such as war. Unless the survival of the population is in question, the huge range of doing better or doing worse in the national economy cannot be seen as existentially threatening to it. As in the political sector, supranational referent objects from specific regimes to the global market itself can be existentially threatened by things that might undermine the rules, norms and institutions that constitute them. In a liberal system it is these that are the most obvious referent objects for security.

Societal security is about relationships of collective identity. It concerns the sustainability, within acceptable conditions for evolution, of traditional patterns of language, culture and religious and national identity and custom. In the societal sector, the referent object is large-scale collective identities that can function independently of the state, such as nations and religions. Given the peculiar nature of this type of referent object it is extremely difficult to establish hard boundaries that differentiate existential from lesser threats. Collective identities naturally evolve and change in response to internal and external developments. Such changes may be seen as invasive or heretical, and their sources pointed to as existential threats, or they may be accepted as part of the evolution of identity. Given the conservative nature of 'identity,' it is always possible to paint challenges and changes as threats to identity, because "we will no longer be us," no longer the way we were, or the way we really ought to be to be true to our identity. Thus, whether migrants or rival identities are securitized depends on whether the holders of the collective identity take a relatively closed—or a relatively open—minded view about how their identity is constituted and maintained. The ability to maintain and reproduce a language, a set of behavioural customs, or a conception of ethnic purity can all be cast in terms of survival.

Environmental security is about relationships between human activity and the planetary biosphere. It concerns the maintenance of the local and the planetary biosphere as the essential support system on which all other human enterprises depend. In the environmental sector the range of possible referent objects is very large, extending from relatively concrete things such as the survival of individual species (tigers, whales, humankind) or types of habitat (rain forest, lakes) to much fuzzier, larger scale things such as the maintenance of the planetary climate and biosphere within the narrow band that human beings have come to consider normal during their few thousand years of civilization. Underlying many of these referent objects is a baseline concern about the relationship between the human species and the rest of the biosphere, and whether that relationship can be sustained without risking either or both of a collapse of the achieved levels of civilization, and a wholesale disruption of the planet's biological legacy. The interplay amongst all of these things is immensely complicated. At either the macro or the micro extremes there are some pretty clear cases of existential threat (the survival of species, the survival of human civilization) that can be securitized. In between, somewhat like in the economic sector, lies a huge mass of problems that it is more difficult, though not impossible, to construct in existential terms.

Understanding security in terms of these five sectors is a helpful way of thinking about comprehensive concepts of security. Limiting the meaning of security to existential issues requiring emergency measures is a good way of containing the proliferation of securitization that marked the 1980s. It is also useful in making explicit that security is not the end goal, but only a way station on the road to the ideal of normal politics, and that whether or not to pose issues in security terms is a political choice whose consequences need to be evaluated. Claiming security status is an attractive way of seeking to gain political priority. But as shown by the experience of excessive securitization from the McCarthy episode in the US, to the all-consuming securitization in North Korea, achieving it may have serious negative consequences.

## 5. Current Security Concepts

Within the wider understanding of comprehensive security, one finds the following concepts in use.

### 5.1 Collective Security

Collective security had its heyday during the interwar years when it was the core concept behind the League of Nations. The central idea of collective security is to institutionalise a permanent arrangement of the balance of power in which the entire international community agrees to oppose military aggression by any member. The logic of the scheme is that no state can stand up to all of the other members of the system together, and that aggression will therefore be permanently deterred (an assumption made difficult when there are nuclear powers in the system). The necessary conditions for collective security are very demanding. First, all states must accept the *status quo* sufficiently to renounce the use of force for any purpose other than defence of their own territory. Second, all states must agree on a clear definition of aggression so that paralysis can be avoided if cases arise. Third, all states, and especially the major powers, must be willing to commit their own armed forces and/or funds (or to create, pay for, and find means of controlling, an international armed force) to prevent aggression even if it is remote from, or opposed to, their immediate interests. Fourth, all states must prevent actively any breaches of sanctions that might assist the declared outlaw. Attempts by the League of Nations to implement collective security failed because of inability to meet these conditions. The United Nations Security Council is a mechanism for collective security, and its operation in 1991 against Iraq's invasion of Kuwait might be seen as an instance of successful implementation of the idea. Collective security is sometimes used to refer to more limited subglobal arrangements such as NATO.

### 5.2 Common Security

The term common security was introduced into public debate by the Report of the Palme Commission in 1982. That a term like common security was promoted by a high profile group of politicians and government officials is important for two reasons. First, it represented an attempt to shift the focus of popular idealist thinking away from the amorphous utopianism of peace, and towards the more concrete realities of security. Second, by reasserting the centrality of interdependence as a major theme in thinking about security, it attempted to combat the tendency of much Cold War strategic thinking to be cast in the self-centred, and often ethnocentric, terms of *national security*. The ethnocentric focus of national security made it attractive in policy political terms, but only at the cost of supressing the interdependence dimension which is implicit in the idea of security as a whole. Like most good political ideas, common security suggests a strong normative orientation in terms of core values, while at the same time leaving broad scope for interpretation about how those values might be realized. The idea indicates clearly the basis for a synthesis of idealist and realist concerns. It represents a commitment to talk in terms of realist preoccupations with security as an objective of state policy, but only if the idealist concerns with interdependence and common interests in survival are given equal weight. This concept played a significant role in the last stages of the Cold War, and given the increasing salience of interdependence in current security debates, is likely to remain important.

## 5.3 Cooperative Security

Cooperative security is best seen as a weaker Asia-Pacific regional variant of common security. It emerged during the 1990s in response to the ending of the Cold War security framework in the region, and the attempt to start building regional institutions (ASEAN Regional Forum, APEC) in an area remarkable for the absence of them. Japan can take some credit for originating the idea, but its main public advocates have been Australia and Canada. Like common security, cooperative security is rooted in the ideas that acknowledging interdependence is a central key to winding down hostilities, and that security is about more than just military relations. But given the rather difficult political relations in the region, cooperative security embodies a rejection of the heavily institutional and rule-based European approach. Instead it stresses less formal processes of dialogue, low entry barriers to inclusion in these processes, and avoidance of confrontation. These features make it vulnerable to criticisms that it is at best superficial and hollow, and at worst a form of appeasement of expansionist and/or undemocratic governments. But its supporters claim that it reflects a unique Asian way of doing things that should not be judged by European standards.

## 5.4 International Security

The term international security is frequently used, but lacks a clear meaning. If it refers to the security of the international system as a whole, then its content is too abstract for use in most national policy debates. The international system as a whole has no mass political constituency willing to act on its behalf, though it is beginning to have elite defenders concerned about the maintenance of international regimes and institutions ranging from trading and financial arrangements, through arms control agreements such as the nuclear non-proliferation regime, to the legal and political frameworks of international society itself. If international security refers simply to the sum of national securities, then it lacks a clear indication of the interdependence theme.

## 5.5 Security Community

The term security community (or more strictly, pluralist security community) was coined by Deutsch et al., (1957). It refers to a group of states whose international relations have evolved to the point where they neither expect, nor prepare for, the use of force in relations with each other. Originally, the concept had only a narrow application, referring to relations amongst the Nordic states, the members of the European Community, and the Canada-US relationship. With the end of the Cold War, it can now be applied to almost the whole of the West, including Japan, and is one of the keys to understanding the change in the role of war in the international system.

## 5.6 Comprehensive Security

The term comprehensive security is used by a number of East Asian states to describe their national security policies. The specific content of the term thus varies from case to case, though there is a common thread that comprehensive security refers to an agenda that contains more than military issues, and in which military security concerns may not be the main ones. This concept originated in Japan during the 1970s, where one of its functions was to get around the term national security, whose military associations were difficult to handle in the Japanese political context (Dewitt 1994 pp. 2-3). It comprised a variety of concerns about mostly external threats to Japan, including food and energy supplies, earthquakes, and politico-military relations with the US, China and the former Soviet Union, and promoted both domestic and international policies. It seems to have been useful to Japan in translating many aspects of security policy into economic issues, thus enabling it to steer around the still uncomfortable military domain. In Southeast Asia, several countries use the concept, but mostly to justify more inward-looking perspectives than in the case of Japan (Dewitt 1994 pp. 3-4). For states such as Malaysia, Singapore and Indonesia, comprehensive security links closely to development strategies designed to consolidate the national polity and economy. It is closely tied to ideas of self-reliance and avoidance of dependency on outside powers.

In these usages, comprehensive security is simply a variant on the original 1940s idea of national security as something that embraced political, economic and societal issues as well as military ones. The Japanese version is compatible with interdependence-based concepts such as collective and common security, but the Southeast Asian variants are much less so.

See also: *Collective Security and Collective Self-defense; Human Rights and Environmental Rights: Their Sustainable Development Compatibility*

*Bibliography* ————————————————————

Barnett R W 1984 *Beyond War: Japan's Concept of Comprehensive National Security*. Pergamon/ Brssey's, Washington

Buzan B 1991 Is international security possible. In: Booth K (ed.) *New Thinking about Strategy and International Security*

Buzan B, Wæver O, Wilde J de 1997 *Security: A New Framework for Analysis*. Lynne Rienner, Boulder Co.

Chipman J 1992 The future of strategic studies: Beyond grand strategy. *Survival* 34

Deutsch K et al., 1957 *Political Community and the North Atlantic Area*. Princeton University Press, Princeton

Deudney D 1990 The case against linking environmental degradation and national security. *Millennium* 19(3)

DeWitt D 1994 Common, comprehensive and cooperative security. *Pacific Review* 7

Gilpin R 1981 *War and Change in World Politics*. Cambridge University Press, Cambridge

Gray C S 1994 *Villains, Victims and Sheriffs: Strategic Studies and Security for an Inter-War Period*. University of Hull Press, Hull

Independent Commission on Disarmament and Security Issues 1982 *Common Security: A Programme for Disarmament*. London

Kennedy P 1989 *The Rise and Fall of the Great Powers*. Fontana, London

Krause K, Williams M C 1996 Broadening the agenda of security studies: Politics and methods. *Mershon Int'l Stud. Rev.* 40

Stockholm International Peace Research Institute (SIPRI) 1985 *Policies for Common Security*. Taylor and Francis, London

Walt S M 1991 The Renaissance of Security Studies. *Int'l Stud. Q.* 35

Wæver O 1995 Securitization and desecuritization. In: Lipschutz R (ed.) *On Security*. Columbia University Press, New York

BARRY BUZAN

# Conciliar Movement

The states of medieval Europe, for the most part dynastic in character, owed their unity as a civilization to the common institution of the Church. Churchmen dominated education, administration, the civil law, and diplomacy, possessed tax-levying powers on behalf of the papacy, and shared, in an often uneasy relationship, authority with the temporal rulers. At the head of the Church stood the Pope, the supreme arbiter in matters of faith and morals, and claiming the overlordship of Christendom (see *Peace in the Middle Ages*).

By the fourteenth century, however, this traditional dual order was in danger of breaking down. The papacy proved increasingly unable to fulfil the functions expected of it, whether in the realm of spiritual leadership, or as the focus and symbol of Christian unity. Such was the political turmoil in Rome that the popes from 1309 to 1377 took refuge in Avignon, where they fell under the influence of the French kings. In 1378, a year after the pope's return to Rome, and a vacancy occurring, the cardinals elected Urban VI, who soon proved so harsh and brutal an autocrat, so hated in his rule, that they switched allegiance to Robert of Geneva who, as 'Clement VII,' set up court once more in Avignon. Thus began 'the Great Schism' with each of the rival popes at Rome and Avignon claiming to be the one true pope, each creating his own cardinals, and each having his own following among the princes of Europe. The Emperor, together with Hungary, Scandinavia, England and, in time, England's ally, Portugal, as well as the Italian states, supported Urban; France and Scotland (England's enemies), Castile and Aragon, and those German princes under French influence, backed Clement. Not only this division of Christendom into rival camps, but the despotic and capricious rule of successive popes, together with the corruption and intrigue inseparable from papal elections and papal politics, proved intolerable to the more spiritually-minded.

In England, John Wyclif (1324-84), a leading Oxford divine, reacted to these manifold scandals by repudiating the whole medieval ecclesiastical order. He denounced prelacy, advocated a national church and use of the vernacular, proclaimed as false the doctrine of the Mass, declared the Scriptures to be the supreme authority, and held that divine grace alone, as exhibited in his character and behaviour, rendered a churchman worthy of obedience (see *Religion and Peace*). These proto-Protestant doctrines took a ready hold in Bohemia where they were championed by John Hus (1369-1415), a priest and teacher of the University of Prague.

Meanwhile, in the early years of the fifteenth century, the crisis in the divided papacy was coming to a head. The lead in resolving it was taken by the University of Paris, the universities seeing themselves, after the priestly power, the *Sacerdotium*, and the princely, the *Regnum*, as the third power in Christendom, the *Studium*. Their suggested method of ending the Schism was by the simultaneous abdication of both popes followed by a fresh election. Yet, despite promises to abdicate, the two popes, Benedict XIII at Avignon, and Gregory XII at Rome, clung on, until in exasperation their respective cardinals deserted them and together called a General Council of the Church to meet at Pisa in 1409. Parts of Europe still adhered to the rival popes, but France, England, Poland, Portugal, most of Germany and much of Italy, supported the cardinals and sent 500 delegates to Pisa.

The Council of Pisa (1409-10) summoned both popes to appear before it, and on their failure to do so declared them deposed. It then commissioned the cardinals to hold a new election and their choice fell upon the Archbishop of Milan who took the title 'Alexander V.' There were now three popes instead of two. To make matters worse, when Alexander died in the following year, 1410, the Pisan cardinals elected as his successor Baldassare Cossa, a former freebooter and papal extortioner who, because he exercised great power in central Italy, was a leading force in the Council. His election, as 'John XXIII,' was as politically inevitable as it was ecclesiastically scandalous.

With central Italy in political turmoil, the papal issue as intractable as ever, the pope who was to have resolved the Schism entirely lacking in moral credibility, and a dangerous English-born heresy beginning to flourish in central Europe, there was a growing demand among all who upheld the traditional order for a real General Council of the Church, a parliament of all Western Christendom, to take the situation in hand and restore order, unity and authority. The initiative was taken by Sigismund, King of the Romans and Emperor-elect, who pressured John XXIII into summoning a Council to meet at Constance, a city within his own territories.

To the Council of Constance (1414-18) were summoned cardinals, bishops, abbots, doctors, and representatives of all the monarchs and universities of Catholic Europe. These were mainly conservative reformers, concerned primarily to combat ideas and remove abuses that posed a threat to the order and system of which they were part. They were faced with three great tasks: to combat heresy, to end the Schism, and to initiate a permanent reform of the Church. Through the adoption of an English proposal, the Council was organized on lines characteristic of a medieval university, being divided into four 'nations.' The French constituted one 'nation,' the Italians another, and the Germans (with the Scandinavians) a third. Owing to the absence of the Spaniards, who still adhered to 'Benedict XIII' (himself a Spaniard), the English, who had traditionally been part of the German 'nation,' insisted in participating (with the Scots) as a 'nation' of their own. When in 1417 the Spaniards, having renounced Benedict, sent delegates to the Council, they objected that so small a country as England, with its comparatively few bishops, should take their place as representing a quarter of Christendom, a stance in which they received the backing of the French. Sigismund, however, upheld the English claim, valuing them as allies against the three Latin 'nations.' The upshot was that the Spaniards were admitted as a fifth 'nation.' Each 'nation' possessed one vote in the deliberations of the Council.

The Council rapidly proceeded against heresy. John Hus was induced to come to Constance with Sigismund himself promising safe conduct. But once there, he was arrested, tried and burnt (July 1415) on the principle '*cum haereticis fides non servanda*' ('there is no need to keep faith with heretics'). The following year his friend and follower, Jerome of Prague, who had gone to Constance to defend him, suffered the same fate. Wyclif himself had died a generation earlier (1384), but his works were condemned, his books ordered to be burnt and his body destroyed.

Besides extirpating heresy, Sigismund was also intent upon the reform of the Church, a chief obstacle to this being John XXIII, the notorious 'Pisan' pope. John, who had reluctantly come to Constance, had thought that the preponderance of Italian delegates would protect him, but, with the decision to vote by 'nations,' he was outmanoeuvred, the Italians being reduced to merely one vote in four. Seeing the tide of opinion turning against him, he fled from Constance, but was later apprehended, and, after being indicted for piracy, murder, rape, sodomy and incest, was formally deposed (May 1415), and incarcerated during the lifetime of the Council. There remained the 'Roman' pope, Gregory XII, and the 'Avignon' pope, Benedict XIII. Gregory, now having virtually the whole of Christendom against him, finally abdicated (July 1415), after first giving the Council his fiat of legitimacy. Benedict had withdrawn to his native Spain, where he was sought out by Sigismund. On the Emperor-elect's failure to persuade him to abdicate, he was condemned by the Council as an incorrigible schismatic and solemnly deposed (July 1417). Thus was ended the Great Schism after thirty-nine years.

The Council was now in a position to determine the future of Christendom: it could institute reforms and then elect a pope who would be bound by them, or elect a pope first. Sigismund and his German 'nation' were reformist; the three Latin 'nations' were papalist. Hitherto the English had been reformist, but now Henry V of England, calculating that political advantage was to be gained both from freeing Sigismund from the distractions of the Council (he wished to have him as a military ally), and from earning the support of a restored papacy, went over to the papalist camp and declared for an immediate election. The cardinals were to vote alongside the five six-man delegations of the 'nations,' a two-thirds vote amongst the former and in each of the latter being required. The choice fell upon an Italian, who took the title 'Martin V.' In vain did Sigismund press for the papal coronation to be deferred until reforms had been promulgated. The most that had been achieved was the adoption of the decree *Frequens* (October 1417) guaranteeing the holding of future Councils, the first after five years, the next after seven, and thereafter at ten-yearly intervals.

The election of Martin V in November 1417 proved a turning point in the Conciliar Movement, for despite the decree *Sacrosancta* (April 1415), declaring that a General Council of the Church held its authority from Christ alone and so was superior to the Pope, there was little a transient body could do once a shrewd, strong-minded priest-politician had again taken over the levers of papal power. Significantly, Martin's first pronouncement was that it was 'impious' to appeal to a Council against a papal decision. Although not averse himself to certain reforms, his overriding concern was the recovery of the power of the Pope, both as an Italian prince and as the spiritual and ecclesiastical overlord of Christendom.

The real issue was, who was to rule Christendom,

Council or Pope? Martin took every opportunity to weaken the Conciliar cause. When the next Council met, first at Pavia and then at Siena (1423-24), it was thinly attended and had no significant princely backing. The Pope's party sowed dissension among the 'nations,' and then the Pope himself dissolved the Council on the excuse of the small attendance. Its only effective act was to decree that the next Council met at Basle in 1431. Martin reluctantly confirmed this move, and with the need to suppress the Hussites, who were successfully fighting for their cause in Bohemia, summoned the Council shortly before his own death in February 1431.

The Council of Basle (1431-49) saw the developing conflict with the Pope come to a head. It was better attended than its predecessor, and accepted the need to compromise with the Hussites. This alarmed the new pope, Eugenius IV, who dissolved it in December 1431. The Council, however, growing in numbers, and supported by Sigismund, together with France, England, Burgundy and Castile, refused to disperse, rejected papal absolutism, and sent Eugenius an ultimatum to withdraw his bull of dissolution. After vacillating the Pope gave way. The demands of the more extreme reformers, such as confiscation of the papal revenues and the power to grant indulgences, eventually brought a reaction; the Council split into two hostile groups and Eugenius summoned those who remained loyal to him to meet at Ferrara. The majority declared him deposed and in 1439 elected in his place their own nominee as 'Felix V.' The rulers of France and Germany used these troubles to strengthen their own grip on church affairs, and even before the election of a new, more acceptable pope, Nicholas V, in 1447, had made their peace with the papacy. The Council, bereft of support, was expelled from Basle in 1448, and the following year, after recognizing Nicholas V, dissolved itself.

So ended a forty-year attempt to give the Christian West an international parliament. Martin Wight, the English historian and International Relations theorist, saw the Conciliar Movement of 1409-49 as the first of the four great experiments in ecumenical government, the others being the Congress System (1815-22) (see *Congress System*), the League of Nations (1920-46) (see *League of Nations*) and the United Nations (1945- ) (see *United Nations: Achievements and Agenda*). Although it was ecclesiastical in character owing to the prevailing culture and thought-world of the late Middle Ages, there are interesting parallels with its secular successors. The division into the five great 'nations' is suggestive of the way the Security Council is constituted, and the holding of the Councils every few years in a different city was to be repeated in the workings of the Congress System. Indeed the Councils, which generally had a secular political side, set the pattern for the great peace congresses of later centuries.

But it is, perhaps, in the League of Nations that the parallels are most striking. Both Councils and League arose because of a crisis in the system: in the case of the first, a Great Schism in the papacy and so in Christendom; in the case of the second, a 'great schism' in the European states-system with the rivalry of its two embattled alliances culminating in the cataclysm of 1914-18. In each case there was a response from the class whose interests were mainly threatened by the breakdown: the conservative church and university clerisy in the early fifteenth century; the bourgeois intelligentsia in the early twentieth. Each recognized the threat posed by the revolutionary alternative: the incipient Protestantism of Wyclif and Hus in the one case; Communism and the Third International in the other. And in both cases the experiment petered out in futility because in neither case did the class of conservative reformers (usually dismissed today as 'the chattering classes') possess that power which they thought was their due and without which it was impossible to dominate, and so save, the system. Although the advocates of the conciliar reform of the Church had correctly diagnosed the dangers which were to shatter it only a century later, it is likely that nothing, not even a restructured papacy, could have averted the outcome. In late medieval Europe the centrifugal forces were too strong: the nations-state system was struggling to be born out of the womb of the *Respublica Christiana*. It is this which explains the political realities not only behind the Schism and the Councils, but behind the Reformation itself: a revolution from which a unified Christendom was never to recover.

See also: *Globalization; Internationalization; Council of Europe*

*Bibliography* ————————————————

Allmand C 1992 *Henry V.* Methuen, London
Bell M I M 1921 *A Short History of the Papacy.* Methuen, London
Cheyney E P 1936 *The Dawn of a New Era 1250-1453.* Harper, New York and London
Fisher H A L 1936 *A History of Europe.* Book I, Chap. XXX Arnold, London
Hay D 1966 *Europe in the Fourteenth and Fifteenth Centuries.* Longmans, London
Hefele C J von 1915 *Histoire des Conciles,* Vols. VI, VII (trans. of *Konciliengeschichte*). Letouzey et Ané, Paris
Jacob E F 1953 *Essays in the Conciliar Epoch*, 2nd edn. Manchester University Press, Manchester
Kitts E J 1908 *In the Days of the Councils.* Constable, London
Kitts E J 1910 *Pope John XXIII and Master John Huss of Bohemia.* Constable, London
Loomis L R (trans.) Munday J H, Woody K M (eds.) 1961 *The Council of Constance: The Unification of the Church.* Columbia University Press, New York (Contemporary documents, diaries etc.)
Pastor L 1938 *The History of the Popes from the Close of the Middle Ages*, 6th edn. Kegan Paul, London
Previté-Orton C W, Brooke Z N (eds.) 1936 *The Cambridge Medieval History* Vol. VIII *The Close of the Middle Ages.* Cambridge University Press, Cambridge
Previté-Orton C W 1952 *The Cambridge Shorter Medieval History.* Cambridge University Press, Cambridge, Book X
Tanner J R, Previté-Orton C W, Brooke Z N (eds.) 1932 *The Cambridge Medieval History* Vol. VII *Decline of Empire and Papacy.* Cambridge University Press, Cambridge
Waugh W T 1949 *A History of Europe from 1378 to 1494*, 3rd edn. Greenwood Press, Westport Conn.
Wight M 1978 *Power Politics.* Leicester University Press, Leicester
Wight M 1977 *Systems of States.* Leicester University Press, Leicester
Wylie J H 1900 *The Council of Constance to the Death of John Huss.* Longmans, London

BRIAN E. PORTER

# Concordat of Worms

The Concordat of Worms was a compromise settlement agreed to by Emperor Henry V and Pope Calixtus II in 1122, ending the Investiture Conflict. It thus drew a curtain on half a century of brutal struggle, struggle which had left much of central Europe in shambles, dealt a perhaps fatal blow to the political unification of Germany, and deeply involved the Roman Catholic Church in the secular politics of medieval Europe. Before the Investiture Conflict began, the German emperors were unquestionably the strongest rulers in Europe. Their realm included not only all of modern Germany, but the Low Countries, Switzerland, Austria, and substantial parts of modern France, Italy, and Czechoslovakia as well.

Moreover, the emperors enjoyed revenues and powers which other medieval rulers, their actions sharply circumscribed by the might and belligerence of the feudal warlords who were their vassal, could only envy. Eleventh century Germany was, of course, far from being a modern, centralized state, but it was by far the most vigorous and powerful political unit of its time.

One extremely important aspect of the German emperors' power was their firm control over the Church within their domains. The Church, with its vast holdings of land and wealth, its educated and talented clergy, and its high place in public trust and respect, was a vital part of the imperial political system. The emperors selected the bishops and abbots who led the Church within the empire, and by carefully appointing able and loyal men to fill these positions they made sure that the immense resources of the Church would be used to buttress their own authority.

The Church accepted this situation calmly through the tenth century, and reaped many advantages from it. Not only did the emperors shower their loyal and helpful Church with ever-increasing amounts of wealth and privileges, but the Church, longing for peace, found the emperors to be reliable allies. It was in the emperors' interest, of course, to have their subjects settle their disputes in the imperial courts rather than wage war against one another. Thus the Church found that helping the emperors was a way to decrease the violent warfare that was such a curse to medieval Europe.

However, the Church's position on the proper relationship between its own officials and political rulers began to change dramatically in the eleventh century. A reform movement centered on the Burgundian monastery of Cluny was affecting the thinking of an increasing number of clerics. The reformers argued that it was wrong for a layperson, even a king or an emperor, to choose or to have any authority over clergymen. Since clergymen were responsible for the health of the soul, while rulers were merely charged with ensuring the physical security of people's lives and property, and since the soul was infinitely more important than the physical body, clergy should have authority over rulers, rather than vice versa. The fact that many of the bishops and abbots appointed by the emperors and other European rulers were more notable for their cunning and political ambitions than for piety and virtue confirmed the reformers in their belief that the situation was an affront to God. The German emperors, in particular, aroused their ire because the emperors had taken it upon themselves to name not only their own clergymen, but the popes as well.

Emperor Henry III died in 1056, leaving as successor his son Henry IV, who was still a small child. During Henry IV's long minority, the reformers gained more and more power in the Church, establishing a College of Cardinals to elect the pope in defiance of imperial pretensions, and insisting that bishops and abbots should be elected by their fellow clergymen rather than by rulers such as the emperor. In 1075 the great reforming pope, Gregory VII, struck a blow at imperial control of the Church by forbidding lay investiture of clerics. Investiture was the ceremony by which a man was formally installed in the office of bishop or abbot. It was traditionally marked by the emperor giving him a ring and a staff, the symbols of his new spiritual authority. This carried the message that the spiritual authority of the clergy was something bestowed on them by the emperor, thus legitimizing the emperor's right to choose and to control the clergy. Gregory, in insisting that only clergymen could invest someone with spiritual authority, was in reality attacking the entire system of imperial control over the Church.

Henry IV, now a grown man, reacted angrily to Gregory's decree, declaring him deposed as pope. He could hardly have accepted a ruling which would cripple the basis of his political position so severely. Gregory, in turn, determined to free the Church from its bondage to political authority, declared Henry deposed as emperor. This was war, and by 1077 the two irascible leaders were fighting with armies as well as words. Though many of the German bishops remained loyal to the emperor who had appointed them, many German princes chose to take up arms on behalf of the papacy. Alarmed by the growth of imperial power at their own expense, they welcomed the chance to weaken the emperors by depriving them of their control over the Church.

Though Gregory died in 1085 and Henry in 1106, the war that they had begun ground on and on without them, devastating much of Germany and Italy. The real victors turned out to be neither popes nor emperors, but the feudal nobles of Germany. They seized the opportunity which the breakdown of order presented to make themselves virtually absolute masters of their own lands. Germany, which had been the most politically centralized state in Europe at the beginning of the eleventh century, became fragmented into dozens of autonomous princely states. Germany's inability to achieve political unification until the late nineteenth century can be traced back to this disastrous struggle.

By 1122 the German nobles were weary of the war and eager for a period of peace in which to consolidate their gains, so they put pressure on both sides to accept a compromise settlement. The Pope, Calixtus II, and his German representative, Archbishop Adalbert of Mainz, were reluctant to give up their demands for a total end to lay involvement in the selection of the clergy, but the threat of the loss of their allies forced them to agree to make concessions. Finally, on September 23, 1122, the papacy and Henry IV's successor, his son Henry V, accepted the compromise terms of the Concordat of Worms. Under these terms, the emperor agreed to restore to the Church all land and other wealth which had been seized during the wars. He also agreed that the investiture of prelates with ring and staff—the conferring of spiritual authority—would no longer be done by himself or any other layperson.

The papacy also gained a guarantee that henceforth bishops and abbots would be elected by groups of local clergymen, rather than appointed by lay rulers. However, it was stipulated that the emperor or his representatives could be present at such elections and could adjudicate any disputes which arose in connection with them. It was also stipulated that, before a prelate could be consecrated, he would have to be invested with the symbols of his temporal authority, that is, the jurisdiction over the landholdings and political power that went with his office, by the emperor.

Under the terms of the Concordat, then, the emperors relinquished the symbols of spiritual authority, but maintained the reality of their power. Rarely did

the local clergy ever dare to elect anyone except the emperor's chosen candidate while under the threatening eye of the emperor. If they did, the emperor could nullify their choice simply by refusing temporal investiture. In effect, then, the emperors continued to choose the bishops and abbots within the Empire. Not surprisingly, the compromise did not satisfy many clerics, and within 40 years after its signing, pope and emperor were at war again. The Concordat of Worms should thus be considered a truce in a conflict which would rage on for several centuries rather than a definitive settlement. Despite its imperfections, though, by the sharp distinction which it drew between political and spiritual authority, the Concordat did help lay the basis for the Western idea of the separation of Church and State.

See also: *Peace in the Middle Ages*

*Bibliography*

Brooke C N L 1958 *The Investiture Disputes*. Historical Association, London
Tellenbach G 1970 *Church, State, and Christian Society at the Time of the Investiture Contest*. Humanities Press, New York
Tierney B 1964 *The Crisis of Church and State, 1050-1300*. Prentice-Hall, New York

GARRETT L. MCAINSH

# Confidence Building in International Diplomacy

Since wars begin in the minds of men, it is in the minds of men that the defenses of peace must be constructed. [Preamble to the Constitution of the United Nations Educational, Scientific, and Cultural Organization (UNESCO)]

Confidence building is an extension of diplomacy. It is a fundamental process; a prerequisite to the peaceful settlement of disputes. It is peacebuilding. This article aims to illustrate how in present-day international politics the true art of diplomacy has been lost and why a new and broader based diplomacy is required to overcome the misperceptions and prejudices which dominate political thinking and actions today.

Abba Eban, former Israeli Foreign Minister, has written (1983) that "there have been so many upheavals in the international system that diplomacy

reels under the shock of change. Negotiation, which used to be protected by privacy, is now exposed to public scrutiny." He goes on, "one result has been the erosion of the ambassadorial function." Gone are the days when US President Thomas Jefferson could remark to his Secretary of State that since they had not heard from their ambassador in Paris for two years they should consider writing him a letter if they still had not heard from him before another year had passed.

Ambassadors no longer enjoy the independence or have the initiative to act on their own experience in matters of major international relations. Telecommunications and the importance of national public opinion have bred a different style of diplomacy—"PR diplomacy." Traditional on-site diplomacy has been replaced by what the Secretary-General of NATO, Lord Carrington, once called "megaphone diplomacy"— the use of rhetoric, threats, propaganda, and the media to win hearts and minds. The art of diplomacy has become the art of expediency. No confidence building can be expected to flourish under such destabilizing conditions. What makes this form of summitry diplomacy so much more disquieting is that it is conducted by people who, when they come to office, are in the main inexperienced in international affairs or in the art of diplomatic negotiation.

Good international relations depend upon mutual trust and confidence, and these in turn can only be acquired if there is adequate communication. If trust and confidence are lacking and instead there are fear and distrust, the chances of peaceful coexistence become remote. The tensions and misunderstandings which as a result prevail create obstacles to communication and in themselves endanger peace. Weapons replace logic and lead to an upward spiral in military expenditure and growth and to the ultimate arms race in sophisticated weapons technology. Only by creating confidence will it be possible to halt the upward trend of the arms race and embark upon a process of de-escalation.

Diplomacy must be an act of communication. It is an exercise in "getting to yes," as Roger Fisher and William Ury explain in their book of the same title. The art of "getting to yes" in international negotiations is to start with those issues on which it is easiest to agree and to proceed from there, step by step. Dealing with the easier questions first makes discussion of succeeding issues easier because of the increased sense of confidence and rapport derived from the earlier exchanges. A firm base of understanding and objectivity has first to be established before approaching the more sensitive and complex problems which form the major obstacles to settling differences. However crucial these issues might be to the resolution of such differences, there is a better chance of their being resolved at a later rather than an earlier stage in the negotiations, when the necessary degree of confidence has been established.

It is unfortunate that with the erosion of ambassadorial influence the importance of diplomacy has been demoted. Instead we place our faith in nuclear weapons to provide US with security and peace. Many people believe that strength through armaments is the best negotiating tool and guarantee of peace and security. But many others believe that the build-up of armaments only increases insecurity and the likelihood of war. It was claimed that Europe had been at "peace" for 40 years because of the existence of the nuclear deterrent. If "peace" meant the absence of war then the statement could be accepted; but

peace means much more than that. It involves peaceful international relations, communication, interaction, and, above all, freedom from fear, distrust, tension, and threat. Peace is a state, not an act. It provides stability as well as security and peaceful coexistence between peoples. It is doubtful whether the world is any safer today than it was 50 years ago. The incidence of wars throughout the globe in the past 50 years is proof enough and refutes the claim that peace has prevailed throughout that time (see *Local Wars Since 1945*).

Peace will not come as a result of the single act of abolition of nuclear weapons. They are only the symptoms, not the causes, of international unrest. If the symptoms are to be effectively removed, the causes have to be resolved first. There therefore has to be a process of confidence building before positive disarmament agreements can be expected. This will require a peacebuilding process.

The acts of peacemaking and peacekeeping are usually recognized as being the two dimensions of the peaceful settlement of disputes—the one political, the other military. They provide the basis on which United Nations peace missions and operations are conducted. Yet the third dimension of peacebuilding—the rebuilding and restructuring of intercommunal and international relations—has rarely been attempted. Peacemaking and peacekeeping can have no lasting effect so long as the structural causes of a conflict remain unresolved.

Peacebuilding is by no means a purely political exercise in reconciliation. It needs the broadest possible base involving the whole spectrum of society. It requires a holistic approach reaching into every avenue of intersocial activity so that peoples rather than just governments are involved. International relations are rather like a jigsaw puzzle or a stained glass window. They have many components which, when pieced together, create the complete pattern.

Reconciliation is only possible if there is communication; so every opportunity to talk has to be taken. But there are two levels of talking, the formal negotiations on the one hand and the less formal dialogue and exchanges on the other. The former are the kind that take place in Geneva, Stockholm, and elsewhere—so far reaping little harvest—while the latter have been only spasmodically explored. Yet both are complementary. While the regular negotiations are concerned with defining and agreeing treaties, a wide range of initiatives across the breadth of international interests can help to ease the rigidity (and remove the obstacles) which halt progress at the negotiating table. Every communicating door should be opened and be kept open. Extraneous and controversial issues, however pertinent, should not be allowed to divert attention away from the peacebuilding process and better international understanding. The right kind of diplomacy is going to be required, and it has to be formulated on the philosophy of "getting to yes."

But the initiatives at governmental and ministerial level are only a part of the peacebuilding, confidence-building process. They are the most important because in the final analysis it is at that level that the decisions will have to be taken and agreements reached. However, a significant contribution to their ultimate success can be made by ordinary people undertaking their own confidence-building initiatives, sometimes described as "people's diplomacy" or "people's détente."

The Final Act of the Helsinki Accord (1975) sets out a blueprint for the kind of initiatives which can be taken to improve international relations. One part of the document, known as Basket 3, deals specifically with confidence building. Baskets 2 and 3 contain a catalogue of proposals for cooperation in humanitarian and other fields, among them:

(a) inter-travel between states with improvements in conditions for tourism on an individual or collective basis;

(b) meetings among young people with increased exchanges and contacts involving working, training, and learning together;

(c) expansion of sporting links;

(d) improvement in the general cooperation within the field of information, including films and broadcasting, and in the media generally;

(e) extending the opportunities for cooperation and exchanges in the fields of culture, arts, literature and education;

(f) the furtherance of access and contact between competent bodies and enterprises, specialists in all fields of common interest, including joint studies; and finally, but not least,

(g) the proposals stress the importance of exchanges which encourage youth and adults to work together on "those major problems of mankind whose solution calls for a common approach and wider international cooperation."

The Final Act provides the motivation and the guidance for people's diplomacy. (But the Helsinki Accord does not stand alone on confidence building. The two UN Special Sessions on Disarmament (1978/82) addressed the subject, and in Article 93 of the Final Statement emphasis is placed on the fact that "commitment to confidence building measures could significantly contribute to preparing for further progress in disarmament.")

People's diplomacy or détente—call it what you will—is the essence of the Helsinki Accord. There is no limit to its potential, and it involves professionals, technologists, artists, business personnel, and many common interest groups. Young people particularly have a prominent role in this diplomacy. But to be positive and constructive, all such contacts must involve interaction so that it is the "doing" as well as the "speaking" together which can promote the understanding and trust.

Contacts such as those outlined in the Helsinki Accord have existed over a long period, but it is only recently that they have come to be linked with international confidence building. The International Physicians for the Prevention of Nuclear War (1985 Nobel Peace Prize Winners) in 1981 united East and West European doctors in a public warning against the immediate and long-term results of nuclear war (see Nobel Peace Prize Laureates: *International Physicians for Prevention of Nuclear War (IPPNW)*). An example has already been set by a small group of British psychologists who, jointly with the Hungarian Peto Institute for the Motor Disabled, were promoting an in-depth analysis of the Institute's program of treatment for brain-damaged victims, particularly children suffering from spina bifida. Yet the Peto Institute records a 78 percent success rate in patients learning to cope with their disabilities in their homes and at work. By working together this initiative could bring hope to many millions of sufferers from spasticity, multiple sclerosis, Parkinson's Disease, and so on. This may seem a far cry from international diplomacy, but the initiative falls within the parameters of the Helsinki Accord and can contribute to the confidence-building process.

A stable and secure Europe means a more stable and secure world; but it will require a comparable peacebuilding effort to create the necessary confidence and cooperation in North-South and South-South relations.

The Brandt (1979) and Palme (1982) Commissions set out blueprints for what is required to provide economic and social stability and common security respectively for the Third World. Insufficient attention has been paid to their recommendations; yet they provide the only in-depth examination of the problems. The industrial nations need to abandon their policies of exploitation, self-interest, and "knowing what is best" for the underdeveloped countries. Instead, these countries should be encouraged to forge their own collective security structures with their neighboring states, based on social and economic arrangements, a sharing of responsibility, and common interest cooperation. Peacebuilding founded on relationships of this kind would reduce the dependency of those countries upon weapons and armed forces for their security and stability.

So it is that world peace and security will ultimately depend not so much on nuclear arsenals and deterrence policies of states than on the initiatives and efforts of governments and people in creating confidence in international relations. This will require a change of attitude by governments towards the capacity of ordinary people to play a role in building peace, and a willingness to devolve to them the responsibility to assume such a role. Much greater use should be made of the wide experience of those who have both the potential and specialist knowledge to make a major contribution in all aspects of international relations and understanding. At the same time this requires a realization on the part of such people that by interacting together they have an added responsibility to use the opportunities so presented to further the confidence-building process.

Much greater use should also be made of new opportunities for transglobal communication through satellite link-ups. The United States has led the way with televised rock concerts, discussion programs, and joint productions of peace musicals, like "Peace Child," which united young people from Minneapolis and Moscow in a joint TV presentation.

The process of confidence building is also one of mutual learning. Unless we are prepared to learn from every culture—whether "developed" or "undeveloped"—the peacebuilding effort is likely to fall on barren ground.

Peace is everybody's business, and whether it is built in the council chambers and corridors of the United Nations, or in the cabinets of governments, or whether it develops from a people's diplomacy, it is a holistic commitment for everyone. New perceptions and perspectives of international understanding are needed at all levels if a confidence is to be generated which will create a new basis on which the "defenses of peace can be constructed."

Martin Luther King, in a Christmas message, said, "No individual can live alone; no nation can live alone, and as long as we try, the more we are going to have war in this world . . . . We must either learn to live together as brothers or we are all going to perish together as fools." Three thousand years earlier, King Soloman had written, "Men live in the constant warfare of ignorance and call this monstrous evil Peace."

Both messages deserve careful consideration.

See also: *Problem Solving in Internationalised Conflicts*

*Bibliography* ———————————

Brandt Commission 1979 *North-South: A Programme for Survival*. Pan Books, London
Broinowski A (ed.) 1982 *Understanding ASEAN*. Macmillan, London
Burnett A 1985 Propaganda cartography. In: Pepper D, Jenkins A (eds.) 1985 *The Geography of Peace and War*. Basil Blackwell, Oxford.
Ebab A 1983 *International Diplomacy: International Affairs in the Modern Age*. Weidenfeld and Nicholson, London
Fisher R, Ury W 1982 Getting to Yes. Hutchinson, London
Foell E, Nenneman R (eds.) 1986 *How Peace Came to the World*. MIT Press, Cambridge, Massachusetts
Garrison J, Shivpuri P 1983 *The Russian Threat: Its Myths and Realities*. Galway Books, London
Mueller R 1982 *New Genesis*. Doubleday, New York
Palme Commission 1982 *Common Security: A Programme for Disarmament*. Pan Books, London
Prins G 1984 *The Choice: Nuclear Weapons versus Security*. Chatto and Windus, London

MICHAEL HARBOTTLE

# Conflict and Peace: Class versus Structural School

## 1. Introduction

While peace is the essential condition for *maintenance development*, conflict may be necessary for, either, *accelerated developmental change*, or *retreat* from the maintenance development. Peace can be of both *positive* and *negative* type, and conflict also can be of nonviolent and violent characters. *Positive peace* leads to progressive or revolutionary change, but *negative peace* accepts the situation of class and structural violence, with certain reforms, in a negotiated way (see *Positive versus Negative Peace*). Nonviolent conflict accepts the existing situation of class and structural inequality and inequity in the interest of the *maintenance-progress*, while violent conflict opts for radical or regressive change, depending on the character and strength of the participating actors.

The class concept of peace is based on the Marxian concept of dialectical and historical materialism (see *Marxist-Leninist Concepts of Peace and Peaceful Coexistence*). The structural concept of peace, which is still in the course of formation and consolidation, is based on the Nordic and Western abstract and analytical framework of structural violence, injustice, behaviour, etc., initiated, mainly, by Johan Galtung.

On the concept of peace and conflict, there exist dogmatic, pragmatic and neo-leftist interpretations among the Marxists of the socialist establishments, i.e., of the socialist societies, and those of the non-socialist societies. There also appeared the liberal and neo-liberal interpretations within the structural school of conflict and conflict have become more peace-publicist than peace-analyst. The non-establishment Marxists, i.e., the Marxists of the non-socialist world, engage more in conflict and peace actions than in conflict and peace theories and research. The exponents of the structural school, because of structural pressure of the juridical and economic sanctions type, confined themselves to conflict and peace research as well as education of an abstract nature, doing away with peace actions and, therefore, efforts for structural and social change. So, there is a lack of inter-relation and coordination between and among them, not only from the view of concept, but also from the standpoint of understanding and action.

This paper proposes to deal only with the conceptual differences and contradictions between the class school and the structural school, regarding conflict formation and peace attainment, and different aspects as well as their prospects. Again, both the concepts of conflict and peace treated here, refer to *social conflict* and *social peace*, which affect and concern society's life, social condition, social process and society's march, in general. *Armed conflict*, with the exception of revolution, and *peace under the arms race, arms preparation and under the umbrella of arms*, have their genesis in power-rivalries, system-rivalries, hunger for geo-political territory, hunger for sources of basic and strategic raw materials; tribal, religious, linguistic and cultural rivalries; big power chauvinism, hegemonistic and arrogant actions, etc. Of course, they do have negative social consequences for the loser nations, but the negative consequences of social conflicts and contradictions are long-standing and far-reaching which slowly poison the oppressed social classes, strata, groups, etc. *Peace under the umbrella of arms and super-powers, is a peace with nerve-breaking tension*, and so it cannot assure *peace for progress* for a nation concerned. Social peace, under the conditions of dynamic and dialectical process, and horizontalised action of both the mobilisational and participatory functions of all the members of the society, can assure the achievement of the desired social goals.

## 2. Origin and Process: From Conflict to Peace

Conflict is generated from the time and space-gap between two or more differing social processes, interests, systems, trends, etc. Each participating actor in a conflict tries to prove and attain its superiority and rightfulness over the other or others, in logic and fact, theory and empirical analysis, ideology and action (see *Conflict Formation, Elements in*). Peace is the outcome or end-result of the conflict or

**Figure 1**
Inter-relations between conflict and peace

| *Problems/Realities/ Causes for Conflicts/ Contradictions* | *Means for Solution* | *Goals/End/Resulting Peace* |
|---|---|---|
| Conflicts of | | |
| a) Class-interest: | Nonviolent, or | Negative peace, or |
| b) Strata or struc- | negotiated | acceptance of class or |
| ture-interest: | Violent: | structural violence |
| | a) Revolutionary, or self-generated | Positive, or attained peace |
| | b) Reactionary or suppressed | Imposed peace, or negative peace |

conflicts, attained, either, through action, or, through superiority of the causes (see *Theoretical Traditions of Peace and Conflict Studies*). Before going into a deeper analysis on both conflict formation and peace-attainment; I would like to produce a diagram here showing the relation and process, from conflict to peace (see figure 1).

The Marxists believe that conflicts and contradictions come from the differences in class and social interest and they get consolidated through ideology and action. The structuralists believe that conflicts and contradictions arise because of structural violence effected by the social elite or social top-dogs on the rest of the social strata or social under-dogs. They also believe that the elite (the decision-maker for the entire society), has excessively centralised the decision-making and operational functions of the sociey, for its own interest of power and privilege. That is why the structurally-dominated and oppressed strata struggle for the decentralisation of the participation in and implementation of actions, which can do away with structural violence (see *Structural Violence and the Definition of Conflict*). The class-interest concept is a broad one, while the strata-interest concept is more particular and limited, whose origin lies within the class concept. Which *special stratum* has appeared in each of the capitalist or industrial-commercial-financial bourgeois class, feudal and semi-feudal class, working class and the peasantry, in the last fifty years, controls and guides both the productive and distributive, participatory and mobilisational, and controlling and guiding functions within every class. If we consider the class concept as the macro-concept, the strata or the structural concept is the micro concept. The main-actors of conflicts and contradictions under the class concept are the "Haves" or the dominant classes, and the "Have-nots" or the proletariat. The actors of the conflicts and contradictions under the structural concept are the "More-haves" and the "Less-haves."

The conflicts and contradictions of class interest cannot be solved in a negotiated way or a nonviolent way, or under the condition of peaceful co-existence between and among classes. Hence, the means for solution towards attaining classlessness or equality and equity is revolutionary violence. If the revolutionary mass-forces win over the reactionary forces, we can term that stage as *Positive* or *Attained Peace*. If the reactionary forces win over the progressive forces and a status quo situation can be arrived at, we can term it as *Negative Peace or Imposed Peace*.

The exponents of the structural school opts for nonviolent or negotiated means as a way or solution to reach to the goal of social peace. But, peace obtained through nonviolence and negotiation cannot remove the structural inequalities, injustice and violence. Therefore, it is *Negative Peace* which recognizes and accepts structural violence, and under such a type of peace, the social elite and the techno-bureaucrat strata accumulate the economic, political and military power to maintain the so-called "stable" or "stabilised" peace in the society (see *Peace Theory: An Introduction*).

Absence of war and war-like tensions, social tensions, direct exploitation, *direct* violence, structural violence of the nature of inequity and inequality, direct dominance, direct negation of autonomy, and self-reliant and self-sustained development of a region, nation or individual fall within the category and boundary of negative peace. There are *indirect* violence, exploitation, dominance and negation of self-determination, whose malicious and mal-effects are tremendous on the society and the social beings. If these *indirect and negative* aspects are not completely eradicated, one cannot see how positive peace can appear. *Positive Peace* can be achieved only through a dynamic process of societal and human development, in which the society is to be understood as the collectivity of social members of equal rights and duties, and a social individual is to be understood as an integral part of the whole social collectivity, not an ego-centric one. A *horizontal* social and human development, on the basis of appropriate and equivalent correlation, is the goal of positive social change under the condition of positive peace. Poverty, hunger, malnutrition, untimely death, poor health, ignorance, etc., which are the fundamental problems facing the mankind in a vast part of our globe, need an earlier attention for a solution towards achieving positive and dynamic peace. They constitute the fundamental social needs; and the peace researchers, educators and the activists of the South are putting more accent on these aspects and issues (see *Human Security*). The Marxists of the socialist establishments have centered their efforts *around the economic aspects* of these fundamental problems, and contend that the model of "development from above" for both the production and distribution will solve the problems. Running after the development model of the Western growth-economy, the Marxists of the socialist establishments try to find a solution to the above basic problems, within their own societies, on the basis of *growing consumerism*. The Western peace researchers and activists, generally, ran away from these fundamental human problems and instead, concentrated on the aspects of studies on the nature of non-fundamental needs like: free flow of ideas, right to impression and expression, political and economic right to travel, and some other aspects like psychological and cultural problems at cross and multi-national levels, international relations, arms control and disarmament, theories on super-powers, organizational and functional behaviour of the international governmental and nongovernmental organisations including the United Nations, and future studies and the prognosis of the world's future after the year 2000 (see *Future of Humanity*). It seems to be very paradoxical to think of a solution to problems which do not concern the life and living of two-thirds of the population of the globe whose basic needs are not yet satisfied. The research on and the action for the future is good, but what about the action and work on the problems of the present?

*Class struggle*, in the first instance, leads to system change, and then gradually to social change. But the social change takes a longer course and period after the system change caused by social revolution. In this course and process, there take place the birth and growth of *structural strata* within the post-revolution societies. This very creation of social strata can be observed from:

(a) the created bureaucracy and technocracy at the administration and party level,

(b) the special social groups, privileged in respect of possession of power for production, distribution and consumption functions of the society, and

(c) the framing-up of subjective, and restrictive measures for control and guidance, in the name of the interest of the proletariat or the working masses.

The post-revolutionary activities in a society is to proceed through a correlated action of both ideological and of socio-economic development. If the ideological action gets the upper hand over socioeconomic developmental action, it will lead to social dissatisfaction and conflict. On the other hand, if the action of socio-economic development proceeds ahead of the ideological action and development it will fall victim to the window-display of the Western consumers' society. It can generate counter-conflict. The socialist societies of today, including China, are the examples of this trap. The imbalance between the two can lead either to counter-revolution or cultural revolution. While counter-revolution can lead a society several steps backward, re-revolution can correct the mistakes and put it to proper direction, or even, one step forward.

*Class harmony* is the basic ideology of *Nonviolence*. The ideology of nonviolence promotes the ideas and actions of *voluntary change of hearts* of the people belonging to different social classes within the same social structure towards reduction of exploitation and tension, establishment of social justice, reduction of inequality, and wider expansion of human rights (see *Nonviolence, Philosophy and Politics of*). These changes are meant to occur under the conditions of peaceful co-existence. But peaceful co-existence among different social classes and social strata cannot give birth to classlessness or stratalessness, end of exploitation and social inequality, and change in the class and strata behaviour and action. Nonviolent change of state power in 1947 and nonviolent social action since then in India, did not help the end of exploitation and corruption. On the contrary, the preachings of nonviolence by all types of Gandhians in the country, helped the *consolidation* of the national bourgeoisie as a class in India, which was still at the stage of formation during the pre-independence days. Nonviolence or negative peace, also, does not help the abolition of the existing production relation which in the course of time becomes conservative and old, and establishment of the new production relation (see *Nonviolence*).

### 3. West-East and North-South Conflict Situations and Peace Efforts

Economic factors, whether in the gaining or in the losing side, are the fundamental reasons of social contradictions and conflicts. Economic rectification of these conflicts and contradictions, through revolutionary means in the positive interest of the masses or the social majority, is the prime objective of social peace. This very true finding of the Marxist analysts can also be shared by the structuralists. So the conflict situation and peace efforts between the West and the East, apart from the confrontation of ideology and system-arguments, are based, in the ultimate analysis, on economic factors. The same analysis between the North and the South, based on the grounds of affluence and deprivation, over-consumption and under-consumption, neo-colonisation and neo-proletarisation, are also attributable to economic factors (see *North-South Conflict*).

Apart from the ideology and system differentiation, with both the goals and means, the main ground of conflict between the West and the East is centered around the gap of technology, the sources for procurement of raw materials, and the medium of distribution: whether on the basis of purchasing power or fundamental human needs. The conflict between the North and the South is a conflict between the combined power of capital and technology, and supply of raw materials as well as cheaper labour in some cases. The efforts of the *det'ente*, the New International Economic Order, or other types of international orders can produce only temporary compromises, understandings and *peace-like* atmosphere, but not a positive peace (see *New International Economic Order (NIEO)*). Until and unless the gaps mentioned above, between both the West and the East, and the North and the South are removed through dynamic actions of mutual *equal* interdependence, no one can talk of a genuine peace. But as long as the technology will be handled as private property and means of exploitation, instead of social property and means of satisfying the social needs of the entire mankind, both the capital and technology will continue to be over-valued against the continuous under-valuation of raw materials and labour, and the conflicts and contradictions at the West-East and the North-South levels will not cease.

While "divide and rule" has been the pronounced policy of some of the industrially developed countries of the North towards the South, most of the economically under-developed nations of the South became entrapped in it, either for extreme nationalism and tribalism or territorial hunger. So, the South became a market of arms for the North which developed and develops further arms technology and production of arms (see *Maldevelopment*). While millions in the South suffer from starvation, malnutrition and untimely death, its elite, the decision-maker, spends millions of national currency for arms purchase. Its social effect is very negative, naturally. Again, as the North does not *generally* sell the arms technology to the South, there is a latent conflict developing between the arms technology-possessor North and the arms and arms technology-needy South.

The United States, in its recent effort for peace in the Middle-East, is contributing much towards the concept of "*Imposed Peace*." The right to a state for the Palestinians, which was a major point in the Arab-Israeli confrontation and the Egyptian-Israeli war, has totally been sacrificed. Instead, the United States imposed a peace on both Egypt and Israel, with a 15 billion dollar credit for sale of US arms and finished industrial products as well as foodstuffs. In essence, it is nothing but a *forward commerce* for the United States, as a result of which the American arms industry and other processing industries could get assurance for a market in the future, particularly at a crucial point of economic crisis, manifested by rising unemployment, inflation, and social unrest. So, the meaning of this "pax Romana" is the expansion of

market for the United States, and we can also say that the lost market in Iran is regained in Egypt and Israel.

*Imposed peace* is the peace mentioned above, pressed by either a non-actor or an indirect actor on the two or more direct actors in the conflict. Only the decision-makers of the actor-nations and non-actor nation or nations enjoy participatory functions here, while the masses are obliged to accept the decisions. Under such sort of peace the conflicts as well as the conflict situations remain latent. Like structural violence, we can also see *Structural Peace*, when it is reached through *adjustment of interest, compromise, concession, mild reforms at different stages of intra-nation levels*. The scope of conflict in the future remains hidden or disguised at all levels of structural peace. *The main root of present-day conflict lies in the fact that the goals of development and all other related concerns have been transferred from the human-actors to the non-human actors, from the problems of masses to other areas.*

## 4. Marxist and Non-Marxist Interpretation of Conflict and Peace under Peaceful Co-existence

There exist differences which make conflicts and contradictions among the world nations in respect of socio-economic system, level of socio-economic development, consciousness development, mode of life, culture and heritage, etc., more or less *continuous* by nature. They coexist, their process is continuous, and so they tolerate each other in their inter-relations of today, regarding the behavioural aspects. That is why there appeared the conceptual elements like *peaceful co-existence, peaceful competition* at inter-system and intra-system levels. Thus *the situation of peaceful co-existence is the situation at the level of conflicts and contradictions*. According to dialectical analysis, there cannot be peaceful co-existence between two opposites, between two conflicting processes, or between two contradictory elements. The process of struggle between these two types of contraries continues for a longer time until *the new* appears. This time-factor can be regarded as the factor or period of *co-existence within the conflict situation* (see *Peaceful Coexistence*). Its defect is that it does not sharpen the class struggle, system struggle and the struggle of contradictions. The US-USSR relationship of the last decades and the recent Sino-United States relationship affirm this statement. There had been explanations from the acting parties regarding their *slow-going process or action with low tension-maintenance*. The explanations of *strategies and tactics* are very often, brought into picture here. It is argued that *the goals and strategies* remain unchanged while the *means and tactics* differ and get modified according to the tridimensional objectivity: the *situation*, need of *time* and adaptable capacity of the *space*. But no one can deny that the *tactics and the means* to reach the goals, under continuous changes and modifications, can exercise effects on the *strategies* and even on the goals. Thus takes place convergence, while convergence, in its turn, avoids *annihilation and struggle* on the one hand, and embraces *assimilation* on the other. Under the condition of convergence, *peace* becomes *outwardly pronounced* and *conflict* remains *hidden*. At the stage of peaceful co-existence, the course of *material development* in both the systems is best assured. But what about human development then? The production and distribution of needs and non-needs satisfying goods and services improve, undoubtedly, during this period, but certainly not the ideological and consciousness levels of the masses. Many times two fundamental questions were raised: (a) Does a man eat to live or live to eat? and (b) Does ideology remove poverty or poverty-situation enriches ideology? Conflicts and contradictions had and have always been present in both the above situations, and, there has never appeared a *balanced relation* between the two. Of course, under the *conditions of dialectics*, the idea of balance or equivalence does not arise.

There has always been discussion that the Marxists center research and developmental activities around *material conflict* and material peace. Perhaps, it is true to some extent. The Marxist ideology believes that the *non-material conflicts and peace* are very abstract, while mental conflict and mental peace owe their origin to *material poverty and material happiness*, in general. There has also been overdevelopment and over-fulfillment of the material needs generate oversaturation, which ultimately leads to decadence. Decadence from the condition of material peace tries to find out solution in the non-material aspects. But it is not the failure of Marxism to analyze these aspects and find out solution. The problem lies within the over-development and over-consumption. So, why over-development, over-consumption and over-saturation? The morality of the material content of a thing or a situation is that it tries to maintain the continuous consciousness-formation about the respective thing or the situation as well as the society. The members of the society who act on the matter or situation are to process or transform the matter or the situation in such a way as not to go beyond the normal needs-satisfaction at the sufficiency level. If this development process or transformation goes beyond

the broad social interest, it generates overdevelopment and oversufficiency, which may also be termed as maldevelopment and maldigestion. So, peace formation demands elimination of the polarisation tendency of overdevelopment over underdevelopment, otherwise the deepening of crisis and contradiction between the overdeveloped societies and the underdeveloped societies cannot be avoided.

To determine the inter- and intra-societal conflicts, the sociologists of different ideologies, in various countries, have started finding out reasons as such:

(a) Marxists: in chauvinism, hegemonism, social imperialism, etc., at big nation, small nation, and national majority, and national minority levels. Revisionism and dogmatism are also two other main causes.

(b) Western Liberals: in dominance-dependence relationship at superpower-dominated nations level, in top-dog-under-dog relationship at social structure, and centre-periphery relationship at world structure levels.

(c) Latin American Sociologists and Economists: in the built-up structure of dependency (dependencia in Spanish) relationship.

(d) Afro-Asian Sociologists and Economists: in the structural violence caused by unequal exchange based on the over-valuation of capital and technology, i.e., the result of the past labour, as against the undervaluation of raw materials and labour, i.e., the creation and source of the present labour. Unequal human relationship is also another reason.

There exist both truth and exaggeration in all the above approaches as well as findings. But all these findings lead to one essence, that of dominance and dependence.

In theory-building or concept-formation on both conflict and peace, we generally face two very distinctive approaches: (a) Functional Approach and (b) Psychological Approach. While the functional approach deals with the *practical problems* of conflict and peace, the psychological approach gives only intellectual pleasure. The function of the structural bureaucracy consists of the *maintenance of conflict at present with efforts and promises for peace in the future*. Within the functional approach, the believers of a class concept are again divided into two groups: (i) one group believes in the achievement of social change through slow process or *peaceful co-existence*, which in practice is similar to *evolutionary revolution* and (ii) the other group opts for obtaining social change through quick process of *revolutionary violence*. This is the present-day global situation, in which *conflict maintenance* has become a function of the politicians as well as the national and international bureaucracy, while *conflict solution* has become an option for the common masses (see *Evolutionary Movement Toward Peace*).

## 5. Ideology of Conflict and Peace

Social conflicts and contradictions help the development of social and ideological consciousness. A social individual, as a member of the society and as a participant-actor in the social conflicts and contradictions, becomes aware of his own situation of the social class to which he belongs and of the problems which concern him and his own class and strata. On the basis of this awareness, the respective social classes or strata determine their strategies and tactics of action within the social process and revolution.

If we consider peace as positive, it is *not passive*. The main characteristics of positive peace are its 'dynamicity' and 'dialecticity.' Positive peace presupposes the action of continuous process in which the old disappears making room for the new, conservatism is replaced by progressivism, and old and obsolete values are replaced by the new and timely necessary values. While social process is continuous, the process of peace and its action are also continuous. And within the course of process and action, the values of peace are verified and modified with the need and urge of both time and space (see *Peaceful Societies*).

Conflict generates from the gap (a) *between and among goals,* (b) *between and among means,* and (c) *between and among goals and means.* Within this tri-dimension, the values also differ. Good and bad are two very simple and moralistic words to characterize the qualities of values. Values in conflict and in peace can be of *material and moral*, socially *fundamental* and socially *non-fundamental*, self-created and externally-imposed, and dominance and self-determination types. These values guide the main areas of conflict and peace ideology.

It is an interdisciplinary subject and so we prefer to term it as the science of sciences, whose main goal is to serve the humankind, to assure human development and to channelise all the activities in the human interest. The science of conflict and peace also intends to establish an ecological balance in the developmental relation between man and nature. Mankind of today, with better and highly developed conscience, started understanding that unless the *man-nature* relationship proceeds *in the horizontal level and direction*, we cannot avoid the catastrophical effects of both the over-development and under-development, wastage and under-subsistence, and affluence and poverty. Men of science from sociology, economics, political science, philosophy, psychology, biology, physics, chemistry, mathematics, medicine, anthropology, ecology, etc., are now actively engaged in peace research and peace action, in order to find out the proper solution for Man's Development and Man's Future.

The combined topic of conflict and peace research is still in the stage of interpretation at the conceptual level. Serious research efforts started exactly three decades ago. Because of its interdisciplinary character it covers a wide range and variety of subjects. So the theory-building on this topic is not a very easy task, and at the same time, there cannot be any unique or uni-directional theory on conflict and peace problems. Some conceptual, modelic and empirically analytical works have already been accomplished in different parts of the world starting from Japan to Canada and Argentina and covering the countries from Northern Europe to Australia. There appeared many approaches, out of which the following are important ones:

(a) The Social Justice Approach of Northern and Western Europe and North America, with Johan Galtung as the pioneer.

(b) Third World Self-Reliant and Self-identification Approach.

(c) Disarmament, Action and Arms Race Reduction Approach of the World Peace Council and its Affiliated National Peace Councils.

(d) Peace through Nonviolence Approach of the Indian Gandhians as well as the Indian and Western Neo-Gandhians.

(e) Social Change and Peace through Social Revolution Approach of the Marxist-Leninists.

At this stage, we can simply say: Let hundred conceptual frameworks appear and get improved, let thousands participate in and verify them with problems and realities.

I have presented here some critical and comparative elements towards the conceptual framework on conflict and peace, particularly of the structural and class schools of thought. With the solution of some conflicts, the newer conflicts appear, and so the mode of analysis and solution also differs from those of the former conflicts. So, it is a continuous process in which newer elements try to improve it with newer elements, or put forward new concepts for new solutions. Therefore, it will be absurd to try to draw any definite conclusion here.

See also: *Theoretical Traditions of Peace and Conflict Studies; Conflict: Inherent and Contingent Theories; Perpetual Peace; Socialism and Peace; Social Conflicts and Peace; Social Progress and Human Survival; Conflict Formation, Elements in*

AMALENDU GUHA

# Conflict Formation, Elements in

## 1. Introduction

Conflict is the result of both the gap and contradiction between two and among various social processes, components, tendencies, and interests. Conflicts are generated both in time and in space, and may be of various characters—like national, international, social, economic, political, cultural, and class strata. When a conflict refers to the time factor, it means a struggle between the New and the Old aimed at finding out the most appropriate solution in favour of each. When it refers to the space factor, it manifests itself in finding out a proper action or a process to be followed in order to establish the superiority of the system, law, or an action of one geo-political territory over the other. Social conflicts manifest themselves in the struggle between two or among various contradictory social interests, ideas, rules, and processes of both the antagonistic and non-antagonistic nature (see *Social Conflicts and Peace*). At the territorial and systems levels, there appear, now and then, contradictions and conflicts of the nature of chauvinism or hegemonism. Imposition of the relationship of both dominance and dependence sows the seeds of conflict. At the systems level, conflicts are of fundamental nature, in which each tries either to establish or to defend its superiority or supremacy over the other (see *Peace, Systems View of*). Conflicts of non-fundamental nature, sometimes, may seek to find solution of a conformist nature. At the societal level, the Marxists find the root of social conflicts in the structure of class; but the structural school argues that the root of social differentiation and hence of conflict lies in the establishment and maintenance of structural violence and centre-periphery relationship, both at the social and geo-political levels. The Marxists propose class struggle as the means of resolution of conflicts and contradictions, while the structuralists believe mainly in the negotiated solutions among different social strata (see *Conflict and Peace: Class versus Structural School*).

Among the Marxists also, there exist differences as regards the means of finding solution for social conflicts in spite of the fact that there exists a fairly strong uniformity about the goals. The East European socialist system and China and the Euro-Communists of West Europe used to accept the condition of peaceful co-existence at the level of their own society as the best strategy and tactics for achieving social goals. The Marxists in the socially, politically, and economically oppressed societies believe and act on the theory of class struggle. Marx's approach of class struggle in order to undo socio-economic injustice was based on the idea of annihilation of the class enemies by the proletariat. The ideological content of peaceful co-existence was first proposed and discussed at the Bandung Conference of the Afro-Asian nations in 1955, in which Chou En-lai, with Mao's guidance and blessings, took an active part (see *Peaceful Coexistence*). Later, Khrushchev, Brezhnev, and several party leaders and State leaders of East Europe embraced it as the most suitable condition, applicable both at the inter-nation and intra-nation levels. The theory of peaceful coexistence, both directly and indirectly, embodies the principle of assimilation. Assimilation, at the level of inter- and intra-classes, leads to liberalism and reformism.

The Marxists of the less-developed countries, who are involved in a national liberation movement against semi-colonialism, neo-colonialism, and military dictatorship, believe in the Marxian theory of class struggle as the means to resolve social conflicts. The Marxists of the established socialist societies prefer and accept the condition of peaceful co-existence as the basis of socio-economic order, both at the intra-nation and inter-nation levels. The Marxists in the developed countries and in the national bourgeois democracies, who are trying to capture State power, either solely or in coalition with some other political parties, opt for peaceful co-existence with different social classes of different interests, because the very existence of social peace can assure the very desired condition of parliamentary democracy. The believers in the process of peaceful co-existence and the theory of assimilation argue on the time and space factors of the dimensions of the dialectical system. The Establishment communists of the East European and other socialist countries used to argue that class struggle was essential and valid only at the time of revolution and that peaceful co-existence is necessary at the time of construction and development after the social revolution in any country (see *Socialism and Peace*). But the question is: Can a society solve the conflicts between and among classes and strata in a few years after a revolution? Certainly not, as it is a long process and, perhaps that is why we feel the necessity of a permanent revolution. It is very difficult to draw a line of demarcation between the antagonistic contradictions and the non-antagonistic contradictions. With the solution of the old conflicts and contradictions, the new conflicts and contradictions arise, and their nature, even in the case of a socialist country, cannot be called non-antagonistic. The emergence of a classless and a strataless society does not take place in a short span of time. It needs a long process, a long experiment, and a long time. The situation of the proletariat or the oppressed people is almost the same in all the countries belonging to the non-socialist system. So is the relation of contradictions and conflicts between and among classes and social strata. The nature of class conflicts and structural exploitation and their solution in each country depends on the specific objective situation obtaining in that country (see *Social Conflicts and Peace*). Therefore, the historical materialists leave the whole problem and issue of the treatment of social conflicts and revolution in the hands of the exploited people of the country under question on the ground that revolution and the resolution of social conflicts cannot be exported. The dialectical materialists nullify the above argument on the ground of passivity in attitude and action on the part of the historical materialists and some of the established socialist countries. There is always an organic relationship between the dialectical materialism and historical materialism. This aspect needs a little more practical attention, application, and verification.

The dimensions of conflict are vast and so are the elements contributing to conflict formation and conflict theory (see *Evolutionary Movement Toward Peace*). In this paper we propose to deal with only the following elements which generate conflicts.

## 2. Subjective/Objective Elements

Subjective elements are self- or ego-centered and do not take into account the objective situation and surroundings. The objective elements are realistic and their origin lies in a specific situation. In a society in which the social minority consisting of the social majority of the working class and the peasantry because of ownership and control of the power mechanism and the means of production, we can simply say that these are the very subjective elements constituting the causes of conflicts. When the exploited and deprived classes and the peripheries prepare themselves for resistance and offensive measures to undo the damage caused by the subjective elements, we may call them objective elements. In the sphere of social affairs, the suppression of tolerance-resistance relationship does not always come from the *majority-minority axis*. It may also generate from the *majority-minority axis*, particularly in the cases when (a) the majority tribes and castes suppress the rights and activities of the minority tribes and castes; (b) the majority language and culture groups oppress the development of languages, literature, culture, and tradition of the minority languages and culture groups; and (c) the majority religious groups oppress the maintenance and growth of the religious activities of the minority religious groups (see *Religion and Peace*).

Therefore, the determinants of the subjective and objective elements of a social reality depends on how far and how much they can interact or counteract on each other. While the interaction of the elements leads to some sort of adjustments, their counteraction leads to conflicts. Again, both the subjective and objective elements are relative, in respect of time and space, because of the *gap* in action of both the time and space in social development.

Coming back to the determinants of the elements of subjectivity and objectivity and their character of relativity, we may mention that if the social majority, say the combined forces and action of the working class and the peasantry, hinders the ego-centric and exploitative developmental activities of the social minority, say the alliance of the industrial and feudal bourgeoisie, the very act can be termed as the act of objectivism, and not of subjectivism (see *Neocolonialism*). The conflict between the *decision-makers* and the *decision-implementors*, which is of structural nature, in both the capitalist and the socialist societies, is also the conflict of subjective-objective category, because of the gap in the participatory function.

The subjective-objective elements in social action and education play an important role in the formation of social consciousness. Here the conflict is between "duty to the society" and "right from the society." Both can become either subjective or objective in their relationship at the level of the two main different socio-economic systems. The struggle for right in an exploitative society is objective and the compulsion to duty is subjective. The duty in a socialized society is objective by nature and struggle for an individual or special group privileges or right is of subjective nature. The contradiction between the right and the duty, at the intra-system level, has so far been of an antagonistic nature, because of its very vertical relationship. It can become of dialectical nature, provided a gradual horizontalized relationship of interaction between them could be established. The trade unions in the capitalist socio-economic system, which are mainly based on economism, do struggle mainly for a redressal of economic grievances of the working class and so concentrate their action on the economic front for economic rights. The trade unions of the socialist economic system are based on overdosed *socio-patriotism* and centre their activities around the fulfillment and over-fulfillment of social duties. At the inter-systems level, again, the relationship between the right-based economism and the duty-based socio-patriotism is of vertical nature and the way to solve this contrast and conflict is yet to be found.

## 3. Class/Structure Elements

Both class conflicts and structural conflicts are conflicts of interest. Class conflicts arise at the different historical stages of social formation and the structural conflicts appear in course of the formation and consolidation of Establishments. Classes are bigger groups of people in which one group or an alliance of two or more appropriate the labour and the result of labour of other groups, because of ownership of the means and ends of production and because of the control over the military and security mechanism for appropriation and its perpetuation.

The theory of social structure or social stratification is the theory introduced by the liberal sociologists of the West. This theory affirms that every society is stratified into several strata or layers, the determinants of which are such factors as the size of income, social prestige, and style of living; and through the process and action of social mobility some members of one social stratum can pass to the other social stratum. The nature of contradictions and conflicts among different social strata is of passive interaction and not of active counteraction. The stratification theory does not subscribe to a belief in the abolition of the society's division of classes, i.e., in the establishment of a classless society or a society of homogeneity.

Class conflicts lead to social revolution and social

revolution, in its turn, to a new mode of production after abolishing the old one, which in due course establishes new relations of production (see *Revolution*). The exploitation, both at the class and centre-periphery levels, has increased manifold and become acute in recent years in both the developed and the developing parts of the world. In spite of that, with the exception of a few Asian and African countries like Cambodia, Laos, Vietnam, Mozambique, Ethiopia, and Angola, there did not take place any social revolution. The main reasons for this are: (a) acquisition and concentration of enormous and sophisticated offensive and defensive military means by the class-in-power and power structure; (b) offering of occasional concessions, both of economic and political nature to the working class and the peasantry, in the form of wage-increase, minority participation in the management, production bonus, and concessional agrarian reforms; and (c) concentration of the trade union activities, i.e., the struggle of the working class only on economism which is only a temporary solution, rather than on social revolution which is a permanent solution.

In a capitalist economic system, both in the developed and the underdeveloped worlds, the intelligentsia has always played an important and decisive role in the class conflicts, both in its formation and in its reconciliation. At the stage of conflict formation, it took on the role of propaganda, agitation, and organization, while at some later stages, the role of compromise, and concession either in order to avoid social violence or to strengthen its own economic interests and consolidate the role of its leadership. Hence it has both the revolutionary and counterrevolutionary roles in conflict formation and conflict management. In the East-European socialist world, the intelligentsia is a social stratum which controls and guides both the mode and relation of production, very often holding a dominant position, since the model of social development in this world is a model of *development from above*, in which the goals and means of development of the entire society as well as its well-being are decided by the intelligentsia. Thus there also exist conflicts and contradictions between the intelligentsia on the one hand and the working class and the peasantry on the other. Because of a "disciplined" social order, these conflicts and contradictions remain disguised. In the under-developed capitalist world the peasantry has been reduced to a minority because of higher flux to other economic sectoral activities as a result of a higher degree of mechanization and rationalization of agriculture, and it is still the most sacrificing class for the establishment of socialism in the socialist world as it was in the past and does still contribute with high surplus products. The peasantry in the economically developed societies is a farming class which can dictate its terms to the working class and other social classes, as regards the supply and guidance of consumption of agricultural products, since the small peasantry, in course of time, has gradually disappeared. Because of a lower rate of development of industry and other socio-economic sectors, there could not take place a flux of population from the agrarian sector to these ones leaving the greater majority of population dependent on it. On the other hand, there did not take place the very desired radical agrarian reforms to horizontalise or socialise the ownership of land while the agriculture itself, did not receive much investment for its improvement. The marketing operational activities are also mostly left in the hands of the commercial bourgeoisie in this world. So it is the most exploited class in the developing societies and its scope of conflict with the national and comprador bourgeoisie is the most significant one. It will give rise to new conflict situations.

There also exist conflicts between the participatory and mobilizational functions and behaviour in the social development process. Because of the centralization action of the decision-making and the administrative power being concentrated in the hands of a few persons, function of the common masses is absent. The masses are mobilized in all the centralized systems. The masses have only the participatory function of implementing or fulfilling the decisions taken from above. The West did not talk of democratic centralism at all, but the East talked of its theoretical aspects very much while it has centralized the democracy in action in the name of dictatorship of the proletariat, though nobody knows how long this centralization process of dictatorship of the proletariat will continue. The leadership of the working class and the peasantry does not mean the concentration of all the socio-economic and political power in the hands of a few persons. The whole process is, therefore, verticalised and, when a few persons take all the decisions affecting all walks of a nation's life, it cannot be said that those very decisions contain the character of socio-objectivity. So there appears a gap between the subjective outlooks of the decision-makers and the objective reality of the decision-implementors. In the bourgeois democratic societies of the West, the contradiction between the mobilisers and the mobilized, between the decision-makers and the implementors, occasionally gives birth to open conflicts—but in the socialist societies of today the con-

tradiction under the same circumstances gives birth to only hidden conflicts (see *Marxist-Leninist Concepts of Peace and Peaceful Coexistence*).

Because of huge concentration of capital and technology, the developed capitalist centre could attain huge economic power during the last twenty years and this economic power enabled it to exercise control over the underdeveloped peripheries as well as over its own economic orbit. In this process of centre-periphery exploitative relationship the Multinational Corporations form the nerve-point or the centre of the Centre, which builds up the whole structure of the present-day economic imperialism, on which the consolidated former East European socialist systems and until recently self-reliant China have become dependent for advanced means of production and technology (see *Multinational Corporations and Peace*). The economic imperialism of today has succeeded in crossing the geo-political barriers through expansion of market in all the existing socio-economic systems. So the ideological and political contradictions between and among systems had to sacrifice themselves to economic conformism and confrontation had to submit to conciliation.

## 4. Dominance/Dependence Elements

Dominance and dependence had, since the abolition of the primitive egalitarian communal system and the emergence of the era of "right with the might," been the predominant elements of conflict formation and conflict theory. Dominance always has one character, that of imposition over others; but dependence has two specific characteristics: (a) imposed dependence, and (b) accepted dependence. Imposed dominance has always been excercised and pressed by the dominant actor or actors on the weaker actor or actors for the purpose of exploitation, control, and rule. Accepted dominance is the result of either (i) surrounding economic, political, or social circumstances which compel a certain territory, party, or actor to accept it; or (ii) incapability of own environment, sources and resources, of both the moral and material categories, of the same, to remain self-dependent or self-reliant.

Dominance, from the standpoint of class analysis, is the result of division of societies into antagonistic classes and is manifested in the exploitative relations of production, i.e., ownership over the means of production. Dominance, both at intra- and inter-national levels is the exercise of social, economic, political, and cultural power by the dominant classes over the dominated ones, by virtue of ownership over the means of production (see *Power*). This is, again exercised through legislative, executive, judicial, and military measures.

From the point of view of structural analysis, dominance is exercised through the means of structural imperialism which is the outcome of the centre's systematised exploitation and subjugation of the periphery through octopolistic and monopolistic multilateral activities of the multinational corporations, capitalist institutions, and capitalism-controlled international organisations, with the active assistance of the centre-states (see *Imperialism*).

At the analysis-level of the factors of production, we find acute contradiction between the owner of capital and technology on the one hand and supplier of raw material and labour on the other. In the capitalist economic system of today, the combined forces of capital and technology exercise dominance over both the raw material and labour. From the human and logical points of view, the prime objective and function of capital and technology, i.e., machinery and the results of research and development for improvement of the means of production is to (a) reduce the intensity of labour and make the function or use of labour in production much easier, and (b) effect the improved, economical, and rational use of raw materials towards product-improvement, and (c) production-maximization for satisfying the material needs of the society in the best way. So, in order to avoid the conflicting relationship between both the above groups of factors of production, their vertical relationship of dominance for extraction of maximum possible surplus values is to be gradually horizontalised. But the task is neither voluntary nor can be made easy.

In order to hide the exploitative and subjugative character of the dominance-dependence relationship, the proponents of the idea of a New International Economic Order started using the term "interdependence" which in its true sense should mean the reciprocal or mutual dependence on the basis of equality (see *New International Economic Order (NIEO)*). But this very type of interdependence cannot be found at present. What we come across now are either (a) positive, or (b) negative interdependence. It becomes positive for the gainer in the agreement and negative for the loser. More clearly, the interdependence becomes positive for one party in the contract which has controlling interest over the other contracting party or parties, and this controlling interest consists of: (a) obtaining of profit from the sale of processed and semi-processed products at maximum possible range and procurement of raw materials and other natural resources at the minimum possible price, i.e.,

at the under-valued price; (b) expansion of market for own products, means of production and technology, as well as military weapons; (c) enforcement of economic, political, social, and cultural dominance; (d) control and guidance of the means of transport and communication; and (e) control of, and infiltration into, the mass media, etc. (see *Interdependence, International*).

The negative interdependence is just opposite to it, which the dominated party in the contract has to accept. So, in essence, it does not change the contents of contradictions prevailing in the dominance-dependence relationship.

During the period of colonialism, the metropoles destroyed the bases of industry in the colonies; while they developed both the processing and semi-processing enterprises in their own territories. This action bound the colonies in *double dependency* to the metropoles: (i) once for *marketing* of the colonies' raw materials, and again, (ii) for *receipt* of finished and semi-finished products produced from their own raw materials, to satisfy their own societies' material needs. Now, with the abolition of colonialism, the *epoch of neo-colonialism* has started. The present-day multinational corporations and the oligopolies are using the same old type of exploitation in a much more refined and effective way. Double-dependency means the *double-dominance* for the dominant centre. The dependent periphery is twice drained of its resources: once through the sale of raw materials at the under-valued price, i.e., at a price below worth; and, then through the purchase of processed products, the purchase price of which includes surplus-values.

## 5. Penetration/Counter-penetration Elements

As the Cold War had been a slow-going, nerve-breaking, and strenuous process, so has been the process of penetration and counter-penetration. Infiltration into a society from outside and causing dislocation of the means and goals of its social life and own values is the prime function of penetration. If a society or a socio-economic system, with the motto of taking revenge for the penetration from another society or socio-economic system, counter-infiltrates into the former and creates disequilibrium in its socioeconomic and politico-cultural areas, we can term it as an act of counter-penetration. Both the penetrative and counter-penetrative actions can be either progressive or reactionary and active or passive. Their range of action is wide. Starting from the ideological field, as in the case of the Cold War, it can extend to the concrete level of naked and cruel intervention in the internal affairs, as in the case of the North-South Dialogue (see *North-South Conflict*).

When, on the request of the progressive social forces of an oppressed and bourgeoisie-dominated country, an active political and ideological penetration from the progressive forces of another country takes place, one can characterize this type of penetration as objective and progressive one, because the very goal of this type of infiltration is the social, economic, political, cultural, and humanistic emancipation of the great social majority in the oppressed country. Of course, the bourgeois democracy, national democracy, and social democracy, which form the very core of the present-day's sophisticated capitalism, reject this argument on the ground of "intervention from outside," just ignoring the class, social, and objective characters of this type of infiltration (see *Nonintervention and Noninterference*). If the reactionary ideology, political action, economic subversive activities, and antisocial approaches from a reactionary regime or system penetrate into a progressive social regime or system, we can characterize it as a negative one.

Now let us analyse the characteristics of a counterpenetration. When the reactionary and dominant forces of a reactionary country make multilateral penetration into a country striving for social emancipation and progress; and, if the penetrated country, in order to undo the ills done to her through penetration, makes a counter-penetration into the former one, we can characterize this act as a progressive one. Thus, in order to judge the objectivity and the aspects of contradiction between penetration and counter-penetration, one has to be very careful. When the relationship between penetration and counter-penetration becomes acute, it gives birth to conflict.

With the plea of military aid and economic loan, the developed countries, during the last two decades, did make infiltration into the administrative organization, cultural and political institutions, educational and mass information media, and social organizations of the developing countries. But the penetration of the Multinational Corporations, with their gigantic financial, managerial, and tactical resources into the industrial, commercial, and financial enterprises of the developing countries, through purchase of shares and making agreement for extension of technical and management know-hows in exchange of economic control, is the most significant one, whose effect is most detrimental to the social and economic interests of the later ones. Some oil-rich countries of the Third World like Saudi Arabia, Kuwait, and Iran have

started the action of counter-penetration into the capitalist economic system and share markets. This action is manifested in the purchase of shares in big industries, agricultural land, hotels, recreation centres, etc., and, by such sort of counter-penetrative action, these countries are helping directly; (a) the development of capitalism and its exploitation further; (b) ease the tension and some aspects of the long-run economic crisis, started since the oil crisis in 1973; (c) explantation of the developing countries through the expansion of market for finished products, means of production and technology of the capitalist industries, financed by the oil Sheiks, at the cost of under-investment and non-investment in their own countries' socio-economic sector.

Therefore, the character of this type of counterpenetration is reactionary.

## 6. Elements of Chauvinism/Hegemonism/Arrogance

Chauvinism is the expression of extreme nationalism. In the capitalist social system, chauvinism gives birth to national democracy and fascism (see *Chauvinism*). If it is practiced in the Socialist system, it leads to social imperialism.

Hegemonism is the exercise of the power and force of superiority, dominance, and influence of one class or political party over the others at the inter-nation level, or the same by one State over another State or other States at the inter-State level (see *Hegemony*). The concept of hegemony is a concept of superstructure, which in the most profound manner, relates the various forces of superstructure and economic structure. The terminology "big-nation arrogance" has appeared very recently and was used by Albania to mean China's arrogance towards her manifested through the stoppage of technical and economic aid and through ideological attack. It combines the elements of both chauvinism and hegemonism.

The United States of America, which has become a Super Power during the last three decades, has continuously and systematically been using the multilateral chauvinistic attitude and activities towards some other developed countries and most of the underdeveloped countries. In the socialist world, the former Soviet Union, another Super Power, had been accused, directly by China and indirectly by Romania and Yugoslavia of carrying out "big-brother chauvinism" against other small socialist nations (see *Brezhnev Doctrine*).

Political and economic supremacy is the main reason of the development of chauvinism of the capitalistic type. But the main reasons of the development of chauvinism in the socialist system are as follows:

(a) failure to solve the problems of economic development gaps among the member States within the system;

(b) failure to understand the difference in cultural life and values of customs and traditions among different countries within the same system, and efforts to impose one particular prototype development model of one country over the others;

(c) pursuance of nation-building attitude in the development policies rather than international ones.

The intra-nation hegemonism is the result of:

(d) failure to solve the inter- and inner-class contradiction;

(e) failure to find out correlation between theory and practice and between documents and arguments, towards solving the class contradictions;

(f) failure to solve the growing socio-economic privilege-differences between the social elite and the masses, between consumerism and deprivation, and between physical and intellectual labour;

(g) failure to solve the problem of wage-differentiation at different social-structure levels.

The inter-nation hegemonism consists of some elements of chauvinism. Hegemonism, at the international level, means the exercise of the dominant role by one State over the other, by virtue of its economic, political, social, cultural, ideological, and military dominance (see *Hegemony*). Hegemonism can be of two types: class hegemonism and structural hegemonism. If a social class, and under the condition that it is the social majority and can give advanced solution to the current social, cultural, economic, and ideological problems, does exercise the relation of supremacy over other classes in society and thus leads the whole society, we can characterize this as a progressive phenomenon. For example, the working class and the peasantry hegemony over the bourgeoisie and the feudals is a progressive, promotional, and creative phenomenon. At the structural level, the hegemony becomes political hegemony, because of the special social strata's power of control over the means and ends. The ultimate results is structural violence which may generate structural conflict as and when time will be ripen.

Classlessness, structurelessness, and statelessness are the essential conditions which can solve all types of contradictions generating and developing chauvinism, hegemonism, and arrogance.

## 7. Elements of Imbalance/Balance/Overbalance/ Counterbalance

These elements grow from the feelings of rivalry and mutual distrust and suspicion between and among nation-states and are used as defensive, offensive, and counter-offensive strategies and means against each other. These elements had been used by the economic, political, and military Super Powers (the United States and the former Soviet Union); emerging Super Powers (Japan, the European Economic Community with West Germany in the leadership); and China and some other Powers in the developed and underdeveloped countries like Iran, Saudi Arabia, India, Brazil, and Libya in their defensive, offensive, counter-defensive and counter-offensive strategies and activities. Though the main domain where it is practiced is the military, its sphere of activities also extends to the economic and political domains.

At the East-West or inter-system level, the United States, the European Community and the NATO nations, Japan and Australia suspected that the former Soviet Union and the former COMECON as well as the former Warsaw Pact member nations did possess advanced military potentials, technology, and sources of research and development, for both the defensive and offensive purpose and that is why they pursued the actions of balance at the initial stage and later, those of overbalance and counter-balance. The former Soviet Union and the socialist countries *en bloc*, with the exception of China, argued that they had to develop their military technology and potentials, research and development for the purpose of being on par with the developed capitalist bloc and then to counteract any eventual attack from that bloc. Had the Soviet bloc not developed the above military strategy, the system would have been wiped off the map of the world systems, since there had always been provocations and repeated trials of exporting counter-revolutions (see *East-West Conflict*).

Talks of peace can be successful only when both the blocs, or the systems, or the countries concerned *en bloc*, are equally, or almost *equally powerful* and do really agree to conclude non-aggression agreements towards achieving lasting peace. Otherwise, for the development of the strategies and means of military balance, overbalance, and counterbalance, the social and economic development of not only the rich countries, but of the poorer ones, will also have to be sacrificed.

## 8. *Elements of North-South Divergence/Confrontation*

The main point of contradiction between the West and the former East European countries which was based on mutual mistrust is on the way of gradual disappearance because of the collapse of the Centralised Socialist System and victory as well as expansion of the Neo-Market Capitalism. While the East-West divergence has gradually been transformed into convergence, the contradiction and divergence between the North and the South was and is based mainly on the sources and resources, or between the capital and technological ownership on the one hand and raw materials and labour on the other hand. The contrast between the two are gaining the momentum of counter-distinctiveness. From the structural and functional points of view the capitalism of today may be classified into two categories, namely, (a) the multinationalised neo-market economic capitalism and (b) concession-giving social-democratized capitalism. The neo-market economy-guided neo-capitalism practiced in most of the North falls within the first category while the social democratic capitalism of Northern Europe belongs to the second category.

Both the North and the South are undergoing two respective distinctive phases of over-consumerism and deprivation of the basic human needs satisfaction. Besides the technological dependency of the South over the North the North-South divergence and confrontation is centred around the Power of Capital + Technology of the North and Helplessness of Underpriced Raw Materials + Underrated Labour. The development of capital and the development of capital and technology in the developed countries is the result of (a) accumulation of the past and present labour, both inside the countries and the former colonies as well as the present neo- and economic colonies in the Third World, and (b) demand for (i) maximization of surplus values, (ii) product-improvement, (iii) rational utilization of raw materials, (iv) minimization of production cost, etc. The growth-economy of the developed countries creates demand for more consumption goods, whether to be fully consumed or partly spoilt, and it ultimately creates the demand for more raw materials. But, the reserves of the minerals, raw materials, specially of the twelve most basic strategic ones, are being gradually exhausted, because of their exploitation for a long time. Moreover, the exploitation of the old mines is no more economic in spite of advanced technical and technological inputs. Therefore, the supply of these basic raw minerals, to the extent of about 50 per cent, the developed or the so-called First World is to depend on the former-Second and the Third Worlds, in order to maintain their present industrial consumption level only. Again, because of the higher extraction and production costs of raw materials of both the minerals and agricultural origin, the raw materials of the developed countries are becoming more and more expensive. In most cases, the mineral raw materials in the developed capitalist countries are being extracted from high depths. As most of the mines with richer contents have already been exhausted, now those with lower contents are to be explored and their processing costs are also becoming higher, while the turnover is very low. On the contrary, raw materials can be obtained from the under-developed countries at prices below worth and below the international market prices, because the labour in the less developed countries is being paid below the worth of his physical skill and intensity inputs. Obviously, the raw materials of the developing countries are cheaper not because of the fact that they are either of the lower quality or they contain lower intrinsic values than those of the developed countries but because of the undervaluation of the labour inputs in them. Hence it becomes more profitable for the developed countries and their Multinational Corporations to procure raw materials from abroad than to have them from inside their own countries. This is the essence of political economy of raw materials of the developed and the developing countries. It also presents the possibility of a very clear conflicting situation between the capital + technology of the developed countries on the one hand and raw materials + underpaid labour of the less developed countries on the other.

A genuine production and export cooperation of the raw material producing countries, in the forms of Raw Material Producer's Associations and Raw Material Exporter's Associations, on the pattern of OPEC and OPEAC, can produce a sort of alternative to the present conflicting situation described above. But, excepting in the case of oil, the bargaining power of other raw materials producing and exporting countries of the less developed countries, such as copper, tin, rubber, coffee, tea and jute failed miserably, because of either huge stock-piles of the same in the developed countries, or because of a threat of synthetics and probable alternatives to the above raw materials. Moreover, there are raw materials consumers' and importers' associations too, who still hold the better edge of the market mechanism. Though the collective or regional cooperation can assure the best possible regional self-reliance with more or less self-sufficiency, the less developed countries could not yet proceed to that direction whole-heartedly.

Let us now turn to the political economy of the oil-income of the oil producing developing countries. The OPEC and the OPEAC have collectively succeeded in raising the sale price of crude oil by about 60 US dollars per ton since the oil crisis of 1973. But, during the same period, the Multinational oil giants of the West could raise the price of refined petroleum products from the very ton of crude oil by about 120 US dollars by virtue of the ownership over the means of transporting crude oil and refilling it as well as control over the market mechanism. Thus we can fund here that the gains of the Multinational oil giants increased minimum twice to that of the oil producing and exporting developing countries. The situation could be otherwise if the less developed oil producing and exporting countries could, through collective efforts, develop their own refining capacities and could market only the finished products instead of the present form of crude oil.

There was a large expectation that the oil money of the oil-exporting developing countries could be used for their own development purposes. But it was misused and misinvested as mentioned earlier. The oil-rich developing countries promised much development aid including the sale of crude oil at a price lower than the international market price to the other non-oil-producing developing countries. But, in reality, the volume of aid to the above needy and less developed countries, as compared to their oil income, was very insignificant, while the other condition was never attended to. So the ever-growing oil-income of the oil-rich developing countries is the subject-matter of open conflict between the ownership elite and the common masses, at the international level, and is becoming a dominant factor of hidden conflict between the oil-rich and oil-less developing countries.

### 9. Elements of Labour Aristocracy/Discrimination

The revolutionary Marxist slogan of "Workers of all the Countries: Be United" does not work very much now, in spite of the fact that the common interest of the work very much now, in spite of the fact that the common interest of the working class is the same everywhere (see *Socialist International*). This is due to the fact that there has arisen differentiation in the interest of the working class from country to country, system to system, skilled job occupation, upper to lower strata, enterprise to enterprise and working conditions. In some Western countries, labour has

become an active associate or partner with the owner of capital and technology for exploitation of the neo-colonies or the Third World. It has been possible because of grant of concession by the owner of capital to labour, and this is how the labour aristocracy could be formed in the Western world as against the gradual pauperization of the working people in the South.

As mentioned earlier, the labour movement of today suffers much from economics. The social and ideological goals and struggles have much been sacrificed to the struggle for only economic benefits. Moreover, the labour of today is much more concession-oriented and less radical-ideology and outlook-oriented. At the center-periphery level, if there takes place a labour-strike in a periphery country which supplies either raw-materials, or labour-consuming cheaper component parts to the more complex industries of the centre, the economist-minded labour-aristocrats of the centre do not solidarise with the former; and, instead stage protest action on the ground that the industry in the centre is threatened with either full or a partial closure. This type of action and contrasting attitude among the workers can be observed at the Multinational Corporations' centre and their peripheral subsidiaries level also. At the intra-nation level also, their exists the attitude-differentiation as regards the working wage-earner, in both the developed capitalist and the under-developed countries. It is so because of the attitudinal contract between the immediate demands and the long-standing or ultimate demands in the working class movements of today. Here, by *immediate demands,* we mean the current economic demands and improvement of working conditions and, by *long-range or ultimate demand or goal,* we mean the change in the relations of production, i.e., radical social change. Much has been talked about the dialectical relation between the two towards obtaining proper correlation between them both, through action, to abolish their contradictions, but very little has been achieved so far.

The trade unions in the West are facing a strong challenge, in respect of relationship between the indigenous workers and the immigrant workers and fixation of policies and strategies of action towards it. It cannot be disagreed that in most of the Western countries, the foreign workers are unwanted. The recent long ranging economic crisis and resultant massive unemployment in the West made the situation of the immigrant workers perform the hardest and dirtiest jobs, generally refused and rejected by the indigenous workers; and, at the same time, discrimination in respect of payment of wages apart from social discrimination to some extent, yet they are attended with cool reception by a section of people in the West (see *Nationalism*). Here, the elements of conflict are between the tendency of neo-nationalism and tolerance because of economic helplessness and lack of an alternative to it; between national unemployment and job-occupation by the immigrant workers; between national economic crisis and unwanted economic and social burden generated by the employment of immigrant workers; and between indigenous social problems and the imported social problems etc. As a class, the labour is and should be homogeneous but the appearance of strata within the working class, both at the national and international levels, has started creating contradictions and problems in the working class movement. In the conflict theories of tomorrow, it will occupy an important role.

## 10. Elements of Internationalism/Nationalism

Internationalism and cosmopolitanism in words and patriotic nationalism in deeds is the practice of the day (see *Cosmopolitanism*). There does not exist any international system, though the transnationalists try to define and explain it in the very context. The world is divided into socio-economic systems with both goals and means differentiation into socio-economic systems and each system, again, consists of several countries with variation of culture, tradition, specific historical and economic conditions, language, etc. Whether in the capitalist, or, in the socialist, or in the developing countries, the socio-economic, political-cultural ideologies and activities are mainly based on the patriotic nationalism. The very seeds of nationalism are sown in the minds of their people from the childhood through the educational, cultural, religious and the publicity media. So it acts as a brainwashing mechanism on every national of every country through multilateral and repetitive functions. The cross-cultural activities, transnational action repetitive functions. The cross-cultural activities, transnational action of impression and expression arrangement of international travels, organization of multinational philanthropic social developmental activities help the development of international mentality and attitude among the people of various nationalities (see *Internationalization*). But ideology stands in the way of system-level intercourse of impression and expression as well as other functions. The East-West detente could not have been successful because of the problem of infiltration and counter-infiltration (see *Détente*). The spirit of internationalism had been introduced in the educational media of the socialist system in order to prepare their citizens for developing a wider outlook. But unfortunately, their state and party leadership applied it very dogmatically. The educational media of the West contained the spirit of self-centrism and economist very much. There is a theory in the socialist world that if all the nations attain the same level of socio-economic development, then only the way towards internationalism will be paved (see *World Economy, Social Change and Peace*). But an indicator of that specific level of development is yet to be elaborated. The indicator of growth-economy will not help to solve this aspect. But the development of social consciousness and humanism is the basic criterion which can remove the barrier between nationalism and internationalism. It is true that with the abolition of nation-state system, territorial boundary and other artificial barriers, the main contradictions between nationalism and internationalism can be solved. But it will take a long time and there are people who do not believe that this stage will ever come (see *Internationalization*).

## 11. Concluding Remarks

Conflict has opposite directional actions and effect. It may lead either to progress or to regress and reaction. It depends on the force or strength, both physical and moral, argumentative and mobilisational, ideological and implementative, strategies and tactics of action. As the just cause and reasons of progress do contain moral forces, their occasional setbacks in a conflict situation should not be taken as the ultimate defeat. In the course of time, it is bound to regain the necessary strength to defeat the regressive and reactionary forces. The existence of conflict gives rise to the need for peace. Therefore, in order to understand peace, we have to first understand the conflict situation in its analytical form of cause and effect. We have analyzed only some elements of conflict formation and conflict theory above. Since the causes and effects of conflict are multilateral, their treatment in the theoretical and empirical analytical direction should also be multi-directional. Research on conflict theory is not very old and so we hope that this new interdiscipline will receive a more careful attention of the researchers in future.

See also: *Conflict Resolution, Process of; Emerging Tool Chest for Peacebuilders; Theoretical Traditions of Peace and Conflict Studies; World Peace Order, Dimensions of a*

AMALENDU GUHA

# Conflict Impact Assessment (CIAS)

## 1. Limits of Conflict Prevention

In 1994 PIOOM[1] registered 22 high intensity conflicts (wars with more than 1000 deaths in one year); 39 low intensity conflicts (with 100-999 political violence victims per year), and 40 serious disputes (less than 100 political victims per year). Such data clearly indicate that there is still a wide gap between the international aspirations and reality. If a distinction is made between *proactive and reactive conflict prevention*, we notice that most of today's efforts are of a reactive nature. Proactive conflict prevention refers to measures taken before the conflict has escalated; reactive conflict prevention refers to measures taken after the conflict has escalated. The aim of the latter is to contain and reduce the intensity, the duration and the geographic spill-over of the armed violence. Proactive conflict prevention is a more cost-effective way of handling conflicts. After crossing the threshold of violence the conflict dynamic becomes not only more destructive, but also very costly and difficult to transform. How does one account for the failure of proactive conflict prevention? Many explanations have been given.[2] The three most important explanations relate to problems with respect to prognosis, perceived interests and know-how.

To prevent surprises, many governments and international organizations have paid considerable attention to the improvement of *early warning systems*. Also universities and research institutes have been very active in developing and testing alarm bells and warning signals. Six types could be distinguished: signal, trend, added value, scenario, sequential, and strategic models. Signals are events or developments which historically tended to be predictors of conflict escalation.[3] Signals could be: arms buildup, mobilization of troops, dehumanization campaigns, inability or unwillingness of the potential aggressor to negotiate a settlement, internal unrest within the potential defender. The second model basis its forecasts on an extrapolation of perceived trends. Illustrative are Melko's peace and war cycles and his expectation that at least until the middle of the 21st century the northwestern part of the world will be characterized by peace.[4] The value added model has not only an empirical but also a theoretical base. A classic illustration of this approach is the security community model of Karl Deutsch. The chances of creating a security community (see *Peace and Regional Integration*) are assessed by checking the realization of a series of preconditions, such as:

the compatibility of values, a we-ness feeling, democratization, economic growth, the expectation of mutual benefits, mobility, effective governance, constructive transformation of ethnic and nationalist conflicts, arms control, etc.[5] Sequential models differentiate between background, intervening, response, and trigger variables. Also very useful are the scenario models. The development of best, better, more of the same, worse and worst case scenarios raises the awareness of unexpected developments. Finally, the strategic model identifies the points in the conflict dynamic in which interventions are expected to make a difference in outcomes. Despite all those efforts and the development of better early warning systems, reactive conflict prevention still prevails. Africa is covered with alarm bells and flashing lights. Early warning is a necessary but not a sufficient precondition for implementing an effective conflict prevention policy.

A second necessary condition is the perception of the potential intervenors that proactive conflict prevention is advancing their *interests* (see *Intervention; Arbitration, International*). As long as the conflict is not perceived as threatening vital interests, the response tends to be too little, too late and of a low risk nature. The main interest of the European Community in Bosnia has for a long time been to contain or quarantine the conflict. Human suffering and moral considerations, amplified by the media, could jolt the international community into action. However, moral considerations by themselves seem to be not sufficient to provoke adequate proactive conflict prevention measures.

The third factor which inhibits proactive conflict prevention, is the lack of *know-how*. For the most serious problems in society one finds research and training programs. For problems related to health, universities provide for the education of medical doctors; for legal problems there are excellent law schools; for economic problems there are master programs in Business Administration, etc. For dealing with large scale violence, with some exceptions, no comprehensive academic training is available. Until recently conflict management was considered the exclusive domain of professional diplomats and soldiers. The training was provided for by departments of foreign affairs, the military academy or on the job. The conflicts they were expected to handle were predominantly interstate conflicts. The traditional approaches of conflict have proven to be of limited relevance for coping with non interstate conflicts.

The management of the new types of conflicts requires a more sophisticated analysis of conflict dynamics, an acquaintance with a wide battery of conflict prevention instruments and with constructive conflict transformation. It requires not only skills in *peace-making* and *peace reinforcement/keeping*, but also in peace (re)building (see *Conflict Resolution, Process of*). As one of the newest additions of the diplomatic vocabulary, the term *peace building* tends to be loosely defined. Peace building refers to the creation of an objective and subjective context which enhances a constructive transformation of conflicts and to a sustainable peace (see *Emerging Tool Chest for Peacebuilders*). A sustainable peace is a legitimate peace, supported by the major stake holders or the people involved. Such a peace is build on the concept of conflict transformation, underscoring the goal of moving a given population from the status of extreme vulnerability and dependency to that of self-sufficiency and well-being.[6] In more specific terms, conflict progression refers to the movement from latent to manifest conflict, to confrontation, negotiation and finally to the peaceful relationships of a security community.[7] Peace building requires two sets of efforts relating to: (re)construction and (re)conciliation.

The most visible efforts are the structural measures which are meant to improve the life conditions, reduce discrimination, provide ways and means for settling or resolving disputes. In more concrete terms those efforts refer to the installation and reinforcement of democratic structures, including the organization and supervision of elections; to the strengthening of the legal system; to economic reconstruction, to rebuilding the educational infrastructure; to the resettlement of refugees and health services.

Less visible, but as essential, are the (re)conciliation measures. These measures intend to create a new moral-political climate in which the conflicting parties are committed to the restoration of ruptured relationships and to the construction of a new future. This implies not only reconciliation with the present (a peace agreement settling particular issues), but

also a reconciliation with the past (healing of historical wounds) and a reconciliation with the future. A reconciliation with the past, present and the future, is necessary for achieving a sustainable peace. Another essential component of the new moral-political climate is the creation of a compatible value system. This requires a (re)conciliation of such competitive and interdependent values as: truth, peace, welfare, justice, mercy, freedom and beauty.[8] This kind of reconciliation aims at creating a social context in which all those values and needs are validated, rather than a value system in which some must win out over the others. A last component of the new moral-political climate is the creation of a we-ness feeling. This implies efforts to enhance multiple loyalties.

## 2. Early Warning of What?

Tracing the causes of the failure of conflict prevention, one is struck by the importance of problems of a conceptual nature. The surprises, lost opportunities, chronic crisis management, the lack of a coherent and effective conflict prevention policy, all point to a series of conceptual problems. With respect to the early warning efforts four problems can be distinguished (see Table 1). First, there is a tendency to focus most attention to the hard-tangible-quantifiable variables and to *overlook the soft variables* which influence the conflict dynamic, such as perceptions, expectations, analytic styles, preferred world-orders and strategic approaches. A second problem is the predominant attention given to *forecasting threats, dangers or worst-case developments*. A disproportional low amount of attention goes to the warning of opportunities to intervene pro-actively. As a consequence most of the wars could be analyzed as histories of missed opportunities (see Part 3). The third problem concerns the assessment of the costs and benefits of alternative policy options. The *cost-benefit analyses tend to be very rudimentary*, without sight of several important cost-factors (see Part 4). Finally, if policy impact assessments are made, they tend to be of a *uni-dimensional nature*. Not enough

*Table 1*
Problems of early warning systems

| | | |
|---|---|---|
| focus on threats | <——————— | focus on opportunities |
| rudimentary cost-benefit analysis | <——————— | comprehensive analysis of costs and benefits |
| hard-quantifiable variables | <——————— | soft variables |
| one- dimensional analysis | <——————— | multi-dimensional / cross-impact analysis |

attention is paid to assessing the impact of conflict prevention measures on other domains, levels or time-frames (see Part 5).

## 3. Missed Opportunities

During the Cold War most of the research efforts were directed to threat and worst-case analysis. A disproportional low amount of attention went to the assessment of opportunities for constructive conflict transformation. The same is true today. Most research money is spent on the development of systems for the early warning of threats, dangerous escalations or worst case scenarios. Practically no attention is being paid to the development of early warning systems identifying the points in conflict processes in which particular interventions would enhance a constructive transformation of the conflict. A great deal of the recent conflicts could be described as histories of missed opportunities. The term 'missed opportunity' refers to moments or periods during the conflict where measures could have been taken, which would have had a significant positive impact on the conflict dynamics. A glance at the conflict in ex-Yugoslavia indicates several missed opportunities (see Table 2).

Several explanations could be given to explain this sad history of missed opportunities: (a) the lack of foresight; (b) the overload of the political and diplomatic agenda at the beginning of the war caused by the implosion of the USSR, the Gulf War and the efforts of the European Union to strengthen the integration-Maastricht Treaty, and; (c) the diminished interest in Yugoslavia caused by its reduced geopolitical importance after the Cold War and the fact that the country lies beyond 'Little Europe.' To increase the chances of successful conflict prevention much more attention should be paid to the development of early warning systems indicating to politicians when and how to intervene effectively.

## 4. Accounting for Costs and Benefits

The development of a more effective proactive conflict prevention system also requires a better insight in the economy of war and peace. This area of research has been neglected seriously. It is for example practically impossible to find an accurate and comprehensive accounting of the costs of the destruction in a particular war and of the respective

**Table 2**
Ex-Yugoslavia: a history of missed opportunities

---

*Before Outburst of Violence*

- (a) Deteriorating economic situation : 1982-89
- (b) Media war offensive of Milosovic '88
- (c) Repression Kosovo '89
- (d) Disarmament in Slovenia and Croatia before war started
- (e) War games of the Yugoslav National Army (YNA)
- (f) International community preferred unitary state and was not prepared to listen to Slovenian and Croatian points of view—implicit green light for the YNA to intervene

*Early in war*

- (a) No credible military response to the destruction of Vukovar and Dubrovnik
- (b) Recognition of Slovania and Croatia not successfully linked to overall peace and cooperation agreement

*During the war*

- (a) The arms embargo reinforced the asymmetric character of the war
- (b) No credible stick . . . the no-fly zone became only operational in Feb '94
- (c) Peace proposals reinforced might is right options, and not a just peace.

peace-rebuilding efforts. A complete assessment includes not only the human and economic costs, but also the social, political, ecological, cultural, psychological and spiritual destruction (see Fig. 2).

Lacking also, is research about the 'vulture factor' or the persons or groups who profit from the armed violence. Their identification is very important, because wars tend to last as long as major groups or decision-makers expect benefits. Neglected also, are studies comparing the costs of proactive and reactive conflict prevention. Such data could help to convince policy-makers about the cost-effectiveness of proactive conflict prevention. In addition, the publication of the cost and benefits of war and the obligation of decision-makers to account for the destruction and profits, could make them think twice before engaging in future wars. An early warning of the cost and benefits of conflict policy options envisaged, could lead to a more 'enlightened' assessment of the interests involved.

## 5. Conflict Impact Assessment: CIAS

Research should also be focused on the assessment of the impact of intervention measures on the conflict dynamic. Most conflict prevention policies are compilations of well intentioned, uni-dimensional measures. Not enough attention is paid to possible negative externalities. Generally peace keepers play a positive role, but in some situations they have became an obstacle for peace-making and effective peace-reinforcement. The Khmer Rouge parasitized on the refugee camps in Thailand. Food aid can be used to sustain warmongering groups. The threat with a war crimes tribunal can under certain circumstances protract a violent conflict. Democratization pressures could be a blessing, but could also enhance centrifugal forces and lead to anarchy and end up in a dictatorial system. In all cases, causal loops are not discussed systematically and comprehensively. The

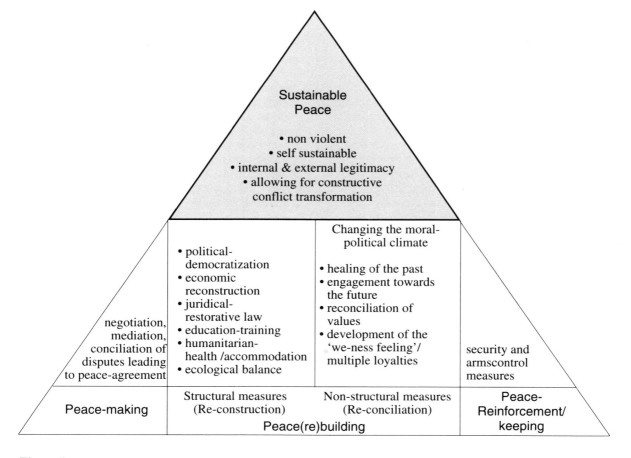

*Figure 1*
Requirements for a sustainable peace

***Figure 2***
Costs of wars

chances of proactive conflict prevention could be significantly raised by requiring conflict impact assessments (CIAS).

The aim of a conflict impact assessment system is (a) to assess the positive and/or negative impact of different kinds of intervention or of the lack of intervention on the dynamics of the conflict, (b) to contribute to the development of a more coherent conflict prevention and peace building policy, (c) to serve as sensitizing tool for policy-shapers and policy-makers, helping them to identify weaknesses in their approach (for example: blind spots, incoherence, bad timing, inadequate priority setting, etc., (d) to further the economy of peace building.

Despite the self evident need of a conflict impact assessment system one senses resistance and reservations with respect to the development and the implementation of such a tool. Some reservations are based on the conviction that conflict dynamics are much too complex to be tracked by a CIAS. Others fear that an adequate assessment will be a time consuming exercise and inhibit the flexibility. There is also the apprehension by some, stated less explicitly, that a CIAS, would expose the negative impact of ones policies on the chances of reaching a sustainable peace, and thereby make the pursuit of self-interest in conflict zones more difficult. All those comments suggest some limits with respect to the development and implementation of an assessment system. The overall aim of such a tool is to sensitize the decision makers and opinion leaders about the complexity of peace making, peace building and peace keeping, and to help them to formulate or design a more coherent, efficient and effective peace policy.

A conflict impact assessment system requires:

> • a clear and compelling definition of the peace one wants to achieve and a valid conceptual framework indicating the conditions enhancing or inhibiting the realization of the aim,
> • a comprehensive assessment of the needs or of the presence or absence of the above mentioned conditions in the conflict region,
> • a coherent action plan,
> • an effective implementation of the action plan,
> • a recognition of the ownership and legitimate control of the conflict transformation,
> • an awareness and dismantling of mental walls inhibiting the satisfaction of all the above.

### 5.1 A Clear and Compelling Definition of the Peace One Wants to Achieve

One of the causes of the failure of conflict prevention is the existence of an incoherent peace policy. In many cases the incoherence results from the pursuit of different aims or of different kinds of peace. It is impossible to develop an effective conflict prevention policy when there is no consensus or clarity about what is meant by conflict prevention or the kind of peace one wants to pursue. Do the policy makers perceive peace as an endpoint or as a process? Are they satisfied with negative peace (the absence of military violence) or do they want positive peace? Are they aiming for a suspension of violence (a peace break) or a sustainable peace? The definition of peace is a moral-political decision. From an analytic point of view however clarity and precision is very important. An analyst should insist on working with a clear operational definition. Without an explication of kind of peace one wants to see realized, it will be difficult to evaluate singular peace initiatives or the peace policy as a whole. To make a long-term difference, one must envision the peace one wants to achieve. Only in that way will it be able to establish criteria for judging where it is heading. Equally important is to have a good idea of the conditions to be fulfilled to achieve the peace. Establishing a sustainable peace process requires much more than providing humanitarian aid or containing violence.

### 5.2 A Comprehensive Needs Assessment in the Conflict Region

The design of an effective conflict prevention policy requires not only a clear operational definition of the peace, but also a comprehensive assessment of the needs in the region; in other words we have to find out if the necessary conditions for a sustainable peace process are present or not. Such need assessment helps to distinguish strong areas which have been adequately covered, weak areas which needs much more effort, and blind spots. In Burundi, practically nothing has been done to overcome the security dilemma with which the ethnic groups have been confronted; development projects grind to a halt when security cannot be provided; no inclusive peace making process seems to have started. Salient among the blind spots is the debilitating political-psychological climate dominated by fear, hostility, stress, cynicism, pessimism.

### 5.3 A Coherent Action Plan

The third requirement for implementing a more effective conflict prevention policy is the design of a coherent action plan for building a sustainable peace. Most peace plans today are concoctions of well intentioned, uni-dimensional measures (political, legal, humanitarian, economic . . .). Not enough attention is paid to the cross-impact of these measures on the conflict dynamic. For analytical purposes several types of impact may be distinguished:

*(a) Positive—Negative*

Certain interventions could be listed as satisfiers, counterproductive measures, pseudo-satisfiers and inhibiting satisfiers.[9] Satisfiers are measures which clearly advance projected goals, such as democratization, development . . . . Counterproductive measures tend to have a paradoxical nature. When applied with for example, the intention to increase security (arms race), they not only impair the overall security, but also the adequate satisfaction of other peace-building conditions. Pseudo-satisfiers are measures that generate a false sense of achievement of a given need (formal democracy, stereotypes). Inhibiting satisfiers are those that oversatisfy a given requirement for peace, therefore seriously curtailing the possibility of satisfying other requirements.

*(b) Weak—Strong*

In addition to the direction, positive or negative, an assessment has to be made of the strength of the impact.

*(c) Duration of the Impact*

The impact could be of a permanent or a temporary nature.

*(d) Singular Versus Synergetic Satisfiers*

Single satisfiers are measures or initiatives which sat-

isfy a particular requirement for building a sustainable peace (economic, legal, educational . . .). With respect to other requirements they are neutral (professional armies). Synergetic satisfiers are those measures that satisfy a given requirement, while simultaneously stimulating or contributing to the fulfillment of other requirement (popular education). The cross-impact could relate to different sectors (political, military, economic, legal, educational . . .), levels (personal, local, regional, national, international . . .), actors (man and woman) and time frames.

*(e) Exogenous and Endogenous Satisfiers*

Exogenous satisfiers are measures which are prescribed, imposed, induced ritualized or institutionalized. They are generated from outside or at the top. Endogenous satisfiers or measures on the other hand, are elicited from the stakeholders or the people who have to live with the outcome.

*(f) Timing of the Impact*

The impact could be felt immediately, or be a short-, medium- or long-term impact.

Also more systematic attention should be given to the complex interdependence of different intervention domains (political, economic, legal, military), levels, time-frames and layers or depths (see Table 3). Everybody has the mouth full of words like peacemaking, peace-building and peace-keeping; these are all necessary building stones. In conflict areas, piles of peace building stones can be found. But where is the peace architecture. Where does one start? What are the priorities? How does one effectively combine time and means to build a sustainable peace process?

### 5.4 An Effective Implementation of the Action Plan

Implementing a peace plan effectively remains a major conceptual problem. It requires the will to make the necessary means and time available, co-ordination and leadership. Delivering the necessary means is to a great extent related to the perceived interests of the donor countries. When vital interests are at stake, it seems to be easier than when it concerns a far from bed type of conflict. How does one convince the opinion leaders that one should be involved and that proactive conflict prevention is more cost-effective than reactive conflict prevention? A second set of questions relates to: who will be the prime mover(s)? How will the peace efforts be co-ordinated? Should it be one person or a team who will handle the conflict? Should the team consist of outsiders or also include partial insiders? When do coordination efforts result into a creative synergetic process and when do they become stifling? Finally, more attention should be paid to the role of 'leadership' in conflict transformation. What kind of leadership is appropriate for conflict transformation?

### 5.5 Recognition of Ownership and Legitimate Control of the Process

It has become part of the litany for peace-builders that the conflicting parties should be the owners of their conflict; that one should not steal them; that one needs a mandate to provide peace services; that one ought to work with local partners, etc. The problem of ownership is also alive in the academic discussion about the pros and cons of inclusive versus exclusive, illicitive versus prescriptive, and exogenous versus endogenous approaches of conflict transformation. It is also related to the entry and exit issue of a conflict. The underlying assumption of this concern is that a peace process can only be sustained when it is supported by the internal and external stake holders. But who are these stake holders? Should the efforts be concentrated on the elite or also involve

the people? What does it mean to empower the people? Should the extremists be invited to the negotiation table? How and to what extend should external parties whose security and interests are linked up with the conflict have a say in the conflict transformation process and the peace agreement. What are the guidelines for governmental and non-governmental third parties whose expertise and other kinds of support are needed for peace-making, peace-building and arms control.

### 6. Awareness and Dismantling of Mental Walls

Finally, one should be aware of the mental walls which stand in the way of developing the necessary flexibility, open-mindedness and creativity to help to transform conflicts constructively. Among the natal obstacles we can distinguish: Several socio-psychological walls stand in the way of developing the necessary flexibility: (1) myths, illusions and taboos; (2) reductionism and intolerance of complexity (3); elite orientedness; (4) the propensity to react rather than proact; (5) a destructive socio-political climate;

*Figure 3*
Cross-impact of the domains, levels, lead times, and deeper layers of a conflict

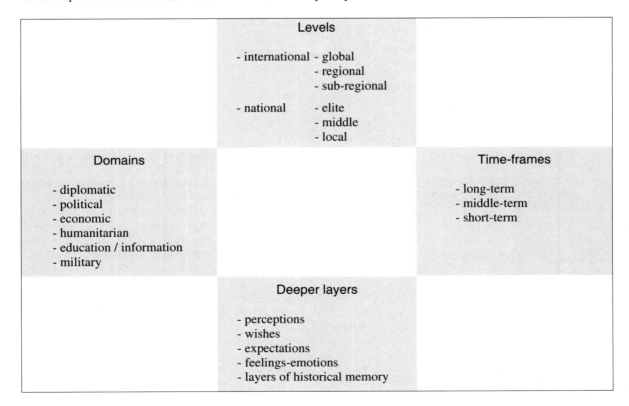

(6) lack of innovative thinking the development of new tools (hope-raising measures, field diplomacy[10] . . .). One of the most severe challenges to cope with the entrenched conflicts is to unlearn or discard the inappropriate ways of thinking and to see conflict transformation as a learning process for all involved (see *Psychology of Peace*).

The world is getting fed up with today's failures of conflict prevention. It is tired of well-intentioned and one-dimensional people who know exactly what has to be done. It is tired of people walking around with a briefcase full of solutions looking for problems to fit those solutions. We should start respecting the capacity to re-search our ways and means for building peace (see *Theoretical Traditions of Peace and Conflict Studies*).

See also: *Conflict Formation, Elements in; Conflict: Inherent and Contingent Theories; United Nations and NATO in Former Yugoslavia*

## Notes

This is a revised version of a paper 'Conflict Impact Assessment' (CIAS) presented at the IPRA Conference, in the Commission for Conflict Resolution and Peace Building, Brisbane, Australia, July 1996. I am grateful to Jos De la Haye, researcher at the Center for Peace Research and Strategic Studies (CPRS) for his valuable cooperation.

1. PIOOM, *Newsletter and Progress Report*, Vol. 7, Winter 1995.
2. W Bauwens & L Reychler, *The art of conflict prevention*, Brassey's, London, 1994.
3. J Dunnigan and W Martel, *How to stop a war?: The lessons on two hundred years of war and peace*, 1987, Doubleday, New York.
4. Melko, Matthew, The remission of violence in the world, *International Journal on World Peace*, Vol. II, No 2, April-June, 1985, pp. 48-61.
5. Luc Reychler. A Pan-European Security Community: Utopia or realistic perspective?, in *Disarmament*, United Nations, 1991.
6. J. P. Lederach, *Building peace: sustainable reconciliation in divided societies*, UN University, Tokyo, Japan, 1994.
7. See L.Reychler, *Field Diplomacy: a new conflict paradigm?*, IPRA conference, Brisbane 1996.
8. *Ibid.*
9. The use of the term satisfier has been inspired by Manfred A.Max-Neef, *Human scale development: conception, application and further reflections*, 1991, New York and London, The Apex Press.
10 Luc Reychler, "Field diplomacy: a new conflict paradigm?," paper presented at the IPRA conference in Brisbane, Australia, July 1996.

LUC REYCHLER

# Conflict: Inherent and Contingent Theories

The main thrust of this article will be concerned with a discussion of inherency and contingency in the context of contemporary social conflict theory. First, though, contingent and inherent theory will be defined. Secondly, it will be argued that the distinction between these two types of theory runs through the history of human thinking about power and society, and spans across the social sciences today. Thirdly, an examination will be made of the arguments advanced by Eckstein with respect to two theories of conflict, and it will be suggested that social science can make no decisions about the inherent or contingent nature of society or human nature.

An event is "contingent if its occurrence depends upon the presence of unusual (we might say aberrant) conditions that occur accidentally" (Eckstein 1980 p. 138). Hence, if parties get into positions of goal incompatibility, it is not due to some inherent factor in the nature of groups or in the nature of human beings, but rather is due to the circumstances in which they find themselves. The interests of different parties may collide, but it is not inevitable that they should collide; better information, or less mis-perception, or more rational behavior may have prevent-ed the collision. Conflict may occur through a scarcity of and competition for resources, or through maldistribution of ample resources, but it may not be a necessary condition of human societies that these conditions pertain. Similarly, as in frustration-aggression theory, aggression is not innate, but only the potential for it, this potential being activated by certain kinds and levels of frustration (Dullard et al., 1980).

On the other hand, an event is "inherent either if it will always happen (e.g., entropy) or if the potentiality for it always exists and actuality can only be obstructed" (Eckstein 1980 p. 139). An inherent view of conflict, then, would suggest that it is a normal and natural factor in society. To be more useful, we might perhaps bring the notion of violence into the definition of inherent theories of conflict. Goal incompatibility is almost inevitable in any complex highly differentiated society, but a difference of opinion is not the same as a violent conflict. Peace researchers in general are not concerned with the eradication of conflict, but rather with the eradication of violent expressions of conflict. An inherent theory of conflict in this light would mean a theory where violence is seen as normal and to be expected. A distinction should be made between "endemic" violent conflict and "inherent" views of conflict. Malaria is in some parts of the world endemic, in the sense that it is an ever-present disease, but it is not inherent: it can be eradicated by the appropriate medication and drainage projects. The frequency of violent conflict should not lead us to assume that it is an inherent factor in human society, if it in fact stems from other conditions which are themselves manipulable. If, however, the conditions which give rise to violence are themselves inherent—as some would argue that differential access to social goods is in all societies beyond the hunting and gathering stage—then the fact that violence is not itself inherent is of no account. The difference between endemic and inherent notions of violent conflict lies, then, both in the perceived nature of society and humanity, and in the potential manipulability of the environment within which violence flourishes.

According to Eckstein, the inherency-contingency distinction is "the most fundamental problem requiring solution if a progressive development of theory about a subject is going to develop" (Eckstein 1980 p. 135). It is noteworthy that the importance attributed here is in the context of science, and that in his definition of inherency Eckstein points to entropy as an inherent tendency that can be "obstructed." The emphasis attached to the discovery of inherent and contingent factors relates to the discovery of general laws in society. If it can be argued that there are inherent social processes, then a technology of society becomes possible. However, two points should be noted. The possibility of establishing generalizations of a probabilistic nature is not wholly dependent upon the establishment of inherency, but these generalizations would tend to be temporally and culturally limited and subject to change. Thus there can be a "science" of society without inherency. Further, even given inherency, prediction and manipulability may not be much advanced. The law of gravity, for example, states that objects will fall to earth at a given rate. However, things never do fall at that rate because of all the intervening variables that affect the rate of fall, such as air pressure, winds, and so on. The law would only operate in ideal conditions, that is, in a vacuum. Similarly, even if inherency could be demonstrated, the complex interaction of causes and effects in highly differentiated societies would mean that the ideal conditions never pertain. Take, for example, Roberto Michels' "iron law of oligarchy." Organization as such is never wholly isolated from the disturbance emanating from the wider environ-

ment, or from the unpredictable consequences flowing from particular personalities. Like a leaf falling from a tree on a windy day, a tendency may exist, but prediction as to its course may be very low. If this is so in the relatively simple world of natural science, how much less should we worry about inherency in social science when people by virtue of reason and will can act to change the "natural" course of things.

The inherency-contingency distinction, while not phrased in these terms, runs through the history of social thought about society and power. It is one of that class of philosophic ideas known as "type and token" questions. Throughout the ages the same type of question has arisen, while many different tokens have been proffered by way of answer. Plato was clearly leaning towards an inherency view; his myth of metals can be seen as ideological propagation to persuade and legitimize the subordination of the many to the few (Conford 1966). The tendency had to be checked by both force and ideology. During the French Revolutionary period inherency and contingency theories were articulated, argued as statements of fact but serving ideological purposes. On one side of the English channel, Jean-Jacques Rousseau, the Enlightenment philosopher, was arguing that the corrupt nature of humanity was due to the social conditions acting upon it. This is one of the messages contained in both the *Discourse on the Origins of Inequality,* and *The Social Contract.* The corollary of this was that if the environment were changed, then so also would be human nature (see *Rousseau, Jean Jacques*). The theme was revolutionary and has come down to modern times via Marxist and humanitarian thought. On the English side of the channel, on the other hand, the Irish rhetorician Edmund Burke was arguing a very different case, which became the basis for British Conservatism until the inception of the "New Right" ideas which swept to power in the 1979 General Election. Burke saw a dangerous side to humanity, held in check only by law, custom, and civilization, which if removed would throw it back on its scanty resources with chaos and anarchy resulting. Law, custom, and civilization were the "obstructions" which inhibited the emergence of a terrible reality; in them was embodied the accumulated wisdom of the past which could only be abandoned at peril. In the former case, human nature was seen as undesirably molded by a poor environment, while in the latter the undesirable characteristics of human nature were held in check by the environment.

Coming closer to our own time the same debate continues. Freud, particularly in his later years, saw the antisocial desires of humans as inborn, with the only check on these atavistic impulses towards power and dominance being the socialization processes through which the individual passed (see *Freud, Sigmund*). Konrad Lorenz, a Nobel Prize ethologist, concluded on the basis of a comparative biological study (Lorenz 1963) that humans belonged to that class of animals which had no inbuilt inhibitions against violence and killing. Like Burke, he stressed the necessity of social forms to constrain the emergence of this behavior. Obversely, in a tradition stretching from the English philosopher John Locke (1964 pp. 67-68), the behaviorist school ejects all notion of drives and instincts and argues that environment is all. An extreme statement of this *tabula rasa* view of human nature comes from Watson (1924 p. 104):

> Give me a dozen healthy infants, well-formed, and my own specified world to bring them up in and I'll guarantee to take any one at random and train him to become any type of specialist I might select—doctor, lawyer, artist, merchant-chief, and, yes, even beggarman and thief, regardless of his talents, penchants, tendencies, abilities. vocations, and race of his ancestors.

Hence, there are no inherent tendencies either in the human or society other than the various causes that act upon humanity.

Within international relations theory, inherency has a strong base. Morganthau, the doyen of the realist school, argues in *Politics Among Nations* (1973) that each nation will strive for dominance as a means to achieving security and attaining its national interest. Peace is forever a temporary phenomenon, to be achieved through diplomacy, alliances (see *Alliance*), and a balance of power (see *Balance of Power*). But these are "obstructions" again, for conflict will occur and much of that conflict will be in the form of war. In denial of this thesis John Burton, one of the progenitors of the World Society model, and successor to the functionalist school, sees the world in a very different light, where the imperative to war comes not from the nature of the nation-state and its external relations, but from the way in which the environment acts upon the individual. Individuals have needs which they strive to fulfill, and it is the frustration of these needs, either personally or collectively, that leads to violent conflict. But conflict, according to Burton and his followers, is not inherent, because the values which would satisfy human needs are not in short supply. Hence the needs for identity, participation, or security, for example, can be gained without loss to other parties. Thus, if the social environment were changed, and in particular the manner in which

parties view each other, then violent conflict would cease (Burton 1972, 1982).

The debate over inherency or contingency should not be thought of as a dry sterile debate, to be confined to the dusty corners of university libraries. Rather, it is an argument that affects the fate of every man, woman, and child on Earth, for it is about the nature of humanity, society, and the appropriate forms of social control. If those who wield power believe in the view of human nature expressed by Lorenz, Freud, and Burke, then social control becomes very important, with a tendency to repression: human desires cannot be satiated, and every concession is a step down the slippery slope to anarchy. Lorenz, Freud, and Burke were, of course, far more subtle and sophisticated than this, but in the translation from test to practice the finer qualifications are lost and the simple message will become the model for action in the realm of practical politics and control. If, on the other hand, the powerful believe in a contingency view, the implied imperatives are very different. The rulers, to avoid disruption and dissent which may threaten their control, will attempt to meet the demands of the people. Hence, on the one hand society is typified by repression and oppression, while on the other it is responsive and open to demands. In many cases it will not in fact matter which theory, if either, is correct, for rulers will act on a belief that one view is correct. In the words of W. I. Thomas, "What men believe is real, is real in its consequences." It becomes very important, therefore, to ensure that neither inherency nor contingency become accepted as *the* scientific view of humanity unless there is certainty, for the consequences of error would be considerable. In the contemporary world to label something as "scientific" is to validate it in the public consciousness. The products of science are among the most certain knowledge we have, and to claim scientific status for a particular view of humanity and society would have political effects which are not warranted by the actual state of knowledge.

Eckstein, in the belief that the establishment of inherency and contingency is the most important issue facing conflict theorists, argues that "collective action" theories (otherwise known as the resource mobilization approach) are an example of inherency theory, while the relative deprivation approach is an example of contingency theory. Relative deprivation may be defined as the actors' perception of discrepancy between their value expectations and their value capabilities (Gurr 1970 p. 24), or, more simply, between what they feel they ought to have and what they actually have got. Discontent thus arises because of a felt need or want (see *Relative Deprivation*). The resource mobilization approach, on the other hand, "emphasizes both societal support and constraint of social movement phenomena. It examines the variety of resources that must be mobilized, the linkages of social movements to other groups, the dependence of movements upon third parties for success, and the tactics used by authorities to control or incorporate movements . . ." (Zald and McCarthy 1979 pp. 1-2), while contending groups struggle for power. On the way they maneuver, form and break coalitions, try alternative strategies, win, and lose (Tilly 1978 p. 99). According to Eckstein's "Explanation-sketches" of what contingency and inherency theories should look like (1980 pp. 142-43, paraphrased below), the two types of conflict theory should conform to this dichotomy.

## 1. Contingency Approach

(a) Individuals are basically pacific.

(b) Under special conditions the pacific impulses may be diverted.

(c) The major problem for conflict theory is to explain the frequency of violence.

(d) When special conditions arise, other human dispositions may be activated.

(e) Collective violence is affective rather than coolly calculated.

(f) The tendency to violence may be affected by cultural learning.

(g) Two further minor factors affecting the use of violence are the coercive balance between forces and other factors facilitating the successful use of violence.

## 2. Inherency Approach

(a) The fundamental disposition of individuals is towards power and dominance; violence is only an extreme but normal expression of this tendency.

(b) There are alternative channels for seeking power, of which collective political violence is merely one.

(c) The major problem is explaining why violence does not occur more often.

(d) The choice of violence is a question of tactical consideration.

(e) Tactical choices are influenced by cost-benefit calculations.

(f) Cultural factors play a relatively minor role, and will both inhibit and promote the use of violence.

(g) Factors such as the coercive balance of forces and facilitating conditions are of major importance.

The general argument here will be that Eckstein, while articulating a sparkling and provocative perspective, has made a fundamental error in that what is essentially a change in research strategy is seen by him as a major scientific and philosophic schism. The clue to this error can be seen in his plea for theories of greater simplicity. He particularly attacks Hibbs (1973) and Gurr (1970), and by implicating others, for providing models of such complexity that no decision can be made on the basis of them between peace-seeking and power-seeking humanity. Eckstein attributes this complexity to "an overdose of induction" (1980 p. 162), while the reality is that whether the researcher starts with one approach or the other, the nature of the subject material drives him or her to complexity by incorporating at least some aspects of the other approach. A basic difference between the relative deprivation approach and the resource mobilization (collective action) approach is the level of analysis, the former taking the individual as the basic unit of analysis, while for the latter the group is the basic unit of analysis. However, in order to make relative deprivation useful as a theory of social conflict, group factors have at some stage to be introduced, while to make collective actions understandable, individual motivations have also to be considered. Thus what starts off as a simple explanatory framework becomes complex, not because of the weakness or error of the researcher, but because social reality is complex and can be oversimplified only at the cost of gross distortion.

To emphasize this point, let us look at the three basic options open to the collective action theorist with respect to motivation. It is taken as read that a theory of motivation is needed even while it is action on the group level which is studied: groups do not act, only individuals do. The first option open which comes nearest to avoiding any theory of motivation is to assume that the level of social discontent is constant and generalized and requires only opportunity in the form of lowering costs of action, an appropriate elite leadership, and so on, to find expression. We may refer to this as the "gusher" model: the pressure is always there and it only requires a geosocial fault or a weakness in the cap of social control for discontent and aggression to flood out. As a theory of motivation this view is, of course, wholly untestable. Opportunity is known to exist when discontent takes social form, and discontent can only take social form when there is opportunity; hence the argument becomes wholly circular, ignoring the possibility that opportunity may be created (see Goldstone 1980). Further, the gusher model ignores a whole tradition of social research which has established the fact of differential mobilizability of populations. A second option is to "black-box" psychological factors, or to treat as simple facts things which for the specialist in that area are full of complexity (Gluckman 1964 p. 173). Hence the chemist may ignore quarks and charm, not because he or she is unaware of them, but because he or she believes they have little relevance at his or her level of research. However, simplifying by black-boxing is only an acceptable procedure if the inputs and outputs are constant in relation to each other; thus for an electronics engineer the internal complexities of a resister would be irrelevant for a larger model if the output were predictable from the input. Individuals in society are both inputs and outputs, but cannot be black-boxed because prediction is affected by learning processes. The final option is to accept the painful inevitability of theoretical amalgamation; at some point social analyses have to take on board theories of motivation.

A similar argument can be made with respect to relative deprivation theory. Cast at the level of the individual, though with a social dimension involved through the processes of referencing, there is no possibility of this approach "explaining" collective violence without also incorporating as additional factors sociological explanatory variables. Hence, as Bowers et al., (1980a, 1980b, 1981a, 1981b) and Webb et al., (1983) have argued, no amount of relative deprivation makes for social discontent without *processes* of articulation and mobilization. Further, the development of a dissenting group may be both the result of relative deprivation and also the cause of further relative deprivation in a recursive cycle.

The conclusion of this very brief discussion of a complex empirical and theoretical issue is that Eckstein's attempt to place these theories in opposition with regard to inherency and contingency fails primarily because their differentiation cannot be maintained under examination. Hence Eckstein's laudable attempts to provide tests, akin to Popperian "crucial experiments," to decide between the two theories and thus establish the inherency or contingency of violent conflict must also fail; it is like testing the two sides of a coin to discover which is most like the real coin—both sides make up the coin.

Having rejected Eckstein's attempt to provide a decision procedure for eliciting the "real" nature of humanity by the processes of science, the question must then be raised as to whether science can ever provide a definitive answer to the problem of human nature. The conclusion reached here is that while science—including social science—can do many things there are some questions that are forever beyond its grasp. Science essentially does not seek essences. Plato, Rousseau, Burke, Marx, Maslow, or Burton claim to discern the "real" nature of humanity, but only through a process of philosophic abstraction while science looks only at the attributes of phenomena and the relations between them. It is up to humanity itself to take the products of science and interpret them as it wills, much as Spinoza looked at the laws of natural science and saw in them the substance of God. It would also seem improbable that a view of human nature could be established that was impervious to human learning and reaction (Popper 1960 ch. v-vii). Further, in sociological analysis the apparently clear distinction between contingency and inherency may be a false dichotomy in practice if the number and effectiveness of actual or potential "obstructions" to the emergence of inherency is sufficiently high. Finally, while there *may* be some constancies in human behavior, the malleability and adaptability of the human subject would seem to preclude any ultimate statement as to what a human being "really" is.

See also: *Aggression; Conflict Resolution, History of; Structural Violence and the Definition of Conflict; War: Environmental and Biological Theories*

*Bibliography*

Bowers D A, Mitchell C R, Webb K 1980a Dynamic models of conflict between two communities. *J. Appl. Syst. Analysis* 7

Bowers D A, Mitchell C R, Webb K 1980b Modeling bicommunal conflict. *Futures* 12

Bowers D A, Mitchell C R, Webb K 1981a Modeling bicommunal conflict: Structuring the model. *Futures* 13

Bowers D A, Mitchell C R, Webb K 1981b Modeling bicommunal conflict: Simulation and validation. *Futures* 13

Burton J W 1972 *World Society.* Cambridge University Press, Cambridge

Burton J W 1982 *Dear Survivors.* Francis Pinter, London

Conford F M 1966 *The Republic of Plato.* Oxford University Press, Oxford

Dollard J et al., 1980 *Frustration and Aggression.* Greenwood Press, Westport, Connecticut

Eckstein H 1980 Theoretical approaches to explaining collective political violence. In: Gurr T R (ed.) 1980 *Handbook of Political Conflict: Theory and Research.* Free Press, New York

Gluckman M 1964 *Closed Systems and Open Minds: The Limits of Naivete in Social Anthropology.* Oliver and Boyd, Edinburgh

Goldstone J 1980 The weakness of organization: A new look at Gamson's strategy of social protest. *Am. J. Social.* 85

Gurr T R 1970 *Why Men Rebel.* Princeton University Press, Princeton, New Jersey

Hibbs D A 1973 *Mass Political Violence: A Cross National Causal Analysis.* Wiley, New York

Locke J 1964 *An Essay Concerning Human Understanding.* Collins, London

Lorenz K 1974 *On Aggression.* Harcourt, Brace and Jovanovich, New York

Morganthau H J 1973 *Politics Among Nations: The Struggle for Power and Peace.* Knopf, New York

Popper K R 1960 *The Poverty of Historicism.* Routledge and Kegan Paul, London

Rousseau J-J 1963 *The Social Contract and Discourses.* Dent, London

Tilly C 1978 *From Mobilization of Revolution.* Addison -Wesley, Reading, Massachusetts

Watson J B 1924 *Behaviourism.* University of Chicago Press, Chicago, Illinois

Webb K et al., 1983 Etiology and outcomes of protest. *ABS* 26(3)

Zald M N, McCarthy J D (eds.) 1979 *The Dynamics of Social Movements.* Winthrop, Cambridge, Massachusetts

KEITH WEBB

# Conflict Resolution, History of

Conflict resolution as a concept has been promoted over the years by members of the Society of Friends (Quakers) (see *Quakerism*) and others. When "Conflict Resolution" was introduced at the University of London in 1965 as an extension of the conventional strategic, power politics, International Relations course, it was given a specific meaning. This new section dwelt on the possibilities of analytical problem solving in inter-state relationships rather than dealing with potential military conflict situations by balance of power and alliance means. Why had Germany and Japan gone to war against Britain? Why was a revolt in Vietnam not deterred by the threat of force from the leading world power of the time and from the United Nations? If deterrence did not deter, what were the options? After some years of debate and discussion Conflict Resolution became an alternative to the traditional Morgenthau (1948) power politics approach to International Relations (see *Power*).

This problem solving approach, with its analytical focus on human motivations and relationships, was soon seen to apply to all social and political levels, thus offering an alternative to the power-based law-and-order approach to the problems of societies. A body of theory and a Conflict Resolution literature quickly evolved. Conflict Analysis and Resolution emerged as a separate social science area of study. To cope with its comprehensive, a-disciplinary approach, frequently independent institutes and centres were established within universities, rather than separate departments or sections within departments.

By reason of its comprehensive nature, Conflict Resolution is now emerging as a political philosophy, with widespread social and political implications.

## 1. The Post-World War II World Society

The Charter of the United Nations (see *United Nations Charter*) was drafted at San Francisco in 1945. At that time conventional wisdom held that the emerging global society should be a centralized federal system. The central authority was to have final power in the preservation of peace. There were certain international legal norms to be observed. There was to be a Court to interpret these. There was to be a body, the Security Council, comprising the five major powers, plus ten others elected by the General Assembly. The Security Council was given enforcement powers. Member states were to contribute forces for the purpose.

The world society was, in short, to be constructed and administered along the lines of the prevailing single nation state. Majority rule, law and order, the common good, were among the conceptual notions that made up the political philosophy of the time.

## 2. Philosophical Failure

It was not then acknowledged that the common good was, both at the domestic level and at the international level, the common good as interpreted by the powerful. It was assumed, and widely accepted, that authorities which have effective control within their territories are, by dint of this control, politically legitimized authorities.

We now know from experience that this power conception of legitimization is false. In the absence of consensus support, the maintenance of law and order through coercion by a central authority, can be a source of violence and protracted conflict which spills over into the international system.

The UN was thus flawed from the outset in two ways. Many of its members are non-legitimized authorities and, as such, the source of serious domestic conflicts. And the UN is flawed by its own non-legitimacy. The General Assembly has no means of control in respect of matters of international concern. Only the Security Council can apply law and order, and the permanent members of that body each has the right of veto.

It is hard to believe now, but at the time at which the Charter was drafted, few people, perhaps none at San Francisco, had any clear ideas on the handling of conflict situations outside this traditional power framework. The national central authority coercive model was what was in the minds of all as the ideal for an international institution. The goal was to prevent aggression of the World War II German, Italian and Japanese type. Few were educated to ask why this aggression had occurred, what were the background circumstances, and were there problems that could have been resolved.

It was not until the early 1965 that there was any effective challenge to the normative and authoritarian approach of power theory. When it came, it came in the field of industrial relations. Scholars and consultants (such as Blake, Shepard and Mouton, 1964), pointed to the need for interaction between management and workers if there were to be cooperation and increased productivity. This coincided with work in decision-making theory which focused attention on the advantages of feedback processes, rather than on unqualified power and hierarchical approaches to decision making (Karl Deutsch 1963).

### 3. A Shift in Thinking

A group of lawyers in Britain associated with the David Davis Memorial Institute published in 1966 their considered view that the institutions available to states, judicial settlement, mediation, conciliation, negotiation and the other means contemplated within the UN Charter and within classical power political philosophy, were adequate as means by which to maintain peaceful international relationships. The League of Nations (see *League of Nations*) had failed because of an unwillingness on the part of states to use the instruments available, but the powers given to

the United Nations Security Council had changed this.

The academic community became sharply divided between those who adopted this traditional power view, and those who sought to determine the nature of conflict and how to resolve it through an understanding of it by the parties concerned.

In England in the late 1960s one outcome of this quite bitter academic debate was an attempt by some teachers of International Relations at University College, London, to falsify the belief that parties in conflict were unwilling to cooperate in resolving conflicts. Their hypothesis was that parties in conflicts would endeavor to avoid the costs of escalation of conflicts and to resolve them if they were placed in an exploratory and analytical framework in which they could explore possible options.

Obviously some new process would be required, some analytical process, that would avoid power bargaining from stated positions and would be exploratory once the goals and objectives of all sides had been revealed. Clearly, this would require an appropriate third party, preferably a panel of four or five facilitators, who could inject interdisciplinary knowledge and information, not about the conflict at issue, but about conflicts and human behavior generally which the parties could apply to their conflict (see *Arbitration, International*). This would need to be without publicity so as to avoid charges of weakness by leaders who were willing to negotiate with the enemy, and possibly change perceptions and policies.

One test case in the mid-60s concerned a conflict in South East Asia, involving Indonesia, Malaysia and Singapore, which the British Prime Minister of the day, Harold Wilson, had tried to mediate. The parties had all refused to accept his invitation—which he had made public. With his knowledge and consent the London group invited the three heads of government to send nominees to meet in London for an off-the-record analytical and exploratory dialogue. They responded immediately. The nominees met for ten days in a face-to-face situation controlled by a panel of five scholars. The agenda was an analysis of the situation, with no preliminary proposals. There was no bargaining or negotiation. All three discovered that they shared the same fears and aspirations, possible infiltration sponsored by the other parties, of their economies by foreign nationals. After some days they could communicate readily. They returned home. Fighting stopped and diplomatic relations were reestablished without any public statements. (For an account of this intervention, see "Civilizations in Crisis" in *International Journal of Peace*

*Studies* Vol 1 No 1.)

This exercise was followed by others which again falsified the proposition that conflicting parties would not meet together. The same processes were tested at the industrial level and at the community level. Much was learned by these experiences, which were shared by many scholars working in the field. Confidentiality became an important consideration. There were none of the usual academic reports of experiments. Once it was accepted by the parties that there would be no publicity or reporting of any observations made during discussions, at least for many years, changes in attitudes and policies could be made, without any possibility of accusations of being "weak" or climbing down. The degree to which parties reperceived the total situation, and the values and motivations of their "enemy," came as a welcome surprise to those facilitating and observing.

### 4. The Development of Theory

A theory of behavior was now required which would not merely explain why parties were unwilling to meet within existing international institutions, but which would also indicate what kind of institutions and processes would be acceptable and helpful.

Paul Sites, in 1973, introduced a previously neglected behavioral dimension into the study of human relationships. He attributed "power," not to governments, but to individuals and groups of individuals. He observed that they use all means at their disposal to pursue certain human needs. The individual or group has an inherent need for a social role, an identity and identification with others, and social recognition as an individual or ethnic group. He argued that there are certain societal needs that *will* be pursued regardless of consequences. This, in his view, was the source of ultimate power and explained why authorities are powerless in many situations, both domestic and international, to deter or to enforce their decisions.

It was then possible to make a clear distinction between human needs, such as those listed by Sites and which are an ontological part of the human organism, and interests, such as commercial and material interests. It followed that in any conflict situation there are differences (interests) that can be negotiated, but there are also differences (human needs and some cultural values) that are not for trading at any price. The latter, being ontological needs, are shared by all parties. When there is a direct interaction they are readily recognized by all as shared sources of conflict to be removed.

It was necessary, therefore, in resolving any conflict situation, to work towards political structures that enable the full development of the individual and of the identity group to which the individual belongs. Ethnic conflicts could not be settled by "democratic" majority government, and other options had to be explored (see *Ethnic Conflicts and International Relations*). Indeed, the major role of panels associated with conflict resolution processes would be to be innovative in translating the shared needs and values that are revealed by the dialogue into political structures, institutions and behaviors that would promote their fulfillment.

There is one other strand in the development of conflict resolution theory that should be noted. We are here dealing with what must be regarded as the most complex field of study that man will ever come across: the behavioral relations of humans as persons and as groups. It happened that, during this period of development of behavioral theory, the philosophy of science was also developing. What was previously described as scientific method was found to be not so scientific, and indeed, useful and reliable only in limited circumstances. The debate between Popper (1957) and Kuhn (1962) revealed shortcomings in controlled experiments and in empirically based theorizing. It also demonstrated that a formal deductive approach that relied upon falsification was impractical, as such testing was usually not possible in open systems.

Further insights emerged after Peirce's work on "abduction" (1980)—the questioning of the consensus assumptions. Those engaged in conflict resolution analysis were persuaded, by the behaviors and responses revealed in a conflict situation, to conclude that traditional concepts of law and order, of the common good, of majority decision making, of the right to rule and to expect obedience, were probably at the root of a great deal of social conflict. Clearly this was the case in situations where there was an absence of political legitimization. The attempt to impose structures that denied to people their identity and their development in all aspects, and the attempt to impose the norms of the powerful, were dysfunctional and a source of conflict.

### 5. Recent Developments: Interests and Needs

The theory of needs led logically to the development of a process that would enable parties in conflicts to ascertain the hidden data of their motivations and intentions, and to explore means by which human-societal needs held in common could be satisfied. As these needs were universal, and as they related to security, identity and other developmental requirements that are not in short supply, the process soon revealed that conflict resolution with win-win outcomes was possible.

Many research and teaching institutes in different cultures have now sought to test both theory and practice in actual situations. The Foreign Service Institute of the US Department of State has published reports on the process (1986). An extensive literature on conflict resolution now exists (Banks and Kelman 1984; Burton 1979 and 1990; Dukes 1996; Mitchell and Banks 1996; Sandole and Van der Merwe 1993 and many others).

In summary, classical thinking led us to believe that conflict was about negotiable interests only. For that reason it was thought that the individual could be socialized and, if necessary, deterred by punishments. What both conflict theory and resolution processes revealed was that protracted conflicts are primarily over non-negotiable human needs such as those listed by Sites. This being the case, it is impossible to socialize the individual into behaviors that run counter to the pursuit of security, identity and other aspects of development (Burton 1997). The warning flag is out: conflicts, such as wage disputes, and conflicts over opposing cultural and national "human values," may not really be over negotiable interests. They may relate to needs that are not for trading, such as being treated on the shop floor as a person and not a machine. Indeed, it may well be that conflicts are protracted unnecessarily just because inalienable values (identity) are translated into interests (wages) merely to fit into the traditional processes of bargaining and negotiation. When analytical processes are available, the hidden data are revealed and can be dealt with.

A new conceptual frame requires a new language. As suggested, there is a need to redefine disputes and conflicts. A "dispute" may be a matter for negotiation, but a "conflict" has its sources in values that are not subject to bargaining or negotiation. "Prevention" by police action is a quite different concept from "prevention," that is getting to the source of problems so that they do not occur. There are many terms with special meanings within this non-power philosophy (Burton 1996).

## 6. Settlement Processes as a Cause of Protracted Conflict

At the international policy level, however, there has been little change. National defense is the main priority of state policy. Superiority of power remains the goal of states—which leads to adversary diplomacy and politics, and to arms escalation. States, and the UN as the institution of states, still see the global society in the classical framework.

In the absence of any national institutions or international agency with the role of conflict resolution, leaders of powerful governments intervene. They seek credits for their initiatives, and informal, confidential exchanges become impossible. Publicity forces parties to adhere to their positions to avoid being accused by local interest groups of weakness in changing their positions.

There are, in addition, structural conditions which make any significant change towards conflict prevention unlikely. Whenever there are political changes which remove a source of serious international conflict, as for example, changes in the former Soviet Union, other serious situations seem to emerge, for example, the denial of "human rights" in China and its reactions to Western policies, and existing "preventive" structures are once again justified and extended. The practical reality is that national armies, intelligence agencies and the global arms industry combine to make up an interest group more extensive and powerful than any other likely combination of problem-solving structures (Saul 1993 and Timberg 1996).

## 7. The Problem of Change

The evolution of civilizations has required change and adjustment to change, yet "survival of the fittest," the struggle by leaders and potential leaders for recognition, identity and a social role, results in many built-in mechanisms for preservation against change. Leadership and elites seek to conserve existing roles and institutions by whatever military and political means are at their disposal until overcome by more powerful forces. Societies have always been in conflict because some sections have drives for change stemming from pursuit of their human needs, while others fear it and its threat to their interests.

The facilitated conflict resolution processes that have now evolved are effective to the extent that parties to conflicts are helped to cost accurately the consequences of change or no change, to cut down the delays that occur in change, and to speed up the evolutionary process toward greater fulfillment of societal needs. Societies are moving towards insights and processes in which bargaining of needs against interests can be avoided, and in which the parties concerned can define needs and interests, and cost the consequences of preserving interests at the expense of needs.

Translated on to the global scene the great powers fear change lest it prejudices their relative power positions. Yet all sides know that change in political systems is not merely inevitable, but also desirable. The US does not particularly desire to defend repressive feudal systems in Central America and elsewhere throughout the globe, but it fears the consequences of unpredictable political change. China fears the responses of existing "great powers" to its emergence as a major developing economy. Analytical interaction has not yet taken place. If there were a means of reliably bringing about change with desired outcomes, many situations in the world society would no longer attract great power interventions.

## 8. An Emerging Political Philosophy

The shift of Conflict Analysis and Resolution as a study from the resolution of specific conflicts to the "provention" of conflicts by getting at their institutional sources is a shift towards an altered political philosophy. It is a shift from adversarial political, industrial legals and other institutions towards problem-solving processes.

This makes Conflict Analysis and Resolution a challenge to all social sciences, which have to date failed adequately to include a human dimension. Economics treats unemployment as a function of economic development, treating the unemployed as robots to be employed or not according to financial needs governing inflation and investment. Sociology was founded on the assumption that the human being is malleable and can, if socially motivated or coerced, adjust to institutional requirements. Politics is still within the traditional power frame and continues to define "democracy" as majority rule, the majority frequently being elected by a minority of voters, and excluding many class and ethnic groups.

Once a human dimension is included in social analysis it becomes clear that many traditional assumptions are false, and no more than historical myths. The long-term trend from feudalism, through industrial relations and political classes towards continuing and increasing conflict has now placed civilizations in crisis. A holistic approach is required to all problems: conflict, crime, violence, corruption and other sources of personal insecurity.

The analytical challenge is finally a challenge to political philosophy. Democratic systems are founded on adversarial institutions: adversarial party politics, adversarial industrial relations, adversarial legal systems and processes, and others which are power

based and do not take into account the human needs which have been found to require satisfaction if there are to be non-conflictual relationships.

In the light, however, of structural conditions which ensure the continuing production and sales of weapons of war, and professions which rest on continuing threats to security, national and international movements towards conflict resolution, to be credible, must be within the prevailing defense, intelligence, and industrial structure. It may be possible to modify or eliminate some adversarial processes in party political processes, in industrial relations, in law and order, in families, etc., but more than this becomes no more than idealism, at least until these preliminary changes become accepted and future generations are educated in a non-power environment.

## Bibliography

Banks M, Kelman H C 1984 *Conflict in World Society: A New Perspective on International Relations.* Wheatsheaf Books Ltd, Sussex

Blake P R, Shepard H A, Mouton J S 1964 *Managing Inter-Group Conflict in Industry.* Gulf Publishing Co

Burton J W 1979 *Deviance, Terrorism and War: The Processes of Solving Unsolved Social and Political Problems.* St. Martin's Press, NY

Burton J W 1990 *Conflict Resolution and Prevention.* St. Martin's Press, NY

Burton J W 1996 *Conflict Resolution: Its Language and Processes.* The Scarecrow Press, Lanham, MD; London

Burton J W 1997 *Violence Explained.* Manchester University Press

David Davis Memorial Institute 1966 *Report of a Study Group on Peaceful Settlement of International Disputes.* London

Karl D 1963 *The Nerves of Government.* The Free Press, NY

Kuhn T 1962 *The Structure of Scientific Revolutions.* The Chicago Press

Mitchell C, Banks M 1996 *Handbook of Conflict Resolution: the Analytical and Problem-solving Approach.* Pinter, London

Morgenthau H 1948 *Politics among Nations: The Struggle for Power and Peace.* Knopf, NY

Peirce C S 1980 Induction in Peirce, I. In: Mellor D H (ed.) *Science, Belief and Behavior.* Cambridge University Press

Popper K 1957 *The Poverty of Historicism.* Routledge & Kegan Paul, NY

Sandole D J D, Hugo van der M 1993 *Conflict Resolution: Theory and Practice.* Manchester University Press

Sites P 1973 *Control, the Basis of Social Order.* Dunellen Publishers

Tinberg R 1996 *The Nightingale's Song.* Simon and Schuster

Saul J 1993 *Voltair's Bastards: The Dictatorship of Reason in the West.* Penguin Books

United States Department of State, Foreign Service Institute.

1986 *Perspectives on Negotiation*

JOHN W. BURTON

# Conflict Resolution, Process of

## 1. Introduction

Conflicts of today, whether of a socio-economic, political, cultural or ecological nature are different from those of the armament nature in the recent past. They are, perhaps, more complex with multi-dimensional determinants, and thus because of their inter-linkage actors and actoral behaviour their solution needs more perseverant, painstaking, attentive or cautious and especially confidence-building treatment. Therefore the traditional processes of conflict-resolution need to change according to the needs of present contemporary and emerging social conflicts (see *Social Conflicts and Peace*). Skilled and tactful mediation and conciliation are necessary for finding out realistic solutions. Since there can be different determinants and elements in conflict-formation so there can also be different ways and means as well as processes for conflict resolution. While conflict-maintenance is a negative and passive process, conflict-management towards solution can be characterised as a positive and progressive one; and development from divergence to convergence can be regarded a positive phenomenon in the process of conflict resolution. In cases where the dimension of conflict is large and multi-attitudinal, the process of mediation and conciliation can be long and vast. Among the confidence-building measures and necessary pre-conditions for conflict-resolution a state and stage of common and mutual security of feelings need to be created.

It should be pointed out here, that in understanding a conflict and its process towards solution, there is a need for a thorough background and historical analysis. Some of the component elements or parts of a conflict do have organic linkages and the analysis of each part cannot be taken separately. Thus a separate or partial analysis cannot give a conglomerated solution to the whole problem. Although it should be also recognised that a partial solution to a complex and integrated conflict-situation can pave the way to solving the problems of other component parts. One can term it as the stage-level theory or aspect of conflict settlement. The partial nuclear arms reduction by the superpowers, the USA and the former USSR, can be exemplified as a concrete case to prove the validity of the above statement for proceeding towards a General Disarmament. But partial solution is not equitable to partial analysis.

Besides the logical aspects of arguments, approaches and evidences which contribute much to the process of mediation, conciliation and settlement of conflicts one cannot exclude the role of suddenness, accidental, unilaterality and unwarranted positive decisions. Logic cannot explain magic or unexpectation, but unexpectations can also happen in case of conflict-settlement in the same way as irrationality wins over the rationality in conflict-formation.

The study, besides reflecting on different aspects and prospects of the process of conflict-resolution as well as different models of conditions, pre-conditions and aftermaths of mediation and conciliation, will also deal with the theoretical and practical topologies, cooperative and competitive conflict management and settlement models as well as the emerging effective alternative trends in the behavioral process of conflict resolutions. Since there exists the structural process of conflict-formation, there can be found also the destructural process of conflict-resolution.

Conflicts can be of (i) intra-nation and (ii) inter-nation types. Intra-nation conflicts take place within the same nation-state boundary or geopolitical territory while inter-nation conflicts may take place among two or more nation-states within the same geographical region or regions, beyond regional or continental boundaries. Intra-nation conflicts may be either of social, a civil war or armament nature. Social conflicts do have class character in the majority of the cases, but some of them also have an origin in the problems and complexities of religion, language, culture, racism, tribalism, ethnicity, provincialism, economic and political chauvinism (see *Conflict Resolution, History of*). Inter-nation conflicts are mainly due to power-chauvinism or issues of dominance (Guha. A. 1989). These can also be related to boundary problems, religious problems, and to economically and politically motivated neo-colonialism. But all of these determinants have one basic root and that is power-hegemony. The main motivations and forms of expression of hegemonism can be traced in fig. 1.

## 2. Conflict Formation: Cardinal Reasons

Coercion constitutes the very essence of hegemonism and can be of economic, political, social, cultural, power-demonstrating or maintaining military-type in nature. For example, the former Soviet Union, Rumania, People's Republic of China, and Bulgaria, had long been practicing political-motivated, multi-directional measures of homogenisation by integrating the national and ethnic minorities into a national majority. Of course, as a result of Glasnost and Perestroika policy-measures a democratisation process from the Centre has started taking place in the former Soviet Union (see *Glasnost and Perestroika*), but Mao's "Let hundred flowers bloom and thousand schools of thoughts contend" idea is far away from materialisation in Chinese soil. The COCOM terms and conditions of the US monopoly and dominance over technology and its export-embargo to East Europe and certain Third World countries will be the basis of conflict between the United States and its political allies, Western Europe and Japan. The old colonial powers like the UK and France will still colonize territories, and control the post-1950 liberated new-state-nations, through the linkage-system, in the same way as the United States has been practicing the application of the COCOM agreement.

## 3. Types, Areas and Dimensions of Conflict-Involvement

Both the direct and indirect types of armed conflicts and conflict involvements in area levels like system, region, and nation-state may extend from the local level of dimension to a multi-level and international one. Different types of conflict are classified in fig. 2, distinguishing between the centre and subcentre of the conflict, and its periphery. Social conflicts mainly originate at the national-state level and these can be of the characteristics shown in fig. 3.

Different strategies are to be adopted at different moments and stages of conflicts, and the creation of appropriate conditions and tactics depend much on them. The resolution of all types of tractable and non-tractable territorial and centre-peripheral conflicts should have two prime motivations:

(a)  equitable co-existence and

(b)  cooperative co-existence,

instead of the competitive one. Competition generates rivalry and hatred, co-operation creates tolerance, rationality and good neighborhood. Any effort to justify or legitimise the motivations of conflicts and the conflicts themselves means their permanentisation.

The process of conflict resolution should always be guided by both (a) goals (motivations) and (b) the means/prospects. Unless there exist well-defined and decided goals, the means, no matter how much and how far better these may be, cannot be effective in conflict resolution. Again, appropriate effective means are to be devised in order to suit the goals. Of course, there always has to be an effective interaction between both the goals and the means.

### Figure 1
Forms and motivations of hegemony

|  | Power Hegemony | | |
|---|---|---|---|
| Forms: | Homogenization | Sanction | Legitimisation of Power-Asymmetry |
| Motivations: | East Europe Political, Cultural and Linguistic dominance of the majority over the minority | Europe Technological dominance as per COCOM agreement | USA, UK dominance over Falklands Islands and French dominance over Caledonia |

### Figure 2
Definition of conflict orientations

| Conflict Classification | Class/Strata Involved in Conflict |
|---|---|
| Centre-periphery | Dominant class and the marginalised class and social strata |
| Centre-subcentre | Dominant class and social sub dominated but allied class social strata |
| Intra-peripheries | Between and among marginalised classes and social strata |
| Subcentre-periphery | Between sub-dominated class/social strata and the marginalised class/strata |

## Figure 3
Peace stages and processes (I)

| System level | Type involvement | | |
|---|---|---|---|
| | Direct (Bilateral) | Third Party (Trilateral) | Multiparty (Multilateral) |
| Regional | USA-Nicaragua USA-Cuba<br><br>India-Pakistan<br><br>China-India<br><br>Chad-Iibya<br><br>Iran-Iraq | Red Khmer-Sihatnuk Royal Nationalist-Vietnamese involvement in Cambodia<br><br>Sri Lanka (Sinhalese vs Tamils and India) | Korean War (North Korea, South Korea, China, USSR, USA, Japan)<br><br>Afghanistan USSR, USA, Pakistan, Iran & rival Afghans |
| Nation State | Sri Lanka Civil War: Sinhalese-Tamil<br><br>India Armed Unrest: Khaliathani Sikhs-Hindus & others<br><br>USSR Civil Unrest: Armenia<br><br>China Civil Unrest: Tibetans-Chinese in Tibet<br><br>Canada Aborigine Indians-White | Dictatorship vs People in some countries in Asia, Africa and Latin America and the direct and indirect involvement of the United States under the pretense of protecting own rights | |

## Figure 4
Peace stages and processes (II)

| | STAGES of and for Peace | | |
|---|---|---|---|
| | Primary | Secondary | Final |
| PROCESS<br><br>of and for<br><br>peace | Creation of atmosphere for negotiation | Consultation | Cooperation |
| | Understanding the conflict situation | Mediation | De-escalation (status-quo and non-spread of aggression) |
| | Bringing the parties to the stage of discussion and the table of and for evaluation | Re-consultation and clarification Loss & Gain Give & Take Strategies & Tactics | Evaluation of + & - aspects or gains and sacrifice of points. |
| | | Conciliation at the point and stage of confrontation | Compromise & final understanding & conclusion of final agreement |

## 4. Process of and for Peace

While conflicts can be defined with both the subjective and objective backgrounds and argumentation, the process of and for peace has to be started with only the objective understanding of each situation (Guha. A. 1980). Such process can be characterised as stage process which can be traced as in fig. 4. In the process of consultation and mediation for conflict-resolution one can find the operation of structural, bargaining, and compromising power, as defined in fig. 5. Both the Structural and the Bargaining powers may generate confrontation at the talks for negotiation, but the Compromising power paves the way for conciliation.

Because of the direct and indirect involvements by the superpowers, and by other powers with direct interests in the trilateral/tripartite and multilateral/multipartite conflicts, it has become much more difficult to categories them (Jackson, S. et al., 1978). Most of the conflicts of our time, are therefore the victims of multi-party involvements or participation, which begs the question of how to proceed towards conflict resolution. One needs, naturally, to analyze the preconditions and conditions of the moments of conflict before proceeding to the process of finding out solution (Eckhardt, W. and Azar, E. 1979).

## 5. Pre-conditions and Conditions of Acceptable Conflict Resolution

Conflicts once started try to find out both the objective and subjective arguments in their favour and legitimise them in order to either (a) prolong them, or (b) to win over the adversaries (Holst, K. 1966). Conditions for processing the resolution of conflicts need the understanding of the pre-conditions and phases of the conflicts. We may identify the pre-conditions or moments in time and the processing conditions through fig. 6. In analysis of the processing actoral behaviour for peace, there are (a) subjective and (b) objective actors of conflict-formation which generate the respective confrontation and concilia-

tion. The motivational roots of these actors may be presented as in fig. 7.

While the subjective actors generate mistrust, misperception, suspicion and finally, confrontation, the objective actors like self and mutual interest (self in the sense of promotion of own national/social class interest in an atmosphere of peace and peaceful co-existence) lead to conciliation. However, conciliation should not be regarded as a weakness as the hegemonistic partner in the conflict might think. The actors which lead to conciliation do, generally, contribute to the understanding of the causes and effects of resolution to each of the conflicting partners more objectively and precisely [2].

Conflict management towards some resolution has some practical and problematic aspects:

(a) can the perception and fear of violence be avoided [1]?

(b) can the suspicion of coercive or contractual consent be avoided?

(c) can the initiative be taken from within rather than from outside?

(d) can the convergence of expectations be achieved?

(e) how to avoid deadlock and what types of measures should be taken in such situation?

(f) how to prepare a conciliatory mentality from the point of departure of winning mentality?

(g) how to achieve the minimisation of fear about the strength of the adversary?

The above, of course, needs the persuasion of time, space and objectives (goals).

## 6. Process of Conflict Resolution

Since the causes of conflict may be of both the objective and subjective types, the process of conflict resolution may also be both of the objective and subjective nature, because these are dependent on (a) motivations and (b) action programmes (Burton, J.

*Figure 5*
Definition of power types

| Power Type | Meaning |
|---|---|
| Structural | the controlling and dominating power |
| Bargaining | the power of being placed at superior position |
| Compromising | the power of acceptable understandability |

### Figure 6
Momental pre-conditions and processing conditions for conflict-resolution

| Conditions for processing the resolution of conflict | Raw Moment | Hard Moment | Crisis Moment | Ripe Moment |
|---|---|---|---|---|
| | Creation of tensionless standing | Removal of misunderstanding | Avoidance of destabilization | Confidence building |

⎿➔ Pre-conditions of conflict

### Figure 7
The processing actoral behaviour from conflict to peace

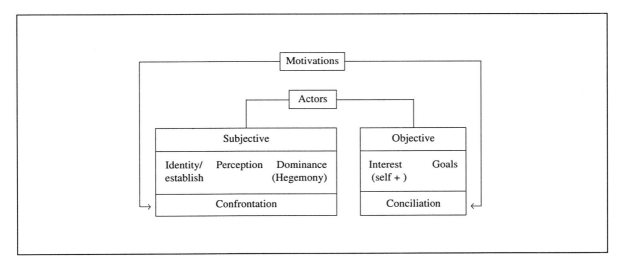

### Figure 8
Conflict resolution process

| Motivations | Motivation type | Conflicting Parties<br>Bi-parties    Multi-parties |
|---|---|---|
| Objective: | Indirect | Mediation |
| | Direct | Consultation talks/deals |
| Subjective: | Indirect | Skilled impartial consultation input of neutral position setting creation of positive atmosphere |
| | Direct | Favorable attitude formation for conflict resolution/realistic diagnosis for conflict formation/ prescription for conflict resolution |

*Figure 9*
Factoral relationship between the conflicting parties and the degree of controversy
(Subject-object relationship)

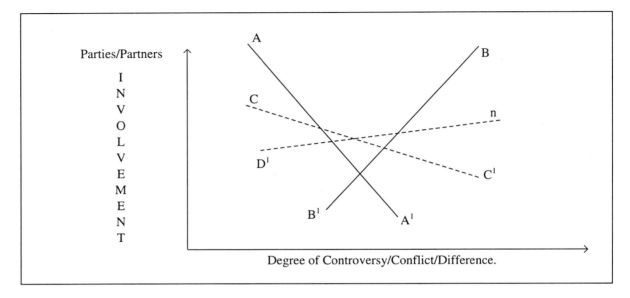

1969). The process of conflict resolution may be put as in fig. 8.

In order to implement the concepts of fig. 8 in a realistic way one is to take into consideration the following cardinal points:

(a) value-judgement for value-realization (Guha, A., 1991),

(b) understanding the incompatibility in order to create the ground for compatibility,

(c) judgement of conflict-stage and conflict analysis for taking standpoint in mediation/conciliation,

(d) means for realisation of balance to be taken in negotiation (Guha, A. 1989),

(e) means for realization of balance from imbalance, etc.

Conflict can be characterized as a dynamic process of both the subjective and objective elements with cognitive and perceptive behavioral aspects (Guha, A. 1979). This is valid for both the armament and social conflicts. In the process of conflict resolution two factors need cognitive and evaluative attention: (a) parties or partners involvement and (b) degree of difference and controversy. The inter-relationship between these two factors can be put as in fig. 9. The stronger the relationship between the involved partners and the degree of controversy (the difference) is

to the vertical, so the process of conflict resolution becomes more difficult. Again, when the relationship between them is more horizontal the process becomes much easier.

From fig. 9 we can see that the relationship between the parties/partners involved in the conflict and the degree of difference or controversy:

(i) is more vertical and complex in cases of A-A[1] and C-C[1], and

(ii) is more horizontal and nearmost in cases B-B[1] and D-D[1].

From the typological point of view, conflict resolution and conflict-maintenance process may be either of (i) cooperative or of (ii) competitive nature. The cooperative process is more constructive and is based on the value of equity. The competitive process is more coercive and is based on the principle of hegemony. Their motivations and characteristics maybe concretised as in fig. 10.

From this figure one can observe that:

(i) the competitive process of conflict resolution and management cannot be a lasting one because of its vertical nature, while:

(ii) the cooperative process may contribute to more stable and lasting solution because of its more horizontal nature.

*Figure 10*
Characteristics and conceptual framework of conflict resolution

| Type of Process | Characteristics | Conceptual Clarity |
|---|---|---|
| Cooperative | | |
| (a) | Perceptive + Cognitive | Sensitivity to commonness and similarity |
| (b) | Attributive | Confidence (Mutual/Common) and Friendliness and Helpfulness |
| (c) | Communicative | Accuracy, Relevance and Openness |
| (d) | Goal | Solution with mutual/common consent and conscience |
| Competitive | | |
| (a) | Perceptive + Cognitive | Sensitivity Development to Differences and Distrust |
| (b) | Attributive | Suspicion, Aggressiveness (Enmity), Hegemonistic Dominance and Coercive |
| (c) | Communicative | Misrepresentation, Wrong Interpretation, Half-truth and Concealment |
| (d) | Goal | Solution through Pressure and Coercion, Escalation and Prolongation |

Of course, the cooperative process of conflict resolution and management may suffer from some hindrances of diverse nature like:

(a) Cognitive: Schematic Rigidity, Stereo-type of Solution and less Objectivity if the resolution is pre-determined,

(b) Misperceptive: Imbalance of Actoral Behaviour related to objective-subjective evaluation, and

(c) Imaginative: Wrong Judgement.

These hindrances of the cooperative process of conflict resolution become the fundamental premises of the competitive-type of conflict resolution.

### 7. Can there be an Alternative Process of Conflict Resolution and How?

Willingness to resolve any conflict and hence fixing the goals for conflict resolution paves the way for finding out appropriate methods and means for it. When a situation of peacelessness or of conflict arrives, the parties or partners-in-cause must try to avoid direct conflict by applying rationality and opening the door for conscious mediation and conciliation (Guha, A. 1988).

While this is the condition for the pre-conflict situation, the pre-condition for conflict situation should be (i) the creation of non-conflict stage with a strong will to avoid conflict and (ii) to sit down immediately at the negotiation table, without thinking much of material and hegemonistic gains. Humanistic moral victory should constitute the very foundation of a genuine alternative conflict-resolution strategy. Subjective arguments to maintain and prolong conflict-situation and conflicting action should be avoided. The conscientious objectives to resolve conflicts, and to achieve them, the creation of objective process can become the very core of the new process of conflict resolution. The roots of each conflict being different, there cannot be any prescribed or pre-determined process of conflict resolution. Each conflict is to have its own diagnosis from its very causes or premises. The negotiators in conflict resolution should have authority not only to negotiate but to create resoluble binding decisions.

### 8. Destructural Process of Conflict Resolution: How?

The modern structural analysts and theorists of conflict formation do, rightly, conceive that the conflicts are, mostly, generated by the Centre (the structure), where Centre can be defined as such:

(a) at Global territorial level: the Superpowers (and the sub-Superpowers in alliance) in case of both the armed and economic/political conflict arena (Guha, A. 1984),

(b) at National territorial level: the dominating and functional power at the national centre over the national sub-centre and peripheries in respect of armed, economic-political, boundary, linguistic, ethnic, tribal and other problems,

(c) at Global dominance level: economic, political and strategic power cartel/alliance for imposing dominance or enforce dependence of all varieties over the dependent peripheries, and

(d) at Social level (national and international): Dominating social strata/class alliance over the helpless dependent social strata and class/classes.

Destucturalisation and decentralised or destructuralised efforts and actions are the positive responses for solving structural conflicts. Whether at the global or at the national level, the relationship between the centre and the periphery is always vertical and any type of vertical relationship is the root of all types or varieties of conflicts. Both the peripheries and the sub-centres are dominated from the centre by direct contacts, and peripheries are never allowed to unite to take any defensive and offensive types of strategies and measures against the centre (see *Colonialism; Neocolonialism*). All types of territorial, economic, political, social and cultural destructuralisation/decentralisation, with horizontal interests and hence goals motivation, can generate the basis of equitable end equal human and material relation. On the basis of equity and equality the peripheries can establish common communication and common background of goals and means, in common interest. And by this way they can solve the existing conflicts and conflicting situation between, and among, themselves and hence avoid any such emerging conflict or situation in the future. The peripheral unity or the unity of the destructured societies can put a check on the structural violence of the centre.

See also: *Conflict: Inherent and Contingent Theories; World Peace Order, Dimensions of a; Peace, Systems View of*

*Notes*

1. *Conflict Quarterly*, Centre for Conflict Studies, University of New Brunswick, Canada, 1991
2. *Conflict Studies*, the Institute for the Study of Conflicts, London, 1988 and 1989

*Bibliography*

Burton J 1969 *Conflict and Communication*. Free Press, New York
Eckhardt W, Azar E 1979 Major world conflict formation. *Gandhi Marg* I(3) (June) Gandhi Peace Foundation, New Delhi
Guha A 1979 *Peace Education and Peace Research: East-West and North-South Confrontation in Theory and Practice, in Peace, Development and New International Economic Order*. IPRA Secretariat, Tampere, Finland
Guha A 1980 *Concept on Conflict and Peace*. Gandhi Marg, Gandhi Peace Foundation. New Delhi
Guha A 1984 Conflict and Cooperation between the United States and the Euro-Nato in the Seventies and Eighties: Economic, Military and Political Dimensions. *Scandinavian Journal of Development Alternatives* III(1) (March), Stockholm
Guha A 1985 *Conflict and Peace: Theory and Practice*. Institute for Alternative Development Research, Oslo
Guha A 1986 *Premises and Perspectives of Conflict Resolution between Mainland China and Taiwan*. Institute of International Relations, Taipei
Guha A 1989 *Elements in Conflict Formation*. Gandhi Marg, Gandhi Peace Foundation, New Delhi
Guha A 1991 *Disarmament Education: Why and How?* (Speech at the UNESCO Conference on Disarmament Education, 1979), in Approaching Disarmament Education, London
Holsti K J 1966 Resolving International Conflicts: A Taxonomy of Behaviour and Some Figures on Procedures. *J. Conflict Resolution* 3
Jackson S, Bruce R, Snidal D, Sylvan D 1978 Conflict and coercion in dependent state. *J. Conflict Resolution* 22(4) (December)

AMALENDU GUHA

# Confucianism and Neo-Confucianism

With the advent of the Neo-Confucian thinkers in the Sung Dynasty (960-1279) there came a reintegration of Confucian themes into a metaphysically more profound understanding of the universe. "The Great Harmony" of Chang Tsai (Chang Heng-Ch'u 1020-

77) was an intellectual achievement which consolidated Confucian ethics and principles of governing into a harmonious unity which comprehended the universe. Having constructed a rationalistic and naturalistic theory on the basis of the universal presence

of the principle of vital individuation, *ch'i*, Chang could claim a metaphysical grounding for a universally comprehensive ethical value of benevolence, *jen*. In his *Western Inscription (Hsi Ming)* Chang proclaimed:

> Heaven is my father and Earth is my mother, and even such a small creature as I find an intimate place in their midst . . . .
> *All people are my brothers and sisters, and all things are my companions* . . . . Even those who are tired, infirm, crippled, or sick; those who have no brothers or children, wives or husbands, are all my brothers who are in distress and have no one to turn to.

From the foundation of this comprehensive harmony Chang developed a justification for benevolent government and the pursuit of the self-cultivated virtue of benevolence which extended to embrace the whole of humanity and creation. These themes had precedents in the earlier Confucian texts from which Chang had drawn his inspiration.

In particular, the concern for benevolent government and the peace it engendered had been explicitly refined in the writings of Mencius (371-289 BC). Within the dialogues of *Mencius*, the "Kingly Way" (*wang-tao*) is proffered as an alternative to the bellicose tendencies of King Hui of Liang (Book 1, Part A, section 3). Being too "fond of war," King Hui had actually developed a rationale for his aggressive military maneuvers: if the crops failed, he would simply encroach on his neighbors in order to provide provisions and new land for his people.

Mencius' response situates the "Kingly Way" in direct opposition to hegemony (*pa-tao*). These aggressive actions interfere not only with peoples but also with the harmony which they should maintain within the balance of Heaven, Man, and Earth. If the natural resources are not exploited and their natural cycles of fruition are not disrupted, there would be no lack of nourishment; if more care was directed to the education and discipline of the people, particularly in their respectful relations between each other, the problems of hunger and shelter could be overcome. A benevolent government persists in responsible communication with all its people, in sensitive directives to preserve the natural environment, and in educational structures and imitable actions of the ruler which promote the welfare of all. These are the principles of government which cause peace to predominate.

The interrelations between Heaven and the people establish the possibilities for the continuity of government. An earlier Confucian classic, the *Book of Documents*, identifies the Mandate of Heaven (which designates the ruler who is to take hold of the governing responsibilities) with the mandate of the people. If the people are nourished, guided, and educated, they will naturally respond in support of the ruler; the state will increase in peace and in numbers. In this way the pursuit of peace aggrandizes the harmony between the ruler, the people, and the flux of Nature.

In view of this concern for harmony, another Neo-Confucian scholar, Ch'eng Hao (1032-85) thoroughly worked out the role of "Heavenly Principle" (*t'ian-li*). The complete development of one's nature (*chin-hsing*) in accordance with the Heavenly Principle brings about the union of man with all things. Recognizing the reality of both good and evil in the realm of human beings, Ch'eng Hao asserted that the harmony of which Chang Tsai had spoken could only be actualized in the refinement of oneself. Once self-refined, one could envelop more and more of the ambient world within the expanding sympathy of benevolence until the whole was unified. The extension of one's nature provided the praxis for achieving unity. Certainly Ch'eng Hao's approach did not carry the rational development of Chang Tsai's vision that "all people are my brothers and sisters," but it did suggest that the issues of self-cultivation were intimately involved with the actualization of that ideal. From the vantage point of cosmological differentiation he mapped out the extent to which a person's being was the adhesive which could unite all things.

The Confucian virtue of benevolence had earlier been associated with governmental achievements which had united otherwise separate and antagonistic groups. In the *Analects* Confucius referred to the government of Duke Huan of Ch'i as exemplary in this regard (14:16-17). Duke Huan is noted as the first of the Five Leaders among the feudal lords who organized and maintained the protection of the Chinese against external invasions. It is not, however, this military achievement which receives Confucius' attention; rather it is the peacemaking effort of one of Duke Huan's famous statesmen, Kuan Chung which is identified as an action befitting benevolence.

> Kuan Chung helped Duke Huan to become the leader of the feudal lords and to save the Empire from collapse. To this day, the common people still enjoy the benefit of his acts . . . .
> It was due to Kuan Chung that Duke Huan was able, without a show of force, to assemble the feudal lords nine times. Such was his benevolence!

It is Confucius' insight that powerful government need not be judged on the basis of its military prowess and arrogant display of power, but rather upon its ability to orchestrate peace even in the face of malevolence.

The great synthesis of Neo-Confucian thought employed both the pervasiveness of the principle of vital instantiation, *ch'i*, and the grounding *ch'i* had in the metaphysical principle, *li*, which gave structure to its physical counterpart. All this was created by Chu Hsi (1130-1200). Chu recognized the power of the metaphysical unity claimed by Chang Tsai and realized the practical significance of the role of self-cultivation in actualizing benevolent government which promoted peace.

Three basic measures for achieving good government were articulated by Chu. First, he urged that ministers should "invite the able and sagely, reject the vicious and the crooked, and open one's mind to all men under heaven for securing order under heaven." Government which is open to the advice of those who have displayed cultivated benevolence will recognize that the achieved unity of the people is the standard it must pursue in order to maintain peace. This unity is made possible through "open[ing] one's mind to all men under heaven." The essential principle of sensitive dialogue between ruler and the ruled is established as a cornerstone for peace.

Secondly, Chu urged that the ruler should be unselfish and public minded, rectifying his mind so that he can listen and get close to the righteous while detaching himself from the petty. The reaffirmation of the model role of the ruler in self-cultivation, a central motif of the Confucian tradition, is in the manner integrated into the goal of peaceful and prosperous government.

Finally, Chu believed that "learning and clarifying the true meanings and principles of things will enlighten the minds of people and enable more people to know principles. In this way one need not worry about failure in government." Here the Confucian trust in the value of education in its effect on stability is restated in the light of Chu's own metaphysical commitment to the principle *li*.

Chu Hsi's achievement came in his synthesis of these elements of governmental policy which summarize the pursuit of peace within the Confucian and Neo-Confucian traditions.

See also: *Confucius; Mencius*

*Bibliography* ———————————————

Asai S 1982 *Mōshi no Reichi to Ōdō Ron* [Mencius' Theories on Ritual/Wisdom and the Kingly Way]. Kōbundō Shuppansha, Tokyo

Cheng C Y 1977 Toward constructing a dialectics of harmonization: Harmony and conflict in Chinese philosophy. *J. Chinese Philosophy* 4(3)

Cheng C Y 1981 Legalism versus Confucianism: A philosophical appraisal. *J. Chinese Philosophy* 8(3)

Chiang K H 1982 Shih Lun Chang Tsai te "T'ien Jen Ho Yi" Ssu Hsiang [On "Heaven and Man become One" in Chang Tsai's thought]. *Jen Wen Tsa Chih* [Journal of Humane Literature] 6

De Bary W T 1983 *The Liberal Tradition in China*. Columbia University Press, New York

Fang T H 1981 *Chinese Philosophy: Its Spirit and Its Development*. Linking, Taipei

Feng Y L 1981 Chang Tsai te Che Hsueh Ssu Hsiang chi ch'i tsai Tao Hsueh chung te Ti Wei [Chang Tsai's philosophical thinking and his position in Neo-Confucianism]. *Chung Kuo Che Hsueh* [Chinese Philosophy] 5

Fingarette H 1981 How the "Analects" portrays ideal authority and its mode of operation. *J. Chinese Philosophy* 8(1)

Hsiao K C 1979 *A History of Chinese Political Thought*. Princeton University Press, Princeton, New Jersey

Jochim C 1981 Naturalistic ethics in a Chinese context: Chang Tsai's contribution. *Philosophy East and West* 31(2)

Kasoff I E 1984 *The Thought of Chang Tsai (1020-1077)*. Cambridge University Press, Cambridge

Schirokauer C 1978 Chu Hsi's political thought. *J. Chinese Philosophy* 5(2)

Tillman H C 1981 The development of tension between virtue and achievement in early Confucianism: Attitudes toward Kuan Chung and Hegemon (Pa) as conceptual symbols. *Philosophy East and West* 31(1)

Tu W M 1979 Ultimate self transformation as a communal act: Comments on modes of self-cultivation in traditional China. *Journal of Chinese Philosophy* 6(2)

CHUNG-YING CHENG

# Confucius

Confucius (Kong Fu Zi) was one of a handful of men who have exercised a great influence upon human history by virtue of their intellectual gifts and achievements. In China, as well as in many other countries in the East, he was held in the highest respect for generations. In the West, his influence was also tremendous. Reichwein says that "Confucius became the patron saint of the eighteenth century Enlightenment" (*China and Europe* p. 77).

Confucius was born in 551 or 552 BC in the small state of Lu, a part of modern Shandong Province, China. We cannot be certain about his ancestry but it is probable that there were aristocrats among his forebears. His father died when he was very young and he was brought up in poverty by his mother. In his youth he held minor offices—keeper of granaries and superintendent of parks and herds—to earn a living. He set his heart on learning at 15 and thus became a man of erudition in later days.

He lived in a time where "the world had fallen into decay, right principles had disappeared, ministers overthrew the throne, and sons murdered their fathers." He had an ambition to serve in high office in the hope that he could undertake the work of reformation and restore the social order and morality of humankind. However, he made no progress in his own state of Lu which at the time was controlled by usurpers. Then for more than 10 years he travelled from state to state, accompanied by some of his disciples, seeking a ruler who would use his philosophy in his government, but he never found one. By 484 BC, he returned to Lu and spent the last period of his life as a private teacher, giving instruction to his students in the principles of right conduct and right government, hoping that those who obtained careers in government would be more successful than he himself had been in putting his ideas into effect. In his last years he was greatly saddened by the death first of his son and then of his favorite disciple, Yan Hui, at an early age. He himself died in 479 BC. A biography of Confucius can be found in the *Records of the Grand Historian* (*Shih ji*), written at the beginning of the first century BC by Si-ma Qian but the information is, to some extent, unreliable. Because Confucius gained the reputation of a sage, apocryphal stories about him abounded from very early times. Therefore, to have a clear picture of Confucius, we must rely on the *Analects* (*Lun yu*), supplemented by the *Mencius* (*Meng zi*) and the Zuo-zhuan, and discard the elaborate traditional legends of his life.

Confucius' teachings cover a wide range of topics—from universal truth to daily social behavior. This article, however, deals solely with Confucius' theories that are directly related to the thoughts on peace.

First and foremost, Confucius emphasized that benevolence (*sen*), is the most important moral quality a person must possess. With this moral quality, one can become as good a person as possible or, at least, not impose on others what one does not desire oneself. Furthermore, "the truly virtuous man, desiring to establish himself, seeks to establish others; desiring success for himself, he strives to help others

succeed" (*Analects* VI: 28). Confucius believed that people are essentially social beings and society is nothing more than the interaction of these people. The moral person must be a cooperating member of the society. If everyone is benevolent and cooperative, society will be in peace.

Confucius laid stress on the system of ethics: the natural love and obligations between members of the family as the basis of a general morality. Parents should be kind and benevolent to their children and children should fulfil filial duties to their parents. If a man is a good father or a good son at home, he can be counted on to behave correctly in society. So, love for people outside one's family is looked upon as an extension of the love for members of one's family.

Confucius considered the rites (*li*) a key part of education. The rites are a body of rules governing action in every aspect of life and they are the repository of past insights into morality. It is therefore important that one should observe them. Psychiatrists believe that our education today, though it cultivates the intellect to a high degree, often fails signally to discipline emotions. Confucius considered intellectual cultivation to be of little worth if it is not accompanied by emotional balance. To produce such balance, he depended on education in *li*. He said, "If one tries to guide the people by means of rules, and keep order by means of punishments, the people will merely seek to avoid the penalties without having any sense of shame. If one leads them with virtue and to maintain order by the education in *li*, the people will feel their moral obligation to correct themselves" (*Analects* II: 3).

Confucius declared that the ultimate purpose of government is the welfare of the common people (*min*). To this end, the government should be administered by the most capable men in the country. Such capability has nothing to do with birth, or wealth, or position, but is solely a matter of character and knowledge. This philosophy was developed later by Mencius (372-289 BC) who advocated a benevolent government and emphasized that the ruler was set up for the benefit of the people. However, Confucius was not a pacifist. He believed that there are times when force must be used, by moral men, in order to prevent themselves and the world from being enslaved by those for whom force is the only argument and the only sanction. But he considered force the last resort and that it must always be subordinate to the power of justice.

To sum up, Confucius' teachings are chiefly based on a moral philosophy. In his eyes, benevolence (*sen*) was conceived of as the totality of all moral virtues. To practice *sen*, a person must behave correctly at home and in society, and love his or her fellow people. The society, as well as the world, will be in good order and in peace, when everyone is disciplined by means of *li* and the country is administered by capable people who work for the benefit of the people in the full conviction of morality.

See also: *Confucianism and Neo-Confucianism; Mencius*

*Bibliography* ————————————————

Chang C 1959 *Confucianism and the Modern Civilization.* Taipei

Ch'en T 1964 *The Teachings of Confucius.* Taipei
Ch'ien M 1975 *A Brief Biography of Confucius.* Taipei
Chung C 1983 *Studies on Confucius.* Beijing
Creel H G 1949 *Confucius, the Man and the Myth.* New York Taipei
Confucius 1979 *Analects.* Penguin, Harmondsworth
Dawson R S 1981 *Confucius.* Oxford University Press, Oxford
Ho P H 1995 *Five Essays on Confucianism.* Hong Kong
Nivison D S, Wright A F (eds.) 1959 *Confucianism in Actions.* Stanford University Press, Stanford, California
Smith D M 1973 *Confucius.* London
Yip C 1977 *The Moral Philosophy of Confucius.* Taipei

KENNETH P. H. HO

# Congress of Vienna

The congress which assembled in Vienna towards the end of September 1814 was primarily concerned with the reorganization of the European states system in the aftermath of the revolutionary and Napoleonic wars. It had to deal with a multitude of problems relating to the redrawing of frontiers, the establishment of new administrations, and the restoration of old dynasties. Much of its work, which was completed by the *acte final* of June 9, 1815, was done by specialist committees. But its proceedings were dominated by the spokesmen of the principal victorious powers, Austria, Prussia, Russia, and the United Kingdom, and of the defeated France. These included the Emperor Alexander I of Russia, who attended the congress in person, Lord Castlereagh, the British foreign secretary, the Prince von Hardenberg, the Prussian chancellor, the Prince von Metternich, the Austrian foreign minister, and the Prince de Talleyrand, the foreign minister of France.

The attention of the peacemakers was focused upon a Europe which had been divided by war for the greater part of 22 years. During that time the spirit, though not all the ideals, of the French Revolution had been carried far beyond the boundaries of the First Republic, and Napoleon had established his hegemony over most of the continent. By 1810, France's frontiers extended northwards to the Baltic, and southwards to encompass Piedmont, Tuscany, and Rome. New French departments had been created in Istria and Dalmatia, and new dependencies had been brought into being in the shape of a confederation of the Rhine, a kingdom of Italy, and a grand duchy of Warsaw. Moreover, the thrones of Spain and Westphalia had been presented to Napoleon's brothers, and his brother-in-law, Joachim Murat, had secured that of Naples. In this process the archaic Holy Roman Empire had been abolished, ancient principalities and republics had been swept aside, and the lands of the Habsburgs and the Hohenzollerns had been severely reduced in their extent. It was in these circumstances quite natural that France's conquerors should have envisaged the restoration of a European equilibrium which would ensure that no major power should again dominate the others, and which would be capable of enduring any fresh revolutionary challenge.

Already, since their victory at Leipzig in October 1813, the allies had concluded agreements amongst themselves and with Napoleon's successors which were of fundamental importance for the structure of international relations in Europe, and for the territorial settlement. Thus on March 9, 1814 Castlereagh had persuaded Austria, Prussia, and Russia to join with the United Kingdom in the Treaty of Chaumont, a consolidating alliance which bound its signatories to continue the war until the defeat of France, and to take up arms again in the event of renewed French aggression. Castlereagh hoped that he would thereby be able both to overcome differences between the allies during the last stages of the war, and to effect the future containment of France. This last aspiration was also apparent in the support which the coalition powers gave to the restoration of the Bourbons to the throne of France, and in the terms of the peace settlement which they subsequently imposed upon the French. It was assumed that Louis XVIII, the brother of the ill-fated Louis XVI, would be able to survive the relinquishment of territorial gains made since the

Revolution, and that he would possess sufficient authority to avoid becoming dependent upon any other power.

The first peace of Paris, which the allies (including Portugal, Spain, and Sweden) concluded with Talleyrand on May 30, 1814 was nonetheless moderate in the territorial demands which it made upon France. Its new frontiers were thus to conform with a generous interpretation of those which it had known in 1792. And overseas it regained most of those colonial territories which the British had occupied. At the same time the settlement anticipated the proceedings at Vienna in so far as it foresaw the incorporation of the former Austrian Netherlands in an enlarged Dutch kingdom an enhanced Prussian presence in the Rhineland, the confederating of the German states, the reestablishment of an independent Switzerland, Austrian and Sardinian annexations in Italy, and the British retention of Malta. In effect France would henceforth have to reckon with a continuing alliance amongst its recent enemies, and the emergence of stronger political entities on its northern and eastern frontiers. The hope of Castlereagh and his colleagues was that the French could be deterred from further interference in areas where they had traditionally sought to exercise an influence.

Many matters of detail, such as the division of the left bank of the Rhine, remained unsettled by the first peace of Paris. Nevertheless, it was a triumph for Castlereagh's diplomacy since it met his principal objectives in western Europe, and left him free to concentrate on the potentially more divisive problems of the east. There the main threat to the balance of power seemed in the eyes of Castlereagh and Metternich more likely to come from the Russians than the French. Napoleon's defeat and his retreat from Germany had been made possible by Russia's employment of its massive reserves of manpower, and its armies had thrust deep into the heartland of Europe. In the spring of 1813 Metternich had tried to sponsor a mediated settlement which would, whilst freeing Germany from the French, have left France powerful enough to counterbalance Russia. Eighteen months later he had to reckon with Alexander I's determination to hold on to most of the grand duchy of Warsaw, and to make himself king of Poland. It was also probable that Alexander would have the support of Frederick William III of Prussia, who was tempted by a Russian proposal that he should have Saxony as compensation for the nonreturn to Prussia of lands originally acquired in the Polish partitions of 1793 and 1795. Such a bargain, which would have strengthened Austria's two northern neighbors, was

anathema to Metternich. The most he could agree to was the possibility of Prussia securing Saxony, or of Russia keeping the grand duchy. He could not accept both of these territorial accessions.

Castlereagh was likewise opposed to Alexander's scheme. Wedded to the notion of a strong central Europe, which would be able to withstand French and Russian pressures, he cooperated with Metternich in trying to separate Prussia from Russia. But while Hardenberg was prepared to accept a project which would have made the Vistula Russia's western frontier in Poland, his royal master was incapable of resisting the wishes of the Czar. Frederick William regarded Alexander as his savior, and the aggrandizement of Prussia in Germany was a more attractive proposition than the restoration of Polish territory. This left Castlereagh and Metternich with only limited room for maneuver. There was little chance of their being able to dislodge the Russians from Poland, and Prussia's demands on Saxony, whose unfortunate king had delayed too long in joining the alliance against Napoleon, threatened to undermine the coalition. Indeed, the dispute over Saxony allowed Talleyrand, who had initially been excluded from the discussions of the four major allies, to offer his assistance to Metternich.

Faced with the likelihood of a continued deadlock on the Saxony issue, and with Hardenberg talking openly of the possibility of war, Castlereagh and Metternich accepted a proposal from Talleyrand for an alliance. This, however, was essentially a tactical move which, though it added to France's prestige, was intended to persuade the Prussians to compromise on Saxony. In this respect the Austrians and the British were successful. Prussia's negotiating position was weakened when early in January 1815 Alexander agreed to a Polish settlement which left him with all the former grand duchy except Posen, which returned to Prussia, and Cracow, which was transformed into a free city. And on February 6 the Prussians gave way and accepted the northern half of Saxony, along with the promise of a very considerable addition to their territories in the Rhineland and Westphalia.

These arrangements did little to check Russia's advances towards the west. Alexander had already acquired Finland from the Swedes, and Bessarabia from the Turks, and the kingdom of Poland which he added to his dominions was only slightly smaller than Napoleon's grand duchy. Moreover, although the survival of an independent Saxony was of some comfort to the Austrians, Prussia's position in northern Germany was substantially improved. Prussia's gains were to some extent balanced by Austria's recovery of territories lost to the Bavarians and the French. But the final German settlement was less than satisfactory from Castlereagh's point of view. The Germanic confederation, which was intended to embrace all the German states, including much of Prussia and the western half of Austria, thus emerged from self-appointed German committee of the congress as a very loose union of 34 princes and four free cities. It was provided with a diet composed of representatives of the states under the presidency of Austria. No effort was made, however, to set up any genuinely federal institutions, or to achieve agreement on a common currency. The strong center that Castlereagh had desired in Europe would henceforth depend upon Austria's capacity to provide leadership in Germany, and Prussia's willingness to cooperate.

In retrospect it seems surprising that Austria should have been expected to fulfill this role. The Austrian empire, which had only come formally into existence in 1804, had neither the demographic advantages of Russia, nor the economic ones of the United Kingdom and although its position in central Europe was consolidated by the acquisition of Lombardy-Venetia and the coastal littoral of Istria and Dalmatia, its new responsibilities in Italy placed a further strain upon its limited resources. Thus the Emperor Francis became the virtual protector of Tuscany, whose grand duke was his brother, of the duchies of Parma and Modena, whose new rulers were respectively his daughter and his grandson, of the church lands, which returned to the Pope, and of the Spanish Bourbons, who were eventually restored to Naples. True, and enlarged kingdom of Sardinia, which comprised, besides the island itself, Liguria, Nice, Piedmont, and Savoy, was intended to assist Austria in the defense of Italy against the French. But the house of Savoy, like that of Hohenzollern, was in the end to prove to be more of a rival than an ally of the Habsburgs.

The Italian settlement was only achieved after long and difficult negotiations at Vienna. One of the main problems arose from the fact that in January 1814 Murat had agreed to desert Napoleon and to ally with Austria in return for a promise that he might keep his Neapolitan throne. Thus, when at Vienna Talleyrand demanded the application of the principle of legitimacy and the return of the Bourbons to Naples, Metternich, though not unsympathetic to this course, found it expedient to procrastinate. His patience was rewarded, for when in March 1815 Murat learned that Napoleon had escaped from his island exile on Elba, he rallied to the emperor's support and attempted to raise Italy against the Austrians. It was a gallant, but

futile, gesture, and after the French defeat at Waterloo on June 18, Murat was captured and executed.

Napoleon's 100 days also led to the revision of the peace of Paris. French enthusiasm for his cause had seemed to demonstrate that moderation in the treatment of France had failed, and there were appeals from the Bavarians, the Dutch, and the Prussians for a more punitive treaty. But Castlereagh continued to favor a conciliatory approach. Any considerable dismemberment of France would, he feared, weaken the government of the re-restored Louis XVIII and upset the balance of power that he had striven to establish. If further restrictions were to be placed upon the French, then he favored temporary to permanent measures. He was backed by Alexander and Metternich, and the terms of the second peace of Paris, which was concluded on November 20, 1815, though unacceptable to Talleyrand, could hardly be regarded as harsh. France was thus compelled to part with strips of territory on its northern frontiers (including the Saar valley), to pay an indemnity of 700 million francs, and to accept an allied army of occupation for three to five years. At the same time, Austria, the United Kingdom, Prussia, and Russia, concluded a Quadruple Alliance, which provided for the maintenance of the peace settlement, and for periodic conferences between their sovereigns or foreign ministers in order to ensure the execution of the treaty, and to permit consultations on matters of common interest.

Unlike the Holy Alliance, which, at the instigation of Alexander I, Austria, Prussia, and Russia concluded in September 1815, and which emphasized the need for monarchical solidarity against revolution and war, the Quadruple Alliance was not based upon any religious or ideological principle. Nor was its membership open to other powers. It was a practical attempt to carry over into the postwar world some of the experiences of coalition diplomacy. It also sought to maintain the ascendancy of the Great Powers. Indeed, one of the main criticisms which was later levelled against the Vienna settlement was that it had been achieved by the Great Powers to the detriment of the interests of the smaller European states. The peacemakers were accused of having been reactionary in their approach, and of having applied the principle of legitimacy, rather than that of nationality, in recasting Europe.

Such charges were valid, but contradictory. The interests of small countries were certainly subordinated to the requirements of the Great Powers and to their desire to establish a viable balance of power. Saxony was compelled to provide Prussia with compensation for its losses in Poland, and no attempt was made to revive either the Genoese or the Venetian republic. The claims of many German princes to the restoration of their estates were similarly ignored, and the Roman catholic church was unable to recover the territories of the prince-bishops of Germany and the Low Countries with which Napoleon had conveniently dispensed. In these last instances, however, both the rights of small claimants and the principle of legitimacy were set aside. The peacemakers of 1814-15 recognized the virtues of Napoleon's rationalization of central Europe, and the Germanic confederation gave a very limited recognition to German nationhood.

Nationalism was, nevertheless, to assist in the destruction of the territorial settlement of Vienna. One of its first victims was the new kingdom of the Netherlands, which Castlereagh had considered vital to the containment of France. Just 15 years after the signing of the final act, an insurrection in Brussels commenced the process which led to the separation of Belgium from the rest of the Netherlands. Moreover, national and liberal revolts elsewhere in Europe both then and in 1848-49, and the establishment of the Second Empire in France, portended further changes. In 1859 the French and the Sardinians drove the Austrians from Lombardy, and in 1860 most of Italy was united under the Savoyard dynasty. The following decade witnessed similar developments in Germany, where Bismarck identified Prussia with the national cause, and after wars with Denmark (1864), Austria (1866), and France (1870-71) he founded a German empire from which the Austrians were excluded. Prussia's victories allowed the Italians to acquire Venetia and to deprive the Pope of Rome and the other remnants of the patrimony of St. Peter. In the meanwhile, France obtained Savoy and Nice, and lost Alsace-Lorraine.

Long before these events transformed the map of Europe the congress system had collapsed. Revolution and friction in the Near East, an area which lay outside the scope of the Vienna settlement, divided the former allies, and between 1854 and 1856 the United Kingdom and France fought and defeated Russia in the Crimea. Moreover, the idea of a balance of power based upon a roughly equitable distribution of strength between individual Great Powers was supplanted after 1871 by one linked to shifting alliances and alignments. It is, however, easy to overlook some of the more enduring achievements of the congress. Quite apart from such agreements as those reached on diplomatic precedence and the navigation of Europe's waterways, the peacemakers of 1814-15 provided a framework for a concert of European Great Powers which survived in some of its essentials until 1914. And despite the failure of their attempt to institutionalize that concert, diplomats and politicians continued to subscribe to the notion of a European community of states. During the nineteenth century Great Power status was to be synonymous not just with the possession of great economic and military potential, but also with a willingness to share in the corporate responsibility for maintaining order in Europe. Such a system could neither eliminate Great Power rivalries, nor prevent armed conflict. Nevertheless, it could limit their impact, and it gave to Europe a kind of unity which it took two world wars and another revolution to destroy. Since 1945 world states-men and -women have only rarely been able to aspire to that sense of a common purpose that imbued those of the Congress of Vienna and their heirs. The aristocratic values of 1815 were lost in the transition from a Continental balance of power to a global balance of terror.

See also: *Balance of Power*

*Bibliography*

Bridge F R, Bullen R 1980 *The Great Powers and the European States System, 1815-1914.* Longman, London

Crawley C W (ed.) 1965 *The New Cambridge Modern History, Vol. 9: War and Peace in an Age of Upheaval, 1793-1830.* Cambridge University Press, Cambridge

Gulick H V 1967 *Europe's Classical Balance of Power.* Norton, New York

Kissinger H A 1957 *A World Restored: Metternich, Castlereagh and the Problems of Peace, 1812-1822.* Weidenfeld and Nicolson, London

Palmer A W 1972 *Metternich.* Weidenfeld and Nicolson, London

Sked A (ed.) 1979 *Europe's Balance of Power, 1815-1848.* Macmillan, London

Webster C K 1931 *The Foreign Policy of Castlereagh 1812-1815: Britain and the Reconstruction of Europe.* Bell and Sons, London

Webster C K 1934 *The Congress of Vienna.* Bell and Sons, London

KEITH HAMILTON

# Congress System

The Congress System is the name generally given to the series of "summit meetings" held by the major Allied Powers from the end of the Napoleonic Wars in 1815 until 1822. Their purpose initially was to guard against any revival of revolution in France and to superintend the peace settlement. Great Britain, Austria, Prussia and Russia had already in the Treaty of Chaumont (March 1814) pledged themselves to make no separate peace with Napoleon but jointly to achieve his defeat, to continue their cooperation after the war, and to form, for twenty years, a defensive alliance against any future French aggression. The process was taken further in the Quadruple Alliance of November 1815.

Much had happened in the meantime. Following Napoleon's surrender in April 1814 and his exile to Elba, had come his triumphal return to Paris in March 1815 and "the Hundred Days." The Congress of Vienna was then in session, the Act of the Congress, or general treaty of peace, being signed on 9 June. On 18 June came Napoleon's final defeat at Waterloo. The first Treaty of Paris of may 1814 was replaced by a second Treaty of Paris, with harsher terms for France, on November 20, 1815.

The Quadruple Alliance was signed in Paris on the same day as the Treaty, and was intended to provide for the security of Europe for the foreseeable future. By its terms the four Allies agreed to maintain the Treaty of Paris, to exclude forever the Bonapartes from the French throne, to keep an army of occupation in France for the time being, and, in Article VI:

> to renew their meetings at fixed periods, either under the immediate auspices of the Sovereigns themselves, or by their respective Ministers, for the purpose of consulting upon their common interests and for the consideration of the measures which at each of those periods shall be considered the most salutary for the repose and prosperity of nations, and for the maintenance of the peace of Europe.

This Article, drafted by Castlereagh, the British Foreign Secretary, was the basis of the Congress System. Like the Treaty of Chaumont, the System was a product of his initiative and reflected his belief not only that continuing inter-Allied cooperation was needed to counter any new threat from France, but that conflicts and tensions between the Great Powers could best be resolved through the habit of talking and working together (see *Power*). In particular he saw the System as a means to "contain" Russia, the greatest military power on the Continent, and to defuse the rivalry between Russia and Austria.

The first major question the Powers needed to address concerned their policy towards France. Wellington saw that the presence of the Allied army of occupation, which he commanded, through irritating French public opinion was weakening the position of the French monarchy which had been newly restored in the person of Louis XVIII. He therefore, in January 1817, recommended that it should be reduced by 30,000 men. A little over a year later, in March 1818, the British cabinet suggested withdrawal of the Army altogether, but that a special force should be based in the Netherlands. The Allies decided to call a Congress to discuss these matters.

It met at Aix-la-Chapelle, in the Rhine Province of Prussia, at the end of September 1818. The participants were the sovereigns of Russia, Austria, and Prussia, and their ministers, and Castlereagh and Wellington for Great Britain. Of these, the most prominent negotiators were Czar Alexander, Metternich (the Austrian Chancellor) and Castlereagh. France was invited to send a representative and Louis XVIII shrewdly chose the Duc de Richelieu, who as an *émigré* had formerly been Governor of Odessa, and who soon won the Czar's complete confidence.

The Congress swiftly disposed of the French issue. The French indemnity to the Allies of 265 million francs having been paid or guaranteed, and Louis XVIII now with an army of his own to maintain his regime, the army of occupation, it was agreed, could be withdrawn by the end of November. The next step was to admit France under Article VI of the Quadruple Alliance as a fifth member of the system. The four original Allies, however, renewed the Alliance as a reinsurance against France. This was done in a Secret Protocol to avoid hurting French sensibilities, although the Duc de Richelieu was privately informed, moves to bring in other Powers, notably Spain, were successfully resisted by Castlereagh. He wanted an Alliance based exclusively on the Treaties, not a general Congress that might become a vehicle for the "Holy Alliance" policies of the Continental monarchies (see *Alliance*).

The "Holy Alliance," a product of the mystical enthusiasm of Czar Alexander I, had been concluded between the Czar, the Emperor of Austria, and the King of Prussia, on 26 September 1815. It was a pledge of the three monarchs, who described themselves as "fellow countrymen," to rule their peoples in accordance with Christian principles, and to support one another in these endeavors. All the other Christian sovereigns of Europe were invited to adhere to it. The whole scheme was patriarchal and dynastic and entirely contrary to the spirit of constitutionalism and nationalism which was increasingly permeating the countries of western Europe, if not always their governments. The British cabinet refused to become involved on the grounds that adherence to treaties was a governmental act, and not the personal prerogative of the sovereign. The other Powers subscribed to the Holy Alliance, partly as a means of humoring or even subtly restraining the Czar, and partly as an excuse for taking such anti-revolutionary measures they deemed to be in their best domestic or international interests.

The ideological difference was already apparent at Aix-la-Chapelle. If, under the Holy Alliance, international society was to be based on dynasties, then the natural concomitant would have been a general guarantee of thrones and territories. This was the Czar's proposal. Castlereagh would have none of it. Not only would it have given the Russians an excuse to march their huge armies all over Europe in order to suppress revolution, but it would, besides encouraging the most reactionary forms of government, have involved Great Britain in endless Continental commitments and entanglements. Owing to British objections, Prussia and Austria backed down from a general guarantee, but Castlereagh felt he had to go some way to accommodate the Czar. The result was two instruments signed on November 15, 1818, the first being the Secret Protocol mentioned above, and the second a Declaration, to which France was invited to adhere, restating the principles of the Powers' cooperation, and notably the preservation of peace on the basis of the Treaties and the need for periodic meetings, when the occasion arose, to discuss matters of common interest. Even this proved almost too much for the British cabinet, especially a faction led by Canning, where there was dislike of the very idea of repeated Congresses, besides which, in the new Parliament and the country, Castlereagh was coming under increasing attack for his whole policy of working with the autocrats of the Holy Alliance.

Events of the next few years revealed the widening gap between Great Britain and the other Powers. The former, even under the ultra-Tory administration of Lord Liverpool, was a commercial and constitutional state in which the spirit of liberalism, partially suppressed during the Napoleonic Wars, was once more a growing force. On the Continent, however, the anti-revolutionary reaction was still in the ascendant. In the Carlsbad Decrees, August 1819, Metternich imposed police state repression upon the whole German Confederation and when, in July 1820, revolution broke out in Naples, a state with which Austria had a treaty relationship, he turned to the Czar for support. Alexander, already alarmed by a revolutionary outbreak in Spain, proposed a new Congress of the Powers to consider the situation in the Italian peninsula.

The Congress met at Troppau (the modern Opava) in Austrian Silesia, from October 20 until December 30, 1820. It was more purely a Holy Alliance affair than its predecessor, the participants being the Russian, Austrian and Prussian sovereigns and their ministers, with Metternich as the driving force. The British government, seeing the Neapolitan revolution as primarily a local matter, and therefore not requiring international intervention (which except in the possible case of France it was in principle against) was represented by an observer only. The French too, after British persuasion, limited themselves to observer status. The British and French were in consequence excluded from the innermost deliberations which produced the Troppau Protocol. This declared:

> States which have undergone a change of government, due to revolution, the results of which threaten other States, *ipso facto* cease to be members of the European alliance, and remain excluded from it until their situation gives guarantees of legal order and stability. If, owing to such alterations, immediate danger threatens other States, the Powers bind themselves, by peaceful means, or if need be by arms, to bring back the guilty State into the bosom of the Great Alliance.

To Castlereagh this was a reiteration of the right of interference in the domestic affairs of others which he had successfully countered at Aix-la-Chapelle and he subjected the Troppau Protocol to a devastating criticism, holding that it had no basis in the Treaties, was contrary to international law, and would not only undermine sovereignty but place Europe under a species of police dictatorship. He much regretted that he had not been present to exercise his customary influence on the Czar.

Before anything further could be done the Troppau Congress was adjourned and, for the convenience of the King of Naples and other Italian heads of state who were invited to attend it, transferred to Laibach (now Ljubljana) in Austrian Carniola. It opened on January 26, 1821, and again the British and French sent only observers. A mandate was at once given to the Austrians to send their army into Naples, a step from which Stewart, the British ambassador at Vienna and observer at the Congress, was careful to dissociate his government. The Neapolitan revolution swiftly collapsed as did another insurrection, also put down by Austrian troops—to be aided, if necessary, by 100,000 Russians—in Piedmont.

Castlereagh meanwhile, in a published diplomatic circular, was quick to make the British position clear: the objection was not to the Austrian action, which might be justified on grounds of that power's security, but that it was done in the name of the Alliance, thus implicitly including Great Britain. As before, he could in no way countenance generalized international intervention.

Before the Laibach Congress dispersed, it was decided that a new Congress should be held at Verona, in Austrian Venetia, in October 1822. Here the chief business was the revolutionary situation in Spain, and what action to take. This time Castlereagh had intended to be present, but his sudden death in August 1822 transformed the diplomatic situation. His successor, Canning, had little interest in European diplomacy by conference and his whole outlook was more liberal and nationalist than that of his aristocratic predecessor. Wellington took the place of Castlereagh although working to the instructions that the latter had drawn up.

After the defeat of revolution in Italy, the restive liberals of Spain who had placed their despotic king under constitutional restraint, appeared to pose the chief remaining threat to the monarchical order upheld by the Powers of the Holy Alliance. The Czar's eagerness to march a great Russian army across Europe into Spain so alarmed everyone that Metternich was able to thwart the idea at the Congress of Verona, but it strengthened the claim of France, now swinging towards ultra-conservatism, to do the job herself. In April 1823, proclaiming her adherence to the principles of Troppau and Laibach, but in truth eager to behave loke an independent Great Power again, with the right to dominate what she considered to be her sphere of interest, France sent an army of 100,000 into Spain, and by October had restored Ferdinand VII (like Louis XVIII, a Bourbon) to absolute rule. This action was resented by all the Allies except Russia. Metternich, distrusting France as an unstable, ambitious Power, at first sought to bring down the Spanish revolutionaries by diplomatic means alone, but then, failing in this, tried to bring the French intervention under the control of the Alliance. These tactics lost him Great Britain. Wellington, in Verona, and in accordance with his instructions, had expressed total opposition to the interference of the Alliance in Spain, and now it seemed that the results of the six-year Peninsular Campaign, by which Wellingto himself had liberated Spain from French rule, were being undone. Although unable to save the Spanish liberals, Canning made it clear that he would use the British navy to prevent any attempt by the Holy Alliance Powers to regain for the Spanish monarchy its former colonies in Latin America. The Monroe Doctrine was but a corollary to this decision.

French intervention in Spain also marked the end of the Congress System, for there was no successor to Verona. True, the Great Powers of Europe never entirely lost the habit of conferring together when it suited their purposes, as witness the Congress of Paris (1856), the Congress of Berlin (1878), even the Munich Conference (1938); but the series of gatherings thought up by Castlereagh and brilliantly exploited by Metternich ended in 1822. Partly this was owing to the death of Castlereagh, and that of Czar Alexander only three years later. Both, in contrast to their successors, and despite acute political differences, were at heart internationalists. But there was a deeper reason. The Powers were in process of realigning themselves as the fear of an aggressive, revolutionist France, which had originally brought them together, faded. Post-Congress Europe fell naturally into two ideological camps: on the one hand Great Britain and France (on its return to liberalism), and on the other the three great autocracies of the East. This, broadly, was to remain the pattern until the Metternichian system was brought down by the upheavals of 1848.

The English historian and International Relations theorist, Martin Wight, saw the Congress System of 1815-22 as the second of four great experiments in ecumenical government, taking the Conciliar Movement (1409-49) as the first. Does it deserve this attribution? Like the League of Nations and United Nations which followed it, it emerged from the aftermath of a major war, the creation of those who as allies had cooperated to achieve victory. But unlike its two twentieth century successors, it had no constitution (other than, perhaps, Article VI of the Quadruple Alliance), secretariat, or seat of deliberations, and lasted the shortest span of the four, a mere seven years. All of this leads some historians to doubt whether it was a "system" at all. Moreover, right from the beginning there were very different ideas amongst the statesmen who participated in it as to what they were involved in, or what their objectives were.

To Castlereagh, who has some claim to be regarded as the chief founding father, for it was he who inserted in the Quadruple Alliance the famous Article VI stipulating regular meetings, the object was the harmonization of interests through diplomatic intercourse and personal contact, and in the Congress of Aix-la-Chapelle, the only one which he attended, his intention was effectively fulfilled. But a closer look at the four congresses reveals that what the system became was rather different from what its initiator intended it to be. Unlike the British, who had achieved their own constitutional revolution over a century earlier, in 1688-89, the Continental monarchies feared revolution wherever it might appear and in whatever form it might take. Like a fire it had at once to be doused, lest the sparks should start it up in another place. The result was that the "Holy Alliance" leaders, and supremely Metternich through his sheer diplomatic skill, and with the additional advantage that all but the first of the congresses were held on Austrian territory, took over the Congress System for their own anti-revolutionary purposes. Castlereagh, who might have succeeded in keeping it as a "forum" rather than a "government," was handicapped both by having the additional burden of holding a fragile administration together (as well as being Foreign Secretary he was chief government spokesman in the House of Commons) and by having farther to travel than most of his Continental colleagues. The effect of Castlereagh's absence and consequent loss of influence was, however, that Wight's assessment was well merited, and indeed, in his famous study of the period, *A World Restored*, Henry Kissinger claims that for five months the Congress of Laibach became, in effect, the government of Europe. Yet even before this, the Congress of Aix-la-Chapelle was being accredited almost with the functions of a European government, competent to decide on such matters as the suppression of the Barbary Pirates and the Slave Trade, the rights of European Jews, recognition of the spanish Colonies, the treatment of Napoleon at St Helena, the financial obligations of Sweden, the appeal of the Elector of Hesse to be made a king (refused), a petition of the citizens of Monaco against their Prince, and the ancient claim of the British to be accorded salutes in the Channel.

In comparing the Congress System with the other three great ecumenical institutions, although it resembles the Conciliar Movement (see *Conciliar Movement*) in that the meetings were *ad hoc* and each in a different city, it is in the Security Council, the heart of the United Nations, that the System has its strongest echo. Each was a continuation of the wartime alliance. Each was dominated by the Great Powers. Each was soon riven by ideological differences. The absence of Castlereagh during the Italian crisis had comparable consequences to the absence of the Soviet delegation during the Korean crisis (see *Cold War*), allowing the others to utilize the system for their own purposes. But this is a parallel in form only; the true successor of the "Holy Alliance" police state system was the Soviet bloc, and the right to repress dissent wherever it appeared and was within reach, was to re-emerge, a century and a half later, as the Brezhnev Doctrine (see *Brezhnev Doctrine*).

The Congress System was made possible by a comparatively rare mood in European history: one of monarchical and aristocratic triumph and fellow feeling after the defeat of the greatest threat the old order had ever had to face. Castlereagh had tried to build on this mood a structure for future peace and stabili-

ty. The greatest authority on his diplomacy, Sir Charles Webster, wrote:

> Politics, and especially international politics, so rarely produce men who rise above a weak opportunism, that the spectacle of a man trying almost single-handed to put into practical shape a new conception of international diplomacy is one that compels admiration. Few men could have obtained even the measure of success which was his, and that was only won by almost unparalleled devotion to duty. Castlereagh undoubtedly gave up his life to the cause of international peace. (Webster 1934 p. 502)

The effort was an impossible one, for the future lay with liberalism and nationalism—reflected in British public opinion, expressed most effectively by Canning, and inspiring the politically dispossessed and restless everywhere—with which the monarchical and aristocratic order could have no real accommodation. Castlereagh's increasingly anomalous position, together with overwork, led to his mental breakdown and tragic death. Only he could have breathed fresh life into the Congress System and with his own passing, passed, within a few months, his own creation.

## Bibliography

Aspinall A, Smith E A  (eds.) 1959 *English Historical Documents 1783-1832*. Eyre and Spottiswood, London

Barlett C J 1966 *Castlereagh*. Macmillan, London

Cresson W P 1922 *The Holy Alliance: The European Background of the Monroe Doctrine*. Oxford University Press, New York

Fisher H A L 1936 *A History of Europe*. Arnold, London

Hayes P 1975 *The Nineteenth Century 1814-80*. (Modern British Foreign Policy Series). A. and C. Black, London.

Hinde W 1973 *George Canning*. Collins, London

Hinde W 1981 *Castlereagh*. Collins, London

Kissinger H A 1957 *A World Restored: Metternich, Castlereagh and the Problems of Peace 1812-22*. Houghton Mifflin, Boston Mass

Longford E 1972 *Wellington: Pillar of State*. Weidenfeld and Nicolson, London

Metternich R (ed.) 1881 *Memoirs of Prince Metternich Volume III, 1816-22* (trans.). Bentley, London

Palmer A 1974 *Alexander I: Tsar of War and Peace*. Weidenfeld and Nicolson, London.

Palmer A 1972 *Metternich*. Weidenfeld and Nicolson, London

Sauvigny G de B de 1962 *Metternich and his Times* (trans.). Darton, Longman and Todd, London

Schroeder P W 1962 *Metternich's Diplomacy at its Zenith 1820-1823*. University of Texas Press, Austin, Texas

Seton-Watson H 1967 *The Russian Empire 1801-1917*. Clarendon Press, Oxford

Seton-Watson R W 1945 *Britain in Europe 1789-1914*. Cambridge University Press, Cambridge

Sked A (ed.) 1979 *Europe's Balance of Power 1815-1848*.

Macmillan, London

Ward A W, Gooch G P (eds.) 1923 *The Cambridge History of British Foreign Policy: Volume II 1815-66.* Cambridge University Press, Cambridge

Webster C 1929 *The European Alliance, 1815-1825.* University of Calcutta, Calcutta

Webster C 1934 *The Foreign Policy of Castlereagh 1815-22: Britain and the European Alliance*, 2nd edn. Bell, London

Woodward E L 1938 *The Age of Reform 1815-70.* Oxford University Press, Oxford

BRIAN E PORTER

# Conscientious Objection

Formalized claims of conscientious objection against war are basically recent phenomena that have accompanied the growth of modern war, national military service, and modern political orders, though they have obvious roots in the past, that is, the conscience-based war refusal of early Christians. In the seventeenth century, the Quaker witness created awareness of individual conscience. It was a new phenomenon in politics. One particular exemplification of this recognition in the modern state has been the steady of unspectacular rise of "conscientious objection," a term that was first used in the 1890s (at first in relation to objection to vaccination).

It is important to distinguish between the specific legal category, "conscientious objector" or "CO," as formally recognized by some modern states, and the broader historical and sociological category of "conscientious objection," that is, including all those who have resisted conscription or military service on the *claimed* basis—wholly or partly—of "conscience," whether recognized by a state or not, and whether accompanied by an application or submission to a state or not.

Much confusion, both in the literature and in assessing numbers of conscientious objectors in a society, is caused by the deployment of the former, more narrow, legalistic definition. There are four major subcategories of objectors:

(a) those who seek acceptance as "conscientious objectors" within a state's given legal meaning and who are accepted—on whatever basis or conditions;

(b) those who apply for such status but who are *not* recognized or accepted;

(c) those who conscientiously reject military service, but refuse to *apply* for such a status, on the grounds for example, that such a state demand is illegitimate or that it would imply an acceptance of the state's right to conscript, or to fight a particular war, or to impose military service involuntarily; and

(d) those who do not apply for conscientious objector status because no such status is recognized and to apply for it would be futile, or would not be an obvious or known form of action.

The Society of Friends, or Quakers, have long been associated with conscientious objection (see *Quakerism*). But they were not alone. From early Christian times there has been in very many religious communities the desire to resist war, or at least to distance the religious group and the individual from the institution of war and the performance of military service. This laid one of the moral and political foundations for the more modern "civic right" of conscientious objection, a claim which secular liberal individualists, socialist war resisters, members of other churches (including other peace sects), and international organizations came to support in different ways, at different times, and to different degrees. By the twentieth century it was often claimed as a basic human right. During the First World War, this element was to prove of crucial importance in sustaining the peace movement and anticonscription in wartime, and in building the new antiwar movements at the end of the war. Independent of peace movements since that time, conscientious objection to conscription has been spreading as a basic claim by individuals (human right) in most parts of the modern world.

Just as the rights of religious toleration were granted when religious sects were no longer seen as subversive of secular authority or salient to questions of power, the right of conscientious objection to vaccination was introduced with little fuss during the 1890s, but it was later cited as a precedent in the subsequent debates on involuntary conscription.

Compulsory military service had been much less extensive in the absolute monarchies than under subsequent modern regimes, and many informal methods of accommodation had existed (such as commutation) rather than formal "rights." Indeed, to some extent such exemptions continued after the introduction of conscription, sometimes in the formal guise of special conscientious objector status for certain groups.

Whilst legal or customary exemption of groups and individuals long predated formal "conscientious objection" itself, such exemption was often because of religious scruples, and often specified particular groups. In a number of cases such special privileges simply evolved into grounds for a legal right of conscientious objection to military service. The spread of religious toleration, and the granting of such exemptions to sects, were thus interrelated. But for those who could not claim allegiance to a recognized peace church, like the Quakers or another body with special status, adherence to conscience or a "higher law" usually meant application of state law: trial, often followed by prison, and sometimes death.

At first, for example, in the United States, membership of a recognized religious body was almost the only guarantee of avoiding conscription, but what had been informal and exceptional became systematized into law: as military service became universal, so did statutes covering the status of the conscientious objector. As a result, since their seventeenth century origins, conscientious scruples have increasingly confronted the "rule of law," as opposed to the personal will of rulers. The anarchic implications of this for a militarily defended state are clear enough; active pacifism only became permissible through the conscientious objector loophole as long as it never seriously impinged on a state's ability to mobilize for war—a safety valve in liberal societies, but one quickly closed off in others.

Conscientious objection, when it is in effect merely the exemption of relatively inward-looking religious sects which are numerically small, socially isolated, and politically quietist (Adventists, Brethren, and some Mennonites) involves no real confrontation with state power. As a result, membership of such sects often gave legal as well as social protection: indeed until the First World War, whilst objectors with such affiliations might sometimes receive brutal treatment, they did also have a certain privileged status and often formal exemptions.

The objection to the right of any state to dispose at will of the lives of its subjects in foreign wars came first; opposing the state's right to impose the "duty" of killing was a secondary objection. It could be argued that without these two state "rights" however, the modern state would itself not survive. Such "anarchist" or "subversive" implications of pacifism were disguised by the "conscientious objector" formula. (When couched in religious terms such objections remained continuous with a quasi-monastic or purist exceptionalism.) From the seventeenth to nineteenth centuries such traditional corollaries came to be ignored, and claims for exemption were asserted on simple grounds of the religious "rights" of groups and the religious freedom of individuals. In part, group-based resistance to conscription was legitimized simply because the clear division between "public" and "private," between state and society, had not yet fully emerged.

Of course, such claims against the state as the right of exemption from military service also reflected a more general struggle over rights and freedoms between a central authority and subsidiary power; if the right to object to military service is to be seen retrospectively as an extension of classic liberties like these, it has also emerged through specific phases since the first development of modern conscription systems.

Expressive as well as oppressive functions of the state grow together; permissive and prohibitive legislation, rights and duties, are interlinked. The oddly complementary *duty* of military service, and the *right* of "conscientious objection" are paralleled in other areas of social life. Since many sections of the peace movement are skeptical of the state, they see the claims of the conscientious objector as an irrelevant, individualistic activity that fails to challenge the source of war and violence. As a formal "right," conscientious objection historically emerges as a counterpart of universal conscription (and, some would argue, of universal suffrage). Since the new systematic and comprehensive systems of law and administration are based on equity and universality, claims for exemptions can no longer be dealt with on an arbitrary, localized, or ad hoc basis; there have to be universalistic criteria and general rulings on the performance of "military duty." As each state introduces conscription, it has to assess the place of conscience in its new scheme. The exemptions granted to French Anabaptists during the Revolutionary Wars were seen as a somewhat haphazard accommodation with group consciences, and not a systematic legalization of conscientious objector status. Early Norwegian innovations in the field of conscientious objection, as in some others, were humane and in advance of their time, but the model legal provisions and protections established after 1812 did not all survive into the twentieth century.

Oddly enough—given the subsequent association between conscientious objector rights, liberal legislation, and democratic polities—the first rationalized, formal treatment of conscientious objection emerged in an autocracy. Under Russian Czarism, formal procedures were established for assessing conscientious objector claims, and civilian service options were organized for those (mostly Mennonites) whose applications or status were approved. Claims of objectors grew substantially with the resistance of Russia's religious minorities to conscription after 1874. Following the mass resistance and emigrations of the Doukhobors there were, between 1914-16, 837 officially recorded cases of conscientious objectors; in addition the Mennonites were placed in nine alternative labor camps. An increasingly acceptable solution for most religious conscientious objectors was civilian service, first substantially expanded in Russia after 1890. Czarism pioneered the idea of these civilian public service camps, unattached to the military (later to be copied in the United States, the United Kingdom, France, and elsewhere) to cope with objectors both to military authority and combatant status.

After 1917, civilian service was not available in the United States, however, but once recognized formally as conscientious objectors, individuals were eligible for some sort of "noncombatant" service. The claims of conscience were not easy to prove. Many wartime tribunals found the absolutists' refusal of noncombatant and alternative service incomprehensible. This position was usually adopted by those who made no formal application to the state for exemption from military service, conditional or otherwise; it has been a stance taken by those committed to political or religious positions of an absolutist kind, and was adopted by anarchists, Nazarenes, and Jehovah's Witnesses with the most consistency.

Nonregistrants, who refused to cooperate with the legal preliminary to conscription or selective service, have been sent to jail in most Western countries, whether or not conscientious objector provisions exist. The absolutist stand was adopted by A. J. Muste, one of the leading figures in the United States peace action. His well-known and often reprinted essay on "holy disobedience" publicly advocated noncooperation with military service, and no compromise with either registration or alternative service (see *Muste, Abraham Johannes*). In the United States between May 1917 and May 1918, over 64,000 conscientious objection applications were made (in comparison with nearly three million inductions and 171,000 "draft evaders"), of which 56,000 were legally recognized.

Conscientious objection in Britain in the First World War, although described as only a "minor but intractable problem," was one which was said to concern the Prime Minister (Asquith) even during military crisis. Fewer than one in five British conscientious objectors in the First World War would accept

military control; most of the 16,500 "official" cos who went to prison were either socialists or Christian pacifists, or both.

Insofar as conscientious objector laws and their implementation could not meet the claims of each and every conscience—genuine or spurious—a "criminality of conscience" came into being. If claims were accepted at face value, it would become a universal solution for those who wished to evade "civic duties." The Anglo-American tribunals of the post-1914 period were thus presented with almost insoluble dilemmas, which were typically confronted in an arbitrary, piecemeal, and extemporizing fashion.

Accounts of tribunal proceedings stress the uneven and uncertain operation of the law—or of arbitrary human judgment, an uncertainty compounded in the case of selective objection, where political arguments are brought into play. Can the state "tolerate the potential anarchy" of the individual's claim to judge the morality of each war as a civic right? Also, there is considerable evidence of class or racial, as well as political, bias in the operation of tribunals judging conscientious objectors; this often derived from the cos' lack of experience or literacy. At first the intensification of state opposition to conscientious objection mainly took the form of propaganda, but in addition it became increasingly difficult in many countries to obtain or provide information on exemptions or on the legal rights of objectors (where such laws existed).

In many places propaganda for objection on grounds of conscience had continued to be banned or curtailed. In 1917 and 1918 the United States Congress had passed Espionage and Sedition Acts aimed at all elements opposing enlistment or hindering war mobilization, including civil liberties groups giving co information. Pacifists and peace groups have often supported conscientious objectors by giving such information during wartime, whether or not supporting the refusal to participate in war.

The state's monopoly of coercion over those selected as agents of its violence was affirmed with relentless insistence in the First World War. No rights of objectors existed under the German Empire (1870-1918). Under the Reich, dissenters from the war of 1914 were placed in mental institutions; this included an unknown number of German conscientious objectors of whom some were socialists and Seventh Day Adventists. In most countries, individuals who developed their objection after induction usually faced courts martial and severe sentences, including flogging or execution. Conscientious objectors in France during the First World War were put under military law, and often sentenced to death or long terms of imprisonment as "deserters": 20-year sentences were not uncommon. First World War COS were often manhandled, sometimes brutally. The torture of objectors and the occasional killings of the American Civil War were repeated in 1917-18. Even in "liberal" Britain, as a direct result of their objection, or their experiences in prison, an estimated 73 died, 40 were driven insane, and over 30 were sentenced to death. Thus, even democracies have not questioned the extensiveness of state power or the comprehensive nature of its sovereignty. However, although civic or political rights which are seen to undermine the authority of operation of the state (as does any mass resistance to war mobilization) are unlikely to be granted, in diverse areas, from vaccination to military service, modern democracy has recognized moral claims against, and beyond the state, often involving recourse to "higher laws."

In order to reconcile these two contradictory aspects of the modern liberal state, those who have campaigned for the *right* of objection (as opposed to a privilege or concession) have often stressed the individual, moral, and private character of such objection.

Political objection to military service was actually given legal status in Norway in 1922, through socialist pressure. But except for limited experiments in the former Soviet Union (1917-20), Scandinavia, and Switzerland, formal conscientious objection had never had much recognition even in Europe. Generally, communist or state socialist regimes have *not* granted conscientious objector status, yet immediately after the coup the Bolsheviks did briefly experiment with extremely liberal conscription laws. But by 1929 the last known pacifist groups associated with war resistance and conscientious objection in the former Soviet Union were closed down by the state. The conscientious objector then disappeared from Soviet history: the 1939 conscription laws specifically denied any need or "right" of conscientious objection on the grounds that all applications had ceased by the 1930s!

One of the first modern communist governments to give some recognition to religious objections to military service was, perhaps surprisingly, the German Democratic Republic. Since the early 1950s, the German Democratic Republic has provided noncombatant service as an option, and conscientious objectors associated with the Protestant churches became an active force after 1980.

The Second World War saw a more liberal context for the Western conscientious objector. In the United States, a quasi-civilian service became available in the Second World War, ostensibly under the auspices of the churches, but its status was ambiguous and was dismissed by most conscientious objectors as an "insignificant witness." In the United Kingdom 67,000 males officially registered as conscientious objectors; whilst this partly reflected the size of the mass pacifist movements of the 1930s, it was under one percent of those actually registering (80 percent were upheld as official COs) but about 6,500 people were imprisoned for objection. Once again, official figures reveal only the tip of an iceberg; the total numbers of *formal* CO applications in the United States were in the region of 85,000, but the number of objectors was higher.

Even after 1945, Continental Europe generally remained unsympathetic to conscientious opposition to war; France in particular remained untouched and was the last major Western democracy to make any concessions. With the proliferation of national regimes which between 1945 and 1972 raised membership of the United Nations from 71 to 122, as new sovereign nations joined almost all of them brought in compulsory military service, and by the 1950s the system of conscripting states seemed to have achieved a level of acceptability as a permanent feature of global society, increasingly spreading to women as well as men.

Whilst conscientious objector status was generally gaining ground in the Anglo-American context by the Second World War, such legalized objection was still highly unusual in the rest of the world; indeed even by the end of 1968, despite the United Nations Declaration on Human Rights, only 16 out of 140 sovereign states had any legal provisions for conscientious objectors (with nine of these in Europe). These years were also significant, in the European context, insofar as the debate about conscientious objection as a right, was carried into the arena of formal international and legal debate at the Council of Europe.

During 1966, the Council of Europe began to research and debate the issue of conscientious objection for its member states, seeking to establish some parity of treatment for resisters in different countries, and either amnesty or legal rights for those imprisoned. Various resolutions and reports prepared in the mid-1960s were debated, which were partly based on the assumption that the treatment of conscientious objectors should be raised to the standards of those member states which had liberal CO provisions, rather than that some median or lower common standard should be achieved. Even though only objection to *combatant* service, and provision of alternative service, was considered, these were pointers towards standardization of status in Western Europe. Although the resolutions of 1967 were ambiguous, they helped bring the issue to wider public attention. They also helped internationalize the problems of conscientious objectors and their linkages.

An increasing number of Roman Catholic objectors emerged (e.g., in Italy) in the 1960s, and a statement of the Vatican Council of 1963 considering their cases demanded humane treatment. The phenomenon of selective objection (to particular wars) which had first emerged with the socialist opposition to the First World War, also grew influential after 1960, especially in the former Federal Republic of Germany and the United States, and in the context of the Vietnam War. In the 1960s both the United States and the German figures also show an increasing ratio of political to religious objection.

A new phase for conscientious objection began in 1964, before the major Indochina escalation took place, when Daniel Seeger was freed by the United States Supreme Court on the grounds that the clause in the draft law demanding that conscientious objectors believed in a "supreme being" was unconstitutional and violated several amendments. In the Vietnam context, United States CO inquiries and applications increased tenfold. Although by no means just from pacifists or religious or absolutist objectors, expansion of CO inquiries in the United States had by 1965 again reached its 1947 (predemobilization) total.

Partly due to liberal conscription laws, partly due to wartime experiences, the rise of conscientious objection in the former Federal Republic of Germany was more spectacular than in any other Western country. The German constitution of 1949 had guaranteed the rights of conscientious objectors. By 1968, claims had risen to almost 12,000 COs out of 177,000 drafted, and there were also 4,000 applications from soldiers.

In the same period, the spread of nuclear weapons itself posed the issue of war resistance in a new way: the act of individual conscientious objection, particularly where, as in Britain, conscription had been removed, no longer seemed a relevant form of noncooperation with modern warmaking. Only for those working within the defense hierarchy or in arms manufacture, research, and development, could such conscientious dissociation be a relevant act.

In summary, the situation for conscience, especially in wartime, which grew worse with the mass nineteenth century conscriptions, in many places reached its lowest point during and after the First World War. Generally speaking, after 1914, the treatment of conscientious objectors in wartime changed for the worse. Since the 1940s, it slowly—outside authoritarian

and totalitarian regimes, and including most Third World states—tended to improve, and this improvement has been most marked in the West since the 1950s. At the same time, the basis or motivation for conscientious objection has tended to change and widen in the direction of a more secular and political—though still largely ethical—stance: increasingly this is expressed in terms of absolutist rejection of military service or has moved in the direction of selective objection to particular wars; in both cases it has often involved conscious noncooperation with conscripting authorities.

Despite a somewhat contradictory, uneven picture, on balance the evidence suggests that recognition of objection is still gaining ground, despite an adverse world climate and increasing numbers of military regimes. Despite liberalized treatment of conscientious objectors there is no sign that the most extreme form of objection, nonregistration, or refusal to recognize any part of the system connected with military conscription, is disappearing. But in no state has the selective objector clearly established a claim to exemption.

Despite the peace movements' deepening skepticism about the "liberal" state, there is a recognition that conscientious objection of all kinds retains its salience partly under the wing of an inherited religious toleration, and that political objection continues to be accepted (if at all) on sufferance. It is clear that the institutional germs of modern liberalism included facets that were to become critical to the subsequent organization of "peace movements" and the claims of conscientious objectors.

Views on the relevance of the claim of conscientious objection to peace vary widely within and outside the peace movement. To some individual pacifists, wars will cease when people refuse to fight them; to others this view implies a collective refusal, not an individual objection. To yet others, conscientious objection may dangerously weaken the will or ability of liberal states to defend peace and democracy with conscripted armies. In general, it may be said that conscientious objectors have been a significant prophetic minority within the larger peace movement and have, through their witness and unpopular stances, been a leaven in that movement, providing inspiration, example, and leadership in many groups and organizations concerned both with disarmament and peace and with human rights issues, whether pacifist or not. The tenacity of their often largely symbolic resistance has kept alive the view that all war may be an unacceptable human institution with which civilized peoples should no longer associate.

See also: *Conscription; Pacifism*

*Bibliography* ————————————

Boulton D 1967 *Objection Overruled.* McGibbon Kee, London

Brock P 1970 *Twentieth Century Pacifism.* Van Nostrand, New York

Cain E 1970 Conscientious objection in Britain, France and the US. *Comp. Politics*

Ceadel M 1980 *Pacifism in Britain, 1914-45.* Oxford University Press, Oxford

Nuttall G 1958 *Christian Pacifism in History.* Oxford University-ty Press, Oxford

Prasad D, Smythe T (eds.) 1970 *Conscription: A World Survey.* War Resisters' International, London

Peterson H, Fite G 1957 *Opponents of War.* Washington, DC

Rae J 1979 *Conscience and Politics.* Oxford University Press, Oxford

Schlissel L (ed.) 1972 *Conscience in America.* Dutton, New York

Young N 1977 *The Nation State and War Resistance.* Ann Arbor, Michigan

NIGEL YOUNG

# Conscription

Conscription is the compulsory enrollment of men (and sometimes women) into a country's armed forces. In the United States it is called "the draft." Universal conscription—the recruitment of all able-bodied men between certain ages—has been rare. Normally conscription has been selective, even during war. Occasionally men and women have been conscripted to carry out civilian tasks.

## 1. Conscription and the State

Conscription is not simply an issue concerning how best to provide manpower for a country's defense. It also involves profound political and philosophical questions relating to an individual's obligation to the state, and to the state's ability to regiment and demand the obedience, perhaps unto death, of the individual. Not surprisingly, it has often been a controversial issue, particularly in liberal-democratic societies where compulsory military service represents both the furtherance and the rejection of certain cherished values. Arguments about an individual's rights and duties to the state are inevitably sharpened when the possibility of the ultimate sacrifice is demanded.

The notion that all members of a community have a duty to defend it is an ancient one. Records of conscription date back to ancient Egypt. In modern times the idea of universal duty to defend the community has often been associated with the spread of egalitarian beliefs. Radical opponents of this view—those who refuse to bear arms on behalf of the state—are known as conscientious objectors. Sometimes the latter have been able to opt for civilian rather than military service. The legal provision for conscientious objectors has varied considerably, but even where it has been allowed as a right, it has often been implemented

unsympathetically (see *Conscientious Objection*).

The factors which determine whether a country adopts conscription or some other type of military service are varied. Of primary importance are a country's political culture and its geopolitical situation (the size and location of its enemies, the type of wars it thinks it might have to face, and the likelihood of attack). Countries surrounded by potential enemies and with authoritarian traditions, like Germany before 1945, have adopted conscription far more readily than have relatively secure liberal democracies such as the United Kingdom and the United States. Military demands apart, totalitarian regimes have also favored conscription because it has been thought to aid social regimentation, political indoctrination, youth control, and loyalty to the state. Whatever their ideology, most states have required conscription to meet the demands of war, especially total war. Once conscription has been decided upon, decisions have then to be made about length of service and the method of recruitment. Normally service has been shorter in armies than in the more technical branches of the forces (though as modern armies become more technologically sophisticated, problems have begun to emerge in giving conscripts adequate training given the limited time available). Recruitment may be universal or, if the potential intake is greater than estimated needs, it may be selective or done randomly by lot (as in the United States during the later part of the Vietnam War).

For a country to rely for the raising of manpower on volunteer forces its government must be able to offer sufficiently attractive pay and conditions to continue to attract and hold men and women of varied skills from civilian life. Historically, countries have favored different systems, but most have filled out their armed forces with a combination of regular volunteers, short-term conscripts, and a body of reserves made up of trained citizens. Each system has its advantages and disadvantages in terms of cost, fighting ability, mobilization potential, and usability in different types of war.

## 2. History of Conscription

Universal military conscription in modern times began with the French Revolution. Napoleon's military needs, together with the goal of *egalite*, led to the *levee en masse*, producing the "nation in arms." Without such a system it would have been impossible for Napoleon to have sustained his extensive ambitions. The nation in arms was one of the factors that led to war becoming less limited and less controllable. After Napoleon's defeat in 1815 France abolished conscription, but a modified system was soon revived. Following another French defeat in 1871, this time by Prussia alone, universal military service was reinstated, though in practice there were many exemptions. At the start of the nineteenth century, Prussia had followed France's lead in creating a nation in arms with impressive effect, and by the end of the century had replaced France as Europe's major military power. In 1808 Prussia had adopted a system of conscription without distinction of class or right of exemption. The army became *die Schule der Nation*; it provided a common experience for Prussian men for a period of three years, and so helped to foster national unity and a common spirit. In addition the effectiveness of the Prussian military system was successfully tested in battle during the wars against Denmark (1860), Austria (1866) and France (1870-71). Meanwhile in Czarist Russia a much more brutal system operated. The army there proved to be a prison rather than a school; conditions were primitive, duties were onerous and rights were few.

Before the First World War conscription had become the norm in continental Europe. This was not the case, however, with the secure democracies of Britain and the United States. In the United States, though, the recruitment system from the colonial period to the Civil War had been based on a compulsory militia: with a few exceptions, all able-bodied men between certain ages were required for military training and service when necessary. During the War of Independence the short-service militia forces had to be strengthened by volunteers and, in some states, by a compulsory draft. In 1792 the Militia Law affirmed a universal military obligation on all free white male citizens; in practice exceptions were allowed, and universal national conscription was

never put into operation. Following independence, the militia system fell into decline and the United States armed strength came to depend on volunteers; however, even quite generous pay and conditions proved insufficient to attract the levels of manpower the government required, for example during the War of 1812.

The American Civil War (1861-65) was initially fought between a mixture of militia and volunteer forces on both sides, but as the losses in the war quickly grew both the Union and Confederate governments passed laws which made all men liable for military service, though in each case there was plenty of scope for exemption, and the practice of substitution allowed a conscripted man to pay someone else to carry out his duty. Service could also be discharged by direct payment. Despite—and to a degree because of—such loopholes, there was widespread opposition to the draft, and occasional riots took place; nevertheless, the system of universal conscription had become established in principle in the United States, though in practice service proved to be far from universal. At the end of the Civil War conscription was abolished, and the United States fought the Spanish-American War of 1898 with volunteers.

The recruiting problems of the United States became increasingly apparent as the nation's role in world affairs expanded, notably as a result of its involvement in the First World War. The National Defense Act of 1916 established the National Guard as a state military force, based on volunteers, which could be called into federal service by the President. Given the inadequacies of the established system of volunteers, the pressure for universal military training and service grew, resulting in the Selective Service Act of 1917. All men above 21 (later 18) were required to register. Selection then followed in which there were exemptions and deferments. But the Act did enable a massive infusion of new blood into the Allied effort, and so helped to bring the deadlock of the Western Front to an end.

Britain, like the United States, traditionally relied upon volunteer forces. Throughout the nineteenth century this proved adequate even for the demands of a greatly expanding empire. Given the long periods served away from the UK, garrisoning the empire, and the military advantages of professional British forces against poorly trained "natives," a small volunteer force supplemented by local troops was seen as more effective than a larger conscripted force. This volunteer system however proved inadequate for the demands of twentieth century attritional war in Europe, and it was thought necessary to introduce conscription in Britain in 1916. This system was quickly abandoned at the end of the First World War, but it was reintroduced in 1939 as the danger of an even greater European war loomed—the first time conscription had been employed in "peacetime" in Britain.

Conscription everywhere reached its height in the Second World War. Never before had the man-and-woman power of nations been mobilized to such an extent and to such an effect. Communist Russia proved alone in using women for front line duties; other belligerents conscripted women either to replace men in civilian tasks or for non-combat roles in the armed forces. Total war demanded total national effort. The effects were felt not only in the military sphere: there were also important sociological implications arising out of such national effort, for example in terms of ideas about the employment of women, and about social welfare after the war.

Following the Allied victory in 1945, most major powers retained some form of conscription. For West European powers such as Britain and France, this was necessary to meet the growing military demands of both the Cold War and the retreat from empire. The countries of Eastern Europe, which had been liberated from Nazism by the former Soviet Union and then coerced into Soviet-style communism, also adopted conscription. The former Soviet Union itself maintained its vast armies by recruiting all able-bodied men between certain ages. Former Axis powers such as Italy instituted systems of conscription, as did the former Federal Republic of Germany. Some countries conscripted women as well as men, most notably Israel when, after its foundation in 1948, the egalitarian, outnumbered, and encircled new state had to fight for its life.

A major exception to the widespread employment of conscription after the war was Japan. Following the period of militarism and imperialism which had put Japan on the road to Hiroshima and utter defeat, Japan's postwar Constitution forbade the creation of military forces in the traditional sense. Instead it raised volunteer "Self-Defense Forces" after 1954. The outcome in practice appeared very much like traditional armed forces, but they remained a small factor in terms of the country's emerging significance (see *Japan: Debates on Peace (1950s-1980s)*).

In the United States recruitment policy for the armed forces was unsettled after 1945; various systems of military service have been employed, and attitudes towards them have fluctuated considerably. In 1947 the wartime selective service system expired, and with it conscription. But when voluntary recruit-

ing failed to meet the demands of the Cold War, a new Selective Service Act (1948) was passed by Congress. The demands of being a world power, intensified by major if "limited" wars such as those in Korea and Vietnam, maintained a heavy demand for military manpower (see *Limited War*). As the casualty lists in Vietnam grew, and with them the unpopularity of the war, so did the unacceptability of the draft. Selective service lasted until 1973 when peacetime conscription was terminated and the United States adopted an all-volunteer military service. Criticism was periodically addressed at this system, on the grounds that it did not meet all the country's Cold War defense needs—facing the huge land-forces of the Warsaw Pact and China—but the draft remained unpopular.

With diminishing global responsibilities and an increased reliance on nuclear deterrence, the British government announced in 1957 that conscription (National Service) would end in 1960. France, however, decided to maintain conscription, as well as develop its nuclear *force de frappe*. All the British Commonwealth countries came to adopt a voluntary system, although some such as Australia and New Zealand maintained wartime national service for a few years after 1945, while in apartheid South Africa conscription was limited to the white population. Restricting the system to a particular section of the community has not been common, but it has not been unique to apartheid South Africa. In Israel, for example, it has been restricted to Jewish and Druze citizens (but both women and men). As a result of changing attitudes to the role of women in many societies, this will be another of the contentious issues involved in future discussions about conscription in different countries.

With the end of the Cold War, conscription in European states came under increased pressure. There was no longer the perception of a threat to national survival, the direct costs of conscription became relatively high given the reductions in defence spending (although relatively high unemployment rates means that the opportunity costs in tying up manpower are less pressing), and conscription remains extremely unpopular amongst the young. The latter has been especially evident in Germany, where a growing number are opting for community rather than military service. Finally, as the military focus of West European states shifts from the remote if apocalyptic threat of a continent-wide war involving nuclear weapons, to one of limited expeditionary deployments, the risk of soldiers being killed in conflicts which are not seen as vital national interests militates against the use of conscripts: it is one thing for a volunteer to be killed far from home in a conflict of at best indirect significance to national security, it is something else for a conscript to be killed in such a conflict.

## 3. Implications of Conscription

Arguments for and against conscription, and how it should be applied in practice, echo down the years and are still heard today. The main arguments used in support of conscription are as follows: the market-place does not always provide sufficient volunteer forces for national defense; conscription is a cheap form of recruiting compared with volunteers; a period in the armed forces instills a sense of national consciousness and discipline in those who experience it; military service fosters a sense of duty towards the state and an awareness of social obligations; conscription may be used to create a sense of national unity amongst disparate sub-national groupings; military training improves an individual's maturity and develops his or her professional skills; national service is the duty of every citizen; a period in the armed services offers a common and levelling experience for a national community; conscription civilianizes the armed forces and so helps to curb elitism and militarism; universal service helps to bridge the gap between military professionals and society as a whole; military training increases public awareness about defense issues; a nation-in-arms projects an image of national determination; and conscription provides that body of trained reserves which is essential in an unstable world. Although conscription has always been seen as having advantages for authoritarian regimes in relation to their ability to mobilize, regiment and to a certain extent control their country's manpower, it has also sometimes been seen as a natural adjunct of democratic rights and duties, the idea of "one man, one vote, one gun."

The main arguments against peacetime conscription reflect a similar mixture of politics, principle, and pragmatism: conscription is seen as morally objectionable in a liberal democratic society (nobody should be compelled to learn to fight and kill); it is argued that professionals—volunteers—do a better military job than conscripts, while conscripts merely distract and dilute the work of the professionals; during the Cold War, war in Europe was thought likely to have gone quickly nuclear, and hence the building up of mass armies was seen to be unnecessary; the post-Cold War demands of complex emergencies require highly trained, capable and motivated troops

willing to be placed at risk in conflicts perhaps only indirectly related to vital national interests—situations seen as inappropriate for conscripts; conscription is regarded as costly, in a direct financial sense, in terms of the dislocation it causes to a country's economic life, and also is socially disruptive; finally, for the individual, national service is often an unpleasant and tedious experience—a form of physical taxation on the citizen.

Arguments such as those above, and variations on them, have been particularly relevant in those Anglo-Saxon countries where conscription has not been a firmly established national tradition. The contending arguments are based on quite different assumptions about people and society, the duties incumbent on citizens in democracies, and analyses of the military needs of particular countries. For many states, however, conscription has never been a major issue; principle, politics, and pragmatism have led them more easily to its acceptance. This has normally been the case in the twentieth century with the countries of continental Europe, though whether this acceptance continues, if the post-Cold War environment continues to avoid the threat of major war remains to be seen.

So long as the threat of war remains a rational concern for governments, the raising of military manpower will continue to be an obligation, and for many countries conscription will remain the optimum means of reaching desired force levels. But if the threat of major inter-state war recedes, as changes in the international political system and in warfare itself increase the costs and reduce the benefits of armed conflict, then governments may no longer require all or most of their able-bodied male citizens to fight to defend their national rights and territory. Furthermore, as the sophistication both of military hardware and of battle increases, so conscripts may be deemed unsuitable for modern, high technology wars given their limited training. Moreover the nature of threats is changing away from inter-state war towards intra-state conflicts and non-military threats (such as environmental degradation). Conscript forces are much less useful in these situations. Whatever the future of conscription in practice, two historical facts stand out above all, and are of enormous anthropological and potentially political significance. The first is that governments have occasionally found it necessary to place the whole weight of state power behind conscription, in order to get young men to train to fight. The second is that it has rarely if ever been popular. Together, these facts throw into question the common assumption that

young men in the mass are either biologically pro-
grammed or are predisposed by gender to embrace
the realities of the life of the warrior.

See also: *Militarism and Militarization; Civilian-
based Defense*

*Bibliography* ―――――――――――――――

Anderson M 1976 *Conscription: A Select and Annotated Bibli-
ography.* Hoover Institution Press, Stanford, California
Cohen E A 1985 *Citizens and Soldiers: The Dilemmas of Mili-
tary Service.* Cornell University Press, Ithaca, New York
Foot M R D 1961 *Men in Uniform.* Praeger, New York
Gerhardt J M 1971 *The Draft and Public Policy: Issues in Mili-
tary Manpower Procurement, 1945-1970.* Ohio State
University Press, Columbus, Ohio
Haeckel E 1970 *Military Manpower and Political Purpose.*
Adelphi Paper, No. 72. International Institute for Strate-
gic Studies, London
Janowitz M 1981 *Civil-Military Relations.* Beverly Hills, Sage
Kelleher C M 1978 Mass armies in the 1970s: The debate in
Western Europe. *Armed Forces and Society* 5(1)
O'Sullivan J, Meckler A M (eds.) 1974 *The Draft and Its Ene-
mies.* University of Illinois Press, Urbana, Illinois
Shaw M 1991 *Post-Military Society: Militarism, Demilitarisa-
tion and War at the End of the Twentieth Century.* Cambridge, Polity
von Bredow, Wilfried 1992 Conscription, conscientious objection and civic service: The military institutions and political culture of Germany: 1945 to the present. *J. Political
and Military Sociology* 2(2)
Walzer M 1970 *Obligations: Essays on Disobedience, War and
Citizenship.* Simon and Schuster, New York

KEN BOOTH; COLIN MCINNES

# Constructing a Cooperative Security Structure in Asia: A Korean Perspective

## 1. The Necessity for Cooperative Security

Sovereign states can not escape from the security
dilemma. Throughout history, security has been the
primary aim of states. The concept of cooperative
security is distinct from that of collective defense
through the balance of power, and is likewise
differentiated from the concept of collective security,
which focuses upon deterrence, especially on the
power politics of the Cold War era (see *Comprehensive Security*). Cooperative security is a possible
solution for a New World Order in the post-Cold
War era.

For cooperative security, we must adopt two
assumptions. First, there can be no winners in this
age of severe nuclear threat. Second, many issues
other than security, such as the arms race, resource
shortages, environmental pollution, local area disputes, race and ethnic problems, border disputes and
drugs etc., can not be solved by a limited number of
countries, and have a strong influence upon international peace and stability (see *World Peace Order,
Dimensions of a*).

Ultimately, security is achieved not by sacrificing
the other party but only through a cooperative
approach. In other words, cooperative security
should be pursued not with the logic of a zero-sum-
game, but with that of a non-zero-sum-game. So, the
basic characteristics of cooperative security in the
New World Order can be explained by the following
five points:

First, cooperative security is an attempt to solve
security problems among countries through mutual
trust and cooperation rather than by maintaining
deterrence as was used in the past as a useful strategic concept. So, peaceful coexistence, and equality
must be accepted by the nations in Asia, as in the
OSCE in Europe (see *Peaceful Coexistence*).

Second, compared to the military alliance and collective security systems, which functioned to solve
conflicts and disputes in the past, cooperative security operates to prevent and preempt conflict through
dialogue and cooperation. Thus, preventive diplomacy becomes very important. For preventive diplomacy to succeed, it is crucial that nations work together
to build trust and institutionalize arms control (see
*Problem Solving in Internationalized Conflicts*). Allan
G. Jung argues that as in Europe, nations in Asia
should establish an organization to provide security
and promote cooperation. First, he argues that it is
necessary to establish regular inter-state meetings to
overcome potential security problems. In addition, he
suggests institutionalizing a Special Envoy Mechanism and constructing a Regional Crisis Management
Center.

Third, states should discuss the relationship
between politics and military in terms of security and
other related issues such as economy, terrorism, and
drugs (see *Social Progress and Human Survival*).

Fourth, to achieve cooperative security, states must

actively exchange information through multilateral contacts, exchange of military information and personnel, and advance notification of military exercises on the basis of mutual trust building.

Fifth, states must prefer international and peaceful solutions of conflict to power politics.

Briefly speaking, North East Asian multilateral security cooperation is needed to manage regional crises, to prepare safety programs, such as special hotlines between national capitals, to regulate military expenditure, to prevent the emergence of a new hegemon, to lead the transition from bilateralism to multilateralism, and to pursue stability in the Korean Peninsula. A North East Asian multilateral cooperation is also necessary to ensure a Nuclear-Free Korean Peninsula, a proposition which is supported by neighboring countries under two different models, the passive security approach and the structural perspective for guaranteeing security (see *Nuclear-Weapon-Free Zones: A History and Assessment*). Adherents to the former school take the 1978 UN General Assembly Resolution, which was adopted by each nuclear power state at the special UN General Assembly on disarmament, as their precedent. The latter group, however, seeks to expand the nuclear-free zone to encompass all of North East Asia.

For Korea, multilateral security serves as a useful alternative to the weakening Korea-US military alliance. The emergence of preventive diplomacy is related to the appearance of the concept of collective security during the Cold War era. Non-traditional types of security threats such as economic conflict, overpopulation, the spread of drugs, environmental pollution, and ethnic disputes have proliferated in the international relations of the post-Cold War era (see *Global Neighborhood: New Security Principles*). Such new threats require states to adopt more constructive and flexible intervention strategies, since the traditional forms of security, such as readiness and deterrence have proven to be ineffective. There are several potential sources of security threat in East Asia. Unequal economic levels and rates of development can lead to conflict between nations. The most threatening development, however, is the arms race between China and Japan. In addition, various ever present border disputes and ethnic hostility plague the region, such as the border conflict between Russia and Japan, the wrangle between the Philippines, China, Vietnam, Taiwan, and Malaysia over the control of the Spratly Islands, and the bitter emotions between the Koreans and Japanese stemming from past Japanese colonization.

Finally, even though a variety of maladies plague

the region, including environmental pollution resulting from industrial development, the nations in East Asia lack the diplomatic tradition to overcome these problems. These nations need to develop the diplomatic capacity to employ international institutions to settle disputes, such as those mentioned earlier, before they are transformed into full scale military conflict. In a paper titled "Cooperative Security in North East Asia" presented at the Bangkok ARF (see *ASEAN Regional Forum*) on May 5, 1994, the Korean government emphasized the principles of preventive diplomacy, and pledged to respect national sovereignty, to abstain from making trade threats or intervening in international affairs, to support regional integration, and non-aggressive, peaceful, dispute resolutions, to coexist with her neighbors in peace, and to respect other nation's culture and the rights of their citizens. The Korean government has even suggested establishing a crisis-hotline to promote effective preventive diplomacy.

To achieve effective security, related dialogue and cooperation between the nations of North East Asia, even before an international institution is established, a 'Second Track' process should be activated by encouraging links between NGOs, scholars, and other societal institution in different countries (see *Field Diplomacy: A New Conflict Paradigm*).

Therefore, it is clear that further research needs to be conducted on how potential armed conflict can be averted through peaceful means and preventive diplomacy, as was achieved through the CBM Treaty, which established an early warning system.

## 2. Direction of Cooperative Security System

Europe reached an agreement which laid the foundation for peace at the European security meeting in Helsinki in 1975, with the attendance of 33 European nations, and the USA and Canada. Even in 1972, the US acceded to Soviet suggestions for arms reduction of the Nixon-Breznev summit talks. At the summit, the US attempted to persuade the Soviets to participate in the mutually-balanced forces reduction dialogue (MBFR) and to put human rights on the agenda of the CSCE (see *Security and Cooperation in Europe*).

The Helsinki agreement uses the respect for sovereignty and for international borders as an overwhelming principle to govern relations between member states and to provide security in Europe (see *Helsinki Process*).

In order to build trust and security between member states, and to promote arms reduction efforts, the Helsinki agreement introduced measures that required members to notify neighboring countries of large scale exercises, and promoted the exchange of inspectors.

Subsequent meetings of the European Security, such as the Paris Meeting in 1990, have succeeded in bringing about more systemic institutionalization, and contributed to the protection of human rights and greater trust between nations in Europe Today.

In Asia, too, there have been several calls for the establishment of an Asia-wide security cooperation institution, including Kraznoyaski' suggestion for an Asia-wide Security Cooperation Meeting in 1988, Sevardnadze's call for an All-Asia Forum in 1990, and the construction of the North-East Asian Cooperation Area in 1991, after Gorbachev promulgated the Vladivostok Resolution in September 1986 (see *Regionalism in Asia Pacific, Organizational Forms of*).

The US, South Korea, Japan and Taiwan did not actively respond to these Soviet-sponsored initiatives, which were regarded as Soviet attempts to check the influence of America's dominant naval power.

Japan has actively pursued multilateral security dialogue with her neighbors to meet the changing international environment and the emergence of new problems in North East Asia, complementing the system of already established bilateral ties.

Japan had been against adopting multilateral security ties until 1990 for several important reasons. First, Japan had used the US-Japan security treaty as a pillar of national security after the World War II. Japan feared that adopting a multilateral security approach might negatively affect long established ties with the US. Japan was also concerned that adopting a multilateral approach would lead to interference by countries outside the region in such bilateral issues as the problems with Russia over the control of cities in the area directly north of Japan, making the resolution of these problems even more difficult. In addition, the US had previously displayed displeasure towards Japan adopting a multilateral security policy in Asia.

Japan showed signs of change, however, when the Japanese Foreign Minister, Nagayama, suggested discussing the Asia-Pacific security issues at the meeting of officials at an extended meeting of ASEAN Foreign Ministers in 1991 (see *Association of Southeast Asian Nations (ASEAN)*).

In 1992 Prime Minister Miyazawa built upon Nagayama's earlier efforts, by emphasizing the need for Asian nations to follow the lead of European countries and hold a meeting to discuss multilateral security cooperation. Later, during his visit to ASEAN countries, in 1993, Miyazawa proposed holding Asia-Pacific Regional Security Meetings.

Japan's intention is to use regional security meetings to meet a changing international security situation in North East Asia to expand Japanese regional influence in response to possible future shifts in the US Security Treaty and China's arms build-up and increasing military influence.

It appears that Japan is setting her sights upon the whole Asia-Pacific region, and not simply the smaller North East Asia area as a target for a multilateral security cooperative body, as Japan is attempting to take advantage of established institutions like the ASEAN-PMC.

Japan appears to possess a larger interest in her traditional strategy of comprehensive security diplomacy, to try to check the power of South Korea, China and South East Asian countries, and extend Japanese influence throughout the whole Pacific region, rather than focusing her interest strictly on the North East Asian nations which directly affect her security.

At present, in contrast to American, Russian and Japanese official support for North East Asia multilateral security cooperation, China is refusing to take part in such a multilateral security institution, instead regarding bilateral negotiations as more important. China worries that joining such an institution will make it vulnerable to criticism by member countries of its military build-up and the possibility that Taiwan might be admitted, when this institution becomes operational. Basically, although China recognizes that the present post-Cold War World Order is evolving into a multi-polarity, the US still remains as a hegemon. China regards President Clinton's criticism of human rights in China, Japan's dispatch of peace-keeping troops to Cambodia, and calls establishing a multilateral security cooperation system as direct and indirect threats to China's national interest and security. This explains why China has adopted a hostile attitude toward a multilateral security cooperation system, regarding it as the strategy of neighboring countries to besiege China.

China's position has begun to change, however, as China has realized the importance of easing the worries of neighboring countries of Chinese military expansion. Particularly, China has begun to realize that without adequate measures to deter the Japanese desire to expand militarily to reach super-power status, a multilateral security cooperation system might not necessarily be contrary to China's security interests.

In fact, the Chinese Foreign Minister, Chun Ki Chim expressed official support for a multilateral dialogue led by ASEAN during his visit to Seoul and Tokyo in May, 1993, and for the formation of a North East Asia Economic Community encompassing Korea, China and Japan, and in the long term, North Korea (see *Regionalism, Economic Security and Peace: The Asia-Pacific*).

Several other countries have also called for the formation of such an institution, and there have been proposals for bodies such as the North East Asia Peace Committee by Korea in 1988, the North East Asia 8-country Regular Committee by Mongolia in 1989, the North Pacific Cooperative Security Dialogue (NPCSD) by Canada, and the CSCA by Australia in 1990. The US has been hesitant to support the establishment of multilateral security cooperation meetings, however, fearing that the MSCM might jeopardize American vested security interests, which the US has promoted through established bilateral alliances established through treaties with Korea and Japan. The US, has considered security alternatives, such as a North East Asian Multilateral Security Cooperative Arrangement, in order to lessen the economic burden of maintaining world security following the collapse of USSR, and to prepare effective measures to resolve conflicts without breaking the established strategic order.

The then Secretary of State, James Baker, during his visit to several South East Asian nations in July 1992, expressed that Korea is an area in North East Asia which is in need of an arms reduction initiative, where it is possible for European style trust-building, and ultimately, conventional arms reduction. He further suggested that the US should adjust to the changing regional security situation in North East Asia by holding multilateral security meetings with China, Russia, and other regional powers, on select issues, while maintaining established bilateral alliance relationships, as the US had in Europe with the coexistence of US-led NATO and the CSCE as a pan-European security forum in Europe.

In July, 1997, Steven Solarz, US congressman, remarked that "if the US's participation is guaranteed, the US will consider the construction of a collective security arrangement centered on the Korean peninsula in Asia-Pacific region." In addition, a *New York Times* editorial dated August 10, 1992, argued that a collective security system is more desirable than a US-led security system for the promotion of stability in Asia.

Soon after these remarks, the US changed its policy to be more accommodating of multilateralism, with Clinton's advocating the establishment of a 'New Pacific Community' in July, 1993. In the post-Cold War era, the US has retreated from the previous policy of active interventionism, instead has been adopting the role of international cooperative balancer undertaking limited intervention abroad. Such a limited interventionist approach is more congruent to the functioning of a multilateral cooperation system. The US has momentarily postponed plans for US military reduction in North East Asia due to new factors such as the North Korean nuclear issue.

So, for the time being, while the US will continue to adhere to a US-centered North East Asia policy, when the East Asian security situation becomes more stable, and US domestic issues become more pressing, it is likely that the Americans will more actively pursue a policy more supportive of an Asian collective security cooperative system. The US especially has an interest in preventing the rise of an East Asian hegemon, and therefore prefers a multilateral security cooperation system to stabilize and institutionalize the regional balance of power (see *Multilateralism*). Recently, the US has been open to multilateral discussion of broad issues including political and military issues, and the US continues to regard Asia-Pacific economic cooperation through APEC as very important. APEC presently functions as a device to promote Asia-Pacific economic cooperation, and it was profound that the US Secretary of Defense Perry suggested extending APEC role to function as a regional security forum, at the APEC Summit Talks in November, 1995 (see *Asia Pacific Economic Cooperation (APEC)*).

Thus, while the US has expressed interests in an Asia-Pacific multilateral security system, up to now it has appeared to explore multilateral security cooperation through the established ARF and APEC, instead of creating a new security cooperation body.

Other reasons for the US's active participation in multilateral security meeting is to check the Asia-centered EAEC led by Malaysia, and arrest the growing military power of Japan and China.

North Korea has opposed multilateral security cooperation, worrying that constructing an international institution might bring increased foreign pressure upon it on such issues as human rights, nuclear and conventional weapons, and its isolation from the international community. North Korea has criticized the idea of multilateral security cooperation as an American attempt to root out the Socialist State and to strengthen US imperial domination of Asia.

North Korea also opposed the creation of 'North East Asia Peace Council,' suggested by South Korea and others in 1989. The North Korean Foreign Minister stated in January 13, 1991, that the European security cooperation model is not relevant to the

Asian situation, and criticized South Korea's proposal, saying that it was a betrayal to the Korean people and part of a treacherous US-led conspiracy. Although North Korea has been open towards a "Pan-asia Collective Security Meeting" proposal and the "Vladivostock Resolution" of the former-President of the then USSR, after seeing the establishment of friendly ties between South Korea and the USSR gaining momentum, through the Korea-USSR Summit Talks in San Francisco, in June 1990, North Korea objected to multilateral relations saying that the proposal for an Asia-Pacific multilateral security cooperation system led by former USSR. was practically impossible. North Korea did not show any particular objection to the 'North Pacific Security Dialogue' organized by Mr. Clark, in Canada in July 1990 or the 'Asian Security Cooperation Meeting' arranged by Mr. Evans, in Australia in July, 1991, however.

Although North Korea showed an openness to talks on multilateral security cooperation system to solve tension in North East Asia by participating in the Preparatory Meeting for 'North East Asia Security Cooperation Meeting' held in San Diego, California in July, 1993, it boycotted the October main Meeting of the NEASCM due to heightened tensions with the US, Japan and South Korea concerning the nuclear issue.

The possibility, however, of North Korea's participation is increasing with the coming of the 21st century for several reasons: First, the successful resolution of nuclear conflict between the US and North Korea has reduced tensions. In addition, the North should shift its policy from the previous defensive approach to a more open, diplomatically aggressive policy, to take advantage of the increasing friendly relationship between the US, Japan, and the North. So, it is possible that North Korea will respond actively to the notion of multilateral security cooperation system.

Second, North Korea's military alliance with the CIS and China has virtually collapsed which had provided crucial support for the North's security. Especially if China continues to support the North Korean regime, and the Russian Communist Party regains power and improves relations with North Korea, the North may regard the MSCS as a means to check South Korea's strategy of unification through absorption. Third, even assuming that North Korea continues to oppose a multilateral security cooperation system, some North Korean security analysts argue that the North will ultimately participate. In the past, North Korea opposed entrance into the UN following the 'One Chosun' policy. The North finally embraced the unconditional affiliation policy to escape from international isola-

tion, and decided to affiliate with the South, a result of a changing international situation. Applying similar logic, North Korea can not help but participate in multilateral security cooperation system after the MSCS begins to operate.

Although ASEAN has officially announced a neutral stance in general, each ASEAN member country has had security linkages with the outside world. In particular, the Philippines and Thailand have had security relations with US, and Malaysia and Singapore signed a five-country security agreement with the United Kingdom, Australia, and New Zealand. ASEAN countries have exerted individual efforts to increase military expenditure and expand military power, contrary to the world trend of de-militarization following the end of Cold War.

On the other hand, ASEAN, at the Third ASEAN Summit Talks in Singapore in January, 1992, decided to discuss Asia-Pacific security issues through ASEAN-PMC with seven ASEAN dialogue partners: the US, Japan, Canada, Australia, New Zealand, South Korea, and the EC, immediately following the annual ASEAN Foreign Minister Meeting. Singapore agreed to establish an ASEAN Regional Forum (ARF), with eighteen participating countries, including ASEAN-PMC member countries as well as China, Russia, Vietnam, Laos, and Papua New Guinea in July 1993. Through this motion, the Security Cooperation Body for Asia-Pacific multilateral security issues was established with the official launching of ARF with 18 member countries in Bangkok in July, 1994.

The establishment of ARF has far reaching importance because of the membership of such enemies during the Cold War era as Russia, China, Vietnam and Laos. It also increases the possibility of improving relationships between these countries by promoting direct trade and contacts through increased multilateral cooperation. In early 1994, North Korea, too, had expressed interest in participating in ARF. It is easy for many countries to enter ARF, because the entrance vote to ARF is not based on unanimity but on majority.

At present, a multilateral order is emerging in the Asia-Pacific economic and security multilateral cooperation council. Inter-governmental relations are promoted by APEC, the Expanded ASEAN Foreign Minister Meeting, and non-governmental organization (see *Track II Diplomacy*). Relations are furthered through the Asia Pacific Round Table in 1987, NPCSD in 1990, and CSCAP in 1992.

In order to move forward with multilateral cooperation in Asia, the following points should be included in the agenda of North East Asia security cooperation meeting, especially relating to the issue of arms control and reduction. First, military trust building should be strengthened to prevent accidental and surprise military attack in the region. Second, effective measures should be contrived to regulate such weapons of mass-destruction as nuclear, biological and chemical weapons. Third, limitation on marine power expenditure is necessary because countries in the region are linked by the sea.

In the application of the European model to the unique geo-political situation of North East Asia, the agenda should include reduction of marine power and CSBMs in particular, as part of an overall military CSBM and military power reduction. Conventional arms reduction is needed, as well. On the other hand, North East Asia multilateral security cooperation should deal with nuclear and conventional arms issues simultaneously, because unlike Europe, the North East Asian multilateral security meeting does not regulate and has not reduced the number of nuclear weapons. The NEAMSCS should include the following points in discussion of nuclear issues in order to help bring about a nuclear free North East Asia: control and reduction of strategic nuclear and inter-mediate range missile, guarantee of no-first use (see *Nuclear Weapons, No First Use of*) of nuclear weapons among nuclear states, guaranteed provision of passive security by nuclear states to non-nuclear states, and equal and consistent standards relating to plutonium storage and nuclear re-treatment measures.

Hence, to replace the vertical and hierarchical order that currently exists in North East Asia with balanced order supported by multilateral cooperation, it is necessary to apply the ten principles of Helsinki Agreement to create horizontal and balanced order. Namely, member countries need to faithfully meet these following Helsinki principles: equality and respect for sovereignty, bans on the use of military force and threat, non-aggression towards borders, respect for territory, peaceful solution of disputes, non-intervention in domestic issues, respect for basic freedom and human rights, equal rights and self-determination, cooperation among nations, and the duty to uphold and follow international law.

There are currently four problems that impede the implementation of a North East Asia security cooperation system. First, each country's strategic interest differs according to its security environment and its position in the regional power-structure. Second, there is a problem as to the future boundary of a regional cooperative group, whether it should include nations in the Pacific region, including such a wide ranging group of countries as Russia and Australia, or the nations of the NPCAD (North Pacific Country's Security Dialogue) with the North East Asia boundaries proposed by South Korea and Mongolia.

Third, as bilateral and subregional compromises took place prior to signing of the CSCE, Asian nations should first seek to resolve regional disputes before the real progress on the North East Asia multilateral security cooperation system can take place.

Fourth, contrary to the political and military focus of the CSCE (see *Organization for Security and Cooperation in Europe (OSCE)*), an Asia-Pacific multilateral security cooperation has a higher possibility of success by focusing upon economic cooperation, as APEC has sought to achieve. Asian countries then must search for an appropriate linkage between the established economic system of cooperation and a system of security cooperation.

In considering these problems, to increase the possibility of North East Asia security cooperation meeting Asian nations should gradually pursue cooperation, first in non-military issues, and then later in the military and political arena. They also need to increase transparency to promote military trust building, and discuss issues such as establishing subregional military cooperative dialogues. In addition, the concerned nations should institutionalize 'Open-Sky' and 'Open-Sea' agreements, construct hot-lines between related countries and crisis management centers, provide advance notification of military exercises, and need to carry out further research on problems such as non-use of military force, control of arms proliferation and mass-destruction weapons, organizational and structural arms control, and establishing a nuclear-free zone.

## 3. Korea's Leadership in the North East Asia Security Cooperation System

Korea, surrounded by super-powers, should use its unique position to lead neighboring countries in North East Asia security cooperation system, in order to preempt regional conflicts, and create a fertile security environment for peaceful reunification, since military power in itself is not enough to meet security threats.

Recently, meetings between Japan, China, and the US are frequently held. Japan has suggested dialogue on politics and security issues between the three nations. It has followed a two-step approach toward China, in which the two countries first undertake civilian exchanges, after which government official dialogue will commence. China displayed opposition to the plan, however, and was worried about stronger ties between the US and Japan, produced by a revision of the US-Japan defense treaty.

Japan has also moved to establish a three-country security committee, composed of policy-consultant research centers in the three countries, to promote an international dialogue concerning Asia-Pacific security and military problems. As was suggested in 1995, the Korean government should build upon the three-country security council movement by actively pursuing diplomacy to create a North East Asia security council with the participation of North Korea and South Korea, and their four neighbors.

While the US and Russia were relatively warm to the creation of the North East Asian security council, China appears to prefer bi-lateral security dialogue of the concerned parties to the North East Asian security council. So, the Korean government needs to mobilize the support from the US, Japan and Russia, and should attempt to convince the Chinese to take part by noting the strong points of the multilateral security cooperation council.

All of the countries in North East Asia, including China, are unified in the need to maintain the balance of power in the region in the face of increased threat (see *Balance of Power*). There are several reasons for the increased threat in the region, and likewise the increased necessity for a North East Asia security cooperation dialogue. First, the North-South relationship has been aggravated due to North Korea's nuclear development project, even after the US-North Korea Geneva agreement (see *North Korea's Nuclear Activities and US-North Korea Accord of 1994*). Second, conflicts over the control on the sea in North East Asia have intensified. Third, the US, Japan and China have had severe difficulty drawing up the regional boundaries of a security cooperative body, especially over whether Taiwan should be included or not. Fourth, while the US, Japan, and neighboring Asian countries worry about an increasing Chinese threat, China is trying to rid itself of checks upon its power.

At present, the international institutions addressing multilateral security cooperation dialogue in North East Asia are 'ARF' and 'NEACD.' The ARF, created in 1994, is in the process of developing regular annual meetings, but its potential to develop as the direct security cooperation institution for North East Asia is limited by its large number (18) of participating member countries throughout the Asia-Pacific region. The NEACD operates with the participation of government officials and civilian scholars from Korea and four neighboring countries, with the exception of North Korea which only participated in the preparatory meetings held in 1993.

But, the NEACD's development as a real government-level council has stagnated. So, the Korean government must reaffirm its neighboring countries that the US-Japan-China dialogue should not be limited to the super powers only, because conflict between North and South Korea is directly related to peace throughout all of North East Asia. At the same time, the Korean government should take leadership initiatives to offer logical proposals to promote multilateral security cooperation as a necessary institutional device for keeping peace in North East Asia, after North and South Korea agree to recognize one another and North Korea establishes separate diplomatic relationships with the US, and Japan. This is especially important, because of the likelihood of a conflict starting between North and South Korea of spreading to regional major powers.

While there are some analysts who argue that it is too optimistic to expect that such a multilateral security regime can operate as a cooperative and discussion device to bring about painless settlement of opposing national interests, when there exists an imbalance in power in the international system and nation states remain as the unit, it appears that there is no objection to the proposition that the best chances for future Korean security can be gained from the establishment of a strong multilateral security cooperation structure.

At present, if the current four-country conferences are successful, a subsequent six-country meeting including Japan and Russia is desirable to help bring about North East Asian multilateral security cooperation. It is also possible to make the NEACD an official organization, by encouraging North Korean participation, regardless of the outcome of the four-country talks. Another possibility is for the ARF to use the four-party meetings as a starting point to institutionalize regular meetings among the countries directly related to North East Asia security. Moreover, Korea should use APEC as a channel for dialogue not only concerning economic issues but also security cooperation issues.

In order to construct a multilateral security cooperation structure in North East Asia, it is necessary for the concerned nation's to adopt a gradual approach, and explore rational measures agreeable to all member countries, because the NEA does not yet possess the tradition of multilateral security cooperation. Korea's four neighboring countries: the US, Japan, China and Russia possess mutual distrust and a history of war. In addition, recently the US, Japan and China have demonstrated that none would allow either of the others to attain hegemony in the region, and each has sought to pursue active economic participation and exercise strong military influence.

Each nation's reluctance to engage in a multilateral security cooperation structure results from a lack of mutual trust. For this reason, Korea must take the initiative to promote cooperative trust building. As a middle power, Korea is uniquely suited to the role of instigator of multilateral cooperation, since its actions will not be viewed as threatening by neighboring countries.

The US and China are not appropriate for the role, since they are engaged in checking each other from pursuing hegemony in North East Asia. Japan, as well, is not suited to be a leading proponent of multilateral security cooperation system because of her role as the past imperial architect of the 'Great East Asia Co-prosperity Zone.' Modern Russia, in a sense, has the possibility of leading the movement to multilateral cooperation, because, relatively, it is not pursuing regional hegemony. On the other hand, though, Russia is prevented from taking on such a role by its present domestic problems and weakness.

Even though Korea is somewhat limited in performing the role as leading proponent for multilateral cooperation, due to her alliance with the US and her involvement in the 'North-South Conflict,' Korea is the only practical choice as a leading country, since the neighboring countries have virtually conceded to the point that the special US-Korea relationship, and the presence of US forces on the Korean peninsula is inevitable to keep the peace in North East Asia, and currently North Korea is unable and unwilling to lead the construction of a multilateral security cooperation structure.

It seems plausible that in the future North Korea will warm to the pursuit of economic development and security guarantees through North East Asian multilateral security cooperation, because the North appears to favor some measures, such as the KEDO for the construction of the light water nuclear power plant, in which many countries will participate, and the participation, since 1990 of related countries in discussion of Korean reunification.

For a sequential, gradual approach to achieving North East Asian security cooperation, it is necessary to follow the following three guidelines. First, each country can pursue its national interest through North East Asia economic cooperation. Second, it is necessary that the nations of East Asia build political trust in one another. For example, Japan must humbly recognize her past history, the nations in the region must reach a mutual understanding, and the US and China

need to adopt a cooperative spirit of compromise to put a stop to the excessive rival for hegemony between the two nations which has led to mutual disadvantage. Third, nations in the region must take measures to enhance military trust building, by creating transparency in military exercises, by checking the spiraling expansion of military power through arms control agreements, and by mutual exchange of defense papers, for instance.

Initially, dialogue for multilateral security cooperation should be based upon informal meetings rather than through official institution building as was done with ASEAN, and should rely upon dialogue rather than rules. In addition, member countries must adopt economic solutions, not military solutions, to solve even security conflicts, and should work towards accumulating a tradition of multilateral cooperation in North East Asia.

See also: *Integration Theories; Integration, Regional; Peace and Regional Integration; Regionalism in Asia-Pacific, Organizational Forms of*

*Bibliography*

Kim K J Aternatives for constructing multilateral council for peace and security in North East Asia. *Research Series.* The Institute of Comparative Security

Ban K M 1995 The threats and response in Northeast Asia. Paper presented at the Asean Regional Forum Seminar on Preventive Diplomacy, Seoul

Hong G D *Prospect for Multilateral Security Cooperation Council.* Research Center for Peace and Unification of Korea

Lee C K 1993 *The North East Countries.* The Hoam Press, Seoul

Jeong E S 1993 CSCE as a Case of Multilateral Security and Cooperation. *International Issues* (November)

Jury G A 1995 The Asean Regional Forum (ARF) on preventive diplomacy. Paper presented at the Asean Regional Forum Seminar on Preventive Diplomacy, Seoul

Nishihara M 1994 Multilateralism in Asia Pacific: The view from Tokyo. *Asian Defence Journal* (September)

Prospect for the Change in the US-North Korea Relationship and The US-South Korea Relationship. Report Paper, Research Center for Peace and Unification of Korea

*Series on the Situation Analysis.* The US's Policy toward North East Asian Regional Cooperation, Research Institute of National Security Affairs

Song Y S 1992 The idea and prospect for North East Asia peace structure. *Report Paper.* Research Center for Korean National Defense

CHUNGWON CHOUE; KI-JONG LEE

# Construction of the Principle of Toleration and Its Implications for Contemporary Democratic States

It is an important premise of John Rawls's revised interpretation of the basis of his theory of justice (by some distance the most influential twentieth century work of political philosophy: Rawls 1971, 1985, 1993), that it recapitulates the political lesson drawn by Western Europe from the traumatic experience of its sixteenth and seventeenth century wars of religion. In Rawls's view his theory really is the appropriate modern liberal theory of the fundamental constitutive principle of a modern representative democratic polity (Fontana 1994; Manin 1994), and the society and economy which should go with this. It is thus offered as an exposition of the moral rationale for an actually existing form of society. It remains, however, eminently causally questionable how realistic this is as an explication of the implications of any features of this society as it actually does exist (Dunn 1985, 1990, 1993, 1994). I propose to approach the assessment of this pressing question by considering the conceptual (and political) process of the construction of the principle of toleration in early modern Europe.

Before doing so, it is crucial to note a verbal ambiguity in English of the term toleration itself (an ambiguity not matched in the Latin terminology—*toleratio, tolerantia*—in which much of the key literature of toleration was initially composed). In the English of this epoch, as largely today, the term toleration carries both the sense of an external political and social practice and the sense of a dispositional virtue appropriate to such a practice. But the term tolerance by contrast carries solely the second sense. I shall use tolerance accordingly whenever I wish to pick out virtues and attitudes, and reserve the key term toleration for the discussion of legal, political and institutional arrangements. This is important since the view that there is a dependable elective affinity between the modern representative democratic republic as a state form and a distinctive array of supportive and energizing attitudes, strongly associated with Alexis de Tocqueville and especially popular in the United States, is not empirically well-founded and cannot reasonably be pre-assumed in discussion with an East Asian audience.

Let me distinguish, within the principle of toleration, two weakly aligned components. The first of these is a thesis about the order of public right: that political authority has no entitlement to constrain either (a) religious practice as such, or (b) moral or religious belief as such (belief about certain key existential issues), or (c) belief as such in its entirety, and all pertinent verbal or symbolic expression of such belief. The first and minimal claim yields a right to freedom of worship. The second yields a claim to freedom of thought about how to worship. The third, on a reasonably bold interpretation, yields a general claim to freedom of speech itself, as a putative precondition for realising the second and thus in practice (and crucially) the first. You can think of these three domains as concentric circles of expanding claims to self-righteous self-determination, spreading out from a highly concrete and specifically religious core to a potentially wholly secular circumference. But it is extremely important to note that the conceptual (and political) process of constructing the principle of toleration in early modern Europe remained explicitly religious in its interpretative scope throughout (if perhaps not always in wholly good faith). In all instances the principle is a thesis about the rights and duties of rulers and subjects. In the core case, it is a thesis about the right of the latter to worship as they deem fit and of the right and duty of the former to permit them to do so. In the intermediate version it expresses the right of the latter to believe on religious issues whatever they do believe and a duty of the former not to molest them for so doing. In its fullest version it vindicates the right of the latter to believe and to express whatever they happen to believe on any issue whatever, the right of promiscuously free speech, and the duty of the former to acknowledge that right and indeed defend its application in practice.

The second component is a thesis about the practical merits (political, social, economic, cultural, moral) of an essentially adverbial virtue: the virtue of tolerance, the disposition to accept gracefully, if often without undue enthusiasm, the real beliefs, sentiments, discourses, and practices of human others, whose lives interact causally with one's own, and who share a common social and political space—to view them at worst with resignation, and at most with a certain core of appreciation (or at least respect), and at any rate to treat them with a minimum of *restraint*, independently of the sentiments one does happen to have towards them.

Where did this principle come from? It came, in the first instance, aversively from a long, bloody and appallingly painful history of intensely self-righteous and often brutal religious warfare (driven by the ambition of credal cleansing), and from the practical recognition that this brutality could only be brought to a permanent and dependable end by the acceptance of such a principle, and by the cultivation and development of the virtue which practically expresses and secures it: makes it collectively and individually liveable.

It came, in the second instance, altogether more positively and actively, from a cumulative dynamic of increasingly urgent practical thought about how this grim experience could indeed be ended permanently, and about the imaginative mechanisms and sordid practical interests which had reinforced it so relentlessly and for so long.

In this sense, the principle was a product of religious, moral and political *thinking*, spurred by religious, moral, political, military, and in the broadest sense also social and economic, experience.

It would be possible to present the integral logic of this process of political, religious and moral reflection, and political, moral and even *religious* learning, in a wide variety of ways, without palpably distorting it. It was a multidimensional process, with no clear edges; and there could not be a canonical way of summarizing it.

One especially illuminating way of presenting is to ask the following questions:

(a) What was the principal imaginative *barrier* to reaching the conclusions which were in the end reached by the great European theorists of toleration in the late seventeeth and eighteenth centuries—above all John Locke and Pierre Bayle? Why did it require *so much* thought to reach what to many now seem such palpably obvious and bewilderingly simple conclusions?

(b) How compelling were the arguments which eventually secured the twin conclusions, about the fundamental order of right, and about the adverbial virtue of mutual imaginative and practical forebearance which best expresses and sustains that order?

(c) How far did the arguments themselves (or the virtues which expressed and sustained them in practice) depend for their force on distinctive properties of the culture and theoretical belief systems of Western Europe at that time? How far were either or both culturally relative? (There is no need to underline the importance of this question in relation to the claims of the modern constitutional democratic republic to form a uniquely cosmopolitan paradigm of contemporary political legitimacy: Dunn 1992; Fukuyama 1992; Huntington 1993; Fontana 1994.) And how

far, accordingly, can they really hope to retain a comparable analytical cogency or imaginative (and thus motivational) force, for the denizens of other cultures, whether these be for the present principally located elsewhere, or whether they are already located (as they surely also are, and will continue to be in increasing numbers) in Western Europe itself, and in the major territories of its diaspora (most crucially, for the present, the United States of America)?

(d) (Much harder to formulate felicitously, or separate out neatly, and at least equally hard to answer with any confidence). How far did the adoption and maintenance of the political and legal practice of religious toleration derive, in the European cases, from grubby and unfanciful political calculation of its comparative advantage, from considered normative reflection about its religious, moral and political hazards and rewards, or from cumulative changes in the actually existing sentiments of different groups within European populations themselves towards each others' co-presence: from irritability and intolerance towards calm, indifference, tolerance, or even mutual appreciation?

I have nothing of merit to say about this question, except that it is of obvious analytical importance, that it has been abominably neglected by European historians, at least since the days of Lord Acton, and that if one knew the answer to it, this might prove of fairly peremptory political relevance. (For example, if the answer was simply that the adoption and maintenance of the practice of toleration in late seventeenth-, eighteenth- and early nineteenth-century Europe came largely from changes in the sentiments of European populations towards each other, and these changed sentiments, in turn, came relatively directly from pleased recognition of the practical advantages of incorporation into a steadily expanding international product market, that answer would handsomely support some of the blandest and least searching elements in the thought world of the most advanced capitalist states today. While I'm in no position to *refute* this simple fancy, I'm bound to say, however, that I do not find it remotely convincing.) A proto-GATT vision of the world market, or even of a paneuropean market, as a simple and accessible public good, might provide quite a sound basis for practices of toleration and attitudes of tolerance. But the analytical strain of vindicating the validity of that judgment in a contested political space even today is a pretty clear refutation of the plausibility of its having discreetly enforced itself upon demotic (or even elite) consciousness in late seventeenth century Europe, without anyone at the time much noticing it. For the very different perspective of those who were actively interested in the matter at the time (see especially Hont 1990). It is a better guess that any such vision is likelier to be a causal product over time of the preexistence of practices of toleration and tolerant attitudes than it is to be a causally sufficient condition for generating either the practices or their accompanying supportive attitudes.

I shall therefore confine what I have to say substantively about the construction of the principle of toleration to the first three of these questions, and then apply my conclusions, in the crudest fashion, to the institutional structures and presumed causal dynamics of the canonical modern form of legitimate rule, the representative democratic constitutional republic.

Let me take first the issue of what was the principal *barrier* to drawing what seems the obvious (and exclusively decent cosmopolitan) conclusion over how groups of human beings with sharply divergent religious beliefs should live with one another.

Many seventeenth century Europeans would have said that the principal barrier to reaching such conclusions, across the bloody centuries of religious warfare and the less bloody, if still to us pretty unprepossessing and protracted, period of subsequent *infâme*, lay either in the nasty core of actually existing human motivation (cruelty, self-righteousness, utter indifference to the misery of others), or in the insistent sinister interest of persecuting rulers and clerics, who prompted or reassured them in their persecutions. One can scarcely doubt that each of these insistences was eminently to the point. Much religious persecution (perhaps even most religious persecution) must have stemmed from, or at least been fanned by, Reason of State, Reason of the Church, or, in more reductive terms, the reasons of those who directly controlled the State or Church; and the optic of modern political and social theory tempts us, with some violence, to attribute the explanatory residue, insofar as we see it as intelligible at all, to the core of unreason—practical irrationality and chaotic negative passion—of the same range of human agents and agencies. (I know, for example, of no serious defence of the thesis that religious intolerance, while it lasted, was best understood as a structural prerequisite under existing production relations for the imperious impulse of human productive powers to expand.)

While all this is quite sensible as far as it goes, it goes in my view an extremely short distance. It is unblinkingly superficial.

To go deeper, we must see the key obstacles to identifying and vindicating the principle of toleration as lying less in the penetralia of the human psyche, or in the structure of political and economic interests in sixteenth- or seventeenth-century Europe, than in the intense plausibility of the claim that it was the *duty* of sincere Christians to persecute their backsliding fellow believers into believing what was religiously true, and thus indispensable for the salvation of their mortally endangered souls (cf. Dunn 1991); and for background beliefs (see Dunn 1984). The key thesis which the principle of religious toleration needed to refute was that it was the religious duty of Christian rulers and ecclesiastical leaders to force the saving truth upon those who would otherwise be damned to all eternity. (Religious tolerance was no more a point of principle for the pagan world into which Christianity first intruded: Garnsey 1984; Paschoud 1990; but for a more nuanced treatment see Brown 1997, ch. 2. What was distinctive about the Christian context in which modern doctrines of religious toleration were forged was the peremptoriness of the duty of proselytism.)

Vindicating the principle of toleration proved, therefore, not merely politically or emotionally, but also *cognitively*, a pretty uphill struggle. It was a very difficult conclusion to establish (or even render plausible), if one set out from the premises common to the leaders of European societies. These rulers naturally differed as to who precisely should persecute whom for the good of their own souls. (*Quisque sibi orthodoxus*, in Locke's formula: everyone is orthodox in their own eyes: Locke 1689 (1968) p. 58, 80, 112—or, as we might say, everyone *believes* his own beliefs.) But, as the theorists of toleration underlined with increasing acerbity as the seventeenth century wore on, these differences were far more apparent than real. They cloaked an almost unwavering commonality of assumptions, which depended crucially for their plausibility on their quite unnoticed indexicality—their inadvertent, yet overwhelmingly agent—convincing, egocentricity.

I shall approach the second question of how compelling were the arguments of those who sought to secure the twin conclusions of the objective rightness of the practice of toleration, and the moral and religious merit of its accompanying and supportive virtue, by stating very simply the version of them set out in John Locke's *Epistola de Tolerantia* (1689), partly because of its sheer historical prominence, and partly because it brings out so clearly the logic of late seventeenth-century conclusions on behalf of toleration.

I shall try, too, to show quite what a subtle question, in Locke's case, the third issue (the degree to which his arguments depended for their plausibility on features of the culture of late seventeenth century Europe, and of England more particularly) remains even today.

Finally, I shall align this last analysis with the question of how quite this practice and the virtue which aptly informs it fit with the fundamental properties of the modern constitutional representative democratic republic, with its precarious claim to embody the solution, for the present, to the riddle of Man's political history.

Let me take first the structure of Locke's argument:

(a) The rights of rulers and the duties of subjects have to be interpreted, if they are to be understood correctly, within a comprehensive theory of Christian right, and of the good for Christians (Natural Law: the centuries-old theoretical matrix of the *Lex Naturae*), which specifies and explains the rights and duties of each.

(b) The theory, for this purpose, has to be aimed in the first instance at the putative sites of authority within the human historical world subsequent to the life and death of Jesus Christ—the pertinent political and ecclesiastical institutions, or in slightly anachronistic modern form, the State and the Church.

(c) Its fundamental premise is the priority of one type of duties (both for rulers and subjects) over any other type: namely the duty to act in a manner believed by the actor in question best to serve the overwhelming need to save their own soul.

(d) A key theoretical property of the Christian religion is the individuality of salvation and damnation, and the indispensability of belief and sentiment on the part of the bearer of each particular soul for the salvation or damnation of that soul.

(e) The main case for religious persecution was the duty of other Christians (and especially of Christians with the heavy responsibility of enjoying superior opportunities for so doing—Louis XIV of France would be the paradigm case) to edify the more benighted souls amongst their human fellows.

(f) The key block to this case was the claim that such edification could knowably never be a sufficient condition, and might plausibly never be a necessary condition, for the dawning of the light. If this block could be sustained, it would at least

severely weaken the case for Christian persecution so memorably set out by St Augustine in (see *St. Augustine*) his great (and odious) sermon on the Cana Wedding Text: "Go out into the highways and hedgerows and compel them to come in." (A text, one should note, which still served as the epitome of persecutory orthodoxy for the Huguenot refugee Pierre Bayle in his classic *Commentaire philosophique sur les paroles de Jesus-Christ "Contrains-les entrer,"* a text also prompted by the revocation in 1685 of the Edict of Nantes and the ghastly persecutions which followed this.) If sustained, this block would transform confessional persecution from a plain duty to (at best) a spiritually hazardous and epistemically speculative hypothesis.

(g) Locke, like Bayle, attacked the style of Louis XIV's persecution of the Huguenots, arguing with great rhetorical force that it was a singularly unconvincing exemplification of what it was to be a good Christian in action: cruel, heartless, bigoted, inflexibly self-righteous, and monumentally practically stupid—seen soberly, as palpably fatuous as it was drenched in human vice.

(h) He also attacked the conceptions both of Church and State which underlay it (*La France Toute Catholique sous le Règne de Louis le Grand*), Absolute Monarchy and the Holy Catholic Church, the teleologically comprehensively Catholic and orthodox absolute monarchy of the Roi Soleil, supposedly sanctioned by a *politique*, in Bossuet's phrase, *tirée des propres paroles de l'Écriture sainte*. In place of these queasy conceptions, Locke insisted trenchantly on the analytical, moral and indeed religious need to see both Church and State simply as human voluntary associations with dramatically different goals—in the first case, the goal of an irretrievably personal and individual salvation, and in the second the impartial collective defence of the civil goods—life, liberty, estate and personal rights—of each individual subject.

(i) But the foundation of Locke's case was the block to the task of self-righteous coercive edification which I have already mentioned: the thesis that it is ex-hypothesi impossible for a Christian to enter the gates of Heaven under compulsion or out of fear of purely human threats and intimidation.

(j) Why so? Locke does not deny that human beliefs are in substantial measure *caused* (though he is understandably equivocal, and probably not in the end wholly consistent, over the issue of whether or not they are caused in their entirety: comprehensively externally determined). What he denies is that they can be directly and immediately *chosen*: caused by the immediate present tense choice of the believer in question. Because I cannot at time T choose my own beliefs, you too cannot, however terrifyingly you threaten me, or indeed mutilate or savage me, *cause* me at time T to choose to believe what you wish me to believe. Hypocrisy, the insincere expression of prudently feigned belief, can be compelled with relatively little effort. But belief itself, the real thing, (which is the only thing which in this context it makes any sense to *wish* to generate), cannot.

(k) It is worth underlining that this argument is not necessarily especially *convincing*, even on its own terms, to the sincere and self-righteous religious persecutor—and not merely because such persecutors are unlikely seriously to attend to it. Not only does it seem a shade sophistical and lacklustre in comparison with the overwhelming appeal of dragooning France back into the holistic orthodoxy and comprehensive and unitary political subordination, so disturbingly disrupted by Huguenot military successes a century earlier. It also looks potentially completely beside the point. Only the most impetuous and short-breathed of persecutors would rest the rationale of their efforts on the expectation, or even the hope, of instantaneous conversion. What they could reasonably hope for, by the drastic shift in pertinent pay-off matrices which they engineer, is conversion of the majority over time and in the long run: the crushing of heretical imaginative self-confidence, and the will to think for themselves over the generations to come, or, where this failed, at least the effective erasure of the offending religious dissidence from the visible terrain of the Kingdom. In this sense the smoking hamlets of the Cévennes were an epitome of a political and religious project, *mutatis mutandis*, which in Tokugawa Japan earlier in the century had effectively extirpated a nascent Christian movement, literally burying it in the blood, stench and anguish of its martyrs, and driving it underground for over two centuries (Elison 1988).

(l) Locke held, thus, that coercive proselytization was likely to be evil and unchristian in its motivation, and that it was certain to prove absurd in its ultimate self-understanding. He also thought that it was as predictably ineffectual, as it was politically ill-considered in the light of its real

and predominantly unintended consequences: the endless proliferation of self-righteous internecine conflict which it insistently provoked. But his clearest argument against it was that it was necessarily a violation of right: a contravention of the entitlements of persecuted subjects, and a misconstruction of their rights and duties on the part of persecuting rulers.

The principle of toleration and the practice of tolerance, so understood, are interpretations of the fundamental structure of political rights and duties in a legitimate political order, and of the proper basis for public policy in maintaining good relations between subjects with sharply varying interpretations of their own most pressing existential responsibilities, in this instance towards a world to come. Within this still profoundly Christian, if endlessly riven, world of late seventeenth century Europe, this interpretation goes through not just for Christian rulers in face of other Christians who interpret Christianity differently, but also in relation to subjects who worship quite other Gods or interpret their worship of these in ways which are impossible for Christians themselves to countenance—as Locke himself says, to Mahometans, to Jews, even to American Indians.

What it does not go through to, however, and this is of immense importance, is atheists: those who do not believe that there is a God at all, and who are injudicious enough to say so.

Why?

Not, assuredly, because Locke was fool enough to suppose that atheists too do not at time T believe what they believe or indeed say, but rather because what they say is in his eyes, (unlike those of Pierre Bayle (Dunn 1991)), ghastly in itself and almost limitlessly unnerving in its prospective consequences, should it induce others to come to share their belief. As he put it, in William Popple's enormously influential English translation of the *Epistola*: "the taking away of God even only in thought, dissolveth all."

(m) What is protected, therefore, is a specifically religious freedom—the right to worship as one happens to believe that one's own salvation requires. It is not an unqualified and self-subsistent freedom of thought (a right to believe whatever one happens to believe), let alone an unfettered right to freedom of expression, or a right to privacy (a right to say in public whatever one happens to believe, or to behave in private just as one deems fit, wherever that way of behaving is not in itself a direct assault on the rights of other human beings).

As I have tried to show elsewhere (Dunn 1984; 1991), it is transparently clear, if you care to examine the evidence, that Locke himself did not accept the existence of any such general right of freedom of thought or speech. He gives quite good arguments for supposing that it is likely to prove futile to try to change men's or women's beliefs by threatening them; and he insists trenchantly that nothing about the history of human political or religious practice suggests that the holders of coercive power are likely to offer sound guidance on how to pursue the truth. But he very explicitly does not allocate to subjects a right to think or speak just as they please.

His reasons for refusing to do so are clear and of very great force. They rest on a distinction between two classes of belief—theoretical beliefs and practical beliefs. It is not a self-certifying property of any belief at time T whether or not it is a theoretical as opposed to a practical belief (as one can tell decisively from the case of atheism). Locke claimed (and believed) that atheists have no good reason to behave well towards their fellow human beings, and that the diffusion of atheism was therefore a sure means of diffusing untrustworthiness and general moral turpitude across a human population. Despite Dostoievsky, and in a very different vein Nietzsche, most modern thinkers regard this claim as ludicrous (as did Pierre Bayle in Locke's own day). But the force of Locke's argument does not depend on the quality of his own causal judgment.

Theoretical beliefs are an inappropriate target for coercive power, both because it is extraordinarily unlikely to succeed in changing them (and even less likely to succeed in changing them as it wishes), and because it does not have the slightest *need* to change them. But practical beliefs are always, ex hypothesi, a perfectly eligible target for coercive power, because they do bear directly on the question of what human beings have good reason to do; and wherever, in the judgment of the political sovereign, the conduct which they make rational is itself a threat to the rights of their fellow citizens, it may well be appropriate to respond to them in a forcefully punitive manner. Indeed, where a sovereign genuinely believes them to constitute such a threat, he (or she) cannot consistently suppose that the practical believer does have a right to express or hold the beliefs in question, and indeed has a clear duty of his (or her) own to punish them for doing so. What sovereigns are for, and what they must try their best to do, is to preserve the rights of all their subjects. It is not necessary to read Catherine MacKinnon (1987), or to reflect carefully on the debate over the consequences of watching horror videos, to appreciate that this is not an issue which has gone away since Locke's day. The modern legal and philosophical apparatus for addressing it has become extraordinarily intricate. But I doubt myself if any decisive conceptual advance on Locke's simple contrast between theoretical and practical beliefs has yet been made.

(n) My claim is that Locke's analysis of the place of the practice of toleration within the order of right is an explicitly Christian vindication, (although by no means a vindication for Christians alone), of a distinctively religious right; that it does not sanction, and was not seen by Locke himself as sanctioning, a general entitlement to freedom of speech or thought; and that its force, even for the purposes for which it was devised, depends, and depends rather abjectly, on a rich and culturally specific theory of religious and ethical right.

(o) If this was all that there was to say about the matter, Rawls's vision of a post-Kantian constructivist theory of justice as potential basis for a rationally self-understood modern representative constitutional democracy would be dead in the water.

(p) To see that it is not quite all that needs to be said, we must, I think, look back at the trajectory of strictly political and social learning of Western Europe in the long epoch of the wars of religion, and remember how squarely that cumulative political lesson stands behind and motivates the brilliant intellectual construction of Locke and Bayle.

(q) What was learnt from this protracted and often singularly odious episode was the benefit for statecraft of extending practices of toleration, the hideous costs of persisting in persecution, and the merits for groups in vividly religiously plural societies of coming to regard the attitudes of other groups in their vicinity in an altogether calmer and less malignant manner.

No modern writer has quite captured how these lessons were in fact learnt, so I shall simply offer the crudest of formulae for the logic through which bitter experience imposed these plain and salutary conclusions. The key, most brilliantly set out in Bayle's writings (Dunn 1991; and see now Lennon 1997; Wootton 1997), is the principle of reciprocity and the obfuscatory force of egocentricity. What had to be dissipated was the blinding obviousness of first-person self-righteousness. What had to be learnt was the seeing, however momentarily, of one's own actions (or those of the groups to which one most crucially belonged) as these would appear to others, and not merely as they appeared to oneself. This is an exceedingly simple, and also a very old and deep, theme in the lengthy and usually somewhat ineffectual moral self-education of the peoples of Western Europe. It has been widely registered in other cultures. And, as we all know, even in the European case, it does not initially *derive* from Europe itself. It is not the sort of lesson which is ever learnt comprehensively and permanently, either individually or collectively. It does not, on the whole, readily commend itself to those who have not already had occasion to learn it the hard way for themselves. But it is as deep a lesson about the politics of civility, decency and hope as any human community has yet learnt. I see no reason whatever to regard its rational force as in any way culturally relative.

(r)  Where does that leave the relationship between the theoretical principle of toleration, the decidedly less theoretical virtue of tolerance, and the political forms and cultural self-understanding of the modern representative democratic republic?

Here, I must be very brisk, and hence dogmatic:

(a)  I doubt if it leaves Rawls's revised and mutedly communitarian theory of justice (Rawls 1985, 1993) as a well-grounded view, either of how the denizens of such a republic do at present regard one another in most instances, or of how they have good reason to regard one another, or of how the political leaders of such republics would be well advised to think of the bases on which these can be governed for the better.

At the level of attitude and virtue, some humans are very tolerant (wise, quizzical, unsurprised, forgiving), and some societies are at least fairly tolerant (if usually in pretty discontinuous and rationally weakly related ways). Some states, too, notably the USA, have written the more ambitious modern secular transpositions of the duty to tolerate robustly into their (quite effectively enforced) public law. But in all of these paradigm exemplars of tolerance, contingency is of the essence; and matters are as they happen to be, rather than having come to be so by some dependable and external structural guarantee—imaginative, legal or political: through the peremptory force of some steadily present external reason (cf. Williams 1981).

(b)  Rawls's proposal began as a proposal principally about how the denizens of a modern representative democracy have good reason to regard one another, and how, on this basis, they have good

reason to design the fundamental features of their political and economic order (Rawls 1971). It remains deeply at odds with the viewpoint of self-righteous egocentricity (outside purely private life). But the political history of the United States since 1971 does not suggest that it carries overwhelming persuasive power even for Americans (and perhaps less now even than at the time of publication).

Why has this proved to be true?

(c)  In my view, the key reason why it has proved to be so is that Rawls's theory proposes to individual agents, if and when it comes to be applied, too large a shift in sentiments on too diffident and uncompelling a base. It prescribes, in effect, that, at least as public actors, each citizen should accord to the life plans of others just as deep a respect as they dare to claim for their own life plan from other people. To *pretend* to do this might indeed be a maxim of democratic prudence. But to do it in fact, in the context of political action, demands a degree of imaginative self-restraint, a radical self-abnegation in face of the projects of others, of which most human beings are simply incapable, and which almost none feel spontaneously inclined to accord. The project of aligning popular attitudes with a comprehensive order of public right which runs through the entire political, legal, economic and social texture of a particular population is a heroic venture in the construction of collective moral rationality. But it remains deeply at odds with the real economic organization, the actual political dynamics, and the great bulk of popular attitudes, in every society in the world today (cf. Dunn (ed.) 1990). In my view it involves a complete misunderstanding of what the modern representative constitutional democratic republic is really like, and of why it has come to dominate the struggle for legitimate political authority in so much of the world in the last few decades (cf. Dunn 1992; Dunn 1994a in Fontana 1994).

(d)  In my view the political practice of toleration—still crucially in many settings like India (or perhaps Northern Ireland) in relation to religion, but also in relation to alien folkways, aesthetics and ideological bombast, is indeed a powerful and salutary political lesson, and fully retains its power when addressed to populations who in no way share the cultural antecedents of the Europe of Locke and Bayle. But it is a much *thinner* practice than Rawls appears to imagine. It rests not on the conception of a society as a moral order, even in *form* and even of a skeptically constructivist character, but simply on a recognition of the long-term political merit of aligning the claims of authority and the practice of power with principles on which those who differ acutely about what is good or right, and find many aspects of each other acutely offensive, can yet, on balance and on reflection, reasonably agree. It is, above all, a *prudential*, rather than a moral, principle. (For the importance of this contrast in relation to modern democratic states, see Dunn 1990 ch. 12.)

*Bibliography*

Brown P 1997 *Authority and the Sacred*. Cambridge University Press, Canto pd ed Cambridge

Dunn J 1984 *Locke*. Oxford University Press, Oxford

Dunn J 1985 *Rethinking Modern Political Theory*. Cambridge University Press, Cambridge

Dunn J 1990 *Interpreting Political Responsibility*. Polity Press, Cambridge

Dunn J (ed.) 1990 *The Economic Limits to Modern Politics*. Cambridge University Press, Cambridge (Korean Trans. Young Joe Park, Seoul 1992)

Dunn J 1991 Freedom of conscience: Freedom of thought, freedom of speech, freedom of worship? In: O P Grell, J Israel, N Tyacke (eds.) *From Persecution to Toleration*. Clarendon Press, Oxford

Dunn J (ed.) 1992 *Democracy: The Unfinished Journey, 508BC to 1992*. Oxford University Press, Oxford

Dunn J 1993 *Western Political Theory in the Face of the Future*, 2nd edn. Cambridge University Press, Cambridge

Dunn J 1994a *Stato nazionale e comunita umanà*. Edizioni Anabasi, Milan

Dunn J 1994b The identity of the Bourgeois Liberal Republic. In: Fontana (ed.) *The Invention of the Modern Republic*

Elison G 1988 *Deus Destroyed: The Image of Christianity in Early Modern Japan*. Harvard University Press, Cambridge, Mass

Fontana B (ed.) 1994 *The Invention of the Modern Republic*. Cambridge University Press, Cambridge

Fukuyama F 1992 *The End of History and the Last Man*. Hamish Hamilton, London

Garnsey P 1984 Religious toleration in classical antiquity. In: W J Shiels (ed.) *Persecution and Toleration*. Studies in Church History 21, Oxford University Press, Oxford

Hont I 1990 Free trade and the economic limits to national politics: Neo-Machiavellian political economy reconsidered. In: J Dunn (ed.) *The Economic Limits to Modern Politics*. Cambridge University Press, Cambridge (Korean Trans (ed.) Young Joe Park, Seoul 1992)

Huntington S 1993 The Clash of Civilizations? *Foreign Affairs* 72

Lennon T M 1997 Bayle, Locke and the Metaphysics of Toleraton. In: M A Stewart (ed.) *Studies in Seventeenth Century European Philosophy*. Clarendon Press, Oxford

Locke J 1689(1968) *Epistola de Tolerantia* [A Letter Concerning Toleration]. J Gough, R Klibansky (ed.) Clarendon Press, Oxford

MacKinnon C 1987 *Feminism Unmodified*. Harvard University Press, Cambridge, Mass

Manin B 1994 *Principes du gouvernement représentatif*. Calmann-Levy, Paris

Paschoud F 1990 L'Intolérance chrétienne vue et jugée par les païens, *Cristianesimo nella Storia* II

Rawls J 1971 *A Theory of Justice*. Harvard University Press, Cambridge, Mass

Rawls J 1985 Justice as fairness: Political, not metaphysical. *Philosophy and Public Affairs* 14

Rawls J 1993 *Political Liberalism*. Columbia University Press, New York

Williams B 1981 *Moral Luck*. Cambridge University Press, Cambridge

Wootton D 1997 Pierre Bayle, Libertine? In: M A Stewart (ed.) *Studies in Seventeenth Century European Philosophy*. Clarendon Press, Oxford

JOHN DUNN

# Containment

"Containment" refers to the policy adopted by the United States between 1947 and 1989 designed to limit the expansion of the power and ideology of the former Soviet Union by all 'means short of war.' Containment effectively dominated US global thinking for over forty years, and though criticized by some—especially during the turbulent years of the Vietnam War—the strategy overall tended to be endorsed by most Americans. Indeed, according to its supporters, containment not only frustrated communist expansion, but over time, forced China and the former Soviet Union to abandon their aggressiveness and accept the international *status quo*. Some have even suggested that the successful containment of the USSR contributed in no small way to the final collapse of the Soviet system in the late 1980s (see *Cold War*).

## 1. The "X" Article

The policy of containment emerged out of a reassessment of Soviet intentions and behavior by the US government in the 18-month period following the surrender of Japan in August 1945. The originator of the concept, if not the actual policy, was George F. Kennan. A lowly-ranked Foreign Service officer based in the Moscow Embassy in the latter part of the war, Kennan rapidly rose through the ranks to become the State Department's foremost Soviet expert. In 1947 he was appointed Head of its Policy Planning Staff and assigned the task of coordinating the European Recovery Programme (or Marshall Plan). In that year the concept of "containment," and with it the rationale for future US foreign policy, was given its first public airing in a famous article anonymously authored by Kennan in the July issue of the important foreign policy magazine, *Foreign Affairs*. The essay, entitled 'The Sources of Soviet Conduct' and written by Kennan under the pseudonym "X," remains one of the most significant pieces of writing in the history of diplomacy. It has also remained one of the most controversial.

The bulk of Kennan's article consists of a somber analysis of Soviet conduct, and says relatively little in fact about US policy and how the United States ought to respond to the Soviet challenge. But it is the latter for which the article is best remembered, especially Kennan's famous call for a 'long-term, patient but firm and vigilant containment of Russian expansionist tendencies.' Soviet pressure against the West, Kennan wrote, is 'something that can be contained by the adroit and vigilant application of counterforce at a series of constantly shifting geographical and political points, corresponding to the shifts and maneuvers of Soviet policy.' However, war was not inevitable he believed, nor was indefinite containment. As Kennan argued, it was possible for the United States, 'to influence by its actions the internal developments, both within Russia and throughout the international Communist movement, by which Russian policy is largely determined.' By 'coping successfully with the problems of its internal life and with the responsibilities of World Power,' he thought that the United States could frustrate the ambitions of the Kremlin. Since a 'mystical, Messianic movement' such as communism could not face endless frustration, it would have to adjust 'to the logic of that state of affairs.' The result, eventually, would be 'either the break-up or the gradual mellowing of Soviet power.' It proved a remarkable forecast.

Kennan's analysis was thus both pessimistic at one level (insofar as he seemed to be ruling out the possibility of co-operation with the Soviet Union) but optimistic at another (insofar as he assumed that over the long term the USSR might be impelled to change its ways). Moreover, though he was deeply wary about Soviet intentions, he never overestimated its capabilities. It was, he noted, 'by far and away' the weaker of the two superpowers. Nor did he make facile comparisons between Hitler and Stalin. Stalin was neither a revolutionary romantic nor a military adventurist in his view. Unfortunately, this is not how the US foreign policy establishment came to regard the USSR. In their judgement, Moscow was engaged in a serious bid for world domination. This was not Kennan's assessment, and he increasingly found himself at odds with the new Cold War consensus in Washington. Indeed, over time he went on to develop a devastating critique of US policy in the Cold War, arguing that the "X" article had been misinterpreted and his views misrepresented by successive administrations. His words fell on stony ground however, and by the time he left the Foreign Service in the early 1950s, his original, more flexible concept of containment had given way to a rigid confrontational stance in which the "follow-up" aspects of containment of seeking to engage and change the former Soviet Union had been abandoned.

Given his role as both author and critic of the doctrine of containment, there has been a lively debate as to what Kennan actually meant in his "X" article. Even sympathetic critics accept that there is room for misunderstanding on questions such as the extent to which he thought Soviet expansion was driven by ideology or the search for security, or whether containment implied primarily economic and political or military counter-pressure. Some of the problems were caused by Kennan himself, because of the language he employed and his failure (or inability) to join in the discussion which followed the publication of the article. He later attempted to clarify the situation with the publication of his two volume *Memoirs* in 1967 and 1972. But far from settling matters, his own intervention in the debate only managed to stimulate even more discussion. That said, the weight of opinion generally vindicates Kennan's claim that the "X" article was an unfortunately incomplete representation of his views, and that the containment policies adopted by US administrations during the Cold War were more expansive, less discriminating, and more militarized than he had ever intended.

## 2. Two Decades of Containment

The "X" article was published at a critical moment,

when the US was reassessing its relationship with the former Soviet Union. In the face of what many viewed as Stalin's increasing belligerence, US policy through 1946 moved in an increasingly anti-Soviet direction. And when Britain proved too weak to support Greece and Turkey in early 1947, President Harry S. Truman recognized that the United States would have to act decisively. Truman decided to use the situation however to articulate a bold new foreign policy. The 'Truman' Doctrine of March 12, 1947 was the outcome (see *Truman Doctrine*). The simple message outlined by Truman in his famous speech before Congress was that 'it must be the policy of the USA to support free people who are resisting subjection by armed minorities or outside pressures.' Though his address was immediately concerned with mobilizing support and aid to prop up weak regimes in Greece and Turkey (neither of which could conceivably be described as being 'free' at the time), it was read by both critics and supporters alike as marking the end of one era and the beginning of another. Isolationism (see *Isolationism: United States*) was now officially dead. The ending of the Second World War would not lead to 'American boys' being brought back home, or to the United States again taking a backseat in international affairs: the deepening frosts of the Cold War and the exigencies of a bipolar world required a long-term US commitment to counter the perceived challenge from the former Soviet Union.

If the eastern Mediterranean was the immediate catalyst for the policy of containment, within a short space of time western Europe and the Middle East had been added to the list of regions threatened by communist subversion: and after the triumph of communism in China in 1949, the policy then expanded to cover the whole Eurasian land mass. It was in the Far East however, on the Korean peninsula, where the first war was fought in the name of containment. This limited, but extraordinarily brutal conflict, had significant long-term implications: it legitimized an already planned programme of conventional rearmament; it led to the US decision to develop the H-bomb; it fanned the flames of anti-communism in US politics; it strengthened the hand of those calling for West German membership of NATO (see *North Atlantic Treaty Organization (NATO)*); and it made unlikely—if not impossible—any early rapprochement between the People's Republic of China and the United States (in the event it took another quarter-of-a century before the two countries even established formal diplomatic relations).

The Korean War also illustrated that the practice of containment was always bound to be difficult given the variety of challenges the United States faced as it sought to build up positions of strength to counter what it perceived as communist expansion. A variety of policies would have to be employed therefore in pursuit of this larger goal: these included the extension of economic support to Western Europe and developing countries, the construction of a formidable military arsenal, the establishment of a ring of US bases around the perimeter of Soviet power, the deployment of an equally extensive western intelligence network to counter Soviet subversion, and the creation of a series of bilateral and multilateral alliances—NATO, CENTO and SEATO (see *Alliance*). In the 1950s this extensive alliance policy attracted particular criticism, and came to be as dubbed as "pactomania" for the apparent addiction with which the United States accumulated allies in an effort to strengthen local positions, deter communism and draw clear lines in what had now become a global conflict. These alliances included former enemies, undemocratic and sometimes unstable regimes; but Realpolitik was thought to demand the suppression of such scruples in order to contain the ambitions of the former Soviet Union and the People's Republic of China (see *Balance of Power*).

In spite of these various measures, containment, by definition, seemed to imply a strictly defensive posture. For this reason, it was sometimes criticized for being unduly passive, thus condemning a large segment of humankind indefinitely to enslavement under communism. This view was most forcefully articulated by the Republican party after its defeat in the 1948 presidential election, and in particular by John Foster Dulles (see *Dulles, John Foster*), General Eisenhower's foreign policy adviser in the 1952 presidential campaign. Dulles, who went on to become Secretary of State, argued that the US had to move 'beyond containment' so as to keep alive the hope of 'liberation' for those subjected to communist rule—especially the 'captive peoples' in Eastern Europe. While a policy of liberation was never formally adopted, it did lead to a rhetorically more aggressive stance. Indeed, there is some evidence to suggest that this contributed in no small part to encouraging the anti-Soviet insurgency in Hungary in 1956. Here, the people rose up against Stalinist rule hoping, it seems, that the United States would come to their rescue. In the event, Eisenhower was not prepared to risk war with the USSR, and the movement was brutally crushed by Soviet tanks. Significantly, after this disaster, the US dropped all talk of liberating the peoples of Eastern Europe and began to develop what became known as a strategy of 'peaceful engagement.'

If critics on the right attacked the concept of containment for being too defensive, others complained that it provided the US with a rationale for interference in the internal affairs of other countries. Some radical analysts have even gone so far as to suggest that containment was merely a useful 'device,' whose real purpose was to justify US expansion and counter-revolutionary intervention in the Third World. This 'arrogance of power'—as Senator Fulbright later termed it—was displayed on more than one occasion after 1947 (see *Power*). First, and most dramatically perhaps, the US undermined the popular nationalist government of Mohammed Mossadeq in Iran in 1953 and replaced him with the pro-western Shah of Persia. Then, in Guatamala, in 1954, President Eisenhower engineered a coup against the radical government of Jacobo Arbenz. In 1961 President Kennedy supported an attempted invasion of Cuba to depose the revolutionary Fidel Castro. And in 1965, President Johnson sent 22,000 US troops into the Dominican Republic, ostensibly to prevent the overthrow of that country's government by pro-Castro rebels (see *Intervention*).

If the US stance in the Third World could be characterized as dominant and assertive, its relationship with the USSR might best be described as adversarial but cautious. The goal here was not so much to eliminate the former Soviet Union, but to create conditions that would encourage the gradual socialization of the USSR and China into the traditional norms of the international system. In this sense containment can be understood as the Western equivalent of the Soviet doctrine of "peaceful coexistence" (see *Peaceful Coexistence*). In many ways, the two had much in common. Both looked forward to the eventual collapse of the other; both recognized the intractability of the struggle; and both agreed that the relationship had to be carefully managed if nuclear war was to be avoided. This is why the Cuban missile crisis of 1962 was such an important event in the history of containment. On the one hand, it dramatised the real dangers inherent in the Cold War; on the other it showed the extent to which fear of nuclear annihilation imposed caution on the leaders of the two superpowers.

A necessary adjunct of the doctrine of containment in an age of nuclear overkill was the strategy of "limited war." This assumed the seriousness of the communist threat, but recognized that conflicts arising from the Cold War (as in Korea and later in Vietnam) had themselves to be contained in order to pre-vent them leading to a nuclear exchange. This notion was in turn underpinned by an equally important concept: the "domino theory" (see *Domino Theory*). This stated that if any strategically placed nation succumbed to communism, then its neighbours were also likely to fall—literally like dominoes. Most analysts would argue that the theory was implicit in Truman's original 1947 speech. However, the term was first used by President Eisenhower in 1954 to justify US involvement in South-East Asia. In the spring of that year the long struggle between France and the communist Vietminh had reached a climax, with France facing the prospects of complete defeat. Eisenhower and Dulles however were determined to avoid a loss of Indochina to communism. Comparing the nations of East Asia to a row of falling dominoes, Eisenhower warned that Burma, Thailand and Indonesia would be the next victims if communism were permitted to triumph in Indochina. When, just over 20 years later, Indochina did 'fall' to communism, it seemed to some at least as if Eisenhower's fears had been vindicated. Others drew rather different conclusions however, and insisted that the real lesson to be learned was that the domino theory had led the United States to fight a long and brutal war, in a region where it had few interests, for unachievable political goals, against a foe it could never defeat.

## 3. Vietnam and After

Whether we view Vietnam as a tragedy waiting to happen, or a necessary but unwinnable war, it certainly exposed the expansive version of the doctrine of containment. This in turn resulted in a widespread attack upon its fundamentals by a new generation of Americans who only a few years earlier had heard President Kennedy announce in his Inaugural Address of 1961 that the US would 'pay any price, bear any burden, meet any hardship, support any friend, oppose any foes, in order to assure the survival and success of liberty.' Vietnam also carried complex lessons for US policy, both in terms of defining its vital interest in the world, and in determining its future military strategy. More immediately though it led to the election of Richard M. Nixon, a Cold War warrior of the old school who had made his name in the late 1940s hunting down alleged communists in the State Department. An early critic of Kennan's less belligerent version of containment, there was little in Nixon's make-up or background to suggest that he would challenge the basics of containment.

Yet even the conservative Nixon had to adjust to the changing forces in world politics, and assisted by his National Security advisor—Henry Kissinger—he devised a strategy that many have termed "containment on the cheap" and others a "constrained" version of containment. At the heart of this strategy was a recognition that as a result of the US defeat in Vietnam, the Soviet challenge to its nuclear superiority and a growing restlessness in the Third World, the United States had to find different (and less costly) ways of maintaining its dominant international role. This did not mean an abandonment of containment, or a recognition of the legitimacy of communism. Instead, it involved a less hostile relationship with the former Soviet Union and China—in the hope that both would work with the United States in order to preserve global order—and the strengthening of various pro-American Third World regimes who would then be better placed to resist 'aggression' without necessarily calling upon direct US intervention (see *Aggression*).

This new grand strategy—known as the 'Nixon' doctrine—led to a number of significant initiatives. At the rhetorical level, US officials began to argue that the world had moved beyond confrontation and had entered into a new "era of negotiations." In terms of burden-sharing, Nixon suggested that 'Asian boys' would now have to start fighting their own 'Asian Wars.' There was, in addition, a dramatic US opening to China that culminated in Nixon's famous visit to Beijing in 1972. This was followed shortly thereafter by the signing of treaties stabilizing relations across the inter-German and East-West divide in Europe (see *East-West Conflict*). Washington also began the Strategic Arms Limitations Talks in 1969 which concluded with the USA and the Soviet Union signing an important arms control agreement (SALT I) in 1972. Finally, under Kissinger's careful direction, the US concluded a series of potentially important trade deals with the USSR, in the hope—as he admitted at the time—of drawing the former Soviet Union out of economic autarchy and into a closer, more cooperative relationship with the capitalist world.

Nonetheless, there was always some resistance to the new policies within the US; especially to the strategy of establishing a more constructive relationship with the USSR. Indeed, long before President Nixon's inglorious exit from power in 1974, a powerful coalition comprising the military, sections of the Democratic party around Senator Jackson, and those concerned with the fate of Soviet Jews and intellectual dissidents in the USSR, had virtually destroyed his policy of détente. Other events also conspired to weaken the case for better relations with the Soviet Union. First, there was the MAD logic of the arms race. Arms control may have slowed the race down. But it did not bring it to an end, and inevitably the action-reaction dynamic of the nuclear competition fostered a high level of superpower mistrust. Second, while China may have managed to 'come in from the cold' after 1972, many in the US continued to see the hand of the former Soviet Union behind a wave of new revolutions in the Third World. This in turn spawned new doctrines (such as the 'Carter Doctrine') whose underlying premise was that Moscow has embarked upon an aggressive course whose goal was to eliminate western influence from key Third World regions. Finally, came Soviet intervention in Afghanistan in 1979. Whilst motivated more by a desire to support a besieged ally on its southern flank than to expand to the Indian Ocean (see *Indian Ocean: The Duality of Zone of Peace Concept and Politics of Security Revisited*), the Soviet intervention—like the North Korean attack of 1950—only confirmed US mistrust and provided extra ammunition to those already calling for a 'revitalization of containment' against the USSR.

## 4. The Revitalization of Containment

The shift back to Cold War confrontation, which began under Carter but accelerated under President Reagan after 1980, meant an abandonment of detente and the policies associated with it: arms control, expanding East-West trade and the tacit acceptance by both superpowers that each had legitimate security concerns in Europe (see *Détente*). These were substituted with an altogether more aggressive US posture, based on the old Cold War belief (now adopted by the New Right) that the only thing the Russians understood and respected was raw power, and that the only way to deal with the USSR was from a clear position of military strength. Reagan however was not content just to reassert US power after a period of perceived decline, but to mobilize US assets in what looked to many as a determined and concerted effort to force the former Soviet Union onto the defensive. Indeed, so aggressive were his policies—particularly towards Soviet allies in the Third World and in the broad area of nuclear strategy—that it appeared to some at least that he was aiming to undermine the Soviet system altogether. In a number of key statements, Reagan made it plain that this was precisely his purpose. As he argued in a speech to the British Parliament in the early 1980s, Soviet communism was doomed in at least two senses: doomed to expand and doomed to decay. The United States should therefore set itself the two-fold task of in the short term limiting Soviet international influence, and in the longer term of accelerating its decline.

The enunciation of what became known as the 'Reagan Doctrine' thus combined together a powerful restatement of classic Cold War beliefs about the inevitability of conflict with the former Soviet Union, together with a clear commitment to rolling back communism wherever possible. This more assertive policy expressed itself in many ways, though most obviously in the support given by the Reagan Administration to those countries and groups seeking to reverse the apparent gains made by the former Soviet Union in the Third World in the 1970s. It was also reflected in the massive Reagan military build up. Publicly justified in terms of redressing the military balance between the superpowers, it clearly had another purpose—which was less to close military 'gaps' (that did not exist), or mythical 'windows of vulnerability' (which were not open), than to put pressure on what many in the Reagan administration genuinely believed was a Soviet system on its last legs. Running throughout the Reagan policy, finally, was a concerted ideological drive to portray the superpower relationship in stark moral terms with the US on one side embodying all that was fine and good in the world, and the former Soviet Union on the other representing all that was evil.

The strategy pursued by the Reagan administration was certainly controversial, especially in Western Europe where the provocative US military build-up (symbolized for millions by the deployment of Cruise and Pershing II missiles) provoked resistance on the streets. But even in the United States itself there were many who were deeply unhappy with the new strategy, and sought to deflect it by pointing to its lack of military logic and its dangerously confrontational rhetoric. This did not spawn a peace movement on the scale of the Vietnam years, but the popular demand for a nuclear 'freeze' did force the Reagan administration onto the defensive (see *Nuclear Weapons Abolition*). Reagan faced an even greater test in his efforts attempts to destabilize revolutionary regimes in the Third World. While Congress had no particular sympathy for the Sandinistas in Nicaragua, or for the various left-leaning governments in black Africa, it was not prepared to sanction internationally dubious (and sometimes illegal) efforts to undermine them. Reagan's strategy also could not overcome the fact that the US and the world had changed since the early days of containment.

Vietnam in particular had made Americans extremely wary of getting dragged into uncertain overseas commitments. Many moreover were skeptical that there was in fact a rising Soviet threat which demanded a robust American response. Perhaps when communism had been in an ascendant phase immediately after the war, the call for tough and expensive measures made some sense. In an era of communist ideological fatigue and Soviet economic decline, they did not.

## 5. Beyond Containment

Paradoxically, the biggest problem for Reagan was not to be found in Western Europe, or at home, but in the land of his communist adversary. Here, quite unexpected changes after 1985 rapidly eroded all preexisting notions about the nature of the Soviet system. Thus, it had always been assumed that the USSR was bound to contest the West. However, during the latter half of the 1980s it did precisely opposite and started to back away from confrontation. It had also been taken for granted that the USSR was quite unreformable. But Gorbachev managed to challenge this particular truth as well through his policies of *perestroika* and *glasnost* (see *Glasnost and Perestroika*). He also undermined long-held Western notions about the eternal character of the Soviet threat by making significant concessions in the field of both conventional and nuclear weapons. Moscow moreover started winding down its support for revolutionary forces in the Third World. It even withdrew its battered army from Afghanistan. Finally, in 1989, the former Soviet Union then did what it was not supposed to do at all, and allowed Eastern Europe to slip quietly (and without serious opposition) from out under its control (see *Eastern Europe, Transformation of*).

Gorbachev's 'new thinking' elated many but confused some—in particular those in the United States and the West who had either assumed that the former Soviet Union could not reform, or that if it did, that this would only make it a more capable and attractive adversary (see Nobel Peace Prize Laureates: *Mikhail S. Gorbachev*). There were even a few who saw the whole thing as an enormous strategic deception whose only purpose was to weaken Western resolve in general and US resolve in particular. For all these different reasons, there were plenty in Washington who viewed Gorbachev not as a welcome breath of fresh political air, but a more dangerous version of the same old foe—"a Bolshevik with a smile." Yet by 1989, even the skeptics had to concede that something quite fundamental had changed and that containment no longer made very much sense. Some greeted this with a sigh of relief and looked forward to what President Bush optimistically hoped would one day become a 'new world order.' Others reflected back nostalgically on the past and wondered whether we would all soon be missing the Cold War. A few however began to count all the costs. True, the former Soviet Union had finally mellowed—as Kennan predicted it would. But in the meantime over twenty million had died, the world had come to the brink of a nuclear holocaust at least once, billions of dollars had been spent on weapons, and brutality rather than democracy had become the rule rather than the exception in the Third World. Containment might have been a success, but it came with a very heavy price tag. One can only hope that future generations will remember this when they repeat the truism that the West 'won' the Cold War.

*Bibliography*

Brands H W 1989 *The Specter of Neutralism: The United States and the Emergence of the Third World.* Columbia University Press, New York

Gaddis J L 1982 *Strategies of Containment: A Critical Appraisal of Postwar American National Security Policy.* Oxford University Press, Oxford

Gaddis J L 1997 *We Now Know: Rethinking Cold War History.* Clarendon Press, Oxford

Halliday F 1982 *The Making of the Second Cold War.* Verso, London

Herring G C 1985 *America's Longest War: The United States and Vietnam, 1950-75.* Knopf, New York

Hogan M J 1987 *The Marshall Plan: America, Britain, and the Reconstruction of Western Europe.* Cambridge University Press, New York

Jones H 1989 *"A New Kind of War": America's Global Strategy and the Truman Doctrine in Greece.* Oxford University Press, New York

Kennan G F ("X") 1947 The sources of Soviet conduct. *Foreign Affairs* 25

Kennan G F 1967 *Memoirs: 1925-50.* Little, Brown, Boston

Kennan G F 1972 *Memoirs: 1950-1963.* Little, Brown, Boston

Leffler M P 1992 *A Preponderance of Power : National Security, the Truman Administration and the Cold War.* Stanford University Press, Stanford

Lippman W 1947 *The Cold War: A Study in US Foreign Policy.* Harper, New York

Mastny V 1996 *The Cold and Soviet Insecurity: The Stalin Years.* Oxford University Press, New York

Yergin D 1977 *Shattered Peace: The Origins of the Cold War and the National Security State.* Houghton Mifflin, Boston, Massachusetts

KEN BOOTH; MICHAEL COX

# Contemporary International Terrorism, Nature of

## 1. Introduction

Over the last twenty years, a plethora of both experts and novices have attempted to provide an overview of international terrorism.[1] Most of these authors focus on a variety of issues connected with this particular form of political violence. This material is presented in a variety of written forms. One of the most popular media is "the nature of terrorism chapter," appearing in edited books such as this one. There is, however, a wide discrepancy in definitions,[2] coverage of topics, sources of information, and quality of interpretation with this type of writing. This article attempts to comment on the last three differences, present updated statistics, point out common interpretations of these data, critique these accepted interpretations, and, where possible, suggest improvements or additional insights in these types of studies. In general, the author will focus on topics that have most consistently appeared in this genre of writing.

## 2. The Nature of Terrorism Chapter as a Genre of Writing

The nature of terrorism as a subject matter is covered in approximately six types of writing: monographs, textbooks, government publications, consultant reports, academic and quasi-academic journals, and book chapters.

A number of monographs—most of which are in their second and revised printing—covering a wide variety of issues on international terrorism have been produced and are slowly being regarded as classics in the field.[3] Three books published in 1988, all of which attempt to provide a broad review of terrorism, were actually designed or marketed as textbooks.[4] Concomitantly, many publicly available reports produced by government agencies (e.g., the US State Department) or private consulting companies (e.g., the Rand Corporation) are a functional equivalent of these monographs and textbooks.[5] Periodically, academic or quasi-academic journals will also feature articles on the nature of terrorism.[6] Finally, a series of book chapters, appearing in edited books similar to this one, giving an overview of the subject of international terrorism, have become commonplace. Chapters by Jenkins, Singh, and Mickolus,[7] Fearey, Russell, and Wilkinson;[8] Jenkins, Shultz and Sloan, and Mastrangelo are examples of this latter category.[9]

### 3. Coverage, Sources of Information, and Quality of the Nature of Terrorism Chapters and the Aim of the Paper

From a cursory content analysis of the nine book chapters, which collectively might represent a genre of writing in the terrorist field, the author detects wide variability in subject matter, sources of information, and quality of analysis.

### 3.1 Coverage

The subtopics addressed in these book chapters can be divided into three areas of concentration. First and most rare (only one author focuses on each one of these subjects) are: the provision of a typology of political violence; a history of political terrorism; a discussion of the threat terrorism poses to legal systems; the effectiveness of terrorism; a review of terrorist strategy; a discussion of objectives of terrorists; weapons used by terrorists; methods for combating terrorism; US policies in terrorist incidents; international cooperation against terrorism; individual terrorist profiles; and a listing of causes of terrorism.

Second and relatively common (two authors discuss these themes) are: types of groups engaging in terrorism; typologies of terrorism; discussions of the future of terrorism; the American experience with terrorism; support for terrorist groups; and the provision of a recent chronology of terrorist attacks.

Third and most prominent (three to six authors focus on these issues) are treatments of: different definitions of international terrorism; the number of events/annual trends; targets; tactics of terrorists; regional variation/geographical spread; and a review of governmental responses to terrorism.

While there is probably no essential logic to the subject matter selection, outside of editorial mandates, I will focus on the material that has been most frequently treated (those mentioned more than once). Missing, from the present review, however, is a section on definitions of international terrorism, a chronology of terrorist incidents, and a review of governmental attempts to respond to terrorism. The writer's rationale for excluding these subjects stems from the fact that the definitional issue is treated in the previous chapter, the utility of chronologies in chapters of this type is limited, and governmental reactions are dealt with in a series of chapters following this one.

Consequently, this chapter reviews the empirical research with respect to past and recent trends in international terrorism focusing on eight aspects: a typology of international terrorism; the number of events/annual trends; the regional and geographical spread of terrorism; the tactics of terrorists; the targets (human and nonhuman) of terrorist attacks; the different groups engaging in terrorism; the support for terrorist groups; and the future of terrorism.

### 3.2 Sources of Information

In terms of sources of information, these "nature-of-terrorism" chapters are equally divided among those largely based on data, those mainly based on secondary sources (monographs, journal articles, chapters from edited books, and State Department publications), and those that utilize both data and secondary sources. When a data source is cited in these chapters, it is commonly based on statistics from the Risks International Data Base and the Rand Corporation Data Base; only two use data from the Central Intelligence Agency (CIA) data set. Furthermore, only one of these chapters discusses data collection methods and none of them analyzes the potential drawbacks of the data.

Prior to the mid-1970s, most of the information on international terrorism was presented in case studies of particular movements, groups, and individuals[10] that used terrorism and of countries that experienced terrorism. This material was generally descriptive, atheoretical and nonempirical. In the mid-1970s however, we saw a greater attempt among scholars, private research agencies, and governmental departments to systematically collect data on terrorist actions and perpetrators. The majority of these efforts were quantitative studies, which unlike the descriptive ones, allow us to speak with greater precision about the phenomenon. The most basic statistics for the study of terrorism are events data, discrete incidents as units of analysis. This method has been used in the creation of roughly thirteen large-scale comparative studies of political conflict.[11] Most of these projects did not have a separate variable for terrorism but included these acts under other types of violence. This state of affairs changed during the middle of the last decade; events data methodology was eventually applied to international terrorism, beginning with Edward Mickolous.[12]

Since the mid-1970s, there has been an increase in attempts to systematically collect data on terrorism.[13] This mode of analysis has allowed researchers to understand mainly the frequency of terrorism, and occasionally to test hypotheses. Nevertheless, these data sets suffer from a number of problems: their definitions of terrorism, which are believed to be too broad; their limited public availability; their focus on regional totals rather than on country totals; their lack of distinction between domestic and international events; and their inclusion of acts of violence which are not terrorism.[14]

Over the last few years, many of the incident-level data sets on terrorism have merged with others, have become closely held, or no longer exist. Meanwhile new ones have entered the academic/corporate/state marketplace. For example, upon examination of the current status of the nine terrorist events data listings compiled by William Fowler,[15] one discovers that the BDM Corporation data set no longer exists, and the whereabouts of the Democratic Worldwatch system is unknown.[16] In addition, no information is publicly available on the CIA's File on International Terrorist Events (FITE) system, the State Department's Threat Analysis Group's data base, and the Defense Intelligence Agency Significant Terrorist Incident Files (STAG) system.[17] With regard to the data sets created by state agencies, one can only assume that these data sets have either ceased to exist or are closely guarded state secrets. This inaccessibility of data presents a number of validation problems for researchers trying to gain an accurate picture of the frequency of various attributes of international terrorism. Periodically, tallies of raw yearly totals will be given to the academics or the media from these governmental agencies.[18] Although of some utility, these data are not comprehensive enough, the coding categories are not delineated, and secondary analysis of these events is not possible since the actual complete chronology is not publicly available.

Three data sets, listed by Fowler, have managed to withstand the economic demands that maintaining a data set entails. These projects include: the Rand Corporation data set, the Control Risks and Risks International data sets; and the International Terrorism: Attributes of Terrorism Events (ITERATE) I, II, and III data sets. The economic obstacles are most evident when one observes that the first two have been created by private research organizations and the latter, at least ITERATE I and II, by Mickolus with funding from the CIA. While all of these data sets have been criticized on several accounts,[19] they have

many practical advantages.

First, the Rand Corporation is an independent, "nonprofit" think tank which performs contract research for various sponsors. It has gained a reputation for conducting wide-ranging studies on subnational, low-intensity conflict, and international terrorism. Not only has it published a number of chronologies and developed some ground-breaking research on terrorism, it has also constructed a number of data bases on various areas pertaining to international terrorism.[20] While Rand's data sets are not publicly available for others to analyze, some of the reports generated with these data make it into the public domain.

Second, the Control Risks Group maintains a data set on domestic and international terrorism. Formed in 1975, it serves the security needs of businesses and multinational executives. These country files contain data on terrorist and criminal behavior. Updated monthly, the Data Solve Information system from Control Risks Information Services is available in several formats including on-line videotext. While publicly available, the cost of the service is high, thus limiting its accessibility. To remedy this situation, the Group has a policy of giving information free of charge to students conducting research on terrorism, this is only in the form of aggregate totals.[21] All this explains the low frequency with which articles detailing past years' rate of terrorism make it into either an academic journal, quasi-academic journal or an edited book.

Finally, the ITERATE data sets have become the best-known public data sets, most widely used by researchers studying international terrorism. Roughly 150 variables per case are computer coded. The data set consists of a hostage file, fate file, and skyjack file, with all subfiles linked to the master. Originally, this data base was developed from two Rand chronologies and from press accounts in *The New York Times, The Washington Post,* and other media. By 1980, it listed more than 200 sources. ITERATE has three major advantages: it is publicly available for a minimal cost (ITERATE I and II are available to member institutions of ICPSR); and both a readily accessible chronology and a code book have been prepared so that researchers can check the validity of coding.[22]

Although new computer-based data sets on international terrorism have been started by a number of academics, information on these projects is scant. Some of the more widely discussed collections are those initiated by Paul Wilkinson to the University of St. Andrews, Ariel Merari at the Jaffee Center for Strategic Studies,[23] John B. Wolf at the John Jay College of Criminal Justice,[24] Alex P. Schmid at the University of Leiden, and A. J. Jongman at the Polemological Institute of Groningen State University.

Despite the previously mentioned drawbacks with most data sets, the majority of data bases on international terrorism show the same general patterns. Thus for purposes of this chapter statistics are based mainly on information from State Department sources. Specifically, the State Department, through the Office of the Ambassador at Large for Counter-Terrorism, issues an annual "Patterns of Global Terrorism" report. When appropriate State Department information was not available, the author relied on Rand reports.

### 3.3 Quality

No chapter on the nature of terrorism can adequately cover all the subjects previously inventoried. Moreover, the choices of data sets used as statistical evidence in each of the above-mentioned chapters, while troublesome in some respects, are mainly a reflection of their availability or of corporate/agency loyalties. These inherent difficulties aside, many of the nature-of-terrorism chapters are much too superficial. The more salient complaints are that they are generally précis of State Department reports with little critical analysis or commentary. Not only are the definitions used too simplistic, the studies are chart-laden with little interpretation and, in most cases, are dated. Adding to the problem is the fact that, while discussions are generally aimed at international terrorism, examples of domestic terrorism are used to buttress arguments/examinations on international terrorism. To worsen the situation, examples of terrorist groups are limited to two or more commonly known groups. The chapters that clearly involve some analysis are those that have been reprinted, albeit with some modifications, such as those written by Jenkins, Mickolus, or Wilkinson. The remaining part of the chapter, then will offer some critical insights in the eight areas previously mentioned.

### 4. A Typology of International Terrorism[25]

One of the earliest typologies of terrorism was developed by E.V. Walter.[26] Although several authors have since grappled with the issue of an appropriate typology for terrorism, this researcher could not locate any attempts to develop a typology of international terrorism.

Schmid and Jongman, for example, outline roughly ten bases for classifying different types of terrorism;

list five definitions of international terrorism put forward by other authors; and focus on: actor-based, political orientation, multidimensional, and purpose-based typologies. The first typology distinguishes between state and nonstate actors. The second differentiates between terrorism from "above or below," and right-wing versus left-wing terrorism. The third subsumes distinctions based on Thorton's and Bowyer-Bell's work.[27] The authors conclude that "one of the problems with typology building is the absence of a commonly agreed-upon definition of terrorism." However, that does not stop them from constructing their own: an actor-based typology using state and nonstate actors as the major participants.

### 5. Number of Events/Annual Trends

The prevailing impression given by the mass media, public officials and experts concerned with international terrorism is that it is on the increase. In so far as we can tell, the increase in terrorism is genuine and is not an artifact created by both better coverage of these events or more media attention. From 1968 to 1989 there have been a total of 10,914 international terrorist events ranging from a low of 125 (1968) incidents to a high of 855 (1988).[28] Over the past twenty-two years there has been a ragged increase with several peaks and valleys. This should not be surprising; throughout history terrorism has frequently occurred in cyclical upsurges.[29] This pattern is partly due to general factors involved in causation and decline.[30] In 1989, the most recent year for which data was available at time of writing, the total number of international terrorist incidents (528), was almost 38 percent less than in the previous year (855). In fact, since 1968, terrorism has only increased at an average rate of almost seven percent a year.

More important than the actual figures is the public's perception that international terrorism is increasing.[31] The majority of research examining the attribute of frequency focuses on the attitudes of opinion leaders,[32] the general public, or students, and explores the complex relationship between terrorism and the media and terrorism and propaganda.[33] Many of these studies are done, however, on the country experiencing terrorism,[34] on terrorist organizations, or on domestic terrorism specifically. Moreover, many are limited to one year, or are conducted after major terrorist incidents.[35] Many are also impressionistic with little reliance on modern survey techniques. In other words, very little sophisticated, systematic crossnational research is done on the relationship between international terrorism and perceptions of increase.

Additionally, while 1968 is generally regarded as the beginning of "contemporary" international terrorism (hence the rationale for 1968 as the start date of most data sets),[36] this has not been documented in a statistical manner. Monthly and daily level breakdowns are generally coded in most data sets, but they are not mentioned in most data reports, though information on end-of-month anniversaries, which tend to be times when many events take place, would help security personnel budget their resources more efficiently. Furthermore, events such as threats and hoaxes should be eliminated from data sets as they are underreported in the news media, difficult to operationalize, and too easy for non-terrorists to carry out.

Finally, although terrorism has created a considerable amount of controversy and has cost governments and corporations considerable amounts of money, perhaps there is a tolerable level of terrorism with which a society can live. By way of comparison, it is worth noting that during the 1960s and 1970s citizens in advanced industrialized countries were constantly reminded through the media, educators, and personal experience of the fact that street crime was increasing. This created a furor of public indignation and governmental responses which instigated the "War on Crime." While the rate of crime has increased since these times, the public indignation has quelled. But, with respect to terrorism, few researchers have seriously explored the question of whether or not there are tolerable levels of violence.

## 6. Geographic Spread

The increase in the volume of terrorist activity has been matched by its geographic spread. Each year the number of countries experiencing some sort of terrorist activity has gradually increased. In the late 1960s, international terrorist incidents occurred in an average of twenty-nine countries each year. This number climbed to thirty-nine in the early 1970s and forty-three in the late 1970s. For the first three years of the 1980s, the average number of countries experiencing international terrorist incidents was fifty-one, and for the period 1983 to 1985, the average was sixty-five.[37]

Although terrorism is experienced throughout the world, a considerable number of nations currently experience a disproportionate amount of the world's terrorism. About twenty countries account for between 75 to 90 percent of all reported incidents. The top ten countries that experience the most amount of terrorism (approximately 75 percent) are in descending order of importance: Israel (including the Gaza strip and the West Bank), Pakistan, Colombia, Spain, Lebanon, West Germany, Zimbabwe, South Korea, Peru, and France.[38]

In 1989, terrorists hit citizens or facilities of seventy-four states in a total of sixty countries.[39] While the general increase in countries experiencing terrorism is acknowledged, since World War II there has been a proliferation in the number of new countries. Thus the assumption of increase must be weighted by this caveat. None of the reports take this into account.

Despite the fact that regions experiencing the most amount of terrorism change each year, there is a degree of consistency. In 1989 the largest number of events (193) took place in the Middle East, followed by Latin America (131), and then Western Europe (96). The largest changes between 1988 and 1989 were in Asia and the Middle East, where incidents of international terrorism decreased almost 29 and 62 percent respectively. Of course, events such as the Persian Gulf Crisis could reverse the trend in the Middle East. Overall, Western Europe, the Middle East, and Latin America account for over half of all international terrorist attacks since 1968. Regions such as Africa, Asia, Eastern Europe, and North America stand a distant second.

## 7. Targets

Over the past twenty-one years, the spectrum of terrorist targets has expanded. At the beginning of the 1970s terrorists concentrated their attacks mainly on property, whereas in the 1980s they increasingly directed their attacks against people.[40]

Some of the property that has been attacked includes: embassies, factories, airliners, airline offices, tourist agencies, hotels, airports, bridges, trains, train stations, reactors, refineries, schools, restaurants, pubs, churches, temples, synagogues, computers, and data processing centers.[41] A considerable amount of writing has been devoted to the problem of attacks on nuclear facilities. However, most of the actions carried out by antinuclear extremists and terrorists were aimed at halting or delaying the construction of nuclear facilities rather than at the destruction of existing ones.[42]

Americans, French, Israelis, British and Turks account for approximately half of all the nationalities victimized by terrorists. Some of those who have been attacked include diplomats, military personnel, tourists, businessmen, students, journalists, children, nuns, priests and the Pope.

According to State Department statistics, since 1968 the majority of victims or facilities that have been targeted are miscellaneous (4,933). Otherwise, in descending order of frequency, victims or facilities can be classified under business (2,701), diplomatic (2,403), government (1,016), and military (788).

A distinction should be made regarding soft versus hard targets. Once a target becomes hardened (e.g., more security precautions have been instituted especially on embassies or airports) terrorists will switch to softer targets (such as cruise ships like the *Achille Lauro*). Because soft targets require less skill and sophisticated tactics to attack than do hard targets, they are attacked more often.

Between 1968 and 1989 there were a total of 24,520 casualties from international terrorism. Out of this number, almost 29 percent (7,714) resulted in deaths; the number of deaths ranged from a low of thirty-four (1968) to a high of 825 (1985). In 1989 there was a total of 787 casualties including 390 deaths. Only 15 to 20 percent of all terrorist incidents involve fatalities and of those, 66 percent involve only one death. Less than one percent of the thousands of terrorist incidents that have occurred in the last two decades involve ten or more fatalities; incidents of mass murder are truly rare. This has led some commentators to suggest that "terrorists want a lot of people watching and not a lot of people dying."[43]

## 8. Tactics

Terrorists operate with a fairly limited repertoire of attacks. Six basic tactics have accounted for 95 percent of all terrorist incidents including: bombings, assassinations, armed assaults, kidnappings, hijackings, and barricade and hostage incidents. In short, terrorists blow up things, kill people, or seize hostages. Every terrorist incident is merely a variation on these three activities.[44]

Tactics, like fashions, are time-specific and temporary. This is largely due to advances in technology on the terrorist side and to increases in countermeasures by those charged with the control and prevention of terrorism. First, terrorist use of letter bombings reached its apex in 1972; explosive bombings in 1974; seizure of embassies and kidnapping diplomats in the mid-1970s; incendiary bombing in 1976; and hijacking means of transportation reached its apex in 1970. Seizing embassies declined as security measures made embassy takeovers more difficult, and as governments resisted the demands of terrorists holding hostages and became more willing to use force to end such episodes, which incidentally increased hostage-takers risk of death or capture. The number of hijackings has dropped because of security proce-

dures and the general unwillingness of countries to grant asylum to hijackers. Letter bombs appear to follow no pattern; the 1972 and 1973 peak years show a wave of bombings by Irish and Palestinian groups rather than a worldwide phenomenon conducted by many organizations. It appears that although most bombs are sent from the same post office on the same day, the targets are worldwide. Because of their general unreliability in successfully harming the chosen victim (many letter bombs are intercepted by police or explode in post offices, injuring innocent workers and leading to negative publicity for the terrorists) as well as the technical sophistication required to make them, other terrorists groups do not seem to have picked up the practice of using letter bombs.

Second, bombings of all types continue to be the most popular terrorist method of attack. Approximately 52 percent of all international terrorist events are bombings. This is followed, in terms of numbers, by armed attacks, arson, and kidnappings. In addition, assassinations, bombings combined, arson, and attacks on diplomats have increased in the last few years.

Third, while the majority of bombs are simple incendiary devices, terrorists have made and often use more sophisticated explosive devices. A variety of more elaborate detonators, with anti-tampering devices built in, have also been put into use. A distinction should also be highlighted between symbolic and victim-intended bombings. The former, and clearly the largest number of events, are not intended to produce casualties but only to dramatize a group's objectives. The latter are more rare but fatal when they do occur. Unfortunately, there is no way that independent researchers can objectively distinguish between these types of events.

Fourth, terrorists also have a preference for powerful rapid fire (automatic) concealable weapons. They buy these either legally or on the black market, or steal them from commercial establishments or government arsenals.

Fifth, some terrorist groups have used Soviet made SA-7 heat seeking rockets (1973 attempt at the Rome airport), RPG-2 and RPG-7 grenade launchers (1975 Orly airport incident), and RPG-7-W antitank weapon (1981 attack against General Kroesen, US Army, in Heidelberg, West Germany).

Finally, terrorist use of nuclear, chemical (CW), biological (BW), or toxic weapons (TW) is a topic of constant concern.[45] During the last fifteen years there has been a growing criminal rather than terrorist activity in the nuclear theft/threat domain. While some terrorist organizations have considered using nuclear devices, many of the crimes are not politically motivated and cannot properly be considered acts of political terrorism. In the majority of cases "ordinary" thieves have stolen nuclear material (e.g., uranium ore or low enriched uranium). None of these incidents has involved any attempt to acquire nuclear material for possible use in a weapon though.

Most reviews on the nature of terrorism have shied away from discussions concerning terrorist use of chemical, biological and toxic weapons. Chemical weapons, particularly poisonous gas, have been used rarely in conventional warfare since the First World War. Some of these include mustard, nerve, and cyanide gases. They kill after being inhaled, ingested, and/or absorbed through the skin. While chemical weapons have not been used in terrorist actions, some terrorist organizations have shown capability. In 1978 Palestinian terrorists attempted to sabotage Israel's citrus crop by injecting deadly mercury in oranges. In the United States, the Symbionese Liberation Army were using cyanide-dipped bullets and considering biological warfare.[46] While use of chemical weapons is a violation of the Geneva Protocol of 1925, as recently as 1988 Iraq was charged with using chemical weapons against Iran and its own minority Kurdish population.

Given this, the use of biological/toxin weapons by terrorists has recently spawned a great deal of academic interest. Raymond Zilinskas writes:

BW systems consist of living pathogenic organisms, commonly bacteria or viruses, and their delivery vehicles . . . . The effects of BW are multiplied through contagion—the spread of the agent through air, food, water, or direct contact. Extremely small doses of BW agents can cause severe damage.[47]

While BW were used in World Wars I and II, they have not been used by terrorists although their capability is evident. For example, in November 1980 a police raid on the Paris hideout of the Red Army Faction uncovered sophisticated lab equipment, notes on biological warfare and plans for a germ warfare assassination attempt on a prominent figure.[48]

Toxic weapon agents, on the other hand, are "proteinaceous chemical substances produced by living organisms." They only affect the person who ingests, inhales, or absorbs the toxin; toxins are not spread from person to person. One of the more popular is botulinum toxin. One of the best known cases of the usage of this type of weapon was the assassination of Bulgarian dissident Georgi Markov by Bulgarian secret service agents who shot him with pellets impregnated with the toxin Ricin.

The number of reported incidents of terrorists using nuclear threats, CW, BW, and TW is low. Many of these events are criminal (usually extortion threats) and not political in nature. Two reasons mitigated the wide adoption of these four types of weapons. The first is the fear among terrorists that they themselves will be contaminated/exposed, and the second is the backlash from the public. Nevertheless, these weapons are cost-effective and technology about them is becoming more sophisticated. Moreover, most of these can be easily concealed, transported, and deployed by persons protected (in the case of BW and TW) by vaccines and having only minimal technical training.

## 9. Terrorist Groups

Most of the currently active terrorist groups show no signs of abandoning their struggle. Some of them have been working for a decade or more, replacing their losses, preparing for new attacks, and turning into a semipermanent subculture.

In a recent analysis of the longevity of seventy-six terrorist organizations, Martha Crenshaw showed that many groups have exhibited remarkable stability and tenacity but that almost half of the organizations which existed at some time no longer exist or no longer use terrorism. However, at least ten groups have been in operation for twenty years (including Fatah, the Popular Front for the Liberation of Palestine-General Command (PFLPGC), and Euzkadi Ta Askatasuna (ETA)).[49]

There are no notably active new organizations (formed in the last five years). The last serious group (the *Celles Communistes Combattants* in Belgium) was formed in 1984 and lasted for a year. Nevertheless, new causes and new groups have emerged and have taken their struggle internationally. Some of these include Armenian-related terrorism, Sikh-related terrorism, and issue-oriented groups opposed to nuclear power, abortion, technology, pollution, animal vivisection, and farm foreclosures. The new groups that appear are generally "smaller, more tightly organized at the operational level, sometimes less structured at the national level, harder to penetrate, harder to predict, and always more violent."[50]

There is a debate over whether or not there is a single European terrorist organization. Clearly there was cooperation among a network of groups, but it seems to have ceased since the roundup of the *Action Directe* leaders in 1987.[51] Despite bilateral cooperation among terrorist groups, most terrorism continues to be primarily a national problem.

Studies on the terrorist phenomenon in Western Europe have emphasized the nature and the significance of the generational changes which the terrorist movements undergo over the years. The Italian and the German experiences with terrorism suggest, for instance, that newer generations replace older terrorist leaders approximately every four years. These generational changes are largely due to the death or the imprisonment of the preceding generation of terrorists. The replacement of the first generation leadership, in turn, exercises strong influence on the behavior of future terrorist groups. While the first generation terrorist leaders are likely to be well versed in ideology and theory, later generations turn out to be progressively less interested in ideology and more inclined to be action-oriented. They also tend to be less scrupulous in the employment of violent and often ruthless terrorist tactics against their perceived enemies.[52]

Finally, terrorism is increasingly being committed by hardened (criminally, psychologically, and socially) but inexperienced youth with their own agendas. This type of individual contrasts with earlier terrorist profiles which suggested that the average terrorist was in his mid- to late-twenties and came from middle- to upper-middle-class background. Relatively recent events including the car and truck bombs in Lebanon (1983) and the *Achille Lauro* hijacking (1985) were carried out by terrorists under the age of twenty. This trend is explained by the problems of youth growing up in violent environments (e.g., the refugee camps of Lebanon, or the polarized communities of Ulster).[53]

## 10. Support of Terrorist Groups

Over the past two decades a considerable amount of attention has been focused on the support of terrorist groups. This has led to what have been called conspiracy theories of terrorism. Without a doubt, states (through their armies, intelligence agencies, etc.), terrorist organizations, emigrant populations, and philanthropists support terrorists and terrorist groups to further their own goals. This support includes financing, training, securing intelligence, providing false documents, donating or selling weapons and explosives, and providing sanctuary or safe houses.[54]

Over the last seven years, however, there has been an abundance of literature cataloguing real, possible, and imagined acts of state-sponsored terrorism or, as it is sometimes called, "Surrogate Warfare." Originally the responsibility for international terrorism was attributed to Iran, Iraq, Libya, the former Soviet Union, Syria, and Vietnam. By 1989 the US State Department had officially identified nine states that either engaged in terrorist actions or aided terrorist organizations (e.g., training or financing, etc.): Afghanistan, Cuba, Iran, Iraq, Libya, Nicaragua, North Korea, former South Yemen, and Syria. On the basis of public statements by American officials, several more nations can be added to the list, including: Algeria, Bulgaria, Czechoslovakia, East Germany, Kuwait, North Korea, Saudi Arabia, former Soviet Union, Vietnam, and to varying degrees the entire Arabic bloc of nations. Past East German support for the West German Red Army Faction has been confirmed by recent arrests and relations there.[55]

On the other hand, there are several problems with these assertions. First, this phenomenon is not new. For example, after World War I, Croatian Ustacha received most of its support from Fascist Italy and Hungary; the Inner Macedonian Revolutionary Organization (IMRO) received funds from Fascist Italy, Hungary, and Bulgaria; and the Rumanian Iron Guard allegedly received funds from Poland.[56]

Second, use of former Soviet, Soviet satellite, or "outlaw nation" weaponry does not mean that terrorists are being directed, trained, or supplied by these countries; these weapons can be obtained/purchased on the black market through a number of channels (e.g., the Afghanistan war, Belgian arms dealers, etc.).

Third, terrorist organizations are increasingly becoming self-reliant. James Adams argues that support from Libya, Syria, and Iraq played an important role in assisting terrorists; he asserts, however, that it always came with strings attached, leading terrorists to resent the control their sponsors tried to have over their actions and political views. As a result, terrorist groups have rapidly moved to become self-sufficient and hence depend less on outside countries for support. For example, in 1983 approximately $600 million in current account income was generated for the Palestinian National Front, and of this less than $100 million came in the form of donations from wealthy Palestinians or Arab nations. In fact, the PLO has investments in Wall Street, the City of London and elsewhere. The PLO's financial policy has left them with a wide ranging financial portfolio that includes banks, property, factories, and other semi-legitimate or conventional businesses.[57]

It was also popularly believed that the major source of income for the IRA was the United States, where cash was funnelled through Irish Northern Aid (NORAID). However, out of an income of around £5 million in 1987, the IRA received less than £150,000 from the United States and even less is expected in future years. Some money comes in the form of smuggling, and protection rackets to local shop owners, the public and industrialists. To launder money generated from protection the IRA moved into the taxi business in 1972. To undercut the competition a sustained campaign was launched against the city-run bus system, that involved systematic stoning and acts of arson. Moreover, in the early 1970s the IRA committed a series of frauds on building sites involving tax exemptions and opened a number of illegal drinking establishments.[58]

Fourth, noticeably absent from most studies or pronouncements about state-sponsored terrorism is any, even in passing, reference to the terrorist actions of the armies and national security agencies of Western countries or the actions of Soviet bloc countries that predated the period of contemporary terrorism.[59] The revelations by ex-intelligence agents, senate investigations, and investigative journalists have disclosed a wide-ranging number of terrorist, and terrorist-like activities committed by security agencies or with their assistance.[60] Care must be taken, however, in labeling all covert operations as terrorist.[61] Although assassination is clearly a method used by terrorists and national security agencies alike, it does not necessarily follow that these assassinations were acts of terrorism. In most cases they were meant to remove from power people who were perceived to be a threat to state interests, rather than to terrorize.[62]

## 11. The Future of International Terrorism

There is much consensus over the future course of international terrorism. In general, some future trends may include: increased links among terrorist groups; more extravagant attention-seeking destructive acts; new weapons finding their way into the terrorist arsenal; increase in the use of terrorism by governments as surrogate warfare; and, the possibility that terrorists will use more destructive technologies like nuclear, biological, chemical and toxic weapons.[63]

Missing from these pronouncements however, are explanations of the methods that futurists use to comment on the likelihood of any of these trends: e.g., trend extrapolation, scenarios, mapping, use of expert opinion, and models, games and simulations.[64] Scholars are entitled to know how their colleagues and other futurists reach the conclusions they provide. More needs to be explained in this regard.

## 12. Conclusion: Moving Beyond the Genre

International terrorism does not exist in a vacuum.

One must compare the nature and trend of this type of terrorism with others and with other forms of violent political conflict and life-threatening phenomena occurring in the international arena. In all respects, international terrorism has not been as deadly as other modes of political conflict during the same period (e.g., state terrorism or war)[65] or other sources of damage (e.g., natural disasters). Nevertheless, the perceptions of terrorism need to be further analyzed in a more accurate, and unbiased manner. While terrorist activities still occur relatively infrequently compared to other types of violence, the disruption, destruction, and loss of life that even a few incidents of terrorist activity can bring upon a state and its citizens more than justify the continuing search to understand this phenomenon.

See also: *Psychological Causes of Oppositional Political Terrorism: A Model*

## Notes

1. See the select bibliography.
2. The question of definition has been explored by Thomas Mitchell. Mitchell offers a definitional framework which is consistent with the one I use, although I prefer (with some qualifications) the original definition offered in Alex P. Schmid, *Political Terrorism: A Research Guide to Concepts, Theories, Data Bases and Literature* (New Brunswick, NJ: Transaction Books, 1983). In addition to features common to other definitions, Schmid describes terrorism as a method of combat, and emphasizes the extranormal nature of terrorist victimization, which creates an audience beyond the target of terrorism. See also Jeffrey Ian Ross and Ted Robert Gurr, "Why Terrorism Subsides: A Comparative Study of Canada and the United States," *Comparative Politics*, 21, no. 4 (July 1989), pp. 406-7.
3. See, for example, Grant Wardlaw, *Political Terrorism: Theory, Tactics, and Counter-Measures* (New York: Cambridge University Press, 1982); Paul Wilkinson, *Terrorism and the Liberal State* (2nd ed.) (New York: New York University Press, 1986): Walter Laqueur, *The Age of Terrorism* (Toronto: Little Brown, 1987); Michael Stohl, *The Politics of Terrorism* (3rd ed., revised and expanded) (New York: Marcel Dekker, 1988); and Alex P. Schmid and Albert J. Jongman, *Political Terrorism: A New Guide to Actors, Concepts, Data Bases, Theories, and Literature* (New Brunswick, NJ: Transaction Books, 1988).
4. James Poland, *Understanding Terrorism* (Englewood Cliffs, NJ: Prentice-Hall, 1988); Donna Schlagheck, *International Terrorism: An Introduction to the Concepts and Actors* (Lexington, MA D.C. Heath Company, 1988); and Leonard B. Weinberg and Paul B. Davis, *Introduction to Political Terrorism* (Hightstown, NJ: McGraw-Hill, 1988).
5. Some of the better known reports attempting to provide an outline of the phenomenon are Robert A. Oakley, "International Terrorism: Current Trends and US Response" Washington, DC: United States Department of State, Current Policy no. 706, 1985; Brian M. Jenkins (ed.), *Terrorism and Beyond: An*

*International Conference on Terrorism and Low-Level Conflict,* R-2714 (Santa Monica, CA: Rand Corp., 1982); and Brian M. Jenkins, *New Modes of Conflict,* R-3009 (Santa Monica, CA: Rand Corp., 1983).

6. See, for example, Michael J. Barrett, "Patterns in Terror," *Journal of Defense and Diplomacy* 4, no. 3, (March 1986), pp. 40-43; Chris Rootes, "Living with Terrorism," *Social Alternatives* 1, nos. 6/7, (1980), pp. 46-49; J. Bowyer Bell, "Old Trends and Future Reality," *Washington Quarterly* 8, no. 2, (1985), pp. 25-36; Brian M, Jenkins, "Reflections on Recent Trends in Terrorism," *Miliary Intelligence* 10, no. 4, (1984), pp. 31-34; Brian M. Jenkins, "Trends in International Terrorism," *World Affairs Journal* 3 (Spring 1984), pp. 40-48; James B. Motley, "Terrorist Warfare: A Reassessment," *Military Review* 65, no. 5, (1985), pp. 45-57; Walter Laqueur, "Reflections on Terrorism," *Foreign Affairs,* Fall 1986, pp. 86-100; and Paul Johnson, "The Seven Deadly Sins of Terrorism," *NATO Review* 28, no. 5, (1980), pp. 28-33.

7. The relevant chapters are: Brian M. Jenkins, "International Terrorism: A New Mode of Conflict" in David Carlton and Carlo Schaerf, eds., *International Terrorism and World Security* (New York: John Wiley, 1975), pp. 13-49. Many of Jenkins' writings have appeared slightly revised as "publicly available" Rand reports, as chapters in edited books or as journal articles; Baljit Singh, "An Overview" in Yonah Alexander and Seymour Maxwell Finger, eds., *Terrorism: Interdisciplinary Perspectives* (New York: John Jay Press, 1977), pp. 5-17; Edward F. Mickolus, "Statistical Approaches to the Study of Terrorism" in *Terrorism: Interdisciplinary perspectives,* pp. 209-69. Variations of this chapter have appeared as Edward F. Mickolus, "An Events Data Base for Analysis of Transnational Terrorism" In Richards J. Heuer, eds., *Quantitative Approaches to Political Intelligence: The CIA Experience* (Boulder, CO: Westview Press, 1978); Edward F. Mickolus, "Trends in Transnational Terrorism," in Marius H. Livingston, ed., *International Terrorism in the Contemporary World* (Westport, CT: Greenwood Press, 1978), pp. 44-73; Edward F. Mickolus, "Tracking the Growth and Prevalence of International Terrorism" in Patrick J. Montana and George S. Roukis, eds., *Managing Terrorism* (Westport, CT: Quorum Books, 1983); and Edward F. Mickolus, "International Terrorism" in Michael Stohl, ed., *The Politics of Terrorism* (Second ed., revised and expanded) (New York: Marcel Dekker, 1983), pp. 221-53.

8. Robert A. Fearey, "Introduction to International Terrorism" in *International Terrorism in the Contemporary World,* pp. 25-35; Charles A. Russell, "Appendix A: Terrorism-An Overview, 1970-78" in Yonah Alexander and Robert A. Kilmarx, eds., *Political Terrorism and Business* (New York: Praeger, 1979), pp. 281-96; Paul Wilkinson, "Terrorism: International Dimensions" in William Gutteridge, ed., *Contemporary Terrorism* (New York: Facts on File, 1976). A revised version of this chapter appears as Paul Wilkinson, "Terrorism: International Dimensions" in William Gutteridge, ed., *Contemporary Terrorism* (London: Institute for the Study of Conflict, 1986), pp. 29-56.

9. Brian M. Jenkins, "International Terrorism: Trends and Potentialities" in Alan D. Buckley and Daniel D. Olson (eds.) *International Terrorism: Current Research and Future Directions* (Wayne, NJ: Avery Publishing, 1980), pp. 101-7. Richard H. Shultz, Jr. and Stephen Slona, "International Terrorism: The Threat and the Response" in Richard H. Shultz, Jr. and Stephen Sloan, eds., *Responding to the Terrorist Threat* (New York: Pergamon, 1980), pp. 1-17; Eugene Mastrangelo, "International Terrorism: A Regional and Global Overview, 1970-1986" in

Yonah Alexander, ed., *The 1986 Annual on Terrorism* (Dordrecht, Netherlands: Martinus Nijhoff, 1987); see also, Ted Robert Gurr, "Some Characteristics of Political Terrorism in the 1960s" in Michael Stohl, ed., *The Politics of Terrorism* (New York: Marcel Dekker, 1979), variations of which have appeared as Ted Robert Gurr, "Some Characteristics of Political Terrorism in the 1960s" in Michael Stohl, ed., *The Politics of Terrorism* (Second ed., revised and expanded) (New York: Marcel Dekker, 1983); or Frederick Cavanagh, "Political Terrorism" in John T. O'Brien and Marvin Marcus, eds., *Crime and Justice in America* (New York: Pergamon, 1979), pp. 187-207. The chapter by Gurr is limited to "internal" and not "international" terrorism. The piece by Cavanagh covers a variety of forms of terrorism and equates one with the other. Additionally, government reports such as the State Depatrment's "Patterns of Global Terrorism" are excluded from this listing, even though they have appeared as chapters in edited volumes.

10. See Schmid and Jongman, p. 42, for a brief discussion on the different terminology with respect to groups.

11. On the other hand, very few data sets have been created that systematically code the attributes of terrorist groups or individuals who engage in terrorism. See Inter-University Consortium for Political and Social Research, *Guide to Resources or Political and Social Research 1987-1988* (Ann Arbor, MI: ICPSR, 1988) for a readily accessible listing of these data sets.

12. See, for example, the works by Edward Mickolus already cited, plus his Combatting International Terrorism: A Quantitative Analysis," unpublished Ph.D. dissertation, Yale University, 1981.

13. For a descriptive review of the different types of events data bases on terrorism currently available, see Schmid and Jongman. For an empirical review of these and more data bases, see Jeffrey Ian Ross, "Survey of Data Bases on Political Terrorism," unpublished manuscript (1989).

14. For a discussion of problems with events data in general and events data elated to terrorism, see Jeffrey Ian Ross, "Domestic Political Terrorism in Canada, 1960-1985: An Empirical Analysis," Masters Thesis, University of Colorado at Boulder, 1988; Jeffrey Ian Ross, "An Events Data Base on Political Terrorism in Canada: Some Conceptual and Methodological Problems," *Conflict Quarterly,* 8, no. 2 (Spring 1988), pp. 47-65.

15. While Fowler reviewed a total of nine data sets, one of them specifically focused on assassinations. See William W. Fowler, "Terrorism Data Bases: A Comparison of Missions, Methods, and Systems," N-1503-RC (Santa Monica, CA: Rand Corp., 1981).

16. Personal communication with Dr. Paul S. Ello, Vice President, International Policy Research, BDM Corporation, 1 November 1988, confirmed the discontinuation of their data set. I have tried unsuccessfully to locate the Democratic Worldwatch system. It is the only data set which is not listed in Fowler's appendix, and Fowler, who is no longer with Rand, could not be located. Mickolus says that he has never heard of the Democratic Worldwatch System (personal conversations Spring 1989).

17. The status of these data sets is virtually unknown. Requests for information brought only one response—from the CIA. The request for information, however, was denied.

18. In general the CIA produced reports that provided annual statistics beginning with United States, Central Intelligence Agency, Directorate of Intelligence, *International Terrorism in 1976* (CIA, 1977); and followed by United States, Central Intelligence Agency, National Foreign Assessment Center, *Interna-*

*tional Terrorism in 1977* (CIA, 1978); *International Terrorism in 1978* (CUA, 1979); *International Terrorism in 1979* (CIA, 1980); and *Patterns of International Terrorism: 1980* (CIA, 1981). In 1982 this task was taken over by the State Department in their "Patterns of Global Terrorism" reports. The frequency of these reports is somewhat sporadic. For example, the report analyzing 1985 was published in October 1986 and the one analyzing 1986 was published in January 1988. Useful but too narrow in scope are the "Significant Incidents of Political Violence Against Americans" published by the Bureau of Diplomatic Security of the United States Department of State.

19. The ITERATE I and II pilot data set, initiated by the CIA, was turned over to the State Department in the early days of the Reagan Administration. Allegations have been made that its coding scheme was redesigned to suit the foreign policy objectives of the Reagan Administration. The entire data set was back-dated resulting in a doubling of the number of incidents since 1968. Charles Mohr, "Data on Terrorism Under U.S. Revision," *New York Times,* 24 April 1981, p. A17 and George Lardner, "CIA Report Adds Thousands of Incidents to Statistics on International Terrorism." *Washington Post,* 16 June 1981, p. A10. For an additional discussion of problems associated with the ITERATE and other data sets, see Schmid and Jongman, p. 145, and Ross, "Domestic Political Terrorism in Canada" (1988).

20. See, for example, Fowler, "Terrorism Data Bases" (1981) and "An Agenda for Quantitative Research on Terrorism," P-6591 (Santa Monica, CA: Rand Corp., 1980); Bonnie Cordes, Brian M. Jenkins, Konrad Kellen with Bass. Relles, Sater, Juncosa, and Fowler, "A Conceptual Framework for Analyzing Terrorist Groups," R-3151 (Santa Monica, CA: Rand Corp., 1985).

21. Occasionally the reports of a third private analysis company, Risks International, make their way into *Terrorism: An International Journal.* See, for example, Martin C. Arostegui, "Special Reports of Risks International" *Terrorism* 7, no. 4, (1985), pp. 417-30.

22. ITERATE has been used for a variety of purposes, including the study of the global diffusion patterns of transnational terrorism; terrorist trend analysis; comparison of terrorist campaigns; evaluation of policy prescriptions for crisis management; evaluation of deterrence possibilities of terrorism; improving hostage negotiation techniques; and evaluation of the effects of publicity on terrorist behavior, for example Edward S. Heyman, *Monitoring the Diffusion of Transnational Terrorism* (Gaithersburg, MD: IACP, 1980). For an early listing of various uses of ITERATE and other aggregate data, see "Appendix B: Statistical and Mathematical Approaches to the study of Terrorism: A study of current work" in Yonah Alexander and Seymour Maxwell Finger, eds., *Terrorism: Interdisciplinary Perspectives,* pp. 253-56. ITERATE has been described in greater detail in Mickolus' own writings.

23. See Doron Bal, *et al., INTER 84: A Review of International Terrorism in 1984* (Tel Aviv University: Jaffee Center for Strategic Studies, 1985) and Ariel Merari, *et al., INTER 85: A Review of International Terrorism in 1985* (Jerusalem and Boulder: Jerusalem Post/Westview Press, 1986).

24. See John B. Wolf, "Analytical Framework for the Study and Control of Agitational Terrorism," *The Police Journal* 49, (July-Sept. 1976), pp. 165-71.

25. The material for this section is largely based on Schmid and Jongman, pp. 39-60.

26. E. V. Walter, *Terror and Resistance* (London: Oxford University Press, 1969).

27. Thomas Perry Thornton, "Terror as a Weapon of Politi-

cal Agitation" in Harry Eckstein, ed., *Internal War: Problems and Approaches* (New York: The Free Press of Glencoe, 1964), pp. 82-88; J. Bowyer Bell, *A Time of Terror* (New York: Basic Books, 1978).

28. United States, Department of State, *Patterns of Global Terrorism: 1989* (Washington, DC: Department of State, April 1990).

29. See, for example, Zeev Ivianski, "Individual Terror as a Phase in Revolutionary Violence in the Late 19th and the Beginning of the 20th Century," Ph.D. Dissertation. University of Jerusalem, 1973 (Hebrew) as quoted in Laqueur, *Age of Terrorism;* and Paul Wilkinson, "The Anatomy of Terrorism" in Royal United Services Institute, eds., *Ten Years of terrorism* (New York: Crane, Russak & Company, 1979), pp. 7-21.

30. See, for example, Martha Crenshaw, "The Causes of Terrorism," *Comparative Politics,* Vol. 13, No. 4, 1981, pp. 379-97, and "How Terrorism Ends," paper presented at the Annual Meeting of the American Political Science Association, Chicago, September 4, 1987; Jeffrey Ian Ross, "The Structural Causes of Domestic Political Terrorism in Advanced Industrialized Countries: A Causal Model," paper presented at the International Studies Association Annual Meeting, St. Louis, April 1, 1988; "Domestic Political Terrorism in Canada," (1988); and Ross and Gurr "Why Terrorism Subsides," *Comparative Politics* (1989).

31. According to Jenkins, "International Terrorism: Trends and Potentialities" in Buckley and Olson, *International Terrorism: Current Research and Future Directions,* p. 104, "[p]ublic perceptions of the level of terrorism in the world appear to be determined . . . not by the level of violence but rather by the quality of the incidents, the location, and the degree of media coverage."

32. According to a 1984 Gallup poll, 11 percent of opinion leaders surveyed placed terrorism among the five most serious problems facing the United States. More than 14 percent of the leaders interviewed anticipated that terrorism would be one of the five major threats by the year 2000. Finally they also believed that terrorism will increase (*The Gallup poll,* 1984). This finding, however, suggests that terrorism has far less impact than we have thought heretofore.

33. See, for example, Maurice Tugwell, "Politics and Propaganda of the Provisional IRA" in Paul Wilkinson, ed., *British Perspectives on Terrorism* (London: Crane, Russak and Company, 1981), pp. 149-70.

34. See, for example, D. G. Boyce, "Water for the Fish: Terrorism and Public Opinion" in Yonah Alexander and Alan O'Day, eds., *Terrorism in Ireland* (New York: St. Martin's Press, 1983), pp. 13-40.

35. See Christopher Hewitt, "Terrorism and Public Opinion: A Five Country Study," paper presented at the American Political Science Association Meeting, Atlanta, 3 September 1989 for an examination of the cross-national relationships between domestic terrorism and public opinion in five countries. He analyzes concern over terrorism, images of terrorist, support for terrorist goals, and approval of antiterrorist measures. Hewitt concludes that "Public opinion towards terrorism is a product of complex historical situations, and that support for terrorist goals, and perceptions of the terrorists is minimally affected by the terrorist campaign itself."

36. See Bowyer Bell, *A Time of Terror,* Chapter 3; Shultz and Slona, 1980, pp. 2-4; and Jenkins, *New Modes of Conflict* (1983), pp. 8-9 for typical discussions of the rationale for 1968 as the beginning of contemporary terrorism. This argument suggests that 1968 is taken as a starting point largely because

of events in the Middle East—the Palestinian groups moving into the vacuum created by the defeat of the Arab armies in 1967; the failure of these groups to ignite an insurgency in the occupied territories, and the consequent striking out at a new range of international targets (especially the PFLP attacks on airliners). Secondly, rural insurgency movements throughout the world suffered serious setbacks. Consequently, they moved to urban areas. Finally, radical student movements in Western countries spawned a number of terrorist groups.

37. Brian M. Jenkins, "Areas of Consensus, Areas of Ignorance" in Burr Eichelman, David Soskis, and William Reid, eds., *Terrorism: Interdisciplinary Perspectives* (Washington, DC: American Psychiatric Association, 1983), pp. 154-80.

38. *Patterns of Global Terrorism: 1989, op. cit.*

39. *Ibid.*

40. Arguments why terrorists are killing more people are developed by Brian M. Jenkins, "The Future Course of International Terrorism," *TVI Report* 6, no. 2, (Fall 1985), special supplement, pp. S-3-S-7. Also released as "Future Course Trends in International Terrorism," P-7139 (Santa Monica, CA: Rand Corp., 1985). One reason why there has been a shift from physical targets is the improved hardening of targets. For example, security improvements on embassies have been or are being made. See James Bishop, "Toward Safer Embassies," *TVI Report* 7, no. 3, (1987), pp. 3-4.

41. These are often referred to as places of assembly. Moreover, while terrorists have blown up computers and set fires in data processing centers, they have not yet tried to penetrate computers in any sophisticated fashion to disrupt or destroy data. On the other hand, there has been a number of "viruses" installed in corporate, institutional, and government computer programs by criminals and hackers. See, for example, John Markoff, "Cyberpunks Seek Thrills in Computerized Mischief," *New York Times* 26 November 1988, p. 1, 7, for a recent account of this incident.

42. In a 1978 interview, a former member of West Germany's terrorist movement stated that members of the Red Army Faction discussed the possibility of nuclear extortion (Jenkins, *New Modes of Conflict*, 1983), p. 11. Meanwhile "[a] series of terrorist bombings and threats have been directed against European firms that have contracts to provide Pakistan with a similar unclear capability. And when France withdrew its nuclear technicians from Pakistan, Muslim terrorists launched a series of attacks against French diplomatic officials to try to force France to resume work on the nuclear plant" (Jenkins, *op cit.*, pp. 11-12). Finally, in 1984, the ETA staged several attacks on nuclear power plants while they were under construction in the Basque region (Weinberg and Davis, p. 198).

43. Jenkins, "International Terrorism: Trends and Potentialities," (1980), p. 104, arbitrarily defines mass murder as "something approaching 100 or more potential deaths." This perception of low mass murder rates may be challenged by the recent number of multi-casualty incidents (*e.g.,* Lebanon and Ulster car bombs, mass slaying in Punjab and Sri Lanka, and the Air India tragedy). See also, Brian M. Jenkins, "Terrorism in the 1980s," P-6564 (Santa Monica, CA: Rand Corp., 1980), p. 5.

44. Jenkins, "The Future Course of International Terrorism" (1985), p. 17.

45. See, for example, Bruce Hoffman, "Terrorism in the United States and the Potential Threat to Nuclear Facilities," R-3351 (Santa Monica, CA: Rand Corp., 1986).

46. Both of these incidents were referred to in Peter Goodspeed, "Biological Terrorism—A New Nightmare," *Toronto Star*, January 12, 1984 p. A1, A5.

47. The majority of work in this area has been carried out by Raymond A. Zilinskas. This section draws heavily from his paper, "Determining the Threat of Terrorist Use of Biological/Toxin Weapons: Real or Fanciful," presented at the American Political Science Association, Washington, DC, 2 September 1988.

48. Goodspeed.

49. Crenshaw, "How Terrorism Ends."

50. Brian M. Jenkins, "Some Reflections on Recent Trends in Terrorism," P-6897 (Santa Monica, CA: Rand Corp., July 1983), p. 3

51. For a more in-depth discussion see, for example, Gerd Langguth, "Euroterrorism: Fact or Fiction," *TVI Report* 7, no. 3, (1987), pp. 8-12; and Jeffrey Ian Ross, "Recent Terrorist Attacks on NATO: Their Occurrence, Perpetrators, Causes, and Control" for NATO Information Day, University of Colorado-Boulder, 11 March 1988.

52. Jenkins, *Terrorism and Beyond,* pp. 63-66.

53. Robin Wright, "The Rage of the Children," *TVI Report* 7, no. 3, (1987), pp. 35-39.

54. For a more complete discussion of conspiracy theories of terrorism, see Peter C. Sederberg, *Terrorist Myths: Illusion, Rhetoric and Reality* (Englewood Cliffs, NJ: Prentice-Hall, 1989), chapter 5; see also Laqueur, *Age of Terrorism,* chapter 8; Claire Sterling, *The Terror Network* (New York: Holt, Rinehart and Winston, 1981), and Schmid and Jongman.

55. *Patterns of Global Terrorism: 1989*; see also S. T. Francis, *The Soviet Strategy of Terrorism* (Washington, DC: The Heritage Foundation, 1981); and Stephen Posony and L. F. Bouchey, *International Terrorism: The Communist Connection, with a Case Study of West German Terrorist Ulrike Meinhof* (Washington, DC: American Council for World Freedom 1978). The collapse of the East German Communist régime in 1989-90 led to the arrest of RAF members living there, and to official confirmation by the successor régime of extensive support for international terrorism by the former East German secret service. See *Globe and Mail,* 8, 16 June 1990; *The Economist*, 23 June 1990; *Newsweek*, 2 July 1990, *Time,* 13 August 1990.

56. Laqueur, *Age of Terrorism*, p. 20 and 97.

57. James Adams, *The Financing of Terrorism* (New York: Simon and Schuster, 1986).

58. On American financing of the Provisional IRA through NORAID and other channels, see Adams, pp. 135-55; and Michael McKinley, "Lavish Generosity: the American Dimension of International Support for the Provisional Irish Republican Army, 1968-1983," *Conflict Quarterly,* 7, no. 2 (Spring 1987), pp. 20-42; on racketeering and other forms of crime as a source of funds, see Adams, pp. 20-42; on racketeering and other forms of crime as a source of funds, see Adams, pp. 156-84; and Paul K. Clare, *Racketeering in Northern Ireland: a new Version of the Patriot Game* (Chicago: University of Illinois, 1989), pp. 16-32.

59. One exception in this regard with respect to American involvement in state-sponsored terrorism is Michael Stohl, "States, Terrorism, and State Terrorism: the Role of the Superpowers," in Robert O. Slater and Michael Stohl, eds., *Current Perspectives on International Terrorism* (London: Macmillan, 1988), pp. 155-205.

60. See, for example, Victor Marchetti and John Marks, *The CIA and the Cult of Intelligence* (New York: Dell Publishing, 1974); Philip Agee, *Inside the Company* (Toronto: Bantam Books, 1975); John Stockwell, *In Search of Enemies* (New

York: Norton, 1978); United States Senate, Select Committee on Intelligence, *Alleged Assassination Plots* (New York: Norton 1976); and Bob Woodward, *Veil: The Secret Wars of the CIA* (New York: Pocket Books, 1987). The majority of investigations that have come to public attention have been American activities. Whether this reflects actual incidence or better detection is a matter of debate. But clearly, the national security agencies of other countries have also engaged in similar activities. The DGSE, the French secret service was responsible for the July 10, 1985 sinking of the Rainbow Warrior, the flagship of Greenpeace, an international environmental group, in Auckland, New Zealand. For a more complete description of this incident, see John Dyson, *Sink the Rainbow!* (London: V Gollancz, 1986). Likewise the Soviet secret services assassinated emigrés, defectors, and other opponents abroad from the 1920s to the 1960s.

61. See Noam Chomsky and Edward S. Herman, *The Washington Connection and Third World Fascism* (Boston: South End Press, 1979) for an over-application of this term. See Jeffrey Ian Ross, "Controlling the Coercive Power of the Democratic State: Towards a Theory," presented at the Annual Meeting of the Western Social Science Association, 29 April 1988, Denver, for a clarification of terms surrounding state and oppositional terrorism.

62. The *Report of the National Commission on the Causes and Prevention of Violence* (New York: Bantam Books, 1970), pp. 3-7, identified five types of assassinations; Feliks Gross, "Political Assassination" in M. H. Livingston, ed., *International Terrorism in the Contemporary World* (Westport, CT: Greenwood Press, 1978), pp. 307-15 who identifies three "Political Assassinations"; see also the Senate Committee report, *Alleged Assassination Plots*, and John Ranelagh, *The Agency: The Rise and Decline of the CIA* (New York: Simon and Schuster, 1987), pp. 336-45. The most thorough historical analysis of the causes, role, and consequences of assassinations is Franklin Ford, *Political Murder: From Tyrannicide to Terrorism* (Cambridge, MA: Harvard University Press, 1985).

63. See pronouncements such as Brian M. Jenkins, "Future Trends in International Terrorism," P-7176 (Santa Monica, CA: Rand Corp., 1985) and "The Future Course of International Terrorism," P-7139 (Santa Monica, CA: Rand Corp., 1985); or J. Bowyer Bell,"Old Trends and Future Reality," *Washington Quarterly* 8, no. 2, (1985), pp. 25-36. For a comprehensive and recent treatment, see David Charters, "Terrorism and Political Crime: The Challenge of Policing in the Global Village, in Donald J. Loree (ed.) *Future Issues in Policing* (Ottawa: Minister of Supply and Services, 1989), pp. 79-106.

64. See Edward Cornish, *The Study of the Future* (Washington, DC: The World Future Society, 1983), Chapter 8, for an excellent discussion of these methods.

65. See Barbara Harff and Ted Robert Gurr, "Toward Empirical Theory of Genocides and Politicides: Identification and Measurement of Cases since 1945," *International Studies Quarterly* 32, (1988), pp. 359-71, for an empirical review of cases of genocide. See Barbara Harff and Ted Robert Gurr, "Genocides and Politicides Since 1945: Evidence and Anticipation" in *Internet on the Holocaust and Genocide* Issue 13, (December, 1987), pp. 1-5, for a comparison of deaths by terrorism with those of natural disasters.

JEFFREY IAN ROSS

# Cosmopolitanism

Cosmopolitanism is derived from two Greek words: *kosmos* which meant both "world" and "order" and *polis* which originally meant "fortified castle" and later "city-state." The term kosmopolites stood already in Greece for "citizen of the world," someone who considered humankind as a whole as more important than his or her own state or native land. Cosmopolitanism is thus often used as a blameword, implying the accusation that someone is a traitor to his or her country. But it can also be used as a praiseword indicating that someone is sophisticated, knows the ways of the world, and is open to other cultures, customs, and ideas than those of his or her own nation. A cosmopolitan in that sense is someone who regards the whole world as the native land and has no national prejudices, a citizen of the world.

In fact, strong identification with a particular nation is a recent development. Until the eighteenth century the aristocracy did not identify with the people living in their state but with other aristocracies, whereas the majority of the people identified with local communities, with towns or villages. The idea of the nation became powerful in the nineteenth century in the aftermath of the French Revolution. Gradually all social classes within the state came to identify with each other as members of one nation and were integrated into the political system of the state. In the nineteenth century the working classes were, one can say, torn between national identification and cosmopolitanism or internationalism. Marx and Engels could still write: "The working man has no fatherland, one cannot take away from him what he does not have." On that premise socialist movements and parties combined in Internationals (see *Socialist International*). Until 1914 socialists hoped that an internationally united working class would be able to prevent war. But Bebel already saw the flaw in this reasoning, namely that those countries which had the most strongly organized working class would be at the mercy of attack from countries which had much less well-organized proletariats. The 1914 experience has shown, however, that the integration of the working classes into nation-states was much stronger than class identification across boundaries.

If social classes cannot, who can then be the carriers of a cosmopolitan ideology? Voltaire once said that neither the poor nor philosophers could have a native land, because philosophers loved all of humanity. Can we consider intellectuals to be the primary carriers of cosmopolitanism? That is certainly not by definition the case because it is precisely intellectuals that have been the strongest carriers of nationalist ideas. On the other hand, intellectuals are most open to "foreign" influences and can become more easily alienated from their own governments and national cultures than others. They can therefore formulate broader perspectives on the world than on their own nation. Intellectuals are perhaps best able to have empathy and understanding for other cultures, especially for literature and art. In fact it may be said that art (literature and music included) and science are by their nature and development the most cosmopolitan of all human endeavors. Science and the arts—in fact the two most important aspects of culture—have no respect for state boundaries. Knowledge is the property of all human beings, as they have in principle the same capacities for understanding language and arithmetic, for connecting events in time and in space— even though some may do this better than others. There is but one intersubjective body of human knowledge which is relatively autonomous from the different cultures and nations of the world. In the long run, for example, all states will in principle be able to produce video tape recorders or nuclear weapons. However, it is precisely the latter possibility that is responsible for an increasing nationalization of scientific activity. The military application of scientific results puts a premium on secrecy and on placing obstacles to the spread of scientific knowledge. But, in the same way as the production of nuclear weapons has now become openly available knowledge, so will all other results of scientific discovery—with the exception perhaps of specific military-technological applications (see *Military Research and Development, Role of*). For that reason the nationalization of scientific activity cannot prevent science itself from being and remaining a cosmopolitan culture. Nevertheless a more cosmopolitan attitude by scientists is necessary to make it possible for all of humankind to profit more from the benefits of science and to be better protected from its harmful effects, especially nuclear war.

In the social sciences, however, nationalization of scientific activity can be more harmful, because no agreed-upon general theoretical synthesis is available which can guarantee that the social sciences will become more of a cosmopolitan activity. Here language is already an obstacle but even more so are national and political ideologies. In a large number of states in the world today it is not even possible to freely practice social science and freely publish the results of scientific activity. Ideological influences, whether nationalist or political, still impinge heavily on the social sciences. The development of a cosmopolitan attitude is therefore a very important precondition for the further development of the social sciences as a common human acquisition of knowledge. But it is not easy to move beyond ideology, especially in the branch of the social sciences which deals with problems of war and peace. There the particular ideologic perspectives of the Great Powers often set the terms of the debate. It is still very difficult for peace researchers to fully detach themselves from the perspectives of their own nation-states. One can therefore safely say that cosmopolitanism is a precondition for the development of a more adequate analysis of the problems of war and peace. Peace research must be cosmopolitan to fulfill its purpose.

That there in fact is a tendency in the direction of cosmopolitanism can best be seen in the development of art. In art, movements toward cultural synthesis clearly occur. The development of popular music is a good example. The most important innovation in the music of the twentieth century has been jazz. Jazz originally developed as a synthesis of African and European music, at first created by American blacks, descendants of African slaves. From the original New Orleans and Chicago jazz, played by blacks, a white variety quickly developed in the form of Dixieland. Black musicians could not keep a monopoly on their music. An interesting attempt was made by a group of musicians of whom Charlie Parker, Dizzie Gillespie, Max Roach, and Miles Davis became the most famous. They wanted to play a music so difficult that "whitey" would not be able to keep up. What they created was called "Re-bop" or "Be-bop" or just "Bop" for short. It did not take long, however, for white musicians to learn to play their music. Jazz since then has developed as a form of musical synthesis which turned out not to be bound to any specific ethnic group, country, or culture. There are, for example, excellent Swedish, Brazilian, and Japanese jazz musicians who all add something to the wider synthesis. But cosmopolitanism in music went even further. Out of jazz and blues developed rock and modern pop music in general. But that in turn became influenced by the synthesis of jazz and Dixieland music that developed in Third World countries, such as Bossa Nova in Brazil, Reggae in the Caribbean, and High-life in West Africa. We now observe an enormously complicated movement of musical styles between different parts of the world. Popular music, both in its commercial and in its artistic varieties, has developed into a truly cosmopolitan form of music. One can observe similar movements in the other arts which demonstrate that cosmopolitanism does not have to be uniform. In fact the movement toward cultural synthesis has led to a great variety and pluriformity of art forms. For that reason it is perhaps better not to think too much in terms of a sharp dichotomy between cosmopolitanism and nationalism (see *Nationalism*). Both can be seen as aspects of a continuing movement toward larger units of integration.

At the same time that nation-states developed, the broader process of global integration was speeded up, both through increasing economic interdependencies and through the two world wars of this century. The increasing aversion to war combined with the awareness that nuclear war may well lead to the end of human civilization as we know it, make people increasingly look at problems from a global or world perspective. That kind of cosmopolitanism is not incompatible with valuing national identity. Perhaps the most important manifestation of increasing cosmopolitanism is the increasing acceptance of and concern for human rights (see *Human Rights and Peace*). Human rights form a clear demonstration of the fact that there can be "duties beyond borders," based upon the awareness of a "world society." Such a cosmopolitan "one world" conception recognizes the rights of human beings as members of humankind irrespective of state or national boundaries. However, here too, the struggle between nationalism and cosmopolitanism manifests itself. States can invoke their claim to domestic jurisdiction (Article 2.7 of the Charter of the United Nations) and block interference from outside with the human rights of its citizens in the name of the lack of respect for their national pride which such interference implies. The recognition of the existence of globalized human rights, however, cannot be undone. The different kinds of cosmopolitanism discussed here may in the longer run become important conditions for a durable world peace.

See also: *Global Integration*

*Bibliography*

Fainsod M 1966 *International Socialism and the World War.* Octagon, New York
Hoffmann S 1980 *Duties beyond Borders.* Syracuse, New York
Kohn H 1961 *The Idea of Nationalism.* Macmillan, New York
Pettman R 1979 *State and Class: A Sociology of International Affairs.* Croom Helm, London
Rieff P (ed.) 1970 *On Intellectuals: Theoretical Studies and Case Studies.* New York

G. VAN BENTHEM VAN DEN BERGH

# Costa Rica: Neutrality

The foreign policy of Costa Rica during most of this century has been characterized by its isolation from the Central American context. Costa Rica refused to participate in the internal and external affairs of the other nations of the isthmus and, at the same time, it wished to prevent other Central American countries from interfering in its internal matters. This did not mean that the country was not concerned about the problems of the area. The onset of the Second World War induced the president in office to send messages to his Central American colleagues emphasizing the need for a solid friendship in the face of the world conflict.

After a brief civil war in 1948, the victors' leader, José Figueres, decided to abolish the armed forces as a permanent institution—a truly unprecedented deed in the history of nations. The policy, elevated to constitutional norm shortly after, was in effect the culmination of the peaceful civilian tradition and spirit that has characterized Costa Rica's population throughout history. In fact, and contrary to what has been common in most other Latin American countries, the army had never had any relevance in the country's politics and had always been respectful of the constitution and the national institutions.

Since the late 1970s the Central American region has been the theater of a series of political and military conflicts. Although Costa Rica has not taken part in these conflicts, they affected the traditional stability and peace of the country. Geopolitical, internal, and external motivations induced the government to find a way of keeping the country out of international complications and the growing armed turmoil of the rest of Central America. Thus, on September 15, 1983, Independence Day, Luis Alberto Monge, President of the Republic of Costa Rica (1982-86), announced his decision of proclaiming "the Permanent, Active and Unarmed Neutrality" of Costa Rica, vis-à-vis the armed conflicts of Central America. On November 17 that same year, amid a celebration which included national and international political and religious personalities, the President read the Neutrality Proclamation, fully supported by the Government Council (Ministers' Council), and in use of the powers invested in him by Article 140 of the political constitution of the Republic and according to the principles of the Charter of the United Nations and the Charter of the Organization of American States. "The peace of Costa Rica is endangered because the Central American Isthmus is on the verge of war," exclaimed President Monge, remembering that the region had suffered armed conflicts for half a decade, which had resulted in the burden of 100,000 deaths and a million homeless.

The Neutrality Proclamation establishes a very important principle in Costa Rican foreign policy, namely, a peacemaking instrument in one of the most conflict-ridden areas of the world. The Proclamation is within the framework of the best pacifist and democratic traditions of the country. In the present circumstances of the region, the requisites and compromises incumbent upon Costa Rica as a result of its neutral status constitute an engagement to reinforce the country's civil attitudes, which have characterized the nation since 1821.

As a legal institution, Costa Rica's neutrality is peculiar, inasmuch as it did not originate in an international treaty. The Proclamation was in effect a practical decision to avoid armed involvement in the conflicts so prevalent in the region. However, Costa Rica, despite its neutrality and its previous decision to disarm, continues to participate as a full member in various regional and international organizations, as well as in the Inter-American Treaty of Reciprocal Assistance (Rio Treaty), which is a treaty for a defensive alliance. In fact, Costa Rica relies for its defense on the different mechanisms of international law, which guarantee the principle of collective security as established in the Charter of the United Nations and the Charter of the Organization of American States, and in various regional agreements.

Previous to the Neutrality Proclamation, Costa Rica achieved in 1980 the establishment of the Uni-versity for Peace, aimed at the research of the proper means to further the cause of world peace through education (see *University for Peace*). Also, in December 1981 the First World Congress on Human Rights was held in this country. It proposed as one of its main objectives "to achieve the international reconnaissance of a Perpetual Neutrality Statute for Costa Rica, similar to the 1815 Swiss Statute or the Austrian of 1955," and regarded this aim as the best mechanism for juridical protection and efficient defense to maintain the peace and the security of the democratic system.

The world is undergoing a full historical transformation within the framework of classical international law. There was previously only one kind of neutrality conceived during wartime, that according to the rules of the Hague Conventions. Today the concept of neutrality has been broadened, and it implies a form of peaceful coexistence amid a world of military pacts and nuclear imperialisms. Neutral countries today contribute actively to the solution of national and international conflicts; therefore the modern concept of neutrality is an inseparable element of peace, since it is a neutrality for peacetime.

See also: *Neutrality; Neutrality, Permanent*

*Bibliography* ─────────────────────

*Aspects juridiques de la Neutralité* 1964 Editions de l'Association Internationale des Juristes Démocrates, Brussels
Monge L A 1984 *Presidential Proclamation on the Permanent, Active and Unarmed Neutrality of Costa Rica*. Imprenta Nacional, Costa Rica
Rhenán-Segura J 1984 *Costa Rica: L'Exception démocratique*, Rev. Amérique Latine No. 20. Centre de Recherche sur l'Amérique Latine et le Tiers Monde, Paris

JORGE RHENÁN-SEGURA

# Council of Europe

## 1. Description

The Council of Europe (based in Strasbourg) is an international organization with a general political mandate to provide for cooperation between the countries of the European region with a view to their achievement of "greater unity." It has at the moment 40 member countries—including the members of the European Union, and the former East European countries of the Soviet Bloc. Not only is it juridically separate, but it has an increasingly distinctive character, developed partly in consequence of the growth and extension of Community institutions in the last 22 years culminating in the formation of the European Union. Whereas the latter reflect an integrationist vision of the future of Europe and are driven primarily by economic concerns, the Council of Europe embodies a gradualist "intergovernmental" approach and seeks increasingly to link the provision it makes for cooperation between its members to the criteria which determine and limit its membership. At the heart of these criteria is a very precise conception of the principles which should govern relations between the state and the individual citizen. As set forth on the Statute signed in London in 1949, these principles—which are declared to form "the basis of all genuine democracy"—are "individual freedom, political liberty and the rule of law." They are presented as derivable from a common European heritage of "spiritual and moral values." The quintessential concept was to find expression the following year in Articles 1 and 25 of the European convention on Human Rights, which provides an international procedure for any person within the jurisdiction of a signatory state to lodge complaints against the government. This was—and remains—a remarkable innovation in international law, to such an extent that this "right of individual petition" was made optional at the time the Convention was concluded in 1950. But at the time of writing it is accepted by 18 of the Council of Europe's 21 member countries, and it represents the purest distillation of the organization's philosophy of the primacy of the individual in his or her relations with the state.

The Council of Europe is thus a value-driven institution, which distinguishes it in its primary motivation from most other international political institutions. Alone excluded from its mandate are the military aspects of defense. It works through a committee of foreign ministers representing governments and a parliamentary assembly whose members come from national parliaments. The latter are thus closely involved in national parliamentary life and have in consequence the potential for influence on the governments of their countries which members of the "European parliament" (of the European Union) sometimes lack. The Committee of Ministers takes decisions on recommendations drawn up by the Parliamentary Assembly, or on proposals from its committees of governmental experts and/or conferences of specialized ministers. More than 100 conventions and agreements have been concluded. The Organization's contribution to peaceful international relationships can best perhaps be exemplified as follows: by its work towards the strengthening of international law on the field of human rights; by its focusing of trans-European parliamentary opinion on problems and issues of balanced world economic and technological development; and by its promotion of a concept of European cultural identity which may yet serve to ease the tensions arising from intra-European political divisions.

The Council of Europe's "Convention for the Protection of Human Rights and Fundamental Freedoms" (which came into force in 1953) has established not only principles of international control of the actions of national governments in this sphere, but also a new status in international law accorded to the individual. The latter has direct access, when domestic remedies have been exhausted, to an international control system, consisting of an investigatory Commission and a Court, the aim of which is to ensure observance of the civil and political rights set forth in the "Universal Declaration" proclaimed by the UN General Assembly on 10 December 1948. There is no comparable system of international control elsewhere in the world—though encouraging developments are now taking place in other regions, notably under the Inter-American Convention and in Africa. The surprising criticism has been made that the regional ambit of the Council of Europe's system of protection in some way detracts from the universality one would like to see accorded to respect for human rights—not only in rhetoric but in realization. This criticism is belied, however, by the interest shown in the Council of Europe's system from all quarters of the globe—not only by lawyers but by active politicians. Moreover, the constitutions of many countries which have become independent since 1953 contain guarantees of human rights directly inspired by the European Convention. Its effect is thus felt in regions of the world far beyond Europe. It must perhaps be observed that the concept of limited national state sovereignty in regard to the protection of the political and civil rights of individual (derived moreover from a country's shared heritage of "spiritual and moral values") is difficult to reconcile with the concept of the state as the expression of the collective rights of peoples to particular forms of socioeconomic development and culture: the discourse on human rights of the Council of Europe is thus not always concordant with that developed from time to time within the UN system. The element of "representative democracy" in the Council of Europe's composition is integrally linked to the operation of the human rights machinery. The parliamentary Assembly elects the judges of the European Court from lists of candidates nominated by governments. It proposes candidates, for election by the Committee of Ministers, to the Human Rights Commission. The "Social Charter" of the Council of Europe (1961) aims to ensure respect for basic economic and social rights, but the international machinery is supervisory and not juridical. Its aims, however, have been advanced by the European code (1964) and Convention (1972) on Social Security and by the European convention on the Legal Status of Migrant Workers (1977).

The Parliamentary Assembly's committees on economic affairs and development and on science and technology have combined their efforts on recent years to focus European parliamentary attention on problems and issues of balanced world development. The former organizes annual debates on reports from the Paris-based Organization for Economic cooperation and Development (OECD)—debates which are attended by parliamentarians from the non-European countries of OECD and in which the development aid policies of the industrialized countries and the unending quest for more effective forms of North-South dialogue play a prominent part. Likewise, from the time of its contribution to the historic UN Conference on Science and Technology for Development (UNC-STD, Vienna 1979), the committee on science and technology has sought to mobilize European support for the strengthening of financial mechanisms within the UN system for the harnessing of science and technology to the needs of developing countries: the guiding policy objective being the attainment of "self-reliance." It has also sought to elicit initiatives from within Europe for practical steps (e.g., by the European Space Agency) towards the realization of an "international satellite monitoring agency"—as conceived by France and supported by the UN General Assembly. In a different vein, the "parliamentary and scientific conferences" of the committee on science and technology have worked towards a broadening of European self-perceptions at the philosophical as well as political levels—the fifth (Helsinki 1981) and the sixth (Tokyo 1985) both addressing the quadripolar problematique of science/technology/democracy/civilization. Of continuing concern has been the potential effect of scientific and technical advance on the rights of the individual—leading in recent years to significant Council of Europe initiatives (from within its intergovernmental program) on data protection and privacy, on the integrity of each person's genetic inheritance, and on the future of audiovisual communications and the mass media.

## 2. Brief History and Recent Development

Europe that awoke in the days following the Liberation was in a sorry state, torn apart by five years of war. States were determined to build up their shattered economies, recover their influence and, above all, ensure that such a tragedy could never happen again. Movements of various persuasions, but all dedicated to European unity, were springing up everywhere at the time. All these organisations were to combine to form the International Committee of the Movements for European Unity. Its first act was to organise the Hague Congress, on May 7, 1948, remembered as "The Congress of Europe."

More than a thousand delegates from some twenty countries, together with a large number of observers, among them political and religious figures, academics, writers and journalists, attended the Congress. Its purpose was to demonstrate the breadth of the movements in favour of European unification, and to determine the objectives which must be met in order to achieve such a union. A series of resolutions was adopted at the end of the Congress, calling, amongst other things, for the creation of an economic and political union to guarantee security, economic independence and social progress, the establishment of a consultative assembly elected by national parliaments, the drafting of a European charter of human rights and the setting up of a court to enforce its decisions. All the themes around which Europe was to be built were already sketched out in this initial project. The Congress also revealed the divergences which were soon to divide unconditional supporters of a European federation (France and Belgium) from those who favoured simple inter-governmental co-operation, such as Great Britain, Ireland and the Scandinavian countries.

On the international scene, the sharp East-West tensions marked by the Prague coup and the Berlin blockade were to impart a sense of urgency to the need to take action and devote serious thought to a genuine inter-state association. Two months after the Congress of Europe, Georges Bidault, the French Minister for Foreign Affairs, issued an invitation to his Brussels Treaty partners, the United Kingdom and the Benelux countries, and to all those who wished to give substance to The Hague proposals. Robert Schuman, who replaced him a few days later, confirmed the invitation. France, supported by Belgium, in the person of its Prime Minister Paul Henri Spaak, called for the creation of a European Assembly, with wide-ranging powers, composed of members of parliament from the various states and deciding by a majority vote. This plan, assigning a fundamental role to the Assembly seemed quite revolutionary in an international order hitherto the exclusive preserve of governments. But Great Britain, which favoured a form of intergovernmental cooperation in which the Assembly would have a purely consultative function, rejected this approach. It only softened its stance after lengthy negotiations.

Finally, on January 27-28, 1949 the five ministers

for foreign affairs of the Brussels Treaty countries, meeting in the Belgian capital, reached a compromise: a Council of Europe consisting of a ministerial committee, to meet in private; and a consultative body, to meet in public. In order to satisfy the supporters of co-operation the Assembly was purely consultative in nature, with decision-making powers vested in the Committee of Ministers. In order to meet the demands of those partisans of a Europe-wide federation, members of the Assembly were independent of their governments, with full voting freedom. The United Kingdom demanded that they be appointed by their governments. This important aspect of the compromise was soon to be reviewed and, from 1951 onwards, parliaments alone were to choose their representatives.

On May 5, 1949, in St. James's Palace, London, the treaty constituting the Statute of the Council of Europe was signed by ten countries: Belgium, France, Luxembourg, the Netherlands and the United Kingdom, accompanied by Ireland, Italy, Denmark, Norway and Sweden. The Council of Europe was now able to start work. Its first sessions were held in Strasbourg, which was to become its permanent seat. In the initial flush of enthusiasm, the first major convention was drawn up: the European Convention on Human Rights, signed in Rome on November 4, 1950 and coming into force on September 3, 1953.

The new organisation satisfied a very wide range of public opinion, which saw in it an instrument through which the various political tendencies, and the essential aspirations of the peoples of Europe, could be expressed. This was indeed the purpose for which it was founded, as clearly stated in Chapter I of its Statute: "The aim of the Council of Europe is to achieve a greater unity between its Members for the purpose of safeguarding and realising the ideals and principles which are their common heritage, and facilitating their economic and social progress." In order to achieve its objectives, certain means were made available to the Council and were listed in the Statute, which specified that: "This aim shall be pursued through the organs of the Council by discussion of questions of common concern and by agreements and common action in economic, social, cultural, scientific, legal and administrative matters and in the maintenance and further realisation of human rights and fundamental freedoms."

In accordance with the compromise reached, the Statute made no mention of drawing up a constitution, or of pooling national sovereignty, in order to achieve the economic and political union called for by The Hague delegates. Consequently, the need was soon felt to set up separate bodies to address the urgent questions arising on the political and economic fronts. Shortly after the accession of the former Federal Republic of Germany, Robert Schuman approached all the Council of Europe countries with a proposal for a European Coal and Steel Community, to be provided with very different political and budgetary means. The six countries most attached to the ideal of integration—Belgium, France, Italy, Luxembourg, the Netherlands and the Federal Republic of Germany—joined, and on May 9, 1951 signed the very first Community treaty. Strengthened by the experience and commitment which had brought the "Greater Europe" into existence, the "Smaller Europe" was now making its own leap into the unknown of European construction.

In the years between 1949 and 1970, eight new countries joined the founder members: in order of accession Greece, Iceland, Turkey, Germany, Austria, Cyprus, Switzerland and Malta. In this period, the organisation gradually developed its structure and its major institutions. Thus, the first public hearing of the European Court of Human Rights took place in 1960. These years also saw the introduction of the first specialized ministerial conferences; by the early 1970s they had been extended to cover a wide range of areas. The first, in 1959, brought together European ministers responsible for social and family affairs. On October 18, 1961, the European Social Charter was signed in Rome: a text which the Council sees as the counterpart of the European Convention on Human Rights in the social domain.

The Charter came into force on February 26, 1965. It sets out 19 rights, including the right to strike and the right to social protection, but does not have such effective machinery as the Human Rights Convention. Nevertheless, it is gradually developing into a common body of social rights that apply right across Europe. The same era saw the institution of the Council for Cultural Cooperation in 1961, which non-Council of Europe member states were allowed to join from the outset. One example was Finland, which only joined the Council itself 28 years later. Similarly, the European Pharmacopoeia was founded in 1964 and the European Youth Centre in 1967.

The Council of Europe's first major political crisis came in 1967 when the Greek colonels overthrew the legally elected government and installed an authoritarian regime which openly contravened the democratic principles defended by the organisation. On December 12, 1969, just a few hours before a decision would have been taken to exclude Greece, the colonels' regime anticipated matters by denouncing the European Convention on Human Rights and withdrawing from the Council of Europe. It did not return until five years later, on November 28, 1974 after the fall of the dictatorship and the restoration of democracy. In the meantime, the Cypriot crisis, which broke out in the summer of 1974 and culminated in the partitioning of the island after Turkish military intervention, represented a fairly negative experience for the Council of Europe, whose discreet efforts to broker a solution, alongside those of the United Nations' Secretary General, were not crowned with success.

A new crisis arose in 1981 when the Parliamentary Assembly withdrew the Turkish parliamentary delegation's right to their seats in response to the military coup d'etat a few weeks earlier. The Turkish delegation only resumed its place in 1984 after the holding of free elections. Greece's return marked the disappearance of the last authoritarian regime in western Europe. Portugal had made its Council of Europe debut on September 22, 1976, two years after its peaceful revolution of April 1974, bringing an end to 48 years of Salazarist dictatorship, while the death of General Franco in 1975 eventually led to Spain's accession on November 24, 1977.

The Council of Europe's permanent role on the European political and institutional scene was sealed on January 28, 1977 with its move from its provisional premises to the Palais de l'Europe, designed by the French architect Bernard. Liechtenstein's accession on November 23, 1978, San Marino's on November 16, 1988 and Finland's on May 5, 1989 more or less completed the absorption of west European states while the Council of Europe was already laying the foundations for a rapprochement with the countries of central and eastern Europe.

A further, critical stage in the Council of Europe's life started in 1985 with the first movements to introduce democracy to central and eastern Europe. In January of that year Hans-Dietrich Genscher, Chairman of the Committee of Ministers, invited his colleagues to take part in an extraordinary session devoted entirely to East-West relations. This process of reflection, that took account of the trend emerging in Eastern Europe—in Romania and Poland, and in the former Soviet Union, where Mikhail Gorbachev had just come to power—gave rise to the notion of a European cultural identity, which became the subject of a resolution in April 1985. Convinced that unity in diversity was the basis of the wealth of Europe's heritage, the Council of Europe noted that their common tradition and European identity did not stop at the boundaries between the various political systems; it stressed, in the light of the CSCE Final Act, the advan-

tage of consolidating cultural co-operation as a means of promoting a lasting understanding between peoples and between governments. The Eastern European countries grasped this outstretched hand with enthusiasm.

Rapprochement had at last become not only possible but necessary. The Council of Europe was naturally delighted by the process of democratisation set in motion in the East, together with the economic and social reforms introduced in the name of *perestroika*. It was the Council's role and purpose to support this trend, to help make it irreversible, and to fulfil the expectations of the countries calling upon it for assistance. Not of course by renouncing its principles but, on the contrary, by making them a precondition for any form of co-operation.

The arrival of the Russian Federation in February 1996 meant that the institution had finally become fully pan-European. Henceforth, more than 700 million citizens would be concerned in building the new Europe. The Council's activities are now having to adapt to an environment that is not only wider and more diverse but also more complex and less stable. This is changing the nature of its co-operation programmes.

Support and monitoring activities are being strengthened. More attention is being paid to what happens on the ground, for example, via confidence measures or campaigns to combat intolerance. New priorities are emerging such as migration, corruption, the right to be granted nationality, social exclusion and minorities. The dual machinery for protecting human rights was to be replaced on November 1, 1998 by a single Court, housed in the Human Rights Building designed by the British architect Richard Rogers and inaugurated in June 1995.

At the same time several other European or North Atlantic institutions have been increasing their co-operation with the countries of central and eastern Europe, offering the prospect of closer integration. The work under the auspices of the intergovernmental conference of the European Union and NATO summit held in Madrid, show that European co-operation will continue to develop.

As it approaches its fiftieth anniversary, the Council of Europe, with its forty members, will also be required to clarify how it sees its future role as a focus for democratic security and the proponent of a European model of society. A second summit was held for this purpose on October 10-11, 1997. The Strasbourg Summit, held at the Council of Europe headquarters and hosted by the French Presidency, gave the forty Heads of State and Government an opportunity to assess the positive contribution which the Council had made to stability in Europe by admitting new countries, running programmes to help them make the transition to democracy and monitoring all its members' compliance with their obligations. The Summit adopted a Final Declaration and an Action Plan, fixing the Organisation's priorities in the years ahead, and gave reform of its structures the green light.

See also: *Human Rights and Peace; European Union; Integration, Regional*

*Bibliography*

Council of Europe 1970 *Manual of the Council of Europe.* Steve's and Rothman, London
Council of Europe 1985a *Committee of Ministers' Resolution*
(85) 6 *on European Cultural Identity.* Council of Europe, Strasbourg
Council of Europe 1985b *European Convention on Human Rights.* Council of Europe, Strasbourg
Council of Europe 1998 History of the Council of Europe. http://www.coe.fr/eng/present.htm
*Forum* (Quarterly Bulletin of the Council of Europe)
Laszlo E, Vitanyi I 1985 *European Culture and World Development.* Pergamon, Oxford
Leuprecht P 1984 Quel droits de l'homme? *Le Monde Diplomatique* (April), Paris
Robertson A H 1961 *The Council of Europe.* Steve's, London
Vasak K 1977 A 30-year struggle. *UNESCO Courier* (11)
Völkerrecht 1982 *Lehrbuch: Teii 2.* Staatsverlag der Deutsche Demokratischen Republik, Berlin

JOHN HEARTLAND; PEDRO B. BERNALDEZ

# Crime Trends and Crime Prevention Strategies

Crime is a major social problem which is bent on disrupting the stability and welfare of society. If not controlled properly and effectively, crime may lead a whole nation into chaos and terror.

## 1. Nature of Crime

The nature of crime is so complex that it is rather difficult to describe. Crimes vary in degree from one locality to another. It may take place on the spur of the moment or as a result of an elaborate plan. The latter case is commonly known as "organized crime."

A study of crime trends and crime prevention strategies is of paramount importance for the eventual control and possible elimination of this social problem. Such study may be divided into the following ten major areas of criminology:

*1.1 Approach to Crime*—how it is reported to official sources and acted upon officially.

*1.2 Present Criminal Laws*—how they relate to social, economic and political systems as well as to the social values of the respective societies.

*1.3 Characteristics of Criminals*—how they compare with non-offenders involved in crimes related to sex, race, nationality, employment, pathological conditions of the mind and body, and so forth.

*1.4 Variation of Crime*—how it differs from one locality to another due to existing circumstances.

*1.5 Sources of Crime*—how it originates and develops in every way.

*1.6 Criminal Careers*—how organized crime develops among highly educated people, successful businessmen, and respectable government officials.

*1.7 Closely Affiliated Problems*—how alcoholism, drugs, prostitution, gambling, vagrancy, and begging may generate other crimes.

*1.8 Effectiveness of Law Enforcement*—how responsible government officials proceed to control and eventually eliminate crime.

*1.9 Rehabilitation Programs*—how detained offenders are educated to secure desirable behavior after they leave prison.

*1.10 Experiments in Crime Prevention*—how to detect potential criminals and give them needed assistance before they fall prey to crimes.

## 2. Analyzed Criminal Behavior

Criminologists and behavioral scientists must identify, describe and classify the various delinquent and criminal behaviors of society.

The magnitude of the crime depends on how it is performed. It also depends on the criminal's awareness of the nature of the crime itself. Two men, for example, may commit the same identical deplorable action. Yet, one may be guilty of crime while the other may not. If Publius wants to get rid of Clement, he goes out to search for him. Publius finds him, shoots him, and kills him. Publius becomes a criminal wanted for murder.

On the other hand, Peter goes hunting in his usual forest. He sights a deer far away and shoots her. By mistake he hits and kills Oscar who was lying hidden beneath a tree. Peter does not become a criminal. In addition, evidence could be furnished that he was not even negligent in the very least. At times, of course, it may be difficult to distinguish between the criminal and the innocent person. But a difficulty, however great, does not constitute an impossibility when it comes to the search for a right solution.[1]

Parental neglect and desertion during infancy and childhood may lead to early thefts and prostitution. Such acts, like other various kinds, vary in gravity when taken within the context. One who steals a typewriter to sell it and make money should not be judged on the same level of one who steals bread to survive by avoiding starvation.

Professional criminals base their philosophy on the belief that "crime pays." Hence, such criminals falsify, cheat, overcharge and do anything possible within their power to "get money." Machiavelli's philosophy—*the end justifies the means*,—becomes the very foundation of their lives. Nothing counts apart from their personal interests. In this way, they become very dangerous to society and every step should be taken to stop such a trend whenever it exists.

Certain types of crime tend to become prevalent in a country due to manifold circumstances that may not easily be explained. For example, armed robbery in the United States, and lately in Russia as well, is emerging as a professional technique.

Holdups are considered to be the result of careful planning and efficient execution. Such an organized crime is planned in four steps: (a) Determine the exact location of the holdup, then decide upon the day and time; (b) Get together the team of men who are going to be involved making sure everyone knows his job well; (c) Rehearse the details of the plan over and over again so as to develop perfect self-confidence; and (d) Execute the job with a successful getaway. All this reveals a good contrast with the traditionally known "cowboy job" who acts on the spur of the moment with no plans or precautions and who is often caught in the act.

Criminal behavior is more difficult to analyze when it stems from highly influential persons including those in the government. At times, legitimate business is invaded and stirred up by "corrupt" politicians in order to procure the public with needed distraction from illegal actions such politicians are themselves engaged in. This approach constitutes an abuse of power which is in itself one of the most abhorrent crimes in human history. As revealed in the Kefauver Committee report to the US government, top men in organized crime have successfully become immune to criminal justice. They can literally do what they want since law enforcement and prosecution in their case are non-existent for all practical purposes.

The Kefauver Committee analyzed the mentioned criminal behavior of government officials and law-enforcement officers in four different forms as follows:

2.1 Direct bribes are made to law-enforcement officials so that they will not interfere with special criminal activities.

2.2 Political pressuring of important political leaders is used to protect criminal activities or criminal gangs.

2.3 Law-enforcement officials are found in the possession of unusual and unexplained wealth.

2.4 Law-enforcement officials participate directly in the business of organized crime.

## 3. Search for Causes

Scholars have sought to explain crime for many years. Until the eighteenth century, the sources of crime were attributed to the devil or to naturally sick minds. During the last century a new theory developed based on *rationalism*. In accordance with such a theory, the human was presumed to have the power to choose right from wrong. Man's behavior was supposed to be guided by what brought him pleasure. At the same time, he was to turn away from things that brought him pain and penalties. Modern criminal law is based on this assumption.

Another theory, based on positivism, attributed the cause of crime to elements which must be sought in heredity and the physical makeup of man as well as in his environment. In this century, some sociologists attributed the causes of crime to social organization which is constantly creating problems of self-identity and cultural understanding.[2]

Most psychiatrists in the United States concluded that repetitive and serious criminality is often related to personality disorders of psychogenic origin (see *Psychology and Peace*). These disorders are usually revealed in the individual's emotionally unstable and aggressive personality as well as in his sexual deviation. In addition, it was indicated that persons suffering from personality disorders do not make good adjustment to life situations. Consequently, such persons become easily to detect as potential criminals since they are constantly revealing any of the following three elements: (1) *Inadequate personality* revealed in the individual's being aloof, detached, cold, depressed, suspicious and jealous; (2) *Personality trait disturbance* revealed in the individual's emotionally unstable personality which is usually aggressive and compulsive; (3) *Sociopathic personality disturbance* revealed in the individual's antisocial reaction, sexual deviation and addiction to alcohol and drugs.

In the early 20th century, attention was focussed on the social, economic and political conditions which were thought to be partly responsible for criminality and delinquency. According to Enrico Ferri, a famous Italian criminologist, social factors which revealed considerable influence on criminality and delinquency were *the density of population, public opinion, manners and religion, family circumstances, the system of education, industrial pursuits, alcoholism, economic and political conditions, public administration, justice and police and, in general, legislative, civil and penal institutions.*

According to many criminal sociologists, the bad or unfavorable environmental conditions operate as a pressure on the person. As a result, they may force the individual into delinquency and crime. In addition, some sociologists stated that criminal behavior is learned in interaction with other persons especially in intimate personal groupings.

## 4. Problem of Juvenile Delinquency

The main factor of juvenile delinquency is vandalism. According to the US Government reporter, vandalism *is a form of protest, an explosion of suppressed resentment, or the release of feelings of aggression by children who, given a large measure of freedom in an atmosphere of violence and destruction, are unable to control their impulses because they lack the quality of self-discipline.*

Public property is often the object of attack: schools, buildings, parks, road signs, trees, shrubs, and benches. Parked automobiles have had tires slashed, windows broken, convertible tops cut, and upholstery destroyed.

In most countries, the delinquency problem has a sensational value for the newspapers, magazines, radio and television, all of which give it a big play. The sad part of the story lies in the fact that in terms of results very little seems to be achieved. Among other juvenile crimes mostly on the news are drug-

addiction, abnormal sex offenses, organized crimes, and labor rackets.

Some kind of master plan needs to be developed to help reduce considerably the juvenile problem. Our society's priorities need to be reorganized. In the meantime, the following steps may be taken:

4.1 The problem of juvenile delinquency needs to be brought into proper perspective. A united front, based on common understanding of the problem, needs to be set up between the uniformed public, police, press, lawyers, educators, social workers, psychiatrists and sociologists. All of these, as well as others, must seek general public support of various measures of prevention and treatment.

4.2 All those involved in the welfare of juveniles—teachers, ministers, pediatricians, psychologists—should work out a plan of action that would enable the child feel as an integral part not only of the family but also of the community with important specific roles to fulfill.

4.3 Special attention should be given to children who reveal a great potential for crime. The old saying: *prevention is better than cure*, applies here perfectly well.

4.4 Money needs to be appropriated for state and nationwide crime prevention projects which could be operated by private agencies or even individuals with expertise.

4.5 Present juvenile delinquency laws need reevaluation. The age could be placed at 14 to 18 years. Certain present illegalities such as truancy and running away from home should shift from the juvenile court to the responsibility of a specialized agency or individual.

4.6 A system of education needs to be adopted where parents and the general public become more cooperative in stopping juvenile crimes. Education for crime prevention may prove itself to be more effective than deterrence through punishment for crimes committed.

4.7 Finally, there is a need to synchronize and integrate all the services and procedures which deal with the delinquent youth, following his taking into custody first by the police and later turned over to the court.[3]

## 5. Crime Control and Treatment

Modern society is vitally concerned with curbing crime and in keeping it at a minimum. Crime control seeks to hold the volume of crime in check by keeping it from spreading and breaking out into new places. In this way, it protects society from the aggressions of abnormal and habitual offenders.

To ensure the effectiveness of crime control, the local police must be organized into an alert combat force. The public, as well as government officials, need to cooperate with police departments in making them a viable force of susceptibility to corrupt politicians, to underworld interests and to organized crime. Apart from the police, the courts play a big role in crime control. One of the greatest problems that exits in this area lies in the fact that most courts are staffed with the kind of people not properly prepared for the job.

Statistical studies indicate that a large portion of adult offenders are really uncorrected juvenile offenders. In recent times, it was pointed out that in the State of California 87 percent of crimes committed in one year alone were committed by those who were formerly in jail. All this indicates that very little is being done to rehabilitate the inmates properly and effectively.

In conclusion, crime remains a serious social problem which cannot be taken lightly. Seminars and workshops, organized for potential criminals, on the development of the *Self-Image, Life-Acceptance and Future Achievement* may prove to be an effective and decisive step in crime prevention strategies. Every country needs to make good use of every means at its disposal and take drastic actions for the solution of this problem, the sooner the better.

See also: *Cultural Roots of Peace; Education for Global Citizenship; Global Neighborhood: New Security Principles; Human Security; Peace and Peace Education: A Holistic View; Peace and Social Development*

*Notes*

1. R J (ed.) 1996 *Criminal Justice?—The Legal System vs. Individual Responsibility*. The Foundation for Economic Education, 30 South Broadway, Irvington-on-Hundson, 10533, New York, NY, USA

2. Colin 1990 *Access to Inner Worlds*. Celestial Arts, P.O. Box 7327, Berkeley, CA 94707, USA

3. 1990 *Deskbook Encyclopedia of American School Law*. Data Research Inc., P.O. Box 490, Rosemount, Minnesota 55069, USA

*Bibliography*

Dator J, Roulstone M G (ed.) 1988 *Who Cares? And How?—Futures of Caring Societies*. Secretariat World Futures Studies Federation, University of Hawaii at Manoa, Honolulu, Hawaii

Hazlitt H 1996 *The Foundations of Morality*. The Foundation for Economic Education, New York, NY

Micou A M, Lindsnaes B 1993 *The Role of Voluntary Organizations in Emerging Democracies*. Copenhagen K, Denmark

Nathanson S 1993 *Patriotism, Morality and Peace*. Rowman & Littlefield Publishers, Inc.

Webster-Doyle T 1991 *Peace, the Enemy of Freedom: The Myth of Nonviolence*. Atrium Society

CHARLES MERCIECA

# Crisis

The period since the end of the Second World War has sometimes been described as "the age of crisis" in international relations. Some of the most dramatic and dangerous crises had involved the two Superpowers during the Cold War. For example, one of the top-ranking participants in the Cuban missile crisis of 1962 estimated that the probability of a nuclear war between the former Soviet Union and the United States was one in three. Such dangerous episodes have by no means been limited to the major powers. During recent decades the Middle East has been wracked by repeated crises, a number of which have resulted in wars. Such local or regional crises may ultimately result in much wider conflicts, as demonstrated most dramatically by the rapid escalation of the dispute between Serbia and Austria-Hungary in 1914 into the First World War.

Not all crises result in war; even such dangerous confrontations as those over Berlin in 1948-49 or over missiles in Cuba were ultimately resolved peacefully. Nor do all wars arise from crises which get out of control; other factors are probably needed to explain the invasions of Poland and Finland in 1939, of Afghanistan in 1979, of Iran by Iraq in 1979, or of Grenada in 1984. Nevertheless, the relationship between crisis and war is sufficiently close that anyone wishing to understand fully the causes of war and the conditions of peace must take crisis into account.

This article focuses on the diversity of analytical approaches to international crises rather than on a historical description of specific crises. After examining various definitions of the widely used term, it describes various approaches to analyzing crises. A companion article focuses upon prescriptive theories for coping with crises (see *Crisis Management*).

## 1. Definition of Crisis

One of the first requirements for understanding any phenomenon is a workable definition. Unfortunately, "crisis" is a much overused term that has become burdened with a wide range of meanings, some of them quite imprecise. In common usage, crisis is often used as a synonym for virtually every problem of even moderate difficulty. Even in foreign policy research and diplomatic history, diversity is more in evidence than uniformity. As one of the pioneers in crisis research, Charles McClelland, observed in 1977:

So many studies of crisis have been published in the last fifteen years from so many different angles of inquiry that it is more difficult than it once was to be sure about the denotations and connotations of the term. Not only is there a heavy popular usage of the word in ordinary discourse but also there are indications that historical change has brought about an expansion of the variety of situations that are called readily by the crisis name.

In order to resolve this problem, analysts have sought to establish precise definitions of crisis. These efforts fall into two very broad groups. Common to the first is a systemic perspective in which crisis represents a significant change in the quantity, quality, or intensity of interactions among nations. This approach "looks on the whole configuration of parties participating back and forth" and observes changes in the patterns of interaction. Special attention is given to any significant change or turning point. This might be a dramatic increase in the number of border incidents, verbal challenges, or physical threats. After a crisis, the number and type of these exchanges may return to a more "normal" state. Accordingly, one way to identify crises is through search for changed interaction patterns between nations.

A second approach to defining a crisis—the decision-making perspective—focuses on the policy makers rather than the international system. From this perspective a situation is a crisis when it is so defined by those who must cope with it. It is thus possible that in a confrontation between two nations, decision makers in one believe themselves to be facing a crisis, whereas those in the other do not. Although differences may be found among those who adopt a decision-making approach to crisis, one

definition that has gained a number of adherents states that a crisis is a situation characterized by surprise, a high threat to important values, and short decision time. The definition is not without its critics, but most of them tend to disagree only with one or another of the three criteria, usually either surprise or decision time. An alternative but not wholly different definition specifies that a crisis occurs when decision makers perceive that there exists a serious threat to national interests, bargaining reputation, or ability to remain in power; any action other than capitulation will give rise to a significant prospect of war; and there is a need to act under time constraint.

## 2. Crisis Theories

Most of the extensive literature on crisis extends far beyond the problem of definition and concentrates its attention on actual behavior during crisis situations. This proceeds from a wide variety of theoretical and empirical perspectives that may be grouped into four rather distinct, descriptive theories.

The first of these is the organizational response model. It is directed at decision-making groups and the bureaucratic organizations which may shape and constrain policy choices in crisis. Studies at the level of the decision-making group reveal that the concomitants of crisis—for example, smaller groups or greater cohesion—can have both positive and negative consequences for the quality of decision processes. Leadership skills often determine whether, for example, group cohesion becomes a source of constructive cooperation or whether it takes on a pathological form such as "groupthink." Organizational theorists have often regarded crises as occasions in which greater than normal rationality prevails because decisions are made at the top of organizational hierarchies by persons less constrained by narrow parochial views. Moreover, limited time reduces opportunities to adopt bargaining and incremental strategies that may reduce the quality of decisions. However, others have shown that not even in crisis situations is decision making free of the organizational processes and bureaucratic politics that may constrain rational choice.

A second approach may be found in the hostile interaction model, which examines the antecedents and consequences of interactions among nations in crises, with special attention paid to the role of perceptions in exacerbating, sustaining, or mitigating the pattern of relations between contending parties. According to this model, those involved in a crisis perceive accurately any hostility directed toward them, and they respond in kind. Crisis is thus viewed as an occasion that is likely to trigger a "conflict spiral." Stated somewhat differently, this conception of crisis highlights the processes by which hostility breeds more hostility, and it focuses less attention on the means by which such a pattern of interactions may be arrested.

The cost calculation model emphasizes the strategic and tactical choices associated with maximizing gains and minimizing losses in crisis management. Crises that pose significant threats to such central goals as national existence are likely to engender greater caution in decision makers, as well as more vigorous efforts to reach peaceful settlements. Conversely, in crises posing threats of lesser magnitude, policy makers will feel less constrained and, therefore, they may be more willing to resort to high-risk strategies and tactics; for example, they may undertake actions that convey unalterable commitments or loss of control in an effort to force concessions from the adversary. The hostile interaction and cost calculation models thus differ in some significant ways, especially with respect to the prospects for attenuating escalation in a crisis.

The individual stress model emphasizes the impact of crisis-induced stress on certain aspects of cognitive performance that are critical in decision making. Theories and research at the individual level often identify some potentially negative effects of intense and protracted crisis on decision processes and outcomes. It should be noted, however, that this model is not merely a variant of a frustration-aggression theory. The probable consequences of intense and protracted stress are by no means confined to or even most clearly manifested by the release of aggressive impulses.

Other theories address themselves to the consequences of crisis. These are also marked by substantial diversity. Among those with systemic perspective, crisis has been viewed both as a prelude to war and as a substitute for war that offers a means of effectuating needed change. There are also competing views on the consequences of multiple crisis. The first, suggested by Quincy Wright among others (see *Wright, Quincy*), states that the more frequent the crises, the greater the likelihood that war will result. "If $p_1$, $p_2$, $p_3$, etc., indicate the probability of war in successive crises in the relations of two states and P indicated the probability of war for n crises, then $p = 1-(1-p_1)(1-p_2)(1-p_3) \ldots (1-p_n) \ldots$ . Even though p is very small, as n approaches infinity the probability of war approaches certainty." This might be labeled the "actuarial" view of crises. An insurance company typically charges a higher premium for the person who drives 30,000 miles a year than one who logs only a quarter of that distance on the basis that greater exposure to the highways will increase the probability of a claim. The Wright formulation assumes that each crisis can be thought of as a discrete event and that there is little or no learning from one episode to another; that is, the participants can be thought of as beginning each time with a "crisis management tabula rasa." Thus, the cumulative probability of crises leading to war increases with each incidence of such an event.

An alternative position denies that decision makers begin with a blank slate with the onset of each crisis. Because the participants learn from their experiences, McClelland has suggested that crises become "routinized." "Outputs received from occurrences and situations in the international environment and from sequences of international interaction are processed by the advanced modernizing social organizations according to their perceived characteristics: if these outputs are recognized as familiar and expected experiences met repeatedly in the remembered past, they will be treated in a highly routine fashion." The participants gain experience in ways of coping with environment and adversaries and, although threats and challenges may continue to characterize relations between parties, uncertainty is reduced. Thus, "repeated exposure to acute crises may reduce the probabilities of an outbreak of general war."

In most respects the latter thesis appears to be more realistic than Wright's somewhat mechanical formulation. Nevertheless, it is possible that it assumes too optimistically that there is only one type of learning from history, rather than many variants. The concept of "routinization of crises" assumes that learning will enhance the ability of decision makers to cope with crises in a manner that reduces rather than increases the probabilities of war. However, there is at least some evidence that decision makers do not always draw "lessons" from history in a sophisticated manner that enhances their ability to cope with complex decision-making problems. This process may therefore not invariably operate to enhance the quality of crisis management. The key phrases are "recognized as familiar and expected experiences" and "treated in a highly routine fashion." The dangers are that the diagnosis of a historical parallel may be superficial; that historical models or analogies may be used to shortcut adequate search and analysis of the problem; and that they may provide a set of prescriptions that are applied prematurely and too mechanically (i.e., in a "highly routine fashion") to crises that bear a superficial rather than a fundamental similarity to those from which the "lessons" are drawn. Put somewhat differently, the use of historical models and analogies may result in a short-circuiting of the very processes (diagnosis, search, analysis) that are necessary to determine whether the historical parallels are valid or not.

Perhaps this cursory review of a large literature is sufficient to establish the point that even if there are fewer than a hundred flowers contending for the attention of those undertaking crisis studies, consensus remains an elusive goal rather than an established condition. Stated somewhat differently, the scholar, policy maker, or reformer who searches through the cumulated knowledge about international crisis with expectations of finding broad agreement on key concepts that are linked together in well-established theories, and solidly buttressed by empirical evidence, is not likely to be wholly satisfied.

Lest this appraisal paint an overly pessimistic picture, it is also worth pointing to some signs of genuine progress toward the goals of cumulative knowledge. There is a convergence around, and refinements of, certain key terms and definitions in the literature. There is also a growing willingness to undertake comparative studies in which a single crisis is viewed from several, rather than a single, theoretical perspective, or in which two or more crises are examined in a systematic and rigorous comparative manner. Moreover, there is evidence that the crisis literature that has been heavily skewed toward studies of postwar crises involving one or more of the Superpowers, is now being significantly broadened by research which includes both pre- and post-1945 cases as well as small and middle-range powers. Finally, the concept of crisis itself is being subjected to cross-cultural comparisons in order to understand the involvement of more than one decision system in the anticipation, avoidance, control, and termination of international crises. These several developments suggest promising prospects for policy makers, social scientists, and peace activists concerned with crisis.

See also: *Crisis Management; International Conflicts, De-escalation of*

*Bibliography*

Allison G T 1971 *Essence of Decision: Explaining the Cuban Missile Crisis.* Little, Brown, Boston, Massachusetts
Bell 1971 *Conventions of Crisis: A Study in Diplomatic Management.* Oxford University Press, Oxford
George A L, Hall D, Simons W 1971 *The Limits of Coercive Diplomacy.* Little, Brown, Boston, Massachusetts
Hermann C F (ed.) 1972 *International Crises: Insights from Behavioral Research.* The Free Press, New York
Holsti O R 1972 *Crisis, Escalation, War.* McGill-Queens University Press, Montreal
Janis I 1972 *Victims of Groupthink: A Psychological Study of Foreign-policy Decisions and Fiascoes.* Houghton Mifflin, Boston, Massachusetts
Jervis R 1976 *Perception and Misperception in International Politics.* Princeton University Press, Princeton, New Jersey
Lebow R N 1981 *Between Peace and War: The Nature of International Crisis.* Johns Hopkins University Press, Baltimore, Maryland
McClelland C A 1977 The anticipation of International Crises: Prospects for theory and research. *Int. Stud. Q.* 21
Snyder G H, Diesing P 1977 *Conflict Among Nations: Bargaining, Decision Making and System Structure in International Crises.* Princeton University Press, Princeton, New Jersey
Williams P 1977 *Crisis Management.* Wiley, New York
Wright Q 1965 *A Study of War,* 2nd edn. University of Chicago Press, Chicago, Illinois

OLE R. HOLSTI

# Crisis Management

Some years ago, Robert McNamara stated that "There is no longer any such thing as strategy, only crisis management." Although this may be something of an overstatement, it reflects two facts of contemporary international life. Ours is accurately described as an "age of crisis," and the fate of humankind may well depend on the ability of policy makers to manage effectively the international crises that could trigger off a global conflict.

Many theories of foreign and national security policy incorporate the optimistic assumption that the more crucial the situation, the higher the quality of both policy-making processes and the resulting decisions. This point is perhaps best illustrated by theories of nuclear deterrence (see *Deterrence; Nuclear Deterrence, Doctrine of*), which presuppose rational and predictable decision processes, even during intense and protracted international crises. They assume that threats and ultimata will enhance calculation, control, and caution, while inhibiting recklessness and risk taking. Deterrence theories, in short, tend to be sanguine about the ability of policy makers to be creative when the situation requires it—and never is that requirement greater than during an intense international crisis. This is an oversimplified summary of the rich literature on deterrence. Nevertheless, there is a substantial element of truth in Karl Deutsch's assertion that "the theory of deterrence . . . first proposes that we should frustrate our opponents by frightening them very badly and that we should then rely on their cool-headed rationality for our survival."

To what extent are these premises valid? What is the impact of crisis on policy making? What steps can be taken to enhance the ability of policy makers to deal more effectively with crises? This article focuses on crisis management from a decision-making perspective, with special emphasis on the performance of policy makers who must make crucial decisions under conditions of high stress. It thus supplements a companion article elsewhere in this volume on the broader topic of "crisis" (see *Crisis*).

The most important aspect of crises for our purposes is that these situations are characterized by high stress for the individuals and organizations involved. That a threat to important values is stress-inducing requires little elaboration. The element of surprise is also a contributing factor; there is evidence that unanticipated and novel situations are generally viewed as more threatening. Finally, crises are often marked by almost around-the-clock work schedules, owing to both the severity of the situation and the absence of extended decision time. Lack of rest and excessively long working hours are likely to magnify the stresses inherent in the situation. These attributes of crisis raise a number of questions that are important for crisis management. Most generally, how do policy makers respond to the challenges and demands of crises? Do they tend to approach such situations with high motivation, a keen sense of purpose, extraordinary energy, and an enhanced capacity for creativity? Or, is their capacity for coping with complex problems sometimes impaired, perhaps to the point suggested by Richard Neustadt's phrase (1970) "the paranoid reaction characteristic of crisis behavior?"

## 1. The Impact of Crisis on Decision Making

Although one must be cautious about accepting uncritically the memoirs of policy makers who have experienced major international crises, they can provide at least anecdotal insight into crisis management. Some leaders have been quite optimistic about their abilities to manage even severe international crises. In memoirs written some years before he assumed the presidency, Richard Nixon (1962) wrote

of crises as "mountaintop experiences" in which he often performed at his best: "Only then [in crises] does he discover all the latent strengths he never knew he had and which otherwise would have remained dormant." He added that:

It has been my experience that, more often than not, taking a break is actually an escape from the tough, grinding discipline that is absolutely necessary for superior performance. Many times I have found that my best ideas have come when I thought I could not work for another minute and when I literally had to drive myself to finish the task before a deadline. Sleepless nights, to the extent that the body can take them, can stimulate creative mental activity.

Herman Kahn (1965) has appraised the effects of crisis on decision making in a similar vein suggesting, for example, that "a decision maker may, in a crisis, be able to invent or work out easily and quickly what seems in normal times to both the 'academic' scholar and the layman to be hypothetical, unreal, complex, or otherwise difficult."

These observations appear to confirm the conventional wisdom that in crisis decision making, necessity is indeed the mother of invention. However, the recollections of others who have experienced intense and protracted crises suggest they may be marked at times by great skill in crisis management, and in other instances by decision processes and outcomes that fail to meet even the most permissive standards of effective policy making. Some recall the "sense of elation that comes with crises," whereas others admit to serious shortcomings in their own performance during such situations. Indeed, the Watergate episode suggests that Nixon's performance during the culminating crisis of his presidency was at best erratic, certainly falling far short of his own self-diagnosis as described above. Perhaps even more sobering is Robert Kennedy's recollection (1969) of his colleagues' performance during the Cuban missile crisis: "That kind of [crisis-induced] pressure does strange things to a human being, even to brilliant, self-confident, experienced men. For some it brings out characteristics and strengths that perhaps they never knew they had, and for others the pressure is too overwhelming."

But anecdotes do not provide a sufficient basis for addressing the questions posed earlier. Psychological evidence generally suggests that severe and protracted stress erodes the cognitive abilities needed to cope effectively with complex tasks. One might object, however, that such experimental findings are of limited relevance in the "real world" of international crises because they do not adequately take into account the executive's prior experience in coping with crises. Will not experience, when combined with selective recruitment and promotion, weed out those who cannot stand "the heat in the kitchen" well before they reach top leadership positions? Because individuals differ in abilities to cope with crises and stress, the point at which increasing stress begins to hamper cognitive performance, and the rate at which it does so, is not the same for all persons. But only the most optimistic will assume that the correlation between the importance of the executive's role and ability to manage intensely stressful crises approaches unity.

A second possible objection to reliance on evidence about the impact of crisis-induced stress on individuals is that foreign policy leaders rarely need to face crises alone. They can instead draw upon support and resources from both advisory groups and the larger organizations of which they are a part. This point is valid, but on further examination it is not wholly comforting. There is some evidence that during crises advisory groups may be vulnerable to such malfunctions as "groupthink." There may, moreover, be a tendency to consult others less as the pressure of time increases, as well as to rely more heavily upon those who support the prevailing policy assumptions. Finally, leaders differ not only in their "executive styles" but also in their abilities to employ advisory groups effectively—that is, in ways that may help them to counteract some of the potentially adverse consequences of crisis. Even the same executive may demonstrate great skill during one crisis and equal ineptitude in another instance. John F. Kennedy's use of advisers during the missile crisis and the Bay of Pigs fiasco are illustrative in this respect.

When we turn our attention to research on foreign policy crises, the evidence about the impact of stress on crisis management is mixed. Shlaim (1963) found that the stress experienced by American policy makers during the Berlin blockade crisis (1948-49) did not erode their ability to perform vital decision-making tasks. Lentner's study (in Hermann 1972) of State Department officials revealed that only about a third of the respondents felt a reduction in perceived alternatives as a result of crisis. In their impressive analysis of a dozen international crises—including Fashoda (1898), Bosnia (1908-09), Munich (1938), Iran (1945-46), and Berlin (1948-49)—Snyder and Diesing found no evidence of adverse consequences arising from high stress. Yet they did report that misperception, miscalculation, and other cognitive malfunctions were common occurrences during the

crises. Drawing on his research on Israeli behavior during the crises of 1956, 1967, and 1970, Brecher (1974) found strong support for the hypotheses that time will be perceived as more salient, decision makers will become more concerned with the immediate rather than the distant future, and that they will perceive the range of alternatives open to themselves to be narrow. The negative consequences of stress on crisis management also emerge from Holsti's study (1972) of the 1914 crisis.

These mixed results are not surprising, nor should they result in premature and overly optimistic assumptions about crisis management. Interest in the effects of stress on crisis management does not depend on finding that *every* crisis resulted in substandard decision-making performance, any more than concern for the consequences of smoking must await evidence that all smokers develop lung cancer. The much more interesting and important questions emerge precisely at the point of recognizing that the dangers and opportunities inherent in crises can give rise to various patterns of coping, some effective, others much less so. At that point our attention is directed to a series of further questions—for example, what are the decision-making structures, personal attributes of leaders, strategies of crisis management, and other variables that are associated with more or less effectiveness?

## 2. Prescriptive Theories of Crisis Management

Given the potentially catastrophic consequences of crises that escalate beyond the control of policy makers—as in 1914—it is not surprising that a good deal of social science research on the topic has been directed toward developing prescriptive theories of crisis management. Despite a shared desire to help officials cope more effectively with crises, there are at least two somewhat different schools of thought on the matter. These parallel to some extent the two elements in the Chinese character for crisis—danger and opportunity.

The first perspective tends to place greater emphasis on the opportunities than the dangers in crises. The goal is to prevail over the adversary. The primary task of crisis management is to communicate one's interests and demands as unambiguously as possible in order to prevent miscalculation on the part of adversaries. With a clear exposition of these interests, it is assumed that the adversary will either back down (thereby ending the crisis on favorable terms), or demonstrate a calculated willingness to escalate the conflict (and thus revealing no interest in resolving it except on the adversary's own terms).

Some have suggested strategies of crisis management that include a cautious application of coercive diplomacy to protect vital interests. Others have proposed also using such techniques as "burning one's bridges" and similar forms of seemingly irrational behavior that are intended, by conveying an unambiguous message of one's unyielding resolve and commitment, to force the adversary to yield. In summary, according to this viewpoint the dangers of crises are best dealt with by firmness, a policy that may also provide opportunities for gains at the expense of the adversary. For example, some critics of the Kennedy Administration have argued that the missile crisis, had it been dealt with more forcefully, provided an opportunity for removal not only of the Soviet missiles but also of the Castro regime.

A rather different prescriptive approach to crisis management places emphasis not only on protecting one's vital interests, but also on avoiding actions that might drive an opponent into a mutually undesirable escalation of the conflict. Theorists described in the previous paragraph believe that the primary danger of crisis management is that unwise concessions or compromises will mislead a thoroughly rational opponent into making further demands (the "appeasement model") (see *Appeasement Policy*); the opposing view is that an overly rigid policy might lead the adversary, whose rationality is probably not without limits under circumstances of crisis-induced stress, to escalate the conflict in ways that could ultimately be catastrophic to both sides. According to this view, then, it is important not to push the adversary into a corner in which its alternatives are reduced to two— humiliating defeat or escalation.

Effective crisis management would appear to rely upon some elements of both approaches. Capitulation may bring a crisis to an end without escalation, but policy makers can scarcely be expected to accept that as a panacea, especially when vital interests are at stake. At the same time, a relentless drive to force the adversary into a humiliating defeat may, at best and with good luck, succeed in some situations. However, it can hardly be a prescription for all circumstances and all times because the adversary may regard escalation, even if that entails a high risk of ruinous costs and probable defeat, as preferable to capitulation.

Among those who have attempted to provide more specific guidelines for crisis management there has been some convergence. For example, Alexander George's "requirements for controlled, measured use of force and effective crisis management" in the context of the United States are: presidential control of military options; pauses in military operations; clear and appropriate demonstrations; military actions coordinated with political-diplomatic action; confidence in the effectiveness and discriminating character of military options; military options that avoid motivating the opponent to escalate; and avoidance of impression of resort to large-scale warfare. These overlap to some extent with Holsti's list: sensivity to the adversary's frame of reference; avoidance of steps which seal off "escape routes"; use of a combination of sticks and carrots to reduce the adversary's incentives to escalate; sensitivity to the point that, especially in crisis diplomacy, actions speak louder than words; efforts to slow the pace of events; and maintenance of control over not only broad strategic decisions, but also over the details of implementation. Richard Ned Lebow (1971), Irving Janis (1972), Phil Williams (1977), Coral Bell, Thomas Milburn (1972), and others have also proposed prescriptive theories of crisis management.

Although there may be some agreement on certain aspects of crisis management, serious students of the issue are acutely aware of the many limitations of their prescriptive theories.

(a) Even the best prescriptive theories do not offer panaceas that can be used mechanically in all circumstances.

(b) There is no assurance that policy recommendations, even if based on the best social science research, will be accepted by decision makers.

(c) Prescriptive theories of crisis management cannot offer much help if one of the parties is determined to gain a total victory. They can only offer some assistance when all of those caught up in a crisis share at least some interest in resolving it short of total war.

See also: *Crisis; International Conflicts, De-escalation of; Avoiding Conflict by Preventive Diplomacy: West New Guinea, 1951*

*Bibliography*

Bell C 1971 *Conventions of Crisis: A Study of Diplomatic Management.* Oxford University Press, Oxford
Brecher M 1993 *Crisis in World Politics: Theory and Reality.* Pergamon Press, New York
Deutsch K W 1963 *Nerves of Government.* Free Press, New York
George A L, Hall D, Simons W 1971 *The Limits of Coercive Diplomacy.* Little, Brown, Boston, Massachusetts
Hermann C F (ed.) 1972 *International Crises: Insights from*

*Behavioral Research*. Free Press, New York

Holsti O R 1972 *Crisis, Escalation, War.* McGill-Queens University Press, Montreal

Janis I 1972 *Victims of Groupthink: A Psychological Study of Foreign Policy Decisions and Fiascoes.* Houghton Mifflin, Boston, Massachusetts

Kahn H 1965 *On Escalation: Metaphors and Scenarios.* Praeger, New York

Kennedy R 1969 *Thirteen Days.* Norton, New York

Lebow R N 1981 *Between Peace and War: The Nature of International Crisis.* Johns Hopkins University Press, Baltimore, Maryland

Lentner H H 1972 The concept of crisis as viewed by the US Department of State. In: Hermann C F (ed.) 1972

Milburn T W 1972 The management of crisis. In: Hermann C F (ed.) 1972

Neustadt R 1970 *Alliance Politics.* Columbia University Press, New York

Nixon R 1962 *Six Crises.* Doubleday, New York

Schelling T C 1963 *The Strategy of Conflict.* Oxford University Press, New York

Shlaim A 1983 *The United States and the Berlin Blockade, 1948-1949: A Study in Crisis Decision Making.* University of California Press, Berkeley, California

Smoke R 1977 *War: Controlling Escalation.* Harvard University Press, Cambridge, Massachusetts

Snyder G H, Diesing P 1977 *Conflict among Nations: Bargaining, Decision Making and System Structure in International Crises.* Princeton University Press, Princeton, New Jersey

Stein J, Tanter R 1980 *Crisis Decision Making: Rationality and Israel's Choices.* Ohio State University Press, Columbus, Ohio

Williams P 1977 *Crisis Management.* Wiley, New York

OLE R. HOLSTI

# Critical Security Studies

Critical Security Studies represents an important departure in the academic study of security, strategy and peace. The approach owes its genesis to two coincidental developments: the end of the Cold War; and major debates within the social sciences as to their nature, purpose and method. Both developments ask fundamental questions about some of the central tenets that underpinned traditional Security Studies and Peace Studies alike (see *Theoretical Traditions of Peace and Conflict Studies*). The vibrant and often contentious exchanges that have resulted from this period of geopolitical transformation and intellectual uncertainty look set to continue well beyond the end of the 1990s. Nevertheless, the contours of a new approach are now clearly emerging. Critical Security Studies, as it has come to be known, is nothing if not ambitious. Its proponents not only offer a thorough-going critique of both the theory and practice of the hitherto dominant, traditional approach to security (usually called Strategic Studies or National Security Studies). They also aim to provide intellectual support and justification for alternative security practices that can emancipate humanity from the fear and insecurity which dominate the lives of people across the world.

## 1. The Critique of Traditional Security Studies

Traditional Security Studies was in many ways a direct product of the Cold War (see *Cold War*). Despite ritualistic references to such great military thinkers of the past such as Sun Tzu and Clausewitz,

the subject was almost exclusively concerned with superpower rivalry, and in particular its nuclear manifestations. It was the perceived exigencies of Cold War competition that encouraged Security Studies to flourish in Western academia and research institutes. Furthermore, from the late 1940s onwards, such was the symbiotic nature of the relationship between security specialists in academia and defence establishments in government and industry that some posited the existence of a military-industrial-academic complex; each element had vested interest in promoting a militarised conception of relations between states.

The ethical issues raised by this entanglement were trenchantly highlighted in the 1960s by such writers as Anatol Rapoport and Philip Green, but equally as problematic for the future of human security was the state-centric conceptualisation of the subject (see *Human Security*). Making sovereign states conceived in rather simplistic unitary terms, the exclusive 'referent object' for the understanding of security issues had far-reaching implications. Because Cold War Security Studies was *about* states, for example, with the security of individuals were subsumed under the ambit of the state, and were often sacrificed to the demands of *realpolitik*. The more secure the apartheid state of South Africa became, for example (in terms of strong borders and increased legitimacy for the regime) the less secure became the lives of the majority of the population. Security Studies, implicitly or explicitly, generated information and analysis *for* states, and specifically for the ruling elites within them. Security Studies within Universities became an arm of statism.

Moreover, Cold War Security Studies conceived state security in almost exclusively militarised terms. Security was equated with military security. True, during the era of détente and oil shocks from the late 1960s to the mid-1970s, a broader range of issues was allowed on the agenda, in recognition of the growing sensitivity of economic and environmental concerns. However, this constituted more of a parenthesis rather than a break; things returned quickly to security-business-as-usual with the re-intensification of the Cold War in the late 1970s.

Traditional Security Studies was never without its critics. As already noted, some questioned whether close involvement with government was compatible with scholarly independence. But criticism was not confined to academia. Events such as the 'Ban the Bomb' marches in Britain in the late 1950s, support for the 'nuclear freeze' in the United States in the 1980s, and growing demands in Western Europe for 'pan-European' perspectives, illustrated that cross-cutting differences over the theory and practice of security existed even within the West.

In the early 1980s, the widespread fear and disaffection created by the Second Cold War led to two inter-related and hugely significant developments. First, the introduction of Cruise and Pershing II missiles into western Europe led a massive resurgence in peace activism that challenged some of the central nostrums of security policy. The newly invigorated peace movement also inspired and was inspired by a second development, namely the growth of 'alternative defence' thinking, which challenged the establishment and its experts on their own grounds.

The crucial insight upon which 'alternative defence' (see *Alternative Defense*) was based was that the zero-sum notions of security prevalent during the Cold War were actually destabilising, and a major source of *insecurity* in international relations. Thus for alternative defence thinkers, real peace and security was not just the absence of war, but rather depended on the establishment of the conditions for social justice and mutual understanding—a view also shared by Peace Research. Alternative defence thinking concentrated on seeking means whereby the so-called 'security dilemma' could at least be mitigated. Consequently they developed such concepts as common security, non-offensive defence, a nuclear freeze, military confidence building, democracy and disarmament, 'détente from below,' and alternative security orders. Surprisingly perhaps, it was ultimately in the Eastern bloc that these ideas were to have most impact. The

principles and precepts of 'alternative defence' directly influenced the 'new thinking' that emerged in the former Soviet Union after 1986 under its new leader Mikhail Gorbachev (see Nobel Peace Prize Laureates: *Mikhail Gorbachev*). Despite being condemned in many Western capitals for being hopelessly deluded and idealistic, alternative defence thinkers played a crucial role in the ending of the Cold War.

## 2. *Towards a Critical Security Studies*

Given the symbiotic relationship between the Cold War and Security Studies, it is not surprising that the end of the former led to a crisis in the latter. Not least among the factors that have led some to call for a fundamental rethink of the way security is conceptualised has been the inability of 'security specialists' to respond adequately in the face of the new—or old, but hitherto neglected—issues which have emerged since the late 1980s. These issues have forced all but the most hidebound to reconsider what we actually mean when we use the term 'security,' and what is the appropriate 'referent object' for security discourse. Proponents of Critical Security Studies have combined an eagerness to explore these crucial issues with a commitment also to reconsider the methodology by which security should be studied. Again, the influence of the alternative defence thinkers of the early 1980s is important here. They had been concerned to support and influence those social movements that had emerged to protest the continuing superpower arms spiral. In doing this they had broken fundamentally from traditional security specialists who had often claimed a spurious objectivity and detachment for their work while in reality their teaching and research legitimised the prevailing status quo by making it into a 'false necessity.'

Through their rejection of simplistic notions of 'detachment' and 'objectivity,' alternative defence thinkers were precursors of a much more widespread move in the social sciences to question the very nature and purpose of social research. While such questioning has been vigorous, there has been little consensus as to what might constitute acceptable answers. This is reflected in Critical Security Studies where there is disagreement, for example, between those who follow such post-structuralist thinkers as Foucault and Derrida on methodological issues, and those who are more persuaded by the arguments of Critical Theorists such as Habermas. Nevertheless, whatever their differences, all proponents of Critical Security Studies seem to regard the ultimate aim of their work as aiding in the transformation of prevailing patterns of power and domination in favour of those who are currently disempowered and disenfranchised. In the case of thinkers influenced by Critical Theory, this intent is recognised in terms of an explicit commitment to human emancipation.

As well as introducing a new level of methodological awareness and sophistication into Security Studies, proponents of Critical Security Studies have also re-worked the key concept of 'security' in important ways. In doing so they have provided new answers to such central questions as: What is security? Whose security should we be concerned about? And, what is the purpose of studying security? The answers to these questions provide the basis for the claim of supporters of Critical Security Studies that it represents 'the next stage' in this new era of world politics.

## 3. What is Security?

As we have already seen, traditional Security Studies understood security in almost entirely military terms. This may have had a certain logic during the period nuclear, mutual assured destruction (MAD). However, even then, this understanding did not produce a conceptualisation of security that spoke the concerns of the vast majority of the world's population living in the Third World: for them a broader conception of security always made more sense. In the wake of the end of the Cold War, the narrowly militarised understanding of security simply became anachronistic (see *World Peace Order, Dimensions of a*). The vocabulary of nuclear deterrence, arms control, limited war and superpower crisis management had minimal relevance in a world in which the salient security concerns increasingly related to ethnic conflict, refugee flows, famine, peaceful settlement of disputes, the politics of identity, confidence-building, humanitarian intervention, conventional war, and so on. A narrowly militarised understanding fails to grasp the complexity of the 'new' issues on the security agenda, not to mention their life-and-death relevance to many people on the planet.

Barry Buzan's seminal study *People, States and Fear* (1983), was the first sustained attempt from within Security Studies to re-draw a broader notion of security that moved beyond a purely military focus. Although still arguing within a state-centric framework, Buzan argued that by paying disproportionate attention to the military dimension, analysts ignored other issues which were of equal importance when it came to understanding how policy-makers and populations alike perceive their security interests. In response, he proposed to broaden the concep-

tualisation of security to include four other 'sectors' in addition to that of the military: these were political, economic, societal and environmental sectors. This influential formulation has been criticised. Some traditionalists argue that adopting a broader conception of security will dilute the coherence of Security Studies. Some radical critics are wary of the danger that labeling issues such as environmental degradation as 'security concerns' will lead to their militarisation. However, these arguments have been forcefully countered by those who favour the 'broadening of security.' On the one hand they have pointed out that the parsimoniousness of the traditional approach has blinded analysts to the inter-relationship between different threats, or in Buzan's terms, between the different sectors. Thus one of the consequences of rejecting any attempt to narrow the analysis through an arbitrary definition is to allow for a more variegated and realistic assessment of the dynamics of security. Interestingly, a broader notion of security also echoes what is increasingly becoming state practice. Even Britain, for example, now distinguishes between 'defence policy,' which focuses exclusively on the military dimension, and 'security policy,' which takes a broader view incorporating economic and trade issues.

In response to worries that 'broadening security' runs the risk of militarising the new issues incorporated into the security agenda, supporters argue that broadening is itself part of a move to promulgate a different understanding of security: this understanding rejects the zero-sum notions prevalent during the Cold War.

In addition to supporting moves to broaden notions of security, proponents of Critical Security Studies have also called for its 'deepening.' Deepening involves the recognition that security is a derivative concept. That is, our conceptions of security depend on the particular philosophical world-view we have. Traditional Security Studies was based on an often-implicit understanding of a world characterised by a continual struggle for power among sovereign states competing in an anarchical international system. According to this understanding, inter-state conflict is endemic and is destined to remain so, and this should establish the character of Security Studies. However, while this view may have achieved the status of 'common-sense' among Cold War security specialists, this is far from being the only possible world-view. When conceptions of security are derived from alternative perspectives—those of Feminists, Marxists, world order thinkers and so on—very different understandings of 'security' emerge.

Recognising the derivative nature of security, Critical Security Studies has sought to expose and criticize the world-view that has underpinned traditional Security Studies and explore the understandings of security that can be built on the basis of possible alternatives. To this end Critical Security Studies is concerned to explore regional security questions, including those of a military character, and promote thinking about practical policies to advance the security of people as individuals and groups.

## 4. Whose Security?

One of the most pervasive of the assumptions underlying traditional Security Studies is state-centrism. State-centrism privileges the role of the state in world politics, regarding it as the sole legitimate focus for decision making and loyalty. The state became the only referent object of Cold War Security Studies. Strategic problems were analysed in terms of their impact on states. 'National security' was stressed as opposed to the security of individuals, groups of one sort or another, civil society, world society or common humanity. The justification for this was the doctrine that the state provides security for its own citizens. However, even a cursory examination of the empirical reality of world politics exposes the fact that this is a hopelessly idealised view. States tend to prioritise threats to their own security and often end up neglecting those posed to individuals, groups within the state, and certainly humanity as a whole. Indeed, in many cases, the state itself is one of the main threats to the security of its own population. This fact is all too well confirmed by the widespread pattern of state-sanctioned political oppression, human rights violations and torture.

Rather than continue to privilege states as the referent object for Security Studies, proponents of the Critical approach such as Ken Booth have insisted on viewing states as means rather than ends in themselves. That is, while states may in some cases be providers of security, and are certainly a crucially important element in the politics of security, this does not mean that they should be privileged as referents for the theory and practice of security. In his article 'Security and Emancipation,' Booth argues that the ultimate referent for security should be individual human beings. This formulation has not won universal acceptance even in the critical camp. Some, for example, have suggested that 'civil society' is a more appropriate referent. However, given that making individuals the 'ultimate' referent for discussion of security concerns does not preclude—in fact, encour-

ages—consideration of the boarder contexts in which human beings live their lives, the logic of favouring the individual referent is particularly strong.

## 5. What Sort of Security Studies?

In addition to challenging the way in which security has been conceptualised, Critical Security Studies also offers an alternative understanding of the meaning and purpose of studying security in the context of universities. As we have noted, behind a veil of spurious detachment and objectivity, traditional Security Studies has served the interests of statism and official thinking. Ultimately the subject has legitimised and supported the interests of those who benefit from the *status quo*, on both a local and global scale. Critical Security Studies follows in the tradition of alternative defence thinking by regarding itself as thought in the service of 'bottom-up' progressive social change. Robert Cox has famously argued that 'all theory is for someone and for some purpose.' If this is the case then Critical Security Studies is primarily for those made insecure by the prevailing order. In Critical Theory terms, its purpose is to aid in the process of their emancipation.

## 6. Critical Security Studies and the Future

The traditional, Cold War approach to security has attracted many critics, though it is still resilient in many institutions. Critical Security Studies is perhaps best understood as an attempt to bring together these various strands of criticism and to weld them into a coherent whole. A variety of different approaches have important contributions to make to the Critical Security Studies project: the work of the Peace Researchers in widening the concept of violence and emphasising the positive conception of peace; the work of alternative defence thinkers in focusing on 'common security' and ways of mitigating the security dilemma; the work of critics within Security Studies in broadening the security agenda; the role of Third World specialists in emphasising the role of the structure of the international economic system in engendering insecurity in the South; the insights of feminists in underlining the relationship between the personal, the political and the international, and demonstrating the centrality of identity politics to the understanding international phenomena; the analyses of Critical Theorists in exposing traditional approaches to theory and in outlining a theoretical approach explicitly oriented towards human emancipation; and, the work of World Order theorists (WOMPERs) in outlining alternative visions of attainable and sustainable world orders (see *World Order Models Project (WOMP)*).

By bringing these strands together and giving them more methodological sophistication, a new direction and greater coherence, Critical Security Studies hopes to become an important voice informing and legitimising those political practices which promote security, community and emancipation to the whole of humanity.

*Bibliography*

Booth K 1991a Security and emancipation. *Rev. Int'l Stud.* 17(4)

Booth K 1991b A Security regime in Southern Africa: Theoretical considerations. *Southern African Perspectives* 30 (February), Centre for Southern African Studies, University of the Western Cape

Booth K (ed.) 1999 *Security, Community and Emancipation: An Introduction to Critical Security Studies*. Lynne Rienner Publications, Boulder, Colo

Buzan B 1991 *People, Sates and Fear: An Agenda for International Security Studies*, 2nd edn. (first edition published in 1983), Harvester Wheatsheaf, London

Buzan B, Wæver O, de Wilde J 1998 *Security: A New Framework for Analysis*. Lynne Rienner Publications, Boulder, Colo

Cox R W 1981 Social Forces, States and World Orders: Beyond International Relations Theory. *Millennium: J. International Relations* 10(2)

Krause K, Michael C W 1997 *Critical Security Studies: Cases and Concepts*. Minnesota University Press, Minneapolis

Wæver O, Buzan B, Kelstrup M, Lemaitre P 1993 *Identity, Migration and the New Security Agenda in Europe*. Pinter, London

Wyn J R 1999 *Strategy, Security and Critical Theory*. Lynne Rienner Publications, Boulder, Colo

Wyn J R, Tooze R (eds.) 1999 *Critical Theory and World Politics*. Lynne Rienner Publications, Boulder, Colo

RICHARD WYN JONES; KEN BOOTH

# Crucé, Emeric

Emeric Crucé (c. 1590-1648) was an obscure French scholar, possibly a monk, who in 1623 published an intriguing essay on the way to achieve a stable and lasting peace throughout the world. Virtually nothing is known of his life, but his book, *The New Cyneas*, is of great interest. Its title refers to a story told by the Roman historian Plutarch about an ancient Thessalonian statesman named Cyneas. According to plutarch, Cyneas's arguments on the folly of war so impressed King Pyrrhus that he made him one of his chief advisers.

Crucé addressed his work to the kings and rulers of the earth, on the grounds that questions of war and peace were in their hands, rather than in those of their subjects. He began by advising these rulers to look first to the order and prosperity of their own states, arguing that restless and miserable populations served as fertile ground for all sorts of violence and chaos. In an age when internal disorders in France, Holland, and Germany had produced prolonged and vicious international conflicts, his concern was eminently justified. He urged princes to make their subjects happy by avoiding religious persecution and despotic acts, by encouraging commerce and education, and by maintaining sound currency. If they did these things, he maintained, their subjects would have no wish to disturb the peace by rebelling, and tranquillity and international peace could be more easily preserved.

Crucé also enjoined rulers to encourage international trade by cooperating on such projects as the construction of canals connecting one nation with another and the suppression of piracy. Anticipating such later figures as Richard Cobden (see *Cobden, Richard*), he argued that such measures would not only improve their subjects' standard of living, but by fostering economic interdependence and increasing contacts between peoples, would be a significant deterrent to war.

The centerpiece of Crucé's plan for peace was his suggestion that the kingdoms and other realms of the world send ambassadors to a permanent court of arbitration. This court would be designed to resolve all disputes which might arise between nations, thus making war unnecessary. For such a body to work, he insisted, all of its decisions would have to be accepted as binding by everyone. In Crucé's words, "all the said Princes will swear to uphold as inviolable law whatever would be ordained by the majority of voters in the said assembly, and to pursue with arms those who would wish to oppose it." The prospect of being attacked by the entire world, he hoped, would deter even the most impetuous princes from trying to take by war that which was denied to them by the international assembly. Crucé further argued that this assembly could not only resolve disputes without war, but could prevent serious grievances from arising in the first place by promoting mutual understanding between rulers and by serving as a watchdog to nip potential problems in the bud.

Crucé was not the first person to argue for an international assembly to preserve the peace—his countryman Pierre Dubois (see *Dubois, Pierre*) predated him by nearly four centuries—but his ideas contain several noteworthy features which cannot be found in earlier schemes. First, he appears to have appreciated the advantages of a permanent body watching over international peace, as opposed to an assembly which would be called into session only after a problem had reached the point of threatening the peace. Second, he clearly recognized the importance of an advance pledge of acceptance of binding arbitration, and of concerted action against any breaker of that pledge.

Furthermore, all previous plans for peacekeeping leagues of princes which had come from Western writers had limited membership to Christian states. Indeed, their stated purpose was invariably to create a strong Christian commonwealth at peace with itself which could wage effective war against the hated infidel. Crucé, however, based his entire belief in the value of peace on the concept of the brotherhood of man, regardless of race or creed. "Why should I, a Frenchman," he asked, "wish harm to an Englishman, a Spaniard, or a Hindoo? I cannot wish it when I consider that they are men like me . . . and that all nations are bound together by a natural and consequently indestructible tie, which ensures that [no] man can consider another a stranger."

Crucé's proposed league would include even Christendom's most dreaded enemies, the Turks. Cruce, in fact, proposed that the Turkish ruler be given precedence above all secular Christian princes, placing him second only to the pope. He also hoped to attract the Persians, Chinese, Ethiopians, Mongols, and Russians, giving their rulers rank behind the rulers of Europe's Holy Roman Empire, France, and Spain, but ahead of every other Western prince. At a lower rank, he placed the rulers of Japan, Morocco, and India, and voiced the hope that these men as well

as the rulers of other African and Asian states yet unknown would all join his league. To facilitate such a membership he proposed that the assembly meet in the Italian city of Venice, since its position on the Mediterranean Sea made it accessible to Africa and Asia, as well as to Europe.

Cruce was clearly a man ahead of his time. Though his book was issued in a second edition in 1624, indicating that it had attracted some interest, it soon dropped out of sight. In one of the few mentions of it by one of Cruce's contemporaries, the great philosopher Leibniz remarked some decades after its publication that he recalled having read the book in his youth, but had no idea of how to obtain a copy. Indeed, by the nineteenth century, only three copies of *The New Cyneas* were known to exist. Not until the twentieth century was he given recognition for his pioneering work on international institutions, and seen as one of the intellectual forefathers of such modern institutions as the World Court, the League of Nations, and the United Nations.

*Bibliography*

Balch T W (ed.) 1909 *The New Cyneas of Émeric Cruce.* Allen, Lane, and Scott, Philadelphia, Pennsylvania
Butler G 1970 *Studies in Statecraft.* Kennikat, Port Washington, New York
Cruce É 1972 *The New Cineas.* Garland, New York
Louis-Lucas P 1919 *Un Plan de paix générale et de liberté de commerce au XVIIe siècle: Le Nouveau Cynée d'Émeric Cruce.* Sirey, Paris
Pajot H 1924 *Un Rêveur de paix sous Louis XIII: Émeric Cruce, parisien.* Presses Universitaires de France, Paris
Souleyman E V 1941 *The Vision of World Peace in Seventeenth and Eighteenth Century France.* Putnam, New York
Van den Dungen P 1980 *The Hidden History of a Peace "Classic:" Émeric Cruce's 'Le Nouveau Cynée.'* Housmans, London

GARRETT L. MCAINSH

# CTBT **in Indian Perception**

*1. Introduction*

In recent years, never perhaps in relations between states, has any drafting of a treaty been so universally espoused and been the subject of so much discussion and negotiation as the CTBT. Notwithstanding it is also an unparalleled irony of history that only one

country, e.g., India, which has been consistently espousing the cause of suspension and halting of atomic weapons tests since her earliest days of first Prime Minister Nehru, by giving her dissenting note vetoed the treaty and thereby blocked the mandated transmittal to GA which subsequently endorsed the treaty by an overwhelming majority.

Such a solitary Indian attitude, obviously contrary to the wishes of the rest of the world, may appear in common eye an obstructionist and unhelpful behaviour of India. However it is worth noting that while the rest of the world was totally not appreciative of this Indian stand, the Indian nation stood as one, with the exception of a microscopic minority of few columnists belonging to the American lobby in India.

In the circumstances 'Indian Perception of the CTBT' necessitates a thorough analysis.

## 2. CTBT: Was It a Fresh Framework?

Though the CTBT negotiations started from January 1994 at the UNGA level yet the world media focussed world attention of the new nomenclature of 'Comprehensive' only after the GA resolution of December 12, 1995 leading common people to regard it as a fresh framework. The above representation is not historically true. Any one conversant with the functioning of UN knows it very well that the 'Comprehensive Test Ban' proposal owes its origin to the 1956-57 fruitless USA-USSR joint deliberative proposal. After this there started the era of Trilateral Proposals (USA, UK and USSR) and the consequent GA resolutions viz A/RES/2372 (XVIII) and A/RES/2028 (XX). As such talks were suspended during the following Cold War days and came to be revived only in the Nineties after the termination of the Cold War so the comprehensive terminology went in disuse. As the world during the last three decades has been familiar with only Nuclear Treaties, e.g., TBT of 1963, SALT-I of 1974 SALT-II of 1979 and Washington Summit Treaty of 1987, so the proposed CTBT came to be looked upon world-wide as a fresh framework. Thus it was not a novel phenomenon but a revival of the old CTB talks.

## 3. CTBT Stipulations (1992-95)

Coming into power by Mr. Clinton and India having the New Prime Minister Rao resulted in a brief interlude of mutual reconciliation enabling the two countries to co-sponsor the CTBT resolution in 1993 and repetition of the same in the 1994. But the same condition of relationship could not continue and in 1995 India declined to co-sponsor the CTBT resolution.

The CD was to decide the political and legal basis for the CTBT. An approved draft by all the 44 participating nations with nuclear reactor programmes was to be enacted to reach the GA by September 18, 1996. The CTBT was to enter into force by January 1997. If one member country did not approve the draft it was to be considered as vetoed. If an approved draft was not pos-

sible a detailed report had to be submitted. "The nuclear countries have agreed to have a Review Conference after three years of the signing of the Treaty." They had further agreed upon "The procedures to penalize the defaulters after the treaty came into force and also as to how the defaulter will be identified and what physical verifications will be necessary for legal action."

The CTBT in its operative body of the text "Binds the non-nuclear states not to manufacture or acquire weapons and reciprocally it also binds the nuclear states not to give to non-nuclear states either nuclear weapons or help in producing such weapons." Under another operative provision "each of the parties to the treaty undertakes to pursue negotiations in good faith in (a) affective measures regarding cessation of the nuclear arms race and (b) on a treaty on general and complete disarmament."

## 4. CTBT Negotiations

Initially the CTBT negotiations were held at the Ad Hoc Committee's level in which not only the non-aligned and non-nuclear states voiced their disagreements but even nuclear powers, like France, China and Russia, also voiced some reservations (see CTBT Negotiations: Analysis and Assessment). It is just possible India was emboldened by their attitudes. But India could not visualise the American diplomatic manipulative skill in managing the consent and accomodation of the French agreement of June 1995 about receiving the research data on advanced laboratory and computer testing and meeting the Chinese demand for the technological adjustments about the procedures of verifications as well as the securing of Russia's acceptance of the 'Zero-yield Test' provision. Side by side the acceptance of the Tripartite proposal of the EIF clause XIV making the signing of the treaty obligatory by the threshold states, by America by giving up its original idea of ratification by a simple majority of 40 or more states, got the support of other nuclear powers.

These very facts of American 'Appeasement' and 'Accomodation' enabled America in ensuring the overwhelming support of the participating countries to the modified CTBT draft (see Appeasement Policy; Problem Solving in Internationalized Conflicts).

## 5. CTBT Draft

The Chairman of the CD and Ad Hoc Committee Mr. Ramaker prepared the June 28, 1996 consensus draft on the above stated modified lines, particularly including the EIF clause XIV for being placed before the ensuing plenary session of the CD. Prior to it a consternation had been caused in the CD due to the Indian categorical denial of accepting the 'so called consensus draft as it stood then' in its statement of June 20, 1996.

Prior to this firm stand of India America had been optimistically expecting India to fall in line with the American stand and in the last hour to agree to the CTBT draft. The past behaviours of the Rao government of India had largely been responsible for such an optimistic American expectation. Co-sponsoring the American resolution of 1993 for CTBT and renewal of same in 1994, slackening the defense budgets for defense after the Rajiv government, connivance in not showing keen interest in 'Agni' and 'Prithvi' missile programme and more particularly withdrawal by India of its resolution regarding the treaty for the complete elimination of the nuclear weapons from the 1994 UNGA had been responsible for the above stated American hope. President Clinton had written a personal letter to the new Indian Prime Minister Mr. Devegowda imploring him to sign the proposed draft.

Despite all these, as well as the American undiplomatic threats to India, the Indian ambassador to the UN as well as the Indian Foreign Secretary made it clear in the Ad Hoc Committee that India would veto the proposed draft.

In the circumstances the P-5 powers held informal consultations among themselves in the third week of August 1996, before the plenary session of the CD to draw up a strategy on how to mobilise support in defeating the obstructionist attitude of India as shown in spoiling their tedious negotiating efforts for enabling the transmittal of the CTBT draft from the CD to the resumed 50th session of the UNGA.

## 6. Logically Proper Course of Action

As the draft documents, stitched together by the CD Chairman, more or less in accordance with the wishes of the USA and the other nuclear weapon states, had been vetoed by India so the proper course of action on the part of the CD would have been to refer back the issue again to the Ad Hoc Committee for further negotiations and to report the news of the lack of consensus to the GA along with the text of national statements of the participating countries made at the Ad Hoc Committee level, implying that negotiations had not been as yet over.

## 7. UNGA Adopts the CTBT

With a view to negotiating the Indian blocking of the transmittal of the CTBT draft from the mandated CD to the resumed 50th session of the GA the P-5 had succeeded in finding the way out, i.e., 'the alternate route,' by persuading Australia to play the 'procedural trick' of moving a resolution calling upon the GA to approve its national statement, including the June 28 draft as prepared by the President of the CD, and signing the treaty and later on to become parties to it at the earliest.

In fact what the delegates had before them was not what had been asked for but instead a technically 'stalled' or 'flawed' draft presented by Australia and co-sponsors clearly to bypass the requirement of consensus. This procedural trick of taking the draft away from the CD and refering the same to GA was obviously a violation of the basis of the CD itself besides constituting an unusual bypassing of the UN rules of procedure.

The delegates were exhorted not only to vote for the resolution but also to oppose the moving of any formal amendments. This P-5 move, under the US tutelage, was motivated primarily because they no longer needed to conduct nuclear explosions in view of the laboratory testing and computer simulations facilities available only to them. Besides the immediate American driving force behind the move was Clinton's Presidential election in which he wanted to show the approval of the move as a foreign policy victory despite the Republication party's reservations over the CTBT.

The compelling abiding American interest behind the CTBT negotiations was to get the treaty in the bag before 'Super Tuesday' so that president Clinton gets to score points with the electorate.

In this context, the basic motives of the P-5 powers are quite understandable but what is not easily understandable is India's reluctance to go all the way in GA on such a crucial issue by not moving any formal amendments either on substantive or procedural grounds. It has been argued that this decision of India was prompted by a desire to avoid further confrontation and increased isolation. It may be a valid argument but it could have been equally applied to the Geneva discussions where India fought a long courageous battle. However even at this level India clearly and very firmly vowed not to sign the treaty. Though even at this stage. Many countries had expressed their reservations against the implementation of this treaty but the CTBT was passed by an overwhelming majority on September 10, 1996—158 countries voting for, five abstaining and only three, including India, voting against. Those who approved the treaty generally agreed with the Australian 'slightly unusual way' of placing the resolution but while not liking the Indian attitude of 'one state trying to seek to prevent the rest of them from doing something as something was better than nothing' they voted for the resolution.

## 8. In Defence of the CTBT

Defending the CTBT would be based on the following:

(a) It was indisputably a normative measure favouring nuclear arms reduction and disarmament and commitment not to conduct nuclear test explosions.

(b) It was an important achievement both to block a conspicuous competition and to retain the momentum of a step-by-step complex of processes that together could lead to the complete elimination of nuclear weapons.

(c) It was a move in the right direction as it was to bring about moratorium on tests by nuclear weapons powers.

(d) To abandon the CTBT at this stage would be a great reversal for the arms control as it would defuse the momentum for disarmament.

(e) It was the first international treaty purporting to ban both outer-space and the underground tests.

(f) Even a flawed treaty is better than none at all.

(g) That nuclear test ban and complete elimination of nuclear weapons must be kept apart.

(h) The demand of linkage of the CTBT with a fixed time bound programme was impractical.

(i) The hawkish propaganda that 'the rest of the world was coerced by the US to sign it' was disproved by the fact of its support by even the enemies of the US like Iraq and Iran.

(j) President Clinton as the first signatory called it as "the great step in the reduction of nuclear non-proliferation and nuclear disarmament."

## 9. General Criticisms of the CTBT

### 9.1 Procedural

(a) After India's veto in the AC and CD the transmittal of the Draft to the GA was undoubtedly an anti-climax and charade. (b) The resultant Australian game plan, with the connivance of P-5, particularly under the tutelage of the USA, was definitely a fraudulent violation of the CD mandate and a purposive flagrant disregard of the UN rules of procedure. (c) The mandate of the GA was to 'evolve through negotiations' but from all accounts the weapons states in general

and the US in particular had behaved as a cabal and not bothered to even discuss, leave alone negotiate, the core issues with the negotiating body.

### 9.2 Substantive

(a) The CTBT does not fulfil the expectations with which the GA had mandated the CD as it was always conceived as a capping measure. (b) It is spuriously labeled as 'Comprehensive' as in reality it is shaped more by the technological preference of only the P-5 states. (c) It is not a genuinely transparent treaty as it has many loopholes and suffers from defects. (d) It is highly discriminatory because it makes a distinction between the nuclear and non-nuclear powers. (e) Similarly it is iniquitous also because it tends to perpetuate and reinforce the divide between them by maintaining the status-quoist monopoly of the nuclear powers. (f) It is an ineffective treaty because it does not mention that the tests be continued through the medium of laboratories and computers. Not to talk of the elimination of the nuclear weapons by it, most probably by itself, it can not prevent even the first generation horizontal proliferation though it aimed at vertical proliferation. (g) By the implied verification system, it will be virtually impossible for it to detect and penalize the clandestine defaulting tests. (h) The EIF provision in it is definitely of coercive nature and violative of the Article 18 of Vienna Convention. Besides it amounts to the implementation of the widely criticized and discredited doctrine of 'Limited Sovereignty.' (i) Unless fixed time bound programme leading to the total distinction of the whole nuclear stockpile is incorporated in it, this treaty does not mean anything. (j) It would be setting up an unjust international regime of nuclear hegemony in the name of the balance of terror of the nuclear holocaust.

## 10. Indian Objections at the CD

Keeping in mind the points of objections raised during the AC level talks the Chairman of the AC and CD Mr. Ramaker prepared a consensus draft to be presented at the CD. This draft, stitched together by him, was more or less in accordance with the wishes of the USA and the other nuclear weapons states. As this draft did not suit India so India firmly expressed that it would not sign the same as it stood then. The Indian objections were as follows:

(a) The mandate for the CTBT was to "evolve through negotiations, a treaty that effectively contributed to non-proliferation in all its aspects, horizontal and vertical, qualitative and quantative, and the process of disarmament." But the draft totally fails on both negotiating mandate criteria and the disarmament as from all accounts the weapon states, in general and the United States in particular, have not bothered to even discuss, leave alone negotiate, the core issues with India.

(b) "India was at Geneva with clean hands." In order to achieve a nuclear weapon free world within a time framework we seek a transparent comprehensive CTB free of loopholes." GA treaty that will check the nuclear weapon states to continue developing and refining their nuclear arsenals through non-explosive means. India seeks to ban not merely any nuclear weapon explosion or any other nuclear test explosion but also any release of nuclear energy caused by the assembly or compression of fissile or fusion material by chemical explosive or other means.

(c) In India's perception the real aim of the CTBT was to prevent the non-nuclear powers, particularly the threshold states, like India which had the capacity to make atom bomb to enter into the atomic programme.

(d) In India's view one cannot have a spurious treaty which heaps all the control, all the limitations and all the prohibition on non-nuclear countries while at the same time giving a license, even indirect encouragement, to the existing nuclear weapons powers themselves to proliferate and to continue with their manufacture of nuclear weapons and delivery vehicles.

(e) In India's view at least some measures be taken which are fundamental and germane to this disease of proliferation and that the cause of proliferation be dealt with not only its consequences. The CTBT was not an end in itself but a means to an end. In India's view if one wishes to diagnose a disease one must see the history of the disease. We should be really caring for the real essence of the cause and not only for the symptoms.

(f) In fact the draft of CTB was centred unfortunately not on disarming those who were armed but on preventing those who were unarmed from arming themselves. It has given a de facto, if not de-jure, legitimacy to nuclear apartheid that those who have acquired the major stockpiles of nuclear weapons are the ones who are exempting themselves from any commitment to give up nuclear weapons. It may be noted that P-5 states are so technologically advanced that they do not need

to test. Therefore India seeks to ban even explosive based laboratory tests.

(g) The peculiar circumstances in which certain countries are placed not taken into account. India's special problem of security against nuclear threat or nuclear blackmail not considered at all.

## 11. *Indian Objections at the GA*

India expected the reconsideration of the issue as the result of her veto at the CD level. Surprisingly P-5 connived in finding way out of 'Alternate Route' of 'Australian Procedural Trick' only to negate India's blocking of the transmittal. This fraudulent hijacking of the stalled and flawed treaty for endorsement and voting at the GA level was regarded as a violation of the basis of CD and a flagrant repudiation of UN rules.

## 12. *Subjective Indian Reservation*

(a) Jilted love—Despite accommodating American wishes (1992-94) India received the American reward of Brown amendment, meddling in Kashmir affairs and purposive refusal of accepting well documented Chinese help to Pakistan in undertakings related to atomic weapon programmes. (b) CTBT not a genuinely motivated global peace oriented move but only a myopic and lopsided strategic and diplomatic move of capping India's nuclear option, particularly after the incorporation of Entry Into Force clause XIV. (c) Grim kernel of truth was that despite the appeasement of France and accomodation of Russian and Chinese wishes American contemptuously neglected rightfully deserving core concerns of India. (d) No self-respecting nation can compromise with the American way treating India as being pushed around as a camp follower in the hope of getting some crumbs from the American high table. (e) Psychological revulsion against Arm Twisting and bulldozer attitude of American thinking that India would be unable to notice the real ways of the P-5. (f) "Not now, not later approach is in conformity with the consistent approach in the past and the Indian way of looking at questions and taking our own decisions.

## 13. *Conclusion*

India has done the right thing by refusing to be dragooned into signing the CTBT fearlessly raising the voice of reason against the setting up of an unjust international regime of nuclear hegemony and desiring the world to know that the treaty as proposed at

Geneva was not a genuine CTBT. At no other point in history has so crucial a decision or mankind been taken so arbitrarily by so few nations while the others watched with secret misgivings.

See also: *Campaign for Nuclear Disarmament; Arms Control, Evolution of; Arms Race, Dynamics of*

RAM NARESH TRIVEDI

# CTBT Negotiations: Analysis and Assessment

On September 24, 1996, a treaty banning all nuclear test explosions was opened for signature in New York. It was described by President Bill Clinton of the United States as "the longest sought, hardest fought prize in arms control history" (see *CTBT Negotiations: Analysis and Assessment*). Indeed, the question of nuclear explosions had been on the agenda of bilateral (United States-Soviet Union), trilateral (Great Britain-United States-Soviet Union), and multilateral arms control negotiations ever since 1954, when India proposed a so-called "standstill agreement" on nuclear testing (see *India: Historical Concepts and Institutions of Peace*). The Indian proposal was put forward after a major radiation accident which followed an American nuclear test in the Pacific (see *CTBT in Indian Perception*).

During the subsequent four decades of deliberations and negotiations for the cessation of nuclear testing, three treaties were concluded circumscribing the environment for test explosions and reducing the force (yield) of the explosions. Since none of these treaties had made a mitigating impact on the nuclear arms race, international pressure for a comprehensive test ban (CTB) continued. For a long time, the CTB talks dealt almost exclusively with technical means to verify compliance with a projected ban rather than with the specifics of the ban itself. The Western Powers insisted on control measures which were obviously unacceptable to the former Soviet Union. Whereas the former Soviet Union refused to accept control measures which were obviously indispensable for the credibility of a CTB. In the atmosphere of the Cold War, characterized by unremitting nuclear competition, the sterile dispute over verification provided a convenient excuse for the great Powers to block an agreement which they were clearly not keen to achieve. After years of fruitless bargaining, the United States declared that since nuclear testing was important for the security of the Western Alliance, a CTB could only be a long-term objective to be sought in the context of nuclear arms reductions, maintenance of a reliable nuclear deterrent and expanded confidencebuilding measures. The former Soviet Union was thus relieved from making public its own reluctance to stop nuclear testing.

The situation changed radically in 1992, when the

United States Congress, following the example of Russia, and France, declared a nine-month suspension of nuclear testing. Congress also resolved that the American testing programme should be terminated by September 30, 1996, after a limited number of explosions, designed primarily to improve the safety of nuclear weapons, had been carried out. In 1993, the Clinton Administration decided that the United States would use means other than test explosions to ensure the safety of its nuclear arsenal, and extended its moratorium on testing. Russia and the United Kingdom followed suit. Thus, a way was opened for bona fide negotiations on a CTB (see *Comprehensive Nuclear Test Ban Treaty (CTBT)*). They started at the Conference on Disarmament (CD) in January 1994, and some two years later the 50th United Nations General Assembly (UNGA) called upon the CD to complete the text of the treaty as soon as possible in 1996, so as to enable its signature by the outset of the 51st session of the Assembly.[2]

The CD set up an ad hoc committee with a mandate to negotiate a nuclear test ban. In addition to the so-called rolling text of the CTB treaty (CTBT), subject to continuous changes, the Conference had before it drafts submitted by Australia and Iran. The main contentious points were:

(a) the scope of the obligations of the parties;

(b) entry into force of the treaty;

(c) the duration of the treaty; and

(d) verification of compliance.

On 28 June 1996, the Chairman of the ad hoc committee proposed a draft CTBT which included compromise formulations for the controversial issues.[3]

This paper analyses the four problems (noted above) encountered by the negotiators and explains how they were solved. It ends with an assessment of the treaty.

*1. Scope of the Obligations under the CTBT*

From the beginning, the CD negotiators agreed that nuclear-weapon test explosions should be banned at any place in the atmosphere, outer space, underwater and underground. However, since "nuclear explosion" was not defined, a controversy arose as to whether a CTB should or should not cover the so-called hydronuclear experiments (HNEs) which release small amounts of nuclear energy.[4] For some, "small" meant a yield equivalent to a few kilograms of high explosives; for others, it meant a yield equivalent to tens or even several hundred tons of high explosives—which is more than the explosive force of certain battlefield nuclear weapons. At one point during the negotiations, France and the United Kingdom wanted to reserve the right in "exceptional circumstances" to conduct nuclear explosions without restrictions on yield, but they later withdrew this demand.

To a certain degree, HNEs may be useful to check the safety of a nuclear weapon and to assess the significance of unforeseen physical changes in the weapon. However, their technical value is small compared to the political benefits of reaching a CTB. The tests so far conducted by the nuclear Powers must have already ensured a high degree of safety of nuclear weapons; no accidental nuclear explosion has occurred since the beginning of the nuclear age. A few detonations of the non-nuclear explosive component of nuclear weapons did take place, causing the dispersal of radioactive materials, but the risks of such occurrences were considerably lowered when the conventional explosive initiating the fission or fission-fusion reaction was replaced in most weapons with an "insensitive" high explosive less prone to accidental detonation. Moreover, many nuclear weapons are equipped with permissive action links permitting the use of weapons only by authorized personnel, as well as with use-denial mechanisms disabling the weapons when their use is attempted by unauthorized persons. Improvement of these devices does not require explosive testing and can be made without affecting the weapon design.

Nor is nuclear-explosive testing indispensable to ensure the reliability of ageing stockpiles. This can be achieved through visual and electronic examination of warheads disassembled in the course of routine maintenance operations and possible correction of faulty components. In the so-called JASON Report, prepared for the United States Department of Energy, a group of American physicists and nuclear-weapon designers concluded that age-affected warheads could be remanufactured using the original materials. The present weapon designs are deemed to be sufficiently robust to tolerate the inevitable changes that would occur in remanufacture.[5] What cannot be done without test explosions is the development of entirely new or significantly modified designs of nuclear weapons. However, if development testing were permitted, the test ban would be deprived of its arms control value.

To ensure that a CTBT would contain no loopholes which would allow further improvement of nuclear weapons, India proposed that the treaty prohibit not only nuclear test explosions, but also "any release of nuclear energy caused by the assembly or compression of fissile or fusion material by chemical explosive or other means."[6] It favoured, together with Indonesia, Egypt, Iran and a few other countries, the outlawing of all tests of nuclear devices, whether explosive or not.[7] Such proposals were unacceptable to the nuclear Powers which argued that activities intended to maintain the safety and reliability of nuclear weapons, not involving nuclear explosions, should continue. They also proved unacceptable to certain non-nuclear-weapon nations, in so far as they would amount to prohibiting activities serving civil-

*Figure 1* Nuclear explosions, July 16, 1945–September 24, 1996

| | United States | USSR/Russia | United Kingdom | France | China | India | Total |
|---|---|---|---|---|---|---|---|
| Atmosphere and Underwater | 217 | 219 | 21 | 50 | 23 | – | 530 |
| Underground | 815 | 496 | 24 | 160 | 22 | 1 | 1518 |
| Total | 1032 | 715 | 45 | 210 | 45 | 1 | 2048 |

After 1961, all British tests were conducted jointly with the United States at the Nevada Test Site; thus the number of American explosions is actually higher than that indicated above.

Sources: Stockholm International Peace Research Institute, United States Department of Energy and National Resources Defence Council.

ian purposes, in particular, laboratory-scale experiments to develop means of producing commercial energy by creating nuclear fusion.

On August 10, 1995, France—thus far the main proponent of HNES—declared that it would accept a prohibition on "any nuclear-weapon test explosion or any other nuclear explosion."[8] This declaration, which reproduced the language formally proposed by Australia,[9] was understood as a renunciation of the postulate to exempt small-yield explosions from a future global nuclear test ban. At the same time, the United Kingdom announced its acceptance of the Australian text on the scope of the CTBT.[10] One day later, the United States made an announcement which set the goal of achieving a "true zero yield" CTB[11] and, on October 23, 1995, after a meeting between Presidents Clinton and Yeltsin, it was reported that Russia supported a treaty banning all nuclear explosions, whatever their yield.[12]

There remained the problem of nuclear explosions meant for peaceful (civilian) purposes, which China (with practically no support from other delegations) proposed to exclude from the scope of a CTBT. However, such explosions—though permitted under the 1968 Non-Proliferation Treaty (NPT) for nuclear-weapon States—can not be tolerated under a CTB, because there are no means to distinguish them from explosions conducted for military purposes. Moreover, the potential benefits of such explosions have not been demonstrated. To meet the Chinese request, at least partially, it was agreed that a CTBT Review Conference should, upon request by any party, consider the possibility of permitting the conduct of underground nuclear explosions for peaceful purposes. If the conference decided by consensus that such explosions might be permitted, it would have to commence work with a view to recommending to the parties an appropriate amendment to the treaty. The probability of reaching such a decision is low, as is the probability of amending the treaty; amendments may be adopted only by a positive vote of a majority of parties with no party casting a negative vote (article VII). Nonetheless, the compromise regarding peaceful nuclear explosions, which China considers to be merely a "temporary" solution, is unfortunate. It may reopen the debate on an issue which has a potential of subverting not only the test ban but also the NPT, for it could be understood as justifying research and development in the field of nuclear explosives (short of actual explosions) not only by the nuclear Powers, but by other States as well.

Nevertheless, the agreed language on peaceful nuclear explosions led to the undertaking not to carry out "any nuclear weapon test explosion or any other nuclear explosion," and to prohibit and prevent any such explosion at any place under the jurisdiction or control of the parties. Each party must refrain from causing, encouraging or in any way participating in the carrying out of such explosions (Article I).

To deter potential violators, several representatives demanded that a ban be imposed not only on the conduct of nuclear explosions, but also on preparations for such explosions. This demand, related to the proposal for closing down all nuclear test sites, was categorically rejected by the United States, Russia and China,[13] even though, in doing so, the nuclear Powers would not lose the capability to resume explosive testing, if for some reason they ceased to be bound by the treaty. Only France decided to close its testing site.

## 2. Entry into Force of the CTBT

Setting a mere number—without qualification—of ratifications needed for a CTBT to enter into force was considered by many as inappropriate, because those actually testing or capable of testing could remain unconstrained.[14] To avoid such a situation, it would be necessary to obtain ratifications from all of the recognized nuclear Powers, as well as from the nuclear-threshold States which conduct significant nuclear activities but refuse to join the NPT and to accept full-scope nuclear safeguards administered by the International Atomic Energy Agency (IAEA). All other nuclear-capable non-nuclear-weapon States are already prohibited by the NPT or the nuclear-weapon free-zone treaties from acquiring and, *ipso facto*, from exploding nuclear weapons, and are subject to full-scope IAEA safeguards. Their participation in a CTB is, of course, desirable but not indispensable. With this approach, the number of States whose ratifications would be necessary for a CTBT to become effective could have been reduced to eight: China, France, Russia, the United Kingdom and the United States (as the recognized nuclear Powers), and India, Israel and Pakistan (as the nuclear-threshold States). Alternatively, when it became clear that not all nuclear-threshold countries would subscribe to the CTBT, one could have required ratification only by the five nuclear Powers. No other country would then be in a position, by withholding its ratification, to prevent the treaty from entering into force.[15] Verification arrangements could be introduced gradually, following increases in the number of adherents; they need not and cannot be global from the very beginning.[16]

The straightforward solutions, as indicated above, were not seriously considered by the CTBT negotiators. The solutions that were discussed at great length provided for a number of ratifications much higher than eight, which, in most cases, included the eight countries mentioned. According to one formula, all participants in the Conference on Disarmament would have to ratify the treaty. According to other formulas, all of the several dozen States possessing or building nuclear power or research reactors, or all countries providing facilities for monitoring the test ban, would have to ratify. According to yet another formula, countries which have ratified the treaty could subsequently decide to waive, individually or collectively, any requirement for its entry into force stipulated in the text (including the requirement of ratification by all eight of the countries in question), thus making the treaty effective immediately only for them.

In an effort to reconcile the divergent positions, the Chairman of the ad hoc committee proposed that the treaty should enter into force 180 days after the date of deposit of the instruments of ratification by all States listed in an annex to the treaty, but not earlier than two years after its opening for signature—the time estimated for the establishment of the verification machinery (Article XIV.1). The annex enumerated forty-four States, those which were members of the CD as of June 18, 1996 (date of the effective expansion of the CD membership from 38 to 61) and which formally participated in the work of the 1996 session of the CD,[17] and which, according to the IAEA publications of December 1995 and April 1996, possessed nuclear power or research reactors. The nuclear-threshold States were included in this number as meeting the above criteria. However, India stated categorically that it would not subscribe to the draft treaty under consideration, and dissociated itself from the envisaged monitoring system. The treaty was not—in its opinion—conceived as a measure towards universal nuclear disarmament and was, therefore, flawed. (Several other, mainly non-aligned, countries complained that the goal of nuclear disarmament was not adequately stated in the treaty preamble and insisted that the nuclear Powers should accept a timetable for the elimination of nuclear weapons; they did not however, find this omission serious enough to reject the draft.) Moreover, India considered the treaty language unacceptable as it would affect its "sovereign right to decide," in the light of its national interest, whether or not it should accede to the treaty.[18] This was understood as a warning that entry into force of the CTBT could be blocked by India for an indefinite period of time. (Opinion polls in India showed strong support for

India's keeping its nuclear-weapon option open.)[19] As a matter of fact, any country, out of the forty-four mentioned above, could do so, even for reasons not related to the subject-matter of the treaty.

Recognizing the above predicament, the draft stipulated that in case the treaty did not become effective three years after "the date of the anniversary of its opening for signature," the Secretary-General, the depositary of the treaty, would, upon request of the majority of States that had deposited their instruments of ratification, convene a conference of those States (Article XIV.2). The conference would consider and decide by consensus (but would not be authorized to change the entry into force provision) what measures "consistent with international law" might be taken to accelerate the ratification process. The procedure envisioned could be repeated each year in the hope of persuading the recalcitrant countries to join the treaty. India interpreted this as a threat of sanctions against nonparties, but the Chairman of the ad hoc committee explained that the clause in question did not refer to the United Nations Security Council action under Chapter VII of the United Nations Charter, and the United States Secretary of State said that the United States would not impose sanctions against countries remaining outside the treaty. It is more likely that States which had ratified the treaty would—in accordance with international law (Article 25 of the 1969 Vienna Convention on the Law of Treaties)—decide to apply it provisionally, pending its entry into force. The nuclear-threshold countries could, of course, withstand international pressure, as they have done in opposing the NPT—a treaty which entered into force more than a quarter of a century ago and which is now adhered to by over 180 States. However, a CTBT signed and ratified by a large number of States will have an international norm-setting value even before it enters into force. In fact, all five nuclear Powers are already bound by their unilaterally declared moratoria on nuclear-explosive testing. Moreover, once a State signs a treaty it is obliged under international law to refrain from acts which would defeat the object and purpose of the treaty, until such time as it has made its intention clear not to become party to it (Article 18 of the above-mentioned Vienna Convention) (see *Nuclear Weapons Abolitions*).

### 3. Duration of the CTBT

The widely shared view was that a CTBT should be of unlimited duration. This corresponded to the pledges made by the parties to the NPT to stop nuclear-weapon tests for all time. As in other arms control agreements, the possibility to withdraw from the treaty was provided for—but only in extraordinary circumstances when the country's supreme interests were in jeopardy. The withdrawing party would then have to give prior notice with an explanation and justification for its action (Article IX). The American suggestion to make unilaterally decided withdrawals a simple formality (without citing reasons of supreme national interests) already at the time of the first review conference, was strongly criticized and had to be retracted. Indeed, a provision for an "easy exit" from the treaty would jeopardize its survivability. However, this American retreat might be of no consequence, should some future problems with the nuclear-weapon stockpile of the United States—such as an uncertainty about the safety of reliability of weapons—justify withdrawal from the CTBT, as envisaged in the *Comprehensive Test-Ban Treaty Safeguards* of the United States.[20] Also Russia said that it would withdraw from the treaty to conduct tests if there were no other means to confirm confidence in the safety or reliability of the key types of its nuclear weapons.[21] Such interpretations of "supreme interests" could facilitate arbitrary decisions not subject to international scrutiny.

## 4. Verification of Compliance

To ensure the implementation of the treaty and provide a forum for consultation and cooperation among parties, the CTBT Organization is to be established with a seat in Vienna. The Organization will be an independent body, but it may maximize cost efficiencies through cooperation with other international organizations, such as the IAEA. It will have the following organs: the Conference of States Parties, the Executive Council and the Technical Secretariat (Article II).

The task of the Conference will be to review compliance with the treaty and promote its object and purpose. The Executive Council, a body destined to play a prominent political role in the decision-making, is to consist of fifty-one members from six geographical regions.[22] The Technical Secretariat must carry out verification and other functions entrusted to it. It will comprise a Director-General, appointed by the Conference upon recommendation of the Executive Council, and such scientific, technical and other personnel as may be required.

The International Monitoring System (IMS) necessary to check compliance with the CTBT will consist of facilities—listed in an annex—for seismological,

radionuclide, hydroacoustic and infrasound monitoring. The IMS is to be supported by the International Data Centre (IDC), attached to the Technical Secretariat, where processing of data would take place (Article IV B and Protocol Part I). Some doubts were expressed about the usefulness of infrasound monitoring and about the cost effectiveness of radionuclide monitoring in detecting underground explosions.[23] It was nevertheless felt by most negotiators that the synergy of different monitoring technologies should enable verification of events with a yield well below one kiloton—the adopted seismic threshold of detectability.[24] Moreover, electromagnetic pulse monitoring or satellite monitoring could be subsequently incorporated in the IMS in accordance with a procedure envisaged in the treaty. As confidence-building measures, the parties were expected to assist in the resolution of compliance concerns arising from possible misinterpretation of verification data relating to chemical explosions (Article IV E and Protocol Part III).

Suspicious events, not clarified through consultations, could be subject to international on-site inspection—an admittedly exceptional occurrence. A request for such inspection was to be based on "information collected by the IMS, on any relevant technical information obtained by national technical law," or on a combination thereof. The Executive Council would have to act within ninety-six hours of receiving a request for an inspection. According to the Chairman's draft, the decision giving a green light for a requested on-site inspection would have to be made by a majority of all members of the Council. (The American proposal, that on-site inspections should proceed automatically unless two-thirds of the Executive Council had voted against it, was withdrawn.) If the on-site inspection request were found to be frivolous or abusive, the requesting party might be required to pay the cost of any preparations made by the Technical Secretariat. Possible further penalties included the suspension for a period of time of the party in question's rights to request an on-site inspection and to serve on the Executive Council (Article IV D and Protocol II).

Reacting to the proposed procedures, China (supported by Pakistan, Iran and a few other countries) expressed the opinion that espionage must be specifically excluded from the purview of national technical means of verification allowed to be used to trigger on-site inspections. However, most delegations appeared satisfied with the assurances contained in the draft that "verification activities shall be based on objective information" and "shall be carried out on the basis of full respect for the sovereignty" of States parties (Article IV A). China, moreover, insisted that to initiate an on-site inspection a two-thirds majority decision of the Executive Council should be required instead of a simple majority.[25]

In cases where a party failed to fulfill a request to redress a situation, raising problems with regard to its compliance with the provisions of the treaty, the Conference could decide to restrict or suspend that party from the exercise of its rights and privileges. In cases where damage to the object and purpose of the treaty could result from non-compliance with the basic obligations of the treaty, the Conference might recommend some (unspecified) collective measures "in conformity with international law." Alternatively, the non-compliance issue might be brought to the attention of the United Nations (Article V).[26]

The likelihood that the CTBT—which in practical terms affects only a handful of nations—would be violated is not high. A single small explosion, difficult to detect, may not be sufficiently important from the military point of view to justify the risk of exposure, whereas a larger explosion or a series of small ones could probably be detected with the technical and other means which are already in possession of several countries. The international verification machinery seems, therefore, to be excessively complex and costly.[27]

Ten years after entry into force of the treaty, a conference of the parties should review its operation and effectiveness. At intervals of ten years thereafter (or earlier, if necessary), further review conferences might be convened. Considering that the Conference of State Parties, the principal organ of the CTBT Organization, is to meet annually in regular sessions, and that it may make recommendations and take decisions on "any questions, matters or issues within the scope of the treaty," the rationale of having additional meetings of parties, with essentially the same objectives, is unclear.

A Preparatory Commission, composed of all signatory States, will carry out preparations for the implementation of the CTBT and prepare the first session of the Conference of States Parties. It will have the standing of an international organization.[28]

## 5. Conclusion of the CTBT Negotiations

In August 1996, a majority of the CD participants arrived at the conclusion that the ad hoc committee Chairman's draft treaty of June 28, 1996 represented the maximum common ground among the negotiators. They were, therefore, prepared to accept the text without further changes. Amendments suggested by a few delegations were discussed but were not subject to negotiations, with one exception: to satisfy the Chinese delegation's demand regarding verification procedures, it was agreed that the decision to launch an on-site inspection would have to be made by at least thirty affirmative votes of the members of the Executive Council. This agreement, reached between the United States and China outside the CD, was included in the Chairman's concluding statement and, subsequently, in the revised draft treaty.[29]

According to the CD rules of procedure, all decisions of the Conference must be taken by consensus. Since India was opposed to the draft treaty and decided to use its right of veto, the text of the treaty—although supported by most CD participants[30]—could not be recognized as a product of the Conference. Even the transmittal to the United Nations of a special CD report on the CTB negotiations, which would note the failure of the Conference to reach consensus, was vetoed by India (with the support of Iran). In this situation, a group of States, led by Australia, decided to turn directly to the United Nations. On September 10, 1996, the General Assembly resolved to adopt the CTBT text and asked the United Nations Secretary-General to open it for signature. The vote in the Assembly was 158 to three (India, Bhutan and Libya), with five abstentions (Cuba, Lebanon, Mauritius, Syria and Tanzania). Nineteen Member States delegations were absent or not allowed to vote as they were in arrears in the payment of their financial contributions to the Organization. Pakistan, which voted for the resolution, said that it would not sign the treaty until India did so, but India declared that it would never sign. The unprecedented procedure which was used to bypass the Conference on Disarmament, thus far considered to be the sole multilateral disarmament negotiating body, is bound to affect the future of this body. However, the Conference on Disarmament, which was set up in the period of the Cold War, and which now—after the expansion of its membership—resembles a deliberative body rather than a negotiating body, will have to be revamped anyway. New arms control mechanisms, more effective and adapted to present-day realities, are needed.

## 6. The Significance of the CTBT

The degree of importance attached to a CTB by different countries or groups of countries has varied over the years, reflecting major changes in the world's political situation as well as the evolving strategic interests of the nuclear weapon states. However, the main concerns of the world community about nuclear testing have remained unchanged. They relate mainly to the proliferation of nuclear weapons, the race for qualitative improvement of nuclear arsenals and the contamination of the human environment.

For the cause of inhibiting the proliferation of nuclear weapons, the CTBT will not carry the same importance now as it would have carried in the early years of the nuclear age. Today, fission atomic devices of a relatively simple design can be manufactured without testing by any State with an indigenous modern technological base or the financial resources to buy the necessary technology. Developing thermonuclear devices without testing would be difficult but not impossible. None the less, by imposing the same obligation on all parties, the CTBT may strengthen the NPT as it will eliminate an important asymmetry between the rights and obligations of the nuclear haves and have-nots. This will be of real value after all nuclear-threshold countries have formally joined the treaty.

If in the present international situation an emerging nuclear-weapon State decided to test a newly developed nuclear device, it would do so chiefly for political reasons—to demonstrate to the world that it had acquired a workable nuclear weapon and to ask for some special international status. However, when a recognized nuclear Power conducts test explosions, it does so primarily to validate modifications in the existing designs of nuclear warheads. The main pur-

poses of these modifications are to achieve greater efficiency and economy in the use of fissionable and fusionable materials and, at the same time, make the weapon assembly compatible with the means of delivery, as required by current military needs. Simulation with supercomputers cannot meet all these objectives.[31] Warheads of designs not tested through explosions are not deemed sufficiently reliable to be deployed. At least one explosion, at or near full yield, of a new or significantly redesigned warhead is considered indispensable by technical experts and the military establishments of the nuclear Powers. Testing is needed not only to modernize the first two generations of nuclear weapons—the fission and fusion explosive devices—but also to develop socalled "third generation" nuclear weapons. These constitute a refinement of the techniques involved in fission/ fusion processes for the purpose of achieving special weapon effects. It is thus evident that the cessation of nuclear testing will bring arms control benefits by putting a stop to substantial qualitative improvements of nuclear weapons. The test ban should also make it unlikely that something completely new, unpredictable and exotic would suddenly emerge in the nuclear field.

One of the central purposes of the 1963 Partial Test-Ban Treaty prohibiting atmospheric tests was to reduce the radiation hazards from nuclear explosions. This has been achieved, but venting of radioactivity

***Figure 2*** Major events related to nuclear explosions

| July 16, 1945 | The atomic era begins with an atomic test explosion carried out by the United States at Alamagordo, New Mexico. |
|---|---|
| August 6, 1945 | The United States launches an atomic bomb, based on uranium, on Hiroshima, Japan. |
| August 9, 1945 | The United States launches an atomic bomb, based on plutonium, on Nagasaki, Japan. |
| August 5, 1963 | The Partial Test-ban Treaty (PTBT) banning nuclear test explosions in the atmosphere, outer space and underwater is opened for signature. (In force since October 10, 1963) |
| July 1, 1968 | The Non-Proliferation Treaty (NPT) banning the acquisition of nuclear weapons by non-nuclear-weapon States is opened for signature (In force since March 5, 1960.). |
| July 3, 1974 | The Threshold Test-Ban Treaty (TTBT) prohibiting underground nuclear-weapon test explosions with a yield exceeding 150 kilotons is signed by the United States and the Soviet Union (In force since December 11, 1990.). |
| May 28, 1976 | The Peaceful Nuclear Explosions Treaty (PNET) regulating nuclear explosions outside the nuclear-weapon test sites (and therefore presumed to be for peaceful ends) is signed by the United States and the Soviet Union (In force since December 11, 1990.). |
| September 10, 1996 | The United Nations General Assembly adopts, with an overwhelming majority of votes, the text of the Comprehensive Test-Ban Treaty (CTBT) banning all nuclear test explosions. |
| September 24, 1996 | The CTBT is opened for signature. |

from underground nuclear tests has not been avoided. In some cases, radioactive fallout was detected beyond the national borders of the testing States. The CTBT will put an end to further contamination of the human environment. It will also free for productive purposes those resources which are spent on the development of nuclear weaponry.

Meaningful progress towards the elimination of nuclear weapons is improbable as long as nuclear test explosions are not definitively and universally banned. It is, therefore, essential that the CTBT enter into force without undue delay.

See also: *Disarmament and Development; Security and Cooperation in Europe; New World Order and New State-Nations Arms Control, Evolution of*

## Notes

1. United Nations document, A/RES/50/65, 12 December 1995.
2. Conference on Disarmament Document, CD/NTB/WP.330/Rev.1.
3. Dozens of such experiments were made in the United States during the 1958-1991 United States-Soviet nuclear-testing moratorium. They were not considered by the American Administration to be nuclear explosion tests.
4. F. v. Hippel, A Pentagon Arms Plan Goes France One Better, *International Herald Tribune*, 29-30 July 1995.
5. Conference on Disarmament Document, CD/NTB/WP.244.
6. Ibid., CD/NTB/WP.243.
7. Ibid., CD/PV.713.
8. Ibid., CD/NTB/WP.222.
9. Ibid., CD/PV.714.
10. Ibid., CD/1340.
11. Reuters, *News Reports*, 23 October 1995.
12. The nuclear Powers argued that they needed the test sites to conduct certain non-prohibited activities. In the United States, the Nevada Test Site is to be used for subcritical experiments with plutonium. (Statement by the United States Assistant Secretary of Defence, USIS Geneva, Daily Bulletin, 31 May 1996.)
13. India, the main proponent of such a solution, suggested that the CTBT should enter into force after the deposit of the instruments of ratification by any sixty-five States.

14. The 1963 Partial Test-Ban Treaty entered into force when the United States, the United Kingdom and the Soviet Union deposited their instruments of ratification.
15. Those opposing the five-Power ratification requirement included China, Russia and the United Kingdom. The reasons for this opposition are not clear, as the retention of the nuclear-testing option for some time by any of the present nuclear-threshold States could not pose a direct danger to the security of the nuclear Powers.
16. Excluding Yugoslavia, formally a member of the CD but has not participated in its work in recent years.
17. Statement by the Permanent Representative of India at the Conference on Disarmament, 20 June 1996, and by the External Affairs Minister in the Indian Parliament, 15 July 1996.
18. *International Herald Tribune*, 24-25 August 1996.
19. The White House Office of the Press Secretary, *Fact Sheet*, 11 August 1995.
20. Conference on Disarmament documents, CD/1395, 13 May 1996; CD/PV.734, 31 July 1996.
21. Some Middle Eastern delegations expressed dissatisfaction with the inclusion of Israel in their region for the purpose of allocating Executive Council seats.
22. Statement by the Representative of Belgium at the Conference on Disarmament, 24 August 1995.
23. Few delegations expressed interest in monitoring outer space as a potential environment for nuclear-explosive testing.
24. Statements by the Ambassadors of China and Pakistan at the Conference on Disarmament, 1 August 1996.
25. Pakistan did not think that the United Nations Security Council should have a role in the enforcement of compliance with the CTBT (Conference on Disarmament document, CD/PV.741, 25 June 1996).
26. The capital costs of establishing the IMS are estimated to be between 70 and 82 million US dollars, and the annual running costs at about 20 million (*UNIDIR Newsletter*, No. SI, 1/96).
27. Conference on Disarmament document, CD/NTB/WP.333/Rev. 1.
28. Ibid., CD/NTB/WP.330/Rev.2.
29. Ibid., CD/1425
30. In his announcement that in 1998 the United States would place on-line "the world's most powerful computer," the Director for Defence Policy and Arms Control of the United States National Security Council said that simulating explosions with this supercomputer would help the United States to maintain the safety and reliability of the existing stockpile of nuclear weapons without resorting to actual explosions, but not to build new types of weapons.

JOZEF GOLDBLAT

# Cultural Democracy

The notion of democracy in many respects means the same as peace. There is peace in the social sense when different groups of people live and act according to their own systems of values and norms, have the freedom to express their will and participate in the activities of the entire society, while preserving and evolving their own characteristic features. And these constitute, at the same time, the criteria of

democracy, especially that of cultural democracy.

The notion of democracy is multifaceted in its nature. Its interpretation and use vary in different historical periods and different spheres of social life. Its criteria are not entirely identical when used in such senses as economic democracy, political democracy, or cultural democracy.

The issues of cultural democracy were for a long

time kept in the background behind those of political and economic democracy. Cultural democracy has acquired greater emphasis in recent decades only— initially in the sphere of protecting the rights of minority groups. The point is that cultural democracy in this context has an important function in diffusing democratism.

In the debates on the various interpretations of democracy, the principle of majority and minority has always been an important argument. The partisans of the principle of majority (for instance, those of the French Revolution) professed that democracy is the will of the people, and the decisions of the majority must override those of the minority. The followers of the principle of minority (for instance, those of British liberalism) interpret the right of the minority to preserve its own opinion undisturbed as the criterion of democracy.

These two principles, naturally, hold different weight in different situations. In certain spheres, laws must be enacted and a uniform order must prevail; hence in the field of law the principle of majority has a predominant role. The situation in culture is the opposite where (disregarding now very exceptional cases) there is no place for majority decisions; the diversity and the development of culture are maintained by pluralism. In this sense culture can be regarded as the school or rather as the laboratory of democracy in several respects. The extent to which cultural democracy can evolve is limited by the form and degree of the political democracy of the given society, but this limit is not rigid and mechanical: cultural democracy may, in many respects, extend beyond political democracy (either legally or illegally, against the given power) and may prepare for the evolution of democratic relations and conditions in the political sphere.

In the same sense we may say that cultural democracy is also the laboratory of peace; wherein consensus and separation necessarily coexist. Every cultural activity means the acceptance of the community and of identity but it is also an individual choice, and the more this is so, the greater the value of the culture in question. Hence, the assimilation and practice of culture invariably mean the practicing of conditions of peace.

## 1. The Two Themes of Cultural Democracy

The broad notion of cultural democracy is not a uniform one because it comprises at least two endeavors differing in their tendencies and directions. These endeavors can be referred to as the democratization of culture and the democratism of culture. The former means the development and diffusion of culture, that is sociocultural activities in the broadest sense of the term which start from above going downward but which pass on cultural values to everybody. The democratism of culture (cultural democracy in the narrowest sense of the term) on the other hand, starts from below going upward, and its key words are participation and creativity, in fact the creativity of the masses—identity detected in culture. This means that cultural democracy cannot be limited to culture in the strict sense of the term (even less so to activities associated with the arts) but has to encompass the entire lifestyle. In the final analysis, cultural democracy means a lifestyle of participation which tries to improve the quality of life through participation in social activity and to find, in this way, its "identity" and community.

Since we have separated the democratization of culture from cultural democracy, it is necessary to link them up again. Cultural democracy is empty without the democratization of culture (of values) since its only aim is to let everybody live with such culture as he or she chooses; it does not create real opportunities for choosing from among the values produced by society. On the other hand, the democratization of culture is dry and bloodless without cultural democracy because forwarding, as it does, the values of culture to all, it fails to create opportunities actively to assimilate them. That is why in the long run they can only be conceived together.

It is necessary to make this statement again and again because it is not always evident. It is usual to come across the idea of distributing culture according to the share of votes in the spirit of democratization of culture, as well as the idea of looking upon the cause of cultural democracy as solved by a wide spectrum of values. At the same time there is a view that puts the protection of values in second place behind the cultural amateur activities of the masses.

Cultural democracy means both at the same time. It is important to realize, on the one hand, that in a certain sense culture is from the very outset a democratic process: you can, for instance, order someone to listen to certain music but you cannot order him or her to like it. On the other hand, it is also important to know that under the conditions of modern society, democracy is necessarily limited because the chances of liking or not liking a piece of music are determined by social circumstances (childhood, education, family environment, schooling, profession, place of residence, the course of life) that make a person susceptible to the assimilation of some kinds of culture and not susceptible to the adoption of other kinds.

True enough, this state of determination is only valid statistically (that is, there are individual exceptions), yet it *is* valid statistically. Hence democracy cannot prevail without culture being democratized.

## 2. *Cultural Democracy and Cultural Liberalism*

It is of paramount importance to distinguish between democracy and liberalism, for many look upon liberalism as democracy.

The cultural policy of liberalism indeed has democratic features. In its classical form liberalism seems to pursue no cultural policy at all: letting things happen under the impact of spontaneous processes and regulating their evolution merely through general laws. This, however, is very much a cultural policy and it is a determined one, too. This can be explained by taking into account two considerations.

One is that liberalism relies on the regulating system of the laws of the market, a system that very consistently prevails in culture (provided it is regarded as something wider than the universal relation system of cultural supply and demand). A really democratic cultural policy cannot rest satisfactorily with this alone because it must not accept, in every respect, the apparent or visible demand as valid, being aware that large sections of the population have latent desires which can be aroused and being ready to take the necessary steps to arouse them. Liberal cultural policy, however, consciously relies on the regulating power of the market.

The other consideration, which is of no less importance than the former, is that liberalism was born in countries where the bourgeois development of the preceding centuries had not taken place in the spirit of liberalism but in the frame of rather authoritarian systems (such as absolutist monarchy). Control over culture did not remain unattended even after the victory of the bourgeois system. The churches' role remained unaltered, representing strictly determined value systems, and the bourgeois state welcomed the ideological and cultural power the Church had preserved: it could be tolerant without running any risks, undertaking only a regulatory function while the ideological and cultural unity it required was ensured by the churches (including the schools operating in an ecclesiastic spirit as well as other cultural organizations). The state consciously relied on all this even when acting as though its only concerns were liberalism and the freedom of culture.

The appearance of the third factor, that is, of the cultural industries, exerted its impact in this same direction. The system of cultural institutions known in classical capitalism consisted of the theater, the museum, the concert hall, book publishing, scientific societies, schools, and universities. This discrete and isolated institutional system was meant to serve "high culture" for the most part, and only a few elements thereof were turned toward the population. Beginning in the second half of the nineteenth century, cultural industries started gradually to develop, oriented toward diverse sections of the population and creating for them a specific culture, different in value and character from the earlier autonomous "high culture." The technical inventions of the twentieth century served to intensify this process (for, instance, through mass communications). The operation of the system thus created suits liberalism (because it functions according to the laws of the market) but is far from complying with democracy because, by the abundance of the products it turns out, it establishes an authoritarian power leaving no chance for real choices. That is why the role of "mass culture" thus created is with good reason compared by its critics to that of religion: parallel to the weakening of the power of the Church, part of its function has been assumed by the "consumers' culture" since it offers not only consumable products but—together with it—also a rather rigid value system.

In spite of all this, the cultural policy of liberalism contains quite a number of democratic elements. One of its important features is its tolerance of minorities, with the simultaneous manifestation of different endeavors leaving the choice to the population (which, for the reasons explained above, is not a real possibility of decision making). In fact the whole creative intelligentsia and autonomous culture produced and represented by them constitute such a minority. Within these boundaries, however, it definitely displays tolerance.

Cultural democracy is distinguished from cultural liberalism not by being less than the latter and not even by being different from it, but by being *more*. Cultural democracy encompasses the protection of the rights and independent cultural practices of all kinds of cultural minorities; cultural pluralism in the broadest sense of the term, and not merely in a mechanical manner but by offering the possibility of real and full choice to all members of society. To this end it is necessary to develop consciously the democratization of culture and, on the other hand, to enlarge participation and creativity.

In this sense one of the focal issues of cultural democracy is its relation to traditions. As in social development, so also in cultural development, no stride forward can be made without assimilating and diffusing the achievements of previous periods. In culture this means, first and foremost, the transmission of traditions created by the development of the past centuries (such as modern large-scale industry, the universal system of commodity production, urban life, and civilization) as well as a corresponding highly differential cultural life. Value is the guiding principle throughout. Any socioeconomic and cultural progress can only be conceived on this basis, by accepting these relations and by transforming them.

Cultural democracy interpreted in this sense is not a state but a process. Its evolution is an integral part of the historical development of democracy but has so far reached perfection nowhere, that is, it has materialized only partially. Yet development points in this direction everywhere, proving that society has set this task as its aim.

See also: *Cultural Identity; Development: Cultural Dimensions*

*Bibliography*

Bell D 1975 *The Cultural Contradictions of Capitalism.* Basic Books, New York
*Culture* 1983 Vol. IX No. 33 (1) (issue devoted to Cultural Policies)
Laszlo E, Vitányi I (eds.) 1985 *European Culture and World Development.* Pergamon-Corvina, Oxford-Budapest
Mennel S 1976 *Cultural Policies in Towns.* Council of Europe, Strasbourg
Mennel S 1981 Cultural policy and models of society. *Loisir et Societé* 4 (2)
Minihan J 1977 *The Nationalization of Culture.* New York University Press, New York
Peterson R A 1979 Revitalizing the culture concept. *Annual Review of Sociology* 5
Purcell E 1973 *Crisis of Democratic Theory.* University of Kent Press, Lexington, Massachusetts
Shore H 1982 *Perspectives on Art and Cultural Development.* Australian Institute for Technology Adelaide
Starr J M (ed.) 1985 *Cultural Politics.* Praeger, New York
White L A 1977 *The Concept of Cultural Systems.* Columbia University Press, New York
Williams R 1960 *Culture and Society 1780-1950.* Chatto and Windus, London

IVÁN VITÁNYI

# Cultural Identity

The concept of identity and the sphere of related problems are of relatively recent origin in sociology and cultural policies. The origin of the term is a psychological one, meant to suggest identity with one's ego. Even considering its primary meaning, this notion is a complex and a relative one since the psychological identity of any person is semantically at least as diverse as the personality itself. Almost all research in the field of applied psychology has for the past decades come to the conclusion that normal human activity, work, self-realization, creative desires, the will to acquire knowledge, participation in communities, the capacity for unselfish love in communities of primary and secondary character, that is human happiness, require the harmony and existence of the social and personal ego.

What can one identify oneself with? With a nation, a state, a people, a class, a layer, ideals, one's own self? In fact, with everything and with many more phenomena than it is possible to enumerate here. At any rate, the object of identification, viewed from the social angle, may refer to some minority or to the majority. Whether minority or majority, the relevant community may be a national, an ethnic, a professional, or a class community. The possibility of this variety of foci of identification has been brought about by modern societies; every new possibility involves new problems.

Before the appearance of advanced industrial social forms, identity was no problem since everybody identified with himself or herself and with his or her position in society. Systems of strict rules and rituals governed the distances between the different social strata and classes, the relations of communication and this trend protected the citizens from alienation, from the problems of identity. In more advanced societies, these same rites only materialize at the level of formality—and do not act as protective factors.

The problems arising in modern society are referred to by different terms in different disciplines. Are such terms as alienation used in philosophy and sociology, or neurosis used in psychology, not different aspects of confusion in identity? The same question arises in a new light when symptoms of disintegrating identity can be perceived in a dual sense in developing countries emerging in the wake of the liquidation of the colonies.

(a) In the newly formed African countries, the linguistic, cultural, and state borders are artificial: at the same time the disintegrating tribal framework has not yet been replaced by a popular, national consciousness evolving at a more abstract level.

(b) It is precisely the struggle against colonial life, the desire for survival, that maintains and activates the cultures of the individual ethnic groups, their sense of belonging together through their joint intention to cease being colonies.

The latter has always been a very natural symptom in the course of history: its remnants can be traced, for instance, in different ethnic groups living in the Americas.

But what are the causes of the problem of cultural identity? It is possible to say that the term cultural identity itself is a pleonasm, since every identity has a cultural character: you can only identify yourself with your own role, community, and people if you identify yourself with its culture. Identification cannot be achieved unless there is something to identify oneself *with*, and this something is invariably and unequivocally the given culture. It follows that cultural identity is a notion, or rather a sphere of notion, just as wide as culture itself taken in the broader sense of the term. This applies to the entire gamut of activities beginning from behavioral, communicational, emotional, relaxational, and entertainment customs and habits through linguistic, literary, and musical forms of expression in higher culture to the etiquette of collective, social, and political intercourse—in fact, to everything that makes up the popular, national, ideological, and spiritual life of a group entity.

The problem is more complex for both the individual and society than one would think precisely on account of its wide diversity. Although in a different dimension, it also recurs in advanced modern societies with the same diversity as in developing countries fighting for their national entity.

Identity understood in this sense has come into the focus of scientific and cultural-political thinking in the past years or decades. In different formulations, identification belongs to the same semantic group as creativity, cultural democracy (see *Cultural Democracy*), participation, struggle against alienation, and cultural pluralism, that is, in the same group as the free expression of the culture of various social layers, groups, and minorities (ethnic groups, in the first place).

When examining the problem from the angle of culture, one more phenomenon needs to be analyzed with special care, namely the opposite trends of homogenization (uniformization) and differentiation (pluralism).

Cultural homogenization is the outcome of modern society, of mechanized big industry, and of the international exchange of commodities as well as of modern cities, technologies, and consumer goods. In all parts of the world where modern mechanized large-scale industrial production has evolved, culture has also produced new forms: on the one hand those of high-level autonomous culture (book publishing, theater, and concert life, for example, which have accumulated tremendous values but necessarily for a small number of people) and, on the other hand, those of entertaining culture meant for all and sundry, produced and diffused by a newborn and prosperous industry. Viewed from the angle of identification this has created a twofold contradiction.

The first contradiction stems from the above-mentioned anomaly concerning the social position of autonomous and entertaining culture. Since high-level, autonomous culture is accessible to the few only, the cultural foundation of identification for large sections of the population is not the integration of values but a homogenization leveling downward. This contradiction has made its appearance even in the most advanced countries in a wide circle—perhaps in a relatively wider field than in the moderately advanced countries—and has become a major obstacle to cultural development.

The second contradiction has cropped up in countries not belonging to the Euro-American centrum of economico-industrial development. When these countries began universal development—much later than the central countries—they found themselves obliged (that is, were compelled in their colonial position) to adopt the cultural forms of the advanced countries. This, however, constantly involved the danger of impairing or abandoning the national-ethnical and any kind of autochthonous identity. This resulted in a peculiar dilemma. Those who wished to achieve progress were compelled to give up their traditions, their ethnico-national cultural identity. And those who wished to preserve this identity were exposed to the possibility of having to oppose progress or, at least, to deviate from the path of progress.

Nowadays this problem is usually mentioned in the first place in connection with developing, formerly colonial, countries. But this is characteristic not merely of the developing countries, but—in a somewhat different form and to a somewhat different degree—also of such European countries as could embark upon the road of economic development only at a later date.

When dealing with various kinds of identity, national identity, that is the ideal of a creative participation in national culture, acquires particular emphasis, as the most important element of cultural identity. It would, however, be a mistake to think that this is the only underlying element of identity. The real problem is that in modern society identification is stratified in many ways; in fact the more advanced industrialization and urbanization are, the more stratified identification is. The psychological identification of the individual with him/herself—identification with smaller communities, with the family, in the first place—participation in major social units, identity with ethnic groups and with the nation (these two are sometimes identical, but are often different where there are different ethnic groups within a political nation), identification with the social system, and finally with humankind make up a coherent concatenation which extends over an area wider than the nation since it necessarily comprises cooperation with other nations, the adaptation of the nation to others national communities.

There is no doubt that the fundamental problem of identity is this stratification. In modern society everybody belongs to many kinds of groups according to his or her origin and way of life, to occupation and ideology, to his or her ethnic group and social class. The conscious realization of this diversity, the evolution of a harmonious system, is everybody's task, and not an easy one at that. Its realization in artistic form is usually achieved by the greatest geniuses.

As an example we could quote the entire history of high culture (of high arts) since every important creation belonging to it is a commensurate alloy, corresponding to the age, of the national and international character. But in order to throw light on the problem from today's angle, and in order to choose an idiom accessible to everybody, an artistic modality, the conception underlying the oeuvre of two great creative geniuses. Béla Bartók and Zoltán Kodály, will be described. This can be done with good reason because they were not only musicians but both professed a wide conception of cultural policy.

How can this conception be characterized? It relies, first and foremost, upon the total and organic unity (alloy) of tradition and progress. When Hungary joined universal (then) European musical life, the full assimilation of the West European musical tradition appeared to be the first prerequisite of membership. On the other hand, the Hungarian national identity was expressed through folklore, and particularly through the centuries-old practice of peasant music. This contradiction seemed to be irresolvable: Hungarian folk music preserved traditions which had sprung from the peoples of Eastern Europe and of Asia and

not form the peoples of Western Europe. The two kinds of music were not interrelated. Bartók, however, found the solution to this contradiction and created a new kind of music that was to rely on, and comply with, both Hungarian traditions and Western European achievements. This is why Bartók's music came to be associated even in the history of Western music with modern, revolutionary avant-garde trends. This experience is valid not only for Hungary but—*mutatis mutandis*, that is, by way of a model—for all other peoples newly joining universal development.

The other main feature of the conception is the unity of the characteristics of national identity and of internationalism. Bartók relied on popular and national traditions but never interpreted them in a narrow sense and never tried to find what separated nations but rather what linked them together. That is why he was concerned, at the same level, with the folk-music traditions of Hungarian neighbors: Slovaks, Romanians, Yugoslavs, and Bulgarians. Thus to expound the "specificity and universality" of culture, there is no better example than this composer. He can stand as the best emblem for the statement that in a wider sense national identity comprises community with other peoples and even identity.

The third element of the conception is that music, when diffusing culture in the broader sense of the term, makes equal use of the means of institutional culture (concerts, and so on), of school pedagogy, and of participation programs based on cultural democracy. What matters is that these means should develop in full harmony because all three stand on an equal footing.

Bartók and Kodály evolved a conception that encompasses, even today, the tasks of preserving and developing cultural identity. The eight decades that have elapsed since their appearance on the scene have proved the validity of this belief. What seemed to be then a specifically Hungarian or, at most, Central or East European cause, has since proved to be one of the most important problems of the cultural (and social) development of the world.

First of all it has become evident by now that cultural identity cannot and must not be mentioned without its dialectical conceptual counterpart—cultural cooperation, that is cultural dialogue, when speaking about peace. If there were only one person on this globe, if there were one single community, one single parent, one single nation, identity would be meaningless. Identity with one's own self would be evident and natural. Yet the human and social notion of identity comprises also dissimilarity, (on the basis of Spinoza's famous principle: *omne determinatio est negatio*). Negation, however, is not understood here in the everyday sense of the term but means actual dialogue, that is people's identity evolves best when they communicate and not when they separate.

In the present state of the world, at the actual level of development of the countries and peoples of the globe, such a fertile and mutual dialogue is of particular importance because it may become the foundation of cooperation securing for all participants the best chance for development.

Consequently, all national cultural policies oriented toward peace will have to pursue the aim of solving the above-mentioned contradictions. They will have to make efforts to develop culture of a high standard progressing in its value and form together with the cultural development of the world, and relying, at the same time, on their own traditions. Such a cultural policy will express and feed the identity of its own people and that of others. That is how it creates a culture whose national character is, in the deepest sense of the term, international, one that accepts the traditions of other peoples, chiefly those of neighbors, and cherishes the common values of global culture.

Cultural policy has to be able to create a chain of identities comprising identity with small communities, ethnic groups, and with the political nation, but reject all kinds of separation, including belief in the superiority of its own group or nation and the colonial subordination of other groups (nations and classes). Considering the situation in this complexity it becomes obvious that identity is indeed one of the chief problems of our age. The preservation and development of the identity of all peoples and all nations is the basis of cooperation between states, peoples, and nations.

*Bibliography* ——————————————————

De Levita D J 1965 *The Concept of Identity*. Mouton, Paris

Erikson E H 1950 *Childhood and Society*. Norton, New York

Erikson E H 1968 *Identity: Youth and Crisis*. Norton, New York

Gordon C, Gergen K J (eds.) 1968 *The Self in Social Interaction*. Wiley, New York

Hewitt J P 1976 *Self and Society: A Symbolic Interactionalist Social Psychology*. Allyn and Bacon, Boston, Massachusetts

Klapp O E 1969 *Collective Search for Identity*. Holt, Rinehart and Winston, New York

Laszlo E, Vitányi I (eds.) 1985 *European Culture and World Development*. Pergamon Press, Oxford

Lendvai E 1983 *The Workshop of Bartók and Kodály*. Editio Musica, Budapest

Maslow A 1943 A theory of human motivation. *Psychol. Rev.* 50

Parsons T 1973 Culture and social structure revisited. In: Schneider L, Bonean C (eds.) 1973 *The Idea of Culture in the Social Sciences*. Cambridge University Press, Cambridge

Parsons T, Shils A 1961 *Toward a General Theory of Action*. Harvard University Press, Cambridge, Massachusetts

Sági M, Vitányi I 1983 Rediscovery and re-animation of folkart in modern industrial societies. *International Science Journal* 95 35(1)

UNESCO 1985 *Cultural Pluralism and Cultural Identity*. Final Report of the UNESCO Study of Cultural Development in Countries containing different National and/or Ethnic Minorities. UNESCO, Paris

MÁRIA SÁGI

# Cultural Roots of Peace

Peace is an important part of the traditional system of values of many cultures. It is such a value in Hindu cultures, as exampled by Gandhi in recent history; Buddhism and the cultures linked to it have peace and harmony as part of their everyday life; traditional Chinese culture is a peaceful one; many African cultures have peace as a basic value; Christianity in its original stage takes love and nonaggression as the bases for its culture; and some of the ancient cultures of Latin America and Central America have a vision of peace. Why, then, has the principle of peace so often been cancelled out or overthrown by one of conflict, war, and antagonism through the centuries and especially in the last 35 years?

We are now faced with the fact that we have built a culture of war where competition in the economic field is the norm, where technology is very often turned against both nature and humankind. It is imperative that humankind now learns to foster a culture of peace so as to avoid destruction, perhaps total destruction.

Are we forced to build a culture of peace by the great danger of the present in relation to the future of ourselves, of our children, and of our grandchildren? There again, is it a historical process or more particularly a response to the force of recent events and specific technological developments, especially in the nuclear area?

Is a culture of peace developed through the birth of

more and more institutions and organizations which aim to build a future of peace—even though governments choose to ignore the activities of such great movements working in areas neglected by official negotiations?

Is a culture of peace emerging in the developing countries which now have stronger links with their own cultural backgrounds? Can these developing countries retain their cultural identity in the face of foreign influence upon them? Or do such changes perhaps lead only to war-directed values?

Is a culture of peace created because education is changing and so many of the people involved in it know that there has to be more movement toward greater understanding and solidarity among people? In particular, is there not increased consciousness today of the need for peace on the part of the young?

Will a culture of peace develop because people are becoming more and more aware of their rights and are determined to retain this increased consciousness, whether it is of cultural identity in developing countries, of women's identity and capacity, of children's rights, or of old people's rights? Is a culture of peace more likely to emerge because women are now participating to a greater extent in the world's affairs and even in decision making?

Can a culture of peace arise from the need for communication among people and the existence of ever-more adequate means to foster such communication, such as radio, television, computers, and so on? How in fact do such means contribute to furthering the cause of peace? Do they perhaps lead in the opposite direction?

It can be argued that significant changes are occurring in all these different fields, even if it is, as yet, unclear in some cases whether the cause of peace is in fact being advanced. Further analysis of the changes outlined above is necessary to determine which are conducive to peace and should be promoted, and also to develop new avenues in those areas which do seem to foster a culture of peace.

It has been said that war is connected with a need for identity or for belonging to an identifying body on the part of both the individual and the group. This need leads to nationalism and hence to international conflicts. Most modern theorists regard war as a cultural product and not a biological one. Since the Second World War, modernization in both the developed and the developing countries has tended to reinforce and escalate the need for national identification through recognition of borders. But the possibility of nuclear war changes the situation: the need for recognition through identity becomes subordinate to the nuclear threat. As a consequence, peace becomes an obligatory objective.

But what cultural roots are most likely to grow in the direction of peace? There are certainly changes occurring in the world today from a high priority of materialistic values to a high priority of nonmaterialistic values, which are being described by many authors such as Inglehart (1977). It is suggested that these changes, as reflected in many of the developments listed above, constitute the true cultural roots of a future lasting peace. Further, two leading agents of these changes are women and youth.

## 1. The Role of Women

Women can be the carriers of cultural roots of peace in different cultures. In fact women have for generations been peacebuilders, within the family and within the community. Their role in creating peace in a wider arena can be considered a possibility arising from the emergence of women in the public field in the last decades. This emergence goes hand in hand with a growing awareness of women all over the world in terms of their capability and their responsibility at the social and political levels. Even so, the new role of women in society has yet to be accepted fully, even by women themselves.

If women in the different professions—teachers, medical doctors, researchers in the natural and social sciences—rethought their capacities, in particular those relating to peace work and peacebuilding, much could be solved in terms of political behavior and decision. If, instead of acting with men's attitudes and behaviors, women involved in active politics brought to bear their capacity for mediation and negotiation as builders of peace, they could be a greater influence at the different levels of political life, which is usually so competitive and conflictual. Women, in fact, have spurned competitiveness for a long time, and they become competitive only when giving up their basic tendencies to live in peace with others.

This last may be taken as a normative statement, as it has been backed by research, although it has to be admitted that it is more applicable to the public than to the private arena, especially in cultures where relations among women, such as that of the mother-in-law to the daughter-in-law, may in fact lead to social conflict. Granted such differences, the capacity of women to solve conflicts and to understand the need for conflict resolution can be shown by the participation of women in nongovernmental organizations which have the main aim of contributing to the building of peace. Elise Boulding (1977) has indeed shown this very clearly in her book *Women in the 20th Cen-*

*tury World*. She says: "Women are weak now, but they will become stronger in the future as more attention is paid to network skills. A much closer collaboration between women and scholars and activism is needed to develop the new networks." And: "What women have is the potential for alternative thinking, but it has to be encouraged and trained . . . ."

## 2. The Role of Youth

Another social group capable of forwarding the cause of peace is youth. Up to a point in the lives of young people, competitiveness and conflict do not seem to be as apparent or as strong as in the "adult" world. Given this fact, together with the increased consciousness of the young today about the dangers of nuclear war, it may be that they can achieve solidarity in working for peace. In fact, the peace movement may be viewed as representing not only an awareness of the nuclear threat, but also a search on the part of its members for identity within the group—identity not emerging in conflict or competitiveness. The young in particular, not yet embroiled in society's conflicts and competitive struggles, seem to be in need of identity. They may find this identity within the peace movement, which has related groups across many countries, all striving toward a more peaceful and united world. This hypothesis has of course to be verified, but it springs from a common intuition that the world seems to be heading for disaster and that a new direction has to be followed.

See also: *Cultural Identity; Sexual Equality and Peace*

## Bibliography

Boulding E 1977 *Women in the 20th Century World*. Sage, Beverly Hills, California

Inglehart R 1977 *The Silent Revolution: Changing Values and Political Style Among Western Publics*. Princeton University Press, Princeton, New Jersey

Homann R, Masini E (eds.) 1984 *Cultural Roots of Peace*. Duttweiler Institute

International Federation of Catholic Universities (FIUC) 1984 *The Peace Movements*, Proc. Symp. organized by FIUC and Club of Rome, Salzburg, February 18-21, 1983. Research Center of FIUC, Rome

Masini E 1984 The futures of peace: Cultural perspectives. *Opening speech to the VIII World Conference on Future Research* organized by World Futures Studies Federation in Costa Rica, December 1984

ELEONORA BARBIERI MASINI